AN

ARABIC-ENGLISH LEXICON

AN

ARABIC-ENGLISH LEXICON

BY

EDWARD WILLIAM LANE

IN EIGHT PARTS

PART 6 غ - ف

القَامُوسُ مَدُّ

AN

ARABIC-ENGLISH LEXICON,

DERIVED FROM THE BEST AND THE MOST COPIOUS EASTERN SOURCES;

COMPRISING A VERY LARGE COLLECTION
OF WORDS AND SIGNIFICATIONS OMITTED IN THE ḲÁMOOS,
WITH SUPPLEMENTS TO ITS ABRIDGED AND DEFECTIVE EXPLANATIONS,
AMPLE GRAMMATICAL AND CRITICAL COMMENTS,
AND EXAMPLES IN PROSE AND VERSE:

COMPOSED BY MEANS OF THE MUNIFICENCE OF THE MOST NOBLE

ALGERNON,
DUKE OF NORTHUMBERLAND, K.G.,
ETC. ETC. ETC.,

AND THE BOUNTY OF

THE BRITISH GOVERNMENT:

BY EDWARD WILLIAM LANE,
HON. DOCTOR OF LITERATURE OF THE UNIVERSITY OF LEYDEN, CORRESPONDENT OF THE INSTITUTE OF FRANCE, ETC.

IN TWO BOOKS:

THE FIRST CONTAINING ALL THE CLASSICAL WORDS AND SIGNIFICATIONS COMMONLY KNOWN
TO THE LEARNED AMONG THE ARABS:
THE SECOND, THOSE THAT ARE OF RARE OCCURRENCE AND NOT COMMONLY KNOWN.

BOOK I.—PART 6.

غ — ف

EDITED, WITH A MEMOIR,
BY
STANLEY LANE POOLE.

KALPAZ

ISBN: 978-93-5128-814-5(Set)
ISBN: 978-93-5128-828-2(PB)

First Published in 1877
Indian Reprint in 2017

Published by

Kalpaz Publications
C-30, Satyawati Nagar,
Delhi – 110052
E-mail: kalpaz@hotmail.com
Website: kalpazpublications.com
Ph.: +91-9212142040

Cataloging in Publication Data—DK

Courtesy: D.K. Agencies (P) Ltd. <docinfo@dkagencies.com>

Lane, Edward William, 1801-1876, **author.**

Madd al-qa˜mu˜s = An Arabic-English lexicon : derived from the best and the most copious eastern sources, comprising a very large collection of words and significations omitted in the Kamoos, with supplements to its abridged and defective explanations, ample grammatical and critical comments, and examples in prose and verse : composed by means of the munificence of the most noble algernon, Duke of Northumberland, K. G., etc. etc. etc., and the bounty of the British Government / by Edward William Lane.

volumes cm

English and Arabic.

Parts 6-8 edited with a memoir by Stanley Lane Poole.

"First published in 1863"—Title page verso.

"In two books: the first containing all the words and significations commonly known to the learned among the Arabs : the second, those that are of rare occurrence and not communly known."
ISBN 9789351288145 (set :

1. Arabic language—Dictionaries—English. 2. English language—Dictionaries—Arabic. I. Lane-Poole, Stanley, 1854-1931, editor. II. Title. III. Title: Arabic-English lexicon.

PJ6640.L36 2017 DDC 492.7321 23

غ

The nineteenth letter of the alphabet: called غَيْنٌ. It is one of the letters termed حَلْقِيَّة [or faucial], (L, TA,) its place of utterance being the upper part of the fauces, near to that of ح, (TA in art. غين,) the same place as that of خ, (L, TA,) [from which it differs in being pronounced with the voice, for] it is of the letters termed مَجْهُورَة [or vocal], (L, TA, and Ḳ in art. غين,) and of those that are termed مُسْتَعْلِيَة [q. v.]; one should not reiterate the voice in uttering it, so as to exceed what is right, nor neglect exactness in respect of its place of utterance, so as to render it obscure, but should make it thoroughly distinct, and clear: it is not an augmentative letter: and [it is said that] it is not substituted [for another letter]: (Ḳ in art. غين:) [but this is a mistake; for] it is substituted for two letters; for خ, in غَطَرَ بِيَدِهِ, aor. يَغْطِرُ, meaning خَطَرَ, aor. يَخْطِرُ, mentioned by IJ and several others, (MF, TA,) and in غَطَرَ بِذَنَبِهِ for خَطَرَ; (TA in art. خطر;) and for ع, in لَغَنَّ for لَعَنَّ, mentioned by Ibn-Umm-Ḳásim and others, (MF, TA,) [and in نَشُوغٌ for نَشُوعٌ,] and in اِرْمَغَلَّ for اِرْمَعَلَّ, and also in الغَيْنُ as signifying "thirst" and "the clouds." (TA in art. غين.) ═ [As a numeral, it denotes *A thousand.*]

غب

1. غَبَّتِ الإِبِلُ, (Ṣ,) or المَاشِيَةُ, (Mṣb, Ḳ,) aor. ـِ, inf. n. غِبٌّ (Ṣ, Mṣb, Ḳ) and غُبُوبٌ, (Mṣb, Ḳ,) *The camels,* (Ṣ,) or *cattle,* (Mṣb, Ḳ,) *came to water,* (Ṣ,) or *drank,* (Mṣb, Ḳ,) *on alternate days; one day and not the next day.* (Ṣ, Mṣb, Ḳ.) — Hence, (IAth, TA,) غَبَّ said of a man means *He came visiting at intervals of some days,* or *after some days.* (AA, IAth, TA.) [See also غِبٌّ: and see غُبَيْشٌ.] — And غَبَّ عَنِ القَوْمِ, (Ks, Ṣ, Mṣb, Ḳ,) aor. ـُ, the verb in this case being of the class of قَتَلَ, [but this is contr. to analogy, as well as to the derivation,] inf. n. غِبٌّ, with kesr, *He came to the people,* or *party, day after day:* (Mṣb:) or, as also ↓ اغبّ القَوْمَ, *he came to the people,* or *party, on alternate days, coming one day and not the next:* (Ks, Ṣ, Ḳ:) or *he came to them once in two days* or *more.* (TA.) It is said in a trad., أَغِبُّوا ↓ فِى عِيَادَةِ المَرِيضِ وَأَرْبِعُوا *Visit ye the sick on alternate days and after intervals of two days:* (Ṣ, TA:) not every day, lest he find your visits to be troublesome. (TA. [See also art. ربع.]) And you say, أَغْبَبْتُهُ ↓, inf. n. إِغْبَابٌ, meaning *I visited him* [*once*] *in every week.* (A.) — And hence غَبَّتْ said of a fever. (Mṣb.) غَبَّتِ الحُمَّى and أَغَبَّتْ ↓ signify the same; (Ṣ:) you say, غَبَّتْ عَلَيْهِ الحُمَّى, *The fever came upon him,* (Mṣb,) or *attacked him,* (Ḳ,) *one day and intermitted one day;* (Mṣb, Ḳ;) as also أَغَبَّتْهُ ↓ and أَغَبَّتْ ↓ عَلَيْهِ. (Ḳ.) [See also غِبٌّ.] — You say also, غَبَّ عِنْدَنَا, (Ṣ, L, Ḳ,) and اغبّ ↓, (L, Ḳ,) *He passed the night,* or *a night, at our abode.* (Ṣ, L, Ḳ.) Hence the saying, رُوَيْدَ الشِّعْرَ يَغِبَّ [so accord. to the TA, حَتَّى being understood, accord. to the explanation of Meyd, but in the CḲ, and in one of my copies of the Ṣ, and in Freytag's Arab. Prov. i. 522, يُغَبَّ,] (Ṣ, Ḳ,) i. e. *Leave thou the poetry until some days shall have passed,* that thou mayest see what will be its result, whether it will be praised or dispraised: (Meyd, TA:) or it may be from غَبَّتْ said of a fever, and may thus mean, *leave thou the poetry to be kept back* from people, [or *to be intermitted,*] i. e. do not repeat it to people in an uninterrupted manner, lest they become weary. (Meyd. [See also art. رود.]) — And [hence] غَبَّ, (T, Ṣ, L, Mṣb, Ḳ,) aor. ـِ, (L, Mṣb,) inf. n. غِبٌّ and غَبٌّ and غُبُوبٌ and غُبُوبَةٌ, (L,) said of food, (L, Mṣb,) and of dates, or especially of flesh-meat as some say, (L,) *It remained throughout a night,* whether it became corrupt or not: (L, Mṣb:) and, said of food, *it became altered* [*for the worse*] *in its odour:* (L:) or, said of flesh-meat, *it became stinking;* (T, Ṣ, Ḳ;) as also اغبّ ↓: (T, Ḳ:) and *it* (a thing) *became corrupt.* (TA. [See also 2.]) — غَبَّتِ الأُمُورُ means *The affairs,* or *events, came to,* or *arrived at, their ends, conclusions, latter* or *last parts* or *states, issues,* or *results.* (Ṣ, TA.) — And غَبَّ الشَّىْءُ فِى نَفْسِهِ, aor. ـِ, inf. n. غِبٌّ, [app. meaning *The thing came into his mind,*] is a phrase mentioned by Th. (TA.)

2. غَبَّبَ فِى الحَاجَةِ, (Ṣ, O,) inf. n. تَغْبِيبٌ, (Ḳ,) *He was remiss;* or *did not exert himself,* or *act vigorously* or *strenuously;* (Ṣ, O, Ḳ;) *in the needful affair:* (Ṣ, O:) [and] so تغبّب ↓ فيها [if not a mistranscription]. (Thus in a copy of the A.) [Hence,] كَتَبَ إِلَيْهِ يُغَبِّبُ عَنْ هُلْكِ المُسْلِمِينَ, (TA,) or عَنْ هَلَاكِ المسلمين, (thus in the O,) ‡ *He wrote to him not acquainting him with the great number that had perished of the Muslims:* (O, TA:) a metaphorical mode of expression; as though he were remiss, or fell short, in making known the essential state of the case. (TA, from a trad.) — And غبّب signifies also *It* (a thing) *became very corrupt.* (TA. [See also 1, last sentence but two.]) ═ غَبَّبَ الشَّاةَ, (O, L,*) inf. n. as above, (L, Ḳ,) *He* (a wolf) *seized the sheep,* or *goat, by its throat,* (O, Ḳ,) *and fixed his canine teeth in it:* (O:) or *attacked the sheep,* or *goat, and broke its neck:* and also *left it with some remains of life in it.* (L.) And غبّب الذِّئْبُ فِى الغَنَمِ *The wolf made,* or *did, mischief among the sheep,* or *goats.* (TA.) — And [hence, app.,] غبّب عَنِ القَوْمِ, (Ṣ, O,) inf. n. as above, (Ḳ,) *He repelled from,* or *defended, the people,* or *party:* (Ṣ, O, Ḳ:) so say Ks and Th. (TA.)

4: see 1, in seven places. — You say also, لَا يُغِبُّنَا عَطَاؤُهُ *His gift will not come to us on alternate days,* but will come every day. (Ṣ, O, Ḳ.*) — And اغبّت الحَلُوبَةُ *The milch camel yielded milk on alternate days.* (A.) And اغبّت الإِبِلُ *The camels did not yield milk every day.* (TA.) — See again 1, last sentence but two. ═ اغبّ الإِبِلَ *He watered the camels on alternate days:* (Ṣ, O, Mṣb:*) from غِبٌّ [q. v.]. (Ṣ, O.) ═ And أَغَبَّنِى is said by Th to signify وَقَعَ بِى [app. meaning *He fell upon me* in fight]. (TA.)

[**5.** تغبّب is app. from الغِبُّ in the sense of العَاقِبَةُ, and thus syn. with تَعَقَّبَ signifying *He looked to the consequence, end, issue,* or *result,* of an affair: see its part. n. مُتَغَبِّبٌ, below.] — See [also] 2, first sentence.

8. اِغْتَبَّتِ الخَيْلُ; see اغتمّت.

R. Q. 1. غَبْغَبَ *He acted dishonestly in buying and selling.* (AA, TA.)

غُبٌّ A sea dashing so that it goes far, or runs, upon the land: (JK, K, TA:) pl. غُبَّان. (TA.) —— And Depressed land: pl. [of pauc.] أَغْبَابٌ and [of mult.] غُبُوبٌ (K, TA) and غُبَّان. (TA.)

غِبٌّ [a subst., like ظِمْءٌ,] A coming (of camels, S, O) to water on alternate days; coming to the water one day and not the next day: (S, O, K:) or after [being kept from it] a day and two nights: or pasturing one day and coming to the water the next day; and this is the غِبّ of the ass. (TA.) [And وِرْدُ الغِبِّ signifies The coming of camels to the water in the second of two nights (as is shown by the context of a passage in which it occurs in the S and O and K voce طَلَقٌ), or in the second of two days.] But the saying of a rájiz,

وَحُمَّرَاتٌ شُرْبُهُنَّ غِبُّ

means And hummarahs [a species of birds] whose drinking is every hour or every little while (كُلَّ سَاعَةٍ). (S, O.) —— Also [for سَيْرُ غِبٍّ] A journey of two days [whereof one is without any watering of the camels; i. e. in the case of which they are watered only on the first and third of three days]. (TA in art. نبج.) —— And A visiting once in every week: (S, O, K:) so says El-Hasan: (S, O:) or at intervals of some days: after some days: (AA, IAth: [see also its verb:]) from the same word used in relation to camels. (IAth.) One says, زُرْ غِبًّا تَزْدَدْ حُبًّا [or, accord. to common usage, حِبًّا, to assimilate it to غِبًّا, Visit once a week, or at intervals of some days; not frequently, or not every day: so thou shalt have more love: a prov., respecting which see Freytag's Arab. Prov. i. 587; where غُبًّا is put for غِبًّا]. (S, O.) [See another ex. voce تَرَجَّلَ, last sentence.] The saying of Zeyd-el-Fawáris

يَرَانِى العَدُوُّ بَعْدَ غِبِّ لِقَائِهِ

means [The enemy will see me] after the day of meeting with him by a day. (Ham p. 732.) —— And The coming, or attacking, of a fever one day and intermitting one day: from the same word used in relation to camels. (S, O, Msb.) —— And A tertian fever; that attacks one day and intermits one day: (K, TA:) you say حُمَّى غِبٌّ [a tertian fever]; using it as an epithet: (TA:) and حُمَّى الغِبِّ. (Msb in art. ثلث.) —— And The end; conclusion; latter, or last, part or state; issue; or result; syn. عَاقِبَةٌ, (S, A, MA, O, Msb, K,) and آخِرٌ; (S,* O,* TA;) of an affair, (S, A, O, Msb,) of any kind, (S, O,) or of a thing; (K;) as also ▼ مَغَبَّةٌ, (MA, O, Msb, K,) and ▼ مَغَبٌّ. (MA.) And [hence] غِبَّ means After; syn. بَعْدَ: thus in the phrases غِبَّ الأَذَانِ [After the call to prayer] and غِبَّ السَّلَامِ [After salutation or the salutation]: and one says,

غِبَّ الصَّبَاحِ يَحْمَدُ القَوْمُ السُّرَى

[After daybreak, the party commend night-journeying: but more commonly, عِنْدَ الصَّبَاحِ: see art. سرى]. (TA.) —— مَآءٌ غِبٌّ means Distant water: (A, TA:) and مِيَاهٌ أَغْبَابٌ distant waters. (A, K, TA.)

غُبَّةٌ A sufficiency of the means of subsistence: (O, K, TA:) and so غُفَّةٌ. (TA.) —— And غُبَّةُ, (S, O,) without ال, (K,) [and imperfectly decl.,] is the name of An eaglet that belonged to the Benoo-Yeshkur, (S, O, K,) and to which a certain story, or tradition, relates. (S, O.)

غَبَبٌ and ▼ غَبْغَبٌ The flesh that hangs down under the part beneath the chin and lower jaw: (K:) or what hangs down beneath that part of an ox or cow [i. e. the dewlap], and beneath the beak of the cock: (S, O:) and the wrinkled skin of the part where the lower hairs of the chin grow: and the former word, what hangs down under the part beneath the lower jaw of the ox or cow and of the sheep or goat: and the غبغب is [what hangs down under the part beneath the lower mandible] of the cock and of the bull [i. e. the wattle of the cock and the dewlap of the bull]: (Lth, TA:) and this is also used in relation to an old woman: (Ks, TA:) and, metaphorically, in relation to the chameleon: and in like manner in relation to the stallion-camel, [as meaning the part below the under jaw,] as the camel has really no غبغب: (TA:) [the pl. of غَبَبٌ is أَغْبَابٌ: see طِمْطِمٌ.]

غَبِيبٌ: see غَابٌّ. —— Also A small and narrow water-course, from the hard and elevated part of a mountain, or of a tract of land: or in plain, or level, land: (TA:) and a watercourse that is not deep, and in which are [trees of the species called] طَلْح: pl. [of pauc.] أَغِبَّةٌ and [of mult.] غُبَّان. (JK.) —— [And An affair or a business ("res, negotium"). (Freytag, from the Deewán of Jereer.)]

غَبِيبَةٌ Milk (S, O, K) of sheep or goats (S, O) drawn in the early morning, upon which other is milked at night, and which is then churned (S, O, K) on the morrow: (S, O:) [and] accord. to IAar, camel's milk such as is termed مَرُوبٌ [q. v.]: and the milk that is termed رَائِبٌ [q. v.]: (TA:) A'Obeyd is related on the authority of Sh to have assigned this last meaning to عَبِيبَة. (TA, voce عَبِيبَةٌ.)

غُبَيَّةٌ and غِبْيَةٌ: see عُبَيَّةٌ, in art. عب.

غَابٌّ [part. n. of غَبَّ]. You say إِبِلٌ غَابَّةٌ and غَوَابُّ Camels coming to water, or drinking, on alternate days. (As, S, O, K.) —— And Flesh-meat that has remained throughout a night: (S, O:) or stinking flesh-meat: (TA:) or food, and dates, and, as also ▼ غَبِيبٌ, flesh-meat, that has remained throughout a night, whether it have become corrupt or not: (L:) and applied also to bread. (S and K in art. بيت.) —— And نَجْمٌ غَابٌّ means A fixed star [app. because of its twinkling, or shining with intermitted light]. (A.)

غَبْغَبٌ: see غَبَبٌ. —— Also A place where victims are sacrificed: (O, TA:) or الغَبْغَبُ, (S, O, K, TA,) particularly, (TA,) a small mountain, (S, O, K, TA,) which is the place of sacrifice, (S, O,) in Minè: (S, K:) or the place in which was El-Lát, at Et-Táif: or the place where they used there to sacrifice to El-Lát: or غَبْغَبٌ is an appellation of any place of sacrifice in Minè. (TA.) —— And الغَبْغَبُ is the name of An idol (صَنَمٌ), (O, K, TA,) which they used to worship in the Time of Ignorance, and upon which (عَلَيْهِ) they used to sacrifice; (O, TA;*) and IDrd says that some called it العَبْعَب [q. v.], with the unpointed ع: (O:) or a stone which was set up before the idol, for, or [dedicated] to, Menáf, opposite the corner of the Black Stone [of the Kaabeh]; and there were two [whereof each was] thus called. (TA.)

تَغِبَّةٌ False testimony: (K, TA:) of the measure تَفْعِلَةٌ, [being originally تَغْبِبَةٌ,] from غَبَّ الذِّئْبُ فِى الغَنَمِ, or from غَبَّ signifying "it became very corrupt." (IAth, TA.)

رَجُلٌ مُغِبٌّ [A man having a tertian fever, as is indicated in the TA,] is mentioned on the authority of AZ, in the form of an act. part. n. (TA.) —— And المُغِبُّ means The lion. (O, K.)

مَغَبٌّ } see غِبٌّ, last sentence but two.
مَغَبَّةٌ }

مُغَبِّبَةٌ A ewe, or goat, that is milked on alternate days. (IAar, S, K.) —— And مُغَبَّبٌ A bull having a غَبَبٌ [or dewlap]. (Ham p. 293.)

[مُتَغَبِّبٌ app. A man looking to the consequence, end, issue, or result, of an affair; like مُتَعَقِّبٌ: see a verse in the Ham p. 154, and the verse next preceding it: and see its verb, above.]

غبث

1. غَبَثَ, (S, O,) aor. ـُ, (TK,) inf. n. غَبْثٌ, (S, O, K,) He moistened, and beat up, or mingled, [the preparation of curd called] أَقِط with clarified butter. (Fr, S, O, K.) [See also عَبَثَ, of which it is a dial. var.; and عَبَثَتِ المَرْأَةُ, and عَبَثَ الأَقِطَ.]

9. اِغْبَثَّ, inf. n. اِغْبِثَاثٌ, He, or it, was, or became, أَغْبَث, (S, O, K,) i. e., of a colour inclining to that of dust, (S,) or dust-coloured. (O.)

غُبْثَةٌ [formed by transposition from بُغْثَةٌ] A colour inclining to that of dust: (TA:) or dust-colour. (O.)

غَبِيثَةٌ [The preparation of curd called] أَقِط moistened, and beaten up, or mingled, with clarified butter. (Fr, S, O, K.) [See also عَبِيثَةٌ, of which it is a dial. var.] —— And I. q. عَبِيثَةٌ in its [other] meanings. (O,* K.)

أَغْبَثُ i. q. أَبْغَثُ, (S, O, K,) from which it is formed by transposition, (S, O,) Of a colour inclining to that of dust: (TA:) or dust-coloured. (O.)

غبر

1. غَبَرَ, (Ṣ, Mṣb, Ḳ,) aor. ُ, (Ṣ, Mṣb,) inf. n. غُبُورٌ, (Mṣb, Ḳ,) *He, or it,* (a thing, Ṣ) *remained, lasted,* or *continued:* (Ṣ, Mṣb, TA:) and (Mṣb) *he* (a man, JK) *tarried, stayed,* or *waited.* (JK, Zbd, Mṣb, Ḳ.) — And *He,* or *it, passed, passed away,* or *went away.* (Mṣb, Ḳ.) It is sometimes used in this latter sense; (Mṣb;) and thus it has two contr. significations. (Mṣb, Ḳ.) — And *It was future.* (KL.) = See also 9. = غَبِرَ: see 5, last two sentences. — Also, this last, aor. َ, (Ṣ, Ḳ,) inf. n. غَبَرٌ, (Ṣ,) said of a wound, (Ṣ, Ḳ,) *It was,* or *became, in a corrupt state:* (Ḳ:) or *it became in a healing state, and then became recrudescent:* (Ṣ:) or *it was always recrudescent:* and *it became in a healing state upon,* or *over, corruptness:* (IḲṭṭ, TA:) or *it healed externally while in a withering state internally.* (L.) — And [hence, perhaps,] غَبِرَ said of a man, † *He bore rancour, malevolence, malice,* or *spite;* or *hid enmity,* or *violent hatred, in his heart.* (IḲṭṭ, TA.)

2. غَبَّرَ النَّاقَةَ: see 5. — [Hence, app., as inf. n. of the pass. verb,] التَّغْبِيرُ signifies *The milk's becoming drawn up* or *withdrawn* [from the udder]. (TA.) = غَبَّرَهُ, inf. n. تَغْبِيرٌ, *He sullied,* or *sprinkled, him,* or *it, with dust.* (Ḳ.) — See also 4, in two places. — [Hence,] تَغْبِيرٌ signifies also *A reciting of poetry,* or *verses, in the praising,* or *glorifying, of God, in which the performers trill,* or *quaver, and prolong, the voice;* whence the epithet مُغَبِّرَةٌ; as though the persons thus called, being affected with a lively emotion, danced, and raised the dust: thus accord. to Lth: (TA:) or the *saying* لَا إِلٰهَ إِلَّا ٱللّٰهُ, (IDrd, IḲṭṭ, Ḳ, TA,) *in the praising,* or *glorifying, of God:* (Ḳ, TA:) or it signifies, (IDrd, TA,) or signifies also, (IḲṭṭ, Ḳ, TA,) the *reiterating the voice in reciting* [*the Ḳur-án*] *&c.* (IDrd, IḲṭṭ, Ḳ, TA) Esh-Sháfi'ee is related to have said that, in his opinion, this تغبير was instituted by the زَنَادِقَة [pl. of زِنْدِيقٌ, q. v.], in order that they might turn away [others thereby] from the [simple] praising, or glorifying, of God, and from the reciting of the Ḳur-án. (Az, TA.) = غَبَّرَ ضَيْفَهُ, inf. n. as above, *He gave his guest, to eat,* غُبْرَان [meaning *dates thus termed*]: (TA:) the verb thus used is like نَبَّجَ [and نَسَّجَ &c.]. (L, TA.) = مَا غَبَّرَتْ إِلَّا لِطَلَبِ المِرَآءِ is a saying mentioned by AZ [app. meaning *She did not oppose and then acquiesce save for the purpose of obstinate disputation*]: see غَبَرٌ. (TA.)

4. اغبر *He* (a man) *raised the dust;* (Ṣ, Mṣb, Ḳ;) as also ▼غَبَّرَ, (Ṣ, Ḳ,) inf. n. تَغْبِيرٌ. (Ṣ.) [Hence,] ▼غَبَّرَ فِى وَجْهِهِ [so, evidently, but written in the TA without any syll. signs, lit. *He raised the dust in his face;* meaning,] † *he outwent him; outstripped him; went,* or *got, before him.* (TA.) — And اغبر فى طلب الحاجة † *He strove, laboured, exerted himself,* or *employed himself vigorously* or *diligently, in seeking after the thing that he wanted;* (ISk, Ṣ, Ḳ;) *he hasted, made haste,* or *was quick, in doing so;* as though, by reason of his eagerness and quickness, he raised the dust. (TA.) — أَغْبَرْتُ فِى الشَّىْءِ † *I set about,* or *commenced, doing the thing.* (IḲṭṭ.) — أَغْبَرَتْ عَلَيْنَا السَّمَآءُ † *The sky rained upon us vehemently.* (Ṣ,* Ḳ,* TA.) = See also 9.

5. تغبّر النَّاقَةَ *He milked the camel, drawing what remained in her udder;* (Z, Ṣgh, Ḳ, TA;) as also ▼غَبَّرَهَا. (Ḥam p. 527.) — Hence the following saying, of a people who had increased and multiplied, on their being asked how it was that they had increased: كُنَّا لَا نَلْتَبِئُ الصَّغِيرَ وَلَا نَتَغَبَّرُ الكَبِيرَ † *We used not to take the first seed of the young, nor the remainder of the seed of the old;* meaning the marrying them, from eagerness to procreate. (TA. [But لَا is there omitted in both clauses, and نَلْتَبِسُ is put by mistake for نَلْتَبِئُ.]) [See also art. لبأ.] — And hence, (TA,) تغبّر مِنَ المَرْأَةِ وَلَدًا (Ṣ, Ḳ) † *He got offspring from the woman* [*she being old*]. (Ḳ.) It is related that a certain man, (Ṣ, Ḳ, TA,) an Arab of the desert, (Z,) 'Othmán, accord. to the Ḳ, but correctly, as in the Genealogies of Ibn-El-Kelbee, Ghanm (غَنْمٌ) with gheyn moved by fet-ḥ, and a quiescent noon, (TA,) the son of Ḥabeeb (Ḳ, TA) the son of Kaab the son of Bekr the son of Yeshkur the son of Wáïl, (TA,) married a woman advanced in age, (Ṣ, Z,) Rakáshi the daughter of 'Ámir, (Ḳ,) and it was said to him, "She is old:" (Ṣ,* Ḳ,* TA:) whereupon he said, لَعَلِّى أَتَغَبَّرُ مِنْهَا وَلَدًا (Ṣ, Ḳ) *May-be I shall get from her offspring:* (TA:) and when a son was born to him, he named him غُبَّرٌ, (Ṣ, Ḳ,) like عُمَّرٌ; (Ṣ;) and he became the father of a tribe. (TA.) = تغبّر also signifies *He,* or *it, became sullied,* or *sprinkled, with dust;* (TA;) as also ▼غَبِرَ. (L.) You say also ▼غَبِرَ التَّمْرُ *The dates,* or *dried dates, became dusty.* (TA.)

9. اغبرّ, (Ṣ, Ḳ,) inf. n. اِغْبِرَارٌ, (Ṣ,) *It was,* or *became, dust-coloured; of a colour like dust;* (Ṣ, Ḳ;) as also ▼غَبَرَ, (Ḳ,) inf. n. غُبُورٌ and غُبْرَةٌ; (TA;) and ▼اِغْبَارَّ, (Ḳ,) inf. n. اِغْبِيرَارٌ. (TA.) — *It* (a day) *became very dusty.* (Aboo-'Alee, Ḳ.)

غُبْرٌ *A remain, remainder, remnant, relic,* or *residue,* (Ṣ, Ḳ,) of a thing; (Ḳ;) generally, of the blood of the menses, (Ḳ,) and of milk in the udder: (Ṣ, Ḳ:) as also ▼غُبَّرٌ: (Mṣb, Ḳ:) or ▼غُبَّرٌ is a pl. of غُبْرٌ: [but if so it is extr.:] (TA:) or the pl. of غُبْرٌ is أَغْبَارٌ: (Ṣ, Ḳ:) and ▼غُبَّرٌ is pl. of ▼غَابِرٌ [used as an epithet in which the quality of a subst. is predominant]; (A'Obeyd, TA;) and signifies *remains,* &c.: (A'Obeyd, Ṣ, TA:) and ▼غُبَّرَاتٌ is a pl. pl.; i. e., pl. of ▼غُبَّرٌ. (A'Obeyd, TA.) You say بِهَا غُبْرٌ مِنْ لَبَنٍ *In her* (the camel) *is a remain of milk.* (Ṣ.) And ▼غُبَّرُ الحَيْضِ signifies *The remains* [of the blood] *of the menses;* (Ṣ;) as also غُبْرَةٌ. (Ḥam p. 37.) And غُبَّرُ المَرَضِ *The remains of the disease.* (Ṣ.) And in like manner, غُبَّرُ اللَّيْلِ (Ṣ) *The last part,* and *the remains, of the night.* (TA.) It is said in a trad. of 'Amr Ibn-El-'Áṣ, مَا تَأَبَّطَتْنِى الإِمَآءُ وَلَا حَمَلَتْنِى البَغَايَا فِى غُبَّرَاتِ ▼ المَآلِى [*Female slaves did not carry me under their armpits,*] i. e., female slaves did not have the office of rearing me, *nor did prostitutes carry me in the remains of the rags used for the menses.* (TA.) And in another trad., فَلَمْ يَبْقَ إِلَّا غُبَّرَاتٌ ▼ مِنْ أَهْلِ الكِتَابِ, or ▼غُبَّرُ أَهْلِ الكِتَابِ, accord. to different relations, i. e. *And there remained not save remains of the people of the Scripture,* or *the remains &c.* (TA.) And in a trad. of Mo'áwiyeh, بِفِنَائِهِ أَعْنُزٌ دَرُّهُنَّ غُبْرٌ [*In the court of his house were some she-goats whose flow of milk was a mere remain* of what it had been,] meaning, *little.* (L.) [See also غَابِرٌ.]

غِبْرٌ † *Rancour, malevolence, malice,* or *spite;* or *concealed enmity and violent hatred:* (Ḳ, TA:) like غِمْرٌ. (TA.)

غَبَرٌ *A remaining, lasting,* or *continuance;* (TA;) and so ▼مَغْبَرٌ. (Ḥam p. 225.) — [And by some of the grammarians it is used as signifying The *future:* see also غَابِرٌ.] = Also *A certain disease in the interior of the foot of a camel.* (Ḳ.) — And *A morbid affection* in a vein, *that will hardly,* or *in nowise, be cured.* (TA.) [See also غَبِرٌ.] — دَاهِيَةُ الغَبَرِ (said by A'Obeyd to be from the phrase جُرْحٌ غَبِرٌ [q. v.], TA) means *A calamity,* or *misfortune,* (JK, Ṣ, Ḳ,) *of great magnitude,* (Ṣ,) *which,* (JK, Ṣ,) or *the like whereof,* (Ḳ,) *is such that no way of escape therefrom will be found:* (JK, Ṣ,* Ḳ:*) or *a trial,* or *an affliction, that will hardly,* or *in nowise, depart:* (TA:) or *a person who opposes thee, disagreeing with thee, and then returns,* or *has regard, to thy saying;* (Ḳ, TA;) whence the saying, mentioned by AZ, مَا غَبَّرَتْ إِلَّا لِطَلَبِ المِرَآءِ. (TA. [See 2, last sentence.]) — صَمَّآءُ الغَبَرِ, occurring in a verse of El-Hirmázee in praise of El-Mundhir Ibn-Járood, to whom it is applied, is expl. by Z as meaning *The serpent that dwells near to a small water in a place where it collects and stagnates, and that will not be approached.* (TA.) And [it is said that] الغَبَرُ signifies *Water little in quantity.* (O.) = Also *Dust,* or *earth;* syn. تُرَابٌ. (Ḳ.) [See also غُبَارٌ.]

جُرْحٌ غَبِرٌ *A wound in a corrupt state:* (Ḳ:) or *that becomes in a healing state upon,* or *over, corruptness, and then becomes recrudescent after having healed.* (TA.) — Hence, عِرْقٌ غَبِرٌ *A vein constantly becoming recrudescent;* (Ṣ, TA;) called in Pers. [and hence in Arabic] نَاسُور [q. v.]. (TA.) = نَاقَةٌ غَدِرَةٌ غَبِرَةٌ *A she-camel that remains,* or *lags, behind the other camels in being driven.* (L in art. غدر.)

غُبْرٌ *A kind* [or *species*] *of fish;* as also ▼غُوبَرٌ. (O, Ḳ.)

غَبْرَةٌ *A sullying,* or *sprinkle, of,* or *with, dust.* (TA.)

غُبْرَةٌ *Dust-colour; a colour like dust:* (Ṣ, L, Ḳ:) and *a dusty hue of complexion* arising from grief or anxiety and the like. (L.) — See also غُبَار.

غَبَرَة : see غُبَار : — and see also أَغْبَرُ, latter half.

غَبْرَآءُ : see غُبَيْرَآءُ. [For other meanings, see the masc., أَغْبَرُ.]

غُبْرَانٌ *Two ripe dates upon one base;* pl. غَبَارِينُ : (Ḳ, TA:) so says A'Obeyd: or *two, or three, full-grown unripe dates upon one base;* and it has no pl. of its own radical letters: or, accord. to AḤn, *several small green dates that come forth upon one base.* (TA.)

غُبْرُورٌ *A certain small bird of the passerine kind,* (O, L, Ḳ, TA,) *dust-coloured:* (O, L, TA:) so says AḤát in the "Book of Birds:" pl. غَبَارِيرُ: (O:) it is the same as is mentioned in an earlier part of this art. in the Ḳ by the name of † غُبْرُونٌ, which is a mistranscription. (TA.)

غُبْرُونٌ : see what next precedes.

غُبَارٌ and † غَبَرَةٌ signify the same, (Ṣ, L, Ḳ,) as also † غُبْرَةٌ; (IAar, Ḳ;) i. e. *Dust;* syn. رَهَجٌ: (L:) or the first, *dust raised and spreading:* (L:) or *what remains of dust raised and spreading:* (B, TA:) and the second, the *moving to and fro of dust.* (L.) — You say طَلَبَ فُلَانًا فَمَا شَقَّ غُبَارَهُ † [*He pursued after such a one but did not cleave his dust;*] i. e., *he did not overtake him.* (TA.) And مَا يُشَقُّ غُبَارُهُ, and مَا يُخَطُّ غُبَارُهُ, † *He is not to be outgone, outstripped,* or *got before.* (TA.) [See also بَاعَ فُلَانٌ عَلَى بَيْعِ فُلَانٍ, in art. بيع.] — لَا غُبَارَ عَلَيْهِ † [*There is no dust upon it;* meaning, *it* (a phrase or the like) *is clear,* or *perspicuous,* or *free from obscurity;* like the saying لَا عَفَرَ فِيهِ, or لَا عَفَرَ لَهُ]. (TA, in many places.)

غُبَيْرٌ *A sort of dates.* (Ḳ, TA.)

غُبَيْرَآءُ [dim. of غَبْرَآءُ]: see أَغْبَرُ, in two places. — Also *A certain plant* [or *tree*], (Ḳ,) *well known,* (Ṣ,) *growing in the plains;* (TA;) [the *service-tree,* or *sorb:* or *its fruit:* so called in the present day: as is also the "inula undulata:"] and so † غَبْرَآءُ: (Ḳ:) so called *because of the colour of its leaves; the fruit of which, when it appears, becomes intensely red:* (TA:) or the former is the *tree,* and the latter is the *fruit:* or the converse is the case: (Ḳ:) the sing. and pl. are alike: all this says AḤn, in his "Book of Plants." (TA.) — Also *A kind of beverage,* (شَرَاب, Ṣ, Ḳ, or نَبِيذ, Mṣb,) *which intoxicates, made by the Abyssinians,* (Ṣ,) *from* ذُرَة [or *millet*]; (Ṣ, Mṣb, Ḳ;) also called سُكُرْكَة: (Mgh, Mṣb, Ḳ:) or *wine* [or *cider*] *made from the well-known fruit of the same name* [*the service-apple*]. (Th, TA.) [See also مِزْرٌ.] It is said in a trad., إِيَّاكُمْ وَالْغُبَيْرَآءَ فَإِنَّهَا خَمْرُ الْعَالَمِ (Ṣ, Mgh, TA) *Avoid ye the beverage called* غبيراء; *for it is* like *the wine* that is commonly known *of all men:* there is no distinction to be made between the two drinks (Mgh, TA) with respect to prohibition. (TA.) In another trad., it is called غُبَيْرَآءُ السُّكَّرِ; to distinguish it from a kind of غبيراء made of dates, or dried dates. (Mgh.)

غُبُرٌ and غُبَّرَاتٌ : see غُبْرٌ, passim.

غَابِرٌ *Remaining; lasting; continuing:* (Az, Ṣ, IAmb, Mgh:) this is the sense in which it is used by the Arabs: (Az:) or it is the meaning most commonly obtaining among them: (IAmb:) *tarrying; staying; waiting:* pl. غُبَّرٌ: (Ḳ:) and the pl. of غَابِرَةٌ is غَوَابِرُ. (TA.) You say قَوْمٌ غُبَّرٌ [*A people remaining, &c.*]. (TA.) And غُبَّرُ النَّاسِ *The later of mankind.* (TA.) And هُوَ غَابِرُ بَنِى فُلَانٍ *He is the relic of the sons of such a one.* (TA.) And الغَابِرُ مِنَ اللَّيْلِ *What remains of the night.* (TA.) And جَوْفُ اللَّيْلِ الغَابِرُ *The last division of the night.* (Mgh.) And العَشْرُ الغَوَابِرُ مِنْ شَهْرِ رَمَضَانَ *The remaining,* or *last, ten* nights *of the month of Ramaḍán.* (TA.) And قَطَعَ اللّٰهُ غَابِرَهُ وَدَابِرَهُ [*May God cut off the last, and what remains, of him,* or *it:* or *may God extirpate him*]. (TA.) See also غُبْرٌ. — *Passing; passing away; going away: past:* syn. مَاضٍ; (Az, Ṣ, IAmb, Mgh;) or ذَاهِبٌ: (Ḳ:) so accord. to some of the lexicologists: (Az:) or so used sometimes, as, for instance, by the poet El-Aạshà: (IAmb:) thus it bears two contr. significations. (Ṣ.) You say, أَنْتَ غَابِرٌ غَدًا وَذِكْرُكَ غَابِرٌ أَبَدًا [*Thou passest away to-morrow, but thy fame remaineth for ever*]. (TA.) — [*Future* time. See an ex. in the first of the verses cited voce حَيْثُ. The meaning of "remaining" seems equally appropriate in that verse: but غابر is often used by grammarians in the last of the senses expl. above.]

غَوْبَرٌ : see غُبْرٌ.

الغَابِرَةُ means البَاقِيَةُ [*The lasting,* or *everlasting, state of existence*]; (Ḳ, TA;) i. e. الآخِرَةُ [*the latter,* or *last, state*]. (TA.)

أَغْبَرُ *Dust-coloured; of a colour like dust:* (Ṣ:) [fem. غَبْرَآءُ: and pl. غُبْرٌ.] — الأَغْبَرُ † *The wolf;* (Ḳ, TA;) because of his [dusty] colour: like الأَغْثَرُ. (TA.) — And الغَبْرَآءُ † *The female of the* حَجَل [or *partridge*]. (Ḳ.) — Also (الغَبْرَآءُ) ‡ *The earth;* (Ṣ, IAth, Mṣb, Ḳ;) because of its dusty colour; or because of the dust that is upon it: (TA:) opposed to الخَضْرَآءُ, which means "the sky," or "heaven." (IAth.) — And you say, جَآءَ عَلَى غَبْرَآءِ الظَّهْرِ † *He came on foot:* (Z, TA:) [i. e.] *he came upon the earth,* or *ground;* and so جَآءَ عَلَى غُبَيْرَآءِ † الظَّهْرِ: (M, TA:) or the latter means, *he returned without his having obtained,* or *attained, anything:* (T, TA:) or *he returned without his having been able to accomplish the object of his want.* (El-Aḥmar, TA.) And تَرَكَهُ عَلَى غُبَيْرَآءِ † الظَّهْرِ † *He left him in the possession of nothing:* (M, TA:) accord. to Zeyd Ibn-Kethweh, it is said by one who has contended in an altercation with another and overcome him so as to become master of all that was in his hands: in all the copies of the Ḳ, [probably in consequence of an omission by an early transcriber,] it is expl. as meaning *he returned disappointed,* or *unsuccessful;* and so تركه على غَبْرَآءِ الظهر. (TA.) — بَنُو الغَبْرَآءِ † *The poor, needy,* or *indigent;* (Ṣ, IB, Ḳ, TA;) [to which is strangely added in one of my copies of the Ṣ and the *guests;*] so called because of their cleaving to the dust: (IB, TA:) and غَبْرَآءُ النَّاسِ likewise means *the poor of mankind:* or, as some say, the former means *strangers from their homes:* (TA:) or *strangers,* (Ḳ,) or *persons,* (TA,) *who assemble together for* [*the drinking of*] *beverage,* or *wine, without mutual acquaintance:* (Ḳ, TA:) or *persons who contribute equally to the expenses which they have to incur in journeys:* all of these meanings have been assigned to it in explaining a verse of Ṭarafeh: [see EM p. 85:] and it is also expl. in the A as meaning *persons of whom one knows not to what family,* or *tribe, they belong:* (TA:) and [it is said that] ابْنُ غَبْرَآءَ signifies *the thief,* or *robber.* (T in art. بنى.) — غَبْرَآءُ also signifies † Land *abounding with coverts of the kind termed* خَمَر [q. v.]: (TA:) and *land abounding with trees;* (Ḳ;) or so أَرْضٌ غَبْرَآءُ; (TA;) as also † غَبَرَةٌ. (Ḳ.) — Also † *Herbage in plain,* or *soft, land.* (Ṣgh, Ḳ.) [This is said in the TA to be more probably with ث; but I do not find any meaning like this assigned to غَثْرَآءُ.] — And † *A species of plant.* (Ṣ. [App. that called غُبَيْرَآءُ, q. v.]) — وَطْأَةٌ غَبْرَآءُ † *A footstep,* or *footprint, that is becoming obliterated,* or *effaced:* (Ṣ, A, Ḳ:) or *such as is recent.* (Ḳ. [See also دَهْمَآءُ, voce أَدْهَمُ.]) — And عِزٌّ أَغْبَرُ † *Might departing;* (Ḳ, TA;) *becoming effaced.* (TA.) — سَنَةٌ غَبْرَآءُ † *A year of drought;* (IAth, Ḳ;) *a year in which is no rain:* (TA in art. شهب:) pl. غُبْرٌ: so called because of the dustiness of the tracts of the horizon therein from paucity [or want] of rain, and of the ground from there being no herbage. (IAth.) — And جُوعٌ أَغْبَرُ † *Severe hunger* or *famine.* (TA.)

مُغْبَرٌ : see غُبْرٌ, first sentence.

مُغْبِرٌ A camel *the interior of whose foot is in a withering state.* (Aṣ, TA.)

مُغَبِّرَةٌ *A party of men praising,* or *glorifying, God, by saying* لَا إِلٰهَ إِلَّا اللّٰهُ, and *reiterating the the voice in reciting* [*the Ḳur-án*] *&c.:* (Lth, Ḳ, TA:) accord. to Zj, (TA,) so called because of their exciting men to be desirous of the غَابِرَة, which means the بَاقِيَة [or lasting, or everlasting, state of existence], (Ḳ, TA,) and to be undesirous of the evanescent, which is the present, state. (TA.) [See 2.]

مِغْبَارٌ A palm-tree (نَخْلَةٌ) *that becomes overspread with dust.* (AḤn, Ḳ.) — And A she-camel *that abounds with milk after the abounding therewith of those that have brought forth with her.* (Ḳ.)

مُغْبُورٌ *i. q.* مُغْثُورٌ [q. v.]: (Kr, Ḳ:) the latter is the more approved term. (TA.)

غبس

1. غَبِسَ, (Ḳ,) aor. ـَ, (TḲ,) inf. n. غَبَسٌ; (TA;) and غَبُسَ, aor. ـُ, inf. n. غُبْسٌ and غُبْسَةٌ; (IḲṭṭ,

TA;) and ▼ أَغْبَسَ, (Ḳ,) in some copies of the Ḳ, erroneously, اِغْبَسَّ; (TA;) and ▼ اِغْبَاسَّ; (Aṣ, Ḳ;) *It* (the night, TA) *was*, or *became, dark.* (Ḳ.) [See also غَبِشَ.] — غَبَسَ وَجْهَهُ *He blackened his face.* (TA.)

4: see 1. — اغبس الذِّئْبُ, inf. n. إِغْبَاسٌ, [*The wolf was*, or *became, of the colour termed* غَبَس, *and* غُبْسَة.] (TA.)

11: see the first paragraph.

غَبَسٌ The *darkness of the end*, or *last part, of the night;* as also غَبَشٌ: (Lth:) or the *darkness of the beginning*, or *first part*, of the night; and غبش, that of the end, or last part, thereof: (TA:) or the former has the first of the above-mentioned significations; as also غَلَسٌ; and غبش, the second of those significations. (El-Khaṭṭábee, MF.) [See also غَبَشٌ.] And *Darkness* [absolutely]; as also ▼ غُبْسَةٌ: or ▼ both signify *whiteness in which is a duskiness* or *dinginess:* (Ḳ:) or the former, (Ṣ,) and ▼ the latter, (A,) *a colour like that of ashes;* (Ṣ, A;) i. e., *whiteness in which is a duskiness* or *dinginess:* (Ṣ:) or ▼ the latter, *a hue between dust-colour inclining to black and dust-colour properly so called:* (IDrd:) or *a colour between black and yellow.* (TA.) [See also غَلَسٌ.]

غُبْسَةٌ: see غَبَسٌ, in four places.

لَا آتِيكَ مَا غَبَا غُبَيْسٌ means *I will not come to thee ever:* (Ṣ, Ḳ:) but the origin of this saying is unknown: (Ḳ:) IAạr said that he knew it not: (Ṣ:) or, accord. to him, it means, *while time lasts:* it seems that he did not know it at first, and then thus explained it: (T, TA:) accord. to some, غُبَيْسٌ is an abbreviated dim. of أَغْبَس, and means *the wolf;* (Ṣ, Ḳ;*) and غَبَا is originally غَبَّ, the ا being substituted for one of the letters of duplication, as in تَقَضَّى for تَقَضَّضَ; (Ṣ;) and the saying means *I will not come to thee as long as the wolf comes now and then* (يَأْتِى غِبًّا) *to the sheep* or *goats.* (Ṣ, Ḳ.*)

أَغْبَسُ *Ash-coloured;* (Mgh;) *of a colour like that of ashes;* (Ṣ;) *of a dingy*, or *dusky, white;* applied to a wolf: (Ṣ, Ḳ:) or it is an epithet applied to any wolf: or, applied to a wolf, *light*, or *active, and greedy:* fem. غَبْسَآءُ: (TA:) pl. غُبْسٌ. (Ḳ.) — Applied to an ass, *Black.* (TA.) — وَرْدٌ أَغْبَسُ, applied to a horse, [app., *Of a dusky bay colour;*] i. q. سَمَنْد; (Mgh, Ḳ;) *what the Persians call by the latter term:* (Ṣ, TA:) it is [a colour] desired by them. (TA.)

غبش

1. غَبِشَ, aor. ـَ, (inf. n. غَبَشٌ; TḲ) and ▼ أَغْبَشَ; *It* (the night) *had somewhat remaining of it:* (Ḳ, TḲ:) or *was dark in its end*, or *last part*, (O, Ḳ, TḲ,) *with a darkness intermixed with whiteness:* (TḲ:) or both of these verbs; (TA;) or غَبِشَ, (aor. ـَ; TA) and ▼ أَغْبَشَ; (A'Obeyd, O, TA;) *it* (the night) *was*, or *became, dark*, (A'Obeyd, O, TA,) *in its end.* (O.) [See also غَبِسَ, below: and see غَبَسَ.] — غَبَشَهُ, (aor. ـِ, TA) i. q. غَشَمَهُ [*He wronged him*, &c.]. (Aboo-Málik, O, TA. [See also 5.]) — And *He deceived him*, عَنْ حَاجَتِهِ [*of the object of his want*]. (Lḥ, O, TA.)

4: see 1, in two places.

5. تغبّشهُ *He wronged him:* (O, Ḳ: [see also 1:]) or *he made a false claim upon him:* (Ḳ, TA:) or so تغبّشهُ بِدَعْوَى بَاطِلَةٍ: (O:) so says Aṣ: (O, TA:) and تعبّشهُ is a dial. var. thereof. (TA.)

غَبَشٌ The *darkness* [or *duskiness*] *of the end*, or *last part, of the night;* (Ṣ, Ḳ;) as also ▼ غُبْشَةٌ: (Ḳ, TA:) or *of the part next to daybreak:* or *when daybreak commences:* and sometimes *in the beginning*, or *first part, of the night:* (TA:) or the *remains of darkness mixed with the whiteness of daybreak, so that the true dawn* (الخَيْطُ الأَبْيَضُ) *becomes distinguished from the false dawn* (الخَيْطُ الأَسْوَدُ); as also غَبَسٌ and غَلَسٌ: (Az, TA:) or *a remaining portion of the night;* (Ṣ, Ḳ;) as also غَبَشُ الصُّبْحِ: (Mgh:) or *intense darkness:* pl. أَغْبَاشٌ. (Ṣ, Mgh, Ḳ.) أَغْبَاشُ اللَّيْلِ and غَامِسُ, both signify *The remains of the night.* (Yaạḳoob, TA.) [See also غَبَسٌ.]

غَبِشٌ: see أَغْبَشُ.

غُبْشَةٌ: see غَبَشٌ. — Also *Intense blackness with smoothness;* like دُلْمَةٌ; in the colours of beasts or horses and the like. (TA.)

غَابِشٌ *A wronger*, &c., syn. غَاشِمٌ, (AZ, O, TA,) in the Ḳ, erroneously, غَامِسٌ, (TA,) of others: (AZ, O, TA:) and *a dishonest adviser*, syn. غَاشٌّ, (Ḳ, TA,) of them: (TA:) and *a deceiver.* (Ḳ, TA.)

أَغْبَشُ A *dark* night; as also ▼ غَبِشٌ. (IDrd, Ḳ.) — A beast or horse or the like *of the colour termed* غُبْشَةٌ: fem. غَبْشَآءُ. (TA.)

غبط

1. غَبَطَهُ aor. ـِ, (Ṣ, Ḳ,) inf. n. غَبْطٌ, (Ṣ,) *He felt with his hand his* (a ram's) أَلْيَة [i. e. *rump*, or *tail*, or *fat of the tail*,] *in order to see if he were fat or not:* (Ṣ, Ḳ:) and *he felt it* (his back) *with his hand in order to know whether he were lean or fat:* (Lth, Ḳ:*) and in like manner the verb is used in relation to a she-camel. (TA.) — غَبَطَهُ, aor. ـِ; (ISk, Az, Ṣ, Mṣb, Ḳ;) and غَبِطَهُ, aor. ـَ; (Ibn-Buzurj, Ṣgh, Ḳ;) inf. n. غَبْطٌ (ISk, Az, Ṣ, Mṣb, Ḳ) and غِبْطَةٌ, (Ṣ, Ḳ,) or the latter is a simple subst.; (Mṣb;) *He regarded him* [*with unenvious emulation*, i. e.] *with a wish for the like of his condition*, (ISk, Az, Ṣ,) meaning a good condition, (Az,) or *for the like of that which he had attained*, (Mṣb,) or *for a blessing*, (Ḳ,) *and that it might not pass away*, (ISk, Ḳ,) or *without desiring that it should pass away*, (Az, Ṣ, Mṣb,) *from the latter person:* (ISk, Az, Ṣ, Mṣb, Ḳ:) the doing so is not حَسَدٌ, (Az, Ṣ, Mṣb,) for this implies the desire that what is wished for may pass away from its possessor; (Az, Mṣb;) or it is a kind of حَسَد, of a more moderate quality: (Az:) or غِبْطَةٌ and غَبْطٌ have the signification shown above, and are also *syn. with* حَسَدٌ; (Ḳ;) this latter meaning is assigned to غَبْط by IAạr; and it is said that the Arabs use غَبْط in the sense of حَسَد metonymically; (TA;) [so that غَبَطَهُ and غَبِطَهُ may also mean ‡ *he envied him;* &c.; see an ex. in a prov. cited voce بَطْنٌ; but it is said that] حَسَدٌ, when it is for courage and the like, is syn. with غِبْطَةٌ, and then it implies admiration, without a wish that the thing admired may pass away from its possessor. (Mṣb in art. حسد.) You say, غَبَطَهُ بِهِ, (Ṣ,) and عَلَيْهِ, (IAth,) and فِيهِ, (Mṣb,) *He regarded him with a wish for the like of it*, meaning a thing or state which he had attained, *without desiring that it should pass away from the latter person.* (Ṣ, IAth,* Mṣb.) Mohammad was asked, "Does الغَبْط injure?" and he answered, "Yes, like as الخَبْط injures:" or, accord. to the relation of A'Obeyd, "No, save as الخَبْط injures the [trees called] عِضَاه:" (Az, TA:) [see خَبَطَ:] by الغبط meaning, accord. to some, الحَسَد: (TA:) or a kind thereof, of a more moderate quality; injurious, but not so injurious as الحسد whereby one wishes that a blessing may pass away from his brother; الخبط meaning the beating off the leaves of trees; after which they become replaced, without there resulting any injury therefrom to the stock and branches: moreover, الغبط sometimes occasions the smiting of its object with the evil eye. (Az, TA.) [See also غِبْطَةٌ, below.] — Accord. to IḲṭṭ, غَبَطَ signifies also *He lied;* but perhaps it is a mistranscription for عَبَطَ, which has this meaning; for it is not mentioned by any other. (TA.)

2. It is said in a trad., جَآءَ وَهُمْ يُصَلُّونَ فَجَعَلَ يُغَبِّطُهُمْ; thus it is related, meaning, [*He came to them while they were praying, and he began*] *to incite them to wish for the like* of that action: if related without teshdeed, [يَغْبِطُهُمْ,] the meaning is, *to regard them with a wish for the like condition*, because of their forwardness to prayer. (Nh, Ḳ.)

4: see 8. — اغبط الرَّحْلَ عَلَى ظَهْرِ البَعِيرِ, (Ṣ,) or على الدَّابَّةِ, (Ḳ,) *He kept the saddle constantly* (Ṣ, Ḳ) *upon the back of the camel*, (Ṣ,) or *upon the beast*, (Ḳ,) *not putting it down from him.* (Ṣ.) — إِغْبَاطٌ also signifies The *continuing constantly riding.* (ISk.) And أَغْبَطُوا عَلَى رِكَابِهِمْ فِى السَّيْرِ *They kept the saddles on their travelling-camels night and day, not putting them down, in journeying.* (ISh.) — Hence, (A, TA,) أَغْبَطَتْ عَلَيْهِ الحُمَّى ‡ *The fever continued upon him;* (Ṣ, Ḳ, TA;) *as though it set the* غَبِيط *upon him, to ride him;* like as you say, رَكِبَتْهُ الحُمَّى, and اِرْتَحَلَتْهُ, and اِمْتَطَتْهُ: (A, TA:) or *clave to him:* (TA:) or *did not quit him for some days;* as also أَغْمَطَتْ, and أَرْدَمَتْ. (Aṣ.) — And أَغْبَطَتِ السَّمَآءُ ‡ *The sky rained continually.* (Ṣ, Mṣb, Ḳ, TA.)

And أَغْبَطَ عَلَيْنَا المَطَرُ ‡ *The rain continued upon us incessantly, rain following close upon rain.* (Aboo-Kheyreh.) — And أَغْبَطَ النَّبَاتُ ‡ *The herbage covered the land, and became dense, as though it were from a single grain.* (Ḳ, TA.)

8. اغتبط *He was, or became, regarded [with unenvious emulation, i. e.,] with a wish for the like of his condition, without its being desired that it should pass away from him:* (Ṣ:) or *he was, or became, in such a condition that he was regarded with a wish for the like thereof, without its being desired that it should pass away from him:* (Táj el-Maṣádir, TA:) or *he rejoiced,* or *became rejoiced, in being in a good condition;* (Ḳ;) or *in blessing bestowed upon him:* (TA:) or *he was grateful,* or *thankful, to God for blessing,* or *bounty, bestowed upon him:* (L:) and the same, (Ḳ,) or ↓ أُغْبِطَ, inf. n. إِغْبَاطٌ, accord. to the L, (TA,) *he was, or became, in a good state* or *condition; in a state of happiness;* (L, Ḳ;) *and of enjoyment,* or *wellbeing.* (L.) You say, لَقِيَ مَا يُغْتَبَطُ عَلَيْهِ [*He met with, or experienced, that for which one would be regarded with unenvious emulation,* i. e., *with a wish to be in the like condition, without its being desired that it should pass away from him*]. (TA in art. فوز.) — The saying,

خَوَّى قَلِيلًا غَيْرَ مَا آغْتِبَاطِ

cited by Th, but not expl. by him, is held by ISd to mean [*He* (referring to a camel) *lay down,* or *did so making his belly to be separated somewhat from the ground*], not resting *upon a wide* غَبِيط [q. v.] *of ground,* but upon a place not even, and not depressed. (TA.)

غَبْطٌ [originally an inf. n.]: see غِبْطَةٌ. — Also, and ↓ غِبْطٌ, *Handfuls of reaped corn* or *seed-produce:* pl. غُبُوطٌ, (Ḳ, TA,) and, it is said, غُبُطٌ: or [rather] accord. to Eṭ-Ṭáifee, غُبُوطٌ signifies the *handfuls which, when the wheat is reaped, are put one by one;* and غَبْطٌ is the sing.: or, as AḤn says, غُبُوطٌ signifies the *scattered handfuls of reaped corn* or *seed-produce;* one of which is termed غَبْطٌ. (TA.)

غِبْطٌ: see the next preceding paragraph.

غُبْطَةٌ *A strap in the* [*leathern water-bag called*] مَزَادَة, (Ibn-'Abbád, O, Ḳ,) *like the* شِرَاك [*of the sandal*], (Ibn-'Abbád, O,) *which is put upon the extremities of the two skins* [*whereof the* مزادة *is mainly composed*] *and then strongly sewed.* (Ibn-'Abbád, O, Ḳ.)

غِبْطَةٌ *A good state* or *condition;* (Ṣ, L, Mṣb, Ḳ;) *a state of happiness;* (L, Ḳ;) *and of enjoyment,* or *wellbeing;* (L;) as also ↓ غَبْطٌ, in the saying, اَللّٰهُمَّ غَبْطًا لَا هَبْطًا, meaning, *O God,* we ask of Thee *a good state* or *condition* [&c.], (Ṣ, Ḳ,) and we put our trust in Thee for preservation *that we may not be brought down from our state,* (Ṣ, TA,) or *that we may not be abased and humbled:* (TA:) or *place us in a station for which we may be regarded* [*with unenvious emulation,* i. e.,] *with a wish to be in the like condition without its being desired that it should pass away from us,* (Ḳ,* TA,) and *remove from us the stations of abasement and humiliation:* (TA:) or [we ask of Thee] *exaltation, not humiliation;* and *increase of* thy *bounty, not declension nor diminution.* (TA.) [See also 1, second sentence.]

سَمَآءٌ غَبْطَى ‡ *A sky raining continually* (Jm, Ḳ) *during two or three days;* (Jm;) as also غَمْطَى. (TA.)

غَبُوطٌ A she-camel *whose fatness is not to be known unless she be felt with the hand.* (Ḳ, TA.)

غَبِيطٌ *A* [*camel's saddle of the kind called*] رَحْل, (Ṣ, Mṣb,) *for women,* (Ṣ,) *upon which the* [*vehicle called*] هَوْدَج *is bound:* (Ṣ, Mṣb:) or *an elegant kind of* رَحْل, *depressed in its middle:* (TA:) or *a vehicle like the pads* (أُكُف [in the CḲ, erroneously, أَكُفّ]) *of the* [*species of camels called*] بَخَاتِىّ, (Ḳ,) *which is tented over with a* [*framework such as is called*] شِجَاز, *and is for women of birth:* (Az, TA:) or, as some say, *of which the pad* (قَتَب) *is made not in the* [*usual*] *make of pads* (أَقْتَاب): (TA:) or *a* رحل *of which the pad* (قَتَب) *and the* [*curved wooden parts called*] أَحْنَآء *are one* [i. e., app., *conjoined*]: (Ḳ:) pl. غُبُطٌ. (Ṣ, Mṣb, Ḳ.) The pl. is also applied to the *pieces of wood in camels' saddles;* and to such are likened Persian bows, (Ṣ, TA,) because of their curvature. (IAth.) — [Hence,] † *Depressed land* or *ground:* (Ṣ, Ḳ:) or *a wide and even tract of land of which the two extremities are elevated,* (Ḳ,) *like the form of the camel's saddle so called, of which the middle is depressed:* (TA:) also † *a channel of water furrowed in a tract such as is termed* قُفّ, (Ḳ, TA,) *like a valley in width, having between it and another such channel meadows and herbage:* pl. as above. (TA.)

غَابِطٌ act. part. n. of 1, (Ṣ, Ḳ,) as expl. in the first sentence: (Ṣ:) — and also as expl. in the second sentence: (Ḳ:) pl., accord. to the Ḳ, غُبُطٌ, like كُتُبٌ; but correctly, غُبَّطٌ, like سُكَّرٌ, as in the L. (TA.)

فَرَسٌ مُغْبَطُ الكَاثِبَةِ ‡ *A horse high in the withers; likened to the form of the* غَبِيط; accord. to Lth: in the A, *as though he had on him a* غبيط. (TA.) — أَرْضٌ مُغْبَطَةٌ, with fet-ḥ, (Ḳ,) i. e., in the form of the pass. part. n., not with fet-ḥ to the first letter, (TA,) *Land covered with dense herbage, as though it were from a single grain.* (AḤn, Ḳ.) — سَيْرٌ مُغْبَطٌ † *Journey continued without rest;* as also مُغْمَطٌ. (ISh.)

حُمَّى مُغْبِطَةٌ ‡ *Continual fever.* (TA.)

مَغْبُوطٌ and ↓ مُغْتَبَطٌ *Regarded* [*with unenvious emulation,* i. e.,] *with a wish for the like condition, without its being desired that it should pass away from him:* (Ṣ, TA:) *in a good state,* or *condition; in a state of happiness; and of enjoyment,* or *wellbeing;* as also ↓ مُغْتَبِطٌ. (TA.)

مُغْتَبَطٌ and مُغْتَبِطٌ: see the next preceding paragraph.

غبق

1. غَبَقَهُ, (Ṣ, O, Ḳ,) aor. ـُ (Ṣ, O, TA) and ـِ, (TA,) inf. n. غَبْقٌ; (O, TA;) and ↓ غَبَّقَهُ, inf. n. تَغْبِيقٌ; (TA;) *He gave him to drink an evening-draught,* or *what is termed a* غَبُوق. (Ṣ, O, Ḳ, TA.) لَا أَغْبِقُ قَبْلَهُمَا أَهْلًا وَلَا مَالًا, in a trad. respecting the companions of the cave [to which allusion is made in the Ḳur ix. 40], in which the verb is thus written by El-Yooneenee with kesr to the ب, means *I did not give to drink to* any one [of *family nor of cattle*] the share [of *the evening-draught*] *of milk of them two.* (TA.)

2: see the next preceding paragraph. One says also غَبَّقَ الإِبِلَ, and الغَنَمَ, *He gave to drink to the camels,* and *the sheep* or *goats, in the evening:* or *he milked them in the evening:* and اغتبق ↓ النَّاقَةَ *he milked the she-camel after sunset.* (TA. [See also 5.])

5. تغبّق *He milked in the evening.* (Lḥ, O, Ḳ. [See also what next precedes.]) — And *He drank in the evening.* (TA. [See also what next follows.])

8. اغتبق, (Ṣ, O, Ḳ,) inf. n. اِغْتِبَاقٌ, (TA,) and مُغْتَبَقٌ may be an inf. n. as well as a n. of place, (O, Ḳ,) *He drank an evening-draught,* or *what is termed a* غَبُوق. (Ṣ, O, Ḳ. [See also what next precedes.]) — And اغتبق لَبَنَهَا *He drank her* (a camel's) *milk in the evening.* (TA.) — See also 2.

غَبْقَةٌ *A single case of the evening-drink,* or *of what is termed* غَبُوق. (TA.)

غَبَقَةٌ *A string,* or *cord,* (IDrd, O, Ḳ,) or *a plaited thong* (عَرَقَة), (IDrd, O,) *which is tied to the transverse piece of wood upon the hump of the bull* [in the TA *of the camel,* or, accord. to the T, *of the bull,*] *when he* [*draws the plough that*] *turns over the ground for cultivation, or is used for the drawing of water* [*to irrigate land* in the manner expl. voce سَانِيَةٌ], *in order that the piece of wood may be firm.* (IDrd, O, Ḳ.)

غَبْقَانُ, applied to a man, and غَبْقَى [for which the CḲ has غَبْقَآء], applied to a woman, (O, Ḳ, TA,) epithets similar to صَبْحَانُ and صَبْحَى, (O,) irregularly formed, for فَعْلَانُ is not to be formed from اِفْتَعَلَ nor from تَفَعَّلَ, (TA,) *Who has drunk an evening-draught,* or *what is termed a* غَبُوق. (Ḳ.)

غَبُوقٌ *An evening-draught;* i. e. *a draught, drink,* or *potation,* [and particularly *of milk,* but also applied to one *of water,* and *of wine, &c.,*] *that is drunk in the evening,* or *the last,* or *latter, part of the day.* (Ṣ, O, Ḳ. [See also صَبُوحٌ.]) See an ex. in a verse of Khuzaz Ibn-Lowdhán cited voce كَذَبَ. One of the Arabs said to a companion of his, إِنْ كُنْتَ كَاذِبًا فَشَرِبْتَ غَبُوقًا بَارِدًا [*If thou be lying, then mayest thou drink a cold evening-draught*]; meaning, may there not be milk for thee, so that thou shalt drink water not mixed with anything; this being called by him غبوق by way of comparison: or meaning, may that be to thee in the place of غبوق. (TA.)

And one says, لَقِيتُهُ ذَا غَبُوقٍ [lit. *I met him at a time of drinking the evening-draught*], meaning, *in the evening*; a phrase used only adverbially; like ذَا صَبُوحٍ: (TA:) and ذَاتَ الغَبُوقِ [which has a similar meaning]. (T in art. ذو.) —— Also, and with ة, A she-camel *whose milk one drinks in the evening*: or, accord. to Lḥ, *that is milked after sunset*: epithets like صَبُوحٌ and صَبُوحَةٌ. (TA.)

مُغْتَبَقٌ an inf. n. [of 8, q. v.]: and also a n. of place [signifying *A place in which one drinks the draught termed* غَبُوق]. (O, Ḳ.)

غبن

1. غَبَنَهُ, (Ṣ, MA, Mṣb, Ḳ,) aor. ـِ, (Mṣb, Ḳ,) inf. n. غَبْنٌ (Ṣ, MA, Mṣb, Ḳ, KL) and غَبَنٌ, or the former is [the inf. n. used in this case, i. e.] in selling [and the like], and the latter is in judgment, or opinion, (Ḳ, agreeably with a positive statement in the Ṣ,) *He cheated, deceived, overreached,* or *defrauded, him,* (Ṣ, MA, Ḳ, KL, TA,) in selling; (Ṣ, MA, Ḳ, TA;) *he endamaged him,* or *made him to suffer loss* or *damage* or *detriment,* (Mṣb, KL, TA,) in selling, (KL, TA,) &c., (KL,) or in the price, or otherwise: (Mṣb:) [or] *he overcame him* in selling and buying. (Mṣb.) And غُبِنَ *He was cheated,* or *deceived* [&c. in a purchase]: (Ṣ, Ḳ, TA:) and ▼ انغبن [in like manner signifies] *he became* [*cheated* or *endamaged* or] *overcome* in selling and buying. (Mṣb.) And it is said that غَبَنَ فِى البَيْعِ, inf. n. غَبْنٌ, signifies *He was unmindful,* or *inadvertent,* [or perhaps غَبَنَ is here a mistranscription for غُبِنَ, signifying thus, and therefore meaning *he was made to suffer loss,*] *in selling* or *in buying.* (TA.) And one says also, غُبِنَ الرَّجُلُ أَشَدَّ الغَبْنَانِ, [*The man was cheated* or *deceived* &c. *with the utmost degree of cheating* &c.]. (Ibn-Buzurj, TA.) غَبْنٌ يَسِيرٌ [*A petty overreaching* or *endamaging*] *is one of which the rate is such as has been estimated* [*as allowable by custom*] *by one estimator, not by every one*: and غَبْنٌ فَاحِشٌ [*An exorbitant overreaching* or *endamaging*] *is one of which the rate is such as has not been estimated* [*as allowable by custom*] *by any one.* (Dict. of Technical Terms used in the Sciences of the Musalmans.) [الغُبْنُ وَالغَبْنُ mentioned by Freytag as occurring in the Fákihet el-Khulafà, and expl. by him as meaning "Fraus omnimoda," should, I doubt not, be الغَبْنُ وَالغَبَنُ, the two inf. ns. mentioned in the first sentence above.] —— غَبَنَهُ, aor. ـِ, inf. n. غَبْنٌ, signifies also *He passed by him* (i. e. a man) *inclining,* or *leaning,* [or *bending down, so as to elude his observation,* i. e.] *so that he* [the latter] *did not see him, and was not cognizant of him.* (TA.) —— [And it is said in the TA that غَبَنُوا النَّاسَ means *None but they obtained it*: whence it appears that فِيهِ or the like has been omitted after النَّاسَ: with this addition, the phrase may be rendered, *they overreached,* or *prevented, the other people in respect of it, by obtaining it themselves.*] —— هٰذَا يَغْبِنُ عَقْلَكَ, said to a man whom another had cheated (غَبَنَ) in a sale, means *This* [man] *attributes defect,* or *imperfection, to thy intellect.* (TA.) —— قَدْ غَبِنُوا خَبَرَهَا, and غَبِنُوا, aor. of the former verb ـِ, and of the latter ـَ, i. e. لَمْ يَعْلَمُوا عِلْمَهَا [meaning *They have not known her case* or *state* or *condition,* or *her qualities*], (ISh, Ḳ,* TA,) is a phrase relating to a she-camel, of which it is said that she is what one would desire a she-camel to be as a beast for riding and in generousness of race, but she is ▼ مَغْبُونَةٌ, [i. e.] one *of which the qualities are not known to be as above mentioned.* (ISh, TA.) —— غَبَنْتَ رَأْيَكَ [if not a mistranscription for غَبِنْتَ (see غَبِنَ رَأْيَهُ in what follows)] means *Thou hast lost,* and *forgotten, thy judgment,* or *opinion.* (TA.) —— غَبِنَ الشَّىْءَ and فِى الشَّىْءِ, aor. ـَ, inf. n. غَبْنٌ and غَبَنٌ, signify *He forgot the thing*: or *he was unmindful, neglectful,* or *heedless, of it*; (Ḳ, TA;) and *ignorant of it*: (TA:) or *he made a mistake in respect of it*; (Ḳ, TA;) as in the saying, غَبِنَ كَذَا مِنْ حَقِّهِ عِنْدَ فُلَانٍ [*he made a mistake in respect of such a thing, of his right, or due, to be required at the hand of such a one*]. (TA.) —— غَبِنَ رَأْيَهُ, inf. n. غَبْنٌ (Ṣ, Mṣb, Ḳ) and غَبَانَةٌ, (Ṣ,* Ḳ,) means *He was,* or *became, deficient in his judgment,* or *opinion*: (Ṣ:) or *he was,* or *became, weak* [therein]: (Ḳ:) or *his intelligence,* or *sagacity,* and *his sharpness,* or *acuteness, of mind, went away*: (Mṣb:) the parsing of this phrase has been [fully] expl. voce سَفِهَ [q. v.]. (Ṣ.) ═ غَبَنَ الثَّوْبَ, (Ṣ, Mgh, Mṣb, TA,) inf. n. غَبْنٌ, (Ḳ,) from مَغْبِنٌ [q. v.], (Mṣb,) *He folded,* or *doubled, the garment,* (T, Mgh, Mṣb, Ḳ,* TA,) it being [too] long, (T, TA,) *and then sewed it*; (Mgh, Mṣb;) like خَبَنَهُ [q. v.] (Ṣ, Mgh) and كَبَنَهُ. (Mgh.) And غَبَنَ الدَّلْوَ *He folded,* or *doubled,* [*the edge of*] *the leathern bucket, to shorten it.* (TA: but only the inf. n. of the verb thus used is there mentioned.) —— And غَبَنَ الشَّىْءَ *He hid,* or *concealed, the thing in the* مَغْبِن [or *armpit* or *groin* or *the like*]; (TA;) as also ▼ اغتبنه. (Ḳ, TA.) —— غَبَنَ الطَّعَامَ is like خَبَنَهُ [i. e. *He concealed, kept,* or *stored, wheat,* or *food, for a time of dearth,* or *adversity*]. (Ṣ.)

3: see 6, first sentence.

5: see 10.

6. تَغَابُنٌ signifies *Mutual* غَبْن [i. e. *cheating* or *endamaging* or *overcoming* in selling and buying: and ▼ مُغَابَنَةٌ signifies the same; or *mutual endeavouring to cheat* &c: see 3 in art زبن]. (Ṣ, MA, Ḳ, KL, TA.) Hence, يَوْمُ التَّغَابُنِ [in the Ḳur lxiv. 9], an appellation of *The day of resurrection*; because the people of Paradise will then overreach (تَغْبِنُ) the people of Hell, (Ṣ, Ḳ, TA,) by the state of enjoyment in which the former will become and the punishment which the latter will experience; or, as El-Ḥasan says, because the former will attribute defect, or imperfection, to the intellects of the latter by reason of the preferring infidelity to faith. (TA.) —— And تغابن له [i. e. لَهُ, but this, I think, is probably a mistranscription for به,] signifies تَقَاعَدَ [i. e. تقاعد به, meaning *He did not pay him his due,*] حَتَّى غُبِنَ [*so that he was cheated* or *endamaged* or *overcome*]. (TA.)

7: see 1, second sentence.

8: see 1, last sentence but one.

10. استغبنهُ and ▼ تغبّنهُ [app. signify *He esteemed him* غَبِين, i. e. *weak in judgment,* and therefore *liable to be cheated* or *endamaged*]. (TA in art. زبن: see 10 in that art.)

غَبْنٌ [mentioned above as an inf. n.,] *Weakness*: and *forgetfulness.* (Ḳ.) ═ And *What is cut off from the extremities of a garment, and thrown down,* or *let fall.* (TA.)

غَبِينٌ *Weak in his judgment,* or *opinion*; (Ṣ, Ḳ, TA;) and *in intellect,* and *in religion*; (TA;) and ▼ مَغْبُونٌ signifies the same. (Ḳ, TA.)

غَبَانَةٌ [mentioned above as an inf. n. (see غَبِنَ رَأْيَهُ),] *Weakness of judgment,* or *opinion.* (Ṣ.)

غَبِينَةٌ [The *act of cheating, deceiving, overreaching,* or *defrauding*; or *of endamaging*; in selling or the like;] a subst. (Ṣ, Mṣb, Ḳ) from [the inf. n.] غَبْنٌ, like شَتِيمَةٌ from شَتْمٌ, (Ṣ,) [or] from غَبَنَهُ (Mṣb, Ḳ) used in relation to selling, (Ḳ,) or in relation to a price &c. (Mṣb.)

غَابِنٌ *Remiss,* or *languid, in work.* (Ḳ.)

مَغْبِنٌ sing. of مَغَابِنُ, (Mgh, Mṣb, Ḳ,) which signifies The أَرْفَاغ, (Ṣ, Mgh, Mṣb, Ḳ,) and the آبَاط, (Mgh, Mṣb, Ḳ,) [i. e. the *groins* and the *armpits,* and *the like*; (see رُفْغٌ;)] or the *places of flexure,* or *creasing, of the skin*: the sing. is expl. by Th as signifying *any part upon which one folds his thigh.* (TA.)

مَغْبُونٌ pass. part. n. of 1 signifying as expl. in the first sentence of this art. [q. v.]. (Ṣ, Mṣb, Ḳ.) —— See also غَبِينٌ. —— مَغْبُونَةٌ applied to a she-camel: see 1, latter half.

غبو

1. غَبِىَ, aor. يَغْبَى, inf. n. غَبًا and غَبَاوَةٌ, [the latter of which is the more common,] *He had little* [or *no*] *intelligence.* (Mṣb.) —— And غَبِىَ الشَّىْءَ, (Ṣ, Ḳ, TA, in the CḲ [erroneously] غَبَى,) or الأَمْرَ, (Mṣb,) and غَبِىَ عَنِ الشَّىْءِ (Ṣ, Ḳ) or عَنِ الأَمْرِ, (Mṣb,) aor. as above, (Ṣ,) inf. n. غَبَاوَةٌ (Ṣ, Ḳ) and غَبًا, (Ḳ,) *He did not understand* (Ṣ, Mṣb, Ḳ) *the thing* (Ṣ, Ḳ) or *the affair.* (Mṣb.) And غَبِىَ عَنِ الخَبَرِ *He was ignorant of the information.* (Mṣb.) —— And in like manner, غَبِىَ عَلَىَّ الشَّىْءُ, inf. n. غَبًا, [*The thing was not understood,* or *not known, by me*; or] *I knew not the thing*: (Ṣ:) [or] غَبِىَ الشَّىْءُ مِنْهُ i. e. خَفِىَ [*the thing was hidden from him*], (Ḳ, TA,) *so that he did not know it*: (TA:) and غَبًا is used in the dial. of Ṭeiyi for غَبِىَ in the sense of خَفِىَ: (A and TA in art. غبس:) or it is for غَبَّ, like

تَقَضَّى for تَقَضَّضَ. (Ṣ in that art. [See غُبَيْشٌ: and see also غَبْيَةٌ, in art. غبى.])

5. تغبّاهُ: see 10.

6. تغابى i. q. تَغَافَلَ, (Ṣ, MA, TA,) i. e. *He was, or he feigned himself, unmindful*, &c. (MA.) So in the phrase تغابى عَنْهُ: (TA: [see تَغَافَلَ and تَغَفَّلَ:]) and one says تغاباهُ [also, app. in the same sense]. (IAar, TA in art. عمش.)

10. استغباهُ and ♦ تغبّاهُ [app. *He esteemed him unintelligent, or one having little intelligence*]. (TA in art. زبن: see 10 in that art.)

فِيهِ غَبْوَةٌ and ♦ غُبْوَةٌ and ♦ غُبًى *In him is unmindfulness, forgetfulness, neglectfulness, heedlessness, or inadvertence.* (Ḳ.)

[غَبَاةٌ *Stupidity.* (Freytag, from El-Meydánee.)]

غَبًا: *Low, or depressed, ground.* (Ḳ, TA.) And *A thing that is hidden, or concealed, from one.* (TA.) — And *Earth, or dust, that is put over a thing to conceal it from one.* (TA.) [See also art. غبى.]

غَبِىٌّ *Having little,* (Ṣ, Mṣb,) or *no,* (Ḳ,) *intelligence:* (Ṣ, Mṣb, Ḳ:) or *one who does not understand deceit, or guile,* and *the like:* (T, TA:) or *unmindful, forgetful, neglectful, heedless,* or *inadvertent:* (TA:) and *ignorant:* (Mṣb:) pl. أَغْبِيَآءُ (IAth, Mṣb, TA) and أَغْبَآءٌ: (IAth, TA:) accord. to J and others, (TA,) it belongs to this art.; (Ṣ, TA;) but Aboo-'Alee derives it from شَجَرَةٌ غَبْيَآءُ, [see أَغْبَى in art. غبى,] as though his ignorance hid from him to whom it is applied what is plainly apparent to others. (TA.) — [And *A hunter, or sportsman, concealing himself.* (Freytag, from the Deewán of the Hudhalees.)]

غُبًى: see غَبْوَةٌ.

غَبَاوَةٌ an inf. n. of غَبِىَ [q. v.]. (Ṣ, Mṣb, Ḳ.) — هُوَ ذُو غَبَاوَةٍ means *He is one to whom things, or affairs, are unapparent, or obscure;* or *from whom they are hidden, or concealed.* (TA.)

غُبْوَةٌ: see غَبْوَةٌ.

أَغْبَى: see the next article.

غبى

2. غَبَّاهُ عَنِ الشَّىْءِ, (TA,) inf. n. تَغْبِيَةٌ, (Ḳ, TA,) *He covered, veiled, or concealed,* (Ḳ,* TA,) *him, or it, from the thing.* (TA.) — And غَبَّى البِئْرَ *He covered the head* [or *mouth*] *of the well, and then put over it earth, or dust.* (TA.) — غبّى شَعْرَهُ, (TA,) inf. n. as above, (Ḳ, TA,) *He shortened his hair:* (Ḳ,* TA:) of the dial. of 'Abd-el-Ḳeys, and sometimes used by others: (TA:) and *he eradicated it* (Ḳ, TA) *at once.* (TA.)

4. اغبت السَّمَآءُ, inf. n. إِغْبَآءٌ, *The sky rained such rain as is termed* غَبْيَةٌ [q. v.]. (AZ, Ṣ.)

غَبْيَةٌ *A rain that is not copious,* (Ṣ, Ḳ,) *but exceeding such as is termed* بَغْشَةٌ [q. v.]: (Ṣ:) or *a vehement shower* (Ḳ, TA) *of rain:* (TA:) pl. غَبَيَاتٌ. (Ṣ.) — [And app. † *A shower of arrows.*] شَرُّ الغَبَيَاتِ غَبْيَةُ النَّبْلِ [which seems clearly to mean † *The worst of showers is the shower of arrows*] is a saying mentioned by Aṣ. (TA.) — Also *An abundant pouring of water:* — and likewise † *of* سِيَاط [i. e. *strokes of the whip,* or *lashes*]: (Ḳ, TA:) thought by ISd to be thus termed as being likened to the غَبَيَات of rain. (TA.) — And, as being likened to the rain thus termed, ‡ *A running after another running:* [but] A'Obeyd says, it is *like a leap in pace or going.* (Ṣ. [In three copies of the Ṣ, I find الغَبْيَةُ كَالوَثْبَةِ فِى السَّيْرِ as the explanation given by A'Obeyd: in one of my copies of the Ṣ, الغَبْيَةُ كَالزَّبْيَةِ: and in the TA, الغبية كالزبية في السير: I have followed the first of these readings, as I cannot doubt its being the right.]) — Also *Dust of the earth, that has risen,* or *that has spread,* or *diffused itself;* (Ḳ, TA;) as also ♦ غَبَآءٌ; thus correctly; but in [some of] the copies of the Ḳ, غِبَآءٌ, like كِسَآءٌ; [and accord. to other copies غُبًا;] it is *like dust in the sky:* or, as some say, it is the *earth, or dust, with which the head* [or *mouth*] *of the well is stopped up, upon the cover.* (TA.) [See also art. غبو.] — One says also, جَاؤُوا عَلَى غَبْيَةِ الشَّمْسِ, meaning غَيْبَتِهَا [i. e. *They came at,* or *in the time of, the setting of the sun*]; (Ḳ, TA;) in which instance it is thought by ISd to be formed by transposition. (TA. [See also 1 in art. غبو.])

غَبَآءٌ: see the next preceding paragraph: — and see also art. غبو.

غُصْنٌ أَغْبَى, and شَجَرَةٌ غَبْيَآءُ, *A branch,* and *a tree, tangled, confused,* or *dense.* (Ḳ.) — أُدْخُلْ فِى النَّاسِ فَإِنَّهُ أَغْبَى لَكَ means [*Enter thou among the people, for it will be*] *most concealing for thee.* (TA.)

سَمَآءٌ مُغْبِيَةٌ *A sky raining such rain as is termed* غَبْيَةٌ [q. v.]. (AZ, Ṣ.)

مُغْبَاةٌ i. q. مُغَطَّاةٌ: so in the saying, حَفَرَ مُغْبَاةً [*He dug a pitfall* which he afterwards *covered over with earth*]: and [hence] one says, فُلَانٌ دَفَنَ لِى مُغْبَاةً ثُمَّ حَمَلَنِى عَلَيْهَا [lit. *Such a one covered over a pitfall for me, then urged me to go upon it*], meaning † *such a one caused me to fall in* [or *by means of*] *a stratagem that he had concealed.* (TA.) — Also i. q. مَفْوَاةٌ [A land (أَرْضٌ) *abounding with* فُوَّة i. e. *madder*]. (TA.)

غت

1. غَتَّهُ, (Ṣ, Ḳ,) aor. ـُ, inf. n. غَتٌّ, (TḲ,) *He fatigued, or wearied, him,* (كَدَّهُ,) بِالأَمْرِ [*by,* or *with, the affair*]. (Ṣ, Ḳ.) — And *He forced him to do a thing against his will, so that he afflicted, distressed, or oppressed, him.* (TA.) And you say, غَتَّ الدَّابَّةَ شَوْطًا أَوْ شَوْطَيْنِ *He fatigued, or wearied, the beast by urging it to run a heat, or two heats.* (Ḳ, TA.) — Also *He grieved him;* (Ḳ, TA;) and *afflicted, distressed, or oppressed, him.* (TA.) And غُتَّ *He was grieved* [&c.]. (Sh, TA.) — And *He overcame him, or silenced him,* بِالكَلَامِ [*by speech,* i. e. *by what he said*]. (Ḳ, TA.) [Hence] it is said in a trad. respecting prayer, يَا مَنْ لَا يَغُتُّهُ دُعَآءُ الدَّاعِينَ *O Thou whom the praying of those who pray does not overcome.* (TA.) And [hence, perhaps,] one says, غَتَّ الضَّحِكَ, (aor. and inf. n. as above, TA,) *He concealed laughter,* (Ṣ, Ḳ, TA,) *by putting his hand, or his garment, over his mouth.* (TA.) — Also *He squeezed his throat, or throttled him:* (Ḳ:) and *he squeezed his throat for the period of one breath, or of two breaths,* or, as some say, *more than that.* (TA.) It is said in a trad. respecting the mission [of Moḥammad], فَأَخَذَنِى جِبْرِيلُ فَغَتَّنِى *And Gabriel took me, and squeezed me vehemently, so that I experienced distress as when one is forcibly plunged into water:* inf. n. غَتٌّ: and غَطٌّ signifies the same. (TA.) — غَتَّهُ فِى المَآءِ, (Ṣ, Ḳ, TA,) aor. and inf. n. as above, (TA,) is *syn. with* غَطَّهُ; (Ṣ, Ḳ, TA;) meaning *He immersed, or plunged, him, or it, into the water.* (TA.) — And one says, غَتَّهُمُ اللّٰهُ بِالعَذَابِ, inf. n. as above, *God plunged them,* or *may God plunge them, with consecutive plungings, into punishment.* (TA.) — And غَتَّ, aor. and inf. n. as above, *He took successive draughts, keeping the vessel to his mouth.* (AZ, TA.) And غَتَّ المَآءَ, (Ḳ, TA,) and غَتَّ فِى الإِنَآءِ, (TA,) *He drank, taking draught after draught,* or *gulp after gulp, without removing the vessel from his mouth.* (Ḳ, TA.) — And غَتَّ الشَّىْءَ الشَّىْءَ *He made one part of the thing to follow another part thereof,* (Ḳ, TA,) whether in drinking or in speaking [&c.]. (TA.) — It is said in a trad., respecting Moḥammad's pool, يَغُتُّ فِيهِ مِيزَابَانِ i. e. *Two spouts were pouring forth into it with an uninterrupted pouring:* or it is said to mean, *two spouts were running into it with a murmuring sound;* accord. to which latter explanation we must read يَغِتُّ: and some say that it is يَغُطُّ. (Az, L, TA.) [See also another reading voce عَبَّ.] — And one says, غَتَّهُ بِجُشَمِهِ *He threw his breast upon him.* (TA in art. جشم.) — غَتَّ, aor. ـِ, *It was, or became, bad, or corrupt;* said of food; and likewise of speech. (Aboo-Bekr, TA.) [See also غَثَّ.]

2. غَتَّتَ الطَّعَامَ, inf. n. تَغْتِيتٌ *He made the food bad, or corrupt;* as also ♦ اغتّهُ. (Aboo-Bekr, TA.)

4: see what next precedes.

غَتٌّ [inf. n. of 1, q. v. — And] *The interval between two draughts, or gulps, while the vessel is kept to the mouth.* (TA.)

غتم

1. غَتِمَ, aor. ـَ, inf. n. غَتَمٌ, *He had an impotence, or an impediment, or a difficulty, in his*

speech, or utterance; and a barbarousness, or vitiousness, therein, especially in speaking Arabic; i. e., a want of clearness, perspicuousness, distinctness, chasteness, or correctness, therein. (Mṣb.) ═ غَتِمَ, said of food (طَعَام), It was, or became, wholesome, or beneficial. (TA.)

4. اغتم الزِّيَارَةَ, (Ḳ, TA, in the CḲ [erroneously] اغْتَمَرَ,) He visited much, so as to weary. (Ḳ, TA.) One says, لَا تُغْتِمِ الزِّيَارَةَ فَتُمِلَّ [Do not thou visit much, so as to weary]. (TA.) — And they said, كَانَ العَجَّاجُ يُغْتِمُ الشِّعْرَ i. e. El-'Ajjáj used to make poetry cause much wearying: and it is said in the A, أَغْتَمَ آلُ العَجَّاجِ الرَّجَزَ i. e. The family of El-'Ajjáj recited much poetry of the metre termed رَجَز; and he among them. (TA.)

8. اغتم He suffered from indigestion (Ḳ, TA) in consequence of much eating; and became affected by what is termed ↓ غَتْم [app. meaning heat of the stomach so intense as to take the breath] arising from the distress occasioned by repletion. (TA.)

غَتْمٌ Intense heat that almost takes away the breath. (Ṣ, Ḳ.) A rájiz says, (Ṣ,) namely, Mes'ood Ibn-Ḳeyd [?] El-Fezáree, (TA,) describing camels, (Ṣ in art. فول,)

• حَرَّقَهَا حَمْضُ بِلَادٍ فِلِّ •
• وَغَتْمُ نَجْمٍ غَيْرِ مُسْتَقِلِّ •

[The pasturage termed حمض of tracts of country not rained upon and not having fresh herbage rendered them thirsty, and the intense and almost-suffocating heat of a star not high (above the horizon), i. e. not having become high so as to be concealed by the rays of the sun]; i. e. [a star] not high (غَيْرِ مُرْتَفِعٍ) because of the constancy of the heat attributed to it [at the time of its auroral rising]; the heat becoming intense only at the time of the [auroral] rising of الشِّعْرَى, [meaning Sirius, the star to which allusion is here made,] which is in [correctly after] الجَوْزَآء. (Ṣ. [See الشِّعْرَى.]) — See also 8.

غُتْمٌ Thick pieces [or clots or lumps] of milk. (TA.)

غُتْمَةٌ An impotence, or an impediment, or a difficulty, in speech, or utterance; and a barbarousness, or vitiousness, therein; i. e. a want of clearness, perspicuousness, distinctness, chasteness, or correctness, therein; meaning, in speaking Arabic; syn. عُجْمَةٌ. (Ṣ, Mgh, Mṣb, Ḳ.)

غُتْمِىٌّ: see أَغْتَمُ. — Hence, applied to milk, [and so, accord. to Reiske, as stated in Freytag's Lex., ↓ أَغْتَمُ,] Thick; the pouring forth of which is without any sound. (IAạr, Ḳ.) — And One who is heavy in spirit: from غَتْم signifying as expl. above. (TA.)

حِيَاضُ غُتَيْمٍ, like زُبَيْرٍ, (so in copies of the Ḳ,) [or حياض غُتَيْمَ, for it is] a proper name for المَنِيَّة, (TA,) meaning Death, (Ḳ, TA,) like شَعُوبُ, imperfectly decl. [as being a proper name and of the fem. gender]; so says Z; and, accord. to Lḥ, الغُتَيْمُ signifies the same, but ISd says, "I know it not save as from him." (TA.) One says, أَوْرَدَهُ حِيَاضَ غُتَيْمٍ [He brought him to death]: and in like manner, وَقَعَ فِى أَحْوَاضِ غُتَيْمٍ [He fell into death], expl. by Lḥ as meaning he died. (TA.)

أَغْتَمُ, (Ṣ, Mgh, Mṣb, Ḳ,) and ↓ غُتْمِىٌّ (Ṣ,* Ḳ,* TA,) [and ↓ أَغْتَمِىٌّ, occurring in the فاكهة الخلفآء, p. 151, l. 18, as mentioned by Freytag, who explains it as meaning "barbarus,"] One who does not utter anything with clearness, perspicuousness, or distinctness, or with chasteness, or correctness; (Ṣ, Mgh, Mṣb, Ḳ, TA;) i. q. أَعْجَمُ: (TA:) fem. of the first, غَتْمَآءُ, applied to a woman: (Mṣb, TA:) pl. of the first غُتْمٌ (Ṣ, Mgh, Mṣb, Ḳ) and أَغْتَامٌ, (Mgh,) or this latter is pl. of the second. (TA.) — See also غُتْمِىٌّ.

أَغْتَمِىٌّ: see the next preceding paragraph.

مَغْتُومٌ, Burned by the heat. (TA.)

غث

1. غَثَّ, aor. ـِ; and غَثَّ, (originally غَثُثَ, TA) aor. ـُ; (Ṣ, O, Ḳ;) said of flesh-meat; (Ṣ, O;) and غَثَّتْ; said of a شَاة [i. e. sheep or goat]; (Ṣ, O, Mṣb;) inf. n. غَثَاثَةٌ and غُثُوثَةٌ, (Ṣ, O, Ḳ,) or غَثٌّ; (Mṣb;) and ↓ اغثّ, (Ḳ,) or اغثّت, (Ṣ, O,) or both; (TA;) It was, or became, lean, or meagre: (Ṣ, O, Ḳ:) or غَثَّت, said of a شَاة, it was, or became, weak. (Mṣb.) — [Hence the saying,] غَثَّ الحَدِيثُ ‡ The talk, or discourse, was, or became, [meagre, or] bad, or corrupt; (Ṣ, A, O, Ḳ;) as also ↓ اغثّ. (Ṣ, Ḳ.) [See غَثٌّ.] — And لَا يَغِثُّ عَلَيْهِ شَىْءٌ † [Nothing is bad in his opinion; so that] he does not say of anything that it is bad, and therefore leave it. (Ṣ, Ḳ.) And مَا يَغِثُّ عَلَيْهِ أَحَدٌ † [No one is to be disregarded in his opinion; so that] he does not leave any one unasked by him. (T, A, O, Ḳ.) And غَثَّتْ عَلَيْنَا مَكَّةُ فَلَا بُدَّ لَنَا مِنْ خُرُوجٍ † [Mekkeh has become unpleasing (as though insipid) to us, so that there is for us no avoiding going forth]. (A.) — And غَثَّ, (Ṣ, O, Ḳ,) aor. ـِ, inf. n. غَثٌّ and غَثِيثٌ, (Ṣ, O,) is said of a wound, meaning It flowed with thick purulent matter, as also ↓ اغثّ, (Ṣ, O, Ḳ,) and with dead flesh. (Ṣ and O in explanation of the former verb.)

2. غثّثت الإِبِلُ, (El-Umawee, O, TA,) inf. n. تَغْثِيثٌ, (El-Umawee, O, Ḳ,) The camels became fat (El-Umawee, O, Ḳ, TA) by little and little: (O, Ḳ, TA:) [or became somewhat fat; for] one says, غَثَّ بَعِيرِى ثُمَّ غَثَّثَ My camel became lean; then he became somewhat fat. (A, TA.)

4: see 1, in three places. — You say also, اغثّ فِى مَنْطِقِهِ ‡ He [was meagre in his diction; or] spoke badly, or corruptly. (Ṣ, TA.) And اغثّ فِى كَلَامِهِ † He said that in which was no good. (A, Mṣb.) ═ And اغثّ اللَّحْمَ He bought the flesh-meat lean. (Ṣ, O.)

5. أَتَغَثَّثُ مَا أَنَا عَلَيْهِ حَتَّى أَتَسَمَّنَ means † I do what is of an inferior kind that I may find much; as also ↓ أَسْتَغِثُّهُ: (A, TA:) or أَتَغَثَّثُ مَا أَنَا فِيهِ حَتَّى أَسْتَسْمِنَ, meaning † I deem my doing to be little that I may obtain thereby much recompense. (O.)

8. اغتثّت الخَيْلُ (as also اغتفّت and اغتبّت, O) The horses found, or lighted upon, somewhat of the [herbage called] رَبِيع, (O, Ḳ, TA,) and became fat in consequence thereof after having been lean. (TA.)

10. استغثّ الجُرْحَ He extracted from the wound the thick purulent matter therein, (Ṣ, Ḳ,) and the dead flesh, and treated it curatively. (Ṣ.) ═ See also 5.

R. Q. 1. غَثْغَثَ, (O,) inf. n. غَثْغَثَةٌ, (Ḳ,) He remained, stayed, dwelt, or abode, (O, Ḳ,) in a place. (O.) ═ [And it seems to signify also He washed clothes without an implement of the kind called مِقْصَرَة (q. v.): for —] غَثْغَثَةٌ signifies also † Weak fighting, without a weapon: (O, Ḳ:) likened to the غَثْغَثَة of the garment, or piece of cloth, [which is] when it is washed with the hands [app. meaning with the hands only]. (O.)

غَثٌّ Lean, or meagre; (Ṣ, A, O, Ḳ;) as also ↓ غَثِيثٌ; (Ṣ, O, Ḳ;) both applied to flesh-meat; and the former, with ة, to a شَاة [i. e. sheep or goat]: (Ṣ, O:) pl. غِثَاثٌ. (MA.) — Hence, i. e. as being likened to flesh-meat thus termed, كَلَامٌ غَثٌّ † Speech, or language, that is [meagre,] without grace, or beauty. (Ḥam p. 757.) One says, فِى الكَلَامِ الغَثُّ وَالسَّمِينُ † [In speech, or the speech, is what is meagre and what is vigorous; or] what is good and what is bad [or rather what is bad and what is good]. (Mṣb.) And حَدِيثُكُمْ غَثٌّ وَسِلَاحُكُمْ رَثٌّ † [Your talk, or discourse, is meagre, or bad, and your weapons are old and worn out]. (A.) And قَوْمٌ غَثَثَةٌ † [A people, or party, meagre, or bad, in speech: غَثَثَة being pl. of غَثّ, like as بَرَرَة is of بَرّ]. (A. [The meaning that I have given is there indicated by the context.])

غَثَّةٌ A lean, or meagre, شَاة [i. e. sheep or goat]. (TA.) [See also غَثٌّ.] ═ And A sufficiency of the means of subsistence: (O, Ḳ:) like غُفَّةٌ and غُبَّةٌ. (O.)

الغَثْغَثُ and ↓ الغُثَاغِثُ The lion. (O, Ḳ.)

غِثَاثٌ [if not a mistranscription for the inf. n. غَثَاثَةٌ] Leanness, or meagreness, of a camel [&c.]. (A, TA.)

غَثِيثٌ: see غَثٌّ: ═ and see what here follows.

غَثِيثَةٌ, (Ṣ, O,) or ↓ غَثِيثٌ, (A, Ḳ,) The thick purulent matter, (Ṣ, A, O, Ḳ,) and dead flesh,

(Ṣ, O,) *of a wound.* (Ṣ, A, O, Ḳ.) — And [hence, probably,] the former word, † *A corrupt,* or *disordered, state of mind.* (Ṣ, A, O, Ḳ.) So in the saying, لَبِسْتُهُ عَلَى غَثِيثَةٍ فِيهِ [meaning † *I consorted with him* (see لَبِسَ) *notwithstanding a corrupt,* or *disordered, state of mind in him*]. (Ṣ, O, L, TA. [In a copy of the A, لَسْتُ عَلَى غَثِيثَةٍ, meaning † *I am not in a corrupt,* or *disordered, state of mind:* but the former, I doubt not, is the right reading.]) ═ Also A palm-tree (نَخْلَةٌ) *that produces ripe dates without sweetness.* (O, Ḳ.) — And *Foolish,* or *stupid, in whom is no good:* (O, Ḳ:) or *foolish,* or *stupid:* and also one *who speaks that in which is no good.* (TA.)

الغَثْثُ : see الغُثَاغِثُ.

غثر

1. غَثَرَتِ الأَرْضُ بِالنَّبَاتِ *i. q.* مَادَت (thus in the JK [app. meaning *The land became flourishing and fresh with herbage*]): or مَادَتْ (thus in the O and Ḳ [i. e. without ء; but the former, I think, is evidently the right: the meaning which I have given may be from غَثَرٌ, q. v., and therefore tropical: and it may be inferred from what here follows that the verb is correctly, or originally, غَثِرَت, fem. of ♦ غَثْرَى]). The epithet applied to such land is ♦ مُغْثِرِيَةٌ. (JK, O, Ḳ.)

4. اغثر *It* (the [species of tree, or shrub, called] رِمْث [&c.]) *exuded what is termed* مُغْثُور [q. v.]; (Ḳ;) as also اغفر. (TA.) — See also عَبَرٌ, last sentence.

11. اغثارّ *It* (a garment, or piece of cloth,) *had much* غَثَر i. e. *nap,* or *villous substance,* (Ḳ, TA,) and *wool.* (TA.)

Q. Q. **1.** غَثْرَى : see the first paragraph.

Q. Q. **2.** تَمَغْثَرَ *He gathered* مُغْثُور [q. v.]. (Ḳ.) You say, خَرَجَ النَّاسُ يَتَمَغْثَرُونَ, like يَتَمَغْفَرُونَ, *The people went forth to gather* مَغَاثِير [pl. of مُغْثُور]. (TA.)

غَثَرٌ The *nap,* or *villous substance,* of a garment, or piece of cloth; (Ḳ, TA;) and the *wool* thereof. (TA.)

غَثَرَةٌ *Abundance:* (TA:) [and particularly] *abundance of herbage,* and *of the goods, conveniences,* or *comforts, of life; ampleness* [thereof]. (Ḳ, TA.) — And *A portion of* property. (TA.)

غُثْرَةٌ *A dust-colour inclining to* خُضْرَة [which here app. means *a dingy ash-colour*]: (Ṣ, TA:) or, as some say, [simply] *dust-colour:* (TA:) or it is *like duskiness* (غُبْشَة) *mixed with redness.* (Ḳ, TA.)

غَثْرَةٌ : see أَغْثَرُ, last sentence.

غَثَارٍ, or غَثَارُ, accord. to the CḲ غَثَّارُ : see أَغْثَرُ.

الغَثْوَثَرُ and الغَوْثَرُ : see أَغْثَرُ, former half.

غَيْثَرَةٌ *A threatening.* (Ḳ.) — And *Fight,* or *conflict;* and *commotion,* or *tumult:* so in the saying, تَرَكْتُ القَوْمَ فِى غَيْثَرَةٍ and غَيْثَمَةٍ [*I left the people,* or *party, in fight,* &c.]: (Aṣ, TA:) or, accord to IAạr, it means the *treading,* or *trampling,* of the people, or party, *one upon another,* (مُدَاوَسَةُ القَوْمِ بَعْضِهِمْ بَعْضًا,) *in fight,* or *conflict:* you say, بَيْنَ القَوْمِ غَيْثَرَةٌ شَدِيدَةٌ [*Among the people,* or *party, is a vehement treading,* &c.]. (Ṣ, TA.) ═ See also أَغْثَرُ, last sentence, in two places.

أَغْثَرُ, (Ṣ,) and [the fem.] غَثْرَآءُ, (Ḳ,) *Dust-coloured:* (Ḳ, TA:) or *of a dingy,* or *dusky, colour:* (TA:) or [*of the colour termed* غُثْرَة, which is] *nearly the same as dust-coloured.* (Ṣ, Ḳ, TA.) 'Omárah says,

• حَتَّى اكْتَسَيْتُ مِنَ المَشِيبِ عِمَامَةً •
• غَثْرَآءَ أُغْفِرُ لَوْنَهَا بِخِضَابِ •

[*Until I attired myself with a dusky turban of hoariness, the colour of which I concealed with hair-dye*]. (TA.) — أَغْثَرُ is applied as an epithet to a ram *That is not red* [or *brown*] *nor black nor white;* (IAạr, TA;) meaning *of a dusky,* or *dingy, colour.* (TA.) And it is so applied to a wolf. (IAạr, TA.) And الأَغْثَرُ signifies *The wolf;* (TA;) as also الأَغْبَرُ. (TA in art. غبر.) — And [in like manner] الغَثْرَآءُ signifies *The hyena,* or *female hyena;* (Ḳ, TA;) because of its colour; (TA;) as also ♦ غَثَارِ, (O, Ḳ, TA,) like قَطَامِ, (O, TA,) determinate; (Ḳ, TA;) [accord. to the CḲ غَثَّارُ, which is wrong;] and accord. to IAạr ♦ غَثَارُ, imperfectly declinable. (TA.) — And الأَغْثَرُ signifies also *The lion;* and so ♦ الغَثْوَثَرُ: (Ḳ:) or the latter, as also ♦ الغَوْثَرُ, *the lion that is in a confused,* or *perplexed, case.* (O.) — And *A certain bird,* (Ḳ, TA,) *having confused,* or *disordered, plumage,* (TA,) *long in the neck,* (Ḳ, TA,) *in the colour of which is* غُثْرَة [q. v.], *and which is of the aquatic kind.* (TA.) — أَكَلَتْهُمُ الغَثْرَآءُ [which may be rendered *The hyena,* or *female hyena, devoured them*] means † *they perished.* (Z, TA.) — غَثْرَآءُ applied to [garments of the kind called] أَكْسِيَة [pl. of كِسَآء] (Ḳ, TA) and قَطَائِف [pl. of قَطِيفَة] and the like, and to an عَبَاءَة, (TA,) signifies *Having much wool* (L, Ḳ, TA) *and nap,* or *villous substance.* (L.) — الأَغْثَرُ also signifies *The* [*green substance that overspreads stale water, called*] طُحْلُب. (Ṣ, TA.) — Also † The *ignorant* man: and the *stupid* man: likened to the hyena, or female hyena, which is one of the most stupid of beasts, and of which one of the appellations is الغَثْرَآءُ. (IDrd, TA.) — And الغَثْرَآءُ and الغُثْرُ, (Ṣ, Ḳ, TA,) which latter is the pl. of الأَغْثَرُ, (Ṣ, TA,) † *The low, base, vile, ignoble, mean,* or *sordid,* or *the refuse,* or *rabble, of mankind;* as also ♦ الغَثَرَةُ, (Ṣ, Ḳ, TA,) said to be originally ♦ الغَيْثَرَةُ, (Ṣ, TA,) which signifies the same: (Ṣ, Ḳ, TA:) and غَثْرَآءُ is also expl. as meaning *a mixed assemblage of people* (Ḳ, TA) *of the low, base, vile, ignoble, mean,* or *sordid,* or *of the refuse,* or *rabble, of mankind;* (TA;) and so ♦ غَيْثَرَةٌ: (AZ, TA:) or *a mixed assemblage of people of various tribes:* or the *unknown common people:* or the *commonalty,* or *generality, of men.* (TA.)

مِغْثَرٌ } مِغْثَارٌ } see what next follows.

مُغْثُورٌ (Ṣ, M) and ♦ مِغْثَرٌ (Yaạḳoob, Ṣ, Ḳ) and ♦ مِغْثَارٌ (TA) [*A sort of manna;*] *a thing* [or *substance*] *which is exuded by the* [*species of tree, or shrub, called*] رِمْث, (Ṣ, Ḳ,) *and by the* عُرْفُط, (Ṣ,) *and the* ثُمَام, *and the* عُشَر, (Ḳ,) *resembling gum, and sweet,* (Ṣ,) *like honey:* (Ṣ, Ḳ:) *it is eaten;* (TA;) *and sometimes it flows upon the ground, like* دِبْس; *and it has an unpleasant smell:* مُغْثُورٌ is a dial. var. of مُغْفُورٌ [q. v.]: (Ṣ, TA:) the pl. is مَغَاثِيرُ. (Ḳ.)

أَرْضٌ مُغْثِرِيَةٌ : see **1**. — وَجَدَ المَآءَ مُغْثَرِيًا عَلَيْهِ means *He found the water to be thronged:* (Ḳ, TA:) or, accord. to Ṣgh, (TA,) you say, وَجَدْتُ المَآءَ مُغْثَرِيًا بِالوِرْدِ *I found the water to be thronged by the coming thereto.* (O, TA.)

غثى and غثو

1. غَثَا الوَادِى, (Mṣb, Ḳ,) aor. يَغْثُو, (Mṣb,) inf. n. غَثْوٌ; (Mṣb, Ḳ;) and غَثَى, aor. يَغْثِى, inf. n. غَثْىٌ; (Ḳ;) the latter mentioned by IJ, but the former is that which is [commonly] known to the lexicologists; (TA;) *The valley,* or *water-course, was,* or *became, full of* غُثَآء [q. v.]: (Mṣb: [and the like is indicated in the Ḳ:]) or *had in it abundance of camels'* or *similar dung* (بَعْر) *and leaves and reeds* or *canes.* (TA.) — غَثَا اللَّحْمُ, inf. n. غَثْوٌ, *The flesh-meat was bad by reason of its leanness.* (IKṭṭ, TA.) — غَثَتِ النَّفْسُ, (Ṣ, Mṣb, Ḳ,) aor. تَغْثِى, (Ṣ, Mṣb,) inf. n. غَثْىٌ and غَثَيَانٌ; (Ṣ, Mṣb, Ḳ;) and, accord. to Lth, غَثِيَت, aor. تَغْثَى, inf. n. غَثًا, but Az says that this is post-classical; (TA;) *i. q.* خَبُثَتْ; (Ṣ, Ḳ, TA;) and جَاشَتْ; (TA;) i. e. [*The soul,* or *stomach, heaved;* or *became agitated by a tendency to vomit;* or] *became agitated so that the person nearly vomited, by reason of a mixture pouring forth to the mouth of the stomach:* (Mṣb, TA:) or, as some say, غَثَيَانٌ signifies *a flowing of the mouth which sometimes,* or *often, occasions vomiting.* (TA.) — غَثَتِ السَّمَآءُ بِالسَّحَابِ, (Ḳ, TA,) aor. تَغْثِى, (TA,) *The sky was,* or *became, clouded,* or *covered with clouds:* (Ḳ, TA:) or *began to be so.* (TA.) ═ غَثَا السَّيْلُ المَرْتَعَ, aor. يَغْثُوهُ, inf. n. غَثْوٌ; thus accord. to J, [in the Ṣ,] but accord. to the Ḳ and ISd, غَثَى, mentioned in art. غثى; and in [some of] the copies of the Ḳ, المَرْبَع is erroneously put for المَرْتَع; (TA;) *The torrent drew* [or *washed*] *together the pasture, and deprived it of its sweetness;* as also ♦ اغثاهُ. (Ṣ, Ḳ.) — And hence, by way of comparison, (TA,) غَثَى الكَلَامَ, aor. يَغْثَاهُ; (Ḳ, TA;) and غَثِيَهُ, aor. يَغْثِيهِ; (Ḳ, TA;) the former verb of the class of رَمَى, and the latter of the class of رَضِىَ; inf. n. غَثْىٌ;

(TA;) ‡ *He mixed, or put together confusedly, the speech,* or *language.* (Ḳ,* TA.) —— And غَثَى المَالَ, and النَّاسَ, *He beat the cattle,* and *the people,* and *dealt blows among them.* (Ḳ,* TA.) —— غَثِيَتِ الأَرْضُ بِالنَّبَاتِ *The land became abundant in herbage:* (Ḳ, TA:) or *began to be so.* (TA.) —— And غَثِىَ شَعَرُهُ, inf. n. غَثًى, *His hair became matted,* or *compacted together:* mentioned in art. غثى by IḲṭṭ: perhaps a dial. var. of عَثِىَ, with the unpointed ع; mentioned before. (TA.)

4: see the preceding paragraph, latter half.

غُثَآءٌ (Ṣ, Mṣb, Ḳ) and غُثَّآءٌ (Ṣ, Ḳ) The *rubbish,* or *small rubbish,* or *particles of things,* or *refuse, and scum, and rotten leaves mixed with the scum,* (Zj, Ṣ,* Mṣb,* Ḳ, TA,) *borne upon the surface* (Ṣ, Mṣb, TA) of a torrent: (Zj, Ṣ, Mṣb, Ḳ, TA:) or *dried-up* [or *decayed*] *and broken pieces* [or *leaves and stalks*] *of herbage, that are seen upon a torrent:* so in the Ḳur lxxxvii. 5: [see أَحْوَى in art. حو:] (TA:) pl. أَغْثَآءٌ. (Ṣ, TA.) —— [Hence,] one says, مَالُهُ غُثَآءٌ وَعَمَلُهُ هَبَآءٌ وَسَعْيُهُ جُفَآءٌ † [*His property is as rubbish borne by a torrent* (see Ḳur xxiii. 43), *and his work is as motes that are seen in the rays of the sun* (see Ḳur xxv. 25), *and his labour,* or *earning, is a thing that is unapparent*]. (TA.) —— [Hence, also,] غُثَآءُ النَّاسِ † *The low,* or *vile,* and *the refuse, of mankind.* (TA.)

الأَغْثَى *The lion.* (Ḳ.)

غد

1. غَدَّ and غُدَّ, said of a camel: see 4.

2. غَدَّدَ: see 4. —— غَدَّدَ, inf. n. تَغْدِيدٌ, *He took his* [غُدَّة, i. e.] *lot, portion,* or *share.* (Ḳ.)

4. أَغَدَّ (Ṣ, A, O, L, Mṣb, Ḳ) and أُغِدَّ, (O, L, Ḳ,) and ↓ غُدَّ, (Az, O, L, Ḳ,) this last heard by Az from the Arabs, (L,) [in the CḲ ↓ غَدَّ, but (though the phrase غُدَّتْ إِبِلُهُمْ occurs there afterwards) غُدَّ may be less correct than غَدَّ, for the part. n. of the former was disallowed by Aṣ,] and ↓ غَدَّدَ, (Az, O, Ḳ,) *He* (a camel) *had the disease termed* غُدَّة [q. v.]; (Az, Ṣ, O, L, Mṣb, Ḳ;) or *had* غُدَد [pl. of غُدَّة] *between the flesh and the skin.* (L.) —— Hence, (A,) أَغَدَّ signifies also ‡ *He* (a man, Aṣ, Ṣ, A, O) *was,* or *became, angry,* (Aṣ, Ṣ, O, L,) or *swollen by reason of anger, as though he were a camel having the disease termed* غُدَّة: (A:) and أَغَدَّ عَلَيْهِ *he was angry with him;* (Ḳ;) or *he swelled against him and was angry with him.* (L.) —— And أَغَدَّ القَوْمُ *The people,* or *party, had their camels affected with the disease termed* غُدَّة. (Ṣ, O, L, Ḳ.)

غَدٌ: see art. غدو.

غُدَّةٌ (IDrd, Ṣ, O, L, Mṣb, Ḳ) and ↓ غُدَدَةٌ (Ṣ, O, L, Ḳ) [*A ganglion;* i. e.] *any hard lump in the tendinous parts;* (L, Ḳ;) [*a lump of*] *flesh arising from disease, between the skin and the flesh, which may be made to move about:* (Mṣb:) and *any small nodous lump* (عُقْدَة) *in the body* (IDrd, O, L, Ḳ) *of a man,* (IDrd, O, L,) *surrounded by fat:* (IDrd, O, L, Ḳ:) pl. غُدَدٌ [properly pl. of غُدَّة, and also a coll. gen. n. of which غُدَدَةٌ is the n. un.]: (Ṣ, O, L, Mṣb, Ḳ:) غُدَّةٌ [is applied in the present day to *a ganglion:* and *a bubo:* and *a wen:* and all these may be meant by its being said that it] also signifies *a* [*swelling such as is termed*] سِلْعَة, (L, Ḳ,) *overspread by fat.* (L.) —— And غُدَّةٌ signifies likewise The *plague,* or *pestilence,* (طَاعُون,) *in camels;* (Aṣ, Ṣ, O, L, Ḳ;) as also ↓ غُدَدٌ: (Ḳ:) or the *same in camels as the* طاعون *in man:* (Mṣb:) *it attacks them in the groins, and seldom do they recover from it:* (L:) or *it is only in the belly;* (Ḳ, TA;) and when it extends to the camel's نَحْر [or part where he is stabbed, or stuck, when he is slaughtered], and to his groin, or arm-pit, the epithet دَابِرٌ [so in the TA, but in the O دَارِئٌ, which I believe to be the right reading,] is applied to him: so says ʼAṣr: (TA:) or *it is also in the fat parts;* (Lth, O, L;) *and between the flesh and the skin.* (L.) —— And *What is between the fat and the hump* [of the camel]. (Ḳ.) ═══ Another signification of غُدَّة is *A part,* or *portion,* of property; (L, Ḳ;) as in the saying, عَلَيْهِ غُدَّةٌ مِنْ مَالٍ [*He owes a part,* or *portion, of some property*]: (L:) pl. غَدَائِدُ, (L, Ḳ,) and, in some of the copies of the Ḳ, غِدَادٌ. (TA.) And [these two pls.] غَدَائِدُ and غِدَادٌ signify also *Lots, portions,* or *shares:* (L, Ḳ:) thus, accord. to Fr, the former of them means in a verse of Lebeed cited and expl. voce عَدِيدَةٌ; but the reading better known is عَدَائِدُ: accord. to Az, غَدَائِدُ in this instance signifies *redundances.* (L.)

غُدَدٌ: see the next preceding paragraph.

غُدَدَةٌ: see غُدَّةٌ. —— [The pl.] غُدَدَاتٌ is expl. by AHeyth as signifying *Redundances of fatness:* and *redundances of goodly* [*fur, such as is termed*] وَبَر. (L.)

غَادٌّ: see مُغِدٌّ, in two places.

مُغَدٌّ: see the paragraph here following.

مُغِدٌّ A camel *having the disease termed* غُدَّة; (Aṣ, Az, Ṣ, O, L, Ḳ;) as also ↓ مُغَدٌّ (L) and ↓ مَغْدُودٌ, (Az, L, Ḳ,) or this is not said, (Aṣ, O, Ḳ,) but it was heard by Az from the Arabs, (O, L,) and ↓ مُغَدِّدٌ (Az, L) and ↓ غَادٌّ: (O, L, Ḳ:) مُغِدٌّ, without ة, is also applied to a she-camel: and its pl. is مَغَادٌّ: (L:) the pl. of ↓ غَادٌّ is غِدَادٌ. (O, L, Ḳ.*) —— [Hence,] ‡ An *angry* man: (Aṣ, Ṣ, L:) or *swollen by reason of anger,* (A, L,) *as though he were a camel having the disease termed* غُدَّة. (A.) One says, رَأَيْتُ فُلَانًا مُغِدًّا and ↓ مُسْتَغِدًّا ‡ *I saw such a one swollen with anger.* (L.)

مُغَدِّدٌ: see the next preceding paragraph.

مِغْدَادٌ † A man, (Ṣ, O, L, Ḳ,) and a woman, (O, L, Ḳ,) *much,* or *often, in anger:* (Ṣ, O, L, Ḳ:) or *always angry:* (O, Ḳ:) or *angry in disposition or nature.* (O, L.)

مَغْدُودٌ:
مُسْتَغِدٌّ: } see مُغِدٌّ.

غدر

1. غَدَرَهُ, (Ḳ,) and [more commonly] غَدَرَ بِهِ, aor. ـِ (Ṣ, M, IḲṭṭ, Mṣb, Ḳ) and ـُ; (M, IḲṭṭ, Ḳ;) and غَدِرَ, aor. ـَ, (Lḥ, Ḳ,) but ISd doubts the correctness of this last; (TA;) inf. n. غَدْرٌ, (Ṣ, Mṣb, Ḳ,) of غَدَرَ; (Ṣ, Mṣb, TA;) and غَدَرٌ (TA, and so in the CḲ in the place of غَـدْر,) and غَدَرَانٌ, (Ḳ, TA,) which are both of غَدِرَ; (TA;) *He acted perfidiously, unfaithfully, faithlessly,* or *treacherously, to him;* (M, Ḳ;) *he broke his compact, contract, covenant,* or *the like, with him;* (Mṣb;) *he neglected the performance,* or *fulfilment, of his compact,* &c., *with him:* (Ṣ:) غَدْرٌ is the *contr. of* وَفَآءٌ, (Ḳ,) or *of* وَفَآءٌ بِعَهْدٍ: (M:) or it signifies the *being remiss* in a thing, and *neglecting* it. (B.) ═══ غَدَرَ, aor. ـِ, (T, O, Ḳ,) inf. n. غَدْرٌ, (T, O,) *He drank the water of the* غدير [q. v.]: (T, O, Ḳ:) and, accord. to the Ḳ, غَدِرَ, *he drank the water of the sky;* but this is a sheer mistake, occasioned by a misunderstanding of a saying in the T; here following: (TA:) Az says that غَدَرَ meaning as expl. above should accord. to analogy be غَدِرَ, like كَرِعَ meaning "he drank the كَرَع," i. e. the water of the sky: (O, TA:) moreover, a distinction is strangely made in the Ḳ between the water of the غدير and the water of the sky. (TA.) ═══ غَدَرَتْ وَلَدَهَا, said of a woman, is *like* دَغَرَتْهُ [q. v.]. (TA.) ═══ غَدِرَ, [aor. ـَ, inf. n. غَدَرٌ,] *He remained,* or *lagged, behind;* as also ↓ تَغَدَّرَ, accord. to Aṣ, who cites the following verse of Imra-el-Ḳeys:

عَشِيَّةَ جَاوَزْنَا حَمَاةَ وَسَيْرُنَا
أَخُو الجَهْدِ لَا نَلْوِى عَلَى مَنْ تَغَدَّرَا

[*In the evening when we passed beyond Ḥamáh, and our journeying was laborious, we not waiting for such as lagged behind*]: but accord. to one relation it is تَعَذَّرَ, which means [the same, or] "held back, or withheld himself, for a cause rendering him excused." (TA.) You say غَدِرَ عَنْ أَصْحَابِهِ *He remained,* or *lagged, behind his companions.* (TA.) And غَدِرَتِ النَّاقَةُ عَنِ الإِبِلِ, (Ṣ, Ḳ,) and الشَّاةُ عَنِ الغَنَمِ, (Ṣ,) *The she-camel remained,* or *lagged, behind the other camels,* (Ṣ, Ḳ,) *not coming up to them,* (TA,) and so *the sheep,* or *goat, behind the other sheep,* or *goats.* (Ṣ.) And غَدَرَ فُلَانٌ بَعْدَ إِخْوَتِهِ *Such a one remained after the death of his brothers.* (TA. [But غَدَرَ, here, is app. a mistake for غَدِرَ, unless both forms be allowable.]) ═══ غَدِرَ اللَّيْلُ; (Ḳ;) or غَدِرَتِ اللَّيْلَةُ, aor. ـَ, inf. n. غَدَرٌ; and ↓ أَغْدَرَتْ;

(Ṣ;) *The night became dark:* (Ḳ:) or *became intensely dark.* (Ṣ.) ═ غَدِرَتِ الغَنَمُ, (Ḳ,) inf. n. غَدَرٌ, (TA,) *The sheep, or goats, became satiated in the place of pasture in the first of the growth thereof.* (Ḳ.) ═ غَدِرَتِ الأَرْضُ *The land abounded with* غَدَر [q. v.]. (Ḳ.)

2. غدّر *He cast* men, or *made* them *to fall, into what is termed* غَدَر [q. v.]; and ▼ اغدر may signify the same. (O.)

3. غَادَرَهُ, inf. n. مُغَادَرَةٌ (Ṣ, Ḳ) and غِدَارٌ; (Ḳ;) and ▼ اغدرهُ; (Ṣ, Ḳ;) *He left him,* or *it;* (Ṣ, Ḳ;) *he left him,* or *it, remaining.* (Ḳ.) It is said in the Ḳur xviii. 47, لَا يُغَادِرُ صَغِيرَةً وَلَا كَبِيرَةً *It will not leave,* or *omit,* or *it will not fall short of,* (TA,) *a small sin nor a great sin.* (Jel.) And in a trad., يَا لَيْتَنِى غُودِرْتُ مَعَ أَصْحَابِ نُحْصِ الجَبَلِ *Would that I had* [*been left behind,* and had] suffered martyrdom *with the people of the foot of the mountain* of Oḥud, who were slain there, and the other martyrs: said by Moḥammad. (A'Obeyd.) [See also a verse of 'Antarah cited voce مُتَرَدَّمٌ; and another, of Kuthciyir, voce عَشَبٌ.] ▼ اغدر also signifies *He left behind.* (TA.) You say اغدر ▼ النَّاقَةَ, and الشَّاةَ, *He* (the pastor) *left the she-camel behind the other camels,* and *the sheep,* or *goat, behind the other sheep,* or *goats.* (Ṣ.) And أَعَانَنِى فُلَانٌ فَأَغْدَرَ ▼ لَهُ ذٰلِكَ فِى قَلْبِى مَوَدَّةً i. e. [*Such a one aided me, and that*] *left remaining* [*in my heart a love for him*]. (Lḥ, TA.)

4: see 3, in four places: ═ and see also 1: ═ and 2.

5: see غَدِرَ.

10. استغدر *It* (a place) *had in it pools of water left by a torrent* or *torrents.* (Ḳ.) — And اسْتَغْدَرَتْ هُنَاكَ غُدُرٌ *Pools of water left by a torrent* or *torrents became formed there.* (Ṣ.)

غَدَرٌ; pl. غُدُورٌ: see غُدْرَةٌ, in three places. — [Hence,] one says, أَلْقَتِ النَّاقَةُ غَدَرَهَا *The she-camel cast forth what her womb had left remaining in it of blood and foul matter* [*after her bringing forth*]. (TA.) And أَلْقَتِ الشَّاةُ غُدُورَهَا *The ewe,* or *she-goat, cast forth the water and blood and other remains in her womb after bringing forth.* (TA.) — And فِى النَّهْرِ غَدَرٌ *In the river,* or *rivulet, is slime remaining when the water has sunk into the earth.* (TA.) ═ غَدَرٌ signifies also *A place such as is termed* ظَلِفٌ [app. as meaning *hard, and that does not show a footmark,* or *rugged and hard*], *abounding with stones:* (Ṣ, O, TA:) or *a place abounding with stones, difficult to traverse:* (TA:) or *any difficult place, through which the beast can hardly,* or *in nowise, pass:* (Ḳ:) or *soft ground, in which are* [*trenches, or channels, such as are termed*] لَخَاقِيق: (TA:) or *burrows,* (Lḥ, Ṣ, Ḳ, TA,) and *banks,* or *ridges, worn and undermined by water,* (Lḥ, TA,) *and uneven* لَخَاقِيق *in the ground:* (Lḥ, Ṣ, Ḳ, TA: [and the like is also said in the TA on the authority of Aṣ:]) and *stones* (Ḳ, TA) *with trees;* thus accord. to AZ and IḲṭṭ: (TA:) and *anything that conceals one, and obstructs his sight:* pl. أَغْدَارٌ. (TA.) — [Hence,] one says, مَا أَثْبَتَ غَدَرَهُ, meaning مَا أَثْبَتَهُ فِى الغَدَرِ [*How firm is he in traversing the rugged and hard and stony place!* &c.]: this is said of the horse: and also † of the man when his tongue is firm in the place of slipping and of contention or litigation: (Ṣ, TA:) or, accord. to Lḥ, it means † *how firm,* or *valid, is his argument,* or *plea, and how seldom does harm in consequence of slipping and stumbling befall him!* or, accord. to Ks, *how firm is what remains of his intellect or understanding!* but ISd says that this explanation did not please him. (TA.) And فَرَسٌ ثَبْتُ الغَدَرِ *A horse firm,* or *steady, in the place of slipping.* (Ibn-Buzurj, TA.) And رَجُلٌ ثَبْتُ الغَدَرِ ‡ *A man firm,* or *steadfast, in fight,* or *conflict,* (Ṣ, Ḳ, TA,) or *in altercation* or *disputation,* or *in speech,* (Ṣ accord. to different copies,) or and *in altercation* or *disputation,* (Ḳ, TA,) and *in speech;* (TA;) and also *in everything that he commences.* (Ḳ, TA.) And accord. to Ibn-Buzurj, one says, إِنَّهُ لَثَبْتُ الغَدَرِ, meaning † *Verily he is strong in talking,* or *discoursing, with men,* and *in contending,* or *disputing, with them.* (L.) [See also ثَبْتٌ.]

غَدِرٌ [part. n. of غَدِرَ]. — See غَادِرٌ, last sentence but one. ═ And see also غَدُورٌ. ═ You say also لَيْلَةٌ غَدِرَةٌ and ▼ مُغْدِرَةٌ (Ṣ, Ḳ) meaning *A dark night;* (Ḳ;) as also ▼ غَدْرَآءُ: (IḲṭṭ, TA:) or *an intensely-dark night,* (Ṣ,) *in which the darkness confines men in their places of alighting or abode, and their shelter, so that they remain behind:* or, as some say, such a night is termed ▼ مُغْدِرَةٌ because it casts him who goes forth therein into the غدر [i. e. غَدَر]. (L, TA.)

غُدَرُ and غُدَرٌ: see غَادِرٌ, in six places: ═ and for غُدُرٌ, see also غَدِيرٌ.

غَدْرَةٌ [an inf. n. un., signifying *An act of perfidy, unfaithfulness, faithlessness,* or *treachery*]: see two exs. voce غَادِرٌ.

غُدْرَةٌ and ▼ غُدُرَةٌ, (Ḳ,) or ▼ غِدْرَةٌ, (ISk, Az, TA,) and ▼ غَدَرَةٌ and ▼ غَدَرٌ, (Lḥ, TA,) and ▼ غُدَارَةٌ, with ḍamm, (Ḳ,) or ▼ غِدَارَةٌ, (as written in the L,) *A portion that is left,* or *left remaining,* of a thing; (Ḳ,* TA;) *a remain, remainder, remnant, relic,* or *residue:* (Lḥ, ISk, Az, L:) the pl. of غُدْرَةٌ is غُدُرَاتٌ (Ḳ) [and accord. to analogy غُدْرَاتٌ and غُدَرَاتٌ] and app. غُدَرٌ; (TA;) and that of ▼ غِدْرَةٌ [or ▼ غَدَرَةٌ] is غَدَرٌ and غَدَرَاتٌ; (ISk, Az;) and that of ▼ غَدَرٌ is غُدُورٌ. (TA.) You say, عَلَى فُلَانٍ غَدَرٌ مِنَ الصَّدَقَةِ *Such a one owes arrears of the poor-rate.* (ISk.) And عَلَى بَنِى فُلَانٍ غُدْرَةٌ ▼ مِنَ الصَّدَقَةِ and ▼ غَدَرٌ *The sons of such a one owe an arrear of the poor-rate.* (Lḥ, L.) And بِهِ غَادِرٌ ▼ مِنْ مَرَضٍ *In him is a relic of disease;* like غَابِرٌ. (TA.)

غُدُرَةٌ, and the pl. غُدَرٌ: see غُدْرَةٌ, in three places.

غِدْرَةٌ: see غُدْرَةٌ, in two places.

غَدَرَةٌ, and the pl. غَدَرٌ: see غُدْرَةٌ, in three places.

غَدْرَآءُ *Darkness.* (Ḳ.) — See also غَدِرٌ. ═ أَرْضٌ غَدْرَآءُ *Land abounding with places of the kind termed* غَدَر. (IḲṭṭ, TA.)

غَدَّارٌ: see غَادِرٌ.

غَدُورٌ: see غَادِرٌ, in two places. ═ Also *A she-camel that remains,* or *lags, behind the other camels:* (Ḳ, TA:) in some of the copies of the Ḳ غَدُورَةٌ, with ة; but the former is the right. (TA.) And نَاقَةٌ غَدِرَةٌ ▼ غَبِرَةٌ *A she-camel that remains,* or *lags, behind the other camels, in being driven.* (Lḥ.)

غَدِيرٌ *A pool of water left by a torrent:* (A'Obeyd, Ṣ, M, Ḳ:) of the measure فَعِيلٌ in the sense of the measure مُفَاعَلٌ, from غَادَرَهُ, or مُفْعَلٌ, from أَغْدَرَهُ; or, as some say, of the measure فَعِيلٌ in the sense of the measure فَاعِلٌ; (Ṣ;) because it is unfaithful to those who come to it to water, failing when much wanted: (Ṣ,* TA:) but it is a subst.; [not an epithet; or an epithet in which the quality of a subst. predominates, and only used as a subst.:] you do not say هٰذَا مَآءٌ غَدِيرٌ: (Lḥ:) or *a place in which rain-water stagnates,* whether *small* or *large, not remaining until the summer:* (Lth:) or *a river:* (Mṣb:) [but this is extr.:] pl. [of pauc. أَغْدِرَةٌ, (occurring in a verse cited voce إِلَّا, &c.,) and of mult.] غُدْرَانٌ (Ṣ, Mṣb, Ḳ, TA) and غُدُرٌ (Ṣ, Nh, L, TA,) which last is sometimes contracted into غُدْرٌ: (TA:) in the Ḳ, the last pl. is said to be of the measure of صُرَدٌ; [i. e. ▼ غُدَرٌ;] but this is inconsistent with what is said in other lexicons, as shown above: and it is also said in the Ḳ that غُدَرٌ signifies the same as غَدِيرٌ, in the sense first given above; but it appears that this is a pl. of غُدْرَةٌ; and that, in the Ḳ, we should read, for كَالغَدِيرِ, وَالغَدِيرُ, and place this before, instead of after, its explanation. (TA.) — Hence, ‡ *A piece of herbage;* (TA;) as also ▼ غَدِيرَةٌ: pl. غُدْرَانٌ: (Ḳ, TA:) this is the only pl. (TA.) — Hence also, (TA,) ‡ *A sword;* (Ḳ, TA;) like as it is called لُجٌّ. (TA.) — And ▼ غَدِيرَةٌ also signifies A she-camel *left by the pastor* (Ṣ, Ḳ) *behind the other camels;* and in like manner, a sheep, or goat. (Ṣ.)

غُدَارَةٌ or غِدَارَةٌ: see غُدْرَةٌ.

غَدِيرَةٌ: see غَدِيرٌ, last two sentences. ═ Also *A portion,* or *lock,* or *plaited lock, of hair, hanging from the head;* syn. ذُؤَابَةٌ: (Ṣ, Ḳ:) accord. to Lth, every عَقِيصَة is a غَدِيرَة; and the غَدِيرَتَانِ are the *two portions,* or *locks,* or *plaited locks, of hair* (ذُؤَابَتَانِ) *which fall upon the breast:* (TA:) pl. غَدَائِرُ: (Ṣ, Ḳ:) or غدائر *pertain to women, and are plaited;* and ضَفَائِر, to men. (TA.) ═ غَدِيرَةُ الحَائِكِ means *The hollow, in the ground, in which the weaver puts his legs,* or *feet:* also called الوَهْدَةُ. (Mgh in art. وهد.)

غُدَّار : } see غَادِرٌ; the first and third, in two places.
غِدِّيرٌ :
غَدَّارَةٌ :

غَادِرٌ and ♦ غُدَرٌ [respecting which see below] (Ṣ, Ḳ) and ♦ غَدُورٌ and ♦ غَدَّارٌ and ♦ غِدِّيرٌ (Ḳ) are epithets applied to a man [and signifying, the first, *Perfidious, unfaithful, faithless,* or *treacherous;* or *acting perfidiously,* &c.; and the rest, *very perfidious,* &c.]: (Ṣ, Ḳ:) and ♦ غَدُورٌ and ♦ غَدَّارٌ and ♦ غَدَّارَةٌ are epithets applied to a woman [and signifying as above]: (Ḳ:) but ♦ غُدَرُ is mostly used in calling to a man and reviling him: (Ṣ:) you say to a man, يَا غُدَرُ [*O very perfidious man*]; (Ṣ, Ḳ;) and in like manner, يَا آبْنَ مَغْدَرٍ ♦, and ♦ يَا مَغْدِرُ, and ♦ يَا مَغْدَرُ, and ♦ يا ابن مغدرٍ, all determinate; (Ḳ, TA;) and to a woman, ♦ يَا غَدَارِ, like قَطَامِ: (Ḳ:) [accord. to some, ♦ غُدَرُ is only used in this manner, and is therefore without tenween; for] it is said that رَجُلٌ غُدَرُ is not allowable, because غُدَرُ is determinate: but Sh says رَجُلٌ غُدَرٌ, writing it, says Az, with tenween, contr. to what Lth says; and this is correct; a word of the measure فُعَل being imperfectly decl. [only] when it is a determinate subst., like عُمَرُ and زُفَرُ: and IAth says that غُدَرُ is altered from its original form, which is غَادِرٌ, for the sake of intensiveness: (TA:) in the pl. [sense] you say يَا آلَ غُدَرَ, (Ṣ,) or يَا لَغُدَرَ [for يَا آلَ غُدَرَ], (see the letter ل, and see آلٌ, in art. اول,)] like يَا لَفُجَرَ. (TA.) It is said in a trad., يَا غُدَرُ ♦ أَلَسْتُ أَسْعَى فِي غَدْرَتِكَ [app. meaning, *O thou very perfidious: am I not striving,* or *labouring, in respect of thine act of perfidy, to rectify it?*]. (Ṣ: but in one copy, غُدْرَتِكَ.) And in another trad., relating to El-Ḥodeybiyeh, يَا غُدَرُ ♦ وَهَلْ غَسَلْتَ غَدْرَتَكَ ♦ إِلَّا بِالْأَمْسِ [*O thou very perfidious: and didst thou wash away thine act of perfidy save yesterday?*]: said by 'Orweh Ibn-Mes'ood to El-Mugheereh. (TA.) And in another trad., ♦ اِجْلِسْ غُدَرُ [*Sit thou, O very perfidious*]; for يَا غُدَرُ: said by 'Áïsheh to El-Ḳásim. (TA.) — [Hence,] ♦ سِنُونَ غَدَّارَةٌ ‡ *Years in which is much rain and little herbage;* from [the inf. n.] الغَدْرُ; i. e. *that excite people's eager desire for abundance of herbage, by the rain, and then fail to fulfil their promise.* (TA.) — [And ♦ غَدِرٌ is app. syn. with غَادِرٌ; for] غَدِرَةٌ occurs in a trad. applied to land (أَرْض), as though meaning † *Not producing herbage bountifully;* or *giving growth to herbage, and then soon becoming blighted,* or *blasted;* wherefore it is likened to the غَادِر, who acts unfaithfully. (TA.) ═ See also غُدْرَةٌ, last sentence.

مَغْدَر and مَغْدِر: see غَادِرٌ, each in two places.

لَيْلَةٌ مُغْدِرَةٌ: see غَدِرٌ, in two places.

غدف

1. غَدَفَ لَهُ فِي العَطَآءِ, (aor. ـِ, inf. n. غَدْفٌ, TḲ,) *He was profuse to him in giving.* (Ibn-'Abbád, O, Ḳ.)

4. اغدفت قِنَاعَهَا *She* (a woman, Ṣ) *let down,* or *let fall, her* [*head-covering called*] قناع *upon her face.* (Ṣ, Ḳ.) 'Antarah says,

إِنْ تُغْدِفِي دُونِي القِنَاعَ فَإِنَّنِي
طَبٌّ بِأَخْذِ الفَارِسِ المُسْتَلْئِمِ

(Ṣ,) i. e. *If,* O my beloved, *thou let down before me the head-covering,* meaning if thou veil thyself from me, *I am expert in capturing the mail-clad horseman:* then how should I lack power to capture thee? (EM p. 236.) — [Hence,] اغدف اللَّيْلُ ‡ *The night let down its curtains* [*of darkness*]. (Ṣ, Ḳ.) — And اغدف الشَّبَكَةَ عَلَى الصَّيْدِ *He* (a sportsman, or fowler, or the like,) *let fall the net upon the object,* or *objects, to be captured.* (Ṣ, Ḳ.) Hence, (TA,) it is said in a trad., إِنَّ قَلْبَ المُؤْمِنِ أَشَدُّ آرْتِكَاضًا مِنَ الذَّنْبِ يُصِيبُهُ مِنَ العُصْفُورِ حِينَ يُغْدَفُ بِهِ (Ṣ, TA,) i. e. [*Verily the heart of the believer is more vehemently agitated in consequence of the offence that he purposes than the sparrow*] *when the net is made to cover it,* whereupon it struggles to escape: (TA:) or مِنَ الخَطِيئَةِ [i. e. *in consequence of the sin* that he is tempted to commit]. (So in the O, instead of من الذنب يصيبه.) — اغدف بِهَا † *He compressed her,* (Ibn-'Abbád, O, Ḳ,) i. e., a woman: (Ibn-'Abbád, O:) or, as in the A, *he went in to her.* (TA.) — اغدف said of the sea [app. from the same verb said of the night] ‡ *It became confusedly agitated in its waves;* expl. by the words اِعْتَكَرَتْ أَمْوَاجُهُ. (TA.) — And † *He slept.* (AA, TA in art. سدف.) — And, accord. to Lḥ, (O,) اغدف said of the circumciser (O, Ḳ, TA) of a boy (O) means *He cut off entirely the prepuce;* (O, Ḳ, TA;) like أَسْحَتَ; (O, TA;) but ISd holds that the latter has this meaning, and the former means *he left somewhat thereof:* (TA:) one says to the circumciser, لَا تُغْدِفْ وَلَا تُسْحِتْ, (O, TA,) but this means *Leave not thou much of the skin, nor cut off entirely.* (TA.)

8. اغتدف مِنْهُ *He* (a man, O) *took from him* (another man, O) *much.* (Ibn-'Abbád, O, Ḳ.) — And اغتدف الثَّوْبَ *He cut the garment,* or *piece of cloth.* (Ibn-'Abbád, O, Ḳ.)

12. اِغْدَوْدَفَ *It* (the night) *came with its darkness.* (TA.)

غَدَفٌ *A state of ease,* and *plentifulness,* or *ampleness:* so in the saying, القَوْمُ فِي غَدَفٍ مِنْ عَيْشِهِمْ (O, Ḳ*) or مَعِيشَتِهِمْ (TA) [*The people,* or *party, are in a state of ease,* &c., *in respect of their means of subsistence*]: thus in the O and TṢ: but in the L, فِي غُدَافٍ ♦ من معيشتهم. (TA.)

غُدْفَةٌ *A thing in the form of the* [*head-covering called*] قِنَاع, *worn by the women of the Arabs of the desert.* (TA.)

غِدْفَةٌ The *apparel of the king.* (TA.)

غُدَافٌ The *crow,* (Ṣ, O, Ḳ, TA,) or, as some say, the *large crow,* (TA,) *of the summer,* or *hot season:* (Ṣ, O, Ḳ, TA:) or, accord. to some, in an absolute sense, the *crow:* (TA:) or the *large crow that is full in the wings:* (JK:) or the *black crow:* (MA:) pl. غِدْفَانٌ. (Ṣ, O.) — And *A vulture having abundant plumage* (Ṣ, O, Ḳ) is sometimes thus called: (Ṣ, O:) pl. as above. (Ḳ.) — And *Long,* (Ṣ, O, Ḳ, TA,) *abundant,* (TA,) *black hair.* (Ṣ, O, Ḳ, TA.) — Also *A black* wing. (Ṣ, Ḳ, TA.) And Anything *intensely black* is termed غُدَافٌ, and ♦ أَسْوَدُ غُدَافِيٌّ. (TA.) ═ See also غَدَفٌ.

غُدَافِيٌّ: see the next preceding paragraph.

مغدف, [app. مُغْدِفٌ, or perhaps taken from a mistranscription for مُغْدِقٌ,] as an epithet applied to means of subsistence (عَيْش), signifies *Smooth and ample.* (TA.) [Freytag mentions مُغْدَوْدِفٌ and مُغْدَوْدِقٌ, each having the fem. with ة, as signifying *Copious,* applied to rain: both from the "Fákihet el-Khulafà," p. 141, l. 3; where the word is مغدقة, evidently مُغْدِقَة, and rhyming with مُطْبِقَة.]

غدق

1. غَدِقَتِ العَيْنُ, (Ṣ, O, Mṣb, Ḳ,) aor. ـَ, inf. n. غَدَقٌ, (Mṣb,) *The spring,* or *source, abounded with water;* (Ṣ, O, Mṣb, Ḳ;) as also ♦ اغدقت, inf. n. إِغْدَاقٌ. (Mṣb.) And غَدِقَ المَطَرُ, inf. n. as above; (Mṣb;) and ♦ اغدق, (O, Mṣb, Ḳ,) inf. n. إِغْدَاقٌ; (Mṣb;) and ♦ اِغْدَوْدَقَ; (Ḳ;) and ♦ غَيْدَقَ; (Abu-l-'Omeythil, TA;) *The rain was,* or *became, copious.* (O, Mṣb, Ḳ, TA.) And غَدِقَتْ سَنَتُنَا [*Our year was,* or *became, rainy*]. (O.) And غَدِقَ, aor. and inf. n. as above, *There was abundance of rain,* or *dew,* or *moisture,* or *of water,* in the place. (Zj, TA.) — غَدَقٌ is also used in relation to herbs, or herbage, as meaning The *being plentifully irrigated,* or *flourishing and fresh, juicy,* or *moist.* (En-Naḍr, AḤn, TA.) — And you say, غَدِقَتِ الأَرْضُ, and ♦ اغدقت, meaning *The land abounded,* or *became abundant, with herbage,* or *with the produce of the earth.* (TA.) — And غَدَقَتِ الأَرْضُ, aor. ـِ, being of the class of ضَرَبَ, *The land became moistened by abundant water.* (Mṣb.)

4: see the preceding paragraph in three places.

12: see 1, second sentence.

Q. Q. 1. غَيْدَقَ: see 1, second sentence. — Also ‡ *He* (a man, Ibn-'Abbád, O) *had much saliva;* (Ibn-'Abbád, O, Ḳ, TA;) or, accord. to the L, *much slaver.* (TA.)

غَدَقٌ [an inf. n.: and used in the sense of the part. n. ♦ غَدِقٌ, meaning] *Abundant,* or *copious;* applied to water; (Ṣ, O, Mṣb, Ḳ, TA;) not restricted to rain; (TA;) as also ♦ مُغْدِقٌ and ♦ مُغْدَوْدِقٌ, both applied to rain, and the latter [or both] applied to water [in general]; and ♦ غَيْدَاقٌ likewise, applied to water, and, as AA says, to rain: or غَدَقٌ is applied to rain as meaning *abundant*, or *copious*, [*so as to be*] *general in its extent*. (TA.) It is said in the Ḳur [lxxii. 16], لَوِ ٱسْتَقَامُوا عَلَى ٱلطَّرِيقَةِ لَأَسْقَيْنَاهُمْ مَآءً غَدَقًا [*If they should go on undeviatingly in the way* which they are pursuing, *we would water them with abundant water*]; (O, TA;) to try them thereby; the طريقة here being that of infidelity; so says Th, and in like manner Fr; but others say that it is that of the right direction: (TA:) 'Ásim Ibn-Abi-n-Najood read ▼غَدِقًا. (O, TA.) In the saying, in a trad., اَللّٰهُمَّ ٱسْقِنَا غَدَقًا ▼مُغْدِقًا, the last word is used as a corroborative [the meaning being *O God, water us very abundantly*]. (TA.) — See also غَيْدَاقٌ.

غَدِقٌ: see غَدَقٌ, in two places. You say also عَيْنٌ غَدِقَةٌ *A spring*, or *source*, *abounding with water*. (Mṣb.) And أَرْضٌ غَدِقَةٌ *Land that is moist and irrigated in the utmost degree; abounding with water*. (TA.) And عُشْبٌ غَدِقٌ *Herbs*, or *herbage*, *plentifully irrigated*, or *flourishing and fresh, juicy*, or *moist*. (En-Naḍr, AḤn, TA.)

عَيْنٌ غُدَيْقَةٌ: see عَيْنٌ, near the end of the paragraph.

غَيْدَقٌ: } see each in two places in the next paragraph.
غَيْدَقَانٌ: }

غَيْدَاقٌ: see غَدَقٌ. — [Hence,] عَيْشٌ غَيْدَاقٌ *A life ample in its means*, or *circumstances*; *plentiful*; as also ▼غَيْدَقٌ: and هُمْ فِى غَدَقٍ ▼ مِنَ ▼غَيْدَاقِ العَيْشِ and [*They are in an ample*, or *a plentiful, state of life*]. (TA.) And عَامٌ غَيْدَاقٌ *A year abounding in herbage, fruitful*, or *plentiful*; and so سَنَةٌ غَيْدَاقٌ, without ة [to the latter word]. (TA.) — And إِنَّهُ لَغَيْدَاقُ الجَرْىِ and العَدْوِ *Verily he is wide-stepping in respect of running*. (TA.) — And شَدٌّ غَيْدَاقٌ *A vehement running*. (TA.) — غَيْدَاقٌ applied to a horse signifies طَوِيلٌ [app. meaning *Long-bodied*]. (O, Ḳ.) — And, applied to a man, (Ṣ, O, TA,) *Generous*; (Ṣ, O, Ḳ, TA;) *bountiful*; *large*, or *liberal, in disposition*; *munificent*; (TA;) and so ▼غَيْدَقَانٌ; (Ḳ,* TA;) or this, some say, signifies *abundant, ample*, as applied to anything. (TA.) — Also, and ▼غَيْدَقٌ, (Ṣ, O, Ḳ,) and ▼غَيْدَقَانٌ, (O, Ḳ,) *Soft*, or *tender*; applied to a youth, or young man; (Ṣ, O, Ḳ;) and to youth, or youthfulness, (O, Ḳ,) as also غداقى [app. a mistranscription for ▼غَيْدَاقِىٌّ]: (TA:) and it is said that غَيْدَاقٌ applied to a boy signifies *that has not attained to puberty*. (TA.) — And غَيْدَاقٌ signifies also The *young one of the* [*lizard called*] ضَبّ, (AZ, Ṣ, O, Ḳ,) after the state in which it is termed حِسْل [q. v.]. (AZ, Ṣ, O.) — And [the pl.] غَيَادِيقُ signifies *Serpents*. (Ṣ, O, L, Ḳ.)

غَيْدَاقِىٌّ: see the next preceding paragraph.

مُغْدِقٌ: see غَدَقٌ, in two places. [مُغَدَّقٌ mentioned by Freytag as signifying "copious," applied to rain, is a mistake: see the last paragraph of art. غدف.]

مُغْدَوْدِقٌ: see غَدَقٌ, first sentence.

غدو

1. غَدَا, (Ṣ, M, Mṣb, Ḳ,) aor. يَغْدُو, (Ṣ, M, Mṣb,) inf. n. غُدُوٌّ (Ṣ, M, Mgh, Mṣb, Ḳ) and غَدْوٌ (M, TA, and so accord. to the CḲ instead of غُدُوٌّ [which is the only inf. n. commonly known]) and غُدْوَةٌ, (Ḳ,) *He went*, or *went away, in the time called* غُدْوَة, (Mgh, Mṣb,) i. e. [*the early part of the morning*,] *the period between the prayer of daybreak and sunrise*: this is the primary signification: (Mṣb:) or *i. q.* بَكَرَ [*he went forth early in the morning*; *in the first part of the day*; or *between the time of the prayer of daybreak and sunrise*]; so in the phrase غَدَا عَلَيْهِ [*he went forth early in the morning*, &c., *to him*, or *it*]; (Ḳ;) as also ▼اِغْتَدَى: (Ṣ,* Ḳ:) and ▼غَادَاهُ signifies the same as غَدَا عَلَيْهِ; (Ṣ;) or the same as بَاكَرَهُ [which is syn. with بَكَرَ عَلَيْهِ as expl. above; and signifies also, like بَكَرَ عَلَيْهِ, *he hastened to it*, or *to do it*, at any time, morning or evening]: (ISd, Ḳ, TA:) الغُدُوُّ is *the contr. of* الرَّوَاحُ [inf. n. of رَاحَ]. (Ṣ.) Hence, in the Ḳur [lxviii. 22], أَنِ ٱغْدُوا عَلَى حَرْثِكُمْ [*Saying, Go ye forth early*, &c., *to your land's produce*]: and the saying of a poet,

وَقَدْ أَغْتَدِى ▼ وَالطَّيْرُ فِى وُكُنَاتِهَا

[*And sometimes*, or *often, I go forth early*, &c., *while the birds are in their nests*]. (TA.) — Afterwards, by reason of frequency of use, it became employed as meaning *He went*, or *went away*, or *departed*, at any time. (Mgh,* Mṣb, TA.) Hence the saying, (Mgh, Mṣb,) of the Prophet, (Mṣb,) in a trad., (Mgh,) اُغْدُ يَا أُنَيْسُ, (Mgh, Mṣb,) meaning *Depart thou, O Uneys*. (Mṣb.) — [Freytag has erroneously assigned to it another meaning, i. e. "Nutrivit;" misled by his finding تَغْدُوْ put for تَغْذُو in art. طلى in the CḲ.] = غَدِىَ: see 5.

2. غَدَّيْتُهُ, (Ṣ, Mṣb, Ḳ,) inf. n. تَغْدِيَةٌ, (Mṣb, Ḳ,) *I fed him with the meal called* غَدَآء [q. v.]. (Ṣ,* Mṣb, Ḳ.)

3: see 1, first sentence. One says, أَنَا أُغَادِيهِ وَأُرَاوِحُهُ expl. in the first paragraph of art. روح.

5. تَغَدَّى [*He ate the meal called* غَدَآء, q. v.; properly,] *he ate in the first part of the day*; (Ṣ,* Mṣb,* Ḳ;) as also ▼غَدِىَ, (IḲṭṭ, Ḳ, TA,) inf. n. غَدًا. (TḲ: but in the TA written غداء.) When it is said to thee, تَغَدَّ [*Eat thou the* غَدَآء], thou sayest, مَا بِى مِنْ تَغَدٍّ [*I have no desire for eating the* غَدَآء]; and not مَا بِى غَدَآءٌ, for [the] غَدَآء is the meal itself. (Ṣ, Mṣb. See also 5 in art. عشو.) تَغَدَّى فِى رَمَضَانَ means تَسَحَّرَ [i. e. *He ate the meal, or drank the draught of milk, called* سَحُور, q. v.]. (TA.) — And تَغَدَّتِ الإِبِلُ means *The camels pastured in the first part of the day*. (AḤn, TA.)

8: see 1, first and second sentences.

[10. اِسْتَغْدَى accord. to Freytag is *syn. with* تَغَدَّى; but for this I do not find any authority.]

غَدٌ, meaning The *morrow*, the *day next after the present day*, (Mṣb,) is originally ▼غَدْوٌ, (Ṣ, Mṣb, Ḳ,) the و being elided, (Ṣ, Mṣb,) without any substitution, (Ṣ,) and the د being made a letter of declinability. (Mṣb.) And one says غَدًا meaning [I will do such a thing, &c.,] *to-morrow*: and بَعْدَ غَدٍ *the day after to-morrow*. (MA.) See also غَدَاةٌ. — And its signification has been extended so that it is applied to a remote time that is expected, (Mṣb, TA,) and to a near time. (Nh, TA.) — It is not used in its complete form except in poetry: (Nh, TA:) Lebeed, (Ṣ, TA,) or Dhu-r-Rummeh, (TA,) has thus used it in his saying,

وَمَا النَّاسُ إِلَّا كَالدِّيَارِ وَأَهْلُهَا
بِهَا يَوْمَ حَلُّوهَا وَغَدْوًا ▼ بَلَاقِعُ

[*And mankind are no other than the like of dwellings, the occupants thereof being in them during the day in which they have alighted in them, and to-morrow they are vacant*]: (Ṣ, TA:) or, accord. to the M, one says, هٰذَا غَدُكَ and ▼هٰذَا غَدْوُكَ [*This is thy morrow*]. (TA.) — It has no diminutive. (Sb, Ṣ in art. امس.)

غَدْوٌ: see the next preceding paragraph, in three places.

غَدَاةٌ: see غُدْوَةٌ, in four places: though [properly] fem., and not heard as made masc., it may be made masc. if meant to be understood as signifying the "first part of the day:" (IAmb, Mṣb:) it is originally غَدَوَةٌ, because its pl. is غَدَوَاتٌ. (IHsh, TA.) One says, آتِيكَ غَدَاةَ ▼غَدٍ [*I will come to thee in the early part of the morning*, &c., *of to-morrow*]. (Ṣ, TA.) بِٱلْغَدَاةِ وَٱلْعَشِىِّ in the Ḳur [vi. 52 and xviii. 27] means *After the prayer of daybreak and* [*after*] *the prayer of* [*the period of the afternoon called*] *the* عَصْر: or, accord. to some, [it means *in the morning and the evening*, or rather *in the forenoon and the afternoon*, for they say that] it denotes constancy of religious service: Ibn-'Ámir and Aboo-'Abd-er-Raḥmán Es-Sulamee read بِٱلْغُدْوَةِ ▼ وَٱلْعَشِىِّ; but the former is the common reading; and A'Obeyd says, we think that they read thus following the handwriting, for it is written in all the copies of the Ḳur-án with و, like الصَّلٰوة and الزَّكٰوة, and this is not an indication of the reading [which they have adopted], as the و in الصلوة and الزكوة is not pronounced [otherwise than as an ا of prolongation except that it requires the fet-ḥah that follows to be uttered with a somewhat broad sound]. (TA.) هُوَ ٱبْنُ غَدَاتَيْنِ means *He is a son of two days* [i. e. *he is two days old*]. (TA.) — The dim. is ▼غُدَيَّةٌ: (TA:) or this is the dim. of ▼غُدْوَةٌ: (EM p. 56:) one says, أَرْكَبُ

إِلَيْهِ غُدَيَّةً [*I will ride to him*, or *it, in a short period of an early part of a morning*, &c.]: and one says also, أَتَيْتُهُ ▼ غُدَيَّانَاتٍ [*I came to him*, or *it, in short periods of early parts of mornings*, &c.]; an anomalous [pl.] dim. like عُشَيَّانَاتٌ; both of which are mentioned by Sb. (TA.)

غَدْوَةٌ *A journey in the first part of the day*: [an inf. n. un. of غَدَا:] opposed to رَوْحَةٌ. (TA.) — See also the next paragraph. — And see غَدَاةٌ.

غُدْوَةٌ, (Ṣ, Mṣb, Ḳ, &c.,) and ▼ غَدْوَةٌ, said by MF to be well known, and ▼ غِدْوَةٌ, said by him to be rare, or disapproved, (TA,) The *early part of the morning*; the *first part of the day*; (Ḳ;) or the *period between the time of the prayer of daybreak and sunrise*; (Ṣ, Mṣb, Ḳ;) as also ▼ غَدَاةٌ, and ▼ غَدِيَّةٌ, (Ḳ, TA,) the last [in the CḲ غَدْيَةٌ, but correctly] a dial. var. of غُدْوَةٌ, like ضَحِيَّةٌ a dial. var. of ضَحْوَةٌ: (IAạr, TA:) or ▼ غَدَاةٌ is syn. with ضَحْوَةٌ [meaning the *early part of the forenoon, after sunrise*; accord. to some; *when the sun is yet low*; or, accord. to others, *when the sun is somewhat high*]: (Mṣb:) [it may therefore be generally rendered *morning, before*, or *after, sunrise*:] the pls. are غُدًى, which is pl. of غُدْوَةٌ; (Ṣ, Mṣb, TA;) and غَدَوَاتٌ, (Ṣ, Mṣb, Ḳ, TA,) which is pl. of ▼ غَدَاةٌ; (Ṣ, Mṣb, TA;) and ▼ غُدُوٌّ, (Ḳ, TA,) which is a pl. of غُدْوَةٌ, formed by rejecting the ة [of the sing.], or, accord. to the M, an anomalous pl. of ▼ غَدَاةٌ, or, as J says, [in the Ṣ,] referring to the phrase بِالْغُدُوِّ وَالْآصَالِ, in the Ḳur [vii. 204 and xiii. 16 and xxiv. 36], بِالْغُدُوِّ there means بِالْغَدَوَاتِ, and is a verb [i. e. an inf. n.] used to denote the time, as [is طُلُوع] in the saying أَتَيْتُكَ طُلُوعَ الشَّمْسِ meaning فِى وَقْتِ طُلُوعِ الشمس; (TA;) and غُدَيَّاتٌ, (IAạr, Ḳ, TA, [in the CḲ, erroneously, غَدِيَاتٌ,]) which is pl. of ▼ غَدِيَّةٌ; (TA;) and غَدَايَا, (Ḳ, TA,) which is likewise a pl. of ▼ غَدِيَّةٌ, accord. to IAạr, and, if so, regularly formed from غَدَايِوُ, in the same manner as has already been expl. in the case of عَشَايَا [pl. of عَشِيَّةٌ, q. v. voce عَشِىٌّ]; by some said to be a pl. of غُدْوَةٌ, but this has been controverted by IHsh in the Expos. of the "Kaạbeeyeh" and by its commentator ['Abd-El-Ḳádir] El-Baghdádee; (TA;) or غَدَايَا is not used except in conjunction with عَشَايَا; (Ḳ, TA;) one says, إِنِّى لَآتِيهِ بِالغَدَايَا وَالعَشَايَا [*Verily I come to him in the early parts of mornings and in the late parts of evenings*], for the purpose of conformity. (Ṣ, TA.) Zj says that when غُدْوَةٌ means *The* بُكْرَة [or *early part of the morning*, &c.,] *of the present day*, or *of a particular day*, it is imperfectly decl.: and AḤei says that it is thus accord. to the opinion commonly obtaining, as is also بُكْرَةُ, each as being a generic proper name, like أُسَامَةُ; and that when you mean to generalize, you say, غُدْوَةٌ وَقْتُ نَشَاطٍ [*An early part of a morning is a time of briskness, liveliness*, or *sprightliness*]; and when you mean to particularize, لَأَسِيرَنَّ اللَّيْلَةَ إِلَى غُدْوَةَ [*I will assuredly journey to-night until the early part of the morning*]: (TA:) [in the latter case also] one says, أَتَيْتُهُ غُدْوَةَ [*I came to him in the early part of the morning of this*, or *of a particular, day*]; غدوة being here imperfectly decl. because it is determinate, like سَحَرَ; but it is of those adv. ns. that may be used otherwise than as adv. ns.: you say, سِيرَ عَلَى فَرَسِكَ غُدْوَةُ and غُدْوَةٌ [i. e. *Journeying was performed on thy horse*, or *mare, in the* غُدْوَة *of this*, or *of a particular, day*, and *in a* غُدْوَة,] and غُدْوَةُ and غُدْوَةٌ [i. e. *the journey of the* غُدْوَة *of this*, or *of a particular, day*, and *the journey of a* غُدْوَة, *was performed* (lit. *was journeyed*) *on thy horse*, or *mare*, غُدْوَةُ and غُدْوَةٌ being for مَسِيرَةُ غُدْوَةَ and مَسِيرَةُ غُدْوَةٍ, like as شَهْرٌ in the Ḳur xxxiv. 11 is for مَسِيرَةُ شَهْرٍ]; what is with tenween, of these, being indeterminate, and what is without tenween being determinate. (Ṣ. [In one of my copies of the Ṣ, سُيِرَ is put in the place of سِيرَ: that the latter is the right is shown by the addition of غُدْوَةٌ and غُدْوَةُ; for each of these must be what is termed نَائِبٌ عَنْ فَاعِلٍ i. e. a substitute for an agent.]) See also غَدَاةٌ, in two places.

غِدْوَةٌ: see the next preceding paragraph.

غَدَوِىٌّ: see غَدِىٌّ. — Also *Whatever* [*offspring*] *is in* [*any of*] *the bellies of pregnant animals* (AO, Ḳ, TA) *of camels* and *of sheep* or *goats*: (AO, TA:) or peculiarly *of sheep* or *goats*; (Ḳ, TA;) thus in the dial. of the Prophet: (TA:) or it [virtually, in a trad. mentioned in what follows,] means the *selling a camel*, or *other* [*animal*], *for what the stallion begets*: or the *selling a sheep for the offspring begotten by the ram*: (Ḳ:) in all of which senses غَدِىٌّ and غَدَوِىٌّ are [said to be] syn.: (Ḳ in art. غدو:) or غَدَوِىٌّ, (TA,) or غَدَوِىٌّ, or, as some relate a verse of El-Farezdaḳ in which it occurs, غَدَوِىٌّ, (Ṣ in art. غدو,) means the *selling a thing for the offspring begotten by the ram* [or, as appears from what follows, *by the stallion-camel*] *in that year*: غَدَوِىٌّ being a rel. n. from غَدٌ: as though they rendered one desirous by saying, "Our camels will bring forth and we will give thee to-morrow (غَدًا):" (Ṣ in art. غدو, and TA:) what is thus termed is forbidden in a trad.: a man used to buy, for a camel or a she-goat or money, what was in the bellies of pregnant animals; and this is a hazardous proceeding, and was therefore forbidden. (Nh, TA.) See also art. غدو. — And see عَدَوِيَّةٌ, in art. عدو.

غَدْيَانُ *Eating the meal called* غَدَاء: (Ṣ, Ḳ:*) fem. غَدْيَا, of the measure فَعْلَى, applied to a woman; (Ṣ;) or غَدْيَاءُ: (so in copies of the Ḳ:) they are originally with و [in the place of the ى], on the ground of preference, as is said in the M: and غَدْيَانَةٌ is mentioned by Z, as applied to a woman, coupled with عَشْيَانَةٌ. (TA.)

غَدَاءٌ The *morning-meal, that is eaten between daybreak and sunrise*; i. e. the *meal*, or *repast, of the* غُدْوَة; (Ḳ;) or *of the* غَدَاة; (Mṣb;) the *meal*, or *repast, that is the contr. of the* عَشَآء: (Ṣ:) [it may therefore be rendered *breakfast*: but it is now commonly applied to *dinner*, which is eaten soon after the prayer of noon, and which is a lighter repast than the عَشَآء, i. e. supper:] الغدوة [app. ▼ الغُدْوَةُ] as meaning الغَدَاءُ is vulgar: (TA voce عَشْوَةٌ:) the pl. of غَدَاءٌ is أَغْدِيَةٌ. (Ḳ.) And The [*meal*, or the *draught of milk, called*] سَحُور is thus termed; because it is to the person fasting the like of what it is to him who is not fasting. (TA.) — Also The *pasture of camels in the first part of the day*. (TA.)

غُدُوٌّ: see غُدْوَةٌ.

غَدِىٌّ *Of*, or *relating to, the morrow*; the rel. n. from غَدٌ; as also ▼ غَدَوِىٌّ; (Ṣ, Ḳ;) the latter allowable. (Ṣ.) — See also عَدَوِيَّةٌ, in art. عدو.

غَدِيَّةٌ: see its syn. غُدْوَةٌ, in three places.

غُدَيَّةٌ: and غُدَيَّانَاتٌ: } see غَدَاةٌ, last sentence.

الغَادِى *The lion*: (Ḳ, TA:) because he goes forth in the early part of the morning against the prey. (TA.)

غَادِيَةٌ *A cloud that rises* (Ṣ, Ḳ) *in the* صَبَاح (Ṣ) or *in the* غُدْوَة (Ḳ) [i. e. *in the first part of the day*]: or *a rain of the* [*period of the morning called*] غَدَاة: (Ḳ, TA:) thus says Lḥ: the pl. is غَوَادٍ. (TA.) [See a verse in the Ḥam p. 429.]

مَغْدًى and ▼ مَغْدَاةٌ [*A place to which people go*, or *to which they return, in the period of the morning called* غُدْوَة]; opposed to مَرَاحٌ and مَرَاحَةٌ]. — [Hence] one says, مَا تَرَكَ فُلَانٌ مِنْ أَبِيهِ مَغْدًى وَلَا مَرَاحًا, and ▼ مَغْدَاةً وَلَا مَرَاحَةً, expl. in art. روح. (Ṣ in art. روح, and Ḳ in the present art.)

مَغْدَاةٌ: see the next preceding paragraph, in two places.

غذ

1. غَذَّ, aor. ـِ (Ṣ, O, L, Ḳ, &c.) and ـُ, (Ḳ,) but the former aor. only is known, (MF,) inf. n. غَذٌّ, (Ṣ, O, L,) *It* (a wound) *flowed with what was in it*; as also ▼ اغذّ: (Ḳ:) or *flowed with thick purulent matter*; (Ṣ, O;) as also ▼ اغذّ [and غَثَّ and اغثّ: (O, L:) or *flowed with purulent matter, thick* or *thin*: (Az, O, L:) or *became swollen*: (Lth, L, Ḳ:) or this is a mistake; the true signification being that next preceding. (Az, O, L.) You say, تَرَكْتُ جُرْحَهُ يَغِذُّ [*I left his wound flowing with thick*, or *thin, purulent matter*]. (Ṣ.) — Also *It* (a vein) *flowed with blood without stopping*; (O, L;) and so ▼ اغذّ. (L.) — [And, accord. to Freytag, as on the authority of Meyd, *He delayed*, or *loitered*, and *remained behind*, in (فى) a journey.] = And غَذَّهُ *He diminished*, or *impaired, to him*; or *made him to*

lose; syn. نَقَصَهُ; (O, Ḳ;) as also ▼ غَذْغَذَ مِنْهُ. (O, Ḳ.) You say, مَا غَذَذْتُكَ شَيْئًا i. e. مَا نَقَصْتُكَ [*I did not diminish to thee,* &c., or *I have not diminished to thee,* &c., *aught*]. (O.)

4. اغذّ: see 1, in three places. — اغذّ فِى السَّيْرِ, (Ṣ,* O,* L, Ḳ,) inf. n. إِغْذَاذٌ; (Ṣ, O, L;) and اغذّ السَّيْرَ; (L, Ḳ;) *He hastened in the pace* or *journeying;* (Ṣ, O, L, Ḳ;) and *he hastened the pace* or *journeying.* (L, Ḳ.) — And Abu-l-Ḥasan Ibn-Keysán thinks, from the use of the phrase سَيْرٌ مُغِذٌّ, that one says also, اغذّ السَّيْرُ, meaning *The pace,* or *journeying, was quick.* (L.)

R. Q. 1. غَذْغَذَ: see 1, last sentence but one.

R. Q. 2. تَغَذْغَذَ *He leaped, sprang,* or *bounded.* (O, Ḳ.)

غَذِيذَةٌ *Thick purulent matter* (Ṣ, O, L, Ḳ) of a wound; as also غَثِيثَةٌ. (Ṣ, O, L.) Yaạḳoob says that the ذ of the former is a substitute for the ث of the latter; (L;) and so says Ibn-es-Seed. (TA.)

غَاذٌّ [act. part. n. of 1, q. v.: as such signifying A vein *incessantly bleeding.* (L.) — Also *A recrudescence* (عَرَبٌ [inf. n. of عَرِبَ], so in the O, in copies of the Ḳ غَرْبٌ, and in the CḲ غَرَبٌ, [app. a mistranscription suggested by another explanation of غَاذٌّ which will be found in what follows,]) *in any part of the body.* (L, Ḳ.) AZ says, what we call العَرَبُ, the Arabs term الغَاذُّ. (O.) One says of a camel that has had a gall on the back which has healed but is, or becomes, moist [or exuding], بِهِ غَاذٌّ [*He has a gall which has healed but is moist,* or *constantly discharging,* or *exuding*]. (Ṣ, O, L.) — And *A vein,* or *duct, in the eye,* [also called غَرْبٌ,] *which flows incessantly.* (L, Ḳ.) In this sense, and in that immediately preceding, it is a subst. like كَاهِلٌ and غَارِبٌ. (L.) — And قَطَعَ ٱللّٰهُ غَاذَّ فُلَانٍ signifies الحِسُّ الغَاذُّ: one says, i. e. حِسَّهُ [app. meaning *May God cause to cease the sound of such a one*]. (Ibn-'Abbád, O.)

الغَاذَّةُ *The part that is in a state of commotion,* [or *that pulses,*] *of the top of the head of a* [*young*] *child;* as also الغَاذِيَةُ [which belongs to art. غذو]. (IAạr, Ḳ, TA.)

أَغَذُّ *More,* or *most,* or *very, quick, and brisk,* or *sprightly.* (L.)

سَيْرٌ مُغِذٌّ *A quick pace* or *journeying:* a phrase like لَيْلٌ نَائِمٌ. (L. [See also 4: and see an ex. voce مُورِدٌ, in art. ورد.])

مُغَاذٌّ A camel *that loathes water.* (Ṣ, O, L, Ḳ.)

غذو

1. غَذَوْتُهُ, (Ṣ, Mṣb, Ḳ, TA,) aor. أَغْذُوهُ, (Mṣb,) inf. n. غَذْوٌ, (Ḳ,) *I fed him,* or *nourished him,* (Ṣ, Mṣb, Ḳ, TA,) [for instance,] a child, (Ṣ, TA,) with milk; (Ṣ, Mṣb, TA;) and غَذَيْتُهُ signifies the same, unknown by J, and therefore disallowed by him, (Ḳ and TA in art. غذى,) but known by ISd; (TA in that art.;) and so ▼ غَذَّيْتُهُ, (Ṣ,* Mṣb, Ḳ, TA,) inf. n. تَغْذِيَةٌ, (Ṣ, TA,) [but, accord. to SM,] in an intensive sense. (TA.) And غَذَاهُ الطَّعَامُ, aor. and inf. n. as above, *The food* [*nourished him,* or] *had an agreeable, a wholesome,* or *a beneficial, effect upon him, and sufficed him;* namely, a child. (Mṣb.) — And [hence,] غُذُوا بِلِبَانِ الكَرَمِ ‡ [*They were fed,* or *nourished, by sucking the milk of generosity;* meaning *they derived generosity from their parents*]. (TA.) ═ غَذَا بَوْلَهُ, and غَذَا بِهِ, (Ḳ,) aor. and inf. n. as above, (TA,) *He* (a camel) *interrupted his urine;* (Ḳ, TA;) as also ▼ غذّاه, (Ṣ, Ḳ, TA,) inf. n. تَغْذِيَةٌ. (Ṣ, TA.) And غَذَا الكَلْبُ بِغَذْىٍ [or بِغَذًا] *The dog emitted urine in repeated discharges.* (TA.) ═ غَذَا, said of urine, *It became interrupted:* (Ṣ, Ḳ, TA:) the verb being intrans. as well as trans. (TA.) — And, (Ṣ, M, Ḳ, TA,) aor. يَغْذُو, inf. n. غَذْوٌ and غَذَوَانٌ, (M, TA,) *It flowed;* (Ṣ, M, Ḳ, TA;) said of water, (Ṣ,) or, as some say, of anything, [or] of water or blood or sweat. (TA.) [Thus,] as IḲṭṭ says, the verb has two contr. significations. (TA.) *It flowed with blood;* (Ṣ, Ḳ;) aor. as above, inf. n. غَذْوٌ; (Ṣ;) said of a vein; as also ▼ غَذَّى, inf. n. تَغْذِيَةٌ. (Ṣ, Ḳ.) And *It flowed continually;* aor. as above; said of a wound. (TA.) — And † *He went quickly,* or *swiftly;* (Ṣ, M, Ḳ, TA;) aor. as above, inf. n. غَذْوٌ and غَذَوَانٌ; said of a horse. (TA.)

2: see the preceding paragraph, first sentence. — [Hence,] النَّارُ تُغَذَّى بِالحَطَبِ ‡ [*The fire is fed with firewood*]. (TA.) — And التَّغْذِيَةُ signifies also التَّرْبِيَةُ [app. as meaning *The rearing* a child &c.: though it also means "the feeding, or nourishing"]: (Ṣ, Ḳ:) or in an intensive sense. (TA.) ═ See, again, 1, in two places.

5. تغذّى quasi-pass. of 2: (Mṣb, Ḳ:*) see 8. — [Hence,] one says of a man, خَيْرُهُ يَتَغَذَّى كُلَّ يَوْمٍ ‡ *His goodness increases every day.* (TA.)

8. اغتذى *He was,* or *became, fed,* or *nourished;* (Ṣ, Mṣb, Ḳ;) as also ▼ تغذّى. (Mṣb, Ḳ.) You say, اغتذى بِهِ *He was,* or *became, fed,* or *nourished, with it;* (Ṣ, Mṣb;) namely, food, and beverage, (Ṣ,) or milk. (Mṣb.)

10. استغذاه *He threw him down on the ground with vehemence.* (Ḳ.)

غَذًا or غَذًى [accord. to different copies of the Ḳ, the former agreeable with a general rule, though the latter is said in the TA to be the right,] The *urine* of the camel, (Ḳ, TA,) and of the dog. (TA. [See 1.])

غَذَوَانٌ [an inf. n. of غَذَا said of water, and of a horse, and hence, app.,] † *Swift:* (TA:) or *brisk, lively,* or *sprightly, and swift;* applied to a horse: (Ṣ, Ḳ, TA: [see also غَذَوَانٌ:]) or *that interrupts his urine,* or *emits it in repeated discharges,* (يَغْذُو بِبَوْلِهِ,) *when he runs.* (TA.) — And (applied to a man, TA) † *Long-tongued,* or *clamorous and foul-tongued; foul, unseemly,* or *obscene* [*in speech*]: fem. with ة: (Ḳ, TA:) the latter, applied to a woman, expl. by Fr as signifying فَاحِشَةٌ [i. e. *foul,* &c., as above]. (TA.)

غَذَوِىٌّ: see غَذِىٌّ, in four places: — and see also عَذَوِيَّةٌ, in art. عدو.

غِذَآءٌ *Aliment,* or *nutriment;* consisting of *food* and of *drink;* (Ṣ, Mṣb;) the *means of the growth,* or *increase, and of the sustenance,* or *support, of the body:* (Ḳ:) pl. أَغْذِيَةٌ. (KL.) [One says رَجُلٌ حَسَنُ الغِذَآءِ *A man good in respect of food;* i. e., *who feeds on good food:* and سَيِّئُ الغِذَآءِ *bad in respect of food; who feeds on bad food.*] — It is also applied, by the poet Eiyoob Ibn-'Abáyeh, to † The *water for irrigation* of palm-trees. (TA.) ═ Also pl. of غَذِىٌّ. (Ṣ, &c.)

غَذِىٌّ *A lamb,* or *kid;* syn. سَخْلَةٌ; (Ṣ, Mṣb, Ḳ;) or, as some say, *a lamb* (حَمَلٌ); (Mṣb;) and the pl. is غِذَآءٌ: (Ṣ, Mṣb, Ḳ:) and *syn. with* غَذَوِىٌّ in senses expl. in art. غدو: as also ▼ غَذَوِىٌّ: (Ḳ:) or غَذِىُّ المَالِ and ▼ غَذَوِيُّهُ signify *the younglings of cattle, such as lambs* or *kids* and *the like;* (Ṣ, Mṣb;) accord. to Khalaf El-Aḥmar, (Ṣ,) or IF; so that they are *of camels* and *of kine* and *of sheep* or *goats:* (Mṣb:) accord. to IAạr, ▼ غَذَوِىٌّ is *syn. with* بهيم [an evident mistranscription for بَهْمٌ, q. v.]: and signifies *such as is fed:* (TA:) and he was told, he says, by an Arab of the desert, of Belhujeym, that the ▼ غَذَوِىٌّ is *the lamb* (حَمَل), or *the kid, that is not nourished with the milk of its mother, but with another's milk;* accord. to which explanation it is different from the غَذِىٌّ; and so it is accord. to Az; but, as IF says, some imagine الغَذَوِىُّ to be from الغَذِىُّ, which signifies *the* سَخْلَة [as expl. in the beginning of this paragraph]. (Mṣb, TA.) The dim. of غَذِىٌّ is ▼ غُذَىٌّ. (Ṣ.) — See also عَذَوِيَّةٌ, in art. عدو.

غُذَىٌّ dim. of غَذِىٌّ, q. v. (Ṣ.)

غَاذِى مَالٍ † *A good manager* or *tender* [*of cattle*]: (Ḳ, TA:) as though he fed them, or reared them. (TA.) ═ And الغَاذِى signifies also The wound *that will not cease to bleed.* (TA.)

الغَاذِيَةُ *A certain vein;* (Ḳ, TA;) so called because of its flowing with blood. (TA.) — And *The part that is in a state of commotion,* [or *that pulses,*] *of the top of the head of a* [*young*] *child, as long as it continues soft;* for when it becomes hard, and becomes bone, it is termed يَافُوخ: pl. الغَوَاذِى: mentioned by AZ: (TA:) also called الغَاذَّةُ. (IAạr, Ḳ in art. غذ.)

الغَيْذَا, of the measure فَيْعَلٌ [when indeterminate], from غَذَا "it flowed," occurring in a trad. as meaning *The clouds*, is said by Z to be the only word of this measure having the final radical letter infirm except الكَيْهَا, [which I do not find in its proper art.,] meaning "the large, or bulky," she-camel [like كَهَاةٌ and كَيْهَاةٌ]. (TA.)

غذى

1. غَذَيْتُهُ: see 1 (first sentence) in art. غذو.

غر

1. غَرَّهُ, aor. يَغُرُّ, inf. n. غُرُورٌ (Fr, Ṣ, Mṣb, Ḳ) and غَرٌّ, (Az, Ḳ,) which latter is preferable to the former, [though less common,] because the inf. n. of a trans. verb is scarcely ever of the measure فُعُولٌ, (Az,) and غِرَّةٌ (Lḥ, Ḳ) and غَرَرٌ, (IḲṭṭ, TA,) *He* (the devil, TA) *deceived him; beguiled him;* (Ṣ, Ḳ;) *made him to desire what was vain, or false.* (Ḳ.) You say غَرَّتْهُ الدُّنْيَا *The world deceived him, or beguiled him, by its finery, or show, or pomp.* (Mṣb.) It is said in the Ḳur [lxxxii. 6], مَا غَرَّكَ بِرَبِّكَ *What hath deceived thee, and led thee into error, so that thou hast neglected what was incumbent on thee to thy Lord?* (Aboo-Is-ḥáḳ:) or *what hath deceived thee respecting thy Lord, and induced thee to disobey Him, and to feel secure from his punishment?* (TA:) or *what hath deceived thee, and emboldened thee to disobey thy Lord?* (Bḍ. [But see بِ as syn. with عَنْ.]) مَا غَرَّكَ بِفُلَانٍ signifies [*What hath deceived thee, and emboldened thee against such a one?* or] *how is it that thou art emboldened against such a one?* (Aṣ, Ṣ, Mṣb, TA.) [See also 4.] And مَنْ غَرَّكَ بِفُلَانٍ, (TA,) and مِنْ فُلَانٍ, (Ṣ, TA,) *Who hath made thee to pursue a course without being rightly directed, or a course not plain,* (مَنْ أَوْطَأَكَ عَشْوَةً, Ṣ, TA,) *with respect to such a one,* (Ṣ,) or *with respect to the case of such a one?* (TA. [See again 4.]) [Also غُرَّ مِنْ فُلَانٍ, i. e. غُرَّ غُرُورًا صَادِرًا مِنْ فُلَانٍ, *He was deceived by such a one; he was deceived with deceit proceeding from such a one.* See غَرِيرٌ, as syn. with مَغْرُورٌ.] And غَرَّ فُلَانٌ فُلَانًا *Such a one exposed such a one to perdition or destruction* [app. *by deceiving him*]. (TA. [See also 2, and 4.]) Also *Such a one acted with such a one in a manner resembling the slaying with the edge of the sword.* (TA. [See 3 in art. عطو.]) ═ غَرَّ فَرْخَهُ, (Ṣ, O, Ḳ,) aor. ـُ, (Ṣ, O,) inf. n. غَرٌّ (Ṣ, O, Ḳ) and غِرَارٌ, (O, Ḳ, [or the latter is inf. n. of غَارَّ only,]) *It* (a bird, Ṣ, O, Ḳ,* or a pigeon, TA) *fed its young one with its bill:* (Ṣ, O, Ḳ:) and غَارَّ ↓ أُنْثَاهُ, (Aṣ, Ṣ, Ḳ,) inf. n. غِرَارٌ (Ṣ) or مُغَارَّةٌ, (TA,) *he* (the [collared turtle-dove called] قُمْرِىّ) *fed his female with his bill.* (Aṣ, Ṣ, Ḳ.) — Hence, in a trad., كَانَ يَغُرُّ عَلِيًّا بِالعِلْمِ (O, TA) (TA) † *He* (the Prophet) *used to nourish 'Alee with knowledge like as the bird feeds its young one.* (O, TA.*) And one says, غُرَّ فُلَانٌ مِنَ العِلْمِ مَا لَمْ يُغَرَّهُ غَيْرُهُ † *Such a one has been nourished, and instructed, with that wherewith other than he has not been nourished, and instructed, of knowledge.* (TA.) ═ غَرَّ, aor. يَغِرُّ, (Ṣ, Mṣb,) with kesr; (Ṣ;) or غَرَّ, sec. pers. غَرِرْتَ, aor. يَغَرُّ; (Ḳ, TA;) inf. n. غَرَارَةٌ; (Ṣ, Mṣb, Ḳ;) *He* (a man, Ṣ, Mṣb, or a youth, or young man, Ḳ) *was inexperienced in affairs;* (Ṣ, Ḳ;) *he was ignorant of affairs; negligent,* or *heedless, of them.* (Mṣb.) You say كَانَ ذٰلِكَ فِى غَرَارَتِى وَحَدَاثَتِى, i. e. فِى غِرَّتِى, *That was in* [the time of] *my inexperience and youth.* (Ṣ.) [See also 8.] — And غَرَّ, (Ḳ,) sec. pers. غَرُرْتَ, (IAạr, T, TA,) aor. يَغَرُّ, with fet-ḥ, (IAạr, T, Ḳ,) inf. n. غَرَارَةٌ, (IAạr, T, TA,) *He acted in a youthful* or *childish manner:* (IAạr, T, TA:) or *he so acted after having soundness of judgment, produced by experience.* (Ṣgh, Ḳ.) But this is at variance with what J cites from Fr, in art. شد, that the aor. of an intrans. verb of this class of the measure فَعَلَ, should be of the measure يَفْعِلُ, with kesr to the ع. (TA.) ═ غَرَّ, (IAạr, IḲṭṭ, Ḳ,) in one place written by IAạr غَرِرَ, to show that it is of the measure فَعِلَ, and that the sec. pers. is غَرِرْتَ, (TA,) aor. يَغَرُّ, (IAạr, IḲṭṭ, Ḳ,) inf. n. غَرَرٌ (IAạr, Ḳ) and غُرَّةٌ, (IAạr, IḲṭṭ, Ḳ,) or the latter, as ISd thinks, is not an inf. n., but a subst., (TA,) and غَرَارَةٌ, (Ḳ,) *He* (a horse, IAạr, IḲṭṭ, and a camel, IAạr) *had what is termed a* غُرَّة *upon his forehead:* (IAạr, IḲṭṭ:) *it* (his face) *had what is so termed:* (Ḳ:) *it* (his face) *became white.* (IAạr, Ḳ.*) — غَرَّ, aor. يَغَرُّ, *He* (a man) *became eminent,* or *noble.* (TA.) — And غُرَّةٌ signifies also A grape-vine's *quickly becoming tall.* (Ḳ.) ═ See also R. Q. 1. ═ غَرَّ عَلَيْهِ المَآءَ *He poured upon him, or it, the water:* like قَرَّ. (TA.) And غُرَّ فِى حَوْضِكَ *Pour thou into thy watering-trough.* (TA.) And غُرَّ فِى سِقَائِكَ *Fill thou thy skin by putting it into the water and throwing the water into it with thy hand, not abstaining until thou fillest it:* thus as related by Az accord. to the usage of the desert-Arabs. (TA.)

2. غَرَّرَ بِنَفْسِهِ, (Ṣ, Ḳ, TA,) and بِمَالِهِ, (TA,) inf. n. تَغْرِيرٌ and تَغِرَّةٌ, (Ṣ, Ḳ,) *He exposed himself,* (Ḳ, TA,) and *his property,* (TA,) *to perdition,* or *destruction,* or *loss,* (Ḳ, TA,) *without knowing it:* (TA:) *he endangered, jeoparded, hazarded,* or *risked, himself,* (Ṣ, TA,) [and *his property,*] *and was negligent,* or *heedless, of the end, issue,* or *result, of an affair.* (TA.) [See also 1.] ═ غُرِّرَ *He* (a horse) *was marked with a* غُرَّة [i. e. *a star,* or *blaze,* or *white mark, on the forehead* or *face*]: you say بِمَ غُرِّرَ فَرَسُكَ *With what kind of* غُرَّة *is thy horse marked?* and the owner answers, With a شَادِخَة, or with a وَتِيرَة, &c. (Mubtekir El-Aạrábee, TA.) ═ غَرَّرَتْ ثَنِيَّتَا الغُلَامِ *The central incisors of the boy showed their points for the first time:* (Ṣ:) or غَرَّرَ الغُلَامُ *the first of the teeth of the boy showed its point;* as though the غُرَّة, i. e. whiteness, of his teeth appeared: and غَرَّرَتْ أَسْنَانُ الصَّبِىِّ *the teeth of the boy were disposed to grow, and came forth.* (TA.) — And hence, (TA,) غَرَّرَتِ الطَّيْرُ *The birds desired,* or *endeavoured, to fly, and raised their wings.* (Ḳ, TA.) ═ غَرَّرَ القِرْبَةَ (Ṣgh, Ḳ, TA) and السِّقَآءَ (TA) *He filled the water-skin.* (Ṣgh, Ḳ, TA.)

3. غَارَّتِ النَّاقَةُ, (Aṣ, ISk, Ṣ, Ḳ,) aor. تُغَارُّ, inf. n. غِرَارٌ, (ISk, Ṣ,) *The she-camel became scant of milk:* (Aṣ, Ṣ, Ḳ:) or *deficient in milk:* (TA:) or *she took fright, and drew up her milk,* (ISk, Ṣ,) *after yielding milk freely:* (ISk, TA:) or *the she-camel, having yielded milk abundantly on her teats' being stroked, and not being promptly milked, drew up her milk, and would not yield it plentifully until it collected again in her udder in the interval before the next period of milking.* (Az.) [This signification of the verb is said in the TA to be tropical: but I rather think it to be proper; as the next is derived from it.] — غَارَّتِ السُّوقُ, aor. تُغَارُّ, (AZ, Ṣ,) inf. n. غِرَارٌ, (AZ, Ṣ, Ḳ,) ‡ *The market became stagnant,* or *dull, with respect to traffic;* (AZ, Ṣ, Ḳ;) *contr. of* دَرَّتْ. (AZ, Ṣ.) — [See also غِرَارٌ, below.] ═ غَارَّ أُنْثَاهُ, said of the قُمْرِىّ: see 1.

4. اغرّه *He, or it, emboldened him, or encouraged him;* [*by deceiving him;*] syn. أَجْسَرَهُ: so says AHeyth; and he cites the following verse:

> أَغَرَّ هِشَامًا مِنْ أَخِيهِ ٱبْنِ أُمِّهِ
> قَوَادِمُ ضَأْنٍ يَسَّرَتْ وَرَبِيعُ

meaning [*The teats of sheep that have yielded abundance of milk and of young, and spring herbage,* i. e.] the abundance of his sheep and their milk, *have emboldened Hishám against his brother, the son of his mother,* [to pursue a wrong course towards him, and] to forsake him, thinking himself independent of him: the poet makes قوادم to belong to sheep, whereas they properly belong to the udders of camels, using the word metaphorically. (TA.) [But I incline to think that the أ in أَغَرَّ is the interrogative particle, and that its explanation is أَجْسَرَ, with the same particle; and the more so as I have not found any authority, if this be not one, for أَجْسَرَ in the sense of جَسَّرَ: so that the meaning of the verse is, *Have the teats,* &c.? and it shows that غَرَّهُ مِنْهُ, not أَغَرَّهُ, means جَسَّرَهُ عَلَيْهِ, like غَرَّهُ بِهِ. See 1.] — Also *He caused him to fall into peril, danger, jeopardy, hazard,* or *risk.* (TA.) [But perhaps this meaning is also derived from a misunderstanding of the verse quoted above. See again 1.]

8. اغترّ *He became deceived,* or *beguiled;* (Ṣ, Ḳ;) *made to desire what was vain,* or *false;* (Ḳ;) بِشَىْءٍ *by a thing.* (Ṣ.) [See also 10.] — *He was negligent, inattentive, inadvertent, inconsiderate, heedless,* or *unprepared;* (Ṣ, Ḳ;) *he thought himself secure, and therefore was not on his guard.* (Mṣb.) [See again 10.] ═ اغترّهُ *He, or it, came to him when he was negligent, inadvertent, heedless,* or *unprepared;* (T, Ṣ, TA;) as also ↓ استغرّهُ: (T, Ḳ, TA:) or *he sought to avail himself of his negligence, inadvertence, heedlessness,* or *unpreparedness;* as also اغترّ بِهِ. (TA.)

10. استغرّ *i. q.* اغترّ [which see in two places: but in what sense, is not said]: (Ḳ, TA:) said of a man. (TA.) ═ استغرّه: see اغترّه.

R. Q. 1. غَرْغَرَ, (IḲṭṭ,) inf. n. غَرْغَرَةٌ, (Ḳ,) *He gargled with water;* (IḲṭṭ, Ḳ;) and in like manner *with medicine;* (IḲṭṭ;) *made it to reciprocate in his throat,* (IḲṭṭ, Ḳ,) *not ejecting it, nor suffering it to descend easily down his throat;* (IḲṭṭ;) as also ▼ تَغَرْغَرَ. (Ḳ.) — غَرْغَرَتِ القِدْرُ *The cooking-pot made a sound in boiling.* (TA.) And غرغر اللَّحْمُ *The flesh-meat made a sound in broiling.* (Ḳ.) [See an ex. in a verse of El-Kumeyt cited voce مَرْضُوفَةٌ.] — غرغر *He gave up his spirit,* [app. *with a rattling sound in the throat,*] *at death;* (Ḳ;) as also ▼ غَرَّ. (TA.) — غرغر بِصَوْتِهِ *He* (a pastor) *reiterated his voice in his throat.* (Ṣ.) ═ غَرْغَرَهُ *He slaughtered him by cutting his throat* with a knife. (Ḳ,* TA.) — *He pierced him in his throat* with a spear-head. (IḲṭṭ, Ḳ.) ═ And غَرْغَرَةٌ signifies also The *breaking* of the bone of the nose, and of the head of a flask or bottle. (Ḳ.)

R. Q. 2. تَغَرْغَرَ: see R. Q. 1. — تغرغر صَوْتُهُ فِى حَلْقِهِ *His* (a pastor's) *voice became reiterated in his throat.* (Ṣ.) — تغرغرت عَيْنُهُ بِالدَّمْعِ *The water came and went repeatedly in his eye.* (TA.)

غَرٌّ, (Ṣ, O, Ḳ, TA,) with fet-ḥ, (Ṣ, O, TA, [in the CḲ erroneously said to be with ḍamm,]) *A crease, wrinkle, ply, plait,* or *fold,* (Ṣ, O, Ḳ, TA,) in skin, (O,* Ṣ,) accord. to Lth, from fatness, (TA,) or in a skin, (Ḳ,) and in a garment, or piece of cloth; (Ṣ, O, Ḳ;) syn. كَسْرٌ, (Ṣ, O,) or كَسْرٌ مُتَثَنٍّ, (Ḳ,) and مَكْسِرٌ: (Ṣ,* O:) pl. غُرُورٌ. (Ṣ, TA.) [Hence,] غُرُورُ الفَخِذَيْنِ *The furrows* [or *creases* or *depressed lines*] *between the muscles of the thighs.* (TA.) And غُرُورُ الذِّرَاعَيْنِ *The duplicatures* [or *creases*] *between the* [*sinews called*] حِبَال [pl. of حَبْلٌ q. v.] *of the fore arms.* (TA.) And غَرُّ الظَّهْرِ *The duplicature* [or *crease*] *of the* مَتْن [or *flesh and sinew next the backbone*]: or, as ISk says, غَرُّ المَتْنِ signifies *the line of the* متن. (TA.) And غُرُورُ القَدَمِ *The creases of the foot.* (TA.) And one says, طَوَيْتُ الثَّوْبَ عَلَى غَرِّهِ *I folded the garment,* or *piece of cloth, according to its first,* or *original, folding.* (Ṣ, O, TA. [In the TA said to be tropical; but for this I see no reason.]) And hence طَوَيْتُهُ عَلَى غَرِّهِ meaning † *I left him as he was, without making known his case:* a saying proverbially used in relation to one who is made to rely upon his own opinion. (Ḥar p. 233. [In Freytag's Arab. Prov., ii. 38, it is not well rendered nor well explained.]) Hence also the saying of 'Áisheh, respecting her father, mentioned in a trad., فَرَدَّ نَشَرَ الإِسْلَامِ عَلَى غَرِّهِ i. e. † *And he reduced what was disordered of El-Islám to its* [*primitive*] *state* [*of order*]: (O:) meaning that he considered the results of the apostacy [that had commenced], and counteracted the disease thereof with its [proper] remedy. (TA.) — Also *A fissure,* or *cleft, in the earth* or *ground.* (Ḳ.) — And *A rivulet:* (IAạr, TA:) or *a narrow stream of water in land:* (Ḳ, TA:) so called because it cleaves the earth: pl. غُرُورٌ. (TA.) — غُرُورٌ signifies also The *streaks,* or *lines, of a road.* (TA.) — And الغَرَّانِ signifies *Two lines by the two sides of the lower part of the* عَيْر [or *ridge in the middle of the iron head,* or *blade, of an arrow* &c.]. (AḤn, TA.) — See also غِرَارٌ, last sentence. — Also, the sing., The *extremity* of a tooth: pl. as above. (O.) ═ And The *food wherewith a bird feeds its young one with its bill:* (Ḳ, TA:) pl. as above. (TA.) — Its pl. is used in a verse of 'Owf Ibn-Dhirweh in relation to the journeying of camels, in the phrase اِحْتَسَى غُرُورَ عِيدِيَّاتِهَا, meaning † *He jaded their* عِيدِيَّات [an appellation given to certain excellent she-camels]; as though he supped their غُرُور. (TA.)

غِرٌّ *Inexperienced in affairs;* (Ṣ, Ḳ;) *ignorant of affairs; negligent,* or *heedless, of them;* (Mṣb;) applied to a man, (Ṣ, Mṣb,) or to a youth, or young man; (Ḳ;) as also ▼ غَارٌّ (Mṣb) and ▼ غَرِيرٌ; (Ṣ, Ḳ;) and applied to a young woman; as also ▼ غِرَّةٌ and ▼ غَرِيرَةٌ: (Ṣ, Ḳ:) or these three epithets, applied to a girl, signify *young, inexperienced in affairs, and not knowing what women know of love:* (A'Obeyd:) the pl. of غِرٌّ is أَغْرَارٌ (Ṣ) and غِرَارٌ; (TA;) and of ▼ غَرِيرٌ, أَغِرَّاءُ, (Ṣ, Ḳ) and أَغِرَّةٌ [which is a pl. of pauc.]. (Ḳ.) [And غِرَّةٌ is also used as a pl.] Paradise says, يَدْخُلُنِى غِرَّةُ النَّاسِ *The simple, of mankind, who prefer obscurity, and discard the affairs of the present world, and provide themselves for the world to come, enter me.* (TA, from a trad.) — Also *Youthful,* or *childish, in conduct;* applied to a man, and to a girl, or young woman. (IAạr, T.) — And One *who submits to be deceived.* (Ḳ.)

غُرَّةٌ *Whiteness; clearness of colour or complexion.* (L, TA.) So in the phrase ▼ أَغَرُّ غُرَّةً [app. meaning *More,* or *most, fair-complexioned*]; occurring in a trad. applied to virgins: or the phrase is ▼ أَغَرُّ ▼ غِرَّةً, meaning *more,* or *most, remote from the knowledge of evil.* (L.) — [*A star,* or *blaze,* or *white mark, on the forehead* or *face of a horse;*] *a whiteness on the forehead of a horse,* (Ṣ, Mgh, Mṣb, Ḳ,*) *above the size of a* دِرْهَم; (Ṣ, Mṣb;) or *of the size of a* درهم; (Mgh;) as also ▼ غُرْغُرَةٌ: (Ṣ, Ḳ:) or it is *a general term* [*for a star* or *blaze*], *including different kinds, as the* قُرْحَة *and the* شِمْرَاخ *and the like:* or, *if round, it is termed* وُتَيْرَة; *and if long,* شَادِخَة: or as, ISd thinks, the *space itself, of the face, that is occupied by whiteness;* not the whiteness: pl. غُرَرٌ. (TA.) [See also أَغَرُّ.] — In a dog, *A white speck,* or *a small white spot, above each of the eyes:* so in a trad., in which it is said that the black dog having two such marks is to be killed. (TA.) ═ Also ‡ The *first,* or *commencement,* of the month; (Mṣb;) the *night,* of the month, *in which the new moon is first seen:* (Ḳ:) so called as being likened to the غُرَّة on the forehead of a horse: (AHeyth:) pl. غُرَرٌ: (AHeyth, Mṣb:) which is also applied to the *first three nights of the month.* (A'Obeyd, Ṣ, Mṣb.) One says كَتَبْتُ غُرَّةَ الشَّهْرِ كَذَا *I wrote on the first of the month thus.* (TA.) — [And hence,] † The *first,* or *commencement,* of El-Islám; (TA;) and of anything. (Ṣ.) — The *whiteness* of the teeth; and the † *first* [*that appears*] of them. (Ḳ.) — † The *head* [app. *when first appearing*] of a plant. (TA.) — † [The *sight,* or *spectacle,* or] *whatever appears to one,* of light, or daybreak: you say thereof, بَدَتْ غُرَّتُهُ [*The sight,* or *spectacle, thereof appeared*]. (Ḳ.) — † The *aspect* of the new moon: (Ḳ:) because of its whiteness: (TA:) or the *phasis* of the moon *in the first night* [*of the month*]. (TA in art. هل.) — † The *face* of a man: (Ḳ:) or his *aspect;* syn. طَلْعَة. (TA.) — † [And The *forehead* of a man. So used, as opposed to قَفًا, in the Life of Teemoor, i. 170, ed. Mang., cited by Freytag; and so used in the present day; but whether in classical times, I know not.] — تَطْوِيلُ الغُرَّةِ, in performing the ablution termed وُضُوء, means † *The washing of the fore part of the head with the face, and the washing of the side of the neck:* or, as some say, *the washing of somewhat of the fore arm and of the shank with the hand and the foot.* (Mṣb.) — And غُرَّةٌ also signifies † *A noble,* or *an eminent, man,* (Ḳ,) or *a chief,* or *lord,* (Ṣ,) of a people: (Ṣ, Ḳ:) pl. غُرَرٌ. (Ṣ.) — And ‡ The *best,* (Ḳ,) *and chiefest,* (TA,) of goods, or household furniture: (Ḳ:) pl. as above: (TA:) the *best* of anything: (Ṣ:) the *best,* (Mgh,) or *most precious and excellent,* (Aboo-Sa'eed,) of property; as, for instance, *a horse,* and *an excellent camel,* (Aboo-Sa'eed, Mgh,) and *camels,* (TA,) and *a male slave,* (Aboo-Sa'eed, Ṣ, Mgh, Mṣb, Ḳ,) and *a female slave,* (Ṣ, Mṣb, Ḳ,) or *a clever female slave:* (Aboo-Sa'eed, Mgh:) its application to a slave, male or female, [among articles of property,] is most common. (TA.) It has this last signification (a male or female slave) in a trad. in which it relates to the compensation for the destroying of a child in the womb: (TA:) as though this term were applied, by a synecdoche, to the whole person; (Ṣ;) the word properly signifying the "face;" in like manner as the terms رَقَبَة and رَأْس are employed: (Mgh:) Aboo-'Amr Ibn-El-Alà is related to have said that it there means *a white male slave* or *a white female slave:* but this is not a condition accord. to the doctors of practical law; for they hold the term to mean *a male* or *female slave whose price amounts to the tenth part of the whole price of blood:* (IAth:) or *to the twentieth part thereof:* (Ḳ, T:) or it means *a slave of the best sort.* (Mgh.) The Rájiz says,

كُلُّ قَتِيلٍ فِى كُلَيْبٍ غُرَّهْ
حَتَّى يَنَالَ القَتْلُ آلَ مُرَّهْ

Every one slain in retaliation for Kuleyb is as a slave, until the slaying reach the family of Mur-

rah. (TA.) —— Also † *Goodness,* and *righteous conduct:* so in the saying, إِيَّاكُمْ وَالْمُشَارَّةَ فَإِنَّهَا تَدْفِنُ الغُرَّةَ وَتُظْهِرُ العُرَّةَ [*Avoid ye contention,* or *disputation, for it hides goodness,* &c., *and manifests what is disgraceful*]. (TA.) ═ [It is also an inf. n.: see 1, latter part.]

غِرَّةٌ *Negligence; inattention; inadvertence,* or *inadvertency; inconsiderateness; heedlessness;* or *unpreparedness:* (Ṣ, Mgh, Mṣb, Ḳ:) [pl. غِرَّاتٌ and غِرَرٌ: see an ex. of the former in a verse cited voce شَفَعَ, and exs. of both in a verse cited voce دَرَى.] It is said in a prov., الغِرَّةُ تَجْلِبُ الدِّرَّةَ *Inadvertence brings the means of subsistence:* (TA:) or *paucity of milk causes to come abundance thereof:* applied to him who gives little and from whom much is hoped for afterwards. (Meyd. [See Freytag's Arab. Prov. ii. 179: and see also غِرَارٌ.]) [Hence,] عَلَى غِرَّةٍ [*On an occasion of negligence,* &c.; *unexpectedly*]. (Ḳ in art. عرض; &c.) [And عَنْ غِرَّةٍ *In consequence of inadvertence:* see an ex. in a verse cited voce زَلِقَ.] Also *Inexperience in affairs.* (Ṣ.) غِرَّةٌ and غَرَارَةٌ signify the same. (A'Obeyd.) [The latter is an inf. n.: see 1.] See also غُرَّةٌ, second sentence. —— غِرَّةٌ بِٱللّٰهِ means *Boldness against God.* (Mgh.) ═ [See also غُرّ.]

غُرَى: see أَغَرُّ, near the end.

غَرَرٌ *Peril; danger; jeopardy; hazard;* or *risk.* (Ṣ, Mgh, Mṣb, Ḳ.) It is said in a trad., نَهَى عَنْ بَيْعِ الغَرَرِ *He* (Moḥammad) *forbade the sale of hazard,* or *risk;* (Ṣ, Mgh, Mṣb;) *of which it is unknown whether the thing will be or not;* (Mgh;) *such as the sale of fish in the water, and of birds in the air:* (Ṣ, Mgh:) or, accord. to 'Alee, *in which one is not secure from being deceived:* (Mgh:) or *of which the outward semblance deceives the buyer, and the intrinsic reality is unknown:* (TA:) or *that is without any written statement* (عُهْدَة), *and without confidence.* (Aṣ, Mgh.) —— حَبْلُ غَرَرٍ means غَيْرُ مَوْثُوقٍ بِهِ [i. e., app., *A bond,* or *compact, in which trust,* or *confidence, is not placed*]. (TA.) ═ See also غَرِيرٌ.

غِرَارٌ *Paucity of milk* of a camel: (Ḳ:) or *deficiency thereof.* (Ṣ.) [See 3.] It is said in a prov., respecting the hastening a thing before its time, سَبَقَ دِرَّتُهُ غِرَارَهُ [lit., *His abundant flow of milk preceded his paucity thereof*]: (Aṣ:) or سَبَقَ دِرَّتَهُ غِرَارُهُ [lit., *his paucity of milk preceded his abundance thereof;* agreeably with an explanation of Z, who says that it is applied to him who does evil before he does good: see Freytag's Arab. Prov. i. 613: and see also غِرَّةٌ]. (So in my copies of the Ṣ.) —— Hence, † *Paucity* of sleep. (Aṣ, A'Obeyd, Ṣ.) —— [Hence also,] in prayer, ‡ *A deficiency in,* (Ḳ,) or *an imperfect performance of,* (Ṣ,) *the bowing of the body, and the prostration,* (Ṣ, Ḳ,) *and the purification.* (Ḳ.) And in salutation, The *saying* (*in reply to* السَّلَامُ عَلَيْكُمْ) وَعَلَيْكُمْ, *not* وَعَلَيْكُمُ السَّلَامُ: (T, TA:) or the *saying* سَلَامٌ عَلَيْكُمْ (Ḳ) or سَلَامٌ عَلَيْكَ (M) [without ال prefixed to سلام: as though it were a deficient form; but it is the form specially sanctioned by the Ḳur-án]: or the *replying by saying* عَلَيْكَ, *not* عَلَيْكُمْ. (Ḳ.) This is said in explanation of a trad., لَا غِرَارَ فِى صَلَاةٍ وَلَا تَسْلِيمٍ [*There shall be no deficiency in prayer, nor in salutation*]: but accord. to one relation, it is لاغرار فى صلاة ولا تَسْلِيمَ, meaning, that the person praying shall not salute nor be saluted: in the former case, تسليم is an adjunct to صلاة: in the latter, it is an adjunct to غرار, so that the meaning is, *There shall be no deficiency nor salutation in prayer.* (TA.) —— Also ‡ *Little* sleep (Ṣ, Ḳ) &c. (Ḳ.) El-Farezdaḳ uses the expression نَوْمُهُنَّ غِرَارٌ *Their sleep is little.* (TA.) —— And particularly † *Littleness of consideration;* denoting *haste.* (TA.) You say, أَتَانَا عَلَى غِرَارٍ † *He came to us in haste.* (Ṣ.) And لَقِيتُهُ غِرَارًا † *I met him in haste.* (TA.) —— And مَا أَقَمْتُ عِنْدَهُ إِلَّا غِرَارًا † [*I remained not at his abode save*] *a little while.* (TA.) And لَبِثَ غِرَارَ شَهْرٍ *He* (a man, Ṣ) *tarried the space of a month.* (Ṣ, O, TA.) And لَيْتَ اليَوْمَ غِرَارُ شَهْرٍ i. e. [*Would that the day were*] *of the length of a month.* (So in some copies of the Ṣ, and in the O: in other copies of the Ṣ, لَبِثَ القَوْمُ غِرَارَ شَهْرٍ [like the phrase immediately preceding].) —— And, accord. to Aṣ, غِرَارٌ signifies *A way, course, mode,* or *manner.* (Ṣ, O, TA.) One says, رَمَيْتُ ثَلَاثَةَ أَسْهُمٍ عَلَى غِرَارٍ وَاحِدٍ [*I shot three arrows*] *in one course.* (Ṣ, O, TA.) And وَلَدَتْ فُلَانَةُ ثَلَاثَةً بَنِينَ عَلَى غِرَارٍ, (Ṣ,) or عَلَى غِرَارٍ وَاحِدٍ, (TA,) i. e. [*Such a woman brought forth three sons,*] *one after another,* (Ṣ, TA,) *without any girl among them.* (TA.) And بَنَى القَوْمُ بُيُوتَهُمْ عَلَى غِرَارٍ وَاحِدٍ [app. *The people,* or *party, reared their tents,* or, perhaps, *their houses, in one line,* or *according to one manner*]. (Ṣ, O.) —— Also The *model,* or *pattern, according to which iron heads* (Ṣ, Ḳ) *of arrows* (Ṣ) *are fashioned,* (Ṣ, Ḳ,) *in order to their being made right.* (Ḳ.) One says, ضَرَبَ نِصَالَهُ عَلَى غِرَارٍ وَاحِدٍ (Ṣ, TA) i. e. [*He fashioned his arrow-heads according to*] *one model,* or *pattern.* (TA.) —— And The حَدّ [app. meaning *point,* or perhaps the *edge of the iron head* or *of the blade,*] of a spear and of an arrow and of a sword: [see also ذُبَابٌ:] and غِرٌّ ↓ also signifies the حَدّ of a sword: (Ḳ, TA:) or الغِرَارَانِ signifies *the two sides* of the [arrow-head called] مِعْبَلَة: (AḤn, TA:) or *the two edges* of the sword: [see, again, ذُبَابٌ:] and غِرَارٌ, the حَدّ of anything that has a حَدّ: (Ṣ, O:) and the pl. is أَغِرَّةٌ. (Ṣ.)

غَرُورٌ *Very deceitful;* applied in this sense as an epithet to the present world; (Mṣb;) or *what deceives one;* (Ḳ;) such as a man, and a devil, or other thing; (Aṣ, TA;) or such as property or wealth, and rank or station, and desire, and a devil: (B, TA:) and غُرُورٌ ↓ signifies *a thing by which one is deceived,* of worldly goods or advantages: (Ṣ:) or the former signifies the *devil,* specially; (Yaạḳoob, Ṣ, Ḳ;) because he deceives men by false promises and by inspiring hopes; or because he urges a man to do those things which are causes of his being loved but which are followed by that which grieves him: (TA:) and this last sense it has, accord. to ISk, in the Ḳur xxxi. 33 and xxxv. 5: (Ṣ:) also the *present world;* (Ḳ;) as an epithet in which the quality of a subst. predominates: and this sense is assigned to it by some as used in the passages of the Ḳur-án to which reference has just been made. (TA.) [It is masc. and fem., agreeably with analogy.] ═ Also *A medicine with which one gargles:* (Ṣ, Ḳ:) a word similar to لَدُودٌ and لَعُوقٌ and سَعُوطٌ (Ṣ) and سَفُوفٌ. (TA.)

غُرُورٌ *False,* or *vain, things; vanities:* (Zj, Ḳ:) as though pl. of غَرٌّ, inf. n. of غَرَّهُ: (Zj:) or pl. of غَارٌّ ↓; (Zj, Ḳ;) like as شُهُودٌ is pl. of شَاهِدٌ, and قُعُودٌ of قَاعِدٌ: (Zj:) or *what is false,* or *vain; a deception; a thing by which one is deceived.* (AZ.) See also غَرُورٌ.

غَرِيرٌ *Deceived; beguiled; made to desire what is vain,* or *false;* (A'Obeyd, Ḳ;) and so مَغْرُورٌ ↓. (Ḳ.) And you say likewise, أَنَا غَرِيرٌ ↓ مِنْكَ, in the sense of مَغْرُورٌ [*I am deceived by thee*]. (TA.) And مَغْرُورٌ ↓ signifies also A man *who marries to a woman in the belief that she is free, and finds her to be a slave.* (TA.) —— See also غِرٌّ, in three places. —— It is said in a prov., أَنَا غَرِيرُكَ مِنْ هٰذَا الأَمْرِ, meaning *I am one possessing knowledge in this affair so that when thou askest me of it I will inform thee respecting it without being prepared for it and without consideration:* so says AZ: and Z says the like; i. e. *I* [*am one who*] *will answer thee if thou ask me unexpectedly respecting this affair by reason of the soundness of my knowledge of the true state of the case:* or [it means *I am a deceived informant of thee respecting this affair;* for] as Aṣ says, the meaning is, thou art not deceived by me, but I am the person deceived; the case being this, that false information came to me, and I acquainted thee with it, and it was not as I told thee; I having only related what I had heard. (TA.) And one says, أَنَا غَرِيرُكَ مِنْهُ i. e. *I caution thee* [or *I am thy cautioner*] *against him;* (Ḳ, TA.) [i. e.,] مِنْ فُلَانٍ [*against such a one*]; (Ṣ, O;) meaning, as Aboo-Naṣr says in the "Kitáb el-Ajnás," [*that*] *there shall not happen to thee, from him, that whereby thou shalt be deceived;* (Ṣ, O, TA;) as though he said, *I am thy surety,* or *sponsor, for that.* (AM, TA.) —— [Hence, app., it is said that] غَرِيرٌ signifies also *A surety, sponsor,* or *guarantee.* (Ḳ, TA.) —— And عَيْشٌ غَرِيرٌ ‡ *A life in which one is not made to be in fear:* (Ṣ, Ḳ, TA:) like عَيْشٌ أَبْلَهُ: (TA:) pl. غُرَّانٌ. (Ḳ.) —— Hence, perhaps; or from الغِرَّةُ [app. as meaning "inexperience"], which is sometimes approved; (Ḥar p. 607;) or because it [sometimes] deceives; (TA;) غَرِيرٌ also signifies ‡ *Good disposition* or *nature.* (Ṣ, O, Ḳ, TA.) One says of a man when he has become old, and evil in disposition, أَدْبَرَ غَرِيرُهُ وَأَقْبَلَ هَرِيرُهُ

‡ *His good disposition has regressed, or departed, and his evil disposition has advanced, or come:* (Ṣ, Meyd, O, TA:) or *what deceived and pleased has gone from him, and what is disliked on his part, of evilness of disposition &c., has come.* (Meyd.)

غِرَارَةٌ, (Ṣ, Mṣb, Ḳ,) not غَرَارَةٌ, (Ḳ,) for the latter is vulgar, (TA,) *A sack,* syn. جُوَالِقُ, (Ḳ,) *for straw &c.,* (Ṣ,) *resembling what is called* عِدْلٌ: (Mṣb:) [J says,] I think it is an arabicized word: (Ṣ:) pl. غَرَائِرُ. (Ṣ, Mṣb.)

غَارٌّ *Deceiving; beguiling; causing to desire what is vain, or false; a deceiver.* (TA.) — See also غُرُورٌ. — And *Negligent; inattentive; inadvertent; inconsiderate; heedless; unprepared.* (Ṣ, Ḳ.) See also غِرٌّ.

غَرْغَرَةٌ *A sound with which is a roughness,* (Ḳ,) *like that which is made by one gargling with water.* (TA.) — The *sound of a cooking-pot when it boils.* (Ḳ.) — The *reciprocation of the spirit in the throat.* (Ṣ.) — *A word imitative of the cry of the pastor* (Ḳ, TA) *and the like.* (TA.) [See also R. Q. 1.]

غُرْغُرَةٌ: see غُرَّةٌ: — and see أَغَرُّ.

أَغَرُّ *More, or most, negligent, inattentive, inadvertent, inconsiderate, heedless,* or *unprepared.* (Mgh.) See also غُرَّةٌ, second sentence. — And *White;* (Ṣ, Ḳ;) applied to anything: (Ḳ:) pl. غُرٌّ (TA) and غُرَّانٌ (Ṣ) [and perhaps غُرُورٌ, as in an ex. voce ذِرْوَةٌ: but see what is said of this pl. in a later part of this paragraph]. You say رَجُلٌ أَغَرُّ الوَجْهِ *A man white of countenance.* (TA.) And قَوْمٌ غُرَّانٌ, (Ṣ,) and غُرٌّ, (TA,) *White people.* (Ṣ.) And امْرَأَةٌ غَرَّآءُ *A woman* [*white of countenance:* or] *beautiful in the front teeth.* (TA voce قَرَّآءُ.) See, again, غُرَّةٌ, second sentence. And الأَيَّامُ الغُرُّ *The days of which the nights are white by reason of the moon; which are the 13th and 14th and 15th;* also called البِيضُ. (TA.) And يَوْمٌ أَغَرُّ مُحَجَّلٌ: see art. حجل. And اللَّيْلَةُ الغَرَّآءُ † *The night of* [i. e. *preceding the day called*] *Friday.* (O.) — Also A horse *having a* غُرَّة [i. e. *a star,* or *blaze,* or *white mark, on the forehead* or *face*]: (Ṣ, Mgh, Mṣb, Ḳ:) or *having a* غُرَّة *larger than a* دِرْهَم, *in the middle of his forehead, not reaching to either of the eyes, nor inclining upon either of the cheeks, nor extending downwards; it is more spreading than the* قُرْحَة, which is of the size of a درهم, or less: or *having a* غُرَّة *of any kind, such as the* قُرْحَة or *the* شِمْرَاخ or *the like:* (L, TA:) and in like manner a camel *having a* غُرَّة: (IAạr:) fem. غَرَّآءُ. (Mṣb, Ḳ.) [See an ex. in a prov. cited voce بَهِيمٌ: and another (from a trad.) voce مُحَجَّلٌ.] — [Hence] الغَرَّآءُ † *A certain bird,* (Ḳ, TA,) *black,* (TA,) *white-headed:* applied to the *male* and the *female:* pl. غُرٌّ; (Ḳ, TA;) which is also expl. in the Ḳ as signifying *certain aquatic birds.* (TA.) — And أَغَرُّ, (Ḳ, TA,) applied to a man, (TA,) † One *whose beard occupies the whole of his face, except a little:* (Ḳ, TA:) as though it [his face] were a [horse's] غُرَّة. (TA.) — And ‡ *Generous; open,* or *fair,* or *illustrious, in his actions;* (Ḳ;) applied to a man: (TA:) *eminent; noble;* as also ▼ غُرْغُرَةٌ: (Ṣ, Ḳ:) or *fair-faced:* or *a lord,* or *chief, among his people:* (Mṣb:) pl. غُرٌّ, (T, M,) accord. to the Ḳ غُرُورٌ, but the former is more correct, (TA,) and غُرَّانٌ. (T, M, Ḳ.) And ▼ غُرَّى signifies † *A woman of rank, eminence,* or *nobility, among her tribe.* (Ṣgh, Ḳ, TA.) — يَوْمٌ أَغَرُّ means ‡ *An intensely hot day:* (Ḳ, TA: afterwards expl. in the Ḳ as meaning [simply] *a hot day:* TA:) and in like manner one says هَاجِرَةٌ غَرَّآءُ, and ظَهِيرَةٌ غَرَّآءُ, (Ḳ, TA, expl. by As as meaning, *white by reason of the intense heat of the sun,* TA,) and وَدِيقَةٌ غَرَّآءُ. (Ḳ, TA.) — And ▼ سَنَةٌ غَرَّآءُ † *A year in which is no rain.* (L in art. شهب.)

مَغْرُورٌ: see غَرِيرٌ, in two places.

مُغَارٌّ (Ṣ, Ḳ) and مُغَارَّةٌ (TA) A she-camel *having little milk:* (Ṣ, Ḳ:) or *having lost her milk by reason of some accident or disease;* as some say, *on disliking her young one, and rejecting the milker:* (TA:) or *taking fright, and drawing up her milk,* (ISk, Ṣ,) *after yielding it freely:* (TA:) pl. مَغَارُّ, (Ṣ, Ḳ,) imperfectly decl. [being originally مَغَارِرُ]. (Ṣ.) — Hence, (TA,) ‡ *A niggardly,* or *tenacious, hand:* (Ḳ:) but accord. to the A and the TṢ, you say رَجُلٌ مُغَارُّ الكَفِّ, meaning *a niggardly,* or *tenacious, man.* (TA.)

غرب

1\. غَرَبَ, aor. ـُ, (TA,) inf. n. غَرْبٌ, (Ḳ, TA,) *He,* or *it, went, went away, passed away,* or *departed.* (Ḳ,* TA.) — And *He retired,* or *removed,* (Ḳ,* TA,) عَنِ النَّاسِ [*from men,* or *from the people*]. (TA.) — And غَرَبَ, (Ṣ, Ḳ, TA,) aor. and inf. n. as above; (TA;) and ▼ غرّب; (A, TA;) and ▼ تغرّب; (Ḳ, TA;) *He,* or *it, became distant,* or *remote;* or *went to a distance.* (Ṣ, A, Ḳ, TA.) One says, اُغْرُبْ عَنِّى *Go thou,* or *withdraw, to a distance from me.* (Ṣ.) — And غَرَبَ and ▼ غرّب *He,* or *it, became absent,* or *hidden.* (Ḳ.) The former is said of a wild animal, meaning *He retired from view,* or *hid himself, in his lurking-place.* (A.) — And غَرَبَتِ الشَّمْسُ, (Ṣ, Mṣb, TA,) aor. ـُ, (Mṣb,) inf. n. غُرُوبٌ (Ṣ, Mṣb, TA) and مَغْرِبٌ [which is anomalous] and مَغْرِبَانٌ [which is more extr.], (TA,) *The sun set:* (Ṣ, Mṣb, TA:) and غَرَبَ النَّجْمُ *The star set.* (TA.) — غَرْبٌ [app. as an inf. n. of which the verb is غَرُبَ] signifies also † The *being brisk, lively,* or *sprightly.* (Ḳ.) — And † The *persevering* (Ḳ, TA) in an affair. (TA.) — غَرِبَتِ العَيْنُ, inf. n. غَرَبٌ, *The eye was affected with a tumour such as is termed* غَرَب [q. v.] *in the inner angle.* (TA.) — غَرُبَ, aor. ـُ, inf. n. غَرَابَةٌ or غُرْبَةٌ and غُرْبٌ, said of a man: see 5. — غَرُبَ, (Ḳ, TA,) inf. n. غَرَابَةٌ, said of language, (A, TA,) *It was strange,* or *far from being intelligible; difficult to be understood; obscure.* (A,* Ḳ, TA.) And in like manner, you say, غَرُبَتِ الكَلِمَةُ [which also signifies *The word was strange* as meaning *unusual*]. (A, TA.) — غَرِبَ, aor. ـَ, (Ḳ, TA,) inf. n. غَرَبٌ, (TA,) *He,* or *it, was,* or *became, black.* (Ḳ, TA.) — غَرِبَتْ said of a ewe or she-goat, *She was,* or *became, affected with the disease termed* غَرَب *meaning as expl. below.* (Ṣ.) — See also غَرْبٌ in another sense.

2\. غرّب, inf. n. تَغْرِيبٌ: see 1, in two places: and 4, likewise in two places: — and see also 5. — Also *He went into the west:* (TA in this art.:) *he directed himself towards the west.* (TA in art. شرق.) One says, غَرِّبْ شَرِّقْ [*Go thou to the west: go thou to the east:* meaning *go far and wide*]. (A, TA.) [See also 4.] — *He made,* or *caused,* him, or it, *to be,* or *become, distant, remote, far off,* or *aloof:* (Mgh:) *he removed, put away,* or *put aside,* him, or it; as also ▼ اغرب. (TA.) — And غرّب, (Mṣb,) inf. n. as above, (Ṣ, Mgh, Mṣb,) *He banished* a person *from the country,* or *town,* (Ṣ,* Mgh,* Mṣb, TA,) in which a dishonest action had been committed [by him]. (TA.) — And *He divorced* a wife. (TA, from a trad.) — And غَرَّبَهُ الدَّهْرُ, and غَرَّبَ عَلَيْهِ, *Fortune left him distant,* or *remote.* (TA.) — تَغْرِيبٌ signifies also, accord. to the Ḳ, The *bringing forth white children:* and also, *black children:* thus having two contr. meanings: but this is a mistake; the meaning being, the *bringing forth both white and black children:* the bringing forth either of the two kinds only is not thus termed, as Saạdee Chelebee has pointed out. (MF, TA.) — Also The *collecting and eating* [*hail and*] *snow and hoar-frost;* (Ḳ;) i. e., غُرَاب. (TA.) — See also غَرْبٌ.

4\. إِغْرَابٌ signifies The *going far* into a land, or country; as also ▼ تَغْرِيبٌ. (Ḳ.) And you say, غَرَّبَتِ ▼ الكِلَابُ *The dogs went far in search,* or *pursuit, of the object,* or *objects, of the chase.* (A, TA.) — See also 5. — And اغرب signifies *He made the place to which he cast,* or *shot, to be distant,* or *remote.* (A.) — Also, (TA,) inf. n. as above, (Ḳ, TA,) *He* (a horse) *ran much:* (Ḳ:) or اغرب فِى جَرْيِهِ, said of a horse, (A, TA,) *he exceeded the usual bounds,* or *degree, in his running:* (A:) or *he ran at the utmost rate.* (TA.) — And اغرب فِى الضَّحِكِ, (A, Ḳ,) and ▼ اسْتَغْرَبَ فِيهِ, (Ṣ, A,* Ḳ,*) and ▼ اُسْتُغْرِبَ (Ḳ, TA) i. e. فى الضحك, and ▼ اِسْتَغْرَبَ ضَحِكًا occurring in a trad., and اغرب الضَّحِكَ, and ▼ اُسْتُغْرِبَ عَلَيْهِ الضَّحِكُ, (TA,) *He exceeded the usual bounds,* or *degree, in laughing;* (A, Ḳ, TA;) or *he laughed* [*immoderately,* or] *violently,* or *vehemently,* and *much:* (Ṣ, TA:) or *i. q.* قَهْقَهَ [q. v.]: (TA:) or اغرب signifies *he laughed so that the* غُرُوب [or *sharpness and lustre* &c.] *of his teeth appeared:* (L, TA:) or اغرب فى الضحك means *he exceeded the usual bounds,* or *degree, in laughing, so that his* *eye shed tears* [which are sometimes termed غَرْب]. (Har p. 572.) In the saying, in a certain form of prayer, أَعُوذُ بِكَ مِنْ كُلِّ شَيْطَانٍ مُسْتَغْرِبٍ ▼ [*I seek protection by Thee from every devil* &c.], the meaning of مستغرب is thought by El-Harbee to be *exorbitant in evilness, wickedness,* or *the like;* as though from الاِسْتِغْرَابُ فِى الضَّحِكِ : or it may mean *sharp,* or *vehement, in the utmost degree.* (TA.) — And اغرب, (Ṣ, Mṣb,) inf. n. as above, (Ḳ,) *He did,* or *said, what was strange,* or *extraordinary.* (Ṣ, Mṣb, Ḳ.) You say, تَكَلَّمَ فَأَغْرَبَ *He spoke, and said what was strange,* and *used extraordinary words:* and يُغْرِبُ فِى كَلَامِهِ [*He uses strange,* or *extraordinary, words in his speech*]. (A, TA.) — Also, (TA,) inf. n. as above, (Ḳ,) *He came to the west.* (Ḳ, TA.) [See also 2.] == اغرب also signifies *He had a white child born to him.* (TA.) — And إِغْرَابٌ signifies *Whiteness of the groins,* (Ḳ, TA,) *next the flank.* (TA.) You say, of a man, اغرب meaning *He was white in his groins.* (TḲ.) == See also غَرْبٌ. == اغرب as trans.: see 2. — إِغْرَابٌ said of a rider signifies His *making* his horse *to run until he dies:* (Ḳ:) or, accord. to Fr, one says, اعرب عَلَى فَرَسِهِ meaning "he made his horse to run:" [or اعرب فَرَسَهُ has this meaning: (see 4 in art. عرب:)] but he adds that some say اغرب. (O in art. عرب.) — And اغرب, (Ṣ, TA,) inf. n. as above, (Ḳ, TA,) *He filled* (Ṣ, Ḳ, TA) a skin, (Ṣ, TA,) and a watering-trough or tank, and a vessel. (TA.) Bishr (Ibn-Abee-Kházim, TA) says,

• وَكَأَنَّ ظُعْنَهُمْ غَدَاةَ تَحَمَّلُوا •
• سُفُنٌ تَكَفَّأُ فِى خَلِيجٍ مُغْرَبِ ▼ •

[*And as though their women's camel-vehicles, on the morning when they bound the burdens on their beasts and departed, were ships inclining forwards* (or *moving from side to side like the tall palm-tree*) *in a filled river* (or *canal*)]. (Ṣ.) — Hence, (TA,) إِغْرَابٌ signifies also *Abundance of wealth, and goodliness of condition:* (Ḳ, TA:) because abundance of wealth fills the hands of the possessor thereof, and goodliness of condition fills [with satisfaction] the soul of the goodly person. (TA.) [Therefore the verb, meaning *He was endowed* (as though filled) *with abundance of wealth and with goodliness of condition,* is app. أُغْرِبَ; not (as is implied in the TḲ) أَغْرَبَ: the explanation of the verb in the TḲ is, *his wealth was,* or *became, abundant, and his condition was,* or *became, goodly.*] — One says also (of a man, Ṣ) أُغْرِبَ (with ḍamm, Ḳ) meaning *His pain became intense,* or *violent,* (Aṣ, Ṣ, Ḳ, TA,) *from disease* or *some other cause.* (TA.) — And أُغْرِبَ عَلَيْهِ, accord. to the Ḳ, signifies *A foul,* or *an evil, deed was done to him;* and [it is said that] أُغْرِبَ بِهِ signifies the same: but in other works, [the verb must app. be in the act. form, for] the explanation is, *he did* [*to him*] *a foul,* or *an evil, deed.* (TA.) — And أُغْرِبَ said of a horse, *His blaze spread* (Ṣ, Ḳ) *so that it took in his eyes, and the edges of his eyelids were white:* and it is used in like manner to signify that *they were white by reason of what is termed* زَرَقٌ [inf. n. of زَرِقَ, q. v.]. (Ṣ, TA.) See its part. n., مُغْرَبٌ.

5. تغرّب : see 1, third sentence. — تغرّب and اغترب ▼ are syn., (Ṣ, Mṣb, Ḳ,) signifying *He became* [*a stranger, a foreigner;* or] *far,* or *distant, from his home,* or *native country;* (Ṣ,* Mṣb, Ḳ;) [*he went abroad, to a foreign place* or *country;*] and so غَرُبَ ▼, aor. ـُ, inf. n. غَرَابَةٌ, (Mṣb,) or غُرْبَةٌ (MA) [and app. غُرْبٌ, this last and غُرْبَةٌ being syn. with تَغَرُّبٌ and اِغْتِرَابٌ, and being like قُرْبٌ and قُرْبَةٌ inf. ns. of قَرُبَ]; and غَرَّبَ ▼ بِنَفْسِهِ, (Mgh,* Mṣb,) inf. n. تَغْرِيبٌ, (Mṣb;) and أَغْرَبَ ▼, (Aboo-Naṣr, Ṣ,) or this last signifies *he entered upon* الغُرْبَة [*the state,* or *condition, of a stranger,* &c.]. (Mṣb.) — And تغرّب signifies also *He came from the direction of the west.* (Ḳ.)

8. اغترب : see 5. — Also *He married to one not of his kindred.* (Ṣ, Ḳ.) It is said in a trad., اِغْتَرِبُوا وَلَا تُضْوُوا (TA) [expl. in art. ضوى].

10: see 4, in four places. == استغربهُ *He held it to be,* or *reckoned it,* غَرِيب [i. e. *strange, far from being intelligible, difficult to be understood, obscure;* or *extraordinary, unfamiliar,* or *unusual;* and *improbable*]. (MA.)

غَرْبٌ [an inf. n. of غَرَبَ, q. v., in several senses. — As a simple subst.,] *Distance,* or *remoteness;* and so غَرْبَةٌ ▼. (A, Ḳ.) غَرْبَةُ ▼ النَّوَى [in one of my copies of the Ṣ غُرْبَةُ] means *The distance,* or *remoteness, of the place which one purposes to reach in his journey.* (Ṣ, TA.) — [And hence, used as an epithet, *Distant,* or *remote.*] You say نَوًى غَرْبَةٌ [in one of my copies of the Ṣ غُرْبَةٌ] *A distant,* or *remote, place which one purposes to reach in his journey.* (Ṣ, A.*) And دَارُ فُلَانٍ غَرْبَةٌ *The house,* or *abode, of such a one is distant,* or *remote.* (TA.) And دَرَاهِمُ غَرْبَةٌ *Distant money* [so that it is *not easily attainable*]. (TA.) And عَيْنٌ غَرْبَةٌ *A far-seeing eye:* and إِنَّهُ لَغَرْبُ العَيْنِ *Verily he is far-seeing;* and of a woman you say غَرْبَةُ العَيْنِ. (TA.) == And الغَرْبُ is *syn. with* المَغْرِبُ ▼, (Ṣ, M, Mṣb, Ḳ,) which latter is also pronounced المَغْرَبُ ▼, with fet-ḥ to the ر, but more commonly with kesr, (Mṣb,) or accord. to analogy it should be with fet-ḥ, but usage has given it kesr, as in the case of المَشْرِقُ; (TA;) [both signify *The west;*] الغَرْبُ is *the contr. of* الشَّرْقُ; (M, TA;) and المَغْرِبُ ▼ [is *the contr. of* المَشْرِقُ, and] originally signifies *the place* [or *point*] *of sunset,* (TA,) as also مَغْرِبَانُ ▼ الشَّمْسِ; (Ḳ;) and is likewise used to signify *the time of sunset;* and also as an inf. n.: (TA:) and المَغْرِبَانِ ▼ signifies *the two places* [or *points*] *where the sun sets;* i. e. *the furthest* [or *northernmost*] *place of sunset in summer* [W. 26° N. in Central Arabia] *and the furthest* [or *southernmost*] *place of sunset in winter* [W. 26° S. in Central Arabia]: (T, TA:) *between these two points are a hundred and eighty points, every one of which is called* مَغْرِبٌ; and so between the two points called المَشْرِقَانِ. (TA.) == غَرْبٌ signifies also The *first part* (Ṣ, Ḳ) of a thing (Ḳ) [and particularly] † *of the run* of a horse. (Ṣ.) — And The حَدّ [or *edge*] (Ṣ, Ḳ) of a thing, as also غُرَابٌ ▼, (Ḳ,) or of a sword and of anything; (Ṣ;) and thus [particularly] the غُرَاب ▼ of the فَأْس [or adz, &c.]. (Ṣ, Ḳ.) — And † *Sharpness* (Ṣ, A, Mṣb, TA) of a sword, (TA,) or of anything, such as the فَأْس [or adz, &c.], and of the knife, (Mṣb,) and (Mṣb, TA) † of the tongue: (Ṣ, A, Mṣb, TA:) and [as meaning † *sharpness of temper* or *the like, passionateness, irritability,* or *vehemence,*] of a man, (TA,) and of a horse, (Ṣ, TA,) and of youth: (A, TA:) [from the same word signifying the "edge" of a sword &c.: whence the saying, أَرْهِفْ غَرْبَ ذِهْنِكَ لِمَا أَقُولُ (mentioned in the A and TA in art. ارهف,) meaning ‡ *Sharpen the edge of thine intellect for what I say:*] and غَرْبَةٌ ▼ signifies the same. (TA.) And *Vehemence of might* or *strength,* or *of valour* or *prowess,* of men; syn. شَوْكَةٌ. (TA.) [And hence, app., † *Briskness, liveliness,* or *sprightliness:* and † *perseverance* in an affair: see the first paragraph.] — Also, [used as an epithet,] † *Sharp,* applied to a sword [and the like], and to a tongue. (TA.) And, applied to a horse, † *That runs much:* (Ṣ, Ḳ:) or *that casts himself forward, with uninterrupted running, not desisting until he has gone far with his rider.* (TA.) == And *A large* دلو [or *leathern bucket*], (Ṣ, Mgh, Mṣb, Ḳ, TA,) *made of a bull's hide,* (Mgh, TA,) *with which one draws water on the* [*camel,* or *she-camel, called*] سَانِيَة [q. v.]: (Mṣb:) of the masc. gender: pl. غُرُوبٌ. (TA.) So expl. in the following words of a trad.: أَخَذَ الدَّلْوَ عُمَرُ فَاسْتَحَالَتْ غَرْبًا ['*Omar took the* دلو, *and it became changed into a* غرب]; i. e. when he took the دلو to draw water, it became large in his hand: for the conquests in his time were more than those in the time of Aboo-Bekr. (IAth, TA.) — And *A* [*camel,* or *any beast, such as is called*] رَاوِيَة, (Ḳ, TA,) *upon which water is carried.* (TA.) — And accord. to the Ḳ, *A day of irrigation:* but [this is app. a mistake: for] Az says that Lth has mentioned the phrase فِى يَوْمِ غَرْبٍ, meaning thereby *in a day in which water is drawn with the* [*large bucket called*] غَرْب, [*for irrigation,*] *on the* [*camel,* or *she-camel, called*] سَانِيَة. (TA.) == And *Tears* (Ḳ, TA) *when they come forth from the eye:* (TA:) or غُرُوبٌ signifies *tears;* (Ṣ;) and is pl. of غَرْبٌ. (TA.) A poet says,

• مَا لَكَ لَا تَذْكُرُ أُمَّ عَمْرٍو •
• إِلَّا لِعَيْنَيْكَ غُرُوبٌ تَجْرِى •

[*What aileth thee, that thou dost not mention Umm-'Amr but thine eyes have tears flowing?*]. (Ṣ, TA.) And it is said of Ibn-'Abbás, in a trad., كَانَ مِثَجًّا يَسِيلُ غَرْبًا i. e. ‡ [*He was an eloquent orator, flowing with*] *a copious and uninterrupted* *stream of knowledge*, likened to غَرْبٌ as meaning "tears coming forth from the eye." (TA.) — And *A flowing*, (مَسِيلٌ, K,) or *vehement flowing*, (اِنْهِمَالٌ, A, K,) in one copy of the K اِنْهِلَالٌ [which means *a flowing*], (TA,) *of tears from the eye:* (A, K:) and *a single flow* (فَيْضَةٌ) of tears, and of wine. (K.) — And *A certain vein*, or *duct*, (عِرْقٌ,) *in the channel of the tears*, (S, Mgh,) or *in the eye*, (A, K,) *that flows* [*with tears*] *uninterruptedly;* (S, A, Msb, K;) *like what is termed* نَاسُورٌ. (S, Mgh.) One says of a person whose tears flow without intermission, بِعَيْنِهِ غَرْبٌ. (As, S, Mgh.) And [the pl.] الغُرُوبُ signifies *The channels of the tears.* (S.) — Also The *inner angle of the eye*, and the *outer angle thereof.* (S, A, K.) — And *A tumour in the inner angles of the eyes;* (Mgh, K;) as also ▼غَرَبٌ. (Mgh.) — And *A pustule* (بَثْرَةٌ) *in the eye*, (K, TA,) *which discharges blood, and the bleeding of which will not be stopped.* (TA.) — And *Abundance of saliva* (K, TA) *in the mouth;* (TA;) and the *moisture thereof*, i.e., *of saliva:* (K:) pl. غُرُوبٌ. (TA.) And The *place where the saliva collects and remains:* (K, TA:) or the غَرْب in a tooth is the *place where the saliva* thereof *collects and remains:* (TA:) or غَرْبٌ, (TA,) or its pl. غُرُوبٌ, (S, TA,) signifies the *sharpness*, and مَآء [meaning *lustre*], (S, TA,) of the tooth, (TA,) or of the teeth: (S, TA:) accord. to the T and M and Nh and L, غُرُوبُ الأَسْنَانِ signifies *the places where the saliva of the teeth collects and remains:* or, as some say, *their extremities and sharpness and* مَآء [which may here mean either *water* or *lustre*]: or *the* مَآء *that runs upon the teeth:* (TA:) or *their* مَآء, *and shining whiteness:* (A, TA:) or *their fineness*, or *thinness, and sharpness:* or غُرُوبٌ signifies *the sharp*, or *serrated, edges* of the fore teeth: it is also, as pl. of غَرْبٌ, expl. as signifying the مَآء *of the* فَم [by which may be meant either the *water of the mouth* or the *lustre of the teeth*, for الفَمُ properly signifies "the mouth" and metonymically "the teeth"], and the *sharpness of the teeth:* and accord. to MF, as on the authority of the Nh, [but SM expresses a doubt as to its correctness,] it is also applied to the *teeth* [themselves]. (TA.) [See also شَنَبٌ, in two places.] ═ سَهْمُ غَرْبٍ, and ▼أَصَابَهُ سَهْمُ غَرْبٍ and ▼سَهْمُ غَرَبٍ, and سَهْمٌ غَرْبٌ and ▼سَهْمٌ غَرَبٌ, (S, Msb,* K,) the second of which, i. e. ▼سَهْمُ غَرَبٍ, accord. to IKt, is the most approved, (MF,) mean *An arrow of which the shooter was not known* [*struck him*]: (S, Msb, K:) or, accord. to some, سهم غرب signifies *an arrow from an unknown quarter;* سهم ▼غَرَبٍ, *an arrow that is shot and that strikes another.* (TA.) ═ And غَرْبٌ signifies also *A certain tree of El-Hijáz*, (K, TA,) *green*, (TA,) *large*, or *thick, and thorny*, (K, TA,) *whence is made* [or *prepared*] *the* كُحَيْل [i. e. *tar*] *with which* [*mangy*] *camels are smeared:* [or it is a coll. gen. n., for] its n. un. is with ة: so says ISd: قَطِرَانٌ is كحيل, of the dial. of El-Hijáz: and he [app. ISd] says also, the أَبْهَل [q. v.] is the same as the غَرْب, because قطران is extracted from it. (TA.) Hence, as some say, (K, TA,) the trad., (TA,) لَا يَزَالُ أَهْلُ الغَرْبِ ظَاهِرِينَ عَلَى الحَقِّ [*The people of the* غرب *will not cease to be attainers of the truth*, or *of the true religion*]: (K, TA:) or the meaning is, *the people of Syria*, because Syria is [a little to the] west of El-Hijáz: or *the people of sharpness, and of vehemence of might* or *strength*, or *of valour* or *prowess;* i. e. *the warriors against unbelievers:* or *the people of the bucket called* غَرْب; i. e. *the Arabs:* or *the people of the west;* which meaning is considered by 'Iyád and others the most probable, because, in the relation of the trad. by Ed-Dárakutnee, the word in question is المَغْرِب. (L, TA.)

غُرْبٌ: see غُرْبَةٌ.

غَرَبٌ *Silver:* or a [*vessel such as is termed*] جَام *of silver;* (S, K;) [i. e.] *a* [*drinking-cup* or *bowl such as is termed*] قَدَح *of silver.* (L, TA.) A poet says,

فَدَعْدَعَا سُرَّةَ الرَّكَآءِ كَمَا
دَعْدَعَ سَاقِى الأَعَاجِمِ الغَرَبَا

cited in the S as being by El-Aashà; but it is said in the L, IB says, this verse is by Lebeed, not by El-Aashà, describing two torrents meeting together; meaning, *And they filled the middle of the valley of Er-Rekà*, also, but less correctly, called Er-Rikà, *like as the cup-bearer of the* اعاجم [or *foreigners*] *fills the silver* قَدَح with wine: the verse of El-Aashà in which [it is said that] غَرَب occurs as meaning "silver" is,

إِذَا ٱنْكَبَّ أَزْهَرُ بَيْنَ السُّقَاةِ
تَرَامَوْا بِهِ غَرَبًا وَنُضَارَا

i. e. *When a white wine-jug is turned down so as to pour out its contents* [*among the cup-bearers*], *they hand it*, i. e. the wine in the cups, *one to another* [while it resembles *silver or gold*]: (L, TA:) غَرَبًا is here in the accus. case as a denotative of state, though signifying a substance: [and so نُضَارًا:] but it is said that غَرَبٌ and نُضَارٌ signify species of trees from which are made [drinking-cups or bowls such as are termed] أَقْدَاح [pl. of قَدَحٌ]: and it is said in the T that نُضَار signifies a species of trees from which are made yellow أَقْدَاح. (TA.) — [In explanation of the last of the applications of غَرَبٌ mentioned above, it is said that] it signifies also *A species of trees* (T, S, ISd, TA) *from which are made white* [*drinking-cups* or *bowls of the kind termed*] أَقْدَاح; (T, TA;) *called in Pers.* إِسْبِيذْ دَار [or إِسْپِيدَار]: (S:) [generally held to mean the *willow;* like the Hebr. עֲרָבִים; or particularly the species called *salix Babylonica:* a coll. gen. n.:] n. un. with ة. (ISd, TA.) [Avicenna (Ibn-Seenà), in book ii. p. 279, mentions a tree called غرب, but describes only the uses and supposed properties of its bark &c., particularizing its صَمْغ; whence it appears that he means the غَرَب, not the غَرْب.] — It also signifies *A* [*vessel of the kind termed*] قَدَح [perhaps such as is made from the species of trees above mentioned]: (K, TA:) and its pl. is أَغْرَابٌ. (TA.) — And *Gold.* (K.) — And *Wine.* (S, K.) — And The *water that drops from the buckets between the well and the watering-trough* or *tank*, (S, K,) *and which soon alters in odour:* (S:) or *any water that pours from the buckets from about the mouth of the well to the watering-trough* or *tank, and that soon alters in odour:* or the *water and mud that are around the well and the watering-trough* or *tank:* (TA:) and (as some say, TA) the *odour of water and mud:* (K:) so called because it soon alters. (TA.) [Hence] one says, لا تغرب, [thus in the TA, so that it may be ▼لَا تُغْرِبْ or ▼لَا تَغْرُبْ or ▼لَا تُغَرِّبْ,] meaning *Spill not thou the water between the well and the watering-trough* or *tank, so as to make mud.* (TA.) ═ Also *A certain disease in sheep* or *goats*, (S, K,) *like the* سُعَاف *in the she-camel, in consequence of which the hair of the* خُرْطُوم [i. e. *nose*, or *fore part of the nose*,] *and that of the eyes fall off.* (S.) — And [*A colour such as is termed*] زَرَق [q. v.] *in the eye of a horse*, (K, TA,) *together with whiteness thereof.* (TA.) — See also غَرْبٌ, latter half, in five places.

غَرِيبٌ: see غُرُبٌ.

غُرْبَةٌ: see غَرْبٌ, former half, in three places.

غُرْبَةٌ (S, K) and ▼غُرْبٌ (K) [as simple substs. The *state*, or *condition, of a stranger* or *foreigner;* but originally both are, app., inf. ns. of غَرُبَ, like قُرْبَةٌ and قُرْبٌ of قَرُبَ, signifying] the *being far*, or *distant, from one's home*, or *native country;* (K;) *i. q.* اِغْتِرَابٌ (S, K) and تَغَرُّبٌ. (K.) ═ Also, the former, *Pure*, or *unmixed, whiteness.* (IAar, TA.) [See مُغْرَبٌ.]

غَرْبِيٌّ [*Of*, or *relating to, the west*, or *place of sunset; western*]: see غَارِبٌ. — [Also,] applied to trees (شَجَرٌ), *Smitten*, or *affected, by the sun at the time of its setting.* (K.) [Respecting the meaning of its fem. in the Kur xxiv. 35, see شَرْقِيٌّ.] ═ And *A sort of dates:* (K:) but accord. to AHn, the word is غَرَابِيٌّ [q. v.]. (TA.) — And The [*sort of*] نَبِيذ *that is termed* فَضِيخ [i. e. *a beverage made from crushed unripe dates without being put upon the fire*]: (K, TA:) or [*a beverage*] *prepared only from fresh ripe dates; the drinker of which ceases not to possess self-restraint as long as the wind does not blow upon him; but if he goes forth into the air, and the wind blows upon him, his reason departs:* wherefore one of its drinkers says,

إِنْ لَمْ يَكُنْ غَرْبِيُّكُمْ جَيِّدًا
فَنَحْنُ بِٱللّٰهِ وَبِٱلرِّيحِ

[*If your gharbee be not excellent, we* (*put our trust*) *in God and in the wind*]. (AHn, TA.) — And *A certain red* صِبْغ [i. e. *dye*, or perhaps *sauce*, or *fluid seasoning*]. (K.)

غِرْبِيبٌ *One of the most excellent kinds of grapes;* (K;) *a sort of grapes growing at Et-Táif, in-*

tensely black, of the most excellent, and most delicate, and blackest, of grapes. (TA.) [See an ex. in a verse cited voce عَجْمِيَّةٌ.] —— Applied to an old man, *Intensely black* [app. *in the hair*]: or *whose hair does not become white*, or *hoary:* (TA:) or, so applied, *who blackens his white*, or *hoary, hair with dye:* (Ḳ, TA:) occurring in a trad., in which it is said that God hates such an old man: pl. غَرَابِيبُ. (TA.) —— أَسْوَدُ غِرْبِيبٌ means *Intensely black:* but if you say غَرَابِيبُ سُودٌ, you make the latter word a substitute for the former; because a word corroborative of one signifying a colour cannot precede; (Ṣ, Ḳ;) nor can the corroborative of any word: (Suh, MF:) or, accord. to Hr, غَرَابِيبُ سُودٌ [in the Ḳur xxxv. 25], relating to mountains, means Streaks *having black rocks.* (TA.)

غُرَابٌ *A certain black bird,* (TA,) *well known;* (Ḳ, TA;) [the *corvus*, or *crow;*] *of which there are several species;* [namely, the *raven, carrion-crow, rook, jackdaw, jay, magpie,* &c.:] and it was used as a proper name, which, as is said in a trad., he [i. e. Moḥammad] changed, because the word implies the meaning of distance, and because it is the name of a foul bird: (TA:) the pl. [of mult.] is غِرْبَانٌ (Ṣ, Mṣb, Ḳ) and غُرْبٌ (Ḳ) and (of pauc., Ṣ) أَغْرِبَةٌ (Ṣ, Mṣb, Ḳ) and أَغْرُبٌ; (Mṣb, Ḳ;) and pl. pl. غَرَابِينُ. (Ḳ.) When the Arabs characterize a land as fertile, they say, وَقَعَ فِي أَرْضٍ لَا يُطَيَّرُ غُرَابُهَا ‡ [*He lighted upon a land of which the crow will not be made to fly away;* because of its abundant herbage: see also طَيَّرَ]: and وَجَدَ تَمْرَةَ الغُرَابِ † [*He found the fruit of the crow*]; because that bird seeks after and chooses the most excellent of fruits. (TA.) They also say, طَارَ غُرَابُ فُلَانٍ ‡ [*The crow of such a one flew away*], meaning *the head of such a one became white*, or *hoary*. (A, TA. [See also a similar phrase below.]) Also, فُلَانٌ أَبْصَرُ مِنْ غُرَابٍ [*Such a one is more sharp-sighted than a crow*]: and أَحْذَرُ [*more cautious*]: and أَزْهَى [*more proud*]: and أَشْأَمُ [*more inauspicious*]: &c.: they say that this bird is more inauspicious than any other inauspicious thing upon the earth. (TA.) In the phrase غُرَابٌ غَارِبٌ ▼, the epithet is added to give intensiveness to the signification. (TA.) غُرَابُ البَيْنِ has been expl. in art. بين. —— الغُرَابُ is the name of † *One of the southern constellations,* [i. e. *Corvus,*] *consisting of seven stars* [*in the enumeration of Ptolemy*], *behind* البَاطِيَةُ [which is *Crater*], *to the south of* السِّمَاكُ الأَعْزَلُ [i. e. *Spica Virginis*]. (Ḳzw.) —— أَغْرِبَةُ العَرَبِ is an appellation of † *The blacks* [lit. *crows*] *of the Arabs; the black Arabs:* (Ḳ, TA:) likened to the birds called اغربة, in respect of their complexion: (TA:) *in all of them the blackness was derived from their mothers.* (MF, TA.) The أَغْرِبَة in the Time of Ignorance were 'Antarah and Khufáf Ibn-Nudbeh (asserted to have been a Mukhaḍram, TA) and Aboo-'Omeyr Ibn-El-Ḥobáb and Suleyk Ibn-Es-Sulakeh (a famous runner, TA) and Hishám Ibn-'Oḳbeh-Ibn-Abee-Mo'eyṭ; but this last was a Mukhaḍram: and those among the Islámees, 'Abd-Allah Ibn-Kházim and 'Omeyr Ibn-Abee-'Omeyr and Hemmám [in the CḲ Humám] Ibn-Muṭarrif and Munteshir Ibn-Wahb and Maṭar Ibn-Abee-Owfà and Taäbbaṭa-Sharrà and Esh-Shenfarà and Ḥájiz; to the last of whom is given no appellation of the kind called "nisbeh," (Ḳ, TA,) in relation to father, mother, tribe, or place. (TA.) —— رِجْلُ الغُرَابِ signifies † *A certain herb, called in the language of the Barbar* إِطْرِيلَال, (Ḳ, TA,) *and in the present day* زِرُّ الأَخِلَّةِ, (MF,) *resembling the* شِبِتّ [q. v., variously written in different copies of the Ḳ,] *in its stem and in its* جُمَّة [or *node whence the flower grows*] *and in its lower part,* or *root, except that its flower is white, and it forms grains like those of the* مَقْدُونِس [app. *scandix cerefolium* or *apium petroselinum*], (Ḳ, TA,) *nearly:* (TA:) a drachm of its seeds, bruised, and mixed with honey (Ḳ, TA) deprived of its froth, (TA,) is a tried medicine for eradicating [the species of leprosy which are called] the بَرَص and the بَهَق, being drunk; and sometimes is added to it a quarter of a drachm of عَاقِرْ قَرْحًا, (Ḳ, TA,) which is [commonly] known by the name of عود القرح [i. e. عُودُ القَرْحِ, both of these being names now applied to pyrethrum, i. e. pellitory of Spain, but the latter, accord. to Forskål (Flora Ægypt. Arab. p. cxix.), applied in El-Yemen to the cacalia sonchifolia, or to a species of senecio]; (TA;) the patient sitting in a hot sun, with the diseased parts uncovered: (Ḳ, TA:) [see also رِجْل: now applied to the *chelidonium hybridum* of Linn., *chelidonium dodecandrum* of Forsk.: (Delile's Floræ Ægypt. Illustr. no. 502:) in Boethor's Dict. Français-Arabe, both the names of رجل الغراب and اطريلال are given to the plants called *cerfeuil* (or *chervil*) and *corne de cerf* (or *buck's-horn plantain*, also called *coronopus*).] —— Also (i. e. رِجْلُ الغُرَابِ) *A certain mode of binding the udder of a camel,* (Ṣ, Ḳ,) *tightly,* (Ṣ,) *so that the young one cannot suck;* (Ḳ;) *nor will it undo.* (TA.) [Hence] one says, صُرَّ عَلَيْهِ رِجْلُ الغُرَابِ, meaning ‡ *The affair was,* or *became, difficult,* or *strait, to him:* (A,* Ḳ:) or *his life,* or *subsistence, was,* or *became, so.* (TA.) [And in like manner one says also أُصَرَّ, accord. to the TA: but this I think doubtful; believing that أُصَرَّ is a mistranscription for صَرَّ, meaning that one says also صَرَّ عَلَيْهِ رِجْلَ الغُرَابِ i. e. *He bound him with a bond not to be undone,* or *that would not undo;* or *he straitened him.* See, again, رِجْل; and a verse there cited as an ex.] ═══ الغُرَابَانِ signifies *The two lower extremities of the two hips,* or *haunches, that are next to the upper parts of the thighs:* (Ḳ, TA:) or *the heads,* and *highest parts, of the hips,* or *haunches:* (TA:) or *two thin bones, lower than what is called the* فَرَاشَة [or, app., فَرَاش, q. v.]: (Ḳ, TA:) or, in a horse and in a camel, *the two extremities of the haunches,* namely, *their two edges, on the left and right, that are above the tail, at the junction of the head of the haunch,* (Aṣ, Ṣ, TA,) *where the upper parts of the haunch, on the right and left, meet:* (TA:) or *the two extremities of the haunch that are behind the* قَطَاة [or *fore part of the croup*]: (IAṣr, TA:) pl. غِرْبَانٌ: Dhu-r-Rummeh says, referring to camels,

* تَقَوَّبَ عَنْ غِرْبَانِ أَوْرَاكِهَا الخَطْرُ *

meaning تَقَوَّبَتْ غِرْبَانُهَا عَنِ الخَطْرِ [*The prominences of their haunches were excoriated from the lashing with the tails*], the phrase being inverted, for the meaning is known; (Ṣ in this art.;) or تَقَوَّبَ may be for قَوَّبَ [i. e. the saying means *the lashing with the tails excoriated the prominences of the haunches*]: (Ṣ in art. خطر:) or غِرْبَانٌ signifies the *haunches* themselves, of camels: and is employed [by a synecdoche] to signify *camels* [themselves]: (IAṣr, TA:) and [the sing.] غُرَابٌ is also expl. as meaning the *extremity of the haunch that is next the back.* (L, TA.) —— غُرَابٌ signifies also The *whole of the back of the head.* (Ḳ, TA.) You say, شَابَ غُرَابُهُ, *The hair of the whole of the back of his head became white,* or *hoary.* (TA. [See a similar phrase above in this paragraph.]) —— See also غَرْبٌ, former half, in two places. ═══ And *A bunch* of بَرِير [or fruit of the أَرَاك, q. v.]: (Ḳ:) or *a black bunch* thereof: pl. غِرْبَانٌ: (TA:) or غِرْبَانٌ signifies *the ripe fruit of the* أَرَاك.البَرِير (Ṣ.) ═══ And *Hail,* and *snow,* (Ḳ, TA,) and *hoar-frost:* from مُغْرِبٌ signifying the "dawn;" because of their whiteness. (TA.)

غُرُوبٌ pl. of غَرْبٌ [q. v.]. —— [Golius assigns to it the meaning of وِهَادٌ, which he renders "*Depressiores terræ;*" as on the authority of J: but I do not find this in the Ṣ.]

غَرِيبٌ (Ṣ, Mṣb, Ḳ) and غُرُبٌ ▼ (Ṣ, Ḳ) and غَرِيبِيٌّ ▼ (AA, TA) signify the same, (Ṣ, Ḳ, TA,) [*A stranger,* or *foreigner;*] one *far,* or *distant, from his home,* or *native country;* (Mṣb;) a man *not of one's own people:* (TA:) a man *not of one's own kindred; an alien with respect to kindred;* (Ṣ in explanation of the first;) pl. of the first غُرَبَاءُ; (Ṣ, TA;) and غُرُبٌ [also] is a pl. of غَرِيبٌ, like as قُرُبٌ is of قَرِيبٌ: (TA in art. زلف:) fem. of the first غَرِيبَةٌ; pl. غَرَائِبُ. (L, TA.) أَذَاعَتْ غَزْلَهَا فِي الغَرَائِبِ, a phrase used by a poet, means *She distributed her thread among the strange women:* for most of the women who spin for hire are strangers. (L, TA.) And one says وَجْهٌ كَمِرْآةِ الغَرِيبَةِ [*A face like the mirror of her who is a stranger*]: because, the غَرِيبَة being among such as are not her own people, her mirror is always polished; for she has none to give her a sincere opinion respecting her face. (A.) And لَأَضْرِبَنَّكُمْ ضَرْبَ غَرِيبَةِ الإِبِلِ ‡ [*I will assuredly beat you with the beating of the strange one of the camels*] is a saying of El-Ḥajjáj threatening the subjects of his government; meaning, as a strange camel, intruding among others when they come to water, is beaten and driven away. (IAth, TA.) And [hence] قِدْحٌ غَرِيبٌ means † [*An arrow, without feathers or head,*] *such as is not of the same trees whereof are the rest of the arrows.* (TA.) — غَرِيبٌ signifies also Language that is *strange;* [*unusual, extraordinary,* or *unfamiliar;*] *far from being intelligible; difficult to be understood;* or *obscure.* (Msb, TA.) Hence, مُصَنَّفُ الغَرِيبِ [*The composition on the subject of the strange kind of words &c.*]. (A, TA.) [Hence also الغَرِيبَانِ *The two classes of strange words &c.,* namely, those occurring in the Kur-án, and those of the Traditions.] And كَلِمَةٌ غَرِيبَةٌ *A word,* or *an expression, that is* [*strange,* &c., or] *obscure:* (A, TA:) غَرِيبَةٌ applied to a word [and often used as an epithet in which the quality of a subst. is predominant] is opposed to فَصِيحَةٌ: and its pl. is غَرَائِبُ. (Mz 13th نوع.) — [And hence it often signifies *Improbable.*] — Applied to a trad., it means *Traced up uninterruptedly to the Apostle of God, but related by only one person, of the* أَتْبَاعُ التَّابِعِينَ or *of those termed* تَابِعُونَ or *of those termed* أَتْبَاعُ أَتْبَاعِ التَّابِعِينَ. (KT.) = [The fem.] غَرِيبَةٌ, in a verse of Aboo-Kebeer El-Hudhalee, as some relate it, is expl. by Skr as meaning *Black;* syn. سَوْدَآءُ. (TA voce عَزِيزَةٌ [q. v. It is perhaps used by poetic license for غِرْبِيبَةٌ, fem. of غِرْبِيبٌ.])

غَرِيبَةٌ fem. of غَرِيبٌ [q. v.] — [Hence, as a subst.,] الغَرِيبَةُ signifies ‡ *The hand-mill:* so called because the neighbours borrow it, (A, K, TA,) and thus it does not remain with its owners. (A, TA.)

غُرَابِىٌّ *A sort of dates.* (AHn, K, TA. [See also غُرْبِىٌّ.]) In some copies of the K, for تمر is put ثمر: the former is the right. (TA.)

غَرِيبِىٌّ: see غَرِيبٌ.

غَارِبٌ [The *western side* of a mountain &c.]. You say, هٰذَا غَارِبُ الجَبَلِ and ▼ غَرْبِيُّهُ [*This is the western side of the mountain*], and [in the opposite sense] هذا شَارِقُ الجَبَلِ and شَرْقِيُّهُ. (TA in art. شرق.) = Also The كَاهِل [or *withers*], (A, K, TA,) of the camel; (TA;) or the *part between the hump and the neck;* (S, A, Msb, K, TA;) *upon which the leading-rope is thrown when the camel is sent to pasture where he will:* (Msb:) pl. غَوَارِبُ. (Msb, K.) — Hence the saying, (S, &c.,) حَبْلُكِ عَلَى غَارِبِكِ [*Thy rope is upon thy withers*]; (S, A, Mgh, Msb, K, TA;) used (Msb, TA) by the Arabs in the Time of Ignorance (TA) in divorcing; (Msb, TA;) meaning ‡ *I have left thy way free,* or *open, to thee;* (TA;) *go whithersoever thou wilt:* (S, A, Mgh, Msb, K, TA:) originating from the fact of throwing a she-camel's leading-rope upon her withers, if it is upon her, when she pastures; for when she sees the leading-rope, nothing is productive of enjoyment to her. (As, S, TA.) — الغَارِبَانِ signifies *The fore and hind parts of the back* [and *of the hump*]: and بَعِيرٌ ذُو غَارِبَيْنِ, *A camel whereof the part between the* غاربان [or *fore and hind parts*] *of the hump is cleft;* which is mostly the case in the بَخَاتِىّ, whose sire is the فَالِج [or large two-humped camel of Es-Sind] and his dam Arabian. (TA.) — And غَارِبٌ signifies also The *fore part of the hump:* thus in the following saying, in a trad. of Ez-Zubeyr: فَمَا زَالَ يَفْتِلُ فِى الذِّرْوَةِ وَالغَارِبِ حَتَّى أَجَابَتْهُ عَائِشَةُ إِلَى الخُرُوجِ i. e. † [*And he ceased not to twist* the fur of] *the upper part and the fore part of the hump* [*until 'Áïsheh gave him her consent to go forth*]; meaning, he ceased not to practise guile with her, and to wheedle her, until she gave him her consent: originating from the fact that, when a man desires to render a refractory camel tractable, and to attach to him the nose-rein, he passes his hand over him, and strokes his غارب, and twists its fur, until he has become familiar: (L, TA:) or غَارِبٌ signifies the *upper portion of the fore part of the hump.* (Lth, TA.) — Also ‡ The *upper part of a wave:* (Lth, TA:) غَوَارِبُ المَآءِ means ‡ *the higher parts of the waves of water;* (S, K, TA;) likened to the غوارب of camels: (S, TA:) or *the higher parts of water.* (TA.) — And † The *highest part* of anything. (Msb, TA.) = See also غُرَابٌ, first quarter.

مَغْرِبٌ and مَغْرَبٌ: see غَرْبٌ, first quarter, in four places. You say, لَقِيتُهُ مَغْرِبَ الشَّمْسِ (K, TA) and ▼ مَغْرِبَانَهَا (K,* TA) and مَغْرِبَانَاتِهَا (TA) and ▼ مُغَيْرِبَانَهَا (S, K) and مُغَيْرِبَانَاتِهَا (S,* K) *I met,* or *found, him,* or *it, at sunset.* (K, TA.) [It is said that] ▼ مُغَيْرِبَانٌ is a dim. formed from a word other than that which is its proper source of derivation; being as though formed from ▼ مَغْرِبَانٌ. (S, L. [Hence it seems that this last word as given above was unknown to, or not admitted by, the authors of these two works.]) — مَغْرِبٌ signifies also *Anything* [meaning *any place*] *that conceals, veils,* or *covers, one:* pl. مَغَارِبُ, which is applied to the *lurking-places* of wild animals. (Az, TA.)

مُغْرِبٌ: see 4, latter half. — Also *White;* (S, K;) as an epithet applied to anything: or that *of which every part is white;* and this is the ugliest kind of whiteness. (K.) And *White in the edges of the eyelids;* (S, K;) as an epithet applied to anything: (S:) a camel *of which the edges of the eyelids, and the iris of each eye, and the hair of the tail, and every part, are white:* (IAar, TA:) and a horse *of which the blaze upon his face extends beyond his eyes.* (TA.) And عَيْنٌ مُغْرِبَةٌ *An eye which is blue* [or *gray*], *and of which the edges of the lids, and the surrounding parts, are white:* when the iris also is white, the ▼ إِغْرَاب is of the utmost degree. (TA.) — Also The *dawn of day:* (K, TA:) so called because of its whiteness. (TA.)

عَنْقَآءُ مُغْرِبٌ (A, K) and مُغْرِبَةٌ and مُغْرِبٍ, and العَنْقَآءُ المُغْرِبُ, (K,) *A certain bird, of which the name is known, but the body is unknown:* (A, K:) or *a certain great bird, that goes far in its flight:* or they are words having no meaning [except the meanings here following]. (A, L, K.) [See also art. عنق.] — *Calamity,* or *misfortune.* (K.) طَارَتْ بِهِ عَنْقَآءُ مُغْرِبٌ means *Calamity,* or *misfortune, carried him off,* or *away.* (TA.) [See, again, art. عنق.] — And The *summit of an* [*eminence of the kind called*] أَكَمَة: (K:) or أَكَمَةُ العَنْقَآءِ المُغْرِبِ signifies *the summit of an* أَكَمَة *on the highest part of a tall,* or *long, mountain:* so says Aboo-Málik, who denies that it means a bird. (TA.) — And [The people, or the woman,] *that has gone far into a land,* or *country, so as not to be perceived nor seen:* (K:) thus is expl. in the T العَنْقَآءُ المُغْرِبُ, as transmitted from the Arabs, with the ة suppressed in like manner as it is in لِحْيَة نَاصِل meaning "an intensely white beard." (TA.)

مَغْرِبَانٌ; pl. مَغْرِبَانَاتٌ: see غَرْبٌ, first quarter: and see also مَغْرِبٌ, in two places.

مَغْرِبِىٌّ and مَغْرِبِىٌّ, or, accord. to some, the former only, but the latter is now common, *Of the west; western:* now generally meaning *of the part of Northern Africa west of Egypt,* or *of North-Western Africa:* as applied to a man, its pl. is مَغَارِبَةٌ.]

مُغَرَّبٌ and مُغْرَبٌ شَأْوٌ مُغَرِّبٌ [*A term,* or *limit,* &c.,] *distant,* or *remote.* (S.) — And خَبَرٌ مُغَرِّبٌ *Fresh,* or *recent, information,* or *news, from a foreign,* or *strange, land* or *country.* (TA.) One says, هَلْ جَآءَكُمْ مُغَرِّبَةُ خَبَرٍ *Has any information,* or *news, come to you from a foreign,* or *strange, land* or *country?* (Yaakoob, S, TA:) and هَلْ مِنْ مُغَرِّبَةِ خَبَرٍ (A'Obeyd, A, Msb, TA) and مُغَرِّبَةِ خَبَرٍ (A'Obeyd, Msb, TA) *Is there any information from a distant place?* (A;) or *any occasion of such information?* (Msb;) or *any new information from a distant land or country?* or, accord. to Th, مغربة خبر means *new,* or *recent, information.* (TA.) [See an ex. voce جُنُبٌ: and see also مُغْرِبٌ.] — المُغَرِّبُونَ, mentioned in a trad., (Hr, Nh, K, TA,) in which it is said, إِنَّ فِيكُمْ مُغَرِّبِينَ, (Hr, Nh, TA,) is expl. [app. by Mohammad] as meaning *Those in whom the jinn* [or *demons*] *have a partnership,* or *share:* so called because a foreign strain has entered into them, or because of their coming from a remote stock: (Hr, Nh, K, TA:) and by the jinn's having a partnership, or share, in them, is said to be meant their bidding them to commit adultery, or fornication, and making this to seem good to them; so that their children are unlawfully begotten: this expression being similar to one in the Kur xvii. 66. (Nh, TA.) — And مُغَرِّبٌ signifies also One *going,* or *who goes, to,* or *towards, the west.* (S.) [See an ex. voce مُشَرِّقٌ.]

مُغَيْرِبَانٌ; pl. مُغَيْرِبَانَاتٌ: see مَغْرِبٌ, in two places.

مُسْتَغْرِبٌ: see 4, former half.

غربل

Q. 1. غَرْبَلَهُ, (Ṣ, MA, O, Ḳ,) inf. n. غَرْبَلَةٌ, (TA,) *He sifted it*; (MA;) i. q. نَخَلَهُ; (Ḳ;) namely, flour, &c., (Ṣ, O,) or earth, or mould. (MA.) — And [hence, app.,] *He dispersed it*, or *scattered it*. (Sh, TA.) — And *He cut it*, or *severed it*; syn. قَطَعَهُ: (Ṣ, O, and so in the CḲ:) or *he cut it in pieces*; syn. قَطَّعَهُ. (So in several copies of the Ḳ and in the TA.) — And غربل القَوْمَ *He slew*, and *crushed* [lit. *ground*], *the people*, or *company of men*. (Ḳ.) Hence the saying, in a trad., كَيْفَ بِكُمْ إِذَا كُنْتُمْ فِى زَمَانٍ يُغَرْبَلُ النَّاسُ فِيهِ (O,* TA) i. e. [*How will it be with you when ye shall be in a time when men*] *shall be slain*, and *crushed*? (TA:) or the meaning is, *when the best of them shall be taken away and the worst of them shall remain*; like as is done by the sifter of wheat? (O, TA:) or, in the opinion of Suh, as he says in the R, *when they shall be searched to the utmost, and pursued one after another*? agreeably with the saying of Mekhool Ed-Dimashkee, دَخَلْتُ الشَّأْمَ فَغَرْبَلْتُهَا غَرْبَلَةً حَتَّى لَمْ أَدَعْ عِلْمًا إِلَّا حَوَيْتُهُ [*I entered Syria, and searched it to the utmost in such a manner that I left not a science but I acquired it*]. (TA.) — And غَرْبَلَ القَتِيلُ *The slain man became swollen*, or *inflated, and raised his legs*. (TA.)

غِرْبَالٌ [*A sieve*;] *a certain thing well known*; (Ṣ, O;) the *thing with which one sifts*: (Ḳ:) pl. غَرَابِيلُ. (O.) — And (O, Ḳ, TA) hence, as being likened thereto in respect of its circular shape, (TA,) *A tambourine*: (O, Ḳ, TA:) whence the trad., أَعْلِنُوا النِّكَاحَ وَاضْرِبُوا عَلَيْهِ بِالْغِرْبَالِ [*Publish ye the marriage, and beat for it the tambourine*]. (O, TA.) — And ‡ *One who makes known what has been told him, in a malicious, or mischievous, manner, so as to occasion discord, or dissension*. (Ḳ, TA.)

غُرْبِيلٌ a word said to signify *A sparrow*: occurring in the saying, in a trad. of Ibn-Ez-Zubeyr, أَتَيْتُمُونِى فَاتِحِى أَفْوَاهِكُمْ كَأَنَّكُمُ الغُرْبِيلُ [*Ye came, or have come, to me opening your mouths as though ye were the sparrow*]. (TA.)

مُغَرْبَلٌ [*Sifted*. — And hence, app.,] *Dispersed*, or *scattered*. (TA.) — And *The low, base, vile*, or *mean*, (Ḳ, TA,) of men; as though he had come forth from the غِرْبَال [or sieve]. (TA.) — And *Slain and swollen* or *inflated*. (A'Obeyd, Ṣ, O, Ḳ.) — And مُلْكٌ مُغَرْبَلٌ *Dominion passing away*. (O, Ḳ.)

غرث

1. غَرِثَ, aor. ـَ, (Ṣ, A, O, Ḳ,) inf. n. غَرَثٌ, (Ṣ, O,) *He hungered*: (Ṣ, A, O, Ḳ:) or, as some say, *in the slightest degree*: and some say, *vehemently*. (TA.) — And accord. to Aboo-'Amr Esh-Sheybánee, one says, غَرِثُوا بِإِبِلِ فُلَانٍ, meaning *They took the camels of such a one wrongfully*: and a man says to another, وَيْلَكَ غَرِثْتَ بِى وَتَرَكْتَ حَقَّكَ [app. meaning *Woe to thee: thou hast wronged me, and hast left*, or *neglected, thy right*]. (O.)

2. غرّث, (Ṣ, A, O,) inf. n. تَغْرِيثٌ, (Ṣ, A, O, Ḳ,) *He made hungry; made to hunger*. (Ṣ, A, O, Ḳ.) You say, غرّث كِلَابَهُ *He made his dogs hungry*. (Ṣ, O.)

غَرْثَانُ *Hungry*: [or, accord. to some, *in the slightest degree*: and accord. to some, *vehemently*: (see the verb:)] you say قَوْمٌ غَرْثَى [using the fem., i. e. *a hungry people* or *party*], (Ṣ, A,* O, Ḳ,) and غَرَاثَى, (Ṣ, O, Ḳ,) and also with kesr to the ث [i. e. غَرَاثِى] accord. to a copy of the Ṣ, (TA,) and غِرَاثٌ: (Ṣ, A, O, Ḳ:) the fem. is غَرْثَى; (Ṣ, A, O, Ḳ;) pl. غِرَاثٌ. (Ṣ, O, Ḳ.) And you say امْرَأَةٌ غَرْثَى الوِشَاحِ, meaning ‡ *A woman slender in the waist*: (Ṣ, A, O, Ḳ:) because she does not fill her وشاح [q. v.] which is therefore as though it were hungry. (Ṣ, O.)

غرد

1. غَرِدَ: see the next paragraph, in three places.

2. غرّد, inf. n. تَغْرِيدٌ, *It* (a bird) *sang*, or *warbled*, or *uttered its voice*; as also ▾ غَرِدَ: (Aṣ, L:) *it*, or *he*, (a bird, Ṣ, A, Ḳ, and a man, Ṣ, as is implied in a verse there cited, and L,) *prolonged its*, or *his, voice*, and *singing, and modulated it sweetly*, or *warbled*; (Lth, Ṣ, A, Mṣb;) and so ▾ غَرِدَ, inf. n. غَرَدٌ; (Ṣ, L, Mṣb;) and ▾ تغرّد: (Ṣ:) or *raised its*, or *his, voice, and prolonged it, modulating it sweetly*, or *warbling*; (L, Ḳ;) as also ▾ غَرِدَ, aor. ـَ; and so ▾ تغرّد, and ▾ اغرد: (Ḳ:) and *it* (a pigeon) *cooed*: *it* (the [bird called] مُكَّآء) *whistled*: *it* (the cock) *crowed*: *it* (the fly) *buzzed*, or *hummed*: *he* (the ass) *uttered a hoarse*, or *rough, sound*; as also ▾ تغرّد. (L.) غرّد is trans. as well as intrans.; or it may be rendered as though trans. by the suppression of the preposition [لِ]. (L.)

4: see 2. — أَغْرَدَنِى, said of a turtle-dove, means *It gladdened me by its cooing*. (El-Hejeree, L.)

5: see 2, in three places.

10. استغرد الرَّوْضُ الذُّبَابَ *The meadows*, or *gardens, by their luxuriance* (نَعْمَة, as in the L and in some copies of the Ḳ, in other copies of the Ḳ نَغْمَة, TA), *excited the flies to buzz*, or *hum*. (L, Ḳ.)

Q. Q. 3. اِغْرَنْدَاهُ, (Ḳ,) and اِغْرَنْدَى عَلَيْهِ, (AZ, Ṣ, Ḳ,) inf. n. اِغْرِنْدَآءٌ, (AZ, Ṣ,) *He overcame him*; (A'Obeyd, Ḳ;) *he set upon him*, or *assailed him*, or *overcame him, with reviling and beating and violence*; (AZ, A'Obeyd, Ṣ, Ḳ;) like اِغْلَنْتَى, (AZ, A'Obeyd, Ṣ,) and اِسْرَنْدَى. (TA. [See the last of these verbs, in art. سرد, and the verse there cited.])

غَرْدٌ: see غَرِدٌ. — Also *A* [*booth of reeds*, or *canes, &c., such as is called*] خُصّ. (Ibn-'Abbád, O, Ḳ.)

غَرْدٌ: see غَرِدٌ. — Also, (Ks, AḤn, Ṣ, Ḳ,) and ▾ غَرْدَةٌ, (AḤn, Ḳ,) or غَرْدٌ and غَرْدَةٌ are like تِبْنٌ and تِبْنَةٌ [the former a coll. gen. n. and the latter its n. un.], (Ṣ,) and ▾ غَرَدٌ (Fr, AḤn, Ṣ, Ḳ) and ▾ غَرَدَةٌ, (AḤn, Ḳ,) or غَرَدٌ and غَرَدَةٌ are like تَمْرٌ and تَمْرَةٌ [the former a coll. gen. n. and the latter its n. un.], (Ṣ,) and ▾ غِرْدٌ (Ḳ) and ▾ غِرَدَةٌ, (AḤn, L,) [or this last is the n. un. of that next preceding it, which is a coll. gen. n.,] and ▾ غَرَادٌ (AA, Ḳ) and ▾ غَرَادَةٌ, (AḤn, Ḳ,) or this last is the n. un. of that next preceding it, [which is a coll. gen. n.,] (AA, L,) and ▾ مُغْرُودٌ, (Fr, AHeyth, Ḳ,) with ḍamm, (Ḳ,) of the measure مُفْعُولٌ, which is a measure very rare, (Fr, AHeyth, TA,) or this is ▾ مَغْرُودٌ, (L, and thus in my copies of the Ṣ,) with fet-ḥ to the م, accord. to Aṣ, (L,) *A species of* كَمْأَة [or *truffles*]: (Ks, AḤn, Ṣ, Ḳ:) or *small* كمأة: or *bad* كمأة: (AḤn, L:) pl. (of غَرْدٌ, Ṣ, or of غَرَدٌ, Fr, Ṣ) غِرَدَةٌ, (Fr, Ṣ, Ḳ,) like as قِرَدَةٌ is of قِرْدٌ, (Ṣ,) or of جَبْأَةٌ of جَبْءٌ, (Fr, Ṣ,) [or, accord. to some, this is a quasi-pl. n., (see جَبْءٌ,)] and (of both of these, Ṣ) غِرَادٌ, (Ṣ, Ḳ,) like as ذِئَابٌ is pl. of ذِئْبٌ, and كِلَابٌ of كَلْبٌ, (Ṣ,) and (of مَغْرُودٌ [or مُغْرُودٌ], Ṣ) مَغَارِيدُ. (Ṣ, Ḳ.)

غِرَدٌ: see the next preceding paragraph.

غَرِدٌ (Lth, Aṣ, Ṣ, L, Mṣb, Ḳ) and ▾ غَرْدٌ, (M, L, Ḳ,) which is thought by ISd to be a contraction of the former, (L,) and ▾ مُغَرِّدٌ (L, Ḳ) and ▾ غَرِيدٌ, (L, TA,) or ▾ غَرِّيدٌ, (TA,) and ▾ غِرِّيدٌ [which has an intensive signification], applied to a bird, (Aṣ, Ṣ, A, Ḳ,) and to a man, (L,) *Singing, warbling*, or *uttering the voice*: (Aṣ, L:) or *prolonging the voice*, and *the singing, and modulating it sweetly*, or *warbling*: (Lth, Ṣ, L, Mṣb:) or *raising the voice, and prolonging it, modulating it sweetly*, or *warbling*. (L, Ḳ.) [See also 2.]

غَرْدَةٌ and غَرَدَةٌ and غِرَدَةٌ: see غَرْدٌ.

غَرَادٌ and غَرَادَةٌ: see غَرْدٌ.

غَرِيدٌ, or غَرِّيدٌ: see غَرِدٌ.

غَرَّادٌ an appellation applied by the people of El-'Irák to *A maker of* [*the booths called*] أَخْصَاص [pl. of خُصّ, with which غَرْدٌ is syn.], and *of* [*the fabrics of reeds, or canes, called*] حَرَادِىّ [pl. of حُرْدِيَّةٌ or حُرْدِىٌّ]. (O.)

غِرِّيدٌ: see غَرِدٌ.

اغرود and اغرودة [i. e. أُغْرُودٌ and أُغْرُودَةٌ, in measure like أُسْلُوبٌ and أُحْدُوثَةٌ,] *A song* or *a singing* [or *a warbling*, of a bird, &c.]: pl. أَغَارِيدُ. (Ḥar p. 445.) One says طَائِرٌ مُسْتَمْلَحُ الأَغَارِيدِ [*A bird whose songs*, or *warblings, are esteemed sweet*]. (A.)

مُغَرِّدٌ: see غَرِدٌ.

مُغْرَنْدٍ act. part. n. of Q. Q. 3 [q. v.]. (Ṣ.)

مَغْرُودٌ and مُغْرُودٌ : see غُرْدٌ.

أَرْضٌ مَغْرُودَةٌ *Land abounding with* [*the species of truffles called*] غُرْدٌ : (Ḳ:) or *having in it* مَغَارِيد [pl. of مُغْرُودٌ]. (O.)

رَوْضٌ مُسْتَغْرِدٌ *Luxuriant meadows* or *gardens* [*that excite the flies to buzz,* or *hum:* see 10]. (TA.)

غرز

1. غَرَزَ, aor. ـِ, (Ṣ, Ḳ,) inf. n. غَرْزٌ, (Ṣ,) *He pricked* a thing with a needle, (Ṣ, Ḳ,) and with a stick or the like. (Ḳ in art. نخس.) — *He inserted* a needle into a thing; as also ↓ غرّز: (TA:) *he stuck,* (TA,) or *fixed,* (Mṣb, TA,) a thing, (Mṣb,) or a stick, (TA,) into the ground; (Mṣb, TA;) *he inserted and fixed* a stick into the ground; (Mgh;) *he planted* a tree; [like غَرَسَ;] (TA;) with the same aor., (Mṣb,) and the same inf. n.; (Mgh, Mṣb;) as also ↓ اغرز. (Mṣb.) — [Hence,] غَرَزَ رِجْلَهُ فِى الغَرْزِ, (Ṣ, Ḳ,) or فِى الرِّكَابِ, (A,) aor. and inf. n. as above, (Ṣ,) ‡ *He put his foot into the* غَرْز, (Ṣ, Ḳ,) or *stirrup;* (A;) as also ↓ اغترز [alone, from غَرْزٌ meaning a kind of stirrup]. (A, Ḳ.) — [Hence also,] غَرَزَتِ الجَرَادَةُ ; and ↓ غرّزت, (TA,) or غرّزت بِذَنَبِهَا, inf. n. تَغْرِيزٌ; (Ṣ;) *The locust stuck her tail into the ground to lay her eggs.* (Ṣ, TA.) — And hence, أَقَامَ بِأَرْضِنَا وَغَرَزَ ذَنَبَهُ ‡ [*He stayed,* or *abode, in our land, and remained fixed,* or] *did not quit it.* (A and TA in art. ذنب.) — غَرَزَ and ↓ غرّز are also said of anything when one means *It was tucked up* (شُمِّرَ) into a thing. (TA.) It is said in a trad. of El-Ḥasan, وَقَدْ غَرَّزَ ↓ ضُفُرَ رَأْسِهِ, i. e., *And he had twisted* [*the locks* or *plaits of*] *his hair, and inserted its extremities into its roots.* (TA.) — غَرَزَ, aor. ـِ, (Ṣgh, Ḳ,) inf. n. غَرْزٌ, (TḲ,) ‡ *He obeyed the Sultán after having been disobedient to him:* (Ṣgh, Ḳ:) as though he laid hold of his غَرْز [or stirrup] and went with him. (TA.) — غَرَزَتْ, (Ṣ, A, Ḳ,) aor. ـُ, (Ṣ,) inf. n. غِرَازٌ (A, Ḳ) and غَرْزٌ, (Ḳ,) *She* (a camel, Ṣ, A, Ḳ, and a sheep or goat, and an ass, TA) *had little milk; her milk became little.* (Ṣ, Ḳ.)

2: see 1, in four places. — غرّز النَّاقَةَ *He abstained from milking the she-camel:* (A:) and غرّز الغَنَمَ *he ceased to milk the ewes* or *she-goats, desiring that they should become fat:* (TA:) and غُرِّزَتِ النَّاقَةُ, inf. n. تَغْرِيزٌ, *the she-camel was left unmilked:* or *her udder was dashed with cold water in order that her milk might cease:* or *she was left unmilked once between two milkings:* (Ḳ:) this is when her milk has withdrawn: (TA: [see also 2 in art. غزر:]) or تَغْرِيزٌ signifies the *sprinkling a she-camel's udder with water, then daubing the hand with earth or dust and slapping the udder, so that the milk is driven upwards, then taking her tail and pulling it vehemently, and slapping her with it, and leaving her; whereupon she goes away for a while at random.* (AḤn, TA.) It is said in a trad. of 'Aṭà, that he was asked respecting the تغريز of camels; and answered, "If it be for emulation, [to make them more fat than those of other men,] no; but if from a desire of putting them in a good state for sale, yes:" and IAth says that the تغريز thereof may mean their *increase,* or *offspring,* (نِتَاج,) and *fatness;* from غَرْزُ الشَّجَرِ [the planting of trees]; but that the more proper explanation is that before given [which appears to be one of the explanations here preceding]. (TA.)

4: see غَرَزَ. — اغرز الوَادِى *The valley produced the plant called* غَرَز. (Ḳ, TA.)

8: see غَرَزَ. — اغترز السَّيْرُ ‡ *The journeying,* or *time of journeying,* (السَّيْرُ, Ḳ, or المَسِيرُ, Ṣ,) *drew near:* (Ṣ, Ḳ:) or *his journeying,* or *time of journeying, drew near:* (TA:) from غَرْزٌ [meaning a kind of stirrup]. (Ṣ, TA.) [But the reading adopted by the author of the TA is app. السَّيْرُ; agreeably with what I find in a copy of the A, اِغْتَرَزَتِ السَّيْرَ, expl. by دَنَا مَسِيرُكَ.] — It is said in a trad., that a man asked him [meaning, app., Moḥammad,] respecting the most excellent warring against unbelievers, and that he was silent respecting it until اِغْتَرَزَ فِى الجَمْرَةِ الثَّالِثَةِ, i. e., † *He entered upon* [the period of] *the third* جَمْرَة: [meaning, that the most excellent is when the weather has become hot; because warring is then the most arduous: see جَمْرَةٌ:] like as the foot of the rider enters into the غَرْز [or stirrup]. (TA.)

غَرْزٌ The *stirrup* (Ṣ, Mgh, Ḳ) *of the camel's saddle,* (Ṣ, Mgh,) *made of skin,* (Ṣ, Ḳ,) *sewed;* (TA;) that of iron [or brass] or wood being called رِكَابٌ; (Ṣ;) the *camel's stirrup:* (Mṣb:) IAạr says that *it is to the she-camel like the* حِزَام *to the horse:* but others say, that *it is to the camel like the* رِكَاب *to the mule.* (TA.) You say, اِلْزَمْ غَرْزَ فُلَانٍ [lit. *Keep thou to the stirrup of such a one;* meaning,] ‡ *keep thou to the commands and prohibitions of such a one.* (Ḳ, TA.) And أُشْدُدْ يَدَيْكَ بِغَرْزِهِ ‡ *Cleave thou to him,* (A, Ḳ,) *and leave him not.* (A.) And it is said in a trad., اِسْتَمْسِكْ بِغَرْزِهِ, meaning, ‡ *Cling thou to him, and follow what he says and does, and disobey him not;* like as one lays hold upon the stirrup of the rider and goes with him. (TA.) — Also sing. of غُرُوزٌ, which signifies *Sprigs ingrafted upon the branches of the grape-vine.* (Ḳ.)

غَرَزٌ *A species of panic grass* (ثُمَام), (Ḳ, TA,) *small, growing upon the banks of rivers, having no leaves, consisting only of sheaths* (أَنَابِيب) *set one into another; and it is of the plants called* حَمْض: or, as some say, the [*kind of rush called*] أَسَل: and *spears* are so called as being likened thereto: Aṣ says, it is *a plant which I have seen in the desert, growing in plain,* or *soft, tracts of land:* (TA:) or *its growth is like that of the* [*sweet rush called*] إِذْخِر; *of the worst of pasture:* (Ḳ, TA:) AḤn says, *it is an unwholesome pasture; for when the she-camel that pastures upon it is slaughtered, the* غرز *is found in her stomach separate from the water, not diffused; and it does not beget the cattle strength:* the n. un. is with ة: it has been erroneously mentioned as being called عَرَز, with the unpointed ع. (TA.)

غَرْزَةٌ *A single puncture;* syn. خَرْزَةٌ. (TA in art. خرز.)

غُرْزَةٌ [*i. q.* خُرْزَةٌ; q. v.: see Freytag's Arab. Prov., i. 626: in the present day applied to *A stitch:* expl. by Golius, as on the authority of Meyd, as signifying "*sutura seu consutio vestis, quæ densioribus fit punctorum interstitiis:*" the pl. is غُرَز; not غُرْز, as in the Lex. of Golius.]

غَرِيزَةٌ *Nature;* or *natural, native, innate,* or *original, disposition, temper,* or other *quality* or *property; idiosyncrasy;* [of the measure فَعِيلَةٌ in the sense of the measure مَفْعُولَةٌ; as though signifying *a disposition,* &c., *implanted* by the Creator;] syn. طَبِيعَةٌ, (Lḥ, Ṣ, Mṣb, Ḳ,) and قَرِيحَةٌ, (Ṣ,) and سَجِيَّةٌ, (TA,) and أَصْلٌ; (Lḥ, TA;) *whether good or bad;* as, for instance, *courage,* and *cowardice:* pl. غَرَائِزُ. (TA.)

[غَرِيزِىٌّ *Natural, native,* or *innate.*]

جَرَادَةٌ غَارِزٌ *A locust that has stuck her tail into the ground to lay her eggs;* as also غَارِزَةٌ, and ↓ مُغَرِّزَةٌ. (Ḳ.) — [Hence the saying,] مَا طَلَعَ السِّمَاكُ قَطُّ إِلَّا غَارِزًا ذَنَبَهُ فِى بَرْدٍ † *Es-Simák has never risen aurorally unless in conjunction with cold*]; meaning السِّمَاكُ الأَعْزَلُ, a well-known star in the sign of Libra, [a mistake for Virgo, for it is Spica Virginis, the Fourteenth Mansion of the Moon,] which rises with the dawn on the 5th of Tishreen el-Owwal, [or October O.S., nearly agreeing with my calculation, accord. to which it rose aurorally in Central Arabia, about the commencement of the era of the Flight, on the 4th of October O.S.,] (A,* TA,) when the cold commences. (TA.) — [Hence also the saying,] هُوَ غَارِزٌ رَأْسَهُ فِى سِنَّتِهِ ‡ *He is ignorant,* (Ṣgh, Ḳ,) *and departs from that care of himself which is incumbent on him and pertaining to him.* (Ṣgh, TA.) — Also غَارِزٌ A she-camel, (Ṣ, Ḳ,) [and a ewe or a she-goat,] and an udder, (TA,) *having little milk:* (Ṣ, Ḳ, TA:) or a she-camel *that has drawn up her milk from her udder:* (Aṣ, Ṣ:) pl. غُرَّزٌ (TA) [and غَوَارِزُ, for] you say also غَنَمٌ غَوَارِزُ. (AZ, TA.) — [Hence,] عُيُونٌ غَوَارِزُ ‡ *Eyes that shed no tears.* (AZ, TA.) — [Hence also,] غَارِزٌ applied to a man, ‡ [*Parum seminis habens;* and hence,] *that seldom indulges in* نِكَاح: pl. غُرَّزٌ. (TA.)

تَغْرِيزٌ, sing. of تَغَارِيزُ, (Ḳ,) which signifies *Offsets of palm-trees,* &c., *that have been transplanted.* (Ḳt, Ṣ, Ḳ.)

مَغْرِزٌ The *place of growth,* [or *of insertion,*]

(أَصْل,) of a feather, and the like, [such as a tooth, and also of the neck,] and of a rib, and of the udder; [of which last, and of the neck, and the like, it means the *base*, which is also termed اصل:] pl. مَغَارِزُ. (TA.) — [Hence,] The *place in which the locust lays its eggs.* (TA.) — [Hence also the saying,] ‡ أُطْلُبِ الخَيْرَ فِى مَغَارِزِهِ [*Seek thou good in the persons in whom it is naturally implanted*]; as also فِى مَغَارِسِهِ. (A, TA.)

وَادٍ مُغْرِزٌ *A valley in which is the plant called* غَرَز. (Ḳ, TA.)

مَنْكِبٌ مُغَرَّزٌ *A shoulder-joint stuck close to the* كَاهِل [or *withers*]. (TA.)

جَرَادَةٌ مُغَرِّزَةٌ: see غَارِزٌ, first sentence.

غرس

1. غَرَسَهُ, aor. ـِ, (Ṣ, A, Mṣb, Ḳ,) inf. n. غَرْسٌ, (Ṣ, Mṣb,) *He planted it*, or *fixed it in the ground;* (A, Ḳ;) namely, a tree; (Ṣ, A, Mṣb, Ḳ;) as also ↓ اغرسهُ, (Zj, A, Ḳ,) inf. n. إِغْرَاسٌ. (A.) — [Hence,] ‡ غَرَسَ فُلَانٌ عِنْدِى نِعْمَةً *Such a one established*, or *settled, in my possession, a benefaction*, or *boon.* (TA.) And غَرَسَ المَعْرُوفَ ‡ *He did good*, or *what was beneficent* or *kind.* (IḲṭṭ, TA.)

4: see the preceding paragraph.

غَرْسٌ, [originally an inf. n.,] *i. q.* ↓ مَغْرُوسٌ, (Ṣ, Mgh, Mṣb, Ḳ,) i. e., A tree *planted;* [and used as a subst., meaning *a set;*] (A, Ḳ;) as also ↓ غِرْسٌ, (A,) and ↓ غِرَاسٌ: (Mgh, Mṣb, Ḳ:) pl. [of pauc.] أَغْرَاسٌ and [of mult.] غِرَاسٌ (Ḳ) [and accord. to general analogy غُرُوسٌ: see عِشْقٌ]. And *A twig that is plucked from a garden and then planted:* (TA:) and غِرَاسٌ, (Ṣ, A,) which is its pl., (A,) *shoots*, or *offsets, of palm-trees, which are cut off from the mother-trees*, or *plucked forth from the ground, and planted;* (Ṣ, Ḳ;) as also ↓ غَرِيسَةٌ: (TA:) or ↓ this last signifies *one of such shoots or offsets from the time when it is put into the ground until it takes hold:* (IDrd, Ḳ:*) or *a palm-tree when it first grows:* (Ṣ, Ḳ:) or *a palm-tree recently planted:* (A:) and the same word also signifies *a grape-vine when first planted:* (TA:) and *a date-stone that is sown:* (Abu-l-Mujeeb and El-Ḥárith Ibn-Dukeyn:) and its pl. is غَرَائِسُ (A, TA) and غِرَاسٌ, which latter is extr. (TA.) — [Hence,] غِرْسُ ↓ يَدِكَ and أَنَا غَرْسُ يَدِكَ ‡ [*I am the creature of thy hand*]: and نَحْنُ غَرْسُ يَدِكَ and أَغْرَاسُ يَدِكَ ‡ [*We are the creatures of thy hand*]; غَرْسٌ being an inf. n. [used in the sense of a pass. part. n. both sing. and pl., agreeably with a general rule]; and أَغْرَاسٌ being pl. of غِرْس in the sense of مَغْرُوسٌ. (A.) And فُلَانٌ غَرْسُ نِعْمَتِهِ ‡ [*Such a one is the creature of his* (another's) *beneficence*]. (TA.)

غِرْسٌ: see غَرْسٌ, in two places. = Also The *membrane that encloses the child;* syn. مَشِيمَةٌ: (IAạr, Ṣ in art. شيم:) or the *membrane*, or *thin skin, that comes forth with the child from the belly of its mother:* (Az, TA:) or *that is upon*, or *over, the head of the new-born child:* (A:) or *what comes forth upon*, or *over, the face:* (TA:) or *what comes forth with the child, resembling mucus:* or the *membrane*, or *thin skin, that is upon*, or *over, the face of the young one of a camel at the birth, and which, if left upon it, kills it:* (Ṣ, Ḳ:) pl. أَغْرَاسٌ. (Ḳ.)

غِرَاسٌ The *act of planting* trees. (A.) — [Hence,] ‡ هٰذَا مَسْقَطُ رَأْسِهِ وَمَكَانُ غِرَاسِهِ [*This is the place of his birth*, (lit., *of the falling of his head*,) *and the place of his plantation*]. (A.) = The *time of planting:* (Ṣ, Ḳ:) or this is termed زَمَنُ الغِرَاسِ, (A,) or وَقْتُ الغِرَاسِ. (Mṣb.) = See also غَرْسٌ [of which it is a syn. and a pl.]. — Accord. to Kr, *Abundance of the trees called* عُرْفُط. (TA.)

غَرِيسَةٌ: see غَرْسٌ, in two places. — غَرِيسَةُ is a proper name for *The female slave* [as being planted in a family]. (Sgh, Ḳ.)

مَغْرِسٌ *A place of planting:* pl. مَغَارِسُ. (TA.) — Hence, metaphorically, ‡ *A woman*, or *wife.* (Ḥar p. 502.) — [Hence also the saying,] أُطْلُبِ الخَيْرَ فِى مَغَارِسِهِ ‡ [*Seek thou good in the persons in whom it is naturally implanted*]; as also, فِى مَغَارِزِهِ. (A and TA in art. غرز.)

مَغْرُوسٌ: see غَرْسٌ.

غرض

1. غَرِضَ, aor. ـَ, (Ṣ, Ḳ,) inf. n. غَرَضٌ, (Ṣ, A, Ḳ,) *He was vexed*, or *disquieted by grief, and by distress of mind; he was grieved, and distressed in mind: he was disgusted; he turned away with disgust.* (Ṣ, A, Ḳ.) You say, غَرِضَ مِنْهُ *He was vexed by*, or *at, him*, or *it, and disquieted by grief, and by distress of mind; he was grieved, and distressed in mind, by him*, or *it:* (Mgh in art. غرض, and TA:) *he was disgusted with it*, or *at it; he turned away from it with disgust:* (Mgh:) and *he feared him*, or *it.* (Ibn-'Abbád, Ḳ, TḲ: but the first and second mention only the inf. n. of the verb in this last sense.) And غَرِضَ بِالمُقَامِ, aor. and inf. n. as above, [*He was vexed*, &c., *by continuance, stay, residence*, or *abode*, in a place: *he was disgusted with it*, or *at it.*] (Ṣ.) And إِذَا فَاتَهُ الغَرَضُ فَتَّهُ الغَرَضُ i. e. الضَّجَرُ [*When the object of aim*, or *endeavour, escapes him, so that he cannot attain it, vexation*, or *disquietude by grief, and by distress of mind*, or *disgust, crushes him*]. (A, TA.) — And hence, (A,) aor. as above, (Ḳ,) and so the inf. n., (A, TA,) *He yearned*, or *longed:* (Ṣ, A, Ḳ:) or *he yearned*, or *longed, vehemently*, or *intensely:* (TA:) إِلَيْهِ *for him*, or *it:* (Ṣ:) or إِلَى لِقَائِهِ *for meeting with him:* the verb in this sense being made trans. by means of الى because it imports the meaning of اِشْتَاقَ and حَنَّ [which are made trans. by the same means]: (A, TA:) [for] accord. to Akh, غَرِضْتُ إِلَيْهِ signifies غَرِضْتُ مِنْ هٰؤُلَاءِ إِلَيْهِ [*I turned with vexation*, or *disgust, from these, to him*, or *it*]; because the Arabs connect the verb [with its objective complement] by means of all these particles [mentioned above; namely, ب and من and الى]. (Ṣ.) Mbr reckons غَرَضٌ, as meaning both "being disgusted" and "yearning" or "longing," among words having contrary significations; and so does Ibn-Es-Seed; (MF;) and in like manner, IḲṭṭ. (TA.) [Perhaps these derive the latter meaning from غَرَضٌ signifying "a butt," or "an object of aim," &c.] = غَرَضَ عَنْهُ, (TA,) [in the TḲ غَرَضَهُ,] inf. n. غَرْضٌ, (Ibn-'Abbád, Ḳ,) *He* (a man, TA) *refrained, forbore, abstained*, or *desisted, from him*, or *it; left, relinquished*, or *forsook, him*, or *it.* (Ibn-'Abbád,* Ḳ,* TA.) = غَرُضَ, aor. ـُ, inf. n. غِرَض, *It* (a thing) *was fresh, juicy, moist, not flaccid.* (Ṣ, Ḳ.) = غَرَضَ الشَّىْءَ, aor. ـِ, (Ḳ,) inf. n. غَرْضٌ; (TA;) and ↓ غرّضهُ, (Ḳ,) inf. n. تَغْرِيضٌ; (TA;) *He plucked the thing while it was fresh, juicy, moist*, or *not flaccid:* or *he took it* (أَخَذَهُ, in some copies of the Ḳ جَذَّهُ, which is a mistake, TA) *while it was so.* (Ḳ.) — † *He did the thing hastily*, or *hurriedly, before its time;* syn. أَعْجَلَهُ عَنْ وَقْتِهِ. (Ibn-'Abbád, O, TṢ, Ḳ.*) — غَرَضَ السَّخْلَ, (Ṣ, Ḳ,) aor. and inf. n. as above; (TA;) and ↓ غرّضها; (Ḳ;) † *He weaned the lambs*, or *kids, before their time.* (ISk, Ṣ, Ḳ.) — غَرَضَتْ سِقَآءَهَا, (Ṣ, Ḳ,) aor. and inf. n. as above, (Ṣ,) † *She* (a woman, Ṣ) *churned*, or *agitated, the contents of her milk-skin, and when its butter had formed in little clots but had not collected together, she poured out the milk, and gave it to people to drink.* (ISk, Ṣ, Ḳ.*) — غَرَضْتُ لَهُ غَرِيضًا ‡ *I gave him to drink fresh milk.* (TA.) — غَرَضْتُ لِلضَّيْفِ غَرِيضًا ‡ *I fed the guests with food that had not been kept through the night:* so in the A: but in the Ḳ, أَغْرَضَ ↓ لَهُمْ غَرِيضًا ‡ *he kneaded for them fresh dough, and did not feed them with food that had been kept through the night.* (TA.) = غَرَضَهُ, aor. ـِ, [inf. n. غَرْضٌ,] also signifies *He filled it*, namely, a vessel, (Ṣ, Ḳ,) and a skin, and a watering-trough; (TA;) and so ↓ اغرضهُ. (Ḳ.) — And *He stopped short of filling it completely.* (Ṣ, Ḳ. [See also 2.]) Thus it has two contr. significations. (Ṣ, Ḳ.) A rájiz says,

* لَقَدْ فَدَى أَعْنَاقَهُنَّ المَحْضُ *
* وَالدَّأْظُ حَتَّى مَا لَهُنَّ غَرْضُ *

(Ṣ, TA,) i. e. *Verily the* محض *and the* دأظ [*the pure milk and the fatness and fulness so that there is no deficiency in their skins*] *have ransomed them from being slaughtered and sold.* (TA.) [But see غرض below.] — Also, aor. ـِ, inf. n. غَرْضٌ, *He broke it* (i. e. a thing) *without separating it.* (TA.) = غَرَضَ البَعِيرَ, (Ṣ,) or النَّاقَةَ, (Ḳ,) [aor. ـِ, as appears from the word مَغْرِضٌ, for otherwise, by rule, it would be مَغْرَضٌ,] inf. n. غَرْضٌ, (Ḳ,) *He bound the* غَرْض *upon the camel;* (Ṣ;) as also

▼ اغترضهُ; (TA;) or *he bound the she-camel with the* غُرْضَة, (K,) *or* غرض; (TA;) as also ▼ أَغْرَضَهَا; (K;) and in like manner, غَرَضَ البَعِيرَ بِالغَرْضِ. (TA.)

2. غرّض, inf. n. تَغْرِيض, *He ate fresh flesh-meat.* (K.) — See also غَرَضَ, in two places. ═ One says also, غَرِّضْ فِي سِقَائِكَ *Fill not thy skin* [*completely; leave a portion unfilled in thy skin*]. (S.) — And فُلَانٌ بَحْرٌ لَا يُغَرِّضُ i. e. [*Such a one is a sea*] *that will not become exhausted.* (S, A, TA.) ═ And غرّض signifies also تَفَكَّهَ, (K, TA,) [meaning *He affected jesting,* or *joking,* for it is] said in the L to be from الفُكَاهَة signifying المِزَاح. (TA.)

3. غارض إِبِلَهُ ‡ *He brought his camels to the watering-place early in the morning; in the first part of the day.* (A, O, K.)

4. اغرضهُ *He made him to be vexed,* or *disquieted by grief, and by distress of mind; to be grieved, and distressed in mind: he made him to be disgusted; to turn away with disgust.* (S.) ═ See also 1, latter half, in two places. ═ اغرض النَّاقَةَ: see 1, last sentence. ═ اغرض *He* (a man) *hit,* or *attained, the* غَرَض [i. e. the *butt,* or *object of aim,* &c.]. (IKtt.)

5. تغرّض, (K, TA,) thus in the O, on the authority of Ibn-'Abbád; but accord. to the Tekmileh, ▼ انغرض; (TA;) said of a branch, *It broke without breaking in pieces:* (K, TA:) or, accord. to the L, the latter signifies *It bent and broke without becoming separated.* (TA.)

7: see what next precedes.

8. اغْتَرَضَ: (so in a copy of the A: [and if this be correct, the primary signification seems to be *It* (a thing) *was plucked,* or *taken, while it was fresh, juicy, moist,* or *not flaccid:* quasi-pass. of غَرَضَ in the first of the senses assigned to it as a trans. v. above:]) or أُغْتُرِضَ: (so in the JK and TA: [and if this be correct, it is app. formed by transposition from أُغْتُضِرَ:]) ‡ *He died in his fresh state;* (JK;) [i. e.] *he died a youth,* or *a young man:* [the latter reading seems to be the right, for it is said to be] similar to أُحْتُضِرَ [evidently a mistranscription for أُغْتُضِرَ]. (A, TA.) ═ اغترض الشَّىْءَ *He made the thing his* غَرَض [i. e. *butt,* or *object of aim,* &c.]. (TA.) ═ اغترض البَعِيرَ: see 1, last sentence.

غَرْضٌ and ▼ غُرْضَةٌ *The appertenance of a camel's saddle of the kind called* رَحْل *which is like the* حِزَام *of the* سَرْج (S, K) *and the* بِطَان *of the* قَتَب; (S;) i. e. *girth,* or *fore girth,* (تَصْدِير,) *thereof;* (S;) *the* حِزَام *of the* رَحْل: (A:) pl. of the former, أَغْرَاض [a pl. of pauc.] (S, K) and أَغْرُض [also a pl. of pauc.] (IB) and غُرُوض [a pl. of mult.]: and of the latter, ▼ غُرَض, [or rather this is a coll. gen. n.,] (S, K,) like as بُسْر is of بُسْرَة, (S,) and غُرُض. (S, K.) [Hence the saying of Mohammad,] غُرْض shall not be bound [upon camels by pilgrims] except to three mosques; the sacred mosque [of Mekkeh], and my mosque [of El-Medeeneh], and the mosque [El-Aksà] of Beyt-el-Makdis [or Jerusalem]. (TA.) ═ غَرْضٌ also signifies (accord. to some, in the verse cited in the first paragraph, S, TA) *The place of what thou hast left* (مَوْضِعُ مَا تَرَكْتَهُ), not ماء [i. e. not مَآء] as written in the S [and K], TA,) *and not put into it anything:* (S, K, TA:) and is said by some to be like the أَمْت [q. v.] in a skin. (TA.) — And *A state of folding.* (AHeyth, K.) And A man's *having folds* (غُرُوض) *in the body when he has been fat and then has become lean.* (Sgh, K.) And you say, طَوَيْتُ الثَّوْبَ عَلَى غُرُوضِهِ i. e. غُرُورِهِ [*I folded the garment,* or *piece of cloth, according to its first,* or *original, foldings.*] (Ibn-'Abbád, Z, Sgh, K.)

غُرْضٌ: see the next preceding paragraph.

غَرَضٌ *A butt, a mark,* or *an object of aim, at which one shoots,* or *throws;* (S, O, Msb, K;) *a thing that thou settest up* (مَا أَمْثَلْتَهُ) *to shoot or throw at:* (IDrd:) pl. أَغْرَاض. (Msb, K.) It is said in a trad., لَا تَتَّخِذُوا شَيْئًا فِيهِ الرُّوحُ غَرَضًا [*Ye shall not take a thing in which is the vital principle as a butt*]. (TA.) And hence one says, النَّاسُ أَغْرَاضُ المَنِيَّةِ † [*Men are the butts of destiny,* or *of death*]: and جَعَلْتَنِي غَرَضًا لِشَتْمِكَ † [*Thou madest me,* or *hast made me, a butt for thy reviling*]. (TA.) — And hence, ‡ *An object of aim* or *endeavour* or *pursuit, of desire* or *wish,* or *of intention* or *purpose:* (Msb:) *a scope;* or *any end which one endeavours,* or *seeks,* or *intends,* or *purposes, to attain:* (B:) *an object of want,* and *of desire:* (TA:) *the advantage,* or *good, which one seeks,* or *endeavours,* or *purposes, to attain,* or *obtain, from a thing:* so much used in this tropical sense as to be, in this sense, conventionally regarded as proper. (MF.) You say, غَرَضُهُ كَذَا ‡ *His object of aim or endeavour or pursuit, &c., is such a thing:* (Msb:) or *his object of want,* and *of desire, is such a thing.* (TA.) And فَعَلَ لِغَرَضٍ صَحِيحٍ ‡ *He did,* or *acted, for a just,* or *right, object of aim* &c. (Msb.) And فَهِمْتُ غَرَضَكَ † *I understood,* or *have understood, thine object of aim* &c., or *thine intention;* syn. قَصْدَكَ. (S.) [See another ex. voce غَرِضَ, of which it is also the inf. n.]

غَرِضٌ, when followed by مِنْ, *Vexed,* or *disquieted by grief, and by distress of mind; grieved, and distressed in mind: disgusted;* or *turning away with disgust.* (TA.) — Also, when followed by إِلَى, *Yearning,* or *longing:* (S, TA:) or *yearning,* or *longing, vehemently,* or *intensely.* (TA.)

غُرْضَةٌ: see غَرْضٌ.

غَرِيضٌ A thing that is *fresh, juicy, moist,* or *not flaccid:* (S, A, K:) also applied to flesh-meat. (S.) [See also 1, in three places, in the latter half of the paragraph.] — *Fresh,* or *juicy, dates.* (TA.) — *Rain-water;* as also ▼ مَغْرُوض: (S, K:) because of its freshness. (S, TA.) — *Water to which one comes early in the morning; in the first part of the day.* (TA.) — See also إِغْرِيض, in two places. — Also *Any new,* or *novel, song.* (IB, TA.) — And hence, *A singer;* because of his performing new, or novel, singing: (IB, TA:) or *a singer who performs well,* (K, TA,) *and is of those who are well known;* and so called because of his gentleness, or softness. (TA.)

وَرَدَ المَآءَ غَارِضًا † *He came to the water early in the morning; in the first part of the day.* (S, K.*) And أَوْرَدَ إِبِلَهُ غَارِضًا † *He brought his camels to the watering-place early in the morning; in the first part of the day.* (TA.) And أَتَيْتُهُ غَارِضًا *I came to him in the first part of the day.* (TA.)

إِغْرِيضٌ *The spadix of a palm-tree;* syn. طَلْعٌ; (S, K;) which some call إِغْرِيضَة; (TA;) as also ▼ غَرِيضٌ: (S, K:) or *the spadix of a palm-tree* (طَلْع) *when it bursts from its* كَافُور [i. e. *spathe,* or *envelope*]: (IAar:) or *what is in the interior of the* طَلْعَة [or *spathe of a palm-tree*]: (Th:) or *the thing* [i. e. the *spathe*] *from which the spadix of the palm-tree* (طَلْع) *bursts:* (Ks, A:) to which a woman's garment is likened. (A, TA.) — † *Anything white and fresh* or *juicy* or *moist;* as also ▼ غَرِيضٌ: (S, K:) or *anything white like milk.* (Ks.) — ‡ *Hail:* (Lth, Th:) as being likened to what is in the interior of the طَلْعَة. (Th.) — † *Large rain,* or *large drops of rain, appearing, when falling, as though it,* or *they, were arrow-heads, from a dissundered cloud:* or *the first of what falls thereof.* (TA.)

مَغْرِضٌ *The part of a camel which is like the* مَحْزِم [or *place of the girth*] (S, O, K) *of a* دَابَّة, (S,) [i. e.] *of a horse* (O, K) *and mule and ass;* (O;) which is *the sides of the belly, at the lower part of the ribs; for these are the places of the* غُرْض, *in the bellies of camels:* (S:) and ▼ مُغَرَّض signifies [the same; i. e.] *the place of the* غُرْضَة, (IKh, TA,) *or* غُرْض; (TA;) and also *the belly:* (IKh, TA:) or the former signifies *the head of the shoulder-blade, in which is the* مُشَاش [or *prominent part*], *beneath the cartilage:* or *the inner part of what is between the arm* [and] *the place where the* شَرَاسِيف [or *cartilages of the ribs*] *end:* (TA:) pl. مَغَارِض. (S, TA.)

مُغَرَّض: see the next preceding paragraph.

مَغْرُوضٌ: see غَرِيضٌ.

غرضف

غُضْرُوف and غُرْضُوف [*A cartilage;*] *any soft bone,* (T, S,* O, K, TA,) *such as is,* or *may be, eaten:* (T, O, K, TA:) pl. غَرَاضِيف (O, K, TA) and غَضَارِيف. (O, TA.) The مَارِن (O, K, TA) i. e. [the *soft,* or *cartilaginous, part,*] the *firm part that is harder than flesh and softer than bone,* (TA,) *of the nose,* (O, K, TA,) is thus called. (O.) And [*Any one of*] *the heads of the* *ribs* [i. e. *of the costal cartilages*]. (O, Ḳ.) And The رَهَابَة [or *ensiform cartilage*] *of the chest.* (O, Ḳ.) And The [*fibro-cartilage* or] *part within the* قُوف [or *helix*] *of the ear.* (O, Ḳ.) And The نُغْض [q. v.] *of the shoulder-blade.* (O, Ḳ.) And الغُرْضُوفَانِ signifies *The borders, or extremities, of the upper parts of the two shoulder-blades* of the horse; *what is thin, of the hard substance* (lit. *of the hardness*), *of the bone.* (TA.) And they (غُرْضُوفَانِ [i. e. the وَهُمَا]) are *Two sinews,* or *the like,* (عَصَبَتَانِ,) [perhaps, by a somewhat-strained license, applied here to the *two tarsal cartilages,*] *in the borders, or extremities, of the inferior parts of the two eyes.* (TA.) — And الغُرْضُوفَانِ signifies [also] *The two pieces of wood that are bound on the right and left between the* وَاسِط [or *fore part*] *and the* آخِرَة [or *hinder part*] *of the* [*camel's saddle called*] رَحْل. (O, Ḳ.)

غرف

1. غَرَفَ المَآءَ, (Mṣb, Ḳ,) or غَرَفَ المَآءَ بِيَدِهِ, (Ṣ, O, TA,) aor. ـُ (Ṣ, O, Mṣb, Ḳ) and ـِ, (Ḳ,) inf. n. غَرْفٌ; (Ṣ, O, Mṣb;) and ↓ اغترفهُ, (Mṣb, Ḳ,) or اغترف مِنْهُ, (Ṣ,) or both of these; (O, TA;) *He took* [or *laded out*] *the water with his hand* [*as with a ladle*]: (Ḳ, TA:) and in like manner, غَرَفَ الشَّىْءَ بِالمِغْرَفَةِ [*with the ladle*]. (JḲ.) = غَرَفَ, (Ṣ, O, Ḳ,*) aor. ـِ, (TḲ,) inf. n. غَرْفٌ, (TA,) *He cut, or cut off, the thing.* (Ṣ, O, Ḳ.*) — And غَرَفَ نَاصِيَتَهُ *He clipped his forelock;* (Ṣ, O, Ḳ;) i. e. a horse's. (Ṣ, O.) = غَرَفَ الجِلْدَ, (Ṣ, O, TA,) inf. n. غَرْفٌ, (TA,) *He tanned the skin with* غَرْف [q. v.]. (Ṣ, O, TA.) = غَرَفَ البَعِيرَ, aor. ـُ and ـِ, (O, TA,) inf. n. غَرْفٌ, (TA,) *He put upon the head of the camel a rope,* or *cord, called* غُرْفَة [q. v.]. (O, TA.) = See also 7. = غَرِفَتِ الإِبِلُ, aor. ـَ, (Ṣ, O, Ḳ,) inf. n. غَرَفٌ, (Ṣ, O,) *The camels had a complaint* (Ṣ, O, Ḳ) *of their bellies* (O, Ḳ) *from eating* غَرَف [q. v.]. (Ṣ, O, Ḳ.)

5. تَغَرَّفَنِى *He took everything that was with me:* (Ḳ, TA:) so in the Tekmileh. (TA.)

7. انغرف *It* (a thing) *became cut,* or *cut off.* (Ṣ, O, Ḳ.) — And *It bent,* or *became bent:* (Yaạḳoob, TA:) and some say, *it broke,* or *became broken:* (TA:) [and ↓ غَرِفَ, inf. n. غَرَفٌ, app. has both of these meanings; for] الغَرَفُ, accord. to IAạr, signifies *The bending,* or *becoming bent;* and *the breaking,* or *becoming broken.* (TA.) انغرف said of a bone means *It broke,* or *became broken:* and said of a branch, or stick, or the like, *it became broken, but not thoroughly.* (TA.) — And *He died.* (TA.)

8: see 1, first sentence.

غَرْف and ↓ غَرَف, (Ṣ, Ḳ,) the latter mentioned by Yaạḳoob, (Ṣ,) *A species of trees,* (شَجَر,) *with which one tans;* (Ṣ, Ḳ;) *when dry,* [*said to be*] *what are termed* ثُمَام: (TA: [but perhaps this statement applies particularly to غَرَف, which see below: and see also ثُمَام:]) accord. to A'Obeyd, called غَرْف and غَلْف [q. v.]: AḤn says, the غرف is *a species of trees from which bows are made;* [see عِضَاهٌ;] *and no one tans with it;* but Ḳz says that *its leaves may be used for tanning therewith, though bows be made of its branches:* and Aboo-Moḥammad mentions, on the authority of Aṣ, that *one tans with the leaves of the* ↓ غَرَف, *and not with its branches:* El-Báhilee says that غَرْف signifies *certain skins, not such as are termed* قَرَظِيَّة, [i. e. *not tanned with* قَرَظ, *but*] *tanned, in Hejer, in the following manner: one takes for them sprigs* (هَدَب) *of the* أَرْطَى, *and puts them in a mortar, and pounds them, then throws upon them dates, whereupon there comes forth from them an altered odour, after which a certain quantity is laded out for each skin, which is then tanned therewith; and the term* غَرْف *is applied to that which is laded out, and to every quantity of skin from that mash, to one and to all alike:* but Az says, *the* غَرْف *with which skins are tanned is well known, of the trees of the desert* (البَادِيَة), *and,* he says, *I have seen it;* and what I hold is this, that *the skins termed* غَرْفِيَّة *are thus termed in relation to the species of trees called the* غَرْف, *not to what is laded out:* Aṣ says that الغَرْف, with the ر quiescent, signifies *certain skins that are brought from El-Baḥreyn.* (TA.)

غَـرَف, (O, Ḳ, TA,) accord. to AA, (O,) or IAạr, (T, TA,) *i. q.* ثُمَام [*Panic grass*]; (O, Ḳ, TA;) *not used for tanning therewith;* and accord. to Az, this that IAạr says is correct: AḤn says that *when it becomes dry, and one chews it, its odour is likened to that of camphor:* (TA:) or ثُمَام *while green:* (Ḳ:) or *one of the species of* ثُـمَام, *which resembles rushes* (أَسَل), *of which brooms are made, and with which water-bags of leather are covered to protect them from the sun so that the water becomes cool:* (A'Obeyd, TA:) the n. un. is with ة. (AḤn, O.) And, (O, Ḳ,) accord. to Skr, (O,) The شَثّ, and طُبَّاق, and نَشَم [thus (correctly) in the O, but in the Ḳ بَشَم], and عَفَار [in the CḲ غفار], and عُثْم, and صَوْم, and حَبَج, and شَدْن, and حَيْهَل [or حَيَّهَل], and هَيْشَر, and صُوْم [thus in the O and in some copies of the Ḳ] or ضِوْم [thus in other copies of the Ḳ]: every one of these is called غَرَف. (O, Ḳ.) — See also غَرْف, in two places. — Also The *leaves of trees* (Ḳ, TA) *with which tanning is performed.* (TA.)

غَرْفَةٌ *A single act of taking* [or *lading out*] water with the hand [as with a ladle: and in like manner also with a ladle: see 1, first sentence]. (Ṣ,* Mgh,* Mṣb,* Ḳ.) = And *A single act of cutting,* or *cutting off,* a thing: or *of clipping* the forelock of a horse. (Ḳ,* TA.)

غُرْفَةٌ The *quantity* of water *that is taken* [or *laded out*] *with the hand* [*as with a ladle*]; (JK, Ṣ,* Mgh,* O, Mṣb,* Ḳ;) *as much* thereof *as fills the hand;* (JK;) and ↓ غُرَافَة signifies the same: (O, Ḳ:) before it is so taken it is not termed غُرْفَة: (Ṣ, Ḳ:) the pl. is غِرَاف. (Ṣ, Mṣb, Ḳ.) — And [hence, app.,] *Somewhat remaining,* of milk. (IAạr, TA in art. جزع.) = Also *i. q.* عُلِّيَّة; (Ṣ, O, Mṣb, Ḳ;) i. e. [*An upper chamber;* or] *a chamber in the upper,* or *uppermost, story:* (Ḥar p. 325:) pl. غُـرَف and غُـرَفَات (Ṣ, O, Mṣb, Ḳ) which latter is held by some to be a pl. pl. (Mṣb) and غُرُفَات and غُرْفَات. (Ṣ, O, Mṣb, Ḳ.) — And الغُرْفَة signifies *The Seventh Heaven:* (Ṣ,* O,* Ḳ:) or *the highest of the places of Paradise:* or it is one of the names of *Paradise.* (Bḍ in xxv. 75.) Accord. to the Ṣ [and O], the phrase دُونَ غُرْفَةِ عَرْشِهِ occurs in a verse of Lebeed, as applying to the Seventh Heaven: but what is [found] in his poetry is دُونَ عِزَّةِ عَرْشِهِ. (IB, TA.) = Also *A lock* (خُصْلَة) *of hair.* (O, Ḳ.) — And *A rope,* or *cord, tied with a bow,* or *double bow,* (مَعْقُودٌ بِأُنْشُوطَة,) (O, Ḳ,) *which is put upon the head,* (O,) or *hung upon the neck,* (Ḳ,) *of a camel:* (O, Ḳ:) of the dial. of El-Yemen. (TA.)

غِرْفَةٌ *A mode,* or *manner, of taking* [or *lading out*] water with the hand [as with a ladle]. (Ḳ.) = And *A sandal:* pl. غِرَف: (Ḳ:) of the dial. of Asad. (TA.) [See also غَرِيفَة.]

غَرْفِىٌّ applied to a سِقَآء [or skin for water or for milk], (Ṣ, O, Ḳ,) and غَرْفِيَّةٌ applied to a مَزَادَة [or leathern water-bag], (Ṣ, O,) *Tanned with the species of tree called* غَـرْف: (Ṣ, O, Ḳ:) Aboo-Kheyreh says that the [skins termed] غرفية are of El-Yemen and El-Baḥreyn: and accord. to AḤn, one says ↓ قِرْبَةٌ غَرَفِيَّةٌ and مَزَادَةٌ غَرَفِيَّةٌ; and the pl. غَرَفِيَّات occurs in a verse [in which the ر cannot be quiescent], cited by Aṣ. (TA.) — مَزَادَةٌ غَرْفِيَّةٌ signifies also [*A leathern water-bag*] *full:* or, as some say, *tanned with dates and* [*the tree called*] أَرْطَى *and salt.* (TA.)

غَرَفِيَّةٌ: see the next preceding paragraph.

غِرَافٌ *A certain large measure of capacity;* (Ṣ, Ḳ;) like جِرَاف; (Ṣ;) *also called* قَنْقَل [q. v.]. (Ṣ, Ḳ.) — And pl. of غُرْفَةٌ in the first of the meanings assigned to it above. (Ṣ, Mṣb, Ḳ.)

غَرُوفٌ A well (بِئْر) *of which the water is taken* [or *laded out*] *with the hand.* (O, L, Ḳ.) — And A large bucket (غَرْب) *that takes up much water;* (O, Ḳ;) as also ↓ غَـرِيـف; (Ḳ;) and غَرِيفَة is applied [in the same sense] to a [bucket termed] دَلْو. (Lth, TA.)

غَرِيف: see what next precedes. = Also *i. q.* قَصْبَآء [i. e. *Reeds,* or *canes;* or *a collection,* or *bed, thereof;* or *a place where reeds,* or *canes, grow*]: and [the *kind of high, coarse grass called*] حَلْفَآء [q. v.]: and *i. q.* غَيْضَة [i. e. *a collection of tangled,* or *confused,* or *dense, trees;* &c.]: (AḤn, O, Ḳ, TA: [but for غَيْضَة, which is thus in the Ḳ accord. to the TA, as well as in the O, many (app. most) of the copies of the Ḳ have غَيْفَة, a mistranscription:]) and *water* [*in such a collection of trees,* &c., i. e.,] *in an* أَجَمَة; (Ṣ, O, Ḳ;) thus expl. by Lth; (TA;) said to have this meaning in a verse (Ṣ, O, TA) of El-Aạshà; (O, TA;) but pronounced by Az incorrect: (TA:) and *numerous tangled*, or *confused*, or *dense, trees, of any kind;* (Ṣ, O, Ḳ;) as also ▼ غَرِيفَةٌ: (ISd, Ḳ:) or *a dense collection* (أَجَمَةٌ) *of papyrus-plants and of* حَلْفَآء [mentioned above] (Ḳ, TA) *and of reeds,* or *canes;* (TA;) and sometimes *of the* [*trees called*] ضَال *and* سَلَم: (AḤn, Ḳ, TA:) pl. غُرُفٌ. (O.)

غَرْيَفٌ *A species of trees,* (Aboo-Naṣr, Ṣ, O, Ḳ,) *of a soft,* or *weak, kind,* (Aboo-Naṣr, O, Ḳ,) *like the* غَرَب: (Aboo-Naṣr, O:) or the *papyrus-plant.* (AḤn, O, Ḳ.)

غُرَافَةٌ: see غُرْفَةٌ, first sentence.

غَرِيفَةٌ *A piece of leather, about a span in length, and empty, in the lower part of the* [*receptacle called*] قِرَاب *of a sword, dangling; and* [*sometimes*] *it has notches cut in it, and is ornamented.* (Ṣ, O, Ḳ.) — And *A sandal,* (Ṣ, O, Ḳ,) in the dial. of Benoo-Asad, (Ṣ, O,) and used also by the tribe of Ṭeiyi: (Sh, TA:) [see also غُرْفَةٌ:] or *an old and worn-out sandal.* (Lḥ, Ḳ.) = See also غَرِيف.

غَرَّافٌ A river, or channel of running water, *having much water.* (O, Ḳ.) — And A *copious rain*: occurring in this sense in a verse: or, as some relate it, the word is there عَزَّاف [q. v.]. (TA.) — And A horse *wide in step; that takes much of the ground with his legs.* (AZ, O, Ḳ.*)

غَارِفَةٌ, applied to a she-camel, *Swift;* pl. غَوَارِفُ: and one says also ▼ خَيْلٌ مَغَارِفُ [*Swift horses;* app. likened, in respect of the action of their fore legs, to men lading out water with their hands; for it is added,] كَأَنَّهَا تَغْرِفُ الجَرْىَ: and فَارِسٌ ▼ مِغْرَفٌ [*A swift horseman*]. (O, Ḳ.) = الغَارِفَةُ which is forbidden by the Prophet is a word of the measure فَاعِلَةٌ in the sense of the measure مَفْعُولَةٌ, (O, Ḳ,) like رَاضِيَةٌ in the phrase عِيشَةٌ رَاضِيَةٌ, (O,) and means *What a woman cuts, and makes even,* or *uniform, fashioned in the manner of a* طُرَّة [q. v., but for مُطَرَّرَة, the reading of the Ḳ given in the TA, the CḲ and my MS. copy of the Ḳ have مُطَرَّزَة, and thus too has the O but without the teshdeed], *upon the middle of her* جَبِين [here meaning *forehead*]: (O, Ḳ, TA:) thus says Az: (TA:) or it is an inf. n., meaning الغَرْفُ, like اللَّاغِيَةُ (O, Ḳ, TA) and الرَّاغِيَةُ and الثَّاغِيَةُ; (O, TA;) or, accord. to Az, it is a subst. similar to رَاغِيَة and لَاغِيَة; and the meaning is, *the clipping of the front hair, fashioned in the manner of a* طُرَّة (مُطَرَّرَة), *upon the* جَبِين: or, accord. to El-Khaṭṭábee, the meaning is, the *clipper of her front hair* on the occasion of an affliction. (TA.)

مِغْرَفٌ, and the pl. مَغَارِفُ: see the next preceding paragraph, first sentence.

مِغْرَفَةٌ [*A ladle;* i. e.] the *thing with which is performed the act of lading out* (مَا يُغْرَفُ بِهِ), (Ṣ, O, Mṣb, Ḳ) [*water &c.,* or] *food:* pl. مَغَارِفُ. (Mṣb.)

غرق

1. غَرِقَ, (Ṣ, Mgh, O, Mṣb, Ḳ,) aor. ـَ, (Mgh, Mṣb,) inf. n. غَرَقٌ, (Ṣ, Mgh, O, Mṣb,) *He,* or *it,* (a thing, Mṣb,) *sank,* syn. غَارَ, (Mgh,) or رَسَبَ, (TA,) فِى المَآءِ [*in water,* or *in the water*]: (Ṣ, Mgh, O, Mṣb:) primarily [*he drowned;* i. e. *he sank under water, and*] *the water entered the two apertures of his nose so that it filled its passages and he died.* (TA.) — [Hence,] غَرِقَ فِى البِلَادِ, inf. n. as above, † *He* (a man) *went downwards and disappeared* (رَسَبَ) *in the lands,* or *tracts of land.* (TA.) = غَرَقَ, (thus in the O,) or غَرِقَ, like فَرِحَ, (thus accord. to the Ḳ,) *He drank a* [*draught such as is termed*] غُرْقَة: (O, Ḳ:) so says IAạr. (O.) And غَرَقْتُ مِنَ اللَّبَنِ, (O, and thus in copies of the Ḳ, in the CḲ غَرِقْتُ,) or غَرَقْتُ مِنَ اللَّبَنِ غُرْقَةً, (TA,) *I took a* [*draught such as is termed*] كُثْبَة *of the milk:* (O, Ḳ, TA:) so says Ibn-'Abbád. (O, TA.) = And غَرِقَ *He was,* or *became, without want,* or *need.* (IAạr, O, Ḳ.) = غَرْقًا used in the sense of إِغْرَاقًا, see under 4.

2: see 4, first sentence. — Hence تَغْرِيقٌ became used to signify ‡ *Any killing:* the origin of its being thus used being the fact that the midwife used to drown the new-born infant in the fluid of the secundine in the year of drought, (Ṣ, O, Ḳ, TA,) whether it were a male or a female, (Ṣ, O, TA,) so that it died: (Ṣ, O, Ḳ, TA:) or it is from the phrase غَرَّقَتِ القَابِلَةُ الوَلَدَ meaning ‡ *The midwife was ungentle with the child* [*at the birth*] *so that the* [*fluid called*] سَابِيَآء *entered its nose and killed it:* or, accord. to the A, غَرَّقَتِ القَابِلَةُ المَوْلُودَ means *the midwife did not remove from out of the nose of the new-born infant the mucus, so that it entered into the air-passages of the nose and killed it.* (TA.) Hence the saying of Dhu-r-Rummeh,

إِذَا غَرَّقَتْ أَرْبَاضُهَا ثِنْىَ بَكْرَةٍ
بِتَيْهَآءَ لَمْ تُصْبِحْ رَؤُومًا سَلُوبُهَا

i. e. *When her ropes* [with which her saddle is bound] *kill a youthful she-camel's second young one,* [and she casts it in consequence, *in a desert in which one loses his way,*] *she* [*who is bereft of it*] *does not become one that shows affection for her offspring,* by reason of the fatigue that has come upon her: (Ṣ, O, TA:) for, as is said in the T, where this verse is cited, when the saddle is bound on the she-camel that has been ten months pregnant, sometimes the fœtus becomes drowned in the fluid of the سَابِيَآء, and she casts it. (TA.) — غُرِّقَ, said of a bridle, [and of the scabbard of a sword, as also ▼ أُغْرِقَ, (see مُغَرَّقٌ,)] signifies ‡ *It was ornamented,* or *was ornamented in a general manner,* with silver. (TA.) — See, again, 4. = غَرَّقَ البَيْضَةَ *He removed the* غِرْقِئ [q. v.] *of the egg.* (TA.)

3. غَارَقَنِى كَذَا ‡ *Such a thing was,* or *became, near to me; drew near to me;* or *approached me.* (TA.) And غَارَقَتْهُ المَنِيَّةُ ‡ [*Death became near to him*]. (TA.) — And غَارَقَتِ الوَقْعَةُ ‡ *The onslaught was,* or *became, obligatory.* (TA.)

4. اغرقهُ, (Ṣ, O, Mṣb, Ḳ, TA,) inf. n. إِغْرَاقٌ; (TA;) and ▼ غرّقهُ, (Ṣ, Mṣb, Ḳ, TA,) inf. n. تَغْرِيقٌ; (TA;) [primarily, *He drowned him:* (see 1, first sentence:) generally expl. as meaning] *he sank him,* or *it,* (TA, [see again 1, first sentence,]) فِى المَآءِ [*in water,* or *in the water*]. (Ṣ,* O, Mṣb,* Ḳ, TA.) — [Hence,] اغرق أَعْمَالَهُ † *He annulled his* [good] *works, by the commission of acts of disobedience.* (TA.) — And اغرقهُ النَّاسُ † *The people multiplied against him and overcame him:* and in like manner, أَغْرَقَتْهُ السِّبَاعُ † [*The beasts of prey multiplied against him* &c.]: so says IAạr. (TA.) — The saying of Lebeed, describing a horse,

يُغْرِقُ الثَّعْلَبَ فِى شِرَّتِهِ

is said to mean † *He outstrips the* ثَعْلَب [i. e. the *fox*] *in his sprightliness, and leaves him behind:* [see also 8:] or *he causes the part of the spear-shaft that enters into its iron head to disappear in him who is pierced therewith by reason of the vehemence of his running.* (O, TA.*) — اغرق الكَأْسَ means ‡ *He filled the* كَأْس [or *wine-cup*]. (O, Ḳ, TA.) — See also 2, near the end. — اغرق فِى القَوْسِ [السَّهْمَ being understood] ‡ *He* (the drawer of the bow, i. e., of the string of the bow with the arrow, Ṣ, O, Ḳ, TA, or the shooter, Mṣb) *drew the bow to the full:* (Ṣ, O, Mṣb, Ḳ:) accord. to ISh, الاغراق signifies *the sending the arrow far by vehement drawing* [*of the bow*]: accord. to Useyd El-Ghanawee, *the drawing of the bow so that it brings the sinews that are wound upon the socket of the arrow, as far as the iron head, to the part that is grasped by the hand;* which is termed شُرْبُ القَوْسِ الرِّصَافَ; and one says of him who does so, يَنْزِعُ حَتَّى يَشْرَبَ بِالرِّصَافِ: (TA:) ▼ غرّق, also, signifies the same, (O, Ḳ,) inf. n. تَغْرِيقٌ: (O:) and one says, غرّق النَّبْلَ, meaning *he drew the bow with the arrows to the utmost extent.* (TA.) In the saying in the Ḳur [lxxix. 1], ▼ وَٱلنَّازِعَاتِ غَرْقًا, the last word is put in the place of the proper inf. n. of أَغْرَقَ, for إِغْرَاقًا; (Fr,* Az, O, Ḳ;*) the meaning being *By those angels that pull forth* the souls of the unbelievers from their bosoms *with a vehement pulling.* (Fr, O.) — Hence, i. e. from اغرق السَّهْمَ [or اغرق فِى القَوْسِ], one says, اغرق فِى القَوْلِ, (TA,) or فِى الشَّىْءِ, (Mṣb,) ‡ *He exceeded the usual bounds, degree,* or *mode; exerted himself much, beyond measure,* or *to the utmost;* or *was extravagant,* or *immoderate;* (Mṣb, TA;) *in the saying,* (TA,) or *in the thing.* (Mṣb.) [See also 10.]

8. اغترق الخَيْلَ ‡ *He* (a horse) *mixed among the* [other] *horses, and then outstripped them,* or *outwent them.* (Ṣ, O, Ḳ, TA.) And اغترق حَلْبَةَ الخَيْلِ ‡ *He* (a horse) *outstripped,* or *outwent, the collection of horses started together for a wager*

that were preceding. (AO, TA.) And [hence] one says, خَاصَمَنِى فَاغْتَرَقْتُ حَلْبَتَهُ, meaning † [*He contended with me in an altercation, or he disputed, or litigated, with me, and*] *I overcame him in the altercation, &c.* (TA.) — اغترق التَّصْدِيرَ, (O, Ḳ, TA,) or البِطَانَ, (O, TA,) ‡ *He* (a camel), *his belly being large,* (O, Ḳ, TA,) *and his sides being swollen,* (O, TA,) *took up the whole of the breast-girth,* (O, Ḳ, TA,) or *the belly-girth,* (O, TA,) *so that it was too strait for him;* as also ↓ استغرقهُ. (O, Ḳ, TA.) — And اغترق النَّفَسَ † *He took in the whole of the breath in drawing it in, or back, with vehemence.* (Ṣ, O, TA.) Accord. to the copies of the Ḳ, اغترقت النَّفْسُ, meaning اِسْتَوْعَبَتْ: but this is a mistake: the correct phrase is اغترق النَّفَسَ, the latter word مُحَرَّكَة [and in the accus. case]; and the explanation, اِسْتَوْعَبَهُ فِى الزَّفِيرِ. (TA.) — And تَغْتَرِقُ نَظَرَهُمْ, said of a woman, ‡ [*She engrosses their look;* i. e.] *she occupies them in looking at her so as to divert them from looking at other than her, by reason of her beauty:* (O, Ḳ, TA:) and in like manner one says, تغترق الطَّرْفَ ‡ [*she engrosses the look*]. (O, TA.) [See also what next follows.]

10. استغرق ‡ *He, or it, took, took in* or *comprised* or *comprehended* or *included,* or *took up* or *occupied, altogether, wholly,* or *universally; took in the gross; engrossed;* syn. اِسْتَوْعَبَ. (Ṣ, O, Ḳ, TA.) Hence the phrase of the grammarians, لَا لِاسْتِغْرَاقِ الجِنْسِ [لا ‡ *denoting the universal inclusion of the genus*]. (TA.) [Hence also several other conventional usages of the word]. See also **8** [with which it is interchangeable in several cases]. — اِسْتَغْرَقَ فِى الضَّحِكِ is like, (O, TA,) or syn. with, (Ḳ,) اِسْتَغْرَبَ ‡ [*He exceeded the usual bounds,* or *degree, in laughing; was immoderate in laughing*]. (O, Ḳ, TA.) [And in the same sense the verb is used in other cases. See also **4**, last signification.]

12. اِغْرَوْرَقَتْ عَيْنَاهُ *His eyes shed tears* (Ṣ, O, Ḳ, TA) *as though they were drowned therein:* (O, Ḳ, TA:) or اغرورقت عيناه بِالدُّمُوعِ *his eyes filled with tears but did not overflow.* (ISk, Az, TA.)

Q. Q. 1. غَرْقَأَتْ, as said of a hen, mentioned in this art. in the Ḳ (as being Q. Q.) and also in the TA as said of an egg, see in art. غرقأ.

غَرِقٌ and ↓ غَارِقٌ and ↓ غَرِيقٌ part. ns. of غَرِقَ, (Ṣ, O, Mṣb, Ḳ,) the first and second signifying [*Drowning;* or] *sinking in water without dying;* (Ṣ,* Mṣb;) and the third, [*drowned;* or] *dead by sinking in water;* (Kh, Mṣb;) *i. q.* مُغْرَقٌ or مُغَرَّقٌ; (so in different copies of the Ṣ;) and accord. to the Bari', the third may have both meanings agreeably with analogy; (Mṣb;) [see an instance of its usage in the former sense voce تَغَمْغَمَ; and the first is sometimes used in the latter sense; for] it is said in a trad. that the غَرِق is of those who are [reckoned as] شُهَدَآء [or martyrs: see شَهِيدٌ]; (O, TA;) though it is said that غَرِقٌ signifies *sinking in water* [like as does غَارِقٌ]; and غَرِيقٌ, *dead therein;* or, accord. to Aboo-'Adnán غَرِقٌ signifies *overcome by the water but not having yet sunk;* and غَرِيقٌ, *having sunk* [therein]: (TA:) the pl. of غَرِيقٌ is غَرْقَى. (Mgh, O, Mṣb, Ḳ.*) — It is said in a trad., يَأْتِى عَلَى النَّاسِ زَمَانٌ لَا يَنْجُو فِيهِ أَحَدٌ إِلَّا مَنْ دَعَا دُعَآءَ الغَرِقِ [*A time will come upon men in which no one will become safe but he who prays with the praying of the drowning*]; app. meaning, but he who is sincere in praying, as is he who is on the brink of destruction. (TA.) — And مَاتَ غَرِقًا فِى الخَمْرِ, in another trad., means ‡ *He died going to the utmost point,* or *degree, in the drinking of wine.* (TA.) — أَرْضٌ غَرِقَةٌ means *Land in the utmost state of irrigation.* (IF, A, O, Ḳ.) — غَرِقٌ and ↓ غَرِيقٌ also signify ‡ *A man much* [or *deeply*] *in debt:* and *overwhelmed by trials.* (TA.) — And one says, إِنَّهُ لَغَرِقُ الصَّوْتِ, meaning † *Verily he is frightened so that his voice is stopped short.* (Ibn-'Abbád, O, Ḳ.)

غُرْقَةٌ *A single draught* (شَرْبَة [in the CḲ شُرْبَة]) of milk, &c.: (A'Obeyd, Ṣ, O, Ḳ:) or *a small quantity* of milk, and of beverage, or peculiarly of the former: (TA in art. عرق:) pl. غُرَقٌ. (A'Obeyd, Ṣ, O, Ḳ.)

غِرْقِئٌ: see art. غرقأ: its hemzeh is augmentative (O, Ḳ) accord. to Fr: (O, TA:) and Aboo-Is-ḥáḳ [i. e. Zj] held it to be so: (IJ, MF, TA:) but in the opinion of MF, there is no probable reason for this, either on the ground of analogy or of derivation. (TA.)

غَرِيقٌ: see غَرِقٌ, in two places. — One says also, أَنَا غَرِيقُ أَيَادِيكَ, meaning ‡ [*I am the drowned in the flood*] *of thy favours.* (TA.)

غُرْيَاقٌ *A certain bird:* (IDrd, O, Ḳ:) so they assert: but it is not of established authority. (IDrd, O.)

غَارِقٌ: see غَرِقٌ, first sentence.

غَارِيقُونٌ, (Mgh, Ḳ,) or أَغَارِيقُونٌ, (Ḳ,) an ancient Greek word, [ἀγαρικὸν,] (TA,) *A certain medicine; a thing* [or *substance*] *resembling* أَنْجُذَان; [see حِلْتِيتٌ;] *male and female; in the bitterness of which is a sweetness:* (Mgh:) or *the root,* or *stem,* (أَصْل,) *of a certain plant:* or *a certain thing* [or *substance*] *which originates in worm-eaten trees; an antidote to poisons,* (Ḳ, TA,) *an attenuant of turbid humour, exhilarant,* (Ḳ,* TA,) *and good for sciatica;* and [it is said that] he upon whom it is suspended will not be stung by a scorpion. (Ḳ, TA.)

مُغْرَقٌ: see مُغَرَّقٌ.

مُغْرِقٌ, [as though مُغْرَقٌ, but I think it more probable that it is correctly ↓ مُغَرِّقٌ,] applied to a she-camel, *That casts her young one, in a perfect state or otherwise, and will not be made to incline to it, or to affect it, nor will be milked; not such as yields her milk copiously, nor* [*such as is termed*] خَلِفَة [q. v.]. (TA.)

مُغَرَّقٌ, applied to a bridle, ‡ *Ornamented,* (Ṣ, O, Ḳ,) or *ornamented in a general manner,* (TA,) with silver; (Ṣ, O, Ḳ, TA;) as also ↓ مُغْرَقٌ: (Ḳ:) and likewise applied to the scabbard of a sword. (TA.)

مُغَرِّقٌ: see مُغْرِقٌ.

رَمَضَانُ مُغَارِقٌ [The observance of *Ramadán is obligatory*]. (TA.)

غرقأ

Q. 1. غَرْقَأَتْ, said of an egg (بَيْضَةٌ), *It came forth having upon it* [*only*] *its thin integument* [or *pellicle, called* غِرْقِئ]. (Ḳ.) — And, said of a hen, [in the Ḳ in art. غرق (in which the hemzeh is said to be augmentative)] غرقأت بَيْضَهَا *She laid her eggs in the state described above.* (Ḳ.) [But see what follows.]

غِرْقِئٌ The *integument* [or *pellicle*] (Ṣ, Ḳ) *that is beneath the* قَيْض [i. e. *shell*], (Ṣ,) *adhering to the white,* (Ḳ,) *of the egg.* (Ṣ, Ḳ.) But Fr says its ء is augmentative, for it is from الغَرَق. (Ṣ.) Or The *white* [*of the egg*], *which is eaten:* (Ḳ:) but this explanation is of weak authority. (TA.)

غرقد

غَرْقَدٌ *A species of tree,* (Ṣ, O, L, Ḳ,) *of large size,* (L, Ḳ,) *of the kind termed* عِضَاه, (L,) *said by some to grow in the ground termed* قُفّ: (O, L:) or the *species of tree called* عَوْسَج [or *box-thorn*], *when it has grown large:* (AHn, O, L, Ḳ:) *a species of thorny tree:* (L:) [a coll. gen. n.:] n. un. with ة. (L, O, Ḳ.) ═ It is said in the Ḳ to signify also The *white of an egg:* but as thus expl., it is app. a mistake for غِرْقِئ. (TA.)

غرقل

Q. 1. غَرْقَلَتِ البَيْضَةُ *The egg became rotten;* (Ṣ, O;) *the interior of the egg became corrupt:* and thus غَرْقَلَ signifies said of the بِطِّيخ [i. e. melon, or water-melon]: (Ḳ:) or, said of the بِطِّيخ, *it became hard.* (O.) ═ And غَرْقَلَ *He poured water upon his head at once;* (IAạr, O, Ḳ, TA;) inf. n. غَرْقَلَةٌ. (TA.)

غِرْقِلٌ The *white of an egg;* as also ↓ غِرْقِيلٌ. (Az, TA.)

غِرْقِيلٌ: see what next precedes.

غرل

1. غَرِلَ, aor. ـَ, inf. n. غَرَلٌ, *He was uncircumcised.* (Mṣb.)

غَرِلٌ, A man *flaccid, lax,* or *uncompact, in make.* (Ṣ, O, Ḳ.) — And A *long,* (Ḳ,) or an *excessively long,* (TA,) spear. (Ḳ, TA.)

غُرْلَةٌ The قُلْفَةٌ [or *prepuce*]. (Ṣ, O, Mṣb, Ḳ.) Hence, in a trad. of Aboo-Bekr when he was a boy, رَكِبَ الخَيْلَ عَلَى غُرْلَتِهِ, meaning *He rode horses when he was small in age, before he was circumcised.* (TA.)

غِرْيَلٌ and غِرْيَنٌ signify the same; (AA, AZ, Aṣ, Ṣ, O, Ḳ;) [*Silt, or alluvial deposit, left upon the ground by a torrent;*] i. e. (Ṣ, O) *earth,* or *mould, borne by a torrent, and remaining upon the ground,* (AZ, Ṣ, O, Ḳ,) *much cracked,* (Ḳ,) whether *moist* or *dry:* (AZ, Ṣ, O, Ḳ:) or *fine earth* or *mould, which is seen to have dried upon the ground,* (Aṣ, Ṣ, O, TA,) *and become much cracked,* (Aṣ, TA,) *when a torrent has come and remained some time upon the ground, and then sunk in and disappeared:* (Aṣ, Ṣ, O, TA:) or, accord. to AA, (Ṣ, O, TA,) *what remains of,* or *from, water,* (Ṣ, O,) or *of earth,* or *mud,* (TA,) *in a watering-trough:* (Ṣ, O, TA:) and *a pool of water left by a torrent, in which remain* [*animalcules termed*] دَعَامِيص [pl. of دُعْمُوص, q. v.], *and which one cannot drink.* (AA, Ṣ, O, Ḳ, TA.) And The *sediment remaining in the bottom of a flask,* or *bottle:* (AA, Ṣ, O, Ḳ, TA:) and the *sediment of a dye.* (TA.) And (the former) *Dust;* syn. غُبَارٌ. (O, Ḳ.) And The *mucus of the nose of a solid-hoofed animal of any kind.* (O, Ḳ.)

أَغْرَلُ, with which أَرْغَلُ is syn. in all of the following senses, (TA,) applied to a boy, (Ṣ, O,) *i. q.* أَقْلَفُ [i. e. *Uncircumcised*]: (Ṣ, O, Mṣb, Ḳ:) fem. غَرْلَآءُ: and pl. غُرْلٌ. (Mṣb.) —— And عَيْشٌ أَغْرَلُ *A life ample in its means, or circumstances.* (Ṣ, O, Ḳ.) And عَامٌ أَغْرَلُ *A fruitful,* or *plentiful, year.* (Ḳ.)

غرم

1. غَرِمَ, (JK, Ṣ, Mṣb, Ḳ,) aor. ـَ, (JK, Ḳ,) inf. n. غُرْمٌ (JK, Mṣb, TA) and غَرَامَةٌ (Mṣb, TA) and مَغْرَمٌ, (TA,) *He paid,* or *discharged,* (JK, Ṣ,* Mṣb, Ḳ,*) a thing that was obligatory upon him, (JK,) or a bloodwit, (Ṣ, Mṣb, Ḳ,) and a responsibility, and the like thereof, *after it had become obligatory upon him:* (Mṣb:) [or, accord. to an explanation of الغَرَامَةُ in Ḥar p. 36, *he gave property against his will:* or the meaning intended in the Ṣ and Ḳ (in both of which it is very vaguely indicated) may be, *he took upon himself to pay,* or *discharge,* a bloodwit, &c.: for, sometimes,] غُرْمٌ and مَغْرَمٌ and غَرَامَةٌ signify the *taking upon oneself that which is not obligatory upon him:* (Mgh; and the Ksh gives this explanation of مَغْرَمٌ in lii. 40:) [or *the taking upon oneself a fine* or *the like:* for, sometimes,] مَغْرَمٌ signifies اِلْتِزَامُ غُرْمٍ. (Bḍ in lii. 40. [See also 5, and 8.]) And you say, غَرِمْتُ عَنْهُ مَا لَزِمَهُ مِنَ الدِّيَةِ [*I paid for him,* i. e., *in his stead, what was obligatory upon him, of the bloodwit*]. (Mṣb in art. عقل.) —— And غَرِمَ فِي تِجَارَتِهِ *He lost,* or *suffered loss, in his traffic;* *i. q.* خَسِرَ; *contr. of* رَبِحَ. (Mṣb.) ═ غَرِمَ أَنْفًا: see رَغِمَ [from which it is app. formed by transposition].

2. غَرَّمَهُ *i. q.* أَغْرَمَهُ, q. v. (Ṣ, Mgh, &c.) —— [Hence, app.,] غَرَّمَ السَّحَابُ † *The clouds rained:* [as though they were made to discharge a debt that they owed:] Aboo-Dhu-eyb says, describing clouds,

وَهَى خَرْجُهُ وَٱسْتُجِيلَ الرَّبَا
بُ مِنْهُ وَغُرِّمَ مَآءً صَرِيحَا

† [*The clouds that were the first thereof in rising and appearing became rent, and such of them as were suspended beneath other clouds were looked at in order that it might be seen whether they moved, and they discharged clear water*]. (TA.)

4. أَغْرَمْتُهُ and ↓ غَرَّمْتُهُ, (Ṣ, Mṣb, Ḳ,) inf. n. [of the former إِغْرَامٌ and] of the latter تَغْرِيمٌ, (TA,) both signify the same; (Ṣ, Mṣb, Ḳ;) i. e. *I made him to pay,* or *discharge,* [a bloodwit, and a responsibility, and the like, (see 1,)] *after it had become obligatory upon him:* (Mṣb, Ḳ:*) [or the meaning intended in the Ṣ and Ḳ (in the latter of which it is vaguely indicated and in the former more so) may be, *I made him to take upon himself to pay,* or *discharge,* a bloodwit, &c.: for, sometimes,] اغرمهُ and غرّمهُ signify *he made him to incur the taking upon himself that which was not obligatory upon him:* (Mgh:) [and sometimes the inf. ns.] إِغْرَامٌ and تَغْرِيمٌ signify the *making to be fined;* and, *to be indebted:* (PṢ:) اغرمتهُ in the copies of the Ḳ is a mistake for اغرمتهُ إِيَّاهُ. (TA.) —— إِغْرَامٌ also signifies The *throwing* [one] *into destruction.* (KL.) —— And The *rendering* [one] *eagerly desirous* [of a thing; *fond* of it; or *attached* to it]. (KL.) You say, أُغْرِمَ بِالشَّىْءِ *He became eagerly desirous of the thing; fond of it;* or *attached to it;* syn. أُولِعَ بِهِ. (Ṣ, Mṣb, TA.)

5. تَغَرَّمَ [app. *He took upon himself an obligation, such as the payment of a fine, &c.*]. (Ḥam p. 707. [See also 1, and 8.])

8. اِغْتِرَامٌ The *making obligatory upon oneself what is termed* غَرَامَةٌ, which signifies *difficulty* or *trouble,* and *damage* or *detriment* or *loss,* and *the giving of property against one's will.* (Ḥar p. 36. [See also 1, and 5.])

غُرْمٌ an inf. n. of غَرِمَ [q. v.]. (JK, Mṣb, TA.) —— And *A thing that must be paid,* or *discharged;* (Ḳ, TA;) and so ↓ غَرَامَةٌ, and ↓ مَغْرَمٌ, (Ṣ, Ḳ, TA,) and ↓ مُغْرَمٌ: (Ṣ, TA:) accord. to Er-Rághib, *a damage, detriment,* or *loss, that befalls a man, in his property, not for an injurious action, of his, requiring punishment:* (TA:) *a debt:* (Ṣ, TA:) *a fine,* or *mulct:* (MA:) the pl. of ↓ مَغْرَمٌ is مَغَارِمُ, agreeably with analogy; or this is pl. of غُرْمٌ, anomalously, like as مَحَاسِنُ is of حُسْنٌ. (TA.) [See exs. voce غَلِقَ: and see also غُنْمٌ.]

غَرْمَى A woman *heavy,* or *sluggish;* syn. ثَقِيلَةٌ: (Ḳ:) or, accord. to IAạr, *i. q.* مُغَاضِبَةٌ [*that makes, and is made, angry:* or *that breaks off from,* or *quits, one, in anger,* or *enmity*]. (TA.) ═ It is also *syn. with* أَمَا, as a word denoting an oath [or used in swearing]: one says غَرْمَى وَجَدِّكَ [*Verily,* or *now surely, by thy grandfather,* or *by thy fortune* or *good fortune*]; like as one says أَمَا وَجَدِّكَ: (AA, Ḳ, TA:) and عَرْمَى and حَرْمَى are dial. vars. thereof. (TA.)

غَرَامٌ *A thing from which one is unable to free himself:* [*a thing*] *such as cleaves fast.* (Bḍ and Jel in xxv. 65.) *Lasting evil.* (IAạr, Ṣ, Ḳ.) *Perdition:* (Ḳ:) in the Ḳur xxv. 65, (Ṣ, Ksh,) accord. to AO, (Ṣ,) it means *perdition,* (Ṣ, Ksh,) *persistent,* (Ksh,) *and such as cleaves fast.* (Ṣ, Ksh.) And *Punishment,* or *torment:* (Ṣ, Ḳ:) or, accord. to Zj, the *most vehement punishment* or *torment:* and accord. to Er-Rághib, *hardship,* or *difficulty,* and *an affliction,* or *a calamity* or *misfortune, that befalls a man.* (TA.) —— Also *Eager desire* [بِشَىْءٍ *for a thing*]; *fondness* [for it]; or *attachment* [to it]; syn. وَلُوعٌ: (Ṣ, Ḳ:) or *love that torments the heart.* (Ḥar p. 36.) [See 4, last sentence.]

غَرِيمٌ *A debtor:* (Ṣ, Mṣb, Ḳ:) one says, خُذْ مِنْ غَرِيمِ السُّوْءِ مَا سَنَحَ [*Take thou from the evil debtor what has become easy of attainment*]: (Ṣ:) and ↓ غَارِمٌ signifies the same as غَرِيمٌ; or one *upon whom lies the obligation of a bloodwit* or *the like;* or [it virtually signifies thus, but properly] it is a possessive epithet signifying ذُو غَرَامٍ [or غَرَامَةٍ] or تَغْرِيمٍ. (TA.) And (sometimes, Ṣ) it signifies *A creditor* also: (Ṣ, Mṣb, Ḳ:) thus having two contr. meanings: (Ḳ:) Kutheiyir says,

قَضَى كُلُّ ذِى دَيْنٍ فَوَفَّى غَرِيمَهُ
وَعَزَّةُ مَمْطُولٌ مُعَنًّى غَرِيمُهَا

[*Every debtor has paid, and fully rendered to his creditor; but as to 'Azzeh, her creditor is put off, and wearied*]. (Ṣ.) The pl. of غَرِيمٌ is غُرَمَآءُ (IAth, Mṣb, TA) and غُرَّامٌ, which is a strange [i. e. an anomalous] pl.; (IAth, TA;) or this is pl. of ↓ غَارِمٌ as syn. with غَرِيمٌ [and thus is agreeable with analogy]; or it is pl. of ↓ مُغْرَمٌ [signifying "burdened with debt"], formed by the rejection of the augmentative letter [of the sing.]. (TA.) —— And hence, *An adversary in contention, dispute,* or *litigation; an antagonist; a litigant:* because, by his pressing upon his adversary [like the creditor upon his debtor], he becomes one who cleaves, or clings. (Mṣb.)

غَرَامَةٌ: see غُرْمٌ.

غَارِمٌ: see غَرِيمٌ, in two places.

مَغْرَمٌ; pl. مَغَارِمُ: see غُرْمٌ, in two places.

مُغْرَمٌ *Shackled,* (Ḳ,) or *burdened,* (TA,) *with debt;* (Ḳ;) an epithet applied to a man from الغُرْمُ and الدَّيْنُ. (Ṣ.) See غَرِيمٌ. —— And *A captive of love;* (Ḳ, TA;) i. e., *of the love of women:* (TA:) or one *to whom love cleaves:* (Ḥam p. 558:) or you say رَجُلٌ مُغْرَمٌ بِالحُبِّ [*a man to whom love cleaves,* or *clung to by love*]; from the love of women: (Ṣ:) and هُوَ مُغْرَمٌ بِالنِّسَآءِ *He is one who clings to women,* like as does the غَرِيم [or "creditor" to the debtor]. (Er-Rághib, TA.) And مُغْرَمٌ بِشَىْءٍ *Eagerly desirous of a thing; fond of it; or attached to it;* syn. مُولَعٌ بِهِ; (Mṣb, Ḳ, TA;) and حَرِيصٌ عَلَيْهِ; (Ḥar p. 585;) *not having patience to refrain from it.* (TA.) ═ See also غُرْمٌ.

غرمل

غُرْمُولٌ The *penis,* (Ṣ, O, Ḳ,) in an absolute sense: (TA:) or *a large and flaccid penis before its prepuce is cut off;* (Ḳ;) thus says AZ: (TA:) or it is said to be *of a solid-hoofed animal:* but mention is made in a trad. of the غَرَامِيل of men [in relation to whom, however, it may perhaps be used in this instance by way of comparison]. (TA.)

غرنق

غُرْنَقَةٌ *An amorous playing with the eyes.* (Ibn-'Abbád, O, Ḳ.)

غُرَنَاقٌ: see غُرْنَيْقٌ, last sentence.

غُرْنُوقٌ is held by the author of the Ḳ to be wrongly mentioned by J in art. غرق, on the ground of the saying that the ن is radical; and IJ says that Sb has mentioned غُرْنَيْقٌ among quadriliteral-radical words: but there is a difference of opinion on this point; for AḤei asserts that the ن in غُرْنُوقٌ and in all its dial. vars. is augmentative. (TA.) — See غُرْنَيْقٌ, in two places. — Also sing. of غَرَانِقُ, which signifies † *Certain trees:* (Aboo-Ziyád, O, Ḳ:) or, as also ▼ غُرَانِقٌ, sing. of غَرَانِيقُ, which signifies the *tender sprouts at the root, or lower part, of the* عَوْسَج [or *box-thorn*]: (AA, O, Ḳ:) likened to a tender youth, because of their freshness and beauty: (TA:) or غُرْنُوقٌ signifies *a tender and concealed plant;* (Ḳ, TA;) or, accord. to one copy [of the Ḳ], *a tender, spreading plant:* mentioned by AḤn. (TA.) — And † *A lock of hair much twisted:* (Lth, O, Ḳ:) or, accord. to IAạr, *a forelock:* so in the phrase جَذَبَ غُرْنُوقَهُ [*He pulled his forelock*]: and نُغْرُوقٌ signifies the "hair of the back of the neck." (O, TA.)

غِرْنَوْقٌ: see the next paragraph, in two places.

غُرْنَيْقٌ (Ṣ, Ḳ) and ▼ غُرْنُوقٌ and ▼ غِرْنَوْقٌ (O, Ḳ) *A certain aquatic bird,* (Ṣ, O, Ḳ, TA,) *long in the neck* (Ṣ, O, TA) *and in the legs,* (TA,) *white,* (O, Ḳ, TA,) or *black:* (Ḳ, TA:) [app. the *white stork, ardea ciconia;* or, accord. to some, the *black stork, ardea nigra:*] or, accord. to IAmb, the *males* [or *male*] *thereof:* (TA:) or the first, (O, Ḳ,) as also the second, (Ḳ,) signifies the كُرْكِىّ [or *Numidean crane, ardea virgo*]: (Aṣ, O, Ḳ, TA:) or *a certain bird resembling this:* (ISk, O, Ḳ, TA:) pl. غَرَانِيقُ. (O, TA.) It is related of the Prophet that [when he was reciting the words of the Ḳur (liii. 19 and 20), "Have ye considered El-Lát, and El-'Ozzà, and Menáh, the other third?"] the Devil put into his mouth the saying تِلْكَ الغَرَانِيقُ العُلَى [*Those are the most high* غرانيق, as though meaning *cranes,* for the Numidian crane is remarkable in the East for its superlatively-high flight]; referring, as IAạr says, to the idols, which were asserted to be intercessors with God, wherefore they are likened to the birds that rise high into the sky: (O, TA:*) or غرانيق may in this case be a pl. of one of the sings. expl. in what here follows [but applied to females]. (O.) — غُرْنَيْقٌ (O, Ḳ, TA, and so in copies of the Ṣ) and ▼ غِرْنَيْقٌ (IJ, TA, and so in some copies of the Ṣ in the place of the former) and ▼ غُرْنُوقٌ and ▼ غِرْنَوْقٌ (Ṣ, O, Ḳ, TA) and ▼ غِرْنِيقٌ (Ḳ) and ▼ غِرْنَاقٌ and ▼ غِرْوَنْقٌ (O, Ḳ) and ▼ غُرَانِقٌ (Ṣ, Ḳ) signify † *A tender youth;* (Ṣ;) or *a white, or fair, and comely, or beautiful, youth;* (O, Ḳ;) or *a youth white, or fair, tender, having beautiful hair, and comely:* (TA:) pl. غَرَانِيقُ and غَرَانِقَةٌ (Ṣ, O, Ḳ) and غَرَانِقُ, (Ṣ, Ḳ,) which last may be pl. of غُرَانِقٌ, agreeably with analogy, (IAmb, TA,) or it may be a contraction of غَرَانِيقُ, as such used by a poet. (TA.)

غِرْنِيقٌ and غِرْنَيْقٌ: see the next preceding sentence.

غُرَانِقٌ, applied to a youth, (Ḳ, TA,) and to youthfulness, (TA, and so in the CḲ instead of a youth,) *Perfect,* or *without defect.* (Ḳ, TA.) And, applied to a woman, as also غُرَانِقَةٌ, *Youthful and plump.* (Ḳ.) — See also غُرْنَيْقٌ, last sentence. — لِمَّةٌ غُرَانِقَةٌ and ▼ غُرَانِقِيَّةٌ [*Hair descending below the lobe of the ear,* or *descending upon the shoulders,*] *sleek, such as the wind puts in motion.* (Sh, O, Ḳ.) — See also غُرْنُوقٌ.

غِرْوَنْقٌ: see غُرْنَيْقٌ, last sentence.

لِمَّةٌ غُرَانِقِيَّةٌ: see غُرَانِقٌ.

غرو

1. غَرَا الجِلْدَ, (Ḳ,) first pers. غَرَوْتُ, (Ṣ, Mṣb,) aor. ـُ, (Mṣb, TA,) inf. n. غَرْوٌ, (TA,) *He glued the skin;* i. e., *made it to adhere with* غِرَآء. (Ṣ, Mṣb, Ḳ.) And غَرَيْتُ السَّهْمَ signifies the same as غَرَوْتُهُ [i. e. *I glued the feathers upon the arrow:* see the two pass. part. ns.]. (TA.) [And accord. to present usage, ▼ غَرَّاهُ, inf. n. تَغْرِيَةٌ, signifies *He glued it.*] — غَرَا السِّمَنُ قَلْبَهُ, (Ḳ, TA,) aor. and inf. n. as above, (TA,) *Fatness adhered to his heart, and covered it:* (Ḳ, TA:) mentioned by ISd. (TA.) ═ غَرِىَ بِهِ *It adhered to it* [*as glue or the like*]. (Ksh and Bḍ in v. 17. [And used in this sense in the Ṣ and Ḳ as an explanation of لَزِجَ بِهِ.]) — And [hence], aor. يَغْرَى, (Ṣ, Mṣb, Ḳ,) inf. n. غَرًا (Abu-l-Khaṭṭáb, Mṣb, Ḳ, TA) and غَرَآءٌ, (Ḳ, TA,) like كِسَآءٌ, but in the M like سَحَاب [i. e. غَرَآء], which J [in the Ṣ] pronounces to be a subst., (TA,) *He became attached to it,* or *fond of it; was eagerly desirous of it; he adhered, clung,* or *clave, to it;* or *loved it;* syn. أُولِعَ بِهِ; (Mṣb, Ḳ, TA;) and لَزِمَهُ; (TA;) *without his being incited thereto by another;* (Mṣb, TA;) and ▼ أُغْرِىَ بِهِ signifies the same, (Mṣb,* Ḳ, TA,) as also ▼ غُرِّىَ بِهِ, (Ḳ, TA,) each with ḍamm, (Ḳ,) and the latter with teshdeed, as is stated in the M. (TA.) — See also 3. — And غَرِىَ فُلَانٌ *Such a one persisted,* or *persevered, in his anger.* (Ṣ, TA.) — غَرِىَ said of what is termed عِدٌّ [i. e. of the water thus termed,] (M, and so in some copies of the Ḳ,) or of a غَدِير, [or pool of water left by a torrent,] (so in other copies of the Ḳ [but the former is said in the TA to be the right],) *It became cold,* or *cool,* (M, TA,) or *its water became cold,* or *cool.* (Ḳ.) ═ غَرَوْتُ, (inf. n. غَرْوٌ, Ṣ,* Mṣb,) also signifies *I wondered.* (Ṣ, Mṣb, TA.) [See غَرْوٌ, below.]

2. غَرَّاهُ: see 1, third sentence. — [The inf. n.] تَغْرِيَةٌ is *syn. with* تَطْلِيَةٌ [The *daubing, smearing,* or *rubbing over;* perhaps particularly, or originally, with غِرَآء i. e. glue]. (Ḳ.) — غَرَّاهُ بِهِ: see 4. And غُرِّىَ بِهِ: see 1, latter half.

3. غَارَى بَيْنَ الشَّيْئَيْنِ, (Ṣ, Ḳ,) inf. n. غِرَآءٌ, (Ṣ,) *He made no interruption between the two things:* (Ṣ, Ḳ:) mentioned by A'Obeyd, from Khálid Ibn-Kulthoom: and hence the saying of Kutheiyir,

- إِذَا قُلْتُ أَسْلُو فَاضَتِ العَيْنُ بِالبُكَا
- غِرَآءً وَمَدَّتْهَا مَدَامِعُ حُفَّلُ

[*When thou sayest, "I will be forgetful,"* or *"unmindful," the eye overflows with weeping, uninterruptedly, and copious flowings of tears pour into it and replenish it*]: AO says that the verb is from غَرِيتُ بِالشَّىْءِ. (Ṣ, TA.) — And غَارَى فُلَانًا, (Ḳ, TA,) inf. n. مُغَارَاةٌ and غِرَآءٌ, (TA,) *He wrangled, quarrelled,* or *contended, with such a one:* (Ḳ, TA:) mentioned on the authority of AHeyth, who disallowed ▼ غَرِىَ بِهِ, inf. n. غِرَآء. (TA. [Whether AHeyth disallowed the latter in this sense or in one of the senses mentioned in the first paragraph is not stated.])

4. اغراهُ بِهِ *He made him to become attached to it,* or *fond of it; to be eagerly desirous of it; to adhere, cling,* or *cleave, to it;* or *to love it;* (Mṣb, Ḳ;) syn. وَلَّعَهُ: (Ḳ:) one should not say ▼ غَرَّاهُ بِهِ. (TA. [But one says غُرِّىَ بِهِ: see 1.]) And أُغْرِىَ بِهِ: see 1. — *He incited, urged,* or *instigated, him to do it.* (MA, and Ḥar p. 355.) You say, أَغْرَيْتُ الكَلْبَ بِالصَّيْدِ (Ṣ) *I incited, urged, or instigated, the dog, to, or against, the object,* or *objects, of the chase.* (Kull.) — And اغراهُ بِهِمْ *He set him upon them,* or *over them;* or *made him to have mastery, dominion,* or *authority, over them.* (Jel in xxxiii. 60.) — اغرى بَيْنَهُمُ العَدَاوَةَ: *He occasioned enmity between them:* (Jel in v. 17:) *he cast enmity between them, as though he made it to cleave to them:* (Ḳ, TA:) a tropical phrase. (TA.) And أَغْرَيْتُ بَيْنَهُمْ [in which an objective complement is understood] (Ṣ, Mṣb) *i. q.* أَفْسَدْتُ [meaning † *I excited disorder, disturbance, dis-*

agreement, discord, dissension, strife, or *quarrelling,* or *I made,* or *did, mischief, between them,* or *among them*]. (Msb.) —— اغرى الشَّىْءَ, said of God, *He made,* or *rendered, the thing goodly,* or *beautiful.* (IKtt, TA.)

6. هُمَا يَتَغَارَيَانِ فِى الغَضَبِ [app. *They two wrangle, quarrel,* or *contend, in anger*]. (JK. [See 3.])

لَا غَرْوَ signifies لَا عَجَبَ [meaning *There is no case of wonder*], (Msb, K, and Ham p. 603,) the enunciative of لَا being suppressed, as though the saying were لَا غَرْوَ فِى الدُّنْيَا [*there is no case of wonder in the present world*] or مَوْجُودٌ [*existing*]; (Ham;) as also ▾ لَا غَرْوَى: (K:) or لَيْسَ بِعَجَبٍ [meaning *it is not a case of wonder*]. (S.) One says, لَا غَرْوَ مِنْ كَذَا i. e. لَا عَجَبَ [meaning *There is no case of wonder* arising *from such a thing,* or, using غرو as an inf. n., (see 1, last signification,) *there is no wondering at such a thing*]. (Har p. 488.) And the saying

وَلَا غَرْوَ أَنْ يَحْذُو الفَتَى حَذْوَ وَالِدِهْ

means *And it is not a case of wonder* (لَيْسَ بِعَجَبٍ), i. e. *there is no wondering* (لَا عَجَبَ), *that the* [*young*] *man should follow the example of his father, doing the like of his deed.* (Har p. 86.)

غَرًا : see غِرَآءٌ, in two places. —— Also The غِرْس [q. v.] *that descends* [*from the womb*] *with the child.* (TA.) —— And The *young one of the cow:* (K, TA:) or, as some say, peculiarly, *of* [*the species of bovine antelope called*] *the wild cow:* dual غَرَوَانِ: and pl. أَغْرَآءٌ. (TA.) It is also applied to The *young camel when just born:* and, some say, it signifies *a youngling that is very sappy* or *soft* or *tender:* (TA:) and *anything brought forth* (K, TA) *until its flesh becomes firm,* or *hard.* (TA.) —— And (K, TA) [hence], by way of comparison, (TA,) as also ▾ غَرَاةٌ, † *Lean, meagre,* or *emaciated,* (K, TA,) *in a great degree:* (TA:) pl. أَغْرَآءٌ. (K, TA.) Hence the trad., لَا تَذْبَحُوهُ غَرَاةً ▾ حَتَّى يَكْبَرَ † [*Do not ye slaughter it while very lean,* &c., *until it become full-grown*]. (TA. [See 4 in art. فرع.]) —— Also *Goodliness,* or *beauty.* (S, K. [See غَرِىٌّ.])

غَرَاةٌ [*Excitement of disorder, disturbance, disagreement,* &c.;] the subst. from أَغْرَيْتُ بَيْنَهُمْ [q. v.]. (S.) —— See also غَرًا, in two places.

غَرْوَى : see the next paragraph: —— and see also لَا غَرْوَ.

غَرَآءٌ [*A state of attachment,* or *fondness,* &c.;] the subst. from أُولِعَ غَرِىَ بِهِ [q. v.] as meaning بِهِ : (S, Msb, TA:) or, accord. to the M, this is an inf. n.; and the subst. accord. to the K is ▾ غَرْوَى. (TA.)

غِرَآءٌ and ▾ غَرًا (S, Mgh, Msb, K) [*Glue;*] *a substance with which a thing is made to adhere,* (S, Mgh, Msb, K,) *obtained from fish,* (S, Mgh,) or *made from skins, and sometimes made from fish:* (Msb:) or the *substance with which one smears;* (Fr, K, TA;) and thus the former word is expl. by Sh: (TA:) or *a certain thing that is extracted from fish:* (K:) [and *mucilage, which by concretion becomes gum;* the former word is used in this sense in the K voce صَمْغٌ, q. v.:] and it is said that the *trees* [app. *that produce the mucilage termed* غِرَآء, otherwise I know not what can be meant thereby,] are [called] غَرِىّ [or ▾ غَرًا]; but AHn says that certain persons pronounce the word thus, but it is not the approved way. (TA.) —— رَجُلٌ غِرَآءٌ means *A man who has not a beast* [*to carry him*] (لَا دَابَّةَ لَهُ). (K.)

غَرِىٌّ *Made to adhere;* syn. مُلْصَقٌ. (TA voce عَرِيزٌ.) —— [And hence, † *An adherent.* (See عَرِيزٌ.)] —— Hence also, *Daubed, smeared,* or *rubbed over;* as will be shown in the course of this paragraph. (See also مَغْرُوٌّ.) ——] And The *goodly,* or *beautiful,* (S, K, TA,) *in respect of face,* (TA,) of mankind, (S, K, TA,) and the *goodly,* or *beautiful,* of others than mankind: and [particularly] a *goodly* building: (K, TA:) and hence, —— الغَرِيَّانِ *Two well-known buildings, in El-Koofeh,* (K, TA,) *at Eth-Thaweeyeh, where is the tomb of 'Alee, the Prince of the Faithful, asserted to have been built by one of the Kings of El-Heereh:* (TA:) or *two tall buildings, said to be the tombs of Málik and 'Akeel, the two cup-companions of Jedheemeh El-Abrash;* thus called because En-Noamán Ibn-El-Mundhir used to smear them (كَانَ يُغَرِّيهِمَا) with the blood of him whom he slew when he went forth in the day of his evil fortune [or ill omen, the story of which is well known]. (S, TA.) —— الغَرِىُّ is also the name of *A certain idol* [or *object of idolatrous worship,* app. from what here follows, *a mass of stone,* like as اللَّاتُ is said to have been by some, and like as were several other objects of worship of the pagan Arabs], with which [probably meaning with the blood on which] one used to smear himself, and upon which one used to sacrifice [victims]. (TA.) —— And غَرِىٌّ signifies also *A certain red dye.* (TA.)

غُرَاوَى *i. q.* رُغْوَةٌ [i. e. *Froth*]: (K, TA: [الغُرَاوِى in the CK is a mistranscription:]) app. formed by transposition; for رُغَاوَى has been mentioned [in art. رغو] as syn. with رُغْوَةٌ: (TA:) pl. with fet-h [i. e. غَرَاوَى]. (K, TA.)

هُوَ مُغْرًى بِهِ, from أَغْرَاهُ بِهِ [q. v.], *He is made to become attached to it,* or *fond of it;* &c. (TA.)

مَغْرُوٌّ [pass. part. n. of غَرَا, q. v.; *Glued,* &c. —— Hence, for سَهْمٌ مَغْرُوٌّ, lit. *A glued arrow,* meaning *an arrow having the feathers glued upon it,* i. e.] *a feathered arrow.* (Meyd in explanation of what here follows.) It is said in a prov., أَدْرِكْنِى وَلَوْ بِأَحَدِ المَغْرُوَّيْنِ, meaning [*Reach thou me, though*] *with one of the two* [*feathered*] *arrows:* or, as Th says, *with an arrow or with a spear:* (S:) El-Mufaddal says, there were two brothers, of the people of Hejer, a people to whom the Arabs ascribe stupidity, and one of those two rode an intractable she-camel, and the one that did not ride had with him a bow, and his name was Huneyn; so the one that was riding called to him, and said, يَا حُنَيْنُ وَيْلَكَ أَنْزِلْنِى وَلَوْ بِأَحَدِ المَغْرُوَّيْنِ, [in which انزلنى seems to be a mistranscription for ادركنى,] meaning, with his arrow; whereupon his brother shot at him and laid him prostrate; and his saying became a prov., applied on an occasion of necessity, or difficulty, and of the utter failing of stratagem. (Meyd.) One says also قَوْسٌ مَغْرُوَّةٌ [*A glued bow*] (S, Msb, K) and ▾ مَغْرِيَّةٌ. (S, K.)

قَوْسٌ مَغْرِيَّةٌ : see what next precedes.

غرى

1. غَرَيْتُ السَّهْمَ : see 1 in art. غرو.

قَوْسٌ مَغْرِيَّةٌ : see مَغْرُوٌّ (last sentence) in art. غرو.

غزر

1. غَزُرَ, aor. ـُ, inf. n. غَزَارَةٌ (S, Mgh, Msb, K) and غُزْرٌ (Mgh, L, Msb, K) and غُزُرٌ, (L, K,) or غُزْرٌ is a simple subst., (S, L, TA,) *It* (a thing, S, K, or water, Mgh, Msb) *was,* or *became, much, abundant,* or *copious.* (S, Mgh, Msb, K.) —— غَزُرَتْ *She* (a camel, S, Msb, or a beast, K) *had much milk; abounded in milk; became abundant in milk;* (S, Msb, K;) عَنِ الكَلَإِ *from the herbage;* (TA;) or عَلَيْهِ [by feeding] *upon it;* (K;) as also ▾ أَغْزَرَتْ: (IKtt:) and *it* (a well, and a spring,) *abounded in water:* and *it* (an eye) *abounded in tears.* (K.)

2. تَغْزِيرٌ signifies The *omitting a milking between two milkings, when the milk of the camel is backward.* (S, K, TA.) A similar meaning is mentioned in art. غرز: see 2 in that art. (TA.)

3. غَازَرَهُ, inf. n. مُغَازَرَةٌ, *He gave him a small and mean thing in order that he might give him in return twice as much: he sought to obtain from him more than he gave.* (IAar, TA: but only the inf. n. is mentioned.)

4: see 1. —— أَغْزَرَ اللّٰهُ مَالَهُ [*God caused his camels,* or *sheep,* or *goats, to have much milk*]. (TA.) —— اغزر المَعْرُوفَ *He made the beneficence to be abundant.* (K.) —— اغزر القَوْمُ *The people's camels,* (S, K,) and *their sheep or goats,* (TA,) *became abundant in milk.* (S, K, TA.) —— And *The people became in the state of having much rain.* (IKtt.)

غُزْرٌ [*Abundance in milk:* or *abundance of milk:* of camels &c.:] a subst. from غَزُرَتِ النَّاقَةُ: pl. غُزُورٌ; like as جُونٌ is pl. of جَوْنٌ, and حُشْرٌ of حَشْرٌ. (S.) —— Also *A vessel made of* [*the coarse grass called*] حَلْفَآء and *of palm-leaves:* (IDrd, K:) a well-known Arabic word. (IDrd, TA.)

غَزْرَى [as though fem. of أَغْزَرُ] is applied to a she-camel by Honeyf-El-Hanátim [as meaning

Surpassingly abundant in milk]. (IAạr in TA in art. بهى.)

[غُزْرَانٌ mentioned by Freytag as an epithet applied to camels, meaning *Abounding in milk*, on the authority of the Ḳ, is a mistake; it is mentioned in the Ḳ only as the name of a place.]

غَزِيرٌ, and the fem. غَزِيرَةٌ, *Much; abundant; copious:* (Ṣ, Mṣb, Ḳ:) applied to water, (Mṣb,) and rain, (Ḳ,) and beneficence, (Ṣ,) and knowledge, (TA,) and anything. (Ṣ, Ḳ.) — A she-camel, (Ṣ, Mṣb, Ḳ,) and a sheep or goat or other beast, (TA,) *having much milk; abounding in milk:* (Ṣ, Mṣb, Ḳ:) a well, and a spring, (Ḳ,) and a subterranean channel for water, (Mṣb,) *abounding in water:* (Mṣb, Ḳ:) and an eye *abounding in tears:* (Ḳ:) pl. غِزَارٌ. (Ṣ, Mṣb.)

قَوْمٌ مُغْزَرٌ لَهُمْ, in the pass. form, *A people having abundance of milk; whose camels abound in milk.* (Ḳ.)

مَغْزَرَةٌ, (as written in the L, [and so agreeably with analogy, as meaning *A cause of abounding in milk*; similar to مَبْخَلَةٌ and مَجْبَنَةٌ &c.;]) or مُغْزِرَةٌ, (accord. to the Ḳ,) *a thing* [*from the feeding of a beast*] *upon which the milk becomes abundant.* (L, Ḳ.) — And, (Ḳ, TA,) hence, (TA,) *A certain plant, the leaves of which are like those of the* حُرْف [q. v.], (Ḳ, TA,) *dust-coloured, and small, and which has a red blossom, like that of the pomegranate:* (TA:) *it pleases the cows* (Ḳ, TA) *much,* (TA,) *and they become abundant in milk* [*by feeding*] *upon it:* (Ḳ, TA:) *it is of the* [*season called*] رَبِيع; and is mentioned by AḤn, who says that *all cattle pasture upon it.* (TA.)

مِغْزَارٌ [*Abounding much in milk;* applied to a she-camel &c.]. (The Lexicons passim.)

أَرْضٌ مَغْزُورَةٌ *Land upon which much rain has fallen.* (Ḳ.)

مُغَازِرٌ and ♦ مُسْتَغْزِرٌ *One who gives a thing in order that he may obtain in return more than he gives.* (Ḳ.) One of the Tábi'ees says الجَانِبُ المُسْتَغْزِرُ ♦ يُثَابُ مِنْ هِبَتِهِ *The stranger who seeks to obtain more than he gives shall be rewarded for his gift:* meaning, when the stranger, who is not related to thee, gives thee a thing, he seeks to obtain more than it; so do thou requite him for his gift, and exceed it to him. (TA.)

مُسْتَغْزِرٌ: see مُغَازِرٌ, in two places.

غزل

1. غَزَلَتِ القُطْنَ, (Ṣ, MA, O, Ḳ,) and الكَتَّانَ وَغَيْرَهُمَا, (TA,) or الصُّوفَ وَنَحْوَهُ, (Mṣb,) aor. ـِ, (Ṣ, O, Mṣb, Ḳ,) inf. n. غَزْلٌ, (Ṣ, MA, O, KL,) *She spun the cotton,* (MA, KL, PṢ,) and *the flax, &c.,* (TA,) or *the wool, and the like;* (Mṣb;) and ♦ اغتزلته signifies the same. (Ṣ, Ḳ.) ═ غَزِلَ, (Ṣ, O, Ḳ, TA,) aor. ـَ, (Ḳ, TA,) inf. n. غَزَلٌ, (Ṣ, O, TA,) *He talked, and acted in an amatory and enticing manner, with a woman,* or *with women; he practised* غَزَل [meaning as expl. below, i. e. the *talk, and actions, and circumstances, occurring between the lover and the object of love;* &c.]. (Ṣ,* O,* Ḳ,* TA.) ═ And غَزِلَ is also said of a dog, meaning *He flagged,* or *became remiss, in the pursuit of a young gazelle;* i. e., *when he had come up to it, the latter uttered a cry by reason of its fright, whereupon he turned away from it,* (Ṣ, O, Ḳ, TA,) *and became diverted;* (Ṣ, O, TA;) or, as IAạr says, *when it became sensible of the presence of the dog, it became confounded,* or *perplexed, and clave to the ground, and he* (the dog) *became diverted from it, and turned away:* (TA:) or *he was confounded,* or *perplexed, in pursuing a young gazelle, by its uttering a cry in his face when he came up to it.* (Meyd in explanation of a prov.: see أَغْزَلُ, below.)

3. غَازَلَهَا, (Ṣ, MA, TA,) inf. n. مُغَازَلَةٌ, (Ṣ, O, Ḳ, TA,) *He talked with her,* (Ṣ, O,* Ḳ,* TA,) *and acted in an amatory and enticing manner with her;* (Ṣ, TA;) and in like manner one says of a woman with a man: (Ṣ:) or *he played,* or *sported,* [or *dallied,* or *wantoned,*] *and held amorous talk, with her.* (MA.) — [Hence,] one says, أَطْيَبُ مِنْ أَنْفَاسِ الصَّبَا إِذَا غَازَلَتْ رِيَاضَ الرُبَا ‡ [*More pleasant,* or *delightful, than the breaths of the east wind* (which is to the Arabs like the zephyr to us) *when it has wantoned with the meadows of* الربا, (app. الرُّبَا, the name of a place, mentioned in the Ḳ in art. ربو, there written الرُّبَى, and in the TA in that art. said to occur in poetry,) so as to have brought with it the odours of flowers]. (Ḳ.) And هُوَ يُغَازِلُ رَغَدًا مِنَ العَيْشِ ‡ [app. meaning *He plays the wanton with ampleness and easiness and pleasantness of the means of subsistence*]. (TA.) — And غازل الأَرْبَعِينَ † *He approached* [the age of] *forty* [years]. (Th, Ḳ.)

4. اغزل, (Ḳ,) or اغزلت, (Ṣ, O,) *He,* or *she, turned round,* or *made to revolve,* [or rather *twirled,*] *the* مِغْزَل [or *spindle*]: (Ṣ, O, Ḳ:) [or so اغزل المغزل, or اغزلته, for] one says of the مغزل [or spindle], أُغْزِلَ, i. e. *it was turned round* [or *twirled*]. (Fr, Ṣ.) ═ اغزلت *She* (a gazelle) *had a young one.* (Ṣ, O. [See غَزَالٌ.])

5. تغزّل *He affected,* or *attempted, as a self-imposed task,* (تَكَلَّفَ,) *what is termed* غَزَل [meaning as expl. below, i. e. *the talk, and actions, and circumstances, occurring between the lover and the object of love;* &c.]. (Ṣ, O, Ḳ, TA.) — And sometimes it means *He made mention,* or *spoke,* [generally *in verse,*] *of what is termed* غَزَل. (TA.) [See also شَبَّبَ, inf. n. تَشْبِيبٌ; and نَسَبَ, inf. n. نَسِيبٌ.] One says, تغزّل بِالمَرْأَةِ meaning *He mentioned the woman* [*in amatory language, as an object of love,*] *in his poetry.* (TA in art. غنى.)

6. تغازلوا [*They talked, and acted in an amatory and enticing manner;* or *they played, sported, dallied,* or *wantoned, and held amorous talk; one with another:* see 3]: (Ṣ, O:) from الغَزَل [q. v.]. (TA.)

8: see 1, first sentence.

غَزْلٌ, applied to cotton, (Ṣ, O, Ḳ, TA,) and flax, &c., (TA,) or wool, and the like, (Mṣb,) i. q. مَغْزُولٌ [i. e. *Spun*]: (Ṣ, O, Mṣb, Ḳ, TA:) [or rather *spun thread,* or *yarn of any kind;* for] it is an inf. n. used as a subst.: (Mṣb:) of the masc. gender: pl. غُزُولٌ. (TA.) — And accord. to ISd, The *web of the spider.* (TA.) — And غَزْلُ البَنَاتِ is applied in Egypt to *The sort of food called* إِطْرِيَة. (TA in art. طرو, q. v.)

غَزِلُ نِسَاءٍ *A follower and lover of women;* as also ♦ غِزِّيلُ نِسَاءٍ: (JK:) [or both may be rendered *one who talks, and acts in an amatory and enticing manner;* or *who plays, sports, dallies,* or *wantons, and holds amorous talk; with women:*] ♦ غِزِّيل is of the measure فِعِّيل in the sense of the measure مُفَاعِل; like حِدِّيث and كِلِّيم. (TA.)

غَزَلٌ, as expl. by 'Abd-El-Muṭṭalib El-Baghdádee, in his Exposition of the نَقْدُ الشِّعْرِ of Ḳudámeh, signifies The *talk, and actions, and circumstances, occurring between the lover and the object of love;* differing somewhat from تَشْبِيبٌ, which is a celebrating of the person and qualities of the beloved; and from نَسِيبٌ, which is a mentioning of the state, or condition, of the نَاسِب [himself], and of the object of the نَسِيب, and of all the affairs, or events, occurring between them two, [in the prelude of an ode,] thus including the meaning of تَشْبِيبٌ, and being a mentioning of غَزَل: accord. to Ḳudámeh, it signifies *an inclining to foolish and youthful conduct,* or *a manifesting of passionate love, and becoming notorious for affections to women:* (TA:) or it is the subst. from 3 [as such signifying *talk, and amatory and enticing conduct, with women;* or *play, sport, dalliance,* or *wanton conduct, and amorous talk, with women*]; (Ṣ, Ḳ;) as also ♦ مُغَازَلَةٌ: (Ḳ:) or *play, sport,* or *diversion, with women:* (ISd, TA:) or the *talk of young men and* [or *with*] *young women:* (Mṣb:) or, accord. to the leading authorities in polite literature, and those who have made the language to be their study, [or rather accord. to a loose and post-classical usage,] it signifies, like نَسِيبٌ, *praise of what are apparent of the members of the object of love:* or the *mention of the days of union and of disunion:* or the *like thereof.* (MF.)

غَزِلٌ [is, by rule, the part. n. of غَزِلَ, as such signifying *Talking, and acting in an amatory and enticing manner, with a woman,* or *with women;* &c.: but it is said that it] signifies صَاحِبُ غَزَلٍ; (Ṣ, O;) or مُتَغَزِّلٌ بِالنِّسَآءِ; (Ḳ, TA;) by which is here meant *making mention,* or *speaking,* or *one who makes mention,* or *who speaks,* [generally *in verse,*] *of what is termed* غَزَل [signifying as expl. above, i. e. *the talk, and actions, and circumstances, occurring between the lover and the object of love;* &c.]; thus used as being a possessive epithet, [not as a part. n. of غَزِلَ, because this differs in meaning from تَغَزَّلَ,] i. e. it signifies [properly] ذُو غَزَلٍ: (TA:) or it means *displaying amorous gestures* or *behaviour, and foolish and youthful conduct such as is suitable to women, with the love*, or *passionate love, that he experiences for them, in order that they may incline to him*: (Ḳudámeh, TA:) or it is applied to a man as meaning *a companion of women* because of his lacking strength to be otherwise: from what here follows. (IAạr, TA.) — *Lacking strength*, or *ability, to perform*, or *accomplish, things*: (IAạr, Ḳ, TA;) *remiss*, or *languid, in respect to them*. (IAạr, TA.)

غَزْلِىٌّ [*Of*, or *relating to, spun thread*, or *yarn*;] the rel. n. from غَزْلٌ used as a subst. (Mṣb.)

غَزَالٌ *A young gazelle*, وَلَدُ ظَبْيَةٍ: (Mṣb:) or a شَادِنٌ [or *young gazelle*], (T, Ṣ, O, Mṣb, Ḳ, TA,) or, as some say, the *female*, (TA, [but see what follows,]) *when it becomes active*, or *in motion*, (T, Ṣ, O, Mṣb, Ḳ, TA,) *and walks*; (T, Mṣb, Ḳ, TA;) to which the girl, or young woman, is likened in [the commencing of an ode by what is termed] التَّشْبِيب, wherefore the epithet and the verb [therein] are made masc.; (TA;) *after the becoming a* ثَنِىّ [q. v.]: (T, Mṣb:) or *in the stage after that in which he is termed* طَلًا [q. v.]: (AHát, Mṣb, TA:) or *from the time of his birth until he attains to the most vehement running*; (Ḳ, TA;) *which is when he puts his legs together*, [app. meaning *his fore legs together and so his hind legs*,] *and puts them down together and raises them together*: (TA:) or i. q. ظَبْىٌ [i. e. *a gazelle, of any age*]: (M in art. ظبى: for الظَّبْىُ is there expl. as meaning الغَزَالُ: [but this seems to be a loose rendering:]) the female is called ▼ غَزَالَةٌ; (Mṣb, MF, TA;) though it seems from what is said in the Ḳ [&c.] that الغَزَالُ is applied peculiarly to the male, and that the female is called only ظَبْيَةٌ, as several of the lexicologists have decisively asserted: (MF, TA:) the pl. [of pauc.] is غِزْلَةٌ and [of mult.] غِزْلَانٌ. (Ṣ, O, Mṣb, Ḳ.) — غَزَالُ شَعْبَانَ *A certain insect* (دُوَيْبَّةٌ), (Ḳ, TA,) *a species of the* [*locusts*, or *locust-like insects, called*] جَنَادِب [pl. of جُنْدَبٌ]. (TA.) — دَمُ الغَزَالِ *A certain plant, resembling the* طَرْخُون [or *tarragon*], (O, Ḳ,) *which is eaten*, (O,) *burning*, or *biting, to the tongue*, (O, Ḳ,) *green, and having a red root, like the roots of the* أَرْطَاة [n. un. of أَرْطًى, q. v.], (O,) *with the juice of which girls*, or *young women, make red streaks like bracelets upon their arms*: (O, Ḳ:) thus AHn was informed by some one or more of the Benoo-Asad: (O:) and Aboo-Naṣr says, *it is of the* [*kind called*] ذُكُور. [See also دُمْيَةُ الغِزْلَانِ and دَمُ الغِزْلَانِ and دَمُ الغَزَالِ voce دَمٌ in art. دمو or دمى; and see likewise عَنْدَمٌ.]

غَزَالَةٌ fem. of غَزَالٌ, q. v. — الغَزَالَةُ, also, signifies *The sun*; (Ṣ, O, Ḳ;) because it extends [what resemble] cords, [meaning its rays,] as though it were spinning: (Ḳ:) or *the sun when rising*; (Mṣb, Ḳ;) [therefore] one says طَلَعَتِ الغَزَالَةُ, but not غَرَبَتِ الغَزَالَةُ: (TA:) or *the sun when high*: (M,* Ḳ, TA:) or *the* عَيْن [meaning the *disk*, or, as it sometimes means, the *rays*, or *beams*,] *of the sun*. (Ḳ.) — And غَزَالَةُ الضُّحَى means, (Ṣ, O, Ḳ,) as also غَزَالَاتُهُ, (Ḳ,) [or غَزَالَاتُهَا,] *The beginning of the* ضُحَى [or *early part of the forenoon, after sunrise*]; (Ṣ, O, Ḳ;) [whence] one says, جَآءَ فِى غَزَالَةِ الضُّحَى [*He came in the beginning of the* ضُحَى]; and Dhu-r-Rummeh uses الغَزَالَةَ, in the accus. case, as an adv. n., (Ṣ, O,) meaning *in the time* [or *in the beginning*] *of the* ضُحَى; (O;) or, accord. to IKh, this is for طُلُوعَ الغَزَالَةِ, meaning *at the rising of the sun*: (TA:) or the meaning of the phrases first mentioned in this sentence is *after*, or *a little after*, (accord. to different copies of the Ḳ,) *the spreading of the sun*, [i. e. *of the sunshine*,] *and its entrance upon the* ضُحَى: or *the first part of the* ضُحَى, *until the passing away of a fifth* (or *about a fifth*, TA) *of the day*. (Ḳ.) — Also (i. e. الغَزَالَةُ) *A certain herb*, (Aboo-Naṣr, O, Ḳ,) *of the* [*kind called*] سُطَّاح, *spreading upon the ground, with green leaves, having no thorns nor branches; from the middle whereof comes forth a tall* قَضِيب [or *shoot*], *which is peeled and eaten*, (Aboo-Naṣr, O,) *and it is sweet*, (Aboo-Naṣr, O, Ḳ,) *and has yellow blossoms from its bottom to its top; and it is a pasture*: (Aboo-Naṣr, O:) *every thing* [i. e. *animal*] *eats it*; (Aboo-Naṣr, O, Ḳ;) *and the places of its growth are the plain*, or *soft, tracts*. (Aboo-Naṣr, O.)

غَزَّالٌ *A vender* [and *a spinner*] *of* غَزْل [i. e. *thread*, or *yarn*]. (TA.)

غُزَيِّلٌ: see غَزْلُ نِسَآءٍ, in two places.

غَازِلٌ [act. part. n. of غَزَلَ; *Spinning*]. The pls. غُزَّلٌ and غَوَازِلُ are applied as epithets to women: (Ḳ, TA:) but the former is also applied to men, and is of a measure more usual as that of the pl. of the masc. act. part. n. than of the fem. (TA.)

أَغْزَلُ مِنْ عَنْكَبُوتٍ, from the act of spinning, (Meyd,) or from the act of weaving [the web], (O,) is a prov. [meaning *More practised*, or *skilled, in weaving than a spider*]: and so مِنْ سُرْفَةٍ [*than a* سُرْفَة, q. v.]. (Meyd.) — And one says also, أَغْزَلُ مِنِ ٱمْرِئِ القَيْسِ, (Ṣ, Meyd, O,) likewise a prov., meaning [*More practised*, or *skilled*,] *in the celebrating of the person and qualities of the beloved in verse* [*than Imra-el-Keys*]. (Meyd.) — And [hence,] أَغْزَلُ مِنَ الحُمَّى † [*More frequent in visiting*, or *more habitual*, and *more recurrent, than the fever*]; a saying of the Arabs, by which they mean that it [the fever] is a frequent visiter of the sick person. recurrent to him; as though passionately loving him: thus, correctly, as in the L: in the Ḳ it is said that الأَغْزَلُ applied to the fever (الحُمَّى [though this is fem.]) means *such as is a frequent visiter of the sick person; recurrent*. (TA.) — And أَغْزَلُ مِنْ فُرْعُلٍ [*More confounded and perplexed than a young one of the hyena*]; from الغَزَلُ as signifying "the being confounded and perplexed" like as is the dog (Meyd, O, Ḳ) when pursuing the young gazelle; for it may be that the فرعل becomes in the like state in pursuing the object of its chase: (Meyd:) or فرعل was a man of ancient times, and this saying (which is a prov., Meyd) is like أَغْزَلُ مِنِ ٱمْرِئِ القَيْسِ. (Meyd, O, TA.)

مَغْزَلٌ: see مِغْزَلٌ, in two places: — and see also غَزْلٌ, latter half.

مُغْزَلٌ: see مِغْزَلٌ, in three places.

مُغْزِلٌ A doe gazelle *having a young one*. (Ḳ.)

مِغْزَلٌ and ▼ مُغْزَلٌ (Fr, Th, Ṣ, O, Mṣb, Ḳ) and ▼ مَغْزَلٌ, (Th, O, Ḳ,) the first as pronounced by [the tribe of] Temeem, the second as pronounced by [that of] Ḳeys, and the last the most rare, (TA,) or the second as pronounced by Temeem, (Mṣb,) *A spindle*; i. e. the *thing with which one spins*: (Ṣ, MA, O, Mṣb, Ḳ, KL:) Fr says that ▼ مُغْزَلٌ is the original form, from أُغْزِلَ "it was made to turn round" or "revolve" [or "was twirled"]; (Ṣ, TA;) but the ḍammeh was deemed by the Arabs difficult of pronunciation, and therefore they said مِغْزَلٌ, and in like manner مِصْحَفٌ and مِطْرَفٌ and مِجْسَدٌ and مِخْدَعٌ: accord. to IAth, مِغْزَلٌ signifies the *instrument* [*with which one spins*]; and ▼ مَغْزَلٌ, the *place of the* غَزْل [which means the act of *spinning* and the *spun thread* or *yard*]; and ▼ مُغْزَلٌ, the *place in which* (فِيهِ [or this may here mean *upon which*]) the غَزْل [i. e. *spun thread* or *yarn*] *is put*: (TA:) pl. مَغَازِلُ. (MA.) أَعْرَى مِنْ مِغْزَلٍ is a prov. [meaning *More naked than a spindle*]. (Meyd.) And one says, صَاحِبُ الغَزَلِ أَضَلُّ مِنْ سَاقِ مِغْزَلٍ [*The practiser of the talk and actions &c. usual between the lover and the object of love is more erring than the shank* (i. e. *pin*) *of a spindle*], of which the error is its [aiding in] clothing mankind while it is [itself] naked. (A, TA.) — It is said in a book of certain of the Jews, عَلَيْكُمْ كَذَا وَكَذَا وَرُبْعُ المِغْزَلِ, meaning [*Upon you lie as due from you such and such things and*] *the fourth part of what your women have spun*. (TA.) — And [the pl.] مَغَازِلُ signifies The عَمَد (O) or عُمُد (Ḳ) [app. meaning the *upright wooden supports of the seat*] *of the* [*machine called*] نَوْرَج [q. v.] *with which the reaped grain heaped together is thrashed*. (O, Ḳ.)

مِغْزَلِىٌّ (MA) and ▼ مَغَازِلِىٌّ (Ṣ and Ḳ voce مِضْرَمٌ) *A parer of spindles*. (MA.)

مُغَيْزِلٌ *A slender cord* (حَبْلٌ دَقِيقٌ) [so in copies of the Ḳ, and in the CḲ, but in the latter المُغْتَزَلُ is put for المُغَيْزِلُ: in my MS. copy of the Ḳ, المُغَيْزِلُ جَبَلٌ دَقِيقٌ, and this I think to be the correct reading, meaning *El-Mugheyzil is a certain slender mountain*]: ISd says, I think it to be likened to the مِغْزَل, because of its slenderness; adding that El-Hirmázee has mentioned it. (TA. [A verse cited by El-Hirmázee is there given as an ex.; mentioning the day of المُغْزِل, app. as the day of the separation of a lover from his beloved; and it is a common custom of the Arabs to call the day of an event the day of the place where it occurred.])

مِغْزَلِىٌّ : see مَغَازِلِىٌّ.

غزو

1. غَزَاهُ, [aor. ـُ,] inf. n. غَزْوٌ, *He willed,* or *desired, it; he sought it;* and *he aimed at it, intended it,* or *meant it;* syn. أَرَادَهُ; and طَلَبَهُ; and قَصَدَهُ; [the first of which is often used in the same senses as the second and third;] as also ▼ اغتزاهُ; (Ḳ, TA;) this last mentioned by ISd as syn. with قَصَدَهُ. (TA.) One says, عَرَفْتُ مَا يُغْزَى مِنْ هٰذَا الكَلَامِ i. e. [*I knew,* or, emphatically, *I know,*] *what is willed* or *desired* (مَا يُرَادُ) [*from this speech*]. (Ṣ.) And غَزْوِى كَذَا *My aim,* or *intention,* or *meaning, is such a thing.* (Ḳ.) — [Hence, app.,] غَزَا العَدُوَّ, inf. n. غَزْوٌ (Ṣ, Mgh, Mṣb, Ḳ) and غَزَوَانٌ, (Ḳ, TA,) or, as some say, غُزْوَانٌ, mentioned by Sb, (TA,) and غَزَاوَةٌ, (Ḳ,) [but see what is said of this last at the close of this paragraph,] *He went forth,* (Er-Rághib, TA,) or *repaired,* or *betook himself,* (Mgh,) *to wage war,* (Er-Rághib, TA,) or *to fight,* (Mgh,) *with the enemy;* (Er-Rághib, Mgh, TA;) or *he went to fight with, and plunder, the enemy;* (Ḳ, TA;) *in the country of the latter.* (Mṣb.) [And غَزَا alone, the objective complement being understood, often signifies the same; or *He engaged in a warring,* or *warring and plundering, expedition,* or *in such expeditions.*] — And غَزَا إِلَيْهِ, inf. n. as above, *He tended, repaired, betook himself,* or *went, to,* or *towards, him,* or *it;* syn. قَصَدَهُ. (TA.) = غَزَاوَةٌ, mentioned above, is of a measure which in most instances is that of an inf. n. of an intrans. verb, and it seems to be an inf. n. of which the verb is غَزُوَ, meaning جَادَ غَزْوُهُ [i. e. *Excellent,* or *how excellent, is his engaging in a warring,* or *warring and plundering, expedition,* or *in such expeditions!*]; and to be similar to قَضُوَ meaning جَادَ قَضَاؤُهُ, and ضَرُبَتْ يَدُهُ meaning جَادَ ضَرْبُهَا. (TA.)

2: see what next follows.

4. اغزاهُ *He fitted him out, equipped him,* or *furnished him,* (Ṣ,) or *he sent him,* (Mgh, Mṣb,) or *he urged,* or *incited, him,* (Ḳ,) *to engage in a warring,* or *warring and plundering, expedition,* (Ṣ,* Mgh,* Mṣb,* Ḳ,) *in the country of the enemy;* (Mṣb;) and ▼ غزّاهُ signifies the same. (Ḳ.) = أَغْزَتْ, said of a woman, (Mgh, Ḳ,) *Her husband was absent* [*engaged in a warring,* or *warring and plundering, expedition, in the country of the enemy*]; (Mgh;) or *her husband went* [or *had gone*] *to fight with, and plunder, the enemy.* (Ḳ.) — And, said of a she-camel, *Her impregnation was,* or *became, difficult.* (Ṣ, Ḳ.) = And اغزاهُ *He granted him some delay, and deferred* [*the exacting of*] *the debt that he owed.* (Ṣ, Ḳ.)

8. اغتزاهُ : see 1, first sentence. = اغتزى بِفُلَانٍ *He had such a one peculiarly to himself from among his companions:* (Ḳ, TA:) like اِغْتَزَّ بِهِ. (TA.) A poet says,

* قَدْ يَغْتَزِى الهِجْرَانُ بِالتَّجَرُّمِ *

[*Sometimes,* or *often, the cutting off from friendly intercourse has the accusation of that which is a crime,* or *a fault,* or *an offence, peculiarly assigned to it* (*as the cause*)]: التجرّم here meaning اِدِّعَآءُ الجُرْمِ. (TA.)

غَزَاةٌ : see the next paragraph, in three places.

غَزْوَةٌ The *act of* [الغَزْو i. e.] *repairing to fight with* [or *to fight with and plunder*] *the enemy* [*in the country of the latter*]; as also ▼ غَزَاةٌ, and ▼ مَغْزَاةٌ: (Mgh:) or the first signifies *a single time* [or *act*] *of* الغَزْو [i. e. *a single warring,* or *warring and plundering, expedition*]; (Th, Mṣb, TA;) as also ▼ مَغْزَاةٌ: (Mṣb:) and ▼ غَزَاةٌ is the subst. from غَزَوْتُ العَدُوَّ [as such meaning as expl. above, i. e. the *act of* الغَزْو]: (Ṣ, TA:) or this signifies [*a campaign,* i. e.] the *work* [or *operations*] *of a year:* (Th, TA:) the pl. (of غَزْوَةٌ, Mṣb, [and of ▼ غَزَاةٌ, for this is originally غَزَوَةٌ,]) is غَزَوَاتٌ, and (of ▼ مَغْزَاةٌ, Mṣb) مَغَازٍ, (Mgh, Mṣb,) which latter pl. is applied to the غَزَوَات of Moḥammad. (TA.)

غِزْوَةٌ *i. q.* طِلْبَةٌ [app. as meaning *A mode,* or *manner, of seeking, &c.*]. (TA.)

أَبُو غَزْوَانَ [or غُزْوَانٍ?] *The cat:* because it is ever making war upon the mouse. (يَغْزُو الفَأْرَ أَبَدًا). (Ḥar p. 663.)

غَزَوِىٌّ, accord. to [many, app., of] the copies of the Ṣ; or غَزْوِىٌّ, accord. to ISd, [and so in some copies of the Ṣ,] said by ISd to be altered from the regular form [which is غَزْوِىٌّ]; (TA;) *Of,* or *relating to,* الغَزْو [or *the making a warring,* or *warring and plundering, expedition*]. (Ṣ, ISd, TA.)

غَزِىٌّ : see غَازٍ.

غَزَّآءٌ One *who engages much,* or *often, in warring,* or *warring and plundering, expeditions;* syn. كَثِيرُ الغَزْوِ. (TA.)

غَازٍ One *going,* or *who goes, to fight with, and plunder, the enemy,* (Ṣ,* Mgh,* Mṣb, Ḳ,) *in the country of the latter;* (Mṣb;) [one *engaging,* or *who engages, in a warring,* or *warring and plundering, expedition:* and *a warrior,* in a general sense:] pl. غُزَاةٌ (Ṣ, Mgh, Mṣb) and غُزًّى (Ṣ, Mṣb, Ḳ, TA, in the CḲ غُزًى) and غُزَّآءٌ (Ṣ) and غُزِىٌّ, (Ḳ,) [originally غُزُوِىٌّ,] of the measure فُعُولٌ, (TA,) and ▼ غَزِىٌّ is pl. of [the pl.] غُزَاةٌ, (Ṣ, Mṣb,) or [rather] a quasi-pl. n.; (Ḳ;) and ▼ غَازِيَةٌ signifies *a company,* or *body, of* غُزَاة. (TA.)

غَازِيَةٌ : see what immediately precedes.

المُغْزِى and ▼ الأَغْزَآءُ [app. المغزى and الاغزاء, the former a pl. of which the sing. is not mentioned, and the latter a quasi-pl. n. like المَرْجَلُ from الرَّجْلُ,] *The offspring* (نَتَائِج) [more properly نِتَاج, which agrees with the context,]) *of the* [*season called*] صَيْف, on the authority of IAạr, [meaning *such offspring of camels,* for it is added,] *which are discommended, the young camel thereof being always weak.* (TA.)

مَغْزًى The *intended sense* of a saying; the *meaning* thereof; syn. مَقْصَدٌ [as an inf. n. used in the sense of the pass. part. n. of its verb]. (Ṣ, Ḳ; in the CḲ written مُقْصد.) — See also مَغْزَاةٌ. = And see the paragraph next preceding this.

مُغْزٍ [act. part. n. of 4, q. v.]. — مُغْزِيَةٌ A woman *whose husband is absent;* (Mgh;) [meaning] one *whose husband has gone to fight with, and plunder, the enemy.* (Ṣ,* TA.) See an ex. in a trad. mentioned voce كَابِرٌ. = Also, مُغْزِيَةٌ, A she-camel *that has exceeded the year* [*from the time when she was covered*] *without bringing forth;* like مِدْرَاجٌ: (El-Umawee, Ṣ:) or a she-camel *that has exceeded the year by a month,* (Ḳ, TA,) or *the like thereof,* (TA,) *in pregnancy:* (Ḳ, TA:) so in the M. (TA.) And A she-ass *that is late in bringing forth, but does then bring forth.* (Ṣ.) المُغْزِى مِنَ الغَنَمِ means *Those that are late in bringing forth, by a month,* or *two months, after the others, of the sheep* or *goats, because of their having conceived at a late period.* (TA.) — And مُغْزٍ signifies A she-camel *whose impregnation is difficult:* mentioned by Az. (TA.)

مَغْزَاةٌ : see غَزْوَةٌ, in three places. — Also *A place of* غَزْو [meaning *making a warring,* or *warring and plundering, expedition*]: pl. مَغَازٍ. (TA.) — And المَغَازِى signifies also *The memorable deeds of the* غُزَاة [meaning *those who engage in warring,* or *warring and plundering, expeditions,* pl. of غَازٍ]: (Ḳ, TA:) in which sense, some say, it has no sing., but others say that its sing. is مَغْزَاةٌ or ▼ مَغْزًى. (TA.)

مَغْزِىٌّ [as pass. part. n. of غَزَا] was used as an epithet applied to a man: it is properly with و [i. e. مَغْزُوٌّ]; but there are many instances of the former kind. (TA.)

غسق

1. غَسَقَ, said of the night, aor. ـِ, (Ṣ, O, Ḳ,) inf. n. غُسُوقٌ (O, Ḳ,* TA) and غَسْقٌ and غَسَقٌ and غَسَقَانٌ, (Ḳ,) *It became dark;* (Ṣ, O;) as also ▼ اغسق, (Th, O,) said by Z to be of the dial. of the Benoo-Temeem: (TA:) or both signify *it became intensely dark.* (Ḳ.) Hence, in a trad., غَسَقَ اللَّيْلُ عَلَى الظِّرَابِ i. e. *The night poured down upon the small mountains and covered them with its darkness.* (TA.) — And, said of the moon, *It lost its light, and became black and dark.* (TA.) — And غَسَقَتْ عَيْنُهُ, (Ṣ, O, Ḳ,) aor. ـِ; (O, Ḳ;) and غَسِقَتْ, aor. ـَ; (Ḳ;) inf. n. غَسْقٌ, (Ṣ, O,) or

غُسُوقٌ, (Ḳ,) or both, (TA,) and غَسَقَانٌ; (Ḳ, TA;) † *His eye became dark:* (Ṣ, O, Ḳ, TA:) or † *shed tears:* (Ḳ, TA:) or ‡ *poured forth* [*tears*]: (TA:) or غسقت العَيْنُ means † *the eye overflowed with water.* (AZ, TA.) — And غَسَقَ الجُرْحُ, inf. n. غَسَقَانٌ (Ṣ, O, Ḳ) and غَسْقٌ also, (TA,) *The wound had yellow water flowing from it;* (Ṣ, O, Ḳ;) and so غَسِقَ. (Ḳ, by implication.) And غَسَقَتِ السَّمَآءُ, (O, Ḳ, TA,) aor. ـِ, inf. n. غَسْقٌ and غَسَقَانٌ, (Ḳ, TA,) *The sky rained;* or *let fall a little rain, such as is termed* رَشٌّ: (O, Ḳ, TA:) and [*the rain*] *poured forth;* syn. اِنْصَبَّتْ: (TA:) [and in this latter sense غَسَقَ is app. said of any fluid; for,] accord. to Th, (O, TA,) غَسَقَانٌ is syn. with اِنْصِبَابٌ. (O, Ḳ, TA.) [Hence,] غَسَقَ اللَّبَنُ, (Ḳ,) inf. n. غَسْقٌ (TA) [and app. غَسَقَانٌ], *The milk poured forth from the udder.* (TA.)

4. اغسق: see 1, first sentence. — Also *He entered upon the* غَسَق, (O, Ḳ, TA,) i. e. the *beginning of the darkness.* (TA.) And, said of the مُؤَذِّن, *He delayed,* or *deferred,* the [*call to prayer of*] *sunset to the* غَسَق *of the night.* (Ṣ, O, Ḳ.)

غَسَقٌ The *beginning of the darkness of night:* (Fr, Ṣ, O:) or the *darkness* of the night: (Akh, TA:) or the *darkness of the beginning of the night:* (Ḳ:) or [the *time*] *when the* شَفَق [or *redness in the horizon after sunset*] *disappears:* or the *time of the blending of the* عِشَآءَانِ, [see عِشَآءٌ, last sentence,] which is *when the darkness becomes confused, and obstructs* [*the view of*] *the aspects of things:* or, accord. to Sh, the *entering-in of the beginning of the darkness.* (TA.) = Also *Refuse that is found among wheat, such as* زُوَان [or *darnel-grass, &c.*], *and the like.* (Fr, O, Ḳ.)

غَسَاقٌ and ▼ غَسَّاقٌ, (Ṣ, O, Ḳ, TA,) occurring in the Ḳur [xxxviii. 57 and] lxxviii. 25, accord. to different readings, (Ṣ, O, TA,) The *ichor,* or *watery matter,* (O, TA,) *and thick purulent matter,* (TA,) *that will flow and drip* (O,* TA) *from the skins of the inmates of the fire* [*of Hell*]: (O, TA:) or the *washings of them:* or *their tears:* (TA:) or, as some say, the latter of the words has the first of these meanings: (O, TA:) and the former word signifies *cold,* (O,) or *intensely cold,* (TA,) *that burns by reason of its coldness* (O, TA) *like the hot wind:* (TA:) or, accord. to Lth, *stinking:* (O, TA:) the latter word is expl. by I'Ab and Ibn-Mes'ood as signifying *intense cold:* (TA:) or both signify *cold and stinking.* (Ṣ, O.)

غَسِيقَاتٌ *Intensely red;* [applied to she-camels;] thus expl. by Skr as occurring in a verse of Ṣakhr [?] El-Hudhalee. (TA.)

غَسَّاقٌ: see غَسَاقٌ: — and see also the paragraph here following, near the end.

الغَاسِقُ signifies *The night;* (Zj, TA;) and [hence] وَمِنْ شَرِّ غَاسِقٍ إِذَا وَقَبَ (in the Ḳur [cxiii. 3], Ṣ, O) means [*And from the mischief*] *of the night when it cometh in;* (Ṣ, O, Ḳ;) accord. to El-Ḥasan (Ṣ, O) El-Baṣree: (O:) or *the beginning of the night;* as El-Ḥasan is related to have said: (TA:) or *the night when the* شَفَق [or *redness in the horizon after sunset*] *disappears:* (Ṣ, O, Ḳ:) and the night is said to be so called because it is colder than the day: (O, TA:) [for] الغَاسِقُ signifies [also] *the cold* (البَارِدُ) [like الغَسَّاقُ]: (TA:) or what is meant in the verse of the Ḳur-án cited above is *the accident in the night:* (Er-Rághib, TA:) or الغَاسِقُ signifies *the moon;* (Ḳ;) and this is said to be meant in the verse of the Ḳur-án; (Ṣ, TA;) so the Prophet is related to have said to 'Áïsheh; i. e. the verse means, [*the mischief of*] *the moon when it is eclipsed:* (Th, O,* TA:) or what is meant in that verse is, الثُّرَيَّا [i. e. *the asterism called the Pleiades*] *when it sets* [*aurorally* (see ثُرَيَّا)], because diseases and pestilences are frequent at that period, (O, Ḳ, TA,) and become removed at the period of its [auroral] rising [in the opposite season of the year], (O, TA,) as is related in a trad.: (TA:) or *the sun when it sets:* or *the day when it enters upon the night:* or *the serpent called* الأَسْوَد *when it smites,* or *turns over:* or, accord. to Suh, *Iblees when he suggests evil:* (TA:) or, accord. to I'Ab and several others, *from the mischief of the* ذَكَر *when it becomes erect;* (Ḳ, TA;) a strange explanation: and ▼ الغَسَّاقُ is like الغَاسِقُ; [but in what sense or senses is not said;] each is an epithet in which the quality of a subst. is predominant. (TA.) — غَاسِقٌ also signifies *Flowing;* applied by a poet in this sense to a source, or spring; and having no relation to darkness. (Sh, TA.)

غسل

1. غَسَلَهُ, (Ṣ, MA, O, Mṣb, Ḳ,) aor. ـِ, (Mṣb, Ḳ,) inf. n. غَسْلٌ, (Ṣ, MA, Mgh, O, Mṣb, Ḳ,) and غُسْلٌ is the subst., (Ṣ, Mṣb,) or a subst. (Mgh, Ḳ, TA) from الاِغْتِسَالُ, (Mgh, TA,) or, as some say, the latter is the inf. n. and the former is the subst., (MF, TA,) *He washed it;* with water (بِالمَآءِ): (MA:) غَسْلُ الشَّىْءِ signifies *the removing of dirt, or filth, and the like thereof, from the thing, by making water to run over it.* (Mgh.) You say, غَسَلَ الجِلْدَ كُلَّهُ [*He washed the skin, all of it*], and المَيِّتَ [*the dead body*]: and ▼ غسّل has the like, but an intensive, meaning. (Mṣb.) See also 10. — وَٱغْسِلْنِى بِمَآءِ الثَّلْجِ وَالبَرَدِ [lit. *And wash Thou me with the water of snow and of hail*], in a trad. relating to [forms of] prayer, means † *and cleanse Thou me from sins.* (TA.) And one says, غَسَلَ اللّٰهُ حَوْبَتَكَ i. e. † *May God cleanse thee from thy sin.* (TA.) — مَا غَسَلُوا رُؤُوسَهُمْ مِنْ يَوْمِ الجَمَلِ [lit. *They did not wash their heads &c.,* as one does in cleansing himself from impurity,] means مَا تَخَلَّصُوا and مَا فَرَغُوا [i. e., app., † *they did not become free from* the consequences of *the Day of the Camel* (the famous engagement between the forces of 'Alee and those of 'Áïsheh)]. (TA.) — And one says of a horse, غُسِلَ, like عُنِىَ, meaning *He sweated;* [or *became suffused with sweat;*] (Sh, O, Ḳ;) as also ▼ اِغْتَسَلَ. (Ḳ.) [See an ex. of the former in a verse cited in art. عدو, conj. 3.] — غَسَلَ المَرْأَةَ signifies ‡ *He compressed the woman* (جَامَعَهَا); (Az, Mgh, O, TA;) like عَسَلَهَا, with ع; (Az, Mgh, TA;) much or little; (TA;) and ▼ غَسَّلَهَا signifies the same: (Mgh, O, TA:) or both signify *he did so much.* (Ḳ.) It is said in a trad., (Mgh, O, TA,) respecting [preparation for the prayers of] Friday, (Mgh,) مَنْ غَسَلَ وَٱغْتَسَلَ, as some relate it, or, as others relate it, من ▼ غَسَّلَ واغتسل; the latter of which is said to mean *Whoso compresses* his wife [before his going to the mosque]; (Mgh, O;) and El-Ḳutabee says that most hold this to be the meaning; i. e., lest he should see in his way anything that might divert his heart [from devotion]; (Mgh;) [*and then washes himself;*] and Az held غَسَلَ, without teshdeed to be correct (Mgh, O) in this sense: (Mgh:) or the meaning accord. to the reading of غسّل is, *whoso performs the* [*ablution termed*] وُضُوْء *fully, washing every member* [*of those that are to be washed*] *three times,* (Mgh, O,) *and then washes himself* for the [prayers of] Friday; (Mgh;) and accord. to IAmb, it means *whoso washes himself* after الجِمَاع *and then washes himself* for the [prayers of] Friday: (O:) accord. to the Ḳ, ▼ التَّغْسِيلُ signifies *the exceeding the ordinary bounds in washing the members:* (TA:) he who explains it as meaning *the causing* a woman *to become under the obligation of performing a total ablution,* بِأَنْ وَطِئَهَا, says what is improbable, and departs from the authorities respecting it. (Mgh.) — One says also, غَسَلَ الفَحْلُ النَّاقَةَ, meaning ‡ *The stallion covered the she-camel much.* (Ḳ, TA.) [See also 4.] — And غَسَلَ, aor. ـِ, (Ḳ, TA,) inf. n. غَسْلٌ, (TA,) ‡ *He beat, and caused to suffer pain,* (Ḳ, TA,) بِالسَّوْطِ [*with the whip*]. (TA.)

2: see the preceding paragraph, in four places.

4. اغسل [said of a stallion, and intrans.,] † *He covered much,* or *often;* syn. أَكْثَرَ الضِّرَابَ. (Fr, O, Ḳ.) [See also 1, last explanation but one.]

7. انغسل said of a thing is quasi-pass. of غَسَلَهُ [i. e. it signifies *It became washed,* or *washed off*]. (O, TA.) [See غِسْلِينٌ.]

8. اغتسل (Ṣ, O, Mgh, Mṣb, Ḳ) *He washed* [*himself,* i. e.] *his whole person,* (Mgh,) بِالمَآءِ [*with water*]. (Ṣ, Mgh, O, Ḳ.) And اغتسل لِلْجُمُعَةِ [*He washed himself for the prayers of Friday*]. (IAmb, O.) — And اغتسل بِالطِّيبِ *He daubed,* or *smeared, himself,* or *did so copiously, so as to cause a dripping,* (تَضَمَّخَ, Lḥ, TA,) or *he sprinkled himself,* (تَنَضَّخَ, Ḳ,) *with perfume.* (Lḥ, Ḳ.) — اغتسل said of a horse: see 1.

10. It is said in a trad., العَيْنُ حَقٌّ فَإِذَا ٱسْتُغْسِلْتُمْ ▼ فَٱغْسِلُوا [*The evil eye is a truth; so when ye are asked to wash, wash ye*]: i. e., when he who was smitten by the eye of any one demanded [the performance of what is here meant], he brought to

the smiter therewith a bowl in which was water, and he [the latter] would put his hand into it, and rinse his mouth [with some of it], then spit it out into the bowl; then he would wash his face in it; then he would put in his left hand, and pour upon his right hand; then he would put in his right hand, and pour upon his left hand; [then he would put in his left hand (a clause omitted in my original),] and pour upon his right elbow; then he would put in his right hand, and pour upon his left elbow; then he would put in his left hand, and pour upon his right foot; then he would put in his right hand, and pour upon his left foot; then he would put in his left hand, and pour upon his right knee; then he would put in his right hand, and pour upon his left knee; then he would wash what is termed دَاخِلَةُ الإِزَارِ [expl. in art. دخل]: and he would not put the bowl upon the ground: then he would pour that used water upon the head of the person smitten with the eye, from behind him, with one pouring; and he would be cured, with the permission of God. (TA.)

غَسْلٌ inf. n. of غَسَلَهُ: (Ṣ, MA, Mgh, O, Mṣb, Ḳ:) or, accord. to some, this and ▼ غُسْلٌ have one and the same meaning; and the saying that this is the case is ascribed to Sb: (Mṣb:) or, as some say, the latter is the inf. n., and the former is the subst. (MF, TA.) See also the next paragraph.

غُسْلٌ the subst. from غَسَلَهُ [i. e. a subst. signifying *A washing*]: (Ṣ, Mṣb:) or a subst. (IḲooṭ, Mgh, Mṣb, Ḳ, TA) from الاِغْتِسَالُ, (IḲooṭ, Mgh, Mṣb, TA,) and [as such] signifying *a complete washing* [*of oneself*, i. e.] *of the whole person*: (IḲooṭ, T, Mgh, Mṣb, TA:) it is in consequence of جَنَابَة [q. v.], and of child-birth, and for [the prayers of] Friday, and is the *washing* of the dead; but in other cases, the word ▼ غَسْلٌ, with fet-ḥ, is used: (Ḥam p. 30:) and one says ▼ غُسُلٌ as well as غُسْلٌ, (Ṣ, O,) the former being a dial. var. of the latter: (TA:) El-Kumeyt says, describing a wild ass,

• تَحْتَ الأَلَاءَةِ فِى نَوْعَيْنِ مِنْ غُسُلٍ •
• بَاتَا عَلَيْهِ بِتَسْجَالٍ وَتَقْطَارِ •

[*Beneath the* (tree called) أَلَاءَة, *in two sorts of washing that continued during the night upon him with much pouring and much dropping*]; meaning that the water that was upon the tree poured upon him at one time; and at one time, that of the rain: (Ṣ, TA:) the pl. of غُسْلٌ is أَغْسَالٌ. (Mṣb.) See also غَسْلٌ. — And see غَسُولٌ.

غِسْلٌ *A preparation for washing the head, consisting of* خِطْمِىّ [or *marsh-mallows*] *and other things* (Ṣ, Mgh, O, Mṣb, Ḳ) *of a similar kind*, (Mgh, Mṣb, Ḳ,) [*with water*,] *as* [*leaves of*] *the* [*species of lote-tree called*] سِدْر, (Mṣb,) *and* طِين, (TA,) or طِينَةُ الرَّأْسِ, [meaning *fullers' earth*, which is often used in the bath and elsewhere instead of soap,] (Mgh,) *and* أُشْنَان [or *potash*]: (TA:) [and app. *any wash for the head*:] and ▼ غِسْلَةٌ signifies the same: (Mgh, Ḳ:) and also (this latter) *leaves of the myrtle*: and *perfume*; syn. طِيبٌ: and *what a woman puts into her hair on the occasion of combing and dressing it*: (Ḳ:) غِسْلَةٌ مُطَرَّاةٌ being *myrtle* [*-leaves*] *rendered fragrant with aromatic perfumes, used in combing and dressing one's hair*: one should not say غَسْلَةٌ. (Ṣ, O.) IAạr cites the following verse (Ṣ, O) of ʼAbd-Er-Raḥmán Ibn-Dárah El-Ghaṭafánee, (O,)

• فَيَا لَيْلَ إِنَّ الغِسْلَ مَا دُمْتِ أَيِّمًا •
• عَلَىَّ حَرَامٌ لَا يَمَسُّنِىَ الغِسْلُ •

[*And, O Leylà*, (لَيْلَ being a contraction of لَيْلَى, but in the O it is يا جُمْلُ *O Juml*,) *verily the wash for the head, as long as thou remainest husbandless, shall be unlawful to me: the wash for the head shall not touch me*]: i. e. I will not need the wash for the head by my جِمَاع of other than her: [he says thus] in eager desire of taking her in marriage. (Ṣ, O.) — See also غَسُولٌ. ═ And see also غُسَلَةٌ.

رَجُلٌ غِسْلٌ † *A man who compresses his wife much.* (TA.) [See also غُسَلَةٌ.]

غُسَلٌ: see غُسَلَةٌ.

غُسُلٌ: see غُسْلٌ.

غَسْلَةٌ [*A single act of washing*: pl. غَسَلَاتٌ]. — [Hence,] one says, بَنَوْا هٰذِهِ المَدِينَةَ بِغَسَلَاتِ أَيْدِيهِمْ † [*They built this city*] *by means of their earnings.* (TA.)

غِسْلَةٌ: see غَسُولٌ: — and see also غِسْلٌ. — عَلَى وَجْهِهِ غِسْلَةٌ means *His face is beautiful, with no fat*, or *fatness, upon it.* (TA.) — أَبُو غِسْلَةَ is an appellation of *The wolf*: (O, Ḳ:) and so ابو عِسْلَةَ, with ع. (TA.)

غُسَلَةٌ (Ṣ, Mgh, O, Ḳ) and ▼ غُسَلٌ and ▼ غِسِيلٌ and ▼ غِسِّيلٌ and ▼ مِغْسَلٌ (O, Ḳ) and ▼ غِسْلٌ, (Ḳ,) all, except the last, mentioned by Fr, (O, TA,) applied to a stallion [camel], ‡ *That covers much*: (Fr, Mgh,* O, Ḳ, TA:) or *that does so much without impregnating*: (Ks, Ṣ, Ḳ, TA:) and in like manner applied to a man. (Ḳ.) [See also غِسْلٌ.]

الغِسْلِينُ: see الغُسَالَةُ. — الغِسْلِينُ (in the Ḳur [lxix. 36], TA) *What is washed off of the flesh and the blood of the inmates of the fire* [*of Hell*]; (Akh, Ṣ, O;) [for] *what comes forth from any wound, or sore, when it is washed*, is termed غِسْلِين: (TA:) *what is washed off from the bodies of the unbelievers, in the fire*: (Mṣb:) or *what flows from the skins of the inmates of the fire*, (Ḳ, TA,) *such as thick purulent matter &c.*; thus expl. by Fr and Seer; (TA;) as though it were washed from them: (Sb, TA:) accord. to Mujáhid, *a certain food of the inmates of the fire*; and El-Kelbee says that it is *what the fire has cooked, of their flesh, and has fallen off, and is eaten by them*: (TA:) and, (Ḳ,) accord. to Eḍ-Ḍaḥḥák, (O, TA,) *a species of trees in the fire*; (O, Ḳ, TA;) and so he says of الضَّرِيعُ: (O, TA:) and, (Ḳ,) accord. to Lth, (O, TA,) *what is intensely hot*: (O, Ḳ, TA:) the ى and ن are augmentative. (Ṣ, O, Mṣb.)

غَسُولٌ (Ṣ, O, Ḳ) and ▼ غَسُّولٌ (O, Ḳ) and ▼ غُسْلٌ (Mgh, Ḳ) and ▼ غِسْلٌ and ▼ غِسْلَةٌ (IAth, Ḳ) *Water with which one washes himself*; (Ṣ, Mgh, O, Ḳ;) as also ▼ مُغْتَسَلٌ, occurring [in this sense] in the Ḳur xxxviii. 41: (Ṣ:) or the words preceding this signify *water little in quantity, with which one washes himself*: (TA:) and خِطْمِىّ [or *marsh-mallows*], (Ḳ, TA,) and أُشْنَان [or *potash* (see also غَاسُولٌ)], and *the like thereof*, and *certain of the* [*plants termed*] حَمْض: (TA:) or غَسُولٌ signifies *a thing* [or *substance*] *with which the hand is washed, such as* أُشْنَان *&c.*: (Ḥar p. 86:) or, accord. to the M, *anything with which one washes a head* or *a garment and the like.* (TA.) [See also the pl. غَسُولَاتٌ voce دَلُوكٌ.]

غَسِيلٌ *i. q.* ▼ مَغْسُولٌ [i. e. *Washed*]; (Ṣ, O, Mṣb, Ḳ;) applied to a thing, (Ṣ, O,) and to a dead body; (Lḥ, Mṣb, TA;) and the former is also applied as an epithet to a fem. n., as is also غَسِيلَةٌ; (Ṣ, O, Ḳ;) or this last is used after the manner of substs., like نَطِيحَةٌ and ذَبِيحَةٌ; not as is said in the Ṣ [and O] after the manner of epithets: (IB, TA:) the pl. of غَسِيلٌ is غَسْلَى and غُسَلَاءُ; (Lḥ, Ḳ, TA;) and the pl. of غَسِيلَةٌ [and app. of غَسِيلٌ used as a fem. epithet] is غَسَالَى or غُسَالَى. (Ḳ accord. to different copies.) Ḥandhaleh Ibn-er-Ráhib was called غَسِيلُ المَلَائِكَةِ [*The washed of the angels*], because he died a martyr on the day of Oḥod, and the angels washed him, (Ṣ, O, Mṣb,) accord. to the Prophet, who said that he saw them washing him. (O.) — See also غُسَلَةٌ. — [It is now used as meaning *Clothes*, or *the like, put together to be washed.*]

غُسَالَةُ الشَّىْءِ, (Ṣ, O, Mṣb,) or الغُسَالَةُ, (Ḳ,) *That with which one has washed the thing*: (Ṣ, O, Mṣb:) or *the water with which the thing is washed.* (Ḳ.) [Hence the latter often signifies *The infusion of the thing*; i. e. *the liquid in which the thing has been steeped, and which is impregnated with its virtues.*] — Also, the latter, *What is extracted from the thing by washing.* (Ḳ.) — And الغُسَالَةُ also signifies *What is washed from the garment and the like*; and so ▼ الغِسْلِينُ. (Ḳ.)

غَسْوِيلٌ *A certain plant, growing in places that exude water and produce salt*: (O, Ḳ:) said by IDrd to be *a species of trees.* (O.)

غَسَّالٌ [*A washer* of clothes, and also of the dead: fem. with ة]. (TA.) [See also غَاسِلٌ.]

غَسُّولٌ: see غَسُولٌ.

غِسِّيلٌ: see غُسَلَةٌ.

غَاسِلٌ *A washer* of the dead. (Mṣb.) [See also غَسَّالٌ.] ═ And *A species of trees.* (TA.)

غَاسُولٌ i. q. أُشْنَانٌ [i. e. *Potash: and the plant from which it is prepared; kali,* or *glasswort;* or *mesembryanthemum nodiflorum* (Forskål, Flora Ægypt. Arab. pp. lxvii. and 98), *a species of glasswort*]. (TA.) [See also غَسُولٌ.]

مَغْسَلٌ (Ṣ, O, Mṣb, Ḳ) and مَغْسِلٌ [which is anomalous] (Ṣ, O, Ḳ) and ▼ مُغْتَسَلٌ (Ḳ) *A place in which the dead are washed:* (Ṣ, O, Mṣb, Ḳ:) pl. of the first (Ṣ, Mṣb) and second (Ṣ) مَغَاسِلُ: (Ṣ, Mṣb:) and one says also مَغْسِلُ المَوْتَى. (Ṣ, O, Mṣb.*)

مِغْسَلٌ *A thing* [i. e. *vessel*] *in which* (so in the M, in the Ḳ *with which,*) *a thing is washed.* (TA.) — See also غُسَالَةٌ.

مَغْسُولٌ: see غَسِيلٌ. — Hence one says, كَلَامُهُ مَغْسُولٌ, meaning † *His speech,* or *language, is devoid of nice,* or *subtile, expressions* or *allusions;* as though it were washed from such; or deserving to be washed and obliterated: or it may mean ‡ *trimmed,* or *pruned.* (TA.)

مُغْتَسَلٌ *A place in which one washes himself:* (O, Mṣb, TA:*) dim. ▼ مُغَيْسِلٌ: and pl. مَغَاسِيلُ [which, if correct, is anomalous]. (TA.) — And it is said to signify also what is called in Pers. حَوْض مِسِين [or حوض مسين app. meaning *A tank,* or *the like, of copper*]. (Mgh.) — See also مَغْسِلٌ. — And see غَسُولٌ.

مُغَيْسِلٌ: see the next preceding paragraph.

غسم

1. غَسَمَ *It* (the night) *was,* or *became, dark;* (Aṣ, Ṣ, Ḳ;) as also ▼ اغسم, (JK, Ḳ,) like أَغْسَى. (JK.)

4: see what precedes.

غَسَمٌ The *darkness* (Ṣ, ISd, TA) of night; (ISd, TA;) like غَسَقٌ: (Ṣ, TA:) or *blackness:* (Kr, Ḳ:) and (Ḳ) accord. to En-Naḍr, (Ṣ,) the *confusedness,* or *blending, of the darkness:* (JK, Ṣ, Ḳ:) and the *first rising of the dawn.* (JK.) — And *Dust,* or *dust rising,* or *spreading, like smoke;* syn. هَبْوَةٌ and غَبَرَةٌ (Ḳ) or غُبْرَةٌ [which sometimes signifies the same as غَبَرَةٌ]. (CḲ.)

أَغْسَامٌ; see غَسَمٌ.

لَيْلٌ غَاسِمٌ *Dark night.* (TA.)

فِي السَّمَآءِ أَغْسَامٌ and ▼ غَسَمٌ *In the sky are portions of clouds.* (Ḳ.)

غسو and غسى

1. غَسَا اللَّيْلُ, (Ṣ, Ḳ,) aor. يَغْسُو, (Ṣ,) inf. n. غُسُوٌّ; (Ṣ, Ḳ; accord. to some copies of the Ḳ غَسْوٌ;) and غَسَى, aor. يَغْسِى, (IJ, TA;) and غَسِىَ, aor. يَغْسَى, (Ṣ, Ḳ, TA,) inf. n. غَسًا; of which last form, غَشِىَ is a dial. var.; (TA;) *The night was,* or *became, dark;* as also ▼ اغسى. (Ṣ, Ḳ.) [See also غَسَا.]

4: see what precedes. — اغسى also signifies *He* (a man) *entered upon the time of,* or *a little after, sunset.* (TA.) — And أَغْسِ مِنَ اللَّيْلِ *Journey thou not in the first part of the night, until its darkness depart.* (TA.) — And اغساهُ اللَّيْلُ *The night enveloped him in its darkness.* (Ṣgh, Ḳ.)

غش

1. غَشَّهُ, (Ṣ, A, Mṣb, Ḳ,) aor. ـُ, (Ṣ, Mṣb,) inf. n. غَشٌّ, (Mṣb, TA,) or غِشٌّ, with kesr, (Ṣ,) or the latter is a simple subst., (Mṣb, Ḳ,) *He acted towards him,* or *advised* or *counselled him, dishonestly,* or *insincerely:* (A, Mṣb, Ḳ:) and *he dressed up to him an affair* [*in false colours*]: (Mṣb:) or *he acted towards him with dissimulation; pretended to him the contrary of what he conceived in his mind:* (A, Ḳ:) but this is a needless addition, for it is the same as the first explanation: (TA:) as also ▼ غَشَّشَهُ, (Ḳ,) inf. n. تَغْشِيشٌ: (TA:) or this latter has an intensive signification: it is said to be derived from غَشَشٌ, signifying "a turbid drinking-place." (TA:) It is said in the story of Umm-Zarạ, accord. to one relation, ▼ لَا تَمْلَأُ بَيْتَنَا تَغْشِيشًا, said by some to be from الغشّ, and by others to be from [a usage of] التغشيش as signifying النَّمِيمَة [app. here meaning *the embellishing speech with falsehood*]: but accord. to the approved relation, it is [تَعْشِيشًا,] with the unpointed letter. (IAth.) [See art. عش.] — [Also *He made it to seem what it was not; falsified it; counterfeited it; adulterated it:* so as used often by post-classical authors; and so, probably, in classical times also: see its pass. part. n., below.] — غَشَّ صَدْرُهُ, aor. ـَ, [inf. n., probably, غِشٌّ, q. v.,] *His bosom concealed enmity and violent hatred;* or *bore rancour, malevolence, malice,* or *spite.* (TA.)

2: see the preceding paragraph, in two places.

4. اغشّه, inf. n. إِغْشَاشٌ, *He made him to fall into dishonest,* or *insincere, conduct,* or *advice* or *counsel; into dissimulation;* or *the pretending the contrary of what he conceived in his mind.* (TA.) — And أَغْشَشْتُهُ عَنْ حَاجَتِهِ *I prevented him from obtaining the object of his want;* syn. أَعْجَلْتُهُ. (IḲtt, Ḳ.)

8: see the next paragraph, in two places.

10. استغشّه (Ṣ, Ḳ) and ▼ اغتشّه (Ḳ, TA) *He reckoned him,* or *deemed him, dishonest,* or *insincere, in action,* or *advice* or *counsel; contr. of* اِسْتَنْصَحَهُ (Ṣ, Ḳ) *and* اِنْتَصَحَهُ; (Ḳ;) or, [which means the same,] *i. q.* عَدَّهُ غَاشًّا: (TA:) or *he imagined in him dishonest,* or *insincere, conduct,* or *advice* or *counsel; dissimulation;* or *the pretending the contrary of what he conceived in his mind.* (Ḳ.) A poet says,

أَيَا رُبَّ مَنْ تَغْتَشُّهُ ▼ لَكَ نَاصِحٌ
وَمُسْتَنْصَحٍ بِالغَيْبِ غَيْرُ أَمِينِ

[*O man, many a one whom thou reckonest dishonest in action,* or *advice, is honest therein to thee; and* (*many a*) *one who is reckoned honest in action,* or *advice, in that which is beyond the reach of perception, is not faithful*]. (TA.)

غُشٌّ, (Ḳ, TA,) of the measure فُعْلٌ, or it may be originally of the measure فُعُلٌ, (TA,) applied to a man, (Ḳ, TA,) *i. q.* عَظِيمُ الشَّرَهِ [i. e. *Very greedy*]; not عظيم السُّرَّةِ, as in some copies of the Ḳ; nor عظيم الشُّرَّةِ, as in other copies: a rájiz says,

لَيْسَ بِغُشٍّ هَمُّهُ فِيمَا أَكَلْ

[*He is not one who is very greedy; whose care,* or *solicitude, is in respect of what he has eaten*]. (TA.)

غِشٌّ *Dishonest,* or *insincere, conduct,* or *advice* or *counsel:* (Mṣb, Ḳ:) and the *embellishment of an affair* [*with false colours*]: (Mṣb:) or *dissimulation; pretence of the contrary of what one conceives in his mind.* (Ḳ.) [See also 1.] — And *Rancour, malevolence, malice,* or *spite.* (Ḳ.) — [Also *Adulterating alloy* in coin. (See حُمْلَانٌ.) — And *Adulterated,* or *counterfeit, coin.* (See زَغَلٌ.)]

غَشَشٌ *A turbid drinking-place:* (Az, IAmb, Ṣgh, TA:) الكَدِرُ المَشُوبُ in the Ḳ is a mistake; the right explanation of الغَشَشُ being المَشْرَبُ الكَدِرُ, which is that given by Az and IAmb and Ṣgh. (TA.)

غَشَاشٌ: see the next paragraph.

غِشَاشٌ, applied to a drinking (شُرْبٌ), *Little in quantity,* (Ḳ, TA,) because of turbidness: (TA: [in which it is said to be applied in like manner to a day, يوم; but I think that this is a mistranscription for نَوْمٌ, i. e. sleep:]) or *hasty:* or *not wholesome;* (Ḳ, TA;) because the water is not clear. (TA.) — And The *beginning of the darkness:* and the *end thereof.* (Ḳ.) — لَقِيتُهُ غِشَاشًا, (T, Ṣ, Ḳ,) and ▼ غَشَاشًا, (Ḳ,) *I met,* or *found, him,* or *it, in haste;* (T, Ṣ, Ḳ;) and so على غشاش: (T, TA:) or *at sunset;* (Lth, Ḳ;) but Az disallows this: (TA:) or *in the night;* (Ḳ;) which is nearly the same as what Lth says. (TA.)

غَاشٌّ *Acting,* or *advising* or *counselling, dishonestly,* or *insincerely;* or *acting with dissimulation; pretending the contrary of what one conceives in his mind:* [see its verb:] pl. غَشَشَةٌ and [quasi-pl. n., like as صَحَابَةٌ is of صَاحِبٌ,] غَشَاشَةٌ. (TA.)

شَىْءٌ مَغْشُوشٌ [*A thing made to seem what it is not; falsified; counterfeited; adulterated*]; (Ṣ, Ḳ;) *a thing that is not pure; not genuine;* or *not unadulterated.* (Ḳ.) You say, طَعَامُ فُلَانٍ مَغْشُوشٌ أَعْلَاهُ يَابِسٌ وَأَسْفَلُهُ مَرْشُوشٌ [*The wheat of such a one is made to seem what it is not: its upper part is dry, and its lower part is sprinkled*]. (A.) And لَبَنٌ مَغْشُوشٌ *Milk mixed with water.* (Mgh, Mṣb.) And فِضَّةٌ مَغْشُوشَةٌ *Silver mixed with copper or brass.* (TA.)

غشم

1. غَشْمٌ signifies The *acting*, or *treating*, *wrongfully, unjustly, injuriously*, or *tyrannically*: (Ṣ, Ḳ:) or the *taking* another's *property wrongfully*, &c., or *by force*: and the *taking a course, in journeying* [&c.], *at random, without direction and without knowledge*. (JK.) One says of a governor, غَشَمَ الرَّعِيَّةَ, aor. ـِ, [accord. to the TḲ, the aor. of the verb in the sense here following is ـُ, but this I think a mistake,] inf. n. غَشْمٌ, *He struck*, or *beat, with vehemence, the people under his government, wrongfully, unjustly, injuriously*, or *tyrannically, and took* [*from them*] *what he could*. (TA.) And غَشَمَ النَّاسَ *He asked whom he could of the people*. (Z, TA.) And غَشَمَ الأُمُورَ *He performed affairs*, or *the affairs*, [*in a random manner*,] *confusedly, without discrimination*. (Ḥam p. 37: by implication.) — And غَشَمَهُ, aor. ـِ, *He smeared him* [i. e. a camel] *with tar so that he left nothing* [or *no part of him*] *without tar, pouring it upon what was sound thereof and what was diseased thereof*: and ▼ غَشَمٌ [perhaps as an inf. n., but accord. to the TḲ it is a simple subst., and the inf. n. is غَشْمٌ,] signifies the *act of so smearing*. (Ḳ.) — And غَشَمَ ‡ *He collected firewood by night, cutting whatever he could get, without consideration*, (Ḳ, TA,) or, as in the A, *without discrimination*. (TA.)

غَشَمٌ: see the preceding paragraph. ═ Also *Blackness* [of night: app. a dial. var. of غَسَمٌ; or, perhaps, a mistranscription]. (Ḥam p. 163.)

غَشُومٌ A man *who strikes*, or *beats, people vehemently*, [*and wrongfully*, (see 1,)] *and takes* [*from them*] *everything that he can get*; as also ▼ غَشَّامٌ and ▼ غَاشِمٌ [except that the first and second are app. intensive epithets and the last is a simple part. n.]: and it is likewise applied to a fem., as, for ex., to a hand (يَدٌ): and to a striking, or beating, (ضَرْبٌ,) [app. as meaning *wrongful*,] as is also ▼ غَشَمْشَمٌ. (TA.) [One says,] الحَرْبُ غَشُومٌ [*War is wrongful*], because it reaches other than the committer of a crime, or an offence deserving punishment. (Ṣ.) — Also A she-camel *that will not be turned back from her course*, or *way*. (R, TA.)

غَشِيمٌ, meaning [*Ignorant of affairs*,] *not knowing anything*, is a word of the vulgar. (TA.)

غَشُومِيَّةٌ, meaning *Ignorance of affairs*, is a word of the vulgar, like that next preceding. (TA.)

غَشَّامٌ : } see غَشُومٌ.
غَاشِمٌ : }

غَشَمْشَمٌ: see مِغْشَمٌ. Accord. to some, it signifies One *who acts with much wrongfulness, injustice, injuriousness*, or *tyranny*. (Ḥam p. 104.) — نَاقَةٌ غَشَمْشَمَةٌ *A she-camel strong, resisting*, or *indomitable, in spirit*. (IJ, TA.) And غَشَمْشَمٌ is applied to a he-camel as meaning هَائِجٌ [i. e. *Excited by lust*]. (Meyd in explanation of the prov. here following.) — غَشَمْشَمٌ يُغْشِى الشَّجَرَ, i. e. This, or it or he, is a torrent [*wild in its course*,] *that overwhelms the trees, so that it crushes them and uproots them*, سَيْلٌ preceded by هُوَ or هٰذَا being meant to be supplied, is a prov. applied to a man who cares not what wrong he does. (Meyd.) — See also غَشُومٌ.

غَشَمْشَمِيَّةٌ and إِنَّهُ لَذُو غَشَمْشَمَةٍ *Verily he is one who possesses boldness*, or *daringness, and penetrative energy*. (Ḳ.)

أَغْشَمُ [*More, and most, wrongful, unjust, injurious*, or *tyrannical*: &c.: see 1]. أَغْشَمُ مِنَ السَّيْلِ [*More wild in course than the torrent*] is a proverb. (Meyd.) ═ IAạr cites a verse in which it is applied to a plant as meaning *Dry and old*; but accord. to one relation of that verse, the word is أَغْثَمُ. (TA.)

مِغْشَمٌ One *who goes at random, heedlessly*, or *in a headlong manner, without consideration, whom nothing will turn from that which he desires*, (Ṣ, Ḳ,) *by reason of his courage*; (Ṣ;) as also ▼ غَشَمْشَمٌ: (Ṣ, Ḳ:) or, accord. to Aboo-Riyásh, one *who performs affairs* [*in a random manner*,] *confusedly, without discrimination*: or, as some say, one *who, when the road is unapparent to him, goes at random, without direction and without knowledge*. (Ḥam p. 37.)

غشى and غشو

1. غَشِيَهُ, aor. يَغْشَى, inf. n. غِشَاوَةٌ, *It covered*, or *concealed, him*, or *it*; (TA;) as also ▼ تَغَشَّاهُ. (MA.) And one says, غَشَانِى اللَّيْلُ, i. e. غَشِيَنِى [*The night covered me*, or *concealed me*: or the meaning may be that which next follows]. (JK.) — غَشِيَهُ, (Ḳ, TA,) aor. and inf. n. as above, (TA,) is said of an event (أَمْرٌ), [and of heat, (Ṣ and Ḳ in art. دغم,) and of cold, (Ḳ in that art.,) and of an affection of the mind or body, and of various things, sometimes in like manner of a man, and of a company of men,] in a similar sense; and so ▼ تغشّاهُ; (Ḳ, TA;) both signifying *It came upon*, [or *invaded, so as to surprise*, and *so as to overwhelm*, properly meaning] *as a thing that covered, him*, or *it*. (Ḳ,* TA.) Hence, in the Ḳur [liii. 16], إِذْ يَغْشَى ٱلسِّدْرَةَ مَا يَغْشَى [*When there was coming upon the lote-tree so as to cover it*, or *overspread it, what was so coming*]. (TA.) And in the same [xx. 81], فَغَشِيَهُمْ مِنَ ٱلْيَمِّ مَا غَشِيَهُمْ [*And there came upon them so as to overwhelm them, of the sea, what so came upon them*]. (TA.) And in the same [viii. 11], إِذْ يَغْشَاكُمُ [followed by ٱلنُّعَاسَ, i. e. *When it* (drowsiness) *was coming upon you*, or *overcoming you*]; accord. to one reading; other readings being يُغْشِيكُمُ and يُغَشِّيكُمُ [followed by ٱلنُّعَاسَ]. (TA.) See also غَاشِيَةٌ, in three places. — [A somewhat similar signification of غَشِيَهُ will be found below.] — One says of the night, يَغْشَى بِظُلْمَتِهِ كُلَّ مَا بَيْنَ السَّمَآءِ وَالأَرْضِ [*It covers*, or *conceals, with its darkness, everything that is between the heaven and the earth*]. (Jel in xcii. 1.) And [hence it is said that] غَشِىَ اللَّيْلُ means *The night was*, or *became, dark*: as also ▼ اغشى. (Mṣb, TA.) — [And غَشِيَهُ, and غَشِىَ بَصَرَهُ and ▼ غَشَّاهُ, signify *It*, i. e. light (ضَوْءٌ), *came upon him*, and *upon his eye, with an overpowering effect, so as to obscure*, or *dazzle, his sight*.] — غَشِيَهُ also signifies جَآءَهُ (Ṣ) or أَتَاهُ (Mgh, Mṣb, Ḳ) [which have two meanings, i. e. *He came to him*, and *he did it*; both, perhaps, here meant, for both are well-known meanings of غَشِيَهُ]; and, thus used, the aor. is as above, (TA,) and the inf. n. is غَشَيَانٌ, (Ṣ, TA,) or غِشْيَانٌ, (so in one of my copies of the Ṣ,) or the subst. is ▼ غِشْيَانٌ, (Mṣb,) with kesr, (Mgh, Mṣb,) *syn. with* إِتْيَانٌ. (Mgh.) You say, غَشِىَ فُلَانًا *He came to such a one*; syn. أَتَاهُ; as also غَشَّاهُ, aor. يُغَشُوهُ. (Ḳ.) — [Hence,] غَشِيَهَا, (Ṣ, MA, Mṣb, Ḳ,) inf. n. غَشَيَانٌ or غِشْيَانٌ, (accord. to different copies of the Ṣ,) or the latter and غَشْىٌ, (MA,) or ▼ غِشْيَانٌ is the subst. in this case also, (Mṣb,) and *syn. with* إِتْيَانٌ, metonymically used in the sense of جِمَاعٌ, (Mgh, Mṣb,) ‡ *He compressed her*; (Ṣ, MA, Mṣb, Ḳ;) namely, a woman; (MA, Ḳ;) as also ▼ تغشّاها. (MA, Mṣb, TA.) — And غَشِىَ إِلَيْهِ مَحْجَرًا *He did to him* (أَتَى إِلَيْهِ) *a forbidden action*. (TA in art. حجر.) [Hence,] ▼ غِشْيَانُ المَحَارِمِ [*The doing of forbidden things*]. (Mgh and Mṣb and Ḳ in art. رهق.) And غَشِىَ الشَّىْءَ *He occupied himself with the thing, engaged in it*, or *personally managed* or *conducted it*; syn. لَابَسَهُ and بَاشَرَهُ. (JM.) [And ▼ تغشّى has a similar meaning; for it is said that] الغَشْىُ and التَّغَشِّى primarily signify الإِتْيَانُ and المُلَابَسَةُ: and they took an extended range in using the former, so that one said, ▼ تَغَشَّاهُمْ بِالْعَدْلِ or بِالْجَوْرِ [app. meaning *He ruled them with equity* or *with injustice*]. (Ḥam p. 27.) [And one says, يَغْشَى الحُرُوبَ (see Ḥam p. 27), meaning *He plunges into wars*, or *battles*: see مُغَامِسٌ, and its verb.] — One says also, غَشِيَهُ بِالسَّوْطِ, (Ḳ, in which it is said to be like رَضِيَهُ, and so accord. to some copies of the Ṣ, the phrase in these being غَشِيتُ الرَّجُلَ بِالسَّوْطِ,) or ▼ غَشَّاهُ بِهِ, (accord. to other copies of the Ṣ, the verb in these being written غَشَّيْتُ, and thus accord. to an explanation of قَنَّعَ رَأْسَهُ بِالسَّوْطِ in art. قنع in the Ḳ,) *He struck him* (i. e. a man, Ṣ) *with the whip*; *he flogged him*. (Ṣ, Ḳ.) ═ غُشِىَ عَلَيْهِ, (Ṣ, MA, Mgh, Mṣb, Ḳ,) inf. n. غَشْىٌ, (Ṣ, Mgh,* Ḳ,) or غُشْىٌ, (MA,) or both, (Mṣb,) and غَشَيَانٌ, (Ḳ, TA, and so in some copies of the Ṣ,) or غِشْيَانٌ, (so in other copies of the Ṣ,) and ▼ غَشْيَةٌ, (Ṣ, Mgh,) or this last is an inf. n. of un., (Mṣb,) or it is the subst., (Ḳ,) *He swooned*, i. e. *became senseless*: (MA, PṢ:) or *i. q.* أُغْمِىَ عَلَيْهِ [q. v.]: (Ḳ, TA:) or الغَشْىُ, or الغُشْىُ,

is *a state of inertness* (تَعَطُّل, Mgh, Mṣb) *of the motive and sensitive faculties,* (Mgh,) or *of the motive faculties and of the sensitive will,* (Mṣb,) *on account of the weakness of the heart,* (Mgh, Mṣb,) *and the soul's becoming drawn together thereto by a cause that suppresses it* (يُخْفِيهِ) *within so that it finds not a place of passage, and of the causes thereof is a strangling* [or *stifling*], or *hurtful, cold repletion,* or *vehement hunger,* (Mgh,) or *vehement pain,* (Mgh, Mṣb,) or *cold,* or *excessive hunger,* (Mṣb,) or *an evil affection in some associate, or participating, organ, such as the heart and the stomach:* (Mgh:) some say that it is *the same as* الإِغْمَآءُ [for which see its proper art.]; (Mgh, Mṣb;) thus say the scholastic theologians: (Mgh:) others (the physicians and the lawyers, Mgh) make a difference between these two terms. (Mgh, Mṣb.)

2. غَشَّيْتُ الشَّىْءَ, (Ṣ, Mṣb,) inf. n. تَغْشِيَةٌ, (Ṣ,) *I covered the thing; put a cover,* or *covering, upon it,* or *over it.* (Ṣ, Mṣb.) One says, غَشَّى ٱللّٰهُ عَلَى بَصَرِهِ, inf. n. as above; and ↓ اغشى; (Ḳ, TA;) i. e. *God put a covering upon,* or *over, his eyes.* (TA.) And hence, (TA,) it is said in the Ḳur [xxxvi. 8], فَأَغْشَيْنَاهُمْ فَهُمْ لَا يُبْصِرُونَ *And we have put a covering over them* [*so that they shall not see*]. (Ṣ, TA.) — [See a usage of the inf. n. voce شِيمٌ.] — غشّاهُ said of light: see 1, former half. — See also 4. — غشّاهُ بِالسَّوْطِ: see 1, latter half. — One says also, غَشَّيْتُهُ سَيْفًا, or سَوْطًا, [in my original غشيته, without any syll. sign, but app. as I have written, for I do not find any instance of غَشِىَ as doubly trans., meaning *I equipped him with a sword,* or *a whip,*] like the saying عَمَّمْتُهُ سَيْفًا, or كَسَوْتُهُ سَيْفًا. (TA.)

4. اغشاهُ إِيَّاهُ and ↓ غشّاهُ *He made it to cover it;* or *to be a cover,* or *covering, upon it,* or *over it.* (MA,* TḲ, and Bḍ* and Jel* in vii. 52, &c.) — And [hence,] both signify *He made it,* i. e. an event (أَمْر), *to come upon,* [or *invade, so as to surprise,* or *so as to overwhelm,* properly meaning] *as a thing that covered, him,* or *it.* (Ḳ,* TA.) Both of these verbs are used in this sense in the Ḳur-án accord. to different readings in vii. 52 and xiii. 3, and likewise (as mentioned in the first paragraph of this art., q. v.,) in viii. 11. (TA.) — Also, the former, *He made him,* or *it, to come to him.* (Ṣ, MA, TA.) — See also 2, in two places. — [Hence,] اغشى اللَّيْلُ: see 1, former half.

5: see 10: — and see also 1, first and third sentences: — and again, near the middle, in three places.

10. استغشى ثَوْبَهُ, (T, Ḳ, [agreeably with phrases in the Ḳur xi. 6 and lxxi. 6,]) and (Ḳ) بِثَوْبِهِ, (Ṣ, Ḳ,) and ↓ تغشّى بِهِ, (Ṣ) [see an ex. of the latter verb in a verse of El-Khansà cited in the first paragraph of art. وعى, where it is trans. without a preposition,] *He covered himself with his garment* (Ṣ, Ḳ) *in order that he might not see nor hear:* (Ḳ: [in the CḲ, يُسْمَعَ and يُرَى are put for يَسْمَعَ and يَرَى:]) accord. to Er-Rághib, اِسْتَغْشَوْا ثِيَابَهُمْ means *they put their garments as a covering over their ears;* and is a phrase denoting the refusing to hearken; or, as some say, an allusion to running, like the phrase شَمَّرَ ذَيْلًا, and أَلْقَى ثَوْبَهُ. (TA.)

غَشًا The *whiteness of the head* [or *face*] of a horse and of other animals, *denoted by the epithet* أَغْشَى [q. v.]. (Ṣ.)

غَشْوٌ The نَبِق [generally meaning the *fruit of the lote-tree called* سِدْر; but sometimes the *tree thus called* itself]: (Ḳ:) accord. to the M, [the n. un.] غَشْوَةٌ signifies *a* سِدْرَة. (TA.)

غَشْوَةٌ and غُشْوَةٌ and غِشْوَةٌ: see غِشَاوَةٌ.

غَشْيَةٌ an inf. n. of the verb in the phrase غُشِىَ عَلَيْهِ, (Ṣ, Mgh,) or the subst. thereof, (Ḳ,) or the inf. n. un. thereof [signifying *A swoon*]. (Mṣb.) See 1, last sentence. — غَشْيَةُ المَوْتِ is *The clouding* (lit. *covering*) *of the understanding that befalls a man on the occasion of death.* (TA.) — And غَشْيَةُ حُمًّى signifies *A touch,* or *slight attack, of fever.* (TA.)

غُشْيَةٌ: see غِشَاوَةٌ.

غُشْيَانٌ: see 1, near the middle, in three places.

غِشَآءٌ *A cover,* or *covering;* syn. غِطَآءٌ: (Ṣ, Mṣb:) or it differs from the غطاء in being *of clothing* or *the like:* (TA in art. غطو:) and ↓ غِشَاوَةٌ [q. v.] signifies the same: (Mṣb:) [the pl. of the former is أَغْشِيَةٌ and أَغْشَآءٌ; the former regular; and the latter, (which occurs in this art. in the TA in an explanation of غَوَاشٍ, pl. of غَاشِيَةٌ,) like آدَامٌ as pl. of إِدَامٌ.] The غشآء of the heart is The *cover,* or *covering,* thereof; (Ḳ, TA;) the قَمِيص thereof, likewise mentioned in the Ḳ as being called the ↓ غَاشِيَة; *a covering of skin,* [i. e. the *pericardium,*] *the removal of which therefrom causes death;* and also called the ↓ غِشَاوَة, this being expl. as meaning the *skin* of the heart: (TA:) and so of the horse's saddle; (Ḳ, TA;) which is *a covering of skin* or *other material:* (TA:) [see also غَاشِيَةٌ:] and so of the sword; (Ḳ, TA;) which is its غِلَاف [a term applied to its *scabbard,* and also to *a case,* or *covering, enclosing the scabbard,* or *enclosing the scabbard with its appertenances*]: (TA:) and so of other things. (Ḳ.)

غِشَاوَةٌ (Ṣ, ISd, Ḳ) and غَشَاوَةٌ and غُشَاوَةٌ (ISd, Ḳ) and ↓ غِشْوَةٌ and غَشْوَةٌ and غُشْوَةٌ (Ṣ, Ḳ) and غِشَايَةٌ and ↓ غُشَايَةٌ and ↓ غُشْيَةٌ and ↓ غَاشِيَةٌ (Ḳ) signify *A covering* upon the eyes (Ṣ, Ḳ) and upon the heart: (Ḳ:) you say, عَلَى بَصَرِهِ غِشَاوَةٌ &c. [*Upon his eyes is a covering,* or *film,* app. used only in a tropical sense], (Ṣ, Ḳ,) and عَلَى قَلْبِهِ [*upon his heart*]: (Ḳ:) thus the first of these words signifies, in relation to the eyes, in the Ḳur [ii. 6 and] xlv. 22: in relation to the heart, Az says that it is *a* [*sort of*] *covering of rust* (رَيْن) طَبَع [also termed رَيْن]). (TA.) See also غِشَآءٌ, in two places.

غَشَايَةٌ and غُشَايَةٌ: see the next preceding paragraph.

غَاشِيَةٌ: see غِشَآءٌ and غِشَاوَةٌ. غَوَاشٍ is its pl.: (TA:) occurring in the Ḳur vii. 39, meaning أَغْطِيَة, (Ḳ, TA,) i. e. أَغْشَآءٌ [or *Coverings,* a pl. of غِشَآءٌ]. (TA.) — It is also [The *covering,* like غِشَآءٌ, q. v.], of the horse's saddle. (Ṣ.) — And, (Ṣ,) of the [camel's saddle called] رَحْل, (Ḳ,) it is The *iron that is above the* مُؤْخِرَة or [*hinder part*], (Ṣ, Ḳ, TA,) *also called the* دَامِغَة [q. v.]. (Az, TA.) — Also The *skin with which the* جَفْن [or *scabbard*] *of a sword is covered, from the lower part of its* شَارِب [q. v.] *to its* نَعْل [or *shoe of iron,* or *silver, at the lower end of the scabbard*]: or the *covering that is put upon the hilts, consisting of* [*the skins called*] أَسْفَان [pl. of سَفَن, q. v.]: (Ḳ: [for أَسْفَان, which is the reading in the M, some copies of the Ḳ have أَسْفَار:]) or the *first part,* of the sword, *of what is next to thee* [*when holding the hilt*]: and sometimes it signifies its غِمْد [or *scabbard*], also. (Ḥar. p. 22.) — الغَاشِيَةُ (in the Ḳur lxxxviii. 1, TA) means *The resurrection;* (Ṣ, Ḳ, TA;) because it will overwhelm (↓ تَغْشَى) with its terrors; (Ṣ, TA;) or because it will come upon mankind as a thing covering them, (↓ تَغْشَى الخَلْقَ,) so as to include them universally: (TA:) and, (Ḳ, TA,) some say, (TA,) *the fire* [*of Hell*]; (Ḳ, TA;) because it will cover, or overspread, (↓ تَغْشَى,) the faces of the unbelievers. (TA.) [In like manner also,] غَاشِيَةٌ مِنَ العَذَابِ means *Punishment that is general,* or *universal, in its extent.* (TA.) — And غَاشِيَةٌ signifies also *A calamity,* or *misfortune.* (TA.) — And *A certain disease that attacks in the* جَوْف [i. e. *belly,* or *chest*]. (Aṣ, Ṣ, Ḳ.) One says, رَمَاهُ ٱللّٰهُ بِغَاشِيَةٍ [*May God smite him,* or *afflict him, with a* غَاشِيَة]. (Aṣ, Ṣ.) — Also *Petitioners that come to one* (Ḳ, TA) *seeking,* or *demanding,* or *asking, gifts:* (TA:) and *visiters, and friends, that come to one time after time;* (Ḳ, TA;) and *that resort to one:* (TA:) a man's *resorters;* such as *guests;* and *hangers-on,* or *seekers of favours; servants* [or *dependants*]; and *others.* (Ḥar pp. 95 and 467.)

أَغْشَى, applied to a horse, (Ṣ, Ḳ,) and to other than a horse, (Ṣ,) *Whose whole head, as distinct from his body, is white;* like أَرْخَمُ: (Ṣ:) or *whose face is covered by whiteness:* (Ḳ:) or *having a blaze covering his face, and wide:* (M, TA:) fem. غَشْوَآءُ, applied to a goat. (Ṣ, Ḳ.)

مَغْشِىٌّ عَلَيْهِ *Swooning;* i. e. *senseless;* (MA, PṢ;) *having the affection denoted by the phrase* غُشِىَ عَلَيْهِ [q. v.]. (Ṣ, MA, Mgh, Mṣb, Ḳ.)

غص

1. غَصَّ, (Mṣb, MF,) sec. pers. غَصِصْتَ, (Ṣ, Mṣb, Ḳ,) and غَصَصْتَ, (Mṣb, Ḳ,) the latter extr.,

(TA, [see 1 in art. عض,]) aor. يَغَصُّ, (Ṣ, Mṣb, Ḳ,) when the sec. pers. of the pret. is غَصِصْتَ, (Mṣb,) and يَغُصُّ, (Mṣb, TA,) when the sec. pers. of the pret. is of the other form mentioned above, (Mṣb,) inf. n. غَصَصٌ, (Ṣ, Ḳ,) or غَصٌّ, (Mṣb,) or the former when the aor. is يَغَصُّ, and the latter when the aor. is يَغُصُّ, (TA,) *His throat*, or *fauces, became choked*, or *obstructed*, (Ṣ, Ḳ, MF,) by food: (Ṣ, Mṣb, MF:) [as also, app., ▼ اِغْتَصَّ:] accord. to some of those skilled in the science of lexicology, you say غَصَّ when it is by food, and شَرِقَ when it is by beverage, [or by the spittle, and water, and the like, (see art. شرق,)] and شَجِىَ when it is by a bone, and جَرِضَ when it is with spittle; but every one of these is sometimes used in the place of any other: (MF:) and [thus] you say also, غَصَّ بِالْمَآءِ, meaning, *his throat*, or *fauces, became choked*, or *obstructed, by the water*; or *the water stopped therein, and he was hardly able to swallow it.* (TA.) — [Hence,] غَصَّ بِرِيقِهِ [lit., *His throat*, or *fauces, became choked by his spittle*;] meaning, ‡ *he died.* (TA.) — Hence, also, غَصَّ بِالْغَيْظِ ‡ [*He was*, or *became, choked with wrath*, or *rage*]. (Mṣb.) — [And غَصَّ, alone, seems to signify † *He became grieved*, or *disquieted in mind*; like as does شَجِىَ (q. v.): and it seems to be indicated in the CḲ that ▼ اغتصّ signifies the same: see غُصَّةٌ.] — [Hence also,] غَصَّتْ بِنَا الْأَرْضُ † *The land became straitened* [*as though it were choked*] *by us.* (TA.) And غَصَّ الْمَجْلِسُ بِأَهْلِهِ † [*The sitting-place became straitened*, or *choked*, or *choked up, by its people*]; as also ▼ اغتصّ. (TA.)

4. اغصّهُ, (Ṣ, Mṣb, TA,) inf. n. إِغْصَاصٌ, (TA,) *He* (a man, Ṣ, Mṣb) *caused his throat*, or *fauces, to be choked*, or *obstructed*, (Ṣ,) by food; (Mṣb;) syn. أَشْجَاهُ [which has the above-mentioned meaning and also another to be found below]. (TA.) [And *It* (food &c.) *choked him.*] — Hence, اغصّهُ بِالْغَيْظِ ‡ [*He* (a man) *caused him to become choked with wrath*, or *rage*]. (Mṣb.) — [Hence also,] اغصّهُ بِرِيقِهِ [lit., *He caused his throat*, or *fauces, to become choked by his spittle*;] meaning, † *He caused him to become grieved*, or *disquieted in mind*; (A, TA;) [like أَشْجَاهُ: and it seems to be indicated in the CḲ that اغصّهُ without any addition signifies the same: see غُصَّةٌ.] — [Hence also,] اغصّ عَلَيْنَا الْأَرْضَ † *He made strait to us the land.* (Ḳ, TA.)

8: see 1, in three places.

غُصَّةٌ *A thing lying across in the throat*, or *fauces, so as to cause a choking*, or *an obstruction, thereof*; (IDrd, A,* Ḳ;) *a thing by which one has his throat*, or *fauces, choked*, or *obstructed*; (TA;) *food by which one has his throat*, or *fauces, choked*, or *obstructed*; (Mṣb;) i. q. شَجًا; (Ṣ, Ḳ;) [which has another meaning that will be found below; and both these meanings may be intended by it in the Ṣ; but in the Ḳ, the latter only seems to be intended; for there, between it and the explanation which is here first given, we find intervening the pl., and also, in the CḲ, the words وقد أَغْصَصْتُهُ فاغْتَصَّ;] *a thing by which one is choked* (شَجًا يُغَصُّ بِهِ, Lth, JK, TA) *in the* حَرْقَدَة [meaning the *head of the windpipe*], (Lth, TA,) or *in the throat*, or *fauces*: (JK:) pl. غُصَصٌ. (Ṣ, Mṣb, Ḳ.) It is said in the Ḳur [lxxiii. 13], وَطَعَامًا ذَا غُصَّةٍ (TA) *And food that sticks fast*, (Bḍ,) or *by which one is choked*, (Jel,) *in the throat*, or *fauces.* (Bḍ, Jel.) — And hence, ‡ *Choking wrath* or *rage.* (Mṣb.) — [And † *Grief*, or *disquietude of mind*; a signification often occurring; and app. intended by the explanation شَجًا in the Ḳ. See what is said on this point above.] — Hence also, غُصَصُ الْمَوْتِ [*The chokings*, or *strangulations, of death*: *the death-rattles*: or † *the agonies of death*]. (TA.)

غَصَّانُ: see what next follows.

غَاصٌّ A man *having his throat*, or *fauces, choked*, or *obstructed*, (Ṣ, Mṣb,* Ḳ,) by food; (Ṣ, Mṣb;) as also ▼ غَصَّانُ. (Ṣ [in two copies of which it is written غُصَّانٌ], Ḳ [in two copies of which it is written غَصَّانٌ], Mṣb [in my copy of which, as well as in the TA, it is without any final syll. sign].) — And [hence,] غَاصٌّ بِالْقَوْمِ † An abode, or a place of alighting, *filled* [*and as it were choked up*] *with the company of men*; (Ṣ, A, Ḳ;) and in like manner a mosque; as also ▼ مُغْتَصٌّ. (A.)

مُغْتَصٌّ: see what next precedes.

غصب

1. غَصَبَهُ, (Ṣ, A, Mṣb, Ḳ,) aor. ـِ, (Mṣb, Ḳ,) inf. n. غَصْبٌ; (Ṣ, Mgh, Mṣb;) and ▼ اغتصبهُ; (Ṣ, Mṣb, Ḳ;) *He took it wrongfully, unjustly*, or *injuriously*; (Ṣ, A, Mgh, Ḳ;) or *by force*; (Mgh, Mṣb;) and عَلَيْهِ and مِنْهُ [i. e. *from him*], both meaning the same. (Ṣ.) الغَصْبُ repeatedly occurs in the traditions, signifying *The taking another's property wrongfully, unjustly, injuriously*, or *by violence.* (L.) But as employed in law, it means *The taking property that has a price and is forbidden, without the permission of its owner, without stealthiness*: therefore it does not rightly apply in the case of an animal that has died a natural death or not been slaughtered according to the law, because it is not property; nor in the case of the free person, in like manner; nor in the case of the wine of the Muslim, because it has not a price; nor in the case of the property of him with whom one is at war, because it is not forbidden; the saying "without the permission of the owner" precludes the trust, or deposit; and the saying "without stealthiness" excludes theft. (KT.) — One says also, غَصَبْتُهُ مَالًا and غَصَبْتُ مِنْهُ مَالًا *I took property from him* [*wrongfully*, &c., or] *by force.* (Mṣb.) — And غَصَبَهَا نَفْسَهَا (Mṣb, TA) and ▼ اغتصبها نفسها (Mṣb) ‡ *He violated her*; *forced her*; *had connection with her against her will*; (TA;) or *constuprated her by force.* (Mṣb.) — And غَصَبَ فُلَانًا عَلَى الشَّىْءِ (Ḳ, TA) and ▼ اغتصبه (TA) *He compelled such a one by force to do the thing.* (Ḳ, TA.) — And غَصَبَ الجِلْدَ, (Ḳ, TA,) inf. n. as above, (TA,) † *He removed from the skin its hair and its fur by plucking and peeling, without subjecting it to the process termed* عَطْنٌ, *in the tan, and without* إِغْمَال [i. e. *burying it*] *in moist earth*, (Ḳ, TA,) or [*soaking it in*] *urine* [*to loosen the hair and fur*], *and without folding it up*: so Az heard it expl. by the Arabs. (TA.)

[3. غاصبهُ إِيَّاهُ, accord. to Freytag, signifies *He took it from him by violence*: but for this he has not named any authority.]

8: see 1, in three places. — One says also, of a woman, أُغْتُصِبَتْ نَفْسَهَا, meaning ‡ *She was constuprated by force*; (A, Mgh, Mṣb;) as also أُغْتُصِبَتْ عَلَى نَفْسِهَا. (Mṣb.)

غَصْبٌ and ▼ مَغْصُوبٌ A thing *taken wrongfully, unjustly, injuriously*, (Ṣ, Mgh,) or *by force*: (Mgh, Mṣb:) the former originally an inf. n. (Mṣb.)

غَاصِبٌ One *taking*, or *who takes*, a thing *wrongfully, unjustly, injuriously*, (TA,) or *by force*: pl. غُصَّابٌ. (Mṣb.)

مَغْصُوبٌ: see غَصْبٌ. — مَغْصُوبٌ لَهُ and مِنْهُ A man *from whom a thing has been taken* [*wrongfully, unjustly, injuriously*, or] *by force.* (Mṣb.)

غصن

1. غَصَنَهُ, aor. ـِ, (Ḳ, TA,) inf. n. غَصْنٌ, (TA,) *He drew it to him*, or *towards him*; namely, a غُصْن [or branch]: (Ḳ, TA:) from El-Ḳanánee. (TA.) — And *He took it*; namely, a thing: (Ḳ, TA:) or *he cut it off*: (Ṣ, Ḳ:) or it signifies also *he cut it off*, namely, a غُصْن, *and took it.* (TA.) — And غَصَنَ فُلَانًا عَنْ حَاجَتِهِ, (Ḳ, TA,) aor. ـِ and ـُ, (TA,) *He turned*, or *turned away, and withheld, such a one from the object of his want*: (Ḳ, TA:) Az says that it was thus read to him by El-Mundhiree in the "Nawádir" of IAạr; but that, accord. to Sh, it is [غَضَنَ, i. e.] with ض; and this is correct: (TA:) the former is a mistake. (TA in art. غضن.)

2: see the next paragraph.

4. اغصن الشَّجَرُ, (A in art. فرش,) inf. n. إِغْصَانٌ, *The trees put forth branches.* (KL.) — And اغصن, and ▼ غصّن, said of a bunch of grapes (عُنْقُود), *It was*, or *became, large* (كَبُرَ, thus in some of the copies of the Ḳ, in other copies كَثُرَ, but the former is the right, TA) *in its berries*: (Ḳ:) or *somewhat large therein.* (TA.)

غُصْنٌ *A branch from the stem* [or *from another branch*] *of a tree*; *of the slender thereof* as well as *of the thick*: (Ḳ:) [sometimes signifying *a twig*, or *shoot*:] pl. [of pauc.] أَغْصَانٌ and [of mult.] غُصُونٌ and غِصَنَةٌ. (Ṣ, Ḳ.)

غُصْنَةٌ [*A branchlet*; and *a small twig* or *shoot*;] *a small* غُصْن. (Ḳ.)

أَغْصَنُ A bull *having a whiteness in his tail.* (Ḳ.)

غض

1. غَضَّ طَرْفَهُ, (Ṣ, A, Mṣb, Ḳ,) aor. يَغُضُّ, (Mṣb,* TA,) [and يَغْضُضُ may be used, in the dial. of El-Ḥijáz, instead of its contracted form يَغُضُّ,] imp. غُضَّ, (Ṣ, A,) in the dial. of Nejd, (Ṣ,) and اُغْضُضْ, in the dial. of El-Ḥijáz, (Ṣ,) inf. n. غَضٌّ (Mṣb, Ḳ) and غِضَاضٌ, with kesr, (A, Ḳ,) and غَضَاضٌ and غَضَاضَةٌ, with fet-ḥ, (Ḳ,) *He lowered his eye,* or *eyes;* (Ṣ, A, Mṣb, Ḳ;) as also غَضَّ مِنْ طَرْفِهِ; (Mṣb;) [the من being redundant, accord. to some; but see what is said on this point below:] and *he contracted his eye,* or *eyes;* syn. كَسَرَهُ; [*so as to wrinkle the lids;*] or *he blinked;* i. e. *he contracted his eyelids,* or *drew them near together, and looked:* [this signification is very common:] and *he contracted* (كَسَرَ) *his eye,* or *eyes, and looked towards the ground, not opening his eye* [or *eyes*]: and sometimes it indicates a state of abasement. (TA.) Also غَضَّ alone, inf. n. غَضَاضَةٌ, *He contracted his eyelids;* like أَغْضَى: *he looked languishingly.* (TA.) It is said in the Ḳur [xxiv. 30], قُلْ لِلْمُؤْمِنِينَ يَغُضُّوا مِنْ أَبْصَارِهِمْ, in which some of the grammarians hold من to be redundant; but the meaning is obvious, i. e. [*Say thou to the believers*] *that they shall abridge their look,* or *view,* from what is prohibited to them: (Ṣgh:) or *that they shall restrain somewhat of their look,* or *view.* (TA.) — [And hence,] † *He bore with forgiveness and silence what was disagreeable,* or *hateful,* or *evil.* (Ṣ, A, Ḳ.) — غَضَّ صَوْتَهُ, (Mṣb,) or مِنْ صَوْتِهِ, (Ṣ, TA,) or both, (Mṣb,) in like manner signifies *He lowered his voice.* (Ṣ, Mṣb.) It is said in the Ḳur [xxxi. 18], وَٱغْضُضْ مِنْ صَوْتِكَ, (Ṣ, A,) i. e. *And lower thy voice:* or *diminish the loudness of thy voice.* (TA.) — غَضَّ مِنْ لِجَامِ فَرَسِهِ *He lowered the rein of his horse, in order to lessen his sharpness of temper.* (A, TA.*) — غَضَّ مِنْهُ, (Ṣ, Mṣb, Ḳ,) aor. يَغُضُّ, (Ṣ, TA,) inf. n. غَضٌّ (Mṣb, TA) and غَضَاضَةٌ, (Mṣb,) *He lowered and lessened his estimation, dignity,* or *rank:* (Ṣ, Ḳ, TA:) or *he detracted from his reputation;* or *attributed* or *imputed to him, charged him with,* or *accused him of, a vice, fault,* or *the like:* (Mṣb:) and, inf. n. غَضَاضَةٌ, *he disdained it,* or *scorned it;* as also ▾ اغتضّ منه. ('Alee Ibn-Ḥamzeh, TA.) — Also غَضَّهُ, (Ḳ,) aor. as above, inf. n. غَضٌّ, (TA,) *He lessened it, diminished it,* or *made it defective* or *deficient;* (Ḳ, TA;) and so ▾ غَضْغَضَهُ, (Ḳ,) inf. n. غَضْغَضَةٌ. (TA.) You say غَضَضْتُ السِّقَآءَ *I lessened, diminished,* or *made defective* or *deficient,* [*the contents of*] *the skin.* (Mṣb.) And ▾ غَضْغَضْتُ المَآءَ *I lessened,* &c., *the water.* (Ṣ.) And ▾ فُلَانٌ بَحْرٌ لَا يُغَضْغَضُ *Such a one is a sea,* or *great river, that will not be lessened,* &c.: (Ṣ:) or *that will not become exhausted.* (Ḥar p. 418.) [See also R. Q. 1 below, and R. Q. 2.] And [you make the former verb doubly trans., saying,] مَا غَضَضْتُكَ شَيْئًا *I have not abridged thee, deprived thee,* or *defrauded thee, of anything.* (TA.) And لَا أَغُضُّكَ دِرْهَمًا *I will not abridge thee, deprive thee,* or *defraud thee, of a dirhem.* (TA.) You also say, غَضَّ مِنَ الشَّعَرِ *He shortened the hair.* (M in art. قصر.) And [in like manner] one says, غَضَّ مِنْ رَأْسِهِ, i. q. طَمَرَ رَأْسَهُ. (Ḳ voce طمر, q. v.) — Also *He broke it* (i. e. a branch, or stick, or the like,) *but did not break it thoroughly;* (L, Ḳ, TA;) and so ▾ غَضْغَضَهُ. (L, TA.) — And غَضَضْتُهُ also signifies *I withheld, restrained,* or *prevented, it;* whatever it were. (Ṣ.) [Hence the phrase in the Ḳur xxiv. 30, accord. to an explanation given above.] You say غَضَّ العَذْلَ, or المَلَامَةَ, aor. as above, inf. n. غَضٌّ, *He withheld blame.* (Lth.) And you say to a rider, in asking him to stop a little where you are, غُضَّ سَاعَةً, (TA,) and أُغْضُضْ لِى سَاعَةً, (A, TA,) i. e. *Restrain for me thy beast, and stop,* or *pause, where I am, a while.* (A, TA.) ═ غَضَّ, [first pers. غَضِضْتُ,] aor. يَغَضُّ, (Mṣb;) or the first pers. is غَضُضْتُ and غَضَضْتُ, (Ṣ, Ḳ,) and the aor. of each is يَغَضُّ; (Ḳ;) or, accord. to the T, some say غَضِضْتَ, aor. تَغَضُّ, and some say غَضَضْتَ, aor. تَغِضُّ; (IB, TA;) but the latter of these requires consideration; (TA;) inf. n. غُضُوضَةٌ (IAạr, Ṣ, Ḳ) and غَضَاضَةٌ; (Ṣ, Ḳ;) or the former only, accord. to 'Alee Ibn-Ḥamzeh; but the saying بَضَاضَةٌ and بُضُوضَةٌ, to denote the quality of that which is termed بَضٌّ, strengthens what J says [in the Ṣ] with respect to غَضَاضَةٌ; (IB;) *It* (a thing) *was,* or *became, fresh, juicy, sappy, moist, not flaccid:* (Ṣ, Mṣb:) or *flourishing and fresh;* or *luxuriant:* (IAạr:) or *beautiful and bright:* (Ḳ:) and غَضُضْتِ, aor. تَغَضُّ and تَغِضُّ, inf. n. غَضَاضَةٌ and غُضُوضَةٌ, said of a woman, ‡ *she was,* or *became, fine-skinned,* or *thin-skinned, so that the blood appeared* [*through the skin*]. (Lḥ, TA.)

2. غضّض: see 1, latter half. ═ Also, inf. n. تَغْضِيضٌ, *He ate what is termed* غَضّ, (Ḳ, TA,) i. e. *the* طَلْع [or *spadix of a palm-tree*]: (TA:) or *he became thin-skinned, and plump, and soft,* or *tender:* (O, Ḳ:) or *he became affected with languor and abasement;* (Ḳ, TA;) or, as in the Tekmileh, *with softness,* or *tenderness.* (TA.)

7. انغضّ الطَّرْفُ i. q. انْغَمَضَ: (Ṣ, TA:) [or the former more probably signifies *The eye,* or *eyes, became contracted:* and the latter, *the eye,* or *eyes, became closed.*]

8: see 1, near the middle.

R. Q. 1. غَضْغَضَهُ, inf. n. غَضْغَضَةٌ: see 1, near the middle, in three places. ═ غَضْغَضَ [inf. n. as above] is also intrans. (TA.) See R. Q. 2. — It likewise signifies *It* (for instance a sea, or a large river, TA) *became scanty,* or *little in quantity, and sank into the earth,* or *disappeared in the earth;* or *became scanty,* or *little in quantity;* or *decreased:* (Ḳ, TA:) or *went away.* (TA.) In the TṢ, the inf. n. is expl. by غَيْظ, which is an abominable mistake for غَيْض. (TA.) — And غَضْغَضَةٌ also signifies A man's *speaking indistinctly.* (TA.) — And The *boiling* of a cooking-pot. (IḲṭṭ, TA.)

R. Q. 2. تَغَضْغَضَ *It* (water, and a sea, or great river, Ṣ) *decreased, diminished, lessened,* or *became defective,* or *deficient;* (Ṣ, Ḳ;) as also ▾ غَضْغَضَ, (TA,) inf. n. غَضْغَضَةٌ. (Mṣb.) You say, مَاتَ فُلَانٌ بِبِطْنَتِهِ لَمْ يَتَغَضْغَضْ مِنْهَا شَىْءٌ *Such a one died with his property abundant,* (Ṣ,) or *complete; nothing thereof having been given away by him;* a prov. relating to the death of the niggard. (A'Obeyd.) And 'Amr Ibn-El-'Áṣ said, alluding to the death of Ibn-'Owf, خَرَجْتَ مِنَ الدُّنْيَا بِبِطْنَتِكَ وَلَمْ تَتَغَضْغَضْ مِنْهَا شَيْئًا, meaning *Thou hast died with thy religion unimpaired:* (A'Obeyd:) i. e. he had not been occupied with any office of authority or administration whereby his recompense might be diminished. (Az.) You say also مَطَرٌ لَا يَتَغَضْغَضُ *Rain that will not cease.* (TA.)

غَضٌّ *Fresh; juicy; sappy; moist; not flaccid;* (Ṣ, Mṣb, Ḳ;) applied to a thing, (Ṣ, Mṣb,) whatever it be; (TA;) as also ▾ غَضِيضٌ. (Ṣ, Ḳ.) Hence the trad. مَنْ سَرَّهُ أَنْ يَقْرَأَ القُرْآنَ غَضًّا كَمَا نَزَلَ فَلْيَقْرَأْ قِرَاءَةَ ٱبْنِ أُمِّ عَبْدٍ [*He who is rejoiced,* or *pleased, to read the Ḳur-án freshly, like as it descended, let him read according to the reading of Ibn-Umm-'Abd*]. (TA.) — A calf *recently born:* pl. غِضَاضٌ. (Ḳ.) — Anything (Ṣ) *beautiful and bright;* (Ṣ, Ḳ;) as † youth, and the like: (Ṣ:) or غَضٌّ applied to youth, and غَضَّةٌ applied to a woman, ‡ i. q. بَضٌّ and بَضَّةٌ [*thin-skinned,* or *fine-skinned, and plump;* &c.]: (A:) or the latter, applied to a woman, ‡ *thin-skinned,* or *fine-skinned, so that the blood appears* [*through the skin*]: (Lḥ:) and ▾ غَضِيضَةٌ also is thus applied like غَضَّةٌ. (TA.) You say also, شَىْءٌ بَضٌّ غَضٌّ, and ▾ بَاضٌّ غَاضٌّ *A thing fresh,* &c., *and beautiful and bright;* [*in a flourishing condition;*] *not changed,* or *altered* [*for the worse*]. (TA.) And نَبْتٌ غَضٌّ *A* [*fresh and flourishing and*] *tender plant.* (TA.) And ظِلٌّ غَضٌّ † *Shade which the sun has not reached;* like a plant which the sun has not reached. (TA.) — The *spadix of a palm-tree;* syn. طَلْع; as also ▾ غَضِيضٌ: (IAạr:) or both signify *a tender* طَلْع: (Ḳ:) or *a tender* طَلْع *when it appears:* (TA:) or the latter, *a* طَلْع *when it appears:* (Aṣ, Ṣ:) or the same, *fruit when it first comes forth.* (TA.)

غُضَّةٌ: see غَضَاضَةٌ. ═ Also *A sufficiency of the means of subsistence;* like غُبَّةٌ. (TA in art. غب.)

غَضِيضٌ, applied to an eye, or eyes, (طَرْف,) *Lowered:* (A, TA:) *contracted:* *having the lids contracted,* or *drawn near together, and so looking:* *contracted, and looking towards the ground:* (TA:) *languishing:* (Ḳ, TA:) and so ▾ مَغْضُوضٌ, in all these senses: (TA:) and the former, so applied, [and app. the latter also,] *having the eyelids relaxed*, or *flaccid*. (TA.) You say, ظَبْىٌ غَضِيضُ الطَّرْفِ *A gazelle having languishing eyes.* (Ṣ.) And إِنَّكَ لَغَضِيضُ الطَّرْفِ نَقِىُّ الطَّرْفِ, meaning † [*Verily*] *thou art faithful, not treacherous*; by الطَّرْفِ being meant وِعَاؤُهُ. (TA.) — [*Lowered and lessened in estimation, dignity*, or *rank*: (see غَضَّ مِنْهُ:)] *defective* or *deficient* [*in good qualities*]; (Ḳ;) and, in consequence thereof, (TA,) *low, mean*, or *vile*: (A, Ḳ:) pl. أَغِضَّةٌ (Ḳ) and أَغِضَّآءُ. (TA.) — *Lessened*; *diminished*; *made defective* or *deficient*. (TA.) — See also غَضٌّ, in three places.

غَضَاضَةٌ, [an inf. n., of which the verb is not mentioned in senses agreeing with those here following,] (Ṣ, A, Ḳ,) and ▼ غَضِيضَةٌ and ▼ مَغَضَّةٌ (IAạr, Ḳ) and ▼ غُضَّةٌ, (Ibn-'Abbád, Ḳ,) *A defect, an imperfection, a fault, a vice*, or *the like*: and *lowness, meanness*, or *vileness*: (Ṣ, A, Mgh, Ḳ:) and the first, [or all,] *languor*, or *want of power*. (TA.) You say, لَيْسَ عَلَيْكَ فِى هٰذَا الأَمْرِ غَضَاضَةٌ *There is not*, or *will not be, charged against thee, in*, or *with respect to, this affair, lowness*, &c.; or *any defect*, &c.; (Ṣ, TA;) or *languor*, or *want of power*. (TA.) And مَا أَرَدْتُ بِذٰلِكَ غَضِيضَةَ ▼ فُلَانٍ, and ▼ مَغَضَّتَهُ, *I desired not*, or *meant not, thereby, to attribute any defect, imperfection, fault, vice*, or *the like, to such a one.* (IAạr.)

غَضِيضَةٌ: see غَضَاضَةٌ, in two places.

غَاضٌّ: see غَضٌّ.

مَغَضَّةٌ: see غَضَاضَةٌ, in two places.

مَغْضُوضٌ: see غَضِيضٌ.

غضب

1. غَضِبَ عَلَيْهِ, (Ṣ, Mṣb, Ḳ,) [aor. ـَ,] inf. n. غَضَبٌ (Ṣ, Mṣb, Ḳ*) and مَغْضَبَةٌ, (Ṣ, Ḳ,*) *He was angry with him*; (MA, Ḳ,* PṢ, &c.;) and ▼ تغضّب signifies the same. (Mṣb.) [See الغَضَبُ عليه below.] And غَضِبَ مِنْ لَا شَىْءٍ i. e. [*He was angry*] *for nothing*; meaning, *for no cause*. (Mṣb. [لا شىء, in a case of this kind, is regarded as one word, and is therefore as above, not لَا شَىْءَ: see p. 1626, third col.]) — غَضِبَ لَهُ (meaning *He was angry* with another person *for his sake*, or *on his account*, TA) is said when the person [on whose account the anger is excited] is living: and غَضِبَ بِهِ, when he is dead: (Ṣ, A, Mṣb, Ḳ:) so says El-Umawee, and El-Aḥmar says the like. (Ṣ.) — [And you say, غَضِبَ فِى ٱللّٰهِ *He was angry for the sake of God.*] — And غَضِبَتِ الفَرَسُ عَلَى ٱللِّجَامِ ‡ *The mare champed upon the bit.* (TA.) Abu-n-Nejm says,

تَغْضَبُ أَحْيَانًا عَلَى ٱللِّجَامِ
كَغَضَبِ النَّارِ عَلَى الضِّرَامِ

‡ [*She champs, sometimes, upon the bit, like the fierce burning of the fire upon the quickly-kindling fragments of firewood*]. (A, TA.) [See also 5, last sentence.] — غُضِبَ, like عُنِىَ [pass. in form]; and غَضَبَ; (Ḳ, TA;) the former of which is the more usual; (TA;) *He had the disease termed* غُضَاب [q. v.]. (Ḳ, TA.) — And غضبت عَيْنُهُ, with fet-ḥ and kesr [i. e., app., غَضِبَتْ; or "with fet-ḥ and kesr" may be a mistranscription for "with ḍamm and kesr," so that the verb may be غُضِبَتْ; *His eye had in it what are termed* غُضَاب]. (TA.)

3. غَاضَبْتُهُ *I made him angry, he also making me angry.* (Ḳ.) — And *I broke off from him*, or *quitted him, in anger*, or *enmity*. (Ṣ, Ḳ.) ذَهَبَ مُغَاضِبًا, in the Ḳur [xxi. 87], means *He went away, breaking off* from his people, or *quitting* them, *in anger*, or *enmity*. (Ṣ.)

4. اغضبهُ *He angered him*, or *made him angry*. (Ṣ,* Mṣb,* Ḳ.)

5. تغضّب *He became angered* or *angry*: (Ṣ:) or *he was angry somewhat after* [*having been so*] *somewhat*. (Ḥam p. 522.) See also 1, first sentence. — And تَغَضَّبَتِ القِدْرُ ‡ *The cooking-pot boiled fiercely* عَلَى ٱللَّحْمِ [*upon the flesh-meat*]. (TA.)

غَضْبٌ (Ṣ, Ḳ) Red (Ṣ) *intense in redness*: (Ṣ, Ḳ:) you say أَحْمَرُ غَضْبٌ: so says ISk: (Ṣ:) or غَضْبٌ signifies أَحْمَرُ غَلِيظٌ (Ḳ) i. e. *red that is dense*, or *deep*: (TḲ:) or أَحْمَرُ [i. e. *red*], applied to anything: and غَلِيظٌ [i. e. *thick*, &c.]. (TA.) — Also, and ▼ غَضْبَةٌ, *A hard rock* (Ḳ, TA) *set*, or *fixed, in a mountain, and differing therefrom*: (TA:) or the latter signifies thus: or *a hard, round, rock*. (O.) — And الغَضْبُ signifies *The lion*: and *the bull*: as also [in the latter sense, or perhaps in both senses,] ▼ الغَضُوبُ. (Ḳ.)

غَضَبٌ an inf. n. of غَضِبَ [q. v.]. (Ṣ, Mṣb, Ḳ.) الغَضَبُ is *The contr. of* الرِّضَى: (Ḳ, TA:) it is variously defined: some say that it is *a state of excitement of the blood of the heart for the purpose of revenge*: some say that *pain on account of anything reparable* is غَضَب; and for anything irreparable, أَسَف: some say that it [is *a passion which*] *includes all that is evil*; wherefore the Prophet, to a man who asked of him a precept, said, لَا تَغْضَبْ: and some say that الغضب is [*a passion*] *accompanied by an eagerness to obtain revenge*; and الغَمّ is accompanied by despair of obtaining it: (TA: [see also غَيْظٌ:]) there is a غَضَب that is commended, and a غَضَب that is discommended; the former being that which is for the sake of religion and truth, or right; and the latter being that which is in a wrong case: and the غَضَب of God is his disapproving of the conduct of him who disobeys Him, and whom He will therefore punish. (Ibn-'Arafeh, TA.)

غَضِبٌ: see غَضْبَانُ.

غَضْبَةٌ *A single fit of* غضب [or *anger*]. (O.) — See also غَضْبٌ. — Also *An* [*eminence of the kind termed*] أَكَمَة. (L, TA.) — And *A* بَخْصَة (Ḳ, TA, in the CḲ بَخْصَة), or *protuberance* [*of flesh*], *above*, or *beneath, the eyes, in the form of a flatulent tumour*, (TA,) or *in the upper eyelid, produced by nature*: (Ḳ, TA:) so in the M. (TA.) — And *A thing resembling a* دَرَقَة, (Ḳ, TA,) i. e. *a shield*, (TA,) *of the hide of the camel*, (Ḳ, TA,) *one part of which is folded over another.* (TA.) — And *A* [*garment of the kind called*] جُبَّة, *made of the hides of camels, and worn for fighting*. (O.) — Also The *skin of a mountain-goat advanced in age*. (Ḳ.) The *skin of a fish*. (Ḳ.) The *skin of the head*. (Ḳ.) And The *skin of the part between the horns of a bull*. (Ḳ.) — And *A patch* of the small-pox: so in the saying, أَصْبَحَ جِلْدُهُ غَضْبَةً وَاحِدَةً مِنَ الجُدَرِىِّ [*His skin became one patch of the small-pox*]: (O:) like غَضْنَةٌ. (Ṣ in art. غضن.)

غَضِبَةٌ: see غَضْبَانُ.

غَضْبَى fem. of غَضْبَانُ [q. v.]: (Ṣ, Mṣb, Ḳ:) and pl. thereof. (Ṣ.) [See also غَضُوبٌ.] — It is also said by J, (Ḳ, TA,) and [before him] by Ez-Zejjájee, and also [after him] by ISd, (TA,) to be a name for *A hundred camels*, and not to have tenween, nor the article ال: but this is a mistake for غَضْيَا. (Ḳ, TA.)

القُوَّةُ الغَضَبِيَّةُ [*The irascible faculty*]. (KT, in explanation of التَّهَوُّرُ.)

غَضْبَانُ (Ṣ, Mṣb, Ḳ) [and, in the dial. of Benoo-Asad, as is implied by the fem. in that dial. mentioned in what follows, غَضْبَانٌ,] and ▼ غَضِبٌ and ▼ غَضُوبٌ [which is both masc. and fem.] and ▼ غُضُبٌّ (Ḳ) and ▼ غُضُبَّةٌ (Ṣ, Ḳ) and ▼ غَضِبَةٌ and ▼ غُضَبَةٌ, (Ḳ,) or the last, accord. to MF, is ▼ غُضْبَّةٌ, (TA,) are epithets applied to an angry man: (Ḳ:) [the first seems often to signify simply *Angry*, like غَضِبٌ; but accord. to SM,] all these epithets signify *quickly*, or *soon, angry* [as غُضُبَّةٌ is said in the Ṣ to signify, on the authority of Aṣ]: (TA:) the fem. of the first word is غَضْبَى, (Ṣ, Mṣb, Ḳ,) and (in the dial. of Benoo-Asad, Ṣ) غَضْبَانَةٌ, (Ṣ, Ḳ,) which is seldom used; (Ḳ;) and غَضُوبٌ is also used as a fem. epithet [as stated above], (Ḳ,) and has an intensive signification: (TA:) pl. (of the first word, Mṣb) غِضَابٌ (Mṣb, Ḳ) and (likewise of the first) غَضْبَى (Ṣ) and غَضَابَى (Ṣ, Ḳ) and غُضَابَى. (Mṣb, Ḳ.)

غُضُبٌّ: see the next preceding paragraph.

غَضِبَةٌ and غُضَبَةٌ and غُضُبَّةٌ: see غَضْبَانُ.

غُضَابٌ and غُضَابٌ *Motes* (قَذًى) *in the eye*: (Ḳ, TA:) or, as in one copy of the Ḳ, [and in the O,] *in the eyes*. (TA.) — And *A certain disease*; (Ḳ, TA;) or so the latter word; (O;) *an eruption in the skin*; but *not small-pox*: (TA:) or (so accord. to the TA, but in the CḲ "and") *small-pox*. (Ḳ, TA.)

غَضُوبٌ: see غَضْبَانُ. — Also *Stern*, or *austere*,

in look, or *countenance*; applied to a woman: (Ṣ, O, Ḳ:) and in like manner applied to a she-camel: (O, Ḳ:) or thus applied to a she-camel: and also signifying *a company of women*. (TA.) —— And *A malignant serpent*. (O, Ḳ.) —— See also غَضُوبٌ.

غُضَابِىٌّ A man (TA) *perturbed* (كَدِرٌ) *in social intercourse and in comportment*. (Ḳ. [For وَالْمُخَالَفَةِ in some copies of the Ḳ, I read وَالْمُخَالَقَةِ, as in other copies.])

الأَغْضَبُ *The part between the penis and the thigh*. (Ḳ.)

مَغْضُوبٌ عَلَيْهِ [*An object of anger*]. By الْمَغْضُوبِ عَلَيْهِمْ in the Ḳur [ch. i. last verse], are meant The Jews. (O, TA.) —— مَغْضُوبٌ also signifies *Having* [*the disease called* غُضَاب, i. e.] *the small-pox*. (O, TA.)

غضر

1. غَضُرَ, aor. ـُ, inf. n. غَضَارَةٌ, *It* (anything) *was*, or *became, soft*, or *tender*. (TA. [See also the inf. n. below; and see the part. n., غَضِيرٌ; and غَضِرٌ.]) —— And غَضِرَ, aor. ـَ, inf. n. غَضَرٌ, *He* (a man) *became rich, wealthy*, or *abounding in property*. (Mṣb.) You say, غَضِرَ بِالْمَالِ, (Ḳ, TA,) and in like manner, بِالسَّعَةِ وَالأَهْلِ, aor. ـَ, inf. n. غَضَرٌ and غَضَارَةٌ; (TA;) as also غَضِرَ, like غَنِىَ; (IḲṭṭ, TA;) *He* (a man, TA) *had abundance of the goods, conveniences*, or *comforts, of life*; (Ḳ, TA;) [or *he was*, or *became, rich in wealth and family*;] *after having been poor*. (Ḳ, TA.) —— غَضَرَهُ اللّٰهُ, (Ṣ, Mṣb, Ḳ,) aor. ـُ, (Mṣb, TA,) inf. n. غَضْرٌ, (Mṣb, Ḳ,) *God made him to be rich, wealthy*, or *abounding in property*: (Mṣb:) *to enjoy a pleasant life*: (Ṣ:) or *to have abundance of the goods, conveniences*, or *comforts, of life*. (Ḳ, TA.) —— غَضِرَ, with kesr, said of a place, *It had in it red clay or earth*: so says Az. (O.) —— غَضَرَ عَنْهُ, aor. ـِ, (Ṣ, O, Ḳ, TA,) inf. n. غَضْرٌ [and ▾مَغْضَرٌ likewise, accord. to a verse of Ibn-Aḥmar as cited in the O and TA, but accord. to the reading of that verse in my copies of the Ṣ, it is ▾مَغْضِرٌ, app., if correct, a n. of place]; as also غَضِرَ; (TA;) *He turned aside* or *away*, or *deviated, from it*, or *him*; (Ṣ, O, Ḳ, TA;) and so ▾تغضّر. (O, Ḳ.) One says, مَا غَضَرْتُ عَنْ صَوْبِى *I did not deviate from my course*. (TA.) —— غَضَرَ عَلَيْهِ, (Ḳ, TA,) aor. ـِ, inf. n. غَضْرٌ, (TA,) i. q. عَطَفَ (Ḳ, TA) [app. as meaning *He turned against him*, for it is added] and مَالَ. (TA.) —— And مَا غَضَرَ عَنْ شَتْمِى *He did not hold back*, or *refrain, from reviling me*. (TA.) —— And غَضَرَهُ, (Ṣ, Ḳ, TA,) aor. ـِ, inf. n. غَضْرٌ, (TA,) *It*, or *he, withheld*, or *prevented, him*. (Ṣ, Ḳ, TA.) One says, أَرَدْتُ أَنْ آتِيَكَ فَغَضَرَنِى أَمْرٌ [*I desired to come to thee, and*] *an affair withheld*, or *prevented, me*. (TA.) —— And غَضَرَ الشَّىْءَ *He cut off the thing*, (Ḳ, TA,) لَهُ [*for him*]. (TA.) You say, غَضَرَ لَهُ مِنْ مَالِهِ *He cut off a portion for him from his property*. (Ḳ.) —— And غَضَرَ الجِلْدَ *He tanned well the skin*. (TA.)

2. حَمَلَ فَمَا غَضَّرَ *He charged, and was not cowardly, and did not fall short of what was requisite*. (TA.)

5: see the first paragraph.

8. اُغْتُضِرَ *He died being a youth*, or *young man, in a sound state*: (Ḳ, TA:) like أُخْتُضِرَ. (TA.) [See also 8 in art. غرض.]

Q. Q. 1. غَضْوَرَ *He* (a man, TA) *was angry*. (O, Ḳ.)

مَا نَامَ لِغُضْرٍ is expl. as meaning *He hardly*, or *scarcely, slept*; but is said to be with ع and ص, and has been thus mentioned before [in art. عصر]. (TA.)

غَضْرٌ: see غَضِيرٌ. —— One says also عَيْشٌ غَضْرٌ مَضْرٌ *An easy and a plentiful life*: (Ḳ,* TA:) مضر being here an imitative sequent to غضر. (TA.) —— And غَضْرُ النَّاصِيَةِ applied to a man, (O, Ḳ,) and غَضْرَةُ النَّاصِيَةِ applied to a beast (دَابَّة), (O, Mṣb, Ḳ,) *Blest, fortunate*, or *abounding in good* or *advantage* or *utility*. (O, Mṣb, Ḳ.) —— See also غَضْرَآءُ, in two places.

غَضْرَةٌ *A certain plant*. (Ḳ, TA.) Hence the prov. يَأْكُلُ غَضْرَةً وَيَرْبِضُ حَجْرَةً [*He eats ghaḍrah, and lies down aside*]. (TA. [See also حَجْرَةٌ.])

غَضْرَآءُ: see غَضَارَةٌ, in six places. —— Also Earth, or land, (أَرْضٌ, Ḳ,) or a piece, or portion, of clay or earth, (طِينَةٌ, Ṣ, Mṣb,) *good*, or *fertile*, (طَيِّبَةٌ, Ḳ,) *green*, or *of a dark* or *an ashy dust-colour*: (خَضْرَآءُ عَلِكَةٌ: Ṣ, Mṣb, Ḳ:) and land *in which is clay*, or *soil, of a good kind, without sand*, or *without salt earth*; (Ḳ, TA;) as also ▾غَضِيرَةٌ or ▾غَضْرَةٌ, accord. to different copies of the Ḳ, the latter accord. to the L: (TA:) or, accord. to IAạr, ▾غَضْرٌ, [in the TA غَضْرَآء, which is a mistranscription,] signifies a place *having in it red clay or earth*. (O.) One says, أَنْبَطَ فُلَانٌ بِئْرَهُ فِى غَضْرَآءَ (Ṣ, TA) i. e. *Such a one produced the water of his well by digging in land of soft and good earth of which the water was sweet*. (TA.) —— And Land *in which palm-trees will not grow until it is dug*, (Ḳ, TA,) *the upper part thereof consisting of white* [*soft stones, like dry pieces of clay, such as are termed*] كَذَّان. (TA.)

غَضَارٌ Clay *that is cohesive, and* أَخْضَر [i. e. *green*, or *of a dark* or *an ashy dust-colour*], (Ḳ,) or (O) *of a good kind, without sand*, or *without salt earth*; (O, Ḳ;) and so ▾غَضَارَةٌ: (Ḳ:) or the latter signifies *such clay itself*: (Sh, O:) and the former signifies *baked clay* (Sh, O, Ḳ, TA) *made of* غَضَارَة, (Sh, O,) *green*, or *of a dark* or *an ashy dust-colour*, (أَخْضَرُ, O, TA,) *which is suspended upon a human being as a preservative from the* [*evil*] *eye*. (O, Ḳ,* TA.*)

غَضَوَّرٌ *Sticky clay*, (Ḳ, TA,) *that adheres to the foot, which will hardly*, or *in nowise, go into it* [*app. by reason of its compactness*]. (TA.) —— And *A species of trees* [or *plants*], (Ḳ, TA,) *dust-coloured, that grow large*: n. un. with ة. (TA.) And (TA) *A certain plant*, (Ṣ, O, TA,) *resembling the* ثُمَام [or *panic grass*], (TA,) or *of the species of* أَسَل [or *rushes*], *not beneficial, nor causing increase in the cattle*; (AḤn, O;) *it is said that the cattle pasturing upon it do not form fat thereby*, (O, TA,*) *and that it does not dissolve in their stomachs*: (O:) n. un. with ة. (AḤn, O.)

غَضِيرٌ *Soft*, or *tender*; (TA;) applied to a plant, or herbage; as also ▾غَضْرٌ, and ▾غَاضِرٌ; (O, TA;) all in this sense: (TA:) or so the first, applied to anything: (O, Ḳ, TA:) or this signifies *moist, juicy*, or *fresh*: (AA, O:) and i. q. خَضِيرٌ [*syn. with* أَخْضَرُ i. e. *green*]. (Ḳ.) —— See also غَضْرَآءُ.

غَضَارَةٌ an inf. n., of غَضُرَ and of غَضِرَ. (TA.) [Used as a simple subst.,] *Ease, comfort*, and *affluence*; *easiness of life*; *ampleness of the conveniences of life*, or *of the means of subsistence*; *plenty*; (Ḳ,* TA;) *prosperity*; (TA;) *plenty and prosperity*; (Ṣ;) *a plentiful and pleasant and easy state of life*: (TA:) and ▾غَضْرَآءُ signifies the same. (Ṣ.) One says, إِنَّهُمْ لَفِى غَضَارَةٍ مِنَ العَيْشِ and فِى ▾غَضْرَآءَ من العيش, *Verily they are in a plentiful and prosperous condition* [*of life*]. (Ṣ.) Accord. to Aṣ, one should not say اباد الله غَضْرَآءَهُمْ, but أَبَادَ اللّٰهُ ▾خَضْرَآءَهُمْ, meaning *May God put an end to their prosperity, and their plentiful condition*: (Ṣ:) but Aḥmad Ibn-'Obeyd says that both of these phrases mean *may God destroy the collective body of them*: and another says, *their clay of which they were created*. (TA. [See also خَضْرَآء, voce أَخْضَرُ.]) One says also, إِنَّهُ لَفِى غَضْرَآءِ ▾ عَيْشٍ and خَضْرَآءِ عَيْشٍ i. e. *Verily he is in a plentiful condition of life*. (TA.) And إِنَّهُ لَفِى غَضْرَآءَ ▾ مِنْ خَيْرٍ [*Verily he is in an ample state of prosperity*]. (TA.) —— And, (O, Ḳ,) accord. to Lth, (O,) الغَضَارَةُ is an appellation of *The* قَطَاة [or *sand-grouse*]; (O, Ḳ;) but Aṣ disapproved this: (O:) [or] the قَطَاة is called ▾الغَضْرَآءُ; and the pl. is الغَضَارِىُّ. (Mṣb.) —— See also غَضَارٌ. —— Of غَضَارَةٌ meaning *A certain utensil*, IDrd says, I do not think it to be genuine Arabic: (O, TA:) it signifies *a large* [*bowl such as is termed*] قَصْعَة: [app. from the Pers. غَدَارَه:] pl. غَضَائِرُ. (Mgh.)

غُضَارِىٌّ *A species of locust*; also called the جَرَاد مُبَارَك: a word of uncertain derivation. (Mṣb.) —— Also pl. of غَضْرَآءُ mentioned near the end of the next preceding paragraph. (Mṣb.)

الغَضَوَّرُ *The lion*. (Ṣgh, Ḳ.)

غَاضِرٌ: see غَضِيرٌ. —— Also *Withholding*, or *preventing*. (TA.) —— And A skin *well tanned*. (AḤn, Ṣ, O, Ḳ.) —— And One *who occupies himself early in the morning in the accomplishment of the objects of his want*, or *in his needful affairs*. (AA, O, Ḳ.)

مَغْضَرٌ and مُغْضِرٌ : see the first paragraph.

مُغْضِرٌ : see the following paragraph.

مَغْضُورٌ A man *enjoying a pleasant life*: (Ṣ:) *blest; fortunate; abounding in good*, or *advantage*, or *utility*: (Mṣb, Ḳ:) or *in a state of ease, comfort, and affluence*; or *of plenty*, or *prosperity*; (O, Ḳ, TA;) *and of happiness*: (TA:) as also ▾مُغْضِرٌ: (Ḳ, TA:) pl. of the former مَغَاضِيرُ, as well as مَغْضُورُونَ. (TA.)

غضرف

غُضْرُوفٌ is *syn. with* غُرْضُوفٌ, (Ṣ and Ḳ &c. in art. غرضف, q. v.,) in [all of] its meanings: (Ḳ:) pl. غَضَارِيفُ. (O and TA in art. غرضف.)

غضف

1. غَضَفَهُ, (Ṣ, O, Ḳ,) aor. ـِ , (Ḳ,) inf. n. غَضْفٌ, (TA,) *He broke it*, namely, a branch, or stick, or the like, (Ṣ, O, Ḳ, TA,) and a thing, (TA,) *but not thoroughly*. (Ṣ, O, TA.) [See also 2.] —— And غَضَفَ أُذُنَهُ, (Ṣ, O, Ḳ,) aor. and inf. n. as above, (Ṣ, O,) *He* (a dog) *relaxed his ear*, and *folded*, or *creased*, *it*: (Ṣ, O, Ḳ, TA:) [see, again, 2:] or غَضَفَ أُذُنَهُ, inf. n. غَضْفَانٌ and غَضَفَانٌ, *he* (a dog) *twisted his ear*: and in like manner one says of the wind, [غَضَفَتْهَا,] i. e. *it twisted it*. (TA.) And غضف الوِسَادَةَ *He folded the pillow* [*so as to make creases in it*]. (Ḥam p. 785. [But perhaps this is correctly ▾غضّف: comp. its quasi-pass., 5.]) —— غَضَفَتْ said of [wild] she-asses, (O,) or of a she-ass, (Ḳ,) aor. as above, (O, TA,) and so the inf. n., (TA,) signifies أَخَذَتِ الجَرْىَ أَخْذًا [as though meaning *They*, or *she*, *restrained the running*, i. e. their, or her, running; agreeably with what here follows]: (O, Ḳ, TA:) غَضَفَ, [for غَضَفَ مِنَ الجَرْىِ,] said of a horse &c., means *he lessened*, lit. *took from*, the rate of *the running*, (أَخَذَ مِنَ الجَرْىِ,) *without reckoning*: (L, TA:) Umeiyeh Ibn-Abee-'Áïdh El-Hudhalee says,

* يَغُضُّ وَيَغْضِفْنَ مِنْ رَيِّقٍ *

(O, TA) meaning *He* (the ass) *withholds* somewhat of his running, (يَكُفُّ بَعْضَ جَرْيِهِ,) *and they* (the she-asses) *lessen*, lit. *take from*, *the* [or rather *a*] *first*, or *former*, *rate* of their running, (يَأْخُذْنَ أَخْذًا مِنْ أَوَّلِ جَرْيِهِنَّ,) *without reckoning*: (Skr: see Kosegarten's "Carmina Hudsailitarum," p. 189:) Skr says, in explanation of the citation above from Umeiyeh, that غَضْفٌ signifies the act of *taking* and *lading out* [with the hand] (أَخْذٌ and غَرْفٌ); and on one occasion he says, the *taking easily*; [adding,] one says, غَضَفَ فُلَانٌ مِنْ طَعَامٍ لَيِّنٍ [*Such a one took*, or *laded out* with his hand, *from soft food*]. (TA.) ══ غَضَفَ العَيْشُ, inf. n. غُضُوفٌ, *The life was soft*, or *easy*, *and plentiful*. (TA.) ══ غَضِفَ, [aor. ـَ , inf. n. غَضَفٌ,] *He* (a dog, Ṣ) *was*, or *became*, *relaxed*, or *flabby*, *in the ear*. (Ṣ, Ḳ, TA.) And غَضِفَتِ الأُذُنُ, inf. n. غَضَفٌ, is said to mean *The ear was*, or *became*, *long and relaxed* or *flabby*: or *it advanced upon the face*: or *it retired towards the head*: or *its extremities folded upon the inner part thereof*: or, in a dog, *it turned towards the back of the neck*: or *it became folded*, or *creased*, *naturally*. (TA.) [See also غـضـف, below: and see 7.] —— غَضِفَ اللَّيْلُ : see 4.

2. غضّفهُ, inf. n. تَغْضِيفٌ, *He broke it*. (TA.) [See also 1, first signification.] —— تَغْضِيفٌ signifies also The *making* [a thing] *to hang down*. (O, Ḳ.) —— See also 1, third signification.

4. اغضف اللَّيْلُ *The night became dark and black*; (Ṣ, O, Ḳ;) as also ▾غَضِفَ, inf. n. غَضَفٌ. (Ṣ.) —— اغضفت السَّمَآءُ *The sky became clouded, and prepared to rain*. (O,* Ḳ,* TA.) —— اغضفت النَّخْلُ *The palm-trees had many branches, and bad fruit*: (Ḳ, TA:) or *became laden*, or *heavily laden, with fruit*; or *abounded therewith*. (O, Ḳ, TA.) —— And اغضف العَطَنُ *The usual abiding-place of camels*, or *cattle*, or *their place of lying down at*, or *around*, *the water* or *watering-trough*, *had many thereof*. (Ḳ.)

5. تغضّف *It broke*, or *became broken*; as also ▾انغضف. (TA.) —— And تَغَضُّفٌ signifies The *being*, or *becoming*, *creased*, or *wrinkled*; (O, Ḳ, TA;) like تَغَيُّفٌ. (TA.) And تَغَضَّفَ *He*, or *it*, *inclined*, and *bent*, and *became folded*, or *creased*, *much*, or *in several places*, syn. مَالَ, and تَثَنَّى, and تَكَسَّرَ, (Ṣ, O, Ḳ,*) عَلَيْهِ *upon him*, or *it*. (Ṣ, O.) And تغضّفت الحَيَّةُ *The serpent twisted*, or *coiled*, *itself*. (O, Ḳ.) —— تغضّفت البِئْرُ *The sides of the well fell in ruins*, or *became demolished*: (Ṣ, O, Ḳ:) *the well collapsed*, or *broke down*, عَلَى فُلَانٍ *upon such one*, who had descended into it; (O;) as also ▾انغضفت. (O, Ḳ.) —— تغضّف عَلَيْنَا اللَّيْلُ *The night covered us*. (O, Ḳ.) —— تغضّفت عَلَيْنَا الدُّنْيَا *The world became abundant to us in its good things*; and *favourable to us*. (O, Ḳ.)

7: see 5, in two places. —— انغضفت أُذُنُهُ *His ear became folded*, or *creased*, *not naturally*. (TA.) [See also 1, near the end.] —— انغضف الضَّبَابُ *The* ضباب [or *thin clouds, like smoke*,] *overlay one another*. (TA.) —— انغضفوا فِى الغُبَارِ *They entered into the dust*, or *raised and spreading dust*. (Ṣ, O, Ḳ.)

غَضْفٌ : see غَضَفٌ.

غُضْفٌ [written by Golius غُضُفٌ]: see غَضَفَةٌ.

غَضَفٌ [inf. n. of غَضِفَ (q. v.): and, as a simple subst.,] *Laxness*, or *flabbiness, in the ear*: (Ṣ, O, Ḳ:) or, as in the T, *a laxness*, or *flabbiness*, *of the upper part* [*of each*] *of the two ears, upon*, or *over, the concha thereof, by reason of its width and its largeness*: (TA:) Aboo-'Amr Esh-Sheybánee says, after citing a verse of Abu-n-Nejm, describing a lion, that it signifies *a twisting*, in the ear, *backwards*: accord. to ISh, it is, in the lion, *a laxness*, or *pendulousness*, *of the upper eyelids, upon the eyes*; arising from anger and pride: (O:) and he says that, accord. to some, it is, in the lion, *abundance of the fur, and a folding*, or *creasing, of the skin*. (TA.) And one says, [app. in relation to the lion,] فِى أَشْفَارِهِ ▾غَضْفٌ and غَضَفٌ [app. *In the edges of his upper eyelids is a laxness*, or *pendulousness*]; both meaning the same. (TA.) —— Also *Softness*, or *easiness, and plentifulness*, of life: (Ṣ:) like غَطَفٌ. (O in art. غطف.) ══ And *A species of tree in India, exactly like the palm-tree*, (Lth, O, Ḳ,) *except that* (Ḳ) *its fruit-stones are divested of covering, without a* لِحَآء [or *pulpy pericarp*], *and from its lowest to its uppermost part it has green* سَعَف [or *branches like those of the palm-tree*], (Lth, O, Ḳ,) *covered* [*thereby*]: (Lth, O:) AḤn says, it is *a plant resembling the palm-tree exactly*, (O, L, TA,) *but not growing tall*, (TA,) *having many* سَعَف, *and prickles, and* [*leaves such as are termed*] خُوص, *of the hardest sort, whereof are made large* [*receptacles of the kind called*] جِلَال [pl. of جُلَّةٌ], *that serve for sacks, goods being carried in them by land and by sea*; (O, L, TA;) *it produces from its head unripe dates of disagreeable flavour, not eaten*; *and*, he says, *of its* خُوص *are made mats like carpets*, (L, TA,) *called* سِمَام, pl. of سُمَّةٌ [q. v.], (L,) *one of which may be spread for twenty years*. (L, TA.) ══ See also the next paragraph, in two places.

غَضَفَةٌ *A certain bird*: or a قَطَاة [or *sand-grouse*]: (IDrd, O, Ḳ:) or the قَطَاة *termed* جُونِيَّة: pl. ▾غَضَفٌ [or rather this, if correct, is a coll. gen. n.]: J says that ▾الغضف [thus in the TA, but in my and other copies of the Ṣ ▾الغُضْفُ, for which Golius appears to have found الغُضُفُ,] signifies القَطَا الجُونُ; but IB says that it is correctly القطا الجُونِىُّ. (TA. [See جُونِىٌّ: and particularly what is said at the end of the paragraph thus headed.]) ══ Also *An* [*eminence of the kind called*] أَكَمَةٌ. (O, Ḳ, TA. [For اكمة, in this case, the TḲ has most strangely substituted اكمه, meaning أَكْمَهُ, for it explains it as signifying "blind from the birth;" and this, though an obvious mistake, Freytag asserts to be the right reading and explanation.])

غَاضِفٌ : see أَغْضَفُ, in two places. —— Also [applied to a man] *Soft*, or *easy, and plentiful, in his circumstances*. (Ṣ, O, Ḳ.)

أَغْضَفُ, applied to a dog, *Relaxed*, or *flabby, in the ear*; pl. غُضْفٌ; (Ṣ, O, Ḳ;) occurring in a verse of Dhu-r-Rummeh, cited voce عَذَبٌ; (O, TA;) and the fem. غَضْفَآءُ is applied [to a bitch, and] to an ear: (TA:) or a dog *having the upper part of his ear folded*, or *creased*, *backwards*; and ▾غَاضِفٌ when it is *forwards*. (IAạr, O, Ḳ.) And hence [the pl.] غُضْفٌ, as an epithet in which the quality of a subst. is predominant, is used as an appellation for *Dogs of the chase*. (TA.) —— Applied to a lion, *Having the ear folded*, or *creased*; (Hr, O, Ḳ;) denoting a quality that renders him more abominable: (Hr, O:) or *relaxed*, or *pendulous, in the ears*: (O, Ḳ:) or *whose upper eyelids are lax*, or *pendulous, upon his eyes, by reason of anger* or *pride*; (Ḳ, TA;) so says ISh. (TA.) And accord. to Lth, A beast of prey *whose upper part of his ear is folded*, or *creased, and the lower part thereof relaxed*, or *pendulous*. (TA.) And the fem., غَضْفَآءُ, A she-goat *whose extremities of her ears descend low, by reason of their length*. (TA.) — Also Anything *bending, folding*, or *creasing, and relaxed, flabby*, or *pendulous*: fem. as above. (TA.) And ▼ مُغْضِفٌ is like أَغْضَفُ. (TA.) — And الأَغْضَفُ is one of the names of *The lion*. (TA.) — سَهْمٌ أَغْضَفُ *An arrow of which the feathers are thick*; (Ṣ, O, Ḳ;) *contr. of* أَصْمَعُ. (Ṣ, O.) — لَيْلٌ أَغْضَفُ *A night that is dark* (Ṣ, O, Ḳ) *and black*; (Ṣ, O;) *covering with its darkness*. (TA.) — عَيْشٌ أَغْضَفُ *A soft*, or *an easy, and plentiful, life*; as also ▼ غَاضِفٌ: (Ṣ, O, Ḳ:) like سَنَةٌ غَضْفَآءُ أَغْطَفُ. (Ṣ and O in art. غطف.) And *A fruitful*, or *plentiful, year*. (TA.)

مُغْضِفٌ: see أَغْضَفُ, latter half. — Applied to palm-trees (نَخْلٌ), *Having many branches, and bad fruit*; (O, TA;) thus without ة; (O;) and also with ة. (TA. [See also its verb.]) — And ثَمَرَةٌ مُغْضِفَةٌ *A fruit that has become flaccid, but not completely ripe*: (O:) or *nearly, but not yet, ripe*: (Sh, TA:) or *whereof the goodness has not become apparent*: or, accord. to AA, *hanging upon its tree, flaccid*. (TA.)

غضفر

Q. 1. غَضْفَرَ *He* (a jade, or hackney, TA) *was*, or *became, heavy*, or *sluggish*. (Ḳ, TA.)

غَضْفَرٌ: } see the next paragraph; the former,
غُضَافِرٌ: } in two places.

غَضَنْفَرٌ *Big, thick*, or *rude, in body* or *person*; (Ṣ, Ḳ;) as also ▼ غَضْفَرٌ, which is the original form; the ن in the former being augmentative: (Az, TA:) or simply, *big, thick*, or *rude*; applied to a man: (Lth, TA:) or *rude*, or *coarse*, [in disposition or in make,] *and big*, or *thick*; (TA;) as also ▼ غَضَنْفَرٌ and ▼ غَضْفَرٌ; (Ḳ;) applied to a man: (TA:) or *big*, or *thick*, (AA, TA,) *in make*, (TA,) *and wrinkled*; (AA, TA;) applied to a lion. (TA.) You say also أُذُنٌ غَضَنْفَرَةٌ, meaning, *A big*, or *thick, fleshy, ear*. (AO, L.) — [Hence,] الغَضَنْفَرُ *The lion*; (Lth, Ṣ, Ḳ;) as also ▼ الغُضَافِرُ. (TṢ, Ḳ.)

غُضَنْفَرٌ: see the next preceding paragraph.

غضن

1. غَضَنَهُ, (Ṣ, Ḳ,) aor. ـِ and ـُ, (Ḳ,) inf. n. غَضْنٌ, (Ṣ,) *He*, or *it*, (a man, and a thing, Ṣ,) *withheld, restrained, hindered*, or *diverted, him*. (Ṣ, Ḳ.) One says, مَا غَضَنَكَ عَنَّا *What withheld, hindered*, or *diverted*, or *has withheld*, &c., *thee from us?* (Ṣ.) In the "Nawádir" of IAạr, this verb, which is correctly thus, with ض, is erroneously with ص. (TA.) — غَضَنَتْ بِوَلَدِهَا, and ▼ غَضَّنَتْ, *She* (a camel) *cast her young one*, or *fœtus, in an imperfect state*, (Ḳ, TA,) *before the hair had grown upon it and its make had become* [*perfectly*] *apparent*. (TA. [See also خَدَجَتْ.]) [This is what is meant in the Ṣ where, after the mention of a signification of ▼ التَّغْضِين which will be found below, it is said that this word signifies also الرِّجَاعُ (an inf. n. of رَجَعَتْ, q. v.): hence, app., (though referring to the Ḳ as his authority,) Freytag has given to غَضَنَت, as said of a she-camel, besides the signification mentioned above, another, which is also assigned to رَجَعَتْ; i. e., *she falsely indicated her being pregnant, by raising her tail*, &c.] — See also 5, in four places: — and see 4.

2. غَضَّنَهُ, inf. n. تَغْضِينٌ, *I wrinkled, shrivelled*, or *puckered, it*; syn. of the inf. n. تَشْنِيجٌ. (Ṣ.) One says, دَخَلْتُ عَلَيْهِ فَغَضَّنَ لِى مِنْ جَبْهَتِهِ [*I went in to him and he wrinkled to me a portion of his forehead*]. (TA.) — See also 5: — and see 1, in two places: — and 4.

3. مُكَاسَرَةُ العَيْنَيْنِ signifies المُغَاضَنَةُ [*The contracting of the eyes so as to wrinkle the lids*], (Ṣ, Ḳ, TA,) by reason of doubt, or suspicion. (TA.) One says, غَازَلَهَا بِمُكَاسَرَةٍ, غَاضَنَ المَرْأَةَ, meaning العَيْنَيْنِ [i. e. *He talked*, or *acted, with the woman, in an amatory and enticing manner, with the contracting of the eyes so as to wrinkle the lids*]. (A, TA.)

4. اغضنت السَّمَآءُ *The sky rained continually*; (Ṣ, TA;) as also غضنت [perhaps ▼ غَضَنَتْ, but more probably, I think, ▼ غَضَّنَتْ]. (TA.) And اغضنت السَّحَابَةُ [*The cloud rained continually*]. (Ṣ and TA in explanation of رَيَّمَتْ.) — And اغضن عَلَيْهِ الحُمَّى *The fever continued upon him persistently*. (IAạr, TA.) — اغضن عَلَيْهِ اللَّيْلُ *The night became dark upon him*. (TA.)

5. تغضّن *It was*, or *became, wrinkled, shrivelled*, or *puckered*; syn. تَشَنَّجَ; (Ṣ, MA, TA;) as also ▼ غَضِنَ, inf. n. غَضَنٌ [and app. غُضُونٌ, like قُبُولٌ as an inf. n. of قَبِلَ, though this requires consideration, as will be shown by what follows], said of the face as having this signification, or as signifying *it was*, or *became, wrinkled and speckled*; (MA;) [and so, perhaps, ▼ غضّن, for] التغضين [if not a mistranscription for التَّغَضُّنُ], as also ▼ الغُضُونُ, is syn. with التَّشَنُّجُ; and one says رَجُلٌ ذُو غُضُونٍ ▼ فِى جَبْهَتِهِ meaning تَكَسُّرٌ [i. e. *a man having a wrinkling in his forehead*; but غُضُون may be here used as pl. of غَضْنٌ, and thus meaning *wrinkles*]: and ▼ غَضْنٌ signifies *a bending* (تَلَوٍّ and تَثَنٍّ) of a branch or twig or the like. (TA.) One says also, تَغَضَّنَتِ الدِّرْعُ عَلَى لَابِسِهَا *The coat of mail became folded*, [or *it hung*, or *sat, with folds*,] *upon its wearer*. (TA.)

غَضْنٌ and ▼ غَضَنٌ *A wrinkle, crease, fold, ply, plait*, or *pucker*, (Ṣ, Mgh, Mṣb, Ḳ,) of the skin, (Ṣ, Mgh, Mṣb,) and of anything, (Mṣb,) or in a garment, and in a skin, (Ḳ,) and in a coat of mail, (Ṣ, Ḳ,) &c.: (Ṣ:) pl. غُضُونٌ, (Ṣ, Mgh, Mṣb, Ḳ,) occurring in a verse cited in art. شاب. (TA.) — [Hence,] one says, كَانَ ذٰلِكَ فِى غُضُونِ كَذَا [lit. *That was within the folds*, meaning *in the midst, of such a thing*, or *such an affair* or *event*]; like فِى أَثْنَآءِ كذا. (TA in art. ثنى.) — غُضُونُ الأُذُنِ means *The places of folding of the ears*; syn. مَثَانِيهَا. (Ḳ, TA: in the CḲ [erroneously] مَنابِتُها.) — Also (i. e. غَضْن and ▼ غَضَنٌ, TA) *Difficulty, distress*, or *trouble*; and *fatigue*, or *weariness*. (Ḳ, TA.) The Arabs say to a man, in threatening him, لَأُطِيلَنَّ غَضْنَكَ or ▼ غَضَنَكَ i. e. [*I will assuredly make*] *thy difficulty* &c. [*to be long*]. (AZ, Az, TA.)

غَضَنٌ an inf. n. of غَضِنَ. (MA. [See 5, in two places.]) — See also غَضْنٌ, in three places. — غَضَنُ العَيْنِ signifies *The exterior*, or *apparent*, جِلْدَة [app. meaning *tunic*, i. e. *the sclerotic tunic*,] *of the eye*. (Ṣ, TA.)

غَضْنَةٌ [*A patch of the smallpox*]. One says of a person whose skin has become covered, or wholly covered, (أُلْبِسَ,) with the smallpox, أَصْبَحَ جِلْدُهُ غَضْنَةً وَاحِدَةً [*His skin has become one patch of the smallpox*]: and some say غَضْبَةً. (Ṣ.)

غِضَانٌ the subst. from the verb in the phrase غَضَنَتْ بِوَلَدِهَا [i. e. a subst. signifying The *act denoted by that phrase*, q. v.]. (Ḳ.)

غَضِينٌ A she-camel's young one, or fœtus, *cast in an imperfect state, before the hair has grown upon it and its make has become* [*perfectly*] *apparent*. (TA.)

أَغْضَنُ *Contracting his eye so as to wrinkle the lids, naturally*, or *by reason of enmity*, or *from pride*. (Ḳ.)

غضى and غضو

1. غَضَا, aor. يَغْضُو; and غَضِىَ, aor. يَغْضَى: see 4; the former, in three places. — غَضَا, (Ḳ, TA,) aor. يَغْضُو, thus in the M, (TA,) inf. n. غُضُوٌّ, (Ḳ,* TḲ,) *He*, i. e. a man, [and app. *it*, i. e. a thing,] *was*, or *became, such as is termed* غَاضٍ [q. v.]. (Ḳ, TA. [In the TḲ it is mentioned only as said of a thing: but the context in the Ḳ indicates that it is said of a man, and app. of a thing also.]) — [See also غُضُوٌّ below.] — غَضِيَتِ الإِبِلُ, inf. n. غَضًا, *The camels had a complaint* (M, Ḳ, TA) *of their bellies* (Ḳ, TA) *from eating of the trees called* غَضًا. (M, Ḳ, TA.) — And غَضِيَتِ الأَرْضُ *The land abounded with the trees called* غَضًا. (IḲṭṭ, TA.)

4. اغضى, (Ḳ,) inf. n. إِغْضَآءٌ, (Ṣ,) *He contracted his eyelids; drew them near together*; (Ṣ, Ḳ;) like غَضَّ; (TA in art. غض;) [and] so اغضى عَيْنَهُ; said of a man: (Mṣb:) or *he closed his*

eyelids upon his iris; so in the M; as also ▼ غَضَا, a dial. var. of اغضى, likewise mentioned by ISd; and ▼ غَضَى, aor. يَغْضَى, is also a dial. var. thereof: (TA:) or *he made one of his eyelids to cleave to the other, that he might not see a thing, by reason of shame:* (Ḥar p. 19:) or *he put one of his eyelids upon the other from dislike of a thing.* (Id. p. 492.) [See also 6.] — Hence it is used in relation to forbearance: so that one says, أَغْضَى عَلَى القَذَى *He held,* or *refrained, notwithstanding annoyance, spontaneously, without being asked,* or *without constraint:* (Mṣb, TA:) or اغضى عَلَى قَذًى *he bore annoyance patiently.* (M, TA.) And اغضى عَنْهُ *He feigned himself neglectful of it;* [*he closed his eyes from it;*] *he connived at it;* as also اغمض عنه. (TA in art. غمض.) And [sometimes] الإِغْضَآءُ means *The abstaining from proceeding to extremities.* (Mgh in art. جوز.) — Hence also, اغضى عَلَى الشَّىْءِ *He was silent respecting the thing;* and so ▼ غَضَا, aor. يَغْضُو. (Ḳ, TA.) — And اغضى عَنْهُ طَرْفَهُ means *He closed,* or *turned away, from him,* or *it, his eye,* or *eyes;* syn. سَدَّهُ [in the CḲ شَدَّهُ], or صَدَّهُ: (Ḳ, TA:) so in the M. (TA.) = اغضى اللَّيْلُ *The night was,* or *became, dark;* (Ṣ, Mṣb, Ḳ;) *and covered everything* (Ḳ, TA) *with its darkness;* from ISd; (TA;) as also ▼ غَضَا, aor. يَغْضُو. (Ḳ, TA. [See also غُضُوٌّ.])

6. تغاضى *He contracted,* or *put together, his eyelids, that he might not see an evil,* or *unseemly, thing.* (Ḥar p. 473. [See also 4.]) — And [hence,] تغاضى عَنْهُ *i. q.* تَغَافَلَ [i. e. *He was,* or *he feigned himself, unmindful,* &c., *of him,* or *it*]: (Ḳ, TA:) like تَغَابَى عنه: mentioned by Az. (TA. [See, again, 4.])

غَضًا, said by Th to be written [thus] with ا; but ISd says, I know not why this is; (TA;) [the latter, it seems, holding its last letter to be originally ى, not و;] *A species of trees,* (Ṣ, Mṣb, Ḳ,) *well known,* (Ḳ,) *the wood of which is of the hardest of wood, and therefore there is hardness in its charcoal;* (Mṣb;) *it is of the plants of the sands, and has* [*sprigs,* or *foliage, of the kind termed*] هَدَب [q. v.], *like that called* أَرْطَى; (TA;) *and its fire is of long continuance:* (Ḥar p. 60:) [see also رِمْثٌ: Mr. Palgrave (in his Travels, i. 38,) describes it as a shrub believed by him to be peculiar to the Arabian Peninsula, "*of the genus Euphorbia, with a woody stem, often five or six feet in height, and innumerable round green twigs, very slender and flexible, forming a large feathery tuft, not ungraceful to the eye, while it affords some kind of shelter to the traveller, and food to his camels:*"] the sing. [or rather n. un.] is غَضَاةٌ: (Ḳ:) and AḤn says that sometimes غَضَاتٌ is a pl. [of the n. un.]. (TA.) — Hence, ذِئْبُ غَضًا [*A wolf of trees,* or *shrubs, called* غضا]; (Ṣ, Ḳ;) or, as in the handwriting of Aboo-Zekereeyà ذِئْبُ الغَضَا; and such is the most abominable, or malignant, or noxious, of wolves; for he comes not into close proximity to men save when he desires to attack: or this means *the wolf of the covert of trees:* for غَضًا — signifies also *A covert of trees:* (TA:) and *a* غَيْضَةٌ [i. e. *thicket;* or *collection of tangled,* or *confused,* or *dense, trees;* &c.]. (Ḳ, TA.) — أَهْلُ الغَضَا is an appellation of the people of Nejd, (Ḳ, TA,) because of the abundance of [the trees called] غضا there. (TA.)

بَعِيرٌ غَضٍ *A camel having a complaint of his belly from eating of the trees called* غَضًا: and إِبِلٌ غَضِيَةٌ and غَضَايَا [*camels having such a complaint*]; (Ṣ, Ḳ;) like رَمِثَةٌ and رَمَاثَى. (Ṣ.)

غَضْيَا: see غَضْيَآءُ. — Also, (Ḳ, TA,) determinate, and imperfectly decl., like [its syn.] هُنَيْدَةُ, (TA,) *A hundred camels:* (IAạr, Ḳ, TA:) held by ISk to be so called as being likened to a place producing [an abundance of] غَضًا [i. e. the trees thus called]: AA has mentioned it with the article ال, saying that الغَضْيَا signifies *a hundred.* (TA.)

غَضْيَآءُ A land (أَرْضٌ) *abounding with the trees called* غَضًا. (Ṣ, Ḳ.) — And, as also ▼ غَضْيَا, *A place in which is a collection of the trees called* غَضًا; (Ḳ, TA;) *a place where they grow.* (TA.) — And the former, *Rugged* land or ground. (TA.)

غُضُوٌّ *Intense darkness of the night.* (IḲṭṭ, TA. [Perhaps in this sense an inf. n. of which the verb is غَضَا: see 4, last sentence.]) = And The *eating of the trees called* غَضًا. (IḲṭṭ, TA. [App. in this sense an inf. n. of which the verb is غَضِىَ.]) = And *A state of muchness, abundance, copiousness, fulness,* or *completeness,* of a thing. (Ḳ. [See also 1, second sentence.])

رَجُلٌ غَضِىٌّ عَنِ الخَنَا or عَنِ الفَحْشَآءِ [*A man who refrains from taking notice of that which is foul, abominable, unseemly,* or *obscene,*] may be from غَضَا; or it may be from أَغْضَى, similar to وَجِيعٌ and أَلِيمٌ; but the former derivation is the better. (TA.)

غَضَوِىٌّ a rel. n. from الغَضَا [the trees thus called], and applied to a camel [app. as meaning *That is fond of,* or *wont to feed upon, the trees called* غَضًا]. (Ṣ.)

غَضْيَانَةٌ *A herd of camels of generous race:* (Ḳ, TA:) mentioned by Az, from AA. (TA.)

غَاضٍ *Dark;* applied to night (لَيْلٌ); as also ▼ مُغْضٍ, but this latter is rare: (Ṣ, Mṣb:) and so غَاضِيَةٌ, (Ṣ, Ḳ,) applied to a night (لَيْلَةٌ): (Ṣ:) or, thus applied, accord. to Az, *intensely dark.* (TA.) — And غَاضِيَةٌ signifies also *Bright,* or *shining brightly;* (Ṣ, Ḳ;) applied to a night, (thus in one of my copies of the Ṣ,) or to fire (نَار): (so in other copies of the Ṣ and in the TA:) thus having two contr. meanings. (Ṣ, Ḳ.) — And *Great;* applied to a fire (نار): a signification said by Az to be taken from the fire of the tree called غَضًا, which is of the best of firewood. (TA.) = بَعِيرٌ غَاضٍ *A camel that eats the trees called* غَضًا: and إِبِلٌ غَاضِيَةٌ and غَوَاضٍ [*camels that eat those trees*]. (Ṣ, Ḳ.) = شَىْءٌ غَاضٍ *A thing that is much in quantity, abundant, copious, full,* or *complete.* (Ḳ.) — And رَجُلٌ غَاضٍ *A man having food and clothing;* or *having a good state,* or *condition, in respect of food, and having clothing; sufficed,* or *satisfied.* (Ḳ.)

مُغْضٍ: see the next preceding paragraph.

غط

1. غَطَّهُ فِى المَآءِ, aor. ـُ, (Ṣ, Mṣb, Ḳ,) and ـِ, (Ḳ,) [the latter contr. to analogy,] inf. n. غَطٌّ, (Ṣ, Mṣb,) *He immersed, immerged, dipped, plunged,* or *sunk, him,* or *it, in the water:* (Ṣ, Mṣb, Ḳ:) *he made him to plunge,* or *dive, in,* or *into, the water:* (Ṣ:) [Golius adds, as from Ibn-Maạroof, *head-downwards;* but it is not so in my copy of the KL:] and غَتَّهُ signifies the same. (TA in art. غت.) — And غَطَّهُ, inf. n. غَطٌّ, *He pressed,* or *squeezed, him,* or *it,* (عَصَرَهُ,) *vehemently;* and *i. q.* كَبَسَهُ [q. v.]. (TA.) [And غَتَّهُ, q. v., has a similar meaning.] = غَطَّ, aor. ـِ, inf. n. غَطِيطٌ, said of a he-camel, (Ṣ, Mṣb, Ḳ,) *He brayed;* syn. هَدَرَ: (Ḳ:) or *he brayed,* (هَدَرَ, AZ, Ṣ,) or *made a sound,* (صَوَّتَ, Mṣb,) *in the* شِقْشِقَة [or *bursa faucium*]: when not in the شقشقة, it is termed هَدِيرٌ: you say of the she-camel, تَهْدِرُ; not تَغِطُّ; (AZ, Ṣ, Mṣb;) because she has no شِقْشِقَة: (AZ, Ṣ:) or, as some say, *he brayed, but not in the* شقشقة. (L.) — غَطَّ, aor. as above, (Mṣb, Ḳ,*) and inf. n. as above (Ṣ, Mṣb, Ḳ*) and غَطٌّ, (TA,) said of a person sleeping, (Ṣ, Mṣb, Ḳ,) and of one strangled, or throttled, (Ṣ, Ḳ,) and of an animal slaughtered, (Ḳ,) *He emitted a sound;* (Ḳ;) in which sense it is also said of a lynx, and of a leopard, and of a bustard: (TA:) or *snored,* or *snorted:* (Ṣ, TA:) or *sent back his breath up to his fauces so that it was heard by persons around him:* (Mṣb:) or *emitted a sound with his breath, reiterating his breath where he found not an easy passage* [*for it*]. (TA.) — غَطَّتِ البُرْمَةُ *The stone cooking-pot boiled audibly.* (TA.) — See also غَتَّ, near the end of the paragraph.

3. غاطّ حُوتًا *He vied,* or *contended, with a fish in plunging,* or *diving.* (JK in art. قمس.)

6. تغاطّ القَوْمُ *The people,* or *company of men, vied,* or *contended, one with another, in plunging,* or *diving,* (تَمَاقَلُوا,) in the water. (Ṣ.) And الصِّبْيَانُ يَتَغَاطُّونَ فِى البَحْرِ *The children vie,* or *contend, one with another, in plunging,* or *diving,* (يَتَقَامَسُونَ,) *in the sea* or *great river.* (A in art. قمس.)

7. انغطّ فى المَآءِ *He* (a man, TA) *became immersed, immerged, dipped, plunged,* or *sunk, in the water;* or *he plunged,* or *dived, in the water.* (Ṣ, Mṣb, TA.)

R. Q. 1. غَطْغَطَ البَحْرُ [inf. n. غَطْغَطَةٌ] *The*

waves of the sea became high (غَلَتْ), so in some copies of the Ḳ, or *estuated* (غَلَتْ); so in other copies of the Ḳ, and in the L; (TA;) as also ▼ تَغَطْغَطَ. (O, Ḳ, TA.) — And غَطْغَطَتِ القِدْرُ [The contents of *the cooking-pot*] *made a sound:* or *boiled vehemently.* (Ḳ.) — And غَطْغَطَ عَلَيْهِ, said of sleep, *It overcame him.* (L, Ḳ, TA.)

R. Q. 2. تَغَطْغَطَ: see the next preceding paragraph. — Also *It* (a thing) *became separated,* or *dispersed.* (Sgh, Ḳ, TA.)

غَطَاطٌ The [*bird called the*] قَطَا [i. e. the *sand-grouse*]: (M, Ḳ:) or *a species thereof,* (Ṣ, Ḳ,) or, as some say, *a species of bird not of the* قطا, (TA,) *dust-coloured in the backs and the bellies* (Ṣ, Ḳ, TA) *and the bodies,* (Ṣ, TA,) *black in the inner sides of the wings,* (Ṣ, Ḳ, TA,) *long in the legs and the necks, and slender, not collecting in flocks, two or three at most being found together:* (Ṣ, TA:) n. un. with ة: (Ṣ, Ḳ:) it is said that the قطا compose two species: the short in the legs, yellow in the necks, black in the primary feathers of the wings, of a white hue tinged with red (صُهْب) in the tertials, are the كُدْرِيَّة and the جُونِيَّة: and the *long in the legs, white in the bellies, dust-coloured in the backs, wide in the eyes,* are the غطاط: AḤát says that *in the* أَخْدَعَانِ [by which is here meant, as in some other instances, the *places of the two veins so called in the neck*] *of the* غَطَاطَة *are what resemble two decorations, two lines, black and white; and it is slender,* [but] *exceeding the* مُكَّاء: accord. to Skr, it is *a bird resembling the* قطا. (TA.) ═ See also the paragraph here following.

غُطَاطٌ The *commencement of the dawn:* (Ṣ, Ḳ:) or *a remaining portion of the blackness of the night:* (Ṣ,* Ḳ:) or the *commingling of the darkness of the last part of the night with the light of the first part of the day:* (TA:) and (Ḳ) the سَحَر [or *period a little before daybreak;* as also ▼ غَطَاطٌ. (Th, Ḳ, TA.)

غَطْغَطَةٌ a word imitative of The *cry of the* [*bird called the*] قَطَا: (Ṣ, Ḳ:) — and of The *sound of the* [*vehemently-boiling*] *cooking-pot.* (TA.)

قِدْرٌ مُغَطْغِطَةٌ *A cooking-pot vehemently boiling.* (Ṣ.)

غطرف

Q. 1. غَطْرَفَ *He* (i. e. God) *made persons to be* [غَطَارِيف i. e. *chiefs,* &c., (pl. of غِطْرِيف,) or] *noble.* (Ḥam p. 793.) — [And *He treated violently, unjustly.* (Freytag, from the Deewán of the Hudhalees.)] ═ See also the next paragraph.

Q. 2. تَغَطْرَفَ *He sought chiefdom,* or *lordship;* [&c.;] from غِطْرِيف meaning سَيِّد. (O.) — And *He magnified himself,* or *was proud:* (El-Aḥmar, O, Ḳ:) [and so, app., ▼ غَطْرَفَ, for] غَطْرَفَةٌ and تَغَطْرُفٌ and تَغَتْرُفٌ signify تَكَبُّر: (Ṣ:) [or] *he was proud, haughty,* or *self-conceited, in walk* (IAạr, O, Ḳ) especially. (IAạr, O.)

غَطْرَفَةٌ [app. an inf. n. of غَطْرَفَ, q. v.: and, used as a simple subst., signifying *Self-magnification,* or *pride:* (see Q. 2:) or] *pride, haughtiness,* or *self-conceit:* and *play,* or *sport;* or *such as is vain,* or *unprofitable.* (Ibn-'Abbád, O, Ḳ.)

غِطْرَافٌ: see غِطْرِيفٌ, in two places.

غُطْرُوفٌ: } see the following paragraph.
غِطْرَوْفٌ: }

غِطْرِيفٌ The *hawk,* or *falcon;* syn. بَازٍ: this is said to be the primary signification: (Ḥam p. 793:) or the *young one thereof:* (Ibn-'Abbád, Ṣ, O, Ḳ:) or the *hawk,* or *falcon,* (بَازٍ,) *that has been taken from its nest;* as also ▼ غِطْرَافٌ. (TA.) — And *A* سَيِّد [i. e. *chief,* or *lord,* &c.]: (Ṣ:) or *a* سَيِّد *that is high-born,* or *noble,* (Lth, O, Ḳ,) or *generous:* said to be so called as being likened to the hawk, or falcon: (Ḥam ubi suprà:) and *liberal, bountiful, generous, noble, and youthful:* (ISk, O, Ḳ:) or *a goodly,* or *comely, youth* or *young man:* (TA:) and ▼ غِطْرَافٌ signifies the same: (ISk, O, Ḳ:) pl. غَطَارِفَةٌ (O, Ḳ, TA) and غَطَارِيفُ and غَطَارِفُ. (TA.) Also *Goodly,* or *beautiful;* and so ▼ غُطْرُوفٌ and ▼ غِطْرَوْفٌ: (Ibn-'Abbád, O, Ḳ:) or the last of these signifies *a youth,* or *young man, such as is* ظَرِيف [i. e. *excellent,* or *elegant, in mind, manners,* and *address,* or *speech,* and *in person,* &c.]. (AA, O, Ḳ.) — Also The *common fly;* syn. ذُبَابٌ. (Ibn-'Abbád, O, Ḳ.) — And عُنُقٌ غِطْرِيفٌ *A wide neck:* (O, TA:) as also خِطْرِيفٌ. (TA.)

غطس

1. غَطَسَهُ, (Ṣ, A, Ḳ,) aor. ـِ, (Ṣ, TA,) inf. n. غَطْسٌ; (Ṣ;) or ▼ غَطَّسَهُ, (Mṣb,) inf. n. تَغْطِيسٌ; (TA;) or both; (A, TA;) *He immersed, immerged, dipped, plunged,* or *sunk, him* or *it,* in water. (Ṣ, A, Mṣb,* Ḳ, TA.) — [Hence,] ▼ غَطَّسَنِى فِى بَحْرِ أَنْعُمِهِ † [*He overwhelmed me in the sea of his benefits,* or *favours*]. (A.) ═ غَطَسَ, aor. ـِ, (Mṣb, Ḳ,) inf. n. غَطْسٌ, (Mṣb,) *He,* or *it, became immersed, immerged, dipped, plunged,* or *sunk,* in water; or *he immersed,* or *immerged himself, plunged,* or *dived,* in water. (Mṣb,* Ḳ.) — غَطَسَ فِى الإِنَآءِ *He put his mouth into the vessel and so drank.* (Ibn-'Abbád, Ḳ.) ═ غَطَسَتْ بِهِ اللُّجَمُ *Death took him away:* (Sgh, Ḳ:) a dial. var. of عَطَسَتْ [q. v.]. (TA.)

2: see the preceding paragraph, in two places.

6. تغاطسا *They two vied,* or *contended, each with the other, in plunging,* or *diving,* (A, Ḳ,) in water; (Ḳ;) syn. تَمَاقَلَا (A, Ḳ) and تَغَاطَّا (A) and تَغَامَسَا. (TA.) And تغاطسوا *They vied,* or *contended, one with another, in plunging,* or *diving,* in water; syn. تَغَاطُّوا. (TA.) ═ تغاطس *He feigned himself negligent, inattentive, inadvertent, inconsiderate,* or *heedless, not being really so;* (Sgh, Ḳ;) and تغاطش is a dial. var. of the same: both are from Aboo-Sa'eed Ed-Ḍareer. (TA.) You say, تغاطس عَنْهُ *He feigned himself negligent of it,* &c.; (Aboo-Sa'eed, TA in art. غطش;) and [app. in like manner] تغاطسهُ. (IAạr, TA in art. عمش.)

غَطَّاسٌ *One who dives to the bottom of water to fetch the shells that contain pearls,* &c. (TA.)

لَيْلٌ غَاطِسٌ *Dark night;* as also غَاطِشٌ. (IDrd.)

مَغْطَسٌ *A place in which one plunges,* or *dives.* (TA.)

مَغْنَطِيس and its variations, here mentioned in the Ṣ and L and Ḳ, see in art. مغنطس.

غطش

1. غَطَشَ, aor. ـِ, (A, Ḳ,) inf. n. غَطْشٌ, (TḲ,) [or perhaps غَطَشٌ, q. v.,] *It* (the night) *became dark;* (A, Ḳ;) as also ▼ أَغْطَشَ: (Ṣ, Ḳ:) or غَطَشَ is syn. with سَدَفَ; and hence اغطش ▼ اللَّيْلُ [app. meaning *the night became dark,* or *black*]. (Aṣ, A, TA.) [See غَطَشٌ, below.] ═ غَطِشَ, (Ṣ, TA,) [aor. ـَ,] inf. n. غَطَشٌ, (TA,) *He had an affection resembling weakness of the sight, with a shedding of tears at most times.* (Ṣ, TA.) And غَطِشَ البَصَرُ [*The eye,* or *sight, became weak, and affected with a shedding of tears at most times*]; and so ▼ اغطاشّ, like احمارّ [in measure]: (TA:) and ▼ تغطّشت عَيْنُهُ *His eye became dark,* or *dim,* (IDrd, Ḳ,) *and weak-sighted.* (IDrd.)

4. اغطش: see 1, in two places. — اغطشوا *They entered into,* or *upon, the darkness* [*of night*]. (TA.) ═ اغطش اللّٰهُ اللَّيْلَ *God made the night dark.* (Fr, Ṣ, A,* Ḳ.)

5: see 1, last sentence.

6. تغاطش عَنْهُ *He feigned himself negligent,* or *heedless, of it;* (Aboo-Sa'eed Ed-Ḍareer, Ḳ;) namely, a thing, or an affair; as also تغاطس; (Aboo-Sa'eed;) and [app. in like manner] تغاطشهُ: (IAạr, TA in art. عمش:) or *he feigned himself blind to it;* either *in the eyes* or *intellectually;* syn. تعامى. (TA.) You say also, مَرَرْتُ بِهِ فَتَغَاطَشَ [*I passed by him and he feigned himself heedless,* or *blind*]. (A.)

11: see 1, last sentence.

غَطَشٌ i. q. سَدَفٌ [app. meaning The *darkness,* or *blackness, of night*]: (Aṣ, A, TA:) Aboo-Turáb, (L,) or AZ, (TA,) makes it to be *after the* غَبَش: (L, TA:) and ▼ غُطَاشٌ also signifies the *darkness and confusedness of night.* (TA.) — Also *Weakness of sight, with a shedding of tears at most times:* (Ḳ:) or *an affection resembling this.* (Ṣ, TA.)

غُطَاشٌ: see أَغْطَشُ, in two places.

فَلَاةٌ غَطْشَى, (Aṣ, A'Obeyd, Kr, Ṣ, A,) or غَطْشَاةٌ, (O, Ḳ,) if from غَطَشَ اللَّيْلُ, originally [and properly] like عَمْيَآءُ, but by poetic license it is made perfectly decl., [with tenween,] but if غَطْشَانُ occurred, as meaning "dark," it would be a fem., written [غَطْشَى,] with ى, (O, TA,) or both forms, without and with medd, (TA,) *A desert*, or *waterless desert, that is dark*: (Kr:) or *of which the ways through it are obscure*; (Aṣ, A'Obeyd, A, TA;) *where one cannot find the right way.* (Aṣ, A'Obeyd, Ṣ, Ḳ, TA.) You say, رَكِبْنَا فَلَاةً غَطْشَى وَنَحْنُ كَرِمَالِهَا عَطْشَى [*We travelled upon a desert, or waterless desert, of which the ways through it were obscure, and we were like its sands thirsty*]. (A.)

غُطَاشٌ : see غَطَشٌ.

غَاطِشٌ : see what next follows.

أَغْطَشُ *Dark*; applied to night; as also ▼ غَاطِشٌ and ▼ غَطِشٌ: [fem. غَطْشَآءُ : see غَطْشَى :] and ▼ تَغْطِيشٌ, an inf. n. [of غَطَّشَ] used as an epithet, signifies the same, applied to sight. (TA.) — Also A man *having the affection of the eyes termed* غَطَشٌ; (Ṣ, TA;) as also ▼ غَطِشٌ : (TA:) fem. of the former غَطْشَآءُ. (Ṣ, TA.)

تَغْطِيشٌ : see the next preceding paragraph.

مُتَغَاطِشٌ *Feigning blindness to a thing.* (Ṣ.) [See 6.]

غطف

غَطَفٌ *Ampleness of the means*, or *circumstances*, of life: (Ṣ, O, Ḳ:) like غَضَفٌ. (O.) ═ And *Length, and a folding*, (O, Ḳ,) in the edges of the eyelids, (O,) or *of the edges of the eyelids*: (Ḳ:) or *length, and then a bending* [app. *upwards*] *of the eyelashes*: occurring in a trad., and, as some relate it, with ع; but Er-Riyáshee knew not this, and thought it to be غَطَف: (TA:) or *abundance of the hair of the eyebrow*: (Ḳ:) said by ISh to be *syn. with* وَطَفٌ: (TA:) but by IDrd said to be the *contr. of* وَطَفٌ, and signifying *paucity of the hair of the eyebrows*: (O, TA:) and it is said to be sometimes used as meaning *paucity of the eyelashes.* (TA.) [See also غَضَفٌ.]

[غطفان, in a note to "Abulf. Ann." i. 194, thought by Reiske to be the name of a bird, is app. a mistake for some word relating to the cry of the bird called غَطَاط.]

غَاطُوفٌ A مِصْيَدَة [or *snare, trap, gin,* or *net*]: a dial. var. of عَاطُوفٌ [q. v.]. (TA.)

أَغْطَفُ A life (عَيْشٌ) *ample in its means*, or *circumstances*: like أَغْضَفُ. (Ṣ, O.) ═ And *syn. with* أَوْطَفُ in relation to the edges of the eyelids [*Having what is termed* غَطَفٌ *as meaning* وَطَفٌ]. (TA.)

غطل

1. غَطَلَتِ السَّمَآءُ (JK, O, K) يَوْمَنَا هٰذَا, (JK, O,) and ▼ أَغْطَلَتْ, (JK, O, Ḳ,) *The sky has* [*by its becoming overcast*] *concealed the light of the sun* [*in this our day*]: (JK:) or *its* دَجْن [*or shade of the clouds in a rainy day, or its abundant rain, or its covering of clouds full of moisture, and dark, but containing no rain,*] *has overspread.* (O, Ḳ.) ═ And غَطَلَ ٱللَّيْلُ, aor. ـِ , (Ḳ, TA,) inf. n. غَطْلٌ, (TA,) *The darkness of the night became confused.* (Ḳ, TA.)

4: see the preceding paragraph.

Q. Q. 1. غَطْيَلَ, (O, Ḳ, TA,) with the ط before the ى, (Ḳ,* TA,) *He was*, or *became, abundant in his property*, or *cattle, and his dependents*, or *relations and household*, or *servants*, (O, Ḳ, TA,) *and his weal.* (O, TA.) ═ And غَيْطَلَ, (O, TA,) thus correctly in the following senses, accord. to the Ḳ غَطْيَلَ, but this is a mistake, (TA,) *He made his traffic to be in beasts of the bovine kind, bulls* or *cows*, (O, Ḳ, TA,) which are termed غَيْطَلٌ. (TA.) — And غَيْطَلَ ٱلْقَوْمُ فِى ٱلْحَدِيثِ *The people, or party, pushed on, pressed on,* or *were copious* or *profuse, in discourse*; or *entered into it; and their voices became high*: (Ḳ,* TA:) on the authority of El-Hejeree. (TA.) [Accord. to the Ḳ غَطْيَلَ, which is said in the TA to be a mistake.]

Q. Q. 4. اِغْطَأَلَّ *It became heaped up*, or *it mounted, one part upon another*: (A'Obeyd, O, Ḳ, TA:) and so اِغْطَالَّ, mentioned by IḲṭṭ: (TA:) the former verb occurs in a verse of Ḥassán Ibn-Thábit, said of the sea. (O, TA.) — And, said of the heat, *It rose*, or *became raised.* (R, TA.)

غَيْطَلٌ is pl. of ▼ غَيْطَلَةٌ, [or rather a coll. gen. n. of which the latter is the n. un.,] signifying *Numerous dense* or *tangled trees*: (Ṣ, O:) or the latter word signifies thus: (Ḳ:) or it (the latter) signifies also *dense*, or *tangled, trees*: (Ṣ, O:) or both signify thus: and also *anything confused*, or *mixed*: (Ḥam p. 213:) or the latter has this last meaning: and signifies also *a collection of trees* and *of herbs*; (AḤn, TA;) and *a collection of* [*the common tamarisks, called*] طَرْفَآء; (Ḳ, TA;) as AḤn says on one occasion. (TA.) — And [the former, or perhaps both words,] The *light of the dawn when mingling with the darkness of the night.* (Ḥam p. 213 [q. v.].) — And غَيْطَلُ signifies حَيْثُ تَكُونُ ٱلشَّمْسُ مِنْ مَشْرِقِهَا ٱلضُّحَى كَهَيْئَتِهَا مِنْ مَغْرِبِهَا وَقْتَ ٱلظُّهْرِ, (JK, O, and so in copies of the Ḳ,) or بَعْدَ ٱلظُّهْرِ, (accord. to the text of the Ḳ in the TA,) or وَقْتَ ٱلْعَصْرِ: (so in some copies of the Ḳ, as mentioned in the TḲ:) [the last is evidently the right reading; and the meaning, *The period of the earlier part of the forenoon, after sunrise, when the sun is distant from its place of rising like as it is from its place of setting at the time of the* عَصْر (q. v.): الظهر is probably an old mistranscription.] ═ Also *Beasts of the bovine kind, bulls* or *cows.* (TA.) [See also غَيْطَلَةٌ, last explanation.] — And The *cat*: (Ḳ, TA:) as also غَيْطَلٌ: on the authority of Kr. (TA.)

غَيْطَلَةٌ : see غَيْطَلٌ. — Also *A company*, or *collection*, (Th, Ḳ, TA,) *of men*: (Ḳ, TA:) or *the assembling of men, and their becoming in a dense, or confused, state.* (IAạr, TA.) — And *Darkness*; as also ▼ غَيْطُولٌ; (Ḳ;) or the latter signifies *confusedness of darkness*; (IDrd, O;) or signifies also *dense* (lit. *accumulated*) *darkness.* (Ḳ. [The Arabs describe thick darkness as "darknesses one above another:" see Ḳur xxiv. 40.]) And The *intricate and confused blackness* of night: (Ṣ, O, Ḳ:) or غَيْطَلَةُ ٱللَّيْلِ signifies *the confusedness and denseness of the darkness* [*of night*]: and the pl. is غَيَاطِلُ. (TA.) — Also *A confusion*, or *mixture, of cries* or *shouts* or *noises*; (Ṣ,* O,* Ḳ;) and so ▼ غَيْطُولٌ: (IDrd, O, Ḳ:) غَيْطَلَاتٌ, pl. of the former, signifies *clamours* of men: and the sing., the *numerous cries* or *shouts* or *noises, and the dust*, of war, or battle. (TA.) — And The *overpowering influence of drowsiness*: (O, Ḳ:) [or so غَيْطَلَةُ نُعَاسٍ: pl. غَيَاطِلُ:] one says, رَيَّثَتْهُ غَيَاطِلُ ٱلنُّعَاسِ meaning غَوَالِبُهُ [i. e. *The overpowering influences of drowsiness retarded him*, or *made him late*]. (A, TA.) — And The *means of happiness of the present world* or *state of existence*: (Ḳ:) or غَيَاطِلُ ٱلدُّنْيَا means *those means of happiness*: (O:) or this latter phrase means *the consecutive means of happiness of the present world.* (TA.) And The *eating and drinking and rejoicing, with security.* (Fr, O, Ḳ.) — And ٱلْغَيْطَلَةُ (accord. to Fr, as is said in the O and TA,) signifies ٱلْمَالُ ٱلْمُطْغِى [as though most probably meaning *Property that causes extravagance*]: (O, Ḳ, TA:) [but from what SM remarks respecting it, I can only infer that he holds ٱلْمُطْغِى to be an epithet applied to the cow as signifying "having a youngling," which is termed طَغْيًا or طُغْيًا, (like ٱلْمُعْجِلُ signifying "having a calf," which is termed عِجْلٌ, and several other epithets of the same form,) and in like manner applied to a collective number of cows, though I do not find it mentioned in this sense; i. e., that he understands, and would explain, ٱلْمَالُ ٱلْمُطْغِى as signifying *The cattle*, meaning *cows, having younglings*: but his derivation of it seems to be far-fetched; and perhaps he may have been led to assign this meaning to it by another explanation of غَيْطَلَةٌ with which it is agreeable, and which will be found in the next sentence:] it is not [he says] from طَغَا, aor. يَطْغُو, signifying أَسْرَفَ فِى ٱلظُّلْمِ, as it seems to be at first sight; but from طَغَتْ said of the بَقَرَة وَحْشِيَّة, signifying صَاحَتْ, the like of which is also said of the ثَوْر. (TA.) — غَيْطَلَةٌ signifies also *Such as has milk, of gazelles*, or *antelopes*, and *of beasts of the bovine kind* [perhaps meaning *of the wild species*, i. e. *bovine antelopes*]; (Ṣ, O, Ḳ;) pl. غَيَاطِلُ: (Ṣ, O:) accord. to AO, the بَقَرَة وَحْشِيَّة [or *bovine antelope*]: (Ṣ, O:) Th says that it signifies the بَقَرَة [or *beast of the bovine kind, bull* or *cow*], not particularizing the wild species. (TA.) [See also غَيْطَلٌ, last explanation but one.]

غَيْطُولٌ : see غَيْطَلَةٌ, first quarter, in two places.

غَوْطَالَةٌ i. q. رَوْضَةٌ [generally meaning *A meadow*]. (IAạr, O, Ḳ.)

شَجَرٌ مُغْطَئِلٌّ *Dense*, or *tangled, trees.* (JK.

[See also غَيْطَلٌ.]) And غُصُونٌ مُغْطَئِلَّةٌ Soft, or tender, branches, (O, TA,) having dense leaves. (TA.)

غطم

غِطَمٌّ A great sea, (Ṣ, Ḳ, TA,) abundant in water; (Ṣ, TA;) and ▼ غُطَامِرٌ, (Ḳ, TA,) like قُرَشِبٌ, (TA,) [in the CḲ غُطَيْمٌ,] signifies the same; as also ▼ غَطْمَطِمٌ: (Ḳ, TA:) one says بَحْرٌ غِطَمٌّ. (Ṣ.) — And † A man large (Ṣ, Ḳ) in disposition (Ṣ) or dispositions; (Ḳ;) [i. e.] liberal, or bountiful: (TA:) one says رَجُلٌ غِطَمٌّ. (Ṣ.) — And A numerous company, or collective body: (Ḳ, TA:) one says جَمْعٌ غِطَمٌّ. (Ṣ, TA.) And ▼ عَدَدٌ غُطَامِرٌ, like قُرَشِبٌ, A large number. (TA.) [See also غُطَامِطٌ, in art. غطمط.]

غُطَامِرٌ: see the preceding paragraph, in two places.

غَطْمَطِمٌ: see the first paragraph.

غِطَمٌّ Thick milk. (Ḳ, TA.)

غطمط

Q. 1. غَطْمَطَةٌ [an inf. n. of which the verb is غَطْمَطَ] The dashing together of the waves of the sea; as also ▼ تَغَطْمُطٌ: (Ḳ:) you say, ▼ تَغَطْمَطَ عَلَيْهِ المَوْجُ The waves dashed together upon him so as to cover him. (TA.) — And The sea's being great in the waves, and abundant in the water; as also غُطَامِطٌ; each an inf. n. (IDrd, Ḳ, TA: but omitted in the CḲ.) — And The boiling of a cooking-pot: (Ḳ:) [or its boiling vehemently; for] you say, غَطْمَطَتِ القِدْرُ meaning The cooking-pot boiled vehemently; as also ▼ تَغَطْمَطَتْ: (TA:) and ▼ تَغَطْمُطٌ signifies also the sounding of the boiling of a cooking-pot. (Ḳ, TA.) — And The sounding of a torrent in a valley. (Ḳ.)

Q. 2. تَغَطْمَطَ, and its inf. n.: see the preceding paragraph, in four places. — The inf. n. signifies also The making, or sending forth, a sound (Ṣ, Ḳ) with which, (Ṣ,) or in which, (Ḳ,) is a roughness. (Ṣ, Ḳ.)

غُطَامِطٌ (originally an inf. n., mentioned above: TA:) Waves (مَوْجٌ) dashing together. (Ḳ, TA.)

غُطَامِطٌ (Ṣ, Ḳ) and ▼ غَطْمَطِيطٌ (IDrd, Ḳ) The sound of the sea when the waves are great and the water is abundant: (so accord. to copies of the Ḳ:) or the sound of the boiling of the sea; (so [the former] in a copy of the Ṣ; TA;) or of the boiling of the cooking-pot, and of the waves of the sea: (so in other copies of the Ṣ: TA:) and ▼ the latter word, also, the sound of water. (IDrd, TA.) — And بَحْرٌ غُطَامِطٌ and ▼ غُطَوْمَطٌ and ▼ غَطْمَطِيطٌ A sea great in the waves, and abundant in the water. (Ḳ.) غُطَامِطٌ is applied in a verse of Ru-beh to a number of men [app. as meaning † Multitudinous]. (TA voce غِطْيَمٌ, by which it is followed.)

غُطَوْمَطٌ: see the next preceding paragraph.

غَطْمَطِيطٌ: see غُطَامِطٌ, in three places.

[Accord. to J, the م in the words of this article is augmentative.]

غطو and غطى

1. غَطَا الشَّىْءَ, (Ḳ, TA,) first pers. غَطَوْتُ, aor. ـُ, (Mṣb,) inf. n. غَطْوٌ; (TA;) and غَطَى الشَّىْءَ, (Ḳ, TA,) first pers. غَطَيْتُ, aor. ـِ, (Ṣ, Mṣb,) inf. n. غَطْىٌ; (Ṣ, TA;) and غَطَّى عَلَيْهِ; (Ḳ;) and ▼ غَطَّاهُ, (Ṣ, Ḳ,) inf. n. تَغْطِيَةٌ; (Ṣ;) or this has an intensive signification; (Mṣb;) [but it is very often used in the sense of غَطَاهُ without teshdeed;] and ▼ اغطاهُ; (Mṣb, Ḳ;) He, or it, covered, or concealed, the thing; (Ḳ and TA in explanation of all;) and came, or became, upon it, or over it. (Ḳ and TA in explanation of all except the first.) غَطَّى ▼ عَلَيْهِ الشَّمْلَةَ, a phrase used by Lḥ, is thought by ISd to mean He covered [or enveloped] him with the [garment called] مشملة, i. e. غَطَّاهُ بِهَا. (TA in art. شمل.) — غَطَى اللَّيْلُ فُلَانًا means The night clad [or covered] such a one with its darkness; as also ▼ غطّى. (Ḳ.) [And the former is also said of the night as though intrans.; an objective complement being app. understood: thus,] غَطَى اللَّيْلُ, (Ṣ, Ḳ,) aor. ـِ; (Ṣ, TA;) as also غَطَا, aor. ـُ, (Ṣ, Mṣb, Ḳ,) inf. n. غُطُوٌّ and غَطْوٌ; (Ḳ, TA;) signifies The night was, or became, dark; (Ṣ, Ḳ, TA;) [and Freytag states that ▼ اغطى is used in this sense in the Deewán of Jereer; like اغضى;] or covered, or concealed, everything with its darkness: (Mṣb:) or, as some say, rose, and covered, and clad, everything. (TA.) — اَللّٰهُمَّ اغْطِ عَلَى قَلْبِهِ is a saying of the Arabs, meaning أَغْشِ [i. e. O God, put Thou a covering upon, or over, his heart]. (TA.) — And one says, غَطَاهُ الشَّبَابُ, inf. n. غَطْىٌ and غُطِىٌّ, [but the latter I think doubtful, for it is of a measure extr. as that of an inf. n. of a trans. v.,] meaning أَلْبَسَهُ [i. e. Youthfulness, or young manhood, clad him, or invested him as with clothes]; as also ▼ غَطَّاهُ. (TA.) And [using the former v. as intrans., one says,] غَطَى الشَّبَابُ, (Ṣ, Ḳ, TA, [in the CḲ, erroneously, الشّابُّ,]) aor. ـِ, inf. n. غَطْىٌ (Ṣ, Ḳ) and غُطِىٌّ, thus in the Ṣ and accord. to ISd and IḲṭṭ and Ṣgh, but accord. to the Ḳ غُطُوٌّ, (TA,) meaning امْتَلَأَ [i. e. The sap, or vigour, of youth or young manhood became full, or mantled, in a person]. (Ṣ,* Ḳ, TA.) — And غَطَتِ الشَّجَرَةُ The tree had long branches, spreading over the ground, (Ḳ, TA,) so that it covered what was around it; (TA; mentioned in art. غطى;) like ▼ أَغْطَتْ. (Ḳ, TA.) — And غَطَا المَآءُ, (Ṣ, Ḳ, TA,) and غَطَى, (TA,) The water rose, or rose high, (Ṣ,* Ḳ, TA,) and became abundant. (TA.) And غَطَا عَلَى الشَّىْءِ is said of anything as meaning It rose, and became high, upon, or over, the thing. (Ṣ, TA.) And غَطَيَانُ البَحْرِ signifies The overflowing of the sea, or great river. (TA.) — And غَطَتِ النَّاقَةُ, (Ḳ, TA,) inf. n. غَطْىٌ, (TA,) The she-camel proceeded in her course, (Ḳ, TA,) and stretched forth. (TA.) — And فَعَلَ بِهِ مَا غَطَاهُ is mentioned in the M as meaning سَآءَهُ [i. e. He did to him that which occasioned evil to him; or that which displeased, grieved, or vexed, him]: but this may be a mistranscription, for غَظَاهُ, which is mentioned in the Ḳ in this sense: or the two verbs may be dial. vars. (TA. [See also a similar explanation of غَطَاهُ in the first paragraph of art. شرى.])

2: see the preceding paragraph, in four places.

4: see 1, in three places. — اغطى الكَرْمُ The grape-vine had the sap running in it, (Ḳ, TA,) and increased. (TA.)

5. تغطّى بِهِ (Ṣ, MA) He was, or became, covered with it; [or he covered himself with it;] namely, his garment [&c.]; (MA;) [and so ▼ اغتطى; for] اغتطى signifies the same as تغطّى. (Ḳ.)

8: see what next precedes.

إِنَّهُ لَذُو غَطَوَانٍ Verily he is one possessing might, and power of resistance, in his people, or party; and possessing abundance [of defenders, or of the means of defence &c.]. (Ḳ.)

غِطَآءٌ A cover, or covering; i. e. a thing by which, or with which, a thing or person is covered, or concealed: (Mṣb, Ḳ:*) or a thing by which, or with which, thou art covered, or coverest thyself: (Ṣ:) or a thing by which, or with which, thou art covered or another thing is covered; so in the M: accord. to Er-Rághib, a thing that is put upon, or over, a thing, such as a طَبَق [meaning cover, or lid,] and the like thereof; like as the غِشَآء is of clothing and the like thereof: (TA:) or the cover, or lid, of a cooking-pot or the like: (MA:) pl. أَغْطِيَةٌ: (Mṣb, TA:) it is [said to be] from the phrase غَطَى اللَّيْلُ. (Mṣb.) — And it is metaphorically applied to denote ‡ Ignorance: whence [accord. to some] the saying in the Ḳur [l. 21], فَكَشَفْنَا عَنْكَ غِطَآءَكَ فَبَصَرُكَ اليَوْمَ حَدِيدٌ ‡ [But we have removed from thee thine ignorance; and thy sight, or thy mental perception, to-day, is sharp, or piercing: see حَدِيدٌ]. (TA.)

غِطَايَةٌ A thing, of the stuffing of clothes, with which a woman has covered herself, (Ḳ, TA,) beneath her clothes, (TA,) such as the غِلَالَة [q. v.] and the like: (Ḳ, TA:) [it is said that] the ى therein is substituted for و. (TA.)

غَاطٍ [act. part. n. of 1, Covering, or concealing, &c. — And hence,] لَيْلٌ غَاطٍ Dark night: or night rising, and covering, and clothing, everything. (TA.) — And شَجَرَةٌ غَاطِيَةٌ A tree having long branches, spreading over the ground, so that it covers what is around it, (TA.) — And مَآءٌ غَاطٍ Abundant water. (TA.)

غَاطِيَةٌ [as a subst.] A grape-vine covering the ground: (IB in art. عجب:) occurring in a verse cited in that art.: so called because of its high growth and its spreading: (TA in the present art.:) or a grape-vine having many نَوَامٍ, i. e. branches. (T and TA in art. نمى.)

مُغْطًى A thing covered, or concealed, &c. (TA.) — [Hence] one says, هُوَ مُغْطَى القِنَاعِ, meaning † He is obscure in respect of reputation. (TA.)

مُغْطَاةٌ i. q. مُغْبَاةٌ [meaning A pitfall covered over with earth]. (TA in art. غبى, q. v.)

غف

5. تَغَفَّفَهُ He took the غُفَّة [i. e. what was sufficient for his subsistence] thereof. (TA.) — See also what next follows.

8. اغتفّت الفَرَسُ, (Ṣ,) or الدَّابَّةُ, (O, Ḳ,) inf. n. اِغْتِفَافٌ, (Ṣ,) The mare, or the beast, obtained what was sufficient for its subsistence of the [herbage called] رَبِيع; (Ṣ, O, Ḳ;) as also ↑ تغفّفت: (TA:) or [in the Ḳ "and"] acquired somewhat of fatness: (Ṣ, O, Ḳ:) each of these meanings is mentioned as on the authority of Ks: (Ṣ:) AZ mentions the phrase اغتفّت المَالُ, (Ṣ,) or اغتفّ المال, (O,) and says that the meaning is [the cattle obtained] middling pasture, and middling fatness. (Ṣ, O.) And اغْتِفَافٌ signifies also The taking [with the mouth] fodder, or provender. (TA.) [See also 8 in art. غث.] ═ اِغْتَفَفْتُهُ I gave him somewhat, little in quantity. (O, Ḳ.)

غُفٌّ Such as has become dry of the leaves of رُطْب [or juicy herbage (in the CḲ رَطْب)]: (O, Ḳ:) as also قُفٌّ. (TA.)

غُفَّةٌ A sufficiency of the means of subsistence: (Ṣ, O, Ḳ:) like غُثَّةٌ and غُبَّةٌ. (O in art. غث.) See an ex. in a verse cited voce طَبَعٌ. — And A thing [or portion of pasture or fodder] that a camel takes with his mouth in haste. (Sh, O, Ḳ.) — And Old, and wasted or withered, such as is the worst, of pasture or herbage. (TA.) — And A portion remaining of the contents of a vessel and of an udder. (TA.) — And The mouse; because it is sufficient food for the cat. (IDrd,* O,* Ḳ.)

غَفِيفَةٌ Such as is beautiful and bright, in full maturity and in blossom, of herbs, or leguminous plants. (Ḳ.)

جَآءَ عَلَى غِفَّانِهِ He came at the time thereof: (O, Ḳ:) so says Ibn-'Abbád: (O:) or (Ḳ) it is correctly عِفَّانِه, with the unpointed ع, (O, Ḳ,) originally إِفَّانِه. (O.)

غفر

1. غَفَرَهُ, aor. ـِ, (Ḳ,) inf. n. غَفْرٌ, (Ṣ, Mgh, Mṣb,) He covered, veiled, concealed, or hid, it; (Ṣ, Mgh, Mṣb, Ḳ;) i. e., anything. (TA.) This is the primary signification. (Mgh, Mṣb.) — [Hence] غَفَرَ الشَّيْبَ بِالخِضَابِ He covered, or concealed, the white, or hoary, hair with dye; (Ḳ;) as also ↑ أَغْفَرَهُ. (TA.) — And غَفَرَ المَتَاعَ, (Ṣ, Ḳ,) فِى الوِعَآءِ, (Ḳ,) He put the goods, or utensils, into the bag, or receptacle, and concealed them; (Ḳ;) as also ↑ اغفرهُ. (Ḳ.) — [Hence also] غَفَرَ لَهُ ذَنْبَهُ, (Ṣ, Mṣb,* Ḳ,) aor. ـِ, (Ḳ,) inf. n. مَغْفِرَةٌ, (Ṣ, Ḳ,) or this is a simple subst., (Mṣb,) and غُفْرَانٌ and غَفْرٌ (Ṣ, Mṣb, Ḳ) and غُفُورٌ (Lḥ, Ḳ) and غَفِيرٌ and غَفِيرَةٌ, (Ḳ,) He (God) covered, his sin, crime, or offence; (Ḳ;) forgave it; pardoned it; (Mṣb, Ḳ;) as also ↑ اغتفر ذَنْبَهُ, (Ṣ,) or اغتفر له مَا صَنَعَ he forgave him what he had done: (Mṣb:) or غُفْرَانٌ and مَغْفِرَةٌ, on the part of God, signify the preserving a man from being touched by punishment: and sometimes غَفَرَ لَهُ signifies [he forgave him, or pardoned him: and also] he forgave him, or pardoned him, apparently, but not really; and thus it is used in the Ḳur xlv. 13, accord. to the B. (TA.) As an ex. of the last of the inf. ns. mentioned above on the authority of the Ḳ, the following saying, of a certain Arab, is cited: أَسْأَلُكَ الغَفِيرَةَ وَالنَّاقَةَ الغَزِيرَةَ وَالعِزَّ فِى العَشِيرَةِ فَإِنَّهَا عَلَيْكَ يَسِيرَةٌ [I beg of Thee (O God) forgiveness, and a she-camel abounding in milk, and might among the kinsfolk, or in the tribe, for they are to Thee things easy]. (TA.) [See also the paragraph commencing with غَفِيرَةٌ.] — In the following saying of Zuheyr, the verb is used tropically:

أَضَاعَتْ فَلَمْ تُغْفَرْ لَهَا غَفَلَاتُهَا

meaning [She lost her young one, and] her acts of negligence with respect to her young one were not forgiven her, by the wild beasts, so they ate it. (TA.) — غَفَرَ الأَمْرَ بِغُفْرَتِهِ ↑, (Ṣ,* Ḳ,) and ↑ بِغَفِيرَتِهِ, (Ḳ,) aor. ـِ, (Ṣ,) [lit. He covered the affair with its cover,] means † he rectified the affair with that wherewith it was requisite that it should be rectified. (Ṣ, Ḳ.) [And ↑ اغتفره perhaps signifies the same: see مُرْتَابٌ, in art. راب.] ═ غَفِرَ, aor. ـَ, (Ṣ, Ḳ,) inf. n. غَفَرٌ, (Ṣ,) It (a garment, or piece of cloth,) became villous; as also ↑ اغفارّ, (Ṣ, Ḳ,) inf. n. اِغْفِيرَارٌ. (Ṣ.) ═ غَفَرَ, (Ṣ, Ḳ,) aor. ـِ, inf. n. غَفْرٌ, (Ṣ,) It (a wound) became recrudescent; or reverted to a bad, or corrupt, state; (Ṣ, Ḳ;) as also غَفِرَ, [of which see another meaning in what follows,] aor. ـَ, inf. n. غَفَرٌ. (Ṣ.) And in like manner the former is said of a sick person: (Ṣ:) [i. e.] غَفَرَ signifies likewise He (a sick person) relapsed into disease, after convalescence; as also غَفِرَ: (Ḳ, TA:) and in like manner one says of a wounded person. (TA.) And [hence, app.,] it is also said of an excessive lover, meaning He experienced a return of his desire, (Ḳ, TA,) after consolation. (TA.) — غَفِرَ said of a wound signifies also It healed: thus having two contr. meanings. (IḲṭṭ, TA.) ═ غَفَرَ الجَلَبُ السُّوقَ, (Ḳ, TA,) aor. ـِ, inf. n. غَفْرٌ, (TA,) means رَخَّصَهَا [more correctly أَرْخَصَهَا i. e. The beasts, or other things, brought thither for sale, made the market cheap]. (Ḳ, TA.)

2. غفّرهُ He said غَفَرَ ٱللّٰهُ لَهُ [May God cover his sins, &c.; may God forgive him, or pardon him]. (TA, from a trad.)

4. اغفر: see 1, in two places. ═ أَغْفَرَتْ It (land) produced somewhat of غفر, meaning small herbage: (TA:) [i. e.] it produced herbage like the nap of cloth. (O, L, TA.*) — And It (land) produced its مَغَافِير [pl. of مُغْفُور, q. v.]. (IAth, O, L, TA.) And اغفر It (the [species of tree, or shrub, called] رِمْث, Ṣ, and the عُرْفُط, [&c.,] TA) exuded, or produced, its مَغَافِير. (Ṣ, TA.) ═ Also, i. e. اغفرت, [from غُفْرٌ, q. v.,] She (a mountain-goat) had a young one, or young ones. (O, TA.) ═ And اغفر النَّخْلُ The palm-trees had, upon their unripe dates, what resembled bark, or crust; (O, Ḳ, TA;) which the people of El-Medeeneh term الغفا [or الغَفَى]. (O, TA.)

5. تغفّر and ↑ تَمَغْفَرَ He gathered what is called مغفر and مُغْفُور [see the latter of these two words]. (Ṣ, Ḳ.) He who says مُغْفُور says ↑ خَرَجْنَا نَتَمَغْفَرُ, and he who says مغفر says خرجنا نَتَغَفَّرُ, We went forth to gather مغفور, or مغفر, from its trees. (Ṣ.)

6. تغافرا They two prayed for the covering of sins, &c., or for forgiveness, or pardon, each for the other. (TA.)

8: see the first paragraph, in two places.

10. استغفر ٱللّٰهَ, (Mṣb,) and استغفر الله مِنْ ذَنْبِهِ, (Ṣ, Ḳ,) and لِذَنْبِهِ, (Ṣ,) and ذَنْبَهُ, (Ḳ,) He begged of God forgiveness, or pardon; (Mṣb;) he sought of God the covering, or forgiveness, or pardon, of his sin, crime, or offence, (Ḳ, TA,) by word and by deed; for so God requires one to do; not with the tongue only. (TA.)

11: see the first paragraph.

Q. Q. 2. تَمَغْفَرَ: see 5, in two places.

غَفْرٌ: see غَفَرَ, in two places. ═ See also غُفْرٌ. ═ Also The belly. (Ḳ.) ═ And A certain thing like the [sack called] جُوَالِق. (Ḳ.) ═ And الغَفْرُ is the name of The star [λ] in the left foot of Virgo: (Ḳzw in his Descr. of Virgo:) or three obscure stars, (Ḳzw in his Descr. of the Mansions of the Moon,) or three small stars, (Ṣ, Ḳ,) [most probably, I think, (not φ and ι and κ, as supposed by Freytag, who refers to Ideler's "Untersuch." pp. 169 and 288, but) ι and κ and λ of Virgo, though said to be] belonging to Libra: (Ṣ:) one of the Mansions of the Moon, (Ṣ, Ḳ,) namely, the Fifteenth. (Ḳzw in his Descr. of the Mansions.)

غُفْرٌ The young of the mountain-goat; (Ṣ, Ḳ;) as also ↑ غُفُرٌ; but the former is the more common; (Ḳ;) the latter, rare: (TA:) pl. [of pauc.] أَغْفَارٌ and [of mult.] غِفَرَةٌ (Ṣ, Ḳ) and غُفُورٌ: (Kr, Ḳ:) the female is termed غُفْرَةٌ: and it is said that غُفْرٌ is an appellation of one and of a pl. number: the phrase غُفْرٌ كَثِيرٌ is mentioned [as meaning *many young ones of the mountain-goat*]. (TA.)

غُفْرٌ The *young of the cow* [probably meaning *of the bovine antelope called the wild cow*]. (El-Hejeree, Ḳ.) —— And *A certain* دُوَيْبَّة [by which may be meant a *small beast* or *creeping thing*, or an *insect*]: (IDrd, O, Ḳ:) so, says IDrd, they assert. (O.)

غَفَرٌ (Ṣ, Ḳ, TA) and ▾ غَفْرٌ (Ṣ, TA) and ▾ غِفَارٌ (Ṣ, Ḳ, TA) *Hair like down, such as is upon the shank of a woman*, and *upon the forehead*, and *the like thereof*: (Ṣ, TA:) or the *hair of the neck*, and *of the jaws*, and *of the back of the neck*; (Ḳ, TA;) as also ▾ غَفِيرٌ accord. to the copies of the Ḳ, but accord. to the L and other lexicons غُفْرٌ: and the *small, short, hairs* of the body. (TA.) —— And غَفَرٌ signifies also The *growth of hair in the place of the mane* of a horse or similar beast. (TA.) —— And The *nap*, or *villous substance, upon the surface of a garment*, or *piece of cloth*, (Ṣ, Ḳ, TA,) and *the like thereof*; (TA;) and ▾ غَفْرٌ signifies the same: (Ḳ, TA:) n. un. غَفَرَةٌ [and app. غَفْرَةٌ]: and غَفَرٌ is also expl. as signifying the هُدْب [app. here meaning likewise *nap*, or *pile*, or perhaps the *unwoven end*,] of a garment, or piece of cloth, and [particularly] of the thin and soft sorts of what are termed خَمَائِص and قُطُف [pls. of خَمِيصَةٌ and قَطِيفَةٌ]; but not the extremities of أَرْدِيَة and مَلَاحِف [pls. of رِدَآءٌ and مِلْحَفَةٌ]. (TA.) —— And *Small herbage*: (Ḳ:) [or] *a sort of small, sprouting herbage, of the* [*season called*] رَبِيع, *growing in plain*, or *soft, land, and upon the* [*eminences termed*] آكَام [pl. of أَكَمَةٌ]; *when green, resembling green passerine birds standing; and when it has dried up, resembling such as are red, not standing.* (L, TA.*)

ذُو غَفَرِ القَفَا means *He is one who has* [*hair such as is termed*] غَفَر *upon the back of his neck*: and هِىَ غَفِرَةُ الوَجْهِ *she is one who has* غَفَر *upon her face*. (AḤn, Ḳ,* TA.)

غُفْرَةٌ *A cover; a thing with which another thing is covered.* (Ṣ.) [Hence] one says, غَفَرَ الأَمْرَ بِغُفْرَتِهِ (Ṣ, Ḳ) and ▾ بِغَفِيرَتِهِ (Ḳ) expl. above: see 1.

غِفْرَةٌ حَسَنَةٌ *A good manner of covering, forgiving*, or *pardoning, sins, &c.* (Lḥ, Ḳ.)

غِفَارٌ: see غَفَرٌ, first sentence.

غِفَارٌ *A certain brand*, or *mark made with a hot iron, upon the cheek* [app. *of a camel*]. (TA.)

غَفُورٌ: see غَافِرٌ, in three places.

جَمَّآءُ غَفِيرٌ *A helmet that encloses and embraces the whole head.* (Ḳ.) AO says, in his "Book on the Coat of Mail and the Helmet," that بَيْضَةٌ is a general name for a helmet, which has plates like the bones of the skull, fastened together, edge to edge, by nails. (TA.) —— جَآؤُوا جَمَّآءَ غَفِيرًا, and الجَمَّآءَ الغَفِيرَ, (Ṣ, Ḳ,) and جَمَّآءَ الغَفِيرِ, and جَمًّا غَفِيرًا, and الجَمَّ الغَفِيرَ, and جَمَّ الغَفِيرِ, and الجَمَّآءَ ▾ الغَفِيرَى, and ▾ جَمَّآءَ غَفِيرَةً, and ▾ جَمَّآءَ الغَفِيرَى, and ▾ جَمَّ الغَفِيرَةِ, and ▾ جَمَّآءَ الغَفِيرَةِ, and ▾ الغَفِيرَةِ, and ▾ بِجَمَّآءِ الغَفِيرَةِ, and بِجَمَّآءِ الغَفِيرِ, (Ḳ,) are phrases meaning *They came all together, high and low, none of them remaining behind, and they being many*: (Ṣ, Ḳ:) accord. to Sb, (Ḳ,) it (الجَمَّآءَ الغَفِيرَ, Ṣ, which is the only form that he mentions, TA, [or rather the former of these two words,]) is a subst., (Ṣ, Ḳ,) put in the place of an inf. n., (Ḳ,) i. e. put in the accus. case like an inf. n. of the same meaning, (TA,) i. e., [as when you say] مَرَرْتُ بِهِمْ جُمُوعًا كَثِيرًا [I passed by them they being very many]: (Ḳ:) it is not a verb, [by which is here meant, as in many other instances, an inf. n.,] but is put in the accus. case like an inf. n. of the same meaning, as when you say جَآؤُونِى جَمِيعًا, and قَاطِبَةً, and طُرًّا, and كَافَّةً, [They came to me all together,] and the article ال is prefixed like as it is prefixed in the saying أَوْرَدَهَا العِرَاكَ, meaning أَوْرَدَهَا عِرَاكًا [He brought them (the camels) to the water all together]: (Ṣ:) Sb says that it is one of those denotatives of state which have the art. ال prefixed, and is extr.; and that الغَفِير is an epithet inseparable from الجَمَّآء; meaning that you do not say الجَمَّآء and then be silent: (TA:) others hold it to be an inf. n.: IAmb allows it to be in the nom. case, on the condition that هُمْ is understood [before it; i. e., the complete phrase being جَآؤُوا هُمُ الجَمَّآءُ الغَفِيرُ]: and Ks says that the Arabs put الجَمَّآء الغفير in the accus. case فِى التَّمَامِ [i. e. in the case of its occurring after a proposition rendered complete by the mention of the agent, as when you say جَآءَ القَوْمُ الجَمَّآءَ الغَفِيرَ], and in the nom. case فِى النُّقْصَانِ [i. e. in the case of its occurring when what precedes it is not a complete proposition, and is only rendered complete by it as the agent, as when you say جَآءَ الجَمَّآءُ الغَفِيرُ]. (Ḳ.) —— It is said in a trad., that Mohammad, being asked by Aboo-Dharr, what was the number of the apostles, answered ثَلٰثُمِائَةٍ وَخَمْسَةَ عَشَرَ جَمَّ الغَفِيرِ, meaning, *Three hundred and fifteen: a great number.* (Nh, TA.) ═ See also غَفَرٌ, first sentence.

غِفَارَةٌ: see مِغْفَرٌ, in three places. —— Also *A piece of rag worn beneath the* مِقْنَعَة [q. v.], *by which a woman preserves it from the oil* or *grease* [*on her head*]: (Ṣ: [accord. to one of my copies of the Ṣ, "preserves her head:"]) or *a piece of rag by which a woman preserves her* خِمَار [q. v.] *from the oil* or *grease*: (Ḳ:) or *a piece of rag with which a woman covers the fore part and the hind part* (*but not the middle*) *of her head.* (TA.) —— [And *A cloth that is spread upon the camel-litter.* (Freytag, from the Deewán of the Hudhalees.)] —— And *A patch* (رُقْعَة) *that is put upon the notch*, (Ṣ, Ḳ,) or *a piece of skin which is upon the head*, (TA,) *upon which runs the string*, of the bow. (Ṣ, Ḳ, TA.) —— And *A cloud* (Ṣ, Ḳ) *that is as though it were* (Ṣ) *above another cloud.* (Ṣ, Ḳ.) —— And The *head of a mountain.* (Ḳ.)

غَفِيرَةٌ: see غُفْرَةٌ, and 1. —— مَا فِيهِمْ غَفِيرَةٌ [*There is not in them any disposition to forgive;*] means *they do not forgive any one a sin, a crime*, or *an offence.* (Ṣ, Ḳ.) And مَا عِنْدَهُمْ عَذِيرَةٌ وَلَا غَفِيرَةٌ [*They have not a disposition to excuse nor a disposition to forgive;*] means *they do not excuse nor do they forgive a sin, a crime*, or *an offence, of any one.* (TA.) The rájiz (Ṣakhr-el-Ghei, L) said, (on seeing his companions, with whom he was journeying, fly from the Benu-l-Muṣṭalik, whom they chanced to meet, L,)

* يَا قَوْمِ لَيْسَتْ فِيهِمُ غَفِيرَهْ *
* فَامْشُوا كَمَا تَمْشِى جِمَالُ الحِيرَهْ *

[*O my people, there is not in them any disposition to forgive: therefore march ye as march the camels of El-Ḥeereh*]: (Ṣ, L:) he mentioned particularly the camels of El-Ḥeereh because they carry burdens; and meant, march ye heavily, and defend yourselves, and do not fly. (L.) ═ Also *Abundance*, and *increase*, in family and cattle or other property. (TA, from a trad.) ═ See also غَفِيرٌ, in five places.

غَفِيرَى: see غَفِيرٌ.

غَفَّارٌ: see the next paragraph.

غَافِرٌ (TA) and ▾ غَفُورٌ (Ṣ, Ḳ, TA) and ▾ غَفَّارٌ (Ḳ, TA) are epithets applied to God, (Ḳ, TA,) the second and third of which are intensive; (TA;) meaning, [the first,] *Covering* and *forgiving the sins, crimes*, and *offences, of his servants;* [or simply *forgiving;* and the second and third, *covering* and *forgiving much the sins*, &c., *of his servants;* or *very forgiving.*] (Ṣ,* Ḳ,* TA.) The pl. of ▾ غَفُورٌ is غُفُرٌ. (Ṣ.) And ▾ غَفُورٌ is also applied to a woman, without ة. (TA.)

غُوفَرٌ The *autumnal* بِطِّيخ [i. e. *melon* or *water-melon*]: (Ḳ:) or *a species thereof.* (Ṣgh, Ḳ, TA.) It is said that the بِطِّيخ and the غُوفَر are of those things in the cases of which the giving of the tithe is not incumbent. (Mgh.)

أَغْفَرُ [*Having the quality of covering*, or *the like, in a greater*, or *in the greatest, degree*]. One says أَصْبِغْ ثَوْبَكَ بِالسَّوَادِ فَإِنَّهُ أَغْفَرُ لِوَسَخِهِ *Dye thou thy garment*, or *piece of cloth, with black; for it has the quality of bearing and concealing its dirt in the greatest degree.* (Ṣ,* TA.)

مُغْفُرٌ: see مَغْفُورٌ, in two places.

مُغْفِرٌ, (O, TA,) or مُغْفِرَةٌ, (Ṣ,) or the latter also, (O, TA,) A she-goat of the mountain *having a young one* or *young ones*: (Ṣ,* O,* TA:) pl. مُغْفِرَاتٌ. (Ṣ, TA.)

مِغْفَرٌ *What is worn beneath the helmet*: (Mgh, Mṣb:) or *a piece of mail*, (زَرَدٌ, Ṣ, Ḳ,) *woven* (Ṣ) *from the* دِرْع [or *coat of mail*], (Ṣ, Ḳ,) *according to the size of the head*, (Ṣ,) *worn beneath the* [*kind of cap called*] قَلَنْسُوَة; (Ṣ, Ḳ;) as also ▾ مِغْفَرَةٌ and ▾ غِفَارَةٌ: (Ḳ:) or the رَفْرَف [or *pendent appertenance*] *of the helmet*: (TA:) or *a piece of mail*,

(حَلَق, or حِلَق, as in different copies of the Ḳ,) *which an armed man,* (Ḳ,) or *a man,* accord. to some lexicons, (TA,) *wears in the manner of a* قِنَاع (يَتَقَنَّعُ بِهَا); as also ↓ مِغْفَرَةٌ and ↓ غِفَارَةٌ: (Ḳ:) accord. to ISh, the مغفر is *a piece of mail* (حَلَق) *which a man puts beneath the helmet, hanging down upon the neck:* and *sometimes,* he says, *it is like the* قَلَنْسُوَة*, except that it is more ample; a man throws it upon his head, and it reaches to the coat of mail; then the helmet is put on over it; and this* مغفر *hangs down upon the shoulders: sometimes, also, the* مغفر *is* [*a covering for the head*] *made of* دِيبَاج [i. e. *silk brocade*], and *of* [*the cloth called*] خَزّ [q. v.], *beneath the helmet:* accord. to "the Book of the Coat of Mail and the Helmet," by AO, مغفر and ↓ غِفَارَةٌ are names applied to *a portion of mail* [*forming a head-covering*], which is also called تَسْبِغَةٌ [q. v.]; *and sometimes the rings are exposed to view; and sometimes they line them within, and cover them externally, with* دِيبَاج or خَزّ or [*the kind of silk stuff called*] بِزْيَوْن; *and they stuff it with something* (حَشَوْهَا بما كان); *and sometimes they make above it a* قَوْنَس [or *tapering top*] *of silver &c.:* (TA:) the term مغفر is also applied to the *helmet* itself. (Mgh.) ━ See also مُغْفُور, in three places.

مِغْفَرَةٌ: see مِغْفَر, in two places.

مِغْفَار: see the next paragraph, in two places.

مُغْفُور (AA, T, Ṣ, Ḳ, &c.) and ↓ مِغْفَر (Ks, T, Ṣ, Ḳ) and ↓ مُغْفُر and ↓ مِغْفَار and ↓ مِغْفِير (Ḳ) *i. q.* مُغْثُور; (T, Ṣ, Ḳ;) [*A kind of manna;*] *a produce of the* [*species of tree, or shrub, called*] رِمْث*, and sometimes of the* عُشَر *and the* عُرْفُط *and the* ثُمَام *and the* سَلَم *and the* طَلْح *&c.;* (Ṣ;) the *gum of the* رمث *and* عرفط; (T;) the *gum that is found upon the* رمث*, which is sweet, and is eaten;* (AA;) *a thing that flows,* or *exudes, from the ends of the twigs of the* رمث*, resembling* دِبْس *in its colour;* (ISh, in explanation of the pl. مَغَافِير;) *a gum that flows,* or *exudes, from the* عرفط*, not of pleasant odour;* (IAth;) *a gum resembling* [*the kind of sweetmeat called*] نَاطِف*, exuded by the* عرفط*, which is put into a piece of cloth, then sprinkled with water, and drunk:* accord. to Lth, ↓ مِغْفَار is applied to the *gum of the* إِجَّاصَة: and some say that ↓ مغفر is applied to *gum of a round shape;* صُعْرُور to that which is in shape like a finger; and ذَوْب to that which flows upon the ground: and ↓ مغفر is also applied to *a twig of a gum-tree, from which* [for به (with which), in the TA, I read منه,] *is wiped a white fluid, whereof is made a sweet beverage:* (TA:) pl. [of مُغْفُور and مِغْفَار and مِغْفِير] مَغَافِير, (T, Ṣ, Ḳ,) and [of مُغْفُر and مِغْفَر] مَغَافِر: (Ḳ:) it is also said that مَغَافِير is applied to *a kind of sweet honey, like* رُبّ*, except that it is white.* (TA.) [Hence the saying,]

هٰذَا الجَنَى لَا أَنْ يُكَدَّ المُغْفُرُ

[*This is gathering, not the scraping off* مغفر]: a prov. alluding to the preference of a thing; said to him who obtains much good. (Ḳ.) [See also Freytag's Arab. Prov., ii. 874.]

مِغْفِير: see the next preceding paragraph.

أَرْضٌ مَغْفُورَآءُ *Land containing* [*trees producing*] مَغَافِير. (IDrd, Ḳ.) [See مُغْفُور.]

غفص

3. غَافَصَهُ, (Ṣ, A, Mṣb, Ḳ,) inf. n. مُغَافَصَةٌ and غِفَاصٌ, (TA,) *He came upon him suddenly,* or *unexpectedly;* (A, Mṣb, Ḳ;) *he took him at unawares,* (Ṣ, Mṣb, Ḳ,) *and did an evil action to him.* (TA.) ━ Hence the saying, (Mṣb,) أَخَذْتُهُ مُغَافَصَةً (A, Mṣb, TA) *I took it* (a thing, Mṣb) *striving to overcome.* (Mṣb, TA.)

غَافِصَةٌ *A sudden,* or *an unexpected, calamity,* of time, or fortune: (Ṣgh,* Ḳ,* TḲ:) pl. غَوَافِص. (A.) You say, وَقَاكَ ٱللّٰهُ غَوَافِصَ الدَّهْرِ [*May God preserve thee from the sudden,* or *unexpected, calamities of time,* or *fortune*]. (A.)

غفل

1. غَفَلَ عَنْهُ, (Ṣ, O, Mṣb, Ḳ,) aor. ـُ, (Ṣ, O, Mṣb,) inf. n. غُفُولٌ (Ṣ, O, Mṣb, Ḳ) and غَفْلَةٌ, (Ṣ, O, Mṣb,) or the latter is a simple subst., (Ḳ,) or it is a simple subst. as well as an inf. n., and so may be غُفْلَانٌ, said in the Ḳ to be a simple subst.; and MF says that غَفَلَ, aor. ـَ, of which غَفَلٌ, mentioned in the Ḳ as a subst. syn. with غَفْلَةٌ, may be the inf. n., has been mentioned by some as a dial. var. of غَفَلَ, but had not been found by him in any of the lexicological works notwithstanding much research, so that its correctness requires consideration; (TA;) *He was,* or *became, unmindful, forgetful, neglectful,* or *heedless, of it,* or *inadvertent to it;* (Mṣb;) namely, a thing: (Ṣ, O, Mṣb:) or *he neglected it;* and *was,* or *became, unmindful, forgetful, neglectful,* or *heedless, of it,* or *inadvertent to it:* (Ḳ:) and sometimes it is used as meaning *he neglected it* [*intentionally*], *leaving it, and turning away:* (Mṣb:) and ↓ اغفله signifies the same as غَفَلَ عَنْهُ: or غَفَلَ signifies صَارَ غَافِلًا [*he became unmindful, forgetful, neglectful, heedless,* or *inadvertent*]: and غَفَلَ عَنْهُ and ↓ اغفله signify وَصَّلَ غَفْلَتَهُ إِلَيْهِ [which is app. said merely for the purpose of showing that the former verb is made trans. only by means of عَنْ, and the latter is trans. without any prep.; for وَصَّلَ الفِعْلَ إِلَى and أَوْصَلَهُ إِلَيْهِ مَفْعُولَهُ, which latter phrase is the more usual, mean "he made the verb transitive"]: (Ḳ:) or ↓ اغفله signifies *he neglected it* (i. e. a thing) *though remembering it.* ('Eyn, Sb, Ṣ, O, Mṣb.) It is said in a trad., مَنِ ٱتَّبَعَ الصَّيْدَ غَفَلَ i. e. *He who pursues the object of the chase has his mind busied and possessed by it so that he becomes unmindful* [&c. of other things]. (TA.)

2. غفّله, inf. n. تَغْفِيلٌ, *He made him to become unmindful, forgetful, neglectful, heedless,* or *inadvertent.* (Mṣb.) ━ See also 4. ━ التَّغْفِيلُ signifies [also] *The sufficing* one's companion [*in respect of an affair*] *when he who is the object thereof is unmindful, unoccupied* [*in mind,* or *actually,*] *by anything.* (ISk, Ḳ, TA.) [You say, غفّل صَاحِبَهُ meaning *He sufficed his companion in respect of an affair when he* (the latter) *was unmindful,* &c.] ━ And غفّله, (Mgh, O, Ḳ, but in my copy of the Mgh written without teshdeed,) inf. n. as above, (O, Ḳ,) *He concealed it,* (Mgh, O, Ḳ,) namely, a thing. (Mgh, O.)

3. غافلهُ [app. *He acted with him in the manner of him who is unmindful, forgetful, neglectful, heedless,* or *inadvertent*]. (TA voce سَاهَاهُ, q. v., in art. سهو.)

4. اغفلهُ: see 1, in three places. ━ [Hence,] one says, مَا أَغْفَلَهُ عَنْكَ شَيْئًا [app. lit. signifying *How unmindful of thee is he as to anything!* and therefore virtually] meaning *dismiss doubt* [*from thee respecting him as to anything*]. (TA. [See further explanations of it voce شَىْءٌ.]) ━ And اغفلهُ عَنْهُ *He made him to be unmindful, forgetful, neglectful,* or *heedless, of it,* or *inadvertent to it;* (Ṣ,* O, TA;) namely, a thing. (Ṣ.) [Or] اغفله signifies *He,* or *it, smote him,* or *lighted on him, he* (the latter) *being* غَافِل [i. e. *unmindful,* &c.]: or *he made him to be* غَافِل: or *he called him,* or *named him,* غَافِل: and in like manner ↓ غفّلهُ, inf. n. تَغْفِيلٌ: (TA:) or تَغْفِيلٌ signifies the *calling* [one] *unmindful,* &c.: and the *rendering* [one] *stupid,* or *foolish.* (KL.) ━ And اغفلهُ signifies also *He asked him* [*for,* or *respecting, a thing*] *in the time of his occupation, not waiting for the time of his freedom therefrom.* (TA.) ━ And اغفل الدَّابَّةَ *He left the beast unbranded; did not brand it.* (Ṣ, O.)

5. تغفّل as intrans.: see 6, in two places. ━ تغفّلهُ *He watched for his unmindfulness, forgetfulness, negligence, heedlessness,* or *inadvertence;* (Ṣ, Mgh, O, Mṣb;) as also ↓ تغافل عَنْهُ, (Ṣ, O,) and ↓ استغفلهُ: (TA:) تغافل [as trans.] in this sense [without a prep.] is a mistake. (Mgh.)

6. تغافل *He feigned himself unmindful, forgetful, neglectful, heedless,* or *inadvertent; not being so really.* (Mṣb.) [And] *He was intentionally,* or *purposely, unmindful, forgetful,* &c.; as also ↓ تغفّل: (Ḳ:) or the former has this meaning: but ↓ تغفّل signifies *he was deceived,* or *circumvented, in a state of unmindfulness, forgetfulness,* &c. (TA.) تغافل عَنْهُ: see 5. It means [also] *He was unmindful,* &c., *of him,* or *it:* or *he feigned himself unmindful,* &c., *of him,* or *it.* (MA.)

10. استغفلهُ: see 5.

غُفْلٌ Land *without cultivation:* (Ḳ:) or *without any way-mark:* (Mṣb:) or *without any way-mark and without cultivation:* (Ṣ, O:) or *not rained upon:* (Ks, Ṣ, O:) or *unknown; in which is no known trace,* or *vestige:* and, accord. to the

M, *a desert*, or *waterless desert, that causes one to lose his way, wherein is no sign*, or *mark:* (TA:) pl. أَغْفَالٌ, (Ṣ, TA,) *syn. with* مَوَاتٌ [q. v.]: (Ṣ:) and Lḥ mentions the phrase أَرْضٌ أَغْفَالٌ, as though they made every portion thereof to be what is termed غُفْلٌ: and بِلَادٌ أَغْفَالٌ, meaning [*tracts of country*] *wherein are no way-marks by which to be directed.* (TA.) — Also A road, or way, &c., *in which is no sign*, or *mark, whereby it may be known.* (Ḳ.) — And A gaming-arrow (قِدْحٌ) *upon which is no mark* [or *notch to distinguish it*]; (Ḳ;) *such as has no portion assigned to it, and no fine:* (O, Ḳ:) [or,] accord. to Lh, one says قِدَاحٌ غُفْلٌ, using the sing. form [of the epithet] meaning [*gaming arrows*] *in which are no notches, and to which is assigned no portion and no fine:* they used to be added to give additional weight to the collection of arrows from fear of occasioning suspicion [of foul play], i. e. to increase the number: and they were four; the first [called] المُصَدَّرُ; the next, المُضَعَّفُ; the next, المَنِيحُ; and the next, السَّفِيحُ. (TA.) — And A beast (دَابَّةٌ) *having no brand upon it:* (Ṣ, O, Ḳ:) and a she-camel *that is not branded, in order that the poor-rate may not be* [*considered as*] *incumbent for her:* and ▼ غُفُلٌ is a dial. var. thereof, or is used by poetic license: the pl. is أَغْفَالٌ. (TA.) The pl. (أَغْفَالٌ) is also applied to Camels, or cattle, (نَعَمٌ,) *that yield no milk.* (TA.) — And A مُصْحَف [or copy of the Ḳur-án] *bare of the* [*signs called*] عَوَاشِر [pl. of عَاشِرَةٌ q. v.] *and the like of these.* (TA.) — And A book, or writing, [*that is anonymous,*] *of which the author is not named.* (TA.) And Poetry *of which the author is unknown.* (Ḳ.) And A poet *unknown* (Ḳ, TA) *and unnamed* [or *anonymous*]: pl. أَغْفَالٌ. (TA.) — Also A man *inexperienced in affairs.* (Ṣ, O, Mṣb, TA.) One *whose beneficence is not hoped for, nor his evilness feared;* (Ḳ, TA;) *he being like the shackled that is neglected:* pl. as above. (TA.) And One *having no grounds of pretension to respect* or *honour:* (Ḳ, TA:) or, as some say, *of whom one knows not what he possesses.* (TA.) — And The *fur* (lit. *furs*, or *soft portions of hair*, أَوْبَار, [perhaps because long left unshorn,]) *of camels.* (AḤn, Ḳ, TA.)

غَفَلٌ: see غَفْلَةٌ. — Also [Such as is] *abundant and high* [*in estimation*, app. of the means of subsistence]; syn. كَثِيرٌ رَفِيعٌ: (O, Ḳ: [or the latter word is correctly رَفِيغٌ, (so in the TḲ,) i. e. *ample, and pleasant* or *good*, as applied to the means of subsistence:]) and *a state of ampleness* of the means of subsistence: (O, Ḳ:) thus in the saying, هُوَ فِى غَفَلٍ مِنْ عَيْشِهِ [*He is in a state of ampleness in respect of his means of subsistence:* app. thus termed as being a cause of unmindfulness, or heedlessness]. (O.)

غُفُلٌ: see غُفْلٌ, latter half.

غَفْلَةٌ the subst. from غَفَلَ, (ISd, Ḳ,) or it is an inf. n. (Ṣ, O, Mṣb, TA) and also a simple subst., (TA,) or the subst. is ▼ غَفَلَةٌ, with fet-ḥ to the ف, to distinguish it from the inf. n.; (Mṣb;) as also ▼ غَفَلٌ, (ISd, Ḳ,) or this may be the inf. n. of غَفَلَ, mentioned above as a dial. var. outweighed in authority; (TA;) and ▼ غُفْلَانٌ, (Ḳ,) or this may be an inf. n. like كُفْرَانٌ, and it may be a simple subst.; (TA;) *Unmindfulness, forgetfulness, neglectfulness, heedlessness*, or *inadvertence;* (Mṣb, Ḳ;) [the *state in which is*] *absence of a thing from the mind* of a man; and *unmindfulness*, or *forgetfulness:* and sometimes, *intentional neglect:* (Mṣb:) or غَفْلَةٌ signifies the *forgetting, neglecting*, or *being unmindful*, of a thing: (Abu-l-Baḳà, TA:) or the *want of requisite knowledge* or *cognizance* of a thing: (El-Ḥarállee, TA:) or, accord. to Er-Raghib, *negligence occurring from littleness of consideration and of vigilance:* or, as some say, the *following the soul in that which it desires.* (TA.) [فِى غَفْلَةٍ *In a state of unmindfulness* &c., and عَنْ غَفْلَةٍ *in consequence of unmindfulness* &c., may often be rendered *at unawares.*]

غَفَلَةٌ: see the next preceding paragraph.

غَفْلَانٌ, or غُفْلَانٌ: see غَافِلٌ.

غُفْلَانٌ: see غَفْلَةٌ.

غَفُولٌ A she-camel *that does not take fright and flee*, (Ḳ, TA,) *nor hold back from a young one that she suckles, nor care who milks her.* (TA.)

غَافِلٌ [and ▼ غَفْلَانٌ, or غُفْلَانٌ, *Unmindful, forgetful, neglectful, heedless*, or *inadvertent:* and the former, sometimes, *intentionally neglecting:* pl. of the former غُفُولٌ and غُفَّلٌ]. (Ḳ.)

مُغْفِلٌ *Possessing camels not branded.* (TA.)

مُغَفَّلَةٌ The عَنْفَقَة [or *tuft of hair beneath the lower lip*]; (O, Ḳ, TA;) so says Th, (O,) or Ez-Zejjájee: (TA:) not the two sides thereof as it is said to signify by J: (Ḳ:) so called because many men neglect [the washing of] it. (TA.) It is said in a trad., عَلَيْكَ بِالْمُغَفَّلَةِ [*Keep thou to the* washing of *the tuft of hair beneath the lower lip*]: meaning that one should use heedfulness in washing it, in the performance of the ablution termed وُضُوء. (TA.)

مُغَفَّلٌ [lit. *Made unmindful*, &c.; see its verb: and hence, *a simpleton;* or] *devoid of intelligence, sagacity, skill, or natural understanding.* (IDrd, Mgh, O, Mṣb, Ḳ.)

غفو and غفى

1. غَفَا, and غَفِىَ: see 4. — غَفَا, (Ḳ, TA,) inf. n. غَفْوٌ and غُفُوٌّ, (TA,) also signifies *It* (a thing, TA) *floated upon the water.* (Ḳ, TA.) ═ غَفَى الطَّعَامَ, aor. ـِ, (Ḳ, TA,) inf. n. غَفْىٌ, (TA,) *He cleared the wheat of what is termed* غَفًى, i. e. *a thing such as* [*the noxious weed called*] زُوَان [q. v.], (Ḳ, TA,) *and other refuse;* (TA;) or *the straw;* as also ▼ اغفى. (Ḳ, TA.)

4. اغفى, (Ṣ, Mṣb, Ḳ, &c.,) inf. n. إِغْفَآءٌ; (Ṣ, Mṣb;) and ▼ غَفَا, (Ḳ,) first pers. غَفَوْتُ, (Ṣ, Mṣb,) inf. n. غَفْوٌ and غُفُوٌّ; (Ḳ;) the latter verb said by ISd to occur in the trads., (TA,) but disallowed by ISk (Ṣ, Mṣb, TA) and by others, (Mṣb,) and said by Az to be rare; (Mṣb, TA;) *He slept:* (Ṣ, Ḳ:) or *he slept a light sleep:* (Mṣb, TA:) or *he was*, or *became, drowsy*, or *heavy with sleepiness;* as also ▼ غَفِىَ, aor. ـَ, inf. n. غَفْيَةٌ. (Ḳ.) — And اغفى *He* (a man, TA) *slept upon what is termed* غَفًى, i. e. *the straw, in the place in which the grain thereof was trodden out:* (Ḳ:) mentioned as from IAạr by Az, and by Ṣgh as from AA. (TA.) — And اغفى الطَّعَامُ *The wheat was abundant in its* نُخَالَة, accord. to the copies of the Ḳ, but more properly its نُفَايَة [i. e. *refuse*]. (TA.) — See also 1. ═ اغفى الشَّجَرُ *The trees hung down their branches.* (IḲṭṭ, TA.)

7. انغفى *It* (a thing, TA) *became broken.* (Ḳ, TA.)

غَفْوٌ and ▼ غَفْوَةٌ and ▼ غَفْيَةٌ (Ḳ, TA) and ▼ غُفْيَةٌ and ▼ غِفْيَةٌ (Ṣgh, TA) *A* زُبْيَة [or *hollow dug in the ground*], (Ḳ, TA,) *in which a sportsman lurks:* the first and second mentioned by Lḥ. (TA.)

غَفًى The *refuse that is taken forth from wheat, and thrown away*, (Fr, Ṣ, TA,) *such as* [*the noxious weed called*] زُوَان [q. v.]; (Ṣ;) *a thing that is in wheat, such as* زُوَان, (Ḳ, TA,) *and other refuse:* (TA:) or the *straw* [*thereof*]: (Ḳ, TA:) accord. to IAạr, the *bad, that is thrown away*, of wheat; as also ▼ غَفَآءٌ. (Az, TA.) — Also, (thus accord. to ISd in all the senses here following in this paragraph that are found in the Ḳ, as is said in the TA, and thus in some copies of the Ḳ,) or ▼ غَفَآءٌ, (thus in the copies of the Ḳ followed in the TA,) *i. q.* غُثَآءٌ [i. e. The *rubbish*, or *small rubbish*, or *particles of things*, or *refuse, and scum, and rotten leaves mixed with the scum*, of a torrent]. (Ḳ, TA.) — And *Fragments*, or *broken portions, of wheat:* (Ḳ, TA:) or the *stalks thereof.* (TA.) — And *A blight incident to palm-trees, like dust falling upon the unripe dates, preventing their becoming ripe*, (Ṣ, Ḳ, TA,) *and rendering them tasteless.* (Ṣ [in which the word thus expl. is غَفًى] and TA.) And *A thick crust that comes upon unripe dates:* [see 4 in art. غفر:] or, as some say, *bad dates, that become* [app. *in the skin*] *thick, or coarse, and like the wings of locusts.* (TA.) — And *A disease incident to straw, rendering it bad.* (TA.) — Also *Such as they drive away*, or *expel, of their camels.* (Ḳ, TA.) — And غَفًى signifies also The *bad* of anything. (TA.) — And The *low, vile, mean*, or *sordid;* or the *lower, viler*, &c.; or the *refuse*, or *rabble;* of mankind. (TA.)

غَفْوَةٌ *A light sleep:* occurring in the traditions. (TA.) ═ See also غَفْوٌ.

غَفْيَةٌ and غُفْيَةٌ and غِفْيَةٌ: see غَفْوٌ.

غَفِيَةٌ, like فَرِحَةٌ [in measure], in the phrase خُطَّةٌ غَفِيَةٌ, [in which, app., the former word is خُطَّةٌ, and the meaning of the phrase *An affair*, or *a case*, or *a dubious*, or *momentous, and difficult affair, in which is something evil*, or *to be rejected*,] is a possessive epithet, signifying فِيهَا غَفًى. (TA: immediately after غَفًى expl. as meaning the "bad" of anything.)

غَفَآءٌ and غُفَآءٌ: see غَفًى, first and second sentences.

الغُفَاوَةُ [in the CK الغُفاةُ] *The whiteness upon the* حَدَقَة [or *iris of the eye*], (K, TA,) i. e., *that covers the* حدقة. (TA.)

إِغْفَاءَةُ الصُّبْحِ *The sleep of daybreak*, or *the first part of the day*. (TA.)

غل

1. غَلَّهُ, (S, O, K,*) aor. ـُ, (S,) inf. n. غَلٌّ, (K,) *He made it*, or *caused it, to enter*, (S, O, K,* [in the CK أَدْخَلَ is erroneously put for أُدْخِلَ فِى],) *into a thing*; (O, K;) as also ▼ غَلْغَلَهُ, (K,* TA,) inf. n. غَلْغَلَةٌ; or this last word signifies the *making*, or *causing*, a thing *to enter* a thing *so as to become confused with, and a part of, that into which it enters*: (TA:) — and غَلَّ, (S, O, K,) aor. as above, (S,) and so the inf. n., (TK,) signifies also *It entered* [into a thing]; (S, O, K;) being intrans. as well as trans.; (S, O;) and so does ▼ انغلّ, (S, O, K,) and ▼ تغلّل, and ▼ تَغَلْغَلَ; (K, TA;) said of [what are termed by logicians] substances and of [what are termed by them] accidents. (TA.) — يَغُلُّ said of a ram means *Penem suum inserit* (يُدْخِلُ قَضِيبَهُ) *non sublatâ caudâ*. (S, O,* TA.) And غَلَّ signifies also *Inivit* (حَشَأ, in some copies of the K without the hemzeh,) *feminam*: (K, TA; in which latter is added ولا يكون الّا من ضخمٍ [app. meaning that this is not said of any but such as is big, or bulky]:) mentioned by IAar. (TA.) — غَلَّ الدُّهْنَ فِى رَأْسِهِ *He made the oil to enter amid the roots of the hair of his head*. (K.) And غَلَّ شَعَرَهُ بِالطِّيبِ *He made the perfume to enter amid his hair*. (TA.) — And غَلَّهُ لَهُ *He made it to be unapparent to him* (دَسَّهُ لَهُ), *he* [the latter] *having no knowledge of it*. (TA: in which the pronoun affixed to the verb relates to a dagger, and to a spear-head.) — غَلَّ المَفَاوِزَ *He* (a man) *entered into the midst of the deserts*, or *waterless deserts*. (S, O.) — غَلَّ المَآءُ بَيْنَ الأَشْجَارِ, (S, O, K,) aor. ـُ, (S, O,) *The water ran amid the trees*. (S, O, K.) And تَغَلْغَلَ ▼ المَآءُ فِى الشَّجَرِ *The water entered amid the breaks*, or *interspaces, of the trees*. (S.) — غَلَّ الغِلَالَةَ *He clad himself with*, or *wore, the* غلالة [q. v.] (K, TA) *beneath the* [*other*] *garments*; because he who does so enters into it. (TA.) And ▼ اِغْتَلَلْتُ الثَّوْبَ [in like manner] signifies *I clad myself with*, or *wore, the garment beneath the* [*other*] *garments*. (K.) — غَلَّ فُلَانًا, (K, TA,) aor. and inf. n. as above, (TA,) *He put upon the neck*, or *the hand, of such a one, the* غُلّ [i. e. *ring*, or *collar, of iron*, for the neck, or *pinion* or *manacle* for the hand]. (K, TA.) And غُلَّ *He had the* غُلّ *put upon him*. (S,* TA.) And غَلَلْتُ يَدَهُ إِلَى عُنُقِهِ [*I confined his hand to his neck with the* غُلّ]. (S, O.) And غَلَّ أَسِيرًا بِغُلٍّ مِنْ قِدٍّ وَعَلَيْهِ شَعَرٌ [*He confined a captive with a* غلّ *of thongs upon which was hair*]. (TA.) One says, مَا لَهُ أُلَّ وَغُلَّ, (S, O, K, TA, [in some copies of the S and K, which have misled Golius and Freytag, ما له أَلٌّ وَغَلٌّ,]) a form of imprecation, (K, TA,) meaning [*What ails him?*] *may he be thrust*, or *pushed, in the back of his neck, and become possessed*, or *insane*, (IB, TA in the present art. and in art. ال,) *and therefore have the* غُلّ *put upon him*. (TA in the present art.) And غُلَّتْ يَدُهُ إِلَى عُنُقِهِ [sometimes] means † *His hand was withheld from expenditure*. (TA.) — غُلَّ, (S, K,) aor. يُغَلُّ, inf. n. غَلَلٌ, said of a man, (S,) *He was*, or *became, thirsty*; or *vehemently thirsty*; (K, TA;) or *affected with burning of thirst*, (S, TA,) *little* or *much*; (TA;) or *with burning of the inside*, (K, TA,) *from thirst*, and *from anger and vexation*. (TA.) — And غَلَّ said of a camel, (S, O, K,) originally غَلِلَ, (MF, TA,) aor. يَغَلُّ; and ▼ اغتلّ also; *He was*, or *became, thirsty*; or *vehemently thirsty*; or *affected with burning of the inside*: (K:) or *he did not fully satisfy his thirst*; (S and O in explanation of the former, and TA in explanation of both;) and غَلَّتْ is said of camels in like manner, agreeably with this last explanation: (K:) and ▼ اِغْتَلَّتْ is also said of sheep or goats, (K, TA,) signifying *they thirsted*. (TA.) — غَلَّ صَدْرُهُ, aor. يَغِلُّ, (S, O, K, TA, [in the CK, erroneously, يَغُلُّ,]) with kesr, (S, O,) inf. n. غِلٌّ, with kesr, (O,) *His bosom was*, or *became, affected with rancour, malevolence, malice*, or *spite*: (S, O, K:) and *with dishonesty*, or *insincerity*. (S, O.) [See also غِلٌّ, below.] It is said in a trad., ثَلَاثٌ لَا يَغِلُّ عَلَيْهِنَّ قَلْبُ المُؤْمِنِ i. e. [There are *three* habits, (خِصَال being understood, these, as is said in the O, being "the acting sincerely towards God," and "giving honest counsel to those in command," and "keeping to the community" of the Muslims,)] *while conforming to which the heart of the believer will not be invaded by rancour, malevolence, malice*, or *spite, causing it to swerve from that which is right*; (S,* O;) a saying of the Prophet; thus related by some: accord. to others, ▼ يُغِلُّ, (S, O,) with damm to the ى, (O,) which is from the meaning expl. in the next sentence here following. (S,* O.) — غَلَّ, (S, Mgh, O, Msb, K,) aor. يَغُلُّ, (S, O,) inf. n. غُلُولٌ, (S, Mgh, O, Msb, K,) *He acted unfaithfully*; as also ▼ اغلّ: (S, O, Msb, K:) or thus the latter, (S, Mgh, O, Msb, K,) accord. to ISk (S, Msb) and A'Obeyd, (S,) in a general sense; (Mgh, Msb;) and *he became unfaithful*: (TA:) but the former verb is used only in relation to spoil, or booty; (S, Mgh, O,* Msb, K;) you say, غَلَّ مِنَ المَغْنَمِ meaning خَانَ [i. e. *He acted unfaithfully in taking from the spoil*, or *booty*]; (S, O;) or meaning *he acted unfaithfully in relation to the spoil*, or *booty*: (Mgh:) or غَلَّ, (IAth, Mgh, TA,) aor. as above, (Mgh,) inf. n. غُلُولٌ, (IAth, TA,) or غَلٌّ, (Mgh, [thus in my copy, accord. to which it is trans., as will be shown by what follows,]) signifies also *he stole*; and *was unfaithful in respect of a thing privily*; and such conduct is termed غُلُولٌ because, in the case thereof, the hands, or arms, have the غُلّ [q. v.] put upon them: (IAth, TA:) or it signifies also *he took* a thing *and hid* it *amid his goods*; and it occurs in a trad. as meaning *he took* a شَمْلَة *privily*. (Mgh.) It is said in the Kur [iii. 155], وَمَا كَانَ لِنَبِيٍّ أَنْ يَغُلَّ and أَنْ ▼ يُغَلَّ, accord. to different readers; the former meaning [*And it is not attributable to a prophet*] *that he would act unfaithfully*; and ان ▼ يُغَلَّ meaning, [agreeably with an explanation of أَغَلَّ فُلَانًا in the K,] *that unfaithful conduct should be imputed to him*; or *that there should be taken from his* [*share of the*] *spoil*, or *booty*; (S, O, TA;) [or this may mean, *that he should be found to be acting unfaithfully*; for, accord. to the TA, اغلّ الرَّجُلَ means وَجَدَهُ غَالًّا;] but IB says that a pass. aor. is seldom found in the language of the Arabs in a phrase of this kind. (TA.) And it is said in a trad. لَا إِغْلَالَ ▼ وَلَا إِسْلَالَ i. e. *There shall be no acting unfaithfully nor stealing*: or *there shall be no act of bribery* [*nor stealing*]: (S, O:) or, as some say, *there shall be no aiding* another *to act unfaithfully* [&c.]. (TA.) — غَلَلْتُ لِلنَّاقَةِ *I fed the she-camel with* غَلِيل i. e. *date-stones mixed with* [*the species of trefoil called*] قَتّ. (S,* O, TA.) — غَلَّ: see غَلَّ فِى الإِهَابِ: أَغَلَّ فِى الإِهَابِ. — غَلَّ عَلَى الشَّىْءِ, inf. n. غَلٌّ; and ▼ اغلّ; *He was silent at the thing*: and also *he was intent upon the thing*. (TA.)

2. غلّلهُ, (K,) or غلّل لِحْيَتَهُ, (S, O,) بِالغَالِيَةِ, (S, O, K,) inf. n. تَغْلِيلٌ, (K,) *He perfumed him*, (K,) or *daubed*, or *smeared, his beard, much*, (O,) *with* غَالِيَة: the teshdeed denoting muchness, (S, O,) (S, O, K:) and ▼ تغلّل and ▼ اغتلّ بالغالية and ▼ تَغَلْغَلَ *He perfumed himself with* غالية: (K:) Lh mentions تَغَلَّى بِالغَالِيَةِ, which is either from the word غَالِيَة or originally تَغَلَّلَ, in the latter case being like تَظَنَّيْتُ for تَظَنَّنْتُ, but the former is the more agreeable with analogy: accord. to Fr, one says, ▼ تَغَلَّلْتُ بالغالية, and not تَغَلَّيْتُ: (TA:) As held ▼ تَغَلَّلْتُ from الغالية to be allowable if meaning *I introduced the* غالية *into my beard or my mustache*; (S, O;) and the like is the case with respect to غَلَّلْتُ بِهَا لِحْيَتِى: (S:) accord. to Lth, one says, from الغالية, غَلَّلْتُ and غَلَّيْتُ and غَلَّفْتُ. (TA. [See also 1 in art. غلف; and see art. غلى.])

4. اغلّ إِبِلَهُ, (K,) inf. n. إِغْلَالٌ, (TA,) *He watered his camels ill, so that they did not satisfy their thirst*: (K, TA:) or *he brought*, or *sent, them back from the water without satisfying their thirst*: (O, TA:) thus expl. by Az, who says that it is incorrectly mentioned by A'Obeyd, on

the authority of AZ, [in this sense,] with the unpointed ع. (TA. [But see 4 in art. عل.]) — And اغلّ signifies also اغتلّت غنمهُ (O, K) [accord. to the TA as meaning *His sheep, or goats, thirsted*: but this I think doubtful: see 8]. = اغلّ and its aor. and inf. n. as relating to unfaithfulness, see in the latter half of the first paragraph, in five places. = اغلّت الضَّيْعَةُ, (Mgh, Mṣb, K, [in the CK غَلَّت,]) and الضِّيَاعُ, (Ṣ, O, K,) from الغَلَّةُ, (Ṣ, O,) [*The estate, and estates, consisting of land, &c.,*] *became in the condition of having* غَلَّة [*or proceeds, revenue, or income, accruing from the produce, &c.*]: (Mgh, Mṣb:) or *yielded* غَلَّة: (K, TA:) i. e. *yielded somewhat, the source thereof remaining.* (TA.) — And اغلّ meaning بَلَغَتْ غَلَّتُهُمُ القَوْمُ [i. e. *The* غلّة *of the people, or party, arrived*; as expl. in the PṢ and TA; or *the people, or party, had their* غلّة *brought to them*]. (Ṣ, O, K.) And *The people, or party, became in* [or *entered upon*] *the time of the* غَلَّة. (TA.) — And فُلَانٌ يُغِلُّ عَلَى عِيَالِهِ *Such a one brings the* غَلَّة *to his family, or household.* (Ṣ, O.) = اغلّ الوَادِى *The valley gave growth to what are termed* غُلَّان, (Ṣ, O, K,) pl. of غَالٌّ. (TA.) = اغلّ فِى الإِهَابِ, (Ṣ, O,) *He* (a butcher) *left some of the flesh sticking in the hide, in stripping it off*: (Ṣ, O:) or *he took some of the flesh and of the fat* [*in the hide*] *in the skinning*: (K:) and الإِهَابَ ↑ غلّ *he left somewhat* [*of the flesh, or of the flesh and of the fat,*] *remaining in the hide on the occasion of the skinning*: a dial. var. of أَغَلَّ. (TA.) — And accord. to AA, الإِغْلَالُ signifies *The milking of the she-camel when milk remains* [app. *afterwards*] *in her udder.* (O.) [Perhaps the meaning is *The leaving some remaining* in the udder *on the occasion of milking.*] = اغلّ الخَطِيبُ *The orator, or preacher, said, or spoke, what was not right, or correct.* (TA.) = اغلّ بَصَرَهُ, (Ṣ, O,) or البَصَرَ, (K,) *He* (a man, Ṣ, O) *looked intensely, or intently.* (Ṣ, O, K.) — See also 1, last sentence. = إِغْلَالٌ signifies also The *making an overt, or open, hostile, or predatory, incursion.* (TA.) = And The *clothing oneself with, or wearing, a coat of mail.* (TA.)

5: see 1, first sentence: = and see also 2, in three places.

7: see 1, first sentence.

8. اِغْتَلَلْتُ الثَّوْبَ: see 1, former half. = اِغْتَلَلْتُ الشَّرَابَ *I drank the beverage.* (K.) = لَهُ أُرَيْضَةٌ يَغْتَلُّهَا: see 10. = اغتلّ said of a camel, and اِغْتَلَّتْ said of sheep or goats: see 1, near the middle of the paragraph. (See also the next sentence but one.) = اغتلّ بِالغَالِيَةِ: see 2. = اِغْتَلَّتْ said of sheep or goats, *They became affected with the disease termed* غَلَل [q. v.]. (O, K.)

10. اِسْتِغْلَالٌ signifies The *desiring, or demanding, or* [*tasking* a person,] *to bring* غَلَّة [i. e. *proceeds, revenue, or income, accruing from the produce, or yield, of land,* &c.]. (PṢ.) One says, استغلّ عَبْدَهُ, meaning *He tasked his slave to bring* غَلَّة *to him.* (Ṣ, O, K. [In the explanation in the CK, يُغِلّ is erroneously put for يَغُلّ.]) — And The *taking, or receiving,* [or *obtaining,*] *of* غَلَّة: (PṢ:) or the *bringing of* غلّة *from a place* [or *an estate*]. (KL.) One says, استغلّ المُسْتَغَلَّاتِ ↑ *He took the* غلّة *of the* مستغلّات [i. e. of the *lands, or estates, from which* غلّة *is obtained*]. (Ṣ, O, K.) And لَهُ أُرَيْضَةٌ يَغْتَلُّهَا ↑ like يَسْتَغِلُّهَا [i. e. *To him belongs a small portion of land of which he takes, or receives, or obtains, the* غلّة]. (TA.) — And [hence] one says of a hard man, لَا يُسْتَغَلُّ مِنْهُ شَيْءٌ † [*Nothing, meaning no profit or advantage, is reaped, or obtained, from him*]. (L and TA in art. مرس: see 5 in that art.)

R. Q. 1. غَلْغَلَ, inf. n. غَلْغَلَةٌ: see 1, first sentence. — غَلْغَلَ رِسَالَةً إِلَى صَاحِبِهَا [*He conveyed a message, or letter, to the person to whom it pertained*: see the pass. part. n., below]. (Ham p. 500.) = And غَلْغَلَةٌ signifies also *A breaking* [of the bone of the nose, and of the head of a flask or bottle], like غَرْغَرَةٌ. (TA.) = [See مُغَلْغَلَةٌ. I do not find any instance of the usage of غَلْغَلَ otherwise than as trans.: but in the TK, and hence by Freytag, غَلْغَلَةٌ in a sense in which it is expl. below is regarded as an inf. n., and consequently the verb is said to signify *He went quickly*; which is a meaning of R. Q. 2.]

R. Q. 2. تَغَلْغَلَ: see 1, first quarter, in two places. قَدْ تَغَلْغَلْتَ يَا عَدُوَّ ٱللّٰهِ, said to the مُخَنَّث Heet, when he described a woman, as is related in a trad., is expl. as meaning *Thou hast reached,* in thy looking, of the beauties of this woman, *a point which no looker, nor any one having close communion, nor any describer, has reached* [*beside thee, O enemy of God*]. (TA.) — Also *He went quickly*: (K,* TA:) one says, تَغَلْغَلُوا فَمَضَوْا [*They went quickly, and passed, or passed away*]. (TA.) = تغلغل بِالغَالِيَةِ: see 2.

غُلٌّ *A ring, or collar, of iron, which is put upon the neck*: (Mṣb:) *a shackle for the neck* or *for the hand*: [i. e. *a ring, or collar, for the neck,* or *a pinion* or *manacle for the hand*:] (MA:) or *a* [*shackle of the kind called*] جَامِعَة, (TA, and so in the Ṣ and K in art. جمع,) *of iron,* (TA,) *collecting together the two hands to the neck*: (Ṣ in art. جمع; and Jel* in xxxvi. 7:) [sometimes, *a shackle for the neck and hands, consisting of two rings, one for the neck and the other for the hands, connected by a bar of iron*: (see زَمَّارَةٌ:)] and *a shackle with which the Arabs used to confine a captive when they took him, made of thongs, upon which was hair, so that sometimes, when it dried, it became infested with lice upon his neck*: (TA:) the pl. is أَغْلَالٌ: (Ṣ, O, Mṣb, K:) which repeatedly occurs in the Kur-án and the Sunneh as meaning † *difficult tasks* and *fatiguing works* [as being likened to shackles upon the necks]. (TA.) — [Hence] the Arabs apply it metonymically to denote ‡ *A wife.* (TA.) And غُلٌّ قَمِلٌ [lit. *A lousy shackle for the neck* &c.] is an appellation of † *a woman of evil disposition*; originating from the fact that the غُلّ used to be of thongs, upon which was hair, so that it became infested with lice. (Ṣ.) = Also, and غُلَّةٌ ↑, (Ṣ, O, K,) and غَلَلٌ ↑, (K,) or this is the inf. n. of غُلَّ, (Ṣ,) [and accord. to analogy of غَلَّ as originally غَلِلَ,] and غَلِيلٌ ↑, (Ṣ, O, K,) *Thirst*: or *vehement thirst*: (K, TA:) or the *burning of thirst*; (Ṣ, O, TA;) *little* or *much*: (TA:) or *burning of the inside,* (K, TA,) *from thirst,* and *from anger and vexation.* (TA.)

غِلٌّ and غَلِيلٌ ↑ *Rancour, malevolence, malice,* or *spite*: (Ṣ, O, Mṣb, K, TA:) or *latent rancour* &c.: (JK in explanation of the former:) and *envy*; so each signifies; (TA;) [and so the former in the Kur vii. 41 and xv. 47:] and *enmity*: (TA in explanation of the latter:) and the former signifies also *dishonesty,* or *insincerity.* (Ṣ, O.)

غَلَّةٌ *Proceeds, revenue,* or *income,* (Mgh, Mṣb, K, TA, [in the CK, الدَّخَلَةُ is put for الدَّخْلُ,]) *of any kind,* (Mgh, Mṣb,) *accruing from the produce,* or *yield, of land,* (Mgh, Mṣb, K, TA,) or *from the rent thereof,* (Mgh, Mṣb, TA,) [in which sense مُغَلٌّ ↑ is also used, as a subst., pl. مُغَلَّاتٌ,] or *from seed-produce,* and *from fruits,* and *from milk,* and *from hire,* and *from the increase of cattle,* and *the like,* (TA,) and *from the rent of a house,* (K, TA,) and *from the hire of a slave,* (Mgh, K, TA,) and *the like*; (Mgh, Mṣb;) [generally meaning *corn,* or *grain*; i. e.] *wheat* and *barley* and *rice* and *the like*: (KL:) the غَلَّة of the slave is the *payment imposed by the master, and made to him*: (TA voce ضَرِيبَةٌ:) pl. غَلَّاتٌ (Ṣ, O, Mṣb, TA) and غِلَالٌ. (Mṣb, TA.) — Also *Dirhems* [or *pieces of money*] *that are clipped* (مُقَطَّعَة), *in a single piece thereof* [*the quantity clipped being*] *a* قِيرَاط *or a* طَسُّوج *or a grain*; of which it is said in the "Eedáh," that one's lending غَلَّة in order to have such as are free from defect returned to him is disapproved: (Mgh:) or *dirhems* [or *pieces of money*] *that are rejected by the treasury of the state, but taken by the merchants.* (KT. [Freytag has given this latter explanation, but has erroneously assigned it to غُلَّة.])

غُلَّةٌ *A thing in which one hides himself.* (IAar, TA.) — See also غِلَالَةٌ, in two places: — and غَلَلٌ. = And see غُلٌّ, last sentence.

غَلَلٌ *Water amid trees*: pl. أَغْلَالٌ. (Ṣ, O. [See an ex. voce عَذْبٌ.]) And *Water having no current, only appearing a little upon the surface of the earth, disappearing at one time and appearing at another*: (AA, Ṣ, O:) or, accord. to AHn, *a feeble flow of water from the bottom of a valley* or *water-course, amid trees.* (TA.) Aboo-Sa'eed says,

* لَا يَذْهَبُ كَلَامُنَا غَلَلَا *

[*Our speech shall not pass away as a feeble flow of water*]: meaning that it ought not to be concealed from men, but should be made public. (TA.) = Also *A strainer,* or *clarifier*: occurring in a verse of Lebeed, cited voce رَاوُوقٌ: where it means the فِدَام (Ṣ, O, TA) *on the heads of the* أَبَارِيق, (Ṣ,) or *on the head of the* إِبْرِيق: (O, TA:) or, as some relate the verse, the word is غُلَلٌ, pl. of ▼غُلَّةٌ; (Ṣ, O, TA;) which signifies [the same, i. e.] *a piece of rag bound on the head of the* ابريق [*to act as a strainer*]. (IAạr, TA.) ═ And The *flesh that is left upon the thumb when one skins* [*a beast*]. (TA.) ═ See also غُلٌّ, last sentence. ═ Also, (O, Ḳ,) and ▼غُلَالَةٌ, (O, and so in copies of the Ḳ,) or ▼غُلَالَةٌ, (so in other copies of the Ḳ, and accord. to the TA,) *A certain disease that attacks sheep, or goats,* (O, Ḳ, TA,) *in the orifice of the teat, occasioned by the milker's not exhausting the udder, but leaving in it some milk, which becomes blood,* or *coagulates and is mixed with a yellow fluid.* (TA.)

غَلُولُ الشَّيْخِ *The food of the old man, which he ingests into his belly* [or *stomach*]: (Ṣ, O, Ḳ:) and likewise *the beverage drunk by him.* (TA.) One says, نِعْمَ غَلُولُ الشَّيْخِ هٰذَا [*Excellent,* or *most excellent, is this food of the old man* &c.!]. (Ṣ, O, Ḳ.)

غَلِيلٌ: see غُلٌّ, last sentence. — [Hence,] sometimes, (TA,) † The *burning of love,* and *of grief.* (Ḳ, TA.) — See also غُلٌّ. ═ And see مَغْلُولٌ. ═ Also *Date-stones mixed with* [*the species of trefoil called*] قَتّ, (Ṣ, O, Ḳ, TA,) and in like manner *with dough,* (TA,) *for a she-camel,* (Ṣ, O, Ḳ, TA,) *which is fed therewith.* (Ṣ, O, TA.) ═ See also غَالٌّ.

غُلَالَةٌ, or غِلَالَةٌ: see غَلَلٌ, last sentence.

غِلَالَةٌ *A garment that is worn next the body, beneath the other garment,* (Ṣ, O, Ḳ,) and *likewise beneath the coat of mail;* (Ṣ, O;) also called ▼غُلَّةٌ: (Ḳ, TA:) pl. [of the former] غَلَائِلُ and [of the latter] غُلَلٌ. (TA.) — And *A piece of cloth with which a woman makes her posteriors* [*to appear*] *large,* (O,* Ḳ,* TA,) *binding it upon her hinder part, beneath her waist-wrapper;* (TA;) as also ▼غُلَّةٌ, of which the pl. is غُلَلٌ. (IB, TA.) — And The *pin that connects the two heads of the ring* [*of a coat of mail*]: (O, Ḳ:) pl. غَلَائِلُ. (TA.) And غَلَائِلُ signifies *Coats of mail:* or the *pins thereof that connect the heads of the rings:* or *linings,* or *inner coverings, that are worn beneath them,* (Ḳ, TA,) i. e. *beneath the coats of mail:* and [it is said that] the sing. thereof is ▼غَلِيلَةٌ. (Ḳ, TA.)

غَلِيلَةٌ: see what next precedes.

غَلَّانُ (Ṣ, O, Ḳ) and ▼غَالٌّ, (Ḳ,) applied to a camel, (Ṣ, O, Ḳ,) *Thirsty:* (Ḳ:*) or *vehemently thirsty:* (Ṣ, O, Ḳ:*) or *affected with burning of the inside:* (Ḳ:*) and ▼غَالَّةٌ, and its pl. غَوَالُّ, camels *not having fully satisfied their thirst.* (TA.)

غَالٌّ; and its fem., with ة: see the next preceding paragraph. ═ Also *Low,* or *depressed, ground, in which are trees, and places of growth of* [*the trees called*] سَلَم *and* طَلْح: one says غَالٌّ مِنْ سَلَمٍ, like as one says عِيصٌ مِنْ سِدْرٍ and قَصِيمَةٌ مِنْ غَضًا: (AḤn, Ṣ, O:) or, as also ▼غَلِيلٌ, *a place of growth of* [*the trees called*] طَلْح: or *a low,* or *depressed, valley* or *torrent-bed in the ground,* (Ḳ, TA,) *in which are trees:* (TA:) pl. غُلَّانٌ. (Ḳ.) — And *A certain plant,* (Ṣ, O, Ḳ,) [said to be] *well known:* (Ḳ: [but I have not found it to be now known:]) pl. غُلَّانٌ. (Ṣ, O, Ḳ.)

غَالَّةٌ [as a subst.] *A part broken off from the shore of the sea and become collected together in a place.* (TA.) [Expl. by Freytag as signifying "*Pars maris, quæ in litore abrupta est:*" and as being a word of the dial. of El-Yemen: on the authority of IDrd.]

غلغل, [thus in my original,] applied to the root (عِرْق) of a tree, *Extending far into the earth:* pl. غَلَاغِلُ. (TA.)

غَلْغَلَةٌ *A quick rate of going.* (Ṣ, O, Ḳ,* TA.) [App. a simple subst.; but perhaps an inf. n., of which the verb is غَلْغَلَ, q. v.]

غُلْغُلَةٌ *Clamour and confusion of voices.* (TA.) [Like the Pers. غُلْغُل and غُلْغُلَه.]

مُغَلٌّ, as a subst., pl. مُغَلَّاتٌ: see غَلَّةٌ.

مُغِلٌّ A man *cleaving to rancour, malevolence, malice,* or *spite.* (TA.) — An *unfaithful* man; one *who acts unfaithfully.* (Ṣ,* Mgh, O,* TA.) Hence the saying of Shureyḥ, لَيْسَ عَلَى المُسْتَعِيرِ غَيْرِ المُغِلِّ ضَمَانٌ وَلَا عَلَى المُسْتَوْدَعِ, (Ṣ, Mgh, O, TA,) (TA,) i. e. [*There is no guaranteeship to be imposed upon the asker of a loan, except the unfaithful, nor upon him who is asked to take charge of a deposit,* meaning], except in the case of him who has been unfaithful in respect of the loan and the deposit: or, as some say, by the مُغِلّ is here meant the ▼مُسْتَغِلّ [i. e. *the person employed to bring the* غَلَّة]: but IAth says that the former is the right explanation. (TA.) ═ مُغِلَّةٌ, applied to a garden (جَنَّة), as in a verse cited voce حَرْدٌ, (Ṣ, O,) or to an estate (ضَيْعَة), (Mgh, TA,) *Having,* (Mgh,) or *yielding,* (TA,) غَلَّة [q. v.; *fruitful,* or *productive*]. (Mgh, TA.)

مَغْلُولٌ, applied to a man, *Having the* [*shackle called*] غُلّ *put upon him.* (TA.) It is said in the Ḳur [v. 69], وَقَالَتِ ٱلْيَهُودُ يَدُ ٱللّٰهِ مَغْلُولَةٌ [*And the Jews said, The hand of God is shackled*], meaning, *withheld from dispensing.* (O.) ═ Also, (Ṣ, Ḳ,) applied to a man, (Ṣ,) and ▼غَلِيلٌ, and ▼مُغْتَلٌّ, (Ḳ,) *Thirsty;* or *vehemently thirsty;* (Ḳ, TA;) or *affected with burning of thirst,* (Ṣ, TA,) *little* or *much;* (TA;) or *with burning of the inside,* (Ḳ, TA,) *from thirst,* or *from anger and vexation.* (TA.)

مُغْتَلٌّ: see what next precedes. — [Hence,] أَنَا مُغْتَلٌّ إِلَيْهِ ‡ *I am yearning,* or *longing, for him,* or *it.* (Ḳ, TA.)

رِسَالَةٌ مُغَلْغَلَةٌ *A message,* or *letter, conveyed from town to town,* or *from country to country.* (Ṣ, O, Ḳ.)

مُغَلْغِلَةٌ, with kesr to the second غ, *Hastening;* syn. مُسْرِعَةٌ [which is trans. and intrans.; but generally the latter, like سَرِيعٌ]. (TA.)

مُسْتَغَلٌّ *A place* [or *land* or *an estate*] *from which* غَلَّة *is obtained:* (KL:) [thus used, as a subst., it has for its pl. مُسْتَغَلَّاتٌ:] see 10.

مُسْتَغِلٌّ: see مُغِلٌّ.

غلب

1. غَلَبَهُ, (Ṣ, Mṣb,) [and غَلَبَ عَلَيْهِ,] aor. ـِ, (Mṣb,) inf. n. غَلْبٌ and غَلَبٌ, (Ṣ, Ḳ, TA,) the former of which is the more chaste, (TA,) or the latter is an inf. n. and the former is a simple subst., (Mṣb,) and غَلَبَةٌ, (Ṣ, Ḳ, TA,) [the most common form,] or this is a simple subst. like غَلَبٌ, (Mṣb,) which is perhaps formed from it by the elision of the ة, (Fr, Ṣ,) and مَغْلَبٌ and مَغْلَبَةٌ, (Ḳ, TA,) which last is rare, (TA,) and غَلَابِيَةٌ and [in an intensive sense] غِلِبَّى and غُلُبَّى (Ḳ, TA) and غُلُبَّةٌ (Lḥ, Ḳ, TA, said in the Ṣ to be syn. with غَلَبَةٌ) and غَلُبَّةٌ, with fet-ḥ to the غ, (Ḳ, TA, in the CḲ غَلَبَّة,) and غِلِبَّاءُ, (Kr, TA,) *He,* or *it, overcame, conquered, subdued, overpowered, mastered,* or *surpassed, him,* or *it; gained ascendency* or *the mastery, prevailed,* or *predominated, over him,* or *it;* or *was,* or *became, superior in power* or *force* or *influence, to him,* or *it.* (A, MA, Ḳ, PṢ, TḲ, &c.) [See also 5.] — One says, غَلَبْتُهُ عَلَيْهِ meaning [*I overcame him in contending for it;* i. e.] *I took it,* or *obtained it, from him* [*by superior power* or *force*]. (A.) And غُلِبَ فُلَانٌ عَلَى الشَّىْءِ *Such a one had the thing taken from him by superior power* or *force.* (Mgh.) Hence the saying, لَا تُغْلَبُوا عَلَى صَلَاةٍ قَبْلَ طُلُوعِ الشَّمْسِ وَقَبْلَ غُرُوبِهَا *Be not ye overcome and anticipated* by others *in performing prayer before the rising of the sun and before its setting,* so that the opportunity for your doing so escape you. (Mgh.) — And غَلَبَهُ عَلَى نَفْسِهِ *He forced him,* or *constrained him against his will.* (A, TA.) — [And غَلَبَهُ الأَمْرُ *The affair overcame, defeated,* or *baffled, him.*] — And غَلَبَهُ بِالخَوْفِ *He exceeded him in fear.* (Ṣ in art. خوف.) — And غَلَبَ عَلَى فُلَانٍ الكَرَمُ *Generosity was,* or *became, the predominant quality of such a one.* (TA.) — And غَلَبَ أَنْ يُخْطَمَ [*He refused to have the* خِطَام (or *leading-rope*) *put upon him*]; said of a camel. (TA in art. خطم.) — And أَيَغْلِبُ أَحَدُكُمْ أَنْ يُصَاحِبَ النَّاسَ مَعْرُوفًا meaning أَيَعْجِزُ [i. e. *Is any one of you unable to associate with men kindly?*]. (A.) ═ غَلِبَ, aor. ـَ, (Ḳ, TA,) inf. n. غَلَبٌ, (Ṣ,* TA,) *He was,* or *became, thick-necked:* (Ḳ, TA:) or *thick and short in the neck:* or *thick*

and inclining in the neck: from disease or other cause. (TA.)

2. غَلَّبْتُهُ عَلَيْهِ, inf. n. تَغْلِيبٌ, [I made him to overcome, conquer, subdue, overpower, master, or surpass, him, or it; &c.: see 1: and] I made him to gain the mastery over it, or to obtain possession of it, (namely, a town, or country,) by [superior power or] force. (Ṣ.) —— And غُلِّبَ عَلَى صَاحِبِهِ He (a poet) was judged to have overcome his fellow. (TA.) [See مُغَلَّبٌ.] —— [غَلَّبَ لَفْظًا عَلَى لَفْظٍ آخَرَ, a conventional phrase of the lexicologists, means He made a word to predominate over another word; as in القَمَرَانِ for الشَّمْسُ وَالقَمَرُ; and سِرْنَا عَشْرًا for سِرْنَا عَشْرَ لَيَالٍ بِأَيَّامِهَا: of the former instance you say, فِيهِ تَغْلِيبُ القَمَرِ عَلَى الشَّمْسِ In it is the attribution of predominance to the moon over the sun; and in the latter, فِيهِ تَغْلِيبُ اللَّيْلِ عَلَى النَّهَارِ In it is the attribution of predominance to the night over the day. See more in Kull p. 115.]

3. غَالَبَهُ [He vied, contended, or strove, with him, to overcome, conquer, subdue, overpower, master, or surpass, &c., (see 1,) or for victory, or superiority], inf. n. مُغَالَبَةٌ and غِلَابٌ. (Ṣ, Mṣb, TA.) You say, غَالَبْتُهُ فَغَلَبْتُهُ [I vied, contended, or strove, with him, to overcome, &c., and I overcame him, &c.]. (O.) And Kaab Ibn-Málik says,

* هَمَّتْ سَخِينَةُ أَنْ تُغَالِبَ رَبَّهَا *
* وَلَيُغْلَبَنَّ مُغَالِبُ الغَلَّابِ *

[Sakheeneh (a by-name of the tribe of Ḳureysh) proposed to themselves to contend for victory with their Lord: but he who contends for victory with the very victorious will assuredly be overcome]. (TA.)

5. تغلّب عَلَى بَلَدِ كَذَا He gained the mastery over such a town, or country, or obtained possession of it, by [superior power or] force. (Ṣ, Ḳ.*)

6. تغالبوا عَلَى البَلَدِ [They vied, contended, or strove, one with another, against the town, or country, to take it]. (A.)

10. استغلب عَلَيْهِ الضَّحِكُ Laughter became vehement in its effect upon him. (TA.)

12. اغلولب العُشْبُ The fresh, or green, herbage attained to maturity, and became tangled and luxuriant, or abundant and dense: (Ṣ:) or became compact and dense. (TA.)

غَلَبَةٌ an inf. n. of غَلَبَ, (Ṣ, Ḳ, TA,) or a simple subst. (Mṣb.) [It is much used as a subst., signifying The act of overcoming, conquering, subduing, &c.; (see 1;) victory, conquest, ascendency, mastery, prevalence, predominance, superiority, or superior power or force or influence; success in a contest; or the act of taking, or obtaining, by superior power or force.] —— And pl. of غَالِبٌ. (TA.)

غُلُبَّةٌ:
غَلُبَّةٌ and غُلَبَةٌ and غُلْبَةٌ: } see what next follows.
غِلِبَّى and غُلُبَّى:

غَلَّابٌ (Ṣ, O) and ↓ غُلُبَّةٌ (O) and ↓ غُلَبَةٌ and ↓ غُلْبَةٌ (O, TA) and ↓ غَلُبَّةٌ (O) and ↓ غُلُبَّى and ↓ غِلِبَّى, (Fr, O,) [all of which except the first and second, and app. the fifth, are originally inf. ns.,] A man who overcomes, conquers, subdues, overpowers, masters, or surpasses, much, or often, (Ṣ, O, TA,) and quickly; (O;) [very, or speedily, or very and speedily, victorious:] or the third, accord. to Aṣ, signifies a man who overcomes, or conquers, &c., quickly: (Ṣ:) pl. of the first غَلَّابُونَ. (TA.)

رَجُلٌ غَالِبٌ A man who overcomes, conquers, subdues, overpowers, masters, or surpasses; or overcoming, &c.: pl. غَلَبَةٌ. (TA.) —— اِسْمٌ غَالِبٌ A noun [used predominantly in one of its senses,] such as دَابَّةٌ applied to "a horse," and مَالٌ applied to "camels." (TA in art. سنه.) And صِفَةٌ غَالِبَةٌ [i. e. غَلَبَتْ عَلَيْهَا الاِسْمِيَّةُ, or غَالِبَةٌ اَسْمِيَّتُهَا,] An epithet [in which the quality of a substantive is predominant,] such as حَاجِبٌ applied to "a door-keeper." (TA in art. حجب.) —— [And الغَالِبُ signifies also The most, or the most part; and the generality: whence, غَالِبًا and فِى الغَالِبِ meaning Mostly, or for the most part; in which sense ↓ فِى الأَغْلَبِ is sometimes used: and generally. —— And What is most probable: whence, غَالِبًا and فِى الغَالِبِ meaning Most probably.]

أَغْلَبُ [More, and most, overcoming or conquering &c.: fem. غَلْبَآءُ: and pl. غُلْبٌ]. One says قَبِيلَةٌ غَلْبَآءُ A [most overcoming or] mighty, resistive, tribe. (Ḳ.) And عِزَّةٌ غَلْبَآءُ [Most overpowering might]. (Ṣ.) —— See also غَالِبٌ. ═ Also Thick-necked, (Ṣ, TA,) applied to a man: (Ṣ:) [or thick and short in the neck: or thick and inclining in the neck: (see 1, last sentence:)] fem. غَلْبَآءُ, applied to a she-camel: and pl. غُلْبٌ. (TA.) And Thick, applied to a neck. (Lḥ, TA.) —— [Hence,] حَدِيقَةٌ غَلْبَآءُ ‡ [A garden, or walled garden, &c.,] of tangled and luxuriant, or abundant and dense, trees: (Ṣ:) or of compact and dense trees; as also ↓ مُغْلَوْلِبَةٌ. (Ḳ, TA.) In the phrase حَدَائِقُ غُلْبًا in the Ḳur [lxxx. 30], the epithet is expl. by Bḍ as meaning ‡ Large. (TA.) And the fem. is applied to a [mountain, or hill, such as is termed] هَضْبَة, (Ṣ, TA,) meaning ‡ Lofty and great. (TA.) —— And الأَغْلَبُ means The lion [app. because of the thickness of his neck]. (Ḳ.)

[مَغْلَبَةٌ A place where one is overcome, or conquered. (Freytag, from the Deewán of the Hudhalees.)]

مُغَلَّبٌ Overcome, conquered, &c., repeatedly, several times, or many times; (Ṣ, A, Ḳ, TA;) applied to a poet: (A:) and (so applied, Ṣ, A, TA) judged to have overcome (Ṣ, A,* Ḳ, TA) his fellow, (Ṣ, TA,) much, or often: (A:) thus having two contr. significations: (Ṣ, Ḳ:) an epithet of praise as well as of dispraise: (O:) or, when the Arabs say of a poet that he is مُغَلَّبٌ, the meaning is that he is overcome; but if they say, غُلِّبَ فُلَانٌ, the meaning is, such a one has [been judged to have] overcome: thus they say, غُلِّبَتْ لَيْلَى الأَخْيَلِيَّةُ عَلَى نَابِغَةِ بَنِى جَعْدَةَ, for she overcame him, and he ([En-Nábighah] El-Jaadee) was مُغَلَّبٌ. (Mohammad Ibn-Selám, TA.)

مَغْلُوبٌ [pass. part. of غَلَبَ, Overcome, conquered, subdued, &c. —— And] part. n. of غُلِبَ in the phrase غُلِبَ فُلَانٌ عَلَى الشَّىْءِ expl. above: [see 1:] (Mgh: [and the like is said in the A:]) a poet says,

* فَكُنْتُ كَمَغْلُوبٍ عَلَى نَصْلِ سَيْفِهِ *

[And I was like one whose blade of his sword has been taken from him by superior power or force; or who has had his blade of his sword taken from him &c.]. (Mgh.)

مُغْلَنْبٌ One who overcomes, conquers, or subdues, another; who gains ascendency, or the mastery, over him: (Ḳ, TA:) it is quasi coordinate to [مُحْرَنْجِمٌ, part. n. of] اِحْرَنْجَمَ [which is from حَرْجَمَ]. (TA.)

حَدِيقَةٌ مُغْلَوْلِبَةٌ: see أَغْلَبُ.

غلت

1. غَلَتَ, aor. ـِ, (TḲ,) inf. n. غَلْتٌ, (IAar, O, Ḳ,) He rescinded, or annulled, a purchase or sale. (IAar, O, Ḳ, TḲ.) ═ غَلِتَ, [aor. ـَ,] (Ṣ, O, Mṣb,) inf. n. غَلَتٌ, (Ṣ, O, Ḳ,) i. q. غَلِطَ [He made a mistake, or committed an error, &c.]: (Aṣ, IAar, Ṣ, O:) or the former means in reckoning, or computation; and the latter, in speech, (AA, T, Ṣ, O, Mṣb, Ḳ,) i. e. he said a thing by mistake, meaning to say another thing; (AA, Ṣ, O;) or the latter means in reckoning and in speech. (Lb, TA.) It is said in a trad., لَا غَلَتَ فِى الإِسْلَامِ [There shall be no غَلَت in El-Islám], meaning, [for instance,] a man's saying "I bought of thee this garment, or piece of cloth, for a hundred deenárs" and thy then finding that he bought it for less. (O.)

5. تغلّته He took him in a state of inadvertence, or heedlessness; (Ḳ, TA;) the doing of which (i. e. التَّغَلُّتُ) is said in a trad. to be not allowable; (TA;) as also ↓ اغتلته. (Ḳ, TA.)

8: see what next precedes.

Q. Q. 3. اِغْلَنْتَى عَلَيْهِ He set upon him, or assailed him, or overcame him, with reviling and beating and violence: (AZ, Ṣ, O, Ḳ:) like اِغْرَنْدَى. (AZ, Ṣ, O.) [See اِسْرَنْدَى.]

الغَلْتَةُ, (Ḳ,) or غَلْتَةُ اللَّيْلِ, (O,) The beginning, or first part, of the night. (O, Ḳ.)

غُلْتَةٌ a subst. from [the inf. n.] غَلَتٌ [meaning A mistake, or an error, &c.]. (O, Ḳ.)

غَلُوتٌ One who makes mistakes, or commits errors, much, or often, whether in reckoning, or computation, or in speech. (O,* TA.)

غلث

1. غَلَثَ, aor. ـِ , inf. n. غَلْثٌ, (Ṣ, O, Mṣb,) which is like عَلْثٌ in its meanings, (Ḳ, TA,) for the most part, (TA,) *He mixed* one thing with another; as wheat with barley. (Ṣ, O, Mṣb.) ▬ غَلَثَ السِّقَآءَ: see عَلَثَ, with the unpointed ع. ▬ غَلِثَ, [aor. ـَ ,] (Ṣ,) inf. n. غَلَثٌ, (Ṣ, Ḳ,) [like عَلِثَ,] *He fought vehemently.* (Ṣ, Ḳ.) And غَلِثَ بِهِ *He kept,* or *clave, to him, fighting him.* (Ṣ, O.) [And perhaps, as may be inferred from an explanation of مُغَالِثٌ, one says in like manner غَالَثَهُ, or غالث به; to which latter, Golius assigns a meaning similar to this, or to that which here next follows, as on the authority of J; but I do not find it in the Ṣ.] And غَلِثَ الذِّئْبُ بِالغَنَمِ [like عَلِثَ] *The wolf kept to the sheep,* or *goats, seizing them, and breaking their necks.* (Ṣ, O.) ▬ And غَلِثَ, aor. ـَ , (Ḳ,) inf. n. غَلَثٌ, (TA,) said of a زَنْد, *It failed to produce fire;* as also ♦ اغتلث. (Ḳ.) [See also 1 in art. علث.] ▬ And غلث said of a bird, *It vomited from its crop something which it had swallowed.* (O, TA.)

2. إِنِّى لَأَجِدُ فِى نَفْسِى تَغْلِيثًا means *Verily I find,* or *experience, in myself, disorder,* or *disturbance.* (O.) [See also مُغَلِّثٌ: and see 2 in art. علث.]

3: see the first paragraph above.

5. فُلَانٌ يَتَغَلَّثُ بِى *Such a one devotes himself to me,* or *clings to me with devotion.* (L.) [See also تعلّث, with ع.]

8: see 1. ▬ اغتلث زَنْدًا *He chose a* زند from a tree *without knowing whether it would produce fire or not;* (TA;) *i. q.* اعتلثهُ [q. v.]. (Ḳ, TA.) And فُلَانٌ يَغْتَلِثُ الزِّنَادَ signifies the same as يَعْتَلِثُهَا expl. in art. علث. (TA in that art.) ▬ اغتلث ♦ القَوْمَ غُلْثَةً *He told the people,* or *party, a lie,* or *falsehood, whereby he effected his escape,* or *safety.* (TA.)

Q. Q. 3. اِغْلَنْثَى عَلَيْهِمْ [like اِعْلَنْتَى] *He set upon them,* or *assailed them,* or *overcame them, with beating and reviling* (O, Ḳ) *and violence.* (O.) [See اِسْرَنْدَى.]

غَلْثُ الحُلْمِ *A thing that one sees in sleep, that is not a true dream.* (TA.)

غَلَثٌ *What is mixed: as wheat mixed with barley.* (Mṣb.) [In the present day, it is used as signifying *What is mixed with wheat &c., of those things that are taken forth and thrown away;* like عَلَثٌ. See also غَلِيثٌ.] ▬ [And its pl.] أَغْلَاثٌ is mentioned by Aboo-Ziyád El-Kilábee as a term applied to *Several sorts of plants,* (O, TA,) *not* بَقْل *nor* حَمْض *nor* عِضَاه, (O,) *among which are the* عَكَرِش *and* حَلْفَآء *and* حَاج *and* أَسَل *and* سَنَا *and* عِشْرِق *and* لَصَف *and* يَنْبُوت *and* خِرْوَع *and* تَنُّوم *and* حَنْظَل *and* بَرْدِىّ (O, TA) &c. (O.) [See also عَلَثٌ.]

غَلِثٌ and ♦ مُغَالِثٌ (Ṣ, O, Ḳ, TA) and ♦ غَالِثٌ (TA) *A man who fights vehemently,* (Ṣ, O, Ḳ, TA,) *cleaving to him whom he pursues* [*for blood-revenge* or *the like:* see عَلِثٌ]. (TA.) ▬ And the first, *Possessed,* or *insane.* (O, Ḳ.) ▬ And One *in whom is an odour arising from food and wine* or *beverage, and an inclining of the body from side to side, and a languor,* or *languidness, from drowsiness.* (O, Ḳ.)

غُلْثَةٌ: see 8.

غَلْثَى *A certain bitter tree,* (Ḳ, TA,) *with which one tans;* mentioned by Kr: (TA:) or, accord. to Az, *a certain tree, the fruit of which, if given to beasts of prey, or to vultures, kills them.* (O.) ▬ See also the next paragraph.

غَلِيثٌ and ♦ مَغْلُوثٌ *Mixed.* (Ṣ, O.) Wheat (Ṣ, O, Ḳ) *mixed,* (Ṣ, O,) or *adulterated,* (Ḳ,) *with barley;* (Ṣ, O, Ḳ;) as also عَلِيثٌ. (AZ, TA in art. علث.) ▬ Also, the first, (Mṣb,) and second, (Ṣ, O, Mṣb,) Wheat *mixed with pieces of dry clay and with* [*the weed called*] زُوَان [q. v.]. (Ṣ, O, Mṣb.) ▬ And the first, [as also عَلِيثٌ,] *Bread made of barley and wheat.* (Ṣ, O.) ▬ And *Food having poison mixed with it, by which vultures are killed;* (O, Ḳ, TA;) as also ♦ غَلْثَى, (O and TA in art. علث,) and عَلْثَى; (TA in that art.;) and so لَغِيثٌ. (O.)

غَالِثٌ: see غَلِثٌ.

مُغَلِّثٌ *A moderate pain, that does not cause the patient to lie on his side, and of which the source is not known.* (L.) [See also 2 in this art. and in art. علث.]

مَغْلُوثٌ: see غَلِيثٌ. ▬ Also A [skin such as is termed] سِقَآء *tanned with dried dates* (تَمْر), or *with* [*unripe dates in the state in which they are termed*] بُسْر. (ISk, Ṣ, Ḳ.) [But see عَلَثَ السِّقَآءَ, in art. علث.]

مُغَالِثٌ: see غَلِثٌ.

غلس

2. غلّس, (Mṣb, Ḳ,) inf. n. تَغْلِيسٌ, (Ṣ, Mgh, Mṣb,) *He,* or *it,* (a company of men, Mṣb, Ḳ,) *journeyed in the* غَلَس, or *darkness of the last part of the night:* (Ṣ, Ḳ:) or *went forth in the* غَلَس. (Mgh, Mṣb.) ▬ غلّسوا, (Ḳ,) or غلّسوا المَآءَ, (Ṣ,) *They came to the water in the* غَلَس, or *darkness of the last part of the night,* (Ṣ, Ḳ,) or *beginning of daybreak:* and in like manner you say of birds of the kind called قَطًا, and of [wild] asses. (TA.) ▬ غلّس بِالصَّلَاةِ *He performed the prayer* [*of daybreak*] *in the* غَلَس. (Ṣ,* Mgh, Mṣb.)

4. اغلس *He,* or *it,* (a company of men, Ḳ,) *entered upon the* غَلَس, or *darkness of the last part of the night.* (A, Ḳ.)

غَلَسٌ *The darkness of the last part of the night,* (Ṣ, A, Mṣb, Ḳ,) *when it becomes mixed with the light of the dawn:* (TA:) or *the beginning of the dawn, until it spreads in the tracts of the horizon:* as also غَبَسٌ: both signify *blackness mixed with whiteness and redness;* like the dawn. (Az, TA.) بِغَلَسٍ *In a period of the darkness so called.* (Ṣ, Mṣb, Ḳ.) [See also غَبَشٌ.]

غَلِيسٌ, (Sgh, Ḳ,) or غُلَيْسٌ, (JK,) a proper name for *An ass;* [meaning *a wild ass;*] (JK, Sgh, K;) because he is أَغْلَس in colour. (JK.)

أَغْلَسُ [*Of the colour termed* غَلَس; i. e., *black mixed with whiteness and redness:* see غَلِيس]. (JK.)

وَقَعَ فِى تُغُلَّسَ, (TA, and so in a copy of the Ṣ,) or فِى وَادِى تُغُلَّسَ, (Ḳ, TA, and so in another copy of the Ṣ,) and تُغُلَّس, (TA,) imperfectly decl., like تُخُيِّب (Ṣ, Ḳ) and تُبُلِّك, (Ḳ,) *He fell into calamity,* (AZ, Ṣ, TA,) or *into an abominable calamity,* (Ḳ, TA,) and *that which was vain, unreal, nought,* or *the like:* (AZ, Ṣ, TA:) originating from the fact that غَارَات [or hostile, or predatory, incursions] (Ḳ, TA) generally (TA) took place early, بِغَلَسٍ. (Ḳ, TA.)

غلصم

Q. 1. غَلْصَمَهُ, (Ṣ, TA,) inf. n. غَلْصَمَةٌ, (Ḳ, TA,) *He cut,* or *severed, his* غَلْصَمَة [here app. meaning *larynx,* or *upper part of the windpipe:* compare حَلْقَمَهُ]. (Ṣ, Ḳ,* TA.) ▬ And *He took hold of,* or *laid hold upon,* or *seized, his* غَلْصَمَة [here, likewise, app. meaning as expl. above: see the pass. part. n., below]. (Ḳ, TA.)

غَلْصَمٌ: see the next paragraph.

الغَلْصَمَةُ [*The epiglottis:* and also, app. by extension of the primary signification, *the larynx,* or *upper part of the windpipe:*] *the thing that rises up in the uppermost part of the throat, and is said to throw the meat and drink into the œsophagus,* or *gullet:* (Zj, in his "Khalḳ-el-Insán:") *the piece of flesh* [or *cartilage*] *that is between the head and the neck:* or *the* عُجْرَة [or *projecting thing*] *that is upon the place where the uvula and gullet meet:* (Ḳ:) or [by an extended application] *the head of the* حُلْقُوم [or *windpipe*], (Ṣ, Mṣb, Ḳ,) *with its* [*ducts called*] شَوَارِب [q. v. voce شَارِب] *and its* حَرْقَدَة [app. meaning *pomum Adami*]; (Ḳ;) i. e. *the projecting place* [or *part*] *in the* حَلْق [here app. meaning, as it does in many cases, *throat*]: (Ṣ, Mṣb:) or *the root,* or *base, of the tongue:* (Ḳ:) or *the place where the* حُلْقُوم [or *windpipe,* i. e. *the head thereof,*] *becomes in conjunction with the* حَلْق [or *fauces*] *when the eater swallows a mouthful and it descends from* [over] *the* حُلْقُوم: (TA:) pl. غَلَاصِمُ. (Mṣb.) ▬ Also † *The chiefs, lords, nobles,* or *men of distinction:* and *the congregated* or *collective body* [of a people], or *the mass* [thereof]; syn. الجَمَاعَةُ: (Ḳ:) pl. as above. (TA.) And [hence] one says, هُوَ فِى غَلْصَمَةٍ مِنْ قَوْمِهِ i. e. فِى شَرَفٍ وَعَدَدٍ [meaning † *He is among* (*such as are distinguished by*) *nobility and number, of his* people], (ISk, Ḳ, TA,) [or] meaning, accord. to Aṣ, *he is among the chief portion of his people, and the nobility thereof*: (TA:) [and in the same sense ▼ غَلْصَم is used, without ة, but perhaps only by poetic license:] Abu-n-Nejm says,

أَبِى لُجَيْمٌ وَٱسْمُهُ مِلْءُ الفَمِ

فِى غَلْصَمِ الهَامِ وَهَامٍ غَلْصَمِ

[† *My father is,* or *was, Lujeym, and his fame* (a tropical rendering) *is what fills the mouth;* one *among the chief portion and the nobility of the headmen, and among headmen of a chief portion and of nobility*]. (TA.)

مُغَلْصَمٌ pass. part. n. of Q. 1. — مُغَلْصَمَاتٌ means Women *having the necks bound.* (Ḳ, TA.) A poet says,

غَدَاةَ عَهِدْتُهُنَّ مُغَلْصَمَاتٍ

لَهُنَّ بِكُلِّ مَحْنِيَةٍ نَجِيمُ

[*In the morning when I met with them having their necks bound,* (app. as captives,) *they having in every bend* of a valley or the like *some one slain*]. (TA.)

غلط

1. غَلِطَ, (Ṣ, Mṣb, Ḳ,) aor. ـَ, (Ṣ, Ḳ,) inf. n. غَلَطٌ (Ṣ, M, Mṣb, Ḳ) and أُغْلُوطَةٌ, (JK,) *He made a mistake; committed an error;* or *missed,* or *erred from, the right way* or *mode* or *manner:* (Mṣb:) or *he was unable to find the right way,* (JK, M, Ḳ,) and *knew it not:* (M, Ḳ:) *in an affair;* (Ṣ;) *in anything;* (JK;) *in reckoning,* or *computation,* &c.: (Ḳ:) or *in his speech,* (Ṣ, Mṣb, Ḳ,) *in particular;* (Ḳ;) and غَلِتَ in reckoning, or computation: (Ṣ, and so in some copies of the Ḳ:) but some of the Arabs make these two verbs to be syn. dial. variants. (Ṣ.)

2. غلّطهُ, (Mṣb,) inf. n. تَغْلِيطٌ, (Ṣ, Ḳ,) *He said to him* غَلِطْتَ [*Thou hast made a mistake,* &c.]: (Ṣ, Mṣb, Ḳ:) or *he attributed* or *imputed to him the having made a mistake.* (Mṣb.) — See also 4.

3. غالطهُ, inf. n. مُغَالَطَةٌ (Ṣ, Ḳ) and غِلَاطٌ, (Ḳ,) [*He vied,* or *contended, with him, each endeavouring to cause the other to make a mistake:* a signification well known, indicated in the TA, and agreeable with modern usage.]

4. اغلطهُ, (Ṣ, TA,) inf. n. إِغْلَاطٌ, (TA,) *He caused him to fall into the making of a mistake;* (Ṣ,* TA;) as also ▼ غلّطهُ, inf. n. تَغْلِيطٌ. (TA.)

غَلَطٌ [an inf. n. used as a simple subst., *Mistake; error;* in speech; or in that and also in reckoning, or computation, &c.;] has for its pl. أَغْلَاطٌ; and ISd says, "I see that IJ has made غِلَاطٌ its pl.; but I know not the reason of that." (TA.) ▼ مَغْلَطَةٌ also signifies the same in the saying, وَقَعَ فُلَانٌ فِى المَغْلَطَةِ [*Such a one fell into mistake,* or *error*]. (TA.) — See also مَغْلُوطٌ.

[غَلْطَةٌ *A single mistake,* or *error,* in speech, or in speech &c.: pl. غَلَطَاتٌ.]

رَجُلٌ غَلْطَانٌ [*A man making a mistake,* or *committing an error,* in speech, or in speech &c.]. (TA.)

غَلُوطٌ: see مِغْلَاطٌ: — and see also أُغْلُوطَةٌ.

غَلُوطَةٌ: see أُغْلُوطَةٌ.

غَلَّاطٌ: see مِغْلَاطٌ.

أُغْلُوطَةٌ (Ṣ, Ḳ) and ▼ غَلُوطَةٌ and ▼ مَغْلَطَةٌ (Ḳ) *A question by which one causes to fall into the making of a mistake:* (Ṣ:) or كَلَامٌ يُغْلَطُ فِيهِ [which may be rendered both *language in which one makes a mistake,* and *language in which one is caused to fall into a mistake*]: (Ḳ:) and all, (Ḳ,) or the first and second, (TA,) also signify *a question by which a person,* (Ḳ,* TA,) *a man of learning,* (TA,) *is vied,* or *contended, with, in the endeavour to cause him to make a mistake,* (Ḳ, TA,) *in order that he may become lowered; and by which his judgment,* or *opinion, is sought to be made erroneous:* (TA:) you say, ▼ مَسْأَلَةٌ غَلُوطٌ; but when you make the latter word a subst., you add the ة: (El-Khaṭṭábee:) the pl. of أُغْلُوطَةٌ is أُغْلُوطَاتٌ and أَغَالِيطُ (Ṣ) and غُلُوطَاتٌ, which is formed from the first of these pls. by the suppression of the hemzeh, and is not, as some have said, pl. of غَلُوطَةٌ. (Hr.) Mohammad forbade أُغْلُوطَات, (Ṣ, TA,) or غُلُوطَات, (TA,) because they are unprofitable with respect to religion, and there is scarcely, or never, in them aught save what is unprofitable. (El-'Otbee, TA.)

مَغْلَطَةٌ [properly, or originally, *A cause of falling into mistake;* similar to مَبْخَلَةٌ and مَجْبَنَةٌ &c.]: see أُغْلُوطَةٌ: — and غَلَطٌ.

مُغْلِطَانِىٌّ One *who vies,* or *contends, with others, endeavouring to cause them to make mistakes in their reckoning,* or *computation.* (TA.)

مُغَلَّطٌ: see مَغْلُوطٌ.

مِغْلَاطٌ One *who makes mistakes,* or *commits errors, much,* or *frequently;* expl. by كَثِيرُ الغَلَطِ; (Ḳ;) as also ▼ غَلَّاطٌ (TA) and ▼ غَلُوطٌ. (O in art. غلت.)

مَغْلُوطٌ A book, or writing, *having a mistake,* or *mistakes, made in it;* and in like manner, a reckoning, or computation, as also ▼ غَلَطٌ and ▼ مُغَلَّطٌ. (TA.)

غلظ

1. غَلُظَ, aor. ـُ; (Ṣ, Mgh, O, Mṣb, Ḳ;) and غَلَظَ, aor. ـِ; (Ṣgh, Ḳ;) inf. n. [of the former] غِلَظٌ (Ṣ, Mgh, O, Mṣb, Ḳ) and ▼ غِلَاظَةٌ and ▼ غِلْظَةٌ (Ṣ,* O, Ḳ,* TḲ) and ▼ غُلْظَةٌ and ▼ غَلْظَةٌ, (O, Ḳ,* TḲ,) all are inf. ns. of غَلُظَ, (O,) or the last three, the second and third of which are mentioned in the Bári', on the authority of IAạr, are simple substs.; (Mṣb;) and perhaps غَلْظٌ may be an inf. n. [of the latter verb]; (ISd, TA;) *It* (a thing, Mṣb) *was,* or *became, thick, gross, big, bulky,* or *coarse;* (Mgh, Mṣb, Ḳ;) *it* (a thing) *became* غَلِيظ; as also ▼ استغلظ. (Ṣ.) You say, غَلُظَ جِسْمُهُ *His body was,* or *became, thick,* &c. (Mgh.) And ▼ استغلظ الزَّرْعُ i. q. غَلُظَ, (Jel in xlviii. 29,) *The seed-produce became thick:* (Bḍ:) or *strong:* (Mṣb:) or *well grown and thick:* and in like manner one says of any plant or tree: (TA:) and غَلُظَتِ السُّنْبُلَةُ, and ▼ استغلظت, *the ear of corn produced grain.* (Ḳ.) [And غَلُظَ الثَّوْبُ *The garment,* or *piece of cloth, was thick,* or *coarse.*] And غَلُظَتِ الأَرْضُ, inf. n. غِلَظٌ, and perhaps غَلْظٌ may be also an inf. n. [of this verb, or, more probably, of غَلَظَتْ], *The land was,* or *became, rough,* or *rugged.* (ISd, TA.) [In this sense, also, غَلُظَ is used in relation to various things.] — [Said of a colour, *It was dense,* or *deep:* see غَلِيظٌ.] — Also ‡ *He was,* or *became, characterized by* غِلْظَة, *the contr. of* رِقَّة, *in manners, disposition, action* or *conduct, speech, life,* and *the like;* (TA;) i. e., *rough; coarse; rude; unkind; hard; churlish; uncivil; surly; hard to deal with; incompliant; unobsequious; evil in disposition; illnatured;* or *the like:* (Ṣ, by its explanation of غِلْظَة and غِلَاظَة; and Mṣb:*) and in like manner, [as meaning *it was,* or *became, hard,* or *difficult,* and *the like,* (see غَلِيظٌ,)] it is said of an affair: (TA:) and ▼ تغلّظ is said of a crime; meaning *it was gross,* or *great;* but this is accord. to analogy only; not on the authority of hearsay. (Mgh.) It is said in the Ḳur [ix. 74, and lxvi. 9], وَٱغْلُظْ عَلَيْهِمْ *And use thou roughness towards them:* (Bḍ in lxvi. 9:) and some read وَٱغْلِظْ, with kesr to the ل. (TA.) [See also غِلْظَة, below.]

2. غلّظ الشَّىْءَ, inf. n. تَغْلِيظٌ, *He made,* or *rendered, the thing* غَلِيظ [in the proper sense, i. e., *thick, gross, big, bulky,* or *coarse;* &c.: — and also, and more commonly, in a tropical sense, i. e., ‡ *hard,* or *difficult,* and *the like*]: (TA:) and غلّظ عَلَيْهِ الشَّىْءَ, inf. n. as above, ‡ [*he made the thing hard,* or *difficult,* or *the like, to him;*] and hence دِيَةٌ مُغَلَّظَةٌ, which see below. (Ṣ, TA.) [Hence also,] غَلَّظْتُ اليَمِينَ, inf. n. as above, † *I made the oath strong,* or *forcible; I confirmed,* or *ratified, it;* (Mṣb;) [and so ▼ أَغْلَظْتُهَا; for you say,] حَلَفَ بِإِغْلَاظِ اليَمِينِ ‡ [*He swore, making the oath strong,* &c.]. (TA.) And غَلَّظْتُ عَلَيْهِ فِى اليَمِينِ, inf. n. as above, † *I was hard, rigorous,* or *severe, to him in the oath.* (Mṣb.) — تَغْلِيظ in pronunciation: see تَفْخِيم.

3. مُغَالَظَةٌ is similar to مُعَارَضَةٌ † [The act of *mutually opposing,* and app. *with roughness, coarseness,* or *the like*]: (TA:) and signifies a state of *mutual enmity* or *hostility.* (IDrd, Ḳ.) See غِلْظَة, below, last sentence.

4. اغلظ الثَّوْبَ *He found the garment,* or *piece of cloth, to be thick,* or *coarse:* (Ḳ:) or *he bought it thick,* or *coarse:* (Ṣ, Ḳ:) the former is the more correct: (O:) or the former only is correct. (TṢ.) — اغلظت اليَمِينَ: see 2. — اغلظ [is also

intrans., and signifies] *He* (a man, Ibn-'Abbád) *alighted*, or *alighted and abode, in a rough*, or *rugged, tract of land.* (Ibn-'Abbád, Ḳ.) — اغلظ لَهُ فِى القَوْلِ (Ṣ, Mgh, Mṣb, Ḳ) ‡ *He was*, or *became, rough, harsh, coarse, rude, uncivil*, or *ungentle, to him in speech:* (Mgh, Mṣb, Ḳ:) one should not say غَلَظَ. (TA.)

5: see 1, near the end.

استغلظ: see 1, in three places. = استغلظهُ *He saw it to be, regarded it as,* or *esteemed it, thick, gross, big, bulky,* or *coarse.* (Mṣb.) *He abstained from purchasing it* (namely a garment, or piece of cloth, Ṣ) *because of its thickness,* or *coarseness.* (Ṣ, Ḳ.)

غَلْظٌ *Rough,* or *rugged, land* or *ground;* (ISd, Ḳ;) mentioned on the authority of Ibn-'Abbád; and by AḤn, on the authority of En-Naḍr; but it has been repudiated: and is said to be correctly ↓ غَلَظٌ: ISd says, of the former word, "I know not whether it be [properly] syn. with غَلِيظٌ, or whether it be an inf. n. used as an epithet:" accord. to Kr, it signifies *hard land without stones:* Ks says that غَلْظٌ is syn. with ↓ غَلَظٌ. (TA.)

غَلَظٌ: [see 1: — and] see غَلْظٌ, in two places.

غِلْظَةٌ: } see what next follows.
غُلْظَةٌ: }

غَلْظَةٌ and ↓ غُلْظَةٌ and ↓ غِلْظَةٌ: see 1: these three forms are mentioned by Zj, (TA,) and in the Bári', (Mṣb, TA,) on the authority of IAạr, (Mṣb,) and by Sgh; but the first of them [only] is commonly known: (TA:) they are substs. from غَلُظَ; and signify *Thickness, grossness, bigness, bulkiness,* or *coarseness.* (Mṣb.) [And *Roughness,* or *ruggedness.*] — Also ‡ *Contr. of* رِقَّةٌ, *in manners, disposition, action* or *conduct, speech, life,* and *the like;* (TA;) i. e. *roughness, coarseness, rudeness, unkindness, hardness, churlishness, incivility, surliness, roughness in manners, hardness to deal with, incompliance, unobsequiousness, evilness of disposition, illnature,* or *the like:* (Ṣ, Mṣb:*) and in like manner, *hardness,* or *difficulty,* of an affair. (TA, as shown by an explanation of غَلِيظٌ.) You say, رَجُلٌ فِيهِ غِلْظَةٌ ‡ *A man in whom is roughness, coarseness, rudeness, &c.;* (Ṣ, Mṣb;*) as also ↓ غِلَاظَةٌ. (Ṣ.) And it is said in the Ḳur [ix. 124], وَلْيَجِدُوا فِيكُمْ غِلْظَةً, in which the last word is pronounced in the three different ways shown above, accord. to different readers; meaning ‡ [*And let them find in you*] *hardness,* or *strength,* or *vehemence, and superiority in fight:* (TA:) or *hardness,* or *strength,* or *vehemence, and patient endurance of fight:* (Bḍ:) or *hardness,* or *strength,* or *vehemence, in enmity and in fight and in making captives.* (Mgh.) And you say, بَيْنَهُمَا غِلْظَةٌ ‡ *Between them two is enmity,* or *hostility;* as also ↓ مُغَالَظَةٌ. (IDrd, Ḳ.)

غِلَاظٌ: see what next follows.

غَلِيظٌ (Ṣ, &c.) *Thick, gross, big, bulky,* or *coarse;* (Mgh, Mṣb, Ḳ;) as also ↓ غُلَاظٌ: (Ḳ:) fem. of the former with ة: (TA:) and pl. غِلَاظٌ. (Mṣb, TA.) Applied [to a body, &c.; and, as meaning *Thick,* or *coarse,*] to a garment, or piece of cloth. (Mgh, Ḳ.) You say also, أَرْضٌ غَلِيظَةٌ *Rough,* or *rugged, land.* (ISd, TA.) [And in this sense, of *rough,* or *rugged,* غَلِيظٌ is used in relation to various things.] — Applied to a colour [*Dense,* or *deep:* see غَضْبٌ]. (Ḳ in art. غضب.) — Also, applied to a man, ‡ *Characterized by* غِلْظَة, *the contr. of* رِقَّة, *in manners, disposition, action* or *conduct, speech, life,* and *the like; rough, coarse, rude, unkind, hard, churlish, uncivil, surly, rough in manners, hard to deal with, incompliant, unobsequious, evil in disposition, illnatured,* or *the like:* (Mṣb,* TA:) and so غَلِيظُ الجَانِبِ; [*contr. of* لَيِّنُ الجَانِبِ:] (O and Ḳ in art. فظ:) and غَلِيظُ القَلْبِ *hard-hearted;* (Bḍ in iii. 153;) *evil in disposition,* or *illnatured.* (TA.) Applied also to an affair, meaning ‡ *Hard,* or *difficult.* (TA.) And to punishment, [in the Ḳur xi. 61, &c.,] meaning ‡ *Vehement,* or *severe;* (Mgh;) *intensely painful.* (Mṣb.) And [in like manner] to slaying and wounding. (TA.) And to a compact, or covenant, [in the Ḳur iv. 25, &c.,] meaning ‡ *Strong, confirmed,* or *ratified.* (Mgh, TA.) And to water, meaning ‡ *Bitter.* (TA.)

غِلَاظَةٌ: see 1, first sentence; and غِلْظَةٌ.

أَغْلَظُ comparative and superlative of غَلِيظٌ [in all its senses]. (IJ.)

دِيَةٌ مُغَلَّظَةٌ † [*A bloodwit,* or *fine for bloodshed, made hard, rigorous,* or *severe;*] *one which is incumbent for what is like an intentional homicide;* (Ṣ;) or *for a homicide purely intentional,* and *for that which is intentional but committed in mistake,* and *for that which is committed in the sacred territory,* and *for the slaughter of a kinsman;* (Esh-Sháfi'ee;) *consisting of thirty camels of the description termed* حِقَّة, *and thirty of that termed* جَذَعَة, *and forty between the* ثَنِيَّة *and the* بَازِل, *all pregnant.* (Esh-Sháfi'ee, Ḳ.) And يَمِينٌ مُغَلَّظَةٌ † [*An oath made strong* or *forcible,* or *confirmed,* or *ratified.*] (Ṣ.) — العَوْرَةُ المُغَلَّظَةُ: see عَوْرَةٌ.

مُسْتَغْلَظُ الذِّرَاعِ [*The thick part of the fore arm*]. (TA.)

غلف

1. غَلَفَ, (Ṣ, O, Mṣb, Ḳ,) aor. ـِ, (Mṣb,) inf. n. غَلْفٌ, (O, Mṣb, TA,) *He put* a bottle, or flask, (Ṣ, O, Ḳ, TA,) or a knife, (Mṣb,) &c., (TA,) *into a* غِلَاف [q. v.]; (Ṣ, O, Mṣb, Ḳ, TA;) as also ↓ اغلف, (Ṣ, Mṣb,) inf. n. إِغْلَافٌ; (Mṣb;) or ↓ غلّف, inf. n. تَغْلِيفٌ: (Ḳ, TA:) or ↓ the second signifies, (Mṣb,) or signifies also, (Ṣ,) *he furnished* it *with a* غِلَاف; (Ṣ, Mṣb;) or ↓ غلّف signifies thus: (TA:) ↓ أَغْلَفْتُ القَارُورَةَ is said by Lth to be from الغِلَافُ; and so ↓ غَلَّفْتُهَا, inf. n. تَغْلِيفٌ. (O.) — And accord. to Lth, (O,) one says, غَلَفَ لِحْيَتَهُ بِالغَالِيَةِ, (Ṣ, Mgh, O, Mṣb,) aor. ـِ, (Mṣb,) inf. n. غَلْفٌ, (Ṣ,) meaning *He daubed,* or *smeared, his beard with* [*the perfume called*] غَالِيَة [q. v.], (Mgh, TA,) and likewise with other perfume, and with حِنَّآء; (TA;) and ↓ غَلَّفَهَا: (Mgh, TA:) but accord. to IDrd, the vulgar say so: (O, Mṣb, TA:) he says that the correct phrase is غَلَّاهَا (Mgh, O, Mṣb, TA) بالغالية, (O,) and غَلَّلَهَا: (Mgh, O, Mṣb:) in a trad. of 'Áïsheh, however, كُنْتُ أُغَلِّفُ ↓ لِحْيَةَ رَسُولِ اللّٰهِ occurs as meaning *I used to daub,* or *smear, the beard of the Apostle of God* with غالية, *doing so abundantly:* (TA:) and one says, of a man, ↓ تغلّف (Lth, Th, Ṣ, O, TA) بِالغَالِيَةِ (Th, Ṣ, TA) وَسَائِرِ الطِّيبِ (Th, TA) [i. e. *He daubed,* or *smeared, himself,* or *his beard, with* غالية *and the other sorts of perfume*]; and [in like manner,] ↓ اغتلف (Lth, O, TA) مِنَ الغَالِيَةِ (Lth, O) or مِنَ الطِّيبِ: (TA:) but accord. to the saying of IDrd [mentioned above], these are wrong, and should be only تَغَلَّى and تَغَلَّلَ, and اغْتَلَى and اغْتَلَّ: (O:) or, accord. to Ibn-El-Faraj, one says ↓ تغلّف بالغالية when it is external; and تغلّل بِهَا when it is internal, at the roots of the hair. (O, TA. [See also 2 in art. غل.]) = غَلِفَ, aor. ـَ, inf. n. غَلَفٌ, *He was uncircumcised.* (Mṣb.)

2: see 1, first sentence, in three places. You say also, غَلَّفْتُ السَّرْجَ [*I put a* غِلَاف *upon,* or *to, the horse's saddle*] and الرَّحْلَ [*the camel's saddle:* see also its pass. part. n., below]. (O.) — And الحِنَّآءُ يُغَلِّفُ الرَّأْسَ *The* حِنَّآء [q. v.] *covers the head.* (Mgh.) See also 1, second sentence, in two places.

4: see 1, first sentence, in three places.

5. تغلّف, said of a رَحْل [or camel's saddle, (in some copies of the Ḳ erroneously رَجُل,) and in like manner of other things], *It had a* غِلَاف [q. v.], (Ḳ, TA,) *of leather* or *the like;* (TA;) as also ↓ اغتلف. (Ḳ, TA. [See 2, of which the former is quasi-pass.]) — See also 1, latter half, in two places.

8: see 5: — and see also 1, last quarter.

غَلْفٌ *A species of trees,* (Ṣ, O, Ḳ, TA,) *with which one tans,* (TA,) *like* [accord. to some meaning *the same as*] *the* غَرْف [q. v.]: (Ṣ, O, Ḳ, TA:) *some say that one does not tan therewith unless together with the* غَرْف. (TA.)

غَلَفٌ inf. n. of غَلِفَ [q. v.]: (Mṣb:) [as a simple subst.,] The *state of being uncircumcised.* (Ṣ, O, Ḳ.) — [Also, of the heart, † The *state of being* أَغْلَف: so, app., accord. to the TA: in the L written غَلَفَة.] — And † *Ample abundance of herbage,* or *of the goods, conveniences,* or *comforts, of life.* (TA.)

غَلَفٌ *A certain plant, which is eaten, peculiarly, by the apes,* or *monkeys:* mentioned by AḤn. (TA.)

غُلْفَةٌ i. q. قُلْفَةٌ (Mgh, O, Mṣb, Ḳ) and غُرْلَةٌ; (Mṣb;) i. e. [The *prepuce*;] the *little piece of skin which the circumciser cuts off from the* غِلَاف [or *sheath*] *of the head of the penis.* (Mgh.) — And الغُلْفَتَانِ signifies *The two extremities of the two halves of the mustache, next to the* صِمَاغَانِ [or *two sides of the mouth which are the places where the lips conjoin*]. (TA.)

غِلَافٌ *A thing well known;* (Ḳ, TA;) i. e. *a receptacle used as a repository;* and *a covering,* or *an envelope,* of a thing: (TA:) it is of a sword [i. e. the *scabbard,* or *sheath;* and also *a case,* or *covering, enclosing the scabbard,* or *enclosing the scabbard with its appertenances*]; (Ṣ, O;) and of a knife and the like [i. e. the *sheath*]; (Mṣb;) and of a flask or bottle [i. e. the *case* thereof]; (Ṣ, O;) and [likewise] of a bow; (Ṣ, O, Ḳ;) and of a camel's saddle (Ḳ, TA) and of a horse's saddle, [i. e. *a covering*] *of leather* and *the like;* (TA;) and is such as the *enclosing membrane* (قَمِيص) of the heart; [غِلَافُ القَلْبِ signifying *the pericardium;*] and the *pellicle* (غِرْقِئ) of the egg; and the *calyx* of a flower; and the [*imaginary*] سَاهُور [q. v.] of the moon: (TA:) pl. غُلُفٌ (O, Mṣb, Ḳ) and غُلْفٌ (Ḳ) and غُلُفٌ. (O,* Ḳ.) In the phrase in the Ḳur [ii. 82], وَقَالُوا قُلُوبُنَا غُلْفٌ, as some read it, and, accord. to one reading غُلُفٌ, the last word means † *receptacles for knowledge:* (O, TA:) but others read غُلْفٌ, which is pl. of أَغْلَفُ ▼; (Ṣ,* O,* TA;) meaning † *covered* from hearing and accepting the truth; (TA;) or † *as though they were covered* from that to which thou invitest us. (O.)

أَغْلَفُ [*Enclosed*] *in a* غِلَاف [q. v.]; applied in this sense to a sword, as also [the fem.] غَلْفَآءُ to a bow; (Ṣ, O, Ḳ;) and likewise to anything. (Ṣ, O. [See also مُغَلَّفٌ.]) — And A man *having upon him a sort of garment from beneath which he has not put forth his fore arms.* (Khálid Ibn-Jembeh, L, TA.) — And, applied to a man, *i. q.* أَقْلَفُ; (Ṣ, Mgh, O, Ḳ;) i. e. (Mgh) *Uncircumcised:* (Mgh, Mṣb:) fem. غَلْفَآءُ [see بَظْرٌ]: and pl. غُلْفٌ. (Mṣb.) — Applied also to a heart, meaning † *As though it were covered with a* غِلَاف, *so that it does not learn;* (Ṣ, O, Mṣb, Ḳ, TA;) or *covered from hearing and accepting the truth.* (TA.) See also غِلَافٌ. [And see مُغَلَّفٌ.] — أَرْضٌ غَلْفَآءُ † *A land that has not been depastured, so that there is in it every sort of small and large herbage.* (Sh, O, Ḳ.) And سَنَةٌ غَلْفَآءُ † *A year in which is abundance of herbage;* (Ṣ, O, Ḳ, TA;) and so عَامٌ أَغْلَفُ. (TA.) And عَيْشٌ أَغْلَفُ † *Life that is ample in its means* or *circumstances, unstraitened,* or *plentiful, and easy,* or *pleasant.* (Ṣ, O, Ḳ, TA.)

مُغَلَّفٌ, applied to a horse's saddle and to a camel's saddle, *Having upon it a* غِلَاف [or *covering*] *of leather* or *the like.* (TA.) — And applied also to a heart as meaning [*As though it were*] *covered.* (TA.) [See also أَغْلَفُ.]

غلق

1\. غَلَقَ as syn. with أَغْلَقَ: see the latter. ═ Also, inf. n. غَلْقٌ, *He went away.* (TA.) — And غَلَقَ فِى الأَرْضِ, aor. ـُ, inf. n. غَلْقٌ, *He went far into the land;* (Ibn-'Abbád, O, Ḳ,* TA;) as also فَلَقَ, aor. ـُ, inf. n. فَلْقٌ. (Ibn-'Abbád, O, TA.) ═ غَلِقَ said of a door: see 7. — [Hence,] غَلِقَ الرَّهْنُ, aor. ـَ, (Ṣ, Mgh, O, Mṣb, Ḳ, &c.,) inf. n. غَلَقٌ, (Ṣ, O, Mṣb,) or غُلُوقٌ, (IAạr, TA,) or both, (Sb, TA,) ‡ *The pledge was, or became, a rightful possession* [i. e. *a forfeit*] *to the receiver of it* (Ṣ, Mgh, O, Mṣb, Ḳ) *when not redeemed within the time stipulated;* (Ṣ, O, Ḳ;) or so غَلِقَ الرَّهْنُ فِى يَدِ المُرْتَهِنِ: (Sb, TA:) or غَلِقَ الرَّهْنُ means *the pledge remained in the hand* [or *possession*] *of the receiver of it, the pledger being unable to redeem it:* (IAạr, TA:) accord. to the Bári', it is when a man pledges a commodity and says, "If I do not pay thee within such a time, the pledge shall be thine for the debt." (Mṣb.) This is forbidden in a trad. (Ṣ, Mgh, O, Mṣb, &c.) It is said in a trad. of the Prophet on this subject, لَا يَغْلَقُ بِمَا فِيهِ لَكَ غُنْمُهُ وَعَلَيْكَ غُرْمُهُ [meaning *It shall not become a forfeit to the receiver with what is involved in it:* (or, accord. to an explanation of the first clause in the Mṣb, *it shall not become a rightful possession to the receiver for the debt for which it was pledged:*) *to thee shall pertain the regaining of it, and its increase, and growth, and excess in value, if such there be, and upon thee shall be the obligation of the debt belonging to it, and the bearing of any unavoidable damage that it may have sustained*]: (O:) or لَهُ غُنْمُهُ وَعَلَيْهِ غُرْمُهُ i. e., accord. to A'Obeyd, *to him* (the owner) *it shall return, and to him shall pertain its increase* [*if there be any*], *and if it have become defective,* or *have perished,* [*unavoidably,*] *he shall be responsible for it and shall pay the debt to him to whom it is owed without being compensated by* [*the remission of*] *aught of the debt:* (Mṣb:) or لَكَ غُنْمُهُ وَعَلَيْهِ غُرْمُهُ, which means *to thee* (the pledger) *shall pertain the increase of it* (the pledge), *and its growth, and its excess in value,* [*if it have any,*] *and upon him* (the receiver of it) *shall be the responsibility* [*to make compensation*] *for it if it perish* [*through his fault, in his possession*]. (O. [There are other, somewhat different, readings and explanations of this trad. in the Mgh &c.; but what I have here given, from the O and Mṣb, appear to me to be the most approvable. See also غُنْمٌ: and see art. رهن.]) Zuheyr says,

• وَفَارَقَتْكَ بِرَهْنٍ لَا فَكَاكَ لَهُ •
• يَوْمَ الوَدَاعِ فَأَمْسَى الرَّهْنُ قَدْ غَلِقَا •

† [*And she separated herself from thee with a pledge for which there is nothing wherewith it may be redeemed, on the day of valediction, so the pledge has become a forfeit to its receiver*]: (Ṣ, Mgh, O, TA:) he means that she received his heart as a pledge, and went away with it. (Mgh, TA.) The saying of Ows Ibn-Ḥajar

• أَبُو غَلِقٍ فِى لَيْلَتَيْنِ مُؤَجَّلِ •

means † *The owner of a pledge that has become a rightful possession* [or *forfeit*] *to its receiver, the period for the release of which is two nights:* to this he likens a captivated heart. (TA.) — One says also, of a slave who has received permission to traffic, غَلِقَتْ رَقَبَتُهُ بِالدَّيْنِ † *His* رَقَبَة [meaning *person*] *has become a rightful possession* [or *a forfeit* to his creditor or creditors] *by reason of debt,* when he is unable to free it. (Mgh.) — And غَلِقَ signifies also † *He was unransomed,* or *unredeemed;* said of a captive, and of a criminal. (TA.) — And ‡ *He,* or *it, stuck fast:* (Ṣ, O, TA:) thus in the saying, غَلِقَ قَلْبُهُ فِى يَدِ فُلَانَةَ [*His heart stuck fast in the possession of such a woman or girl*]: (TA:) and احْتَدَّ فَغَلِقَ فِى حِدَّتِهِ [*He became excited by sharpness of temper, and stuck fast in his sharpness of temper*]: (Ṣ, O, TA:) and غَلِقَ is said of anything that sticks fast in a thing, and cleaves to it: thus one says, غَلِقَ فِى البَاطِلِ [*He stuck fast in that which was vain,* or *false*]: and the saying of El-Farezdaḳ

• وَلَوْ كَانُوا أُولِى غَلَقٍ سِغَابَا •

means *Had they been persons who had stuck fast in poverty and hunger, cleaving thereto.* (Sh, TA.) — Also, (Mṣb, TA,) inf. n. غَلَقٌ, (Mgh, Mṣb,) † *He was,* or *became, disquieted,* (Mgh,) or *disquieted by grief;* (Mgh, Mṣb;) or *angry,* (Mṣb, TA,) and *excited by sharpness of temper.* (TA.) Hence يَمِينُ الغَلَقِ † *The oath of anger;* said by some of the lawyers to be so called because he who swears it closes thereby against himself a door preventing him from advancing or drawing back. (Mṣb.) And hence إِيَّاكَ وَالغَلَقَ † *Beware thou of,* or *avoid thou, the being disquieted,* or *disquieted by grief* [or *anger*]: or, as some say, the meaning is, لَا يُغْلَقُ ▼ التَّطْلِيقَاتُ حَتَّى لَا يَبْقَى مِنْهَا شَىْءٌ † [i. e. *The sentences of divorce shall not be closed,* or *concluded, at once,* by one's saying "Thou art trebly divorced," *so that there shall not remain of them aught*]; for one should divorce agreeably with the سُنَّة: (Mgh:) [or, accord. to the TA, إِيَّاكَ وَالغَلَقَ app. means *beware thou of,* or *avoid thou, the state of straitness:*] and الغَلَقُ signifies also *the being in a state of perdition:* (TA:) and *contractedness of the mind or bosom,* (Mbr, JK, TA,) and *paucity of patience.* (Mbr, TA.) — One says also, غَلِقَتِ النَّخْلَةُ, (O, Ḳ, TA,) inf. n. غَلَقٌ, (TA,) ‡ *The palm-tree had worms in the bases of its branches and was thereby stopped from bearing fruit;* (O, Ḳ, TA;) and so أُغْلِقَتْ ▼ عَنِ الإِثْمَارِ. (TA.) — And غَلِقَ ظَهْرُ البَعِيرِ, (Ṣ, O, Ḳ, TA,) inf. n. غَلَقٌ, (Ṣ, O, TA,) ‡ *The back of the camel became galled with galls not to be cured;* (Ṣ, O, Ḳ, TA;) *the whole of his back being seen to be two portions of cicatrized skin, the results of galls that had become in a healing state, and the two sides thereof glistening:* ISh says that in the case of the worst galls of the camel, the furniture, or saddle and saddle-cloth, cannot be [partially] raised from contact with him [so as to be bearable by him]. (TA.)

2: see 4, former half, in three places.

3. مُغَالَقَةٌ signifies † The *contending for a bet, or wager;* syn. مُرَاهَنَةٌ; (O, Ḳ;) originally, in the game called المَيْسِر: whence, in a trad., the phrase ارْتَبَطَ فَرَسًا لِيُغَالِقَ عَلَيْهَا † [*He tied up a mare in order that he should contend upon her in a race for a stake* or *stakes*]. (O.)

4. اغلق البَابَ, (Ṣ, Mgh, O, Mṣb, Ḳ, &c.,) inf. n. إِغْلَاقٌ, (Mgh, Ḳ, &c.,) *He made the door fast with a* غَلَق, *so that it could not be opened unless with a key;* (Mṣb;) [i. e.] *he locked the door;* or *bolted it:* or *he closed,* or *shut, it:* (MA:) *contr. of* فَتَحَهُ: (O, Ḳ:*) and ↓ غَلَقَهُ, (Ṣ, O, Mṣb, Ḳ,) aor. ـِ, (Mṣb, Ḳ,) inf. n. غَلْقٌ, (Ṣ, O, Mṣb,) signifies the same; (Ṣ, O, Mṣb, Ḳ;) mentioned by IDrd, on the authority of AZ; but rare; (Mṣb;) or a mispronunciation; (Ḳ;) or bad, (Ṣ, O, Ḳ,) and rejected; (Ṣ;) and غَلْقٌ is [said to be] the subst. from أَغْلَقَ; (Ṣ, Mgh, Ḳ;) whence the saying of a poet,

وَبَابٍ إِذَا مَا مَالَ لِلْغَلْقِ يَصْرِفُ

[*And a door that, when it turns to be locked,* or *closed, creaks*]: (Ṣ, O, Mgh:*) and one says, غَلَّقْتُ ↓ الأَبْوَابَ [*I locked,* or *closed, the doors*]; the verb being with teshdeed to denote multiplicity [of the objects]; (Sb, Ṣ, TA;) [and] it is so to denote muchness [of the action] or intensiveness, (O,) [for] one says also, غلّق ↓ البَابَ, a chaste phrase; El-Iṣbahánee says that ↓ غَلَّقْتُ signifies *I locked,* or *closed,* (أَغْلَقْتُ,) many doors, or a door *several times,* or a door *well* or *thoroughly;* (TA;) and one says also أَغْلَقْتُ الأَبْوَابَ; (Ṣ, O, TA;) said by Sb to be a good Arabic phrase; (TA;) but this is rare; (O;) El-Farezdaḳ says,

مَا زِلْتُ أَفْتَحُ أَبْوَابًا وَأُغْلِقُهَا

حَتَّى أَتَيْتُ أَبَا عَمْرِو بْنَ عَمَّارِ

[*I ceased not to open doors and to close them until I came to Aboo-'Amr Ibn-'Ammár*], meaning, as AḤát says, Aboo-'Amr Ibn-El-'Alà. (Ṣ, O, TA.) — [Hence] one says, أُغْلِقَ عَلَيْهِ الأَمْرُ † *The affair was* [*as though it were closed against him;* i. e., *was made*] *strait to him.* (TA. [See also 10.]) — And [hence] إِغْلَاقٌ signifies † The act of *constraining:* (Mgh, O, TA:) whence the saying in a trad., لَا طَلَاقَ وَلَا عَتَاقَ فِى إِغْلَاقٍ † [*There is no divorcement* of a wife, *nor liberation* of a slave, *in a case of constraint*]; (Mgh,* O, TA;) for the agent is straitened in his affair, (Mgh, TA,) as though the door were locked, or closed, against him, and he were imprisoned. (TA.) One says, أَغْلَقَهُ عَلَى شَىْءٍ † *He constrained him to do a thing.* (IAạr, Mgh, TA.) — See also 1, last quarter, in two places. — One says also, اغلق الرَّهْنَ ‡ *He made,* or *declared, the pledge to be due* [or *a forfeit* to its receiver]. (IAạr, TA.) And in like manner one says of the arrows termed مَغَالِقُ, [pl. of مِغْلَقٌ,] تُغْلِقُ الخَطَرَ i. e. ‡ *They make the stake,* or *wager,* or *thing played-for, to be due* [or *a forfeit*] to the player (O, TA) who wins, or is successful. (TA.) — And اغلق القَاتِلَ † *He delivered,* or *surrendered, the slayer to the heir,* or *next of kin, of the slain, that he might decide respecting his blood as he pleased.* (O, TA.) And أُغْلِقَ فُلَانٌ بِجَرِيرَتِهِ † [*Such a one was delivered,* or *surrendered,* to be punished *for his crime*]. (TA.) And El-Farezdaḳ says,

أُسَارَى حَدِيدٍ أُغْلِقَتْ بِدِمَائِهَا

† [*Captives in bonds of iron, delivered,* or *surrendered,* to be punished *for their bloods* that they had shed]. (TA.) — And أُغْلِقَ فُلَانٌ † *Such a one was angered.* (TA.) — And الإِغْلَاقُ [or rather إِغْلَاقُ ظَهْرِ البَعِيرِ] signifies † *The galling of the back of the camel by heavy loads:* (Ḳ, TA:) whence the phrase مَنْ أَغْلَقَ ظَهْرَهُ [meaning † *Such as has heavily burdened his back with sins*], applied, in a trad., to one of those for whom the Prophet will intercede; the sins that have burdened the back of the man being likened to the weight of the load of the camel: [but] it is also said that الإِغْلَاقُ was a practice of the Time of Ignorance; that when the camels of any one of them amounted to a hundred, أَغْلَقُوا بَعِيرًا, i. e. † *They displaced the* سَنَاسِن [pl. of سِنْسِنٌ, q. v.] *of one of the vertebræ of a camel, and wounded his hump, in order that he might not be ridden, and that no use might be made of his back;* and that camel was termed مُعَنًّى [q. v. in art. عنو]. (TA.)

[6. تغالقوا *They contended, one with another, for bets,* or *wagers.* See 3.]

7. انغلق; (MA, TA;) and ↓ غَلِقَ, (TA,) inf. n. غَلَقٌ; (KL;) and ↓ استغلق; (KL, TA;) said of a door, (MA, KL, TA,) *It was,* or *became, locked,* or *bolted;* or *closed,* or *shut;* (MA, KL;) or *difficult to be opened:* (TA:) انغلق is the *contr. of* انفتح. (Mṣb.) — See a verse cited voce رَوِيَّةٌ, in art. روأ. [And see also 10.]

10: see 7. — [Hence] one says, اِسْتَغْلَقَتْ رَحِمُ النَّاقَةِ فَلَمْ تَقْبَلِ المَآءَ † [*The she-camel's womb became closed so that it did not admit the seminal fluid*]. (Lth, Ḳ in art. ربع.) — And استغلق عَلَيْهِ الكَلَامُ ‡ *Speech was as though it were closed against him,* (Ṣ, O, Ḳ, TA,) *so that he* [*was tongue-tied,* or] *spoke not:* accord. to the A, it is said of one who is straitened, and required against his will to speak. (TA.) — And استغلق الأَمْرُ † *i. q.* أَعْضَلَ, q. v. (Ṣ and O in art. عضل.) — And استغلق الخَبَرُ † *i. q.* اِسْتَبْهَمَ, q. v. (Mṣb in art. بهم.) — And اِسْتَغْلَقَنِى فِى بَيْعِى, (ISh, O,) or فِى بَيْعَتِهِ, (Ḳ,) ‡ *He made me to be without the option of returning* [*in the selling to me,* or *in his sale*]: (ISh, O, Ḳ, TA:) — and اِسْتَغْلَقَتْ عَلَىَّ بَيْعَتُهُ (ISh, O, Ḳ) ‡ *His sale was to me without the option of returning.* (Ḳ, TA.)

غَلْقٌ is [said to be] the inf. n. of غَلَقَ as syn. with أَغْلَقَ: (Ṣ, O, Mṣb:) and (Ṣ, Ḳ) the subst. from the latter verb [q. v.]. (Ṣ, Mgh, Ḳ.) — As an epithet, (O, Ḳ,) applied to a man, or to a camel, (Ḳ,) or to each of these, (O,) *Old,* or *advanced in age, and lean, meagre,* or *emaciated:* (O, Ḳ, TA:) accord. to the "Nawádir," it is applied to an old man [app. as meaning *lean, meagre,* or *emaciated*]: (TA:) or *red;* (Ḳ;) or in this sense applied to a man, and to a skin for water or milk, and to leather: (Ibn-'Abbád, O:) or, accord. to AA, applied to a skin for water or milk, *vitiated,* or *rendered unsound, in the tanning.* (O.)

مَالٌ غَلْقٌ † *Unlawful property:* (JK:) or *property to which there is no access;* (TA voce رَتْجٌ;) *i. q.* مَالٌ رَتْجٌ. (Ḳ and TA ibid.) One says حَلَالٌ طِلْقٌ: [see art. طلق:] and [in the contr. sense] حَرَامٌ غَلْقٌ † [*Unlawful, inaccessible*]. (TA.)

غَلَقٌ [*A lock;*] *a thing by means of which a door is made fast,* (Ṣ,* O,* Mṣb, Ḳ,*) *not to be opened save with a key;* (Ṣ and Ḳ voce مِزْلَاجٌ;) *a thing that is closed and opened with a key;* (Mgh;) pl. أَغْلَاقٌ, (Sb, Mṣb, TA,) its only pl.: (Sb, TA:) and ↓ مِغْلَاقٌ is syn. therewith; (Ṣ, Mgh, O, Mṣb, Ḳ;) pl. مَغَالِيقُ: (Mṣb:) so too is ↓ مِغْلَقٌ: (Mṣb, TA:) and so ↓ مُغْلُوقٌ: (Ṣ, O, Ḳ:) and so ↓ غَلَاقٌ. (TA.) El-Farezdaḳ has used its pl. metaphorically, [in a sense sufficiently obvious,] saying,

فَبِتْنَ بِجَانِبَىَّ مُصَرَّعَاتٍ

وَبِتُّ أَفُضُّ أَغْلَاقَ الخِتَامِ

meaning خِتَامَ الأَغْلَاقِ, the phrase being inverted by him. (TA.) — Also *i. q.* رِتَاجٌ, meaning *A great door:* whence the phrase مَفَاتِيحُ أَغْلَاقِهَا, by which are meant [*the keys of*] *the* [*great*] *doors thereof.* (Mgh.)

غَلِقٌ [part. n. of غَلِقَ primarily signifying *Being,* or *becoming, locked,* or *bolted;* or *closed,* or *shut.* — And hence,] ‡ A pledge *being,* or *becoming, a rightful possession* [i. e. *a forfeit*] *to the receiver of it, not having been redeemed within the time stipulated.* (TA. [See also the verb.]) — And † A captive, and a criminal, *unransomed,* or *unredeemed.* (TA.) — † A *narrow,* or *strait,* place. (TA.) — † A man *evil in disposition:* or *much,* or *often, in anger;* thus expl. by Aboo-Bekr: or *narrow in disposition, difficult to be pleased.* (TA.) — And ‡ Speech, or language, [*difficult to be understood,*] *dubious,* or *confused.* (Ṣ, Ḳ, TA.) — And نَخْلَةٌ غَلِقَةٌ ‡ *A palm-tree having worms in the bases of its branches and thereby stopped from bearing fruit.* (TA.) — And غَلِقٌ applied to the back of a camel, ‡ *Having incurable galls; the whole of it being seen to be two portions of cicatrized skin, and the two sides thereof glistening.* (TA.)

غُلُقٌ, applied to a door, [*Locked;* or *bolted:* or *closed,* or *shut:*] *i. q.* ↓ مُغْلَقٌ; (Ṣ, O, Ḳ;) of which ↓ مَغْلُوقٌ is a dial. var., but bad, (Ṣ, O,) and rejected. (Ṣ, TA.)

غَلْقَةٌ, (Ṣ, O, Ḳ,) thus as heard by AḤn from El-Bekree and others, (O,) and ↓ غَلَقَةٌ (O, Ḳ) as heard by him from one of the Desert-Arabs of Rabee'ah, the former the more common, (O,) and ↓ غَلْقَى, (Ḳ,) *A certain tree* [or *plant*] *with which the people of Eṭ-Ṭáïf prepare hides for tanning by the treatment termed* عَطْنٌ: (ISk, Ṣ, TA: [see عَطَنَ الجِلْدَ:]) accord. to information given to AḤn by an Arab of the desert, (O,) *a certain small tree,* [or *plant,*] (O, Ḳ, TA,) *resembling the* عِظْلِم [q. v.], (O, TA,) *bitter* (O, Ḳ, TA) *in an intense degree, not eaten by anything: it is dried, then bruised, and beaten, with water, and skins are macerated in it, in consequence of which there remains not upon them a hair nor a particle of fur nor a bit of flesh; this being done when they desire to throw the skins into the tan, whether they be of oxen or of sheep or goats or of other animals; and it is bruised, and carried into the various districts or towns for this purpose:* (O, TA:) *it is found in El-Ḥijáz and Tihámeh:* (Ḳ, TA:) AḤn says, *it is a tree* [or *plant*] *not to be endured for pungency; the gatherer of it fears for his eyes from its exhalation or its juice:* (TA:) *it is of the utmost efficiency for tanning:* (Ḳ, TA:) Lth says, (O, TA,) *it is a bitter tree* [or *plant*]; (O;) *and it is a poison; a mixture being made with its leaves for wolves and dogs, which kills them; and it is used also for tanning therewith:* (O, TA:) and AḤn says, (TA,) *the Abyssinians poison weapons with it,* (Ḳ, TA,) *cooking it, and then smearing with it the weapons,* (TA,) *and it kills him whom it smites.* (Ḳ, TA.) [Accord. to Forskål, (Flora Ægypt. Arab. p. lxvi.,) the names of "Harmal حرمل, and Ghalget ed dib غلقت الديب," by which he means حَرْمَل and غَلْقَة الذِّئْب, are now applied to *Peganum harmala.*]

غَلَقَةٌ: } see the next preceding paragraph.
غَلْقَى: }

غَلَاقٌ: see غَلَقٌ. — It is also a subst. from the verb in the phrase أَغْلَقَ فُلَانٌ بِجَرِيرَتِهِ [q. v.]: 'Adee Ibn-Zeyd says,

* وَتَقُولُ العُدَاةُ أَوْدَى عَدِىٌّ *
* وَبَنُوهُ قَدْ أَيْقَنُوا بِالغَلَاقِ *

[*And the enemies say, "'Adee has perished, and his sons have made sure of being surrendered"*]. (TA.)

إِغْلِيقٌ [like إِقْلِيدٌ, which is more common,] *A key;* pl. أَغَالِيقُ. (TA.) [أَغَالِيقُ may also signify *Locks,* as a pl. pl., i. e. as pl. of أَغْلَاقٌ, which is pl. of غَلَقٌ.]

مُغْلَقٌ: see غَلَقٌ.

مُغْلَقٌ: see غَلَقٌ. — Also, (Ṣ, O, Ḳ, TA,) and ↓ مِغْلَاقٌ is a dial. var. thereof in this sense, (TA,) *An arrow,* (Ḳ,) i. e. *any arrow,* (Ṣ, O,) *used in the game called* المَيْسِر: (Ṣ, O, Ḳ:) or, (Ḳ,) accord. to Lth, (O,) المُغْلَقُ signifies السَّهْمُ السَّابِعُ فِى مُضَعَّفِ المَيْسِرِ [i. e. *the seventh arrow,* app. *belonging to the class, of the arrows of the game of* الميسر, *to which manifold portions are assigned;* for المُضَعَّفُ as used in relation to the game called الميسر I do not find expl. otherwise than as an appellation of "the second of the arrows termed الغُفْل, to which are assigned no portion;" (see art. ضعف, and see also سَفِيحٌ;) and this cannot be here meant, as the seventh arrow (which is commonly called المُعَلَّى) has seven portions assigned to it: therefore it seems that مُضَعَّف is here used, if not mistakenly, in a sense which, though admissible, is unusual in a case of this kind]: (O, Ḳ:) pl. مَغَالِقُ: (Ṣ, O, Ḳ: in the CḲ [erroneously] مَغَالِيقُ:) or المَغَالِقُ is one of the epithets applied to *the winning arrows,* and is not one of their [particular] names; (O, Ḳ;) they being *those that make what is played-for to be a forfeit to the player* (تُغْلِقُ الخَطَرَ لِلْقَامِرِ): so accord. to Az, who says that Lth has made a mistake in his explanation. (O.)

مِغْلَاقٌ: see غَلَقٌ. [Hence] one says, فُلَانٌ مِفْتَاحٌ لِلْخَيْرِ مِغْلَاقٌ لِلشَّرِّ † [*Such a one is a key to that which is good, a lock to that which is evil*]. (TA.) — And i. q. مِرْتَاجٌ [*A thing with which a door is closed,* or *made fast,* (app. *a kind of latch,*) *affixed behind the door, in the part next to the lock*]. (TA. [See art. رتج: and see مِغْلَاقٌ, which seems to have the same, or a similar, meaning.]) — And رَجُلٌ مِغْلَاقٌ, (Mṣb,) and قَوْمٌ مَغَالِيقُ, (TA,) † *A man,* and *a company of men, by means of whom* (عَلَى يَدَيْهِ, Mṣb, and عَلَى أَيْدِيهِمْ, TA,) *the pledge is made a forfeit* (يُغْلَقُ). (Mṣb, TA.) And ذُو مِغْلَاقٍ means الَّذِى تُغْلَقُ عَلَى يَدِهِ قِدَاحُ المَيْسِرِ † [app. *One by means of whom the arrows in the game called* الميسر *are withheld* from the rest of the players; i. e. by his winning]: or, accord. to Z, يُغْلِقُ الحُجَّةَ عَلَى الخَصْمِ † [app. *one who closes the argument against the adversary in a dispute*]. (TA in art. علق.) — See also مُغْلَقٌ.

مَغْلُوقٌ: see غَلَقٌ. — Also A hide *in which* [*the plant called*] غَلْقَة [q. v.] *is put, when it is prepared for tanning by the treatment termed* عَطْنٌ: (ISk, Ṣ, TA:) or a hide *tanned with* غَلْقَة. (O, Ḳ.)

مَغْلُوقٌ: see غَلَقٌ.

غلم

1. غَلِمَ, aor. ـَ, inf. n. غَلَمٌ (Mṣb, Ḳ, TA) and غُلْمَةٌ; (Ḳ, TA;) and ↓ اغتلم, (Mṣb, Ḳ,) only the latter of which, accord. to Aṣ, is said of other than man, though sometimes said of a man; (Mṣb;) *He was,* or *became, excited by lust,* or *appetence:* (TA:) or *overcome thereby:* (M, Ḳ, TA:) said of a man; and in like manner one says of a girl, or young woman: (TA:) or *he was,* or *became, vehemently affected with lust,* or *carnal desire.* (Mṣb.) And ↓ اغتلم said of a camel; (Ṣ, Mgh, Mṣb, Ḳ;) and [accord. to some, contr. to an assertion mentioned above,] غَلِمَ, (Ṣ, Ḳ,) inf. n. غُلْمَةٌ; (Ṣ;) *He was,* or *became, excited* (Ṣ, Mgh, Mṣb, Ḳ) *by lust,* (Ṣ, Ḳ,) or *by vehement lust,* (Mgh, Mṣb,) *to cover.* (Ṣ, Mṣb, Ḳ.)

4. اغلمهُ *It* (a thing) *excited his lust,* or *appetence.* (Ḳ,* TA.) And اغلم said of a beverage, *It strengthened in the venereal faculty.* (TA in art. اول.) — See also 8, in two places.

8. اغتلم: see 1, in two places. — Also *He* (a boy) *attained to the limit of what is termed* الغُلُومَة [app. meaning *the seventeenth year*]. (Er-Rághib, TA.) — Said of a beverage, or wine, ‡ *It was,* or *became, strong in its influence upon the head.* (Mgh, TA.*) — Said of the sea, † *It became stirred up, in a state of commotion,* or *tumultuous; its waves dashing together;* as also ↓ أَغْلَمَ. (TA.) — And الاِغْتِلَامُ and ↓ الإِغْلَامُ signify † *The exceeding the prescribed limit, of good or of evil.* (TA.)

غَلِمٌ, (Mṣb, Ḳ, TA,) and ↓ غِلِّيمٌ, (Ṣ, Ḳ, TA,) but this has an intensive signification, (Ṣ, TA,) and ↓ مِغْلِيمٌ, (Ḳ, TA,) [but this also has an intensive signification,] *Excited by lust,* or *appetence:* (TA:) or *overcome thereby:* (Ḳ, TA:) or *vehemently affected with lust,* or *carnal desire:* (Mṣb:) [or the first may generally be better rendered *in a state of excitement,* or *of vehement excitement, by lust:* and the second and third, *lustful,* or *vehemently lustful:*] the epithets applied to a female are غَلِمَةٌ and ↓ مُغْتَلِمَةٌ and ↓ غِلِّيمَةٌ and ↓ غِلِّيمٌ, (Ḳ, TA,) this last being applied to a male and to a female, (Az, TA,) and [particularly] applied to a he-camel, (TA,) and ↓ مِغْلِيمَةٌ and ↓ مِغْلِيمٌ, (Ḳ, TA,) the last [which is omitted in the CḲ] being, like غِلِّيمٌ, applied to a male and to a female: (Az, TA:) and ↓ غَيْلَمٌ likewise is applied to a girl, or young woman, in the sense of مُغْتَلِمَةٌ. (Ṣ, Ḳ.) It is said in a trad., خَيْرُ النِّسَآءِ الغَلِمَةُ عَلَى زَوْجِهَا [*The best of women is the appetent to her husband*]. (TA.)

غُلُمٌ, with two dammehs, [a pl. of which the sing. is not mentioned,] is expl. by IAạr as signifying مَحْبُوسُونَ [*Persons confined, restricted, imprisoned,* &c.]. (TA.)

غُلْمَةٌ, (Ṣ, Mṣb, Ḳ, TA, &c.,) written by some غِلْمَةٌ, [like a pl. of غُلَامٌ,] is expl. by a number of authors as signifying *Lust, appetence,* or *carnal desire:* and the *desire,* or *eager desire, of* [i. e. *experienced by*] غِلْمَان [meaning *young men*]: (TA:) or it signifies *vehement lust* or *appetence:* (Mṣb:) it is also of women, (Ḳ and TA in art. ترح,) meaning their *lust,* or *appetence:* (TA ibid.:) [and] it is used [also] in relation to a camel, signifying his *lust to cover.* (Ṣ, Ḳ, TA.) [See also 1, where it is mentioned as an inf. n. In the Ḳ, voce قَعْرَة, it is used as meaning The *gratification of venereal lust.*]

غُلَامٌ [*A young man, youth, boy,* or *male child:*] *one whose mustache is growing forth* or *has grown forth*: (Mgh, Ḳ:) or *one from the time of his birth until he attains to the period termed* شَبَاب [meaning *young manhood* (see غُلُومَةٌ)]: (Ḳ:) or *i. q.* اِبْنٌ صَغِيرٌ [meaning *a son that has not attained to puberty*]: (Mṣb:) and also applied to ‡ *such as is termed* كَهْل [i. e. *one of middle age, or between that age and the period when his hair has become intermixed with hoariness*]: (IAạr, Mṣb, Ḳ:) Az states his having heard the Arabs call thus the new-born child and also the كَهْل: (Mṣb:) the female is [sometimes] termed غُلَامَةٌ: (Ṣ, Ḳ;) [i. e.] غُلَامَةٌ occurs in poetry, applied to a جَارِيَة: (Mṣb:) the pl. of غُلَامٌ is غِلْمَةٌ, (Ṣ, Mgh, Mṣb, Ḳ,) a pl. of pauc., (Mṣb,) and أَغْلِمَةٌ, (Ḳ,) [also a pl. of pauc.,] or of these two pls. they used only the former, (Ṣ, IAth, TA,) or some of them did so, (M, TA,) and غِلْمَانٌ, (Ṣ, Mgh, Ḳ,) [a pl. of mult.,] or this is pl. of غِلْمَةٌ: (Mṣb:) the dim. of غُلَامٌ is ↓ غُلَيِّمٌ; (TA;) and that of غِلْمَةٌ is ↓ أُغَيْلِمَةٌ, as if it were the dim. of أَغْلِمَةٌ though [it has been said that] they did not use this last word; but some of them said ↓ غُلَيْمَةٌ, agreeably with analogy. (Ṣ, TA.) — It is also used as meaning ‡ *A male slave*; like as جَارِيَةٌ is used as meaning "a female slave:" — and as meaning ‡ *A hireling* [or *servant*]. (Mgh.)

غُلُومَةٌ and ↓ غُلَامِيَّةٌ (Ṣ, Ḳ) and ↓ غُلُومِيَّةٌ (Ḳ) *The state*, or *condition*, *of such as is termed* غُلَام: (Ṣ, Ḳ:*) the second is expl. by Mohammad Ibn-Ḥabeeb as meaning the *period from birth to the seventeenth year*. (TA voce شَبَاب.)

غُلَيْمَةٌ dim. of غِلْمَةٌ pl. of غُلَامٌ, q. v. (Ṣ, TA.)

غُلَامِيَّةٌ: } see غُلُومَةٌ.
غُلُومِيَّةٌ: }

غُلَيِّمٌ dim. of غُلَامٌ, q. v. (TA.)

غِلِّيمٌ, and its fem., see غَلِمٌ, in three places.

غَيْلَمٌ: see غَلِمٌ. — Also A *beautiful* woman. (TA.) — And A youth, or young man, *broad*, (Ḳ, TA,) in the M *large*, (TA,) *in the place of the parting of the hair of the head, having much hair*; (Ḳ,* TA;) as also ↓ غَيْلَمِىٌّ. (Lth, Ḳ, TA.) — مَا بِالدَّارِ غَيْلَمٌ means [*There is not in the house*] *any one*. (Ḳ.) = Also The *tortoise*: (TA:) or the *male tortoise*. (Ṣ, Ḳ, TA. [In the Mṣb said to be, in this sense, غَيْلَم, like زَيْنَب.]) — And The *frog*. (Ḳ.) [Or so عَيْلَم.] = And The *place whence issues the water in wells*. (Ḳ. [See also عَيْلَم.]) = The word signifying "a comb," and "a [thing with which the head is scratched, called] مِدْرًى," is فَيْلَم, with ف, but has been mistranscribed [غَيْلَم], (Ḳ, TA,) by Lth, as has been notified by Az. (TA.)

غَيْلَمِىٌّ: see the next preceding paragraph.

أَغْلَمُ [*More, and most, exciting to lust*]. It is said that أَغْلَمُ الأَلْبَانِ لَبَنُ الخَلِفَةِ [*The most exciting to lust, of milks, is the milk of the pregnant camel, or such as has completed a year after bringing forth and has then been covered and has conceived*]; i. e., to him who drinks it. (TA.)

أُغَيْلِمَةٌ a dim. of غِلْمَةٌ pl. of غُلَامٌ, q. v. (Ṣ, TA.)

مَغْلَمَةٌ *A cause* [*of lusting*, or] *of vehemence of lusting*: such is said to be the drinking of the milk of the أَيَّل [or إِيَّل i. e. mountain-goat]. (TA.)

مِغْلِيمٌ, and with ة: see غَلِمٌ, in three places.

مُغْتَلِمٌ: see its fem. voce غَلِمٌ. — سِقَآءٌ مُغْتَلِمٌ, (Mgh, TA,) and خَابِيَةٌ مُغْتَلِمَةٌ, (TA,) ‡ [*A skin, and a jar*,] *of which the beverage*, or *wine*, *is strong in its influence upon the head*. (Mgh, TA.*) — The خَارِجِىّ is called مَارِقٌ مُغْتَلِمٌ † [*A deviater from the true religion*,] *an exceeder of the prescribed limit*. (TA.)

غلو

1. غَلَا, aor. يَغْلُو, primarily signifies *He*, or *it*, *exceeded the proper, due, or common, limit*; *was excessive, immoderate*, or *beyond measure*; but the inf. n. differs in different cases, as will be shown in what follows: (Er-Rághib, TA:) it is said of anything as meaning *it exceeded*, or *was excessive*. (Mṣb.) — You say, غَلَا فِى الأَمْرِ, (Ṣ, Ḳ,) aor. as above, (TA,) inf. n. غُلُوٌّ (Ṣ, Ḳ, TA) and غَلَانِيَةٌ; as also ↓ تغالى به; (Ḳ* and TA in art. غلى; [but belonging to the present art., as is said in the TA;]) *He exceeded the proper, due, or common, limit, in the affair*; *was excessive*, or *immoderate, therein*. (Ṣ, Ḳ, TA.) And غَلَا فِى الدِّينِ, aor. as above, inf. n. غُلُوٌّ, *He acted*, or *behaved, with forced hardness*, or *strictness*, or *rigour, in religion, so that he exceeded the proper, due*, or *common, limit*: whence the usage of the verb in the Ḳur iv. 169 and v. 81: (Mṣb, TA:) accord. to IAth, الغُلُوُّ فِى الدِّينِ is *the investigating of the intrinsic states, or circumstances, of things*, [*in religion*,] and [*applying oneself to*] *the discovery of their causes, and of the abstrusities relating to the rites and ceremonies thereof*. (TA.) [See also 3.] — And غَلَا بِالسَّهْمِ, (Ṣ, Mgh, Mṣb, Ḳ,) aor. as above, (Mṣb, TA,) inf. n. غَلْوٌ (Ṣ, Er-Rághib, Mgh, Mṣb, Ḳ) and غُلُوٌّ; (Ḳ;) and ↓ غالى به, (Mgh, Ḳ,) and ↓ غالاهُ, (Ḳ,) inf. n. غِلَآءٌ (Mgh, Ḳ) and مُغَالَاةٌ; (Ḳ;) *He shot the arrow to the furthest distance* (Ṣ, Mgh, Mṣb) *that he was able to attain*: (Ṣ, Mgh:) or *he raised his arms with the arrow, desiring* [*to attain with it*] *the furthest limit*. (Ḳ,* TA.) And غَلَا السَّهْمُ *The arrow rose in its course, and exceeded the* [*usual*] *limit*; (Ḳ, TA;) and in like manner, الحَجَرُ *the stone*. (TA.) — And غَلَا السِّعْرُ, (Ṣ, Mgh, Mṣb, Ḳ,*) aor. as above, (Mṣb, TA,) inf. n. غَلَآءٌ, (Ṣ, Mgh, Ḳ,) or this is a simple subst., (Mṣb,) *The price, or rate, at which a thing was to be sold, was*, or *became, high*; (Mgh, Mṣb, TA;) or *exceeded the usual limit*; (Er-Rághib, TA;) *contr. of* رَخُصَ. (Ḳ.) — And غَلَا بِهَا عِظَمٌ [i. e. عِظَمٌ, lit. *Bigness exceeded the usual limit in her*;] meaning *she became plump*, or *fat*: (TA:) one says, غلا بالجَارِيَةِ عظم, and بالغُلَامِ, [*the girl*, or *young woman, became plump*, or *fat*, and *the boy*, or *young man*,] in the case of their quickly attaining to young womanhood and young manhood. (TA in another part of this art.) — And غَلَا is said of anything as meaning اِرْتَفَعَ [i. e. *It rose in degree*; as is shown by the following ex.]: Dhu-r-Rummeh says,

* فَمَا زَالَ يَغْلُو حُبُّ مَيَّةَ عِنْدَنَا *
* وَيَزْدَادُ حَتَّى لَمْ نَجِدْ مَا نَزِيدُهَا *

[*And the love of Meiyeh ceased not to rise in degree with us, and to increase, so that we found not what more we might give to her*]. (TA.) — See also 8. — And see 6.

2: see art. غلى.

3. غالى فِى أَمْرِهِ, inf. n. مُغَالَاةٌ, signifies [the same, or nearly the same, as غَلَا فِيهِ; i. e.] *He exceeded the usual*, or *proper, bounds*, or *degree, in his affair*; *acted immoderately therein*; or *strove* or *laboured*, or *exerted himself* or *his power* or *efforts*, or *the like, therein*; syn. بَالَغَ [q. v.]. (Mṣb.) — See also 1, near the middle, in two places. — غَالَى بِهِ, and غالاهُ, (Ṣ, Mṣb, Ḳ,) which latter is used by a poet for غالى به, (Ṣ,) *He bought it at a high*, or *an excessive, price*, namely, flesh-meat; (Ṣ, Mṣb;) as also ↓ اغلى به; (Ṣ;) and ↓ اغلاهُ, i.e. water, and flesh-meat [&c.]: (IḲṭṭ, TA: [see an ex. in a verse of Lebeed cited in art. دكن:]) or *he exceeded what was usual in purchasing it, or in offering it for sale, and mentioning the price*. (M, Ḳ, TA.) A poet says,

* نُغَالِى اللَّحْمَ لِلْأَضْيَافِ نِيْئًا *
* وَنُرْخِصُهُ إِذَا نَضِجَ القُدُورُ *

[*We purchase at a high price flesh-meat, for the guests, raw; and we make it to be low-priced when the contents of the cooking-pots are thoroughly cooked*]: he has suppressed the ب [after نغالى], meaning it [to be understood]. (Ṣ, TA.) — And غالى فِى الصَّدَاقِ *He made the dowry*, or *the gift to, or for, a bride, high*, or *excessive, in amount*; [*he was excessive, or exorbitant, therein*;] whence the saying of 'Omar, لَا تُغَالُوا فِى صَدُقَاتِ النِّسَآءِ [*Be not ye excessive, or exorbitant, in respect of the dowries of women*]. (TA. [See also 6.]) — And غالاهُ, inf. n. مُغَالَاةٌ, signifies also *He contended with him for superiority in tallness* or *in beneficence*; syn. طَاوَلَهُ. (TA.)

4: see 3, in two places. — اغلاهُ also signifies *He* (God) *made it to be high*, or *excessive*, (Ṣ, Mṣb, Ḳ, TA,) namely, the price, or rate, at which a thing was to be sold; (Ṣ, Mṣb, Ḳ,* TA;*) *contr. of* أَرْخَصَهُ. (TA.) — And *He found it* [a thing] *to be high-priced*: or *he reckoned it to be so*; as also ↓ استغلاهُ. (TA.) — And *He lightened*, or *thinned, somewhat, its* *leaves*, (Ḳ, TA,) namely, those of a grape-vine, *in order that it might grow high, and become* [*more productive*, or] *in good condition.* (TA.) — See also 6.

5: see art. غلى.

6: see 1, second sentence. — تغالوا فِى الصَّدَاقِ *They were excessive*, or *exorbitant, one towards another, in respect of the dowry*, or *the gift to*, or *for, a bride; contr. of* تَسَاهَلُوا and تَيَاسَرُوا. (TA in art. يسر. [See also 3, last sentence but one.]) — تغالى said of a plant, or herbage, *It grew high*; (M, Ḳ, TA;) *it became tall.* (M, TA.) And, said of the same, *It became tangled*, or *luxuriant*, or *abundant and dense, and large*; as also ↓ غَلَا, and ↓ اغلى, and ↓ اِغْلَوْلَى; (Ḳ;) or this last is said of a grape-vine, signifying *its leaves became tangled*, or *luxuriant*, or *abundant and dense, and its branches*, or *its shoots upon which were the bunches of grapes*, or *the buds of its leaves and berries*, (نَوَامِيه,) *became abundant, and it became tall.* (TA.) — Also, said of the flesh of a beast, *It rose*, or *went away*, (اِرْتَفَعَ,) *and became upon the heads of the bones: and it fell away on the occasion of preparing for racing*, or *the like, by scanty feeding &c.*: (T, TA:) or, said of the flesh of a she-camel, *it went away*; syn. ذَهَبَ; (Ḳ;) or اِرْتَفَعَ and ذَهَبَ. (Ṣ.)

8. اغتلى *He was*, or *became, quick*, or *swift*; *he sped*, or *went quickly*; (Ṣ, Ḳ, TA;) said of a camel: (Ḳ, TA:) and *he rose* [*in the degree of celerity*] (اِرْتَفَعَ) *so as to exceed goodness of rate*, or *pace*; and in like manner one says [اغتلت] of any beast (دَابَّة); as also ↓ غَلَتْ, inf. n. غلو [app. غُلُوٌّ]. (TA.)

10: see 4.

12. اغلولى: see 6.

غَلْوَةٌ The *limit*, or *utmost extent, of a shot* or *throw*; (Ṣ, Mgh;*) [i. e.] any مَرْمَاة: (Ḳ:) [generally, *a bow-shot*; i. e.] the *measure, space*, or *extent, of a single shooting of an arrow*: (Ḥar p. 234:) [or the *utmost measure of a bow-shot*; i. e.] *a shot of an arrow to the utmost possible distance*; also termed غَايَةٌ: (Mṣb:) said to be *from three hundred to four hundred cubits*: (Mgh, Mṣb:) the *twenty-fifth part of a complete* فرسخ [q. v.]: (ISd, Z, Mgh, TA:) or it is reckoned by some as *four hundred cubits*, and by others as *two hundred cubits*: (Mṣb voce مِيلٌ [q. v.]:) pl. غَلَوَاتٌ (Mṣb, Ḳ, TA) and غِلَآءٌ. (Ṣ,* Ḳ, TA.) Hence, (TA,) it is said in a prov., جَرْىُ المُذَكِّيَاتِ غِلَآءٌ, (Ṣ, Ḳ, TA,) or, as some relate it, غِلَابٌ. (TA. See art. ذكو.) [Thus] غَلْوَةٌ is sometimes used in relation to horse-racing. (TA.)

غَلْوَى *i. q.* غَالِيَةٌ. (Ḳ.) See the latter in art. غلى.

غُلَوَآءُ (Ṣ, Ḳ) and غُلْوَآءُ, (Ḳ,) the latter mentioned by AZ, and app. a contraction of the former, (TA,) [and Freytag adds غَلْوَآءُ, for which I find no authority,] *Excess*, or *exorbitance*; (TA;) *syn. with* [the inf. n.] غُلُوٌّ. (Ṣ, Ḳ, TA.) One says, خَفِّفْ عَنْ غُلَوَائِكَ [*Alleviate thine excess*, or *exorbitance*]. (TA.) — And The *quickness*, or *haste*, or *hastiness*, and the *first stage* or *state*, of youth, or young manhood; (AZ, Ṣ, Ḳ;) as also ↓ غُلْوَانٌ. (ISd, Ḳ, TA.) One says, فَعَلَهُ فِى غُلَوَآءِ شَبَابِهِ and ↓ غُلْوَانِ شَبَابِهِ [*He did it in the quickness*, or *haste*, &c., *of his youth*, or *young manhood*]. (TA.) — And غُلَوَآءُ signifies also The *rising*, or *rising high, and increasing*, of a plant, or of herbage. (Mz 40th نوع.)

غُلْوَانٌ: see the next preceding paragraph, in two places.

غَلَآءٌ the subst. from غَلَا السِّعْرُ; [as such signifying *A high price*, or *rate, at which a thing is to be sold*;] (Mṣb;) or it is an inf. n. (Ṣ, Mgh, Ḳ.) [See 1, latter half.] — Also, [i. e.] like سَمَآءٌ [in measure], (Ḳ,) but in the copies of the M ↓ غَلَّآءٌ, with teshdeed, (TA,) A man *who shoots the arrow far.* (Ḳ.) — And *A certain small*, or *short, fish*, (Ḳ, accord. to different copies,) *about a span* [*in length*]: (TA:) pl. أَغْلِيَةٌ. (Ḳ.)

غَلِىٌّ: see غَالٍ, in three places.

غَلَّآءٌ: see غَلَآءٌ.

غَالٍ [act. part. n. of غَلَا: and hence, *Acting*, or *behaving, with forced hardness*, or *strictness*, or *rigour*, in religion, *so that he exceeds the proper, due*, or *common, limit*: (see 1:) and particularly] *an extravagant zealot of the class of innovators*: pl. غُلَاةٌ. (TA in art. سبأ.) — And *Shooting*, or *one who shoots, the arrow to the furthest distance.* (Mṣb.) — And *High*, or *excessive*, (Ṣ,* Mṣb, Ḳ, TA,) applied to a price, or rate, at which a thing is sold; (Ṣ, Mṣb, Ḳ, TA;) as also ↓ غَلِىٌّ. (Ḳ, TA.) Hence one says, بِعْتُهُ بِالغَالِى and ↓ بِالغَلِىِّ *I sold it*, or *bought it, at what was a high*, or *an excessive, price*, or *rate.* (Ḳ, TA.) A poet says,

وَلَوْ أَنَّا نُبَاعُ كَلَامَ سَلْمَى ❊
لَأَعْطَيْنَا بِهِ ثَمَنًا غَلِيًّا ↓ ❊

[*And if we were sold the speech*, or *discourse, of Selmà, we would give for it a high*, or *an excessive, price*]. (TA.) — Also *Fat flesh-meat.* (Ḳ.)

غَالِيَةٌ: see art. غلى.

أَغْلَى *More*, or *most, high* [or *excessive*] in price: hence the saying, أَفْضَلُ الرِّقَابِ أَغْلَاهَا ثَمَنًا [*The most excellent of slaves is the highest thereof in price*]. (Mgh.)

مِغْلًى [in the CḲ مِغْلاء] *An arrow with which one raises the arm* [*in shooting*] *in order to exceed with it the usual limit*, or *nearly to do so*: (Ḳ,* TA:) or, accord. to the M, *that is used in striving to exceed the usual limit*: also termed ↓ مِغْلَاةٌ: pl. مَغَالٍ. (TA.)

مِغْلَاةٌ: see what next precedes. — نَاقَةٌ مِغْلَاةُ الوَهَقِ *A she-camel that goes quickly when her feet of her fore legs and of her hind legs fall in one place*: (Ṣ: [it is there expl. by تَغْتَلِى followed by the words إِذَا تَوَاهَقَتْ أَخْفَافُهَا which I have here rendered accord. to an explanation in art. وهق in the O: but the phrase مغلاة الوهق is there mentioned as an ex. of الوَهَقُ as signifying "the lasso;" whence it appears that the phrase lit. means *that exceeds the limit of the lasso*; agreeably with the explanation of Golius, "rapide currens, et fugiens laqueum sibi injiciendum:"]) or [the meaning is *a she-camel that steps far in vying*, or *keeping pace, with another*; for], in explaining the phrase مِغْلَاةُ الوَهَقِ, IB says that المِغْلَاةُ applied to the she-camel signifies الَّتِى تُبْعِدُ الخَطْوَ; and المُبَارَاةُ الوَهَقُ signifies and المُسَايَرَةُ. (TA voce هِرْجَابٌ.)

أَرْضٌ مُغْلَوْلِيَةٌ *A land having abundant, and dense* or *luxuriant, herbage*; and with ع also; *i. q.* مُغْمِئَةٌ and مُغْمَئَةٌ. (TA in art. غمأ.)

غلى

1. غَلَتِ القِدْرُ, aor. تَغْلِى, inf. n. غَلْىٌ and غَلَيَانٌ, (Ṣ, MA, Mṣb, Ḳ,) *The cooking-pot boiled*; (MA, &c.;) and غَلِيَتْ, aor. تَغْلَى, is an unusual dial. var. thereof, the former being the more chaste; (Mṣb;) or غَلِيَتْ is not allowable. (Ṣ.) — [Hence غَلَى said of a liquor, *It estuated: it effervesced: it fermented*: see نَبِيذٌ.] — And hence] يَغْلِى دَمُهُ [as though meaning † *His blood is fit to be shed*] is a phrase like رَابَ دَمُهُ, [q. v.], said of one who has exposed himself to slaughter: his blood being likened to milk that has become thick, and fit to be churned. (A in art. روب.) — And غَلِىَ الرَّجُلُ, like رَضِىَ in measure [but see what has been said of this form of the verb above], ‡ *The man became vehemently angry.* (IḲṭṭ, TA.)

2: see 4, in two places. — غَلَّى الرَّجُلَ, inf. n. تَغْلِيَةٌ, *He rubbed the man over*, or *perfumed him, with* غَالِيَة. (TA.) And غَلَّى لِحْيَتَهُ (Mgh, O, Mṣb, all in art. غلف) بِالغَالِيَةِ (O, ibid.) *He daubed*, or *smeared, his beard with* غَالِيَة; as also غَلَّفَهَا. (Mgh, O, Mṣb, ibid. [See 1 in art. غلف.]) — And تَغْلِيَةٌ signifies also The *saluting from afar, and making a sign.* (Ḳ.)

4. اغلى القِدْرَ, (Ṣ, MA, Ḳ,) and ↓ غَلَّاهَا, (Ḳ,) *He made the cooking-pot to boil.* (Ṣ,* MA, Ḳ.*) IDrd mentions, among some of the sayings of the people of former ages, ↓ أَنْ مَآءً وَغَلِّهِ [*Pour thou out water, and make it to boil*]. (TA.) And one says, أَغْلَيْتُ الزَّيْتَ وَنَحْوَهُ [*I made the olive-oil and the like to boil*], inf. n. إِغْلَآءٌ. (Mṣb.)

5. تغلّى (Ṣ, Mṣb, Ḳ) بِالغَالِيَةِ (Ṣ, Mṣb) *He* (a man, Ṣ, Mṣb) *perfumed himself*, (Ṣ,* Mṣb, Ḳ,) or *rubbed himself over*, (Ḳ,) with غَالِيَة; (Ṣ, Mṣb, Ḳ;) and ↓ اغتلى signifies the same; (IDrd, O

in art. غلف ;) as also تَغَلَّلَ, (Mṣb, and O in art. غلف,) and اِغْتَلَّ. (O in that art.)

6, in all its senses, belongs to art. غلو, q. v.

8: see 5.

غَلَانِيَةٌ, mentioned in the Ḳ in this art., belongs to art. غلو, being an inf. n. of the verb in the phrase غَلَا فِى الأَمْرِ. (TA.)

غَلَّايَةٌ *A vessel of copper* [or *brass*], *in which water is heated; thus called by the people of Syria; the same that is called* مِحَمّ [q. v.] *and* قُمْقُمٌ *and* قُمْقُمَةٌ. (Mṣb voce قُمْقُمٌ.)

غَالِيَةٌ [*Galia moschata,*] *a sort of perfume,* (Ṣ, Ḳ,) *well known;* (Ḳ;) *a certain compound of perfumes;* (Mṣb;) *musk mixed* or *boiled* [*with other perfumes*]; (MA;) or *a perfume composed of musk and ambergris and camphor and oil of ben:* (KL:) it is said that the first who called it thus was Suleymán Ibn-'Abd-El-Melik; (Ṣ, TA;) and he did so because it is a compound boiled together upon the fire: or it was thus named by Mo'áwiyeh; the case being, that 'Abd-Allah Ibn-Jaạfar went in to him, and the odour of perfume was diffusing itself from him; so he said, "What is thy perfume, O 'Abd-Allah?" and he answered, "*musk and ambergris combined with oil of ben;*" whereupon Mo'áwiyeh said, غَالِيَةٌ, meaning *high-priced:* (TA:) [hence some hold the word to belong to art. غلو; and their opinion is strengthened by the fact that] غَلْوَى signifies the same. (Ḳ in art. غلو.)

غمر

1. غَمَّهُ, (Ṣ, Mṣb, Ḳ, &c.,) aor. ـُ, (Mṣb,) inf. n. غَمٌّ, (Mṣb, TA,) *He covered it,* (Ṣ, Mṣb, Ḳ, TA,) *veiled it,* or *concealed it;* (TA;) namely, a thing: (Mṣb, Ḳ, TA:) this is the primary meaning. (TA.) [Hence,] one says, غُمَّ الهِلَالُ (Ṣ, Mṣb, Ḳ, TA) عَلَى النَّاسِ, (Ṣ, TA,) inf. n. غَمٌّ, (TA,) *The new moon was veiled,* or *concealed,* (Ṣ, Mṣb,) *to the people,* (Ṣ,) *by clouds,* or *otherwise,* (Ṣ, Mṣb,) or *was intercepted by thin clouds,* (Ḳ, TA,) or *otherwise,* (TA,) *so that it was not seen.* (Ṣ, Mṣb, TA.) It is said in a trad., فَإِنْ غُمَّ عَلَيْكُمْ فَأَكْمِلُوا العِدَّةَ, (Mgh,* Mṣb, TA,) i. e. *And if it* [the new moon] *be veiled, &c., to you, then complete ye the reckoning* of Shaạbán, thirty [days], in order that the entering upon the fast of Ramaḍán may be with [inferential] knowledge. (Mṣb.) Az says that غُمَّ and أُغْمِىَ and غُمِىَ all signify the same: (TA:) and all three occur in the trad. above mentioned accord. to different relations thereof. (Mgh.) [See also 1 in art. غمى.] — And [hence] غَمَّ القَمَرُ النُّجُومَ *The moon concealed the stars:* or *almost concealed the light of the stars.* (TA.) — And غُمَّ عَلَيْهِ الخَبَرُ *The information,* or *narration, was dubious, confused,* or *vague, to him; such as to be difficult to be understood;* or *such as not to be understood;* (Ṣ, Ḳ;) like أُغْمِىَ: (Ṣ:) or *was obscure,* or *unapparent, to him.* (Mṣb.) — And غَمَّهُ, (Ṣ, Ḳ, TA,) aor. ـُ, inf. n. غَمٌّ, (TA,) *It* (i. e. هَمٌّ [here meaning "grief," see غَمٌّ below,]) *covered* [or *was as though it covered*] *his heart:* (Ḥar p. 637:) or [accord. to common acceptation] *it,* or *he, grieved him;* or *caused him to mourn* or *lament,* or *to be sorrowful* or *sad* or *unhappy;* syn. أَحْزَنَهُ. (Ḳ, and Ḥar p. 422. [See also 4.]) — غَمَّهُ, in which the pronoun relates to an ass, &c., (Ṣ, Ḳ, TA,) aor. ـُ, inf. n. غَمٌّ, (TA,) means *He put* [*as a covering*] *to his mouth and his nostrils the* ↓ غِمَامَة, (Ṣ, Ḳ, TA,) which is *a thing like the* كِعَام [or *muzzle*], (so in the Ṣ and CḲ,) or *a thing like the* فِدَام [which seems to be here similar in meaning to كعام]: (so in other copies of the Ḳ:) or *he put* [*as a covering*] *to his mouth a nose-bag,* or *the like, to prevent his feeding;* and this is termed a ↓ غِمَامَة: (TA:) [the verb that I have rendered "put to" in these explanations is أَلْقَمَ, of which I do not find in its proper place any signification that would be exactly apposite in this case:] or ↓ غِمَامَة signifies *a sort of bag for the mouth of a camel and the like,* (Ḳ, TA,) *his mouth being put into it:* (TA:) pl. غَمَائِمُ: (Ṣ, TA:) and one says, غَمَّهُ بِالغِمَامَةِ [*he covered his mouth with the* غمامة], aor. and inf. n. as above. (TA.) — غَمَّ الشَّىْءَ, aor. ـُ, also signifies عَلَاهُ [app. as meaning *It rose upon,* or *above, the thing,* as though forming a covering over it]: mentioned on the authority of IAạr, who cites [as an ex.] the saying of En-Nemir Ibn-Towlab, [app. describing a رَوْضَة, or meadow,]

* أُنُفٌ يَغُمُّ الضَّالُ نَبْتَ بِحَارِهَا *

[*Not depastured, the trees called* ضال *rising upon,* or *above, the herbage of its fertile tracts,* or *its tracts near to water*]. (TA.) See also 8. — [غَمَّ is also intrans.: one says,] غَمَّ يَوْمُنَا, (Ṣ, Ḳ, TA,) inf. n. غَمٌّ and غُمُومٌ; (TA;) and ↓ أَغَمَّ; *Our day was,* or *became,* [*sultry,* or] *intensely hot,* (Ṣ, Ḳ, TA,) *so that it took away,* (Ṣ,) or *almost took away,* (TA,) *the breath:* (Ṣ, TA:) or both verbs, said of a day, and of the sky, mean *it brought* غَمّ [or *distress that affected the breath* or *respiration*], *arising from closeness of heat,* or *clouds.* (Mṣb.) — غَمِمَ الشَّخْصُ, of the class of تَعِبَ, [the first pers. being غَمِمْتُ,] inf. n. غَمَمٌ, *The person's hair of his head flowed down so that his forehead and the back of his neck were narrowed.* (Mṣb.) [See also غَمَمٌ below.]

3. غَامَمْتُهُ signifies غَمَمْتُهُ وَغَمَّنِى [*I grieved him,* or *caused him to mourn* or *lament* &c., *and he grieved me,* or *caused me to mourn* or *lament* &c.; or *I grieved him* &c., *being grieved* &c. *by him*]. (Ḳ.)

4. اغمّت السَّمَآءُ *The sky became clouded:* (Ḳ, as indicated by the context:) or *i. q.* تَغَيَّرَت [i. e., *became altered*]: thus in the Ṣ; but some say that it is correctly تَغَيَّمَت [agreeably with the former of the explanations above]. (TA.) See also 1, near the end. — مَا أَغَمَّكَ لِى and إِنِّى is [an expression of wonder, meaning *How great grief,* or *sadness, dost thou occasion to me!*] from الغَمّ signifying الحُزْنُ. (Ḳ, TA.) — [Accord. to the TḲ, أَغَمَّهُ signifies أَحْزَنَهُ; like غَمَّهُ: but this I think a mistake. — And Freytag explains أَغَمَّ as occurring in the Deewán of the Hudhalees signifying "*Demersit:*" but in which of its senses he uses this word he does not specify.]

6. تغامّ *He made a show of* غَمّ [or *grief,* &c.,] *without its being in the heart.* (Ḥar p. 126.)

7. انغمّ *It* (a thing, Ḳ) *was,* or *became, covered,* (Ṣ, Ḳ, TA,) *veiled,* or *concealed.* (TA.) — See also what next follows.

8. اغتمّ *He was,* or *became, grieved,* or *caused to mourn* or *lament,* or *to be sorrowful* or *sad* or *unhappy;* (Ṣ,* Ḳ;) as also ↓ انغمّ: (Ḳ:) both mentioned by Sb. (TA.) — And, said of a plant, or herbage, *It was,* or *became, tall,* (Ḳ, TA,) *and tangled,* or *luxuriant,* (TA,) *and abundant:* (Ḳ, TA:) as also اعتمّ. (TA.) [And in like manner ↓ غَمَّ is expl. by Freytag as occurring in the Deewán of the Hudhalees, said of a plant, meaning *It was tall and luxuriant.*] — And, said of a man, *He withheld himself from going out,* or *forth.* (TA.)

R. Q. 1. غَمْغَمَ, [inf. n. غَمْغَمَةٌ, *He* (a bull) *uttered a cry,* or *cries, in fright;* as also ↓ تَغَمْغَمَ: see غَمْغَمَةٌ below. — And] *He* (a courageous man) *raised his voice in conflict with his antagonist;* (Ḥar p. 531;) [as also ↓ تَغَمْغَمَ: see, again, غَمْغَمَةٌ below.] — And *He* [a man] *spoke while taking a thing into his fauces, so that the hearer,* or *listener, did not understand what he was saying;* (Ḥar ubi suprà;) [or *spoke indistinctly;* agreeably with an explanation of غَمْغَمَةٌ below; as also ↓ تَغَمْغَمَ. — And, said of a bow, *It produced a sound;* agreeably with another explanation of غَمْغَمَةٌ below.] — Also, said of an infant, inf. n. غَمْغَمَةٌ, *He wept over the breast, desiring the milk:* [and the inf. n. is used as a simple subst., and therefore pluralized:] IAạr cites as an ex.,

* إِذَا المُرْضِعَاتُ بَعْدَ أَوَّلِ هَجْعَةٍ *

* سَمِعْتَ عَلَى ثُدِيِّهِنَّ غَمَاغِمَا ↓ *

[*When the suckling women, after the first light sleep in the beginning of the night,* are in such a condition that *thou hearest cryings over their breasts*]; meaning, as he says, that the milk of these women is little in quantity, so that the sucking child weeps over the breast when sucking it. (TA.)

R. Q. 2. تَغَمْغَمَ: see R. Q. 1, in three places: and see its inf. n. غَمْغَمَةٌ, below, in two places. — Said of one drowning (غَرِيق) beneath the water, it signifies *He uttered a cry,* or *cries:* or, as is said in the T, *he was pressed upon by the waves above him:* a poet uses it of Pharaoh when he was overwhelmed [in the sea]. (TA.)

غَمٌّ [an inf. n. used as an epithet in which the

quality of a subst. predominates,] *Grief, mourning, lamentation, sorrow, sadness,* or *unhappiness*; syn. حُزْنٌ; (Mṣb, Ḳ;) so called because it covers happiness and forbearance; (Mṣb;) or غَمّ in the heart is thus called because it veils, or precludes, happiness: (Ḥam p. 21:) [it may therefore be rendered *gloominess of mind*:] or i. q. كَرْبٌ, (Ḳ,) which signifies حُزْنٌ, (Ḳ in art. كرب,) or غَمّ, (Ṣ, in that art.,) [*that affects the breath* or *respiration*, lit.] *that takes away the breath*; (Ṣ and Ḳ in that art.;) as also ▼ غُمَّآءُ (Ḳ) and ▼ غُمَّةٌ, (Ṣ, Ḳ,) the last [expl. in the Ṣ as syn. with كُرْبَةٌ, which is syn. with كَرْبٌ, and] mentioned by Lḥ: (TA:) [see also صَقْعٌ:] it is كَرْبٌ [or *grief*, &c.,] *that befalls the heart because of what has happened*; differing from هَمٌّ, which is كرب that befalls because of annoyance, or harm, that is expected to happen: or, as some say, both are one [in meaning]: the differing is asserted by 'Iyáḍ and [many] others: (TA:) [see also غَضَبٌ:] the pl. of غَمٌّ is غُمُومٌ. (Ṣ, Ḳ.) — It is also an inf. n. used as an epithet in the phrase يَوْمٌ غَمٌّ (Ṣ, TA) i. e. *A day that is* [*sultry*, or] *intensely hot, so that it* [*almost*] *takes away the breath*; and لَيْلَةٌ غَمٌّ [*such a night*], i. e. ▼ غَامَّةٌ: (Ṣ:) or one says يَوْمٌ غَمٌّ and ▼ غَامٌّ and ▼ مِغَمٌّ, (Ḳ, TA,) the last with kesr to the م, (TA,) [in the CḲ ▼ مُغِمٌّ,] meaning *a day of heat*, (Ḳ,) or *of intense heat*: (TA:) or *a day of* غَمّ [i. e. *grief*, &c.]: and [in a similar sense, as is implied by the context immediately preceding,] لَيْلَةٌ غَمٌّ and غَمَّةٌ and ▼ غُمًّى: (Ḳ:) [but] A'Obeyd mentions, on the authority of AZ, ▼ لَيْلَةٌ غُمًّى and ▼ لَيْلَةٌ غَمَّةٌ as meaning *a night in which there is over the sky* [*a covering of clouds*, or] *what is termed* غُمًّى [a word belonging to art. غمى, being in measure] like رُمًّى; (Ṣ;) and [in the like sense] يَوْمٌ غَمٌّ. (So in one of my copies of the Ṣ.) — And one says, كَانَ عَلَى السَّمَآءِ غمٌ [app. غَمٌّ, but this, I think, requires confirmation, for which I have searched in vain,] and غمى [app. ▼ غُمًّى, or perhaps غَمًى, a word mentioned above,] meaning *There was over the sky a collection* [*or an expanse*] *of thin clouds*, or *a* ضَبَابَة [i. e. *mist*, or *the like*], فَحَالَ دُونَ الهِلَالِ [*and it intercepted the new moon*]: and هٰذِهِ لَيْلَةُ ▼ غُمًّى, and some say ▼ غَمًّى, *This is a night* [*of a covering of clouds*, or] *of a* ضَبَابَة [*or mist*, or *the like*], *intervening between the new moon and men; so that the new moon is not seen*: (Mṣb:) and [hence] ▼ صُمْنَا لِلغُمَّى, and ▼ لِلغَمَّى, (Ṣ, Mṣb, Ḳ,) both mentioned by ISk on the authority of Fr, (Ṣ,) and ▼ لِلغُمَّآءِ, (Ṣ, Ḳ,) and ▼ لِلغُمِّيَةِ, (Ḳ, TA, but omitted in the CḲ,) and ▼ لِلغُمَّةِ, (TA,) [i. e. *We fasted after*, or *from the time of*, *the covering of clouds*, or *the mist*, or *the like*, *that concealed the new moon*; (the prep. لِ being here used in the sense of بَعْدَ, or مِنْ وَقْتِ, as in the Ḳur xvii. 80;) virtually] meaning [*we fasted*] *without a sight* [*of the new moon*]: (Mṣb, TA:) a rájiz says,

• لَيْلَةَ غُمًّى ▼ طَامِسٍ هِلَالُهَا •
• أَوْغَلْتُهَا وَمُكْرَهٌ إِيغَالُهَا •

[*In a night of a covering of clouds*, or *of a mist*, or *the like, having its new moon effaced: I journeyed quickly and far in it*, (أَوْغَلْتُهَا being used, app. by poetic license, for أَوْغَلْتُ فِيهَا,) *and disliked was the journeying so therein*]: (Ṣ, TA:) and it is said that لَيْلَةُ غُمًّى [i. e. ▼ غُمًّى and ▼ غَمًّى] signifies also *the last night of the* [*lunar*] *month*; being so called because the case thereof is veiled to people so that it is not known whether it be of the coming [month] or of the past. (TA.)

غَمَّةٌ fem. of غَمٌّ, q. v., used as an epithet.

غُمَّةٌ: see غَمٌّ, first sentence: — and also in the latter half. — Also, † *Perplexity*, and *dubiousness*, or *confusedness*: pl. غُمَمٌ: one says, هُوَ فِى غُمَّةٍ † *He is in a state of perplexity*, and *dubiousness*, or *confusedness*: (Mṣb:) and هُوَ فِى غُمَّةٍ مِنْ أَمْرِهِ † *He is in a state of perplexity* and *darkness* [*in respect of his case* or *affair*]; from الغَمّ signifying "the act of covering" [a thing]. (Ḥam p. 320.) [See also غُمَّةٌ and غُمَّآءُ.] And one says أَمْرٌ غُمَّةٌ † *A dubious, confused*, or *vague, case* or *affair*. (Ṣ, Ḳ.*) [See also غُمًّى.] It is said in the Ḳur [x. 72], ثُمَّ لَا يَكُنْ أَمْرُكُمْ عَلَيْكُمْ غُمَّةً i. e. ‡ [*Then let not your case be to you one of*] *darkness*, and *straitness*, and *anxiety*: (A'Obeyd, Ṣ, TA:) or, as some say, *covered, veiled*, or *concealed*. (TA.) And أَرْضٌ غُمَّةٌ means † *A strait*, or *narrow, land*. (TA.) — Also *The bottom of the interior* of a skin for clarified butter (Ṣ, Ḳ) &c. (Ṣ.) [See also the first sentence in art. غمل.]

غُمَّةٌ i. q. لبسة [app. لُبْسَةٌ, meaning † *Obscureness, confusedness*, or *dubiousness*: see also غُمَّةٌ]. (TA.)

غَمَمٌ is the inf. n. of 1 in the last of the senses expl. above: (Mṣb:) or it signifies The *flowing down of the hair so that the forehead*, (Ṣ, Ḳ, TA,) or, as in the M, *the face*, (TA,) *and the back of the neck, are narrowed*: (Ṣ, Ḳ, TA:) or the *hair that veils*, or *conceals, the* جَبِين [generally meaning the *part above the temple*, but sometimes it means the *forehead*,] *and the back of the neck*. (Ḥar p. 21.) Z says that they dislike what is thus termed, and like what is termed نَزَعٌ [i. e. baldness of the two sides of the forehead]. (TA.)

غَمَامٌ *Clouds*: (Ṣ, Mṣb, Ḳ:) or *white clouds*: (Ḳ:) or *thin clouds*: (Jel in ii. 54:) and ▼ غَمَامَةٌ signifies *one thereof*: (Ṣ, Mṣb, Ḳ:) the former being pl. of the latter, as also is غَمَائِمُ: (Ḳ:) [or rather غَمَامٌ is a coll. gen. n., of which غَمَامَةٌ is the n. un.:] they are so called because they veil the sky, or because they veil the light of the sun. (TA.) — [Hence,] حَبُّ الغَمَامِ signifies *Hail-stones*, or *hail*. (TA.) [See an ex. in a verse cited in art. ان, p. 109.]

غُمَامٌ i. q. زُكَامٌ [*A rheum, such as is termed coryza*]. (Ḳ.)

غُمُومٌ [a pl. of which no sing. is mentioned,] *Small stars, such as are faint*, or *indistinct*. (Ḳ.)

غَمِيمٌ i. q. غَمِيسٌ, (Ṣ, Ḳ,) i. e. *Fresh herbage* (كَلَأ) *beneath such as is dried up*; (Ṣ, TA;) or *green herbage beneath such as is dry*. (TA.) — And *Milk heated until it thickens*: (Ṣ, Ḳ:) because it becomes covered over. (TA.)

غَمَامَةٌ: see غَمَامٌ. — Also ‡ *Herbage*: so in the saying, أَحْمَى فُلَانٌ غَمَامَةَ وَادِى كَذَا i. e. ‡ [*Such a one made to be prohibited to the public*] *the herbage that was the growth of such a valley*: thus called [because produced by the water of the clouds,] in like manner as it is called سَمَآءٌ. (TA.)

غُمَامَةٌ: see the next paragraph.

غِمَامَةٌ: see 1, near the middle, in three places. — Also *A thing with which the eyes of a she-camel are bound*, or *with which her muzzle is bound*: (Ḳ:) or *a piece of cloth with which the nose of a she-camel is stopped* (يُسَدُّ) [or *bound* (يُشَدُّ)] *when she is made to incline to the young one of another*: pl. غَمَائِمُ. (A'Obeyd, TA.) [See also دُرْجَةٌ: and صِقَاعٌ.] — And (by way of comparison [thereto], TA) ‡ The *prepuce of a boy*; as also ▼ غُمَامَةٌ. (Ḳ, TA.)

غَمًّى: see غَمٌّ, in six places. — Also *Dust*; syn. غَبَرَةٌ. (Ḳ.) — And *Darkness*. (Ḳ.) — And † *Hardship*, or *difficulty*, or *distress*, [*as though*] *covering* [or *overwhelming*] *a party in war*, or *battle*. (Ḳ.) See also the next paragraph.

غُمًّى: see غَمٌّ, latter half, in four places. — Also † *A calamity*, or *misfortune*; and so ▼ غُمَّآءُ; (Ḳ, TA;) and ▼ غَمَّآءُ, likewise, is said to be allowable. (TA. [But this last I think doubtful.]) And † *A hard*, or *difficult, affair* or *case, in relation to which one knows not the right course to pursue*; as also ▼ غَمًّى, (Ḳ, TA,) and ▼ غَمَّآءُ. (TA.)

غَمَّآءُ [fem. of أَغَمُّ, q. v.: — and also used as a subst.]: see غَمٌّ, first sentence: — and also in the latter half: — and see also غُمًّى, in two places. — إِنَّهُمْ لَفِى غَمَّآءَ مِنَ الأَمْرِ means [*Verily they are in a state of dubiousness*, or *confusedness*, *in respect of the case*, or *affair*; or] *in a dubious*, or *confused, case* or *affair*. (TA.) [See also غُمَّةٌ and غُمَّةٌ.]

غُمَّآءُ: see غُمًّى.

غُمِّيَّةٌ: see غَمٌّ, latter half.

غَامٌّ, and its fem. غَامَّةٌ: see غَمٌّ, former half.

غَمْغَمَةٌ [mentioned above as an inf. n. (see

R. Q. 1), used as a simple subst.,] signifies The *cries* [or *cry*] of bulls [or wild bulls] in fright: (Ṣ, Ḳ, TA:) and of courageous men in conflict: (Ṣ, Mgh, Ḳ, TA:) and so ▼ تَغَمْغُمٌ: pl. of the former, in both senses, غَمَاغِمُ. (TA.) See also an ex. of the pl. voce غَمْغَمَ. — And *Indistinct speech*; (Ḳ;) as also ▼ تَغَمْغُمٌ: (Ṣ, Ḳ:) غَمْغَمَةٌ is when one hears the voice but does not distinguish the articulation of the words; and when speech resembles that of the عَجَم. (T, in TA, voce رَتَّةٌ.) — Also The *sound* of bows. (TA.)

أَغَمُّ الوَجْهِ وَالقَفَا (Ṣ,) and رَجُلٌ أَغَمُّ, (Ṣ, Mṣb, Ḳ,) *A man whose hair flows down so that the face and the back of the neck are narrowed*: (Ṣ, Mṣb, Ḳ:) and in like manner [the fem.] غَمَّآءُ is applied to a woman. (Mṣb.) — غَمَّآءُ applied to the forelock (نَاصِيَة) of a horse means *Excessively abundant in the hair*: and such is disliked. (Ṣ.) — And سَحَابٌ أَغَمُّ means ‡ *Clouds in which is no gap*, or *interstice*. (Ḳ, TA.)

مُغِمٌّ and مَغَمٌّ: see غُمٌّ, former half. — أَرْضٌ مُغِمَّةٌ (Ḳ, TA) and مَغَمَّةٌ (TA) *A land having abundant* (Ḳ, TA) *and dense* or *luxuriant* (TA) *herbage*. (Ḳ, TA.)

مُغَمْغِمٌ, applied to clouds (غَيْم), and to a sea, *Abounding with water*: (Ḳ:) and in like manner, without ة, to a well (رَكِيَّة), *that fills everything, and submerges it*: (IAạr, TA:) and to what is termed حَشًى [q. v.], (IAạr, Ṣ, TA,) meaning *covering*. (IAạr, TA.)

مَغْمُومٌ [pass. part. n. of غَمَّهُ, i. e. *Covered*, &c.]. — [Applied to unripe dates (accord. to the TA to رُطَب, a mistranscription for بُسْر), like مَغْمُولٌ,] *Put into a jar, and covered over until they have become ripe*. (TA.) — Applied to a new moon, *Veiled*, or *concealed*, *by clouds*, or *otherwise*, (Mṣb,) or *intercepted by thin clouds*, (Ḳ,) *so as not to be seen*. (Mṣb.) — Applied to a man, *Grieved*, or *caused to mourn* or *lament*, or *to be sorrowful* or *sad* or *unhappy*. (TA.) — And *Affected with the malady termed* غُمَام. (Ḳ.)

غمت

1. غَمَتَهُ, aor. ـِ, (Ṣ, O, Ḳ,) inf. n. غَمْتٌ, (Ṣ, O,) *It* (i. e. food) *was*, or *became, heavy upon his heart* [or *stomach*], (Ks, Ṣ, O, Ḳ,) *he having eaten much thereof so that it caused him to suffer indigestion*, (Ks, O,) *and it rendered him like one intoxicated*: (Ḳ:) or, accord. to Sh, *it* (i. e. grease) *rendered him like one intoxicated*, (O, TA,) *in consequence of indigestion*. (TA.) — And *He covered it*; (O, Ḳ;) namely, a thing. (Ḳ.) — And غَمَتَهُ فِى المَآءِ *i. q.* غَطَّهُ [i. e. *He immersed*, or *plunged, him*, or *it, into the water*; like غَتَّهُ]. (IDrd, O, Ḳ.) — And غَمَتَ نَفَسًا *He made a sign*, or *motion, with his head*, (O,) or *he raised his head*, (Ḳ,) [*for the purpose of taking breath*,] *in drinking*. (O, Ḳ.) ═ غَمِتَ *He became like one intoxicated, by grease* [*in his stomach*]: (Sh, O:) or *he suffered from the heaviness of food upon his heart* [or *stomach*] *so that he became like one intoxicated*. (Ḳ.)

غمد

1. غَمَدَهُ, aor. ـِ and ـُ, inf. n. غَمْدٌ; and ▼ اغمدهُ, (Ṣ, Mṣb, Ḳ,) inf. n. إِغْمَادٌ; (Mṣb;) mentioned by AO, (Ṣ,) or by A'Obeyd, (L, TA,) as two chaste forms; (Ṣ, L, TA;) *He put it* (i. e. a sword, Ṣ, Mṣb, Ḳ, or the like, Mṣb) *into its* غِمْد [i. e. *scabbard*, or *sheath*; *he sheathed it*]: (Ṣ, Mṣb, Ḳ:) or *he made for it*, or *furnished it with, a* غِمْد. (Mṣb.) — Hence, غَمَدَهُ بِكَذَا ‡ *He covered him*, or *it, with such a thing*; as though he made the latter a غِمْد to the former. (A.) — See also 5, in two places. ═ غَمَدَ, inf. n. غُمُودٌ, said of a tree of the species called عُرْفُط, † *It had its branches abounding with leaves so that one could not see its thorns*; (L, Ḳ;) as though they were sheathed. (L.) — غَمِدَتِ الرَّكِيَّةُ, (L, Ḳ,) aor. ـَ, inf. n. غُمُودٌ, (L,) ‡ *The well lost its water*. (L, Ḳ.) — And غَمِدَت, (L, Ḳ,) aor. ـَ, (Ḳ,) inf. n. غَمَدٌ, (L,) ‡ *It* (a well) *had much water*: (Aṣ, L, Ḳ:) or *it had little water*. (AO, L, Ḳ.)

2: see 5, in two places.

4: see 1. — [Hence,] اغمد الأَشْيَآءَ ‡ *He put the things one within another*. (Ḳ.) — And اغمد الحِلْسَ ‡ *He put the* [*cloth called*] حِلْس *beneath the camel's saddle*, to preserve the animal's back from being galled by the saddle. (Akh, A,* L.)

5. تغمّد الثَّوْبَ ‡ *He put the garment*, or *piece of cloth, beneath him, to conceal it from the eyes of others*. (A.) — And تغمّد الرَّجُلَ, (JK, L,) and ▼ غمّدهُ, (L,) † *He took the man beneath him* بِخَتْلٍ (تَحْتَهُ, thus in the JK, in the L [*by deceit*, or *guile*]), *to cover him over*, or *conceal him*. (JK, L.) — And تغمّد فُلَانًا, (Ṣ, L, Ḳ,) and ▼ غمّدهُ, (Ḳ,) ‡ *He concealed, as with a veil, what had proceeded from such a one*, or *what such a one had done*. (Ṣ, L, Ḳ.) — And تَغَمَّدَهُ ٱللّٰهُ بِرَحْمَتِهِ, (Ṣ, A, L, Mṣb, Ḳ,) and ▼ غمّدهُ بِهَا and ▼ غمّدهُ فِيهَا, (L,) ‡ *God covered him with his mercy*, (A'Obeyd, Ṣ, A, L, Mṣb, Ḳ,) *as with a veil*; *veiled him therewith*; (A'Obeyd, A, L, Mṣb;) *clad him*, or *invested him, therewith*. (A'Obeyd, L.) — تغمّد الأَعْدَآءَ † *He threw himself upon the enemies*; or *came upon them*, or *over them*; *and overwhelmed them*. (L.) — And تغمّدهُ ‡ *He filled it*, (A, Ḳ,) namely, a measure of capacity, (A,) or a vessel. (Ḳ.)

8. اغتمد اللَّيْلَ ‡ *He* (a man, Ṣ, L) *entered into* [*the darkness of*] *the night*; (Ṣ, A, L, Ḳ;) as though it became as a غِمْد to him; like as one says ادّرع اللَّيْلَ: (Ṣ, L:) and simply اغتمد *he ventured upon, encountered*, or *braved, the night*, (رَكِبَهُ,) to seek food for his family. (Ṣ, L.)

10. اِسْتَغْمَدَتِ السَّمَآءُ فِى السَّحَابِ الكَثِيرِ † [*The sky became obscured amid the many clouds*]. (TA in art. طنفس.)

غِمْدٌ (Ṣ, L, Mṣb, Ḳ, &c.) and ▼ غُمْدَانٌ, (L, Ḳ,) but the latter is not of established authority, (IDrd,) of a sword, (Ṣ, L, Mṣb, Ḳ,) and the like, (Mṣb,) The *scabbard*, or *sheath*; [this is well known to be the correct meaning; it is shown to be so in the Ṣ, voce قِرَابٌ; and is the meaning obtaining in the present day;] syn. غِلَافٌ, (Ṣ, O,) or جَفْنٌ: (L, Ḳ:) [both of these words have the signification mentioned above; but not that only; for غلاف has a wider application; and it is said in the Ṣ, voce قِرَابٌ, that the جفن of a sword is *a case*, or *receptacle, in which is* (*put*) *the sword together with its* غمد *and suspensory belt* or *cord*:] the pl. is أَغْمَادٌ [a pl. of pauc.] (O, Mṣb, Ḳ) and غُمْدَانٌ, (O,) or غُمُودٌ. (Ḳ.)

غُمْدَانٌ: see the next preceding paragraph.

غَامِدٌ, عِيشَةٌ رَاضِيَةٌ a phrase like رَكِىٌّ غَامِدٌ, meaning مَغْمُودٌ,] ‡ *Wells having their water covered by earth*, or *dust*; *contr. of* رَكِىٌّ مُبْدٍ. (A.) And غَامِدَةٌ ‡ A well (بِئْرٌ) *filled up*, or *choked up, with earth*, or *dust*. (Ḳ, TA.) — And غَامِدٌ and غَامِدَةٌ † A ship (سَفِينَة) *filled*, or *laden*; (Ḳ, TA;) as also آمِدَةٌ (TA) and آمِدٌ. (Ḳ, TA.)

مُغْمَدٌ: see what here follows.

مَغْمُودٌ and ▼ مُغْمَدٌ A sword [or the like] *put into its* غِمْد [meaning *scabbard*, or *sheath*; i. e. *sheathed*]. (Ṣ, A.)

غمر

1. غَمُرَ, as in some lexicons, or غَمَرَ, aor. ـُ, accord. to all the copies of the Ḳ [consulted by SM], (TA,) or غَمِرَ, [aor. ـَ,] (as in the CḲ and my MS. copy of the Ḳ,) inf. n. غَمَارَةٌ and غُمُورَةٌ, [agreeably with analogy if غَمُرَ be the form of the verb, which is therefore most probably correct,] (Ḳ,) *It* (water) *was*, or *became, much in quantity, abundant, copious*, [or *deep*,] (Ḳ, B, TA,) *so that it concealed its bottom*. (B, TA.) You say مَا أَشَدَّ غُمُورَةَ هٰذَا النَّهْرِ *How great is the abundance of the water of this river!* (Ṣ.) — [And ‡ *He abounded in beneficence*.] You say رَجُلٌ بَيِّنُ الغُمُورَةِ ‡ *A man bearing evidence of abounding in beneficence*. (Ṣ, Ḳ.) ═ غَمَرَهُ, (Ṣ, Mṣb, Ḳ,) aor. ـُ, (Ṣ, Mṣb,) inf. n. غَمْرٌ, (Mṣb, Ḳ,) *It* (water, Ṣ, Ḳ, or the sea, Mṣb) [*overflowed*,] *came over*, or *rose above*, (Ṣ, Mṣb,) or *covered*, (Ḳ,) *and concealed*, (TA,) *him*, or *it*; (Ṣ, Mṣb, Ḳ;) as also ▼ اغتمرهُ: (Ḳ:) and *he* (a man) *veiled, concealed, hid*, or *covered, him*, or *it*. (Mṣb.) — Hence, غَمَرَهُ القَوْمُ † *The people rose above him*, or *surpassed him, in eminence*, (Ṣ, TA,) *and in excellence*. (TA.) — And رَأَيْتُهُ قَدْ غَمَرَ الجَمَاجِمَ بِطُولِ قَوَامِهِ † [*I saw him to have overtopped the heads of others by the tallness of his stature*]. (TA.) ═ غَمِرَ صَدْرُهُ عَلَىَّ, aor. ـَ, (Ṣ, Mṣb, Ḳ,*) inf. n. غَمَرٌ (Yaạkoob, Ṣ, Mṣb) and غِمْرٌ, (Yaạkoob, Ṣ,) [or the latter is a simple subst.,] *His bosom bore con-*

cealed enmity and violent hatred, or *rancour, malevolence, malice*, or *spite, against me*. (Ṣ, Mṣb, Ḳ.) — غَمِرَتْ يَدُهُ, (Ṣ, Ḳ,) aor. ـَ, (Ḳ,) inf. n. غَمَرٌ, (TA,) *His hand was*, or *became, foul with the smell of flesh-meat*, (Ṣ, Ḳ,) *and with the grease thereof adhering to it*. (Ḳ.) — غَمُرَ, aor. ـُ, (Ṣ, Mṣb,) inf. n. غَمَارَةٌ, (Ṣ, [in my copy of the Mṣb written غُمَار, probably by a mistake of the copyist,]) *He was inexperienced in affairs*: (Ṣ, Mṣb:) Benoo-'Okeyl say غَمِرَ, aor. ـَ. (Mṣb.) You say فِيهِ غَمَارَةٌ and غَرَارَةٌ [*In him is a want of experience in affairs*]. (TA.)

2. غَمَّرَتْ وَجْهَهَا, inf. n. تَغْمِيرٌ, *She* (a woman) *smeared her face with* غُمْرَة [q. v.]; (Ṣ;) as also ▾ اغتمرت, (Ḳ,) and ▾ تغمّرت بِالغُمْرَةِ. (Ṣ, Ḳ.) — غَمَّرَ, inf. n. تَغْمِيرٌ, *He* (a man) *was deemed ignorant*. (TA.) — غَمَّرَ فَرَسَهُ, inf. n. as above, *He gave his horse water to drink in a cup*, (Ḳ,) *in the small cup called* غُمَر, (TA,) *because of the scarcity of water*. (Ḳ.) IAạr mentions the phrase غَمَّرَهُ أَصْحُنًا *He gave him to drink some bowls* of water: making the verb doubly transitive. (TA.)

3. غامس فِيهِ and غامر فِى القِتَالِ signify the same [i. e. † *He plunged*, or *threw himself, into the midst of fight*, or *conflict*]. (TA in art. غمس.) [See also مُغَامِرٌ.] — And غامره † *He engaged with him in fight*, or *conflict, not caring for death*. (Ṣ, O.) — And غامر signifies also † *He contended in an altercation*, or *a dispute*. (O.)

5. تغمّرت: see 2. — تغمّر *He drank from a small cup such as is called* غُمَر: (Ḳ:) *he drank a small quantity of water*: (TA:) *he drank less than would satisfy his thirst*: (Ṣ:) *he drank the smallest draught, less than would satisfy his thirst*: (TA:) *he did not satisfy his thirst with water*; (Ḳ,* TA;) said of a camel, (Ḳ,) and of an ass. (TA.) — And تغمّرت المَاشِيَةُ *The cattle ate what is termed* غَمِير [q. v.]. (Ḳ.)

7. انغمر *He immerged, dipped*, or *plunged, himself*, or *he became immerged, dipped*, or *plunged*, (Ṣ, Ḳ,) in water, (Ṣ, TA,) and in a thing; (TA;) as also ▾ اغتمر. (Ḳ.)

8: see 1: — and 7: — and 2.

غَمْرٌ *Much, abundant, copious*, [or *deep*,] water; (Ṣ, Ḳ;) as also ▾ غَمِيرٌ: (Ḳ:) or *much, abundant, copious*, [or *deep*,] water, *that drowns*, or *submerges*: (ISd, TA:) or *that covers over him who enters into it*: (IAth, TA:) [also used as an epithet in which the quality of a subst. predominates, meaning *much, abundant, copious*, or *deep, water*;] and ▾ غَمْرَةٌ signifies the same as غَمْرٌ [when thus used; or *a submerging deep, a deep place*, or *an abyss*, of water]: (TA:) pl. غِمَارٌ and غُمُورٌ. (Ṣ, Ḳ.) You say بَحْرٌ غَمْرٌ *An abundant sea*: and [in the pl.] بِحَارٌ غِمَارٌ, and غُمُورٌ. (Ṣ.) And of a thing that has become much, you say, هٰذَا كَثِيرٌ ▾ غَمِيرٌ *This is much*. (AZ.) [See also غَامِرٌ.] — The *main of the sea*: (Ḳ:) pl. as above, (TA.) — ‡ *Liberal in disposition*: (Ḳ,* TA:) pl. as above: (TA:) and in like manner, غَمْرُ الخُلُقِ: (TA:) or this last, and غَمْرُ الرِّدَآءِ, signify ‡ *abounding in beneficence*: pl. as above: (Ṣ, Ḳ: [see also رِدَآءٌ:]) and غَمْرُ البَدِيهَةِ ‡ a man *who takes by surprise with large bounty*. (TA.) — ‡ A horse *fleet*, or *swift*, or *excellent, in running*. (Ṣ,* Ḳ,* TA.) — ‡ A garment *ample*, or *full*. (Ḳ,* TA.) — † *A mixed crowd* of men, (Ḳ,) *and their thronging, pressing*, or *pushing, and multitude*; (TA;) as also ▾ غُمْرٌ and ▾ غُمْرَةٌ and ▾ غُمَارٌ and ▾ غِمَارٌ: (Ḳ: [in the TA, instead of the last two words, I find غُمَارَةٌ and غِمَارَةٌ, as from the Ḳ, and غُمَارٌ and غِمَارٌ are afterwards there added: but most probably these only (without ة) are correct:]) and ▾ غُمْرَةٌ and ▾ غُمَارٌ and ▾ غِمَارٌ signify *a crowding*, or *pressing*, of men, (Ṣ, Mṣb,) and of water: (Ṣ:) the pl. of ▾ غُمْرَةٌ is غِمَارٌ. (Ṣ.) You say دَخَلْتُ فِى غُمَارِ ▾ النَّاسِ, and غُمَارِهِمْ, (Ṣ, Mṣb, TA,) and ▾ غُمَرِهِمْ, (TA,) † *I entered among the crowding*, or *pressing, of the people*, (Ṣ, Mṣb, TA,) *and their multitude*; (Ṣ, TA;) as also فِى خَمَرِهِمْ [and خُمَارِهِمْ &c.] (TA.) And أَكُونُ فِى غُمَارِ ▾ النَّاسِ, meaning *I shall be among the dense congregation of the people*, occurs in a trad. (TA.) — See also غُمْرٌ. — لَيْلٌ غَمْرٌ means *Intensely dark night*. (TA.)

غُمْرٌ (Ṣ, Mṣb, Ḳ) and ▾ غَمْرٌ (Ṣ, ISd) and ▾ غُمُرٌ and ▾ غُمَرٌ, accord. to the Ḳ, but this last is unknown, (TA,) and ▾ غَمَرٌ (Ḳ) and ▾ غِمْرٌ, (TA,) originally, A boy *devoid of intelligence*: and hence, (Mṣb,) a man (Ṣ, Mṣb) *inexperienced in affairs*: (Ṣ, Mṣb, Ḳ:) *ignorant*: (TA:) *inexperienced in war and in counsel; not rendered firm*, or *sound, in judgment, by experience*: (L:) one *in whom is no profit nor judgment*: (ISd, TA:) one *in whom is no good nor profit with respect to intelligence or judgment or work*: (AZ, Mṣb:) and ▾ مُغَمَّرٌ signifies the same as غُمْرٌ; (Ṣ, TA;) or *deemed ignorant*: (TA:) the fem. of غُمْرٌ is with ة; (Ṣ, Mṣb;) and so is that of ▾ غَمْرٌ: (TA:) and the pl. of غُمْرٌ is أَغْمَارٌ; (Ṣ, Mṣb, TA;) and this may also be pl. of ▾ غَمْرٌ, like as أَسْبَابٌ is pl. of سَبَبٌ. (TA.) — See also غُمْرَةٌ.

غِمْرٌ *Concealed enmity and violent hatred*, or *rancour, malevolence, malice*, or *spite*. (Ṣ, Mṣb, Ḳ.) [See also غَمِرٌ.] — And † *Thirst*: (Ṣ, Mṣb:) pl. أَغْمَارٌ. (Ṣ.) El-'Ajjáj says,

• حَتَّى إِذَا مَا بَلَّتِ الأَغْمَارَا •

‡ [*Until, when they damped their thirst*]. (Ṣ.) بَلَّتِ الإِبِلُ أَغْمَارَهَا means ‡ *The camels drank a little*. (TA.) — See also غُمْرٌ.

غَمَرٌ *A drowning; being drowned*: so in the phrase مَوْتُ الغَمَرِ *Death by drowning*. (TA.) — See also غُمْرٌ. — The *foul smell of flesh-meat*, (Ṣ, Mgh, Ḳ,) *and its grease adhering to the hand*: (Ḳ:) and the *smell of fish*. (Ṣ.) Hence, مِنْدِيلُ الغَمَرِ (Ṣ, Mgh) *The napkin*, or *rough napkin*, *with which the hand is cleansed therefrom*. (L, TA.) — See also غَمِرٌ, in two places.

غَمِرٌ [part. n. of غَمِرَ]. You say يَدٌ غَمِرَةٌ *A hand foul with the smell of flesh-meat*, (Ṣ, Ḳ,) *and with the grease thereof adhering to it*. (Ḳ.) [See also سَهِكٌ.] — See also غُمْرٌ, in two places. — غَمِرَةٌ as an epithet applied to a she-camel, see voce غَبِرٌ.

غُمَرٌ *A small drinking-cup* or *bowl*, (Ṣ, Ḳ,) *with which people divided the water among themselves in a journey when they had little of it*; and this they [sometimes] did by putting a pebble into a vessel, and then pouring into it as much water as would cover the pebble, and giving it to each man among them: (TA:) or the *smallest of drinking-cups* or *bowls*: (Ḳ:) [see قَعْبٌ; and تِبْنٌ:] accord. to ISh, *it contains twice or thrice the quantity of the measure called* كِيلَجَة: [but this seems to be a large غمر, used for watering a horse; and the words which here immediately follow are app. not added by ISh, but relate to the غمر used by a man for himself or for another man:] the قَعْب is larger than it, and satisfies the thirst of a man: the pl. is أَغْمَارٌ. (TA.) El-Aạshà of Báhileh says, in an elegy on his brother El-Munteshir Ibn-Wahb,

• تَكْفِيهِ حُزَّةُ فِلْذٍ إِنْ أَلَمَّ بِهَا •
• مِنَ الشِّوَآءِ وَيُرْوِى شُرْبَهُ الغُمَرُ •

[*A slice of camel's liver, roasted, if he lighted upon it, used to suffice him; and the* غُمَر *used to satisfy his thirst*]. (Ṣ, TA.) And Moḥammad is related, in a trad., to have said, لَا تَجْعَلُونِى كَغُمَرِ الرَّاكِبِ صَلُّوا عَلَىَّ أَوَّلَ الدُّعَآءِ وَأَوْسَطَهُ وَآخِرَهُ *Make ye me not like the* غُمَر *of the rider: salute me in the beginning of prayer and in the middle thereof and in the end thereof*: meaning that they should not make the salutation of him to be a thing of no great importance, and to be postponed: for the rider puts on his camel his saddle and his travelling-provisions, and last of all hangs upon his saddle his drinking-cup. (IAth, TA.)

غُمُرٌ: see غُمْرٌ.

غَمْرَةٌ *Water that rises above the stature of a man*. (Bḍ in xxiii. 56.) See also غَمْرٌ, first sentence. — Hence, (Bḍ,) فَذَرْهُمْ فِى غَمْرَتِهِمْ, in the Ḳur xxiii. 56, ‡ *Therefore leave thou them in* [*the submerging gulf*, or *flood, of*] *their ignorance*; (Fr, Bḍ;) or *in their error*: (Jel:) or *in their error and obstinacy and perplexity*: (Zj, in explanation of another reading, فِى غَمَرَاتِهِمْ:) and in like manner, فِى غَمْرَةٍ, in the same chap., verse 65, signifies *in overwhelming heedlessness*: (Bḍ:) or *in ignorance*: (Jel:) and in the Ḳur li. 11, *in overwhelming ignorance*: (Bḍ, Jel:) or غَمْرَةٌ signifies [here] *a state of obstinate perseverance in vain* or *false affairs*: (Lth, Mṣb, TA:) and غَمَرَاتٌ is the pl. (Mṣb.) You say هُوَ فِى غَمْرَةٍ مِنْ لَهْوٍ, and شَبِيبَةٍ, and سُكْرٍ, ‡ [*He is in a submerging gulf*, or *flood, of frivolous diversion*, and *of youthful folly*, and *of intoxication*]. (TA.)

And غَمَرَاتُ جَهَنَّمَ signifies [*The fiery depths of Hell*; or] *the places, of Hell, that abound with fire.* (TA.) — [Hence] غَمْرَةُ الخُصُومَةِ † *The main part of the contention.* (TA.) [And غَمْرَةُ الحَرْبِ † *The main part*, i. e. *the thick*, or *thickest, of the fight* or *battle.* (See also غَمَرَاتُ الحَرْبِ in what follows.)] — Hence likewise, غَمْرَةٌ signifies also ‡ *Difficulty, trouble, distress*, or *rigour*, (Ṣ, Mṣb, Ḳ,) and *pressure*, of a thing: (Ḳ:) pl. غَمَرَاتٌ (Ṣ, Mṣb, Ḳ) and غِمَارٌ (Ḳ) and غُمَرٌ. (Ṣ.) Hence, (Mṣb,) غَمَرَاتُ المَوْتِ ‡ *The rigours*, or *pangs*, (شَدَائِدُ,) *of death:* (Ṣ, Mṣb:) or غَمْرَةُ المَوْتِ signifies *the agony*, i. e. *the vehemence of the troubles* or *disquietudes, of death:* (TA:) and غَمَرَاتُ الحَرْبِ, and غِمَارُهَا, † *the rigours of war.* (TA.) — See also غَمْرٌ again, latter half, in three places.

غُمْرَةٌ *A kind of liniment, made from* [*the plant called*] وَرْس, (Ṣ, TA,) *used by a bride, for her person:* (TA:) or [the *plant*] ورس [*itself*]: (TA:) or *saffron*; as also ▼غُمْرٌ: (Ḳ:) or كُرْكُمٌ [which also means saffron and *bastard saffron*]: or *gypsum*; syn. جِصٌّ: or, accord. to Aboo-Sa'eed, *a mixture of dates and milk, with which the face of a woman is smeared, to render her skin fine:* and the pl. is غُمَرٌ. (TA.) [See also خُمْرَةٌ.]

غمرة, [thus in the TA, app. غُمُرَّةٌ, of the class of صُرَعَةٌ &c.,] as an epithet applied to a man, *Valid in judgment* or *opinion, in cases of difficulty.* (TA.)

غِمَارٌ: see غَمْرٌ, latter half, in three places.

غُمَارٌ: see غَمْرٌ, latter half, in four places.

غَمِيرٌ: see غَمْرٌ, in two places. ═ Also *A certain plant:* (Ḳ:) or *green herbage that is overtopped*, or *covered, and concealed, by what is dried up:* (Ṣ, Ḳ:*) or *herbage growing in the lower part*, or *at the root, of* [*other*] *herbage*, (Ḳ,* TA,) *so that the first* [*in growth*] *overtops*, or *covers, and conceals, it:* (TA:) or *any verdure that is little in quantity*, (L, Ḳ, TA,) *either* ريحة [i. e. رِيحَةٌ, meaning *what becomes green after the upper parts have dried*,] or نبات [app. meaning *herbage in general*]: (L, TA:) or the *grain of the* [*species of barley-grass called*] بُهْمَى, (Ḳ, TA,) *that falls from the ears thereof when it dries*; so says AḤn: or *somewhat that comes forth in the* بهمى *in the first of the rain, succulent*, or *sappy, amid such as is dry*; and غمير is not known in anything but the بُهْمَى: (TA:) the pl. is أَغْمِرَآءُ. (Ḳ.) ▼غَمِيرَةٌ [is app. its n. un., but] is said by AO to mean *Dry* [*trefoil, or clover, of the species called*] رَطْبَة *and* قَتّ, *with which horses are foddered when they are prepared, by being reduced to scanty food, for racing* or *for a military expedition.* (TA.)

غُمَيْرَةٌ: see what next precedes.

غَامِرٌ *Much*, or *abundant:* applied in this sense to property. (Ḥam p. 593.) [See also غَمْرٌ.] ═ [*In a state of immersion; immerged.* (See أَتَانٌ; and see also a verse cited voce أَنْ, p. 106, first col.)] — And [hence, perhaps,] غَامِرَةٌ signifies Palm-trees (نَخْلٌ) *not requiring irrigation:* (AḤn, Ḳ:) but Az did not find this to be known. (TA.) [See also مُغْتَمِرٌ.] — Applied to land, (Ṣ, Mṣb, TA,) and to a house, (TA,) [but written with ة when أَرْض is mentioned, or دَار,] it signifies the *Contr. of* عَامِرٌ; (Ṣ, TA;) and thus, (TA,) *waste; desolate; in a state the contrary of flourishing; in a state of ruin*; syn. خَرَابٌ: (Mṣb, Ḳ, TA:) [land to which this term is applied is thus called] because overflowed by water, so that it cannot be sown; or because it is covered with sand or dust; or because water generally exudes from it, so that it produces only reeds and the بَرْدِىّ [i. e. papyrus or other rushes]: by غَامِرٌ is meant ذُو غَمْرٍ; like as one says هَمٌّ نَاصِبٌ meaning ذُو نَصَبٍ: (TA:) or any land *that is not tilled* (لَمْ يُسْتَخْرَجْ) *so as to be fit for sowing* (Ḳ, TA) *and planting:* (TA:) or land *that is unsown, but capable of being sown:* so called because the water reaches it and comes over it: of the measure فَاعِلٌ in the sense of the measure مَفْعُولٌ; (Ṣ, Mṣb;) like the epithets in بِئْرٌ كَاتِمٌ and مَآءٌ دَافِقٌ; and made of the measure فاعل only to correspond to عَامِرٌ as its opposite: (Ṣ, TA:) waste land which water does not reach is not called غَامِرٌ; (Ṣ;) but such is called قَفْرٌ. (Mṣb.) It is said in a trad., [which shows that the last two explanations given above are correct,] that 'Omar imposed a tax of a دِرْهَم and a قَفِيز upon every جَرِيب [of land], both عَامِر and غَامِر: and this he did in order that the people might not be remiss in sowing. (Az, TA.)

أَغْمَرُ [*More*, or *most, abundant, copious*, or *deep:* applied to water. —] *More*, or *most surpassing*, or *excelling:* so in the saying, هُوَ أَغْمَرُهُمْ بِطُولِ قَوَامِهِ *He is the most surpassing of them by the tallness of his stature.* (TA.)

مُغَمَّرٌ A garment, or piece of cloth, *dyed with* [غُمْرَة, or] *saffron.* (M, TA.) — مُغَمَّرَةٌ and ▼مُتَغَمِّرَةٌ and ▼مُغْتَمِرَةٌ A girl *having her face smeared with* غُمْرَة. (TA.) ═ See also مُغْمَرٌ.

مُغْمِرٌ: see مُغَامِرٌ.

مَغْمُورٌ [*Overflowed*, or *covered, and concealed, by water*, &c. —] *Rained upon.* (TA.) — † *Overcome, subdued*, or *oppressed.* (TA.) — † An *obscure* man; *of no reputation:* (Ḳ, TA:) as though others surpassed him. (TA.) You say also, فُلَانٌ مَغْمُورُ النَّسَبِ † *Such a one is of obscure race.* (TA.)

مُغَامِرٌ † One *who plunges*, or *rushes without consideration, into places of peril:* (Ṣ:) one *who throws himself into difficulties, troubles*, or *distresses*; as also ▼مُغَمِّرٌ: (Ḳ:) or one *who enters into difficulties, troubles*, or *distresses, and makes another*, or *others, to do so*; like مُغَامِسٌ. (Ḥam p. 338.) Applied to a courageous man as meaning † One *who incurs the rigours*, or *pangs, of death.* (TA.) And † One *who contends in an altercation*, or *a dispute:* or *who enters into the main part* [or *the thick* or *thickest*] *of an altercation* or *a dispute:* and some say that it is from الغِمْرُ, and means *regarding, and regarded, with rancour, malevolence, malice*, or *spite.* (TA.)

مُغْتَمِرٌ Palm-trees (نَخْلٌ) *imbibing water from a copious source.* (AḤn, Ḳ.) [See also غَامِرَةٌ, voce غَامِرٌ.] — And † *A drunken* man: (Ṣgh, Ḳ, TA:) as though intoxication had drowned his reason. (TA.) ═ See also مُغَمَّرٌ.

مُتَغَمِّرَةٌ: see مُغَمَّرٌ.

غمز

1. غَمَزَهُ, (Ṣ, A, Ḳ,) or غَمَزَهُ بِيَدِهِ, (Mṣb,) aor. ـِ, (Mṣb, Ḳ,) inf. n. غَمْزٌ, (TA,) *He felt him*, (namely, a ram,) *to know if he were fat:* (Ṣ, A, Mṣb, Ḳ:) and غَمَزَهَا *he put his hand upon her* (a camel's) *back, to see how fat she was.* (TA.) — Hence, (Mṣb,) غَمَزَهُ بِيَدِهِ, (Ṣ, Mṣb, Ḳ,) aor. ـِ, (Ḳ,) inf. n. غَمْزٌ, (A, Ḳ,) *He pressed*, or *squeezed, it*, [*with his hand*,] namely, a limb, (A, Ḳ, TA,) and a man's back. (TA.) So in a trad. of 'Omar: دَخَلَ عَلَيْهِ وَعِنْدَهُ غُلَيِّمٌ يَغْمِزُ ظَهْرَهُ [*He went in to him, and with him was a little boy pressing*, or *squeezing*, or *kneading, his back*]. (TA.) And in a trad. respecting the ablution termed الغُسْل, it is said, اِغْمِزِى قُرُونَكِ, meaning *Press thou*, or *squeeze thou, the locks of thy hair*, in washing. (TA.) You also say, غَمَزَ الثِّقَافُ القَنَاةَ *The straightening-instrument pinched and pressed the spear.* (A,* Mgh, TA.*) A poet (namely Ziyád El-Aajam, TA) says,

وَكُنْتُ إِذَا غَمَزْتُ قَنَاةَ قَوْمٍ
كَسَرْتُ كُعُوبَهَا أَوْ تَسْتَقِيمَا

[*And I used, when I pinched and pressed the spear of a people, to break its knots*, or *internodal portions, unless it became straight*]. (Ṣ, TA. It is a prov., respecting which see remarks in art. او.) ═ غَمَزَ, (A, Mṣb,) and غَمَزَهُ, (Ṣ, Mgh, Ḳ,) aor. ـِ, (Mgh, Mṣb, Ḳ) inf. n. غَمْزٌ, (Mṣb, TA,) ‡ *He made a sign*, (A, Mṣb,) and *he made a sign to him*, (Mgh, Ḳ,*) with the eye, (Ṣ, A, Mgh, Mṣb, Ḳ,) or eyebrow, (A, Mgh, Mṣb, Ḳ,) or eyelid [by winking]. (Ḳ.) So in the saying, in a trad., غَمَزَنِى عَلِىٌّ أَنْ قُلْ نَعَمْ ‡ *'Alee made a sign to me* with the eye, or eyebrow, *meaning, Say thou Yes.* (Mgh.) The people of the West say, غَمَزَهُ فُلَانٌ بِفُلَانٍ, meaning, ‡ *Such a one blinked towards such a one, to instigate him against him*, or *in order that he should have recourse to him for protection or the like*, or *seek aid of him.* (Mgh.) — Hence, الغَمْزُ بِالنَّاسِ: (Ṣ:) you say, غَمَزَ بِالرَّجُلِ, aor. ـِ, (Ḳ,) inf. n. غَمْزٌ, (TA,) ‡ *He calumniated*, or *slandered, the man.* (Ḳ.) [See also 4.] — You say also, غَمِزَتْ شَهَادَتُهُ

[† *His testimony was suspected* (see مَغْمُوزٌ), or *impugned*]. (TA in art. زور.) ═ غَمَزَتِ الدَّابَّةُ, (Ḳ,) or غَمَزَ فِى مَشْيِهِ, (Mṣb,) or مِنْ رِجْلِهِ, (Ṣ,) aor. ـِ, (Ṣ, Mṣb, Ḳ,) inf. n. غَمْزٌ, (Ṣ, Mṣb,) † *The beast limped*, or *it halted, with its hind leg; had a slight lameness thereof:* (Ḳ,* TA:) or *he had what resembled* عَرَج [or *natural lameness*] *in his gait:* (Mṣb:) or, as IḲṭṭ says, غَمَزَتِ الدَّابَّةُ بِرِجْلِهَا *the beast gave an indication of a limping*, or *halting*, or *slight lameness, in its hind leg:* whence it appears that this signification may be tropical. (TA.) ═ غَمَزَ said of a disease, or of a vice, or fault, of a man, *It appeared.* (AA, Ḳ.) ═ See also 4.

3. [This verb is mentioned by Golius as *syn. with* عايب, a verb for which I find no authority: and Freytag renders it "Vitii arguit," and refers to a passage in Ḥar (p. 427 of the sec. ed.) where (like as is done by Golius) المُغَامِز and المُعَايِب, as syn., are erroneously put for المَغَامِز and المَعَايِب.]

4. أَغْمَزَتْ *She* (a camel) *had fat*, (O, Ḳ,) or *a little fat*, (ISd, IḲṭṭ, TA,) *in her hump.* (ISd, IḲṭṭ, O, Ḳ.) Hence the epithet ↓ غَمُوزٌ, applied to her. (TA.) ═ اغمز فِى فُلَانٍ ‡ *He blamed*, or *found fault with, such a one; attributed* or *imputed to him*, or *charged him with*, or *accused him of, a vice*, or *fault;* (Ṣ, IḲṭṭ, Ḳ, TA;) *deemed him weak;* (TA;) *lessened his rank*, or *dignity:* (Ṣ, IḲṭṭ, Ḳ,* TA:) *he found in him that for which he should be deemed weak:* (A, TA:) and ↓ اغتمزه *he impugned his character; blamed him; censured him;* or *spoke against him.* (Ḳ.) You say, فَعَلْتُ شَيْئًا فَٱغْتَمَزَهُ ↓ فُلَانٌ ‡ *I did a thing, and such a one impugned my character*, or *found in it that by which my character was impugned.* (Ṣ, TA.) And سَمِعَ مِنِّى كَلِمَةً فَٱغْتَمَزَهَا ↓ فِى عَقْلِهِ ‡ *He heard from me a saying, and deemed it weak:* (A, TA:) and in like manner, أَغْمَزَ فِيهَا *found in it that for which it was to be deemed weak.* (TA.) ═ أَغْمَزَنِى الحَرُّ ‡ *The heat remitted*, or *abated, to me, so that I became emboldened to encounter it, and went upon the road:* (AA, ISk, Ṣ, IḲṭṭ, Ḳ,* TA:) Az says ↓ غَمَزَنِى الحَرُّ, on the authority of AA: (TA:) and AA mentioned اغمرنى الحرّ in this sense, but afterwards doubted, and said, I think that it is with زاى. (TA in art. غمر.) — And أَغْمَزَ † *He* (a man) *became gentle, so that others were emboldened against him.* (IḲṭṭ, TA.) ═ And أَغْمَزَ [for which أَغْمَزَهُ is erroneously put in the CḲ] *He acquired cattle such as are termed* غَمْز [q. v.]: (O, Ḳ, TA:) like أَقْمَزَ. (O.)

5. [This verb is said by Freytag to have a signification belonging to تَغَمَّرَ.]

6. تغامزوا *They made signs, one to another, with their eyes*, (Ṣ, A, Ḳ, B,) or with the eyebrow, (A,) or hand, indicating something blameable or faulty. (B.) In this sense it is expl. as used in the Ḳur lxxxiii. 30. (Ṣ, B.)

8: see 4, in three places.

غَمْزٌ *Cattle* (i. e. *camels*, and *sheep* or *goats*, TA) *of a bad quality.* (Aṣ, Ṣ, O, Ḳ.) — And *A weak man:* (Ṣ, O, Ḳ:) like قَمْزٌ: pl. أَغْمَازٌ, like أَقْمَازٌ of قَمْزٌ. (TA.)

غَمُوزٌ *A she-camel of which one doubts whether she be fat or not and therefore feels the hump:* (A'Obeyd, Ṣ, Ḳ:) pl. غُمْزٌ [or غُمُزٌ, or both?]. (TA.) See 4, first sentence.

غَمِيزٌ: see the next paragraph, in two places.

غَمِيزَةٌ ‡ *A thing for which one's character is to be impugned; for which one is to be blamed, censured*, or *spoken against; a vice*, or *fault;* (Ṣ, A, Mgh, Mṣb, Ḳ;) as also ↓ غَمِيزٌ (TA) and ↓ مَغْمَزٌ (Ṣ, A, Mgh, Ḳ) or ↓ مَغْمَزَةٌ: (Mṣb:) and *weakness in work, and impotence of mind*, (TA,) *and ignorance:* (T, TA:) the pl. of ↓ مَغْمَزٌ is مَغَامِزُ, (TA,) *syn. with* مَعَايِبُ. (Ṣ.) You say, لَيْسَ فِيهِ غَمِيزَةٌ, (Ṣ, A, Mgh, Mṣb, Ḳ,) and ↓ غَمِيزٌ, (TA,) and ↓ مَغْمَزٌ, (A, Mgh, Ḳ,) or ↓ مَغْمَزَةٌ, (Mṣb,) ‡ *There is not in him anything for which his character is to be impugned;* or *for which he is to be blamed;* &c.: (Ṣ, A, Mgh, Mṣb, Ḳ:) or *there is not in it anything for which it is to be coveted:* (Ḳ:) or ↓ مَا فِيهِ مَغْمَزٌ has both of the above-mentioned significations. (A.) And فِى فُلَانَةَ مَغَامِزُ ↓ جَمَّةٌ ‡ *In such a woman are many vices*, or *faults.* (A.) [See مَغْمَزٌ, below.]

جَارِيَةٌ غَمَّازَةٌ *A girl who presses*, or *squeezes*, or *kneads, the limbs well with the hand.* (A, Ḳ,* TA.) ═ اِمْرَأَةٌ غَمَّازَةٌ ‡ *A woman who makes frequent signs with the eye*, &c.; *who has a habit of doing so;* syn. رَمَّازَةٌ. (TA in art. رمز.) — غَمَّازٌ One *who blames*, or *finds fault with, others, much*, or *habitually.* (TA in art. همز.)

غَامِزٌ [meaning *Limping*, or *halting*, &c., and *having a limping*, or *halting*, &c.,] is like ظَالِعٌ: sometimes used as a possessive noun; and [therefore] one does not say غَامِزَةٌ. (O and TA in art. ظلع.)

مَغْمَزٌ [should by rule be مَغْمِزٌ: its primary signification is *A place of feeling, to know if an animal be fat:* hence, *a place of pressing* or *squeezing* a limb &c.: and *a place of pinching and pressing* a spear, to straighten it]. — نُكْتَةٌ لَا مَغْمَزَ لِقَنَاتِهَا وَلَا مَقْرَعَ لِصَفَاتِهَا ‡ [lit. *A nice* or *subtile saying, the spear of which has no place where it requires to be pinched and pressed* to straiten it, *and the rock of which has no rough place requiring to be beaten*, or *for the rock of which there is no beating*,] means, † *that has no crookedness:* مقرع is an inf. n., or means "a place of beating," and صفاة is "a rock;" and the above-mentioned use of these two words is borrowed from the phrase قَرَعَ صَفَاتَهُ, meaning ‡ "he impugned his character; blamed, or censured, him; or spoke against him." (Mgh.) — See also غَمِيزَةٌ, in five places.

مَغْمَزَةٌ: see غَمِيزَةٌ, in two places.

مَغْمُوزٌ ‡ A man (A, TA) *suspected* (Ṣ, A,* Ḳ) *of a vice*, or *fault.* (TA.)

غمس

1. غَمَسَهُ, (Ṣ, A, Mṣb, Ḳ,) aor. ـِ, (Mṣb, Ḳ,) inf. n. غَمْسٌ, (Mṣb, TA,) *He immersed, immerged, dipped, plunged*, or *sunk, him* or *it*, (JK, TA,) syn. مَقَلَهُ, (Ṣ, A, Ḳ,) in water, (JK, Ṣ, A, Mṣb, Ḳ,) or other fluid; (JK,* TA;) as, for instance, a morsel of food in vinegar, and the hand in حِنَّآء, (A,) and a garment, or piece of cloth, [for النَّدَى in the TA, I read الثَّوْب,] in water or in dye. (TA.) — اِخْتَضَبَتْ غَمْسًا, so in the T and the Tekmileh; [and so in the JK;] but in the [O and] Ḳ, اِغْتَمَسَتْ ↓ غَمْسًا; (TA;) *She* (a woman, O, TA) *immersed her hand*, (Ḳ,) or, as in the [O and other] correct lexicons, *her hands*, (TA,) [*in the* حِنَّآء] *so as to dye* [*it* or *them*] *uniformly, without* تَصْوِير [or *figuring*], (O, Ḳ,) for which last word Ṣgh [in the TṢ] writes تصرير, and for which we find in the A نَقْش [meaning the same as the word in the Ḳ]. (TA.) — غَمَسَهُمْ فِى البَلَآءِ ‡ [*It* (an event) *plunged them into trial*, or *affliction*]. (A.) [See also a similar usage of the verb below, voce غَمُوسٌ.] — غَمَسَ حِلْفًا فِى آلِ العَاصِ *He took a share in the compact and confederacy of the family of El-'Áṣ, and swore to it:* for it was their custom to bring, in a wooden bowl, some perfume or blood or ashes, and they inserted their hands into it on the occasion of swearing, one to another, that their compact might be completed by their sharing together in one thing. (TA, from a trad. respecting the Hijreh.) — يَغْمِسُ السِّنَانَ حَتَّى يَنْفُذَ [*He thrusts in the spear-head so that it may pass through*, or *that its extremity may protrude*]. (A.) — غَمَسَ عَلَيْهِمُ الخَبَرَ † *He concealed from them the news*, or *information.* (TA.) — غُمِسَ النَّجْمُ, (so in a copy of the A,) or غَمَسَ, (so in the JK and O and Ḳ,) *The star set.* (JK, A, O, Ḳ.)

2. تَغْمِيسٌ signifies The *making a drinking to be little in quantity:* (O, Ḳ, TA:) or, accord. to Kr, a man's *watering* his camels *and then going away.* (TA.)

3. [غامسهُ, inf. n. مُغَامَسَةٌ, *He vied*, or *contended, with him in plunging*, or *diving, in water:*] مُغَامَسَةٌ is *syn. with* مُمَاقَلَةٌ. (Ṣ, TA.) — مُغَامَسَةٌ also signifies ‡ The *throwing one's self into the midst of war* or *fight*, (Ṣ, TA,) or *of an affair* or *a great affair* or *an affliction:* (TA:) and the *mixing*, or *engaging, in fight* or *conflict.* (TA.) You say, غَامَسَ فِى القِتَالِ ‡ *He plunged*, or *threw himself, into the midst of fight* or *conflict;* or *he rushed headlong into it.* (TA.) And غَامَسَهُمْ ‡ *He mixed*, or *engaged, with them in fight* or *conflict.* (TA). [See also مُغَامِسٌ].

6. تغامسا *They two vied, or contended, each with the other, in plunging, or diving,* in water; syn. تَمَاقَلَا and تَغَاطَسَا. (TA in art. غطس.)

7. انغمس (Ṣ, A, Mṣb) and ▼ اغتمس (Ṣ, A) *He, or it, became immersed, immerged, dipped, plunged,* or *sunk,* in water: or *he immersed* or *immerged himself, plunged,* or *dived,* in water: (Ṣ, A, Mṣb:) or *he did so remaining long* therein. (TA in this art. and in art. رمس.) [See ارتمس.] — [Hence,] ▼ the latter also signifies, [and so app. the former,] † *He hid,* or *concealed, himself.* (T, O.)

8: see 7, in two places. — اِغْتَمَسْتُ غَمْسًا: see 1.

غَمْسٌ, [like نَقْضٌ in the sense of مَنْقُوضٌ, &c., or perhaps a mistranscription for غَمِسٌ, like غَرِسٌ in the sense of مَغْرُوسٌ, and many other instances,] *Immersed, immerged, dipped, plunged,* or *sunk.* (TA.)

طَعْنَةٌ غَمُوسٌ ‡ *A spear-wound,* or *the like, that passes through:* (Ṣ, A, Mṣb, Ḳ:) the epithet properly applies to the person who inflicts the wound, because he thrusts in (يَغْمِسُ) the spear-head so that it passes through, or so that its extremity protrudes: and it is *such as cleaves the flesh:* (A:) or *wide, and passing through; that plunges into the flesh.* (ISd, TA.) — أَمْرٌ غَمُوسٌ ‡ *A difficult,* or *distressful, affair;* (Ṣ, A, Mṣb, Ḳ;) *that plunges people into trial,* or *affliction.* (A, Ḳ.*) — Hence, (A,) يَمِينٌ غَمُوسٌ ‡ *An oath that plunges its swearer* (تَغْمِسُهُ) *into sin,* (Ṣ, Ḳ,) *and then into the fire* [*of Hell*]: (Ḳ:) or *a false oath,* (Mgh, Mṣb,) *known by its swearer to be so;* (Mṣb;) so called because it plunges its swearer into sin, (A, Mgh, Mṣb,) and then into the fire [of Hell]: (A, Mgh:) or *a false oath which one purposely swears, knowing the case to be the contrary thereof,* (Ḳ, TA,) *in order to cut off the rights of others:* (TA:) or *an oath by which one cuts off for himself the property of another:* (Ḳ:) or *an oath in which there is made no exception* [by saying إِنْ شَآءَ ٱللّٰهُ (if God will), or the like]. (TA.) [See also الغَمِيسَةُ.] — رَجُلٌ غَمُوسٌ † *A strong, courageous man;* as also ▼ مُغَامِسٌ: which latter epithet is also applied to a lion. (TA.) And †*A man who, in journeying, does not alight to rest in the night until he enters upon the time of dawn* or *morning.* (TA.) — And نَاقَةٌ غَمُوسٌ *A she-camel whose pregnancy is not plainly known* (Ṣ, O, Ḳ) *until she is near to bringing forth* (حَتَّى تُقْرِبَ). (Ṣ, O.) And (O, Ḳ) accord. to En-Naḍr, (O,) *A she-camel that has a young one in her belly and that does not raise her tail so that the case should become manifest:* (O, Ḳ:) pl. غمس [app. غُمُسٌ, agreeably with analogy, like صُبُرٌ pl. of صَبُورٌ, &c.]. (TA.) And (some say, TA) *A she-camel respecting whose marrow one doubts whether it be in a corrupt and melting state or be fat,* or *thick and fat.* (O, Ḳ.)

غَمِيسٌ *Such as is termed* غَمِيرٌ [q. v.] of herbage; (Ṣ, O, Ḳ, TA;) i. e. *such as has become green in consequence of rain, in the lower parts of that which is dry.* (O.) See also غَمِيرٌ. — And *A thing that has not appeared to men, and that is not known, as yet:* whence the phrase قَصِيدَةٌ غَمِيسٌ [*an ode that has not become known:* the epithet being masc. and fem.]. (O, Ḳ.) — And i. q. أَجَمَةٌ [*A collection of tangled,* or *dense, trees* or *shrubs,* or *of reeds* or *canes;* (see also غَمِيسَةٌ;)] and *anything tangled, confused,* or *dense, in which one hides,* or *conceals, himself:* (T, O, Ḳ,* TA:) in the copies of the Ḳ, أَوْ يَسْتَخْفِى is erroneously written for أَىْ يستخفى as in the T and O. (TA.) — And *A water-course,* or *channel in which water flows,* (Ṣ, O, Ḳ, TA,) or (TA) *such as is small, amid* [*plants such as are termed*] نَبَاتٌ *and* بَقْلٌ, (Ṣ, O, Ḳ, TA,) or, as in the L, *combining* (يَجْمَعُ) [app. *within it*] *trees,* or *shrubs, and* بَقْل. (TA.) — Also *Night:* (O:) or *dark night.* (Ḳ.) And *Darkness.* (O, Ḳ.) — And AO is related by El-Athram to have said, المَجْرُ is what is in the belly of the she-camel; and the second [i. e. the offspring of the مَجْر] is [called] حَبَلُ الحَبَلَةِ; and the third is الغَمِيسُ [i. e. this last signifies *The offspring of the offspring of the* مَجْر: see مَجْرٌ and حَبَلٌ]. (TA.)

غَمِيسَةٌ *A collection of dense reeds* or *canes;* or *a bed,* or *place of growth, thereof.* (TA. [See also غَمِيسٌ.]) — حَلَفَ عَلَى الغَمِيسَةِ *He swore a false oath.* (TA. [See غَمُوسٌ.])

غَمَّاسٌ: see what next follows, in two places.

غَمَّاسَةٌ [*A bird of the kind termed divers,* or *plungeons:* thus called in the present day; expl. by Golius and Freytag as meaning "mergus avis;"] *a certain aquatic bird,* (O, Ḳ,) *that dives,* or *plunges, much:* (O:) pl. [or rather coll. gen. n.] ▼ غَمَّاسٌ: (Ḳ, TA: [in the CḲ, erroneously, غُمَّاسٌ:]) IDrd says, the ▼ غَمَّاس is *a well-known bird.* (O.)

مُغَامِسٌ One *who plunges into wars,* or *battles,* (يَغْشَى الحُرُوبَ,) *and engages in them repeatedly:* (Ḥam p. 27:) or one *who enters into difficulties, troubles,* or *distresses, and makes another,* or *others, to do so;* like مُغَامِرٌ. (Id. p. 338.) See also غَمُوسٌ.

غمص

1. غَمَصَهُ, (Ṣ, A, Mgh, Ḳ,) aor. ـِ inf. n. غَمْصٌ; (Ṣ;) and غَمِصَهُ, aor. ـَ, inf. n. غَمْصٌ; and غَمُصَهُ, aor. ـُ, inf. n. غَمَصٌ; (Ḳ,* TA;) but the first is the most chaste; (TA;) *He despised him; held him in contempt;* (A, Mgh, Ḳ;) *accounted him little,* or *vile; regarded him as nothing;* (Ṣ;) as also ▼ اغتمصهُ. (Ṣ, A, Ḳ.) You say also, رَآهُ فَغَمَصَتْهُ عَيْنُهُ *He saw him and his eye despised him.* (A.) — *He blamed him; found fault with him; imputed to him a vice,* or *fault;* and *despised his right.* (A, Ḳ.) You say, وَجَدْتُ النَّاسَ يَغْمِصُ بَعْضُهُمْ بَعْضًا [*I found the people blaming one another,* &c.]; as also ▼ يَغْتَمِصُ. (A.) And غَمَصْتَهُ بِسُوْءٍ [*Thou imputedst evil to him*]. (TA, from a trad.) And غَمَصْتُ عَلَيْهِ قَوْلًا قَالَهُ *I blamed him,* or *found fault with him, for a saying that he said.* (Ṣ.) — And hence, (TA,) غَمَصَ النِّعْمَةَ, (Ṣ, Ḳ,) and غَمِصَهَا, (Ḳ,) the latter is the form authorized by the T and the Deewán el-Adab, this verb and [its syn.] غمط being there said to be both with kesr to the م, (TA,) *He was ungrateful,* or *unthankful, for the favour* or *benefit;* (Ṣ, Ḳ, TA;) *he despised it, and disacknowledged it.* (TA.) — [Hence also, app.,] غَمَصَ ٱللّٰهُ الخَلْقَ *God diminished the height, and breadth, and strength, and might in war,* or *valour, of mankind; and made them small and contemptible:* occurring in a trad. of 'Alee respecting the slaughter of his brother by a son of Adam. (TA.) — غَمِصَتْ عَيْنُهُ, (Ṣ, Ḳ,) aor. ـَ, (Ḳ,) inf. n. غَمَصٌ, (Ṣ,) *His eye had in it what is termed* غَمَصٌ, q. v. (Ṣ, Ḳ.) — [Hence, perhaps,] غَمِصَ هٰذَا الأَمْرُ عَلَىَّ *This thing,* or *affair, turned against me, and became attended with trouble.* (JḲ.) — [And hence, perhaps,] لَا تَغْمَصْ عَلَىَّ [in the CḲ تَغْمِصْ] *Be not thou angry with me:* so accord. to the O [and the JK]: but accord. to the Ḳ, *do not thou lie against me,* or *utter falsehood.* (TA.)

8: see 1, in two places.

غَمَصٌ *Fluid filth* [or *foul matter*] *in the inner corner of the eye:* (Mgh:) or *what is fluid of* [*the filth,* or *foul matter,* or *white filth, which collects in the inner corner of the eye, and which, when concrete, is called*] رَمَصٌ: (Ṣ, Ḳ:) or *a thing like froth, which the eye emits; a portion whereof is termed* ▼ غَمَصَةٌ: (TA:) or *what resembles white froth, in the side of the eye:* but رَمَصٌ is in the side of the eyelashes: (ISh:) or both these words signify *dirt which the eye emits:* or غَمَصٌ is *what is concrete.* (M in art. رمص.)

غَمِصٌ, a possessive epithet, *A great imputer of vices or faults.* (TA.)

غَمَصَةٌ: see غَمَصٌ.

هُوَ غَمُوصُ الحَنْجَرَةِ *He is a liar.* (Ibn-'Abbád, Ḳ.) — غَمُوصٌ i. q. يَمِينٌ غَمُوسٌ. — الغَمُوصُ: see الغُمَيْصَآءُ.

مَا فِى فُلَانٍ غَمِيصَةٌ *There is not in such a one anything for which his character is to be impugned, or for which he is to be blamed, censured,* or *spoken against; any vice,* or *fault;* i. q. غَمِيزَةٌ. (A.)

غُمَيْصَآءُ dim. of غَمْصَآءُ [fem. of أَغْمَصُ]. (TA.) Hence, (TA,) الغُمَيْصَآءُ [*The star Procyon;*] *one of the* شِعْرَيَانِ, (Ṣ, Ḳ,) whereof the other is الشِّعْرَى العَبُورُ [i. e. Sirius]: (TA:) the former is *also called* ▼ الغَمُوصُ, (Ṣ, Ḳ,) *and* الرُّمَيْصَآءُ, (TA,) *and* الشِّعْرَى الشَّامِيَّةُ: (IAth:) *it is one of the Mansions of the Moon* [*accord. to those who make the term* نَوْءٌ *to signify the auroral setting;*

namely, *the Seventh*]; (TA;) *and is in the* ذِرَاع (Ṣ;) i. e., *it is the greater of the two stars called* الذِّرَاعُ المَقْبُوضَةُ: (IAth:) it is called الغميصاء because of its smallness and its littleness of light [in comparison with the other شعرى], from غَمَصُ العَيْنِ: (TA:) [or the reason of its being so called is this:] the Arabs assert that the شِعْرَيَانِ are the sisters of سُهَيْل [or Canopus]; (IDrd, Ṣ;) and that they [three] were together; but that سهيل descended into the south, and الشِّعْرَى اليَمَانِيَّةُ [which is Sirius] followed it; (IDrd;) this latter, they say, crossed the Milky way, and was therefore named العَبُورُ; and الغميصاء remained in her place, weeping for the loss of the two others until her eye became affected with غَمَص: (IDrd, Ḳ:*) they also assert that thou seest العبور when she rises as though she desired to cross [the Milky Way] (كَأَنَّهَا تَسْتَعْبِرُ); but الغميصاء thou seest not [as yet in any part of Arabia], she having wept until she has become affected with غَمَص. (Ṣ.)

أَغْمَصُ *Having, in his eye, what is termed* غَمَص, q. v.: (Mgh, Ḳ:) or *disordered in the eye; whose eyes are dim,* or *watery;* like أَعْمَشُ: (L and TA in art. عمش:) fem. غَمْصَآءُ: and pl. غُمْصٌ. (TA.)

هُوَ مَغْمُوصٌ عَلَيْهِ *He is censured,* or *blamed,* or *reproached,* (Ṣ, Ḳ,) with respect to his religion, (Ṣ, A, Ḳ,) and with respect to his grounds of pretension to respect. (A.) It is said in a trad., إِلَّا مَغْمُوصٌ عَلَيْهِ النِّفَاقُ, meaning, *Except one censured, &c., with respect to his religion; accused,* or *suspected, of hypocrisy.* (TA.)

أَنَا مُسْتَغْمِصٌ مِنْ هٰذَا الخَبَرِ وَمُتَوَهِّمٌ [*I am suspicious of this information, and opining;*] is said by one when a piece of information rejoices him but he fears that it may not be true; or when he fears it and yet it rejoices him. (TA.)

غمض

1. غَمَضَ, and غَمُضَ, aor. of each ـُ, and inf. n. of each غُمُوضٌ, *It* (a thing) *was,* or *became, unperceived, unapparent, hidden,* or *concealed.* (TA.) — غَمَضَ الحَقُّ, aor. and inf. n. as above; and غَمُضَ; *The way of attaining,* or *obtaining, the right,* or *due, was,* or *became, unapparent,* or *hidden.* (Mṣb.) — غَمُضَ الكَلَامُ, inf. n. غُمُوضَةٌ; (Ṣ, Ṣgh, Ḳ;) and غَمَضَ, aor. ـُ, inf. n. غُمُوضٌ; (IB, Ḳ; [but IB seems to express a doubt of the correctness of the latter form of the verb in this case;]) *The speech,* or *language, was unapparent to the mind, not plain* or *perspicuous, obscure, recondite,* or *abstruse.* (Ṣ, IB, Ṣgh, Ḳ.) — غَمُضَ عَلَيْهِ الأَمْرُ *The affair was not easy to him;* (L, TA;*) and you say also, غَمُضَ الأَمْرُ, inf. n. غُمُوضٌ: and فِيهِ غُمُوضٌ [*In it is a want of easiness*]: but, Lḥ says, they scarcely ever, or never, say فِيهِ غُمُوضَةٌ. (TA.) — غَمَضَ المَكَانُ, aor. ـُ, inf. n. غُمُوضٌ; and غَمُضَ, inf. n. غُمُوضَةٌ and غَمَاضَةٌ; *The place was,* or *became, low,* or *depressed;* (Ṣ, Ḳ;) [because a place that is so is unseen from a distance.] — غَمَضَ الخَلْخَالُ فِى السَّاقِ, inf. n. غُمُوضٌ, *The anklet was,* or *became, depressed in the leg;* lit., *choked therein.* (A, TA.) — غَمَضَتِ الدَّارُ, aor. ـُ, inf. n. as above, *The house was not upon a common thoroughfare-road* or *street.* (Lth, L.) — غَمَضَ السَّيْفُ فِى اللَّحْمِ, (Ibn-'Abbád, A, Ḳ,) aor. ـُ, (Ibn-'Abbád,) *The sword became hidden in the flesh.* (Ibn-'Abbád, Ḳ.) — غَمَضَ فِى الأَرْضِ, (Lḥ, A, Ḳ,) in [some of] the copies of the Ḳ, فى الأَمْرِ, which is a mistake, (TA,) aor. ـُ and ـِ, (Ḳ,) inf. n. غُمُوضٌ, (A,) *He went away in,* or *into, the land,* or *country:* (Lḥ:) or *he went away and disappeared therein:* (A, L:) or *he went away and journeyed therein.* (Ḳ.) — And غَمَضَ, aor. ـُ, also signifies *It* (a thing) *was,* or *became, small.* (IḲṭṭ.) = See also 4, under اغمض عنه, in four places.

2. غَمَّضَ الكَلَامَ, (Ṣ, Ḳ,) inf. n. تَغْمِيضٌ, (Ṣ,) *He made the speech,* or *language, unapparent to the mind, not plain* or *perspicuous, obscure, recondite,* or *abstruse.* (Ṣ, Ḳ, TA.) — غمّض حَدَّ السَّيْفِ, (A, TA,) inf. n. as above, (TA,) *He made the edge of the sword thin* [*so that it might become hidden in the flesh when one smote with it*]; (A, TA;) as also ▼ أَغْمَضَهُ. (Ḳ.) = See also 4, in twelve places.

4. اغمض حَدَّ السَّيْفِ: see 2. — اغمض عَيْنَيْهِ, (Mgh,) or العَيْنَ, (Mṣb,) inf. n. إِغْمَاضٌ; (Ṣ, Mṣb;) and ▼ غَمَّضَهُمَا, (Mgh,) or ▼ غَمَّضَهَا, (Mṣb,) inf. n. تَغْمِيضٌ; (Ṣ, Mṣb;) *He shut,* or *closed,* (Mgh, Mṣb,) [*his eyes,* or] *his eyelids,* (Mgh,) or [*the eye,* or] *the eyelids.* (Mṣb.) — [Hence,] مَا أَغْمَضْتُ, (A, TA,) and ▼ مَا غَمَّضْتُ, (TA,) *I have not slept;* (TA;) and ▼ مَا ٱغْتَمَضْتُ [signifies the same]; (JK;) and so مَا ٱكْتَحَلْتُ إِغْمَاضًا, (ISd, Ḳ,) and ▼ تَغْمَاضًا (Ṣ, Ṣgh, Ḳ) and تَغْمِيضًا, (Ṣ, Ḳ,) [two inf. ns. of 2,] and ▼ غِمَاضًا, and ▼ غُمَاضًا, and ▼ غُمْضًا with ḍamm, (Ṣ, Ṣgh, Ḳ,) [and app. ▼ غَمْضًا, and ▼ غُمُوضًا, for] IB says that غَمْض and غُمُوض and غُمَاض are inf. ns. of a verb not used: (TA:) and مَا ذُقْتُ ▼ غُمْضًا, [in a copy of the A ▼ غَمْضًا,] and ▼ غِمَاضًا, *I have not tasted sleep.* (JK.) [And hence,] ▼ اغتمض البَرْقُ ‡ *The lightning ceased to gleam;* as though sleeping. (TA.) — You say also, اغمض طَرْفَهُ عَنِّى, and ▼ غَمَّضَهُ, *He shut,* or *closed, his eye,* or *eyes, at,* or *upon,* or *against, me:* and اغمض عَلَيْهِ, and ▼ غمّض, *he shut,* or *closed, his eyes at,* or *upon,* or *against, him,* or *it.* (TA.) — And [hence,] اغمض عَنْهُ, and عَلَيْهِ, ‡ [*He shut his eyes at it,* or *upon it,* or *against it*], namely a thing that he had heard: a metonymical phrase, denoting patience. (TA.) And اغمض عنه ‡ *He connived at it; feigned himself neglectful of it; passed it by;* (A, Mgh, Mṣb, TA;) as also ▼ غمّض عَنْهُ, inf. n. تَغْمِيضٌ; and ▼ غَمَضَ; and ▼ اغتمض; namely a thing that he had heard; and an evil action: (A, TA:) and ▼ غمّض عَيْنَيْهِ عَنْهُ *he feigned himself blind to it.* (TA.) And اغمض عَنْهُ فِى البَيْعِ, (Ṣ, Ḳ,) or الشِّرَآءِ, (Ṣ, TA,) ‡ *He acted,* or *affected to act, in an easy,* or *a facile, manner towards him,* (تَسَاهَلَ عَلَيْهِ,) *in selling,* (Ṣ, Ḳ,) or *buying;* (Ṣ;) as also ▼ غَمَضَ عَنْهُ, (Ṣ, Ḳ,) aor. ـِ. (Ḳ.) And أَغْمِضْ لِى فِيمَا بِعْتَنِى, (Ṣ, A, Ḳ, TA,) in [some of] the copies of the Ḳ like اِضْرِبْ, [i. e. ▼ اِغْمِضْ,] but the former is the right reading, (TA,) [though the latter is perhaps allowable, as will presently be seen,] meaning, (A, TA,) or as though it meant, (Ṣ, Ḳ, TA,) ‡ *Give thou to me more of what thou hast sold to me, on account of its badness;* or [so in the A, but in the Ṣ and Ḳ "and,"] *lower thou to me the price thereof;* (Ṣ, A, Ḳ, TA;) as also ▼ غَمِّضْ لِى فِيهِ. (Ḳ, TA.) And اغمض فِى البَيْعِ ‡ *He demanded that another should give him more of the thing sold; and that he should lower the price* [*thereof*]; *and he complied with his demand.* (IAth.) And اغمض فِى السِّلْعَةِ ‡ *He demanded a lowering of the price of the commodity, on account of its badness.* (TA.) It is said in the Ḳur [ii. 270], وَلَسْتُمْ بِآخِذِيهِ إِلَّا أَنْ تُغْمِضُوا فِيهِ, (Ṣ, A,* Ḳ,) or, accord. to one reading, ▼ تُغَمِّضُوا, (TA,) i. e. ‡ *When ye do not take it unless ye lower the price;* (Lth, Zj,* Ḳ;) meaning, عَلَى إِغْمَاضٍ, or بِإِغْمَاضٍ. (Fr.) — [Hence also,] ▼ غَمَّضَ فُلَانٌ عَلَى هٰذَا الأَمْرِ † *Such a one executed, performed,* or *accomplished, this affair;* or *kept,* or *applied himself, constantly,* or *perseveringly, to it;* (مَضَى عَلَيْهِ;) [as though he shut his eyes at it;] *knowing what was in it.* (O, Ḳ.) And ▼ غَمَّضَتِ النَّاقَةُ, (Ṣ, A, Ḳ,) inf. n. تَغْمِيضٌ, (Ḳ,) *The she-camel, being driven away* (رُدَّتْ; as in the Ḳ, and in some copies of the Ṣ, or ذِيدَتْ, as in other copies of the Ṣ, and in the A, as is said in the TA,) *from the watering-trough,* (Ṣ, Ḳ,) *rushed upon the driver,* (الذَّائِد, [in the CḲ, erroneously, الزائد,]) *closing her eyes, and came to the water.* (Ṣ, A, Ḳ.) ▼ تَغْمِيضٌ also signifies The *embarking* [*in an affair*], or *undertaking* [*it*], *blindly.* (TA.) — [Hence also,] أَغْمَضَتِ المَفَازَةُ عَلَيْهِمْ ‡ [*The desert concealed them;*] *they did not appear in the desert,* (A, TA,) *being concealed by the mirage, and in the depressed parts;* (TA;) as though it closed its eyelids upon them. (A, TA.) — اغمض النَّظَرَ ‡ *He considered,* or *judged, well, and gave a good opinion:* (M, TA:) and اغمض فِى النَّظَرِ ‡ *he gave a right opinion:* (A:) or † *he considered,* or *judged, minutely.* (IḲṭṭ.) — أَغْمَضَتِ العَيْنُ فُلَانًا † *The eye despised such a one:* (Ḳ, TA:) or you say أَغْمَضْتُهُ عَيْنِى meaning *I despised him:* — and likewise meaning *I vied,* or *contended, in running with him,* (حَاضَرْتُهُ,) *and outstripped him, after he had outstripped me:* (Ibn-'Abbád, O:) or اغمض فُلَانٌ فُلَانًا means *Such a one vied,* or *contended, in running with such a one,* (حَاضَرَهُ,) *and outstripped him, after*

having been outstripped by him. (K.) — اغمض الْمَيِّتَ, (A, Mgh, TA,) inf. n. إِغْمَاضٌ; (TA;) and ▼ غَمَّضَهُ, (A, TA,) inf. n. as above; (TA;) *He closed the eyelids of the dead man.* (Mgh.)

7. انغمض الطَّرْفُ i. q. اِنْغَضَّ: (Ṣ, Ṣgh, K:) [or the former more probably signifies *The eye,* or *eyes, became closed:* and the latter, *the eye,* or *eyes, became contracted.* See also 8.]

8. مَا ٱغْتَمَضَتْ عَيْنَاىَ *My eyes slept not,* or *have not slept.* (Ṣ,* Ṣgh, K.) See also 4, in the first half of the paragraph, in three places. — أَتَانِى ذٰلِكَ عَلَى ٱغْتِمَاضٍ ‡ *That came to me easily, without trouble,* or *pains-taking.* (Aṣ, A, K.)

غَمْضٌ: see غَامِضٌ, in four places: — see also 4, in the third sentence, in two places.

غُمْضٌ:
غَمَاضٌ:
غُمَاضٌ:
غِمَاضٌ:
غُمُوضٌ:
} see 4, in the third sentence; the first and second in two places.

غُمُوضَةٌ: see what next follows.

مَا فِى هٰذَا الأَمْرِ غَمِيضَةٌ, (Ṣ, O, L, K,) and ▼ غُمُوضَةٌ, (L,) *There is not, in this affair, any fault,* (Ṣ, O, L, K,) لِى [*to be imputed to me*]. (TA, where this is added next after ما.)

غَامِضٌ [*Unperceived; unapparent; hidden,* or *concealed.* (See 1, first signification.)] — *Unapparent to the mind, not plain* or *perspicuous, obscure, recondite,* or *abstruse,* speech, or language. (Ṣ, A, K.) You say also, مَعْنًى غَامِضٌ *A nice, subtile,* or *quaint, meaning.* (TA.) And مَسْأَلَةٌ غَامِضَةٌ *A question in which is matter for consideration, and subtility,* or *nicety.* (TA.) And مَسْأَلَةٌ فِيهَا غَوَامِضُ [*A question in which are obscurities, abstrusities, subtilities,* or *niceties:* the last word being pl. of ▼ غَامِضَةٌ, an epithet in which the quality of a subst. predominates]. (A.) — *Obscure; not well known:* (A:) or *not known:* (Mṣb, K:) applied to rank or quality (حَسَب), (A, K,) or to parentage or relationship (نَسَب): (Mṣb:) pl. أَغْمَاضٌ, like as أَصْحَابٌ is pl. of صَاحِبٌ: or, as some say, this is pl. of ▼ غَمْضٌ. (TA.) — *Obscure,* or *of no reputation; low, mean,* or *vile;* (K, TA;) applied to a man: (TA:) such is termed ▼ ذُو غَمْضٍ, (Ṣ, O, TA,) also. (TA.) [And hence, perhaps,] A man *remiss in the charge,* or *in rushing on the enemy:* (Lth, K:) pl. غَوَامِضُ [which is anomalous, like فَوَارِسُ &c.]. (Lth.) — *Low,* or *depressed;* applied to land, (Ṣ, A, K,) and a place; (A;) [because unseen from a distance;] as also ▼ غَمْضٌ; (Ṣ, A, K;) applied to a place: (Ṣ, A:) or this latter signifies land *very low,* or *very much depressed, so that what is in it is not seen:* (AHn:) and in like manner ▼ مَغْمَضٌ, *a place more depressed* (Ṣ, TA) *than what is termed* غَمْضٌ: (TA:) pl. of the first, غَوَامِضُ: (K:) and of ▼ the second, أَغْمَاضٌ [a pl. of pauc.] (Ṣ, K) and غُمُوضٌ: (Ṣ, A, K:) and of the third, مَغَامِضُ. (Ṣ.) — An anklet *depressed,* lit. *choked,* (غَاصٌّ, [in the CK غاض,]) *in the leg:* (JK, A, L, K:) and, applied to an ankle-bone, *concealed by the flesh:* (TA:) or *fat:* (K:) and in this latter sense applied to a leg, or shank. (K, TA.) — A house *not upon a common thoroughfare-road* or *street;* (Lth, A, L, K;) *retired therefrom.* (A, TA.) ▬ *A young camel;* the *young one of a camel:* pl. غَوَامِضُ: (TA:) which also signifies *camels not accustomed to drawing water.* (JK.)

غَامِضَةٌ; pl. غَوَامِضُ: see the next preceding paragraph.

مَغْمَضٌ; pl. مَغَامِضُ: see غَامِضٌ as applied to land, and a place.

مُغَمِّضَاتُ اللَّيْلِ *The darknesses of night.* (TA.) — See also the following paragraph.

الْمُغَمِّضَاتُ مِنَ الذُّنُوبِ, (O, K,* TA,) or مُغَمِّضَاتُ الأُمُورِ, accord. to different relations of a trad. in which it occurs, (TA,) *Sins,* or *offences, which a man commits knowing them* [*to be such*]: (O, K, TA:) or *enormities which a man commits knowing them* [*to be such*]; as though he closed his eyes upon them, feigning himself blind while he saw them: (TA:) IAth says that accord. to one relation it is with fet-ḥ to the second م, [▼ مُغَمَّضَاتٌ,] and means *small sins,* or *offences;* so called because minute and unapparent, so that a man commits them with a kind of doubt, not knowing that he will be punished for committing them. (TA.)

غمط

1. غَمِطَ, aor. ـَ; and غَمَطَ, aor. ـِ; inf. n. غَمْطٌ, (Ṣ, K,) of both; (Ṣ;) *He despised* men; *held* them *in contempt;* (Ṣ, K;) *accounted* them *little,* or *vile.* (TA.) It is said in a trad., إِنَّمَا ذٰلِكَ مَنْ سَفِهَ الحَقَّ وَغَمِطَ النَّاسَ *That* (Ṣ, TA,) meaning transgression, iniquity, or injustice, (TA,) *is only* (Ṣ, TA) the action of (TA) *such as regards the truth,* or *right, as foolishness,* or *ignorance, and despises men:* (Ṣ, TA:) Ṣgh says that accord. to one relation, it is غَمَصَ: and Az relates it thus; الكِبْرُ أَنْ تَسْفَهَ الحَقَّ وَتَغْمِطَ النَّاسَ [*Pride is thy regarding the truth,* or *right, as foolishness,* or *ignorance, and thy despising men*]. (TA.) — Also the former, (TA,) or both, (K,) *He was ungrateful for* health, and safety, (K, TA,) and a favour, or benefit, or blessing: (Ṣ,* TA:) and both, (Ṣ, K,) *he held in light estimation, was ungrateful for, and despised,* (Ṣ, K,) a favour, or benefit, or blessing, (K, TA,) and his life. (Ṣ, TA.) — And the former, *He denied,* or *disacknowledged,* a right, or due. (TA.)

4. اغمط *It continued; it kept,* or *clave;* (K;) like اغبط. (TA.) Hence, (TA,) أَغْمَطَتْ عَلَيْهِ الحُمَّى, a dial. var. of اغبطت, q. v. (Ṣ, TA.)

8. اغتمطهُ بِالكَلَامِ *He treated him contemptuously with speech:* (O:) and (O) *he overcame,* and *subdued, him therewith;* (O, L, K;) and so اِغْتَطَّهُ. (O, L.) — And اغتمطهُ *He vied,* or *contended, in running with him, and outstripped him, after he had been outstripped* (O, K) *by him;* mentioned by Ibn-'Abbád; (O;) and so اِغْتَطَّهُ; (TA;) and أَغْمَصَهُ. (Ibn-'Abbád and O in art. غمص.

سَمَآءٌ غَمْطَى i. q. غَبْطَى, q. v. (IDrd, K.)

سَيْرٌ مُغْمِطٌ i. q. مُغْبِطٌ, q. v. (ISh.)

غمل

1. غَمَلَ الجِلْدَ, (Ṣ, O,) or الأَدِيمَ, (K,) aor. ـُ, inf. n. غَمْلٌ, *He folded the skin,* or *hide, and buried it, in order that it might become soft,* or *flaccid, and pliant, when its wool was pulled:* (Ṣ, O:*) if neglected for a while, it becomes spoiled, or marred: the epithet applied to it is ▼ غَمِيلٌ; (Ṣ, O;) and غَمِينٌ also: (Ṣ:) or *he spoiled,* or *marred, the skin,* or *hide:* or *he put it in the bottom of some receptacle* (فِى غُمَّةٍ), [*and left it a while,*] *in order that its wool might become detached:* (K:) or *he buried it,* (K, TA,) *having folded it,* (TA,) *in the sand,* (K, TA,) *after moistening* [*it*], (TA,) *in order that it might become stinking, and its hair* [or *wool*] *might be plucked off:* (K, TA:) or, accord. to AHn, *he folded it while it was moist, and left it folded longer than it required, so that it became spoiled,* or *marred:* or, as some say, *he folded it after it was tanned, then covered it a day and a night, so that its hair,* or *its wool, became loose, when it was plucked off:* if left more than a day and a night, it becomes spoiled, or marred: (TA:) and ▼ اغمل signifies [the same: (see غَضِبَ الجِلْدُ:) or] *he left* his skin, or hide, [*buried,* or *put in the bottom of some receptacle, &c., while moist,*] *until it became spoiled,* or *marred.* (TA.) — And غَمَلَ التَّمْرَ, (Ṣ,) or البُسْرَ, (O, K,) *He did in like manner to the dates,* or *the unripe dates, in order that they might become ripe:* (Ṣ, O, K:) and the epithet applied to them is ▼ مَغْمُولٌ; and مَغْمُونٌ. (TA.) — And غَمَلَ العِنَبَ, (K, TA,) aor. and inf. n. as above, (TA,) *He put the grapes together, in quantities one above another,* (K, TA,) in the basket of palm-leaves. (TA.) — غَمَلَ فُلَانًا *He covered such a one,* (K, TA,) *with clothes,* (TA,) *in order that he should sweat.* (K, TA.) — غَمَلَ الجُرْحَ *He put pieces of rag, one above another, upon the wound.* (O, TA.) — غَمَلَ الأَمْرَ *He hid, concealed,* or *covered, the affair,* or case. (TA.) — And غَمَلَ الشَّىْءَ, (K,) inf. n. غَمْلٌ, (O,) *He put the thing into a good, sound, right,* or *proper, state.* (O, K.) ▬ غَمِلَ النَّبَاتُ, (O, K,) inf. n. غَمَلٌ, (TA,) *The plants,* or *herbage, became accumulated, one,* or *one part, overlying another,* (O, K, TA,) *so as to become withered, and decayed.* (TA.) [See also 5.] ▬ غَمِلَ النَّبْتُ, the verb being like فَرِحَ, *The plant,* or *plants,* or *herbage, became in a bad,* or *corrupt, state.* (TA.) — And one says غَمِلَ هٰذَا المَكَانُ

بالنَّبْت [app. meaning *This place became*, or *has become, in a bad*, or *corrupt, state by reason of the herbage*: or *concealed*, or *covered, by herbage*; as may be inferred from an explanation of أَرْض غَمِلَة]. (O.) — And غَمِلَ الجُرْحُ, (TA,) inf. n. غَمَلٌ, (Ḳ,) *The wound became in a bad*, or *corrupt, state, by reason of the bandage*. (Ḳ, TA.)

4: see the preceding paragraph, former half.

5. تغمّل النَّبَاتُ *The plants*, or *herbage, became accumulated, one*, or *one part, overlying another*. (TA.) [See also غَمَلَ النَّبَاتَ.] — And تغمّل *He became*, or *made himself, ample*, or *abundant*, syn. تَوَسَّعَ, (O, Ḳ,) *in wealth*. (O.)

7. انغمل, said of a skin, quasi-pass. of غَمَلَ signifying as expl. in the first sentence of this art. [i. e. *It was*, or *became, such as is termed* غَمِيل, or *in the state denoted by the pass. part. n. of the latter verb*]. (Ḳ.)

غَمْلٌ *A certain tree of the* [*kind called*] حَمْض, *that grows surmounted by a fruit*, or *produce, white like the* [*garments called*] مُلَآء. (AA, O, TA.)

غَمِلٌ [accord. to rule, part. n. of غَمِلَ, q. v.]. — أَرْضٌ غَمِلَةٌ *Land abounding with herbage, having its surface concealed*, or *covered, thereby*. (TA.)

غَمِيلٌ: see 1, first sentence. — Applied to herbage, (Ṣ,* O,*) or to such as is called نَصِىّ, (Ḳ, TA,) *Accumulated, one part above another*, (Ṣ, O, Ḳ,* TA,) *so as to be withered*: (TA:) pl. غَمْلَى, (Ṣ, O, TA,) [which is also expl. as] meaning herbage *tangled and dense, one part above another*. (O voce شُرْبُبٌ.) — And *Low*, or *depressed*, land. (Aṣ, O, TA.)

غُمْلُولٌ *A valley containing trees*, (Ṣ, O, Ḳ,) or *containing numerous trees*, (TA,) *and plants*, or *herbage*, (Ṣ, O,) *tangled*, or *luxuriant*, or *abundant and dense*: (Ṣ:) or *such as is long, of little width, and tangled* or *luxuriant* or *abundant and dense* [*in its trees*]: (Ḳ:) or *a narrow valley having much of such produce*: or *a deeply-depressed tract of land*: or, accord. to ISh, *a tract having the form of a* [*road such as is termed*] سِكَّة, *in the ground, narrow, and having two* [*lateral*] *acclivities, each acclivity two cubits in height, extending to the measure of a bow-shot, producing an abundance* [*of trees* or *herbage*], *and narrower than what is termed a* مَلِيع: (TA:) and [its pl.] غَمَالِيلُ is said to signify *low*, or *depressed, tracts* of land, *covered with herbage*. (O.) — And (in like manner, Ṣ, O) *Anything that is collected together*, (Ṣ, O, Ḳ,) *obscure, and accumulated, one part upon another*, (Ḳ,) *of trees*, or *of clouds*, or *of darkness*, (Ṣ, O, Ḳ,) or *a* رَاوِيَة, or زَاوِيَة, (the former in the CḲ, and the latter in other copies of the Ḳ and in the TA,) [or] so that *a* رَاوِيَة, or زَاوِيَة, (the former in my copies of the Ṣ, and the latter in the O,) is thus called: (Ṣ, O:) [but I think that these two words راوية and زاوية are both mistranscriptions for رَابِيَة, which is mentioned in the Ḳ as one of the meanings of غُمْلُول; i. e. *a hill*:] pl. غَمَالِيلُ. (TA.) — Also, (O, Ḳ,) as is said by AḤn on the authority of some other or others, (O,) *A certain herb*, or *leguminous plant*, (بَقْلَة, O, Ḳ,) *likewise called* قُنَّابَرَى, [thus accord. to the O in art. قنبر, and there said in the TA to be correctly with teshdeed to the ن and with kesr to the ب, but in the present art. written in the O قُنَّابَرَى,] *in Pers.* بَرْغَسْت; *a herb of the desert* (بَقْلَةٌ دَشْتِيَّةٌ), *which come forth early in the* [*season called*] رَبِيع; (O;) *eaten* (O, Ḳ) *by men*, (O,) *cooked*. (Ḳ.)

مَغْمُولٌ: see 1, near the middle. — Also A man *having clothes thrown upon him in order that he may sweat*. (Ṣ, O.) — And Flesh-meat *covered over*; whether cooked by roasting or the like or with broth or gravy; as also مَغْمُونٌ. (TA.) — And Palm-trees (نَخْل) *near together*. (TA.) — And A man *obscure, unnoted*, or *reputeless*. (Aṣ, O, Ḳ.)

غمن

1. غَمَنَ الجِلْدَ, (Ṣ, Ḳ,) aor. ـُ, (Ṣ,) inf. n. غَمْنٌ, (TA,) *i. q.* غَمَلَهُ; (Ḳ;) [see the latter;] *He put together the skin after it had been stripped off, and covered it over until its wool became loose, for the purpose of tanning*: (TA:) or *he covered over the skin* (Ṣ, TA) *for two nights, for the purpose of tanning*, (TA,) *in order that its wool might become loosened from it*: (Ṣ, TA:) and the epithet applied to it is ▾ غَمِينٌ, (Ṣ, Ḳ,) like غَمِيل. (Ṣ.) — And غَمَنَ التَّمْرَ, (Ṣ,) or البُسْرَ, (Ḳ, TA,) has the like meaning, (Ṣ,) *i. q.* غَمَلَهُ; (Ḳ;) *He covered over* [*the dates*, or] *the unripe dates, in order that they might become ripe*: (TA:) and the epithet applied to them is ▾ مَغْمُونٌ, like مَغْمُولٌ. (TA in art. غمل.) — And غَمَنَ فُلَانًا [like غَمَلَهُ] *He threw his clothes upon such a one, in order that he should sweat*. (Ḳ.) = غُمِنَ فِى أُدْخِلَ فِيهَا الأَرْضِ means [app. *It*, or perhaps *he, was put into the earth*; or *made to enter into it*]. (Ḳ.)

7. انغمن *It*, or *he, entered* [into the earth: see غُمِنَ (immediately preceding); of which it is expl. as denoting the consequence]. (Ḳ.)

غُمْنَةٌ [*A mixture of*] *white lead* (إِسْفِيدَاج) *and* [*the cosmetic termed*] غُمْرَة [q. v.] *with which a woman rubs over her face*: (Ḳ:) pl. غُمَنٌ [meaning *sorts thereof*]. (TA.)

غَمِينٌ: see 1, first sentence.

مَغْمُونٌ: see 1, second sentence. — Also, applied to flesh-meat, *i. q.* مَغْمُولٌ, q. v. (TA in art. غمل.) — And Palm-trees (نَخْل) *near together*; like مَغْمُول. (TA.)

غمو

1. غَمَا البَيْتَ, aor. يَغْمُوهُ, inf. n. غَمْوٌ: see 1 in art. غمى.

غَمَا in the phrase غَمَا وَٱللّٰهِ, *i. q.* أَمَا [expl. in art. اما]; (Ḳ, TA;) as also with ع. (TA.)

غَمًا; dual غَمَوَانِ: see غَمًى in art. غمى.

غمى

1. غَمَيْتُ البَيْتَ, (Ṣ, Ḳ, TA,) aor. أَغْمِيهِ, inf. n. غَمْىٌ, (TA,) *I roofed the house*, or *chamber*: (Ḳ, TA:) or *covered its roof* (Ṣ, Ḳ) *with earth &c.* (Ḳ) or *with reeds*, or *canes, and earth*, and *the like*: (Ṣ:) and ▾ غَمَّيْتُهُ signifies the same: (Ḳ:) and غَمَا البَيْتَ, aor. يَغْمُوهُ, (Ḳ, TA,) inf. n. غَمْوٌ, (TA,) signifies *he covered* [*the roof of*] *the house*, or *chamber*, [*in like manner*, or] *with clay*, or *earth, and wood*. (Ḳ, TA.) And غَمَى الشَّىْءَ *He covered the thing*. (Ḥar p. 422.) — غُمِىَ اليَوْمُ, and اللَّيْلُ, *The day*, and *the night, was constantly clouded, so that the sun was not seen therein nor the new moon*: so accord. to Es-Saraḳustee: and he says that فَإِنْ أُغْمِىَ ▾ عَلَيْكُمْ means *And if your day be constantly clouded, so that ye see not the new moon*, then complete ye [the reckoning of the days of] Shaabán: (Mṣb:) or غُمِىَ and ▾ أُغْمِىَ and فَإِنْ غُمَّ عَلَيْكُمْ, thus differently related, all mean, *and if it*, i. e. the new moon, *be covered*, or *concealed*: or *and if there be a covering* [of clouds] *over you*: (Mgh:) [see also 1 in art. غمر:] or أُغْمِىَ ▾ يَوْمُنَا means *Our day was one whereof the covering of clouds was constant*: and أُغْمِيَتْ ▾ لَيْلَتُنَا, *Our night was one whereof the new moon was veiled*, or *concealed*. (Ḳ, TA.) — See also 4.

2: see the preceding paragraph, first sentence.

4: see 1, in four places. — One says also, أُغْمِىَ عَلَيْهِ الخَبَرُ *The information*, or *narration, was dubious, confused*, or *vague, to him*; *such as was difficult to be understood*; or *such as was not to be understood*; like غُمَّ: (Ṣ:) or *was obscure*, or *unapparent, to him*. (Mṣb.) — And أُغْمِىَ عَلَيْهِ, (Ṣ, Mgh, Mṣb, Ḳ,) inf. n. إِغْمَآءٌ; (Mgh, Mṣb;) and غُمِىَ ▾ عليه; (Ṣ, Mṣb, Ḳ;) said of a sick man, (Ṣ, Mṣb, Ḳ,) *He swooned*, i. e. *became senseless*, (غُشِىَ عَلَيْهِ, Ṣ,* Ḳ,) *and then recovered his senses*: (Ḳ:) or إِغْمَآءٌ is *a weakness of the faculties by reason of the overpowering effect of disease*: (Mgh:) or it is *an abstraction*, or *absence of mind, that overtakes a man, with languor of the limbs*, or *members*, or *organs, by reason of a malady*; (Mgh, Mṣb;) thus it is defined by the scholastic theologians; and is *the same as* غُشْى: (Mgh:) or it is *a repletion of the venters of the brain with a cold, thick, phlegm*; (Mgh, Mṣb;) thus accord. to the physicians, who distinguish between it and غُشْى, as do the lawyers: (Mgh:) [see also غُشِىَ عَلَيْهِ:] the patient is said to be مُغْمًى ▾ عَلَيْهِ, (Ṣ, Mgh, and so in some copies of the Ḳ,) and مُغْمِىٌّ ▾ عَلَيْهِ, (Ṣ, Mṣb, and so in some copies of the Ḳ,) and ▾ غَمًى, which last epithet is applied to a single person, (Ṣ, Ḳ,) and to two persons, (Ṣ,) and to a pl. number, (Ṣ, Ḳ,) and to a female [as well as a male], (Ṣ,) or (if you will, Ṣ) you say هُمَا غَمَيَانِ and هُمْ أَغْمَآءُ. (Ṣ, Ḳ.)

كَانَ عَلَى السَّمَآءِ غَمًى, (Ḳ,) or فِى السَّمَآءِ غَمًى, (Mṣb,) and ↓ غُمًى, (Mṣb, Ḳ,) mean [*Upon the sky is, or was,*] *what veiled,* or *concealed, the new moon:* (Mṣb, Ḳ:) not from غُمٌّ: (Ḳ:) this addition in the Ḳ is meant as an indirect slur upon J, for his having mentioned [in this art.] the statement of Fr that one says صُمْنَا لِلْغُمَّى and لِلْغَمَّى, meaning *We fasted when the new moon was veiled,* or *concealed, to us;* and هِىَ لَيْلَةُ الغُمَّى [or الغَمَّى]; the [proper] place of which is [the section of words whereof the last radical is] م: (TA:) [see غُمٌّ, in that art. but accord. to Fei,] one says [also], ↓ صُمْنَا لِلْغُمْيَةِ. (Mṣb. [It is there added that this noun is like مُدْيَة in measure: otherwise I should think that the right reading is لِلْغُمَّةِ, which has been mentioned voce غُمٌّ.])

غَمًى and ↓ غَمَآءٌ (T, Ṣ, Ḳ) The *roof* of a house, or chamber: (T, Ḳ:) or the *covering of the roof,* (Ṣ, Ḳ,) *consisting of earth &c.,* (Ḳ,) or *consisting of reeds,* or *canes, and earth,* and *the like;* (Ṣ;) and غَمًا also signifies [the same, or] the *covering* of a house, or chamber, *consisting of clay,* or *earth, and wood:* (TA in art. غمو:) the dual [of the first and last] is غَمَيَانِ and غَمَوَانِ: and the pl. is أَغْمَآءٌ, (Ḳ, TA,) which is [of the same] like أَنْقَآءٌ pl. of نَقًى [and نَقًا], (TA,) and أَغْمِيَةٌ, (Ḳ, TA,) which is of ↓ غَمَآءٌ. (TA.) — Also, the first, [in the CḲ, erroneously, غَمَاء,] *A covering that is put upon a horse in order that he may sweat.* (ISd, Ḳ.) — See also غُمًى. ═ And see 4, near the end.

غُمًى: see صُمْنَا لِلْغُمْيَةِ.

غَمَآءٌ: see غَمًى, in two places.

غَامِيَآءُ *One of the entrances to the burrow of the jerboa.* (Ḳ.)

مُغْمًى عَلَيْهِ and مُغْمِىٌّ عَلَيْهِ: see 4, near the end.

غن

1. غَنَّ, (MA, Mṣb, Ḳ,) originally غَنِنَ, (Mṣb, MF,) [sec. pers. غَنِنْتَ,] aor. يَغَنُّ, (Mṣb, Ḳ,) inf. n. غُنَّةٌ (MA, KL) and غَنَنٌ, (MA, [and the same seems to be indicated in the Mṣb by its being said that the verb is of the class of تَعِبَ,]) or غُنٌّ, (TḲ, [but this I think a mistake,]) *He spoke* (MA, Mṣb, KL) *in,* (MA,) or *from,* (Mṣb, KL,) or [rather] *through,* (KL,) *his nose,* (MA, KL,) or *his* خَيَاشِيم [app. here meaning the *innermost parts of the air-passages of the nose*]. (Mṣb.) [The author of the Ḳ gives no indication of the proper signification of this verb but that of its implying what he states to be meant by غُنَّة, which see below.] — See also 4, in two places.

2. غَنَّنَهُ, inf. n. تَغْنِينٌ, *It rendered him* أَغَنّ [q. v.]. (Ḳ.) One says, مَا أَدْرِى مَا غَنَّنَهُ *I know not what rendered him,* or *has rendered him* أَغَنّ. (TA.) — And غَنَّن صَوْتَهُ *He made his voice to have in it a* غُنَّة [q. v.]. (Mughnee, art. حَرْفُ النُّونِ.) [See مُغَنٍّ, voce غِنَآءٌ, in art. غنى.])

4. اغنّ said of a man, *He made one to hear his* ↓ غُنَّة, i. e. *soft,* or *gentle, plaintive, and melodious, voice, in singing.* (Ḥar p. 645.) — اغنّ الذُّبَابُ *The flies made a sound* [or *humming*]. (Ḳ.) — اغنّ الوَادِى ‡ *The valley had in it the sound* [or *humming*] *of flies,* [or *resounded therewith,*] *being abundant in herbs,* or *herbage:* (Ṣ:) or *abounded with trees;* as also ↓ غَنَّ. (Ḳ, TA.) — اغنّت الأَرْضُ † *The land had its herbs,* or *herbage, tall, full-grown,* or *of full height, and in blossom.* (TA.) — اغنّ النَّخْلُ ‡ *The palm-trees attained to maturity;* as also ↓ غَنَّ. (Ḳ, TA.) — And اغنّ السِّقَآءُ ‡ *The skin became filled* (Ṣ, Ḳ, TA) *with water.* (Ṣ, TA.) ═ And [it is also trans.:] one says, اغنّ اللّٰهُ غُصْنَهُ ‡ *God made its branch beautiful and bright.* (Ḳ, TA.)

غُنَّةٌ [mentioned above as an inf. n. of غَنَّ but generally expl. as a simple subst. signifying *A sort of nasal sound,* or *twang:*] *a sound that comes forth from the nose;* (Ḥam p. 339;) *a sound* (Ṣ, Mṣb) *in,* (Ṣ,) or *that comes forth from,* (Mṣb,) *the* خَيْشُوم [app. here meaning the *innermost part of the air-passages of the nose*]: (Ṣ, Mṣb:) or *a sound from the* لَهَاة [q. v., app. here meaning the *arches,* or *pillars, of the soft palate,* or the *furthest part of the mouth,*] and the *nose, like* [*that which is heard in the utterance of*] *the* ن *of* مِنْكَ *and* عَنْكَ, for the tongue has not part in it: (Mgh:) or the *flowing* [or *passage*] *of the speech in the* لَهَاة [app. here also meaning as expl. above]: (Ḳ:) or *a mixture of the sound of the* خَيْشُوم [expl. above] *in the pronunciation of a letter:* (Mbr, TA:) ن is that one of the letters in which it is greatest in degree: (Kh, Mgh, Mṣb, TA:) خُنَّة is [a sound] greater in degree than غُنَّة. (TA.) — [Also The *roughness of the voice,* of a boy, *consequent upon the attaining to puberty;* or, as Mṭr says,] الغُنَّةُ signifies also *what is incident to the boy on the occasion of his attaining to puberty, when his voice becomes rough.* (Mgh.) — And *A soft,* or *gentle, plaintive, and melodious, voice, in singing.* (Ḥar p. 645.) See 4. — And The *sound* [or *humming*] *produced by the flying of* flies; (TA;) and ↓ غُنَانٌ [likewise] signifies the *sound* of flies. (Ḳ, TA.) [See مُغِنٌّ and أَغَنُّ. And see also an ex. voce ثُنَّةٌ: and another voce عُنَّةٌ.] — And the poet Yezeed Ibn-El-Aạwar has used it in relation to the sounding of stones: (Ḳ:) [or rather] he has so used the epithet ↓ أَغَنُّ. (TA.)

غُنَانٌ: see the next preceding paragraph, near the end.

أَغَنُّ One *who speaks* [*with a nasal sound,* or *twang,* i. e.] *in* [or rather *through*] *his nose;* (TA;) *who speaks from his* خَيَاشِيم [app. here meaning (as expl. before) the *innermost parts of the air-passages of the nose*]: (Ṣ, Mṣb:) or, accord. to AZ, (Mgh, TA,) *whose speech flows,* (Mgh, Ḳ,*) or *passes forth,* (TA,) *in his* لَهَاة [app. (as expl. voce غُنَّة) the *arches,* or *pillars, of the soft palate,* or the *furthest part of the mouth*]: (Mgh, Ḳ, TA:) fem. غَنَّآءُ, applied to a woman. (Mṣb.) — It is also applied to a gazelle (ظَبْى), meaning *Whose cry issues from his* خَيَاشِيم [expl. above]: J has erred in saying that it is applied to طَيْر [i. e. birds, or flying things]: (Ḳ:) or if by طير he mean flies (ذُبَاب), his saying thus is not a mistake, for it is applied to them [as meaning *making a humming sound*]. (TA.) — [Hence,] وَادٍ أَغَنُّ † *A valley abounding with herbs* or *herbage:* for to such the flies constantly keep, and in their sounds is a غُنَّة. (Ṣ. [See also مُغِنٌّ.]) And (for this reason, TA) one says رَوْضَةٌ غَنَّآءُ i. e. † [*A meadow,* or *garden,*] *abounding with herbs* or *herbage:* or *in which the winds pass with a sound that is not clear,* [i. e. *with a confused, humming,* or *murmuring, sound,*] *by reason of the denseness of its herbs* or *herbage.* (Ḳ, TA.) And [for the same reason one says] عُشْبٌ أَغَنُّ † *Herbs,* or *herbage, tall, full-grown,* or *of full height, and in blossom.* (TA.) — And (hence also, Ṣ) قَرْيَةٌ غَنَّآءُ ‡ [*A town,* or *village,*] *abounding with inhabitants* (Ṣ, Ḳ, TA) *and buildings* (Ḳ, TA) *and herbs* or *herbage* [*so that in it is heard the hum of men and women and of flies &c.*]. (Ṣ, TA.) — حَرْفٌ أَغَنُّ means *A letter from* [*the utterance of*] *which results what is termed* غُنَّة [i. e. *the nasal sound thus termed*]. (TA.) — See also غُنَّة, last sentence.

وَادٍ مُغِنٌّ ‡ *A valley in which is* [*heard*] *the sound* [or *humming*] *of flies; these not being in any valley but such as abounds with herbs* or *herbage;* (Ṣ;) *a valley of which the flies are abundant, by reason of the denseness,* or *luxuriance, of its herbs* or *herbage, so that a* غُنَّة [or *humming*] *is heard, produced by their flying:* the epithet being applied to it, but being properly applicable to the flies. (TA.) [See also أَغَنُّ.]

غنج

1. غَنِجَتْ, (Ṣ, A, MA, O, Ḳ;) aor. ـَ, (Ḳ,) inf. n. غُنْجٌ (Ṣ, MA) and غَنَاجَةٌ; (MA;) and غَنَجَتْ; (MA;) and ↓ تغنّجت; (Ṣ, A, MA, Ḳ;) said of a girl, or young woman, (Ṣ, Ḳ,) or of a woman, (A, MA,) *She used amorous gesture* or *behaviour,* or *such gesture* or *behaviour combined with coquettish boldness, and feigned coyness* or *opposition,* (Ṣ,* A,* MA, O,* Ḳ,* TA,) *and an affecting of languor.* (TA.) [See غُنْج below.]

5: see the preceding paragraph.

غُنْجٌ [mentioned above as an inf. n.] and ↓ غُنُجٌ (Ṣ, O, Ḳ) and ↓ غُنَاجٌ and ↓ غِنَاجٌ, (O, Ḳ,) in a girl, or young woman, (Ṣ, Ḳ,) *Amorous gesture* or *behaviour*, or *such gesture* or *behaviour combined with coquettish boldness, and feigned coyness* or *opposition*, (Bkh, Ṣ,* O,* Ḳ,* TA,) *and an affecting of languor*: (Bkh, TA:) [in the present day generally used to signify *lascivious motion*, or *a wriggling of the body* or *hips, under the excitement of sexual passion*, or *to excite such passion*:] accord. to some, *beauty of the eyes*. (TA.) — And غَنْجٌ and ♦ غِنَاجٌ signify also *Smoke-black* (دُخَانُ النَّوُورِ) [see the latter of these two nouns in art. نور] AA, O, Ḳ) *which a woman performing the operation of tattooing puts upon her green colour in order that it may become black*. (AA, O, TA.)

غَنْجٌ *An old man*: (Ṣ, Ḳ:) or *a man*: (TA:) in the dial. of Hudheyl. (Ṣ, Ḳ.) So in the saying غَنْجٌ عَلَى شَنَجٍ (TA) meaning *A man upon a camel*: (Lth, IDrd, O, all in art. شنج:) or *a man or an old man, upon a heavy camel*: (L in that art.:) a phrase of the tribe of Hudheyl. (TA.) [See غَنَجٌ.]

غُنُجٌ : see غُنْجٌ.

غُنْجَةُ, (O,) or غَنْجَةُ, (TA,) without أَلْ, and imperfectly decl., (O, TA,) *The* قُنْفُذ [or *hedge-hog*], (O,) or *the* قُنْفُذَة [or *female hedge-hog*]. (TA.)

غَنِجَةٌ (Bkh, Ṣ, A, MA, O, Ḳ) and ♦ مَغْنُوجَةٌ (A, MA) and [in an intensive sense] ♦ مِغْنَاجٌ, (O, Ḳ) applied to a girl, or young woman, (Ṣ, Ḳ,) or to a woman, (A, MA,) *Using* or *who uses, amorous gesture* or *behaviour*, &c., *such as is termed* غُنْج. (Bkh, Ṣ, A, MA, O, Ḳ, TA.)

غُنَاجٌ : see غُنْجٌ.

غِنَاجٌ : see غُنْجٌ, in two places.

غَوْنَجٌ A *quick*, or *swift*, camel: mentioned by Kr, but said to be not known on the authority of any other. (TA.)

أُغْنُوجَةٌ *A gesture*, or *an action, of the kind termed* غُنْج : pl. أَغَانِيجُ : Aboo-Dhu-eyb says,

• لَوَى رَأْسَهُ عَنِّي وَمَالَ بِوُدِّهِ •
• أَغَانِيجُ خَوْدٍ كَانَ فِينَا يَزُورُهَا •

[*The amorous gestures* or *actions*, &c., *of a soft* or *tender*, or *goodly-shaped and young, damsel, whom he used to visit among us, turned his head from me, and diverted his love*]. (TA.)

مِغْنَاجٌ : } see غَنِجَةٌ.
مَغْنُوجَةٌ : }

غندب

الغُنْدُبُ : see the paragraph here following.

الغُنْدُبَةُ *A hard portion of flesh* [app. *a gland*] *around* [or app. *on either side of*] *the* حُلْقُوم [which seems to mean here, as it often does, the حَلْق, i. e. *fauces*, or *upper part of the throat*]; (O, Ḳ;) thus expl. by Lth; as also ♦ الغُنْدُبُ; (O;) or ♦ الغُنْدُوبُ : (Ḳ:) pl. غَنَادِبُ : and it is said that the غُنْدُبَتَانِ are [*two things*] *like two ganglions* (شِبْهُ غُدَّتَيْنِ) *in the* تَكْفَتَانِ ; (O, Ḳ;) *in each* نَكْفَة [q. v.] *is a* غُنْدُبَة, *and between the* غندبتان *is the place of swallowing*: (O:) *the* غنادب *and the flesh that is upon them, or above them, around the* لَهَاة [app. here meaning the *arches*, or *pillars, of the soft palate*; or the *furthest part of the mouth*], *compose the* لَغَانِين [pl. of لُغْنُونٌ, q. v.], *which are also called the* نَغَانِغ, pl. of نُغْنُغَةٌ [or نُغْنُغٌ, q. v.]: (TA:) or the غندبتان are *two glands* (عُقْدَتَانِ) *in*, or *at*, (فِى,) *the root of the tongue*: (Ḳ, TA:) and they are said to be *the two amygdalæ of the fauces*; i. e. *the tonsils*: (اللَّوْزَتَانِ : TA:) or *two portions of flesh which are situate on either side of the* لَهَاة [app. meaning as expl. above, i. e. the *arches*, or *pillars, of the soft palate*, or the *furthest part of the mouth*], (Ḳ, TA,) *and between which is a space*: (TA:) and غُنْدُبَتَا العُرْشَيْنِ is expl. as meaning *the two things that conjoin* (اللَّتَانِ تَضُمَّانِ) *the* لَغَانِين, [above mentioned (I read اللغانين instead of العين, an evident mistranscription in my original, for I can only suppose the description to mean *the tonsils, as lodged between, and thus conjoining, the anterior and posterior pillars of the soft palate*,)] *on the right and left*. (TA.)

الغُنْدُوبُ : see the preceding paragraph.

غنظ

1. غَنَظَهُ, aor. ـِ (Ṣ, O, Ḳ, TA) and ـُ, (TA,) inf. n. غَنْظٌ, (Ṣ, O, TA,) *It*, (an affair, or event, Ṣ, O, Ḳ, TA,) and *he*, (a man, O, TA,) *distressed him*. (Ṣ, O, Ḳ, TA.) And *It*, or *he, filled him with wrath*. (TA.) And *It* (anxiety) *clave*, or *kept constantly, to him*; as also ♦ اغنظه. (TA.) [See also غَنْظٌ below.]

3. غانظه, inf. n. غِنَاظٌ, *He acted with him contrariously*, or *adversely, and inimically, each doing to the other that which was distressing*, or *grievous*; syn. شَاقَّهُ. (TA.)

4: see the first paragraph.

Q. Q. 1. غَنْظَى بِهِ *He reviled him*; *made him to hear that which was disliked, hated*, or *abominable*; (Ṣ, O;) like عَنْظَى بِهِ. (Ḳ.)

غَنْظٌ [an inf. n.: used as a simple subst.,] *Grief*, or *distress*, syn. كَرْبٌ, (IDrd, Ṣ, O, Ḳ, TA,) as also ♦ غَنَظٌ, (IDrd, O,) and مَشَقَّةٌ, (TA,) [or] *such as is vehement*, (TA,) [or] *such as is most vehement*: (Ṣ, TA:) and, (Ḳ,) accord. to IF, (O,) *constant anxiety*; (O, Ḳ;) as also ♦ غَنَظٌ : (Ḳ:) and, (Ḳ,) accord. to AO, (Ṣ, O,) a man's *being at the point of death* (Ṣ, O, Ḳ) *by reason of distress*, or *grief, and then escaping therefrom*. (Ṣ, O.) It is related of 'Omar Ibn-'Abd-el-'Azeez, that he mentioned death, and said, غَنْظٌ لَيْسَ كَالغَنْظِ وَكَظٌّ لَيْسَ كَالكَظِّ [i. e. *Distress*, &c., *that is not like* other *distress*, &c., *and grief*, &c., *that is not like* other *grief*, &c.: see كَظٌّ]. (Ṣ, O.) [See also غِنَاظٌ.]

غَنَظٌ : see غَنْظٌ, in two places. — Also *A plant's becoming altered* [*for the worse*] *by heat*. (Ibn-'Abbád, O.)

غِنَاظٌ : see an ex. of its dual in the next paragraph.

غِنَاظٌ inf. n. of 3 [q. v.]. (TA.) — And *Distress*; syn. جَهْدٌ, and كَرْبٌ : El-Fak'asee says, [of a camel,]

• تَنْتَحُ ذِفْرَاهُ مِنَ الغِنَاظِ •

[*His two protuberances behind the ears drip with sweat by reason of distress*]. (TA.) [See also غَنْظٌ.] فَعَلَ ذٰلِكَ غِنَاظَيْكَ, as also ♦ غَنَاظَيْكَ, (Ḳ,) or, accord. to Lḥ, غِنَاظَيْكَ and غَنَاظَيْكَ, with غ and ع, (TA, [in which it is implied that غِنَاظَيْكَ is wrong, but this I think improbable,]) means *He did that in order to distress thee time after time*; (Ḳ;) like غِيَاظَيْكَ and غَيَاظَيْكَ. (Ḳ in art. غيظ.)

غَنِيظٌ *Unripe dates that are cut off from the palm-trees*, (AA, O, Ḳ,) *after they have become yellow* or *red*, or *that are upon the racemes when the fruit of the palm-tree is cut off*, (AA, O,) *and are left* (AA, O, Ḳ) *upon the racemes* (Ḳ) *until they become ripe*. (AA, O, Ḳ.)

غَنَّاظٌ an epithet applied by Ru-beh, or by El-'Ajjáj, to a sword [app. as meaning *That causes*, or *causing, much distress*]. (IDrd, O, TA.)

غِنْظِيَانٌ A man *foul, unseemly*, or *obscene, in speech*; (Aṣ, O, Ḳ, TA;) *coarse, rude*, or *rough*: (O, TA:) or *who mocks at, derides*, or *ridicules, others*: (Ibn-'Abbád, O, TA:) and عِنْظِيَانٌ signifies the same: fem. with ة. (O, TA.)

هُوَ أَغْنَظُهُمْ *He is the most vehemently grieved*, or *distressed, of them*. (TA.)

مَغْنُوظٌ *Distressed*. (Ṣ, TA.) [See also 1, of which it is the pass. part. n.]

رَجُلٌ مُغَانِظٌ (Ṣ, O) *A man acting*, or *who acts, with another, contrariously*, or *adversely, and inimically, each doing to the other that which is distressing*, or *grievous*; syn. مُشَاقٌّ. (O.)

غنم

1. غَنِمَ, (Ṣ, Mṣb, Ḳ,) aor. ـَ, (Mṣb,) inf. n. غُنْمٌ (Ṣ, MA, Mṣb,* Ḳ, KL) and غَنْمٌ, (Ḳ,) or, as some say, the former is a simple subst. and the latter is an inf. n., (TA,) and غَنَمٌ and غَنِيمَةٌ and غُنْمَانٌ, (Ḳ,) *He*, or *they*, (i. e. a man, Mṣb, or a party of men, Ṣ,) *obtained, got*, or *took*, (Mṣb, Ḳ,* TḲ,) *spoil*, (Ḳ,* TḲ,) or a thing [*as spoil*]. (Mṣb, TA.) [And *He acquired*, or *gained*, a thing *without difficulty*, or *trouble*, or *inconvenience*: or in this sense the inf. n. is غُنْمٌ,

which see below, voce غَنِيمَةٌ.] مَا غَنِمْتُمْ in the Ḳur viii. 42 means *What ye take by force* [*in war*] *from the unbelievers.* (Bḍ, Jel.) [See also 8.]

2. غَنَّمْتُهُ, inf. n. تَغْنِيمٌ, *I gave him spoil,* or *a free and disinterested gift;* syn. نَفَّلْتُهُ: (Ṣ:) or غَنَّمَهُ كَذَا, inf. n. as above, *he gave him such a thing as spoil,* or *as a free and disinterested gift;* syn. نَفَّلَهُ إِيَّاهُ. (Ḳ.)

4. أَغْنَمَهُ الشَّىْءَ *He made the thing to be to him spoil.* (TA.)

5: see 8. — One says also, هُوَ يَتَغَنَّمُ الأَمْرَ, meaning *He eagerly desires the affair like as one eagerly desires spoil.* (TA.) = And تغنّم, (TA in the present art.,) or تغنّم غَنَمًا, (AZ, T and TA in art. ابل,) *He took for himself, got, gained,* or *acquired, sheep* or *goats* or *both:* like as one says تَأَبَّلَ إِبِلًا. (AZ, T and TA in art. ابل; and TA* in the present art.)

8. اغتنمهُ, as also ↓ تغنّمهُ, *He reckoned it spoil:* (Ṣ, Ḳ:) or both signify *he took, seized, caught,* or *snatched, it as spoil.* (KL.) — And [hence] one says, اغتنم الفُرْصَةَ *He took,* or *seized,* or [*availed himself of,*] *the opportunity;* or *he hastened to take it;* syn. اِنْتَهَزَهَا. (Ṣ and A and Ḳ in art. نهز.)

غُنْمٌ: see غَنِيمَةٌ, in three places. — It signifies also [The *regaining* (as is shown by an explanation of A'Obeyd cited in the first paragraph of art. غلق), and] the *increase, and growth, and excess in value,* of a pledge. (O in art. غلق, and TA in the present art.) Thus in a trad., in which it is said, الرَّهْنُ لِمَنْ رَهَنَهُ لَهُ غُنْمُهُ وَعَلَيْهِ غُرْمُهُ [*The pledge pertains to him who pledged it; to him pertains the regaining of it, and its increase, and growth, and excess in value, if such there be, and upon him lies the obligation to pay the debt for it, without requiring any abatement thereof if the pledge have unavoidably suffered damage or total loss:* see the explanation of A'Obeyd mentioned above]. (TA.) الغُنْمُ بِالغُرْمِ means *The* غنم *is compensated* (مُقَابَلٌ) *by the* غرم [i. e. *the regaining* of the pledge, *with the increase and the growth and the excess in value* thereof *if such there be, is compensated by the payment of the debt* for it]; for like as the owner [of the pledge] is exclusively entitled to the غُنْم, no one sharing it with him, so he bears the غُرْم, no one bearing it with him: and this is the meaning of their saying, الغُرْمُ مَجْبُورٌ بِالغُنْمِ [which may therefore be rendered *The loss suffered by the payment of the debt is repaired by the regaining* of the pledge; app. a phrase of the lawyers, implying that such is to be considered as the case whatever be the state of the pledge at the time of its being restored unless it have suffered damage through the fault of the pledgee]. (Mṣb.) [See more in the first paragraph of art. غلق.] — See also غُنَامَاكَ. = غنم [app. غُنْمٌ] is mentioned by Suh as the name of *A certain idol.* (TA.)

غَنَمٌ *i. q.* شَآءٌ, (T, Mṣb, Ḳ,) meaning *Sheep* and *goats;* (Mṣb;) [and *both together;*] a gen. n., (Ṣ, Mṣb, Ḳ,) of the fem. gender, (Ṣ, Ḳ,) applied to the *males* and the *females,* and to *both together:* (Ṣ, Mṣb, Ḳ:) it has no sing. from which it is derived, the sing. being شَاةٌ: the dual غَنَمَانِ is used as meaning *two flocks* or *herds* [*of sheep* or *of goats* or *of both together*]; (Mṣb, Ḳ;) each flock or herd having its distinct place of pasture and its pastor: (Mṣb, TA:*) and hence it is said in a trad. that the poor-rate [meaning a portion thereof] is to be given to him to whom the year of drought has left a غَنَم, but not to him to whom it has left غَنَمَيْنِ: (TA:) the pl. is أَغْنَامٌ, (Mṣb, Ḳ,) [properly a pl. of pauc.,] sometimes used, (Mṣb,) meaning flocks or herds of غَنَم, (Mṣb and TA in art. ابل,) and also غُنُومٌ and أَغَانِمُ, (Ḳ,) the last used in an ode of Aboo-Jundab El-Hudhalee: (TA:) the dim. is ↓ غُنَيْمَةٌ, with ة, because quasi-pl. ns. of the class having no sing. from which they are derived, when applied to what are not human beings, are constantly fem.; so one says خَمْسٌ مِنَ الغَنَمِ ذُكُورٌ [*five of sheep, males*], making the n. of number fem., though one means *rams,* when it is followed by مِنَ الغَنَمِ, for the n. of number is masc. and fem. accord. to the word, not accord. to the meaning. (Ṣ.) — In the saying لَا آتِيكَ غَنَمَ الفِزْرِ i. e. حَتَّى تَجْتَمِعَ غَنَمُ الفِزْرِ [*I will not come to thee until the sheep,* or *goats, of El-Fizr congregate*], غنم [with its complement] is made to stand in the place of الدَّهْرَ, [the meaning being, *I will not come to thee ever,*] and is [therefore] put in the accus. case as though it were an adv. n. [of time]. (TA. [This saying with مِعْزَى in the place of غَنَم is mentioned by El-Meydánee in his "Proverbs," and thus in the Ṣ and Ḳ in art. فزر. For an explanation of its origin see Freytag's Arab. Prov. ii. 484.]) — الأَغْنَامُ is the name of † *Certain small stars between the legs of Cepheus and the star* الجَدْىُ. (Ḳzw, in his descr. of Cepheus.) [See شَاةٌ (in art. شوه), last sentence.]

غَنِيمٌ: see what next follows.

غَنِيمَةٌ and ↓ مَغْنَمٌ (Ṣ, Mṣb, Ḳ) and ↓ غَنِيمٌ and ↓ غُنْمٌ all signify فَىْءٌ [as meaning *Spoil, booty,* or *plunder*]: and the *acquisition* of a thing *without difficulty,* or *trouble,* or *inconvenience:* or this is termed ↓ غُنْمٌ, and فَىْءٌ is termed غَنِيمَةٌ: (Ḳ:) or, accord. to A'Obeyd, الغَنِيمَةُ signifies *what is obtained from the believers in a plurality of gods, by force, during war;* (Mgh, Mṣb:) *and of this, a fifth is to be taken,* [*and applied in the manner prescribed in the Ḳur viii.* 42,] *and what remains after the fifth is for those who have obtained it, exclusively;* (Mgh;) *the horseman having three shares, and the foot-soldier having one share:* (Az, TA:) and الفَىْءُ signifies what is obtained from them after the laying-down of arms, (Mgh, Mṣb,) when the country, or place, becomes a country, or place, of Islám; and this is for all of the Muslims, and is not to be divided into fifths: (Mgh:) or the فَىْءُ is what God has given, or restored, of the possessions of the believers in a plurality of gods, to the Muslims, without war, such as the poll-tax, and that for which peace has been made with them; and of this also a fifth is to be applied in the manner prescribed by God, and the remainder is to be expended in the purchase of horses and weapons and other apparatus for the defence of the frontiers: (Az, TA:) and النَّفَلُ is what is given to the warrior in addition to his share; and is when the Imám or the commander says, "He who slays one shall have his spoil;" or says to a detachment, "What ye obtain shall be yours," or "the quarter of it," or "the half of it;" and it is not divided into fifths; and it lies on the Imám to fulfil the promise: or, accord. to 'Alee Ibn-'Eesà, الغَنِيمَةُ is more general in signification than النَّفَلُ; and الفَىْءُ is more so than الغَنِيمَةُ, because it is a name for everything of the possessions of the believers in a plurality of gods that becomes the property of the Muslims: accord. to the lawyers, everything that may be lawfully taken, of their possessions, is فَىْءٌ: (Mgh:) the pl. of غَنِيمَةٌ is غَنَائِمُ; and the pl. of ↓ مَغْنَمٌ is مَغَانِمُ, (Mṣb, TA,) and غُنُومٌ occurs as pl. of ↓ غُنْمٌ. (TA.) غَنِيمَةٌ بَارِدَةٌ see expl. in art. برد.

غُنَيْمَةٌ dim. of غَنَمٌ, q. v. (Ṣ.)

غُنَامَاكَ أَنْ تَفْعَلَ كَذَا (Ṣ, Ḳ,* TA) means *The utmost of thy power,* or *ability,* and *of thy case,* (Ṣ,* TA,) and *that which thou eagerly desirest like as one desires spoil,* (Ṣ,* JM, TA,*) [*is,* or *will be, thy doing such a thing;*] i. q. قُصَارَاكَ: (Ḳ, TA: [see also عُنَانَاكَ, in art. عن:]) and so ↓ غُنْمُكَ: (TA:) and [in like manner] one says, حُسَيْنَاؤُهُ, like غُنَيْمَاؤُهُ أَنْ يَفْعَلَ كَذَا, meaning قُصَارَاهُ [*The utmost of his power,* &c.]. (TA in art. حسن.)

غُنَيْمَاؤُهُ: see what next precedes.

غَانِمٌ *Taking,* or *a taker, of* غَنِيمَة [or *spoil*]. (TA.) — See also two exs. voce شَاجِبٌ.

مَغْنَمٌ: see غَنِيمَةٌ, in two places.

غَنَمٌ مُغَنَّمَةٌ and مُغْنَمَةٌ *Sheep,* or *goats, collected together:* (TA:) or *many* or *numerous:* (Ḳ, TA:) or, accord. to AZ, one of these two epithets, thus applied, [probably the latter, like مُؤَبَّلَةٌ applied to إِبِل, as he seems to say,] signifies [app. *divided into distinct flocks* or *herds,*] *each* [*flock* or *herd*] *having its own pastor.* (TA.)

غنو

غَنْوَةٌ: see the art. here following.

غنى

1. غَنِىَ, (Ṣ, MA, Mṣb, Ḳ,*) from المَال, aor. يَغْنَى, (Mṣb,) inf. n. غِنًى (Ṣ,* MA, Mṣb, Ḳ*) and غَنَآءٌ, (MA, Ḳ,* TḲ, [but the latter is app. held by some to be a simple subst.,]) *He was,* or *became, free from want; in the state,* or *condition, of having no wants;* and also, *of having* *few wants; or in a state of competence, or sufficiency; or rich, or wealthy;* الغِنَى being *the contr.* of الفَقْرُ, as also الغَنَآءُ; (Ḳ, TA;) and thus denoting the absence, or non-existence, of wants, which is [properly, or strictly speaking,] attributable to none but God; and also the paucity of wants; (TA;) or *syn. with* اليَسَارُ: (Ṣ:) and the epithet applied to him of whom this is said is ▼ غَنِىٌّ, (Ṣ:) or ▼ غَانٍ, (Mṣb,) [or both, for] both signify the same [as will be shown below]. (Ḳ.) One says غَنِىَ and ▼ استغنى and ▼ تغنّى and ▼ تغانى and ▼ اغتنى, (Ḳ, TA, [but wanting in the CḲ, and app. in several copies of the Ḳ, though it is said in one place in the Ḳ, as it is in the Ṣ, that تغنّى is syn. with استغنى,]) all having one and the same meaning, and followed by بِهِ [as therewith signifying *He was,* or *became, free from want; in the state,* or *condition, of having no want,* or *need;* or *in a state of competence,* &c.; *by means of it,* or *him;* i. e. *he was,* or *became, sufficed by it,* or *him;* and hence, *he was,* or *became, content,* or *satisfied, with it,* or *him*]. (TA.) لَيْسَ مِنَّا مَنْ لَمْ يَتَغَنَّ ▼ بِالقُرْآنِ, (Mṣb, TA,) a saying of the Prophet, (Mṣb,) mentioned in a trad., (TA,) means من لم ▼ يَسْتَغْنِ [i. e. *He is not of us who is not content,* or *satisfied, with the Ḳur-án*]: so says Sufyán Ibn-'Oyeyneh; not regarding it as meaning the utterance of the voice [in chanting]: and A'Obeyd says that this obtains extensively in the speech of the Arabs; that they say ▼ تَغَانَيْتُ and ▼ تَغَنَّيْتُ in the sense of ▼ اِسْتَغْنَيْتُ. (Az, Mṣb, TA.) And one says, غَنِىَ عَنْهُ, inf. n. غِنًى and غُنْيَانٌ, meaning *He was in no need of it* [or *him*]: as also ▼ أَغْنَى عنه and ▼ استغنى عنه; [which seems to be rarely used in this sense]: and ▼ غُنْيَةٌ signifies the *state of being in no need:* and ▼ غَانٍ, a man *free from need.* (MA.) [And مَا ▼ يَسْتَغْنِى عَنْهُ *He is not without need,* or *not free from want, of it,* or *him.*] And غَنِىَ بِهِ عَنْهُ, (Ṣ, Mṣb,) i. e. عَنْ غَيْرِهِ, (Mṣb,) inf. n. غُنْيَةٌ, (Ṣ,) or ▼ غُنْيَةٌ is the subst., (Mṣb,) meaning ▼ استغنى [*He was sufficed by it,* or *was satisfied,* or *content, with it, so as to be in no need,* or *so as to be free from want, of it,* i. e. *of another thing*]: and the epithet is ▼ غَنِىٌّ. (Mṣb.) And [in like manner] غَنِيَتِ المَرْأَةُ بِزَوْجِهَا عَنْ غَيْرِهِ (Ṣ, Mṣb, Ḳ) (Mṣb,) inf. n. غُنْيَانٌ (Ṣ, Ḳ) and غَنَآءٌ also, (TA,) meaning ▼ اِسْتَغْنَتْ [*The woman was satisfied,* or *content, with her husband, so as to have no want of other than him*]. (Ṣ, Ḳ.) And غَنِيَتْ [alone], (Ḳ, TA,) inf. n. غِنًا [for غِنًى, or perhaps a mistranscription for غَنَآءٌ, as in the next preceding sentence], *She* (a woman) *was,* or *became, such as is termed* غَانِيَةٌ [q. v. voce غَانٍ]. (Ḳ.) — غَنِىَ, (TḲ,) inf. n. غِنًى, (Ḳ, TḲ,) also signifies *He married,* or *took a wife;* [as also ▼ تَغَنَّى; (see Ḥam p. 226 l. 1, where تَغَنَّتْ occurs said of a wo n as meaning *she married;*)] syn. تَزَوَّجَ. (Ḳ,* TḲ. [In the Ḳ, only the inf. n. of the former verb in this sense is mentioned; الغِنَى being there expl. in some copies as signifying التَّزَوُّجُ; and in others, التَّزْوِيجُ.]) Hence the saying, الغِنَى حِصْنٌ لِلْعَزَبِ [*Marriage is a bulwark to him who has no wife;* protecting him from the attacks of seductive women by rendering him free from the want of them]: mentioned by Az. (TA.) — Also, غَنِىَ, (Ṣ, Ḳ,) inf. n. غِنًى, (TA,) *He dwelt,* or *abode,* (Ṣ, Ḳ,) بِالمَكَانِ *in the place:* (Ṣ:) or غَنِىَ القَوْمُ فِى دَارِهِمْ *The people,* or *party, dwelt long in their place of abode:* (T, TA:) or غَنِىَ فِى مَكَانِ كَذَا *He dwelt long in such a place, satisfied,* or *content, therewith, so as to be in no need of any other.* (Er-Rághib, TA.) كَأَنْ لَمْ يَغْنَوْا فِيهَا, in the Ḳur [vii. 90 and xi. 71 and 98], means *As though they had not dwelt therein.* (TA.) [See also the last sentence but two in this paragraph.] — And *He lived;* syn. عَاشَ. (Ṣ, Ḳ.) — And *I. q.* بَقِىَ: (TA:) one says, غَنِيتُ لَكَ مِنِّى بِالمَوَدَّةِ, meaning بَقِيتُ [i. e. *I remained,* or *have remained, constant to thee with my love,* or *affection*]. (ISd, Ḳ, TA: in the CḲ [erroneously] غَنَيْتُ.) — [And *I. q.* كَانَ.] قَدْ أَغْنَى الحَبِيبَ, in a verse of Ibn-Muḳbil, means أَكُونُ المُصَافِىَ الحَبِيبَ [i. e. *Certainly I will be,* or *shall be, the sincere friend*]. (TA.) And غَنِيَتْ دَارُنَا تِهَامَةَ, (Ḳ, TA,) in a verse of another poet, (TA,) means كَانَتْ [i. e. *Our place of abode was Tihámeh*]. (Ḳ, TA.) And one says of a thing when it has perished, passed away, or come to nought, كَأَنْ لَمْ يَغْنَ بِالأَمْسِ, meaning كَأَنْ لَمْ يَكُنْ [i. e. *As though it had not been in existence yesterday*]. (Az, TA.) = غَنِىَ also signifies لَقِىَ: (Ḳ:) [SM doubts this; saying,] thus in the copies; but perhaps it should be بَقِىَ, a signification of غَنِىَ accord. to ISd and the Ḳ [and mentioned above]: (TA:) [it appears, however, to be correct; for it is said that] مَا غَنِيتُ فُلَانًا means لَمْ أَلْقَهُ [i. e. *I did not meet,* or *meet with,* or *find,* or *I have not met,* &c., *such a one*]. (JK.) [Accord. to the TḲ, غَنِىَ followed by بِهِ signifies لَقِىَ: but this is perhaps said conjecturally.]

2: see 4. = غَنَّى, (Ṣ, MA, Mṣb,) inf. n. تَغْنِيَةٌ, (KL,) as syn. with ▼ تغنّى, (Ṣ, MA, Mṣb,*) *He sang,* or *chanted,* (Ṣ,* MA, KL;) or *he trilled,* or *quavered,* or *prolonged his voice and modulated it sweetly, singing,* or *chanting.* (Mṣb in explanation of the former.) You say غَنَّاهُ الشِّعْرَ [*He sang,* or *chanted, to him the poetry*], and غنّى بِهِ [*he sang,* or *chanted, it,* i. e., the poetry], inf. n. تَغْنِيَةٌ; and ▼ تغنّى بِهِ; and غنّى and تغنّى having one and the same meaning. (Ḳ, TA.) ▼ يَتَغَنَّى بِالقُرْآنِ, in a trad. cited in the first paragraph of art. اذن, means, as expl. by Esh-Sháfi'ee, *Reciting* [or *chanting*] *the Ḳur-án with a plaintive and gentle voice.* (Az, Mṣb, TA. [See also that trad. somewhat differently related voce تَرَنَّمَ.]) — غَنَّى is also said of a pigeon, meaning *It* [*cooed,* or] *uttered a cry;* (Ḳ, TA;) and so ▼ تغنّى. (TA.) — غنّى بِالمَرْأَةِ means تَغَزَّلَ بِهَا, (Ḳ, TA,) i. e. *He mentioned the woman* [*in amatory language, as an object of love,*] *in his poetry:* (TA:) and غنّى بِزَيْدٍ *He eulogized Zeyd:* or *he satirized him:* like ▼ تغنّى in these two senses: (Ḳ, TA:) in that of eulogizing and that of satirizing: or, in the opinion of ISd, both of the verbs are used in these two senses and likewise in the sense mentioned immediately before them; meaning that *he did thus after prolonging and modulating his voice; singing,* or *chanting, the same,* i. e. the غَزَل and the eulogy and the satire. (TA.)

3: see غَنَآءٌ. [From what is there said, it seems that غاناهُ signifies *He was in no need of him,* or *it;* like غَنِىَ عَنْهُ and استغنى عنه: compare تَغَانَوْا.] = And app. it signifies also *He spoke,* or *talked, to him,* i. e. to a child, or boy, *saying to him what was pleasing to him;* for it is said that] المُغَانَاةُ means تَعْلِيلُكَ الصَّبِىَّ بِمَا يَهْوَى. (JK.)

4. اغناهُ *He* (i. e. God, Ṣ, Ḳ, TA, [but wanting in the CḲ and app. in several copies of the Ḳ,]) *rendered him,* or *made him to be, in no need,* or *free from want;* (Ṣ,* MA, Ḳ;*) [or *in a state of competence,* or *sufficiency;*] or *possessed of wealth;* (Ṣ,* Ḳ,* TA;) [or *rich,* or *wealthy;* (see 1, first sentence;)] and ▼ غنّاهُ signifies the same; (Ḳ, TA; [but wanting in the CḲ and app. in several copies of the Ḳ;]) or, as some say, this latter is [used] in prayer [app. as meaning *he said to him, May God enrich thee,* or *the like:* compare سَقَّيْتُهُ ("I said to him, May God send down rain to thee"), and عَقَّرْتُهُ (as expl. in art. عقر), &c.]. (TA.) [And اغناهُ عَنْ كَذَا *He,* or *it, caused him to be in no need,* or *free from want, of such a thing.* (See Ḥam p. 152.) And يُغْنِى عَنْ أَنْ تَفْعَلَ كَذَا *It renders needless thy doing such a thing:* lit. *it causes that there shall be no need of thy doing such a thing.*] — And اغنى عَنْهُ كَذَا *Such a thing sufficed him;* or *stood him in stead:* whence the saying in the Ḳur [lxix. 28], مَا أَغْنَى عَنِّى مَالِيَهْ [*My property has not sufficed me, or stood me in stead*]: and [in iii. 8 and lviii. 18 of the same,] لَنْ تُغْنِىَ عَنْهُمْ أَمْوَالُهُمْ [*Their possessions will not suffice them* in lieu of God]: (Er-Rághib, TA:) or this last means, *will not defend them* from God, i. e. from his punishment. (Jel in iii. 8.) And ▼ أَغْنَيْتُ عَنْكَ مُغْنَى فُلَانٍ and ▼ مُغْنَاتَهُ, (Ṣ, Mṣb, Ḳ,*) and ▼ مَغْنَى فُلَانٍ and ▼ مَغْنَاتَهُ, (Ṣ, Mgh, Ḳ,) and ▼ غَنَآءَ فُلَانٍ, (Ḳ,) *I sufficed,* or *satisfied,* or *contented, thee,* or *I have sufficed,* &c., *as such a one;* or *I stood thee,* or *served thee,* or *I have stood* &c., *in the stead of such a one.* (Ṣ,* Mgh, Mṣb, Ḳ.) And مَا يُغْنِى عَنْكَ هٰذَا *This does not suffice,* or *satisfy,* or *content, thee;* or *stand thee,* or *serve thee, in any stead;* and *does not avail,* or *profit, thee.*

(Ṣ.) AZ mentions مَا أَغْنَى فُلَانٌ شَيْئًا, thus, and with ع, [i. e. أَعْنَى,] as meaning *Such a one did not avail,* or *profit, at all, in a difficult,* or *an arduous, affair* or *case;* and *did not suffice for such an affair* or *such a case,* or *for the supply of what was necessary for subsistence.* (Mṣb, TA.) And he says also that he heard a man chide his slave, and say to him, أَغْنِ عَنِّى وَجْهَكَ بَلْ شَرَّكَ, meaning *Free me from,* and *avert from me,* [*thy face, nay, rather,*] *thy evil,* or *mischief:* and hence the phrase شَأْنٌ يُغْنِيهِ, [respecting which see the second sentence in art. عنى,] in the Ḳur [lxxx. 37]. (TA.) [Hence also,] وَمَا أُغْنِى عَنْكُمْ مِنَ ٱللّٰهِ مِنْ شَىْءٍ, in the Ḳur xii. 67, means *But I do not avert from you,* by my saying this, *anything* decreed to befall you *from God:* the second من is redundant. (Jel.) And one says, أَغْنِ عَنِّى كَذَا, meaning *Put thou away from me,* and *remove far from me, such a thing:* properly [أَغْنِنِى عَنْ كَذَا, originally meaning *render thou me in no need of such a thing,*] a phrase of the same kind as عَرَضَ الدَّابَّةَ عَلَى المَآءِ [for عرض المَآءَ عَلَى الدَّابَّةِ]. (Mgh.) — أَغْنَى عَنْهُ as intrans.: see 1, former half. — مَا أَغْنَاهُ [*How free from wants,* or *how rich,* or *wealthy, is he!*]: this and مَا أَفْقَرَهُ are [said to be] anomalous; for their [respective] verbs are استغنى and افتقر, from either of which the verb of wonder may not properly [or regularly] be formed. (Ṣ in art. فقر.) [But see غَنِىَ as syn. with استغنى; and see also art. فقر.])

5: see 1, former half, in three places: — and again in the latter half: — and see also 2, in five places.

6: see 1, former half, in two places. — تَغَانَوْا means *They were,* or *became, free from want, one of another,* or, as we say, *of one another.* (Ṣ, Ḳ.) El-Mugheereh Ibn-Ḥabnà says,

كِلَانَا غَنِىٌّ ▼ عَنْ أَخِيهِ حَيَاتَهُ •
وَنَحْنُ إِذَا مُتْنَا أَشَدُّ تَغَانِيَا •

[*Each of us is free from want of his brother in his life-time; and when we die, we shall be more free from such want*]. (Ṣ.)

8: see 1, second sentence.

10: see 1, in seven places. — استغنى ٱللّٰهَ *He asked,* or *begged, God to render him,* or *make him to be, in no need,* or *free from want;* [or *in a state of competence,* or *sufficiency;*] or *rich,* or *wealthy.* (Ḳ, TA. [But wanting in the CḲ, and app. in several copies of the Ḳ.]) Hence the prayer, اَللّٰهُمَّ إِنِّى أَسْتَغْنِيكَ عَنْ كُلِّ حَازِمٍ وَأَسْتَعِينُكَ [*O God, I ask Thee to render me in no need of any one who refuses to give, and I beg thine aid*]. (TA.)

غَنًى, (Ḳ, TA,) with fet-ḥ, and مَقْصُور, (TA,) i. q. مَئِنَّةٌ; so in the saying, مَكَانُ كَذَا غَنًى مِنْ فُلَانٍ [*Such a place is meet, fit,* or *proper, for such a one;* as though meaning a place of freedom from want]; as also ▼ مَغْنًى مِنْهُ. (Ḳ, TA.)

غِنًى and ▼ غَنَآءٌ signify the same; (MA, Ḳ;) both are inf. ns. of غَنِىَ: (MA:) [see the first sentence of this art.: used as simple substs., they mean *Freedom from need* or *want; competence,* or *sufficiency;* or *richness,* or *wealthiness:*] or غِنًى is the inf. n. of غَنِىَ; (Mṣb;) and ▼ غَنَآءٌ signifies *competence,* or *sufficiency;* (Mgh, Mṣb;) as in the saying, لَيْسَ عِنْدَهُ غَنَآءٌ *He has not competence,* or *sufficiency:* (Mṣb:) or غَنَآءٌ signifies *profit, utility,* or *avail;* (Ṣ;) and you say, رَجُلٌ لَا غَنَآءَ عِنْدَهُ meaning *A man who is not profitable to any one:* (TA voce دَدَانٌ; [and in like manner this phrase, occurring in the Ṣ voce دَدَانٌ, is expl. in the PṢ:]) and ▼ غُنْوَةٌ signifies the same as غِنًى in the saying لِى عَنْهُ غُنْوَةٌ [*I have no need of it,* or *him*]: (Ḳ and TA in art. غنو:) so says Ks: but, as ISd says, the word commonly known is ▼ غُنْيَةٌ; (TA in that art.;) which see in two places in the former half of the first paragraph of this art.: this last word [said in the Ṣ to be an inf. n.] and ▼ غِنْيَةٌ and ▼ غُنْوَةٌ and ▼ غُنْيَانٌ [which is said in the Ṣ and in one place in the Ḳ to be an inf. n.] are substs. having one and the same meaning [*syn.* with غِنًى used as a simple subst.]: and مَا لَهُ عَنْهُ غِنًى [in the CḲ erroneously غَنًى] and ▼ غُنْيَةٌ and ▼ غُنْيَانٌ and ▼ مُغْنًى mean [lit. *He has not freedom from need of it,* or *him;* and hence,] *he has not any means,* or *way, of separating himself from,* or *avoiding, it,* or *him;* syn. بُدٌّ: (Ḳ:) and one says فِى النِّكَاحِ غُنْيَةٌ ▼ عَنِ السِّفَاحِ [*In marriage is freedom from need of fornication*]. (A and Mṣb in art. سفح.) مَا كَانَ عَنْ ظَهْرِ غِنًى, in a trad. respecting alms, means *What is over and above that which suffices for the sustenance of the household,* or *family.* (TA.)

غُنْوَةٌ: see the next preceding paragraph, in two places.

غُنْيَةٌ and غِنْيَةٌ: see غِنًى; the former in three places.

غُنْيَانٌ: see غِنًى, latter half, in two places.

غَنَآءٌ: see غِنًى, in two places; and see also 4, former half. A poet says,

سَيُغْنِينِى ٱلَّذِى أَغْنَاكَ عَنِّى •
فَلَا فَقْرٌ يَدُومُ وَلَا غَنَآءُ •

[*He will render me free from need who has rendered thee free from need of me: for poverty will not always continue, nor competence,* or *richness*]: or, as some relate it, غِنَآءُ, meaning thereby the inf. n. of ▼ غَانَيْتُ: [see 3, above:] but it is said that the proper reading is غَنَآءُ; because this has no other meaning than that of غِنًى: so says ISd. (TA.) — مَا فِيهِ غَنَآءُ ذَاكَ means *There is not in him* [*ability for*] *the setting-up of that, and strength,* or *power, to bear it,* or *carry it,* or *to raise it upon his back and rise with it.* (ISd, Ḳ, TA.)

غِنَآءٌ is an inf. n. of 3. (TA. [See the next preceding paragraph.]) — Also, (TA,) [*Song,* or *vocal music;* i. e.] *an utterance of the voice with a prolonging and a sweet modulation thereof;* (Ḳ, TA;) or *a raising of the voice, and continuing it without interruption;* (Nh, TA;) [*a singing,* and *a chanting;*] it is said in the Ṣ to be مِنَ السَّمَاعِ [meaning that it is *a sort of musical performance*]: (TA:) being *an utterance of the voice,* its analogical form would be with ḍamm [i. e. غُنَآءٌ, like حُدَآءٌ &c.]: (Mṣb, TA:) its pl. is أَغْنِيَةٌ: (MA:) [and ▼ مَغْنًى signifies *the same as* غِنَآءٌ; and *a mode of singing;* and *any particular air,* or *tune;* and *a song,* i. e. *a composition in verse that is sung* or *to be sung:* and its pl. is مَغَانٍ: but perhaps it is post-classical: the pl. occurs in the Ḳ, in art. نصب:] غِنَآءٌ [also] signifies [*a song,* i. e.] *poetry,* or *verse, that is* [*sung,* or *chanted,* or] *uttered with a trilling,* or *quavering,* or *a prolonging and a sweet modulation, of the voice;* (Ḥar p. 286;) and ▼ أُغْنِيَّةٌ is syn. with غِنَآءٌ (Ṣ, Ḥar) in this sense; (Ḥar;) or, as also ▼ إِغْنِيَّةٌ, (Fr, Ḳ, TA,) and ▼ each of them also without teshdeed, (Ḳ, TA,) as mentioned by ISd, but said by him to be not of valid authority, (TA,) signifies *a certain sort of* غِنَآء (Ḳ, TA) *which they sing* or *chant:* (TA:) and the pl. is أَغَانِىُّ (Ṣ, TA) [and أَغَانٍ, this latter being the pl. of each sing. that is without teshdeed]. — الغِنَآءُ is also used by a poet in the place of an inf. n., meaning التَّغَنِّى: he says,

تَغَنَّ بِالشِّعْرِ إِمَّا كُنْتَ قَائِلَهُ •
إِنَّ الغِنَآءَ بِهٰذَا الشِّعْرِ مِضْمَارُ •

[*Sing thou,* or *chant thou, the poetry, if thou be uttering it: verily the singing,* or *chanting, this poetry is a* مضمار (expl. in art. ضمر)]. (TA.)

غَنِىٌّ and ▼ غَانٍ: see 1, former half; each in two places: both signify [*Free from want;* or *in a state of competence,* or *sufficiency;* or *rich,* or *wealthy;* or] *possessing much property* or *wealth:* (Ḳ,* TA:) pl. of the former أَغْنِيَآءُ. (Mṣb, TA.) See an ex. of the former in a verse cited above, conj. 6. One says, أَنَا غَنِىٌّ بِكَذَا عَنْ غَيْرِهِ [*I am sufficed by such a thing,* or *satisfied,* or *content, with it, so as to be free from want of another thing*]. (Mṣb.) — الغَنِىُّ as a name of God signifies [*The Self-sufficient;* i. e.] *He who has no need of any one in any thing.* (TA.)

غَنَّآءٌ *A singer;* (MA;) [as also ▼ مُغَنٍّ; and مُغَنِّيَةٌ *a female singer, a songstress:*] accord. to Ibn-Ya'eesh, a ▼ مُغَنٍّ is thus called لِأَنَّهُ يُغَنِّنُ صَوْتَهُ, i. e. because he makes his voice to have in it a غُنَّة [or sort of nasal sound, or twang]; the word being, in his opinion, originally, مُغَنِّنٌ, with three ن s, the last of which is changed into ى, when one says المُغَنِّى, for the purpose of alleviating the utterance. (Mughnee, art. حَرْفُ النُّونِ.)

غَانٍ : see غَنِىٌّ. — [The fem.] غَانِيَةٌ signifies *A young woman who is sufficed by her husband; or satisfied, or content, with him,* (Ṣ, Mṣb, TA,*) *so as to be in no need,* or *free from want, of any other:* (Mṣb:) and sometimes, also, applied to a woman, (Ṣ,) *such as is sufficed by her beauty,* (Ṣ, ISd, Ḳ, TA,) *so as to be in no need of decoration* (ISd, Ḳ, TA) *with women's ornaments:* (ISd, TA:) or *such as is sought,* or *desired, by men, but does not seek,* or *desire:* (ISd, Ḳ,* TA:) or *such as has abode in the house,* or *tent, of her father and mother; and whom captivity* (سِبَآء) *has not befallen;* (IJ, ISd, Ḳ,* TA;) which is the strangest of the explanations: (TA:) or *such as is youthful and chaste,* whether *having a husband* or *not:* (ISd, Ḳ, TA:) or, accord. to AO, *one that is married:* (Ḥam p. 226:) or, accord. to Az, *such as pleases men, and is pleased by* شَبَاب [which means both *youthfulness* and *youths* or *young men*]: (TA:) pl. غَوَانٍ; (Ḳ;) with the article, الغَوَانِى; [and also غَانِيَاتٌ: (see an ex. in a verse cited in the second paragraph of art. زج:)] in the saying of Ibn-Er-Ruḳeiyát,

لَا بَارَكَ ٱللّٰهُ فِى الغَوَانِى هَلْ
يُصْبِحْنَ إِلَّا لَهُنَّ مُطَّلَبُ

[*May God not bless those young women that are sufficed by their husbands,* or *by their beauty,* &c.: *do they enter upon the time of dawn without their having desire* (lit. *a time* or *place,* meaning *an occasion, of seeking,* or *desire*)?], the ى is made movent by a poetic license: (Ṣ, TA:) and another poet uses الغَوَانِ for الغَوَانِى. (TA.)

أَغْنَآءٌ [a pl. of which the sing. is not mentioned,] The أَمْلَاكَات [meaning *Goods and chattels,* or *paraphernalia,*] *of brides.* (Az, Ḳ.)

أُغْنِيَّةٌ and إِغْنِيَّةٌ, and each of them also without teshdeed: see غِنَآءٌ, latter half.

مَغْنًى: see 4, former half: — and غَنِىٌّ: — and غِنًى, near the end. — Also *A place in which were its occupants,* or *inhabitants:* (Ṣ:) or *a place of abode by which its occupants,* or *inhabitants, were sufficed,* or *with which they were satisfied,* or *content, and from which they then departed,* or *removed:* or *in a general sense;* (Ḳ, TA;) *a place of abode,* absolutely; but this seems to be a distinct application: (TA:) pl. مَغَانٍ; with the article, المَغَانِى. (Ṣ, TA.) — See also غِنَآءٌ.

مُغْنًى: see 4, former half.

مُغْنٍ [act. part. n. of 4,] A man *sufficing,* or *satisfying,* or *contenting.* (TA.) — المُغْنِى as a name of God signifies *He who satisfies,* or *contents, whom He will, of his servants.* (TA.) — And مُغْنِيَةٌ A woman *who satisfies,* or *contents, her husband, so as to render him in no need of looking at other than her.* (Ḥar p. 451.)

مُغْنَاةٌ and مَغْنَاةٌ: see 4, former half.

مُغَنٍّ; fem. مُغَنِّيَةٌ: see غِنَآءٌ, in two places.

غهب

1. غَهِبَ, [aor. ـَ,] inf. n. غَهَبٌ, *He was unmindful, negligent, inattentive, inadvertent, inconsiderate,* or *heedless.* (Ṣ.) You say, غَهِبَ عَنْهُ *He was unmindful,* &c., and *forgetful, of him,* or *it;* (Ḳ, TA;) as also ↓ اغهب. (TA.) And أَصَابَ صَيْدًا غَهَبًا *He hit an object of the chase,* or *objects thereof, inadvertently, unintentionally.* (A'Obeyd, Ṣ, Ḳ, from a trad.) — And غَهِبَهُ *He was ignorant of it;* as also عَهِبَهُ. (TA in art. عهب.)

4: see the preceding paragraph.

8. اغتهب *He* (a man, TA) *journeyed in the darkness:* (Ḳ, TA:) and *went far away therein.* (TA.)

غِهِبَّى الشَّبَابِ and غِهِبَّاؤُهُ, and likewise with the unpointed ع, *The first part,* or *state, of youth.* (Ḳ, TA.)

غَيْهَبٌ *Darkness;* (Ṣ, A, Ḳ;) as also ↓ غَيْهَبَانٌ: (Ḳ:) pl. of the former غَيَاهِبُ. (Ṣ.) — And A horse, and night, *intensely black:* (Ḳ, TA:) or, instead of وَاللَّيْلِ in the Ḳ, we may read وَاللَّيْلُ; so that the meaning may be, a horse *intensely black:* and *night:* agreeably with the A, in which this latter meaning [as well as the former] is assigned to the word; and it is added that one says, أَحْسَنُ مِنْ بَيَاضِ الكَوْكَبِ فِى سَوَادِ الغَيْهَبِ [*More beautiful than the whiteness of the star in the blackness of night*]: (TA:) or it signifies *intense blackness* of the night* and of a camel and the like: you say جَمَلٌ غَيْهَبٌ *a deep-black camel:* (Lth, TA:) and also أَسْوَدُ غَيْهَبٌ and غَيْهَمٌ: (Lḥ, TA:) and رَجُلٌ غَيْهَبٌ *a black man;* likened to the darkness of night: and لَيْلٌ غَيْهَبٌ *a dark night:* (Sh, TA:) and فَرَسٌ أَدْهَمُ غَيْهَبٌ *a horse intensely black:* (Sh, Ṣ, TA:) and it is said in "the Book of Horses" by A'Obeyd that أَدْهَمُ ↓ غَيْهَبِىٌّ signifies [a horse] *of the deepest black hue:* that the fem. is غَيْهَبَةٌ; and the pl., غَيَاهِبُ; and that دَجُوجِىٌّ is less than غَيْهَبٌ in blackness, signifying "of a clear black hue." (TA.) — Also, applied to a man, *Unmindful, negligent, inattentive, inadvertent, inconsiderate,* or *heedless:* (Ḳ, TA:) and *weak,* and *timid:* (TA:) or (Ḳ, TA, but in the CḲ "and,") a *heavy, troublesome* man: or *stupid, dull,* or *wanting in intelligence;* or *inert,* or *wanting in vigour.* (Ḳ, TA.) And *Lacking ability to seek his blood-revenge,* or *retaliation;* as also عَيْهَبٌ. (TA in art. عهب.) — And A [garment of the kind called] كِسَآء *having much wool; very woolly;* (Ḳ, TA;) as also عَيْهَبٌ. (TA.) — And *A male ostrich.* (R, TA.)

غَيْهَبَةٌ *A clamour,* or *confused noise,* (Ḳ, TA,) and *commotion,* (TA,) *in fight,* or *conflict.* (Ḳ, TA.)

غَيْهَبِىٌّ: see غَيْهَبٌ.

غَيْهَبَانٌ: see غَيْهَبٌ. — Also The *belly.* (Ḳ.)

غوى or غو

1. غَوَى, aor. يَغْوِى, inf. n. غَىٌّ (A'Obeyd, Ṣ, Mṣb, Ḳ, TA) and غَوَايَةٌ; (A'Obeyd, Ṣ, TA;) [respecting which latter see what follows;] and غَوِىَ (A'Obeyd, Ḳ, TA, but not in the CḲ,) but this is not commonly known, (TA,) aor. يَغْوَى, inf. n. غَوًى, (A'Obeyd, TA,) accord. to the M and Ḳ غَوَايَةٌ, mentioned above as of غَوَى, (TA,) or this last, which is with fet-ḥ, (Mṣb,) not to be pronounced with kesr, (Ḳ,) is a simple subst.; (Mṣb;) *He erred; deviated from the right way* or *course,* or *from that which was right:* (Ṣ, Mṣb, Ḳ:) and *was disappointed;* or *failed of attaining his desire:* (Ṣ, Mṣb:) and *he laboured, and persisted,* (IAth, Mṣb, TA,) *in that which was vain,* or *false,* (IAth, TA,) or *in ignorant conduct:* (Mṣb:) or *he acted ignorantly from misbelief.* (Er-Rághib, TA.) — See also 4, in two places. — غَوِىَ, aor. يَغْوَى; (Ṣ, Mṣb, Ḳ;) and غَوَى, aor. يَغْوِى; (Ḳ;) inf. n. [of the former] غَوًى; (Ṣ, Ḳ;) said of a young camel, (Ṣ, Mṣb, Ḳ,) and of a lamb or kid, (Ṣ,) *He suffered indigestion from the milk;* (Ḳ, TA;) i. e. (TA) *he drank the milk until he suffered indigestion; and his belly,* or *chest, became in a corrupt state;* (Ṣ, Mṣb,* TA;) or *he drank much thereof, so that he suffered indigestion:* (TA:) or, accord. to ISk, (Ṣ, TA,) *he did not satisfy his thirst with the biestings of his mother,* (Ṣ,) or *he did not drink thereof,* (TA,) *nor satisfy his thirst with the milk* [*after it*], *so that he died of emaciation:* (Ṣ, TA:) or *he* (a kid, AZ, TA) *was withheld from sucking* (AZ, Ḳ, TA) *until hunger injured him* (AZ, TA) *so that he became emaciated,* (AZ, Ḳ, TA,) *and almost perished:* (Ḳ:) or *he obtained not sufficient milk to satisfy his thirst so that he almost perished:* (T, TA:) or, said of a child, and of a young camel, *he found not a sufficiency of milk, so that he did not satisfy his thirst, and was seen to be meagre,* or *emaciated;* thus accord. to ISh; and Sh says that his companions held this to be the correct meaning: (TA:) the epithet applied to the young camel [&c.] is ↓ غَوٍ. (Ḳ.) Z has mentioned the reading in the Ḳur [xx. 119], وَعَصَى آدَمُ رَبَّهُ فَغَوِىَ, expl. as meaning [*And Adam disobeyed his Lord, and*] *suffered indigestion from much eating:* but better than this is what Az and Er-Rághib say; that it is فَغَوَى; and that the meaning is, *and his life became evil to him;* or *he was disappointed;* or *he acted ignorantly;* or some other of the meanings mentioned by the expositors. (TA.)

2: see 4. — غَوَّيْتُ اللَّبَنَ, (Ḳ, TA,) inf. n. تَغْوِيَةٌ, (TA,) *I made the milk to become such as is termed* رَائِب [i. e. *thick,* or *coagulated,* &c.]; (Ḳ, TA;) as though I spoiled it, so that it became thick. (TA.)

4. اغواه; (Ṣ, MA, Mṣb, Ḳ;) and ↓ غوّاه, (Ḳ,) inf. n. تَغْوِيَةٌ; (TA;) and ↓ غَوَاهُ, (Ḳ, TA,) mentioned by El-Muärrij; (TA;) [but] accord. to Aṣ, one should not say otherwise than اغواهُ; (Ṣ, TA;) *He caused him to err; or to deviate from the right course,* or *from that which was right:* (Ṣ,

Mṣb, Ḳ:) and *caused him to be disappointed*; or *to fail of attaining his desire*: (Ṣ:) or *he seduced him, misled him,* or *led him astray*; as also ▼ استغواه. (MA.) A poet, cited by El-Muärrij, says,

• وَكَائِنْ تَرَى مِنْ جَاهِلٍ بَعْدَ عِلْمِهِ •
• غَوَاهُ ▼ الْهَوَى جَهْلًا عَنِ الحَقِّ فَانْغَوَى ▼ •

[*How many an ignorant dost thou see, whom, after his knowledge, love,* or *desire, has urged to turn, in ignorance, from that which was right, and who has turned*: or *has turned, in ignorance, from that which was right, and who has suffered himself to be turned*; for,] accord. to Az, غَوَاهُ الْهَوَى is most correctly rendered as meaning لَوَاهُ and صَرَفَهُ; and انغوى is quasi-pass. thereof. (TA.) The saying in the Ḳur [vii. 15], related as from Iblees, فَبِمَا أَغْوَيْتَنِى means [*Then by,* or *because of,*] *thy having caused me to err*: or, as some say, *invited me to* [*do*] *a thing whereby I have erred.* (TA.) But the saying in the same [xi. 36], إِنْ كَانَ ٱللّٰهُ يُرِيدُ أَنْ يُغْوِيَكُمْ, is said to mean *If God desire to punish you for erring*: or *to decree, against you, your erring* [i. e. *that ye shall err*]. (TA.)

6. تَغَاوَوْا عَلَيْهِ *They collected themselves together,* or *combined, and aided one another, against him*; (Ṣ, TA;) originally, (TA,) in an evil affair; from الغَوَايَة and الغَىّ: (Ṣ, TA:) or *they aided one another against him, and slew him*; (Ḳ;) but this addition "and slew him" is from a trad. respecting the slaying of 'Othmán, in which it is said, فَتَغَاوَوْا عَلَيْهِ وَٱللّٰهِ حَتَّى قَتَلُوهُ [*and they collected themselves together,* &c., *against him, by God, so that they slew him*]: (TA:) or *they came against him from this quarter and from that*; though they did not slay him: (ISd, Ḳ, TA:) or *they collected themselves together, and aided one another, against him, as do those who err,* or *deviate from the right way* or *course*; thus expl. by Z. (TA.) [See also 6 in arts. غى and عو.]

7. انغوى signifies اِنْهَوَى and مَالَ [app. *He declined* from the right way or course; for all of these three verbs seem to be here used in one and the same sense, agreeably with a saying in the JK, [المُنْغَوِى شِبْهُ المُنْهَوِى المَائِلُ: (Ḳ:) [or rather,] accord. to Az, [it signifies *he was,* or *became,* or *suffered himself to be, made to decline,* or *to turn,* from the right way or course, by love, or desire; for he says that] it is quasi-pass. of غَوَاهُ الهَوَى, which signifies أَمَالَهُ and صَرَفَهُ: (TA:) or *he fell into error by yielding to love and desire.* (TḲ: there given as the meaning of the explanation in the Ḳ.) See also 4.

10: see 4, first sentence.

R. Q. 2 if belonging to art. غو, or Q. Q. 2 if belonging to art. غوغ. تَغَاغَى عَلَيْهِ الغَوْغَآءُ [as though originally [تَغَوْغَى: see art. غوغ.

غَوًى *Thirst.* (TA.) — And one says, بِتُّ غَوًى, and ▼ غَوِيًّا, and ▼ مُغْوِيًا, (Ḳ, TA,) in the T ▼ مُغَوًّى, (TA,) [in the CḲ مُغْوِيًا,] meaning مُخْلِيًا (Ḳ, TA) [in the CḲ [مُخَلِّيًا مُوحِشًا (TA) [i. e. *I passed the night empty*]: and so قَوِيًا, and قَاوِيًا, and مُقْوِيًا. (TA.) [See also غَوِىٌّ.]

غَوٍ: see غَاوٍ: — and see also 1, near the end.

غَىٌّ is an inf. n.; as also ▼ غَوَايَةٌ; (A'Obeyd, Ṣ, &c.; [see 1, first sentence;]) or the latter is a simple subst.: (Mṣb:) [both, used as substs., signify *Error*; &c.: ▼ غَيَّةٌ, of which the pl. (غَيَّاتٌ) is mentioned by Freytag as meaning *errors*, from the Deewán of the Hudhalees, is an inf. n. of un., and signifies *an error*, &c.:] and غَىٌّ signifies also *a state of perdition.* (Ḥam p. 643.) See also غَيَّةٌ. — Also *A certain valley in Hell*: or *a river* [*therein*]: (Ḳ, TA:) prepared by God for those who err: it is said that it has one or the other of these meanings in the Ḳur xix. 60: (TA:) or it there means † *punishment*; because it is the consequence of غَىّ [properly thus termed]: (Er-Rághib, TA:) or it there means *evil*: or the *recompense of* غَىّ [i. e. of *error*]: or *deviation from the way of Paradise.* (Bḍ.)

غَوَّةٌ: see the next paragraph.

غَيَّةٌ: see غَىٌّ. ▼ غَوَّةٌ and غِيَّةٌ signify the same. — [Hence,] وَلَدُ غَيَّةٍ, and ▼ غِيَّةٍ, (Ḳ, TA,) but the latter is said by Lḥ to be rare, (TA,) *The offspring of fornication* or *adultery*; (Ḳ, TA;) *contr. of* وَلَدُ رِشْدَةٍ. (TA.) And one says also ▼ اِبْنُ الغَىِّ [meaning *The son of fornication* or *adultery*]. (L in art. بهث.) And هُوَ لِغَيَّةٍ, (Ṣ, Mṣb,) and ▼ لِغِيَّةٍ, said in reviling a person, *He is,* or *was, unlawfully begotten*; (Mṣb;) *contr. of* لِرِشْدَةٍ. (Ṣ.)

غِيَّةٌ: see the next preceding paragraph, in two places.

غَوِىٌّ: see غَاوٍ: — and see also غَوًى. You say of a hungry person, رَأَيْتُهُ غَوِيًّا مِنَ الجُوعِ [*I saw him empty,* or *lean, from hunger*]; like as one says قَوِيًا and ضَوِيًا [or ضَاوِيًا] and طَوِيًا. (TA.)

غَوَايَةٌ: see غَىٌّ, above.

غَيَّانُ [as though originally [غَوْيَانُ: see what next follows.

غَاوٍ, and ▼ غَوِىٌّ, (Ṣ, Mṣb, Ḳ,) and ▼ غَوٍ, (Ṣ, TA,) and ▼ غَيَّانُ, (Ḳ,) [or the first is an act. part. n., and the others are intensive epithets,] *Erring; deviating from the right way* or *course,* or *from that which is right*: (Ṣ, Mṣb, Ḳ:) and *suffering disappointment*; or *failing of attaining his desire*: (Ṣ, Mṣb:) [&c.: (see 1, first sentence:)] and the first signifies also *perishing*: (Ḥam p. 643:) the pl. of the first is غُوَاةٌ, (Mṣb, TA,) like قُضَاةٌ pl. of قَاضٍ, (Mṣb,) and غَاوُونَ. (Ḳ.) الغَاوُونَ in the saying وَٱلشُّعَرَآءُ يَتَّبِعُهُمُ الغَاوُونَ [in the Ḳur xxvi. 224] means *The devils*: or *those, of mankind, who err*: (Ḳ, TA:) or *those who love the poet when he satirizes a people,* or *party,* (Zj, Ḳ, TA,) *by saying that which is not allowable*: (Zj, TA:) or *those who love him for his praising them for that which is not in them.* (Zj, Ḳ, TA.) — And الغَاوِى signifies *The locust,* or *locusts* collectively: (Ḳ, TA:) one says, جَآءَ الهَاوِى وَالغَاوِى, meaning *The wolf and the locust,* or *locusts, came*: (TA:) so says IAạr. (TA in art. هوى, where, in the Ḳ, الهَاوِى is said to signify "the locust" or "locusts.") — رَأْسٌ غَاوٍ is a tropical phrase, meaning, accord. to the Ḳ, *A small head*: but accord. to the A, *a head that turns,* or *looks, aside, much,* or *often.* (TA.)

غَاوِيَةٌ *i. q.* رَاوِيَةٌ, (Ṣgh, Ḳ, TA,) [as meaning] *A camel that carries water*: pl. غَوَايَا: [the sing. and pl. being] like زَاوِيَةٌ and زَوَايَا. (JK.)

غَاغٌ and غَاغَةٌ, the latter mentioned in the Ḳ in this art. as meaning *A certain plant*: see art. غوغ.

غَوْغَآءٌ and غَوْغَآءُ: see art. غوغ.

أُغْوِيَّةٌ *A* [*pitfall such as is termed*] زُبْيَةٌ; (Ḳ, TA;) or *a hollow,* or *pit, dug in the ground, like a* زُبْيَة, *for the wolf, and in which a kid is put; and when he* [the wolf] *looks at it, he falls, desiring to obtain it, and so is taken*: (TA:) and ▼ مُغَوَّاةٌ [likewise] signifies *a* زُبْيَة, (TA,) or *a hollow,* or *pit, dug in the ground, like a* زُبْيَة, (Ṣ,) *for* [*catching*] *beasts of prey*: (TA:) whence the saying, (Ṣ, TA,) which is a prov., (TA,) مَنْ حَفَرَ مُغَوَّاةً أَوْشَكَ أَنْ يَقَعَ فِيهَا [*He who digs a pitfall is near to his falling into it*]: (Ṣ,* TA:) pl. مُغَوَّيَاتٌ. (Ṣ.) — And *A cause,* or *place, of perdition* or *death*; (Ḳ, TA;) as also ▼ مُغَوَّاةٌ: (TA:) or *a calamity,* or *misfortune*; thus in the saying, وَقَعَ النَّاسُ فِى أُغْوِيَّةٍ [*The people fell into a calamity,* or *misfortune*]. (Ṣ.)

مُغْوٍ; whence the phrase بِتُّ مُغْوِيًا: see غَوًى.

مُغْوَاةٌ: see مُغَوَّاةٌ, in two places.

مُغَوًّى, in the phrase بِتُّ مُغَوًّى: see غَوًى.

مُغَوَّاةٌ: see أُغْوِيَّةٌ, in two places. — Also *A land in which one errs from the right way*; syn. مَضَلَّةٌ; (Ḳ, TA; in the CḲ مُضِلَّةٌ;) as also ▼ مَغْوَاةٌ, like مَهْوَاةٌ; (Ḳ, TA; in the CḲ مِغْواة, like مِهْواة;) and so أَرْضٌ مُغَوَّاةٌ: (TA:) the pl. of مُغَوَّاةٌ is مُغَوَّيَاتٌ; (Ḳ, TA;) and that of ▼ مَغْوَاةٌ is مَغَاوٍ. (TA.) — Also *Any well.* (AA, TA.)

غوث

1. غَاثَ: see 4. — [And see also غُوِيثَ.]

2. غَوَّثَ, (Ṣ, Ḳ,) inf. n. تَغْوِيثٌ; (Ḳ;) and ▼ استغاث; (TA;) *He cried out,* (TA,) *and said,* (Ṣ, Ḳ,) ▼ وَا غَوْثَاهُ (Ṣ, Ḳ, TA) [*Alas! a cry for aid,* or *succour!* also pronounced وا غَوْثَاهِ] (accord.

to one of my copies of the Ṣ) and وا غَوْثَاهْ]. You say, ضُرِبَ فُلَانٌ فَغَوَّثَ *Such a one was beaten, and cried* وا غوثاه. (TA.) This is declared by the leading grammarians to be the primary signification of غوّث: then they used it as meaning *He cried out*, or *called, desiring*, or *demanding, aid*, or *succour.* (MF.) ═ See also غَوِيثٌ.

4. اغاثهُ, (Ṣ, Mṣb, Ḳ,) inf. n. إِغَاثَةٌ (Mṣb, Ḳ) and ▼مَغُوثَةٌ [which is anomalous], (Ḳ,) *He aided*, or *succoured, him*; (Mṣb;) *He* (i. e. God, Mṣb) *removed from him trouble*, or *affliction*: (Mṣb, TA:) ▼غَاثَهُ, aor. يَغِيثُهُ, is used in the sense of اغاثهُ, but is rare, and is said [by some] to be from الغَيْثُ, not الإِغَاثَةُ: غاثهُ, aor. يَغُوثُهُ, is mentioned by Az as not heard by him from any one; but ISd mentions غاثهُ, inf. n. غَوْثٌ and غِيَاثٌ, though saying that اغاثهُ is more approved. (TA.) And one says also, أَغَاثَنَا المَطَرُ † [*The rain gave us relief*]. (Mṣb.)

[6. تَغَاوَثُوا, accord. to Freytag, appears to be used in the Deewán of the Hudhalees as signifying *They said, one to another,* وَا غَوْثَاهُ: ═ and أَغَاثَ as *syn. with* تغاوث.]

10. استغاثهُ, (Ṣ, O, Mṣb, Ḳ,) and استغاث به, (O, Mṣb, TA,) the latter disallowed by some, but used by Sb, (TA,) *He sought, desired*, or *demanded, aid*, or *succour, of*, or *by means of, him*, or *it*; *he sought*, &c., [or *called for*,] *his aid*, or *succour.* (O, MF, TA.) — See also 2. [Hence, استغاث العُودُ † *The lute sent forth plaintive sounds*: a modern phrase.]

غَوْثٌ and ▼غُوَاثٌ and ▼غَوَاثٌ, (Ṣ, Ḳ,) the last deviating from the common course of speech, (Ḳ, TA,) with respect to analogy, as will be seen from what follows, (TA,) *A cry for aid*, or *succour.* (Ṣ, Ḳ, KL, PṢ.) One says, أَجَابَ ٱللّٰهُ دُعَاءَهُ وغُوَاثَهُ ▼ and ▼غَوَاثَهُ [*God answered his prayer, and his cry for aid*]. (Fr, Ṣ.) ▼غَوَاثٌ is said by Fr to be the only word significant of a sound, or cry, having fet-ḥ [to the first letter]; other words of this kind being with ḍamm, as بُكَآءٌ and دُعَآءٌ, or with kesr, as نِدَآءٌ and صِيَاحٌ. (Ṣ.) See also 2. — And see غِيَاثٌ.

غُوَاثٌ: see غَوْثٌ, in three places: — and see also غِيَاثٌ. — In the dial. of Ḥimyer it signifies † *Travelling-provision.* (TA.)

غَوَاثٌ: see غَوْثٌ, in two places: — and see also the paragraph here following.

غِيَاثٌ, (Ṣ, Mṣb, Ḳ, &c.,) in which the و is changed into ى because of the kesreh preceding it, (Ṣ,) a form disapproved by some of the lexicographers, but several others assign to it priority, (MF,) a subst. from أَغَاثَهُ, (Ṣ, Mṣb, Ḳ, &c.,) as also ▼غَوَاثٌ, ascribed by Ibn-Ḥajar to the majority, and ▼غُوَاثٌ, mentioned on the authority of Aboo-Dharr, (MF,) and ▼غَوْثٌ; (Mṣb;) signifying *Aid*, or *succour*; (Mṣb;) or *deliverance from difficulty, distress*, or *adversity*, and [*from*] *revenge*; and *aid to release from difficulties, distresses*, or *adverse circumstances.* (MF.) In the T, الغِيَاثُ is expl. as signifying *That with which God aids*, or *succours, one.* (TA.) — And غِيَاثٌ signifies also *An aider*, or *a succourer*: you say, فُلَانٌ غِيَاثُنَا *Such a one is our aider*, or *succourer*; i. q. ▼مُغِيثُنَا: (TA in art. نور:) and God is said to be غِيَاثُ المُسْتَغِيثِينَ [*The Aider of the seekers of aid*]. (O.) — [Hence,] أُمُّ غِيَاثٍ is a name for † *The cooking-pot.* (T in art. ام.)

غَوِيثٌ *Food*, or *other succour, with which one aids a person in necessity.* (O, Ḳ.) ═ Also, (O, Ḳ,) in one copy of the Ḳ ▼تَغْوِيثٌ, (TA,) [both perhaps inf. ns., the former like دَبِيبٌ &c.,] *Vehemence of running* (شِدَّةُ عَدْوٍ). (O, Ḳ.)

مُغِيثٌ: see غِيَاثٌ, last sentence but one..

مَغُوثَةٌ, an [anomalous] inf. n.: see 4.

مَغَاوِثُ *Waters*: (O, Ḳ:) said to be one of those plurals that have no singulars. (TA.)

يَغُوثُ *A certain idol which belonged to* [*the tribe of*] *Medhḥij*: (Zj, ISd, Ḳ, TA:) or *a certain good man, who lived between* [*the times of*] *Adam and Noah, and of whom, after his death, was made an image, which, after a long time, became an object of worship*; like وَدٌّ and سُوَاعٌ and يَعُوقُ and نَسْرٌ, mentioned therewith in the Ḳur lxxi. 22 and 23. (Bḍ.)

غوج

1. غَاجَ, (Ṣ, O, Ḳ,) aor. يَغُوجُ, (Ṣ, O,) said of a man; (TA;) and ▼تغوّج, (O, Ḳ,) likewise, (TA,) or this is said of a horse; (O;) *He affected a bending of his body*, syn. تَثَنَّى and تَعَطَّفَ, (Ṣ, O, Ḳ, TA,) and *inclined from side to side*, in his gait. (TA.) Aboo-Dhu-eyb says,

• عَشِيَّةَ قَامَتْ بِالفِنَآءِ كَأَنَّهَا

• عَقِيلَةُ نَهْبٍ تُصْطَفَى وَتَغَوَّجُ

[*In the evening when she arose, in the yard of the dwelling, as though she were the most excellent portion of booty, to be selected* therefrom, *and affecting a bending of her body, and inclining from side to side*]: i. e. displaying herself to the chief of the army, in order that he might take her for himself. (Ṣ, O.)

5: see the preceding paragraph.

غَوْجٌ, applied to a horse, *Pliant, pliable, limber*, or *lithe*; syn. لَيِّنُ الأَعْطَافِ: pl. غُوجٌ. (En-Naḍr, TA.) — And *A man relaxed by reason of drowsiness.* (TA.) — And *A broad-breasted* camel. (TA.) — And غَوْجُ اللَّبَانِ *A horse ample in the skin of the breast*, (Ṣ, O, Ḳ,) but not unless he be سَهْلُ المَعْطِفِ [i. e. *pliant, pliable, limber*, or *lithe*]: (Ṣ, O, TA:) or *a horse long in the* قَصَب [or *bones of the legs*]: or *that bends, going and coming.* (TA.) — And غَوْجٌ مَوْجٌ, the latter word being an imitative sequent, *A horse fleet*, or *swift*; *excellent in running*; or *that outstrips others.* (TA.)

غَوَّاجٌ *That goes with energy*: an epithet applied by Aboo-Wejzeh to a camel. (O.)

غور

1. غَارَ, (Aṣ, Fr, IAạr, Ṣ, Mṣb, &c.,) aor. يَغُورُ, (Ṣ, &c.,) inf. n. غَوْرٌ (Ṣ, Ḳ) and غُؤُورٌ; (Ḳ;) and ▼اغار, (Fr, Mṣb,) inf. n. إِغَارَةٌ; (Ḳ;) but IAth says that this form of the verb is of rare occurrence, (TA,) and Aṣ disallows it; (Ṣ, Mṣb, TA;) and ▼غوّر, inf. n. تَغْوِيرٌ; (Ṣ, Ḳ;) and ▼تغوّر; (Ḳ, TA;) *He came to the* غَوْر, (Aṣ, Fr, IAạr, Ṣ, Mṣb, Ḳ,) i. e., *low land* or *country*, (Mṣb,) [or *the region so called, in Arabia*:] or غار signifies *he journeyed in the region of the* غور: (Aṣ, TA:) or غار and ▼اغار signify *he took his way towards the* غَوْر. (TA.) There is a difference of opinion respecting the saying of El-Aạshà,

• نَبِىٌّ يَرَى مَا لَا تَرَوْنَ وَذِكْرُهُ •

• أَغَارَ لَعَمْرِى فِى البِلَادِ وَأَنْجَدَا •

[meaning, accord. to the first explanation of اغار, *A prophet who seeth what ye see not, and whose fame has come to the low lands, by my life*, or *by my religion, in the several regions, and has come to the high lands*]: Aṣ says that اغار signifies *has gone quickly*; and انجد, *has risen*; and that the poet does not mean *has come to the low lands* nor *to the high lands*; holding غار only to signify the coming to the low land: but Fr asserts that اغار is a dial. var. of غار; and cites this verse as authority: and some say اغار وانجد, but when they do not conjoin the two verbs they say غار; like as they say هَنَأَنِى الطَّعَامُ وَمَرَأَنِى, but when they do not conjoin these two verbs they say أَمْرَأَنِى: (Ṣ:) Aṣ also mentions another relation of the second hemistich, commencing اغام [app. a mistake for أَقَامَ or some other word]: (IḲṭṭ:) and there is another relation, accord. to which the second hemistich is مَخْرُوم, commencing with غَارَ. (L.) You say also غَارَ وَأَنْجَدَ meaning † *He became famous in the low countries and the high.* (A in art. نجد.) — غار فِى شَىْءٍ, inf. n. غَوْرٌ and غُؤُورٌ (Ḳ) and غِيَارٌ, (Sb, Ḳ,) *He*, or *it, entered* [or *entered deeply*] *into a thing.* (Ḳ.) — [Hence,] غار فِى أَمْرٍ ‡ *He examined minutely* [or *deeply*] *into an affair*; (IḲṭṭ, Mṣb;) as also ▼اغار. (IḲṭṭ.) You say فُلَانٌ بَعِيدُ الغَوْرِ ‡ *Such a one is a deep examiner*: (TA:) or *acquainted* [*deeply*] *with affairs*: or *very rancorous, malevolent, malicious*, or *spiteful.* (Mṣb.) [See also غَوْرٌ, below.] — غار المَآءُ فِى الأَرْضِ, (Ḳ,) inf. n. غَوْرٌ (Lḥ, Ṣ, Ḳ, &c.) and غُؤُورٌ; (Ṣ, TA;) and ▼غوّر, (Lḥ, TA,) inf. n. تَغْوِيرٌ; (Ḳ;) *The water sank*, (Ṣ, IḲṭṭ,) or *went away*, (Mṣb, Ḳ,) *into the ground*, or *earth*: (Ṣ, Mṣb, Ḳ:) or *went away into the sources*, or *springs.* (Lḥ.) — غَارَتْ

الشَّمْسُ, (Ṣ, Ḳ,) aor. تَغُورُ, (Ṣ,) inf. n. غِيَارٌ (Ṣ, Ḳ) and غُؤُورٌ; (Ḳ;) and ▼ غوّرت; (Ḳ;) *The sun set:* (Ṣ, Ḳ:) and in like manner one says [غار and ▼ غوّر] of the moon and of a star. (TA.) — غَارَتْ عَيْنُهُ, aor. تَغُورُ, (Ṣ, Mṣb,) inf. n. غَوْرٌ (Ṣ, TA) and غُؤُورٌ; (Ṣ, Mṣb, TA;) and غَارَتْ, aor. تَغَارُ; (Ṣ, TA;) and ▼ غوّرت; (TA;) *His eye sank,* or *became depressed,* (lit. *entered,*) *in the head;* (Ṣ, TA;) i. q. اِنْخَسَفَتْ. (Mṣb.) — غار النَّهَارُ † *The day became intensely hot* [app., like غَوَّرَ, meaning *when the sun had declined from the meridian*]: (Ḳ:) hence الغَائِرَةُ [q. v.]. (TA.) — See also 2. == غَارَ شَيْئًا, aor. يَغُورُ, *He sought for,* or *after, a thing.* (TA.) == غَارَهُمْ, and غَارَ لَهُمْ, [aor. يَغُورُ,] inf. n. غِيَارٌ, *He* (God) *bestowed upon them* غِيرَة, (Ḳ,) i. e. مِيرَة [*a provision of corn,* or *wheat,* &c.]. (TA.) [See also art. غير.] — *He benefited them;* (Ṣ in art. غير, and TA;) and so غَارَهُمْ بِخَيْرٍ: (Ṣ:) and غَارَهُمْ, aor. يَغُورُ, (Ḳ,) inf. n. غِيَارٌ; (TA;) or غَارَهُمْ بِخَيْرٍ; (TA;) *He* (God) *bestowed upon them abundance of the produce of the earth, and rain:* (Ḳ, TA:) and غَارَهُمْ بِرِزْقٍ *He bestowed upon them means of subsistence.* (TA.) You say also اَللّٰهُمَّ غُرْنَا بِغَيْثٍ, (Ḳ,) and بِمَطَرٍ, and بِخَيْرٍ, (TA,) and غُرْنَا مِنْكَ بِغَيْثٍ, (Ṣ,) *O God, aid us,* or *succour us, with rain* (Ṣ, Ḳ) *from Thee,* (Ṣ,) and *with prosperity.* (TA.) [See also art. غير.] == غَارَ الرَّجُلَ, aor. يَغُورُهُ and يَغِيرُهُ, *He gave the man the bloodwit* [which is termed غَوْرٌ and غِيَرٌ]: (ISk, TA:) and so ▼ غَيَّرَهُ. (TA in art. غير.) == غَارَ عَلَى أَهْلِهِ, aor. يَغَارُ, inf. n. غَيْرَةٌ [or rather غَيْرَةٌ (see art. غير)] and غَارٌ, [*He was jealous of his wife.*] (IḲṭṭ.) غَارٌ and غَيْرَةٌ, (Ṣ, so in my two copies,) or غَارٌ and غِيرَةٌ, with kesr, (Ḳ,) signify the same. (Ṣ, Ḳ.) You say فُلَانٌ شَدِيدُ الغَارِ عَلَى أَهْلِهِ i. e. الغيرة [*Such a one is vehemently jealous of his wife*]. (TA.) See also art. غير.

2. غوّر, inf. n. تَغْوِيرٌ: see 1, in five places. — Also *He slept in the middle of the day;* (Ṣ,* Ḳ, TA;) and so ▼ غَارَ. (Ḳ, TA.) — And *He alighted* (Lth, Ṣ, Ḳ, TA) *to sleep* (Lth, Ṣ, TA) *in the middle of the day.* (Lth, Ṣ, Ḳ, TA.) And غَوِّرُوا بِنَا *Make ye the camels to lie down with us during the vehement midday-heat.* (Jm and TA in art. رمض.) IAạr says that ▼ مُغَوِّرٌ signifies One *alighting in the middle of the day for a little while and then departing* [i. e. *resuming his journey*]. (TA.) And مَا بِتُّ هٰذِهِ اللَّيْلَةَ إِلَّا تَغْوِيرًا occurs in a trad. as meaning [*I did not tarry,* or *have not tarried, this night,*] *save in taking a nap* [*like the sleep in the middle of the day*]. (TA.) — Also *He entered upon the middle of the day.* (Ḳ, TA.) — And *He journeyed in the middle of the day:* (Lth, Ḳ:) or *he* (a rider upon a camel, or upon a horse or other beast,) *journeyed until the declining of the sun from the meridian, and then alighted.* (ISh, TA.) — And غَوَّرَ النَّهَارُ ‡ [app. *The day became intensely hot when*] *the sun declined from the meridian.* (Ibn-Buzurj, TA. [See also غَارَ النَّهَارُ.]) == غَوَّرَهُ, inf. n. as above, *He put it,* or *made it to enter, into a low,* or *depressed, place: he hid,* or *concealed, it;* or *caused it to disappear.* (Ḥar p. 165.) — And غوّر, (TA,) inf. n. as above, (Ḳ, TA,) signifies also *He routed, defeated,* or *put to flight;* and *he drove away.* (Ḳ,* TA.)

3: see 4; and see also 6.

4. اغار عَيْنَهُ [*He made his eye to sink,* or *become depressed, in his head:* see 1]. (TA.) == اغار as intrans.: see 1, in four places. — Also *He went away in,* or *into, the country,* or *land.* (Ḳ.) — And, (Ṣ, Ḳ, &c.,) inf. n. إِغَارَةٌ (Ṣ, Mgh, Mṣb) and غَارَةٌ, (Mgh,) or the latter is a simple subst., [or quasi-inf. n.,] (Mṣb,) *He hastened,* (Ḳ,) or *was quick,* (Mṣb,) *in walking,* or *marching,* or *journeying:* (Mṣb, Ḳ:) *he was quick,* (Ṣ, Mgh, Mṣb, Ḳ,) *and pushed,* or *pressed, on,* or *forward,* (دَفَعَ, Ṣ,) *in his running;* (Ṣ, Mgh, Mṣb;) said of a horse, (Mgh, Mṣb,) and of a fox: (Ṣ, Mgh:) *he* (a horse, Ḳ) *ran vehemently, and was quick,* (Ṣ, Ḳ,) *in a* غَارَة [*or raid, or sudden attack upon a people,* or *their dwellings,*] *&c.* (Ḳ.) Hence the saying, (in a trad. respecting the pilgrimage, TA,) أَشْرِقْ ثَبِيرُ كَيْمَا نُغِيرُ [*Enter thou upon the time of sunrise, Thebeer,* (the name of a mountain near Mekkeh,)] *that we may proceed quickly,* (Ṣ, Ḳ,) or *push,* or *press, on,* or *forward,* (Yaạḳoob, Mṣb,) to the sacrifice of the pilgrimage: (Ṣ, Mṣb, Ḳ:) or to the return from Minè: (Yaạḳoob:) or *that we may plunder* the meats of the sacrifices: or *that we may enter into the low land.* (TA. [See also 2 in art. شرق.]) Hence also the saying, أَغَارَ إِغَارَةَ الثَّعْلَبِ *He was quick, and pushed,* or *pressed, on,* or *forward, like as does the fox.* (Ṣ.) — اغار عَلَى العَدُوِّ, (Ṣ, Mṣb,) and عَلَى القَوْمِ, (Ḳ,) inf. n. إِغَارَةٌ (Ṣ, Ḳ) and غَارَةٌ, (Ḳ,) or the latter is a simple subst., [or quasi-inf. n., as in the case mentioned above,] (TA,) and مُغَارٌ, (Ṣ, TA,) *He made* [*a raid,* or *hostile* or *predatory incursion, into the territory of the enemy;* or] *a sudden,* or *an unexpected, attack* [*upon the enemy,* or] *upon the territory* or *dwellings of the enemy,* [*with a party of armed horsemen,* generally meaning *a predatory incursion,*] *and engaged with them in conflict;* (Mṣb,) or *he urged the horses upon,* or *against, the people;* as also ▼ استغار: (Ḳ, TA:) and in like manner you say ▼ غاور العَدُوَّ, inf. n. مُغَاوَرَةٌ and غِوَارٌ. (Ṣ.) See also 6. And اغار الذِّئْبُ فِى الغَنَمِ *The wolf made an incursion among the sheep* or *goats;* (Ḳ* and TA in art. شع;) as also ▼ استغار. (TA ibid.) — Also اغار عَلَيْهِ *He plundered it; took it by pillage.* (TA.) — And اغار إِلَى بنى فلان, and sometimes بِبَنِى فُلَانٍ, *He came to the sons of such a one to aid,* or *succour, them:* (IḲṭṭ, Ḳ:) or *to be aided,* or *succoured, by them.* (IḲṭṭ.) == اغار, (Ṣ, Ḳ,) inf. n. إِغَارَةٌ and quasi-inf. n. غَارَةٌ, (TA,) signifies also *He twisted hard* (Ṣ, Ḳ) a rope. (Ṣ.) == اغار أَهْلَهُ *He married another in addition to his wife* [and *so caused her to be jealous:* see 1]. (Ṣ.) [See also art. غير.]

5: see 1, first signification.

6. تغاوروا *They made* [*raids,* or *hostile* or *predatory incursions, into each other's territories;* or] *sudden attacks, one upon another,* or *one party upon the dwellings of another party, and engaged in conflict, one with another;* or *urged their horses one upon,* or *against, another;* expl. by ▼ أَغَارَ بَعْضُهُمْ عَلَى بَعْضٍ: (Ṣ, Ḳ:) and so ▼ غاوروا, inf. n. مُغَاوَرَةٌ. (TA.)

8. اغتار *He procured* مِيرَة [*or provision of corn,* or *wheat,* &c.]. (TA.) — And *He derived,* or *obtained, benefit, advantage,* or *profit.* (Ḳ.)

10. *He,* or *it, descended:* (TA:) or *he desired to descend into a low land or country.* (Ḳ, TA.) — See also 4, in two places. == Also *He became fat;* and *fat entered into him:* (Ṣ, TA:) or you say, استغار الشَّحْمُ فِيهِ *fat spread in him;* and *he became fat;* (Ḳ, TA;) the pronoun referring to a horse, which is not mentioned in the Ḳ; but the explanation in the Ṣ is better: or, accord. to Az, استغار is said of the fat and flesh of a she-camel, meaning *it became hard,* and *compact;* like the rope of which one says يُسْتَغَارُ i. e. *it is twisted hard:* or, accord. to some, said of the fat of a camel, it means *it entered his inside.* (TA.) — استغارت said of a wound, (قَرْحَةٌ, Ṣ, in the Ḳ جُرْحَةٌ,) means *It became swollen.* (Ṣ, Ḳ.) == اِسْتَغَارَ اللّٰهَ *He asked,* or *begged, of God,* غِيرَة, (Ḳ, TA,) i. e. مِيرَة [*provision of corn,* or *wheat,* &c.]. (TA.)

غَارٌ *A cave,* or *cavern;* syn. كَهْفٌ; (Ṣ, Ḳ;) *in a mountain;* (Ṣ;) as also ▼ مَغَارَةٌ and ▼ مَغَارٌ (Ṣ, Ḳ) and ▼ مُغَارَةٌ and ▼ مُغَارٌ and ▼ غُوْرٌ: (Ḳ: [but غَارٌ in this sense is omitted in the CḲ:]) or *what resembles a* كهف *in a mountain,* [*only differing in being less large,*] *like a* سَرَبٌ: (TA:) or *what is hewn out in a mountain, resembling a* مَغَارَة: when it is large, or spacious, it is called كَهْف: (Mṣb:) or *what resembles a house,* or *chamber, in a mountain:* (Lḥ, Ḳ:) or *a low,* or *depressed, place in a mountain:* (Th, Ḳ:) or *any low,* or *depressed, land, country,* or *ground:* (Ḳ:) see also غَوْرٌ [and غُؤُورٌ]: or the *hole,* or *burrow, to which a wild animal betakes itself:* (Ḳ: [see an instance in art. سمو, conj. 8:]) and sometimes ▼ مَغَارٌ is applied to the *coverts of gazelles, among trees:* (Ṣ:) the dim. of غَارٌ is غُوَيْرٌ: (Ṣ, Ḳ:) [of which see two exs. (a prov. and a verse) voce بُؤْسٌ:] and the pl. (of pauc., TA) أَغْوَارٌ (IJ, Ḳ) and (of mult., TA) غِيرَانٌ. (Ṣ, Mṣb, Ḳ.) — Also The *portion of the upper part of the mouth which is behind the* فَرَاشَة [*or thin bone* of the palate]: or the *hollow* (أُخْدُود) *which is between the two jaws:* or the *interior of the mouth:* (Ḳ: [for دَاخِلُ الفَمِ, in the CḲ, I read دَاخِلُ الفم, as in the TA:]) or, as some say, the *two parts whereof each is called* نِطْعٌ, [app. meaning the *anterior part of the palate* and the *corresponding part next the lower gums,*] *in the* حَنَكَانِ [or the *palate* and the *part corresponding to it below*]. (TA.) —— And الغَارَانِ signifies *The* [*sockets of the eyes;* or] *two bones in which are the eyes.* (ISd, Ḳ.) —— And *The belly and the pudendum:* (Ṣ:) or *the mouth and the pudendum.* (Ḳ.) Hence the saying of a poet, يَسْعَى لِغَارَيْهِ [*He works,* or *earns, for his belly,* or *his mouth, and his pudendum*]. (Ṣ, TA.) ═ Also (غَارٌ) *An army:* (Ṣ, Ḳ:) or *a numerous army.* (TA.) You say اِلْتَقَى الغَارَانِ *The two armies met.* (Ṣ.) —— And *A company,* or *body, of men:* (TA:) or *a numerous company* or *body of men.* (ISd, Ḳ.) ═ And *I. q.* غَيْرَةٌ, (Ṣ,) or غِيرَةٌ. (Ḳ.) [See 1, last signification.] ═ And *A kind of tree,* (Ṣ, Mgh, Ḳ,) *of large size,* (Mgh, Ḳ,) *having leaves longer than those of the* خِلَاف, (Mgh, TA,) *and a fruit* [or *berry*] *smaller than the hazel-nut, which is black, and which, being divested of its covering, discloses a heart that is employed in medicine* [*that is designed to produce a narcotic or an intoxicating effect: the berries are called* حَبُّ الغَارِ]: *its leaves have a sweet odour,* (Mgh, TA,) *and are employed in perfume:* (TA:) *its fruit is called* [*in Persian*] دَهْمَسْت: (Mgh, TA:) *and it has an oil,* (Ḳ,) *which is called* دُهْنُ الغَارِ: (Ṣ:) [it is the *bay-tree;* or *female laurel-tree;* the *laurus nobilis;* also called the *sweet bay;* of which there are several sorts, as the broad-leaved bay, the narrow-leaved bay, &c.: it is commonly supposed to be the laurus of the ancients:] n. un. with ة. (TA.) —— And The *leaves of the grape-vine.* (Ḳ.)

غَوْرٌ The *bottom,* or *lowest part,* of anything; (Ṣ, Mṣb, Ḳ;) as also ↓ غَوْرَى: (Ḳ:) and its *depth.* (TA.) —— You say, عَرَفْتُ غَوْرَ هٰذِهِ المَسْأَلَةِ ‡ [*I have become acquainted with the bottom of this question*]. (TA.) And فُلَانٌ بَعِيدُ الغَوْرِ (Ṣ) ‡ *Such a one is deep and excellent in judgment; one who examines deeply.* (TA.) [See also 1.] And هُوَ بَحْرٌ لَا يُدْرَكُ غَوْرُهُ ‡ [*He is a sea whereof the bottom shall not be reached*]. (TA.) And مَنْ أَبْعَدُ غَوْرًا فِى البَاطِلِ مِنِّى ‡ [*Who is deeper in knowledge with respect to what is vain,* or *false, than I?*]. (TA, from a trad.) —— *Low,* or *depressed, land, country,* or *ground;* (Ṣ, Mṣb, Ḳ;) [like غَارٌ;] as also ↓ حَوْرٌ. (Ḳ.) —— See also غَارٌ, in the first of its senses expl. above. ═ Applied to water, *i. q.* غَائِرٌ [*Sinking,* or *going away, into the ground,* or *earth*]: (Ṣ, Ḳ:) an inf. n. used as an epithet, like مَآءٌ سَكْبٌ, and دِرْهَمٌ ضَرْبٌ. (Ṣ.)

غَوْرٌ *A bloodwit;* syn. دِيَةٌ: (Ḳ, TA:) a dial. var. of غَيْرٌ: (TA:) or the latter is a pl., of which the sing. is غِيَرَةٌ. (AA, Ḳ in art. غير, q. v.)

غَارَةٌ, a subst. from أَغَارَ; *A going away into a country,* or *land.* (TA.) —— *A quick running,* (Mgh, Mṣb,) or *vehement running,* (TA,) of a horse, (Mgh, Mṣb, TA,) and of a fox; (Mgh;) as also ↓ غُوَيْرٌ, of a fox. (TA.) —— [*A raid;* or *an incursion into the* [te]*rritory of an enemy;* or *a sudden,* or *an unexpected, attack upon an enemy,* or *upon the territories* or *dwellings of an enemy, with a party of armed horsemen, and engagement with them in conflict; an urging of horses upon,* or *against, a people;* generally, *a hostile,* or *predatory, incursion:* or the *making such an incursion:*] a subst. [or quasi-inf. n.] from أَغَارَ عَلَى العَدُوِّ. (Ṣ, TA.) —— And *Plunder,* or *pillage.* (TA.) —— And hence, (Mgh, Mṣb,) [*Horsemen making a raid,* or *a sudden,* or *an unexpected, attack, upon an enemy,* or *upon the dwellings of an enemy, and engaging with them in conflict: horsemen urging their horses upon,* or *against, a people:*] i. q. ↓ خَيْلٌ مُغِيرَةٌ: (Ṣ, Mgh, Mṣb, TA:) and one says also ↓ خَيلٌ مِغيرةٌ, with kesr. (TA.) You say شَنَّ عَلَيْهِمُ الغَارَةَ i. e. *He scattered,* (Ṣ in art. شن, and Mgh* and Mṣb,*) or *poured,* (Ḳ in art. شن,) *upon them* [*the horsemen making a raid,* or *sudden attack, and engaging in conflict,* or *the horsemen urging their horses*]. (Ṣ, Ḳ.) The poet (El-Kumeyt Ibn-Maarroof, TA) says,

وَنَحْنُ صَبَحْنَا آلَ نَجْرَانَ غَارَةً •
تَمِيمَ بْنَ مُرٍّ وَالرِّمَاحَ النَّوَادِسَا •

[*And we gave as a morning-drink to* the people of *Nejrán a troop of horsemen making a raid,* or *sudden attack, upon them,* or *urging their horses against them,* namely the tribe of *Temeem Ibn-Murr, and the piercing spears*]: he means, سَقَيْنَاهُمْ خَيْلًا مُغِيرَةً: and تميم بن مرّ is put in the accus. case as a substitute for غارة. (Ṣ, TA.) ═ حَبْلٌ شَدِيدُ الغَارَةِ means *A rope twisted hard;* or *hard in respect of the twisting;* (Ṣ, TA;) غَارَةٌ being in this case [as in that first mentioned above] a subst. standing in stead of the inf. n. إِغَارَة: (TA:) and so ↓ حَبْلٌ مُغَارٌ; (Ṣ, TA;) applied to a rope that is twisted with another. (TA voce مُسْحَل.) ═ And الغَارَةُ signifies *The navel:* (Ṣgh, Ḳ:) app. so called because of its depth. (Ṣgh, TA.)

الغَوْرَةُ *The sun.* (IAar, Ḳ, TA.) ═ See also غَائِرَةٌ.

غِيرَةٌ *Abundance of the produce of the earth:* and *rain:* and *i. q.* مِيرَةٌ [*a provision of corn,* or *wheat,* &c.]: belonging to this art. and to art. غير. (TA.) ═ [See also 1, last signification.]

غَوْرَى: see غَوْرٌ.

غُوَيْرٌ: see غَارَةٌ, second sentence.

غَائِرَةٌ *i. q.* قَائِلَةٌ [app. as syn. with قَيْلُولَةٌ, i. e. *A sleeping in the middle of the day;* though the primary signification of قَائِلَةٌ is that which here next follows]; (Ṣ, O, Ḳ;) as also ↓ غَوْرَةٌ. (O, Ḳ.) —— And The *middle of the day* [itself]. (Ḳ.) —— And one says, بُنِىَ هٰذَا البَيْتُ عَلَى غَائِرَةِ الشَّمْسِ, meaning ‡ [*This house,* or *tent, was,* or *has been, built,* or *set up,*] *facing the place of sunrise.* (TA.)

مَغَارٌ: see غَارٌ, in two places. —— Also *A place of entrance:* and *a place where a thing is sought for:* you say, إِنَّكَ غُرْتَ فِى غَيْرِ مَغَارٍ *Verily thou hast entered into that which is not a place of entrance:* and *verily thou hast sought in that which is not a place where a thing is sought for.* (TA.)

مُغَارٌ: see غَارٌ. ═ Also *A place of a* غَارَة [or *raid,* or *sudden attack upon an enemy,* or *upon the dwellings of an enemy, with a party of armed horsemen,* &c.]. (TA.) ═ See also غَارَةٌ, last sentence but one. —— Hence, ‡ A horse *strong,* or *compact, in make;* as though twisted: (Az, TA:) or a horse *strong in the joints:* (Lth, TA:) or, applied to a horse, *i. q.* مُضَمَّرٌ [*made lean,* or *light of flesh;* &c.: see 2 in art. عير: and see also مُعَارٌ in that art.]. (Aboo-Sa'eed Ed-Dareer, TA in art. عير.) And A horse *that runs swiftly.* (TA. [But in this last sense, the word should be, accord. to rule, as here next follows.])

مُغِيرٌ A horse *swift in running:* [see also what next precedes:] and ↓ مِغْوَارٌ [likewise] signifies a *swift* horse: or this latter, accord. to Lḥ, *vehement in running:* and its pl. is مَغَاوِيرُ. (TA.) —— خَيْلٌ مُغِيرَةٌ and مِغِيرَةٌ: see غَارَةٌ.

مُغَوَّرٌ: see 2.

مَغَارَةٌ and مُغَارَةٌ: see غَارٌ, first sentence.

مِغْوَارٌ: see مُغِيرٌ. —— Also A *fighting* man; and so ↓ مُغَاوِرٌ: (Ṣ:) or the former signifies one *who occupies himself much in* غَارَات [or *raids,* or *sudden attacks upon enemies, or upon the dwellings of enemies, with armed horsemen,* &c., pl. of غَارَة]; (Ḳ, TA;) as also ↓ مُغَاوِرٌ: (TA:) pl. مَغَاوِيرُ: (Ṣ:) and مَغَاوِرُ may be a contracted pl. of مِغْوَارٌ or a pl. of مُغَاوِرٌ. (TA.)

مُغَاوِرٌ: see the next preceding paragraph, in two places.

غوص

1. غَاصَ فِى المَآءِ, aor. يَغُوصُ, (Ṣ, A, Mṣb,) inf. n. غَوْصٌ (Ṣ, A, Ḳ) and مَغَاصٌ and غِيَاصَةٌ and غِيَاصٌ, (Ḳ,) *He dived in,* or *descended beneath, the water;* (Ṣ, A, Ḳ;) or *entered into the water;* (TA;) *to fetch out what was in it.* (Mṣb [in my copy of which, the particle فى is omitted, app. by a slip of the transcriber].) —— غِيَاصَةٌ [also] signifies The *diving in the sea for pearls;* (Ṣ;) and غَوْصٌ signifies [the same: or both signify] the *fetching out pearls from beneath the water.* (Mgh.) —— [Hence,] you say also, غَاصَ عَلَى الأَمْرِ, (Ḳ,) inf. n. غَوْصٌ, (TA,) ‡ [*He dived for the thing,* or *affair, so as to elicit it;* or] *he knew the thing,* or *affair.* (Ḳ, TA.) And غَاصَ عَلَى المَعَانِى حَتَّى بَلَغَ أَقْصَاهَا وَٱسْتَخْرَجَ مَا بَعُدَ مِنْهَا وَدَقَّ فَهْمُهُ ‡ [*He dived for the meanings so that he reached the uttermost of them, and elicited what was remote of them, and the understanding whereof was subtile*]. (Mṣb.) And فُلَانٌ يَغُوصُ عَلَى حَقَائِقِ العِلْمِ ‡ [*Such a one dives for the verities of science*].

(A, TA.) And مَا أَحْسَنَ غَوْصَهُ عَلَيْهَا ‡ [*How good is his diving for them!*]. (A, TA.) And مَا غَاصَ غَوْصَةً إِلَّا أَخْرَجَ دُرَّةً ‡ [*He did not dive a single diving but he fetched out* what was like *a pearl*, or *a large pearl*]. (A, TA.) — You say also, غَاصَ عَلَى الشَّىْءِ, aor. يَغُوصُ, inf. n. غَوْصٌ, *He pounced*, or *came suddenly*, or *at unawares, upon the thing.* (Mṣb.)

2. غَوَّصَهُ فِى المَآءِ *He made him to dive in*, or *descend beneath, the water;* (A;) *he immersed, immerged, dipped, plunged*, or *sunk, him therein.* (TA.)

غَوْصٌ [originally an inf. n.]: see مَغَاصٌ, in two places.

غَوْصَةٌ [*A single diving in*, or *descent beneath, water:* see 1, last sentence but one]. (A.)

غَوَّاصٌ: see the next paragraph, in four places.

غَائِصٌ *One who dives in*, or *descends beneath*, or *enters into, water;* as also ▼ غَوَّاصٌ [which, however, has an intensive signification, or implies the habit of so doing]: (TA:) and ▼ the latter, (Ṣ, A, Ḳ,) or both, (Az, TA,) particularly *one who dives in the sea for pearls*, (Ṣ, A, Ḳ,) or *for pearl-shells, and fetches them out:* (Az, TA:) pl. غُوَّاصٌ, (A, TA,) of the former, (TA,) and غَاصَةٌ, (A, TA,) [also of the former,] and [of the latter] غَوَّاصُونَ. (TA.) — [Hence the saying,] هُوَ مِنْ صَاغَةِ الفِقَرِ وَغَاصَةِ الدُّرَرِ ‡ [*He is of the moulders of* فِقَر, lit., as thus used, *ornaments fashioned in the form of the vertebræ of the back*, but here meaning *choice phrases* or *sentences; and of the divers for, and producers of,* (*expressions like*) *pearls*, or *large pearls*]. (A, TA.) — [Hence likewise,] ▼ غَوَّاصٌ also signifies ‡ *One who exercises art, craft, cunning*, or *skill, in ordering the means of obtaining subsistence.* (TA.) — And غَائِصٌ also signifies *One who pounces*, or *comes suddenly*, or *at unawares, upon a thing;* (JK, Ṣ, Mṣb;) as also, (JK, Mṣb,) but in an intensive sense, (Mṣb,) ▼ غَوَّاصٌ: (JK, Mṣb:) pl. of the former غَاصَةٌ. (Mṣb.)

مَغَاصٌ *A place where one dives in*, or *descends beneath, water;* (Lth, A, Ḳ;) as also ▼ غَوْصٌ: (Lth, Mgh:) or ▼ the latter signifies particularly *a place* [*where one dives and*] *whence pearls are fetched out.* (JK, Mgh.*) You say also, هٰذَا مَغَاصُ اللُّؤْلُؤِ *This is the diving-place for pearls.* (A.) — Also The *upper part of the* سَاق [or *shank*, &c.]. (JK, Ṣgh, Ḳ.)

غوط

1. غَاطَ, aor. يَغُوطُ, (Ṣ, Mṣb, TA,) inf. n. غَوْطٌ, (Ṣ, Mṣb, Ḳ,) *It entered*, or *sank*, (Ṣ, Mṣb, Ḳ, TA,) into (فِى) a thing; (Ṣ, Ḳ, TA;) as, for instance, the foot into sand; (Ṣ, TA;) and a man into mud, (TA,) or into water; (Mṣb;) and into a valley; (TA, in this art. and in art. غيط; in the former expl. by انْغَمَسَ;) and غَاطَ, aor. يَغِيطُ, (Ṣ, TA,) inf. n. غَيْطٌ, (Ḳ,) signifies the same: (Ṣ, Ḳ:) both also signify *he*, or *it, became hidden*, (Aṣ, and Ḳ in art. غيط,) in the ground. (Aṣ.) You say also, غَاطَتْ أَنْسَاعُ النَّاقَةِ, aor. and inf. n. as above, *The plaited thongs of the she-camel clave to her belly, and so entered*, or *sank, therein.* (TA.) And غَاطَتِ الأَنْسَاعُ فِى دَفِّ النَّاقَةِ *The plaited thongs caused their impressions to be visible in the side of the she-camel.* (TA.) — *It* (a place) *sank*, or *became depressed*, in the ground. (ISh.) And *It* (anything) *descended*, or *sloped downwards*, in the ground. (TA.) — Also, aor. and inf. n. as above, *He dug, excavated*, or *hollowed out.* (TA: and in some copies of the Ḳ, الغَوْطُ is expl. by الحَفْرُ; but the reading given in the TA, in that instance, is الحُفْرَةُ.) — غُطْ غُطْ means *Be thou with the* جَمَاعَة [i. e. the mass, or main body], (IAạr, O, Ḳ,) who are termed the غَاط, (O,) [*be thou with them*, not with the factious,] when فِتَن [i. e. factions, &c.,] come. (IAạr, O, Ḳ.)

2. غَوَّطَ, inf. n. تَغْوِيطٌ, *He gobbled* [food]: (Ibn-'Abbád, O, Ḳ:*) or *gobbled largely*, or *in large mouthfuls:* (Ḳ,* TA:) from غَوْطٌ meaning ثَرِيد. (TA.) — And تَغْوِيطٌ signifies also The *making* a well *deep.* (Ḳ. [See also 4.])

4. أَغْوَطَ *He made deep* a well. (Fr, O, TA. [See also 2.])

5. تغوّط ‡ *He voided excrement*, or *ordure.* (Ṣ, Mṣb, Ḳ, TA. [In the CḲ, أَنْدَى is put by mistake for ابدى.])

6. تَغَاوَطَا فِى المَآءِ *They two vied*, or *contended, each with the other, in plunging*, or *diving, in the water.* (Ḳ,* TA.)

7. انغاط *It* (a branch, or twig, or the like,) *bent.* (O, Ḳ.)

غَاطٌ: see غَائِطٌ. — الغَاطُ signifies also الجَمَاعَةُ [meaning The *mass*, or *main body*, of the people]. (O, Ḳ.) One says, مَا فِى الغَاطِ مِثْلُهُ [*There is not in the mass*, or *main body*, of the people, *the like of him*]. (O, TA.)

غَوْطٌ *A hollow, cavity, pit*, or *the like, dug*, or *excavated, in the ground;* syn. حُفْرَةٌ. (So in the Ḳ, accord. to the TA, on the authority of AA: but in some copies of the Ḳ, الغَوْطُ in this instance is expl. by الحَفْرُ: see 1, last sentence.) See also غَائِطٌ. — And *i. q.* ثَرِيدٌ [*Crumbled bread moistened with broth*]. (O: in the Ḳ ثَرِيدَة.)

غَيْطٌ: see غَائِطٌ, latter half.

غَوْطَةٌ *A* [*low*, or *depressed, place*, or *hollow, such as is called*] وَهْدَة, *in the ground.* (ISh, Ḳ.) [See also غَائِطٌ.]

غُوطَةٌ *A place comprising water and herbage:* whence غُوطَةُ دِمَشْقَ, (Ḥar pp. 130, et seq.,) i. e. the city, or district, of Damascus, (Ḳ,) which is a place abounding with water and trees. (Ṣ.)

بِئْرٌ غَوِيطَةٌ *A deep well.* (TA.)

غَائِطٌ *A wide, depressed piece of ground* or *land*, (ISh, Ṣ, O, Mṣb, Ḳ,) *but not much depressed, and in some instances having acclivities* [*bordering it*]; (ISh;) *sometimes, as they assert, a league* (فَرْسَخ) *in extent, and having in it meadows;* (AḤn;) and ▼ غَاطٌ and ▼ غَوْطٌ signify the same; (O, Ḳ;) or *the last is more depressed than the* غائط: (IDrd, O:) and غائط is also applied to *a valley:* (TA:) the pl. [of pauc.] is أَغْوَاطٌ, (Ṣ, Mṣb, Ḳ,) or this is pl. of غَوْطٌ, (IB,) and [of mult.] غِيطَانٌ, (Ṣ, Mṣb, Ḳ,) which is pl. of both these sings., (IB,) and غُوطٌ (Ṣ, Mṣb, Ḳ) and غِيَاطٌ. (Ḳ.) — Hence, ‡ *A place in which one satisfies a want of nature;* the custom being to do so in a depressed place, where one is concealed. (Ṣ,* Mṣb,* TA.) In the Ḳur [iv. 46, or v. 9], accord. to an extraordinary reading, it is written ▼ غَيْط, [a form now commonly used, and signifying *a garden*, but there meaning a *privy place*,] the original form of which may be غَيِّط, and then غَيْط, [and then غَيْط,] it being contracted; or, accord. to Abu-l-Ḥasan, the ى may be originally و, these two letters being in this instance interchangeable. (IJ.) You say, أَتَى الغَائِطَ, (Ṣ, TA,) and ضَرَبَ الغَائِطَ, (TA,) ‡ *He satisfied a want of nature;* (Ṣ, TA;) *voided excrement*, or *ordure.* (TA.) — And hence, (Ṣ, TA,) ‡ *Human excrement*, or *ordure:* (Ṣ, Ḳ, TA:) because they used to cast it away in a غائط: or because they used to go thither to satisfy a want of nature. (TA.)

غوغ

Q. Q. 2 if belonging to this art., or R. Q. 2 if belonging to art. غو. تَغَاغَى عَلَيْهِ الغَوْغَآءُ [as though originally تَغَوْغَى] *i. q.* رَكِبُوهُ [i. e. *The mixed multitude*, or *the low, base, vile*, &c., *of men, bore*, or *pressed*, or *crowded*, (*as though mounting*,) *upon him*]. (TA in art. غو.)

غَاغٌ The حَبَق [q. v.], (IDrd, Ḳ, TA,) *a species of sweet-smelling plants*, (TA,) i. e. the فُوذَنْج, (IDrd, Ḳ, TA,) an arabicized word from [the Pers. پُودِينَهْ: (TA:) [accord. to the TḲ, the *plant called in Turkish* يارپوز, which is *marjoram:*] ▼ غَاغَةٌ [the n. un.] is said by Lth to mean *a certain plant resembling the* هَرْنَوَى [a word of which both the orthography and the application are disputed]. (TA.)

غَاغَةٌ: see what here precedes: — and see also the paragraph here following.

غَوْغَآءُ [i. e. غَوْغَآءٌ and غَوْغَآءُ, as will be shown by what follows; mentioned in this art. in the Mṣb and Ḳ; and in the Ṣ, and again in the Ḳ and TA, in art. غو;] masc. and fem., [being] perfectly and imperfectly decl., (Ṣ and TA in art. غو,) in the former case like قَمْقَام, the ء being substituted for و, and in the latter case like عَوْرَآء, (Ṣ,) *Locusts after the growth of their wings*, (AO, T, Mṣb, Ḳ,) i. e. (AO, T, Mṣb) *after the state in which they are called* دَبًا or دَبَى; (AO, T, Ṣ, Mṣb;) before which earlier state they are called سِرْوَة [or rather

[بَسْرُه]: (A'Obeyd, T, Mṣb: [see also جَرَادٌ:] or *locusts when they become light*, or *active, so as to fly*; thus accord. to AO, and IAth says the like thereof: (TA:) or *locusts when they have wings, and almost fly, before they raise themselves and fly*; thus says Aṣ: (Ṣ:) or *locusts, when they have become divested of the* [*changing*] *colours, and are becoming in a state of transition to redness.* (Aṣ, Ḳ, TA.) — And *A sort of insects resembling* بَعُوض [or *gnats*], *that do not bite*, (AO, Ṣ, Mṣb, Ḳ,) *nor hurt*, (AO, Ṣ, Mṣb,) *by reason of their weakness.* (AO, Ṣ, Ḳ.) — And, (Ṣ, Mṣb, Ḳ,) accord. to Aṣ, (Ṣ,) or AO, (Mṣb,) as being likened to the locusts thus termed, (Ṣ, Mṣb,) applied to men, (Ṣ, Mṣb, Ḳ,) meaning ‡ *A mixed multitude* of men; as also ▼ غَاغَةٌ: (Ṣ and Ḳ in art. غو:) or the سَفِلَة [i. e. *low, base, vile, ignoble, mean*, or *sordid*; or *lowest* or *lower, basest* or *baser*, &c.;] of men; and *such as haste to do evil*: and it may be from the signification here following, because of the muchness of their clamour, or confused noise, and vociferation. (TA.) — [Like غوغا in Pers., and probably from this latter, if the converse be not the case,] it signifies also *Clamour*, and *a confusion of cries* or *shouts* or *noises*. (TA.)

غول

1. غَالَهُ, (Ṣ, Mgh, O, Mṣb, Ḳ,) aor. يَغُولُهُ, (Mṣb, TA,) inf. n. غَوْلٌ, (Mgh, Mṣb, TA,) *He*, or *it*, [accord. to the TA said of a thing,] *destroyed him*; (Lth, Mgh, Mṣb, Ḳ;) as also ▼ اغتالهُ: (Ḳ:) and (Ḳ) *it* (a thing, Ṣ, O) *took him, seized him*, or *took him away, unexpectedly, at unawares*, or *from an unknown quarter*; (Ṣ, O, Ḳ;) and so ▼ اغتالهُ: (Ṣ: [see also an ex. of this latter voce خَرُوعٌ:]) and accord. to IAạr, غَالَ الشَّىْءُ زَيْدًا signifies *The thing took away Zeyd.* (TA.) One says, ▼ غَالَتْهُ غُولٌ *A* [*cause of*] *destruction destroyed him*: (Ḳ, TA:) or [*destroyed him so that it was not known whither he had gone away*; for] it is said of one who has fallen into destruction (Ṣ, TA) and it is not known whither he has gone away: (TA:) and it also signifies *Death* or *the decree of death* [*destroyed him, or took him away*]. (TA.) One says also when persons have perished in a land, غَالَتْهُمْ تِلْكَ الأَرْضُ [*That land caused them*, or *has caused them, to perish in it*]: and ▼ تَغَوَّلَتِ الأَرْضُ بِفُلَانٍ means *The land caused such a one to perish*; and *to pursue a course that led him astray.* (TA.) And one says of a land (أَرْض), تَغُولُ السَّابِلَةَ, meaning *It casts away the travellers*, or *wayfarers*; *causes them to fall*, or *drop down*; and *removes them far away.* (TA.) — غَالَتِ الخَمْرُ فُلَانًا means † *The wine* that he had drunk *deprived such a one of his reason*: or, *of the soundness of his body*: (AHeyth, TA:) [or *corrupted*, or *vitiated, him*; for] غَالَهُ, aor. يَغُولُهُ, signifies أَفْسَدَهُ; (Ksh and Bḍ in xxxvii. 46;) as well as أَهْلَكَهُ: (Ksh, ibid:) and a poet, cited by AO, says,

• وَمَا زَالَتِ الكَأْسُ تَغْتَالُنَا ▼ •

† [*And the cup of wine ceased not to deprive us of our reason*]. (Ṣ, O.) — تَغُولُ الثِّيَابَ فَتَقْصُرُ عَنْهَا is said of a tall woman [app. as meaning *She exceeds the measure of the clothes, so that they are too short for her*]: such a woman is said to be ▼ ذَاتُ غُولٍ. (TA.) — And one says, مَا غَالَكَ عَنَّا i. e. *What withheld*, or *debarred*, or *has withheld* or *debarred, thee from us?* (O.) — And غُلْتُهُ, inf. n. غِيَالَةٌ and غِيَالٌ and غُؤُولٌ, signifies *I stole it.* (O and TA in art. غيل [though belonging to art. غول].)

2. فَلَاةٌ تُغَوِّلُ, inf. n. تَغْوِيلٌ, [*A desert*, or *waterless desert*,] *of which the roads*, or *ways, are unapparent, so that it causes the people thereof* [*who traverse it*] *to go astray.* (TA.)

3. مُغَاوَلَةٌ is *syn. with* مُبَادَرَةٌ [The *hastening, making haste*, or *striving to be first* or *beforehand, in doing* or *attaining* or *obtaining* a thing], (Ṣ, O, Ḳ, TA,) [or] *in journeying, &c.* (TA.) Jereer says, (Ṣ, O,) or El-Akhṭal, (so in the TA,) mentioning a man upon whom horsemen had made a sudden attack, (Ṣ, TA,)

• عَايَنْتُ مُشْعِلَةَ الرِّعَالِ كَأَنَّهَا •
• طَيْرٌ تُغَاوِلُ فِى شَمَامِ وُكُورَا •

[*I saw those that were spreading themselves of the small parties of horsemen, as though they were birds hastening to nests in* (the mountain of) *Shemám*]. (Ṣ, O, TA.) And it is related in a trad. of 'Ammár, that he was brief in prayer, and said, كُنْتُ أُغَاوِلُ حَاجَةً لِى [*I was hastening to accomplish a want that I had*]. (TA.) And in a trad. of Ḳeys Ibn-'Ásim, [it is related that he said,] كُنْتُ أُغَاوِلُهُمْ فِى الجَاهِلِيَّةِ i. e. *I used to strive to be beforehand with them* (أُبَادِرُهُمْ) *in making a sudden attack* or *incursion, and in doing mischief*, [*in the Time of Ignorance*:] or, as some relate it, it is with ر [i. e. كُنْتُ أُغَاوِرُهُمْ *I used to make sudden attacks* or *incursions upon them*]. (TA.)

5. تَغَوُّلٌ is syn. with تَلَوُّنٌ [which primarily signifies The *becoming altered in colour*; but here, the *varying in state* or *condition*, or *in form* or *appearance*; or, agreeably with explanations of its verb by Esh-Shereeshee, (cited in Ḥar p. 480,) the *becoming altered in state* or *condition*; and the *becoming of various sorts* or *species*]. (Ṣ, O, Ḳ.) One says, تَغَوَّلَتِ المَرْأَةُ, meaning تلوّنت [*The woman varied in state* or *condition*, or *in form* or *appearance*, &c.]: (Ṣ, O, TA:) and in like manner تغوّلت is said of the غُول [q. v.]. (TA.) And *The woman made herself to be like the* غُول. (TA.) And تَغَوُّلُ الفَلَاةِ means *The dubious, and varying, state* or *condition, of the desert*, or *waterless desert.* (TA.) And one says also, تَغَوَّلَ الأَمْرُ ‡ *The affair*, or *case, became altered so as to be unknown*; [for تَنَاكَرَ, in my original, I read تَنَكَّرَ;] and *became dubious*, or *confused.* (TA.) — And تَغَوَّلَتِ الأَرْضُ بِفُلَانٍ: see 1, former half. — And تَغَوَّلَتْهُمُ الغُولُ is said of them who have been made to deviate from, miss, or lose, the right way [by the غُول; i. e. it means *The* غول *made them to deviate* &c.]. (TA.)

[6. تَغَاوَلُوا i. q. تَبَادَرُوا i. e. *They hastened together*; *vied*, or *strove, one with another, in hastening*; *made haste to be*, or *get, before one another*; *strove, one with another, to be first*, or *beforehand*, (comp. 3:) expl. by Freytag as meaning "sese invicem studuerunt capere."]

8. اغتالهُ: see 1, first sentence, in two places. — Also (Ṣ) *He slew him* (Ṣ, Mgh, O, Mṣb) *covertly* (Ṣ,* Mgh, O*) or *on an occasion of inadvertence*; (Ṣ,* O,* Mṣb;) syn. ▼ قَتَلَهُ غِيلَةً. (Ṣ, Mgh, O.) — See also 1, latter half. — لَا يَغْتَالُهُ الشِّبَعُ, said of a hawk, (Ṣ, O, TA,) &c., (TA,) signifies ‡ *Satiety will not deprive him of his strength*, (Ṣ, O, TA,) *and his vehemence of flight*: meaning that he will not become satiated: (TA:) [it is said that] it occurs in a verse of Zuheyr, [but I do not find it in his Deewán,] describing a hawk. (Ṣ, O, TA.) — هٰذِهِ أَرْضٌ تَغْتَالُ المَشْىَ means † *This is a land that renders unapparent in it the footing*, or *marching*, [of travellers,] *by reason of its far extent and its width*: an ex. of the verb [in this sense] occurs in a verse of El-'Ajjáj cited voce نِيَاطٌ, in art. نوط. (Ṣ, O.) ═ [And Freytag adds, in art. غيل, the two following significations: the former, or both, from the Deewán of the Hudhalees: *He overtook him in running*: (compare 3 and 6 in this art.:) ═ and *He filled it so that the space became too contracted to take*, or *hold*.]

غَوْلٌ *Far extent* of a desert, or waterless desert; (Ṣ, O, TA;) because it destroys him who passes along in it: (Ṣ, TA:) or of a land; because it casts away the travellers, or wayfarers, causes them to fall, or drop down, and removes them far away: and accord. to Lḥ, it is said of a land when one journeys in it without stopping. (TA.) One says, مَا أَبْعَدَ غَوْلَ هٰذِهِ الأَرْضِ *How far is the extent of this land!* and إِنَّهَا لَبَعِيدَةُ الغَوْلِ [*Verily it is far in extent*]. (ISh, TA.) And أَرْضٌ ذَاتُ غَوْلٍ *A land far extending, though in the view of the eye of little extent*: (IKh, TA:) and غَيْلٌ applied to land is said to have the same meaning. (TA in art. غيل.) And أَغْوَالُ الأَرْضِ [in which اغوال is app. pl. of غَوْلٌ] signifies *The extremities of the land.* (TA.) — اِمْرَأَةٌ ذَاتُ غَوْلٍ *A tall woman.* (TA.) See 1, last sentence but two. [And see also غَيْلَةٌ, voce غَيْلٌ, in art. غيل.] — [ناقة غول النجاء is a phrase mentioned without any indication of the meaning in the TA: perhaps نَاقَةٌ غَوْلُ النَّجَآءِ, and signifying *A she-camel of an exceeding degree of swiftness.*] ═ In the saying in the Ḳur [xxxvii. 46], لَا فِيهَا غَوْلٌ, [referring to the wine of Paradise,] it means The *evil result of headache*; because it is said in another place, [lvi. 19,] لَا يُصَدَّعُونَ عَنْهَا: (Ṣ, O, TA:) or it [there] means [simply] *headache*: or *intoxication*: (Ḳ, TA:) thus some expl. it as used in that instance: (TA:) or, as expl. by AO, it there means *privation of the intellectual faculties.*

(Ṣ, O, TA.) — See also غُولٌ, latter half. — Also *Distress, trouble,* or *molestation:* (Ḳ, TA:) thus expl. by some as used in the Ḳur ubi suprà. (TA.) — And *Unfaithfulness;* or *unfaithful acting.* (TA.) — أَتَى غَوْلًا غَائِلَةً ♦ means *He did a cunning, bad, action.* (Ḳ.) = Also *Much earth.* (Ṣ, O, Ḳ.) Hence the phrase غَوْلًا مِنَ الرَّمْلِ, [app. meaning *A large quantity of sand,*] in a verse of Lebeed. (Ṣ, O.) — And *A collection of* [*the trees called*] طَلْح, (Ḳ, TA,) *with which nothing participates.* (TA.) — And *A low,* or *depressed, part of the earth,* or *of land.* (Ḳ.)

غُولٌ *A kind of* [*goblin,*] *demon, devil,* or *jinnee, which, the Arabs assert, appears to men in the desert, assuming various forms, causing them to wander from the way, and destroying them;* (JM, and TA* on the authority of IAth;) but this the Prophet denied, saying, لَا غُولَ; by which, however, accord. to some, he did not mean to deny the existence of the غول, but only the assertion of the Arabs respecting its assuming various forms and its being able to cause any one to go astray: (IAth, JM,* TA:) *i. q.* سِعْلَاةٌ [q. v.]: or *a sort of* سعلاة: (Ṣ, O, Mṣb:) or *a male jinnee;* the female being called سعلاة: (Abu-l-Wefee El-Aạrábee, TA:) pl. [of pauc.] أَغْوَالٌ and [of mult.] غِيلَانٌ (Ṣ, O, Mṣb, Ḳ) and غُولَةٌ: (O, TA:) and it signifies also *an enchantress of the jinn:* (Ḳ:) and *a demon,* or *devil, that eats men:* (En-Naḍr, O, Ḳ:) or *any jinnee,* or *devil,* or *animal of prey, that destroys a man:* (TA:) or *a certain beast,* (Ḳ, TA,) *terrible* [*in appearance*], *having tusks,* or *fangs,* (TA,) *seen by the Arabs, and known by them; and killed by Taäbbaṭa Sharrà:* (Ḳ, TA:) and *such as varies in form* or *appearance, of the enchanters* and *of the jinn;* (Ḳ, TA;) on his doing which, as is said in a trad., one should hastily utter the call to prayer, to prevent his mischief by the mention of God: (TA:) or *anything by reason of which the intellect departs;* as also ♦ غَوْلٌ: (Ḳ:) and *anything that takes a man unexpectedly and destroys him:* (Ṣ, O, Mṣb:) [whence] one says, الغَضَبُ غُولُ الحِلْمِ, *Anger* [*is that which*] *destroys,* and *does away with, forbearance,* or *clemency.* (Ṣ, O.) — Also *Destruction:* [or *a cause thereof:*] and *death;* or the *decree of death.* (Ḳ.) See 1, second sentence. — And *A calamity,* or *misfortune;* (Ḳ, TA;) as also ♦ غَائِلَةٌ; (TA;) of which latter the pl. in this sense is غَوَائِلُ; (Ḳ,* TA;) thus mentioned by Ks. (Mṣb.) — And *A serpent:* pl. أَغْوَالٌ: (Ḳ:) accord. to Az, the Arabs call serpents أَغْوَالٌ; and thus this word is said to mean in the verse of Imra-el-Ḳeys,

* لِيَقْتُلَنِى وَالْمَشْرَفِىُّ مُضَاجِعِى *
* وَمَسْنُونَةٌ زُرْقٌ كَأَنْيَابِ أَغْوَالِ *

[*To slay me, while the Meshrefee* sword *was my bedfellow, and so were sharpened, polished* arrow-heads, *like the fangs of serpents*]: (O, TA:*) but AḤát says that this is meant as an exaggeration: (TA:) and it is said that the poet here means *devils.* (O, TA.)

غِيلَةٌ The *slaying covertly,* (Mgh,) or *on an occasion of inadvertence;* a subst. from اِغْتَالَهُ: (Mṣb:) originally with و [i. e. غِوْلَةٌ]. (Ṣ.) See 8: and see also art. غيل.

غَوْلَانٌ *A plant of the* [*kind called*] حَمْض, (A'Obeyd, AḤn, Ṣ, O, Ḳ,) *like the* أُشْنَان [i. e. *kali,* or *glasswort*], (Ḳ,) or, accord. to AḤn, *resembling the* عُنْظُوَان [which is described as a plant of the حمض, or, as some say, the best of the اشنان], *except that it is more slender; and it is a pasture.* (TA.) = Also sing. of غَوَالِينُ, which signifies [The *ribs* of a ship or boat, i. e.] the *things that resemble the* ضُلُوع in a ship or boat. (AA, O, TA.)

غَائِلٌ [act. part. n. of 1]. — [Hence,] أَرْضٌ غَائِلَةُ النِّطَاءِ *A land that destroys its inhabitant by reason of its far extent.* (TA.) — And غَائِلَةٌ [as an epithet applied to a fem. n.] signifies *Caused to become absent,* or *to disappear; hidden,* or *concealed:* or *stolen.* (ISh, TA.)

غَائِلَةٌ [as a subst.] *Bad,* or *corrupt, conduct;* and *evil,* or *mischief.* (Mṣb.) See also غُولٌ, last quarter. [And see art. غيل.] — And [particularly] *Wickedness,* or *disobedience,* of a slave; and his *running away;* (Mgh in art. عدو, and Mṣb;) and *the like thereof:* pl. غَوَائِلُ. (Mṣb.) — And [hence, perhaps, (as denoting a cause for reclaiming the price of a slave,) it is said that] it signifies *A right which another than the seller has to the possession of a slave, whereby the sale is annulled, and the seller is obliged to return the price to the purchaser.* (TA voce خِبْثَةٌ.) — See also غُولٌ, latter half. — [Its pl.] غَوَائِلُ also signifies *Places of destruction.* (TA.) — And you say, أَخَافُ غَائِلَتَهُ, meaning *I fear the result,* and *the evil,* or *mischief, thereof.* (TA.) = Also *A hole,* or *perforation,* of a watering-trough, or tank, (IAạr, O, Ḳ,* TA,) *that causes the water to pass away:* (TA:) pl. غَوَائِلُ. (IAạr, O, TA.)

عَيْشٌ غَوْلٌ: see أَغْوَلُ.

أَرْضٌ غِيلَةٌ *A land far extending.* (Lḥ, TA.) [Mentioned also in art. غيل.]

أَغْوَلُ [*More,* and *most, destructive*]. One says, أَيَّةُ غُولٍ أَغْوَلُ مِنَ الغَضَبِ [*What destroyer is more destructive than anger?*]. (Ṣ, O: immediately following the explanation of the saying, الغَضَبُ غُولُ الحِلْمِ.) — [Hence, perhaps,] عَيْشٌ أَغْوَلُ *A soft,* or *plentiful and easy, life;* (Ibn-'Abbád, O, Ḳ;) as also ♦ غَوْلٌ. (Ḳ.)

مِغْوَلٌ [primarily] *An instrument with which a thing is destroyed.* (Ḥam p. 648.) — And [hence] used as meaning *A knife:* and in common acceptation, *a knife that is put in the midst of a whip which is as a sheath to it:* (Ḥam ibid.:) *a knife to which a whip is a sheath:* (Mgh:) or *a slender sword, having a flat back* (لَهُ قَفًا), (Ṣ, O, Mṣb,) *like the knife,* (Mṣb,) *the sheath of which is like the whip:* (Ṣ, O:) or *an iron* [*weapon*] *that is put within a whip, which thus becomes to it a sheath:* (Ḳ:) or *a whip in the interior of which is a sword:* (A'Obeyd, TA:) said to be thus called because its owner destroys with it his enemy unexpectedly: pl. مَغَاوِلُ: (TA:) and *a thing like a* مِشْمَل [or *short and slender sword over which a man covers himself with his garment*], *except that it is more slender, and longer:* (Ḳ:) and *a long* نَصْل [or *blade*], (AḤn, Ḳ, TA,) *of little breadth, thick in the* مَتْن [which generally means the *part in the middle of which is the ridge,* but may here mean the *back*]: (AḤn, TA:) or *a short sword which a man wears inwrapped beneath his clothes:* (TA:) or *a slender sword, having a flat back* (لَهُ قَفًا): (Ḳ:) or *a slender iron* [*weapon*], *having a sharp edge and a flat back* (وَقَفًا), *which the assassin binds upon his waist in order that he may therewith destroy men.* (TA.) — [Hence,] فَرَسٌ ذَاتُ مِغْوَلٍ ‡ *A mare having a quality,* or *faculty, of outstripping:* (O, Ḳ, TA:) as though she destroyed the [other] horses so that they fell short of reaching her. (TA.)

نَزَلُوا مُغَاوِلِينَ, occurring in a trad. respecting the lie [that was uttered against 'Áïsheh, to which allusion is made in the Ḳur xxiv. 11], means *They alighted* [after] *going far in the journeying.* (TA.)

غو see غوى:

غى

1: see what next follows.

2. غَيَّيْتُ غَايَةً, (Ṣ, Ḳ, TA,) inf. n. تَغْيِيَةٌ; (TA;) [in the CḲ ♦ غَيَّتُهَا, which is wrong, unless they said thus as well as غَيَّيْتُهَا, like as they say رَيَّيْتُ رَايَةً as well as رَيَّتُهَا;] and ♦ أَغْيَيْتُهَا; (Ṣ, Ḳ, TA; but in the last as not found in the Ḳ;) *I set up the banner,* or *standard;* (Ṣ, Ḳ, TA;) from A'Obeyd. (Ṣ.) — And غَيَّى لِلْقَوْمِ *He set up a banner,* or *standard, for the people,* or *party:* or *he made it for them.* (TA.) — And غَيَّتِ الطَّيْرُ *The birds flapped their wings,* or *fluttered, in the air, without moving from their place;* or *did thus around a thing, desiring to alight upon it;* syn. رَفْرَفَتْ. (TA.) [See also 6.] = غَيَّيْتُ غَايَةً signifies [also] بَيَّنْتُهَا [i. e. *I made apparent,* or *manifest,* or *known, an utmost,* or *extreme, extent, term, limit,* or *the like;* or *I set it*]. (Mṣb.)

3. غَايَا القَوْمُ فَوْقَ رَأْسِ فُلَانٍ بِالسَّيْفِ [*The people,* or *party, acted with the sword above the head of such a one*] *as though they shadowed him with it;* [i. e., *flourished it above his head;*] from Aṣ; (Ṣ, Ḳ;*) inf. n. مُغَايَاةٌ. (TA.)

4: see 2. — أَغْيَا السَّحَابُ *The clouds were,* or *became, stationary,* (Ḳ, TA,) عَلَيْهِ *upon,* or *over, him,* or *it; shadowing him,* or *it.* (TA.) = اغيا الرَّجُلُ *The man attained the utmost limit,* or *reach, in eminence,* or *nobility,* and *in command:* and in like manner, الفَرَسُ فِى سِبَاقِهِ [*the horse in his contending in a race*]. (IḲṭṭ, TA.)

6. تَغَايَتِ الطَّيْرُ عَلَى الشَّىْءِ *The birds hovered,* or *circled, round about the thing.* (TA.) [See also 2.] — تَغَايَوْا عَلَيْهِ حَتَّى قَتَلُوهُ signifies *the same as* تَغَاوَوْا. (TA.) [See the latter, in art. غو or غوى.]

غَىٌّ:
غَيَّةٌ and غِيَّةٌ: } see art. غو or غوى.
غَيَّانُ:

غَاىٌ: see the next paragraph, in two places.

غَايَةٌ, originally غيية [i. e. غَيَيَةٌ], (TA,) The *utmost,* or *extreme, extent, term, limit, point,* or *reach;* or the *extremity;* of a thing; (MA, KL, PŞ;) *in respect of time* and *of place;* (MA, PŞ;) syn. مَدًى, (Ş, Mşb, Ķ, TA,) and مُنْتَهًى: (M, TA:) pl. ▾ غَاىٌ, (Ş, Mşb, Ķ,*) [or rather this is a coll. gen. n.,] and [the pl. properly so termed is] غَايَاتٌ. (Mşb.) [Hence, *A goal to which racers run;* as is indicated in the TA. And *A scope; an object to be reached* or *accomplished,* or *that one has in view.* And The *ultimate object* or *intent* of an action or a saying. And The *ultimate import* of a word: thus in the phrase, يُطْلَقُ بِٱعْتِبَارِ غَايَتِهِ *It is used with regard,* or *respect, to its ultimate import:* opposed in this sense to مَبْدَأٌ. And The *utmost degree, maximum, climax,* or *acme, that is,* or *may be, attained.*] And The *utmost of* one's *power* or *ability,* i. e., *of* one's *deed:* thus in the saying, غَايَتُكَ أَنْ تَفْعَلَ كَذَا [*The utmost of thy power* or *ability,* or *of thy deed, is,* or *will be, thy doing such a thing*]. (Mşb.) [And A person or thing, and persons or things, *superlative,* or *consummate,* in eminence or baseness, in goodness or evilness; *that has,* or *have, attained the utmost degree* therein. And, applied to a medicine, &c., *Possessing the utmost efficacy,* or *efficiency,* لِكَذَا *for such a thing.*] — [Also, like مَدًى, *A space that is,* or *that is to be, traversed;* or *an extent,* or the *space between two points* or *limits:* whence ٱنْتِهَآءُ غَايَةٍ, and ٱبْتِدَآءُ غَايَةٍ, *The beginning,* and *the end, of a space between two points* or *limits.*] — And *i. q.* غَلْوَةٌ, meaning [*A bow-shot;* or] *a shot of an arrow to the utmost possible distance.* (Mşb in art. غلو.) — Also *A banner,* or *standard:* (Ş, Mşb, Ķ:) pl. غَايَاتٌ (Mşb, TA) and [coll. gen. n.] ▾ غَاىٌ. (Ķ, TA.) — And *A banner* (رَايَة) *which the vintner used to raise* [or *set up*] *in order that he might be known to be a seller of wine.* (TA.) [See an ex. voce عُقَابٌ.] — And *A cloud that is alone; apart from others:* or *that is falling,* or *alighting.* (TA.) — And *Birds flapping their wings,* or *fluttering, in the air, without moving from their place;* or *doing thus around a thing, desiring to alight upon it.* (TA. [See 2.]) — And The قصبة [app. قَصَبَة, generally meaning *reed,* or *cane,* but what is meant by it here I know not,] *with which small birds* (عَصَافِير) *are taken,* or *caught,* or *sought to be taken* or *caught.* (TA.)

غَائِىٌّ [the rel. n. of غَايَة]. العِلَّةُ الغَائِيَّةُ, with the scholastic theologians, means *The final cause.* (TA.)

غَيَايَةٌ The *light of the rays of the sun;* (Ş, Ķ;) not the rays themselves: (Ş:) or, as some say, the *shade of the sun* [i. e. the *shade that is cast by the sun*] *in the morning and in the evening:* (TA:) pl. غَيَايَاتٌ. (Ş, TA.) — And *Anything that shades a man, over his head, such as a cloud,* (AA, Ş, Ķ,) and *dust,* and *darkness,* and *the like.* (AA, Ş.) — And The *bottom* of a well; (Ş, Ķ;) like غَيَابَةٌ. (Ş.)

غَيَايَآءُ A man *heavy in spirit; as though he were a dark, dense shadow, in which is no brightness.* (TA.)

المُغَيَّا *That to which a limit is set,* or *put:* so in the saying, الغَايَةُ لَا تَدْخُلُ فِى المُغَيَّا [*The limit shall not enter into,* or *be included in, that to which the limit is set*]. (Mgh.) [And,] as used by the lawyers and the scholastic theologians, *The end of the* غَايَة [or *space between two points* or *limits*]: a post-classical term. (TA.)

غيب

1. غَابَ, (Ş, O, Mgh, Mşb, TA,) aor. يَغِيبُ, (Mşb,) inf. n. غَيْبَةٌ [the most common form] (Ş, O, Mgh, Mşb, Ķ) and غَيْبٌ (Ş, O, Mşb, Ķ) and غِيَابٌ, (Ş, O,) or غِيَابٌ, (Mşb, Ķ,) and غُيُوبٌ (Ş, O, Mşb, Ķ) and غُيُوبَةٌ (O, Ķ) and غَيْبُوبَةٌ, (O, Ķ,) accord. to some of the measure فَعْلُولَةٌ, but accord. to others of the measure فَيْعَلُولَةٌ i. e. originally غَيْبُوبَةٌ, (MF,) and مَغِيبٌ (Ş, O, Mşb, Ķ) and مَغَابٌ; (Ķ;) and ▾ تغيّب; (Mşb, Ķ;) *He,* or *it, was,* or *became, absent;* غَابَ being the *contr.* of حَضَرَ; (Ş and Ķ in art. حضر;) or *distant,* or *remote;* (Mgh;) or *hidden, concealed,* or *unapparent;* (TA;) [or *absent from the range,* or *beyond the reach, of perception by sense,* or *of mental perception:* see غَيْبٌ.] You say, غَابَ عَنْهُ, inf. n. غَيْبَةٌ (Ş, Mgh, TA) &c., as above, (Ş, TA,) *He,* or *it, was,* or *became,* [*absent from him;* or] *distant,* or *remote, from him;* (Mgh;) or *hidden,* or *concealed, from him;* [&c.;] as also ▾ تغيّب. (TA.) And أَوْحَشَتْنِى غَيْبَةُ فُلَانٍ [*The absence of such a one has made me to feel lonely*]: and أَطَلْتَ غَيْبَتَكَ [*Thou hast made thine absence to be long*]. (A.) And ▾ أَنَا مَعَكُمْ لَا أُغَايِبُكُمْ [*I am with you: I will not be absent from you*]. (A.) And بَنُو فُلَانٍ يَشْهَدُونَ أَحْيَانًا وَيَتَغَايَبُونَ ▾ أَحْيَانًا (ISk, Ş, TA) i. e. [*The sons of such a one are present sometimes*] *and are absent* (يَغِيبُونَ) *sometimes:* but one does not say ▾ يَتَغَيَّبُونَ [unless with عَنْ following it]: (TA:) [it seems, however, that يتغيّبون, here, is a mistranscription for يَتَغَيَّبُونَنَا or the like; for] one says, ▾ تغيّب عَنِّى فُلَانٌ [*Such a one was,* or *became, absent from me;* or *absented himself from me*]; (Ş, Ķ,* TA;) and ▾ تَغَيَّبَنِى also in a case of necessity in verse, (Ş, Ķ, TA,) but not in any other case, (Ķ, TA,) accord. to the generality of authorities except the Koofees: (TA:) Imra-el-Ķeys says,

* فَظَلَّ لَنَا يَوْمٌ لَذِيذٌ بِنَعْمَةٍ *
* فَقُلْ فِى مَقِيلٍ نَحْسُهُ مُتَغَيِّبِى *

[thus in my copies of the Ş and in the TA; but we should read مُتَغَيِّبِ, whether it mean مُتَغَيِّبِى or not, as is shown by what follows: the verse may be rendered, *So a delightful day, with ease and comfort, betided us: and say thou, of a place of midday-sleep whereof the ill luck was absent from me, . . .*]: but Fr says that the word متغيّب is marfooa, [i. e. that the right reading is مُتَغَيِّبُ, meaning simply *absent,*] that the verse is مُكْفَأٌ [or made faulty in the termination], and that it is not allowable to make that word refer to مَقِيلٍ, like as it is not allowable to say مَرَرْتُ بِرَجُلٍ أَبُوهُ قَائِمٍ. (Ş, TA. [One might be tempted to suppose that we should read فَقِلْ; but this would not suit the context, which see in Ahlwardt's "Divans of the six ancient Arabic poets," p. 119.]) — [غَابَ, inf. n. غَيْبَةٌ, is also said of the mind (القَلْبُ), meaning † *It was,* or *became, absent.* The inf. n. (غَيْبَةٌ) is often used as meaning † *Absence of mind;* and particularly, *from self and others by its being exclusively occupied by the contemplation of divine things:* see an ex. voce سَكِينَةٌ.] — مَا غَابَ عَنْهُ ٱبْنُ أَبِى قُحَافَةَ; and another voce شَوًى † [*Ibn-Abee-Ķoháfeh was not a stranger to it,* i. e. *was not unacquainted with it,*] occurs in a trad. respecting a satirical saying of Ḥassán against [the tribe of] Ķureysh; meaning that Aboo-Bekr [the son of Aboo-Ķoháfeh] was skilled in genealogies and traditions, and that it was he who instructed Ḥassán. (TA.) — And one says also, غَابَ الرَّجُلُ, inf. n. غَيْبٌ and مَغِيبٌ; and ▾ تغيّب; *The man journeyed;* and *went away,* or *far away.* (TA.) — And غَابَتِ الشَّمْسُ, (Ş, Mgh, Mşb, TA,) inf. n. غِيَابٌ and غَيْبُوبَةٌ (Mgh, Mşb, TA) and غُيُوبٌ (Mgh) and غَيْبَةٌ and مَغِيبٌ; (TA;) and ▾ تغيّبت; (Mşb;) *The sun set:* (Ş, Mşb, TA:) and the like is also said of the moon, (Mşb,) and of other celestial bodies. (TA.) — And غَابَ الشَّىْءُ فِى الشَّىْءِ, inf. n. غِيَابَةٌ and غُيُوبَةٌ and غِيَابٌ and غَيَابٌ and غِيبَةٌ, [*The thing became hidden,* or *concealed, in the thing.*] (Ķ.) — See also 8, in two places.

2. غَيَّبَهُ (Ş, Mşb, TA) *He caused him,* or *it, to become absent,* or *to disappear;* or *he hid,* or *concealed, it,* عَنْهُ *from him.* (TA.) See also غَيَابٌ. — And see 8.

3. مُغَايَبَةٌ signifies The *being absent,* &c., *one from the other.* (KL.) See also 1, former half. — Also The *addressing words to another* [*in his absence,*] *not in his presence, not face to face;* (KL;) *contr. of* مُخَاطَبَةٌ. (Ş, TA.) [You say, غَايَبَهُ, inf. n. as above, *He held a verbal communication with him in his absence,* i. e. *by means of a letter* or *letters,* or *by a messenger* or *messengers.*]

4. اغابت *She* (a woman) *had her husband,* (Ş,

Mṣb, TA,) or *one of her family*, (TA,) *absent from her*. (Ṣ, Mṣb, TA.)

5: see 1, in seven places. —— The inf. n. تَغْيِيبٌ occurring in a trad. respecting the contract for the sale of a slave means The *selling a stray slave*, or *one who has been found and whose owner is not known*. (L, TA.)

6: see 1, former half.

8. اغتابهُ [*He spoke evil of him*; or *did so in his absence*, i. e. *backbit him*; (the latter being obviously the primary signification;) *not always, though generally*, meaning *with truth*:] *he spoke evil of him in his absence*; (TA;) or *said of him, in his absence, what would grieve him* (Ṣ, TA) *if he heard it*; (Ṣ;) *with truth*: (Ṣ, TA:) *he carped at him behind the back*, or *in absence, by saying what would grieve him*, (تَنَاوَلَهُ بِظَهْرِ الغَيْبِ ↓ بِمَا يَسُوْؤُهُ,) *of what was* [*reprehensible*] *in him*: (TA:) or *he spoke of him imputing to him what he disliked, of vices, or faults, with truth*: (Mṣb:) when the charge is false, it is termed بُهْتَانٌ: (Ṣ, Mṣb, TA:) or *he attributed*, or *imputed, to him a vice*, or *fault*, or *the like*; and *mentioned him with what was in him of evil*; (Ḳ, TA;) or *said of him what would grieve him*: (TA:) and ↓ غَابَهُ signifies the same: (Ḳ, TA:) [so does ↓ غَيَّبَهُ: (see Ksh in civ. 1:) that اغتابهُ does not always signify *he spoke evil of him*, or the like, *in his absence*, appears from several instances, such as the phrases المُغْتَابُ فِى الوَجْهِ (Ḳ in art. لمز) and المُغْتَابُونَ بِالحَضْرَةِ (IAạr, TA in that art.): nor does it always signify *he spoke evil of him*, or the like, *with truth*; for the verb is used in the Ksh and by Bḍ and Jel in civ. 1 having for its object the Prophet:] IAạr says that ↓ غاب is *syn. with* اغتاب, and signifies *he mentioned* a man *with the imputation of good or of evil*. (TA.) [It may also mean *He expressed*, or *signified, an evil opinion of him by making signs with the side of the mouth*, or *with the eye*, or *with the head*, or *otherwise*; as is indicated in the TA in arts. لمز and همز.]

غَابٌ: see غَابَةٌ, in three places.

غَيْبٌ *Whatever is absent*, or *hidden, from one*; (Ṣ, A, Mṣb, Ḳ, TA;) as though it were an inf. n. used in the sense of the act. part. n. [in which the meaning of a subst. is predominant]; (TA;) and so ↓ غَائِبٌ, which [in this sense] is a subst., like كَاهِلٌ, (Ḳ, TA,) or an act. part. n. used in the sense of a subst.: (MF:) *anything that is absent, or hidden, from the eyes; invisible, unseen*, or *unapparent; whether it be, or be not, perceived in the heart*, or *mind*: (IAạr, TA:) [or *anything unperceivable; absent from the range*, or *beyond the reach, of perception by sense*, or *of mental perception*; or *undiscoverable unless by means of divine revelation*; *a mystery*, or *secret, such as an event of futurity*;] *a thing that has been hidden from men, and with which the Prophet has acquainted them, of the events of the resurrection and of Paradise and of Hell &c.*; thus in the Ḳur ii. 2; (Zj, TA;) and [hence] Zj explains الغَيْبُ as meaning, in the Ḳur lxxxi. 24, *that which has been revealed*: (TA in art. ضن:) pl. غُيُوبٌ. (Mṣb.) [See also the Ksh and Bḍ in ii. 2.] [Hence, عَالَمُ الغَيْبِ *The world of the unseen*; *the invisible world*.] And [hence also] one says, رَجَمَ بِالغَيْبِ [and قَذَفَ بِالغَيْبِ (see art. قذف)] *He spoke of that which he did not know*: (Ḥam p. 494:) and قَالَ رَجْمًا بِالغَيْبِ *He said conjecturally*, [or *speaking of that which was hidden from him* or *unknown by him*,] *without evidence*, and *without proof*. (Mṣb in art. رجم, q. v.) —— And † *Doubt*, or *a doubting*: (Ḳ:) but some disapprove this: some regard it as tropical: and some pronounce it correct: (MF, TA:) pl. غِيَابٌ and غُيُوبٌ. (Ḳ.) A poet says,

أَنْتَ نَبِىٌّ تَعْلَمُ الغِيَابَا *
لَا قَائِلًا إِفْكًا وَلَا مُرْتَابَا *

[*Thou art a prophet, knowing doubts*, or *things doubted*; *not saying a lie, nor a thing suspected*: or, more probably, the meaning is, *the things unseen*]. (TA.) —— Also *A place, in the ground, that hides*, or *conceals, one*: (TA:) *a low*, or *depressed, place in the ground*, or *in a tract of land*: (Ṣ, Ḳ, TA:) or *any place such that one knows not what is in it*: and *a place such that one knows not what is behind it*: (Sh, TA:) pl. غُيُوبٌ. (TA.) Hence the phrase عَنْ ظَهْرِ غَيْبٍ in a verse of Lebeed cited voce ظَهْرٌ, q. v. (TA.) [Hence also] one says, سَمِعْتُ صَوْتًا مِنْ وَرَآءِ الغَيْبِ i. e. [*I heard a sound*, or *voice*,] *from* [*behind*] *a place that I saw not*. (A, TA.) And تَنَاوَلَهُ بِظَهْرِ الغَيْبِ بِمَا يَسُوْؤُهُ: see 8. And تَكَلَّمَ بِهِ عَنْ ظَهْرِ غَيْبٍ (A) or عَنْ ظَهْرِ الغَيْبِ (TA, and A and O in art. ظهر) [app. *He spoke of it by memory*; *in the absence of a book or the like*; as one says in modern Arabic, عَلَى الغَائِبِ. See also ظَهْرٌ.] —— Also The خَمْصَة [i. e. *pit*, or *depression*, as is shown by what here follows, (thus in the A, and in the Ksh in ii. 2, in the TA حُفْرَة, which has a similar meaning,)] *that is in the place where the kidney is situate*, (Ksh, A, TA,) *and which swells up when the beast becomes big in the belly*: so says ISh: (Ksh ubi suprà:) or the خَمْصَة *that is next to the kidney*: (Bḍ in ii. 2: [De Sacy doubted respecting its meaning, but conjectured that it might be thus: see his Anthol. Gramm. Arabe p. 55:]) pl. غُيُوبٌ: one says, شَرِبَتِ الدَّابَّةُ حَتَّى وَارَتْ غُيُوبَ كُلَاهَا, (ISh, Ksh ubi suprà, A, TA,) meaning هُزُومَهَا [i. e. *The beast drank until it concealed the pits of its kidneys*]. (A, TA.) —— And *Fat*: (Ḳ, TA:) i. e. the *fat of the* ثَرْب [q. v.] of a sheep or goat: so called because it is hidden from the eye. (TA.) ═ See also غَائِبٌ.

غُيَّبٌ: see غَائِبٌ, in two places.

غَابَةٌ is originally [غَيَبَةٌ] of the measure فَعَلَةٌ, with fet-ḥ to the ع. (Mṣb.) It signifies *A low, or depressed, place*, or *a hollow in the ground*, (El-Hawázinee, Ḳ, TA,) *before which*, or *in the way to which*, (دُونَهَا,) *is an eminence*. (El-Hawázinee, TA.) —— And (Ḳ) *i. q.* أَجَمَةٌ: (Ṣ, Ḳ, TA:) [i. e.] *A bed of canes or reeds*: (AḤn, Mṣb, TA:) and [*a thicket, wood*, or *forest*; like أَجَمَةٌ;] *a collection of trees*, (AḤn, ISd, TA,) *densely disposed*; so called because it conceals what is in it: (ISd, TA:) or *a tall* أَجَمَة, *having high*, or *very high, extremities* [app. *to its canes* or *reeds*]: (TA:) pl. غَابَاتٌ (Mṣb, TA) and [coll. gen. n.] ↓ غَابٌ. (Ṣ, Mṣb, TA.) —— And † *A long spear* (Ḳ, TA) *that has extremities like those of the* أَجَمَة [expl. above]: (TA:) [but I think that this addition in the TA correctly applies to غَابَةٌ signifying *a number of spears, like a bed of canes or reeds*, or *like a forest*; agreeably with two of the explanations here following:] or *a spear that quivers in the wind*: (Ḳ, TA:) or ‡ *numerous spears, like abundant and dense trees*: (A:) or *an assemblage of spears*; app. so called as being likened to a غابة meaning an أَجَمَة of dense trees: (ISd, TA:) pl. غَابَات and [coll. gen. n.] ↓ غَابٌ. (TA.) One says, أَتَوْنَا فِى غَابَةٍ i. e. ‡ [*They came to us*] *amid numerous spears, like abundant and dense trees*: (A:) or غابة may be used in this case in the sense here following. (TA.) —— And *A company*, or *congregated body, of men*: (Aboo-Jábir El-Asadee, Ḳ, TA:) pl. غَابَاتٌ and [coll. gen. n.] ↓ غَابٌ. (TA.)

غَيْبَةٌ an inf. n. [See 1, in several places.] —— Also, and ↓ غَيَابَةٌ, *A low*, or *depressed, piece of land* or *ground*: so in the phrases وَقَعْنَا فِى غَيْبَةٍ and غَيَابَةٍ [app. meaning *We lighted upon a low*, or *depressed, piece* &c.; or perhaps the meaning may be *we fell into* &c.]. (Ṣ.) —— See also غَيَابَةٌ.

غِيبَةٌ the subst. from اِغْتَابَهُ: (Mṣb:) it signifies [*Evil speech respecting a person*; or *such speech in his absence*; *not always, though generally*, meaning *with truth*:] *evil speech respecting a person in his absence*; (TA;) or *a saying of him, in his absence, what would grieve him* (Ṣ, TA) *if he heard it*; (Ṣ;) *with truth*: (Ṣ, TA:) or *speech respecting a person imputing to him what he dislikes, of vices, or faults, with truth*: (Mṣb:) when it is false, it is termed بُهْتَانٌ: (Ṣ, Mṣb, TA:) or *an imputing to a person a vice, or fault, or the like*; and *a mentioning him with what is in him of evil*; (Ḳ, TA;) or *a saying of him what would grieve him*: (TA:) or it may be *speech imputing good or evil*. (Ḳ,* TA.)

غَيْبَانٌ or غَيَبَانٌ, [accord. to different copies of the Ḳ, between which the TA does not enable us to decide with certainty, as it only states, with respect to the ى, that it is مُخَفَّفَة, which may mean either the contr. of doubled or the contr. of movent, though the former is the more general meaning, (in the TA it is said to be erroneously written in a copy of the Ḳ with a final ت instead of ن,)] and ↓ غَيَّبَانٌ, The *roots of trees*, (Ḳ, TA,) *that are hidden from view*: or, accord. to AḤn, the غيبان and ↓ غَيَّبَان and ↓ غَيَابَةٌ, of plants, or herbage, are, with the Arabs, *what the sun has not shone upon*: and accord. to Aboo-Ziyád El-Kilábee, the غيبان and ↓ غَيَّبَان of plants, or herbage, and also of their roots, are *what is con-*

cealed from the sun, so as to be not shone upon by it. (L, TA.)

غَيْبَانٌ : see the next preceding paragraph, in three places.

غَيَابٌ *A thing that hides,* or *conceals, a thing from one:* (Meyd:) and hence, (Meyd, TA,) *a grave;* (Ṣ, Meyd, TA;) and so ↓ غَيَابَةٌ: (TA:) one says, غَيَّبَهُ ↓ غَيَابُهُ (Ṣ, Meyd, TA) and ↓ غَيَابَتُهُ (TA) meaning دُفِنَ فِى قَبْرِهِ (Ṣ, Meyd, TA) [i. e. *May he be buried in his grave*]: an imprecation of death against the man. (Meyd.)

غَيَابَةٌ The *part* of anything *that veils,* or *conceals, one.* (Ḳ.) And hence, (Ḳ,) The *bottom* of a جُبّ [or well]; (Ṣ, Ḳ,* TA;) or this, accord. to some, is the primary signification; as also ↓ غَيْبَةٌ, accord. to one reading, in the Ḳur xii. 10; (TA;) [and غَيَابَةٌ;] and of a valley; (Ṣ, TA;) &c.: (TA:) pl. غَيَابَاتٌ. (Ḳ, TA.) [And *A covert,* or *place of concealment,* of birds. (See طَلَاوَةٌ.)] See also غَيَابٌ, in two places: and غَيْبَةٌ. — And see غَيْبَانٌ.

غَائِبٌ act. part. n. of 1 [signifying *Absent; distant,* or *remote;* and *hidden, concealed,* or *unapparent;* or *absent from the range,* or *beyond the reach, of perception by sense,* or *of mental perception*]: pl. (applied to men, Ḳ, TA) غُيَّبٌ and غُيَّابٌ (Ṣ, Mṣb, Ḳ) and غَائِبُونَ (Ḳ) and ↓ غَيَبٌ, (Ṣ, Mgh, Ḳ,) or rather the last is a quasi-pl. n., (TA,) and ↓ غَيْبٌ, [which is also properly speaking a quasi-pl. n.,] like صَحْبٌ: (Mṣb [in which غَيَبٌ is not mentioned]:) the ى in ↓ غَيَبٌ remains unchanged, notwithstanding the two fet-ḥahs, because it is likened to صَيَدٌ, and, although it is a pl. [in signification] and صَيَدٌ is an inf. n., it may be used as meant for an inf. n. (Ṣ, TA.) — See also غَيْبٌ, first sentence. — Also *A run in which a horse reserves* [*somewhat of his force for the time of need*]. (A in art. شهد: see شَاهِدٌ.)

مَغِيبٌ [an inf. n.: — and also a n. of place and of time, signifying] The *place* [and the *time*] *of setting* of the sun and of the moon [&c.]. (Mṣb.)

مُغِيبٌ and مُغِيبَةٌ, (Mgh, Mṣb, Ḳ,) or you say مُغِيبَةٌ [only], with ة, and [in the contr. sense] مُشْهِدٌ, without ة, (IDrd, Ṣ,) and مُغْيِبٌ (Ḳ) and ↓ مُغَيِّبٌ, (TA,) A woman *having her husband* (or *one of her family,* TA) *absent from her.* (Ṣ, Mgh, Mṣb, Ḳ, TA.)

مُغَيِّبٌ : see the next preceding paragraph.

غيث

1. غَاثَ ٱللّٰهُ ٱلْبِلَادَ, (Ṣ, O, Mṣb, Ḳ,) aor. يَغِيثُ, inf. n. غَيْثٌ, (Ṣ, O, Mṣb,) *God watered the country,* or *countries, with rain.* (O, Mṣb, TA.) And غَاثَنَا *He* (God) *sent down rain upon us.* (TA.) And غَاثَ ٱلْغَيْثُ ٱلْأَرْضَ, (aor. and inf. n. as above, Mṣb,) *The rain fell upon the earth.* (Ṣ, O, Mṣb, Ḳ.) And غِيثَتِ ٱلْأَرْضُ, aor. تُغَاثُ, (Ṣ, O, Mṣb, Ḳ,) inf. n. as above, (Ṣ, O,) *The land was watered with rain.* (Ṣ, O, Mṣb, Ḳ.) غِيثَ ٱلْقَوْمُ *The people were rained upon; rain fell upon the people* [or *upon their land*]. (TA.) And غِثْنَا مَا شِئْنَا [*We were rained upon as much as we desired*]: (Ṣ, O, Mṣb, TA:) originally غُيِثْنَا. (TA.) — غَاثَ ٱلنَّوْرُ ‡ *The blossom shone.* (O, Ḳ, TA.) — See also 4 in art. غوث.

2. غَيَّثَ, said of a blind man, *He sought,* or *searched,* [or *groped, with the hand,*] *for a thing:* (Kr, TA:) also written [عَيَّثَ] with [the unpointed] ع, and thus correctly, though ISd thought this latter to be a mistranscription. (TA.)

5. تَغَيَّثَ *He became fat:* (Ḳ:) said of a camel. (TḲ.)

غَيْثٌ inf. n. of غَاثَ [q. v.]. (Ṣ, O, Mṣb.) — And [a subst.] signifying *Rain:* (Ṣ, A, O, Mṣb, Ḳ:) or *rain that occupies the space of a* بَرِيد [i. e. *six miles, or twelve miles,*] *in width:* (AA, O, Ḳ:) or *rain that is productive of much good;* [supposed to belong to art. غوث, for it is added,] because mankind are aided thereby; thus expl. in the "Sharḥ esh-Shifè:" pl. أَغْيَاثٌ [a pl. of pauc.] and غُيُوثٌ. (TA.) [Hence a tropical usage in a saying mentioned voce تَجَّاجٌ.] — And [hence] ذُبَابُ غَيْثٍ [or ذُبَابُ ٱلْغَيْثِ (see ذُبَابٌ)] lit. *The fly of rain* or *the fly of the rain*] signifies † *the bee,* or *bees* collectively: so called because the bee seeks after herbage and flowers, which are consequent upon the rain: (IAth, TA:) [for] — غَيْثٌ signifies also ‡ *Herbage* (Lth, Ṣ, A, O, Mṣb, Ḳ) *which grows by means of the water of the sky:* (Lth, A, O, Ḳ:) called thus by the name of its cause. (Mṣb.) — And ‡ *Clouds.* (Ṣ, O, TA.) [See an ex. voce فَرُوقَةٌ.]

غِيَاثٌ, originally غِوَاثٌ, see in art. غوث.

غَيِّثٌ i. q. عَيْلَمُ مَآءٍ [i. e. *Water that is beneath a stratum of rock*]. (TA.) [Hence] بِئْرٌ ذَاتُ غَيِّثٍ *A well having a constant accession of water.* (O, Ḳ.) — And [hence] فَرَسٌ ذُو غَيِّثٍ ‡ *A horse that performs,* (O,) or *that increases* [*his running*], (Ḳ, TA,) *run after run.* (O, Ḳ, TA.)

أَرْضٌ مَغِيثَةٌ, and ↓ مَغْيُوثَةٌ, (the latter being the original form, TA,) *Land watered with rain.* (Ṣ, O, Mṣb, Ḳ.)

غَيْثٌ مُغِيثٌ *A general rain.* (TA.) [But the epithet مُغِيثٌ evidently belongs to art. غوث; and the phrase properly signifies *A rain that gives aid,* or *succour.*]

مَغْيُوثَةٌ : see أَرْضٌ مَغِيثَةٌ.

غيد

1. غَيِدَ, aor. ـَ, (L, Ḳ,) inf. n. غَيَدٌ, (L,) *He had a bending neck, and limber sides:* (L, Ḳ:) or *he had a lax,* or *limber, neck.* (L.) — [And غَيِدَتْ is app. said of a young woman as meaning *She was soft,* or *tender;* or *soft,* or *tender, and limber in the sides.* (See غَيَدٌ below.) — And غَيِدَ *He was,* or *became, drowsy;* or *drowsy and with a bending of the neck.* (See, again, غَيَدٌ below.)]

6. تغايد *He affected a bending of his body,* or *he bent his body, from side to side,* in his gait. (A.) And تغايدت *She* (a woman, L) *affected a bending of her body,* or *bent her body,* (L, Ḳ, TA,) *from side to side,* (TA,) in her gait, *by reason of softness,* or *limberness.* (L, Ḳ, TA.)

غَادٍ A *fresh, tender, juicy* twig: (L:) and so غَادَةٌ applied to a tree (شَجَرَةٌ). (L, Ḳ.) — And the latter, A *soft,* or *tender, goodly, thin-skinned, plump,* and *fresh,* or *flourishing,* young woman: (L:) or, (Ṣ, A, L, Ḳ,) as also ↓ غَيْدَآءُ, (Ṣ, A, Ḳ,) a woman, *soft,* or *tender:* (Ṣ, A:) or *soft,* or *tender, and limber* (L, Ḳ, TA) *in the sides.* (TA.)

غِيدْ غِيدْ, or غِيدِ غِيدِ, (accord. to different copies of the Ḳ,) *Hasten thou; make haste; be quick:* (Ḳ:) a word of the people of Esh-Shiḥr. (TA.)

غَيَدٌ [mentioned above as an inf. n.], in a woman, (Ṣ, Ḳ,) or in a young woman, (L,) *Softness,* or *tenderness,* (Ṣ, L, Ḳ,) *and limberness* (L, Ḳ) *of the sides.* (L.) — And *Drowsiness:* (A:) [or *drowsiness with a bending of the neck:* see أَغْيَدُ.]

غَيْدَانٌ The *prime, spring,* or *first part,* of youth. (Ibn-'Abbád, O, Ḳ, TA.)

أَغْيَدُ A plant, or herbage, *soft,* or *tender, and bending.* (L, Ḳ.) — And ‡ A place *abounding with plants,* or *herbage,* (O, Ḳ, TA,) *bending by reason of softness.* (O.) — Also A man, and a gazelle, *having a bending neck, and limber sides:* or *having a lax,* or *limber, neck.* (L.) And [the fem.] غَيْدَآءُ (L, Ḳ) A woman (L) *who bends her body,* or *affects a bending thereof, by reason of her softness,* or *limberness.* (L, K.) See also غَادٍ. — Also *Drowsy, and having a bending of the neck:* (Ṣ, A, L, Ḳ:) fem. غَيْدَآءُ: (TA:) and pl. غِيدٌ. (L.) ٱلْكَرَى ٱلْأَغْيَدُ, occurring in a verse cited voce صُبَابَةٌ [q. v.], means ‡ *Drowsiness that makes one to bend the neck from side to side.* (L, TA.)

غير

1. غَارَ أَهْلَهُ, (Ṣ, Mṣb,) and غار لَهُمْ, (TA,) aor. يَغِيرُ, inf. n. غِيَارٌ (Ṣ, Mṣb) and غَيْرٌ, (Mṣb, TA,) i. q. مَارَهُمْ, (Ṣ, Mṣb, TA,) i. e. *He brought,* or *conveyed, to his family,* مِيرَة [or *a provision of corn,* or *wheat,* &c.]. (Mṣb.) [See also art. غور.] — And *He benefited them.* (Ṣ, Ḳ,* TA.) 'Abd-Menáf Ibn-Ribạ El-Hudhalee says

* مَا ذَا يَغِيرُ ٱبْنَتَىْ رِبْعٍ عَوِيلُهُمَا *

[*What will their loud weeping benefit,* or *avail, the two daughters of Ribạ?*] meaning that their weeping for their father will not avail them aught in lieu of seeking his blood-revenge. (Ṣ, TA.) You say غَارَهُمْ بِخَيْرٍ, (Ṣ, Ḳ, TA,) aor. and inf. n. as above, (TA,) *He* (God) *bestowed upon them abundance of the produce of the earth, and rain*; (TA in art. غور;) like as you say أَعْطَاهُمْ خَيْرًا: (Ṣ, Ḳ:) and so غارهم برزق [*He bestowed upon them means of subsistence*]. (TA.) And اَللّٰهُمَّ غِرْنَا بِخَيْرٍ (Ṣ, Mṣb) *O God, benefit us with prosperity.* (Mṣb.) And غَارَهُمْ بِمَطَرٍ *He* (God) *watered them with rain,* (Ṣ, Ḳ, TA,) *and bestowed upon them abundance of the produce of the earth.* (TA.) And غَارَ الأَرْضَ الغَيْثُ *The rain watered the land.* (Fr, Ṣ.) [See also art. غور.] ═ غَارَهُ, aor. يَغِيرُهُ, (AO, Ṣ, Ḳ,) inf. n. غَيْرٌ, (TA,) *He gave him the bloodwit;* (AO, Ṣ, Ḳ;) as also غاره, aor. يَغُورُهُ; (AO, Ṣ, TA;) مِنْ أَخِيهِ [*for his brother*]: and so ↓ غَيَّرَهُ. (TA.) [See غِيرَةٌ.] ═ غَارَ عَلَى أَهْلِهِ, (Ṣ,) or على آمْرَأَتِهِ, (Mṣb, Ḳ,) aor. يَغَارُ, inf. n. غَيْرَةٌ, (Ṣ, Mṣb, Ḳ,) with fet-ḥ, (Ṣ, Mṣb, TA,) and غَيْرٌ and غَارٌ (Ṣ, Mṣb, Ḳ) and غِيَارٌ, (Ḳ,) [*He was jealous of his wife*:] *he was jealous for her* (مِنْ فُلَانٍ *of such a one*: Mgh): [*he was careful of her, to avoid suspicion: or he regarded her conduct with disdain, scorn, or indignation*: (see غَيْرَةٌ, below:) or] *he was angry at the conduct,* or *action, of his wife.* (Mṣb.) And غَارَتِ آمْرَأَتُهُ عَلَيْهِ [*His wife was jealous of him*: &c.]. (Mṣb, Ḳ.) [See also art. غور.] And you say also, فُلَانٌ لَا يَغَارُ, meaning لَا يَتَغَيَّرُ ↓ عَلَى أَهْلِهِ [*Such a one is not jealous of his wife*: &c.]. (TA.)

2. غَيَّرَ الشَّىْءَ, (Ṣ, Mṣb, Ḳ,*) inf. n. تَغْيِيرٌ, (Mṣb,) *He made the thing other than it was;* (Ḳ;) *made it cease to have the quality which it had;* (Mṣb;) *altered it; changed it.* (Ḳ.) *He,* or *it, altered,* or *changed, the thing in odour,* or *otherwise, for the worse; corrupted, tainted,* or *infected, it; rendered it ill-smelling, stinking, fetid, rancid, rank, fusty,* or *frouzy.* (The lexicons passim.) It is said in the Ḳur [viii. 55], ذٰلِكَ بِأَنَّ اللّٰهَ لَمْ يَكُ مُغَيِّرًا نِعْمَةً أَنْعَمَهَا عَلَى قَوْمٍ حَتَّى يُغَيِّرُوا مَا بِأَنْفُسِهِمْ [*This was because God changeth not favour which He hath conferred upon a people until they change what is in themselves*: or] *until they change what God hath commanded them to do.* (Th, TA.) — [And *He exchanged the thing for another thing.*] — غيّر الشَّيْبَ *He plucked out the white,* or *hoary, hairs.* (TA.) — غيّر عَنْ بَعِيرِهِ *He put down the saddle from his camel, and put it to rights,* or *adjusted it,* or *repaired it.* (TA.) One says تَرَكَ القَوْمَ يُغَيِّرُونَ *He left the people putting to rights,* or *adjusting,* or *repairing, the camels' saddles.* (Ṣ, TA.) ═ See also 1, latter half.

3. [غَايَرَا, inf. n. مُغَايَرَةٌ, *They differed, each from the other.*] You say بَيْنَهُمَا مُغَايَرَةٌ *Between them two is a difference.* (Mṣb.) [See also 6.] ═ غايرهُ, (Ṣ, Ḳ,) inf. n. مُغَايَرَةٌ, (Ṣ,) *He bartered,* or *exchanged, with him, in buying and selling.* (Ṣ, Ḳ.) And غايرهُ بِالسِّلْعَةِ, inf. n. as above, *He bartered,* or *exchanged, the article of merchandise with him.* (TA.) And غاير السِّلْعَةَ, (TA,) inf. n. غِيَارٌ, (Ṣ, Ḳ, TA,) *He exchanged the article of merchandise.* (Ṣ,* Ḳ,* TA.) El-Aạshà says

فَلَا تَحْسِبَنِّى لَكُمْ كَافِرًا
وَلَا تَحْسِبَنِّى أُرِيدُ الغِيَارَا

[*Therefore do thou by no means think me ungrateful towards you; and do thou by no means think I desire the making an exchange*]. (Ṣ, TA.)

4. اغار أَهْلَهُ [*He made his wife jealous;*] *he married another in addition to his wife, so she became jealous* (غارت): (Aṣ, A'Obeyd, Mṣb, Ḳ:) belonging to this art. and to art. غور. (TA.)

5. تغيّر quasi-pass. of غيّر, (Ṣ, Mṣb,) [*It became other than it was;*] *it ceased to have the quality which it had;* (Mṣb;) *it became altered,* or *changed,* عَنْ حَالِهِ, *from its state* or *condition.* (Ḳ.) *It became altered,* or *changed, in odour,* or *otherwise, for the worse; turned,* or *turned bad; became corrupted, spoiled, tainted, infected, ill-smelling, stinking, fetid, rancid, rank, fusty,* or *frouzy.* (The lexicons passim.) — [And *It became exchanged for another thing.*] — See also 1, last signification.

6. تغايرت الأَشْيَآءُ *The things differed, one from another.* (Ṣ.)

8. اغتار *He procured* مِيرَةٌ [*a provision of corn,* or *wheat,* &c.]. (Ḳ.) You say خَرَجَ يَغْتَارُ لِأَهْلِهِ *He went forth to procure* ميرة *for his family.* (Fr, Ṣgh.) — *He derived,* or *obtained, benefit, advantage,* or *profit.* (TA.) See also art. غور.

غَيْرٌ signifies i. q. سِوًى [*Other*]: and the pl. is أَغْيَارٌ: (Ṣ:) [but غير itself often has a pl. meaning, as will be seen in what follows:] or [accord. to general usage, as will be seen below,] غَيْرُ signifies i. q. سِوَى [*other than; exclusively of;* or *not,* as used before a substantive or an adjective]. (Mṣb, Ḳ: in the CḲ [erroneously] سُوَى.) It is used to qualify a subst.; [governing (as a prefixed noun) the noun that follows it in the gen. case;] and when so used, it is put in the same case as the noun preceding it. (Ṣ.) It qualifies an indeterminate noun: (Mughnee, Mṣb:) you say جَآءَنِى رَجُلٌ غَيْرُكَ [*A man, other than,* or *not, thou, came to me*]: (Mṣb:) and نَعْمَلْ صَالِحًا غَيْرَ الَّذِى كُنَّا نَعْمَلُ [*We will* in that case *do good, other than,* or *not, what we used to do*: (Ḳur xxxv. 34:)]: (Mughnee:) and مِنْ مَآءٍ غَيْرِ آسِنٍ [*Of water other than,* or *not, altered in taste and colour*]. (Ḳur xlvii. 16.) It is a noun necessarily prefixed, as to the sense, to a noun which it governs in the gen. case: but sometimes it is without the latter, when the meaning is understood and it is preceded by لَيْسَ, (Mughnee, Ḳ,) or by لَا: (Ḳ:) [in which case it signifies *Any other person* or *thing; any person* or *thing beside,* or *else*:] you say قَبَضْتُ عَشَرَةً لَيْسَ غَيْرُهَا [*I received ten; not other than they* was received by me; i. e., *not any other thing;* or *not anything beside,* or *else*]; (Mughnee, Ḳ;) the enunciative, مَقْبُوضًا, being suppressed: (Mughnee:) and ليس غَيْرَهَا; (Mughnee, Ḳ;) the noun [of ليس] being understood; i. e., لَيْسَ المَقْبُوضُ غَيْرَهَا: (Mughnee:) and ليس غَيْرَ; in which the affixed noun [for المضاف اليه, in the Ḳ, I read المضاف, as in the Mughnee,] is suppressed, and the noun [of ليس] is also understood: (Mughnee, Ḳ:) and ليس غَيْرُ; (Mughnee, Ḳ;) in which, accord. to Mbr, and the later authors, غير is indecl., being likened to قَبْلُ and بَعْدُ, so that it may be either the noun or the enunciative [of ليس] or, accord. to Akh, it is decl., because it is not a noun of time like قَبْلُ and بَعْدُ, nor of place like فَوْقُ and تَحْتُ, but like كُلّ and بَعْض, so that it is the noun [of ليس], and the enunciative is suppressed; (Mughnee;) or it may be either indecl. or decl., (Mughnee, Ḳ,) accord. to Ibn-Kharoof: (Mughnee:) and ليس غَيْرٌ, and ليس غَيْرًا; (Mughnee, Ḳ;) in both which cases it is decl., as though the affixed noun were mentioned: (Mughnee:) and لَا غَيْرُ; for the saying, [which we find in the Mughnee,] app. taken from a statement of Seer, that this is incorrect, is not good, since it occurs in the following verse, cited by Ibn-Málik;

جَوَابًا بِهِ تَنْجُو آعْتَمِدْ فَوَرَبِّنَا
لَعَنْ عَمَلٍ أَسْلَفْتَ لَا غَيْرُ تُسْأَلُ

[*Aim thou at having an answer by which thou mayest be safe; for, by our Lord, respecting an action which thou shalt have done before, not any other thing,* or *not anything beside,* or *else, thou wilt be asked*]. (Ḳ.) — It does not become determinate by its being prefixed to another noun, because it is very vague: but it is also applied as an epithet to a determinate noun which is near to being indeterminate; as in صِرَاطَ الَّذِينَ أَنْعَمْتَ عَلَيْهِمْ غَيْرِ المَغْضُوبِ عَلَيْهِمْ [*The way of those upon whom Thou hast conferred favour; the other than,* or *those who are not, the objects of anger*; (Ḳur i. 6 and 7;)] because the noun rendered determinate by the art. ال denoting a genus is near to being indeterminate, and because when غير occurs between two contraries its vagueness becomes weakened, (Mughnee, Ḳ,*) or altogether departs: (Ḳ:) or it is here applied as an epithet to a determinate noun because it resembles a determinate noun in its being prefixed to such a noun: (Mṣb:) Az says that غير is here in the gen. case because it is an epithet to الذين; and that it may be an epithet to [what is technically termed in this instance] a determinate noun [as having the article ال prefixed to it] because الذين has not [in itself] a direct meaning (لِأَنَّ الَّذِينَ غَيْرُ مَصْمُودٍ صَمْدُهُ), [it being merely a conjunct noun, the meaning of which is determined by what follows it,] notwithstanding it has the art. ال prefixed to it: Abu-l-'Abbás says that Fr holds الذين to have the office of an indeterminate noun; and غير to be an epithet of it; not of any other noun; but that غير, accord. to some, may be an epithet relating to the nouns implied in انعمت عليهم, these not having a direct meaning: Akh says that غير [with what follows] is a substitute [for الذين with what follows], as though the meaning were صِرَاطَ غَيْرِ المَغْضُوبِ عَلَيْهِمْ [*the way* *of those who are not the objects of anger*]. (TA.) The reading غَيْرَ is also related, on the authority of Ibn-Ketheer, in the accus. case, as a denotative of state, [meaning *they being not the objects of anger*,] relating to the pronoun governed in the gen. case by the prep. [in عليهم]; or by أَعْنِى [*I mean*] understood; or as an exceptive, [accord. to a usage to be explained below,] if the favours be interpreted as conferred in common upon the two classes of persons. (Bḍ.) — As it resembles a determinate noun in its being prefixed to a determinate noun, [as المغضوب in the above-cited passage of the Ḳur,] some have presumed to prefix to it the article ال: but against this it may be urged, that its prefixion to a determinate noun is not to render the expression determinate, but for specification; and ال does not imply specification. (Mṣb.) — In the following verse of Ḥassán,

* أَتَانَا فَلَمْ نَعْدِلْ سِوَاهُ بِغَيْرِهِ
* نَبِىٌّ بَدَا فِى ظُلْمَةِ اللَّيْلِ هَادِيَا

the meaning is, [*A prophet came to us, who appeared in the darkness of night, a director in the right way*,] *and we did not weigh another than him with another than the other*, i. e., *with him*. (Mughnee.) — [وَغَيْرُ ذٰلِكَ is a phrase of frequent occurrence, meaning *Et cætera*.] — غَيْرٌ is also used in the sense of لَيْسَ [He, or it, *is not*]; as in the phrase كَلَامُ ٱللّٰهِ غَيْرُ مَخْلُوقٍ [*The word of God is not created*], syn. لَيْسَ بِمَخْلُوقٍ. (Az, TA.) — It is also used in the sense of لَا [meaning *Not*, as used before a participle]; (Ṣ, Ḳ;) and then it is in the accus. case, as a denotative of state; (Ṣ;) as in the phrase فَمَنِ ٱضْطُرَّ غَيْرَ بَاغٍ, (Ṣ, Ḳ,) in the Ḳur [ii. 168, and other places], (Ṣ,) i. e., جَائِعًا لَا بَاغِيًا [*But whosoever is necessitated*, being hungry, *not transgressing the due bounds*]. (Ṣ, Ḳ.) — It is also used as an exceptive, (Ṣ, Mughnee,) in the sense of إِلَّا [*Except; save; or but*]; (Mṣb, Ḳ;) and then it is put in the same case in which the word following إِلَّا would be put in the same phrase, (Ṣ, Mughnee, Mṣb, Ḳ,) because it is originally a qualificative, and its use as an exceptive is adventitious: (Ṣ:) therefore you say جَآءَ ٱلْقَوْمُ غَيْرَ زَيْدٍ [*The people came, except Zeyd*]; and مَا جَآءَنِى أَحَدٌ غَيْرُ زَيْدٍ and غَيْرَ زَيْدٍ [*Not any one came to me, except Zeyd*]: (Mṣb, Ḳ:) or its case depends upon the governing words, so that you say مَا قَامَ غَيْرُ زَيْدٍ [*No one stood, except Zeyd*], and مَا رَأَيْتُ غَيْرَ زَيْدٍ [*I saw not any, except Zeyd*]: (Mṣb:) but Fr says that some of the Benoo-Asad and Ḳuḍá'ah put غير in the accus. case, when used in the sense of إِلَّا, whether the phrase before it be complete or incomplete; saying مَا جَآءَنِى غَيْرَكَ [*Not any one came to me, except thou*], and ما جاءنى أَحَدٌ غَيْرَكَ [*Not any one came to me, except thou*]: (Ṣ, Mṣb:) and AA says that when غير has the place of إِلَّا, it is put in the accus. case. (Mṣb.) In the saying لَا إِلٰهَ غَيْرُ ٱللّٰهِ [*There is no deity other than God*], غير is in the nom. case because it is the enunciative of لا; but it may be put in the accus. case, as meaning إِلَّا. (Mṣb.) When, as an exceptive, it is prefixed to an indecl. word [and not preceded by a prep.], it may be itself indecl., with fet-ḥ for its termination; as in the following verse;

* لَمْ يَمْنَعِ ٱلشُّرْبَ مِنْهَا غَيْرَ أَنْ نَطَقَتْ
* حَمَامَةٌ فِى غُصُونٍ ذَاتِ أَوْقَالِ

[*Nought prevented the drinking from it, except that a pigeon cooed, upon branches having* اوقال, which app. means *stumps of cut shoots*]. (Mughnee, Ḳ.) [See also an ex. (of غَيْرَ أَنَّ) in a verse cited voce بَيْدَ.] — [It is often used with a prep.; as in بِغَيْرِ حِسَابٍ *Without reckoning*; (Ḳur ii. 208, &c.;) and مِنْ غَيْرِ سُوْءٍ *Without leprosy*. (Ḳur xx. 23, &c.)] = غَيْرٌ (JK, Ḳ) and (JK) ↓ غِيَرٌ (JḲ, Ṣ) signifying The *act of altering*, or *changing*, i. q. تَغْيِيرٌ, (JK,) are substs. from غَيَّرَهُ; (Ṣ with respect to the latter, and Ḳ with respect to the former;) not inf. ns., as having no unaugmented verb. (TA.) — [Hence,] ↓ غِيَرُ الدَّهْرِ, the former of these two words being of the same measure as عِنَبٌ, *The accidents*, or *casualties, of time* or *fortune, which alter*, or *change, things*: (Ḳ:) [or *alteration*, or *change, of time* or *of fortune*; for] IAmb says, with respect to the saying لَا أَرَانِى ٱللّٰهُ بِكَ غِيَرًا [*May God not show me, in thee, alteration of state*], that غِيَرٌ is from تَغَيُّرُ الحَالِ, a subst. like قِطَعٌ [as meaning "a portion of the night"]; or that it may be a pl., of which the sing. is ↓ غِيرَةٌ. (TA.) — [Hence also,] بَنَاتُ غَيْرٍ [or ↓ غِيَرٍ, as in Freytag's Arab. Prov. i. 309,] ‡ *Lying*: or *a lie*, or *falsehood*: syn. كَذِبٌ: (TṢ, Ḳ:) or [rather] *lies*. (JK, A.) You say جَآءَ بِبَنَاتِ غَيْرٍ [or ↓ غِيَرٍ] ‡ *He uttered lies*. (A.)

غِيَرٌ: see غَيْرٌ, last quarter, in four places: — and see also غِيرَةٌ.

غَيْرَةٌ [*Jealousy*;] a man's *dislike of another's participating in that which is his* [the former's] *right*: (Kull p. 268:) or *care of what is sacred*, or *inviolable, to avoid suspicion*: or *disdain*; *scorn*; or *indignation*: syn. حَمِيَّةٌ and أَنَفَةٌ: (TA:) or *anger at the conduct*, or *action, of a wife*. (Mṣb.) [See 1, last signification.]

غِيرَةٌ *A provision of corn, or wheat, &c., which a man procures for himself*; syn. مِيرَةٌ; (Ṣ, Mṣb, Ḳ,) as also ↓ غِيَارٌ: (TA:) [or the latter is probably syn. with مِيرَةٌ used in the sense of an inf. n.:] pl. of the former غِيَرٌ. (Mṣb.) [See art. غور.] — See also غَيْرٌ, last sentence but two. — Also *A bloodwit*; (AA, Ṣ, Ḳ;) syn. دِيَةٌ: (AA, Ṣ:*) and غُورٌ is a dial. var. thereof: (TA in art. غور:) pl. ↓ غِيَرٌ: (AA, Ṣ, Ḳ:) or, as some say, this is a sing., (Ṣ, TA,) of the masc. gender; TA;) and the pl. is أَغْيَارٌ: (Ṣ, TA:) and the دِيَة is said to be termed غِيَرٌ because it is a substitute for retaliation. (TA.)

غَيْرَانُ; fem. غَيْرَى: see غَيُورٌ, in two places.

غِيَارٌ The *cognizance*, or *badge, of the free non-muslim subjects of a Muslim government*; *such as the* زُنَّار [or *waist-belt*] (Mgh, Ḳ) *to the Magians*, (Mgh,) *and the like*: (Mgh, Ḳ:) or, as some say, *the cognizance*, or *badge, of the Jews*. (TA.) — كَلَامٌ بِغِيَارِهِ † *Speech*, or *language, having its own proper guise; not altered therefrom*. (Mṣb in جلف.) = See also غِيرَةٌ.

غَيُورٌ and ↓ غَيْرَانُ (Ṣ, Mṣb, Ḳ) and ↓ غَيَّارٌ (TA) and ↓ مِغْيَارٌ (Ṣ, Ḳ) epithets [all of which are intensive] from غَارَ عَلَى أَهْلِهِ, (Ṣ, Mṣb, Ḳ,) i. e., from الغَيْرَةُ: (TA:) [*Very jealous*: &c.: see غَيْرَةٌ:] and غَيُورٌ and غَيْرَى (Ṣ, Mṣb, Ḳ) and غَيَّارَةٌ (TA) signify the same applied to a woman: (Ṣ, Mṣb, Ḳ:) the pl. of غَيُورٌ is غُيُرٌ, (Ṣ, Mṣb, Ḳ,) masc. and fem., (Ṣ, Ḳ,) and he who says رُسْلٌ [for رُسُلٌ] says غُيْرٌ [or غُيُرٌ?]; (TA;) and of ↓ غَيْرَانُ, غَيَارَى and غُيَارَى; (Ṣ, Mṣb, Ḳ;) and of غَيْرَى also, غَيَارَى (Ṣ, Mṣb, Ḳ) and غُيَارَى; (Mṣb;) and of ↓ مِغْيَارٌ, مَغَايِيرُ. (Ṣ, Ḳ.)

غَيَّارٌ: see the next preceding paragraph.

أَغْيَرُ مِنَ ٱلْحُمَّى [*More jealous than fever*:] because a fever cleaves fast to its patient, like as a very jealous woman cleaves to her husband. (TA.)

أَرْضٌ مَغِيرَةٌ and ↓ مَغْيُورَةٌ, *Land watered*: (Ṣ, Ḳ:) or *rained upon*: (TA:) the former [like the latter] is with fet-ḥ to the م. (Ṣ.)

مُغَيِّرٌ *One who puts down the furniture of his camel from off him, to relieve and ease him*. (TA.)

مِغْيَارٌ: see غَيُورٌ, in two places.

مَغْيُورَةٌ: see ارض مَغِيرَةٌ.

غيض

1. غَاضَ, aor. يَغِيضُ, inf. n. غَيْضٌ (Ṣ, A, Mṣb, Ḳ) and مَغَاضٌ (Mṣb, Ḳ) and مَغِيضٌ, (TA,) *It* (water) *became scanty, or little in quantity, and sank into the earth, or disappeared in the earth*: (Ṣ, and so in some copies of the Ḳ:) or *became scanty, or little in quantity, and decreased*, or *diminished*, or *became deficient*: (A, and so in some copies of the Ḳ:) or *sank into the earth, and went away*: (TA:) or *went away into the earth*; (Mṣb;) [*contr. of* فَاضَ, aor. يَفِيضُ;] as also ↓ انغاض, (Ṣ, Ḳ,) which is of the dial. of El-Ḥijáz. (TA.) — *It* (a thing, Mṣb, a flow of milk, TA, and † the price of a commodity, Ṣ, Mṣb, Ḳ) *decreased*, or *diminished*, or *became deficient*. (Ṣ, Mṣb, Ḳ.) — وَمَا تَغِيضُ ٱلْأَرْحَامُ وَمَا تَزْدَادُ, (Ṣ,* Ḳ,* TA,) in the Ḳur [xiii. 9], (Ṣ,) means *And the wombs' falling short* [*of completion* or *of what is usual*], (Akh, Ṣ, Bḍ,) *and their exceeding* [*therein*], *in respect of the body* [*of the fœtus*], *and the period of gestation, and the number borne*: (Bḍ:) or, as some say, *in respect*

of the menstrual blood: (Bḍ:) or *the wombs' falling short of the nine months* (Zj, O, L, and so in copies of the Ḳ, but in others *seven months,*) *of gestation, and their exceeding the nine* [or *seven*] *months:* (Zj, O, L:) or *the wombs' falling short of completion, so that the fœtus dies, and their exceeding so that the gestation becomes complete:* and accord. to this explanation, the reading of seven months in the Ḳ may be correct: see also Ḳatádeh's explanation of غَيْضٌ, below, which favours this reading. (TA.) — You say also, غَاضَ الكِرَامُ وَفَاضَ اللِّئَامُ (Ṣ, A) ‡ *The generous became few,* (Ṣ, TA,) and *failed,* or *perished,* (TA,) *and the mean became many.* (Ṣ.) = غَاضَهُ, (Ṣ, Mṣb, Ḳ,) aor. as above, inf. n. غَيْضٌ, (TA,) *He* (God, Ṣ, Mṣb) *made it* (i. e. water) *to become scanty,* or *little in quantity, and to sink into the earth,* or *disappear in the earth:* (Ṣ:) or *made it to decrease,* or *diminish,* or *become deficient:* (Ḳ:) or *made it to go away into the earth:* (Mṣb:) and ↓ اغاضهُ signifies the same; (Ṣ, A, Ḳ;) and so does ↓ غَيَّضَهُ, inf. n. تَغْيِيضٌ: (TA:) thus the first of these verbs is trans. as well as intrans. (Ṣ.) [It is said in the Ḳur xi. 46,] وَغِيضَ ٱلْمَآءُ (Ṣ, A) *And the water was made to become scanty,* &c.: (Ṣ:) or *was made to decrease,* or *diminish.* (A,* Bḍ.) And hence the saying of 'Áïsheh, describing her father, وَغَاضَ نَبْعَ الرِّدَّةِ † *And he did away with what appeared of apostacy.* (TA.) You say also, غَيَّضَ ↓ دَمْعَهُ, (Ṣ,* Ḳ,) inf. n. as above, (Ḳ,) *He made his tears to diminish,* (Ṣ, Ḳ,) *and restrained them:* (Ṣ:) or *he took the tears from his eye and dashed them away.* (Th.) A poet says, (TA,) namely, Jereer, (O and TA in art. غبض,)

غَيَّضْنَ ↓ مِنْ عَبَرَاتِهِنَّ وَقُلْنَ لِى
مَا ذَا لَقِيتَ مِنَ الهَوَى وَلَقِينَا

meaning *They made their tears to flow until they exhausted them* [*and they said to me, What is it that thou hast experienced, of love, and we have experienced?*]: ISd says that من here denotes some; or it may be redundant, accord. to the opinion of Abu-l-Ḥasan; for he holds that it may be so in affirmative [as well as negative] phrases, mentioning, as an instance, قَدْ كَانَ مِنْ مَطَرٍ, meaning قَدْ كَانَ مَطَرٌ. (TA.) One relation of this verse gives غَبَّضْنَ; but the former is the right. (O and TA in art. غبض.) — Also *He opened a way, passage,* or *channel, for it* (namely water) *to flow forth to a* مَغِيض [q. v.]. (Mṣb.) — † *He diminished it,* namely the price of a commodity; (Ks, Ṣ, Mṣb, Ḳ;) as also ↓ اغاضهُ. (Ḳ.) — And *He caused him to suffer loss,* or *detriment;* and *wronged,* or *injured, him.* (ISd, TA.)

2. غَيَّضَهُ: see 1, latter half, in three places. = غيّض said of a lion *He frequented,* or *kept to, the* غَيْضَة [q. v.]. (Ṣ, Ṣgh, L, Ḳ.)

4. اغاضهُ: see 1, latter half, in two places.

7: see 1, first sentence.

غَيْضٌ *An abortive fœtus, not completely formed;* (Ḳatádeh, Ḳ;) i. e. *less than seven months old.* (TA.) = ‡ *Little;* or *a small quantity:* as in the saying, or in أَعْطَاهُ غَيْضًا مِنْ فَيْضٍ ‡ *He gave him little from much.* (Ṣ, A, Ḳ.) = *An abundance of the trees called* أَعْلَاث; i. e. طَرْفَآء and أَثْل and حَاج and عِكْرِش and يَنْبُوت. (TA.) [See also غَيْضَة.]

غِيضٌ The طَلْع [or *spadix of a palm-tree*]; (IAạr, IDrd, O, Ḳ, TA;) like غَضِيضٌ and إِغْرِيض: (TA:) or the عَجِيم (AA, O, Ḳ) [thus correctly (in the CḲ عُجْم) evidently, I think, here meaning the *heart* (commonly called جُمَّار q. v.) *of the palm-tree* (the only produce that is eaten except the dates)] *that comes forth,* or *coming forth,* (Ḳ,) or *that has not come forth,* (O,) *from* [*amid*] *its* [*membranous fibres termed*] لِيف [q. v.], *and all of which is eaten.* (AA, O, Ḳ.)

غَيْضَةٌ *A thicket;* syn. أَجَمَةٌ; i. e. *a collection of tangled,* or *confused,* or *dense, trees:* (Mgh, Mṣb:) or *an* أَجَمَة; i. e. *a* ↓ مَغِيض [q. v.] *of water collected together, in which, in consequence thereof, trees grow:* (Ṣ:) or *an* أَجَمَة: and *a place in which is a collection of trees in a* مَغِيض *of water:* (Ḳ:) or particularly, *of* [*trees of the willow-kind called*] غَرَب; *not of all trees;* (AḤn, O, Ḳ;) accord. to the first Arabs of the desert; but this is at variance with what we find in the poems of the Arabs; for Ru-beh, for instance, makes it to consist of fruit-bearing trees and trees not fruit-bearing, and makes it to be a غَابَة: (AḤn, O:) [see also غَيْنَةٌ:] pl. [of pauc.] أَغْيَاض (Ṣ, Ḳ) and [of mult.] غِيَاض (Ṣ, Mgh, Mṣb, Ḳ) and غَيْضَات: (Mṣb:) the first of these being formed with disregard of the augmentative [ة]; not being a pl. pl., for this is not so formed: (TA:) *any* غَرَب *in Nejd adjacent to the cultivated lands, when they are collected therein,* are termed غِيَاض. (O, TA.) [See also غَيْض.]

غَائِض as used in the following verse,

إِلَى ٱللّٰهِ أَشْكُو مِنْ خَلِيلٍ أَوَدُّهُ
ثَلَاثَ خِلَالٍ كُلُّهَا لِى غَائِضُ

is said by some to mean غَائِظ, the ض being substituted for ظ; [so that the verse should be rendered, *To God I complain of three qualities,* or *habits, of a friend whom I love, every one of which is to me such as angers;*] thus says IJ: but ISd says that it may be without substitution, from غَاضَهُ as expl. in the last sentence of the first paragraph of this art.; and thus the meaning may be, *such as causes me to suffer loss,* or *detriment,* and *such as wrongs,* or *injures, me.* (TA.)

مَغِيضٌ is an inf. n. (TA. [See 1, first sentence.]) — And also the pass. part. n. of غَاضَهُ; applied to water. (Mṣb, TA.*) — And a n. of place, signifying *A place where water sinks,* or *goes away, into the earth:* (Mṣb, TA:) or مَغِيضُ مَآءٍ signifies *a place where water enters* [*into the earth*]: and *a place where water collects:* (Mgh:) see also غَيْضَة: pl. مَغَايِض. (Mgh.)

غيط

1. غَاطَ, aor. يَغِيطُ, inf. n. غَيْطٌ: see غَاطَ, aor. يَغُوطُ, inf. n. غَوْطٌ, in art. غوط.

غَيْطٌ: see غَائِطٌ in art. غوط.

غيظ

1. غَاظَهُ, (Ṣ, Mṣb, Ḳ,) aor. يَغِيظُ, (Mṣb, Ḳ,) inf. n. غَيْظٌ, (Mṣb, TA,) *He,* or *it, affected him with* غَيْظ [*or anger, wrath,* or *rage;* &c.; i. e. *angered him;* or *enraged him;* &c.]; (Ṣ, Mṣb, Ḳ, &c.;) as also ↓ غَيَّظَهُ; (IAạr, Th, Ḳ; [in a copy of the Mṣb, تَغَيَّظَهُ, which is doubtless a mistranscription;]) and ↓ غايظهُ; (Ṣ, Ḳ;) and ↓ اغاظهُ; (IAạr, Th, Mṣb, Ḳ;) but this last is not common; (Zj;) or it is not allowable. (ISk, Ṣ.) [See also غَيْظٌ below.]

2: see the preceding paragraph.

3. غايظهُ, inf. n. مُغَايَظَةٌ: see 1: [originally, *He angered him,* or *enraged him,* or *the like, being angered,* or *enraged,* or *the like, by him.* — And hence, because emulation, or the like, often causes mutual anger,] ‡ *He emulated him, vied with him,* or *strove to overcome* or *surpass him, and did like as he did.* (TA.) — مُغَايَظَة also signifies † *An acting in a leisurely manner:* or it is [*a*] *mutual* [*acting in that manner*]. (TA.)

4: see the first paragraph.

5: see 8. — سَمِعُوا لَهَا تَغَيُّظًا, in the Ḳur [xxv. 13] means ‡ *They shall hear it to have a sound of boiling,* (Zj, Bḍ, Jel,) *like the boiling of the breast of an angry man.* (Bḍ,* Jel.) — تَغَيَّظَتِ الهَاجِرَةُ ‡ *The midday,* or *summer-midday, became* [*ragingly* or] *vehemently hot.* (Ḳ, TA.)

8. اغتاظ *He was* or *became, affected with* غَيْظ [*or anger;* or *rage;* &c.; i. e. *he was,* or *became, angered;* or *enraged;* &c.]; (Ṣ, Mṣb, Ḳ;) مِنْ كَذَا *by reason of such a thing;* and sometimes one says, مِنْ لَا شَىْءٍ *by reason of nothing;* (Mṣb;) as also ↓ تغيّظ. (Ṣ, Ḳ.)

غَيْظٌ *Anger; wrath;* syn. غَضَبٌ: (Ḳ) or [*rage,* or *vehement anger;* for] it has a more intensive signification than غَضَبٌ: (IDrd:) or the former is *latent* [*anger*]; and the latter is *apparent:* or the former is *that which affects a person who has not power to exercise it;* and the latter, that which affects a person who has power to exercise it: (TA:) or the former, *latent anger affecting one who has not power to exercise it:* (Ṣ:) or *most vehement anger,* (Mṣb, Ḳ,) *encompassing the liver, by reason of some event that is disliked* or *hated,* and sometimes *by reason of nothing:* (Mṣb:) or the *outbreak, and commencement, of anger.* (IDrd, Ḳ.) — تَكَادُ تَمَيَّزُ مِنَ ٱلْغَيْظِ, in the Ḳur [lxvii. 8], means † *It shall almost burst asunder by reason of vehemence of heat.* (TA.)

فَعَلَ ذٰلِكَ غِيَاظَيْكَ, and غِيَاظَيْكَ, (Ḳ,* TA,) [in the CḲ غِيَاضَيْكَ,] *i. q.* غِنَاظَيْكَ, (Ḳ,) i. e. *He did that in order to distress thee,* [or *anger thee,* or *enrage thee,*] *time after time.* (Ḳ in art. غنظ.)

غَائِظٌ *Affecting with* غَيْظ [or *anger;* or *rage;* &c.; i. e. *angering;* or *enraging;* &c.]: (TA:) pl. غَائِظُونَ. (Ḳur, xxvi. 55.)

أَغْيَظُ [comparative and superlative of غَائِظ]. أَغْيَظُ الأَسْمَآءِ عِنْدَ ٱللّٰهِ مَلِكُ الأَمْلَاكِ means *The most severely to be punished, of persons bearing names, is he who is named the king of kings:* (TA:) [lit. *the most angering,* or *enraging, of names, is the king of kings.*]

مَغِيظٌ *Affected with* غَيْظ [or *anger;* or *rage;* &c.; i. e. *angered;* or *enraged;* &c.]. (Ṣ, Mṣb.)

حَلِيمَةٌ مُغْتَاظَةٌ ‡ [lit. *Calm, angry;* or *the like;* because what it contains is sometimes still and sometimes boiling;] is an appellation given to *a stone cooking-pot.* (A, TA.)

غيف

1. غَافَتِ الشَّجَرَةُ, (Ṣ, O, Ḳ,) aor. تَغِيفُ, (O, Ḳ,) inf. n. غَيَفَانٌ; (Ṣ, O, Ḳ;) and ▼ تَغَيَّفَتْ, (Ṣ, O, Ḳ,*) in the copies of the Ḳ erroneously تغيف; (TA;) as also ▼ أَغْيَفَتْ, inf. n. إِغْيَافٌ; (TA;) *The tree inclined,* (Ṣ,) or *had its branches inclining,* (O, Ḳ,) *to the right and left.* (Ṣ, O, Ḳ.)

2. غَيَّفَ, (O, Ḳ,) inf. n. تَغْيِيفٌ, (Ḳ,) *He fled,* or *turned away and fled;* and *drew back,* or *drew back in fear;* (O, Ḳ;) and *was cowardly.* (Ḳ.) You say, حَمَلَ فُلَانٌ فِى الحَرْبِ فَغَيَّفَ i. e. [*Such a one charged, in war,* or *battle, and*] *was cowardly;* or *retreated, and was cowardly.* (Ṣ.) —— See also 5.

4: see 1. —— اغاف الشَّجَرَةَ, (O, Ḳ,*) inf. n. إِغَافَةٌ, (TA,) *He made the tree to bend,* or *incline,* (O, Ḳ,* TA,*) *by reason of softness,* or *tenderness.* (TA.)

5: see 1. —— تغيّف said of a horse, *He inclined,* or *bent,* (Ṣ, O, Ḳ, TA,) *towards one side,* (Ṣ, O, TA,) *in running.* (TA.) And *He* [app. a man] *walked with an elegant and a proud and self-conceited gait, with an affected inclining of the body from side to side, and in the manner of the tall:* or *he passed along easily and quickly:* or, accord. to AHeyth, *he affected an inclining of the body from side to side, by reason of width of step, and gentleness of pace:* accord. to El-Mufaḍḍal, *he was proud,* or *haughty, in his gait.* (TA.) The phrase مَرَّ البَعِيرُ يَتَغَيَّفُ, mentioned by Aṣ, but not expl. by him, is said by Sh to mean [*The camel passed along*] *going quickly.* (TA.) —— One says also, تغيّف عَنِ الأَمْرِ, meaning *He refrained,* or *drew back, from the affair, in fear;* as also ▼ غيّف; this latter mentioned by Th. (TA.) —— And تَغَيُّفٌ signifies also The *being,* or *becoming, creased,* or *wrinkled:* like تَغَضُّفٌ. (TA in art. غضف.)

غَافٌ *A species of trees,* (AḤn, Ṣ, O, Ḳ,) *growing in the sands, and becoming large, the leaves of which are smaller than those of the apple, which it resembles in character,* or *form,* (AḤn, O,) *having a very sweet fruit,* (AḤn, O, Ḳ,) *of the kind termed* عُلَّف, *like the pods* (قُرُون) *of the bean, and its wood is white;* so, says AḤn, *I have been informed by some of the Arabs of 'Omán,* which is the place of its origin: n. un. with ة: (O:) accord. to some of the Arabs, the *species of trees called* يَنْبُوت, [see this word, of which one description agrees exactly with that given above,] (O, Ḳ,* TA,*) *which is found in 'Omán:* (TA:) accord. to AZ, it is *of the* [*trees called*] عِضَاه, and is *a tree like the* قَرَظ [q. v.], *thorny, of the region of El-Ḥijáz, growing in the* [*high,* or *high and rugged, grounds called*] قِفَاف [pl. of قُفّ]. (TA.)

غَيْفٌ *A flock of birds.* (Ibn-'Abbád, O, Ḳ.)

غَيْفَانٌ and ▼ غَيَّفَانٌ, (O, Ḳ, TA,) the latter like هَيَّبَانٌ, (Ḳ, TA, in the CḲ هَيَّبان,) *i. q.* مَرَحٌ; (O, TA;) in the Tekmileh مَرِح, like كَتِف; and in the copies of the Ḳ مَرْخ; but the first of these is the right; meaning [*A proud and self-conceited carriage, with an affected inclining of the body from side to side,*] *in pace,* or [*manner of*] *going.* (TA.)

غَيْفَانِىّ: see أَغْيَفُ.

غَيَّفَانٌ: see غَيْفَانٌ.

غَيَّافٌ One *whose beard is long,* (O, Ḳ, TA,) *and wide on every side,* (O, TA,) *and very large.* (Ḳ, TA.)

أَغْيَفُ *Having a bending of the neck,* (*like* أَغْيَد,) *but without drowsiness.* (O, Ḳ.) —— And, applied to trees (شَجَرٌ), *quivering,* or *playing loosely, succulent,* or *sappy, soft, tender,* or *supple;* as also ▼ غَيْفَانِىّ; and so غَيْفَآءُ [the fem. of the former] applied to a tree (شَجَرَةٌ). (TA.) —— And عَيْشٌ أَغْيَفُ *A soft,* or *an easy, and a plentiful, life;* (Ibn-'Abbád, O, Ḳ;) like أَغْضَفُ. (Ibn-'Abbád, O.)

غيق

غَاقٌ *A certain aquatic bird;* as also ▼ غَاقَةٌ. (Lth, O, Ḳ.) —— And The *crow,* or *raven:* (ISd, Ḳ:) so sometimes called because of his cry. (ISd, TA.) ═══ غَاقِ is a word imitative of *The cry* [i. e. *caw*] of the crow, or raven: when indeterminate, [meaning *a caw,*] it is with tenween, (IJ, Ṣ, O, Ḳ,) i. e. غَاقٍ. (IJ, TA.)

غَاقَةٌ: see the preceding paragraph.

غيل

1. غَالَتْ وَلَدَهَا, inf. n. غَيْلٌ [q. v.]: see 4. ═══ غَالَ فُلَانًا كَذَا *Such a thing brought evil to such a one.* (TA.)

4. أَغَالَ and أَغْيَلَ, (Mgh,) or أَغَالَ وَلَدَهُ, (Ṣ, Mṣb) and أَغْيَلَهُ, (Mṣb,) *He compressed the mother of his child while she was suckling it.* (Ṣ, Mgh,* Mṣb.) —— And أَغَالَتْ and أَغْيَلَتْ, (Mgh,) or أَغَالَتْ وَلَدَهَا and أَغْيَلَتْهُ, (Ṣ, Mṣb, Ḳ,) *She gave her child to drink what is termed* غَيْل, (Ṣ, Ḳ, TA,) i. e. *the milk of her who was compressed,* or *the milk of her who was pregnant:* (TA:) or [accord. to common usage] *she suckled her child while she was pregnant:* (Mgh, Mṣb:) and ▼ غَالَتْ وَلَدَهَا, aor. تَغِيلُ, inf. n. غَيْلٌ, signifies [the same, or] *she suckled her child while she was being compressed,* or *while she was pregnant.* (TḲ.) [See also 10.] ═══ أَغْيَلَتْ said of sheep or goats, (O, Ḳ,) and of cows, (O, TA,) *They brought forth twice in the year.* (O, Ḳ, TA.) ═══ See also the next paragraph.

5. تغيّل الشَّجَرُ *The trees became tangled,* or *abundant and dense,* (Aṣ, Ṣ, Ḳ,) *in their branches, having leafy coverings* or *shades;* as also ▼ أَغْيَلَ and ▼ اِسْتَغْيَلَ: (Ḳ:) or all signify *the trees became large, and tangled,* or *abundant and dense.* (TA.) —— And تغيّلوا *They became many:* (O, Ḳ:) and (so in the O, but in the Ḳ "or") *their cattle,* or *possessions, became many.* (O, Ḳ.) ═══ تغيّل *He entered the* غيل [i. e. *thicket,* or *covert*]. (O.) And تغيّل الشَّجَرَ *He* (a lion) *entered among the trees, and took them as a* غيل [or *covert.* (TA.)

8. اغتاله *He did evil to him without his knowing whence it came so that he might prepare himself.* (TA.) It is said in a trad., أَعُوذُ بِكَ أَنْ أُغْتَالَ مِنْ تَحْتِى i. e. [*I seek protection by Thee from*] *my being the object of an event's befalling me whence I shall not know;* meaning thereby the sinking [into the ground] and being swallowed up. (TA.) الاِغْتِيَالُ and الغِيلَةُ are syn. in a sense expl. below. (Ṣ, O, Ḳ.) See the latter word below: and see also 8 in art. غول. One says, أُغْتِيلَ, meaning *He was deceived, and taken to a place, and* [*there*] *slain.* (TA.) ═══ اغتال said of a boy, *He became thick and fat.* (Ṣ, Ḳ.)

10. اِسْتَغْيَلَتْ, said of a woman, a verb of which the subst. is غِيلَةٌ [q. v.]: (Ḳ:) [accord. to the context in the Ḳ, in which the meaning is not clearly indicated, it seems to signify *She suckled her child while being compressed,* or *while pregnant;* like أَغَالَتْ وَلَدَهَا for أَغَالَتْ; and this I believe to be the right meaning: or] it signifies *she was compressed while suckling a child,* or *while pregnant.* (TḲ.) ═══ See also 5, first sentence.

غَيْلٌ: see غِيلَةٌ, first sentence, in two places. —— As some say, (Mṣb,) it signifies The *milk with which a woman suckles while she is being compressed,* (Ṣ, Mṣb, Ḳ, TA,) or *while she is pregnant:* (Ṣ, Ḳ, TA:) you say, سَقَتْهُ غَيْلًا, (Mṣb,) or الغَيْلَ, (Ḳ, TA,) i. e. *She gave him to drink such milk.* (TA.) ═══ Also *Water running upon the surface of the earth;* (Ṣ, Mgh, O, Mṣb,

Ḳ;) thus correctly, with fet-ḥ; but ▼ غِيلٌ, with kesr, is a dial. var. thereof, mentioned by ISd: (TA:) both are said to signify *water running amid trees:* (Ḥam p. 555:) IB says that the former signifies thus; and that its pl. is غُيُولٌ: and it is also said to signify *water running in rivers* or *rivulets*, and *in streamlets for irrigation:* (TA:) and by some, to signify *water running amid stones, in the interior of a valley.* (Ḥam ubi suprà.) It is said in a trad., that in the case of that [produce] which is irrigated by the water thus termed (مَا سُقِىَ بِالغَيْلِ, Ṣ, Mgh, O, Mṣb, TA, or غَيْلًا, Mgh) there shall be [given for the poor-rate] the tenth; (Ṣ, Mgh, O, Mṣb, TA;) and in the case of that which is irrigated by the bucket, half of the tenth. (Ṣ, TA.) [See also an ex. voce صُبَابَةٌ.] — And *Any valley in which are flowing springs:* (Ḳ:) or *a place in a collection of tangled,* or *abundant and dense, trees, in which is water running upon the surface of the earth:* (Lth, TA:) and *any place in which is water,* (Ḳ, TA,) *such as a valley and the like:* (TA:) and ▼ غِيلٌ, with kesr, signifies *any valley in which is water;* and the pl. of this is أَغْيَالٌ [a pl. of pauc.] and غُيُولٌ. (Ḳ.) — See also غِيلٌ. = Also A *plump, full,* سَاعِد [or fore arm]; (Ṣ, O, Ḳ;) and so ▼ مُغْتَالٌ: (Ḳ:) the latter said by Fr to be applied to a wrist as meaning *full* because from الغَوْلُ; but this saying is not valid, as غَيْلٌ is found in the same sense. (IJ, TA.) [See an ex. of the former in a verse cited voce طَفْلٌ.] And A *fat, big,* boy; as also ▼ مُغْتَالٌ: (Ḳ:) fem. of the former غَيْلَةٌ; (TA;) which is applied to a woman as meaning *fat;* (Ṣ, Ḳ;) or a *fat, big,* woman. (AO, TA.) — See also غَيْلٌ, in two places. = Also The *ornamental,* or *figured,* or *variegated, border* (syn. عَلَم) *in a garment:* (AA, Ḳ:) pl. أَغْيَالٌ. (AA, TA.) — And *A line that one makes,* or *marks, upon a thing.* (Ḳ.)

غِيلٌ *A thicket;* or *trees in a tangled, confused,* or *dense, state:* (Aṣ, Ṣ, O:) or *an abundance of such trees,* (Ḳ, TA,) *not thorn-trees, amid which one may conceal himself:* (TA:) and ▼ غَيْلٌ signifies the same: (Ḳ:) and the former, *a collection of reeds* or *canes,* and *of* [*the kind of high, coarse, grass called*] حَلْفَآء: (Ḳ:) and *i. q.* أَجَمَةٌ [i. e. *a collection,* or *an abundant collection, of tangled, confused,* or *dense, trees,* or *of reeds* or *canes*]: (Ṣ, O, Ḳ) [and in like manner ▼ غِيلَةٌ, occurring in the Deewán of the Hudhalees, is expl. by Freytag, as signifying "saltus:"] and the *place* [meaning *covert*] *of the lion:* it may not have the termination ة: the pl. is غُيُولٌ; (Ṣ, O;) and غَيَايِلُ is said to be an anomalous pl. of غِيلٌ. (O and TA in art. عيل, voce عَيَّالٌ, q. v.) — See also غَيْلٌ, in two places.

غِيلَةٌ: see غِيلَةٌ. — Also A single act of اِغْتِيَال [q. v. voce غِيلَةٌ]. (TA.) = See also غِيلٌ. = It is also fem. of the epithet غَيْلٌ [q. v.]. (TA.)

غِيلَةٌ and ▼ غَيْلٌ signify the same; (Mgh, O, Mṣb); i. e. The *compressing one's wife while she is suckling:* (Mgh, Mṣb:) thus expl. by AO as stated by A'Obeyd: (Mgh:) and thus the former signifies accord. to El-'Alḳamee; and so says Málik: or, accord. to El-Munáwee, it signifies the *compressing one's wife while she is suckling* or *pregnant:* or, accord. to ISk, a woman's *suckling while pregnant:* (from a marginal note in a copy of the Jámi' eṣ-Ṣagheer of Es-Suyooṭee, in explanation of a trad. mentioned in what here follows, commencing with the words لَقَدْ هَمَمْتُ:) and ▼ غَيْلٌ has this last signification (Mgh, TA) accord. to Ks: (Mgh:) غِيلَةٌ is the subst. from اِسْتَغْيَلَتْ: (Ḳ:) and IAth says that ▼ غَيْلَةٌ is a dial. var. thereof; or, as some say, this denotes *a single act* [*of what is termed* غِيلَة]; or the pronunciation with fet-ḥ is not allowable unless with the elision of the ة. (TA.) One says, أَضَرَّتِ الغِيلَةُ بِوَلَدِ فُلَانٍ, meaning *His mother's being compressed while she was suckling him* [*injured the child of such a one*], and likewise *his mother's being pregnant while she was suckling him.* (Ṣ, O.) [But] in a trad. is related the saying, (of the Prophet, O) "Verily I had intended to forbid الغِيلَة (Ṣ, Mgh,* O, Mṣb, Ḳ) until I remembered that the Persians and the Greeks practise it and it does not injure their children." (Mgh, O, Mṣb.) [See also 4 in art. فسد.] — Also The *act of deceiving,* or *beguiling:* (Ḳ:) and *i. q.* ▼ اِغْتِيَالٌ: (Ṣ, O, K: [see 8, and غِيلَةٌ, as expl. in art. غول:]) accord. to Aboo-Bekr, in the language of the Arabs it signifies the *causing evil,* or *slaughter, to come* to another *from an unknown quarter.* (TA.) One says, قَتَلَهُ غِيلَةً, meaning *He deceived,* or, *beguiled, him, and went with him,* or *took him, to a place, and slew him* (Ṣ, O, Ḳ) *when he reached it:* (Ṣ, O:) or *he slew him at unawares.* (Abu-l-'Abbás, TA.) = Also The شِقْشِقَة [or *faucial bag of the he-camel*]. (IAạr, Ḳ.)

أُمُّ غَيْلَانَ [in Pers. مُغِيلَان] *A species of the* [*trees called*] عِضَاه; (Mgh, Mṣb;) the [*species of lote-*] *trees called* سِدْر; (Ṣ, O, Ḳ, TA;) *the fruit of which is said to be sweeter than honey:* the saying, of some, that it is with kesr to the غ, and that it is thus called because the غيلان [pl. of غُول] are often found before it, is rejected and false: (TA:) Lth and ISh say that it is the *same as the* طَلْح [q. v.]. (TA in art. طلح.)

غَيُولٌ, as stated by IJ, on the authority of Aboo-'Amr Esh-Sheybánee, who had it from his grandfather, is sing. of غُيَّلٌ, (TA,) which is an epithet applied to oxen, or bulls and cows, (AO, IJ, O, Ḳ, TA, [نَفَرٌ in the CḲ being a mistake for بَقَرٌ,]) and to camels, (Ḳ,) signifying *Numerous:* and also [in the Ḳ "or"] *fat.* (AO, IJ, O, Ḳ.) — And, applied to anything, *Alone; solitary:* pl. غُيَّلٌ. (AA, TA.)

غَيِّلٌ, like سَيِّدٌ, (O, TA,) in the Ḳ ▼ غَيْلٌ, but this latter is said by ISd to be of weak authority, (TA,) applied to a garment, *Wide,* or *ample.* (O, Ḳ, TA.) And so غَيِّلَةٌ applied to a land: (O, TA: [mentioned also in art. غول:]) or, as some say, غَيِّلٌ, thus applied, (O, TA,) but accord. to the context in the Ḳ ▼ غَيْلٌ, (TA,) signifies *Such as one judges to be of little extent, though it is far extending:* (O, Ḳ,* TA:) and ذَاتُ غَوْلٍ, so applied, has been mentioned in art. غول as having this meaning. (TA.) And غَيِّلَةٌ applied to a woman signifies *Tall:* (O, TA:) and so does ذَاتُ غَوْلٍ. (TA in art. غول.)

الغَيَّالُ *The lion:* (Ḳ) or *the lion that is in the* غيل [or *covert*]. (O.)

غَائِلٌ *Much,* or *abundant,* dust or earth. (TA.)

غَائِلَةٌ *Rancour, malevolence, malice,* or *spite, that is covert,* or *concealed.* (Ḳ.) And *Evil,* or *mischief;* as also ▼ مَغَالَةٌ: (Ṣ, Ḳ:) thus in the saying فُلَانٌ قَلِيلُ الغَائِلَةِ and ▼ المَغَالَةِ [*Such a one is a person of little evil* or *mischief*]. (Ṣ.) — See also the same word in art. غول.

أَغْيَلُ *Full; big,* or *large.* (TA.)

مُغَالٌ (Mgh, Ḳ) and ▼ مُغْيَلٌ (Ṣ, Mgh, Ḳ) A child *given to drink what is termed* غَيْل: (Ṣ,* Ḳ: [See 4:]) or *suckled while its mother is pregnant.* (Mgh.)

مُغْيَلٌ: see the next preceding paragraph.

مُغِيلٌ (Ṣ, Mgh, Mṣb, Ḳ) and مُغْيِلٌ (Mgh, Mṣb, Ḳ) A woman *giving her child to drink what is termed* غَيْل: (Ṣ, Ḳ: [see 4:]) or *suckling it while she is pregnant.* (Mgh, Mṣb.)

مَغَالَةٌ: see غَائِلَةٌ, in two places.

مُغَيِّلٌ [in the CḲ مُغَيَّل] and ▼ مُتَغَيِّلٌ *Continuing,* or *remaining fixed,* or *stationary, in the* غيل [meaning *thicket,* or *covert,* in the CḲ غَيْل]: and *entering therein.* (Ḳ, TA.)

مِغْيَالٌ A tree (شَجَرَةٌ) *having tangled,* or *abundant and dense, branches, with leafy coverings* or *shades.* (Ḳ.)

مُغْتَالٌ: see غَيْلٌ, latter half, in two places.

مُتَغَيِّلٌ: see مُغَيِّلٌ.

غيم

1. غَامَتِ السَّمَآءُ, (Ṣ, Mṣb, Ḳ,) aor. تَغِيمُ, inf. n. غَيْمٌ; (Mṣb;) and ▼ تَغَيَّمَتْ; and ▼ غَيَّمَتْ, (Ṣ, Mṣb, Ḳ,) inf. n. تَغْيِيمٌ; (Ḳ;) and ▼ أَغَامَتْ (Ṣ, Mṣb, Ḳ) and أَغْيَمَتْ; (Ṣ, Ḳ;) all signify the same; (Ṣ;) *The sky was,* or *became, clouded,* or *covered with clouds.* (Ṣ,* Mṣb, Ḳ.*) = غَامَ, aor. يَغِيمُ, (Ṣ, Ḳ,) inf. n. غَيْمٌ, (KL,) *He was,* or *became, thirsty,* (Ṣ, Ḳ, KL,* [like عَامَ,]) and *affected with internal heat.* (Ṣ, Ḳ) — And غَامَ إِلَى المَآءِ, aor. as above, inf. n. غَيْمَةٌ and غَيَمَانٌ and مَغِيمٌ, is mentioned by IAạr [as signifying *He thirsted for water,* or *the water:* or *he thirsted for it vehemently,* accord. to an explanation of غَيْمَة given below]. (TA.)

2: see 1. — [Hence,] غَيَّمَ ٱللَّيْلُ, (Ḳ,) inf. n. تَغْيِيمٌ, (TA,) ‡ *The night became like the* غَيْم [or *clouds*]; (Ḳ;) *became dark, and came like the clouds.* (TA.) — And غَيَّمَ ٱلطَّائِرُ † *The bird fluttered over one's head, not going to a distance;* on the authority of Th: mentioned by IAạr as with غين and ثاء [evidently mistranscriptions for عين and ثاء: see عَيَّثَ]. (TA.)

4. أَغَامَتِ ٱلسَّمَآءُ and أَغْيَمَت : see 1. — أَغْيَمَ ٱلقَوْمُ [*The people, or party, had a clouded sky;*] *clouds came upon the people,* or *party.* (Ṣ, Ḳ.) — And أَغْيَمَ *He* (a man, TA) *became stationary* (Ḳ, TA) *like the clouds.* (TA.)

5: see the first paragraph.

غَيْمٌ, originally an inf. n., from غَامَتِ ٱلسَّمَآءُ [q. v.], (Mṣb,) *Clouds;* (Ṣ, Mṣb, Ḳ, TA;) n. un. with ة: (Mṣb:) or [*an expanse of clouds covering the sky,*] *when one sees not a sun* (Kr, TA) *by reason of much covering of the sky:* (TA:) [and often meaning *mist:*] pl. غُيُومٌ and غِيَامٌ. (TA.) ═ Also *Thirst:* and *internal heat.* (AA, Ṣ, Ḳ.) [See also غَيْمَةٌ.] — And *Anger, wrath,* or *rage,* (Ḳ, TA,) *which is from internal heat.* (TA.) — And *a certain disease in camels, like that called* قُلَاب [q. v.], *except that it does not kill:* (Ḳ, TA:) it is said that the asterism of the Pleiades (ٱلثُّرَيَّا, q.v.,) does not rise nor set aurorally without there being sickness, mostly in the camels, which are then affected with the disease thus called. (Az, TA.) ═ شَجَرٌ غَيْمٌ *Dense,* or *tangled, trees:* like غَيْنٌ [which is a dial. var. of غَيْم in other senses]. (TA.)

غَيْمَةٌ *Thirst;* so says A'Obeyd: or *vehemence of thirst:* thus in the trad. cited under عَيْمَةٌ [q. v.]. (TA.) [See also غَيْمٌ.]

غَيْمَانُ *Thirsty:* and *affected with internal heat:* fem. غَيْمَى: (Ṣ, Ḳ:) the latter applied to a woman. (Ṣ.)

يَوْمٌ غَيُومٌ [*A cloudy day;*] *a day having* غَيْم [or *clouds,* or *clouds covering the sky*]. (Th, TA.)

مَغْيُومٌ A camel *affected with the disease termed* غَيْم: (Az, Ḳ, TA:) such scarcely ever, or never, dies. (Az, TA.)

غين

1. غَانَ عَلَيْهِ كَذَا, [aor. يَغِينُ, inf. n. غَيْنٌ,] *Such a thing covered, veiled,* or *concealed, him,* or *it:* (Ḥam p. 574:) [and so ↓ أَغَانَهُ; whence] one says, اغان ↓ ٱلغَيْنُ ٱلسَّمَآءَ *The clouds covered,* or *overspread,* or *wholly covered, the sky.* (Ṣ, Ḳ.) And غِينَ عَلَى كَذَا *Such a thing was covered over.* (Ṣ.) [Hence,] غِينَ عَلَى قَلْبِهِ, inf. n. غَيْنٌ; as also ↓ أُغِينَ [in the CḲ (erroneously) أَغْيَنَ]; † *His heart was invaded by desire,* or *appetite, as by a thing that covered it:* or *was covered* [*so as to be rendered unsusceptible*]: or *was enveloped by the like of rust* [or *clouded* or *rendered dull*]. (Ḳ, TA. [For ٱلرَّيْن, meaning "the like of rust" covering the heart, the CḲ has ٱلدَّيْن.]) The saying, in a trad., إِنَّهُ لَيُغَانُ عَلَى قَلْبِى (Ṣ, Mṣb, TA) حَتَّى أَسْتَغْفِرَ ٱللّٰهَ فِى ٱلْيَوْمِ سَبْعِينَ مَرَّةً (TA) is from the phrase غِينَ عَلَى كَذَا signifying as expl. above, (Ṣ,) and means † *Verily my heart is invaded as though it were covered, by unmindfulness from which mankind will not be free so that I beg forgiveness of God in the day seventy times:* (TA:) or it means, being used metonymically, *verily I become diverted from* ٱلْمُرَاقَبَة [meaning *the fear of God,* or, as a conventional term, *the constant knowledge of God's cognition of me in all my states* or *circumstances,*] *by the affairs that are for good relating to the present world;* for these, though matters of importance, are, in comparison with the affairs relating to the other world, as idle sport, in the estimation of the people who follow the rule of ٱلْمُرَاقَبَة. (Mṣb.) — One says also, غِينَتِ ٱلسَّمَآءُ, (Mṣb, TA,) inf. n. غَيْنٌ; as also غَانَت, inf. n. غَيْنٌ; [like غَامَتْ;] (TA;) *The sky became covered* (Mṣb, TA) *with* غَيْن (Mṣb) or غَيْم (TA) [i. e. *clouds,* or *an expanse of clouds*]. ═ غِنْتُ, aor. أَغِينُ, [inf. n. غَيْنٌ,] *I was,* or *became, thirsty.* (Ṣ, Ḳ.) And غَانَتِ ٱلإِبِلُ *i. q.* غَامَت (Ṣ, Ḳ, TA) i. e. *The camels were,* or *became, thirsty.* (TA.) — And غَانَتْ نَفْسُهُ, (Ṣ,) or نَفْسِى, (Ḳ,) aor. تَغِينُ, (Ṣ, Ḳ,) inf. n. غَيْنٌ, (TA,) *His,* or *my, soul* [or *stomach*] *heaved,* or *became agitated by a tendency to vomit;* syn. غَثَتْ. (Ṣ, Ḳ.)

2. غَيَّنَ غَيْنًا ↓ حَسَنَةً and حَسَنًا *He wrote a beautiful* غ. (TA.)

4: see the first paragraph, in three places.

غَانٌ: see غَيْنَةٌ.

غَيْنٌ [mentioned above as an inf. n. is also a subst., as such] *i. q.* غَيْمٌ, (Ḳ, TA,) a dial. var. of the latter word, (Ṣ, Mṣb, TA,) signifying *clouds;* (TA;) [or *an expanse of clouds;*] as in the phrase فِى يَوْمٍ غَيْنٍ *in a day of clouds:* (Ṣ, TA:) or, meaning "clouds," it is from غَانَ عَلَيْهِ كَذَا signifying as expl. in the beginning of this art. (Ḥam p. 574.) — And شَجَرٌ غَيْنٌ *Dense,* or *tangled, trees:* (TA:) like غَيْمٌ. (TA in art. غيم.) ═ Also [like غَيْمٌ signifying] *Thirst.* (Ṣ, Ḳ. [See also 1.]) ═ And [The *letter* غ;] *one of the letters of the alphabet:* (Ṣ, Ḳ:) pl. [of mult.] غُيُونٌ and [of pauc.] أَغْيَانٌ and غَيْنَاتٌ. (TA.) See 2, and art. غ.

غَانَةٌ The *ring at the head of the bow-string.* (Ḳ.) [See عُنْتُوتٌ.]

غَيْنَةٌ *i. q.* أَجَمَةٌ; [like غَيْضَةٌ, q. v.;] so in the M; (TA;) [and it is said that] ٱلغَيْنَةُ ٱلشَّجْرَآءُ is like ٱلغَيْضَةُ ٱلخَضْرَآءُ: or, accord. to Abu-l-'Ameythel [or 'Omeythil], (Ṣ, TA,) غَيْنَةٌ signifies [*A collection of*] *tangled,* or *confused,* or *dense, trees,* (Ṣ, Ḳ, TA,) *in the mountains,* and *in the plain,* or *soft, land,* (TA,) *without water;* (Ṣ, Ḳ, TA;) if with water, called غَيْضَةٌ: (Ṣ, TA:) [and Golius states, as on the authority of Yáḳoot, that ↓ غَانٌ signifies the same as غَيْنَةٌ.]

غِينَةٌ The *fluid that runs from a carcass,* or *corpse,* (Ṣ,) or *from the dead:* and [the *humour,* or *matter, termed*] صَدِيد, q. v. (Ḳ.) ═ See also the next paragraph.

أَغْيَنُ *Green:* (Ṣ, TA:) or *green inclining to blackness:* (so in one of my copies of the Ṣ:) and [its fem.] غَيْنَآءُ is applied to a tree (شَجَرَةٌ) as meaning *green,* (AO, Ṣ, Ḳ, TA,) *abounding with leaves, having tangled,* or *dense, branches,* (AO, Ṣ, TA,) *and soft,* or *tender:* and sometimes it is thus applied to herbs: (TA:) or [applied to a tree] it signifies *great, having wide shade:* from the phrase غَانَ عَلَيْهِ كَذَا, expl. in the beginning of this art.: (Ḥam p. 574:) and أَغْيَنُ signifies [also] *such as is tall,* (Ḳ, TA,) of trees, or, by way of comparison [thereto], of men: (TA:) the pl. is غِينٌ: (Ṣ, TA:) which is expl. by Kr as meaning the *abundance, and collected state, and beauty,* of [the trees called] أَرَاك and سِدْر; but what is well known is that it is pl. of غَيْنَآء applied to a tree; of which ↓ غِينَةٌ, with kesr, has also been mentioned as a pl., though, as ISd says, this is not known in the [genuine] language, nor is it agreeable with the analogy of Arabic. (TA.)

مُغْيِنٌ, in the original form, [for مُغِينٌ, act. part. n. of أَغَانَ,] is used by Ru-beh in the following verse:

أَمْسَى بِلَالٌ كَالرَّبِيعِ ٱلْمُدْجِنِ
أَمْطَرَ فِى أَكْنَافِ غَيْنٍ مُغْيِنِ

[*There was, or came, in the evening, a moisture like the continual rain of winter that has rained in the tracts of overspreading clouds*]. (Ṣ.)

ف

The twentieth letter of the alphabet: called فَآءٌ [and فَا]. (TA.) It is one of the letters termed مَهْمُوسَة [or non-vocal, i. e. pronounced with the breath only, without the voice], and of those termed شَفَوِيَّة [or labial]: (TA:) it is a radical letter, and not augmentative: (TA in باب الالف اللّيّنة:) sometimes it is substituted for ث; thus in the conjunction ثُمَّ, as in the saying جَآءَ زَيْدٌ فُمَّ عَمْرٌو ["Zeyd came, then 'Amr"]; and in الثُّومُ, "the well-known herb so called [?]," for which they say الفُومُ; and in الجَدَثُ, "the grave," or "sepulchre," for which they say الجَدَفُ, but using for the pl. أَجْدَاثٌ, and not أَجْدَافٌ, accord. to IJ, (MF, TA,) [unless, app., by poetic license, for] the latter pl. is used by Ru-beh. (R and TA in art. جدف.) —— فَ is a particle having no government: (Mughnee,* Ḳ,* TA:) or it governs a manṣoob aor.; as in the saying, مَا تَأْتِينَا فَتُحَدِّثَنَا [*Thou dost not come to us, that thou mayest talk to us*]; (Mughnee, Ḳ, TA;) accord. to some of the Koofees; (Mughnee;) but the truth is, that the aor. is here manṣoob by أَنْ, meant to be understood, (Mughnee, TA,) as is said by MF, and the like is said by J, (TA,) though the أَنْ in this case is necessarily suppressed: (I'Aḳ p. 295:) and it is said (Mughnee, Ḳ, TA) by Mbr (Mughnee) to govern the gen. case in the saying [of Imra-el-Ḳeys],

فَمِثْلِكِ حُبْلَى قَدْ طَرَقْتُ وَمُرْضِعٍ *

[*Many a one like thee*, even such as was *pregnant, have I visited by night, and* such as was *suckling*]; but the truth is, that what here governs the gen. case is رُبَّ, meant to be understood; (Mughnee, TA;) like as it often is in the case of وَ, as is said in the Lubáb. (TA.) —— It occurs used in three manners; in one whereof it is an adjunctive to an antecedent, and denotes three things: —— one of these is order; and this is of two sorts; relating to the meaning, as in قَامَ زَيْدٌ فَعَمْرٌو [*Zeyd came, and after him 'Amr*]; and relating to a verbal statement, which is an adjoining of an explicit clause to an implicit antecedent, as in the saying [in the Ḳur ii. 34] فَأَزَلَّهُمَا ٱلشَّيْطَانُ عَنْهَا فَأَخْرَجَهُمَا مِمَّا كَانَا فِيهِ [*And the Devil caused them both to slip*, or *fall, from it* (i. e. from Paradise), *and ejected them from that* state of enjoyment *in which they were*]: (Mughnee, Ḳ:*) —— the second thing that it denotes when used as an adjunctive to an antecedent is proximate sequence, and this is in everything [i. e. in every case] according to the estimate thereof; (Mughnee, Ḳ;*) [meaning, according to the relative, or comparative, estimate of the time implied; for, as is said in an explanation of the words thus rendered, in a marginal note in my copy of the Mughnee, "the long period is sometimes esteemed short by comparison;" or it may be defined as a particle denoting sequence in a case in which is an uninterrupted connection between two events;] one says تَزَوَّجَ فُلَانٌ فَوُلِدَ لَهُ [*Such a one took a wife, and, in uninterrupted connection with his doing so, a child was born to him,*] when there did not intervene between the two events aught save the period of gestation, (Mughnee, Ḳ,*) and so if it were a period protracted [beyond the usual length]; and you say دَخَلْتُ البَصْرَةَ فَبَغْدَادَ [*I entered El-Baṣrah, and, in uninterrupted connection with my doing so, Baghdád,*] when you did not stay in El-Baṣrah nor between the two towns: and this sequence is not necessarily implied by the ف that denotes causality; as is shown by the correctness of one's saying إِنْ يُسْلِمْ فَهُوَ يَدْخُلُ الجَنَّةَ [*If he become a Muslim, he will consequently enter Paradise*]; the delay between the two events [by death &c.] being well known: (Mughnee:) —— [or, accord. to J,] the adjunctive فَ occurs in three cases, in the first of which it denotes order and proximate sequence with association; you say, ضَرَبْتُ زَيْدًا فَعَمْرًا [*I beat Zeyd, and next 'Amr*]: (Ṣ: [the second and third of these cases will be mentioned in the course of this art:]) —— and it is said to occur sometimes in the sense of ثُمَّ, (Mughnee, Ḳ,* TA,*) denoting conjunction in an absolute manner, with delay; (TA;) as in the saying [in the Ḳur xxiii. 14] ثُمَّ خَلَقْنَا ٱلنُّطْفَةَ عَلَقَةً فَخَلَقْنَا ٱلْعَلَقَةَ مُضْغَةً فَخَلَقْنَا ٱلْمُضْغَةَ عِظَامًا فَكَسَوْنَا ٱلْعِظَامَ لَحْمًا [*Then we made the sperm a lump of clotted blood, then we made the lump of clotted blood a bit of flesh, then we made the bit of flesh bones, then we clothed the bones with flesh*]: (Mughnee, Ḳ, TA:) —— and sometimes in the sense of وَ, (Mughnee, Ḳ,* TA,*) denoting conjunction in an absolute manner, without order; (TA;) as in the saying (of Imra-el-Ḳeys, TA), بَيْنَ الدَّخُولِ فَحَوْمَلِ [as though meaning *Between Ed-Dakhool and Ḥowmal*]; (Mughnee, Ḳ, TA;) the right reading of which is asserted by Aṣ to be with وَ; but it is replied that the implied meaning is بَيْنَ مَوَاضِعِ الدَّخُولِ فَمَوَاضِعِ حَوْمَلِ [*amidst the places of*, or *pertaining to, Ed-Dakhool, and the places of*, or *pertaining to, Ḥowmal*; the former places and the latter being contiguous; and we may therefore understand these words as relating to an antecedent command to pause]; this phrase being allowable like the saying جَلَسْتُ بَيْنَ العُلَمَآءِ فَالزُّهَّادِ [*I sat amidst the learned men and the devotees*]: it has been said that مَا is here suppressed before بَيْنَ, and that ف is used in the place of إِلَى; but this usage of ف is strange: (Mughnee:) —— the third thing that it denotes when used as an adjunctive to an antecedent is relation to a cause: (Mughnee, Ḳ,* TA:*) this is the second of the three cases mentioned by J, who says, (TA,) it is when what precedes it is a cause of what follows it; and it denotes adjunction and proximate sequence without association; as in the sayings ضَرَبَهُ فَبَكَى [*He beat him, and he consequently wept,*] and ضَرَبَهُ فَأَوْجَعَهُ [*He beat him, and consequently pained him,*] when the beating is the cause of the weeping and of the pain: (Ṣ, TA:) used in this manner, i. e. to denote relation to a cause, it is generally such as adjoins a proposition, as in [the saying in the Ḳur xxviii. 14] فَوَكَزَهُ مُوسَى فَقَضَى عَلَيْهِ [*And Moses struck him with his fist, and consequently killed him*]; or a qualificative, as in [the saying in the Ḳur lvi. 52-54] لَآكِلُونَ مِنْ شَجَرٍ مِنْ زَقُّومٍ فَمَالِئُونَ مِنْهَا ٱلْبُطُونَ فَشَارِبُونَ عَلَيْهِ مِنَ ٱلْحَمِيمِ [*Shall surely be eating from trees of Zaḳḳoom, and consequently filling therefrom the bellies, and drinking thereon of hot water*]. (Mughnee, Ḳ.) —— Another manner in which it is used [the second of the three manners before mentioned (Mughnee)] is as a connective of an apodosis, i. e., of the complement of a conditional clause, (Mughnee,* Ḳ,* TA,) when this is of a kind not fit to be itself conditional, i. e., to be a protasis. (Mughnee.) It is thus used when the complement is a nominal proposition; as in [the saying in the Ḳur vi. 17] وَإِنْ يَمْسَسْكَ بِخَيْرٍ فَهُوَ عَلَى كُلِّ شَيْءٍ قَدِيرٌ [*And if He cause good to betide thee, He is able to do everything*]: (Mughnee, Ḳ, TA:) this is the third of the three cases mentioned by J, who says, (TA,) this is when it is used for the purpose of inception, in the complement of a conditional clause; as in the saying إِنْ تَزُرْنِى فَأَنْتَ مُحْسِنٌ [*If thou visit me, thou wilt be a welldoer*]; in which what follows فَ is a new proposition, grammatically independent of what precedes it, one part thereof governing another; for أَنْتَ is an inchoative, and مُحْسِنٌ is its enunciative; and the proposition has become a complement by means of the ف: (Ṣ, TA:) — or, (Ḳ,) secondly, (Mughnee,) the complement may be a verbal proposition, like the nominal, and it is one of which the verb is aplastic; as in [the saying in the Ḳur xviii. 37 and 38] إِنْ تَرَنِ أَنَا أَقَلَّ مِنْكَ مَالًا وَوَلَدًا فَعَسَى رَبِّى أَنْ يُؤْتِيَنِ [*If thou seest me to be possessing less than thou in respect of wealth and children, it may be that my Lord may give me*]; and [the saying in the Ḳur ii. 273] إِنْ تُبْدُوا الصَّدَقَاتِ فَنِعِمَّا هِىَ [*If ye make apparent the alms, very good, as a thing, is it*, i. e. the doing so]: (Mughnee, Ḳ:) — or, (Ḳ,) thirdly, (Mughnee,) the verb of the complement may be one belonging to a new proposition, grammatically independent of what precedes it, as in [the saying in the Ḳur iii. 29] إِنْ كُنْتُمْ تُحِبُّونَ ٱللّٰهَ فَٱتَّبِعُونِى [*If ye love God, follow ye me*]: (Mughnee, Ḳ:) — or, (Ḳ,) fourthly, (Mughnee,) the verb of the complement may be a pret., as to the letter and as to the meaning; either properly, as in [the saying in the Ḳur xii. 77] إِنْ يَسْرِقْ فَقَدْ سَرَقَ أَخٌ لَهُ مِنْ قَبْلُ [*If he steal, a brother of his hath stolen before*]: or tropically, as in [the saying in the Ḳur xxvii. 92] وَمَنْ جَآءَ بِٱلسَّيِّئَةِ فَكُبَّتْ وُجُوهُهُمْ فِى ٱلنَّارِ [*And whoever shall have done that which is evil, their faces are inverted in the fire* of Hell], this [latter] verb being used as though signifying what has already happened to denote the certain assurance of the event's happening: (Mughnee, Ḳ:*) — fifthly, when the ف is coupled with a particle relating to futurity; as in [the saying in the Ḳur v. 59] مَنْ يَرْتَدَّ مِنْكُمْ عَنْ دِينِهِ فَسَوْفَ يَأْتِى ٱللّٰهُ بِقَوْمٍ يُحِبُّهُمْ [*Whoever of you revolteth from his religion, God will bring a people whom He loveth*]; and in [the saying in the Ḳur iii. 111] وَمَا تَفْعَلُوا مِنْ خَيْرٍ فَلَنْ تُكْفَرُوهُ [*And what ye do of good, ye shall not be denied* the reward *of it*]: (Mughnee: omitted in the Ḳ; as is also what here next follows:) — sixthly, when the ف is coupled with a particle to which is peculiarly assigned the first place in a proposition, as in the saying,

* فَإِنْ أَهْلِكْ فَذِى حَنَقٍ لَظَاهُ *
* عَلَىَّ يَكَادُ يَلْتَهِبُ ٱلْتِهَابَا *

[a verse similar in itself, and probably in its sequel (which is not quoted), to one by Rabee'ah Ibn-Maḳroom (in Ḥam p. 29), app. meaning *And if I perish, many a one having rage* in his bosom, *whose fire* kindled *against me almost flames with a* vehement *flaming*; فَذِى حَنَقٍ being for فَرُبَّ ذِى حَنَقٍ; for رُبَّ is meant to be understood, and to it peculiarly belongs the first place in the proposition: (Mughnee:) — the ف must also be used when the complement of a conditional clause is imperative; as in the saying إِنْ أَكْرَمَكَ زَيْدٌ فَأَكْرِمْهُ [*If Zeyd treat thee with honour, treat thou him with honour*]: or prohibitive; as in the saying إِنْ يُكْرِمْكَ زَيْدٌ فَلَا تُهِنْهُ [*If Zeyd treat thee with honour, treat not thou him with contempt*]: or negative, either by means of لَنْ [as in an ex. above] or by means of مَا; as in the saying إِنْ أَكْرَمْتَ زَيْدًا فَمَا يُهِينُكَ [*If thou treat Zeyd with honour, he does not treat thee with contempt*]: (TA:) — when the verb of that complement is an aor., affirmative, or negative by means of لَا, the ف may be introduced or omitted: in the former case you may say إِنْ تُكْرِمْنِى فَأَنَا أُكْرِمُكَ meaning تُكْرِمْنِى فَأُكْرِمُكَ [i. e. *If thou treat me with honour, I will treat thee with honour*]; and you may say إِنْ تُكْرِمْنِى أُكْرِمْكَ [which is the more usual] if you do not make it [i. e. اكرمك] the enunciative of a suppressed inchoative [i. e. of أَنَا]: and in the case of the negative by means of لا you may say إِنْ تُكْرِمْنِى فَلَا أُهِينُكَ [*If thou treat me with honour, I will not treat thee with contempt*; and you may omit the ف as is more usual]: (TA:) — and sometimes the ف is suppressed in the case of necessity in verse [on account of the metre]; as in the saying,

* مَنْ يَفْعَلِ ٱلْحَسَنَاتِ ٱللّٰهُ يَشْكُرُهَا *

[*Whoso doth those deeds that are good, God will recompense them*, i. e., the deeds], (Mughnee, Ḳ,) meaning فَٱللّٰهُ: (Ḳ:) or, (Mughnee, Ḳ,) accord. to Mbr, who disallows this even in verse, (Mughnee,) the right reading is

* مَنْ يَفْعَلِ ٱلْخَيْرَ فَٱلرَّحْمٰنُ يَشْكُرُهُ *

[*Whoso doth that which is good, the Compassionate will recompense it*]; (Mughnee, Ḳ;) and it is absolutely disallowable: (Ḳ:) or it occurs in chaste prose, (Mughnee, Ḳ,*) accord. to Akh; (Mughnee;) and hence the saying [in the Ḳur ii. 176] إِنْ تَرَكَ خَيْرًا ٱلْوَصِيَّةُ لِلْوَالِدَيْنِ وَٱلْأَقْرَبِينَ [*If he leave wealth, the legacy shall be to the two parents and the nearer of* other *relations*]; and the trad. respecting that which one has picked up, or taken, of property that has been dropped, فَإِنْ جَآءَ صَاحِبُهَا وَإِلَّا ٱسْتَمْتِعْ بِهَا [*And if the owner thereof come*, restore thou it to him; *and if not*, or *otherwise, benefit thyself by it*]: (Mughnee, Ḳ:) — when the verb of the complement of a conditional clause is a pret. as to the letter but future as to the meaning intended [yet not importing certainty, so that it is not like the saying in the Ḳur xxvii. 92, cited above], the ف may not be prefixed to it; as in the saying إِنْ أَكْرَمْتَنِى أَكْرَمْتُكَ [*If thou treat me with honour, I will treat thee with honour*]: and likewise when it is pret. as to the [proper] signification but [an aor. as to the letter and] future as to the meaning intended; as in the saying إِنْ أَسْلَمْتَ لَمْ تَدْخُلِ ٱلنَّارَ [*If thou become a Muslim, thou wilt not enter the fire* of Hell]. (TA.) — And as the ف thus connects the apodosis with its protasis, so it connects the like of the apodosis with the like of the protasis; as in the saying ٱلَّذِى يَأْتِينِى فَلَهُ دِرْهَمٌ [*Who comes*, or *shall come, to me, for him is*, or *shall be, a dirhem*]: by its being introduced in this case, one understands what the speaker means, that the obligation to give the dirhem is a consequence of the coming: otherwise the saying would be ambiguous. (Mughnee.) Thus also it occurs after a clause commencing with the conditional particle أَمَّا, q. v. (Mughnee in art. أَمَّا; &c.) — It also occurs in the cases here following, prefixed to an aor., which is manṣoob by means of أَنْ, meant to be understood, (Ṣ, TA, and I'Aḳ p. 295,) but necessarily suppressed: (I'Aḳ ibid.:) — thus in the complement of a command; (Ṣ, TA, and I'Aḳ p. 296;) as in ٱئْتِنِى فَأُكْرِمَكَ [*Come thou to me, that I may treat thee with honour*]: (I'Aḳ ibid.:) [and] you say زُرْنِى فَأُحْسِنَ إِلَيْكَ [*Visit thou me, that I may do good to thee*]; (Ṣ, TA;) to which J adds, you do not make the visiting to be the cause of the doing good; what you [would] say being, it is of my way to do good always; but [there seems be an omission here in the copies of the Ṣ, for, as] IB says, if you make أُحْسِن to be marfooa, [not manṣoob,] saying فَأُحْسِنُ إِلَيْكَ, [the meaning is, *for I will do good to thee*, for] you do not make the visiting to be the cause of the doing good: (TA:) the demand, however, in this and similar cases, must not be indicated by a verbal noun, nor by an enunciative; for when it is so indicated, the aor. must be marfooa; as in صَهْ فَأُحْسِنُ إِلَيْكَ [*Be silent, then I will do thee good*]; and in حَسْبُكَ ٱلْحَدِيثُ فَيَنَامُ ٱلنَّاسُ [*The discourse is sufficient for thee, so the people shall sleep*]: (I'Aḳ p. 296:) — also in the complement of a prohibition; (Ṣ, and I'Aḳ p. 296;) as in لَا تَضْرِبْ زَيْدًا فَيَضْرِبَكَ [*Beat not thou Zeyd, for he may beat thee*, or *lest he beat thee*]: (I'Aḳ ibid.:) — and in the complement of a prayer; as in رَبِّ ٱنْصُرْنِى فَلَا أُخْذَلَ [*My Lord aid me, so that I may not be left helpless*]: (I'Aḳ ibid.:) — and in the complement of an interrogation; (Ṣ, and I'Aḳ p. 296;) as in هَلْ تُكْرِمُ زَيْدًا فَيُكْرِمَكَ [*Wilt thou treat Zeyd with honour, that he may treat thee with honour?*]: (I'Aḳ ibid.:) — and in the complement of a petition with gentleness; (Ṣ, and I'Aḳ p. 296;) as in أَلَا تَنْزِلُ عِنْدَنَا فَتُصِيبَ خَيْرًا [*Wilt thou not alight at our place of abode, that thou mayest obtain good?*]: (I'Aḳ ibid.:) — and in the complement of a demanding with urgency the performance of an action; as in لَوْلَا تَأْتِينَا فَتُحَدِّثَنَا [*Wherefore dost thou not come to us, that thou mayest talk to us?*]: (I'Aḳ p. 296:) — and in the complement of an expression of wish; as in لَيْتَ لِى مَالًا فَأَتَصَدَّقَ مِنْهُ [*Would that I had wealth, that I might give alms thereof*]: (I'Aḳ ibid.:) — and in the complement of an expression of hope, in like manner as in the case next before mentioned, accord. to the Koofees universally; as in the saying in the Ḳur [xl. 38 and 39] لَعَلِّى أَبْلُغُ ٱلْأَسْبَابَ أَسْبَابَ ٱلسَّمٰوَاتِ فَأَطَّلِعَ [*May-be I shall reach the tracts*, or *the gates*, *the tracts*, or *the gates*, *of the heavens*, *so that I may look*], accord. to one reading: (I'Aḳ p. 298:) — and in the complement of a negation, (Ṣ, and I'Aḳ p. 295,) i. e., of a simple negation; as in مَا تَأْتِينَا فَتُحَدِّثَنَا [*Thou dost not come to us*, *that thou mayest talk to us*; a saying mentioned before, in the first of the remarks on this particle]. (I'Aḳ ibid.) — It is also prefixed as a corroborative to an oath; as in فَبِعِزَّتِكَ [which may be rendered *Now by thy might*, or *nobility*, &c.], and فَوَرَبِّكَ [*Now by thy Lord*]. (TA.) — The third manner in which it is [said to be] used is when it is redundant, so that its being included in a saying is like its being excluded: but this usage is not affirmed by Sb: Akh allows its being redundant in the enchoative, absolutely; mentioning the phrase أَخُوكَ فَوُجِدَ [as though meaning *Thy brother, he has been found*; but هٰذَا is app. meant to be understood, so that the phrase should be rendered, fully, *this is thy brother, and he has been found*]: Fr and El-Aalam and a number of others restrict its being allowable to the cases in which the enunciative is a command, as in the saying,

* وَقَائِلَةٍ خَوْلَانُ فَٱنْكِحْ فَتَاتَهُمْ *

and in the saying,

* أَنْتَ فَٱنْظُرْ لِأَىِّ ذَاكَ تَصِيرُ *

or a prohibition, as in the saying زَيْدٌ فَلَا تَضْرِبْهُ; but those who disallow its being so explain the first of these three exs. by saying that the implied meaning is هٰذِهِ خَوْلَانُ, [so that the saying should be rendered, fully, *Many a woman is there saying, This is Khowlán* (the tribe so named), *therefore marry thou their young woman*; and in like manner the implied meaning of the third ex. is هٰذَا زَيْدٌ فَلَا تَضْرِبْهُ *This is Zeyd, therefore do not thou beat him*;] and the implied meaning of the second ex. is أُنْظُرْ فَٱنْظُرْ, [so that the saying should be rendered, fully, *Look thou, and look to what result thereof thou wilt eventually come*,] the former انظر being suppressed, and its implied pronoun, أَنْتَ, expressed: the saying

* وَإِذَا هَلَكْتُ فَعِنْدَ ذٰلِكَ فَٱجْزَعِى *

[meaning *And when I perish, on the occasion thereof manifest thou impatience*, or *grief*, &c., the second ف being redundant,] is an instance of poetic license. (Mughnee.) = [As a numeral, ف denotes *Eighty*.]

فا

فَا and فَآءٌ *Names of the letter* ف, q. v. = فَا as a prefixed n. in the accus. case, *syn. with* فَم, see voce فُوهٌ, in art. فوه.

فأ

R. Q. 1. فَأْفَأَ, (T, M, Mṣb,) inf. n. فَأْفَأَةٌ, (T, Ṣ, M, Mṣb, Ḳ,) *He reiterated the letter* ف (Mbr, T, Ṣ, M, Mṣb, Ḳ,) *in his speech*; (Ṣ, M, Ḳ;) or *was as though the letter* ف *predominated upon his tongue*; (T;) or *had an impediment in the tongue, the letter* ف *predominating in the speech*. (M.) You say, فِيهِ فَأْفَأَةٌ [*In him is a fault of reiterating the letter* ف *in his speech*; &c.] (Ṣ, Ḳ.) [See also فَأْفَأٌ.]

فَأْفَأٌ: see what follows.

فَأْفَآءٌ (T, Ṣ, M, Mṣb, Ḳ) and ↓ فَأْفَأٌ, (T, M, Mṣb, Ḳ, [and thus accord. to my copy of the Mgh,]) both mentioned by Lḥ, (T,) A man *in whom is what is termed* فَأْفَأَةٌ, expl. above; (T, Ṣ, M, Ḳ;) or *who reiterates the letter* ف *much when he speaks*; (M;) or *who cannot utter the word unless with an effort, commencing with the like of the letter* ف, *and then pronouncing with effort the letters of the word correctly*: (Mgh:) or one *who reiterates his words much in speaking*: (TA:) fem. with ة. (T, Mṣb.).

فأت

8. اِفْتَأَتَ عَلَىَّ *He said of me what was false*: (AZ, Ṣ, O:) or افتأت عَلَىَّ البَاطِلَ *he forged against me what was false*: (Ḳ:) and افتأت عَلَىَّ مَا لَمْ أَقُلْ *he forged against me what I did not say*. (M.) = And افتأت عَلَيْنَا *He was alone in his opinion against us; none sharing it with him*: (ISh, T, TA:) or افتأت بِرَأْيِهِ *he was alone*, or *singular*, *in his opinion*: (ISk, Ṣ, O, Ḳ:) and in like manner in his affair, or case. (ISk, TA.) This verb, thus used, (not known to Az with a radical hemz in this sense except as mentioned by ISh and ISk, TA,) is mentioned with hemz by AA and AZ and ISk and others: it is therefore not from الفَوْتُ, unless it be an instance of the application of hemz to that to which it does not properly belong, as in the cases of حَلَّأْتُ السَّوِيقَ, and رَثَّأَتِ المَيِّتَ, and لَبَّأْتُ بِالحَجِّ. (Ṣ, O.) [See also art. فوت.] = أُفْتُئِتَ, in the pass form, *He* (a man, O) *died suddenly*: (O, Ḳ:) but this, app., [if not a mistake for أُفْتُلِتَ,] should be اُفْتِيتَ, without hemz, from مَوْتُ الفَوَاتِ. (TA.)

فُؤَيْتٌ, applied to a man and to a woman, One *who follows his*, or *her*, *own opinion only*. (From a marg. note in a copy of the Ṣ. [Thus pronounced by AZ: by others, فُوَيْتٌ, without hemz: see art. فوت.])

فأد

1. فَأَدَهُ, (T, S, M, A, L, Ḳ,) aor. ـَ, inf. n. فَأْدٌ, (M, L,) *He*, or *it*, *hit*, *struck*, *smote*, *affected*, or *hurt*, *his* (a man's, Ḳ) فُؤَاد [or *heart*, &c.]: (Ṣ, M, L, Ḳ:) *he hit*, or *smote*, *him*, (AZ, T,) or *shot*, or *shot at*, *and hit*, or *smote*, *him*, namely a gazelle, (A,) or an animal of the chase, (AZ, T,) *in his* فُؤَاد. (AZ, T, A.) — And, said of a disease, (Ṣ,) and of fear, (A,) *It smote*, or *affected*, *his* فُؤَاد: (Ṣ, A:) or, said of fear, *it rendered him cowardly*. (Ḳ.) — And فُئِدَ, (T, M, A, L, Ḳ,) inf. n. فَأْدٌ; (M, L;) and فَئِدَ; (Ḳ;) *He had a disease in his* فُؤَاد: (T:) or *he had a complaint thereof*: (M, L, Ḳ:) or *he had a pain therein*: (Ḳ:) or *he was*, or *became*, *hit*, *struck*, *smitten*, *affected*, or *hurt*, *therein*. (A.) = فَأَدَ الخُبْزَةَ, (T, Ṣ, M, L,) or الخُبْزَ, (Ḳ,) aor. as above, and so the inf. n., (M, L,) *He put the cake of bread*, or *lump of dough*, (T, Ṣ,) or *the bread*, (Ḳ,) *into the hot ashes*; (T, Ṣ, Ḳ;) *and baked it therein*: (T:) or *he toasted* [or *baked*] (M, L) *the cake of bread*, or *lump of dough*, [or *the bread*,] *in the hot ashes*. (M,* L.) And فَأَدَ اللَّحْمَ, (Ṣ, M, L, Ḳ,) فِى النَّارِ, (M, L, Ḳ,) aor. and inf. n. as above, (L,) *He roasted the flesh-meat* [*in the fire*]; as also ↓ افتأده. (Ṣ, M, L, Ḳ.) — And فَأَدَ لِلْخُبْزَةِ, (Ṣ, L,) aor. and inf. n. as above, (L,) *He made for the cake of bread*, or *lump of dough*, *a place in the hot ashes*, or *in the fire*, *to put it therein* [*for the purpose of baking it*]. (Ṣ, L.) = فَأَدَ لِفُلَانٍ *He acted well*, or *kindly*, *to such a one*, *in his affair*, *in absence*: so in the "Nawádir" of Lḥ. (TA.)

5. تفأّد *i. q.* تَوَقَّدَ [i. e., when said of fuel, *It burned*, *burned up*, *burned brightly* or *fiercely*, *blazed*, or *flamed*]: (M, L, Ḳ:) [and] so when said of the heart [i. e. *It became excited with ardour*, or *eagerness*]. (M, L, Ḳ.*) And *i. q.* تَحَرَّقَ [*It burned much*, as a quasi-pass. v.]: (so in copies of the Ḳ, in SM's copy and in my MS. copy and in the CḲ:) or, as in MF's copy of the Ḳ, تَحَرَّكَ [*it was*, or *became*, *in a state of motion*, or *commotion*]: (TA:) [See what is said of the derivation of فُؤَاد.]

8. افتأدوا *They lighted a fire* (M, A, L, Ḳ) *for the purpose of roasting*. (A) = See also 1, latter half.

فَأْدٌ: [see 1, of which it is the inf. n.: and] see the paragraph here following.

فُؤَادٌ (Ṣ, M, A, Mṣb, Ḳ, &c.) and فُوَادٌ, which is strange, (Ḳ,) but said by Esh-Shiháb to be a dial var., and to be without reason disallowed by AHát; (TA;) of the masc. gender only; (Lḥ, M, L, Ḳ, &c.;) The *heart*; syn. قَلْبٌ [q. v.]; (Ṣ, M, A, L, Mṣb, Ḳ, &c.;) of man, and of an animal other than man: (M, L:) so called because of its تَفَؤُّد (T, M, L, Ḳ) i. e. تَوَقُّد [or ardour]; (M, L, Ḳ;) or because of its pulsation, and commotion; [for which reason also the heart is said to be called القَلْبُ, from التَّقَلُّبُ;] for it is said that the primary meaning of ↓ فَأْدٌ is "motion," and the "putting in motion:" (MF, TA:) or the heart is thus called only when its تَفَؤُّد, i. e. its تَوَقُّد, is regarded: and most authors make a distinction between فُؤَادٌ and قَلْبٌ; the latter of which is said to have a more special signification than the former: (TA:) and the former is said to be [the *pericardium*,] the غِشَآء,

(L, TA,) or the وِعَآء, (TA,) *of the* قَلْب: (L, TA:) or the *middle thereof*: (L:) or the *interior thereof*: (TA:) the قلب being its حَبَّة [q. v.], (L, TA,) or its سُوَيْدَآء: (L:) or فُؤَاد signifies the *appendages of the* مَرِىء [or œsophagus], *consisting of the liver and lungs and* قَلْب [or *heart*]: (Ḳ:) pl. أَفْئِدَةٌ, (Ṣ, M, A, Mgh, Mṣb, Ḳ, &c.,) the only pl. thereof known to Sb. (M, L.) — Also The *mind*, or *intellect*: and this, it is said, may be the meaning of the phrase [in the Ḳur liii. 11], مَا كَذَبَ ٱلْفُؤَادُ مَا رَأَى, (TA,) or ما كَذَّبَ, another reading, i. e. [*The mind*] *did not disacknowledge*, or *deem improbable, what he saw*. (Jel.) [Hence,] حِدَّةُ الفُؤَادِ *i. q.* ذَكَآءٌ [meaning *Sharpness*, or *acuteness, of mind*, in a man: and *sharpness of spirit* in a beast]. (Ṣ in art. ذكو.) [And حَدِيدُ الفُؤَادِ *i. q.* ذَكِىٌّ meaning *Sharp*, or *acute, in mind*, applied to a man: and *sharp in spirit*, applied to a beast:] one says فَرَسٌ حَدِيدَةُ الفُؤَادِ [*A mare sharp in spirit*]; and in like manner نَاقَةٌ [*a she-camel*]: (Ṣ and Ḳ in art. روع:) and رُوَاعُ الفُؤَادِ, and نَاقَةٌ رُوَاعَةُ الفُؤَادِ, *a quick, spirited, vigorous, she-camel; sharp in spirit*; syn. شَهْمَةٌ ذَكِيَّةٌ. (Ḳ in that art.) [And طَارَ فُؤَادُهُ *His mind* or *intellect, fled*: and *his courage*. (See شَعَاعٌ: and طَارَ.)]

فَئِيدٌ: see مَفْؤُودٌ, in two places. — Also, (T, M, L,) applied to bread [or dough], (M, L,) and so ▼ مَفْؤُودٌ, (M, L, Ḳ,) and ▼ مُفْتَآدٌ, and ▼ أُفْؤُودٌ, (Ḳ,) *Baked on the fire*: (T:) or *put into hot ashes*, (L, Ḳ,) *and baked therein*: (L:) or *toasted* [or *baked*] *in hot ashes*. (M, L.) And the first, (T, Ṣ, M, &c.,) applied to flesh-meat, (Ṣ, M, L,) *Roasted*, (T, Ṣ, M, L, Ḳ,) as also ▼ مَفْؤُودٌ, (M, L, Ḳ,) *on the fire*: (T:) or *roasted upon live coals*; as also ▼ مُفْآدٌ [evidently, I think, a mistranscription for ▼ مُفْتَآدٌ]. (L.) — And فَئِيدٌ signifies also *Fire* or *a fire* [*for baking* &c.]. (T, L, Ḳ.)

أُفْؤُودٌ *A place which one makes, for a cake of bread, or lump of dough, in hot ashes, or in a fire, to put it therein* [*for the purpose of baking it*]: (Ṣ, M,* L, Ḳ:*) pl. أَفَائِيدُ. (L.) — See also فَئِيدٌ.

مُفْآدٌ: see فَئِيدٌ.

مِفْأَدٌ (T, Ṣ, M, L, Ḳ) and ▼ مِفْأَدَةٌ (Ṣ, L, Ḳ) and ▼ مِفْآدٌ (T, M, L, Ḳ) The [*iron instrument, with which flesh-meat is roasted, called*] سَفُّود, (T, Ṣ, M, L, Ḳ,) [or] *with which one roasts and bakes*. (L, TA.) And [in the CḲ "or"] the first, (Ṣ, L, Ḳ,) and the second and third also, (accord. to the Ḳ,) the *piece of wood*, or *wooden implement, with which the* [*fire in the kind of oven called*] تَنُّور *is stirred*: pl. مَفَائِدُ. (Ṣ, L, Ḳ.)

مِفْأَدَةٌ: } مِفْآدٌ: } see the next preceding paragraph.

مَفْؤُودٌ *Hit, struck, smitten, affected*, or *hurt*, *in his* فُؤَاد [or *heart*, &c.]: (Ṣ, A, L:) *smitten*, or *affected, by a disease therein*: (Ṣ, L:) or *by pain therein*. (L.) — A man *without a heart; having no heart*; as also ▼ فَئِيدٌ: (Ks, Ṣ, L:) *weak-hearted*: (T, L:) *a coward*; (T, M, L, Ḳ;) and so ▼ فَئِيدٌ: (T, Ḳ:) in this sense it has no verb. (AAF, IJ, M, L.) — See also فَئِيدٌ, in two places.

مُفْتَآدٌ: see فَئِيدٌ, in two places. — Also *A place of fuel*: (T, L:) *a place in which a fire is lighted for roasting*. (A.)

فأر

1. فَئِرَ, aor. يَفْأَرُ, *It* (a place) *became abundant in* فَأْر [i. e. *rats*, or *mice*]. (Mṣb.) — فَأَرَ, (J, O,) aor. as above, (Ḳ,) inf. n. فَأْرٌ, (TḲ,) *He dug*; (Ḳ;) or *dug as does the* فَأْر [i. e. *rat*, or *mouse*]: (M, TA:) and, (Ḳ,) as some say, (M, TA,) *he buried*, and *hid*. (M,* O, Ḳ, TA.)

فَأْرٌ [*A kind of animal*,] *well known*, (M, Ḳ,) [the *genus mus*; the *rat*; the *mouse*; and *the like*]; with ء, (Lth, Ṣ, Mṣb,) and without ء; (Mṣb;) [a coll. gen. n.:] n. un. with ة: (Lth, T:) [in the Ṣ and O and Mṣb, فَأْر is said to be pl. of فَأْرَةٌ, but in the last is added, like تَمْرٌ and تَمْرَةٌ, showing that by pl. is meant coll. gen. n.:] the pl. of فَأْر, (Lth, T, M, Ḳ,) or of فَأْرَة, (O, Mṣb,) is فِئْرَانٌ (Lth, T, M, O, Ḳ, Mṣb) and فِئَرَةٌ: (M, Ḳ:) accord. to IAar, (T, TA,) ▼ فُؤَرٌ, like صُرَدٌ, (O, Ḳ, TA,) is applied to the male: (T, O, Ḳ, TA:) but this last word occurs in the phrase الفَأْرُ الفُؤَرُ, [in which الفأر is evidently used in a sense mentioned below, namely, "the muscles," as is indicated in the T and O,] and, accord. to some, [الفُؤَر is a corroborative epithet, for they say that] this phrase is like يَوْمٌ أَيْوَمُ and لَيْلٌ أَلْيَلُ: (O:) فَأْرَةٌ is applied [accord. to some] to the female; (M;) or [more correctly] to the male and the female, (M, Ḳ,) like as حَمَامَةٌ is applied to the male and the female of the [genus] حَمَام. (M, TA.) — Also *Musk*: (M, Ḳ:) this is sometimes called فَأْر because it is from the [animal, or from a kind of animal, called] فَأْر, as some say. (M.) — And فَأْرَةُ المِسْكِ signifies *The bag, follicle*, or *vesicle*, (نَافِجَة, Ṣ, M, O, Ḳ, or نَافِقَة, T,) *of musk*: (T, Ṣ, M, O, Ḳ:) and is also without ء; (M, Mṣb;) or it should correctly be mentioned in art. فور, [as being called فَارَةٌ] because of the spreading (فَوَرَان) of its odour: or it may be with ء because it has the appearance, or form, of the [animal called] فَأْرَة. (O, Ḳ.) It was said to an Arab of the desert أَتَهْمِزُ الفَارَةَ, (Ḳ, TA, in the CḲ أَتَهْمِزُ الفَأْرَ,) [meaning *Dost thou pronounce* فارة *with hemz?*], and he replied, [understanding the animal so called to be meant,] الهِرَّةُ تَهْمِزُهَا, (Ḳ,) meaning, [*The cat*] *bites it*. (TA.) — [Hence, app., by a synecdoche, فَأْرَةُ المِسْكِ is applied to *The musk-animal*, or *Tibet-musk*; *moschus moschiferus*:] El-Jáḥiḍh says, I asked a perfumer, of [the sect of] the Moạtezileh, respecting [the animal called] فأرة المسك, and he said, *it is not a mouse*, or *rat*, (فأرة,) *but is more like a young gazelle: it is found in the region of Tubbat* [or *Tibet*]; *and is hunted; and the man who catches it binds tightly its navel*, [or rather *its umbilical follicle*,] *which being pendent, the blood collects in it; then it is slaughtered; and when it is quiet, he cuts out the bound navel, and buries it in barley* (شعير) *until the congealed blood becomes converted into strong-scented musk*. (TA.) — And فَأْرَةُ الإِبِلِ signifies *The sweet odour of the camels*, [*likened to that of the vesicle of musk*,] *which diffuses itself from them when they have pastured upon the herbs and their blossoms*, (Ṣ, O,) or, as some say, *upon the* [*plant called*] خُزَامَى [q. v.], (O,) *and then drunk, and returned from the water, with their skins moist*: (Ṣ, O:) so says Yaạḳoob. (Ṣ.) Thus in a verse cited voce ذَفِرٌ. (Ṣ, O. [Therefore فَأْرَةٌ ذَفِرَةٌ should there be rendered *A pungent sweet odour like that of a vesicle of musk*. But see فَارَةٌ, in art. فور.]) — الفَأْرُ signifies also † *The muscles*: (T, O:) and فَأْرُ المَتْنِ † *the flesh on either side of the back-bone*; as also يَرَابِيعُ المَتْنِ. (T. [See also الفَارُ, in art. فور.]) — And *A species of trees*; with and without ء: (M:) and فَأْرَةٌ [as its n. un.] *a tree* [*of that species*]. (Ḳ.) — Also *A certain well-known measure*, or *quantity, of wheat*: in this sense an adventitious word. (O.)

فُؤَرٌ: see فَأْرٌ, first sentence.

فَئِرٌ A place *abounding with* فَأْر [*rats*, or *mice*]. (Ṣ, O.) You say أَرْضٌ فَئِرَةٌ, (O, Ḳ,) and أَرْضٌ ▼ مَفْأَرَةٌ, (Ṣ, O, Ḳ,) *Land abounding with* فَأْر: (Ḳ:) or *land containing* فَأْر. (Ṣ, O,) [In my copy of the Mṣb, I find ▼ مَكَانٌ مَفْأَرٌ.] — Milk, (M, Ḳ,) and food, (TA,) *into which a rat*, or *mouse*, (فأرة,) *has fallen*. (M, Ḳ, TA.)

فَأْرَةٌ n. un. (but said by some to be fem.) of فَأْر [q. v.] — Also, (Ṣ, M, O, Ḳ,) and ▼ فُؤْرَةٌ, (M, Ḳ, in the O written فُؤَرَةٌ,) both with and without ء, (M, O,) *A flatus* (Ṣ, M, O, Ḳ) *that collects* (Ṣ) *in the pastern* (Ṣ, M, O, Ḳ) *of a camel*, (Ṣ,) or *of a beast*, (M, Ḳ,) or *of a horse*; (O;) *which issues* (Ṣ, M, O, Ḳ) *when it is felt*, (Ṣ,) or *when it is stroked, and collects when it is left to itself*. (M, O, Ḳ.)

فُؤْرَةٌ: see the next preceding paragraph.

فِئْرَةٌ and فُئَيْرَةٌ: see فَئِيرَةٌ.

فُؤَارَةٌ: see the paragraph here following.

فَئِيرَةٌ (T, M, O, Ḳ) and ▼ فُؤَارَةٌ (M, Ḳ) and ▼ فِئْرَةٌ (Lth, T, O, Ḳ) and ▼ فُئَيْرَةٌ, and also without ء, (Ḳ,) *Fenugreek* (حُلْبَة) *cooked until its foam boils up, when it is put into a press* (معصر), *and clarified, then dates are thrown upon it, and the woman in the state following childbirth sups it*: (Lth, T:) or *fenugreek* (حُلْبَة) *and dates cooked for the woman in the state following child-*

birth, (M, O, Ḳ,) who drinks it, (M,) and for the sick. (O.)

مَفْأَرٌ; and its fem., with ة: see فَئِرٌ.

فأس

1. فَأَسَ, (Ṣ, M, O, Ḳ,) aor. َ, inf. n. فَأْسٌ, (M, Ḳ,) *He struck* (AḤn, Ṣ, O, Mṣb, Ḳ) him, or it, (Ṣ, O,) or a tree, (AḤn, M,) *with a* فَأْس: (AḤn, Ṣ, M, O, Ḳ:) *he cut* him, or it, (M,) or a tree, (TA,) *therewith:* (M:) *he clave,* (M, O, Ḳ,) or *split,* (T, O,) a piece of wood, (M,) or one's head, (O,) *therewith.* (M, Ḳ.) —— *He hit* (Ṣ, Ḳ) a man (Ṣ) *in the* فَأْس *of the head.* (Ṣ, Ḳ.) ═ *He ate* wheat, or other food. (O, Ḳ,* TA.)

فَأْسٌ *A certain implement of iron,* (M,) *with which one digs;* [i. e., *a kind of hoe;* thus called in the present day; *generally having a blade more long than wide, and a short handle; altogether resembling an adz:*] (Kr, M:) and *with which one cuts;* [i. e., *an adz;* and *an axe;* both also thus called in the present day; more commonly the former; *used for cutting, cleaving, and splitting, trees and wood,* (see فَأَسَ,) *and for hewing, forming,* or *fashioning, wood &c.:* (see also قَدُومٌ:)] (M:) *a thing well known:* (A, Ḳ:) [applied also to *a pickaxe:* (see صَاقُورٌ:)] the ء in this word may be suppressed: (Mṣb:) it is of the fem. gender: (M, Mṣb, Ḳ:) the pl. (of pauc., O) is أَفْؤُسٌ (M, O, Mṣb, Ḳ) and (of mult., O) فُؤُوسٌ, (Ṣ, M, O, Mṣb, Ḳ,) and, accord. to some, فُؤْسٌ. (TA.) —— فَأْسُ اللِّجَامِ [*A certain part of the bit;* namely,] *the* [*tongue of*] *iron that stands up towards* [so I render here the particle فِى] *the* حَنَك [here meaning the *palate,* against which it is made to press when the rein is drawn hard for the purpose of checking the horse]; (IDrd in his book on the Saddle and Bridle, [in one part of which he likens to it the tongue of a buckle,] Ṣ, M, A, O, Ḳ;) *the iron that stands up in the* شَكِيمَة; (T;) or, as some say, *that which is in the middle of the* شكيمة, *between the* مِسْحَلَانِ: (ISh:) the شكيمة is the iron that lies across in the mouth, [i. e., the bit-mouth, or mouth-piece of the bit,] and the مِسْحَل is an iron [i. e. a ring of iron, one of a pair of rings which are inserted each into the other, in the place of our curb-chain,] beneath the حَنَك [here meaning the part between the two sides of the lower jaw]: (IDrd:) or, as some say, [and among them Kr,] *the transverse iron in the bit;* (M;) but this assertion requires consideration. (TA.) You say, فُلَانٌ يَلُوكُ لِسَانَهُ فِى الكَلَامِ كَمَا يَعْلُكُ الفَرَسُ فَأْسَ اللِّجَامِ [*Such a one mumbles his tongue in speaking like as the horse moves about in his mouth the* فأس *of the bit*]. (A.) —— فَأْسُ الرَّأْسِ, (Ṣ, O, Ḳ,) or فَأْسُ القَفَا, (M,) *The edge of the* قَمَحْدُوَة [or *hinder part of the back of the head*], *that projects above the back of the neck;* [i. e., *the small protuberance above the back of the neck:*] (Ṣ, O, Ḳ:) or *the hinder part of the* قمحدوة. (M.) —— فَأْسُ الرَّحَى *The* [*protuberant*] *part of the* [*nether,* or *lower,*] *mill-stone, in the middle of which is* [*fixed*] *the axis.* (Ḳzw, description of Ursa Minor.) —— And hence, الفَأْسُ *The Constellation of Ursa Minor.* (Idem, same place.) —— فَأْسُ الفَمِ *The extremity of the mouth, in which are the teeth.* (M.) —— اِجْعَلْ هٰذَا الأَمْرَ فَأْسًا وَاحِدًا means *Make thou this affair to be* [*uniform,* or] *of one way* or *mode* or *manner.* (ISk, TA in art. بأج.)

فأل

2. تَفْئِيلٌ is of the measure تَفْعِيلٌ from الفَأْلُ: (O, Ḳ,* TA:*) [and is app. *syn. with* تَفَؤُّلٌ, signifying The *auguring,* &c.; or it may signify the *auguring,* &c., *much:* accord. to the TḲ, فَأَّلَهُ بِهِ means جَعَلَهُ يَتَفَأَّلُ بِهِ *he made him to augur,* &c., *by it;* but this, as is very often the case in the TḲ, is app. said only on the ground of conjecture: the only ex. that I have found, to show its true meaning, is that which here follows:] Ru-beh says,

لَا يَأْخُذُ التَّفْئِيلُ وَالتَّحَزِّى
فِينَا وَلَا قَذْفُ العِدَى ذُو الأَزِّ

[which seems evidently to mean, *The auguring,* &c., or *auguring,* &c., *much, and the divining, will not have any effect upon us; nor the enemies' noisy reviling* or *reproaching*]: but AA has related it otherwise, substituting التَّأْفِيكُ [lit. the *lying*] for التفئيل; and has explained it as meaning *the enchanting;* because it is a turning of a thing from its proper way, or mode. (O, TA.)

5. تَفَأَّلَ بِهِ, (ISk, Ṣ, M, MA,) or ↓ تَفَايَلَ, (AZ, T, Mṣb,) or both, (Ḳ, TA, [accord. to the latter of which, it seems that the latter v. is formed from the former v., for the purpose of alleviating the pronunciation, and has become the popular form,]) *He augured,* or *augurated, good, by it,* or *from it;* or *regarded it as a good omen;* i. e., something uttered in his hearing: (AZ, ISk, T, Ṣ, M,* MA, Mṣb, Ḳ:) or so, and likewise *evil;* (AZ, T, Mṣb, Ḳ;) accord. to the usage of some of the Arabs: (T:) [but in the latter case they generally said, تَطَيَّرَ مِنْهُ (q. v.): and in like manner they used these verbs in relation to the cries and flights of birds, and the motions of gazelles, &c.; as is stated in several of the lexicons, voce بَارِحٌ, &c. See also 2 and 8: and see فَأْلٌ.]

6: see the next preceding paragraph.

8. اِفْتِئَالٌ [in my copies of the Ṣ written اِفْتِيَالٌ] is of the measure اِفْتِعَالٌ from الفَأْلُ: (Ṣ, Ḳ,* TA:*) [in the PṢ and TḲ, it is said to be *syn. with* تَفَأَّلَ: it seems, however, that in the ex. here following, its exact signification, and whether it be used in an act. or a pass. sense, is doubtful; and that it is trans. without a prep.:] El-Kumeyt says, describing horses,

إِذَا مَا بَدَتْ تَحْتَ الخَوَافِقِ صَدَّقَتْ
بِأَيْمَنِ فَأْلِ الزَّاجِرِينَ ٱفْتِئَالُهَا

[app. meaning, *When they appear beneath the standards,* (perhaps standards set up as winning-posts,) *the regarding them as of good omen,* or *their being regarded as of good omen,* (by reason of their excellent performance,) *verifies the happiest augury of the diviners:* with respect to its being made fem. in this ex., though not regularly fem. in form, see صَوْتٌ, third sentence]. (Ṣ, TA.) —— [It has also another signification:] Fr says, اِفْتَأَلْتُ الرَّأْىَ is with hemz which is originally [a letter] other than hemz [app. meaning that the v. is originally اِفْتَيَلْتُ, which becomes changed by rule to اِفْتَلْتُ]; and that the signification is the same as that of فَيَّلْتُ الرَّأْىَ, *I declared,* or *esteemed, the judgment,* or *opinion, weak;* or *pronounced it to be bad,* and *wrong,* or *erroneous:* perhaps the substitution of hemz for the medial radical letter is for the purpose of giving to the phrase a double meaning: or the hemz may be the original letter, and the phrase may be used ironically]. (O, TA.)

فَأْلٌ, (T, Ṣ, M, O, Mṣb, Ḳ,) and فَالٌ without ء is allowable, (Mṣb,) *A good omen;* (PṢ;) *contr. of* طِيَرَةٌ: (T, M, Mṣb, Ḳ:) it is when a man is sick, and he hears another say يَا سَالِمُ [O safe]; or seeking, and hears another say يَا وَاجِدُ [O finder]: (ISk, T, Ṣ, O, Ḳ:*) or it is when one hears a good saying, and augurs good by it: (Mṣb:) [therefore] it is said in a trad., كَانَ يُحِبُّ الفَأْلَ وَيَكْرَهُ الطِّيَرَةَ [*He* (the Prophet) *used to like the* فأل, *and dislike the* طِيَرَة]: (T, Ṣ, O:) [or it signifies so, and likewise *an evil omen:* i. e.] it is used in relation to a good saying and to an evil saying, (AZ, T, Mṣb, Ḳ,) by some of the Arabs: (T:) it is said in a trad. [of the Prophet], يُعْجِبُنِى الفَأْلُ الصَّالِحُ [*The good* فأل *pleases me*]; which shows that there is a sort of فَأْل that is good and a sort that is not good: (TA:) and [in like manner] طَائِرٌ is applied to that which is good and that which is evil: (Ḳ in art. طير:) the pl. is أَفْؤُلٌ [properly a pl. of pauc.], (Ṣ, O,) or فُؤُولٌ [a pl. of mult.], (M,) or both: (Ḳ:) El-Kumeyt says,

وَلَا أَسْأَلُ الطَّيْرَ عَمَّا تَقُولُ
وَلَا تَتَخَالَجُنِى الأَفْؤُلُ

[*And I will not ask the birds respecting what they say, nor shall omens,* or *good omens, contend with me as though pulling me in different directions*]. (Ṣ, O.) —— لَا فَأْلَ عَلَيْكَ means *No harm shall befall thee;* (T, O, Ḳ;) and *no evil fortune;* and *no mischief.* (T.)

فَئِيلُ اللَّحْمِ, (O, Ḳ,) or ↓ فَيَّالُ اللَّحْمِ, (T,) or both, (TA,) A man *having much flesh.* (T, O, Ḳ, TA.) [See also فَيْلٌ, in art. فيل.]

الفِئَالُ *A certain game of the boys* (T, Ṣ, O, Ḳ,

TA) *of the desert-Arabs*, (TA,) *with earth*, or *dust*: (T:) *they hide a thing in earth*, or *dust*, *and then divide it, and say, In which of them* (Ṣ, O, Ḳ, TA) *twain* (Ṣ, O, TA) *is it?* (Ṣ, O, Ḳ, TA.) [See also الفِيَالُ, in art. فيل.]

فَيَالُ اللَّحْمِ : see فَثْلُ اللَّحْمِ, above.

مُفَايِلٌ [or مُفَائِلٌ (M and TA in art. فيل)] A boy *playing at the game called* الفِئَال. (Ṣ, O.*)

فالوذ &c.

فَالُوذٌ and فَالُوذَجٌ and فَالُوذَقٌ : see art. فلذ.

فأم

1. فَأَمَ, [or فَأَمَ العُشْبَ, as is shown by an ex. in the Ṣ and TA,] aor. ـَ, [inf. n. فَأْمٌ, TḲ,] *He* (a camel) *filled his mouth with herbage*; (IAạr, Ṣ, Ḳ;) as also فَئِمَ, (Ḳ, TA,) like فَرِحَ; (TA; [in the CḲ فَأَّمَ;]) and ↓ تَفَأَّمَ. (AA, T, Ḳ, TA.) — And فَأَمَ, (T,) or فَأَمَ مِنَ المَآءِ, aor. as above, (Ḳ,) *He satisfied his thirst with drinking of water*. (T, Ḳ.) — And فَأَمَ فِى الشَّرَابِ *He drank with his mouth, not with his hand nor with any other thing, a gulp*, or *a draught*, (نَفَسًا,) *of the wine*, or *beverage*; (T, TA;) said of a man: (TA:) app. from أَفْأَمَ signifying "he filled" a vessel: and صَأَمَ signifies the same. (T, TA.) ═ See also 4.

2: see 4. — تَفْئِيمٌ signifies also The *making wide* a leathern bucket. (T, TA.) — And [app. as inf. n. of فَئِمَ, first signifying The *being made wide*, and then, as a subst.,] *largeness, bulkiness*, or *corpulence, and wideness*. (TA.) — See, again, 4.

4. افأم *He widened*, (Ṣ, M, Ḳ,) *and added to*, a [camel's saddle such as is called] قَتَب, (Ṣ, Ḳ,) and [such as is called] a رَحْل, (Ṣ,) or a [woman's camel-vehicle such as is called] هَوْدَج, *in its lower part*; (M;) and ↓ فأّم, (Ṣ, M, Ḳ,) inf. n. تَفْئِيمٌ, (Ṣ, Ḳ,) signifies the same: and the epithets ↓ مُفْأَمٌ and ↓ مُفَأَّمٌ are then applied thereto. (Ṣ, M, Ḳ.) — [And *He widened* a leathern water-bag *by inserting a third skin between the two other skins*: see the pass. part. n. below, and see also شَعِيبٌ.] — And *He filled* a vessel (T, TA) or a leathern bucket: (TA:) and so أَفْعَمَ. (T, TA.) — أُفْئِمَ حَارِكُهُ *His* (a camel's) *withers became full of fat*: (Ṣ:) [or] so ↓ فَئِمَ حَارِكُهُ, like فَرِحَ [in measure], accord. to the Ḳ, but correctly ↓ فُئِمَ, like عُنِىَ: (TA:) [or the latter verb is app. ↓ فُئِّمَ: for] the epithets applied thereto [whether to the camel or to the withers is not clearly shown] are ↓ مُفْأَمٌ (Ṣ, TA) and ↓ مُفَأَّمٌ, meaning *fat, and wide within*: in the Ḳ, erroneously, مِفْأَمٌ and مِفْأَمٌ, like مِنْبَرٌ and مِحْرَابٌ. (TA.)

6: see 1, first sentence.

قَطَعُوهُ فُؤُمًا, [the latter word] like صُرُدٍ, (Ḳ,) or قَطَعُوا الشَّاةَ فُؤُمًا فُؤُمًا, (so in the T accord. to the TT,) i. e. [*They cut it*, or *the sheep*, or *goat*,] *into a number of pieces*. (T, Ḳ.)

فِئَامٌ *A thing that is spread to sit upon or to lie upon*, (Ṣ, M, Ḳ,) *pertaining to the* [*women's camel-vehicles called*] مَشَاجِر [pl. of مِشْجَرٌ], (M,) or *to* [*those called*] هَوَادِج, (Ḳ,) or *to both of these*: (Ṣ:) or, as some say, *a* هَوْدَج *that is widened in its lower part by something added thereto*: or *a burden equiponderant to another burden, like a sack with a small mouth, with which the vehicle of a woman is covered; one being placed on one side, and another* [app. *close to the former*] *on the other side*: (M:) pl. فُؤُمٌ [with two dammehs]. (Ṣ, M, Ḳ.) — [And *A piece that is added to a leathern water-bag*. (See شَعِيبٌ; under which it is loosely explained: and see 4 in this art.)] ═ Also *A company* of men: (T, Ṣ, M, Ḳ:) a pl. having no proper sing.: (Ṣ, Ḳ:) the vulgar say فِيَامٌ, without ء: (Ṣ:) [or] they say فِيَامٌ: (thus in the T accord. to the TT:) [but ISd says,] فِئَامٌ and فِيَامٌ have this meaning; otherwise I should say that فِيَامٌ is a modified form, for alleviation, from فِئَامٌ. (M in art. فيم.)

أَفْآمٌ [a pl. of which the sing. is not mentioned] The *four parts whence the water pours forth, between the extremities of the cross-pieces of wood* (العَرَاقِى), of the leathern bucket. (Th, M.)

مُفْأَمٌ : see 4, first sentence. — مَزَادَةٌ مُفْأَمَةٌ [A *leathern water-bag*] *widened with a third skin* (T, M) *between the two* [*other*] *skins*: [see شَعِيبٌ:] and in like manner دَلْوٌ مُفْأَمَةٌ [app. meaning *a widened leathern bucket*]. (M.) — And سِقَآءٌ مُفْأَمٌ [*A skin for water* or *milk*] *filled*. (TA.) — See also 4, last sentence.

مُفَأَّمٌ : see 4, first and last sentences.

فانيذ and فانيد

فَانِيدٌ and فَانِيذٌ : see art. فند.

فاو and فأى

1. فَأَوْتُ رَأْسَهُ, inf. n. فَأْوٌ; and فَأَيْتُهُ, inf. n. فَأْىٌ; *I split*, or *clave, his head*, i. e. a man's, with the sword: (AZ, T, Ṣ, M:) or *I struck*, or *smote, the upper part of his skull so that it opened from over his brain*. (Lth, T.) — And فَأَيْتُ القَدَحَ *I split*, or *clave*, or *cracked, the bowl*. (M.) And فَأَوْتُهُ بِالعَصَا *I smote*, or *struck, him with the staff*, or *stick*. (IAạr, M.) فَأْوٌ and فَأْىٌ both signify The act of *smiting*, or *striking*: and the act of *splitting*, or *cleaving*. (Ḳ.)

4. افأى *He* (a man, TA) *lighted upon*, or *became in, what is termed a* فَأْو: or *he inflicted a wound of the head such as showed the whiteness of the bone*, or *such as laid bare the bone*. (Ḳ, TA.)

5: see the next following paragraph.

7. انفأى *It became split*, or *cloven*, (Ṣ, M, Ḳ,) or *cracked*; (M, Ḳ;) said of a bowl [&c.]; (Ṣ, M;) as also ↓ تفأّى: (M, TA:) *it opened*, or *became opened*: (M, Ḳ:) *it opened so as to form a break*, or *breach*: (T, M, Ḳ:) *it became laid open, uncovered*, or *exposed to view*. (T, TA.)

فَأْوٌ *An interval*, (Ṣ, M,) or *a low*, or *depressed, place*, (خَفْض, so in one of my copies of the Ṣ,) *between two mountains*: (Ṣ, M:) and, accord. to Lth, (M,) *a cleft* (M, Ḳ) *in a mountain*, (M,) or *between two mountains*. (Ḳ.) And *A* وَطْء [or *depressed tract*], (M, and so in copies of the Ḳ,) or وَطِىْء, (so in other copies of the Ḳ,) meaning *soft*, or *smooth*, or *plain, place*, (TA,) *between two stony tracts of the kind whereof one is termed* حَرَّة. (M, Ḳ.) And, (M, Ḳ,) as some say, (M,) *A clear, open, space among sands*. (M, Ḳ.) And, (M, Ḳ,) accord. to Aṣ, (M,) *A low*, or *depressed, tract of good land surrounded by mountains*, (M, Ḳ,) and *such as is of an elongated form*, and *such as is not of that form*. (M.) And (as some say, TA) *A narrow place in a valley, leading to a wide space*, (Ḳ, TA,) *of which the upper part has no place of exit*. (TA.) And (as some say, TA) *A smooth place*. (Ḳ, TA.) — Also The *night*; (M, Ḳ;) so says Aboo-Leylà; but of questionable correctness. (M.) — And The *place*, or *time, of sunset*. (Ḳ.)

فِئَةٌ *A party, portion, division*, or *distinct body*; or *a company*, or *congregated body*; syn. فِرْقَةٌ, (T,) or طَائِفَةٌ, (Ṣ,) or جَمَاعَةٌ; (M, Ḳ;) *of men*: (T, M:) [see more in art. فيأ, to which it belongs accord. to some: accord. to others,] it is originally فِئْىٌ or فِئْوَةٌ [app. فِئْوٌ] (T) [or (see art. فيأ); or فِئْيَةٌ (see what follows)]; the ة being a substitute for the [final radical letter, which is و or] ى: (Ṣ:) the pl. is فِئُونَ (Ṣ, M, Ḳ) and فِئَاتٌ. (M, Ḳ.) El-Kumeyt says,

• تَرَى مِنْهُ جَمَاجِمَهُمْ فِئِينَا •

meaning [*Thou wouldst see, in consequence thereof, their skulls* become] *scattered fragments*. (Ṣ.)

فَأْوَى The *head*, or *glans, of the penis*. (M, Ḳ.)

فَائِيَةٌ or فَائِثَةٌ (accord. to different copies of the Ḳ) *An elevated, expanded place*. (Ḳ.)

فاوانيا

الفَاوَانِيَا i. q. عُودُ الصَّلِيبِ, [both of which appellations are now applied to *The common peony, pæonia officinalis*, and this is what is meant in what here follows,] i. e. *the* كهينا, [app. for كُهْيَانَا, which is a Pers. word, meaning the plant above-mentioned,] *a plant less than a cubit* [*in height*], *having a purple flower, not found except in the day of the sun's taking its abode in Libra*; (TA;) [its root has, from ancient times, and in various countries, been held in high repute for medicinal properties; and various fancied virtues (some of which are supposed to be partly dependant upon particular aspects of the moon and certain stars, and several of which are mentioned in the TA,) are ascribed to it:] *it is hot, attenuant, resolutive, diuretic, has the property of stopping hæmorrhage, and is beneficial as a remedy against the* نِقْرِس [i. e. *gout,* or particularly *podagra,*] *and epilepsy* (الصَّرْع), *even by its being suspended* [*on the patient*]. (Ḳ.) [See also بُرُوج, in art. برج.]

فت

1. فَتَّ, (Ṣ, M, O, Mṣb,) aor. ـُ, (M, Mṣb,) inf. n. فَتٌّ, (Lth, T, M, Mṣb, Ḳ,) *He crumbled* a thing, or *broke it into small pieces, with his fingers:* (Lth, T, TA:) or *he broke* (a thing, M) *with his fingers:* (M, Ḳ:) or [simply] *he broke* a thing: (Ṣ, O:) or (M) *he bruised,* or *brayed,* (M, Ḳ,) a thing: (M:) and ↓ فتّت, (M, TA,) inf. n. تَفْتِيتٌ, (O,) signifies the same; (M, TA;) or [rather] *he broke* [a thing, or *crumbled* it *with his fingers,*] *much.* (O.) You say of a man, فَتَّ الخُبْزَ, (A, Mṣb,) aor. and inf. n. as above; (Mṣb;) and ↓ فتّته; *He crumbled the bread with his fingers.* (A.) — [Hence,] one says, ذَا مِمَّا يَفُتُّ كَبِدِى † [lit. *This is of what crumbles,* or *crushes, my liver;* like as we say, "of what breaks my heart"]. (A, TA.) — And كَلَّمَهُ بِشَىْءٍ فَفَتَّ فِى سَاعِدِهِ † *He told him,* or *spoke to him, of a thing, and it* [*crushed,* or] *weakened,* or *enervated, him.* (M, Ḳ,* TA.) And فَتَّ فِى عَضُدِى وَهَدَّ رُكْنِى (O, TA) † *He broke my strength, and dispersed,* or *separated, my assistants.* (TA.) And فَتَّ فِى عَضُدِ فُلَانٍ i. e. فِى أَهْلِ بَيْتِهِ † *He sought to injure such a one by diminishing,* or *impairing,* [*in number* or *power,*] *the people of his house.* (T, O. [See also art. عضد.]) The verb in this phrase is also used in the pass. form. (O.)

2: see the preceding paragraph, in two places.

5: see the paragraph here following.

7. انفتّ *It became crumbled,* or *broken into small pieces, with the fingers:* (M, TA:) or *it became broken with the fingers:* (M, TA:) or [simply] *it became broken:* (Ṣ, O:) or *it became bruised,* or *brayed:* and ↓ تفتّت signifies the same; (M, TA;) or [rather] *it became broken* [or *crumbled with the fingers*] *much.* (Ṣ, O.)

R. Q. 1. فَتْفَتَةٌ [inf. n. of فَتْفَتَ] The *drinking,* of camels, *less than satisfies thirst.* (O, Ḳ.) — [And it is also trans.:] one says of a pastor, فَتْفَتَ إِبِلَهُ *He drove back his camels from the water when they had not satisfied their thirst.* (IAạr, T, O.) — And فَتْفَتَ إِلَيْهِ, inf. n. فَتْفَتَةٌ, *He spoke secretly to him:* one says, مَا هٰذِهِ الدَّنْدَنَةُ وَالفَتْفَتَةُ [*What is this whispering, and secret speaking?*]. (A, TA.)

فُتٌّ *A fissure* in a rock: (IAạr, T, O, Ḳ:) as also ↓ فَتٌّ: (IAạr, T:) pl. فُتُوتٌ. (IAạr, T, O.) — مَا فِى يَدِى مِنْكَ حَتٌّ وَلَا فَتٌّ *There is not in my hand, from thee, aught.* (O.) — أُولٰئِكَ أَهْلُ بَيْتٍ فُتٍّ and ↓ فُتُّ (Fr, T, O, Ḳ*) and ↓ فِتٌّ (Fr, T, Ḳ) *Those are the people of a house dispersed,* or *scattered.* (Fr, T, O, Ḳ.*)

فَتٌّ and فِتٌّ: see what next precedes.

فَتَّةٌ, (M, A, and so in some copies of the Ṣ,) or ↓ فُتَّةٌ, (so in other copies of the Ṣ,) or both, (Ḳ,) or the latter and ↓ فِتَّةٌ, (T, O,) The *thing,* (Ṣ, O,) or *piece of dung,* (T, M, A, Ḳ.) [i. e.] *of dry dung,* (CḲ,) *of the camel,* (T, M, A, Ḳ,) or *of the horse* or *any solid-hoofed animal,* (T,) *that is broken,* or *crumbled,* (Ṣ, M, A, O, Ḳ,) *and put beneath the* زَنْدَة, (T, Ṣ, O,) or *put beneath the* زَنْد, *on the occasion of striking fire,* (M,) [i. e.] *in which one strikes fire.* (Ḳ.) [Hence,] one says, فُلَانٌ لَا يُسَاوِى فَتَّةً, meaning [*Such a one is not worth*] *a crumbled piece of dung of the camel.* (A.) — Also, i. e. فَتَّةٌ and ↓ فُتَّةٌ, (Ḳ,) or the latter [only], (AA, T, O,) *A* كُتْلَة [i. e. *lump,* or *compact portion,*] *of dates.* (AA, T, O, Ḳ.)

فُتَّةٌ and فِتَّةٌ: see the next preceding paragraph; the former in two places.

فُتَاتٌ *Broken bits or particles,* (T, Ṣ, M, A, O, Mṣb, Ḳ,) and (A) *such as have fallen off,* (T, A,) of a thing, (Ṣ, O, Mṣb,) [as] of coloured wool, (T, A,) and of wool in general, (T,) and of musk, and [*crumbs*] of bread. (A.)

فَتُوتٌ: see the next paragraph, in two places.

فَتِيتٌ i. q. ↓ مَفْتُوتٌ [i. e. *Crumbled,* or *broken into small pieces, with the fingers:* or *broken with the fingers:* or simply *broken:* or *bruised,* or *brayed*]; (T, Ṣ, M, O, Mṣb, Ḳ;) as also ↓ فَتُوتٌ. (M, Ḳ.) — And particularly, (Lth, T, Ṣ, M, A, Mgh, O, Mṣb,) and so ↓ فَتُوتٌ, (Ṣ, M, A, Mgh, O,) *Crumbled bread,* (Lth, T, Ṣ, &c.,) *like* سَوِيق. (A, Mgh.) ↓ فَتِيتَةٌ has a more special signification than فَتِيتٌ, [being a n. un., meaning *A mess of crumbled bread,*] (Mgh, Mṣb,) and is said to be eaten by a woman in order that she may become fat. (Mgh.) — And فَتِيتٌ signifies also *A thing that falls,* (Lth, T, M,) *and becomes crumbled,* (Lth, T,) or *breaks off.* (M.)

فَتِيتَةٌ: see the next preceding paragraph.

بَيْنَهُمْ فَتَافِتُ *Between them is secret speaking,* [or *between them are secret speakings,* for فَتَافِتُ is app. pl. of the inf. n. فَتْفَتَةٌ used as a simple subst., (see R. Q. 1,)] *not heard nor understood* [*by others*]. (O, Ḳ.)

مَفْتُوتٌ: see فَتِيتٌ.

فتأ

1. مَا فَتِئَ, (Fr,* T, Mṣb, Ḳ,) aor. ـَ; (Fr, T, Mṣb;) and مَا فَتَأَ, [aor. ـَ;] (Ḳ;) and مَا فَتُؤَ, (Fr,* T, Ḳ,) aor. ـُ; (Fr, T;) *He did not cease* [doing a thing; being incomplete, or non-attributive, verbs]; (T, Mṣb, Ḳ;) as also ↓ مَا أَفْتَأَ; (AZ, T, Ḳ;) this last of the dial. of Temeem; (AZ, T, M;) the first of the dial. of Ḳeys and others: (AZ, T:) you say مَا فَتِئْتُ أَذْكُرُهُ, (AZ, T, Ṣ, O, Mṣb,*) or مَا فَتِئْتُ أَفْعَلُ, (M,) and مَا فَتَأْتُ, (AZ, T, Ṣ, O, M,) aor. ـَ, inf. n. فَتْءٌ (AZ, T, M) and فُتُوْءٌ; (M;) and مَا فَتُؤْتُ, aor. ـُ; (Fr, O;) and ↓ مَا أَفْتَأْتُ; (AZ, T, Ṣ, M, O;) *I did not cease* [*remembering him,* or *doing* such a thing]: (AZ, T, Ṣ, M, O, Mṣb:*) these verbs are used only in negative phrases, in this sense; but sometimes the particle of negation is suppressed, it being, however, meant to be understood; (T, Ṣ, M;) as in تَاللّٰهِ تَفْتَأُ تَذْكُرُ يُوسُفَ, (T, Ṣ, O, Ḳ,) in the Ḳur [xii. 85], (T, Ṣ, O,) meaning مَا تَفْتَأُ, (Ṣ, O, Ḳ,) thus in all the copies of the Ḳ [and in the Ṣ and O], but correctly لَا تَفْتَأُ, [i. e. *By God, thou wilt not cease remembering Joseph,*] accord. to all the grammarians and the expositors of the Ḳur-án: (TA:) for the oath that is not accompanied by the sign of affirmation denotes negation. (Bḍ in xii. 85.) — And فَتِئَ عَنْهُ, (O, Ḳ,) inf. n. فَتْءٌ, (O,) *He forgot it, and abstained,* or *desisted, from it;* (نَسِيَهُ وَانْقَدَعَ عَنْهُ, O, and so in some copies of the Ḳ; in other copies of the Ḳ انقذع or انفدع; [both of which are evidently mistranscriptions;]) namely, an affair, or event: (O, TA:) or this is used only in negative phrases. (Ḳ.) — فَتَأَ, as a complete [i. e. an attributive] verb, signifies *He stilled, quieted,* or *made to cease,* syn. سَكَّنَ, or, as some say, (TA,) *he abated,* or *allayed,* syn. كَسَرَ, *and extinguished:* thus says Ibn-Málik, as on the authority of Fr; and it is correct: AḤei has erred in charging him with having committed a mistake: (Ḳ, TA:) for he says that it is a mistranscription for فَثَأَ, with the three-pointed ث: it is mentioned also by IḲoot and IḲṭṭ: and Fr states that one says, فَتَأْتُهُ عَنِ الأَمْرِ meaning *I made him to cease* (سَكَّنْتُهُ) *from the affair:* and فَتَأْتُ النَّارَ meaning *I extinguished the fire.* (TA.)

4: see the preceding paragraph, in two places.

فتح

1. فَتَحَ, (Ṣ, A, MA, Mṣb, Ḳ, &c.,) aor. ـَ, (Ḳ,) inf. n. فَتْحٌ, (Mṣb,) *He opened,* (MA,) i. q. فَرَجَ, (Mṣb,) and [app. *he unlocked,*] *contr. of* أَغْلَقَ, (Mṣb, Ḳ,) a door; (Ṣ, A, MA, Mṣb;) and so ↓ فتّح, and ↓ افتتح; (Ḳ;) or you say ↓ فَتَّحْتُ الأَبْوَابَ [*I opened the doors*], this verb being with teshdeed to denote multiplicity [of the objects]; (Ṣ;) and ↓ استفتح signifies the same as ↓ افتتح; (Ṣ,* Ḳ;) i. e. each of these signifies *he opened* a door; (TḲ;) you say ↓ اِسْتَفْتَحْتُ الشَّىْءَ and ↓ اِفْتَتَحْتُهُ [*I opened the thing;* and the former signifies also *I sought,* or *demanded, the opening of the thing*]; (Ṣ, TA;) and ↓ جَآءَ يَسْتَفْتِحُ البَابَ [*He came opening the door;* or *seeking,* or *demanding, the opening of the door;* the latter being the more obvious meaning]. (A, TA.) —

[Hence,] one says, فُلَانٌ لَا يُفْتَحُ العَيْنُ عَلَى مِثْلِهِ [*Such a one, the eye will not be opened upon the like of him*]. (A.) — And فَتَحْتُ القَنَاةَ, inf. n. as above, *I opened the conduit*, in order that the water might run, and irrigate the seed-produce. (Mṣb.) — And فَتَحَ بَيْنَ رِجْلَيْهِ [*He made an opening between his legs; he parted his legs*; like فَرَجَ بَيْنَهُمَا]. (Ṣ in art. رهو.) — And فَتَحَ أَصَابِعَ رِجْلَيْهِ [app. *He parted his toes*; if not a mistake for فَتَخَ, as it seems probably to be from the fact of its being expl. as meaning] *he inclined the ends of his toes towards the back*, i. e. *the upper part, of his foot*. (Mgh.) — فَتَحَتْ, said of a she-camel, [and of a sheep or goat (see فَتُوحٌ),] *She had wide orifices to her teats*; as also ▼ افتحت; (Ṣ, Ḳ;) and ▼ انفتحت. (TḲ: but this I do not find in the Ḳ.) — [The following meanings are tropical.] — فَتَحَ, (A, Mṣb, TA,) inf. n. فَتْحٌ; (Ḳ;) and ▼ افتتح; (Ḳ, TA;) ‡ [*He laid open by invasion*, to (عَلَى) such a person, or such a people, (see an ex. voce طَرَقَ,) i. e.] *he conquered, won*, or *took by force*, (Mṣb,) a country (A, Mṣb, Ḳ, TA) of the unbelievers, (A, TA,) or of a people with whom there was war. (Ḳ, TA.) — [فَتَحَهُ لَهُ † *He granted it, permitted it, allowed it*, or *made it to be unrestricted, to him*. See Ksh and Bḍ in xxxv. 2.] — فَتَحَ المُشْكِلَ † *He explained*, or *made clear, that which was dubious*, or *confused*. (Bḍ in vii. 87.) And اِفْتَحْ سِرَّكَ عَلَيَّ لَا عَلَى فُلَانٍ ‡ [*Open*, or *reveal, thy secret to me; not to such a one*]. (A, TA.) — [Hence,] فَتَحَ عَلَيْهِ ‡ *He taught him, informed him*, or *acquainted him*. (TA.) [You say, فَتَحَ عَلَيْهِ بِكَذَا † *He taught him such a thing, informed him of it*, or *acquainted him with it*.] — And hence, (TA,) ‡ [*He prompted him*; i. e.] *he recited to him* (namely, an Imám, A, Mṣb, or a reciter, A, TA) *what he was unable to utter* [*by reason of forgetfulness*], *in order that he might know it*. (Mṣb, TA.*) And فَتَحَ عَلَى مَنِ ٱسْتَقْرَأَهُ ‡ [*He recited something to him who desired him to do so, the latter being unable to do it*]. (TA.) — And, said of God, ‡ *He aided him against his enemy*; or *made him to be victorious, to conquer*, or *to overcome*; syn. نَصَرَهُ. (A, Mṣb.) — فَتَحَ عَلَى فُلَانٍ ‡ *Such a one became fortunate; possessed of good fortune; favoured by the world*, or *by worldly circumstances*. (A, TA.) — فَتَحَ ٱللّٰهُ عَلَيْهِمْ فُتُوحًا كَثِيرَةً ‡ is said of persons who have been rained upon [as meaning *God bestowed upon them many*, or *abundant, first rains*]. (A.) — فَتَحَ بَيْنَهُمْ, (A,) or بَيْنَ النَّاسِ, (Mṣb,) or بَيْنَ الخَصْمَيْنِ, (Ḳ,) inf. n. فَتْحٌ, (T, Mṣb, Ḳ,) and فُتَاحَةٌ (Ṣ,* Ḳ) and فِتَاحَةٌ are syn. therewith [app. as inf. ns.], (Ḳ,) and فُتُوحَةٌ and فِتَاحٌ, (L,) in the dial. of Ḥimyer, (TA,) *He judged* (T, Mṣb, Ḳ, TA) *between them*, (A,) or *between the men*, (Mṣb,) or *between the two litigants*. (Ḳ.) You say, اِفْتَحْ بَيْنَنَا *Judge thou between us*: (Ṣ:) thus in the Ḳur vii. 87. (TA.) And مَا أَحْسَنَ فِتَاحَتَهُ *How good is his judging*, or *judgment!* (A.) — [فَتَحَ الحَرْفَ, a conventional phrase in grammar and lexicology, *He pronounced the letter with the vowel-sound termed* فَتْح: and *he marked the letter with the sign of that vowel-sound*.]

2. فتّح: see 1, first sentence, in two places. — [Also, said of a medicine &c., *It opened* the bowels; *acted as an aperient*: and *it removed* obstructions: see the act. part. n.]

3. فاتحهُ [*He addressed him first*]. One says, المُلُوكُ لَا تُفَاتَحُ بِالكَلَامِ ‡ [*Kings shall not be addressed first with speech*]. (A.) — And, (A, Ḳ,* TA,) inf. n. مُفَاتَحَةٌ and فِتَاحٌ, † *He commenced a dispute, debate, discussion*, or *controversy, with him*: (TA:) or ‡ *he summoned him to the judge, and litigated with him*. (A, Ḳ,* TA.) — And فاتحهُ signifies also ‡ *He bargained with him and gave him nothing*: in the case of his giving him, one says فاتكهُ. (IAạr, TA; and Θ and Ḳ in art. فتك.) — And فاتح † *He compressed* (Ḳ, TA) his wife. (TA.) — [Also † *He rendered* a thing *easy*: — and † *He was liberal*. (Freytag, from the Deewán of the Hudhalees.)]

4: see 1, in the second quarter of the paragraph.

5: see 7, in three places. [Hence,] تفتّح النَّوْرُ *The blossom* [or *blossoms*] *opened*. (MA.) And تَفَتَّحَ الأَكِمَّةُ عَنِ النَّوْرِ *The calyxes burst open* [*from over the blossoms, so as to disclose them*]. (TA.) — [تَفَتَّحَ فِي الكَلَامِ is like our phrase † *He showed off*, or *made an ostentatious display, in speech*, or *talk*.] And you say, تفتّح بِمَا عِنْدَهُ (مِنْ مُلْكٍ وَأَدَبٍ (L, in the Ḳ مِنْ مَالٍ أَوْ أَدَبٍ,) † *He boasted of*, or *boasted himself in*, or *made a vain display of, what he had*, or *possessed, of wealth*, or *of good education*, or *polite accomplishments*: (L, Ḳ:*) and تفتّح بِهِ عَلَيْنَا † *He boasted of it*, or *boasted himself in it, against us*. (L.)

6. تَفَاتَحَا كَلَامًا بَيْنَهُمَا † *They two talked together with a suppressed voice, exclusively of others* [i. e. *so as not to be heard by others*]. (Ḳ.)

7. انفتح quasi-pass. of فَتَحَ, said of a door, (Ṣ, A, Mṣb, TA,) *It opened*, or *became opened* or *open*; (Mṣb;) as also ▼ تَفَتَّحَ: (TA:) or the latter is quasi-pass. of فَتَّحَ, so that you say, تَفَتَّحَتِ ▼ الأَبْوَابُ [*The doors opened*, or *became opened* or *open*]. (Ṣ.) — And انفتح عَنْهُ *It* (anything) *became removed from over it*, or *from before it*, (i. e. another thing,) *so as to disclose it*, or *expose it to view*. (TA.) [And ▼ تفتّح has a similar meaning, but is properly said of a number of things.]

8: see 1, first sentence, in three places; and again, in the second quarter of the paragraph, in two places. — One says also, افتتح الصَّلَاةَ ‡ (A, MA) *He opened*, or *commenced, prayer*: (MA:) اِفْتِتَاحُ الصَّلَاةِ meaning ‡ *The saying* ٱللّٰهُ أَكْبَرُ *the first time* [*in prayer*, i. e., *before the first recitation of the Opening Chapter of the Ḳur-án*]. (TA.) And ٱفْتَتَحْتُهُ بِكَذَا ‡ † *I commenced it with such a thing*. (Mṣb.) And مَا أَحْسَنَ مَا ٱفْتَتَحَ عَامُنَا بِهِ ‡ [*How good is that with which our year has commenced!*]; said when the sign, or token, [or prognostic,] of plenty, or abundance of herbage, has appeared. (A, TA.)

10: see 1, first sentence, in three places. — آتِي بَابَ الجَنَّةِ فَأَسْتَفْتِحُ is a saying of Moḥammad, meaning *I shall come to the gate of Paradise and seek*, or *demand*, or *ask for, the opening* thereof. (El-Jámi' eṣ-Ṣagheer, the first of the trads. mentioned therein, and thus expl. in the margin of a copy of that work.) — استفتحهُ القُرْآنَ † *He desired*, or *asked, him to explain the Ḳur-án*. (MA.) — استفتحهُ الإِمَامُ ‡ [*The Imám desired*, or *asked, him to prompt him*; i. e., *to recite to him what he was unable to utter by reason of forgetfulness*: see فَتَحَ عَلَيْهِ]. (A, TA.) — And استفتح signifies also † *He sought, desired, demanded*, or *asked, aid against an enemy*, or *victory*. (Ṣ, Mṣb, Ḳ.) One says, استفتح بِهِمْ † *He sought*, &c., *aid*, or *victory, by means of them*. (L, from a trad.) And استفتح ٱللّٰهَ ‡ (A, TA) *He desired*, or *asked, God to grant aid*, or *victory*, (TA,) لِلْمُسْلِمِينَ عَلَى الكُفَّارِ [*to the Muslims against*, or *over, the unbelievers*]. (A.) — Also † *He sought, desired, demanded*, or *asked, judgment*. (L.)

فَتْحٌ inf. n. of فَتَحَ [q. v.]. (Mṣb, &c.) — [As a subst.,] ‡ *Conquest* of a country: (Ḳ, TA:) pl. فُتُوحٌ (TA) [and pl. pl. فُتُوحَاتٌ]. يَوْمُ الفَتْحِ means particularly † *The day of the conquest of Mekkeh*: (L:) and also † *The day of resurrection*. (Mujáhid, L.) — † *Aid against an enemy*; or *victory*; syn. نَصْرٌ; as also ▼ فُتَاحَةٌ. (Ḳ.) — † *Means of subsistence, with which God gives aid*: pl. as above. (TA.) — ‡ The *first of the rain called* الوَسْمِيّ; (L, Ḳ;) as also ▼ فُتُوحٌ [which see again in what follows]: (Ḳ:) or the *first of any rain*; as also ▼ فَتْحَةٌ: (L:) pl. of the first فُتُوحٌ, (A,) or ▼ فَتُوحٌ, with fet-ḥ to the ف, (L,) [see the mention of this voce فَتُوحٌ,] but MF strongly reprobates this latter form, and observes that فَعُولٌ as a pl. measure is absolutely unknown. (TA.) One says, أَصَابَتِ الأَرْضَ فُتُوحٌ ‡ [*First rains fell upon the land*]. (A.) — ‡ *Water running* (Ṣ, Ḳ, TA) *from a spring or other source*: (Ṣ, TA:) or *water running upon the surface of the earth*: (AḤn, TA:) or *water for which a channel is opened to a tract of land for its irrigation thereby*: (L:) or *a river*, or *rivulet*, or *canal of running water*. (T, TA.) مَا سُقِيَ بِالفَتْحِ فَفِيهِ العُشْرُ, and مَا سُقِيَ فَتْحًا, (L,) فَتْحًا being here in the accus. case as an inf. n., i. e. مَا فُتِحَ إِلَيْهِ مَآءُ الأَنْهَارِ فَتْحًا, (Mgh, L,*) occurring in a trad., means *In the case of that* (relating to the several sorts of seed-produce, and palm-trees,) *which is* *irrigated by means of the channel opened to conduct to it the water of the river* [or *rivers*], *the tithe* [of the produce shall be taken]. (L.) — The *place of insertion of the tang of the iron head that enters into the shaft* of an arrow: (Ḳ,* TA:) pl. as above. (TA.) — The *fruit of the tree called* نَبْع, *resembling the* حَبَّة خَضْرَآء [or *fruit of the pistachia terebinthus*], (Ḳ, TA,) *except that it is red, sweet, and round; eaten by men.* (TA.) — [As a conventional term in grammar and lexicology, *A certain vowel-sound, well-known:* and ▼ فَتْحَة signifies The *sign of that vowel-sound.*]

فُتُح a word of the measure فُعُل in the sense of the measure مَفْعُول. (Ṣ.) You say بَابٌ فُتُحٌ *A wide, open, door:* (Ṣ, Ḳ:) or *a large, wide, door.* (Mṣb.) And قَارُورَةٌ فُتُحٌ *A wide-headed bottle* or *flask:* (Ṣ, Ḳ:) or *a bottle,* or *flask, having neither a stopper nor a case:* (Ks, Ṣ, Mṣb, Ḳ:) because, if so, it is open. (TA.)

فَتْحَة : see فَتْح, last sentence.

فُتْحَة *An opening,* or *intervening space;* syn. فُرْجَة: pl. فُتَح. (Mṣb.) — See also فُتُح. — Also † *A boasting of,* or *boasting oneself in,* or *making a vain display of, what one has,* or *possesses, of wealth,* or *of good education,* or *polite accomplishments.* (L, Ḳ,* TA.) One says, مَا هٰذِهِ الفُتْحَةُ الَّتِى أَظْهَرْتَهَا † *What is this boasting,* &c., *which thou hast exhibited?* (L.) IDrd thinks it to be not [genuine] Arabic. (L.)

فُتْحَى *Gain, profit,* or *increase obtained in traffic;* syn. رِبْح; [so accord. to the L; accord. to the copies of the Ḳ, erroneously, رِيح i. e. "wind;"] mentioned by Az, on the authority of Ibn-Buzurj: a poet says,

أَكُلُّهُمُ لَا بَارَكَ ٱللّٰهُ فِيهِمُ
إِذَا ذُكِرَتْ فُتْحَى مِنَ البَيْعِ عَاجِبُ

[*Are all of them,* (*may God not bless them,*) *when gain* arising *from selling is mentioned, in a state of wonder?*]. (L.)

فَتُوح A she-camel *having wide orifices to her teats;* (Ṣ, Ḳ;) and so a ewe or a she-goat: pl. فُتُح (TA.) — See also فُتُح, in two places.

فَتَاحَة : see فَتْح, fourth sentence.

فُتَاحَة [see 1, near the end]. — الفُتَاحَةُ, thus in the L and other lexicons, without ى after the ح, but in the Ḳ ▼ الفُتَاحِيَةُ, there said to be with ḍamm and without teshdeed, (TA,) *A certain bird, different from that called* الفَتَّاح, (Ḳ, TA,) *tinged with redness.* (TA.)

فِتَاحَة [see 1, near the end]. — [As a subst.,] ‡ The *office of judge:* one says, فُلَانٌ وَلِىَ الفِتَاحَةَ ‡ *Such a one was appointed to the office of judge.* (A, TA.) — And [‡ *Litigation,* or *altercation:*] one says, بَيْنَهُمَا فِتَاحَاتٌ ‡ *Between them two are litigations,* or *altercations.* (A, TA.)

الفُتَاحِيَةُ : see الفُتَاحَةُ.

فَتَّاح [*An opener:* and *an unlocker.* — And hence, † *A conquerer.* — And], in the dial. of Ḥimyer, (TA,) ‡ *A judge; one who decides between litigants:* (Ṣ, Mṣb, Ḳ, TA:) it is like ▼ فَاتِح, but [this signifies simply *judging,* and the former] has an intensive signification. (Mṣb.) الفَتَّاحُ, as an epithet applied to God, in the Ḳur xxxiv. 25, means † *The Judge:* or, accord. to IAth, † *the Opener of the gates of sustenance and of mercy to his servants.* (TA.) — بَيْتٌ فَتَّاحٌ means *A wide,* or *an ample, house* or *tent.* (El-Fáïk, TA.) — And الفَتَّاحُ signifies *A certain bird,* (Ḳ,) *which is black, and which moves about its tail much,* or *often; white in the base of the tail, beneath it; and there is a sort thereof red;* (TA;) *also called* أُمُّ عُجْلَانَ: (O in art. عجل:) pl. فَتَاتِيحُ, (Ḳ,) to which is added in the Ḳ, "without ا and ل;" but there is no reason why it should not have ال prefixed to it; and perhaps it should be correctly "without ا and ت," i. e. it is not pluralized with ا and ت [as an affix to the sing.], as in the L &c. (MF, TA.)

فَاتِح [*Opening:* &c.]: see فَتَّاح.

فَاتِحَة ‡ The *commencement,* or *first part,* of a thing: (Ṣ, A,* Ḳ:) pl. فَوَاتِحُ. (A.) فَاتِحَةُ الكِتَابِ, (Mṣb,) or فَاتِحَةُ القُرْآنِ, (TA,) [and simply الفَاتِحَةُ,] † *The opening chapter,* or *exordium, of the Ḳur-án,*] is [said to be] so called because the recitation in prayer is commenced therewith. (Mṣb.) One says also, قَرَأَ فَاتِحَةَ السُّورَةِ وَخَاتِمَتَهَا ‡ *He recited the first part,* or *portion, of the chapter of the Ḳur-án and its last part,* or *portion.* (A.) And فَوَاتِحُ القُرْآنِ signifies ‡ *The first parts,* or *portions, of the chapters of the Ḳur-án.* (Ḳ, TA.) [See also مُفْتَتَح.]

مَفْتَح *A place in which things are reposited, stowed, laid up, kept, preserved,* or *guarded; a repository;* syn. خِزَانَةٌ and مَخْزَنٌ: [and *a hoard;* syn. خَزِينَةٌ:] and *treasure;* or *buried property;* syn. كَنْزٌ: (Ḳ, TA:) pl., in both senses, مَفَاتِحُ. (TA.) The pl. as occurring in the Ḳur xxviii. 76 is said to signify *treasures* or *buried property* (كُنُوز) and *hoards* (خَزَائِن) [as pl. of خَزِينَةٌ, not of خِزَانَةٌ]): or *hoards* (خَزَائِن) *of wealth,* which Az says is the most probable meaning: (L, TA:) or it there means *keys,* as pl. of ▼ مِفْتَح; (Ksh, Bḍ;) and it is said that they were of skins, of the measure of the finger, and were borne upon sixty mules, (Ksh, L, TA,) or seventy; but this is not a valid explanation. (L, TA.)

مِفْتَح see the next preceding paragraph, and the next but one following; the latter in two places. — Also *A conduit* (قَنَاة) *of water.* (TA.)

[مُفَتِّح, applied to a medicine &c., *Aperient; having the property of opening the bowels:* and مُفَتِّحٌ لِلسُّدَدِ *deobstruent; having the property of removing obstructions.*]

مِفْتَاح (Ṣ, Mṣb, Ḳ, &c.) and ▼ مِفْتَح (Mṣb, Ḳ) *A key; an instrument with which a lock is opened;* (Mṣb;) [*a key*] of a door, and of anything that is closed, or locked; (Ṣ;) *an instrument for opening,* (Ḳ, TA,) i. e. *anything with which a thing is opened:* (TA:) pl. of the former مَفَاتِيح and مَفَاتِح, said by Akh to be similar to أَمَانِىّ and أَمَانِ; (Ṣ;) or مفاتيح is pl. of مِفْتَاح, and مفاتح is pl. of ▼ مِفْتَح [as well as of مَفْتَح]. (Mṣb.) — مِفْتَاحُهَا الطُّهُورُ, said by the Prophet, in relation to prayer, means ‡ *That which is as though it were the key thereof is the thing* [or *water*] *with which one purifies himself;* being the means of removing the legal impurity that prevents one's addressing himself boldly to the act of prayer. (Mṣb.) — And أُوتِيتُ مَفَاتِيحَ الكَلِمِ, or مَفَاتِحَ الكَلِمِ, accord. to different relaters, occurring in a trad., i. e. *I have been given the keys of words,* means [I have been given] an easy faculty, granted by God, for the acquirement of eloquence and chasteness of speech, and the attaining to the understanding of obscure meanings, and novel and admirable kinds of knowledge, and the beauties of expressions and phrases, which are closed against others, and difficult to be learnt by them. (L.) — And المِفْتَاحُ signifies also † *A certain brand upon the thigh and neck* (Ḳ, TA) *of a camel, in the form of what is* [*properly*] *thus called.* (TA.)

مَفْتُوح An *opened,* or *unclosed,* [and an *unlocked,*] door. (Mṣb.) — [And † *A light,* or *bright,* colour; a meaning probably post-classical. — For other significations, see its verb.]

مَفَاتِيحُ, (unparalleled [in form] among sing. words, MF,) applied to a she-camel, *Fat:* pl. مَفَاتِيحَات: (Ḳ:) mentioned by Seer. (TA.)

مُفْتَتَح is an inf. n. [signifying The act of *opening* and *commencing* &c.]: and a n. of place and of time [signifying *a place of opening* and *commencing* &c. and *a time thereof:* and also the *opening portion* of the Ḳur-án; as shown voce خَاتَم, q. v.]: and is a commonly-known and chaste word: though it has been said that مُخْتَتَم [which has the contr. significations] is not a chaste word: (TA in the present art.:) this, however, is not correct; for it is a chaste word, and of frequent occurrence. (TA in art. ختم.)

يَوْمٌ مُنْفَتِحٌ بِالمَآءِ ‡ *A day* [*of clouds*] *bursting,* or *opening vehemently, with rain.* (A.) — الحُرُوفُ المُنْفَتِحَةُ † *The letters of which the utterance requires the opening of* [*that part of the mouth which is called*] *the* حَنَك; (TA;) *all the letters of the alphabet except* ص, ض, ط, *and* ظ. (Ḳ, TA.)

فتخ

1. فَتِخَ, [aor. ـَ,] inf. n. فَتَخ, *He,* or *it, had*

one, or another, of the qualities denoted by the following explanations of فَتَخٌ: (L:) the primary signification is softness, or suppleness: (Aṣ, Ṣ, L:) in a man, it is width, or breadth, and softness, or suppleness, of the hand and foot: (Ṣ:) or it signifies laxness, and softness, or suppleness, (L, Ḳ,) and width, or breadth, (L,) in the joints: (L, Ḳ:) or softness, or suppleness, in the joints &c.: (L:) or width, or breadth, and length, of the hand and foot: (L, Ḳ:) and in a lion, it is width, or breadth, of the claws, and softness, or suppleness, of the joints: (L:) in camels, i. q. طَرَقٌ [i. e. weakness in the knees; &c.; as inf. n. of طَرِقَ, q. v., the having weakness in the knees; &c.]; (L;) or in camels it is the like of طَرَقٌ: (Ḳ, TA: [in the CḲ, erroneously, طَرْق:]) and in the legs, or hind legs, (فِى الرِّجْلَيْنِ,) it is length of the bone, and paucity of the flesh. (L.) — فَتَخَ, (T, Ṣ, A, Mgh, Ḳ,) aor. ـَ, (TḲ,) inf. n. فَتْخٌ; (Ṣ, TA;) and ▼ فتّخ, (Ḳ,) inf. n. تَفْتِيخٌ; (TA;) He made [or spread] wide his أَصَابِع [here meaning toes], and made them lax: (Ḳ:) or he bent, and made supple, his toes in his sitting [in prayer]: (Ṣ:) or he bent his toes towards the sole of the foot in prostration; so accord. to Yaḥyà Ibn-Sa'eed: (TA:) or he (a person [sitting] in the act of التَّشَهُّد [q. v.]) made his toes supple, and pressed the joints thereof towards the sole of the foot: (A:) or he bent his toes towards the upper side of the foot, (T, Mgh, TA,) not towards the sole thereof. (T, TA.) [See also فَتَخٌ.]

2: see the preceding paragraph, latter half.

4. افتخ He (a man, TA) was, or became, fatigued, (Ḳ,) or relaxed and fatigued, (TA,) and out of breath. (Ḳ, TA.)

5. تَفَتَّخَتْ is said of a woman [as meaning She put on, or wore, a ring of the kind termed فَتَخَة, or rings such as are termed فَتَخ]. (A: in which it is added, وَكَانَتْ نِسَاؤُهُمْ يَتَفَتَّخْنَ فِى أَصَابِعِهِنَّ العَشْرِ [And their women used to wear فَتَخ upon their ten fingers or toes; i. e. upon all their fingers and the thumbs or upon all their toes].)

فَتْخٌ: see فَتَخَةٌ. — Also Any [little bell such as is termed] جُلْجُل, (Ḳ,) thus in all the copies of the Ḳ that we have, but in the L any خَلْخَال [i. e. anklet], (TA,) that does not make a sound. (Ḳ, TA.) — And The inner side of the part between the upper arm and the fore arm; as also ▼ فَتْخَةٌ. (TA.)

فَتْخَةٌ: see what next follows.

فَتَخَةٌ (Ṣ, L, Ḳ, &c.) and ▼ فَتْخَةٌ, (Ḳ,) the latter disapproved by MF, but mentioned by more than one of the leading authorities respecting strange words, (TA,) A خَاتَم [here improperly used as meaning simply ring] without a stone, or gem: (A:) or a ring (حَلْقَة) of silver without a stone, or gem; if having in it a stone, or gem, it is called خَاتَمٌ: or a خَاتَم [meaning ring] (L, Ḳ) of large size, (Ḳ,) upon [a finger of] the hand and [upon a toe of] the foot, (L, Ḳ,) with, and without, a stone, or gem: (L:) or a ring (حَلْقَة), (L, Ḳ,) of silver, (Ḳ,) worn on the إِصْبَع [i. e. finger], (L,) like a خَاتَم: (L, Ḳ:) pl. ▼ فَتَخ [or rather this is a coll. gen. n. of which فَتَخَة is the n. un.] (Ṣ, A, L, Ḳ) and فَتَخَاتٌ (Ṣ, L, Ḳ) and فُتُوخٌ (L, Ḳ) and فِتَاخٌ: (L:) the women sometimes put them upon their toes: (Ṣ:) or they are properly upon the toes: (IB:) the women of the Time of Ignorance used to put them upon their عَشْر [i. e. ten fingers or toes]. (L.) — See also فَتْخٌ.

فُتُوخٌ The joints of the claws of the lion. (Ḳ.) — And a pl. of فَتَخَةٌ [q. v.]. (L, Ḳ.)

أَفْتَخُ Having the quality termed فَتَخٌ [expl. in the first sentence of this art.]: as an epithet applied to a man, wide, or broad, in the hand and foot, with softness, or suppleness: (Ṣ:) or it signifies lax, or relaxed, and soft, or supple, and wide, or broad, in the joints: or soft, or supple, in the joints &c.: (L:) and, applied to a lion, wide, or broad, in the fore and hind feet, with softness, or suppleness: (L, Ḳ:*) fem. فَتْخَاءُ: and pl. فُتْخٌ. (Ṣ, L.) [See an ex. in a verse cited voce رَوْحٌ.] — The fem., applied to a she-camel, means Having what is termed طَرَقٌ [expl. above: see 1]. (L.) And فَتْخَاءُ الأَخْلَافِ, so applied, Whose teats rise towards her belly; denoting a quality discommended; but the like in the woman and in the cloven-hoofed animal is commended. (Ḳ) — Also (i. e. the fem.) Any female bird having lax, or relaxed, wings: afterwards used as a name for the eagle: (MF:) or it is an epithet applied to an eagle; you say عُقَابٌ فَتْخَاءُ, (Ṣ, L, Ḳ,) meaning an eagle having soft, or supple, wings; (L, Ḳ;) because, when it descends, it contracts its wings, and this is only from softness, or suppleness. (Ṣ, L.) — And, applied to a foot, accord. to Aṣ, Soft, or supple: and accord. to AA, having in it a crookedness, or curvature. (TA.) Frogs are فُتْخُ الأَرْجُلِ [app. meaning Soft, or supple, in the hind legs]. (A, TA.) — أَفْتَخُ الطَّرْفِ, applied to a gazelle, (A,) or to a man, (Ḳ,) means Languid in respect of the eye. (A, Ḳ.) — And فَتْخَاءُ signifies also A thing, (Ḳ, TA,) four-sided, (TA,) resembling a مِلْبَن [app. here meaning the thing thus called upon which bricks are carried from place to place], of wood, upon which the gatherer of [wild] honey sits: (Ḳ, TA:) then he is drawn, or pulled, [up] from above, until he reaches the place of the honey [which is generally in a cliff]. (TA.)

أَفَاتِيخُ Certain things, or little things, (هَنَوَاتٌ,) of the [fungi termed] فُقُوع, which, when they first come forth, are thought to be truffles, until they are extracted, whereupon they are known: (Ḳ, TA:) so says AḤn, without mentioning a sing. thereof. (TA.)

فتر

1. فَتَرَ, aor. ـُ and ـِ, inf. n. فُتُورٌ and فُتَارٌ, [the latter is thus accord. to the M, and some copies of the Ḳ, and in the TA is said to be like غُرَابٌ, but in the CḲ and one MS. copy of the Ḳ I find it written فِتَار,] It (a thing, M, TA) remitted, or became allayed, or still, after vehemence; and became gentle after violence. (M, Ḳ, TA.) — فَتَرَ عَنْ عَمَلِهِ, (Mṣb, TA,) aor. ـُ, inf. n. فُتُورٌ, (Mṣb,) ‡ He remitted, flagged, or became remiss, or languid, in his work, or labour: (TA:) he remitted therein after vigour, or vehemence; became gentle therein after violence. (Mṣb.) — Hence, (Mṣb,) فَتَرَ الحَرُّ, (Ṣ, O, Mṣb, TA,) aor. ـُ, (Ṣ, O,) inf. n. فَتْرَةٌ (Mṣb) and فُتُورٌ, (Ṣ, O, Mṣb,) ‡ The heat remitted after vehemence; became gentle after violence: (Mṣb, TA:) the heat remitted, abated, or flagged; became languid and faint: and the verb is used in like manner of other things; (Ṣ;) for instance, of a price: (Fr, in TA, art. قط:) and of a man, signifying he was, or became, [languid, languid and faint, or] lax in the joints; (Ḥam p. 799;) [as also ▼ تفتّر, occurring in the Ḳ in art. خثر, &c.]. And فَتَرَ البَرْدُ ‡ The cold abated, or remitted; or became allayed. (TA.) — And فَتَرَ المَآءُ [The water abated in heat so as to become tepid, or lukewarm, or between hot and cold; (see فَاتِرٌ;)] the water ceased to be hot. (M, Ḳ.) — فَتَرَ جِسْمُهُ, (M, Ḳ,) aor. ـُ, (M,) inf. n. فُتُورٌ, (M, Ḳ,) † His body became [languid; or] lax in the joints, and weak. (M, Ḳ.) — And فَتَرَ الطَّرْفُ † The look of the eye, or eyes, became languishing, or languid; expl. by انْكَسَرَ نَظَرُهُ. (IKṭṭ, TA.) [See طَرْفٌ فَاتِرٌ, below; and see also 4.] — فَتَرَهُ He measured it by the فِتْر: (M, O, Ḳ:) like شَبَرَهُ "he measured it by the شِبْر." (M, O.)

2. فتّرهُ, inf. n. تَفْتِيرٌ, He made it (a thing, M, O) to remit, or become allayed or still, after vehemence; and to become gentle after violence. (M, O,* Ḳ.) — ‡ He made him (a worker) to remit, flag, or become remiss, or languid. (TA.) — فَتَّرَ ٱللّٰهُ الحَرَّ, inf. n. as above, ‡ God made the heat to remit after vehemence; to become gentle after violence: (Mṣb, TA:) made it to remit, abate, or flag; to become languid and faint. (Ṣ.) [And فتّر البَرْدَ ‡ He made the cold to remit, or become allayed. — فتّر المَآءَ He made the water to abate in heat so as to become tepid. See 1.] — فَتَّرَ جَسَدَهُ † It (beverage) heated his body, and made it to become languid, or lax in the joints, and weak: or, as some say, فتّرهُ and ▼ افترهُ both signify the same, i. e., it made him, or it, [a man's body,] to become languid, or lax in the joints, and weak: (TA:) or the latter, it (disease, M, Ḳ, and intoxication, M) rendered him weak, or faint: (M, Ḳ:) and افتر also signifies [without its objective complement's being expressed] it (beverage) rendered its drinker languid, or lax in the joints, and weak; (Ḳ;) or it may have this meaning. (O.) — فَتَّرَ السَّحَابُ, inf. n. as above, ‡ The cloud continued motionless, and prepared to discharge rain: (Ibn-'Abbád, O, Ḳ:) or rained, and discharged all its water, and left off, and continued motionless: (Aṣ, TA:) or became motionless: so

expl. by Hammád Er-Ráwiyeh, in the following verse of Ibn-Mukbil, describing rain, (T,) or a cloud: (TA:)

• تَأَمَّلْ خَلِيلِى هَلْ تَرَى ضَوْءَ بَارِقٍ •
• يَمَانٍ مَرَتْهُ رِيحُ نَجْدٍ فَفَتَّرَا •

[*Look attentively, O my friend; dost thou see the light of a cloud emitting lightning from El-Yemen, from which the wind of Nejd has drawn rain, and which has then continued motionless?*]. (T, TA.)

4. افتر : see **2**, where three significations are mentioned. ═ Also, † *His* (a man's, T, O) *eyelids became weak, so that his eyes,* or *sight, became languishing,* or *languid,* or *not sharp,* (انْكَسَرَ) [see طَرْفٌ فَاتِرٌ, below]). (T, O, K.)

5: see **1**, latter half.

10. استفتر, said of a horse, *i. q.* اِسْتَجَمَّ ‡ [i. e. *He abstained from covering, so that his seminal fluid collected*]: (A, TA:) in the copies of the K, [and in the O,] erroneously, اِسْتَجْوَرَ. (TA.)

فَتْرٌ *A* نَبِيَّة, (O,) [i. e.] *a thing like the* سُفْرَة [q. v.] *made of palm-leaves, upon which flour,* or *meal, is sifted.* (Ibn-'Abbád, O, K.)

فِتْرٌ The *space between the extremity of the thumb and that of the fore finger* (Ṣ, O, Mṣb, K) *when they are stretched out asunder* (Ṣ, O, Mṣb, TA) *in the usual manner* [*for measuring*]: (Mṣb:) pl. أَفْتَارٌ. (TA.)

فُتَرٌ : see فَتْرَةٌ. — الفُتَرُ expl. in the K as signifying "the muscles," and also as signifying "a certain well-known measure, or quantity, of wheat," is a mistake for القُأْرُ, mentioned in both of these senses in art. قأر in the TṢ [and in the O]. (TA. [See art. قأر.])

فَتْرَةٌ *Languor,* or *remissness;* and *weakness, feebleness,* or *faintness;* (Ṣ, O;) *an affection like a weakness, feebleness,* or *faintness:* (T:) and ↓ فُتَرٌ also signifies *weakness, feebleness,* or *faintness.* (M, K.) One says, أَجِدُ فِى نَفْسِى فَتْرَةً *I experience in myself an affection like a weakness,* &c. (T.) — *An interval of time* [*between things:* (Ṣ and K in art. وتر; &c.:) or] *between any two prophets,* (M, K,) or *between two of God's apostles,* (Ṣ, O, TA,) *during which there is a cessation of the apostolic function:* (TA:) or *a cessation of the mission of apostles, and a state of effacement of the signs of their religion:* so in the Kur v. 22. (Mṣb.) ═ See also what next follows.

فُتَّرٌ and ↓ فُتَّرَةٌ *A certain fish,* (O, K,) *speckled, and having upon it a blackness,* (O,) *such that when a man treads upon it, he is affected with a languor* (in some copies of the K *a tremour*) *in his legs,* (O, K,) *so that he becomes drowned,* thus described by Ibn-'Abbád, (O,) or *so that he sweats:* (thus in copies of the K:) it is the رَعَّادَة [or *torpedo*], *found in the Nile of Egypt.* (TA.)

فُتَارٌ [*A languor which is the*] *beginning of intoxication.* (AHn, M, K.)

الفُتُورُ *The soft and rising parts of the frogs of horses' hoofs.* (Ibn-'Abbád, O.)

مَآءٌ فَاتِرٌ, (T, M, O, K,) and ↓ فَاتُورٌ, (M, K,) *Water between hot and cold; lukewarm; tepid;* (T, O;) *water ceasing to be hot.* (M, K.) — طَرْفٌ فَاتِرٌ † *An eye,* or *eyes, in which is a weakness that is deemed beautiful;* (B, TA;) [i. e., *languishing,*] *in which is languish,* or *languidness;* (T;) *not having a sharp look:* (T, M, K;) or *not sharp.* (Ṣ, O.) [See **4**.] — مَشْىٌ فَاتِرٌ *A weak walking.* (O.)

فَاتُورٌ : see the next preceding paragraph.

تَفْتَرٌ *i. q.* دَفْتَرٌ, (O, K,) in the dial. of the Benoo-Asad: (Fr, O, TA:) mentioned in this art. by Ṣgh [in the O]. (TA.)

مُفَتِّرٌ, (so accord. to the O,) or مُفْتِرٌ, (so in the L,) Beverage *which renders languid the drinker;* (O, L, TA;) or *which heats the body, and occasions in it a languor,* or *laxity of the joints, and weakness:* such beverage is prohibited. (L, TA.)

فتش

1. فَتَشَ الشَّىْءَ, (Ṣ, O, Mṣb,) aor. ـِ, (Mṣb,) inf. n. فَتْشٌ; (Ṣ, O, Mṣb;) and ↓ فَتَّشَهُ, (Ṣ, O, Mṣb,) inf. n. تَفْتِيشٌ; (Ṣ, O;) both signify the same; (Ṣ, O, Mṣb;) *He examined, looked into, scrutinized,* or *investigated, the thing;* but the latter verb is that which is commonly used. (Mṣb.) And فَتَشَ عَنْهُ, and ↓ فتّش, *He inquired respecting it, and searched to the utmost after it.* (Mṣb.) فَتْشٌ and ↓ تَفْتِيشٌ signify *The seeking with inquiry* or *examination* or *scrutiny* or *investigation.* (Lth, IF, A, O, K.) You say, ↓ فَتِّشْ وَلَا تُفَتِّشْ *Seek thou with inquiry* &c., *and be not thou lax,* or *remiss.* (A, TA.)

2: see above, in four places.

3. فاتشهُ, inf. n. مُفَاتَشَةٌ, [*He inquired of him,* or *examined him, diligently.*] (Sh, TA in art. ثور.)

[فَتَّاشٌ One *who examines things, looks into them, scrutinizes them,* or *investigates them, much,* or *diligently; who inquires much,* or *diligently, and searches to the utmost; who seeks much,* or *diligently, with inquiry, examination, scrutiny,* or *investigation.*]

فتق

1. فَتَقَهُ, (Ṣ, O, Mṣb, K,) aor. ـُ and ـِ, [the former of which is the more common,] (Mṣb, TA,) inf. n. فَتْقٌ, (Ṣ, O, Mṣb,) *He slit it, rent it, rent it asunder* or *open,* or *divided it lengthwise:* (Ṣ, O, K:) *disjoined it,* or *disunited it:* (TA:) or *undid the sewing of it, unsewed it,* or *unstitched it:* (Mṣb:) *contr. of* رَتَقَهُ: (O, TA:) and ↓ فتّقهُ, (Ṣ, O, Mṣb, K,) inf. n. تَفْتِيقٌ, (Ṣ, O,) is like it in signification, (Ṣ, O, Mṣb, K,) but means he did so *much,* or *many times.* (Mṣb.) It is said of the heavens and the earth, in the Kur [xxi. 31], كَانَتَا رَتْقًا فَفَتَقْنَاهُمَا [expl. in art. رتق]. (O, TA.) — And (hence, TA) الفَتْقُ signifies ‡ *The effecting of disunion and dissension among the community* (T, Ṣ, O, K, TA) *of the Muslims,* (T, TA,) *and the befalling of war* (Ṣ, O, K, TA) *among them,* (Ṣ, O,) *after verbal agreement respecting war on the frontier,* or *some other thing,* (T, TA,) *with the occurring of wounds and bloodsheddings.* (TA.) One says, فَتَقَ فُلَانٌ بَيْنَهُمْ *Such a one effected disunion,* &c., *between them,* or *among them.* (TK.) — And sometimes it means ‡ *The dissolving* of a compact, or covenant. (TA.) — فَتَقَ العَجِينَ *He put leaven such as is termed* فَتَاق [q. v.] *into the dough.* (Lth, O, K.) — فَتَقَ المِسْكَ, (Ṣ, O, TA,) aor. ـُ, (PṢ, [in the TA in the next following instance ـِ, an evident mistranscription,]) inf. n. فَتْقٌ, *He drew forth the odour of the musk* [or *increased its fragrance*] *by the admixture of some other thing:* (Ṣ, O, TA:) and فَتَقَ الطِّيبَ, and الدُّهْنَ, *he rendered fragrant, and mixed,* [or *rendered fragrant by mixing,*] *with aloes-wood &c., the perfume,* and *the oil.* (TA.) ═ فَتِقَتِ المَرْأَةُ, aor. ـَ, (TK,) inf. n. فَتَقٌ, (Ṣ, Mgh, O, K, TK,) *The woman was,* or *became, such as is termed* فَتْقَآء; (Ṣ, Mgh, O, K;) *contr. of* رَتِقَت. (TK.) — And فَتِقَ العَامُ, aor. ـَ, inf. n. فَتَقٌ, ‡ *The year was,* or *became, abundant with herbage.* (Ṣ,* O,* K, TA.) It is related by Abu-l-Jowzà that the people were afflicted with drought, and complained to 'Áïsheh, who directed them to make an aperture towards the sky in the tomb of the Prophet, and they did so, and thereupon it rained so that the herbage grew, and the camels became fat to such a degree that they became swollen, or inflated, in the flanks (تَفَتَّقَتْ); whence it [the year] was called عَامُ الفَتْقِ. (O, TA.)

2: see the preceding paragraph, first sentence: — and see also فَتْقٌ. — فتّق الكَلَامَ ‡ *He rectified the language;* or *trimmed it, and removed its faults,* or *defects:* or, as Zj says, *he made its meaning clear.* (TA.)

4. افتق, said of a man, (TA,) or of a party of men, (O,) *He was one,* or *they were persons, whose beasts were become fat* (O, K, TA) *so that they became swollen,* or *inflated, in the flanks* (تَفَتَّقَتْ) (O, TA) *by reason of the abundance of the herbage:* (TA:) mentioned by AA. (O, TA.) — Said of the upper limb (قَرْن) of the sun [app. when a little above the eastern horizon], *It reached a rent* (فَتْق) *in the clouds, and appeared therefrom.* (ISk, Ṣ, O, K.) And, said of the moon, *It appeared, after concealment, between two black clouds.* (IAar, TA.) — Also, said of a party of men, *They had the clouds parted asunder from* [*over*] *them.* (Ṣ, O, K.) — And أَفْتَقْنَا *We found,* or *lighted on, a* فَتْق, i. e. *a place upon which rain had not fallen when it had fallen upon what was around it.* (Ṣ, O, K.*) And *We had no rain fallen upon our parts of the country when other parts had rain fallen upon them.* (TA.) — And افتق ‡ *He went forth to a* فَتْق, or *an open, and a spacious, place:* (O, K, TA:) a verb, in this sense, similar to أَصْحَرَ and أَفْضَى. (O, TA.)

— Also ‡ *He became harassed by* ▼ فُتُوق, meaning *such evils as poverty and debt* (O, Ḳ, TA) *and hunger* (O, TA) *and disease.* (Ḳ, TA.) — And *He cleaned his teeth with the* فِتَاق, or *stem*, or *lower part, of the raceme of a palm-tree.* (IAạr, O, Ḳ.*)

5: see 7. — تفتّقت المَاشِيَةُ and ▼ انفتقت † *The cattle became swollen*, or *inflated, in the flanks*, by reason of fatness: in consequence of their becoming so, they die; or, sometimes, they become free from the disease: (TA:) one says of a camel, تفتّق سِمَنًا. (Aṣ, Ṣ, O, Ḳ.) And تفتّقت خَوَاصِرُ الغَنَمِ † *The flanks of the sheep*, or *goats, became dilated* by reason of much pasturing upon herbs, or leguminous plants. (TA.) It is said in a description of the Prophet, كَانَ فِى خَاصِرَتَيْهِ ▼ اَنْفِتَاقٌ, (O, TA,) meaning † [*There was in his flanks*] *a flaccidity*, or *laxness*: or *a swollen*, or *an inflated, state*: (O:) or *a dilatation*, which is approved in men, but disapproved in women. (TA.) — تفتّق بالكَلَامِ [see فُتُق] ‡ *He was diffuse*, or *profuse, in speech* [as though bursting therewith]. (TA.)

7. انفتق quasi-pass. of فَتَقَهُ [i. e. it signifies *It became slit, rent, rent asunder* or *open*, or *divided lengthwise: became disjoined*, or *disunited*: or *became unsewed*, or *unstitched*]: (Ṣ,* O, Mṣb, K:*) and ▼ تفتّق is quasi-pass. of فتّقهُ [i. e. it signifies *it became slit*, &c., *much*, or *in many places*, or it is said of a number of things]. (Ṣ,* O, Ḳ.*) — انفتقت آبَاطُهُ is said of a fat child [meaning *His armpits became chapped*, or *cracked*]. (Ṣ in art. ضب.) — انفتق الغَيْمُ عَنِ الشَّمْسِ (O, Ḳ, TA) i. e. [*The clouds became parted asunder*, or] *became removed*, or *cleared away, from* [*before*] *the sun*: (TA:) and عَنِ القَوْمِ [*from over the party of men*]. (Ṣ, O, Ḳ.) — انفتقت عَلَيْهِ بَائِقَةٌ † [*A calamity, misfortune*, or *disaster, burst upon him*]. (Ṣ and Ḳ in art. بوق, &c.) — انفتقت said of a she-camel, *She was seized with a disease*, (AZ, O, Ḳ,) *termed* ▼ فَتَق, (TA,) *between her udder and her navel*, (AZ, O, Ḳ,) *occasioned by fatness*: sometimes in this case she recovers, (AZ, O,) and sometimes she dies. (AZ, O, Ḳ.) — See also 5, in two places.

فَتْق inf. n. of فَتَقَهُ. (Ṣ, O, Mṣb.) — [Used as a simple subst., *A rent, slit*, or *the like*. — And hence, ‡ *A breach in society.*] One says, رَتَقَ فَتْقَهُمْ, meaning ‡ [*He closed up the breach that was between them; he reconciled them*; or] *he reformed*, or *amended, the circumstances subsisting between them.* (TA in art. رتق.) — [Hence also *A rupture; a hernia*;] *a certain malady; a protrusion in the thin*, or *delicate, and soft part of the belly*; (Ṣ, O;) *a malady in the* صِفَاق [meaning *peritonæum*], *consisting in a solution of the integument so that a rent takes place in it, and through this passes a strange body, or substance, that was confined within it before the rent; and there is no cure for it, except for that which happens, rarely, to children*: (Ḳ:) *a disease that befalls a man in his intestines, consisting in a disruption of a place between these and his scrotum, in consequence of which a flatus collects between the two testicles and they become enlarged*; in which case one says, أَصَابَتْهُ رِيحُ الفَتْقِ: or *a severing of the fat* [or *cellular substance*] *that encloses the testicles*: in the "Ghareebáni," it is termed ▼ فَتَق, with fet-ḥ to the ت: (Mgh:) and thus it is said to be by Az, and thus it is expl. by him: (O:) or it is *a rending of the skin between the testicles and the lower part of the belly, in consequence of which* [*some of*] *the intestines fall into the scrotum*: (TA:) accord. to Ibráheem El-Ḥarbee, *a rupture of the bladder.* (O, TA.) — [And *A rent* in the clouds: see 4:] and ▼ فَتَق [likewise] signifies *a gap* of the clouds: pl. فُتُوق. (TA.) — And † *An open, and a spacious, place.* (O, Ḳ.) — And *A place upon which rain has not fallen when it has fallen upon what is around it*; (Ṣ, O, Ḳ;) and ▼ فَتَقَة signifies thus, applied to a land: pl. of the former فُتُوق. (TA.) [Hence,] عَامٌ ذُو الفُتُوقِ *A year of little rain.* (Ṣ, O. See an ex., from a rájiz, in the first paragraph of art. زل.) — And ‡ The *dawn*; (O, Ḳ, TA;) and so ▼ فَتَق: (Ṣ, O, Ḳ, TA:) signifying also the *rising* [or rather *breaking*] of the dawn; as in the saying, أُنْظُرْ إِلَى فَتَقِ الفَجْرِ [*Look thou at the rising*, or *breaking, of the dawn*]: and ▼ الفَتِيق likewise signifies *the dawn*; mentioned by El-Iṣbahánee, and in the B. (TA.) — See also 4, last sentence but one, for a meaning of the pl. فُتُوق.

فَتَق [inf. n. of فَتِقَت said of a woman: — and of فَتِقَ said of a year:] as a subst.: see فَتْق, in three places: — and see also 7.

فُتُق, applied to a woman, signifies ▼ مُتَفَتِّقَةٌ بِالكَلَامِ ‡ [*Diffuse*, or *profuse, in speech*, as though bursting therewith]; (Ṣ, O, Ḳ, TA; [in the CḲ مُنْفَتِقَة;]) or *loquacious*: (TḲ:) or, accord. to ISk, so applied, *that mars* (▼ تُفَتِّق [lit. *rends*]) *in* [*performing*] *affairs.* (TA.)

فَتَقَة: see فَتْق, last quarter.

فَتْقَاءُ, applied to a woman, means *Having the* فَرْج *dehiscent*; [or *wide*; *not constringed*;] ▼ مُنْفَتِقَةُ الفَرْجِ; (Ṣ, O, Ḳ;) *contr. of* رَتْقَاءُ [q. v.]. (Ṣ, O.)

فِتَاق The *parting asunder* (اِنْفِتَاق) *of the clouds from* [*before*] *the sun*, (O, Ḳ, TA,) and *their becoming removed*, or *cleared away, therefrom.* (TA.) — And The *upper limb* (قَرْن), and the *disk* (عَيْن), *of the sun*, (O, Ḳ, TA,) *when it is covered over and then somewhat of it appears.* (TA.) — Also The *base*, or *lowest portion, of the white* [*membranous fibres of the palm-tree which are termed*] لِيف, (O, Ḳ, TA,) *such as have not yet appeared*: (TA:) the face is likened thereto, because of its clearness. (O, TA.) — And (accord. to IAạr, O, TA) The *main stem*, or the *lower part of the main stem when the fruit-stalks have been cut off, of the raceme of a palm-tree.* (O, Ḳ, TA.) — And ‡ The *leaven of dough*: (ISd, TA:) *a large lump of leaven, that soon causes the dough to become mature* (O, Ḳ, TA) *when it is put therein.* (O, TA.) — And *Mixtures of medicaments compounded* (O, Ḳ, TA) *with oil of jasmine or the like thereof, in order that the odour may diffuse itself*: (O, TA:) or *musk compounded with ambergris.* (TA.)

فَتِيق [i. q. ▼ مَفْتُوق i. e. *Slit, rent*, &c.]. نَصْلٌ فَتِيقُ الشُّفْرَتَيْنِ means [*An arrow-head*] *having two forking portions*; (Lth, O, Ḳ;) as though [each] one of them were slit [from the other]: (Lth, O:) [or it may mean *sharp in the two edges*: for] سَيْفٌ فَتِيقُ الغِرَارَيْنِ signifies *A sword sharp* [*in the two edges*]: and سَيْفٌ فَتِيقٌ, *A sharp sword*: (TA:) [whence,] رَجُلٌ فَتِيقُ اللِّسَانِ *A sharp-tongued man*: (Ṣ, O, Ḳ:) or *chaste*, or *eloquent, and sharp, of tongue*: or *chaste*, or *eloquent, of tongue, perspicuous in speech.* (TA.) — الصُّبْحُ الفَتِيقُ ‡ *The shining dawn.* (Aṣ, Ṣ, O, Ḳ.) — See also فَتْق, last sentence but one. — جَمَلٌ فَتِيقٌ ‡ *A camel swollen*, or *inflated, in the flanks, by reason of fatness*; تَفَتَّقَ سِمَنًا: (Aṣ, Ṣ, O, Ḳ:) and نَاقَةٌ فَتِيقَةٌ *a fat she-camel.* (TA.) — And فَتِيق is used in the sense of فَتْق: thus in the saying of 'Amr Ibn-El-Ahtam,

• لَهَا مِنْ أَمَامِ المَنْكِبَيْنِ فَتِيقٌ •

[app. describing a she-camel: I can only conjecture the meaning to be, *Having, in the part before the shoulders, a crease like a gash*, occasioned by fatness]. (O.)

فَاتِق [*Slitting, rending*, &c.]. — [Hence,] one says, هُوَ الفَاتِقُ الرَّاتِقُ meaning † *He is the possessor of command or rule, so that he opens and closes, and straitens and widens* [or rather *widens and straitens*]. (Ḥar p. 208.)

فَيْتَق, of the measure فَيْعَل, (Ṣ, TA,) from الفَتْق [" the act of slitting" &c.], (TA,) *A carpenter.* (Ṣ, O, Ḳ.) — And *A* حَدَّاد [which signifies a *worker in iron*: but it also has the meaning here next following, which may therefore be intended by him who first gave this explanation of فَيْتَق]. (AZ, O, Ḳ.) — And *A* بَوَّاب [i. e. *door-keeper*]. (O, Ḳ.) — And *A king.* (AZ, O, Ḳ.)

مَفْتَق *A place of slitting*, or *of the slit*, of a shirt. (O, Ḳ.)

مَفْتُوق: see فَتِيق.

مُتَفَتِّقَةٌ بِالكَلَامِ: see فُتُق.

مُنْفَتِقَةُ الفَرْجِ: see فَتْقَاءُ.

فتك

1. فَتَكَ بِهِ, (Ṣ, MA, O, Mṣb, Ḳ,) aor. ِ and ُ, inf. n. فَتْك and فُتْك and فِتْك (Ṣ, O, Mṣb, Ḳ*) and فُتُوك (MA, Ḳ*) and فَتَاكَة, (MA,) *He assassinated him*; i. e. *he came to him when he* (the latter) *was inadvertent, and assaulted him and slew him*; (Ṣ, MA,* O;) thus it signifies accord. to an explanation of الفَتْك by A'Obeyd;

and this is the primary signification: (Az, TA:) if he have not given him [for أَعْطَانَا in my original (an obvious mistranscription) I read أَعْطَاهُ] assurance of safety, it behooves him to make that known to him: (A'Obeyd, TA:) *he assaulted him; or he slew him at unawares;* and † افتك is a dial. var. thereof: (Msb:) *he seized an opportunity that he* (another) *offered him* (Ḳ, TA) *by his inadvertence,* (TA,) *and slew him: or he wounded him openly:* (Ḳ, TA:) or it has a more general meaning with respect to both of these acts: (Ḳ,* TA:) Fr says that الفَتْكُ signifies *the man's slaying openly.* (TA.) It is said in a trad., قَيَّدَ الإِيمَانُ الفَتْكَ لَا يَفْتِكُ مُؤْمِنٌ [i. e. *The giving assurance of safety has inhibited* (or, emphatically, *inhibits*) *the slaying at unawares,* &c.: *one who gives assurance of safety shall not slay at unawares,* &c.: the like has been said above: see also an explanation of the former clause of the trad. in art. قيد]. (Ṣ, O.) — And فَتَكَ, aor. ـِ and ـُ, inf. n. فَتْكٌ and فُتْكٌ and فِتْكٌ (O, Ḳ) and فُتُوكٌ, (Ḳ,) *He purposed an affair and executed it:* (O:) or *he embarked in,* or *performed, an affair that occasioned uneasiness, and to which the mind invited;* as also † افتك: (Ḳ:) the latter verb is said by Fr to be a dial. var. of the former. (O.) — [Hence,] فَتَكَ فِى الأَمْرِ, (Ḳ, TA,) inf. n. فَتْكٌ, (TA,) ‡ *He persisted,* or *persevered, in the affair;* syn. لَجَّ, or أَلَحَّ. (Accord. to different copies of the Ḳ; in the TA the former. [The same meaning is also assigned to فَتُكَ.]) — And فَتَكَ فِى الخُبْثِ, [in the CḲ فِى الخُبُثِ,] inf. n. فُتُوكٌ, (O, Ḳ, TA,) ‡ *He exceeded the usual bounds in that which was evil, abominable, foul,* or *unlawful.* (Ḳ, TA.) — فَتَكَ فِى صِنَاعَتِهِ † *He was skilful in his art,* or *craft.* (TA.) — And فَتَكَتْ said of a girl, or young woman, means ‡ *She cared not for what she did nor for what was said to her.* (O, Ḳ, TA.) [See also فَتُكَتْ.]

2. فَتَّكْتُ القُطْنَ, (IDrd, O,) inf. n. تَفْتِيكٌ, (IDrd, O, Ḳ,) *I separated, plucked asunder,* or *loosened, the cotton:* (IDrd, O, Ḳ:*) so in one of the dials.; (IDrd, O;) it is of the dial. of Asd. (TA.)

3. المُفَاتَكَةُ signifies المُمَاهَرَةُ; (O, Ḳ, TA;) so says Ibn-'Abbád, (O, TA,) and so Z; (TA;) i. e. ‡ *The making a show of skill, one with another:* (TḲ:) [but for المُمَاهَرَةُ, the CḲ has المُجَاهَرَةُ:] one says, فَاتَكَ صَاحِبَهُ i. e. مَاهَرَهُ ‡ [*He made a show of skill, app. in competition, with his companion*]. (TA.) — And ‡ *The falling to the thing* (مُوَاقَعَةُ الشَّىْءِ) *with vehemence;* such as eating, (Ḳ, TA,) and drinking, (TA,) and the like. (Ḳ, TA.) And فَاتَكَ الأَمْرَ † *He threw himself,* or *plunged, into the affair;* syn. وَاقَعَهُ: (Ḳ, TA:) and the subst. is † فِتَاكٌ [having the meaning of the inf. n.: but why this is not called the inf. n. (for such it is accord. to analogy) I do not see]. (TA.) — And فَاتَكَ فُلَانًا (inf. n. مُفَاتَكَةٌ, TA) i. q. دَاوَمَهُ ‡ [app. as meaning ‡ *He kept continually,* or *constantly, to such a one:* agreeably with what here follows]. (O, Ḳ, TA.) — فاتكت الإِبِلُ الحَمْضَ † *The camels* [*kept continually,* or *constantly, to the plants called* حَمْض, *desiring them as food and finding them wholesome:* (see the part. n., below:) or] *confined themselves to the* حمض, *not pasturing upon anything therewith.* (TA.) And فاتكت الإِبِلُ المَرْعَى † *The camels consumed with their mouths* [or *devoured*] *the pasture.* (TA.) — فَاتَكَ فُلَانًا *He gave to such a one that which he mentioned as the price of what he had to sell:* in the case of his bargaining with him and not giving him anything, one says فَاتَحَهُ. (IAạr, O, Ḳ.) فَاتَكَ التَّاجِرُ فِى البَيْعِ is expl. in the A as meaning *The trader exceeded the due bounds,* or *acted unjustly, in offering the thing for sale and naming the price.* (TA.)

4: see 1, in two places. — مَا أَفْتَكَهُ means *How persistent,* or *persevering, is he!* (TA.)

5. تفتّك بِأَمْرِهِ *He executed,* or *performed, his affair;* or *kept,* or *applied himself, constantly,* or *perseveringly, to it; not consulting any one.* (ISh, O, Ḳ.)

فِتَاكٌ: see 3, former half.

فَاتِكٌ [act. part. n. of 1; generally meaning *Assassinating;* or *an assassin:*] one *who comes upon* another *suddenly,* or *at unawares,* or *takes* him *by surprise, with some evil,* or *hateful, act,* or [more commonly] *with slaughter:* and accord. to IDrd, one *who, when he purposes a thing, does* [*it*]: (Ḥam p. 43:) any one *who attempts,* or *ventures upon, great,* or *formidable, affairs:* (Az, TA:) *bold,* or *daring;* (Ṣ, O, Ḳ;) *courageous:* (Ḳ:) pl. فُتَّاكٌ. (Ṣ, O, Ḳ.) — [Hence,] فَاتِكُ القَلْبِ † *Penetrating, sharp,* or *vigorous,* and *effective, in mind.* (TA.) — And حَيَّةٌ فَاتِكَةٌ لِلسَّبُعِ ‡ [*A serpent that attacks the beast of prey*]. (TA.) — And جَارِيَةٌ فَاتِكَةٌ ‡ *A young woman who cares not for what she does nor for what is said to her.* (TA.)

تَفْتِيكٌ [app. from the Pers. تَفْتِيك signifying "fine, soft, wool," and "soft, downy, kids' hair,"] *A compress of rags which is put upon a wound in order that the moisture may become absorbed* [*thereby*]: a subst. like تَمْتِينٌ and تَنْبِيتٌ: and post-classical. (TA.)

إِبِلٌ مُفَاتِكَةٌ لِلْحَمْضِ *Camels that keep continually,* or *constantly, to the* [*plants called*] حَمْض, *desiring them as food and finding them wholesome.* (O, TA. [See also 3.])

فتكر

فِتَكْرٌ and فَتَكْرٌ: see what follows.

فِتَكْرِينٌ and فَتَكْرِين (Ṣ, O, Ḳ) and فُتَكْرِين and فَتَكْرِين and † فِتَكْرٌ (O, Ḳ) and † فَتَكْرٌ (Ḳ) *A calamity,* or *misfortune;* (O, Ḳ;) and [in the CḲ "or"] *a wonderful, and great,* or *formidable, affair,* or *event:* (Ḳ:) or the ن is the characteristic of the pl.; and one says, لَقِيتُ مِنْهُ الفِتَكْرِينَ and الفُتَكْرِينَ, meaning [*I experienced from him,* or *it,*] *difficulties,* or *distresses,* and *calamities,* or *misfortunes.* (Ṣ.)

فتل

1. فَتَلَهُ, (Ṣ, M, O, Mṣb, Ḳ,) aor. ـِ, (M, Mṣb, Ḳ,) inf. n. فَتْلٌ; (T, M, Mṣb;) and † فتّلهُ, (M, Ḳ, TA,) [but this has teshdeed given to it to denote muchness of the action, or multiplicity of the objects, (see its pass. part. n. below,)] inf. n. تَفْتِيلٌ; (TA;) *He twisted it,* (T, M, Ḳ, TA,) i. e. a thing, (T, M,) like as one twists (T) a rope (T, Ṣ, O, Mṣb) &c., (Ṣ, O, Mṣb,) and like as one twists a wick. (T.) — [Hence] one says رَجُلٌ مُحْكَمُ الفَتْلِ ‡ [*A man firm,* or *compact, in respect of make;* as though firmly twisted]. (Ḳ and TA voce مَجْدُولٌ. [See the pass. part. n. below.]) — And فَتَلَ ذُؤَابَتَهُ, (Ḳ,) or فَتَلَ فِى ذُؤَابَتِهِ, (O, TA,) ‡ [lit. *He twisted his pendent lock of hair;*] meaning *he made him to turn,* or *swerve, from his opinion,* or *judgment,* or *sentiment,* (O, Ḳ, TA,) *by deceiving,* or *deluding, him.* (TA.) And جَآءَ وَقَدْ فُتِلَتْ ذُؤَابَتُهُ ‡ *He came, having been deceived,* or *beguiled, and turned from his opinion,* &c. (TA.) And مَا زَالَ يَفْتِلُ مِنْ فُلَانٍ فِى الذِّرْوَةِ وَالغَارِبِ يَدُورُ مِنْ وَرَآءِ خَدِيعَتِهِ ‡ meaning, [i. e. *He ceased not to be going about seeking,* or *endeavouring, after the deceiving,* or *beguiling, of such a one*]: (Ṣ, O, Ḳ:) originating from a saying in a trad. of Ez-Zubeyr, cited and expl. voce غَارِبٌ [q. v.]. (O, TA. [See also Freytag's Arab. Prov. ii. 200.]) — فَتَلَهُ عَنْ حَاجَتِهِ, (T,) or عَنْ وَجْهِهِ, (Ṣ, O,) means *He turned him* [*from the object of his want,* or *from his way,* or *course*], like لَفَتَهُ, (T, Ṣ, O,) from which it is [said to be] formed by transposition. (Ṣ, O.) And فَتَلَ وَجْهَهُ عَنْهُمْ [also] means *He turned his face from them,* (M, Ḳ,) like لَفَتَهُ. (M.) — فَتِلَتِ النَّاقَةُ, [aor. ـَ,] inf. n. فَتَلٌ, † *The she-camel was smooth,* or *sleek, and flaccid, in the skin of her armpit, it not having in it* عَرْك *nor* حَازّ *nor* خَالِع [which words see in their proper arts.]. (T, TA.) [See also فَتَلٌ below.]

2: see the preceding paragraph, first sentence.

4. افتل said of [trees of the species termed] سَمُرَة and سَلَم, (Ḳ,) or افتلت said of a سَمُرَة (M, O) and of a سَلَمَة, (M,) *They,* or *it, put forth,* or *produced, the* فَتَلَة [q. v.] *thereof.* (M, O, Ḳ.)

5: see the paragraph here following.

7. انفتل, and † تفتّل, [but the latter, as quasi-pass. of 2, denotes, or implies, muchness, or multiplicity,] *It* [a rope, &c.,] *became twisted.* (M, Ḳ.) — And the former, *He turned away* (T, Ṣ, Mgh) from his prayer, (T,) or from prayer, (Mgh,) or from his way, or course. (Ṣ.) And انفتل رَاجِعًا [*He turned away, returning*]. (Ṣ, O, Ḳ, in art. صوع.)

فَتْلٌ : see its n. un. فَتْلَةٌ : — and see also فَتَلٌ. — Also The *cry*, or *crying, of the* فَتَّال, i. e. بُلْبُل. (IAạr, T, O, TA. [Said in the TA to be an inf. n.: but its verb, if it have one, is not mentioned.])

فَتَلٌ an inf. n. of فَتِلَت [q. v.] said of a she-camel. (T, TA.) [It is also expl. as signifying] ‡ *Wideness between the elbows and sides* of a she-camel: (Ṣ, O, TA:) or *a state of firm*, or *concealed, insertion*, (اِنْدِمَاجٌ,) *in the elbow* of a camel, (M, Ḳ, TA,) *and its being apart from the side*; (M, TA;) as also ✝ فَتْلٌ: (M: [thus in the TT as from the M; being there written فَتْل:]) this [or rather the like of this] in the shank and foot of the camel is a fault. (M, TA.)

فَتْلَةٌ [as an inf. n. un., *A twisting*. — And hence, app., † *An intense firmness of compacture of the flesh* of the fore arm: expl. in the TT, as from the M, by the words شدة عَصَب الدباغ; for which, I doubt not, we should read شِدَّةُ عَصَبِ الذِّرَاعِ: see مَفْتُولٌ. — And *A twist*. — And particularly *A twisted slip, formed by slitting*, of the ear of a she-camel. (See 4 in art. دبر, in the last quarter of the paragraph.) — And, as used in the present day, *A needleful* of thread. — Also] The *seed-vessel of the* سَلَم and *of the* سَمُر, *peculiarly*, (M, Ḳ,) *resembling the pods of the bean*, (M,) *when they first come forth*. (M, Ḳ.) And The *blossom of the* سَمُرَة: (M:) or the *fruit of the* سَمُر and *of the* عُرْفُط: (TA:) or the *blossom of the* [*hind of trees called*] عِضَاه, (O, TA,) *when it has become compactly organized*: (TA:) or it signifies also, (M, Ḳ,) and so does ✝ فَتَلَةٌ, (Ḳ,) or peculiarly this latter, بِالتَّحْرِيك, as AḤn says on the authority of some one or more of the relaters, (O,) the *fruit* (بَرَمَة) *of the* عُرْفُط, (M, O, Ḳ,) *because its filaments, or fringe-like appertenances, are as though they were cotton, and it is white, like the button of the shirt*, or *somewhat larger*: (AḤn, M, O:) or it signifies *one of what are termed* ✝ فَتْلٌ, which means *what are* [*as though they were*] *twisted, of the* وَرَق [properly signifying *leaves* of simple and common kinds] *of trees, such as the* ورق *of the* [*tamarisks called*] طَرْفَآء *and* أَثْل *and the like*; (TA;) or, (M, Ḳ, TA,) as AḤn says, (M, TA,) this word فَتْلٌ signifies *what are not* وَرَق, *but are substitutes for these*: (M, Ḳ, TA:) and, (Ḳ,) as some say, (M,) *what do not expand, of* [*the appertenances of*] *plants, but are* [*as though they were*] *twisted*; (M, Ḳ;) *so that they are like* هُدْب [thus in the TT as from the M, perhaps a mistranscription for هَدَب, q. v.]; *being like the* هدب [i. e. هَدَب] *of the* طَرْفَآء *and* أَرْطَى *and* أَثْل. (M.) — See also فَتِيلٌ, last sentence.

فِتْلَةٌ [*A manner of twisting*]. You say فَتَلَهُ فِتْلَةً شَزْرَةً بَارِحَةً, meaning [i. e. *A manner of twisting contrary to that which is usual*]. (A in art. برح.)

فَتَلَةٌ: see فَتْلَةٌ, near the middle: — and see the paragraph here following, last sentence.

فَتِيلٌ *Twisted*; [applied to a rope, &c.;] as also ✝ مَفْتُولٌ. (M, Ḳ.) — And *A slender cord, of* [*the fibres called*] لِيف, (M, Ḳ,) or *of* [*the bark termed*] خَزَم, or *of* عَرَق [meaning *plaited palm-leaves*], or *of thongs*, (M,) *which is bound upon the ring* (M, Ḳ) *called* عِيَان *which is at the end* (مُنْتَهَى), (M,) or *which is at the place of meeting* (مُلْتَقَى), (Ḳ,) *of the* دُجْرَانِ [*two pieces of wood to which the share of the plough is attached*]. (M, Ḳ.) — [And *A tent for a wound*: a term used by surgeons: see دُسُرُ الجُرْحِ, in art. دسر.] — And *What one twists* [or *rolls*] (Ṣ, M, O, Ḳ) *between his fingers* (M, Ḳ) or *between the two fingers* [meaning *the thumb and fore finger*], (Ṣ, O,) *of dirt* [*that has collected upon the skin when it has not been recently washed*]; (Ṣ, O, Ḳ;) as also ✝ فَتِيلَةٌ. (M, Ḳ.) So says I'Ab in explaining the saying in the Ḳur [iv. 52, and 79 also accord. to some readers, and xvii. 73], وَلَا يُظْلَمُونَ فَتِيلًا [meaning ‡ *And they shall not be wronged by their being deprived of the most paltry right*; or *they shall not be wronged a whit*]: (O, TA:) or the [primary, or proper,] meaning in this phrase is what here follows. (TA; and in like manner Bḍ says in iv. 52.) — And The سَحَاة [or *integument*, meaning the *pellicle*], (M, Ḳ, TA,) or the خَيْط [or *thread*, meaning the *filament*], (Bḍ in iv. 52,) *that is in the* شَقّ [or *cleft, resembling a crease, which extends along one side*] *of the date-stone*: (M, Ḳ, TA: but for شَقّ, the CḲ has شِقّ:) ISk says, the قِطْمِير is the thin integument upon the date-stone, and, he adds, (T, TA,*) the فَتِيل is *what is in the* شَقّ *of the date-stone*. (T, Ṣ, O, Mṣb, TA.) Hence, (M,) one says, مَا أُغْنِى عَنْهُ فَتِيلًا, (M, and so in the Ḳ except that the latter has عَنْكَ instead of عَنْهُ,) meaning [*I do not avail*, or *profit, him*, (or accord. to the Ḳ, *thee*,) or *I do not stand*, or *serve, him* (or *thee*) *in stead*,] *as much as that* سَحَاة, (M,) or *a whit*; (Ḳ;) and in like manner, ✝ فَتْلَةً, (Th, M, Ḳ, [in the CḲ, erroneously, فَتِيلَةً,]) and ✝ فَتَلَةً. (IAạr, M, Ḳ.)

فَتِيلَةٌ *A wick* (Ṣ, O, Ḳ) of a lamp: (T, Mṣb:) pl. فَتَائِلُ and فَتِيلَاتٌ. (Mṣb.) [Hence, حَجَرُ الفَتِيلَةِ *Amiantus*, or *flexible asbestus*, of which wicks are sometimes made. — And in the present day, فَتِيلَةٌ also signifies *A hempen match*. — And *A suppository*.] — فَتَائِلُ الرُّهْبَانِ is the name of *A certain plant, the leaves of which are like* [*those of*] *the senna* (السَّنَا), *and its blossom is yellow*. (TA.) — See also فَتِيلٌ.

الفَتَّالُ *The* [*bird called*] بُلْبُل [q. v.]. (T, O, Ḳ.)

أَفْتَلُ, (Ṣ, M, O, Ḳ,) applied to the elbow, (Ṣ, M, O,) of a camel, (Ṣ, O,) or of a she-camel, (M,) [and app. to a he-camel,] *Having what is termed* فَتَل [expl. above]: (Ṣ, M, O, Ḳ:) fem. فَتْلَآءُ, (T, M, Ḳ,) applied to a she-camel, meaning *having, in her arm, a wide separation from the side*: (T,* TA:) or, so applied, *heavy, and curved in the hind legs*: (M, Ḳ:) [the pl. is فُتْلٌ:] and one says قَوْمٌ فُتْلُ الأَيْدِى [app. meaning *Persons having the arms widely separated from the sides*]. (Ṣ, O.)

ذُبَالٌ مُفَتَّلٌ [*Twisted wicks*]: the epithet in this case is with teshdeed because applied to many things. (Ṣ, O, Ḳ.)

مَفْتُولٌ: see فَتِيلٌ. — [It also signifies ‡ *Compact*, or *firm, in make*; as though twisted; like مَعْصُوبٌ and مَجْدُولٌ:] you say رَجُلٌ مَفْتُولُ السَّاعِدِ *A man strong* [or *firm* or *compact*] *in the* سَاعِد [or *fore arm*]; as though it were twisted. (TA.)

فتن

1. فَتَنَهُ, (T, Ṣ, M, &c.,) aor. ـِ, (M,) inf. n. فَتْنٌ, (Ṣ, M, Ḳ,) [and quasi-inf. n., in this and other senses, فِتْنَةٌ,] *He burned it* (T,* Ṣ,* M, Ḳ*) in the fire. (M.) Hence, [in the Ḳur li. 13,] يَوْمَ هُمْ عَلَى النَّارِ يُفْتَنُونَ (T,* Ṣ, M, Ḳ*) i. e. [*The day*, or *on the day*, accord. to two different readings, (يَوْمُ and يَوْمَ, the latter of which is the more common,)] *when they shall be burned* (T, Ṣ, M, Ḳ) *with the fire* [of Hell]. (T.) And [in the Ḳur lxxxv. 10,] إِنَّ ٱلَّذِينَ فَتَنُوا ٱلْمُؤْمِنِينَ وَٱلْمُؤْمِنَاتِ *Verily they who burned the believing men and the believing women* (T, Ṣ*) in the fire kindled in the trench, or pit; throwing them therein. (T.) This is said to be the primary signification of the verb. (TA.) — And *He melted it with fire*, (T,) or *put it into the fire*, (Ṣ, Mṣb,) namely, gold, (T, Ṣ, Mṣb,) and silver, *in order to separate*, or *distinguish*, (T, Mṣb,) *the bad from the good*, (T,) or *the good from the bad*, (Mṣb,) or *to see what was its* [*degree of*] *goodness*. (Ṣ.) — And hence, accord. to Er-Rághib, الفَتْنُ is used as meaning *The causing* a man *to enter into fire* [app. *by way of trial*, or *probation*], and [*in like manner*] into *a state of punishment*, or *affliction*: (TA:) [and it is also used as meaning *the slaying* another; whence, in the Ḳur iv. 102,] إِنْ خِفْتُمْ أَنْ يَفْتِنَكُمُ ٱلَّذِينَ كَفَرُوا means [*If ye fear that those who have disbelieved*] *may slay you*; and in like manner in the Chapter of Yoonus [i. e. in x. 83], أَنْ يَفْتِنَهُمْ means ان يقتلهم. (T. [In the TA, these two exs. are misplaced, or something has been omitted before them by a copyist.]) — [Hence also,] one says, فَتَنَهُ, aor. ـِ, (Ḳ, TA,) inf. n. فَتْنٌ, (TA,) *He*, or *it, caused him to fall into* الفِتْنَة; (Ḳ, TA;) i. e. *trial*; and *affliction, distress*, or *hardship*; [generally meaning *an affliction whereby some good or evil quality is put to the test*;] (TA;) as also ✝ فَتَّنَهُ; and ✝ افْتَتَنَهُ; (Ḳ, TA;) but this, of which the inf. n. is تَفْتِينٌ, has an intensive signification; (Ṣ;) and ✝ أَفْتَنَهُ; (Ḳ, TA;) which last is rare, or rather, accord. to Aṣ, [though app. not in this sense, but in another, to be mentioned in what follows,] is not allowable: (TA:) the first of these verbs is trans. and intrans.: (Ṣ, Ḳ, TA:) you say also, فَتَنَ, (AZ, T, Ṣ, Ḳ, TA,) aor. ـِ, (AZ, T, Ḳ,) inf. n. فُتُونٌ, (AZ, T, Ṣ, TA,) *He fell into* فِتْنَة [i. e.

trial, or *affliction*, &c.]; (AZ, T, Ḳ;) as also ▼ اِفْتَتَنَ: (Ḳ:) or the former signifies *he shifted from a good, to an evil, state* or *condition*: or, accord. to En-Naḍr, one says ▼ اُفْتُتِنَ and اَفْتَتَنَ, both meaning the same; and this is correct; but فَتَنَ as quasi-pass. of فَتَنْتُهُ [i. e. as intrans.] is of weak authority: (T:) and ▼ اُفْتُتِنَ, said of a man, [as also اِفْتَتَنَ,] and فُتِنَ, signify the same, (Ṣ, M,) accord. to AZ, (M,) i. e. *he was smitten by a* فِتْنَة [or *trial*, &c.,] *so that his wealth*, or *property*, or *his intellect, departed*: and likewise *he was tried*, or *tested*: (Ṣ:) and accord. to AZ, one says, of a man, ▼ اُفْتِتَنَ, [if not a mistranscription for اُفْتُتِنَ, as above,] with ḍamm, meaning فُتِنَ: (TA:) [and فَتَنَهُ has فُتُونٌ also as an inf. n.:] it is said in the Ḳur [xx. 41] وَفَتَنَّاكَ فُتُونًا (Ṣ) i. e. *And we tried thee with a* [*severe*] *trying*: or the noun in this instance is pl. of فَتْنٌ, or of فِتْنَة, formed by disregard of the ة, like حُجُوز and بُدُور which are [said to be] pls. of حُجْزَة and بَدْرَة; so that the meaning is, *we tried thee with several sorts of trying*: (Bḍ:) or, as some say, *and we purified thee with a* [*thorough* or *an effectual*] *purifying* [*like that of gold*, or *silver, by means of fire*]: (TA:) [in many instances] فَتَنَهُ, aor. ـِ, [inf. n. فَتْنٌ,] signifies *He tried*, or *tested, him*; whence, in the Ḳur ix. 127, يُفْتَنُونَ means *They are tried*, or *tested*, by being summoned to war, against unbelievers or the like; or, as some say, by the infliction of punishment or of some evil thing. (M.) فَتَنْتُمْ أَنْفُسَكُمْ, in the Ḳur [lvii. 13], means *Ye caused yourselves to fall into trial and punishment.* (TA.) And وَهُمْ لَا يُفْتَنُونَ, in the Ḳur xxix. 1, is expl. as meaning *While they are not tried in their persons and their possessions so that he who has true faith may be known from others by his patient endurance of trial.* (T.) And the saying, in a trad., إِنَّكُمْ تُفْتَنُونَ فِى القُبُورِ means [*Verily ye shall be tried*, or *tested, in the graves by*] *the questioning of* [*the two angels*] *Munkar and Neheer.* (TA.) [See also مَفْتُونٌ, which is said to be an inf. n., and syn. with فِتْنَة, meaning خِبْرَة, or with فُتُونٌ (mentioned above as an inf. n. of the intrans. v. فَتَنَ), meaning جُنُونٌ; as well as a pass. part. n.] — And فَتَنَهُ, (M, TA,) inf. n. فَتْنٌ, (TA, [or perhaps فُتُونٌ, as in the next following sentence,]) also signifies *He made him* (a man, M) *to turn from*, or *quit*, (M, TA,) *the predicament in which he was*, (M,) or *the right course*: (TA:) whence, in the Ḳur [xvii. 75], وَإِنْ كَادُوا لَيَفْتِنُونَكَ عَنِ ٱلَّذِى أَوْحَيْنَا إِلَيْكَ (M, TA) i. e. [*And verily they were near to*] *their making thee to turn* [*from that which we had revealed to thee*]: thus this saying has been explained. (TA.) [And *He*, or *it, seduced him*; or *tempted him*: thus it may often be well rendered, agreeably with what next precedes and what next follows, and with explanations of its act. part. n. and of فِتْنَة.] And one says, فَتَنَ الْمَالُ النَّاسَ, aor. ـِ, inf. n. فُتُونٌ, [or perhaps فَتْنٌ, as in the next preceding sentence,] meaning *Wealth*, or *property, inclined*, or *attracted, to it, men*, or *mankind*: and فُتِنَ فِى دِينِهِ and ▼ اُفْتُتِنَ, both in the pass. form, *He declined* [or *was made to decline*] *from* [*the right way in*] *his religion.* (Mṣb.) And فَتَنَهُ, aor. ـِ, inf. n. فَتْنٌ and فُتُونٌ, (M, Ḳ,) *He*, or *it, induced in him admiration*, or *pleasure*; (M,* Ḳ,* TA;) as also ▼ أَفْتَنَهُ [respecting which see what here follows]: (M, Ḳ:) and one says, of a woman, فَتَنَتْهُ, (T, Ṣ,) meaning [*She enamoured him*; or *captivated his heart*; i. e.] *she bereaved him of his heart*, or *reason*, (دَلَّهَتْهُ, [thus in several copies of the Ṣ, in one of my copies بَلَّهَتْهُ,] *and* [*so affected him that*] *he loved her*; (Ṣ;) as also ▼ أَفْتَنَتْهُ; (T, Ṣ;) the former of the dial. of El-Ḥijáz, and the latter of the dial. of Nejd; (T, Ṣ;*) but ▼ افتنه, (T, Ṣ,) or افتنهُ, (M,) was disallowed by Aṣ, (T, Ṣ, M,) and he paid no regard to a verse mentioned to him as an ex. thereof, (T,) [or] he ignored a verse cited to him as an ex. of the pass. part. n. from an أُرْجُوزَة of Ru-beh, not knowing it therein; (M;) most of the lexicologists, however, allow both: (T:) Sb says that فَتَنَهُ signifies *he put* [or *occasioned*] *in him* فِتْنَة; and ▼ افتنهُ, *he caused* الفِتْنَة *to come to him* [or *to affect him*]; (M;) or he said that the latter means *he made him to be* فَاتِن: (TA voce حَزَنَهُ:) and one says also, of a man, فُتِنَ بِالْمَرْأَةِ and ▼ اُفْتُتِنَ [both meaning *He was enamoured by the woman*]. (T.) — And one says also, of a man, فَتَنَ, aor. ـِ, inf. n. فُتُونٌ, meaning *He desired* الفُجُور [i. e. *the committing of adultery* or *fornication*]: (AZ, TA:) or فَتَنَ إِلَى النِّسَآءِ, inf. n. فُتُونٌ, *he desired* الفُجُور (T, M, Ḳ, TA) *with women* or *the women*; as also فُتِنَ إِلَيْهِنَّ. (M, Ḳ, TA.)

2: see the preceding paragraph, former half.

3. مُفَاتَنَةٌ [*The occasioning* فِتْنَة (meaning *conflict*, or *discord*, or *the like*,) *with another*]. (TA in art. عرم: see 3 in that art.)

4: see 1, former half, in two places: and also in the latter half, in four places.

5. بَنُو ثَقِيفٍ يَتَفَتَّنُونَ أَبَدًا means يَتَحَارَبُونَ [i. e. *The sons of Thakeef* (the tribe so called) *contend in war, one with another, ever*]. — تَفَتَّنِى: see 5 in art. عجب, where it is said to be syn. with تَصَبَّانِى.

8: see 1, former half, in four places: and also in the latter half, in two places.

فَتْنٌ *A sort*, or *species*; and *a state*, or *condition*; syn. ضَرْبٌ, (T, M, Ḳ,) and فَنٌّ, (T, Ḳ,) and لَوْنٌ, (M, Ḳ,) and حَالٌ. (T, Ḳ.) Hence the saying of 'Amr Ibn-Aḥmar El-Báhilee,

* إِمَّا عَلَى نَفْسٍ وَإِمَّا لَهَا *
* وَالعَيْشُ فَتْنَانِ فَحُلْوٌ وَمُرّ *

[*Either against a soul or for it*; *life being of two sorts*, or *conditions, sweet and bitter*; مُرّ being for مُرٌّ]; (T; and the latter hemistich, without the incipient و, is cited in the Ḳ;) thus as related by some: but as related by Aboo-Sa'eed [Aṣ], he said فَنَّانِ, i. e. ضَرْبَانِ: and as related by Aboo-'Amr Esh-Sheybánee, فِتْنَانِ [with kesr]; and [he seems to have held that the poet meant *two-sided*; for] he says that ▼ الفِتْنُ signifies النَّاحِيَةُ. (T.) — And الفَتْنَانِ, (Ḳ, TA, [in the CḲ, erroneously, الفِتْنَانِ,]) dual of الفَتْنُ, (TA,) signifies *The first and last parts of the day*; or *the early part of the morning and the late part of the evening*: (Ḳ, TA:) because they are two states, or conditions, and two sorts. (TA.)

فِتْنٌ: see the next preceding paragraph.

فِتْنَةٌ *A burning with fire.* (T.) — And *The melting* of gold and of silver (Ḳ, TA) *in order to separate*, or *distinguish, the bad from the good.* (TA.) — And [hence, or] from فَتَنَ signifying "he melted," (T,) or from that verb as signifying "he put into the fire," (Mṣb,) gold, and silver, "for that purpose," (T, Mṣb,) it signifies *A trial*, or *probation*; (IAạr, T, Ṣ, M, Ḳ, TA;) and *affliction, distress*, or *hardship*; (TA;) and [particularly] *an affliction whereby one is tried, proved*, or *tested*: (IAạr, T, Ṣ, Ḳ, TA:) this is the sum of its meaning in the language of the Arabs: (T, TA:*) or the *trial whereby the condition of a man may be evinced*: this, accord. to Zj, may be the meaning in the Ḳur v. 45: (M:) or *a mean whereby the condition of a man is evinced, in respect of good* and *of evil*: (Kull:) [hence it often means *a temptation*:] and ▼ مَفْتُونٌ signifies the same as فِتْنَةٌ, (Ṣ, M, Ḳ,) meaning *a trial*: (Ḳ:) the pl. of فِتْنَةٌ is فِتَنٌ. (Mṣb.) It proceeds from God and from man: (Er-Rághib, TA:) [there are many instances of its proceeding from God in the Ḳur; for ex., in xxxvii. 61,] إِنَّا جَعَلْنَاهَا فِتْنَةً لِلظَّالِمِينَ i. e. [*Verily we have made it to be*] *a trial* [*to the wrongdoers*] is said in relation to the tree Ez-Zaḳḳoom; the existence of which they disbelieved; for when they heard that it comes forth in the bottom of Hell, they said, Trees become burned in the fire; then how can they grow therein? (M.) [And hence] it signifies also *Punishment, castigation*, or *chastisement.* (T, M, Ḳ.) And *Slaughter*: (T:) and *civil war*, or *conflict occurring among people*: (M:) and *slaughter, and war, and faction*, or *sedition, among the parties of the Muslims when they form themselves into parties*: (T:) and *discord, dissension*, or *difference of opinions, among the people.* (IAạr, T, Ḳ.) *A misleading*; or *causing to err*, or *go astray*: (T, Ḳ:) [*seduction*; or *temptation*: or *a cause thereof*; *such as*] *the ornature, finery, show*, or *pomp*, and *the desires*, or *lusts, of the present life* or *world, whereby one is tried*: (T:) and *wealth*, or *children*; (T, Ḳ, TA;) because one is tried thereby: (TA:) and *women*; than whom, the Prophet said, there is no فِتْنَة more harmful to men: (T:) and *a cause of* one's *being pleased* with a thing; (T, M, Ḳ;) as in the saying لَا تَجْعَلْنَا فِتْنَةً لِلْقَوْمِ الظَّالِمِينَ [in the Ḳur x. 85, i. e. *Make not us to be a cause of pleasure* *to the wrongdoing people*]; meaning, make not them to prevail over us, so as to become pleased with their unbelief and to think that they are better than we. (T.) Also *Madness, insanity,* or *diabolical possession;* (T, Ḳ;) and so ↓ فُتُونٌ and ↓ مَفْتُونٌ. (T.) And *Error;* or *deviation from the right way.* (M, Ḳ.) And *Infidelity;* or *unbelief:* (T, M, Ḳ:) thus in the saying, [in the Ḳur ii. 187,] وَٱلْفِتْنَةُ أَشَدُّ مِنَ ٱلْقَتْلِ [*And infidelity,* or *unbelief, is more excessive than slaughter:* and the like is said in ii. 214]. (T.) And *A sin, a crime;* or *an act of disobedience for which one deserves punishment.* (M, Ḳ.) And *Disgrace, shame,* or *ignominy.* (M, Ḳ.) فِتْنَةُ الصَّدْرِ signifies الوَسْوَاسُ [app. as meaning *The devil's prompting,* or *suggesting, of some evil idea*]: فِتْنَةُ المَحْيَا, *The being turned from the* [*right*] *road:* فِتْنَةُ المَمَاتِ, *The being questioned in the grave* [by the two angels Munkar and Nekeer]: فِتْنَةُ الصُّرِّ, *The sword:* and فِتْنَةُ السَّرِّ, *Women.* (TA.) [And الفِتْنَةُ العَمْيَا is a phrase used in the present day as meaning *Incurable evil* or *trouble.*] — [It is also the name now commonly given to The *mimosa farnesiana* of Linn.; (Delile's Floræ Ægypt. Illustr. no. 962;) called by Forskål (Flora Ægypt. Arab. p. lxxvii.) *mimosa scorpioïdes.*]

فِتَانٌ *A covering, of leather, for the* [*camel's saddle called*] رَحْل: (T, M, Ḳ:) pl. فُتُنٌ. (M.)

فُتُونٌ: see فِتْنَةٌ, latter half. [It is an inf. n. of 1 in several senses.]

فَتِينٌ, applied to silver (وَرِق, i. e. فِضَّة), *Burnt.* (Ṣ.) — [Hence,] *Black stones;* as though burnt with fire. (T.) And *A* [*stony tract such as is called*] حَرَّة, (Ṣ,) or *like a* حَرَّة, (Sh, T,) *as though the stones thereof were burnt:* (Sh, T, Ṣ:) or *a black* حَرَّة: (Ḳ:) or *a* حَرَّة *wholly covered by black stones, as though they were burnt:* (M:) pl. فُتُنٌ: (Sh, T, M, Ḳ:) and فَتَائِنُ signifies *black* حِرَار [pl. of حَرَّة]; (TA; [and the same is app. indicated in the T;]) as though its sing. were ↓ فَتِينَةٌ; and some say that this is a sing. [or n. un.], and that فَتِينٌ is the pl. [or coll. gen. n.]; but as some relate a verse of El-Kumeyt which is cited as an ex. of فَتِينَة with the ة elided because ending the verse, it is فِتِينَ, and said to be pl. of فِتَة, like as عِزِينَ is of عِزَة. (T.) — In the dial. of El-Yemen it signifies *Short;* and *small.* (TA.)

فَتِينَةٌ: see the next preceding paragraph.

فَتَّانٌ is an intensive epithet. (TA.) — And signifies *A goldsmith* or *silversmith:* (Ṣ, Ḳ, TA:) because of his melting the gold and the silver in the fire. (TA.) — And الفَتَّانَةُ signifies [*The touch-stone;* i. e.] *the stone with which gold and silver are tried,* or *tested.* (KT.) — And the former, A man *who tries,* or *tempts, much.* (TA.) And الفَتَّانُ, *The devil;* (T, Ṣ, Ḳ;) who tries, or tempts, men, by his deceit, and his embellishing acts of disobedience; (T;) as also ↓ الفَاتِنُ; (M, Ḳ;) [each] an epithet in which the quality of a subst. predominates: (M:) pl. of the former فُتَّانٌ. (T, Ṣ.) And الفَتَّانَانِ, *The dirhem and the deenár;* (Ḳ, TA;) as though they tried, or tempted, men. (TA.) And likewise, (Ḳ,) or فَتَّانَا القَبْرِ, (M,) [*The two angels*] *Munkar and Neheer* [who are said to examine and question the dead in the graves]. (M, Ḳ.) — And *A thief,* or *robber,* (T, Ḳ,) *who opposes himself to the company of travellers in their road.* (T.)

فَاتِنٌ [is the act. part. n. of the trans. v. فَتَنَ; and as such] signifies *Causing to err,* or *go astray,* (T, Ṣ, M,) from the truth: (Ṣ:) hence the saying in the Ḳur [xxxvii. 162], مَا أَنْتُمْ عَلَيْهِ بِفَاتِنِينَ, (T, Ṣ,* M,*) which, accord. to Fr, means, *Ye have not power* [*over him*] *to cause him to err,* except him against whom it has been decreed that he shall enter the fire [of Hell]; فاتنين being made trans. by means of عَلَى because it implies the meaning of قَادِرِينَ, which is thus made trans.: (M:) Fr says, the people of El-Ḥijáz say مَا أَنْتُمْ عَلَيْهِ بِفَاتِنِينَ; and the people of Nejd, ↓ بِمُفْتِنِينَ, from أَفْتَنْتُ. (Ṣ.) — See also فَتَّانٌ. — It is also an epithet from the intrans. v. فَتَنَ; and as such is applied to a heart as signifying *Falling into* فِتْنَة [i. e. *trial,* or *affliction,* &c.; or *in a state of trial,* &c.]. (Ṣ,* TA.)

فَيْتَنٌ *A carpenter.* (Ḳ.)

مَفْتَنٌ: see مَفْتُونٌ. [And see also the different explanations of its verb.]

مُفْتِنٌ: see an ex. of its pl. voce فَاتِنٌ.

مَفْتُونٌ [pass. part. n. of 1; signifying *Burned:* &c.]. — It is applied as an epithet to a deenár as meaning *Put into the fire in order that one may see what is its* [*degree of*] *goodness.* (Ṣ.) — It signifies also *Smitten by a* فِتْنَة [or *trial,* &c.,] *so that his wealth,* or *property,* or *his intellect, has departed:* and likewise *tried,* or *tested:* (Ṣ:) or *caused to fall into* الفِتْنَة; (Ḳ, TA;) i. e. *trial;* and *affliction, distress,* or *hardship;* (TA;) as also ↓ مُفْتَتَنٌ. (Ḳ, TA.) And [particularly] *Afflicted with madness, insanity,* or *diabolical possession.* (T, Ḳ.*) [See also what here follows.] — It is also *syn. with* فِتْنَة; (T, Ṣ, M, Ḳ;) and, thus used, it is an inf. n., like مَعْقُول &c. (T, Ṣ, M.) See فِتْنَة, former half: and again, in the latter half. Hence, (T, M,) as some explain it, (M,) بِأَيِّكُمُ ٱلْمَفْتُونُ, [in the Ḳur lxviii. 6,] (T, M,) meaning *In which of you is madness:* (T:) but some say that the ب is redundant; (M;) thus says AO; (T;) the meaning being أَيُّكُمُ ٱلْمَفْتُونُ [*Which of you is the afflicted with madness*]; (T, M;) but Zj disallowed this: (T:) J says, [in the Ṣ,] that the ب is redundant, as in كَفَى بِٱللّٰهِ شَهِيدًا, in the Ḳur [xiii. last verse, &c.], and [thus in copies of the Ṣ, app. a mistake for "or"] المفتون means الفِتْنَةُ, and is an inf. n. [&c.]: IB says, [in remarking upon this passage of the Ṣ,] if the ب be redundant, المفتون is the man, and is not an inf. n.; but if you make the ب to be not redundant, then المفتون is an inf. n. in the sense of الفُتُون. (TA.) [See also art. ب; p. 142, second col.; and p. 143, third col.]

مَفْتُونَةٌ is [a term] applied to *A number of black camels collected together* (لَابَة سَوْدَاء), as though they were like the [stony tract called] حَرَّة, in blackness; as though they were burnt. (T.)

فتى or فتو

1\. فَتُوَ, aor. يَفْتُو; (Lth, T;) or فَتِىَ, aor. يَفْتَى; (Ṣ, TA;) inf. n. فَتَآءٌ, (Lth, A'Obeyd, T, Ṣ,* TA,) or فَتًى; (TA [and so in one of my copies of the Ṣ; but the former, which see below, is that which is commonly known];) *He was,* or *became, such as is termed* فَتِىٌّ [i. e. *youthful,* or *in the prime of life*]. (Lth, A'Obeyd, T, Ṣ,* TA.) — فَتَوْتُهُمْ, (Ḳ, TA,) aor. أَفْتُوهُمْ, (TA,) *I overcame them,* or *surpassed them, in* فُتُوَّة, i. e. *generosity.* (Ḳ, TA.) [Accord. to the TḲ, one says, ↓ فَاتَوْنِى فَفَتَوْتُهُمْ, meaning *They contended with me for superiority in generosity, and I overcame them,* or *surpassed them, therein;* and the inf. n. of the former verb is مُفَاتَاةٌ.]

2\. فُتِّيَتْ, (ISk, T, Ṣ, M, Ḳ,) inf. n. تَفْتِيَةٌ, (ISk, T, Ṣ, Ḳ,) said of a girl (ISk, T, Ṣ, M, Ḳ) that has nearly attained to puberty, (ISk, T,) *She was prohibited from playing with the boys,* (ISk, T, Ṣ, M, Ḳ,) *and from running with them,* (M,) *and was concealed,* or *kept within,* or *behind, the curtain,* (ISk, T, Ṣ, M,) *in the house,* or *tent;* (M;) and so ↓ تَفَتَّتْ: (ISk, T, Ḳ:) [or] ↓ the latter signifies [or signifies also] *she assumed,* or *affected, a likeness to the young women, being the youngest of them.* (Ṣ, M. [In text of the latter, as given in the TT, تشبّهت بالفتيان is put for تشبّهت بالفَتَيَاتِ, which the context shows to be the right reading.])

3: see 1, last sentence. — المُفَاتَاةُ signifies [also] *The summoning another to the judge, and litigating;* and so ↓ التَّفَاتِى. (TA.)

4\. افتى *He* (a learned man) *notified the decision of the law* [in, or respecting, a particular case]. (Mṣb.) [And the verb in this sense is trans.: you say,] افتاه فِى الأَمْرِ *He notified, made known,* or *explained, to him,* [*what he required to know,* and particularly *what was the decision of the law, in,* or *respecting,*] *the case;* (M, Ḳ, TA;) it being dubious: said of a lawyer. (TA.) And أَفْتَانِى فِى مَسْأَلَة, (T, Ṣ,) inf. n. إِفْتَآءٌ, (T,) *He* (a lawyer) *gave me an answer,* or *a reply,* [*stating the decision of the law,*] *respecting a question.* (T, Ṣ, TA.) And أَفْتَيْتُ فُلَانًا فِى رُؤْيَا رَآهَا *I interpreted,* or *explained, to such a one, a dream that he had seen.* (T, TA.) — Also *He drank with the* فَتِىّ [q. v.]. (IAạr, T, TA.)

5\. تفتّى *He affected,* or *assumed, a likeness to youths,* or *young men:* said of an old, or elderly, man; or one past the prime of life. (TA.) —

See also 2, in two places. — And *He affected, or endeavoured to acquire, generosity:* and also *he affected, or made a show of, generosity:* (KL:) you say تفتّى and ↑ تفاتى [app. as signifying the same: but more properly the former verb has the former of these two significations: and ↑ the latter verb has the latter of the same two significations]: both from الفُتُوَّة. (Ṣ, Ḳ, TA.)

6: see the next preceding sentence, in two places: — and see 3. You say, تَفَاتَوْا إِلَى الفَقِيهِ *They appealed to the lawyer for the notifying of the decision of the law.* (Ṣ, TA.)

10. اِسْتَفْتَيْتُ الفَقِيهَ فِى مَسْأَلَةٍ *I sought, or demanded, of the lawyer, a notification of the decision of the law respecting a question.* (T,* Ṣ,* Mṣb,* TA.) And in like manner the verb is used in the Ḳur iv. 126, and xxxvii. 149. (TA.)

فِتْيَةٌ *A* [*stony tract such as is called*] حَرَّة [for which some copies of the Ḳ have جَرَّة, a mistranscription, as may be seen from a statement voce فِتِينٌ, in art. فتن, q. v.]: pl. فِتُونَ. (Ḳ, TA.)

فَتًى i. q. شَابٌّ, (Ṣ, M, Ḳ, TA, but omitted in the CḲ,) or غُلَامٌ حَدَثٌ, (T,) or شَابٌّ حَدَثٌ: (Mṣb:) it is a subst. [signifying *A youth,* or *young man;* or *one in the prime of life*]: and an epithet [signifying *youthful;* or *in the prime of life*]: (TA:) [as an epithet, similar to فَتِىٌّ, but restricted in application to a human being:] or it signifies, (Mgh,) or signifies also, (Mṣb,) *a strong youth* or *young man:* (Mgh, Mṣb:) it is said that in the Ḳur xviii. 59 and 61, it is applied by Moses to Joshua the son of Nun, because he served him: (M, TA:) the fem. is ↑ فَتَاةٌ: (Ṣ, Ḳ:) — and it also means ‡ *A slave;* (T, M, Mgh, Mṣb, TA;) even if an old man; metaphorically used in this sense; (Mgh, Mṣb, TA;) and in like manner, ↑ فَتَاةٌ means ‡ *a female slave,* (T, M, Mgh, Mṣb, TA,) and *a female servant:* (TA:) the Prophet is related to have said, Let not any of you say عَبْدِى and أَمَتِى, but let him say فَتَاىَ and فَتَاتِى: (T, Mgh:) — and *Generous, honourable, liberal,* or *bountiful:* (Ṣ, Ḳ:) [mostly used as an epithet in which the quality of a subst. predominates; meaning *a generous man:*] *a possessor of* فُتُوَّة [q. v.]: hence the saying, لَا فَتَى إِلَّا عَلِىٌّ [*There is no one endowed with generosity but,* or *other than,* (meaning *like,*) *'Alee*]: (TA:) — the dual of فَتًى is فَتَيَانِ and فَتَوَانِ; (Ḳ, TA;) the former occurring in the Ḳur xii. 36: (TA:) the pl. of فَتًى is فِتْيَةٌ, (Ṣ, M, Mgh, Mṣb, Ḳ,) a pl. of pauc., (Mṣb,) not mentioned in the Ḳ, though occurring in the Ḳur xviii. 9 & 12, (TA,) instead of which they did not say أَفْتَاءٌ, (Sb, M,) and فِتْوَةٌ, (M, Ḳ,) [also a pl. of pauc.,] mentioned by Lḥ, (M,) and (of mult., Mṣb) فِتْيَانٌ (T, Ṣ, M, Mgh, Mṣb, Ḳ) and فُتُوٌّ (T, Ṣ, M, Ḳ) and فُتِىٌّ: (Ṣ, M, Ḳ:) the pl. of ↑ فَتَاةٌ is فَتَيَاتٌ: (Ṣ, M, Mṣb, Ḳ:) the dim. of فَتًى is ↑ فُتَىٌّ; and that of فَتَاةٌ is ↑ فُتَيَّةٌ. (T.) [It is disputed whether the last radical letter of this and other words mentioned in the present art. be originally ى or و.] — الفَتَيَانِ means ‡ *The night and the day;* (Ṣ, M, Ḳ, TA;) like الأَجَدَّانِ and الجَدِيدَانِ: (Ṣ, TA:) or, accord. to Seer, *the morning and the evening,* or *the early part of the morning and the late part of the evening,* or *the forenoon and the afternoon;* syn. الغَدَاةُ وَالعَشِىُّ. (Ḥar p. 377.) And you say, أَقَمْتُ عِنْدَهُ فَتِىَّ مِنْ نَهَارٍ i. e. ‡ *I remained, stayed,* or *abode, with him during a first part of a day.* (TA.)

فَتَاةٌ fem. of فَتًى: see the next preceding paragraph, in three places.

فَتْوَى (T, Ṣ, M, Mgh, Mṣb, Ḳ) and فُتْوَى, (M, Ḳ, TA,) [but the latter is mentioned by few,] and ↑ فُتْيَا, (T, Ṣ, M, Mṣb, Ḳ,) substs. from أَفْتَى, (T, Ṣ,) and as such used in the place of [the inf. n.] إِفْتَآءٌ [i. e. The *giving an answer,* or *a reply, stating the decision of the law, respecting a question*]: (T:) [or rather, as commonly used, *a notification of the decision of the law, in,* or *respecting, a particular case;*] *a notification,* or *an explanation, of a case, given by a lawyer;* (M, Ḳ;) or *an answer,* or *a reply, to a question relating to a dubious judicial decision:* (Er-Rághib, TA:) [fancifully said in the Mgh and Mṣb to be derived from الفَتَى:] the pl. is فَتَاوٍ, and فَتَاوَى is said to be allowable, (Mṣb, TA,) and another pl. is فُتًى, mentioned by IḲooṭ. (TA.)

فُتْيَا: see the next preceding paragraph.

فَتَآءٌ [mentioned in the first sentence of this art. as an inf. n.] *Youth,* or *youthfulness;* or the *prime of life;* (T, Ṣ, M, Ḳ;) and so ↑ فُتُوَّةٌ, (T, M,) as a subst. from فَتًى and from فَتِىٌّ: (M:) or the latter is used in relation to human beings; and the former, to camels [and the like], and also, metaphorically, to human beings: (T:) one says, قَدْ وُلِدَ لَهُ فِى فَتَآءِ سِنِّهِ أَوْلَادٌ [*Children had,* or *have, been born to him in the youthfulness,* or *prime, of his age*]. (Ṣ.)

فُتَىٌّ dim. of فَتًى, q. v., latter half. — Hence, i. e. because of its smallness, (Z, TA,) الفُتَىُّ signifies what is called قَدَحُ الشُّطَّارِ [which may be rendered ‡ *The cup,* or *bowl, of the rogues*]; (IAạr, T, Z, Ḳ, TA;) [*a cup,* or *bowl,*] *with which wine is measured;* (TA;) tropically thus called. (Z, TA.)

فَتِىٌّ *Youthful;* or *in the prime of life;* (Lth, T, Ṣ, M, Mgh, Mṣb, Ḳ;) *contr. of* مُسِنٌّ; (Ṣ, Mgh, Mṣb;) applied to a camel, (T,) or to a beast, (Ṣ, Mgh, Mṣb,) or to anything [i. e. to a beast and to a human being]; (M, Ḳ;) or it is like فَتًى [which is applied peculiarly to a human being], but is sometimes applied to a camel: (M:) [this last statement, however, requires confirmation, which I have not been able to find: the epithet is generally known as applied only to a camel or the like:] the fem. is فَتِيَّةٌ; (Lth, T, M, Mgh, Mṣb, Ḳ;) of which the dim. is ↑ فُتَيَّةٌ: (TA:) and the pl. is أَفْتَآءٌ (T, Ṣ, Mgh, Mṣb, TA) and فِتَآءٌ. (M, Ḳ, TA. [The former pl., though the more common, is not mentioned in the M nor in the Ḳ.])

فُتُوَّةٌ: see فَتَآءٌ. — [Also *Youthful conduct.*] One says, مَالَ إِلَى الجَهْلِ وَالفُتُوَّةِ [*He inclined to ignorant,* or *foolish,* or *silly, and youthful, conduct*]. (Ṣ in art. صبو.) — And *Generosity, honourableness, liberality,* or *bountifulness:* (Ṣ, Ḳ, TA:) used as meaning thus in [treatises on] the law; but not occurring in the Sunneh nor in the Scripture [i. e. the Ḳur-án]: the earliest mentioner thereof was Jaạfar Eṣ-Ṣádiḳ. (TA.)

فُتَيَّةٌ: see فَتِىٌّ, latter half: and see also فُتَىٌّ.

أَفْتَى i. q. أَصْغَرُ [as meaning *Less,* and *least, in years,* or *age*]: from الفتى [i. e. الفَتَى or الفَتِىُّ]. (Ḥam p. 207.)

أُفَيْتِيَةٌ [an irreg.] dim. of فِتْيَةٌ [which is a pl. of فَتًى; like as أُصَيْبِيَةٌ, accord. to Sb, is dim. of صِبْيَةٌ, a pl. of صَبِىٌّ]. (TA.)

مُفْتٍ [*A jurisconsult who notifies the decisions of the law, in,* or *respecting, cases submitted to him,* for the guidance of the قَاضِى and others]. — [And] المُفْتِى is the name of *A certain measure of capacity, called the* مِكْيَال *of Hishám Ibn-Hubeyreh.* (Aṣ, T, M, Ḳ.)

فث

1. فَثَّ جُلَّتَهُ, (T, O, Ḳ,) [aor. ـُ,] inf. n. فَثٌّ, (T,) *He scattered the dates of his* جُلَّة [or *receptacle made of palm-leaves*]. (T, O,* Ḳ.) — And فَثَّ المَآءَ الحَارَّ بِالبَارِدِ, aor. ـُ, (M, TA,) inf. n. فَثٌّ, (TA,) *He abated,* or *allayed, the heat of the hot water by means of the cold:* from Yaạḳoob. (M, TA.) [See also فَثَأَ.]

7. انفثّ, inf. n. اِنْفِثَاثٌ, i. q. اِنْكَسَرَ [accord. to the TḲ used in its proper sense as signifying *It broke,* or *became broken:* but for this I find no authority]. (T, O, Ḳ.) So in the saying, انفثّ الرَّجُلُ مِنْ هَمٍّ أَصَابَهُ [*The man became broken in spirit,* or *languid, from anxiety,* or *solicitude, that befell him*]. (T, O.)

8. مَا ٱفْتَثَّ بَنُو فُلَانٍ قَطُّ means *The sons of such a one have not been overcome,* or *subdued, hitherto,* or *ever.* (AA, O, Ḳ.*)

فَثٌّ *A certain plant, the grain of which is made into bread,* (Ṣ, M, O, Ḳ,) *and eaten,* (Ṣ, M, O,) *in the time of drought,* or *dearth:* (Ṣ, M, O, Ḳ:) in some of the copies of the Ḳ, يُخْتَبَأُ is put for يُخْتَبَزُ: (M, F:) *the bread made of it is coarse,* or *thick, resembling the bread that is baked in hot ashes* [which is generally made in the form of thick round cakes]: (Ṣ, O:) *a grain resembling* [*the species of millet called*] جَاوَرْس, *which is made into bread, and eaten:* (IAạr, T:) it is *a wild grain, which the Arabs of the desert take, in the times of hunger, and pound, or bruise, and make into bread; and it is a bad kind of food, but sometimes, or often, they are content with it for days:* (T:) or, as some say, it is [*a plant*] *of the species called* نَجِيل, *growing in salt lands, of the* [*plants termed*] حُمُوض [pl. of حَمْض], *of which bread is made:* [a coll. gen. n.:] n. un. فَثَّة: (Th, M:) Aboo-Ziyád El-Kilábee says, the فَثّ, like the دُعَاع, *is a herb* (بَقْلَة) *in which comes forth grain, and each of them spreads* [*upon the ground*], *not growing up high; and when they become dry, the people collect what is dry thereof, then pound, or bruise, it, and winnow it, and take forth from it a sort of black grain, with which they fill sacks, and lade the camels: it is a black sort of grain like the* شِهْنِيز [q. v.], *and they make bread of it, and make* عَصِيدَة (يَعْتَصِدُونَ): (O:) in the Bári' it is said to be *a species of tree* or *plant* (شَجَر) *growing in the plain,* or *soft, lands, and on the* [*eminences called*] آكَام, *having a sort of grain like the* حِمَّص [or *chick-peas*], *of which are made bread and* سَوِيق. (Mṣb.) — And accord. to IF, الفَثّ signifies *The* هَبِيد, (O, Mṣb,) meaning *the pulp of the colocynth,* شَحْمُ الحَنْظَلِ, (O,) or *the colocynth-plant,* شَجَرُ الحَنْظَلِ. (Mṣb: and this is one of the meanings assigned to الفَثّ in the Ḳ. [In the TḲ, شَحْمُ الحَنْظَلِ is said to be the correct explanation: but from what will be seen voce هَبِيد, I think it most probable that the right meaning is *The seeds of the colocynth.*]) — IF also says that it signifies The فَسِيل [i. e. *shoot,* or *shoots, of the palm-tree,*] *which is,* or *are, plucked forth* [*entire,*] *from the base thereof.* (O.) = تَمْرٌ فَثٌّ *Dates that are scattered;* (Lth, Kr, M, Ḳ;) *not in a provision-bag or other receptacle;* like بَثٌّ: (Kr, M:) or *dates that are separate, each one from others; not sticking together;* (T, O;) and so فَذٌّ and بَذٌّ and فَضٌّ. (T.)

مَفَثَّة *Multitude:* (T, O, Ḳ:) so in the saying, وُجِدَ لِبَنِى فُلَانٍ مَفَثَّة [*Multitude was found to be attributable to the sons of such a one*] when they were numbered: (T, O:) and مَفَثَّة signifies the same. (Ḳ and TA in art. فت.) — And [i. q. نُزُل:] one says, مَا رَأَيْنَا جُلَّةً أَكْثَرَ مَفَثَّةً مِنْهَا, meaning نُزُلًا [i. e. *We have not seen a receptacle made of palm-leaves, for dates, having more food prepared for the guest than it*]: (T, O:) and كَثِيرُ مَفَثَّةٍ means كَثِيرُ نُزُلٍ [i. e. *Abundant in respect of food prepared for the guest*]. (So in some copies of the Ḳ: in other copies نَزَلٍ. [The TA gives the latter reading; and so, therefore, does the TḲ, which explains it as meaning "increase," and adds that one says طعام كثير مفثة, an ex. app. without any authority; for what I have cited from the T and O shows, I think, that the former reading, and not the latter, is unquestionably right.])

فثأ

1. فَثَأَ القِدْرَ, aor. َ, (T, Ṣ, M, O, Ḳ,) inf. n. فَثْءٌ (T, M, Ḳ) and فُثُوْءٌ, (M, Ḳ,) both inf. ns. from Lḥ, (M,) *He stilled,* or *allayed, the boiling of the pot,* (T, Ṣ, M, O, Ḳ,) *with water,* (Ṣ, O,) i. e. *with cold water,* or *by lading out with the ladle:* (T:) and ثَفَأَهَا signifies the same. (M.) — [Hence] one says, أَطْفَأَ فُلَانٌ النَّائِرَةَ وَفَثَأَ القُدُورَ الفَائِرَةَ ‡ [*Such a one extinguished the discord,* or *rancour,* or *enmity, and stilled the boiling passions*]. (A, TA.) — And فَثَأَ غَضَبَهُ, (M, Ḳ,*) aor. َ, (M, Ḳ,) inf. n. فَثْءٌ, (M,) ‡ *He stilled,* or *quieted,* or *abated, his anger,* (M, Ḳ,* TA,*) *by words,* or *otherwise.* (TA.) إِنَّ الرَّثِيئَةَ تَفْثَأُ الغَضَبَ † [*Verily what is termed* رثيئة *stills,* or *appeases, anger*] is one of their provs., (Ṣ, O, TA,) expl. in art. رثأ. (TA.) — And فَثَأْتُ الرَّجُلَ, (Ṣ, O,) or فَثَأْتُهُ عَنِّى, (T, TA,) † *I averted,* or *turned back, the man from me, by words,* or *otherwise.* (T, Ṣ, O, TA.) And فَثَأَ الشَّىْءَ عَنْهُ, (M, Ḳ,) inf. n. فَثْءٌ, (M,) † *He averted the thing from him.* (M, Ḳ, TA.) And مَا فَثَأَكَ عَنَّا † *What withheld,* or *has withheld, thee from us?* (Ḥar p. 180.) — Also فَثَأَ الشَّىْءَ, (M, Ḳ,) aor. َ, inf. n. فَثْءٌ and فُثُوْءٌ, (TA,) *He allayed the cold of the thing by heating.* (M, Ḳ, TA.) And فَثَأَتِ الشَّمْسُ المَآءَ *The sun abated,* or *allayed, the cold of the water* (M.) And فَثَأَهُ, inf. n. فَثْءٌ, *He heated it;* namely, water, (AZ, T, O,) &c. (T.) And accord. to MF, the phrase فَثَأَ اللَّبَنَ is allowable [as meaning *He boiled the milk so that it frothed up and became curdled,* or *clotted,* or *dissundered:* see what next follows]. (TA.) = فَثَأَ اللَّبَنُ, aor. َ, *The milk was boiled so that it frothed up and became curdled,* or *clotted,* or *dissundered:* (AḤát, M, O, Ḳ:) when this is the case, the milk is termed فَاثِئٌ ▼. (AḤát, O.) = فَثَأَتِ القِدْرُ *The cooking-pot ceased to boil.* (O.) — And فَثِئَ [or فَثَىَ] غَضَبُهُ † *His anger was,* or *became, abated;* (TA;) [and] so انفثأ ▼ غَضَبُهُ. (Ḥar p. 232.) — And مَا تَفْثَأُ تَفْعَلُ † *Thou dost not cease doing* [such a thing]; like مَا تَفْتَأُ. (A, TA.) = فَثَأَ بِسَلْحِهِ: see فَطَأَ.

4. افثأ † *It* (the heat) *became allayed,* or *assuaged;* and *remitted,* or *abated.* (Ṣ, O.) — And أَطْبَقَتِ السَّمَآءُ ثُمَّ أَفْثَأَتْ † [*The sky became overcast, and then cleared*]. (A, TA.) — افثأ بِالمَكَانِ † *He remained, stayed, dwelt,* or *abode, in the place.* (O, Ḳ.*) — عَدَا حَتَّى أَفْثَأَ † *He* (a man, M) *ran until he became tired,* (Ṣ, M, O, Ḳ,*) *and out of breath,* (Ṣ, O,) or *and languid.* (M, Ḳ.) In the saying of El-Khansà,

أَلَا مَنْ لِعَيْنٍ لَا تَجِفُّ دُمُوعُهَا
إِذَا قُلْتَ أَفْثَتْ تَسْتَهِلُّ فَتَحْفِلُ

† [*Now who will be as a helper for an eye of which the tears will not dry up? when thou sayest, "They have become tired of flowing," they pour, and become copious*], she means أَفْثَأَتْ. (M.) = أَفْثَؤُوا لَهُ *They heated stones for him* (i. e. a sick man), *and sprinkled water upon them, and he lay prostrate upon them, in order that he might sweat:* (O, Ḳ:) this they did when they were unable to procure a hot bath. (O.)

7: see 1, last sentence but two.

فَاثِئٌ as an epithet applied to milk: see 1, near the end.

فثج

1. فَثَجَ *i. q.* نَقَصَ [accord. to the TḲ in a trans. sense, for it is there said that فَثَجَ الشَّىْءَ, aor. ُ, inf. n. فَثْجٌ, signifies *He,* or *it, diminished the thing*]; (AA, O, Ḳ;) said in this sense in relation to anything. (AA, O.) — [Hence, app., though perhaps the verb in each of these three phrases may be the aor. of أُفْثِجَ ▼,] بِئْرٌ لَا تُفْثَجُ means *A well that will not become exhausted:* and فُلَانٌ بَحْرٌ لَا يُفْثَجُ *Such a one is a sea that will not become exhausted:* (Ṣ, O:) and مَآءٌ لَا يُفْثَجُ *Water that will not become exhausted;* or, accord. to A'Obeyd, *of which the bottom will not be reached* [app. *by drawing therefrom*]. (TA.) And فَثْجٌ [or فَثْجُ مَآءٍ مِنْ مَوْضِعٍ] means *A drawing of water from a place.* (KL.) — And فَثَجَ المَآءَ الحَارَّ بِالبَارِدِ *He abated,* or *allayed, somewhat of the heat of the hot water with the cold.* (O, Ḳ. [Compare فَثَأَ.]) = فَثَجٌ [as inf. n. of فَثِجَتْ] used in relation to a she-camel signifies [The *being such as is termed* فَاثِجٌ in any of the senses assigned to it below: or simply] the *being pregnant:* as also فُثُوجٌ. (KL.) — And فَثَجَ, (O, Ḳ, TA,) inf. n. فَثْجٌ, (O,) said of a man, (TA,) signifies أَثْقَلَ; (thus in the O and in copies of the Ḳ; [but accord. to the TḲ, أُثْقِلَ, for it is there said that the meaning is *He* (a man) *was,* or *became, burdened,* or *heavy;*]) as also فَثَّجَ ▼, (O, Ḳ,) inf. n. تَفْثِيجٌ. (O.)

2: see what next precedes.

4. افثج *i. q.* تَرَكَ: (O, Ḳ:) you say, أَفْثَجَنِى, meaning *He left,* or *relinquished, me,* (تَرَكَنِى,) *and left me alone:* (O:) and so افسج عَنِّى. (Thus in the O in art. فسج.) = Also, (Ṣ, O, Ḳ,) accord. to Ks, (Ṣ, O,) like أَفْثَأَ, (TA,) and so أُفْثِجَ, (O, Ḳ,) this last, in the pass. form, mentioned by IAạr, (TA,) *He* (a man, TA) *was,* or *became, tired, and out of breath,* (Ṣ, O, Ḳ,) from running. (Ṣ, O.) = See also 1, second sentence.

فَاثِجٌ, applied to a she-camel, *Pregnant;* (Aṣ, Ṣ, O, Ḳ;) and so فَاسِجٌ: (Aṣ, Ṣ:) or *youthful, and having conceived:* (Aṣ, Ṣ:) or *having conceived, and become goodly:* (AO, Ṣ:) or *having conceived, and become fat, being youthful:* (TA:) pl. فَوَاثِجُ. (Ṣ, O.) And, so applied, *i. q.* حَائِل

[i. e. One *not conceiving during a year*, or *two years*, or *some years*], *and fat*: (O, Ḳ:) thus having two contr. significations. (Ḳ.) And, (Ḳ,) accord. to IDrd, (O,) A she-camel *having a large hump, and fat*; (O, Ḳ;) and *so though she be not* حَائِل. (O.)

فثر

فَاثُورٌ A [*basin such as is termed*] طَسْت; (M, L, Ḳ;) thus it means with the vulgar: (L:) or *a* طَسْت *of gold*, or *of silver*: (O:) or the طَسْتَخَان, (T, Ḳ,) or طَشْتَخَان, (O, and so in some copies of the Ḳ,) [i. e. *a large circular tray, of brass* or *other metal, which serves as a table for food*, being generally placed upon a stool, the persons who eat sitting on the floor]; (Lth, T, Z, O, Ḳ;) thus it means with the vulgar: (Lth, T, Z, O:) or *a* خِوَان [or *table upon which food is eaten*], *made of marble*, (Lth, T, Ṣ, M, O, Ḳ,) by the people of Syria, who thus call it, (Lth, T, O,) or *of silver*, (T, Ṣ, M,) and *the like*, (Ṣ,) or *of gold*: (M, Ḳ:) or *of any kind* accord. to some: (TA:) or *a* جَامٌ [q. v.] *of silver*, (T, Nh, TA,) or *of gold*: (Nh, TA:) [but this seems to be virtually a repetition; for it is said that] ▼ فَاثُورِيَّةٌ, occurring in a verse of Lebeed, means أَخْوِنَةٌ [pl. of pauc. of خِوَانٌ] (T, O) and جَامَاتٌ [which is pl. of جَامٌ accord. to IAạr, or of جَامَةٌ accord. to IB, who holds جَامٌ to be likewise a pl. of جَامَةٌ]: (T:) فَاثُورٌ is a word of the people of Syria and El-Jezeereh: (M:) and it signifies (Ṣ, O, L) in the dial. of the people of El-Jezeereh, (L,) *a* مَائِدَة [sometimes meaning *table* in an absolute sense, but properly one *with food upon it*]: (Ṣ, O, L:) [hence,] one says, هُمْ عَلَى فَاثُورٍ وَاحِدٍ, (Lth, T, Ṣ, M, O, L, TA) i. e. عَلَى مَائِدَةٍ وَاحِدَةٍ, (Ṣ, O, L, TA,) and مَنْزِلَةٍ وَاحِدَةٍ, (Ṣ, O, TA,) and بَسَاطٍ وَاحِدٍ, (O, TA, [in both of which the former word is without any vowel-sign to the ب, so that it may be either بِسَاط or بَسَاط,]) or بَسْطٍ واحدٍ, (TT as from the M,) or as though meaning على بساط واحد, thus expl. by Lth, as said of the people of Syria and El-Jezeereh: (TT as from the T:) [it means, app., *They are living upon one kind of fare; upon one footing; upon one level* or *stratum*:] in the copies of the Ḳ, [or in the generality of the copies thereof,] الفَاثُورُ is expl. as signifying المَنْزِلَةُ and النَّشَاطُ; but النشاط is a mistake for البساط. (TA. [My MS. copy of the Ḳ has the right reading (البساط), without any trace of alteration.]) — Also ‡ The *breast*, or *bosom*: (Ḳ:) or *a wide breast* or *bosom*; applied by a poet to that of a woman; as being likened to the خِوَان so called. (M.) — And ‡ The *disk* of the sun (Ṣ,* O, Ḳ) is called its فاثور as being likened to the طَسْت so called. (O.) — And ‡ *A* [*bowl such as is termed*] جَفْنَة; (M, Ḳ, TA;) thus with [the tribe of] Rabee'ah; (M, TA;) for the like reason. (TA.) — And *A* [*vessel such as is termed*] نَاجُود *and* مِصْحَاة (AA, T, O, Ḳ) *and* بَاطِيَة; all which words mean the same thing. (AA, O, TA.) — And, accord. to the R, *A* [*molten piece such as is termed*] سَبِيكَة *of silver*: and some say, *a silver* إِبْرِيق [or *ewer*]. (TA.) ═ Also *A company of men upon the frontier of a hostile country, that go after the enemy, in pursuit*. (Ibn-'Abbád, O, Ḳ.) — And *A spy*; syn. جَاسُوس. (Ibn-'Abbád, O, Ḳ.)

فَاثُورِيَّةٌ: see the preceding paragraph, former half.

فثى

4. افثى *He was*, or *became, tired*, (Ḳ, TA,) and *languid*; from running [&c.]. (TA. [But this is for أَفْثَأَ: see an ex. in a verse cited in art. فثأ.])

فج

1. فَجَّ, (TA,) [sec. pers. فَجِجْتَ, aor. يَفَجُّ,] inf. n. فَجَجٌ, (Ṣ,* O,* Ḳ,* TA,) *He had the feet wide apart*: or, said of a man, *he had the knees wide apart*: and, said of a beast, or quadruped, *he had the hocks wide apart*: (TA:) ▼ فَجَجٌ is more ugly than what is termed فَحَجٌ. (Ṣ, O, Ḳ.) — See also 7. — فَجَّ رِجْلَيْهِ, (TA,) and فَجَّ مَا بَيْنَ رِجْلَيْهِ, (Ṣ, O, Ḳ, TA,) aor. يَفُجُّ, inf. n. فَجٌّ, (Ṣ, O, TA,) *He opened* [or *parted*] *his legs* (Ṣ, O, Ḳ, TA) *widely*; [i. e. *he straddled*;] (TA;) and so ▼ افجّ, (Ḳ,) or افجّ رِجْلَيْهِ, *he parted his legs widely*, said of a man and of a beast; (O;) so too ▼ فاجّ [alone], and فَجَا; (TA;) and one says also ▼ تفاجّ [meaning the same], of one walking, (Ṣ, Ḳ, TA,) and meaning he did thus to make water, (Mgh, TA,) as also ▼ فاجّ, inf. n. فِجَاجٌ and مُفَاجَّةٌ, both of these verbs said of a man; but ▼ تفاجّ signifies *he parted his legs very widely*; (TA;) and ▼ تفاجّت is said of a she-camel, (A, O,) لِلْحَلَبِ [*to be milked*]; (A;) and of a sheep or goat (شَاة). (O.) مَا شَىْءٌ يَفَاجُّ ▼ وَلَا يَبُولُ [*What is a thing that straddles and will not make water?*] is an enigma: it is a thing like a couch, having four legs. (A, TA.) الفَجُّ in the language of the Arabs is *The making an opening*, or *interval*, between two things. (TA.) — And فَجَجْتُ القَوْسَ, (Ṣ, O, Ḳ,) aor. أَفُجُّهَا, (Ṣ, O,) inf. n. فَجٌّ, (TA,) *I raised the string of the bow* [*so as to make it distant*] *from its* كَبِد [q. v.]; (Ṣ, O, Ḳ;) like فَجَوْتُهَا. (Ṣ, O.) — فَجَّ الأَرْضَ, (so in the O,) or ▼ افجّ الارض, (so in the Ḳ,) *He clave the ground*, or *earth*, with the plough, *in a manner not approved*. (O, Ḳ.) ═ فَجَّ said of a horse &c., *He purposed*, or *desired, to run*. (TA.) ═ See also فَجَاجَةٌ.

2. تَفْجِيجٌ The *making* [a thing] *to be crude* [or *not thoroughly cooked*]. (KL.) [See فِجٌّ.]

3: see 1, in three places.

4. افجّ: see 1, former half. — Also, (L,) or أَفَجَّتْ, (Ṣ, O, L, Ḳ,) *He*, or *she*, (i. e. an ostrich) *muted*. ═ And, the former, *He travelled a road such as is termed* فَجّ; (O, L, Ḳ;) said of a man; (O;) as also ▼ افتجّ. (L.) — And *He*, (a man, Ṣ, O,) or *it*, (a thing, Mṣb,) *hastened, went quickly*, or *was quick*; (Ṣ, O, Mṣb, Ḳ;) mentioned by IAạr. (Ṣ.) ═ See also 1, near the end.

6: see 1, in three places.

7. انفجّت القَوْسُ, (A,) inf. n. اِنْفِجَاجٌ, (O,) *The bow had its string distant from its* كَبِد [q.v.]; (A, O;) [and so, app., ▼ فَجَّت, for] ▼ فَجَجٌ, in a bow, signifies the *state of having the string distant from the* كَبِد *thereof*. (Ṣ, O.)

8: see 4.

فَجٌّ *A wide road between two mountains*; (Ṣ, A, O, Ḳ;) and ▼ فُجَاجٌ signifies the same: (O, Ḳ:) or, *in a mountain*: (AHeyth, TA:) or, *in the anterior part of a mountain, wider than a* شِعْب [q. v.]: (TA:) or *a depressed road*: (Th, TA:) or *a conspicuous and wide road*: (Mṣb:) or *a far-extending beaten track* or *road*: (AHeyth, TA: [see an ex. in a verse cited voce عَمِيق:]) or, accord. to ISh, [*a track*] *as though it were a road*; and sometimes it is *a road between two mountains*, (L, TA,) or *having on either side what is termed a* قَاو [a word variously explained], (so in the L,) or *between two walls* (حَائِطَيْنِ), (so in the TA,) *and extending to the distance of two days' journey*, or *three, if a road* or *not a road*; and *if a road, abounding with herbage*: (L, TA:) pl. [of mult.] فِجَاجٌ (Th, Ṣ, O, Mṣb) and [of pauc.] أَفِجَّةٌ, which is extr. [with respect to analogy], (Th, TA,) and أَفُجٌّ. (Mṣb.) ═ See also the next paragraph, in two places.

فِجٌّ, with kesr, The *Syrian* بِطِّيخ [i. e. *melon* or *water-melon*], (Ṣ, A, O, Ḳ,) which the Persians call the *Indian*. (Ṣ, A, O.) — And فِجٌّ, (so in the Ṣ and A and Ḳ,) or ▼ فَجٌّ, (thus in the O, and by implication in the Mṣb, [and thus pronounced in the present day,]) signifies *Unripe*; (Ṣ, A, O, Mṣb, Ḳ;) applied to fruit (A, Mṣb, Ḳ) of any kind, (A,) &c.; (Mṣb;) to anything of melons (بِطِّيخ) and of other fruits; (Ṣ, O;) and so ▼ فَجَاجَةٌ; (O, Ḳ;) but ▼ فَجٌّ and ▼ فَجَاجَةٌ are not mentioned by Ed-Deenawaree [i. e. AḤn; and the latter (which see below) I think doubtful in the sense expl. above]. (O.)

فُجَّةٌ *An opening*, or *intervening space*, (O, Ḳ, TA,) *between two mountains*. (TA.)

فَجَجٌ an inf. n.: (TA:) see 1, first sentence: — and see also 7.

فُجُجٌ [a pl. of which the sing. is not mentioned] *i. q.* ثُقَلَاءُ [*Such as are heavy, slow, sluggish*, &c.], (IAạr, O, Ḳ,) of men. (IAạr, O.)

فُجَاجٌ: see فَجٌّ.

فَجَّاجٌ *A male ostrich which* [they assert, like as they say of the domestic cock, (see عُقْرٌ,)] *lays one egg.* (TA.)

فَجَاجَةٌ [app. an inf. n., of which the verb is ▾ فَجَّ, sec. pers. فَجُجْتَ,] *The state of being unripe*, or *not sufficiently cooked.* (TA.) — See also فِجٌّ, in two places.

فَجَّانٌ The *stem* (عُود) *of the raceme of a palmtree:* mentioned by ISd; and held by him to be of the measure فَعْلَانٌ because this is more common than the measure فَعَّالٌ. (TA.)

فَجْفَاجٌ and فُجْفُجٌ and فَجْفَجٌ: see فَجْفَاجٌ.

فَجْفَجَةٌ *Loquacity*, or *much talking:* or *frivolous babbling:* or *much talking, and boasting of abundance which one does not possess:* or *clamouring:* or *great and disorderly talking.* (TA.)

فَجْفَاجٌ, applied to a man, *Loquacious; a great talker:* (Ṣ:) or *a frivolous babbler:* (TA:) or, as also ▾ فَجْفَجٌ (O, Ḳ) and ▾ فُجْفُجٌ (Ḳ) and ▾ فُجَافِجٌ, (O, but there written فَجَافِجٌ,) *a great talker, who boasts of abundance which he does not possess:* (O, Ḳ:) or *clamourous:* or *a great and disorderly talker:* fem. with ة. (TA.) The poet Aboo-'Árim El-Kilábee applies the first of these epithets to palm-trees (نَخِيل) [as meaning † *Promising much fruit, but not fulfilling the promise*]. (L, TA.)

فُجَافِجٌ: see the next preceding paragraph.

أَفَجُّ A man *having his legs wide apart; who straddles;* (Ṣ,* O,* L, Ḳ,* TA;) as also ▾ مُفِجٌّ السَّاقَيْنِ; (L, TA;) [and ▾ مُفَاجٌّ, for] one says يَمْشِى مُفَاجًّا *he walks with his legs wide apart*, or *straddling:* (Ṣ, A, Ḳ:) or أَفَجُّ signifies *having his thighs wide apart.* (IAạr, TA.) — And قَوْسٌ فَجَّآءُ *A bow of which the curved ends are elevated so that its string is distant from the part where it is grasped by the hand:* (L:) or *of which the string is distant from its* كَبِد [q. v.]; (Ṣ, O, Ḳ;) as also ▾ مُنْفَجَّةٌ: (A, O, Ḳ:) and so قَوْسٌ فَجْوَآءُ. (Ṣ, O.)

إِفْجِيجٌ *A valley:* (O, Ḳ:) or *a wide valley:* (Ḳ:) or *a narrow and deep valley*, (IDrd, O, Ḳ,) in the dial. of the people of El-Yemen, but others apply this appellation to any valley. (O.)

مُفِجُّ السَّاقَيْنِ: see أَفَجُّ. — حَافِرٌ مُفِجٌّ *A solid hoof that is round like a cupola*, syn. مُقَبَّبٌ, (Ṣ, O, Ḳ, TA,) [and] *hard:* (TA:) such is approved. (Ṣ, O.)

مُفَاجٌّ: see أَفَجُّ.

مُنْفَجَّةٌ: see أَفَجُّ. — أَرْضٌ مُنْفَجَّةٌ, and قَوْسٌ مُنْفَجَّةٌ: see *Ground, or earth, that is cleft* [app. with the plough, *in a manner not approved:* see 1, near the end]. (TA.)

فجأ

1. فَجِئَهُ, (Ṣ, Mgh, O, Mṣb, Ḳ,) and فَجَأَهُ, (Ṣ, O, Mṣb, K,) the former of which is the more chaste, (TA,) aor. ـَ, (Mgh, Mṣb, Ḳ,) inf. n. ▾ فُجَآءَةٌ, (Ṣ, O, Ḳ,) or this is a simple subst., (Mṣb,) and فَجْءٌ, (Ḳ, TA,) or ▾ فَجْأَةٌ, (so accord. to the CḲ, and Ḥam p. 44,) or this last also is a simple subst.; (Mṣb;) and ▾ فَاجَأَهُ, (Ṣ, Mgh, O, Mṣb, Ḳ,) inf. n. مُفَاجَأَةٌ (Ṣ, O, Mṣb) and فِجَآءٌ; (Ṣ, O;) and ▾ افتجأه; (Ḳ;) *It* (an affair, or event, Ṣ, O, Mṣb) *came upon him*, or *happened to him, suddenly*, or *at unawares*, (Mgh, Ḳ, TA,) *unexpectedly*, (Mgh,) *without his having knowledge of it*, (Mgh, TA,) or *without any precious cause;* (TA;) or *hastily;* syn. عَاجَلَهُ: (Mṣb:) [*it surprised him;* or *took him by surprise:*] and [in like manner] one says, فَجِئْتُ الرَّجُلَ, and فَاجَأْتُهُ, meaning *I came upon the man suddenly*, or *at unawares.* (Mṣb.) — And فَجَأَ المَرْأَةَ, (O, Ḳ,) aor. ـَ, inf. n. فَجْءٌ, (TA,) *He compressed the woman.* (O, Ḳ.*) — فَجِئَتِ النَّاقَةُ, (IAmb, O, Ḳ,) aor. ـَ, (Ḳ,) inf. n. فَجَأً, (IAmb, O,) *The she-camel became big in her belly.* (IAmb, O, Ḳ.) — And فَجَأَ is said in the A to be syn. with زَادَ [*It increased*, &c.]. (TA.)

3: see above, first sentence. — [Hence,] فُوجِئَ *He was taken away by a sudden death; he died suddenly.* (Ṣ in art. فوت.)

4. افجأ *He found*, or *lighted on*, [or *surprised*,] his friend *doing a disgraceful thing.* (IAạr, TA.)

8: see 1, first sentence.

فَجْأَةٌ: see 1, first sentence: — and see also what here follows.

فُجَآءَةٌ: see 1, first sentence. — Also *A sudden*, or *an unexpected, event; a thing that comes upon one suddenly*, or *at unawares.* (Ḳ, TA.) Hence, مَوْتُ الفُجَآءَةِ [*Sudden death*]: written by some ▾ الفَجْأَةِ, as an inf. n. of unity. (TA.)

المُفَاجِئُ *The lion.* (Ṣgh, in his tract on the names of the lion; and Ḳ.)

فجر

1. فَجَرَ, aor. ـُ, (T, L, Mṣb,) inf. n. فَجْرٌ, (T, Mgh, L, Mṣb,) *He clave*, [a thing]; *cut*, or *divided*, [it] *lengthwise:* this is the primary signification, whence several others, to be mentioned below, are derived: (T, L:) *he clave, and opened.* (Mgh.) *He clave*, or *cut, a subterranean channel for water.* (Mṣb.) *He broke open* a dam of a river or the like, *that the water might break, burst*, or *pour, through.* (T, L.) — And فَجَرَ المَآءَ, (Ṣ, Mgh, O, Mṣb, Ḳ,) aor. and inf. n. as above; (Ṣ, O;) and ▾ فَجَّرَهُ, (Ṣ, O, Ḳ,) inf. n. تَفْجِيرٌ; (O, TA;) but the latter is with teshdeed to denote muchness, or frequency, or repetition, of the action, or its application to many objects; (Ṣ, O, TA;) *He opened a way, passage, vent, or channel, for the water to flow forth; gave vent to it; vented it:* (Ṣ, Mgh, O, Mṣb:) *he made the water to flow, run, or stream:* (Ḳ:) and in like manner, blood, or other fluid. (TA.) [See also 4.] — فَجَرَ, aor. ـُ, inf. n. فُجُورٌ, (Ṣ, O, Mṣb, Ḳ, &c.,) *He*, or *it, inclined; leant; declined;* or *deviated.* (Ṣ, O, TA.) You say, فَجَرَ الرَّاكِبُ, (Ḳ,) aor. as above, (TA,) and so the inf. n., (Ḳ,) ‡ *The rider leant*, or *declined, from his saddle.* (Ḳ.) — [Hence,] *He declined*, or *deviated, from the truth;* (Ḳ,* TA;) as also ▾ افجر. (IAạr, O, Ḳ.) — And *He erred in answering*, or *replying.* (El-Muärrij.) — Hence also, (Ṣ,) *He lied;* (Ṣ, O, Mṣb, Ḳ;) said of a swearer; (Mṣb;) as also ▾ افجر: (IAạr, O, Ḳ:) in this sense the former has also فَجْرٌ for an inf. n., as well as فُجُورٌ: (TA:) *he committed a foul deed; such as swearing a false oath*, or *lying;* in which sense also it has both of these inf. ns. (TA.) — *He committed an unlawful action:* (ISh:) [or, as it is generally explained, and most frequently used,] *he acted vitiously, immorally, unrighteously, sinfully*, or *wickedly; he transgressed; went forth from, departed from*, or *quitted, the way of truth*, or *the right way; forsook, relinquished*, or *neglected, the command of God; departed from obedience; disobeyed;* syn. فَسَقَ; (Ṣ, Mgh, O, Mṣb, Ḳ;) and عَصَى (Mgh, Ḳ) and خَالَفَ: (Ḳ:) and [in like manner] ▾ فاجر, inf. n. مُفَاجَرَةٌ and فِجَارٌ, *he did that which was vitious, immoral, unrighteous, sinful*, or *wicked.* (R, TA.) In the sense of عصى (Mgh, O, TA) and خالف (O, TA) it is also trans.: you say فَجَرَهُ, meaning *He disobeyed him;* (Mgh, O, TA;) *he opposed him.* (O, TA.) — *He launched forth into acts of disobedience;* in which sense it has both of the inf. ns. mentioned above; (Ḳ, TA;) and is [said to be] from فَجَرَ in the first of the significations expl. above. (TA.) — *He disbelieved;* syn. كَفَرَ; (TA;) as also ▾ افجر. (IAạr, O, Ḳ:) and فَجَرَ بِهِ *he disbelieved in it;* syn. كَذَّبَ. (O, Ḳ.*) The following passage of the Ḳur, بَلْ يُرِيدُ الْإِنْسَانُ لِيَفْجُرَ أَمَامَهُ, [lxxv. 5], is said to mean, [*But man desireth*, or *nay, doth man desire*,] *to disbelieve in that which is before him*, [or *that which is to come*,] namely, the resurrection and reckoning and retribution: (O, TA:) or *to continue in his* فُجُور [i. e. *vice, immorality, wickedness, unrighteousness*, or *the like*,] *in the time to come:* (Bḍ:) or *to go on therein undeviatingly:* (El-Ḥasan El-Baṣree, O:) or *to defer repentance, and to do evil deeds first:* (O, TA:) or *to multiply sins, and to postpone repentance:* or *to say I will repent at a future time.* (TA.) — *He did*, or *committed, an action inducing doubt*, or *suspicion* or *evil opinion*, or *doubt combined with suspicion* or *evil opinion.* (IḲṭṭ, TA.) — *He committed adultery*, or *fornication;* (Mṣb, Ḳ;) in which sense it has both of the inf. ns. mentioned above; (Ḳ;) and ▾ افجر signifies the same; (IAạr, Ḳ;) and, this latter, *he committed an act*, or *acts, of disobedience with his genital member.* (IAạr, TA.) You say فَجَرَ بِالمَرْأَةِ *He committed adultery*, or *fornication, with the woman:* and فَجَرَتِ المَرْأَةُ *The woman committed adultery*, or *fornication.* (TA.) — *He pursued a headlong*, or *rash*, or *random, course, and went away, not caring whither.* (El-Muärrij.) — فَجَرَ أَمْرُهُمْ

Their case, or *state of affairs, became bad.* (Ḳ.) — And فَجَرَ signifies also *He became dim,* or *dull, in his sight.* (O, Ḳ.) — And فَجَرَ مِنْ مَرَضِهِ *He became free from his disease.* (O, Ḳ.)

2. فَجَّرَهُ: see 1, near the beginning. — Also *He attributed* or *imputed to him,* or *charged him with,* or *accused him of,* فُجُور [i. e. *vice, immorality, unrighteousness, &c.* (see 1)]; like فَسَّقَهُ: whence the phrase, in a trad. of Ibn-Ez-Zubeyr, فَجَّرْتَ بِنَفْسِكَ [*Thou hast attributed to thyself,* or *accused thyself of, unrighteousness, transgression,* or *the like*]. (TA.)

3. فاجر, inf. n. مُفَاجَرَةٌ and فِجَارٌ: see 1, in the middle of the paragraph. [And see also فِجَارٌ, below.]

4. افجرهُ *He made it* (i. e. a spring, or source,) *to well forth.* (O, Ḳ.) [See also 1.] — And [hence, app.,] † *He made* [his gift] *large;* syn. أَجْزَلَ. (Ibn-'Abbád, O.) — افجر as intrans.: see 1, in four places. — Also افجرهُ *He found him to be a person such as is termed* فَاجِر. (O, Ḳ.) — And افجر is like اصبح; (Ṣ, O;) signifying *He entered upon the time of daybreak,* or *dawn:* (Ḳ, TA:) and *he was near to entering upon that time.* (TA.) One says, كُنْتُ أَحُلُّ إِذَا أَسْحَرْتُ وَأَرْحَلُ إِذَا أَفْجَرْتُ [*I used to alight when I entered upon the last sixth of the night, and depart when I entered upon the time of daybreak*]. (Ṣ, TA.) And أُعَرِّسُ إِذَا أَفْجَرْتُ وَأَرْحَلُ إِذَا أَسْفَرْتُ, i. e., *I alight to sleep when I am near to entering upon the time of daybreak, and I depart when* [*I enter upon the time in which*] *the dawn shines.* (TA, from a trad.) — Also *He brought much property;* (O, Ḳ;) this being termed فَجْرٌ. (O.)

5: see the next paragraph, in four places.

7. انفجر (Ṣ, O, Mṣb, Ḳ) and ↓تفجّر, (Ṣ, O, Ḳ,) but the latter is with teshdeed [as quasi-pass. of 2,] to denote muchness, or frequency, or repetition, or application to many subjects of the action, (Ṣ, O,*) *It* (water) *had a way, passage, vent,* or *channel, opened for it to flow forth; it had vent;* (Ṣ, O, Mṣb;) *it poured out,* or *forth, as though impelled* or *propelled;* syn. إِنْبَعَثَ; (TA;) *it flowed, ran,* or *streamed.* (Mṣb, Ḳ.) — [Hence,] انفجر عَلَيْهِمُ العَدُوُّ ‡ *The enemy* [*poured upon them;*] *came upon them suddenly, in great number.* (L, A.) And انفجرت عَلَيْهِمُ الدَّوَاهِى ‡ *Calamities* [*poured upon them;*] *came upon them from every quarter,* (Ḳ,* TA,) *abundantly and suddenly.* (TA.) — [Hence also,] انفجر بِالكَرَمِ, and ↓تفجّر بِهِ, † [*He was profuse of generosity,* or *liberality*]: (Ḳ:) and ↓تفجّر فِى الخَيْرِ † [*he was profuse in bounty,* or *beneficence*]. (Ṣ, O, TA.) — And انفجر الصُّبْحُ, and ↓تفجّر, [*The dawn broke forth*]: and انفجر عَنْهُ اللَّيْلُ [*The night departed from before it;* namely, the rising dawn]. (Ḳ.)

8. افتجر فِى الكَلَامِ *He forged speech, not having heard it from any one, nor learned it.* (O, Ḳ.)

فَجْرٌ [*Daybreak; dawn;*] the *light of morning;* (Mgh, Ḳ;) because it is a cleaving of the darkness from before the light; (Mgh;) i. e., the *redness of the sun in the darkness of night;* (Ḳ;) the فَجْر in the end of the night is like the شَفَق in the beginning thereof: (Ṣ, O:) it is twofold: the first is called الفَجْرُ الكَاذِبُ [*the false dawn*]; *that which rises without extending laterally,* (المُسْتَطِيلُ, Mgh, Mṣb,) *which appears black, presenting itself like an obstacle* (مُعْتَرِضًا) [*on the horizon*]: (Mṣb:) [see ذَنَبُ السِّرْحَانِ, in art. سرح:] the second is called الفَجْرُ الصَّادِقُ [*the true dawn*]; which is *the rising and spreading* [*dawn*], (المُسْتَطِيرُ, Mgh, Mṣb,) *which appears rising, and fills the horizon with its whiteness;* and this is what is called عَمُودُ الصُّبْحِ; *rising after the former has disappeared; and by its rising the day commences, and everything by which fasting would be broken becomes unlawful to the faster.* (Mṣb.) — Hence, The *time of the* فَجْر. (Mgh.) — And The *prayer of that time:* the prefixed noun being suppressed. (Mgh.) — الفَجْرُ and البَحْرُ [in a saying mentioned voce بَحْرٌ, the former here written الفَجَرُ, and said to be مُحَرَّكَة, but app. by mistake, for it is afterwards written الفَجْرُ,] are metonymically applied to ‡ *The troubles of the present state of existence.* (TA.)

فَجْرٌ † *Donation;* (Ḳ;) *generosity;* (AO, Ṣ, Ḳ;) *bounty,* or *munificence;* (Ḳ;) or *large,* or *ample, bounty* or *munificence;* (AO, TA;) and *goodness,* or *beneficence.* (Ḳ.) — And *Property.* (Kr, Ḳ.) And *Much property.* (O.) And *Abundance* of property. (Ḳ, TA.) Aboo-Miḥjen Eth-Thakafee says,

فَقَدْ أَجُودُ وَمَا مَالِى بِذِى فَجَرِ *

[*And verily,* or *often, I practise liberality,* or *bounty, while my property is not abundant*]. (TA.)

فَجَرٌ: see فَاجِرٌ, latter half.

فَجَارِ is a proper name, [i. e. an attributive proper name,] imperfectly decl., like بَرَّةُ; [and signifies the same as الفَجْرَةُ and فَجَارِ;] and ↓فَجَارِ is altered from فَجْرَة, (IJ, TA,) or from الفَجْرَةُ, (Sb, TA,) and is a subst. in the sense of الفُجُورُ [i. e. *Vice, immorality, wickedness, unrighteousness, sin,* or *transgression,* &c., (see 1,)] (Ṣ,) or a name for الفَجْرَةُ [which signifies the same], (O,) like قَطَامِ, (Ṣ, O,) determinate, (Ṣ,) occurring in a verse of En-Nábighah cited in the first paragraph of art. حمل. (Ṣ, O.) One says, رَكِبَ فُلَانٌ فَجْرَةَ, (Ḳ,* TA, [in the CḲ فَجْرَةً,]) and ↓فَجَارِ, (TA,) *Such a one lied;* (Ḳ, TA;) and *acted vitiously* &c. (فَجَرَ). (TA.) And حَلَفَ فُلَانٌ عَلَى فَجْرَةٍ, and اِشْتَمَلَ عَلَى فَجْرَةٍ, [in the L على فجرهِ, in both instances, but the former is the right reading,] *Such a one commited a foul deed, by swearing falsely,* [relating to the former phrase,] or *by adultery,* or *fornication,* or *lying.* (TA.)

فُجْرَةٌ: see مَفْجَرٌ, in two places.

فُجْرَةٌ The *last of a woman's children;* like as زِنْيَةٌ signifies the "last of a man's children." (TA in art. زنى.)

فَجَارِ: see فَجْرَةٌ, in two places: — and see فَاجِرٌ, last sentence but one.

فِجَارٌ [a pl. of which the sing. is not mentioned] *Roads,* or *ways;* (Ḳ, TA;) like فِجَاجٌ [pl. of فَجٌّ, q. v.]. (TA.) — أَيَّامُ الفِجَارِ is an appellation applied to *Four* أَفْجِرَة; (Ḳ, TA;) the four أَفْجِرَة meaning *days* [i. e. *conflicts*] *of the Arabs;* the single day thereof being termed الفِجَارُ: (Ṣ, O, TA:) they took place at 'Okádh; and those engaged therein transgressed, and held to be allowable everything that should be sacred; as is said in the A: they were called فِجَارُ الرَّجُلِ and فِجَارُ القِرْدِ and فِجَارُ المَرْأَةِ and فِجَارُ البَرَّاضِ; the last, which was the greatest onslaught, being thus called in relation to El-Barráḍ Ibn-Ḳeys, who slew 'Orweh Er-Raḥḥál: (TA:) they were between Ḳureysh with their associates of Kinánch on the one side and Ḳeys-'Eylán on the other side, (Ṣ, O, Ḳ,) in the Time of Ignorance; (Ṣ, O;) and the [final] defeat befell Ḳeys; it occurred in the sacred months; and when they fought therein, they said قَدْ فَجَرْنَا; (Ṣ, O, Ḳ;) therefore Ḳureysh called this war فِجَارٌ; (Ṣ, O, TA;*) فِجَارٌ, like مُفَاجَرَةٌ, being an inf. n. of فَاجَرَ, expl. above, on the authority of the R. (TA.) — And فِجَارَاتُ العَرَبِ signifies *The vyings of the Arabs in glorying,* or *boasting.* (TA.)

فُجُورٌ: see the paragraph here following.

فَاجِرٌ *Inclining, leaning, declining,* or *deviating.* (Ṣ, TA.) *Declining* (سَاقِطٌ) *from the road.* (IAar, TA.) — *Lying; a liar;* because he deviates from the right course: and for the same reason it signifies also مُكَذِّبٌ [as meaning *disbelieving;* or *a disbeliever;* see فَجَرَ بِهِ, in the middle of the first paragraph]. (TA.) And one says يَمِينٌ فَاجِرَةٌ meaning ‡ *A false oath:* (Mgh in art. غمس:) a tropical phrase. (Mgh in the present art.) — فَاجِرٌ and ↓فَجُورٌ, (Ḳ, TA,) the latter of which is applied to a woman as well as to a man, (TA,) and ↓فَاجُورٌ, (Ḳ, TA,) which is mentioned by Ṣgh, (TA,) are all epithets from فَجَرَ, and signify [most frequently *Acting vitiously, immorally, unrighteously, sinfully,* or *wickedly;* or *vitious, immoral,* &c.; *transgressing,* or *a transgressor; quitting,* or *one who quits, the way of truth,* or *justice; forsaking,* or *a forsaker of, the command of God; departing,* or *a departer, from the right way,* or *from obedience; disobedient;* or] *launching forth,* or *one who launches forth, into acts of disobedience:* [but the second and third are intensive epithets:] also *committing adultery* or *fornication;* or *an adulterer* or *a fornicator:* (Ḳ, TA:) and the first signifies also *enchanting,* or *an enchanter:* (Ṣgh, Ḳ, TA:) the pl. of the first is فُجَّارٌ and فَجَرَةٌ; and the pl. of the second and third is فُجَرُ. (Ḳ, TA.) ▼ فُجَرُ is altered from فَاجِرٌ, for the sake of intensiveness, and is [determinate, and] seldom used except in the vocative form of speech: you say [in addressing a number of men] يَا لَفُجَرِ [for يَا آلَ فُجَرَ, like as you say يَا لَغُدَرَ for يَا آلَ غُدَرَ, q. v.; and meaning *O ye very vitious*, &c.]; occurring in a trad. of 'Áïsheh. (TA.) And ▼ فَجَارِ, (Ḳ, TA,) like قَطَامِ, (TA,) is a noun altered from الفَاجِرَةُ (Ḳ, TA) [or from فَاجِرَةٌ]: you say (Ṣ, O, Ḳ) to a woman (Ṣ, O) يَا فَجَارِ (Ṣ, O, Ḳ) meaning يَا فَاجِرَةُ [*O vitious woman, &c.*]. (Ṣ, O.) ═ And فَاجِرٌ signifies also *Having much wealth*, or *property*: (Ḳ, TA:) in this sense, a possessive epithet [from فَجْرٌ, q. v.]. (TA.)

فَاجُورٌ: see the next preceding paragraph.

مَفْجَرٌ (TA) and ▼ مَفْجَرَةٌ and ▼ مُنْفَجَرٌ (Ḳ) and ▼ فُجْرَةٌ (Ṣ, Ḳ) *A place through which water flows* (Ḳ, TA) *from a watering-trough &c.*; (TA;) *a place of opening for water*: (Ṣ, O, TA:) and the second signifies also *low ground into which valleys pour their water*: (M, Ḳ, TA:) pl. مَفَاجِرُ. (TA.) مَفَاجِرُ الوَادِى signifies *The parts, of the valley, into which the torrent disperses itself*: (Ṣ, O, TA:) and ▼ فُجْرَةُ الوَادِى, (Ḳ, TA,) which would seem to be with fet-ḥ [to the ف] from its not being restricted by the mention of any syll. signs, [and is so in the CḲ,] but is correctly with ḍamm, (TA,) *the wide part of the valley, into which the water pours*. (Ḳ, TA.) And مَفَاجِرُ الدِّبَارِ signifies *The places opened for the flowing of the water of the* دبار, pl. of دَبْرَةٌ [q. v.]. (Mgh.)

مَفْجَرَةٌ: see the next preceding paragraph.

مُنْفَجَرٌ: see مَفْجَرٌ. — مُنْفَجَرُ رَمْلٍ ‡ *A road*, or *way, in sands*. (Ṣ, O, TA.)

فجس

1. فَجَسَ, aor. ِ, (Ṣ, TA,) inf. n. فَجْسٌ, (Ṣ, O, Ḳ, TA,) *He behaved proudly*, or *magnified himself*; (Ṣ, O, Ḳ, TA;) as also ▼ تفجّس; (Ṣ,* Ḳ;) or this latter signifies *he magnified*, or *exalted, himself*, (O, TA,) and *boasted*: (O,* TA:) and فَجْز signifies the same as فَجْسٌ, i. e. the "behaving proudly, or magnifying oneself." (TA.) — And *He overcame*, or *subdued*, or *oppressed*. (Ibn-'Abbád, O, Ḳ: but only the inf. n. of the verb in this and the following sense is mentioned.) — *He did an unprecedented act*, and only *one of an evil kind*. (Ibn-'Abbád, O, Ḳ, TA.)

4. افجس *He* (a man) *boasted vainly*, or *falsely*. (IAạr, O, Ḳ.)

5: see 1, first sentence. تفجّس السَّحَابُ بِالمَطَرِ *The clouds burst with rain*: (L, TA:) [app. a dial. var. of تبجّس.]

فجع

1. فَجَعَهُ, (Ṣ, MA, O, Ḳ,) aor. َ, (O, Ḳ,) inf. n. فَجْعٌ (MA, O) and فَجِيعَةٌ; (MA; [or this is a simple subst.;]) and ▼ فجّعهُ, inf. n. تَفْجِيعٌ, (Ṣ, Ḳ,) or the latter verb has an intensive meaning; (O, TA;) *It pained him*; (Ṣ, MA, O, Ḳ;) *afflicted*, or *distressed, him*; *disordered him*, or *rendered him diseased*: (MA:) one says, فَجَعَتْهُ المُصِيبَةُ *The affliction, calamity*, or *misfortune, pained him*: (Ṣ, O:) or فَجْعٌ [expl. as the inf. n. of the pass. verb] signifies a man's *being pained by the loss of a thing that is highly esteemed by him* (يَكْرُمُ عَلَيْهِ); (Lth, O, Ḳ, TA;) such as property or cattle, and offspring, and a relation, or person beloved: (TA:) you say, فُجِعَ بِمَالِهِ (Lth, O, Ḳ) and بِوَلَدِهِ (Lth, O) [*He was pained by the loss of his property or cattle, and his offspring*]: and فَجَعْتُهُ فِى مَالِهِ and أَهْلِهِ [*I pained, afflicted*, or *distressed, him, in*, or *in respect of, his property* or *cattle, and his family*], aor. َ, inf. n. فَجْعٌ. (Mṣb.)

2: see the preceding paragraph.

5. تفجّع *He* (a man, Ṣ, O) *expressed*, or *manifested, pain, affliction*, or *distress*; or *uttered lamentation*, or *complaint*; syn. تَوَجَّعَ; (Ṣ, O, Ḳ, TA;) لَهُ [*by reason of it*]; (Ṣ;) or لِلْمُصِيبَةِ [*by reason of the calamity*, or *misfortune*; (O, Ḳ, TA;) and *writhed*, or *cried out and writhed*; *by reason of it*. (TA.)

فَجُوعٌ: see فَاجِعٌ, in two places.

فَجِيعٌ: see مَفْجُوعٌ.

فَجِيعَةٌ, (Ṣ, O, Mṣb, Ḳ, TA,) of which the pl. is فَجَائِعُ, (Mṣb, TA,) i. q. رَزِيَّةٌ [i. e. *An affliction, a calamity*, or *a misfortune*; or *such as is occasioned by the loss of things dear to one*: or *a great affliction* or *calamity* or *misfortune*]: (Ṣ, O, Mṣb, Ḳ, TA:) accord. to ISd, *such as pains by* [*the loss of*] *what is highly esteemed*: (TA:) and ▼ فَاجِعَةٌ signifies the same; (Ṣ,* O,* Mṣb, Ḳ;*) pl. فَوَاجِعُ. (O, Mṣb.)

مَوْتٌ فَاجِعٌ and ▼ فَجُوعٌ *Death that pains* [or *afflicts* or *distresses*] *men by* [*attendant*] *calamities*: (O, Ḳ, TA:) and in like manner, دَهْرٌ فَاجِعٌ (O, TA) and ▼ فَجُوعٌ [*time*, or *fortune, that pains* &c.]. (TA.) And مَيِّتٌ فَاجِعٌ [*A person dead*, or *dying, that causes pain* or *affliction* or *distress*], and [likewise] ▼ مفجع [app. مُفْجِعٌ], as being from أَفْجَعَ, though this [is a verb which] has not been used: thus in the L. (TA.) — [Hence,] غُرَابُ الفَاجِعُ *The raven of separation* or *disunion* (غُرَابُ البَيْنِ); (O, Ḳ, TA;) so called because [they assert that] it pains [or afflicts] men by separation or disunion: (O, TA:) an epithet in which the quality of a subst. predominates. (TA.) — And one says اِمْرَأَةٌ فَاجِعٌ, (O, Ḳ,) mentioned, but not expl., by IDrd, as though he regarded it [i. e. the latter word] as [a possessive epithet, i. e.] of the same class as تَامِرٌ and لَابِنٌ, (O,) meaning *A woman having* [or *suffering*] *a* فَجِيعَة [q. v.], (O, Ḳ,) i. e. *a* رَزِيَّة. (Ḳ.) And رَجُلٌ فَاجِعٌ and ▼ مُتَفَجِّعٌ *A man grieving*, or *lamenting*, [and] *doing so most intensely*. (TA.)

فَاجِعَةٌ [as a subst.]: see فَجِيعَةٌ.

أَفْجَعُ [*More, and most, pain-giving* or *afflicting* or *distressing*]. (O, TA.)

مفجع [app. مُفْجِعٌ]: see فَاجِعٌ.

مُفَجَّعٌ: see what next follows.

مَفْجُوعٌ A man [*pained, afflicted*, or *distressed*; or] *smitten by an affliction such as is termed* رَزِيَّة [*and* فَجِيعَة, q. v.]; as also ▼ فَجِيعٌ, and [in an intensive sense] ▼ مُفَجَّعٌ. (TA.) You say, هُوَ مَفْجُوعٌ فِى مَالِهِ and أَهْلِهِ [*He is pained*, &c., *in*, or *in respect of, his property*, or *cattle*, and *his family*]. (Mṣb.)

مُتَفَجِّعٌ: see فَاجِعٌ, last sentence.

فجل

1. فَجَلَ, aor. ُ, inf. n. فَجْلٌ; (Mṣb, Ḳ;) and فَجِلَ, (O,) or فَجُلَ, (Ḳ,) aor. َ, (O, Ḳ,) inf. n. فَجَلٌ; (Ḳ;) *He*, or *it, was*, or *became, thick, and soft*, or *flaccid*: (O, Mṣb, Ḳ:) so says Ibn-'Abbád. (O.)

2. فجّلهُ, inf. n. تَفْجِيلٌ, *He made it broad*, or *wide*. (Ḳ.)

8. افتجل أَمْرًا, (Ḳ,) or أَمْرَهُ, (Ibn-'Abbád, O,) *He forged* [*a case or matter* &c., or *his case* &c.]; syn. اِخْتَلَقَهُ; (Ibn-'Abbád, O, Ḳ;) and *invented it*, or *excogitated it*; syn. اِخْتَرَعَهُ. (Ibn-'Abbád, O.)

فُجْلٌ (Ṣ, O, Ḳ) and ▼ فُجُلٌ, (O, Ḳ,) both mentioned by AḤn, (O, TA,) or ▼ فِجْلٌ, (Mṣb,) thus, with kesr, commonly pronounced by the vulgar, (TA,) [The *radish*, *raphanus sativus*; (Forskål's Flora Ægypt. Arab., lxix. no. 327; and Delile's Floræ Ægypt. Illustr., no. 608;)] *a certain* أُرُومَة [or *root of the kind termed rhizoma*], (Ḳ, TA,) *that occasions abominable eructation*; (TA;) *a herb*, (Mṣb,) *well known*: (Ṣ, Mṣb:) said by IDrd to be not a genuine Arabic word; and thought by him to be derived from فَجَلَ signifying as expl. above: (Mṣb:) n. un. with ة, (Ḳ,) i. e. فُجْلَةٌ (Ṣ, O) and فُجُلَةٌ (O) [and فِجْلَةٌ]: *it is a garden-plant, found in abundance; and there is a Syrian sort, said to be produced by putting together the seeds of the colza and* [*those of*] *the* فجل: (TA:) *it* (i. e. *each sort*, TA) *is good for pain of the joints, and jaundice*, (Ḳ, TA,) *and sciatica, and the* نِقْرِس [i. e. *gout*, or specially *in the foot* or *feet*], (TA,) *and pain of the liver* (Ḳ, TA) *arising from cold*, (TA,) *and the biting and stinging of vipers and scorpions*: (Ḳ, TA: [several other supposed properties thereof mentioned in the Ḳ, and many more mentioned in the TA, I omit as unimportant:]) *what is most potent thereof is its seed; then, its peel; then, its leaf; then, its flesh*. (Ḳ, TA.) What is called حَبُّ الفُجْلِ is *Another remedial thing:* (Ḳ:) this فجل is *not of the species of herb mentioned above:* (O, Mṣb, TA:) so says AḤn: the ḥakeem Dáwood says, *it is one of the species of this* فجل, *a wild species, elongated, abounding in the Ṣa'eed of Egypt:* (TA:) [it is the *raphanus oleifer*, mentioned by Delile (Floræ Ægypt. Illustr., no. 609,) as cultivated in Nubia and in Egypt, and called in Arabic "symâgah:"] *from it* (or *from its seed*, TA) *is made the oil of the* فجل (دُهْنُ الفُجْلِ); (Mṣb, Ḳ, TA;) and it is known by the appellation of الشَّيْمَعَة [correctly الشَّيْمَغَة]. (TA.) [Delile, ubi suprà, no. 571, mentions فُجْل الجَمَل, as a name of The *cakile maritima* of Tournefort; the *bunias cakile* of Linn.: and in the same, no. 396, he mentions فُجْل الجَبَل as the Arabic name of The *rumex spinosus* of Linn.; as does also Forskål, in his work cited above, p. lxv., no. 213, and again in p. 76.]

فِجْلٌ: } see the next preceding paragraph.
فُجُلٌ:

فَجَّالٌ *A seller of* فُجْل [or *radishes*]. (TA.)

فَاجِلٌ *i. q.* قَامِرٌ [*Playing*, or *a player, at a game of hazard*]: (O, Ḳ, TA:) so says IAạr: (O, TA:) accord. to some copies of the Ḳ, *i. q.* فَاجِر, which is a mistake. (TA.)

فَنْجَلٌ: see أَفْجَلُ.

فَنْجَلَةٌ (Ṣ, Ḳ) and ▼ فَنْجَلَى (Ḳ) *A manner of walking in which is a laxness*, or *slackness*, (Ṣ, Ḳ,) *like that of the old man.* (Ṣ.)

فَنْجَلَى: see what next precedes.

فَيْجَلٌ: see فَيْجَنٌ, in art. فجن.

أَفْجَلُ and ▼ فَنْجَلٌ [A man] *having a wide space between the feet* (Ḳ, TA) *and the shanks.* (TA.)

فجن

4. افجن *He* (a man, TA) *kept constantly to the eating of* فَيْجَن [i. e. *rue*]. (Ḳ, TA.)

فَيْجَنٌ [Πήγανον; i.e. *rue*;] *i. q.* سَذَابٌ; (Ṣ, Ḳ;) as also ▼ فَيْجِين: (T in art. خفت, and TA in art. خنف:) and so فَيْجَلٌ: (TA:) IDrd [rightly] says, "I do not think it to be a genuine Arabic word." (TA.)

فَيْجِين: see the next preceding paragraph.

فجو

1. فَجَا بَابَهُ, (Ḳ,) [aor. يَفْجُو,] inf. n. فَجْوٌ, (TA,) *He opened his door.* (Ḳ.) — And فَجَا القَوْسَ, (Ṣ, Ḳ,) inf. n. as above, (Ṣ,) *He raised the string of the bow* [or *made it distant*] *from the part called its* كَبِد: (Ṣ, Ḳ:) and so فَجَّهَا. (Ṣ and Ḳ in art. فج.) — And مَا بَيْنَ رِجْلَيْهِ فَجَا, or فَجَا رِجْلَيْهِ, *He parted his legs wide*, or *straddled*; or *did so to make water:* and so فَجَّ. (TA in art. فج.) ═ فَجِيَتْ, (Ṣ, Ḳ, TA, [in the CḲ, and in one of my copies of the Ṣ, erroneously, فَجِئَتْ,]) aor. تَفْجَى, inf. n. فَجًا, (Ṣ, TA,) *The bow had its string raised* [or *distant*] *from the part called its* كَبِد; (Ṣ, Ḳ;) and so ▼ اِنْفَجَتْ. (ISd, TA.) — And فَجِىَ, [in the CḲ, erroneously, فَجِئَ,] aor. as above, (Ḳ, TA,) and so the inf. n., i. e. فَجًا, (Ḳ,* TA,) *He* (a man, TA) *was wide between the thighs*, or *between the knees*, or *between the shanks.* (Ḳ, TA.) [And it is implied in the Ṣ* and Ḳ that it is also said of a camel, meaning *He was wide between the hocks.*] — And فَجِيَتْ said of a she-camel, inf. n. فَجًا, *She was*, or *became, large in the belly:* (Ḳ, TA:) mentioned by ISd, but with an expression of uncertainty as to its correctness. (TA.)

2. فَجَّى, (TA,) inf. n. تَفْجِيَةٌ, (Ḳ, TA,) *He removed; put away*, or *at a distance;* (Ḳ,* TA;) and *pushed, thrust*, or *drove, away;* persons from others; (TA;) syn. of the inf. n. كَشْفٌ; and تَنْحِيَةٌ; (Ḳ, TA;) and دَفْعٌ. (TA.)

4. افجى *He expended amply*, or *largely, upon his family*, or *household.* (Az, Ḳ.) ═ And *He found his friend to be guilty of a vice*, or *a disgraceful*, or *shameful, action.* (Az, TA.)

6. تفاجى *It* (a thing) *had* [*an opening*, or *intermediate wide space, such as is termed*] *a* فَجْوَة. (Ṣ, TA.) [Comp. تَفَاجَّ, in art. فج.]

7. انفجى *It* (a door) *opened.* (Ḳ.) — See also 1.

فَجًا inf. n. of فَجِيَتْ [q. v.] said of a bow: (Ṣ, TA:) — and of فَجِىَ [q. v.] said of a man, (Ḳ,* TA,) or of a camel: (Ṣ,* Ḳ, TA:) — and of فَجِيَتْ [q. v.] said of a she-camel. (Ḳ, TA.)

فَجْوَةٌ *An opening*, or *intervening space*, (Ṣ, M, Mgh, Mṣb, Ḳ,) in a place, (M, TA,) and *an intermediate wide space*, (Ṣ, Mgh,) between two things. (Ṣ, Mgh, Mṣb, Ḳ.*) And *A wide tract* of land or ground; as also ▼ فَجْوَآء: (Ḳ:) or *a wide and depressed tract* thereof; and thus, accord. to Th, the word means in the Ḳur xviii. 16. (TA.) And The *court*, or *yard*, of a house. (Ṣ, Mṣb, Ḳ.) And The *part between the two sides of the solid hoof.* (ISd, Ḳ, TA.) The pl. is فَجَوَاتٌ (Mṣb, Ḳ, TA) and فِجَآءٌ. (Ḳ, TA. [To these pls. the CḲ strangely adds, as another, فَجًا.])

فَجْوَآء [as a subst.]: see the next preceding paragraph. [It is originally the fem. of the epithet أَفْجَى, q. v.]

فُجْوَةٌ: see the following paragraph.

أَفْجَى an epithet, of which the fem. is فَجْوَآء. (Ḳ, TA.) The latter, applied to a bow, *Having its string distant from the part called its* كَبِد; (Ṣ, Ḳ, TA;) as also ▼ فُجْوَةٌ; and so فَجَّآء [mentioned in art. فج]. (Er-Rághib, TA.) — And the former, (Ḳ, TA,) applied to a man, (TA,) *Wide between the thighs*, or *between the knees*, or *between the shanks:* or, applied to a camel, *wide between the hocks:* (Ḳ, TA:) or, accord. to Az, it signifies *having the thighs very wide apart.* (TA.) [Freytag adds "*Ventrosus*," applied to a camel, as from the Ḳ, in which I do not find it.]

[Accord. to the TA, some of the words of this art. have ى for the final radical; but for this distinction there is no reason.]

فح

1. فَحَّتِ الأَفْعَى, aor. ـُ and ـِ, (Ṣ, Ḳ,) the former dev. from a general rule, which requires the aor. of a verb of this class when intrans. to be with kesr only, (Ṣ,) inf. n. فَحِيحٌ (Ṣ, Ḳ) and فَحٌّ and تَفْحَاحٌ, (Ḳ,) [the last an intensive form,] *The viper* [*hissed*, or] *made a sound to proceed from its mouth:* (Ṣ, Ḳ, TA: [see a verse cited voce مِطْحَان:]) or what is meant by this verb is [*it made a sound by*] *the rubbing of one part of its skin against another part:* or (TA) its making a sound to proceed from its skin is termed كَشِيش, (Ṣ, TA,) or حَفِيف: (Aṣ, TA:) some use this verb (فحّت) in relation to any serpent: others, peculiarly in relation to the female of the [serpents called] أَسَاوِد. (TA.) [J gives here a list of intrans. verbs of this class which have the aor. with ḍamm, anomalously, and also with kesr; and a list of trans. verbs of the same class which have the aor. with kesr, anomalously, and also with ḍamm: but both lists are defective; and it would be difficult to make them complete.] — And فَحَّ, (L, Ḳ,) aor. ـِ, inf. n. فَحِيحٌ; (L;) and ▼ فَحْفَحَ; said of a man, † *He blew in his sleep*, (L, Ḳ,) *making a sound like the* فَحِيح *of the viper.* (IDrd.)

R. Q. 1. فَحْفَحَ: see the preceding paragraph. — Also, [inf. n. فَحْفَحَةٌ,] † *He* (a man, TA) *was*, or *became, affected with a hoarseness, roughness, harshness*, or *gruffness, in his voice.* (Ḳ.) [See also فَحْفَحَةٌ, below.] ═ And *He* (a man, TA) *was*, or *became, true and sincere in love*, or *affection.* (IAạr, Ḳ.)

فُحَّةٌ The *heat*, or *burning quality*, of pepper. (Ḳ.)

فُحَّحٌ *Vipers:* (L:) or *vipers in a state of excitement*, (هَائِجَةٌ [perhaps meaning *initum appetentes*], Ḳ, TA,) *made to come forth* [*from their lurking-places:* so called] from the sounds of their mouths. (TA.)

فَحِيحٌ an inf. n. of 1 [q. v.]. (Ṣ, Ḳ, &c.) [Freytag explains it as signifying also The *first braying of the young camel, which, by reason of its acuteness, is likened to the hissing of the serpent.*]

فَحْفَحَةٌ [inf. n. of فَحْفَحَ, q. v.] — Also The *voice's being reiterated in the throat*, or *fauces, resembling hoarseness, roughness, harshness*, or *gruffness.* (L.) — And *Speech*, or *talk.* (Kr, TA.) — فَحْفَحَةُ هُذَيْلٍ means *Hudheyl's pronunciation of* ح *as* ع: [a characteristic of the tribe of Hudheyl, or of some persons of that tribe,] mentioned by Es-Suyooṭee in the Mz and [by the same author in] the Iḳtiráḥ. (MF, TA.)

فَخْفَاخٌ A man (L) *having a hoarse, harsh,* or *gruff, voice.* (L, Ḳ.) — And A man *speaking,* or *talking:* or *talkative.* (TA.) — And الفَخْفَاخُ is the name of *A river in Paradise.* (Ṣ, Ḳ.)

فحث

1. فَحَثَ عَنْهُ, (O, Ḳ,) aor. ـَ, (TA,) inf. n. فَحْثٌ, (O, TA,) i. q. فَحَصَ [*He searched,* or *sought, for,* or *after, it; inquired,* or *sought information, respecting it; searched into, inquired into, investigated, scrutinized,* or *examined, it;* &c.]; (IDrd, O, Ḳ, TA;) namely, a thing; (IDrd, O;) or news, or a story; (TA;) as also ↓ افتحث. (O, Ḳ.)

8: see what immediately precedes.

فَحِثٌ (Ṣ, O, Ḳ) and ↓ فَحِثَةٌ (TA) The [*portion,* or *appertenance, called*] حَفِث (Ṣ, O, Ḳ) *of the stomach of a ruminant animal, also termed the* قِبَّة, *which has* أَطْبَاق: (Ṣ, O: [see more in art. حفث:]) pl. of the former أَفْحَاثٌ. (O, TA.) — And one says, مَلَأَ أَفْحَاثَهُ meaning *He filled his* جَوْف [i. e. *belly*]. (IF, O.)

فَحِثَةٌ: see the next preceding paragraph.

فحج

1. فَحِجَ فِى مِشْيَتِهِ, aor. ـَ, inf. n. فَحَجٌ, (Ṣ,) this is the form of the verb commonly known, like other verbs signifying faults, and that it is the correct form, and not فَحَجَ as it is written in the Ḳ [and O], is indicated by the forms of the inf. n. فَحَجٌ and the epithet أَفْحَجُ; (MF;) as also ↓ تفحّج, (Ṣ,) and ↓ فحّج, (Ḳ,) and ↓ افحج; (TA;) *He had the fore parts of his feet near together, and his heels wide apart,* [i. e. *he turned in his toes, and turned out his heels,*] *in his gait:* (Ṣ, Ḳ:) or ↓ فَحَجٌ signifies the *having the middle of the legs wide apart,* [or *having the legs bowed outwards,*] in a man, and in a beast (دَابَّة): (Mgh, L:) [or the *having the shanks wide apart:* (see فَلَجٌ:)] or the *having the thighs wide apart:* [see also 1 in art. فج:] and the verb is فَحِجَ, inf. n. فَحَجٌ and فحجة [thus written, app. فَحْجَةٌ, which is the inf. n. un.]; the latter inf. n. mentioned by Lḥ. (L.) — And فَحَجَ, (accord. to the Ḳ,) or فَحِجَ, (accord. to MF,) *He magnified himself,* or *behaved proudly.* (Ḳ.)

2: see the preceding paragraph: and see also 5.

4. افحج حَلُوبَتَهُ *He parted the hind legs of his milch camel;* i. e., *made an opening,* or *intervening space, between them;* (Ṣ, O, K;) *in order that he might milk her.* (Ṣ, O.) — افحج also signifies *He refrained,* or *desisted,* or *drew back;* syn. أَحْجَمَ. (O, Ḳ.) And one says, افحج عَنْهُ, meaning *He turned,* or *turned away* or *back, from it,* or *him;* syn. اِنْثَنَى. (O,* Ḳ.)

5. تَفَحُّجٌ signifies The *parting of one's legs,* or *making an opening between them,* (AA, Ṣ, O, Ḳ,) *when sitting;* as also ↓ تَفْحِيجٌ: like تَفَشُّجٌ and تَفْشِيجٌ. (AA, Ṣ, O.) And one says, تَتَفَحَّجُ سَاقَاهُ [*His shanks are parted*]. (Ṣ, O.) See also 1.

7: see the first paragraph.

فَحْجٌ The *mode of walking of him who is termed* أَفْحَجُ. (Ṣ, O.)

فَحَجٌ an inf. n.: (Ṣ, L, TA:) see 1.

أَفْحَجُ *Having the fore parts of the feet near together, and the heels wide apart:* (Ṣ, O, Ḳ:) or *having the middle of the legs wide apart:* (Mgh, L:) fem. فَحْجَآءُ: the former applied to a man [&c.]; and the latter, to a beast (دَابَّة) [&c.]: (Ṣ, Mgh, O, L:) or *having the thighs wide apart:* or *having the legs wide apart:* or *having curved,* or *bowed, legs.* (L.) [See also أَفَجُّ, in art. فج.]

فحس

1. فَحَسَ, aor. ـَ, inf. n. فَحْسٌ, *He took* a thing *from his hand, with his tongue and his mouth;* such as water &c.: (Lth, T, O, Ḳ:) or *he licked up* a thing *with his tongue, from his hand.* (O: but only the inf. n. is mentioned.) — And فَحَسَ السُّلْتَ, aor. as above, (O,) and so the inf. n., (O, Ḳ,) *He rubbed* [*the ears off*] *the* سلت, (O, Ḳ, TA,) a particular species of barley, (TA,) *so that the awn,* or *beard,* [*thereof*] *became removed* (O, Ḳ, TA) *and scattered.* (TA.)

4. افحس *He* (a man) *abraded by degrees,* lit., *thing after thing.* (TA.)

Q. Q. 2. تَفَيْحَسَ *He carried himself in an elegant and a proud and self-conceited manner, with an affected inclining of his body from side to side, in his gait:* (O, Ḳ:*) and so تَفَيْسَحَ. (O.)

فحش

1. فَحُشَ, aor. ـُ, inf. n. فُحْشٌ (Ṣ, O, Mṣb, Ḳ) and فَحَاشَةٌ, (TA,) *It* (a thing, or an affair, or anything, TA, or any evil thing, Ṣ) *was,* or *became, excessive, immoderate, enormous, exorbitant, beyond measure,* (Ṣ, O, TA,) or *overmuch;* (O, Ḳ, TA;) as also ↓ تفاحش: (Ṣ, TA:) *it* (a thing) *was* or *became, foul, evil, bad, abominable,* or *unseemly;* [*gross, immodest, lewd,* or *obscene;*] as also فَحَشَ, aor. ـُ: (Mṣb:) [or *excessively,* or *beyond measure, foul,* &c.: (see فَاحِشَةٌ:)] and ↓ تفاحش *it* (a thing, or an affair,) *increased by degrees* (تَزَايَدَ) *in foulness, evilness, badness,* &c. (A.) And فَحُشَتِ المَرْأَةُ *The woman became foul,* or *ugly, and old.* (IAạr.) — See also 4, in two places.

2: see 4, in two places.

3. فاحشهُ, (T in art. بذأ,) inf. n. مُفَاحَشَةٌ, (T and Ḳ in that art.,) [*He vied with him,* or *strove to surpass him, in foul, unseemly, gross,* or *obscene, speech* or *language:* and *he held such discourse with him:*] the inf. n. is syn. with مُبَاذَاةٌ. (T and Ḳ in that art.)

4. افحش, (Mṣb, Ḳ,) or افحش فِى المَنْطِقِ, (Ṣ,) or فِى الكَلَامِ, (Mgh,) or فِى كَلَامِهِ, (A,) inf. n. إِفْحَاشٌ and ↓ فُحْشٌ, accord. to Lḥ and Kr, but the latter is correctly a simple subst. [used as an inf. n. of this verb], (TA,) *He uttered* فُحْش, (Ṣ, A, Mgh, Mṣb, Ḳ,) i. e., *foul, evil, bad, abominable, unseemly,* [*gross, immodest, lewd,* or *obscene,*] *speech* or *language;* (Mgh, Mṣb;) as also ↓ فَحَشَ فى المنطق, (TA,) and ↓ فحّش فى الكلام, (Mgh,) or فى كلامه, (A,) and ↓ تفحّش فى كلامه: (Ṣ, A:) and ↓ تَفَاحَشَ also signifies the same; and *he manifested, discovered,* or *revealed,* or *he made a show of, such speech* or *language.* (O,* Ḳ,* TA.) You say, افحش عَلَيْهِ فِى المَنْطِقِ [*He uttered such speech or language against him*]; (Ṣ;) and in like manner, ↓ فَحَشَ, (TA,) and ↓ فحّش; (Mgh;) and ↓ تفحّش عَلَيْهِ بِلِسَانِهِ. (TA.) — Also افحش *He was,* or *became, niggardly, tenacious,* or *avaricious.* (Mṣb.)

5: see 4, in two places: — and see 10.

6: see 1, in two places: — and see 4.

10. استفحشهُ [*He deemed it foul, evil, bad, abominable, unseemly, immodest, lewd,* or *obscene:* or *excessively,* or *beyond measure, foul,* &c.]. (Mgh in art. قذر.) And ↓ تفحّش بِالشَّىْءِ *He deemed the thing foul, evil,* &c.: or *excessively,* or *beyond measure, foul,* &c. (TA.)

فُحْشٌ inf. n. of فَحُشَ [q. v.]. (Ṣ, O, &c.) — See also 4. — *Excess, exorbitance,* or *transgression of the proper bounds* or *limits;* (O, TA;) [*in anything;* (see 1;) and particularly] *in speech* or *language;* (TA;) and *in reply:* (A,* O, Ḳ,* TA:) *foul, evil, bad, abominable,* or *unseemly;* [*gross, immodest, lewd,* or *obscene;*] *speech* or *language;* (Mgh, Mṣb, TA;) as also ↓ فَحْشَآءُ. (Mṣb.)

فَحْشَآءُ: see فَاحِشَةٌ, in three places: — and see also فُحْشٌ.

فَحَّاشٌ: see the next paragraph.

فَاحِشٌ Anything, (Mṣb, TA,) or any evil thing, (Ṣ,) *excessive, immoderate, enormous, exorbitant, beyond measure, exceeding the proper bounds* or *limits,* (Ṣ, O, Mṣb, TA,) or *overmuch:* (O, Ḳ, TA:) anything *not agreeable with truth,* and *with rule* or *measure:* (TA:) *foul, evil, bad, abominable,* or *unseemly;* [*gross, immodest, lewd,* or *obscene;*] applied to a thing or an affair, (Mgh, Mṣb,) and to speech or language. (TA.) It is said in a trad., He was asked respecting the blood of fleas, [whether it rendered a garment impure,] and said إِنْ لَمْ يَكُنْ فَاحِشًا فَلَا بَأْسَ بِهِ *If it is not excessive, or beyond measure, there is no harm in it.* (TA.) — A man *who transgresses the proper bounds* or *limits* [*in anything:* and particularly] *in speech* or *language,* (TA,) and *in reply:* (Ḳ,* TA:) *who is foul, evil, bad, abominable,* or *unseemly;* [*gross, immodest, lewd,* or *obscene;*] *in speech* or *language,* (Mgh, TA,) and *in action:* (TA:) and ↓ فَحَّاشٌ signifies the same;

(Ṣ,* A,* Mgh;) or has an intensive signification: (TA:) pl. of the former فُحْشَآءُ, like as جُهَلَآءُ is pl. of جَاهِلٌ, since فُحْش is a sort of جَهْل, and contr. of حِلْم. (IJ.) It is said in a trad., لَا تَكُونِى فَاحِشَةً, meaning *Be not thou a trangressor of the proper bounds or limits in reply:* which words were addressed to 'Áïsheh: (Ḳ, TA:) but accord. to one relation, the words were لَا تَقُولِى فَاحِشَةً. (TA.) [See فَاحِشَةٌ, below.] — A man *evil in disposition.* (IB.) — A man *niggardly, tenacious,* or *avaricious:* (A, TA:) or *very niggardly:* (Ḳ, TA:) or *excessively,* or *inordinately, so.* (Ṣ.)

فَاحِشَةٌ [*An excess; an enormity; anything exceeding the bounds of rectitude:*] *a thing excessively, enormously,* or *beyond measure, foul, evil, bad, abominable,* or *unseemly;* [*gross, immodest, lewd,* or *obscene:*] (Mgh:) or *anything not agreeable with truth:* (Lth, Mgh:) or *a sin,* or *crime, that is very foul, evil, bad, &c.:* or *anything forbidden by God:* (Ḳ:) or *any saying,* or *action, that is foul, evil, bad, &c.:* (TA:) and ▼ فَحْشَآءُ signifies the same as فَاحِشَةٌ; (Ṣ;) or *an enormity,* or *excessive sin, beyond measure foul, evil, bad, &c.;* or *a thing that reason disapproves, and the law regards as foul, evil, bad, &c.:* (Bḍ in ii. 164:) the pl. of فَاحِشَةٌ is فَوَاحِشُ. (Mṣb, TA.) Also, particularly, *Adultery,* or *fornication;* (Ṣ, Mgh, Mṣb, Ḳ;) and so ▼ فَحْشَآءُ: (Bḍ in xii. 24; &c.:) so in the Ḳur iv. 23 and lxv. 1 [as well as in numerous other instances]: or the فاحشة [or excess] there mentioned is the women's going out without permission: (Mgh, Mṣb:) or their using foul language against their husband's relations, by reason of the sharpness of their tongues. (Esh-Sháfi'ee.) And ▼ فَحْشَآءُ particularly signifies *Niggardliness, tenaciousness,* or *avarice,* (A, Ḳ,) *in the payment of the poor-rate:* or the *abstaining* [*altogether*] *from paying it.* (TA.) So in the Ḳur ii. 271. (A, TA.)

أَفْحَشُ [*More,* and *most, excessive,* &c.].

مُتَفَحِّشٌ One *who affects,* or *takes upon himself, the reviling of others.* (TA.) — One *who commits excess* (فَاحِشَة) *which is forbidden.* (TA.)

فحص

1. فَحَصَتِ القَطَاةُ, aor. ـَ, inf. n. فَحْصٌ, (Mṣb,) and مَفْحَصٌ is the same as فَحْصٌ, being used transitively, and not only as a n. of place, (TA,) *The* قطاة [i. e. *sand-grouse*] *dug,* or *hollowed out, in the ground, a place wherein to lay her eggs:* (Mṣb:) and فَحَصَتِ التُّرَابَ, aor. as above, *she* (a قطاة) *made for herself an* أُفْحُوص [q. v.] (A, Ḳ) *in the earth,* or *dust.* (Ḳ.) — Hence you say, (Mṣb,) فَحَصَ عَنْهُ, (Ṣ, A, Mṣb, Ḳ,) aor. ـَ, (A, Ḳ,) inf. n. فَحْصٌ; (Ṣ;) and ▼ تفحّص; (Ṣ, A, Mṣb, Ḳ;) and ▼ افتحص; (Ṣ, A, Ḳ;) *He searched,* or *sought, for,* or *after, it; inquired respecting it; sought for information respecting it; searched into, inquired into, investigated, scrutinized,* or *examined, it:* (Ṣ, A, Ḳ:) or *did so to the utmost:* (Mṣb:) or فَحْصٌ signifies *vigorous searching in the interstices of anything.* (TA.) You say also, عَلَيْكَ بِالفَحْصِ عَنْ سِرِّ هٰذَا الحَدِيثِ ‡ [*Keep thou to searching for,* or *after,* or *into, the secret of this story*]. (A, TA.) — Hence also, the saying of Aboo-Bekr, سَتَجِدُ قَوْمًا فَحَصُوا عَنْ أَوْسَاطِ رُؤُوسِهِمْ الشَّعَرَ, (Az, TA,) or فَحَصُوا عَنْ رُؤُوسِهِمْ [alone], (Ṣ,) *Thou wilt find a people who have made their heads like the nests* (أَفَاحِيص) *of* [*the birds called*] قَطًا: (Az, TA:) or, app., *who have shaven the middle of their heads and left them like the* أَفَاحِيص *of* قَطًا. (Ṣ, TA.) [See also أُفْحُوص.] — فَحْصٌ also signifies The *digging,* or *hollowing out* [the ground &c., in any manner]. (TA.) It is said in a trad., فُحِصَتِ الأَرْضُ أَفَاحِيصَ *The earth was dug into hollows.* (Nh, L.) And you say, فَحَصَ لِلْخُبْزَةِ, aor. ـَ, inf. n. فَحْصٌ, *He made, for the cake of bread,* or *lump of dough, a place in the fire;* (TA;) or *a place in the hot ashes,* or *in the fire, to put it therein* [*for the purpose of baking,* or *toasting, it*]. (L in art. فأد.) [فَحَصَ is often used intransitively as meaning *He made,* or *scraped, a hollow* in the ground, &c.; and so ▼ تفحّص.] And sometimes they said, (Ṣ,) فَحَصَ المَطَرُ التُّرَابَ *The rain turned over the dust,* or *earth,* (Ṣ, A, Ḳ,) *and removed one part thereof from another,* (A, TA,) *making it like the* أُفْحُوص: (TA:) and in like manner, الحَصَى *the pebbles:* (A:) this is when it falls vehemently. (TA.) — فَحَصَ also signifies *He* (a gazelle) *ran vehemently* [app. *so as to dig up the ground with his feet*]; but the word more known is مَحَصَ: (TA:) and *he* (a man) *hastened,* or *went quickly.* (Ḳ.) You say, مَرَّ فُلَانٌ يَفْحَصُ *Such a one passed along hastening,* or *going quickly.* (TA.) And it is said in a trad. of Ḳuss, وَلَا سَمِعْتُ فَحْصًا *Nor did I hear the falling of a foot,* or *the sound of walking.* (TA.) — You say also, فَحَصَ الصَّبِىُّ, meaning, † *The child had his central incisors in a wabbling state:* (Ḳ:) [nearly syn. with حَفَرَ, and still more so with أُحْفِرَ.] — And فَحْصٌ also signifies The *spreading* [a thing] *out* or *open; laying* [it] *open; exposing* or *uncovering* or *discovering* [it]. (TA.)

3. فَاحَصَنِى, (Ḳ,) inf. n. مُفَاحَصَةٌ, (TḲ,) [and app. فِحَاصٌ also,] † [*He did*] as though *he searched after,* or *into, my vice,* or *fault, and my secret, I doing the same with respect to his.* (Ḳ, TA.) — [Hence, app., the saying,] بَيْنَهُمَا فِحَاصٌ † *Between them two is enmity.* (TA.)

5: see 1, in two places.

8: see 1, second sentence.

فَحْصٌ *Even ground; an expanded and open tract:* pl. فُحُوصٌ. (TA.) — And hence, (TA,) *Any inhabited place.* (Ḳ, TA.) — In a trad. respecting the intercession [of Mohammad for his people], where it is said, فَأَنْطَلِقُ حَتَّى آتِىَ الفَحْصَ [*And he went away until he came to the* فحص], الفحص is said to signify *What is before the* عَرْش [*of God*]. (TA.)

فَحْصَةٌ The *dimple* (نُقْرَة) *of the chin* (A, Ḳ) of a child; (A;) and *of each cheek.* (TA.)

هُوَ فَحِيصِى, and ▼ مُفَاحِصِى, † *He is a searcher after,* or *into, my vice,* or *fault, and secret, I being the same with respect to his:* (Ḳ,* TḲ:) both mean the same, like أَكِيلِى and مُؤَاكِلِى. (TA.)

فُلَانٌ فَحَّاصٌ عَنِ الأَسْرَارِ ‡ *Such a one is a great searcher for,* or *after,* or *into, secrets.* (A, TA.)

اِعْلَمْ أَنَّ عِنْدَ ٱللهِ مَسْأَلَةً فَاحِصَةً ‡ [*Know thou that with God is a searching interrogation*]. (A, TA.)

أُفْحُوصٌ (Ṣ, M, A, Mgh, Ḳ) and ▼ مَفْحَصٌ (the same, and Mṣb) The [*nest,* or] *place for laying eggs,* (M, Mgh, Mṣb,) or *for lying in,* (Ṣ, Ḳ,) of a قَطَاة [or sand-grouse], (Ṣ, M, A, Mgh, Ḳ,) and of the domestic hen, and sometimes of the ostrich, (M,) *dug,* or *hollowed out, in the ground,* (Mṣb,) or *made by clearing away and removing from it the dust* or *earth;* (Mgh;) or because she digs it, or hollows it out: (Ṣ, M:) pl. (of the former, TA) أَفَاحِيصُ (Ṣ, A) and (of the latter, TA) مَفَاحِصُ: (A, TA:) [see عُشّ:] you say, لَهُمْ مَفَاحِصَا and بُيُوتٌ كَأَفَاحِيصِ القَطَا [*They have houses like the nests of the* قطا]. (A.) And it is said in a trad., ▼ مَنْ بَنَى لِلّٰهِ مَسْجِدًا وَلَوْ مَفْحَصَ قَطَاةٍ بَنَى ٱللهُ لَهُ بَيْتًا فِى الجَنَّةِ [*Whoso buildeth for God a place of worship, be it* comparatively like *a nest of a* قطاة, (كَمَفْحَصِ قَطَاةٍ, accord. to another relation,) *God buildeth for him a house in Paradise*]. (TA.) And in another, in a charge given to the commanders of the army of Mu-teh, ▼ وَسَتَجِدُونَ آخَرِينَ لِلشَّيْطَانِ فِى رُؤُوسِهِمْ مَفَاحِصُ ‡ *And ye shall find others in whose heads the devil hath taken up an abode, making them like nests for him:* like as one says of a person greatly erring, and obstinately persevering in evil, فَرَّخَ الشَّيْطَانُ فِى رَأْسِهِ, and عَشَّشَ فِى قَلْبِهِ. (TA.) — Also, both words, *Any place dug,* or *hollowed out.* (Nh.) — And the former, *A place made in hot ashes,* or *in a fire, in which a cake of bread,* or *lump of dough, is put* [*to bake or toast*]: pl. as above. (L, in art. فأد; and TA.*)

مَفْحَصٌ, and its pl.: see the next preceding paragraph, in three places.

فَحِيصِى: see هُوَ مُفَاحِصِى.

مُتَفَحَّصٌ [*A place of,* or *ground for, inquiring,* or *investigating*]. (A and TA voce تَعَقَّبَ.)

فحل

1. فَحَلَ الإِبِلَ, aor. ـَ, [inf. n. فَحْلٌ,] *He sent a male* [meaning *a stallion-camel*] *among the* [*she-*] *camels.* (Ṣ, O, Ḳ.) The inf. n. فَحْلٌ [used alone]

means The *putting a he-camel among the she-camels.* (KL.) — And فَحَلَ إِبِلَهُ فَحْلًا كَرِيمًا *He chose for his* [*she-*] *camels a generous male* [or *stallion*]; as also ▾ افتحل. (Ḳ.) — See also the next paragraph.

4. افحلهُ, (Ṣ,) or افحلهُ فَحْلًا, (Ḳ, TA,) *He gave to him,* (Ṣ,) or *lent to him,* (Ḳ, TA,) *a male* [*camel*] (Ṣ, Ḳ, TA) *to cover among his* [*she-*] *camels:* (Ṣ, TA:) and accord. to Lḥ, ▾ فَحَلَ فُلَانًا بَعِيرًا and ▾ افتحلهُ signify *he gave to such a one a he-camel;* like افحلهُ. (TA.)

5. تفحّل *He assumed,* or *affected, a likeness,* or *resemblance, to the* فَحْل (Ṣ, O, Ḳ, TA) i. e. the *male* (TA) [or rather the *manly*]: and *he affected the quality of the* فَحْل [or *manly*] *in clothing and in food, by making both to be coarse;* (O, Ḳ, TA;) as did the chiefs of Syria to 'Omar, when he came thither; (O, TA;) i. e., they met him in their ordinary clothing, not having adorned themselves; [in consideration of his simple habits;] self-adornment being an affair of females and of effeminate men. (TA.) [See also its part. n., below.]

8: see 1: — and see also 4.

10. الاِسْتِفْحَالُ signifies *The practice of persons' giving to a man of big make,* (O, Ḳ, TA,) *and comely appearance,* (O,) *free access to their women, in order that he may beget among them the like of himself;* which the unbelievers (عُلُوج, O, or أَعْلَاج, Ḳ) of Kábul do [or used to do] when seeing such a man, of the Arabs: (O, Ḳ, TA:) so Lth was told, and thus he has expl. the word, after saying that he errs who says اِسْتَفْحَلْنَا فَحْلًا لِدَوَابِّنَا [app. meaning *We sought,* or *demanded, a stallion for our beasts*]. (O, TA.) — استفحلت النَّخْلَةُ *The palm-tree became a* فُحَّال [or *tree of which the spadix might be used for the purpose of fecundation*]. (Ḳ. [See also the part. n., below.]) — And استفحل الأَمْرُ ‡ *The affair, or case, became great,* or *formidable,* (Ṣ, O, Ḳ, TA,) and *hard,* or *difficult.* (TA.)

فَحْلٌ a word of well-known meaning, (Ṣ, O,) *A male* of animals (Mgh, Mṣb, Ḳ) of any kind, (Mgh, Ḳ,) [including mankind: and particularly *a stallion:* generally,] *a male* [or *stallion*] *camel:* (MA:) pl. [of mult.] فُحُولٌ (Ṣ, Mgh, O, Mṣb, Ḳ) and فِحَالٌ (Ṣ, Mṣb, Ḳ) and فُحُولَةٌ (Mgh, O, Mṣb, Ḳ) and فِحَالَةٌ (Ṣ, O, Ḳ) and [pl. of pauc.] أَفْحُلٌ: (Ḳ:) and ▾ فَحِيلٌ signifies the same as فَحْلٌ; (Kr, TA;) and [particularly] *a* فَحْل *of the camels.* (Ṣ, O, TA.) — Hence الفَحْلُ is an appellation of ‡ *Canopus* (سُهَيْل); because it is aloof from the other stars, like the فحل which, when he has covered, goes aloof from the [she-] camels: (Ṣ, O, Ḳ, TA:) or, as some say, it is so called because of its greatness. (TA.) — رَجُلٌ ▾ فَحِيلٌ means the same as فَحْلٌ [i. e. † *A masculine, as opposed to an effeminate, man*]. (Ḳ.) And ▾ إِمْرَأَةٌ فَحْلَةٌ means † *A clamorous* [or, app., *masculine*] *woman.* (Ṣ, O, Ḳ.) — فُحُولُ الشُّعَرَآءِ is an appellation applied to † *The poets* (O, Ḳ) *who have overcome,* (O,) or *who overcome,* (Ḳ,) *in satirizing, those who have vied with them therein;* (O, Ḳ;) like Jereer and El-Farezdaḳ, (O, TA,) who used to be called فَحْلَا مُضَرَ: (TA:) and in like manner ‡ *any one who, when he vies with a poet, is judged to have excelled him* [is called a فَحْل]; (Ḳ, TA; [for فَضَل in the CḲ, I read فُضِّلَ, as in other copies of the Ḳ;]) like 'Alḳameh Ibn-'Abadeh; (TA;) who was surnamed الفَحْل because he took to wife Umm-Jundab when Imra-el-Ḳeys divorced her on the occasion of her judging him [i. e. 'Alḳameh] to have overcome him [Imra-el-Ḳeys] in poetry. (Ṣ, O, Ḳ, TA.) — فَحْلٌ also means [app. † *A vigorous orator:* see هَادِرٌ. — And] ‡ *A relater, reciter,* or *rehearser, by heart,* [of poetry, and of traditions, or narratives learned, or heard, or received, from another or others;] syn. رَاوٍ: pl. فُحُولٌ: (Ḳ, TA:) so in the M. (TA.) — See also فُحَّالٌ, in three places. And see مُتَفَحِّلٌ. — And † *A mat that is made of the woven leaves of the palm-tree thus called,* (Sh,* Ṣ,* O,* Ḳ,* TA,) i. e., *of the palm-tree called* فُحَّال: (Ṣ, O, Ḳ, TA:) pl. فُحُولٌ. (Ṣ, O, TA.) — And † *Rain* is thus called [in a verse of Eṭ-Ṭirimmáḥ Ibn-El-Ḥakeem, being likened to the stallion-camel, because of its fertilizing the earth]. (Ḥam p. 110.)

إِمْرَأَةٌ فَحْلَةٌ: see فَحْلٌ, former half.

فِحْلَةٌ The *quality,* or *state, of being a* فَحْل [or *male;* and particularly, *of being a stallion:* and also † *masculineness,* as a quality of a man, *opposed to effeminacy:* &c.]: (Ṣ, O, Ḳ:) and ▾ فُحُولَةٌ and ▾ فِحَالَةٌ [both of which are also pls. of فَحْل] signify the same. (Ḳ.) [Hence,] بَعِيرٌ ذُو فِحْلَةٍ *A camel fit,* or *meet, for being chosen as a stallion.* (TA.) — Also, i. e. فِحْلَةٌ, with kesr, A man's *choosing a* فحل [i. e. *stallion*] *for his beasts.* (TA.)

فَحِيلٌ: see فَحْلٌ, first sentence. — One says also فَحْلٌ فَحِيلٌ, meaning *A generous stallion-camel, that begets generous offspring.* (Ṣ, Ḳ.*) Er-Rá'ee says,

• كَانَتْ نَجَائِبَ مُنْذِرٍ وَمُحَرِّقٍ •
• أُمَّاتُهُنَّ وَطَرْقُهُنَّ فَحِيلَا •

[*Their mothers were of the generous camels of Mundhir and Moḥarriḳ, and their compressing stallion was a generous one, a begetter of generous offspring*]: (Ṣ [accord. to one of my copies], and TA:) [some copies of the Ṣ have نَجَائِبُ and أُمَّاتِهِنَّ; and so has the O: but] IB says that the verse is correctly related as above. (TA.) — And كَبْشٌ فَحِيلٌ means *A ram that resembles the* فَحْل *of camels in his excellence* (Ḳ, TA) *and his* [*comparative*] *greatness.* (TA.) — See also فَحْلٌ again, third sentence.

فِحَالَةٌ: } see فِحْلَةٌ.
فُحُولَةٌ: }

فُحَّالٌ and ▾ فَحْلٌ The *male palm-tree,* (Ṣ, Mgh, O, Mṣb, Ḳ, TA,) *by means of which the fruit-bearing palm-trees are fecundated,* (Ṣ,* Mgh,* Mṣb, TA,) *and which, when they are on the wind-ward side of the latter trees, fecundate these:* (TA:) [see what follows:] only the former word is mentioned [in this sense] by Lth; and ISd says, (TA,) the former word is used peculiarly as applied to the male palm-tree: (Ḳ,* TA:) AḤn cites AA as saying that ▾ فَحْل is not said except of that which has life, and Aboo-Naṣr says the like; but AḤn adds that people in general disagree from them as to this: (TA:) the pl. of فُحَّالٌ is فَحَاحِيلُ; (Ṣ, Mgh, Mṣb, Ḳ;) and the pl. of ▾ فَحْلٌ is فُحُولٌ (Ṣ, Mgh, O, Mṣb) and فُحُولَةٌ (Mgh, Mṣb) and فِحَالٌ; (Mṣb;) of the first of which pls. of فَحْل, the following saying, (Ṣ, O, Mṣb, TA,) of Oḥeiḥah Ibn-El-Julàḥ, (O, TA,) presents an ex.:

• تَأَبَّرِى يَا خَيْرَةَ الفَسِيلِ •
• تَأَبَّرِى مِنْ حَنَذٍ فَشُولِى •
• إِذْ ضَنَّ أَهْلُ النَّخْلِ بِالفُحُولِ •

[*Receive thou fecundation, O best of young palm-trees: receive thou fecundation from Ḥanadh, and show that thou hast received it:* (فَشُولِى being from شَالَتْ بِذَنَبِهَا said of a she-camel, meaning "she raised her tail, showing thereby that she was pregnant:") *since the palm-owners have been niggardly* of the spadixes *of the male palm-trees*]: (Ṣ, O, Mṣb, TA:) the meaning is, that the people of Ḥanadh were niggardly of the spadixes of their [male] palm-trees, and the east wind blew at the time of the fecundation upon the male trees, bearing off [the pollen of] their spadixes and casting it upon the female trees, so that it served for fecundation: Ḥanadh is a place about four miles from El-Medeeneh: and it is said to be the town of Oḥeiḥah: or to be a water belonging to Suleym and Muzeyneh. (Mṣb.)

شَجَرٌ مُتَفَحِّلٌ ‡ *Trees that do not bear fruit;* like the ▾ فَحْل: (Ibn-'Abbád, A, O, TA:) *that becomes barren.* (A, TA.) [See also what follows.]

نَخْلَةٌ مُسْتَفْحِلَةٌ † *A palm-tree that does not bear fruit.* (Lḥ, TA.) [See also what next precedes: and see 10.]

فحم

1. فَحَمَ, aor. ـَ, inf. n. فُحُومٌ (Ḳ, TA) and فُحُومَةٌ, (Ḳ,* TA,) said of anything, (TA,) *It was,* or *became, black* [app. *like* فَحْم i. e. *charcoal*]. (Ḳ, TA.) [See also فَاحِمٌ.] — See also فَحْمٌ, last sentence. ═ فَحَمَ, (Ks, Ṣ, Mṣb, Ḳ,) aor. ـَ, (Ks, Ṣ, Mṣb, TA,) accord. to the Ḳ ـُ, which is wrong; (TA;) and فَحِمَ; and فُحِمَ; (Ḳ;) *He* (a boy, or child,) *wept until his voice became stopped;* (Ks, Ṣ, Mṣb;) or *until his breath became stopped;* as also ▾ أُفْحِمَ. (Ḳ.) — And, said of a ram, (Ḳ,) or thus فَحِمَ and فَحَمَ, like مَنَعَ and عَلِمَ, (TA,) *He uttered a cry,* or *cries.* (Ḳ, TA.) And (TA) one says of a ram, ثَغَا حَتَّى فَحَمَ *He bleated until*

he became hoarse. (Ṣ, TA.) —— فَحَمَ, aor. ـَ, said of a man, *He was unable to answer,* (Ḳ, TA,) when one had spoken to him. (TA.) —— And فَحَمَتِ القَلِيبُ, aor. ـَ, inf. n. فُحُومٌ, ‡ [*The well, or old well,*] *ceased to have a flow of water.* (Ḳ, TA.)

2. فَحَّمَهُ, (Ṣ, A, Mṣb, Ḳ,) inf. n. تَفْحِيمٌ, (Ṣ, A, Ḳ,) *He blackened it,* (Ṣ, A, Mṣb, Ḳ,) namely, another's face, (Ṣ, A, Mṣb,) *with* فَحْم [i. e. *charcoal*]. (Mṣb.) ═ See also the next paragraph.

4. افحم *He* (a man) *entered upon the time called* فَحْمَةُ العِشَآءِ [q. v.]: like أَعْتَمَ. (TA.) —— And one says, أَفْحِمُوا عَنْكُمْ, (Ṣ,) or أَفْحِمُوا, (Ḳ,) مِنَ اللَّيْلِ, meaning *Abstain ye from journeying in the* فَحْمَة (i. e. the *most intense blackness,* Ṣ) *of the night;* (Ṣ, Ḳ;) as also ↓ فَحِّمُوا, (Ṣ,* Ḳ,) inf. n. تَفْحِيمٌ. (Ṣ.) ═ افحمهُ is said of weeping [as meaning *It stopped his voice, or his breath*]: (TA:) see 1. And *He silenced him,* (Ṣ, Mṣb, TA,) namely, his adversary (Mṣb) in a dispute or the like, (Ṣ, Mṣb, TA,) by an argument or evidence, (Mṣb,) or in some other case. (Ṣ, TA.) And, said of anxiety, or disquietude of mind, *It prevented him,* or *withheld him, from uttering poetry,* or *verse.* (Ḳ.) —— And *He found him to be* مُفْحَم, (Ṣ, Ḳ,) *not uttering poetry,* or *verse.* (Ṣ.) One says هَاجَاهُ فَأَفْحَمَهُ, meaning [*He contended with him in satirizing*] *and he found him to be* مُفْحَم, accord. to the Ḳ: (TA:) and هَاجَيْنَاكُمْ فَمَا أَفْحَمْنَاكُمْ (Ṣ [in which it is implied that the meaning is *We contended with you in satirizing and found you not to be* مُفْحَمُون]): or, accord. to IB, this means, and *we caused you not to hold the tongue from answering,* or *replying;* because المُهَاجَاة is between two persons: but you [may] say هَجَوْتُهُ فَأَفْحَمْتُهُ meaning [*I satirized him*] *and I found him to be* مُفْحَم. (TA.)

8. [الاِفْتِحَامُ is expl. in some copies of the Ḳ as signifying الاِغْتِبَاقُ; in some, الاِعْتِنَاقُ; and app. in the copy used by Golius, الاِعْتِيَاقُ: the first, which is that followed in the TḲ, is evidently, I think, the right; meaning *The drinking an evening draught; such as is termed a* غَبُوق. See also the next paragraph, second and last sentences.]

فَحْمٌ and ↓ فَحَمٌ, (Ṣ, Mṣb, Ḳ,) the latter sometimes occurring, (Ṣ, Mṣb,) like نَهْرٌ and نَهَرٌ, (Ṣ,) [*Charcoal;* this is what is meant by its being said to signify] *extinct coal;* (M, Ḳ;) *a thing well known;* (Ṣ, Mṣb;) as also ↓ فَحِيمٌ; (Ṣ, Ḳ;) or, accord. to ISd, this may be a pl. of فَحْمٌ, [or a quasi-pl. n.,] like as عَبِيدٌ is of عَبْدٌ, and مَعِيزٌ of مَعْزٌ, &c.: (TA:) the n. un. [meaning *a piece of charcoal*] is ↓ فَحْمَةٌ, (Ṣ, Ḳ, TA,) but not فَحَمَةٌ. (TA.) ═ And فَحْمٌ signifies also *The draught that is drunk in* [*any one of*] *the times denoted by the word* فَحْمَةٌ [q. v.]: (Ḳ, TA:) like the غَبُوق and صَبُوح and جَاشِرِيَّة and قَيْل: but it is disapproved by Az. (TA.) —— [Accord. to the TḲ, it is an inf. n. of which the verb is ↓ فَحَمَ, aor. ـَ, signifying *He* (a man) *drank in the* فَحْمَة *of the* عِشَآء: but of this I find not any confirmation.]

فَحَمٌ: see the next preceding paragraph.

فَحِمٌ: see فَاحِمٌ.

فَحْمَةٌ n. un. of فَحْمٌ, q. v. [Hence] one says of a black woman with a red خِمَار [or muffler], كَأَنَّهَا فَحْمَةٌ فِى رَأْسِهَا نَارٌ [*As though she were a piece of charcoal with fire upon its head*]. (TA.) —— [And hence,] فَحْمَةُ اللَّيْلِ The *first part of the night:* (Ḳ:) or *the blackness of the night:* (Mṣb:) or *the most intense blackness of the night:* (Ḳ:) or *the blackness of the first part of the night:* (TA:) or *the most intensely black part of the night:* (Ṣ, TA:) or *the part from the setting of the sun to* [*the time of*] *the sleeping of mankind:* (Ḳ:) so called because of its heat [as well as its darkness]; for the first part of the night is hotter than its last part: (TA:) it is *peculiarly in the* صَيْف [meaning *summer*]; (Ḳ, TA;) *not in the winter:* (TA:) and فَحْمَةُ العِشَآءِ signifies *the darkness of the* عشاء [i. e. of the *nightfall*]: (Ṣ:) or *the intenseness of the blackness of the night,* and *its darkness;* which is *in its first part:* or *the time next after the* عشاء: (TA:) the pl. is فِحَامٌ and فُحُومٌ: (Ḳ, TA:) or the latter of these may mean *darkness;* as though it were an inf. n. of فَحَمَ. (TA.) فَحْمَةُ السَّحَرِ means *The time of the* سَحَر [or *last part of the night*]. (Ḳ.) And فَحْمَةُ بْنُ جُمَيْرٍ is [a proper name of] *The middle of the night.* (Ḳ.)

فَحُومٌ One *who will not utter a reply,* or *an answer.* (TA.)

فَحِيمٌ: see فَحْمٌ: —— and see also فَاحِمٌ.

فَحَّامٌ *A seller of* فَحْم [i. e. *charcoal*]. (TA.)

فَاحِمٌ *Black;* (Ṣ, K, TA;) applied to hair, (Ṣ,) and to anything; (TA;) as also ↓ فَحِيمٌ; (Ḳ, TA;) applied to hair and to anything. (TA.) And *Black that is beautiful* or *comely.* (TA.) —— And one says أَسْوَدُ فَاحِمٌ meaning *Black in an intense degree.* (TA.) ═ Also A ram *uttering a cry,* or *cries;* and so ↓ فَحِمٌ. (Ḳ. [But see 1.]) —— And One *who does not speak at all.* (TA.) —— And, applied to water, ‡ *Still; not flowing* or *running.* (Ḳ, TA.)

مُفْحَمٌ [pass. part. n. of 4, q. v.]: *i. q.* عَيِىٌّ [app. as meaning *Unable to express what he would say*]; (Ḳ, TA;) because his face becomes black from anger, like فَحْم [i. e. charcoal]. (TA.) One *unable to utter verse,* or *poetry.* (Ṣ,* Ḳ.) And A poet *who will not* [or *cannot*] *answer,* or *reply to, him who contends with him in satirizing.* (TA.)

مُفْحِمٌ An answer, or a reply, [&c.,] *that silences.* (TA.)

فحو

1. فَحَا بِكَلَامِهِ إِلَى كَذَا, (Mṣb, TA,) aor. يَفْحُو [like يَعْلُو], the verb being of the class of عَلَا, (so in the Mṣb accord. to the TA,) or يَفْحَى [like يَنْفَعُ], the verb being of the class of نَفَعَ, (so accord. to my copy of the Mṣb,) or, as in copies of the T, يَفْحِى, without teshdeed, the verb being of the class of رَمَى, (TA, [but this is app. a mistranscription for يَفْحَى, as the last radical letter is و,]) inf. n. فَحْوٌ; (Mṣb, TA;) or ↓ فَحَّى بكلامه الى كذا, thus accord. to the Ḳ, agreeably with what is said by J; (TA;) [but one of my copies of the Ṣ has إِنَّهُ لَيُفَحِّى بِكَلَامِهِ إِلَى كَذَا وَكَذَا; the other copy having ↓ لَيَفْحَى;] *He meant,* or *intended, by his saying,* or *speech, such a thing.* (Mṣb, Ḳ, TA. [In the Ṣ, the meaning is only indicated by the context.]) ═ بَكَى حَتَّى فَحِىَ, like رَضِىَ, *He* (a child) *wept until he sobbed.* (TA.)

2. فَحَّى القِدْرَ, inf. n. تَفْحِيَةٌ, *He made the cooking-pot to have a large quantity of* أَبَازِير [or *seeds used in cooking, for seasoning the food:* from فَحًا, q. v.]: (Ṣ,* Ḳ, TA:) or, accord. to Aboo-'Alee El-Ḳálee, *he put,* or *threw, into the cooking-pot,* أَبَازِير, i. e. تَوَابِل. (TA.) It is said, by Z, [but with hardly any reason that I can see,] to be formed by transposition from the letters فوح thus combined. (TA.) ═ See also 1, in two places.

3. فَاحَيْتُهُ, inf. n. مُفَاحَاةٌ, *I talked, discoursed,* or *held a colloquy, with him, and understood what he intended,* or *meant.* (A, TA.)

فَحًا and فِحًى, (Ṣ, Ḳ,) the former of which is the more common, (Ṣ,) The *seeds that are used in cooking, for seasoning the food;* (Ṣ, Ḳ;) as also ↓ فَحْوَآءُ: or the *dry thereof:* (Ḳ:) pl. أَفْحَآءٌ; (Ṣ, Ḳ;) which is said by IAth to signify the [*seeds called*] تَوَابِل *of the cooking-pot, such as pepper* and *cumin-seed* and *the like thereof.* (TA.) And it is said to signify particularly The *onion,* or *onions* collectively. (TA.) Thus in a trad. of Mo'áwiyeh, in which he is related to have said to a party who came to him, كُلُوا مِنْ فَحَا أَرْضِنَا فَقَلَّ مَا أَكَلَ قَوْمٌ مِنْ فَحَا أَرْضٍ فَضَرَّهُمْ مَاؤُهَا [*Eat ye of the seasoning of our land* (meaning of the onions,) *for rarely have people eaten of the seasoning of a land and the water thereof has harmed them*]. (TA: and the like is said in the Ṣ, but not so fully.)

فَحْوَةٌ *i. q.* شَهْدَةٌ [*A portion of honey;* or *a honey-comb;* or *a portion of a honey-comb*]. (Ḳ, TA. [It is added in the latter that it is as though it were formed by transposition from فَوْحَة; which I do not find in this sense in any lexicon.])

فَحِيَّةٌ, like جَرِيَّة; (so in some copies of the Ḳ, and accord. to the TA, in which it is said to be "with fet-ḥ;") or فُحَيَّة, like جُرَيَّة; (so in other copies of the Ḳ; [but I think that both are evidently wrong, because deviating from a common rule of the Ḳ, and for more than one other obvious reason; and that the right reading is ↓ فَحِيَّة, like جَرِيَّة (accord. to those who hold this to be of the measure فَعِيلَةٌ, not فُعْلِيَّةٌ; i. e., that it is originally فَحِيوَةٌ, the و being necessarily changed into ى and incorporated into the preceding ى;] and also ↓ فَحِيَّةٌ; (Ḳ, TA;) the former on the authority of AA, and the latter on that of IAạr; (TA;) *Thin soup:* (Ḳ, TA: [in some copies of the Ḳ, حَسْوٌ is erroneously put for حَسُوٌّ or حَسْوٌ, the readings in other copies:]) or *soup in general.* (Ḳ, TA.)

فَحْوَى and ↓ فَحْوَآءُ, (T, Ṣ, Mṣb, Ḳ, &c.,) the latter sometimes used, (Mṣb,) but AZ is said to have disallowed the pronunciation with the lengthened alif, (TA,) and ↓ فُحْوَآءُ, (Ḳ, TA,) this last mentioned by ISd and Ṣgh on the authority of Fr, (TA,) The *meaning* of a saying, or speech; its *intended sense* or *import;* syn. مَعْنًى; (Ṣ, Mṣb, Ḳ;) and مَذْهَبٌ; (Ḳ;) and لَحْنٌ. (Ṣ, Mṣb.) One says, عَرَفْتُهُ, (Ṣ, A,) or فَهِمْتُهُ, (Mṣb,) فِى, (Ṣ,) or مِنْ, (A, Mṣb,) فَحْوَى كَلَامِهِ and ↓ فَحْوَآءِ كَلَامِهِ, (Ṣ, A, Mṣb) i. e. [*I knew it,* or *I understood it, in,* or *from, the intended sense* or *import of his saying,* or *speech;* or,] in [or *from*] *what I elicited of his meaning,* or *intent, in what he said.* (A.) [See also عَرُوضٌ, near the middle of the paragraph.]

فَحْوَآءُ: see the next preceding paragraph, in two places: — see also فَحًا.

فُحْوَآءُ: see فَحْوَى.

فَحِيَّةٌ and فَحِيَّةٌ: see فَحِيَّةٌ, above.

أَفْحَى i. q. أَبَحُّ [*Having a hoarse, rough, harsh,* or *gruff, voice*]. (Ṣgh, TA.)

فخ

1. فَخَّ, aor. ـِ, inf. n. فَخِيخٌ (Ṣ, Ḳ) and فَخٌّ; and so ↓ اِفْتَخَّ, (Ḳ, TA,) inf. n. اِفْتِخَاخٌ; (TA;) said of one sleeping, *He snored;* or *made a sound in breathing, audible by persons around him;* syn. غَطَّ: (Ṣ, L, Ḳ:) or فَخٌّ in sleep is [the *making a sound*] *less than what is termed* غَطِيطٌ [inf. n. of غَطَّ]: and it signifies also a man's *sleeping, and blowing in sleep.* (L.)

8: see the preceding paragraph.

فَخٌّ *A snare, trap, gin,* or *net, for catching game* or *any kind of wild animals* or *birds;* syn. مِصْيَدَةٌ: (Ṣ, A, L, Mṣb,* Ḳ:) said to be a Pers., or foreign, word, arabicized: (TA:) [from the Pers. فَخ:] AM says that the Arabs called it طُرْقٌ [q. v.; and see also طُبَّقٌ]: (TA:) and ↓ فَخَّةٌ signifies the same: (L:) pl. of the former فِخَاخٌ (Ṣ, A, Mṣb, Ḳ) and فُخُوخٌ. (Ṣ, A, Ḳ.) ‡ وَثَبَ فُلَانٌ مِنْ فَخِّ إِبْلِيسَ [lit. *Such a one leaped from the snare of Iblees*] means *such a one repented.* (A.)

فَخَّةٌ *A sleep in which the sleeper snores,* or *makes a sound in breathing audible by persons around him:* (Ṣ: [see 1:]) or *a sleep in which the sleeper blows:* (L:) or *a sleep after coitus:* (Ḳ:) or *a sleep in which the sleeper rests on the back of his head,* (IAạr, L, Ḳ,) *and blows by reason of satiety:* (IAạr, L:) or *a sleep in the early part of the morning* or *of the forenoon, between the time of the prayer of daybreak and sunrise* or *after sunrise:* and, *when tired.* (A.) One says, هُوَ يَنَامُ الفَخَّةَ [*He sleeps the sleep termed* فَخَّة]. (A.) — See also فَخٌّ.

فخت

1. فَخَتَتْ, said of a woman, *She walked with an elegant and a proud and self-conceited gait, with an affected inclining of the body from side to side.* (Mṣb.) [See also 5.] — And, said of the bird called فَاخِتَة, *It* [*cooed,* or] *uttered a cry* or *sound.* (Ḳ.) — And فَخَتَ *He lied,* or *uttered a falsehood.* (A, TA. [See فَاخِتَةٌ.]) — فَخَتَهُ, aor. ـَ, *He cut it off* (Ḳ, TA) with a sword. (TA.) — فَخَتَ رَأْسَهُ *He smote his head* with a sword, (O, Ḳ, TA,) *and cut it off.* (TA.) — فَخَتَ الإِنَآءَ, (Ḳ, TA,) inf. n. فَخْتٌ, (TA,) *He uncovered the vessel.* (Ḳ, TA.) — And الفَخْتُ signifies also *The* cook's *taking out with the hand a piece of flesh-meat from the cooking-pot:* (Ḳ, TA:) مِنَ القِدْرَةِ, the reading found in copies of the Ḳ, [in the CḲ مِنَ القَدْرَةِ,] is a mistake: it should be مِنَ القِدْرِ, as in the L [and O] &c. (TA.)

5. تفخّت *He walked in the manner of the bird called* فَاخِتَة: thus in the Ḳ: but in most of the lexicons تَفَخَّتَتْ: (TA:) i. e. *she* (a woman) *walked as walks the* فَاخِتَة: (A:) [or,] accord. to Lth, [in the 'Eyn,] signifying مشت مجنبحة: (TA: in the O, مَشَتْ مجنحه; and in the margin thereof, مُجَنْبِحَةً: [the right reading is مَشَتْ مُجَنْبِحَةً; thus in the JK, a lexicon founded upon the 'Eyn:] thought by him to be from the walking of the bird called فَاخِتَة: (O,* TA:) he means, *she strode in her walking, and held out her arms apart from* [*her sides beneath*] *her armpits.* (TA.) — And *He wondered,* syn. تَعَجَّبَ, (O, Ḳ, TA,) *and said, How good,* or *goodly, is he,* or *it!* (O, TA.) And it is said of a man as signifying عُجِبَ تعجّب فى مشيته [app. meaning *He showed self-admiration, &c., in his gait:* but I do not find this signification assigned to تعجّب]. (TA.) — And *He affected lying;* or *lied purposely;* syn. تَكَذَّبَ. (A, TA.)

7. انفخت, said of a roof, *It became perforated.* (O, Ḳ.)

فَخْتٌ The *light of the moon; moonlight:* (Ṣ, A, O, Ḳ:) or the *light of the moon when it first appears:* and hence [as some say] the derivation of فَاخِتَةٌ [as the name of a certain bird], because of its colour: (Mṣb: [see, however, what follows:]) you say, جَلَسْنَا فِى الفَخْتِ [as though meaning *We sat in the moonlight*]: (A'Obeyd, Ṣ, O:) but Sh says, I have not heard الفَخْت except in this instance; and Aboo-Is-ḥáḳ states that some one of the lexicologists says, I know not whether it be a name of the *light of the moon* or of *its darkness:* Abu-l-'Abbás says that the meaning [in the saying above mentioned] is, *in the shade of the moon* [i. e. *in the shade of a moonlight-night;* and to this the colour of the فَاخِتَة may be likened]. (TA.) — Also The [*snare,* or *trap,* &c., *called*] فَخّ, (Ḳ, TA,) *of the sportsman:* (TA:) or [*a thing*] *nearly resembling the* فَخّ. (O.) — And *Holes,* or *perforations, of a round form, in a roof.* (O, Ḳ.)

فَاخِتَةٌ *A certain well-known bird;* (Ḳ;) *of those having neck-rings* [or *collars*]; (Ṣ, O;) *a species of pigeon, marked with a neck-ring:* (TA:) accord. to Ibn-El-Jawáleeḳee, (IB, TA,) the name is derived from الفَخْتُ, (IB, Mṣb, TA,) meaning "the light of the moon," (IB, TA,) or "the light of the moon when it first appears;" because of its colour: (Mṣb:) [hence, and from what will be found stated voce قُمْرِىٌّ, it seems to be *a species of collared turtle-dove, of a dull white colour, marked with a black neck-ring:*] or, as some say, the word is a part. n. from فَخَتَتْ signifying as expl. in the first sentence of this art.: (Mṣb:) the pl. is فَوَاخِتُ. (Ṣ, O, Mṣb.) أَكْذَبُ مِنْ فَاخِتَةٍ [*More lying than a fákhiteh*] is a prov.; because the cry of the فاختة resembles هٰذَا أَوَانُ الرُّطَبِ [*This is the season of the fresh ripe dates*]; and this it utters when the spadix of the palm-tree has not yet come forth. (Meyd. [See also Freytag's Arab. Prov. ii. 383.])

فخذ

1. فَخَذَهُ, (Ṣ, O, L, Ḳ,) aor. ـَ, (TA, and so accord. to some copies of the Ḳ, in which the verb is said to be like مَنَعَهُ,) or ـُ, (so in other copies of the Ḳ,) inf. n. فَخْذٌ, (L,) *He hit,* or *hurt, his* (another's) *thigh:* (Ṣ, L, Ḳ:) or *he broke his thigh:* like as one says رَأَسَهُ and رَجَلَهُ. (O.) And فُخِذَ *He was hit,* or *hurt, in his thigh:* (M, L, Ḳ:) or *his thigh was broken.* (A.)

2: see 5, in two places. — فخّذ عَشِيرَتَهُ † *He called his* عشيرة [or *kinsfolk*] فَخِذ *by* فَخِذ [i. e. *one small body of families after another*], (Ṣ, Mgh,* O, L, Ḳ,*) inf. n. تَفْخِيذٌ: (TA:) from a trad. (Ṣ, O, L.) — And فَخَّذَهُمْ, inf. n. as above; (Ḳ;) or فخّذ بَيْنَهُمْ; (L;) † *He dispersed them, and abstained from aiding them;* syn. فَرَّقَهُمْ وَخَذَلَهُمْ: (L, Ḳ: [but see what follows:]) and فخّذهم (L) عَنْ فُلَانٍ (O, L, Mṣb) (O, L,) inf. n. as above, (O, L, Mṣb,) signifies خذلهم, (L, Mṣb, [in both written without any of the syll. signs,]) or خذلهم عنه [which is evidently the right reading (i. e. *he induced them to abstain from aiding such a one*), and I believe it to be the right reading also in the explanation given immediately before from the L and Ḳ]: (O:) and فخّذ بينهم *he dispersed them.* (O, Mṣb.)

3: see the next paragraph, in two places.

5. تفخّذ المَرْأَةَ *He* (a man, Mṣb) *sat between the thighs of the woman* (Mgh, Mṣb) *as he sits who performs* [or *is about to perform*] *the act of coitus*; as also ▼فاخذها, [inf. n. مُفَاخَذَةٌ;] and ▼فخّذها, inf. n. تَفْخِيذٌ: (Mṣb:) or *he sat above the thighs of the woman*: (Mgh:) ▼التَّفْخِيذُ signifies *the same as* ▼المُفَاخَذَةُ [app. agreeably with the former or the latter of the explanations above]. (Ṣ, O, L.) — And تفخّذ *He retired*, or *held back*, (O, Ḳ,) عَنِ الأَمْرِ *from the affair*. (O.)

10. استفخذ *i. q.* اِسْتَخْذَى, (Fr, O, Ḳ, TA,) i. e. *He was*, or *became, lowly, humble*, or *submissive*; and so اِسْتَخْذَأَ. (TA in arts. خذى and خذأ.)

فَخِذٌ and فَخْذٌ (Ṣ, O, L, Mṣb, Ḳ) and فِخْذٌ (Ṣ, O, L, Ḳ) and فِخِذٌ, (L, TA,) as Ez-Zarkashee says in his Expos. of El-Bukháree, (TA,) for in the case of every faucial medial radical of a word of the measure فَعِلٌ, whether a noun like فَخِذٌ or a verb like شَهِدَ, there are four dial. vars., namely, فَعِل and فَعْل and فِعْل and فِعِل; (Seer, O, TA;) thus it is said in the Tes-heel of Ibn-Málik; and MF says that the first three forms are common to every word of the measure of كَتِف though without a faucial letter; (TA;) *The thigh*; i. e. the *limb* (وصل [i. e. وُصْل, but in the O written وَصْل,]) *between the* سَاق *and the* وَرِك; (Mgh,* O, L, Ḳ;*) so says Lth; (O;) and in this sense, the first of the forms above mentioned is the most chaste: (MF:) it is of the fem. gender: (Mgh, O, L, Mṣb, Ḳ:) pl. أَفْخَاذٌ, (Sb, L, Mṣb, Ḳ,) the only pl. form. (Sb, L.) — Also ‡ *A small sub-tribe*, or *portion of the tribe, consisting of the nearest of the kinsfolk* of a man; (Kh, A,* O, L, Ḳ;*) *less than a* بَطْن; the first [i. e. largest] body being the شَعْب, then the قَبِيلَة, then the فَصِيلَة, then the عِمَارَة, then the بَطْن, and then the فَخِذ: (Ṣ, O, L:) or it is *below the* قَبِيلَة *but above the* بَطْن; and is pronounced with the خ quiescent: (IDrd, O:) or *below the* فَصِيلَة *but above the* بَطْن: (Mṣb:) or *below the* بَطْن *and above the* فَصِيلَة: (Mgh, Mṣb:) this last, accord. to IB and Aboo-Usámeh, is the true order; (TA voce شعب, q. v.;) and AM says that the فَصِيلَة is nearer than the فخذ: (L:) in this sense, the second of the forms above mentioned is the most chaste: (MF:) and in this sense it is of the masc. gender; (A, Mgh, O, Mṣb;) because meaning نَفَر; (Mṣb;) wherefore you say, هٰذَا فَخْذِى. (A:) pl. as above. (A, O, L, Ḳ.) — حُلِبَتِ النَّاقَةُ فِى فَخِذِهَا is a phrase mentioned by Fr, meaning † [*The she-camel was milked*] *in her half-month* [app. *at the period commencing half a month after her parturition*]. (O.)

فَخِذَاءُ A woman *that holds a man firmly between her thighs*, (Mṣb, Ḳ, TA,) *by reason of her strength*. (TA.)

مَفْخُوذٌ A man *hit*, or *hurt, in his thigh*: (M, L:) or *whose thigh is broken*. (A.)

فخر

1. فَخَرَ, (Ṣ, O, Mṣb, Ḳ,) aor. ـَ, (O, Mṣb, Ḳ,) inf. n. فَخْرٌ (Ṣ, O, Mṣb, Ḳ) and فَخَرٌ (Ṣ, O, Ḳ) and فَخَارٌ, (Ḳ,) or this is a simple subst., (Mṣb,) or it is a mistake for فِخَارٌ, accord. to some, and this may be an inf. n. either of فَخَرَ, for there are many instances of the same kind, or of فَاخَرَ, (MF,) or فَخَارٌ, with fet-ḥ, is post-classical, and therefore not allowable, (Th, O,) and فَخَارَةٌ and فِخِّيرَى and فِخِّيرَآءُ; (Ḳ;) and ▼افتخر; (Ṣ, O, Mṣb, Ḳ;) and ▼تفاخر; (L in art. فتح;) [*He gloried*, or *boasted*; i. e.] *he gloried in, boasted of, boasted himself in*, or *praised* or *commended himself for, certain properties*, or *particular qualities*: (Ḳ:) *he enumerated*, or *recounted, the particulars of his ancestral nobility* or *eminence*, or *his own glorious* or *honourable deeds* or *qualities*: (Ṣ, TA:) or *he arrogated to himself greatness and nobility*: (TA:) or *he contended for superiority by reason of honours arising from memorable deeds* or *qualities, and from parentage* or *relationship, and other things relating to himself* or *to his ancestors*: (Mṣb:) or *he contended for superiority by reason of things extrinsic to himself, such as wealth, and rank* or *station*. (TA.) You say فَخَرْتُ بِهِ [*I gloried in it*, or *by reason of it*; &c.]. (Mṣb.) And ▼تفاخر بِمَا عِنْدَهُ *He gloried in, boasted of*, or *boasted himself in, what he possessed*. (L in art. فتح.) And فَخَرَ بَعْضُهُمْ عَلَى بَعْضٍ *One party of them boasted against another* [بِكَذَا *in such a thing* or *quality* &c.]. (Ḳ.) — Also فَخَرَ, inf. n. فَخْرٌ, *He magnified himself by boasting*. (TA.) — فَاخَرَهُ فَفَخَرَهُ, (Ṣ, O, Ḳ,) aor. ـُ, (O, Ḳ, [in two copies of the Ṣ written ـَ, contrary to analogy in a verb signifying surpassing in a contest, accord. to most of the grammarians,]) inf. n. فَخْرٌ: (Ṣ:) see 3. — فَخَرَ فُلَانٌ الْيَوْمَ عَلَى فُلَانٍ فِى الشَّرَفِ وَالْجَلَدِ وَالْمَنْطِقِ *Such a one excelled to-day such a one in nobleness and hardiness and speech*. (ISk, TA.) — فَخِرَ, aor. ـَ, (O, Ḳ,) inf. n. فَخَرٌ, (TA,) *He disdained*, or *scorned*. (IAạr, O, Ḳ, TA.) — فَخَرَهُ عَلَيْهِ: see 4.

2: see 4.

3. ▼فَاخَرَهُ فَفَخَرَهُ, (ISk, Ṣ, O, Mṣb, Ḳ,) inf. n. of the former مُفَاخَرَةٌ (Mṣb, Ḳ) and فِخَارٌ, (Ḳ,) [and aor. of the latter ـُ, or, accord. to some, ـَ, (see 3 in art. خصم,)] *He vied*, or *competed, with him*, or *contended with him for superiority, in* فخر [i. e. *glorying*, or *boasting*, &c., or *in glory*, or *excellence*, i. e. *he emulated*, or *rivalled, him therein, and he surpassed him*, or *overcame him, therein*; and, simply, *he vied with him, and surpassed him*]: (Mṣb,* Ḳ:) or *he contended with him for superiority in generousness* or *nobleness of father and mother*: (ISk, Ṣ:) *and he surpassed him*, or *overcame him, therein*. (ISk, Ṣ, Mṣb, Ḳ.)

4. افخرهُ عَلَيْهِ; (ISk, Ṣ, O, Ḳ;) and ▼فخّرهُ, inf. n. تَفْخِيرٌ; (ISk, Ṣ, O;) or ▼فَخَرَهُ عليه, aor. ـَ, (AZ, O,* Ḳ,) inf. n. فَخْرٌ; (AZ, O, TA;) *He judged him*, or *made him, to excel*, or *to have excelled, him in* فخر [or *glorying*, or *boasting*, or *glory*, or *excellence*]. (ISk, Ṣ, O, Ḳ.) — أَفْخَرَتْ *She* (a woman) *brought forth none but such as was* فاخر [or *goodly*, &c.]. (Lth, O.)

5. تفخّر (Ṣ, TA) and ▼تفاخر (TA) *He magnified himself*; *he was*, or *became, proud, haughty*, or *disdainful*; syn. of the inf. n. of the former تَكَبُّرٌ, and تَعَظُّمٌ; (Ṣ, TA;) and that of the latter تَعَاظُمٌ. (TA.)

6. تفاخروا [*They vied*, or *competed*, or *contended for superiority, one with another, in* فخر, i. e., *glorying*, or *boasting*, or *in glory*, or *excellence*, i. e. *they emulated*, or *rivalled, one another therein*; and, simply, *they vied, one with another*;] *they boasted together, one party against another*. (Ṣ,* Ḳ.) تفاخروا فِيمَا بَيْنَهُمْ *They boasted among themselves of their several causes of boasting*. (Mṣb.) — See also 1, in two places; and 5.

8: see 1, first sentence. — [Hence,] افتخرت زَوَاخِرُهُ ‡ [*Its herbs*] *became tall*. (A, TA.)

10. استفخرهُ *He bought it* فَاخِرًا [i. e. *of a good, a goodly*, or *an excellent, quality*], namely, a garment, or piece of cloth, (Lth, O,) or a thing. (Ḳ.) And in like manner the verb is used in relation to the giving [and app. the taking] in marriage. (O.)

فَخْرٌ [*Glory*: *excellence*: originally an inf. n.: as also ▼فُخْرَةٌ.] You say إِنَّهُ لَذُو فُخْرَةٍ عَلَيْهِمْ, i. e. فَخْر [*Verily he possesses glory*, or *excellence, above them*: or perhaps the meaning of this phrase may be *verily he has a disposition to boast himself against them*]: and مَا لَكَ فُخْرَةُ هٰذَا, i. e. فَخْرُهُ [*Thou hast not the glory*, or *excellence, of this*]. (Lḥ, TA.)

فَخْرٌ and فَخَرٌ *Thickness* of an udder, *with contractedness of the orifices of the teats, and with paucity of milk*. (TA.)

فُخْرَةٌ: see فَخْرٌ, in two places.

فِخْرَةٌ [*A manner of glorying*, or *boasting*]. You say فَخَرَ فِخْرَةً حَسَنَةً [*He gloried*, or *boasted, in a good manner*]. (Lḥ, TA.)

فَخَارٌ [said in the Mṣb to be a simple subst.: see 1].

فَخُورٌ: see فَاخِرٌ. — Also A she-camel *great in the udder, contracted in the orifices of the teats*: (Aṣ, Ṣ, O:) or *great in the udder, having little milk*; (Ḳ, TA;) and likewise applied to a ewe or she-goat: or *that yields thee what she has of milk, and has nothing remaining thereof*. (TA.) — And A *thick* udder, *contracted in the orifices of the teats, and having little milk*: (Ḳ, TA:) erroneously repeated in the Ḳ among words ending with ز. (TA.) — And A palm-tree *great in the trunk, thick in the branches*. (Ṣ, O, Ḳ.) — Also, and ▼فَيْخَرٌ, (O, Ḳ,) which is likewise with ز, (TA,) both applied to a horse, (O, Ḳ,) and the latter to a man also, (O,) *Great in the yard*, (O, Ḳ,) *and long therein*: (Ḳ:) and the latter, applied to a penis, *great*; mentioned by IDrd as with ج: (TA:) and the pl. is فَيَاخِرُ. (Ḳ, TA.)

فَخِيرٌ One *who vies, or competes, or contends, with another in glorying, or boasting*, &c., (O, Ḳ,) or *for superiority in generousness or nobleness of father and mother*; (Ṣ;) *i. q.* مُفَاخِرٌ; (Ḳ;) like خَصِيمٌ (Ṣ, TA) in the sense of مُخَاصِمٌ. (TA.) You say جَآءَ فُلَانٌ فَخِيرُ ثُمَّ رَجَعَ أَخِيرًا [*Such a one came contending with others in glorying, or boasting*, &c.: *then returned last, or meanest*]. (A.) — Also *Overcome in* فَخْر [i. e. *glorying, or boasting*, &c.]. (Ḳ.)

فَخَّارٌ *Baked pottery; baked vessels of clay*: (Mṣb, voce خَزَفٌ:) or *baked clay*: before it is baked, it is called خَزَفٌ and صَلْصَالٌ: (Mṣb in the present art.:) or *i. q.* خَزَفٌ: (Ṣ, O, Ḳ:) or *a kind of* خَزَف *of which earthen vessels, or jars, mugs, &c., are made*: (TA:) or *earthen vessels; vessels made of potters' clay*: pl. of [or rather a coll. gen. n. of which the n. un. is] فَخَّارَةٌ. (Ḳ.)

فِخِّيرٌ: }
فِخِّيرَةٌ: } see the paragraph here following.
فِخِّيرَآءُ: }

فَاخِرٌ an epithet from فَخَرَ in the first of the senses expl. above; as also ▼ فَخُورٌ: (Ḳ:) [the former signifies *Glorying; boasting*; &c.: and the latter, the same as] ▼ فِخِّيرٌ one *who glories, or boasts, much*; (Ṣ, O, TA;) as also ▼ فِخِّيرَآءُ: (O, TA:) and ▼ فِخِّيرَةٌ one *who glories, or boasts, very much*. (O,* TA.) — A thing, (Ṣ, O, Mṣb,) or anything, (Ḳ,) [*superb, grand*; as though glorying, or boasting;] *good; goodly; excellent; of excellent quality*. (Ṣ, O, Mṣb, Ḳ.) — Also † *Dates not yet ripe* (بُسْرٌ) *that grow large, and have no stones*: (Ṣ, O, Ḳ:) as though they boasted against others. (TA.)

فَيْخَرٌ: see فَخُورٌ, last sentence.

فَاخُورٌ *A species of sweet-smelling plants*; (Ṣ, TA;) *i. q.* رَيْحَانُ الشُّيُوخِ; (Ḳ, TA;) thus called by the people of El-Baṣrah; accord. to AḤn, the مَرْو [or *marum*] *having broad leaves*; and said to be *that of which there have come forth, in its midst*, جَمَامِيح [pl. of جُمَّاحٌ, q. v.], *like foxes' tails, with a red, sweet-smelling blossom in the middle thereof*: the physicians assert that it cuts short the [sleep termed] سُبَات. (TA.) — [A meaning assigned by Golius to this word belongs to فَنَاخِرَةٌ.]

مَفْخَرَةٌ and مَفْخُرَةٌ *A thing in which one glories, or boasts himself*; (Ḳ;) *a cause of glorying or boasting*; *a generous quality or action, or a generous quality that is inherited by generation from generation*; syn. مَأْثُرَةٌ: (Ṣ, O:) pl. مَفَاخِرُ. (Mṣb.)

فخم

1. فَخُمَ, aor. ـُ, (Ṣ, M, Ḳ, &c.,) inf. n. فَخَامَةٌ, (Ṣ, &c.,) *He* (a man, Ṣ) *was, or became, large, big, bulky, or thick*. (Ṣ, M, Ḳ, &c.) — And *He was, or became, great in respect of estimation, rank, or quality*. (So accord. to an explanation of the inf. n. in the KL [agreeably with an explanation of the epithet فَخْمٌ].) See also مُفَخَّمٌ, below. — And one says also فَخُمَ الأَمْرُ [meaning *Great in estimation is the thing or affair or event or case!*]. (Ḳ in art. بخ, in which see بَخْ.)

2. تَفْخِيمٌ is *syn. with* تَعْظِيمٌ [as signifying The *magnifying* a man, *honouring* him, or *treating* him *with respect or reverence or veneration*]: (Ṣ, Ḳ, TA:) one says, أَتَيْنَا فُلَانًا فَفَخَّمْنَاهُ meaning [*We came to such a one*] *and we magnified him*, or *honoured him*, and *paid him high respect*: and ▼ تَفَخَّمَهُ signifies [the same as فَخَّمَهُ, i. e.] *He magnified him, or honoured him*, &c.; syn. أَجَلَّهُ, and عَظَّمَهُ. (TA.) — تَفْخِيمُ الحَرْفِ is *the contr. of* إِمَالَتُهُ [i. e. it signifies *The pronouncing of the word with the broad sound of the lengthened fet-ḥ* (*approaching to the sound of "a" in our word "ball"*)]: (Ṣ:) [and also *with a full sound of the letter* ل:] or التَّفْخِيمُ is *the abstaining from* الإِمَالَة; (Ḳ, and Kull p. 127;) and *the contr. of* التَّرْقِيقُ; i. e. *i. q.* التَّغْلِيظُ; and signifies *the inclining of* ا *towards the place of utterance of* و, *as in the word* الصَّلٰوةُ; and *the uttering of* ل *from the lower part of the tongue* [i. e. *with the tongue turned up*], *as in the word* اللّٰه [i. e. *in the word* اللّٰه *not immediately preceded by a kesreh*]: (Kull ubi suprà:) it is [predominantly] peculiar to the people of El-Ḥijáz, like as الإمالة is to the tribe of Temeem. (TA.) — See also what next follows.

5. تَفَخَّمَ signifies *He magnified, or aggrandized, himself*; as is shown by a verse cited in the first paragraph of art. فيل; in which verse it is said in the M that ▼ فَخَّمُوا means تَفَخَّمُوا. — And it is also trans., like 2: see 2, first sentence.

فَخْمٌ [seems to signify primarily *Large, big, bulky, or thick*. And hence,] A man *having much flesh in the balls, or elevated parts, of the cheeks*. (TA.) — [And predominantly,] *Great in estimation, rank, or quality*; (Ṣ, Ḳ, TA;) applied to a man: (Ṣ, TA:) pl. فِخَامٌ: the fem. is فَخْمَةٌ. (TA.) And it is likewise applied to حَسَبٌ [or grounds of pretension to respect or honour]. (TA.) — And to speech, or diction, (مَنْطِق,) meaning *Strong; sound, or correct; or chaste, clear, or eloquent, and comprehensive*; syn. جَزْلٌ. (Ṣ, Ḳ.)

فَخْمَةٌ fem. of فَخْمٌ [q. v.]. (TA.) — And *A great army or military force*. (TA.)

فُخْمِيَّةٌ, like جُهْنِيَّةٌ, (so in the JK, Ḳ, and TA, [in the CḲ and my MS. copy of the Ḳ فُخَيْمَةٌ, like جُهَيْنَةٌ,]) *Self-magnification, pride, or haughtiness*, and *assumption of superiority*. (JK, Ḳ, TA.)

فَيْخَمَانٌ *A person of authority*, (TA,) *one held in honour, from whose judgment events are made to proceed, and without whom no affair is decided*. (Ḳ, TA. [In the explanation of this word in the CḲ, يَصْدُرُ is a mistranscription for يُصْدَرُ.])

أَفْخَمُ *i. q.* أَعْظَمُ [as meaning *Most, or very, great in estimation, rank, or quality*; applied to a man]. (TA.)

مُفَخَّمٌ, occurring in a trad., as an epithet applied to the Prophet, means *Magnified, honoured*, or *regarded with respect or reverence or veneration, in the minds and the eyes* [*of others*: and so it means when applied in a general manner]: not largeness in his bodily make: or, as some say, it means [*characterized by*] ▼ فَخَامَة *in his face*, [i. e.] *its nobleness, and fulness, with beauty, or comeliness, and a quality inspiring reverence or veneration*. (TA.)

فد

1. فَدَّ, aor. ـِ, inf. n. فَدِيدٌ (Aṣ, T, Ṣ, M, L, Ḳ) and فَدٌّ, (M, L,) *He* (a man, Aṣ, Ṣ) *uttered his voice, called out, cried out, or vociferated*: (Aṣ, Ṣ, M, A, L, Ḳ:) or *did so vehemently*: (T, M, L, Ḳ:) or *raised his voice*; (TA;) and so ▼ فَدْفَدَ, said of a man, and of a camel: (L:) or *they* (a number of sheep or goats) *made a sound by running*: or *made a sound by running with their pastors and those driving them with singing*: (Ḳ:) or *he, or it, made a sound like that termed* حَفِيف; (Lth, T, M, Ḳ;) as also ▼ فَدْفَدَ, inf. n. فَدْفَدَةٌ: (M, L, Ḳ:*) and *he* (a man) *ran, making a sound by his running*. (L.) — فَدَّ, aor. ـِ, inf. n. فَدِيدٌ, *It* (a bird) *moved, or flapped*, (حَثَّ,) *its wings, expanding and contracting them*. (M.) — *He ran*, (Ḳ, TA,) *fleeing*. (TA.) [See also R. Q. 1.] — فَدَّتِ الإِبِلُ *The camels crushed the ground with their feet, by the vehemence of their tread*. (M, L.) And فَدَّ, aor. ـِ, inf. n. فَدٌّ and فَدِيدٌ; (L;) and ▼ فَدْفَدَ; (M, L;) *He* (a man) *trod vehemently upon the ground, by reason of exultation, and briskness, liveliness, or sprightliness*. (M, L.) [See also 2.] — هُوَ يُفَدِّدُنِى وَيُعَدِّدُنِى means *He threatens me*. (Ḳ, TA.)

2. فَدَّدَ, inf. n. تَفْدِيدٌ, *He cried out, or vociferated, or did so vehemently, in buying or selling*. (IAạr, T, L, Ḳ.) — And *He* (a man) *walked upon the ground proudly and exultingly*. (IAạr, T, L, Ḳ.*)

R. Q. 1. فَدْفَدَ, inf. n. فَدْفَدَةٌ: see 1, in three places. — Also *He* (a man, TA) *ran, fleeing from an enemy or a beast of prey*. (T, L, Ḳ.) [See also 1, latter half.]

فُدَادٌ: see فَدَّادٌ, last sentence.

فَدِيدٌ an inf. n. of 1 [q. v.]. — Also *Abundance of camels*. (M, L.) — And إِبِلٌ فَدِيدٌ *Many camels*. (M, L.)

فُدَادَةٌ and فَدَادَةٌ: see the next paragraph, last two sentences, in three places.

فَدَّادٌ *Having a strong, or loud, voice*, (Ṣ, M, A, L, Ḳ,) *and rude, coarse, or uncivil, in speech*; (L, Ḳ;) as also ▼ فَدْفَدٌ and ▼ فُدَفِدٌ. (Lh, M, L,

Ḳ.) —— *Having a vehement tread.* (M, L, Ḳ.) Hence, in a trad., قَدْ كُنْتَ تَمْشِى فَوْقِى فَدَّادًا i.e. [*Thou usedst to walk upon me*] *treading vehemently*, as said by the earth, (M, L,) to a dead man buried in it. (L.) —— *Proud,* (Ḳ, TA,) *and exulting.* (TA.) —— And *Possessing camels in number from two hundred* (in some copies of the Ḳ [and in a copy of the T] *from hundreds*, TA) *to a thousand,* (AO, T, Nh, L, Ḳ,) *and therewithal rude, coarse,* or *uncivil, and proud.* (AO, T.) —— Pl. فَدَّادُونَ. (L, Ḳ, &c.) —— The pl. occurs in a trad., in the saying, إِنَّ الجَفَآءَ وَالقَسْوَةَ فِى الفَدَّادِينَ, (T, Ṣ, L,) meaning [*Verily rudeness,* or *coarseness, and hardness, are in*] *the men whose voices are high,* or *loud, in their corn-fields and among their cattle:* (El-Aḥmar, Aṣ, T, Ṣ, L, Ḳ:) or (in the Ḳ "and") *the tenders of camels, and pastors, and tenders of oxen and of asses:* (Th, T, Ḳ:) or (in the Ḳ "and") *the tillers of the ground;* (M, A, Mgh, Ḳ, TA;) because they vociferate in their corn-fields: (A, Mgh:) or (in the Ḳ "and") *the people of the deserts;* (M, Ḳ, TA;) *the men who dwell in the* فَدَافِد [pl. of فَدْفَد, q. v.]; (MF;) because of the roughness of their voices, and their rudeness, or coarseness: (M:) or (in the Ḳ "and") *the possessors of many camels.* (M, Ḳ, TA.) [See also art. فدن.] —— ▼ الفَدَّادَةُ signifies *The frog:* (A, Ḳ:) so called because of its croaking. (A.) —— Also, ▼ فَدَّادَةٌ, (IAạr, Th, M, L, Ḳ,) and ▼ فُدَادَةٌ, (IAạr, L,) or ▼ فَدَادَةٌ, (M, Ḳ,) *A cowardly man.* (IAạr, Th, M, L, Ḳ.) —— Also, ▼ فَدَّادَةٌ, (L,) or ▼ فَدَادَةٌ, (M, Ḳ,) *A certain bird:* (M, L, Ḳ:) n. un. of فَدَّادٌ, (L,) or ▼ فَدَادٌ. (M.)

فَدَّادَةٌ: see the last three sentences of the next preceding paragraph.

فَدْفَدٌ *A desert,* or *waterless desert,* (T, M, L, Ḳ,) *wherein is nothing:* (T, M, L:) or *an even tract of land:* (Ṣ, L, Ḳ:) or *a spacious and pebbly tract of land:* (A:) or *a rugged and pebbly tract of land:* or *a hard place:* (M, L:) or *a hard and rugged place:* (Ḳ:) or *an elevated place* (Aṣ, T, L, Ḳ) *in which is hardness:* (Aṣ, T, L:) pl. فَدَافِدُ. (L.)

فُدْفُدٌ: see فَدَّادٌ, first sentence.

فُدْفُدٌ: see فَدَّادٌ, first sentence. ═ Also *Thick milk:* (IAạr, T:) or *i. q.* هُدَبِدٌ, (Ḳ,) which signifies *very thick* milk: (Ṣ and L and Ḳ in explanation of the latter:) or both signify *sour and thick* milk. (T and L in explanation of the latter.)

فدح

1. فَدَحَهُ, (Ṣ, A, Ḳ,) aor. ـَ, (Ḳ,) inf. n. فَدْحٌ, (TA,) *It* (a debt, Ṣ, A, Ḳ, and an affair, and a load, TA) *burdened him, burdened him heavily, oppressed him,* or *overburdened him:* (Ṣ, A, Ḳ:) ▼ افدحهُ [in this sense], said of debt, has not been heard from any one in the correctness of whose Arabic speech confidence is placed. (Ṣ.)

4: see the preceding paragraph: —— and that here following.

10. استفدحهُ *He deemed it* (i. e. an affair [&c.]) *burdensome, heavily burdening, oppressive,* or *overburdening:* (A, TA:) or *he found it to be so;* as also ▼ افدحهُ. (Ḳ.)

فَادِحٌ A debt, (A,) or an affair, (Ṣ, Ḳ,) [or a load, (see 1,)] *burdening, burdening heavily, oppressing,* or *overburdening.* (Ṣ, A, Ḳ.)

فَادِحَةٌ *A misfortune, an affliction,* or *a calamity:* [pl. فَوَادِحُ:] فَوَادِحُ الدَّهْرِ signifies *the afflictions,* or *calamities, of fortune.* (Ḳ,* TA.)

مُفْدَحٌ: see the following paragraph.

مَفْدُوحٌ A man *burdened, heavily burdened, oppressed,* or *overburdened,* by debt, or by an affair, or by a load: (Ṣ,* L, TA:) ▼ مُفْدَحٌ in this sense is not allowable. (L.)

فدخ

1. فَدَخَ رَأْسَهُ, aor. ـَ, (Ḳ, TA,) inf. n. فَدْخٌ, (TA,) *He broke his head* with a stone: (Ḳ, TA:) and فَدَخْتُ الشَّىْءَ *I broke the thing:* (TA:) [but] the verb is not used except in relation to a thing in which is moisture. (Ḳ, TA.)

فدر

1. فَدَرَ, (Lth, IAạr, T, Ṣ, M, O, Ḳ,) aor. ـُ, (M,) or ـِ, (O, Ḳ,) inf. n. فُدُورٌ (Lth, T, Ṣ, M, O, Ḳ) and فَدْرٌ; (Ḳ;) and ▼ فدّر, (IAạr, T, O, Ḳ,) inf. n. تَفْدِيرٌ; (O;) and ▼ افدر; (IAạr, T, O, Ḳ;) said of a stallion, (IAạr, T, Ṣ, &c.,) primarily of a stallion-camel, (IAạr, T,) *He desisted from covering;* (IAạr, T, Ṣ, O;) or *he desisted from covering, being wearied by much indulging therein:* (Ṣ, O:) or *he flagged,* or *became remiss,* or *languid, in covering,* (Lth, T, M, Ḳ,) *and desisted therefrom:* (M, Ḳ:) the د in فَدَرَ, thus used, may be a substitute for the ت in فَتَرَ: (O:) accord. to IAth, it signifies *he lacked power,* or *ability, to cover.* (TA.) —— فَدَرَ, inf. n. فُدُورٌ, said of a mountain-goat, *He became such as protected himself in the mountain from the hunter:* or *he became large,* or *big, and advanced in age,* or *full-grown;* thus says IḲṭṭ. (TA.) —— And فَدَرَ said of cooked flesh-meat, (Ḳ, TA,) inf. n. فُدُورٌ, (TA,) *It became cold.* (Ḳ, TA.) ═ فَدِرَ, aor. ـَ, inf. n. فَدَرٌ, *He was,* or *became, foolish, stupid,* or *unsound in intellect* or *understanding.* (TA.)

2: see 1, first sentence. ═ هٰذِهِ حِجَارَةٌ تُفَدِّرُ means *These are stones that break into small and large pieces.* (O, Ḳ.)

4: see 1, first sentence.

5. تفدّر, said of a stone, *It,* being struck, *broke in pieces.* (TA.)

فَدْرٌ: see فَادِرٌ, in two places.

فَدِرٌ *Foolish, stupid,* or *unsound in intellect* or *understanding.* (Ṣ, M, O, Ḳ.) —— And Wood *that quickly* [or *easily*] *breaks.* (O, Ḳ.)

فِدْرَةٌ *A piece of flesh-meat:* (M, Ḳ:) or *a compact piece thereof:* (Aṣ, T, Ṣ, O:) or *a piece of cold, cooked, flesh-meat:* (T: [mentioned in the TA as from the M:]) and *a piece of anything:* (TA:) pl. فِدَرٌ. (T, TA.) —— *A lump* of dates [*compacted together*]: (M:) or *a large lump* of dates *compacted together;* as also فِنْدِيرٌ and فِنْدِيرَةٌ, (TA in art. فندر.) —— *A piece* of a mountain: (T, Ḳ:) or *an overtopping,* or *an overhanging,* or *a projecting, piece* of a mountain. (M.) See also فَادِرَةٌ. —— And *A portion* of the night. (M, Ḳ.)

فُدْرَةٌ A man *who goes away by himself;* (Ibn-'Abbád, O, Ḳ;) like فُرْدَةٌ; formed by transposition. (Ibn-'Abbád, O.) [See also فَادِرٌ, last signification.]

فُدَّرٌ *Silver.* (O, Ḳ.) ═ And also, (Ḳ,) or فُدُرٌ, (O,) *A boy,* or *youth, that has nearly attained to puberty:* or *fat,* or *plump.* (O, Ḳ.)

فُدُورٌ: see the next paragraph.

فَادِرٌ, applied to a stallion, [primarily to a stallion-camel, (see 1, first sentence,)] *Desisting from covering;* or *desisting from covering, being wearied by much indulging therein:* (Ṣ, O:) or *flagging,* or *becoming remiss,* or *languid, in covering, and desisting therefrom:* (M, Ḳ:) [or *lacking power,* or *ability, to cover:* (see 1:)] pl. فَوَادِرُ, (Ṣ, O,) or فُدْرٌ. (M, Ḳ.) —— Also, and ▼ فَدُورٌ, (Ṣ, M, O, Ḳ,) and ▼ فَدَرٌ, (M, Ḳ,) applied to a mountain-goat, *Advanced in age,* or *full-grown:* (Ṣ, M, O, Ḳ:) or *youthful, and complete in make:* (M, Ḳ:) or *large,* or *big:* (Ṣ, O:) or *that protects himself in the mountain from the hunter:* (M, Ḳ:) فَادِرٌ applied to a mountain-goat as meaning *advanced in age* is like قَارِحٌ applied to a horse, and بَازِلٌ to a camel, and ضَالِعٌ to an animal of the bovine kind and to a sheep or goat: (Aṣ, T:) accord. to IAth, it is from فَدَرَ said of a stallion as meaning "he lacked power, or ability, to cover:" (TA: [and the like is said in the O:]) the pl. (of فَادِرٌ, M) is فُدْرٌ, (M, and so in some copies of the Ḳ,) or فُدُرٌ, (so in other copies of the Ḳ,) or both, (Ṣ, O, [see an ex. of the latter plural in a verse cited voce تَدَثَّرَ,]) and فَوَادِرُ and (of ▼ فَدَرٌ, M) فُدُورٌ, and (quasi-pl. n., M) ▼ مَفْدَرَةٌ, (M, Ḳ,) like مَشْيَخَةٌ. (M.) ═ And فَادِرٌ, (O, Ḳ,) [thus] without ة, (O,) signifies also A she-camel *that goes away alone, apart from the others;* (O, Ḳ, TA;) like فَارِدٌ. (TA.) [See also فُدْرَةٌ.]

† فَادِرَةٌ *A great,* (T, O, Ḳ,) *hard and solid,* (M, Ḳ,) *mass of rock,* (T, M, O, Ḳ,) *which one sees* (T, O) *upon the head of a mountain;* (T, M, O, Ḳ;) likened to the mountain-goat; (M, O;) as also ▼ فِدْرَةٌ. (TA.) [See also what next follows.]

فِنْدِيرٌ (Ṣ, Ḳ) and فِنْدِيرَةٌ (Ṣ, M, Ḳ) *A great mass of rock that projects,* or *juts out,* (تَنْدُرُ,) *from the head of a mountain:* (Ṣ:) what is thus called is *short of* (دُونَ) *what is termed* فِدْرَةٌ [in relation to a mountain]; (M, Ḳ;) by which may be meant دون in respect of place and projection, not in respect of size. (TA.) [See also فُدْرَةٌ and فَادِرَةٌ: and see more in art. فدر.]

طَعَامٌ مُفْدِرٌ, like مُحْسِنٌ [in measure, app. in some one or more of the copies of the Ḳ like مُحْصَنٌ, for, as is mentioned in the TA, El-Bedr El-Ḳaráfee says that it is anomalous, like مُسْهَبٌ from أَسْهَبَ, and مُحْصَنٌ from أَحْصَنَ], Food that stops from copulation; (Ḳ;) as also ▾ مَفْدَرَةٌ. (Lḥ, Ḳ.)

مَفْدَرَةٌ: see what next precedes: — and see فَادِرٌ. — Also A place of the mountain-goats termed فُدْر. pl. of فَادِرٌ: (Ṣ, O:) [or] مَكَانٌ مَفْدَرَةٌ signifies a place in which are many of those mountain-goats. (M, Ḳ.)

فدع

1. فَدِعَ, with kesr, [aor. ـَ, inf. n. فَدَعٌ,] He was, or became, such as is termed أَفْدَعُ [q. v.]. (O.) And فَدِعَتْ قَدَمُهُ, (O, Ḳ, TA, in the CḲ [erroneously] فَدَعَتْ,) [aor. and inf. n. as above,] occurring in a trad., His foot had the affection termed فَدَعٌ [meaning as expl. below; and in like manner the verb may be used in relation to the hand]. (O, Ḳ, TA.) — See also فَدْعٌ.

2. فدّعهُ, (O, TA, from a trad.,) inf. n. تَفْدِيعٌ, (O, Ḳ,) He caused him (a man, O, TA) to be, or become, such as is termed أَفْدَعُ. (O, Ḳ,* TA.)

فَدْعٌ [app. an inf. n. of which the verb is ▾ فَدَعَ] A breaking, or crushing, syn. شَدْخٌ [q. v.]: and a slight splitting or cleaving or slitting. (TA.)

فَدَعٌ [mentioned above as an inf. n.] Deflection, and distortion: this is [said to be] the primary signification. (TA.) [Generally] A distortion of the wrist or of the ankle-joint, (Ṣ, Mgh, O, Mṣb, Ḳ,) so that the hand or the foot becomes turned towards the inner side: (Ṣ, O, Mṣb, Ḳ:) or the walking upon the back [i. e. the upper surface] of the foot [from an explanation of أَفْدَعُ by IAạr, mentioned in the Mgh and O and Mṣb and TA; but it seems rather to mean a distortion of the foot that occasions the so walking]: (Ḳ: [see also رَوَحٌ:]) or height of the hollow part of the sole of the foot, such that if the person trod upon a sparrow it would not hurt it [from an explanation of أَفْدَعُ by Aṣ, mentioned in the O]: (Ḳ, TA:) or a distortion (عِوَجٌ, Ḳ, TA, [in the O عَرَجٌ,] and مَيْلٌ, TA) in the joints, as though they were dislocated, (Lth, O, Ḳ,) mostly in the wrists and ankle-joints, (Lth,* O,* Ḳ,* TA,) by nature (Lth, O, Ḳ, TA) or by disease, as though the person were unable to extend them: (Lth, O, TA:) or a deflection between the foot and the shank-bone, (O, Ḳ, TA,) and the like in the arm, being a state of dislocation of the joints: (TA:) or it is a colliding of the [inner] ankle-bones, and a wide separation of the feet, (Mgh, TA,) to the right and left. (TA. [See, again, رَوَحٌ.]) In the camel, (Ḳ,) or in the fore legs of the camel, (ISh, O, TA,) it is The state in which one sees the animal to tread upon the part between the phalanges of his foot, so that the fore part of his foot becomes raised; (ISh, O, Ḳ, TA;) and it is nought but a rigidity in the pastern [that occasions this]. (ISh, O, TA.)

فَدَعَةٌ The place of what is termed فَدَعٌ, (Ṣ, O, Mṣb,) in the wrist or ankle-joint. (Ṣ, Mṣb.)

أَفْدَعُ Having a deflection; and distorted. (TA [in which it is implied that this is the primary signification].) [Generally] Having the affection termed فَدَعٌ [q. v.]; applied to a man; (Ṣ, Mgh, O, Mṣb, Ḳ;) and to a he-camel: (O, Ḳ:) fem. فَدْعَآءُ; (O, Mṣb, Ḳ;) applied to a woman; (Mṣb;) and to a she-camel; (O, Ḳ;) and to a female slave as meaning whose hand is distorted in consequence of work. (IDrd, O.) And the masc. is applied to a male ostrich, as meaning Having a distortion of the extremities of the fore parts of his feet; in like manner as when it is applied to a he-camel. (Lth,* O, TA.) And hence, الأَفْدَعُ, as an epithet in which the quality of a subst. predominates, signifies The male ostrich. (TA.) And أَفْدَعُ is applied by Ru-beh to fish (سَمَك) as meaning Bending, crooked, or curving. (O.) And الفَدْعَآءُ is a name of † The well-known asterism called الذِّرَاعُ [q. v., the Seventh Mansion of the Moon; also called فَدْعَآءُ النَّثْرَةِ, because النثرة is the Eighth Mansion]: a poet says,

• يَوْمٌ مِنَ النَّثْرَةِ أَوْ فَدْعَائِهَا •
• يُخْرِجُ نَفْسَ العَنْزِ مِنْ وَجْعَائِهَا •

[A day of the auroral setting of النثرة or of its فدعاء that causes the soul of the she-goat to pass forth from her anus]; meaning, by reason of the intenseness of the cold. (TA.) — The dim. of أَفْدَعُ is ▾ أُفَيْدِعُ. (TA.)

أُفَيْدِعُ: see what next precedes.

فدغ

1. فَدَغَهُ, aor. ـَ, inf. n. فَدْغٌ, He broke it, (Ṣ, O, Mṣb, Ḳ,) or crushed it; (Ṣ, O, Ḳ;) or (Ḳ) it is said when the object is a hollow thing, (Ṣ, O, Mṣb, Ḳ, TA,) or a moist, or soft, thing, (TA,) a person's head, (Ṣ, O, TA,) and a grape, and the like: (O, TA:) and he bruised, brayed, or pounded, it coarsely: and he clave, split, or rent, it slightly. (TA.) — And فَدَغَ الطَّعَامَ He put much clarified butter into the food. (O,* Ḳ,* TA.) — And one says also, فَدَغَ الكَمْأَةَ فِي السَّمْنِ [app. meaning He preserved the truffles in clarified butter]. (O.)

7. انفدغ It (anything dry, or rigid,) became soft, or supple. (O, Ḳ.*)

فَدَغٌ Distortion in the foot: (Ibn-'Abbád, O, Ḳ:) like فَدَعٌ, which is more common. (O.) [See فَدَعٌ.]

مِفْدَغٌ An instrument for breaking, or crushing. (Ḳ, TA.) And applied to a man; like مِدَقٌّ [q. v.]. (TA.)

فدم

1. فَدَمْتُ عَلَى فِيهِ بِالفِدَامِ, [aor. ـِ,] inf. n. فَدْمٌ, I covered his, or its, mouth with the فِدَام [q. v.]: (Ṣ:) or فَدَمَ فَاهُ, and عَلَى فِيهِ, aor. ـِ, and ▾ فدّم, (M, Ḳ, TA,) inf. n. تَفْدِيمٌ; (TA;) he put the فِدَام upon his, or its, mouth: (M, Ḳ:) [app. used in relation to a man and also to an إِبْرِيق or other vessel: but the latter verb, and as trans. without a particle, seems to be more commonly used in relation to both:] one says of Persians or other foreigners, and of Magians, on the occasion of their giving to drink, ▾ فَدَّمُوا أَفْوَاهَهُمْ They bound the فِدَام upon their mouths: (T:) and ▾ فدّم الإِبْرِيقَ, (M, Ḳ,) inf. n. تَفْدِيمٌ, (Ḳ,) He put the فدام upon the mouth of the ابريق. (M, Ḳ.*) — فَدُمَ, (T, M, Ḳ,) inf. n. فَدَامَةٌ (T, Ṣ, M, Mṣb, Ḳ) and فُدُومَةٌ, (Ṣ, M, Mṣb, Ḳ,) He was, or became, such as is termed فَدْمٌ [q. v.]; or he was, or became, heavy, sluggish, or dull; and confounded, or perplexed, and unable to see his right course. (TA.)

2: see the preceding paragraph, in three places. One says also, فدّم البَعِيرَ, meaning He bound upon the camel's mouth the فِدَامَة, (M,) which means the غِمَامَة [q. v.]. (TA.)

فَدْمٌ Impotent (T, Ṣ, M, Ḳ) in speech, (T, M, Ḳ,) and in adducing an argument; (T, M;) [as though his mouth were covered with a فِدَام, for it is said in the Ṣ to be from فَدَمْتُ عَلَى فِيهِ بِالفِدَامِ;] heavy, sluggish, or dull; (Ṣ;) or with heaviness, sluggishness, or dulness, and softness, and paucity of understanding: (M, Ḳ:) or unintelligent: (Mṣb:) and thick; (M, Ḳ;) fat; (M;) foolish, or stupid; rough, rude, or uncivil: (M, Ḳ:) accord. to IAạr, the heavy, sluggish, or dull; as being likened to blood, which is thus called: (T:) and ثَدْمٌ is a dial. var. thereof, or, accord. to Yaạḳoob, the ث is a substitute for the ف: (M:) the fem. is with ة: (M, Mṣb, Ḳ:) and the pl. is فِدَامٌ [agreeably with analogy]. (M, Ḳ: in a copy of the T فُدُمٌ [which I think a mistranscription].) — Also Heavy [and app. thick] blood: and, accord. to IAạr, blood [itself]. (T.) — And A garment, or piece of cloth, (T, TA,) saturated with dye, (T,) or saturated with red dye by its being put again into the safflower time after time. (TA.) And Red that is saturated (M, Ḳ) with redness: (Ḳ:) or of which the redness is not intense. (Thus also in some copies of the Ḳ.) [See also مُفْدَمٌ.]

فَدَامٌ: see the next paragraph, in two places.

فِدَامٌ and ▾ فَدَّامٌ and ▾ فِدَامَةٌ and ▾ فُدُومٌ, (Ḳ,) or ▾ فَدَّامٌ [only], (Ṣ, T, M,) A thing which the Persians or other foreigners, (T, Ḳ,) and the Magians, (Ḳ,) bind upon their mouths on the occasion of their giving to drink; (T, Ḳ;) or a *piece of cloth with which the Magian binds his mouth;* (Ṣ;) or *a sort of thing with which the Persians* or *other foreigners wipe* [app. *the mouth*] *when they give to drink;* one of which is termed ♦ فَدَّامَةٌ. (M. [In the Ṣ it seems to be implied that this last word is syn. with فَدَّامٌ as expl. above.]) —— Also, (Ḳ,) or the first, (T, Ṣ, M,) and also ♦ فَدَّامٌ, (Ṣ,) or and also ♦ فِدَامٌ, (M,) *A strainer,* or *clarifier,* (T, Ṣ, M, Ḳ,) *for a mug* and *an* إِبْرِيق and *the like;* (T;) *a thing that is put in,* or *upon, the mouth of the* ابريق, *for the straining,* or *clarifying, of what is in it:* (Ṣ, M:*) also called ثِدَامٌ. (M.) —— And فِدَامٌ signifies also the same as عِمَامَةٌ: thus in copies of the Ḳ [and in a copy of the M]: but the former word is correctly ♦ فِدَامَةٌ [as is implied in one place in the M]; and the word by which it is explained is correctly غِمَامَةٌ, [as in some copies of the Ḳ,] meaning *A thing that is put upon the mouth of the camel.* (TA. [See 2: and see also the first paragraph of art. غم.])

فِدَامَةٌ: see the next preceding paragraph.

فَدَّامٌ: see فِدَامٌ, in three places.

فَدُّومٌ: see فِدَامٌ.

فَدَّامَةٌ n. un. of فَدَّامٌ: see فِدَامٌ, former half.

مُفْدَمٌ: see مُفَدَّمٌ. —— Also A garment, or piece of cloth, *saturated with red dye:* (Sh, T, Ṣ, M, and some copies of the Ḳ:) or *of which the redness is not intense.* (M, and some copies of the Ḳ.) It is said in a trad. that he [the Prophet] disliked the مُفْدَم for the مُحْرِم, but saw no harm in the مُضَرَّج [q. v.]. (TA.) —— Also Dye *thick and saturated.* (Ṣ.) —— And ذُلٌّ مُفْدَمٌ ‡ *Deeply-stained, intense, vileness* or *ignominy.* (TA.)

مُفَدَّمٌ (T, M, Ḳ) and ♦ مَفْدُومٌ (T) and ♦ مُفْدَمٌ (M, Ḳ) An إِبْرِيق [a vessel for wine] *having a strainer, called* فِدَام, (T, M, Ḳ,) *in,* or *upon, its mouth:* (M, Ḳ:*) and so مُثَدَّمٌ. (M.) It is said in a trad., إِنَّكُمْ مَدْعُوونَ يَوْمَ القِيَامَةِ مُفَدَّمَةً أَفْوَاهُكُمْ بِالفِدَامِ [*Verily ye will be summoned on the day of resurrection having your mouths closed with the* فدام]; meaning, ye will be withheld from speaking with your mouths, so that your skins will speak. (M.)

مُفَدَّمَاتٌ [*Vessels of the kinds called*] أَبَارِيق and دِنَان [pls. of إِبْرِيق and دَنٌّ]. (Ṣ.)

مَفْدُومٌ: see مُفَدَّمٌ.

فدن

2. تَفْدِينٌ signifies The *making* a building *tall.* (Ḳ. [See فَدَنٌ.]) —— And ‡ The *fattening* of camels. (Ḳ, TA.) One says, فَدَّنَهُ, meaning ‡ *He* (the pastor) *fattened him* [i. e. a camel]; *made him like the* فَدَن, i. e. the قَصْر. (TA.)

فَدَنٌ *A* [*pavilion, or building of the kind termed*] قَصْر, (Ṣ, M, A, Ḳ,) *raised high,* or *made lofty:* (M, Ḳ:) pl. أَفْدَانٌ; (M, A;) to which fat camels are likened. (A. [See 2.]) ═ And *A certain red dye.* (M, Ḳ.)

فَدَانٌ: see the next paragraph, in five places.

فَدَّانٌ The *bull;* (M, Ḳ;) and so ♦ فَدَانٌ: (Ḳ:) the *bull with which one ploughs:* (IAạr, TA:) or, (AA, AḤn, Ṣ, M, Mgh, Mṣb, Ḳ,) as also ♦ فَدَانٌ, (Mgh, Mṣb, Ḳ,) the *oxen,* (AA, Ṣ,) or the *two bulls* (AḤn, M, Mgh, Mṣb, Ḳ) *which are coupled together* (AḤn, M, Ḳ) *in* [or *by means of*] *the* [*cord called*] قِرَان (Mgh) [*and*] *which plough,* (Ṣ,) or *with which one ploughs;* (AḤn, M, Mgh, Mṣb, Ḳ;*) and one thereof is not called فَدَّانٌ: (AḤn, M, Ḳ:) or فَدَّانٌ signifies, (Mgh, Ḳ,) and so ♦ فَدَانٌ, (Mgh,) or the former, (Ṣ,) or each, (M, Mṣb,) signifies also, (Ṣ, M, Mṣb,) [the *plough;* or the *apparatus,* or *gear, thereof;* i. e.] the *implement,* or the *apparatus,* or *gear,* (Ṣ, Mgh, Mṣb, Ḳ,) *of the two bulls,* (Ṣ, Mgh, Ḳ,) *for ploughing;* (Ṣ, Mgh, Mṣb;) or the *whole apparatus,* or *gear, of the two bulls* [*which are coupled together*] *in* [or *by means of*] *the* [*cord called*] قِرَان: (M:) but accord. to Abu-l-Ḥasan Eṣ-Ṣiḳillee, ♦ فَدَانٌ, without teshdeed, signifies the *implement,* or *apparatus, with which one ploughs:* and فَدَّانٌ, with teshdeed, has a different meaning, expl. in what follows, relating to land: and IAạr says the like: (TA:) [see also عِيَانٌ:] the pl. of فَدَّانٌ is فَدَادِينُ, (Ṣ, M, Mgh, Mṣb, Ḳ,) meaning *oxen with which one ploughs:* (M, TA:) the pl. of ♦ فَدَانٌ is أَفْدِنَةٌ [a pl. of pauc.] and فُدُنٌ, (M, Mgh, Mṣb, TA,) and the vulgar say فِدن, with kesr. (TA.) —— فَدَّانٌ, with teshdeed, also signifies *A certain commonly-known quantity* [*of land*]; (IAạr, TA;) said by Abu-l-Ḥasan Eṣ-Ṣiḳillee to signify *a limited portion of land, subdivided into four and twenty ḳeerâṭs;* (TA;) [loosely reckoned as the *quantity of land which a yoke of oxen will plough in one day;* thus corresponding to the Latin term *jugerum,* and our *acre;* and commonly defined as consisting of 333 *ḳaṣabehs* (or *rods*) *and one third;* (the ḳaṣabeh being 24 ḳabḍahs; and the ḳabḍah being the measure of a man's fist with the thumb erect, or about 6 inches and a quarter;) but different in different times and in different parts of the same country: hence, perhaps,] it is also expl. as signifying *a place of seed-produce.* (M, TA.)

أَصْحَابُ الفَدَادِينَ is said to signify الفَدَّادُونَ [*The possessors of ploughing oxen*]; like as جَمَّالُونَ signifies "possessors of camels:" but it has been otherwise expl. in [its proper place, as pl. of فَدَّادٌ, in] art. فد. (Ḳ.)

بِنَآءٌ مُفَدَّنٌ *A building that is* [*made*] *tall,* or *lofty.* (M.) ═ And ثَوْبٌ مُفَدَّنٌ *A garment,* or *piece of cloth, dyed with* فَدَن. (TA.)

فدى

1. فَدَاهُ, (T, Ṣ, M, &c.,) aor. يَفْدِيهِ, (Mṣb, Ḳ,) inf. n. فِدَآءٌ (T, Ṣ, M, Mgh, Ḳ, [omitted in my copy of the Mṣb, probably by inadvertence,]) and فَدًى, (Mgh,) or فِدًى, (so in the M, accord. to the TT,) or also both of these, (Fr, T, Ṣ, Mṣb, Ḳ,) the latter of them said by Fr, on one occasion, to be the more common, (T, TA,) [which is the case when it is a subst., like فِدْيَةٌ,] but 'Alee Ibn-Suleymán El-Akhfash [i. e. El-Akhfash El-Aṣghar] is related to have said that this is not allowable except by poetic license, and El-Ḳálee says that الفَدَى was used by the Arabs in conjunction with الحِمَى, [see حِمًى, in art. حمى,] but other forms were used in other cases [among which he seems to mention فَدَآء, with fet-ḥ and the lengthened alif, but the words in which I find this expressed are somewhat ambiguous, and are also rendered doubtful by an erasure and an alteration]; (TA;) and ♦ افتداهُ, (M,) [whence an ex. in a verse which will be found in what follows,] or افتدى ♦ بِهِ (Ḳ, TA) and مِنْهُ, (TA,) [but I do not know افتدى in either of these phrases as having any other than the well-known meaning of فَدَى نَفْسَهُ, which is strangely omitted in the Ḳ;] and ♦ فاداهُ, (Ṣ, Mgh, Mṣb, Ḳ, TA,) inf. n. مُفَادَاةٌ and فِدَآءٌ; (Mṣb, TA;) but some explain this differently [as will be shown in what follows]; (T, Mgh, Mṣb, TA;) *He gave his ransom;* (Ṣ;) *he gave a thing,* (Ḳ, TA, [أَعْطَاهُ in the CḲ being a mistake for أَعْطَى, without the affixed pronoun,]) *or a captive, for him,* (TA,) *and so liberated him;* (Ḳ, TA;) [i. e. *he ransomed him;*] or *he liberated him,* or *ransomed him,* مِنَ الأَسْرِ [*from captivity*]: (Mgh, Mṣb:) or ♦ فاداهُ signifies *he loosed him,* or *set him free, and took his ransom:* (Mgh, Mṣb, TA:) or مُفَادَاةٌ signifies the *giving* a man *and taking* a man [*in exchange*]: and فِدَآءٌ, [as inf. n. of فَدَاهُ,] the *purchasing* him [*from captivity* or *the like*]: (Mbr, T, Mgh, Mṣb, TA:) or the *preserving* a man *from misfortune by what one gives by way of compensation for him;* as also فِدًى: (Er-Rághib, TA:) you say, فَدَيْتُهُ بِمَالِي *I purchased* [i. e. *ransomed*] *him with my property,* and بِنَفْسِي *with myself:* (T:) or, accord. to Nuṣeyr Er-Rázee, the Arabs say, فَادَيْتُ ♦ الأَسِيرَ [*I ransomed the captive*], and فَدَيْتُهُ بِأَبِي وَأُمِّي [*I ransomed him* in a tropical sense *with my father and my mother*], and بِمَالٍ [*with property*], as though thou purchasedst him and freedst him therewith, when he was not a captive; and you may say, فَدَيْتُ الأَسِيرَ meaning *I freed the captive from the state in which he was,* though ♦ فَادَيْتُ is better in this sense: as to the reading تَفْدُوهُمْ [in the Ḳur ii. 79], Aboo-Mo'ádh says, it means *Ye purchase them from the enemy and liberate them;* but the reading ♦ تُفَادُوهُمْ, he says, means *ye contend with them who are in your hands respecting the price and they so contend with you:* (T, TA:) [that ♦ افتداهُ is syn. with فَدَاهُ is shown by what here follows:] a poet says,

فَلَوْ كَانَ مَيْتٌ يُفْتَدَى لَفَدَيْتُهُ •
بِمَا لَمْ تَكُنْ عَنْهُ النُّفُوسُ تَطِيبُ •

[*And if a person dead were to be ransomed, assuredly I would ransom him with what minds would not be willing to relinquish*]. (M, TA.) —— [The inf. ns. of the first of these verbs are much used in precative phrases:] they said, فَدًى لَكَ [for فَدَاكَ فَدًى, and therefore virtually meaning فُدِيتَ *Mayest thou be ransomed*; the ل being لِلتَّبْيِينِ i. e. "for the purpose of notifying" the person addressed]: (TA:) and فَدًى لَكَ أَبِى [for فَدَاكَ أَبِى بِنَفْسِهِ فَدًى, and therefore virtually meaning simply فَدَاكَ أَبِى بِنَفْسِهِ *May my father ransom thee with himself*; so that it may be well rendered *may my father be a ransom for thee*]: (Ṣ:) and فِدَاءٍ, with tenween, some of the Arabs pronounce with kesr [to the ء, i. e. they pronounce فِدَاءٍ with the tenween of kesr], peculiarly when it is next to [meaning immediately followed by] the preposition ل, saying فِدَاءٍ لَكَ, because it is indeterminate; they intending thereby the meaning of a prayer; and Aṣ has cited [as an ex. thereof] the saying of En-Nábighah [Edh-Dhubyánee],

* مَهْلًا فِدَاءٍ لَكَ الأَقْوَامُ كُلُّهُمُ *
* وَمَا أُثَمِّرُ مِنْ مَالٍ وَمِنْ وَلَدِ *

[*Act gently: may the peoples, all of them, and what I make to be abundant of wealth and of offspring, give themselves as a ransom*, or *be a ransom, for thee*: فِدَاءٍ being app. assimilated to an indeterminate imperative verbal noun such as صَهٍ in the phrase صَهٍ يَا رَجُلُ, which is as though one said أُسْكُتْ سُكُوتًا يَا رَجُلُ; thus meaning here لِيَفْدِكَ: but De Sacy mentions, in his "Chrest. Arabe," sec. ed., vol. ii., p. 460, three allowable readings (not the foregoing reading) in this verse, namely, فِدَاءً and فِدَاءُ and فِدَاءِ; and adds that what here follows is said by a commentator to be, of several explanations, that which is the right: والقول الآخر وهو الصحيح ان فداء بمعنى ليُفدك فبناه كما بنى الامر وكذلك تراك ودراك لانه بمعنى اترك وادرك: this, it will be observed, is similar to the explanation which I have offered of فِدَاءٍ لك; for لِيُفدك is app. a typographical mistake for لِيَفدك: and I incline to think that فداءِ, though supposed to be correct and therefore likened to تَرَاكِ and دَرَاكِ, is a mistake of a copyist for فداءٍ; and the more so because I find in Ahlwardt's "Divans of the Six Ancient Arabic Poets" the three readings فداءً and فداءُ and فداءٍ, but not فداءِ]. (Ṣ, TA.) —— وَفَدَيْنَاهُ بِذِبْحٍ [in the Ḳur xxxvii. 107] means *And we made an animal prepared for sacrifice to be a ransom for him, and freed him from slaughter*. (T, TA.) —— فَدَتْ نَفْسَهَا مِنْ زَوْجِهَا and ▼ افتدت [alone] mean *She gave property to her husband so that she became free from him by divorce*. (Mṣb, TA.) —— See also what next follows.

2. فَدَّاهُ, (Ṣ,* Ḳ,) or فَدَّاهُ بِنَفْسِهِ, (Ṣ,* TA,) [or both, for both are correct,] inf. n. تَفْدِيَةٌ; (Ṣ, Ḳ;) and ▼ فَدَاهُ بنفسه, (Ṣ, TA,*) aor. يَفْدِيهِ, inf. n. فِدَآءٌ; (TA;) *He said to him* ▼ جُعِلْتُ فِدَاكَ [*May I be made thy ransom*, i. e., *a ransom for thee*]. (Ṣ, Ḳ, TA.)

3: see 1, former half, in five places. —— In the saying respecting bloodwits, وَإِنْ أَحَبُّوا فَادَوْا, the meaning is, [*And if they like*,] *they free the slayer*, or *his next of kin who is answerable for him, and accept the bloodwit*; because this is a substitute for the blood, like as the ransom is a substitute for the captive. (Mgh.)

4. افداهُ الأَسِيرَ [in the CḲ (erroneously) الاسيرُ] *He accepted from him the ransom of the captive*. (M, Ḳ.) Hence the saying of the Prophet to Ḳureysh, when 'Othmán Ibn-'Abd-Allah and El-Ḥakam Ibn-Keysán had been made captives, لَا نُفْدِيكُمُوهُمَا حَتَّى يَقْدَمَ صَاحِبَانَا [*We will not accept from you the ransom of them two until our two companions shall come*], meaning [by the two companions] Saad Ibn-Abee-Waḳḳáṣ and 'Otbeh Ibn-Ghazwán. (M.) —— افدى فُلَانٌ *Such a one danced*, or *dandled, his child*: (Ḳ, TA:) because of his [often] saying, فَدًى لَكَ أَبِى وَأُمِّى [*May my father and my mother be ransoms for thee*]. (TA.) ══ افدى also signifies *He made for his dried dates a store-chamber*. (Ḳ.) —— And † *He became large in his body*; (IAạr, T, Ḳ, TA;) as though it became like the فَدَآء [q. v.]. (TA.) —— And *He sold dates*. (IAạr, T, Ḳ.)

6. تفادوا *They ransomed one another*. (Ṣ, TA.) —— And † *They guarded themselves, one by another*; as though every one of them made his fellow to be his ransom. (Mṣb, TA.) —— And تفادى مِنْهُ ‡ *He guarded against it*, or *was cautious of it, and kept aloof from it*. (Ṣ, Ḳ,* TA.)

8: see 1, first quarter, in two places; and again, near the middle of the paragraph. —— As intrans., افتدى signifies [*He ransomed himself*;] *he gave a ransom for himself*. (Er-Rághib, TA.) You say, افتدى مِنْهُ بِكَذَا [*He ransomed himself from him with such a thing*]. (Ṣ.) Hence the usage of the verb in the Ḳur ii. 229. (TA.) See 1, last sentence but one.

فِدًى and ▼ فَدًى and ▼ فِدَآءٌ and ▼ فِدْيَةٌ all signify the same, (Ṣ, Ḳ,) i. e. [*A ransom*;] *a thing*, (Ḳ, TA,) or *a captive*, (TA,) *that is given for a man, who is therewith liberated*: (Ḳ, TA:) [the first three are also inf. ns. (and have been mentioned as such in the first paragraph); therefore when you say فِدًى لك ابى and فَدًى لَكَ أَبِى, the words فَدًى and فِدًى may be either inf. ns. or substs.: as substs., the second and third are more common than the first:] فِدْيَةٌ [is also sometimes expl. as an inf. n., but accord. to general usage] signifies as above; (Ḳ, TA;) or *property given as a substitute* [or *a ransom*] *for a captive*: (Mgh, Mṣb, TA:) and *property by the giving of which one preserves himself from evil in the case of a religious act in which he has fallen short of what was incumbent, like the expiation for the breaking of an oath and of a fast*; and thus it is used in the Ḳur ii. 180 and 192: (Er-Rághib, TA:) and its pl. is فِدًى and فِدْيَاتٌ. (Mgh, Mṣb, TA.)

فَدًى: see the next preceding paragraph. [Hence the phrase] جُعِلْتُ فِدَاكَ: see 2. It is also a pl. of its syn. فِدْيَةٌ. (Mgh, Mṣb, TA.)

فِدْيَةٌ: see فِدًى. ══ خُذْ عَلَى هِدْيَتِكَ وَفِدْيَتِكَ, accord. to the Ḳ, but in the Ṣ, خُذْ فِى هِدْيَتِكَ وَقِدْيَتِكَ, mentioned in art. قدى, is a saying meaning [*Take thou to*] *that* [*course*] *in which thou wast*: the author of the Ḳ seems to have followed Ṣgh, who has mentioned it here: (TA in the present art.:) فِدْيَةٌ and قِدْيَةٌ are dial. vars. (TA in art. قدى.)

فَدَآءٌ *An* أَنْبَار, (Ḳ, TA,) i. e. (TA) *a collection, of wheat*: (M, Ḳ,* TA:) or it signifies, (Ḳ,) or signifies also, (M,) *a collection of food, consisting of barley and dates and the like*: (M, Ḳ:) or *an* أَنْبَار, i. e. *a collection, of food, consisting of wheat and dates and barley*: (Ṣ:) and it is said to signify *a place in which dates are spread and dried*, in the dial. of 'Abd-El-Keys. (M.) —— And The حَجْم [or *protuberant*, or *prominent, part*, or perhaps the *bulk*,] of a thing (M, Ḳ) of any kind. (M.)

فِدَآءٌ: see فِدًى.

الفَدَاوِيَّةُ is the appellation of *A class*, or *sect, of the* خَوَارِج *of the* دُرْزِيَّة [or دُرُوز, whom we call the *Druses*; it is a coll. gen. n., of which the n. un. is فَدَاوِىٌّ; the و being a substitute for ء: it is used to signify *those who undertake perilous adventures, more particularly for the destruction of enemies of their party; as though they offered themselves as ransoms* or *victims*; and hence it is applied to the sect called in our histories of the Crusades "The Assassins"]. (TA.)

[مَفْدِىٌّ, originally مَفْدُوىٌ. In the saying بِنَفْسِى فُلَانٌ مَفْدِىٌّ *With my soul*, or *myself, may such a one be ransomed*, مَفْدِىٌّ is often suppressed; being meant to be understood.]

فذ

1. فَذَّ عَنْ أَصْحَابِهِ, [aor. ـِ, inf. n. فَذٌّ,] *He was*, or *became, apart from his companions, and remained alone*. (L.) ══ And فَذَّ, (TA,) [aor. ـُ,] inf. n. فَذٌّ, (Ḳ, TA,) *He drove away* (طَرَدَ) *vehemently*. (Ḳ, TA.)

4. افذّهُ *He made him*, or *it, to be single; sole*; or *one, and no more*; syn. أَوْتَرَهُ; (Ṣ in art. وتر;) and جَعَلَهُ فَذًّا, i. e. وِتْرًا. (TA in that art.) —— And أَفَذَّتْ *She* (a ewe or goat) *brought forth one only*, (El-Aḥmar, T, Ṣ, M, O, L, Mṣb,) *at a breeding*; (Mṣb;) inf. n. إِفْذَاذٌ. (El-Aḥmar, T, M, L.) [See مُفِذٌّ.]

5: see the next following paragraph.

10. استفذّ بِهِ *He was*, or *became, alone; inde-*

pendent of others; without any to share, or participate, with him; in it: (Ḳ, TA:) you say, استفذّ عَلَىَّ بِالأَمْرِ *He was*, or *became, alone*, or *independent, exclusively of me, in the affair*: (O:) and ↓ تفذّذ به also has the former meaning: (Ḳ, TA:) or this latter signifies *He was*, or *became, alone with him*. (O.)

R. Q. 1. فَذْفَذَ *He contracted himself* (تَقَاصَرَ), *to leap, deceiving*, or *circumventing*, (IAạr, T, O, Ḳ,) or *in order to deceive*, or *circumvent, when leaping*; (IAạr, T in art. ذف;) said of a man. (IAạr, T, O.) —— [And accord. to the Ḳ, in art. ذف, *i. q.* تَبَخْتَرَ; like ذَفْذَفَ: but] accord. to IAạr, ذَفْذَفَ has this latter meaning, and فَذْفَذَ signifies as expl. above on his authority. (T in art. ذف.)

فَذٌّ *Single; sole; only; one, and no more*; [and *alone*, or *apart from others*; (see 1;)] syn. فَرْدٌ; (Ṣ, M, Mgh, O, L, Ḳ;) and وَاحِدٌ: (L, Mṣb:) pl. [of mult.] فُذُوذٌ (M, L, Mṣb, Ḳ) and [of pauc.] أَفْذَاذٌ. (M, L, Ḳ.) One says, ذَهَبَا فَذَّيْنِ *They two went away singly*. (Ṣ, O, L.) And جَآءَ القَوْمُ أَفْذَاذًا: see فُذَاذَى. —— And تَمْرٌ فَذٌّ *Dates that are separate, each one from others*; (IAạr, Ṣ, M, O, L, Ḳ;) *not sticking together*; (IAạr, M, L;) as also فَضٌّ; (M;) and فَتٌّ. (T in art. فت.) —— And الفَذُّ is [a name of] *The first of the arrows used in the game called* المَيْسِر: (Ṣ, M, O, L, Ḳ:) it has one notch; and for it is gained one share [of the slaughtered camel] when it is successful, and one share is exacted when it is unsuccessful: (Lḥ, M, O, L:) the arrows are ten: the 2nd is called التَّوْأَم; the 3rd, الرَّقِيبُ; the 4th, الحِلْسُ; the 5th, النَّافِسُ; the 6th, المُسْبِلُ; the 7th, المُعَلَّى; and there are three for which there is no share, namely, الوَغْدُ and المَنِيحُ and السَّفِيحُ. (Ṣ, O, L.) [See الرقيب.] —— كَلِمَةٌ فَذَّةٌ: see فَاذَّةٌ.

فُذَاذًا: see the next paragraph, in two places.

جَآءَ القَوْمُ فُذَاذَى, (O,) or ↓ فُذَاذًا, (Mṣb,) and ↓ فُذَاذًا, and ↓ أَفْذَاذًا, *The people*, or *party, came one by one; singly*. (O, Mṣb.) And أَكَلْنَا فُذَاذَى, (Ḳ, TA,) and فَذَاذَى, (CḲ,) and ↓ فُذَاذًا, and ↓ فُذَّاذًا, *We ate separately*. (Ḳ.)

فُذَّاذًا: see the next preceding paragraph, in two places.

كَلِمَةٌ فَاذَّةٌ, and ↓ فَذَّةٌ, *i. q.* شَاذَّةٌ [i. e. *A word, phrase, proposition*, or *sentence, extraordinary*, or *exceptional, in respect of rule*, or *of usage*]. (M, L.) And آيَةٌ فَاذَّةٌ *A verse of the Ḳur-án that is alone in meaning*. (L.)

أَفَذُّ An arrow *having no feathers upon it*; (T, O, Ḳ;) opposed to مَرِيشٌ: so says Aboo-Málik: others say أَقَذُّ [q. v.], with ق: but he allowed only the former. (T, O.)

مُفِذٌّ A ewe or she-goat *bringing forth one only*, (El-Aḥmar, T, Ṣ, M, O, L, Mṣb, Ḳ,) *at a breeding*: (Mṣb:) [like مُفْرِدٌ and مُوحِدٌ:] one does not apply this epithet to a she-camel, because she never brings forth more than one. (Ṣ, M, O, L, Mṣb.)

مِفْذَاذٌ A ewe or she-goat *that usually brings forth one only*. (T, Ṣ, O, L, Ḳ.)

فر

1. فَرَّ, aor. ـِ, inf. n. فِرَارٌ (T, Ṣ, M, Ḳ, &c.) and فَرٌّ (M, Ḳ) and مَفَرٌّ (Ṣ, M, Ḳ) and مَفِرٌّ, (Ḳ,) or the last is a n. of place [and of time], (Ṣ, M,) *He* (a man, T) *fled*: (T, Ṣ:) or *he turned away* or *aside, to elude, and fled*, (M, Ḳ, TA,) from a thing that he feared. (TA.) أَيْنَ ٱلْمَفَرُّ [in the Ḳur lxxv. 10] means *Whither is the* [*fleeing* or] *turning away* &c.? (M, TA:) or it may mean *when is the time thereof?* (TA:) and اين المَفِرُّ, another reading, *where is the place of fleeing* &c.? (I'Ab, Zj, Ṣ, M, TA,) as also المِفَرُّ, (Zj, Ḳ, TA,) which is an instrumental noun used as a noun of place: (Ḳ, TA:) but the first is the common reading. (TA.) —— فَرَّ مِنْ عَدُوِّهِ, aor. as above, inf. n. فَرٌّ, *He wheeled about widely from his enemy, to turn again*. (Mṣb.) —— And فَرَّ إِلَى الشَّىْءِ *He went*, or *betook himself, to the thing*. (Mṣb.) —— And [hence] طَرَّتْ فَرَّتْ يَدُهُ *His arm*, or *hand, fell off*; like and تَرَّتْ. (O.) ═ فَرَّ الفَرَسَ, (Ṣ, O,) or الدَّابَّةَ, (M, Ḳ,) aor. ـُ, (Ṣ, M, O,) i. e. with ḍamm, (O,) [in copies of the Ḳ ـِ, but afterwards in those copies ـُ, which is the regular and correct form,] inf. n. فَرٌّ (Ṣ, M, O, Ḳ) and فُرَارٌ and فِرَارٌ and فَرَارٌ, (Ḳ,) or فُرَارٌ is a simple subst., and فِرَارٌ is an inf. n., (Meyd, in explanation of the prov. which here follows,) *He looked at*, or *examined, the teeth of the horse*, (Ṣ, O,) or *he exposed to view the teeth of the beast that he might see what was its age*. (M, Ḳ.) Hence, (TA,)

إِنَّ الجَوَادَ عَيْنُهُ فُرَارُهُ

(Ṣ, M,* Meyd, Ḳ,*) and فِرَارُهُ, (M, Meyd, Ḳ,) and فَرَارُهُ, (Ṣ, Ḳ,) sometimes thus pronounced with fet-ḥ, (Ṣ,) ‡ [*Verily the fleet and excellent horse, his aspect* (see عَيْنٌ) *is* (*equivalent to*) *the examination of his teeth*, i. e. he is known by his aspect], is a prov., applied to him whose external state indicates his internal qualities; (Meyd, O, Ḳ;) meaning that one knows his excellence from his عَيْن [i. e. aspect] like as one knows the age of a beast by examining his teeth; (TA;) his external appearance rendering it needless for thee to test him, (Ṣ, Meyd, O, Ḳ,) and to examine (أَنْ تَفُرَّ) his teeth: (Ṣ, O, Ḳ:) and [with the same meaning] one says, فُرُّ الجَوَادِ عَيْنُهُ: (A, TA:) and [in like manner] الخَبِيثُ عَيْنُهُ فُرَارُهُ [*The bad, his aspect* &c.]; (Meyd, O, TA;) i. e. thou knowest his badness by his عَيْن when thou seest him. (TA.) And one says also, فَرَرْتُ فَمَ الفَرَسِ *I opened the mouth of the horse that I might know his age*. (Ḥar p. 28.) And فَرَّ عَنْ أَسْنَانِ الدَّابَّةِ, aor. ـُ, *He examined the teeth of the beast*. (Ḥar p. 233.) —— [Hence the saying of El-Ḥajjáj, فُرِرْتُ عَنْ ذَكَآءٍ, expl. in art. ذكو.] And [hence also] one says, فَرَّهُ عَنْ أَشْيَآءَ ‡ *He examined him respecting things*. (O,* TA.) And فَرَّ الأَمْرَ, (M, TA,) and فَرَّ عَنِ الأَمْرِ, (Ṣ, M, O, Ḳ, TA,) ‡ *He examined, looked into, scrutinized*, or *investigated, the affair; searched into it; inquired*, or *sought information, respecting it*. (Ṣ, M, O, Ḳ, TA.) And فَرَّ فُلَانٌ عَمَّا فِى نَفْسِى ‡ *Such a one interrogated me in order that he might know, from what I should say, what was in my mind*. (TA.) —— And فَرَّ الأَمْرُ جَذَعًا † *The thing returned to its first state; it recommenced*. (M, O, Ḳ.) And فُرَّ الأَمْرَ جَذَعًا † *Commence thou the affair from the first thereof*. (M, in the TT. [But the MS. has in this case, as in that here immediately preceding, الأمرُ: the right reading is evidently الامرَ; as in a similar phrase voce جَذَعٌ, q. v.]) ═ فَرَّ, aor. يَفِرُّ or يَفَرُّ, (accord. to different copies of the T,) *He became intelligent after being weak* [*in mind*]. (IAạr, T, TA.)

3. فَارَرْتُهُ, inf. n. مُفَارَّةٌ, ‡ *I investigated his state*, or *condition, he investigating mine*. (TA.)

4. افرّهُ *He*, or *it, made him to flee*; (Ṣ, O;) or *made him to turn away or aside, for the purpose of eluding, and to flee*: (M, Ḳ:) or (O) *he did to him a deed that made him to flee*; (Fr, AO, T, M, O, Ḳ;) as also افرّ به. (TA.) It is related in a trad. that the Prophet said to 'Adee the son of Ḥátim, مَا يُفِرُّكَ عَنِ الإِسْلَامِ إِلَّا أَنْ يُقَالَ لَا إِلٰهَ إِلَّا ٱللّٰهُ (T, M, O, TA) i. e. *Nothing induces thee to flee from El-Islám except the saying "There is no deity but God:"* many of the relaters say يُفَرِّرُكَ; but Az says that the former is the right. (TA.) —— Hence the saying, افرّ ٱللّٰهُ يَدَهُ *God made*, or *may God make, his arm*, or *hand, to fall off*; like أَطَرَّهَا and أَتَرَّهَا. (O.) —— And أَفْرَرْتُ رَأْسَهُ *I split*, or *clave, his head*, with a sword; like أَفْرَيْتُهُ. (Yz, T, O, Ḳ.) ═ أَفَرَّتْ لِلْإِثْنَآءِ, said of camels, (Ṣ, M, O, Ḳ,) and of horses, (M, Ḳ,) *They shed their milk-teeth and had others come forth*. (Ṣ, M, O, Ḳ.)

5. تَفَرَّرَ بِى *i. q.* ضَحِكَ [*He laughed at me, derided me*, or *ridiculed me*]; (Ḳ, TA;) mentioned by Ṣgh. (TA.)

6. تفارّوا *They fled, one from another*. (Ṣ, O, Ḳ.)

8. افترّ *He laughed in a beautiful manner*, (M, Ḳ,) *beyond what is termed* إِنْكِلَال [inf. n. of إِنْكَلَّ, q. v.]. (M.) One says, افترّ ضَاحِكًا *He showed his teeth laughing*; (Ṣ;) as also افترّ عَنْ ثَغْرِهِ. (T.) It is said of the Prophet, وَيَفْتَرُّ عَنْ مِثْلِ حَبِّ الغَمَامِ, meaning *And he used to smile so as to show teeth the like of hail-stones, without a reiterated*, or *a loud, laughing*. (T.) —— Hence, (TA,) افترّ البَرْقُ

† *The lightning glistened.* (M, Ḳ.) And hence the saying, الصَّرْفَةُ نَابُ الدَّهْرِ الَّذِى يَفْتَرُّ عَنْهُ [*Eṣ-Ṣarfeh is the dog-tooth of time,* or *fortune, which it shows smiling*]: for when Eṣ-Ṣarfeh [which is the Twelfth Mansion of the Moon] rises, [but it should be, when it sets, aurorally, for it so set, in Central Arabia, about the commencement of the era of the Flight, on the 9th of March, O. S.,] the blossoms come forth and the herbage attains its full height. (M, L. [See more in art. صرف.]) —— See also فُرّ. ═ Also *He snuffed up* a thing *into his nose.* (M, Ḳ.)

R. Q. 1. فَرْفَرَهُ, (Ṣ, M, Ḳ, &c.,) inf. n. فَرْفَارٌ, (M,) or فِرْفَارٌ, (TA,) *He put in a state of motion, commotion,* or *agitation; shook;* or *shook about;* (Ṣ, M, Ḳ;) *it,* (Ṣ, Ḳ,) or *him.* (M.) One says of a horse, يُفَرْفِرُ اللِّجَامَ فِى فِيهِ *He puts in a state of motion, &c., the bit in his mouth.* (M. [See also an explanation of the verb as intrans., in what follows.]) —— *He broke it,* i. e. a thing. (M, Ḳ.) —— *He cut it.* (Ḳ.) —— *He clave, split, slit, rent,* or *tore, it.* (TA.) [Thus] فَرْفَرَ signifies *He rent,* or *tore,* [skins such as are termed] زِقَاق [pl. of زِقّ], and other things; (O, Ḳ, TA;) and *slit,* or *rent,* them *much.* (TA. [In two copies of the T, instead of الزِّقَاقَ وَغَيْرَهَا, the reading in the O and Ḳ and TA, I find الزِّقاقَ وغيره.]) —— [*He mangled it.*] One says, الذِّئْبُ يُفَرْفِرُ الشَّاةَ *The wolf mangles the sheep,* or *goat.* (O,* TA.) —— And, (O, Ḳ, TA,) hence, (O,) inf. n. فَرْفَرَةٌ, (TA,) † *He defamed him, and mangled his reputation.* (O, Ḳ, TA.) —— And † *He discommended it,* [as though] *mangling it with discommendation:* the verb occurs in this sense in a trad., having for its object الدُّنْيَا [meaning *the enjoyments,* or *good, of the present world*]. (TA.) —— Also, (inf. n. فَرْفَرَةٌ, TA,) *He called* or *cried,* or *called out* or *cried out, to him.* (M, Ḳ.) ═ فَرْفَرَ as intrans., *He* (a camel) *put his body in a state of commotion,* or *agitation.* (M, Ḳ.) —— *He* (a horse) *struck his teeth with the* فَأْس [q. v.] *of his bit, and moved about his head.* (Ṣ, O, Ḳ.) —— *He hastened,* or *sped, and went with short steps.* (M, O, Ḳ.) —— *He was light, and unsteady,* (Ṣ,* M,* O,* Ḳ, TA,) *in mind;* (TA;) inf. n. فَرْفَرَةٌ. (Ṣ, M, O, TA.) —— *He hastened,* or *was hasty, with foolishness,* or *stupidity.* (IAạr, T, TA.) —— And *He confounded,* or *confused, and was profuse,* فِى كَلَامِهِ [*in his speaking,* or *talking,* or *his speech,* or *talk*]. (M, Ḳ.) —— And [app. *He talked;* for] الفَرْفَرَةُ signifies الكَلَامُ [which is often used as a quasi-inf. n. of كَلَّمَ]. (M.) ═ فَرْفَرَ also signifies *He made the kind of vehicle called* فُرْفَار. (T, Ḳ.) —— And *He kindled* [a fire] *with* [*wood of*] *the species of tree called* فُرْفَار. (T, Ḳ.)

فَرٌّ: see فَارٌّ, in two places.

فُرٌّ [The *best,* or *choice,* of men &c.]. One says, هُوَ فُرُّ قَوْمِهِ, (O,) or فُرُّ القَوْمِ, (Ḳ,) and ▼ فُرَّتُهُمْ, (O, Ḳ,) *He is of the best,* or *choice, of his people,* or *of the people,* (O, Ḳ,) and *of the chief persons thereof,* (O, Ḳ,*) *who show him smiling* (الَّذِينَ ▼ يَفْتَرُّونَ عَنْهُ, perhaps better rendered *who withdraw from him so as to render him conspicuous*): (O, Ḳ:) or هُوَ فُرَّةُ ▼ قَوْمِهِ *he is the best,* or *choice, of his people:* (T:) and هٰذَا فُرَّةُ ▼ مَالِى, (T,) or مَالِهِ, (O,) *this is the best,* or *choice, of my,* or *his, property,* or *camels &c.* (T, O.)

فُرَّةٌ and ▼ افُرَّةٌ and ▼ أُفُرَّةٌ The *beginning,* or *first part,* of the heat: (T, Ṣ, M, O, Ḳ:) or they signify, (T, Ṣ, M,) or signify also, (O, Ḳ,) the *vehemence* thereof: (Ṣ, M, O, Ḳ:) but [Az says,] the second and third are in my opinion from أَفَرَّ, the أ being the first radical letter: and Ks states that some change the أ into ع, saying عُفُرَّةٌ and عَفُرَّةٌ. (T.) مَا زَالَ فُلَانٌ فِى أُفُرَّةِ ▼ شَرٍّ مِنْ فُلَانٍ is a saying mentioned by Lth, (T, TA,) meaning [*Such a one ceased not to be*] *in a vehement state of evil* or *mischief* [proceeding *from such a one*]. (TA.) —— Also *Confusion and difficulty.* (M, Ḳ.) One says, وَقَعَ القَوْمُ فِى فُرَّةٍ and ▼ أَفُرَّةٍ and ▼ أُفُرَّةٍ *The people,* or *party, fell into confusion and difficulty.* (M.) —— See also the next preceding paragraph, in three places.

فِرَّةٌ *A smiling:* [or rather *a manner of smiling:*] one says, إِنَّهَا لَحَسَنَةُ الفِرَّةِ [*Verily she is beautiful in respect of the manner of smiling*]. (TA.)

فُرُورٌ: see فُرَارٌ.

فَرُورَةٌ: see فَارٌّ.

فُرَارٌ and ▼ فَرِيرٌ The *young one of the ewe,* and *of the she-goat,* (M, Ḳ,) and *of the cow,* (M,) or *of the wild cow,* (A'Obeyd, T, Ṣ, M, O, Ḳ,) as also, in this last sense, (O, Ḳ,) and in the first and second senses, (Ḳ,) ▼ فُرْفُرٌ and ▼ فُرْفُورٌ (O, Ḳ) and ▼ فُرُورٌ and ▼ فُرَافِرٌ: (Ḳ:) or they [app. referring to all the foregoing words] signify *lambs:* (Ḳ: [but see what follows:]) the female is termed فُرَارَةٌ: (M:) and فُرَارٌ is pl. also; (T, M, Ḳ;) i. e. it is applied to a pl. number as well as to one; (TA;) it is said to be pl. of ▼ فَرِيرٌ; (T, Ṣ, M, O;) and is of a rare form of pl.; (A'Obeyd, Ṣ, O, Ḳ;*) and it signifies the *small in body of the young ones of the goat-kind;* (M;) or ▼ فَرِيرٌ, as some say, signifies thus: (TA: [but this I think doubtful:]) this last word is said by IAạr to signify the *young one of the wild animal, of the gazelle* and *of the bovine kind* and *the like;* and in one instance he says that it signifies *lambs:* (M:) and, (T, A,) as Aboo-l-'Abbás [i. e. Th] states on the authority of IAạr, (T,) فُرَارٌ (T, M) and فُرَارَةٌ (T) and ▼ فَرِيرٌ (M) and ▼ فُرُرٌ and ▼ فُرْفُورٌ and ▼ فُرَافِرٌ (T, M) signify the *lamb when it is weaned,* (T, M,) *and has become what is termed* جَفْرٌ [q. v.], *and obtained plenty of herbage,* (M,) *and has become fat:* (T, M:) accord. to Ibn-'Abbád, (O,) the last two signify *a lamb* (حَمَلٌ, O, TA, in the Ḳ جَمَلٌ, a mistranscription, TA) *when it eats, and chews the cud:* (O, Ḳ: [see also فُرْفُورٌ below:]) and [it is also said that] فُرَارٌ signifies *great* بَهْم [app. as meaning *lambs* or *kids*], and one thereof is termed ▼ فُرْفُورٌ. (TA.) It is said in a prov.

• نَزْوُ الفُرَارِ ٱسْتَجْهَلَ الفُرَارَا •

[*The leaping of the wild calf,* or with equal propriety الفرار may be here rendered *the kid, excited to lightness the* other *wild calf,* or *kid*]: (T, Ṣ, O, Ḳ:) A'Obeyd says, on the authority of El-Muärrij, [and so says Meyd, and the same is implied in the Ṣ and O,] that الفرار here means *the young one of the wild cow:* (T:) i. e., when the فرار attains to youthful vigour it takes to leaping, and when another sees it [do so] it leaps in like manner: (T, Ṣ, Ḳ:) the prov. is used in relation to him of whose companionship one should be cautious; meaning, if thou become his companion thou wilt do as he does: (T, O, Ḳ:) some relate it otherwise, saying نَزْوَ, meaning نَزَا نَزْوَ الفُرَارِ. (O.) [See also a similar prov. in art. سفه, conj. 5.]

فَرُورٌ: see فَارٌّ. It is applied to a woman as meaning *Wont to flee from that which induces doubt,* or *suspicion,* or *evil opinion.* (Ṣ.) —— See also the next preceding paragraph.

فَرِيرٌ: see فُرَارٌ, in four places. ═ Also The *place of the* مَحَسَّة [thus in a copy of the M (app. مِحَسَّة i. e. *currycomb,* as though meaning the *part that is currycombed*), in the Ḳ *of the* مَجَسَّة (i. e. مَجَسَّة, q. v.), and in the O *of the* مَجَمّ, which last I think to be a mistranscription,] *of the* مَعْرَفَة [or *part,* or *flesh, upon which grows the mane*] of the horse: (M, O, Ḳ:) or the *base* (أَصْل) of the مَعْرَفَة of the horse. (T; and accord. to the TA, mentioned by Ṣgh, and there said to be tropical.) —— And The *mouth:* (O, Ḳ, TA:) mentioned by Z in a manner indicating that it is of the horse or the like. (TA.)

فَرُورَةٌ: see فَارٌّ.

كَتِيبَةٌ فَرَّى [*A military force,* or *troop,* &c.,] *defeated:* (T, O, Ḳ:) as also فَلَّى. (T.)

فَرَّآءُ, applied to a woman, *i. q.* غَرَّآءُ, (O, Ḳ, TA,) meaning *Beautiful in the front teeth.* (TA.)

فَرَّارٌ: see فَارٌّ. —— [Hence,] *Quicksilver;* so called because flowing quickly, and not remaining in a place: thus says Esh-Shereeshee. (Ḥar p. 139.)

فُرَيْرَةٌ, in the dim. form, with teshdeed, [*A spinning-top;*] *a thing with which children play.* (TA.)

فَارٌّ (Ṣ, M) and ▼ فَرٌّ (T, Ṣ, O, Ḳ) and ▼ فَرُورٌ (M, O, Ḳ) and ▼ فَرُورَةٌ (M, Ḳ) and ▼ فَرَّارٌ (M, O, Ḳ) and ▼ فَرُّةٌ (Ḳ) are epithets from فَرَّ signifying as expl. in the first sentence of this art.: (Ṣ, T, M, O, Ḳ:) [the first and second meaning *Fleeing;* or *turning away* or *aside, to elude, and fleeing:* the third, fifth, and sixth, *fleeing, &c., much:* and the fourth, *fleeing, &c., very much:*] but ▼ فَرٌّ is applied to one and to two and to more, and to a female; (Ṣ, O;) it has no dual nor pl. [nor fem. form]; (T;) the sing. [and dual] and pl. [and masc. and fem.] are alike; (M;) as it is an inf. n. used as an epithet; (M, O;) and it may be a pl. [or rather a quasi-pl. n.] of فَارٌّ, (Ṣ, M, O,) like as رَكْبٌ is of رَاكِبٌ, (Ṣ, O,) and صَحْبٌ of صَاحِبٌ, (Ṣ, O, Ḳ,*) or شَرْبٌ of شَارِبٌ: (M:) it is related in the trad. respecting the Flight that Suráḳah Ibn-Málik, when he saw the Prophet and Aboo-Bekr fleeing to El-Medeeneh, and they passed by him, said, هٰذَانِ فَرُّ قُرَيْشٍ أَفَلَا أَرُدُّ عَلَى قُرَيْشٍ فَرَّهَا, (T,* Ṣ,* O,* TA,) meaning [*These two are*] *the* two *fugitives* [*of Ḳureysh: shall I not turn back to Ḳureysh their fugitives?*]. (A'Obeyd, T, TA.)

فُرْفُرٌ: see فَرْفَارٌ: — and فُرَافِرٌ: — and فُرْفُورٌ, in three places.

فِرْفِرٌ: see فُرْفُورٌ, in two places.

فُرَفُرٌ: see the next paragraph.

فَرْفَارٌ *A breaker* [or *mangler*] *of everything*; as also ↓فُرَافِرٌ. (M, Ḳ.) — And The *lion*; because he mangles his antagonist: (Z, TA:) or the *lion that mangles his antagonist* (O, Ḳ*) *and everything*; (O;) as also ↓فِرْفَارٌ and ↓فُرْفُرٌ, (Ḳ,) or ↓فُرَفُرٌ, (O,) and ↓فُرَافِرٌ and ↓فُرَافِرَةٌ. (O, Ḳ.) — And *Light and unsteady in mind:* (Lth, T, M, O, Ḳ:) fem. with ة. (Lth, T, M, O.) — And *Loquacious; talkative; a great talker*; (M, Ḳ;) like ثَرْثَارٌ: (M:) fem. with ة. (Ḳ.) ═ Also *A species of tree,* (T, M, O, Ḳ,) *hard, having much endurance of fire,* (T, O,) *of which are made* [*bowls such as are termed*] قِصَاع (M, O, Ḳ) *and* عِسَاس: (M, O:) AḤn says, it is *a great kind of tree;* (O;) *it becomes tall like the* دُلْب [q. v.]; *its leaves are like those of the almond-tree; it has blossoms like the red rose;* (O, TA;) *and it becomes thick so that great* [*bowls such as are termed*] عِسَاس, *and* أَقْدَاح, *are turned from it:* (O:) *when its tree becomes old, its wood becomes black like ebony:* (O, TA:) *it is a hard wood, that blunts iron; and the bowls thereof are thin and light, and of pleasant odour: small saddles,* called مَخَاصِر, pl. of مِخْصَرَةٌ, *for excellent she-camels, were also made of it, and the curved pieces of wood* (أَحْنَآء) *thereof amounted* [*in price*] *to two hundred dirhems.* (O.) ═ And *A sort of vehicle, or saddle, for women* (T, O, Ḳ) *and for pastors, resembling the* حَوِيَّة *and* سَوِيَّة [described in arts. حوى and سوى]. (T.)

فِرْفَارٌ: see the next preceding paragraph.

فُرْفُورٌ: see فُرَارٌ, in three places. [It is said that] it signifies *A fat* جَمَل (Thus in copies of the Ḳ [an evident mistranscription for حَمَل, i. e. *lamb*, as is indicated in the TA by the addition *such as has become what is termed* جَفْر].) — And † *A youth,* or *young man*; (O, Ḳ, TA;) as being likened to the lamb (حَمَل) that has obtained plenty of herbage and has become fat; (TA; [see فُرَارٌ;]) and so ↓فُرَافِرٌ. (O, Ḳ, TA.) — And *A certain bird*; (Ṣ, O, Ḳ;) as also ↓فُرْفُرٌ (O, Ḳ) and ↓فِرْفِرٌ: (Ḳ:) *a small* عُصْفُور [i. e. *sparrow*, or *passerine bird*]: (ISh, T, M:) so it is said: (M:) and ↓فُرْفُورٌ signifies the عُصْفُور [in an absolute sense]; (M, Ḳ;) as also ↓فُرْفُورٌ: (Ḳ:) accord. to AḤát, Et-Táïfee says that ↓الفُرْفُرُ, of which the pl. is الفَرَافِرُ, signifies *the* نَقَاقِير; thus he says, [using the pl.,] not the نُقَّار [or نَقَّار? (see عُصْفُورٌ)]; and he adds that sometimes it is said that the ↓الفُرْفُرُ is the صِرّ [q. v.]; and some say فِرْفُور with kesr, but he says, I am not confident of its chasteness: (O:) [accord. to Ed-Demeeree, as stated by Freytag, فُرْفُر is the name of *a small aquatic bird like the dove* or *pigeon:* SM says, app. relying upon the correctness of a modern application of the word,] I have seen the فُرْفُور in Egypt, and it is *smaller than the* إِوَزّ [which is applied to the *goose* and sometimes to the *duck*]. (TA.) ═ Also, and ↓فُرَافِرٌ, *Parched meal* (سَوِيق) *prepared from the* يَنْبُوت [a tree described in art. نبت, which see, and see also غَافٌ], (M, O, Ḳ,) i. e. *from the fruit thereof;* (O, Ḳ;) as some say, *from the* يَنبوت *of 'Omán.* (TA.)

فِرْفِيرٌ [*Purple;*] *a certain sort of colour.* (Ḳ.) — And The *violet:* or *violet-colour:* syn. in Pers. بنفشه [i. e. بَنَفْشَه, which is said to have both of these significations]. (KL.) — [And *Purslane*, or *purslain*. (Golius, on the authority of Ibn-Beytár.)]

فِرْفِيرِىٌّ [*Of a purple colour*]. (TA: there applied as an epithet to the flower of the فَاوَانِيَا [or peony].)

فُرَافِرٌ A horse *that moves about,* or *agitates, the bit in his mouth,* (M, O, Ḳ, TA,) to which Z adds, *in order that he may disengage it* [*therefrom,* or] *from his head.* (TA.) — And *i. q.* أَخْرَقُ [*Rough, ungentle,* &c.]; (M, O, Ḳ;) applied to a man. (O, Ḳ.) — See also فَرْفَارٌ, in two places: — and فُرَارٌ, likewise in two places: — and فُرْفُورٌ, also in two places.

فُرَافِرَةٌ: see فَرْفَارٌ, second sentence.

أَفَرُّ and أَفَرَّةٌ: see فَرَّةٌ, in five places.

مَفَرٌّ an inf. n. of فَرَّ. (Ṣ, M, Ḳ. [See the first and second sentences of this art.]) — Also *A time* [and *a place*] *of fleeing:* (TA:) and ↓مَفِرٌّ signifies *a place of fleeing:* (I'Ab, Zj, Ṣ, M, TA:) and so does ↓مِفَرٌّ, (Zj, Ḳ, TA,) an instrumental noun used as a noun of place. (Ḳ, TA.) [See 1, second sentence.]

مَفِرٌّ: see the next preceding paragraph.

مُفِرٌّ [*Making to flee:* &c. See its verb, 4]. — [Hence, app.,] الأَيَّامُ المُفِرَّاتُ † *The days that reveal,* or *make manifest,* [or *cause to fly abroad,*] *news,* or *tidings.* (O, Ḳ.)

مِفَرٌّ [originally an instrumental noun: and hence,] A horse *fit for one's fleeing upon him:* (Ṣ, O, Ḳ:) or *excellent in fleeing.* (Ḳ.) One says فَرَسٌ مِكَرٌّ مِفَرٌّ *A horse well trained, willing, and active, ready to return to the fight and to flee.* (TA in art. كر.) — See also مَفَرٌّ.

مَفْرُورٌ: see what follows.

مَفْرُورٌ and ↓مُفَرٌّ *Examined, looked into, searched into, inquired respecting,* or *interrogated.* (TA. [See 1.])

فرأ

فَرَأٌ (T, Ṣ, M, O, Ḳ) and ↓فَرَآءٌ, (Ḳ,) both of these forms authorized by the Koofees, (TA,) *A wild ass:* (ISk, T, Ṣ, M, O, Ḳ:) or *a youthful wild ass:* (M, Ḳ:) but the absolute [i. e. the former] meaning is that which is commonly known: (TA:) pl. (of mult., TA) فِرَآءٌ (T, Ṣ, M, O, Ḳ) and (of pauc., TA) أَفْرَآءٌ. (M, Ḳ.) Hence the saying, كُلُّ الصَّيْدِ فِى جَوْفِ الفَرَا [*Every kind of game is in the belly* (or might enter into the belly) *of the wild ass*]; (T, Ṣ, M, O, Ḳ;) meaning that every kind of game is inferior to the wild ass: (T, O, Ḳ:) a prov., (T, Ṣ, M, Ḳ,) and therefore [the last word is] without hemz, on account of the final pause; (Ḳ;) but some write it with hemz: (TA:) it is said to have originated from the fact that three men went forth to hunt; and one caught a hare; and another, a gazelle; and the third, a wild ass; and the first and second boasted against the third, who thereupon said as above: it is applied to him who excels his fellows: (Meyd:) or to a man who is, with respect to other men, as the wild ass with respect to other kinds of game: or to the case of a man who, having several wants, one of which is a great one, accomplishes that great want, and cares not for the others' being unaccomplished. (T, TA. [See also Ḥar pp. 468-9.]) And أَنْكَحْنَا الفَرَا فَسَنَرَى [*We have married* our daughter *to the wild ass, and we shall see,*] (T, Ṣ, M, O) is another prov.; (T, Meyd;) in which alif is substituted for the hemzeh, (Ṣ, M,* O,) for the purpose of the agreement [of الفَرَا in rhyme] with سَنَرَى: (M:) said by a man to his wife when a man demanded in marriage his daughter and he refused, but his wife consented, and overcame the father so that he gave her in marriage to him against his wish; then the husband made the intercourse [with her] to be evil, and divorced her: it is applied in cautioning against an evil consequence: (Meyd:) or it is applied to a man when his affair has been endangered and he has seen what he does not like; and it means we have wasted our precaution, and the affair has brought us to an evil result; (Aṣ, T;) or we have considered the affair, and we shall see what it will disclose; (T;) or we have sought after high things, and we shall see what our case will be afterwards. (Th, M.)

فَرَآءٌ: see above, first sentence.

شَىْءٌ فَرِىءٌ *i. q.* فَرِىٌّ [q. v.] (O, Ḳ.* See art. فرى.)

فربج

Q. 3. اِفْرَنْبَجَ, said of a lamb, (Lth, O,) or of the skin of a lamb, (Ṣ, Ḳ, [some of the copies of the latter of which have الجَمَل in the place of الحَمَل,]) and of the skin of a kid, (O,) *It was roasted so that the upper parts of it became dried up.* (Lth, Ṣ, O, Ḳ.)

مُفَرْنَبِج [part. n. of the verb above]. A man said, describing a roasted female kid,

* فَأَكَلْتُ مِنْ مُفَرْنَبِجٍ مِنْ جِلْدِهَا *

[*And I ate of such as was roasted so that the upper parts were dried up, of its skin*]. (O.)

فربيون

فَرْبِيُونٌ, (Ḳ, TA, [in several copies of the Ḳ فَرْفِيُون,]) also called ↓ أَفْرَبْيُون, (TA,) [*Euphorbium; an inspissated sap of a certain African plant;*] i. q. لُبَانَةٌ مَغْرِبِيَّةٌ; *the best of which is that which dissolves quickly in water;* (TA;) *an attenuant medicine, beneficial as a remedy for sciatica, and for cold of the kidneys, and for colic, and for the sting,* or *bite, of venomous* or *noxious reptiles* or *the like, and for the bite of the mad dog, and it causes abortion, and attenuates viscous phlegm.* (Ḳ.)

أَفْرَبْيُون: see the preceding paragraph.

فرت

1. فَرُتَ, aor. ـُ, inf. n. فُرُوتَةٌ [said in the M to be a subst.], *It* (water, T, Mṣb) *was,* or *became, sweet* [or *very sweet* or *most sweet* (see فُرَاتٌ)]. (T, O, Mṣb, Ḳ.) ══ فَرَتَ, (M, Ḳ,) aor. ـِ, (M,) or ـُ, (Ḳ,) inf. n. فَرْتٌ, (M,) *He acted vitiously,* or *unrighteously;* or *committed adultery,* or *fornication;* syn. فَجَرَ. (M, Ḳ.) ══ فَرِتَ, [aor. ـَ,] *He became weak in his intellect, after having possessed ample intelligence.* (IAạr, T, O, Ḳ.)

فُرْتٌ i. q. فُتْرٌ [*The space measured by the extension of the thumb and fore finger*]; (IJ, M, Ḳ;) a dial. var. of the latter word; as though formed by transposition. (M.)

فُرَاتٌ, applied to water, (T, Ṣ, M, &c.,) and فُرَاهٌ, both chaste forms, and well known, like تَابُوتٌ and تَابُوهٌ, (Towsheeh, MF, TA,) *Sweet:* (Ṣ, O:) or *very sweet:* (Ḳ:) or *of the sweetest kind:* (T, M, L:) or *that subdues thirst by its excessive sweetness:* (Bḍ in xxv. 55:) so called, accord. to Z, because it breaks the vehemence of thirst, and allays it; as though from رَفَتَ, and formed by transposition: (TA:) you say مَآءٌ فُرَاتٌ, (Ṣ, M, O, Ḳ,) and in a copy of the Ḳ فَرَاتٌ also, (TA,) and مِيَاهٌ فُرَاتٌ, (Ṣ, M, O, Ḳ,) and فِرْتَانٌ, (M, Mṣb, in copies of the Ḳ فُرْتَانٌ, and in the CḲ فُرَتانٌ,) like غِرْبَانٌ [pl. of غُرَابٌ], when فُرَاتٌ is pluralized, but this is rarely the case. (Mṣb.) — الفُرَاتُ signifies also [*The Euphrates;*] *the river of El-Koofeh;* (Ṣ, Mgh, O,* Ḳ;*) *a great, celebrated river, which issues from the limits of Er-Room, then passes by the borders of Syria &c., and, after meeting with the Tigris, forms therewith one river, and pours forth into the Sea* [or *Gulf*] *of Persia.* (Mṣb, TA.) And الفُرَاتَانِ is an appellation applied to [*The Euphrates and Tigris;* i. e.] الفُرَاتُ *and* دِجْلَةُ: or, accord. to the Ṣ [and O] الفُرَاتُ *and* دُجَيْل [*The Euphrates and Dujeyl,* which latter is a branch of the Tigris]. (TA.) — Also *The sea:* (M, Ḳ:) so in a verse of Aboo-Dhu-eyb describing pearls as found therein. (M.)

فَرْتَنَا, (M, K,) accord. to Ibn-Ḥabeeb from فَرَتَ [q. v.], but accord. to Sb the ن is radical, (M,) or الفَرْتَنَا accord. to IB, (TA in art. فرتن,) *The fornicatress,* or *adultress.* (M and Ḳ in this art.* and in art. فرتن.) And *The female slave:* (Th, and Ṣ and Ḳ in art. فرتن:) or so الفَرْتَنَا: and اِبْنُ الفَرْتَنَا *The son of the female slave that is a fornicatress.* (IAạr, TA in that art.) And اِبْنُ فَرْتَنَا *The low, ignoble, mean,* or *sordid.* (El-Aḥwal, IB, TA.) — Also, فَرْتَنَا, the name of *A certain woman.* (M and Ḳ in art. فرتن.) — And الفَرْتَنَا *The young one of the hyena.* (Ḳ in art. فرتن.)

فرتن

Q. 1. فَرْتَنَ, (T, Ḳ, TA,) inf. n. فَرْتَنَةٌ, (T, TA,) signifies شَقَّقَ كَلَامَهُ وَاهْتَمَشَ فِيهِ [app. meaning *He uttered,* or *endeavoured with repeated efforts to utter, his speech in the best manner, and proceeded slowly therein*]: (T, Ḳ,* TA:) in the copies of the Ḳ, اهتمس, with the unpointed س, is put for اهتمش, which is the right reading. (TA.) — And *He went along with short steps.* (Ḳ.) ══ And *He* (a man) *became angry, and in a state of excitement:* from what here follows [and therefore, app., post-classical]. (TA.)

فُرْتُنَةٌ, with ḍamm, [meaning with two dammehs,] *A state of commotion of the sea arising from the violence of the winds:* app. post-classical. (TA.)

فَرْتَنَا, in which the ن is held by some to be radical, and by others to be augmentative, see in art. فرت.

فرث

1. فَرَثْتُ الكَرِشَ: see 4. — فَرَثَ الجُلَّةَ, (ISk, T, Ṣ, M, O, Ḳ,) aor. ـُ, (T, O,) or ـِ, (M,) or both, (ISk, Ṣ, Ḳ,) inf. n. فَرْثٌ, (T, M,) *He scattered,* or *dispersed,* [*the contents of*] *the* جُلَّة [or *receptacle made of palm-leaves, for dates*]: (T,* Ḳ:) or *ripped the* جُلَّة, *and then scattered,* or *dispersed, its contents,* (ISk, Ṣ, M, O,) *entirely,* (M,) لِلْقَوْمِ [*for the people,* or *party*]. (ISk, Ṣ, O.) — And in like manner, (M,) فَرَثَ كَبِدَهُ, (ISk, T, Ṣ, M, O, Ḳ,) aor. ـُ, (ISk, Ṣ, and so in some copies of the Ḳ,) or ـِ, (O, and so in other copies of the Ḳ,) inf. n. فَرْثٌ; (Ṣ, O;) and ↓ فَرَّثَهَا, (ISk, Ṣ, M, O, Ḳ,) inf. n. تَفْرِيثٌ; (ISk, Ṣ, O, Ḳ;) *He struck,* or *smote, him,* (ISk, T, Ṣ, O,) or *his liver,* (Ḳ,) *he being alive,* (ISk, Ṣ, O, Ḳ,) *so that his liver became scattered.* (ISk, T, Ṣ, O, Ḳ.) And [hence] one says, فَرَثَ الحُبُّ كَبِدَهُ, and ↓ فَرَّثَهَا, and ↓ افرثها, meaning † *Love crumbled* [or *crushed*] *his liver:* [like as we say "it broke his heart:"] (M, TA:) and فَرْث is used in like manner of men, as meaning the *crumbling* of the liver by grief and molestation. (TA.) ══ See also 7. — فَرِثَ, aor. ـَ, (Ḳ,) inf. n. فَرَثٌ, (M, O,) *He was,* or *became, satiated.* (M,* O,* Ḳ.) You say, شَرِبَ عَلَى فَرَثٍ *He drank on an occasion,* or *in a state, of satiety.* (M, TA.) — فَرِثَ القَوْمُ *The people,* or *party, became scattered,* or *dispersed.* (O, Ḳ.)

2: see the next following paragraph: — and see also the preceding paragraph, in two places.

4. افرث الكَرِشَ *He scattered the contents of the* كرش [or *stomach of a ruminant animal*]: (T:) or *he ripped the* كرش, *and threw away what was in it:* (ISk, Ṣ, O:) or ↓ فَرَثْتُ الكَرِشَ عَنِ الفَرْثِ, aor. ـُ, inf. n. فَرْثٌ; and أَفْرَثْتُهَا, and ↓ فَرَّثْتُهَا; *I ripped the* كرش, *and scattered what was in it.* (M, TA.) Accord. to the Ḳ, one says, افرث الكَبِدَ, meaning *He ripped the* كبد [or *liver*], *and threw away the* فُرَاثَة, i. e., *what was in it:* but this is taken from two passages in the M and T, which the author of the Ḳ has confounded. (TA.) — And [hence, app.,] افرث أَصْحَابَهُ † *He exposed his companions* (T, Ṣ, M, O, Ḳ) *to the ruling power,* (T,) or *to the censure of men:* (T, Ṣ, M, O, Ḳ:) or *he pronounced them to be liars, in the presence of a people,* or *party, in order to lessen them in their estimation:* or *he exposed to reproach their secret:* (M:) or *he calumniated,* or *slandered, them.* (IF, O.) And افرث الرَّجُلَ † *He reviled, vilified,* or *vituperated, the man; charged him with a vice, fault,* or *the like; defamed him;* or *detracted from his reputation.* (M, O.) — See also 1.

5: see the paragraph here following.

7. انفرثت كَرِشُهُ *His* (a ruminant animal's) *stomach became ripped and its contents became scattered,* or *dispersed.* (M.) — And انفرثت كَبِدُهُ *His liver became scattered* by a blow, (ISk, T, Ṣ, O, Ḳ,) *he being alive.* (ISk, Ṣ, O, Ḳ.) — اِنْفَرَثَتْ said of a pregnant woman; as also ↓ تَفَرَّثَتْ; (O, Ḳ, but only the inf. ns. are mentioned in the Ḳ;) and ↓ فَرِثَتْ; (T, A, O, Ḳ, but only the inf. n. is mentioned; in a copy of the T written فَرَثَتْ; in the Ḳ, فَرْث, and so in a copy of the A; [accord. to the TḲ, the pret. is فَرَثَتْ, and the aor. تَفْرُثُ; but is probably only inferred from the form of the inf. n. in the Ḳ;]) *She had a heaving of the soul* [or *stomach*], or *a tendency to vomit.* (T, A, O, Ḳ.*) [And] اِنْفَرَثَتْ بِهَا *She* (a woman, in the beginning of her pregnancy,) *was affected with a spitting, and with a heaving of the soul* [or *stomach*], or *a tendency to vomit.* (M.) [See also the last of the following paragraphs.]

فَرْثٌ The سِرْجِين [here meaning *feces*] (Ṣ, A, O, Ḳ) *while remaining* (Ṣ, O) *in the* كَرِش [or *stomach of a ruminant animal*]; (Ṣ, A, O, Ḳ;) *the dregs in the* كرش: (Jel in xvi. 68:) or i. q. سِرْقِين [a dial. var. of سرجين]: and the *of the* كرش; as also ↓ فُرَاثَةٌ, (M,) [i. e.] الفُرَاثَة signifies *what is extracted from the* كرش [like

الفَرْثُ: it is erroneously expl. in the Ḳ: see 4]: (O:) the pl. of فَرْثٌ is فُرُوثٌ. (Ṣ, O.) — And *Anything that is scattered from a bag or other receptacle for travelling-provisions* &c. (M.) ═ Also *A small* [*leathern vessel for water, of the kind called*] رَكْوَة [q. v.]; (T, Ḳ;) a dial. var. of قَرْثٌ: (Ḳ:) or the small رَكْوَة is called القَرْثُ [only], with ق. (O.) ═ See also the last of the following paragraphs.

فُرَاثَةٌ: see the next preceding paragraph.

مَفَارِثُ [a pl. of which the sing. is app. مَفْرَثٌ or مَفْرِثٌ] The *places in which* [*slaughtered*] *sheep and other animals are ripped* [*and eviscerated*] *and skinned.* (O.)

مُتَفَرِّثَةٌ: see the following paragraph, in two places.

إِنَّهَا لَمُنْفَرِثٌ بِهَا, said of a pregnant woman, *Verily she is affected with a heaving of the soul* [or *stomach*], *or a tendency to vomit,* (O, Ḳ,* TA,*) *by reason of the heaviness of pregnancy:* (O:) [or] one says of a woman in the beginning of her pregnancy, ↓ إِنَّهَا لَمُتَفَرِّثَةٌ, meaning [*Verily*] *she is affected with a heaving of the soul* [or *stomach*], *or a tendency to vomit, and the phlegm at the head of her stomach is much in quantity:* so says ISk, on the authority of AA: but [Az, after citing this, adds,] I know not whether it be مُنْفَرِثَةٌ or ↓ مُتَفَرِّثَةٌ: (T, TA:*) and ↓ اِمْرَأَةٌ فَرِثٌ, (M, TA, [in the former, as given in the TT, the latter word is written فرث, without any vowel-sign to the ف,]) it is said, (TA,) means *A woman who spits,* [or *expectorates phlegm,*] *and has a heaving of the soul* [or *stomach*], *or a tendency to vomit, in the beginning of her pregnancy.* (M, TA.)

فرج

1. فَرَجَ بَيْنَ الشَّيْئَيْنِ, aor. ـِ, inf. n. فَرْجٌ, *He made an opening,* or *intervening space,* [*or a gap, or breach,*] *between the two things;* or *he opened the interstice,* or *interval, between the two things:* (Mṣb:) [and فَرَجَ الشَّىْءَ *He opened the thing;* and particularly *by diduction,* or *so as to form an intervening space,* or *a gap,* or *breach; he unclosed it:* and in like manner ↓ فرّج, inf. n. تَفْرِيجٌ; for ex.,] you say, فَرَّجَ مَا بَيْنَ رِجْلَىْ حَلُوبَتِهِ [*He made an opening,* or *intervening space, between the hind legs of his milch camel;* i. e. *he parted her hind legs*]; (Ṣ and O and Ḳ in art. فحج, &c.;) and فرّج بَيْنَ أَصَابِعِهِ *He made openings,* or *intervening spaces, between his fingers.* (MA.) — The saying in the Ḳur lxxvii. 9 وَإِذَا ٱلسَّمَآءُ فُرِجَتْ means [*And when the sky*] *shall be opened so that it shall become portals:* (Ksh:) or *shall become cloven,* or *split,* or *rent.* (Bḍ and Jel.) — And you say, فَرَجَ البَابَ *He opened the door.* (A, TA.) And فَرَجَ فَاهُ *He opened his mouth to die.* (TA.) — And فَرَجَ القَوْمُ لِلرَّجُلِ, aor. ـِ, inf. n. فَرْجٌ, [and فَرَجَ لَهُ, aor. ـِ, inf. n. فَرْجٌ and فُرْجَةٌ, seems from the context to be mentioned in this sense in the L,] *The people,* or *party, made room,* or *ample space, for the man,* in the place of standing or of sitting. (Mṣb.) — And فَرَجَ, aor. ـِ, (O, Mṣb, Ḳ,) inf. n. فَرْجٌ; (O, Mṣb;) and ↓ فرّج, (O, Mṣb, Ḳ,) inf. n. تَفْرِيجٌ; (Ṣ, O;) signify also *He* (God) *removed, cleared away,* or *dispelled,* grief, or sorrow; syn. كَشَفَهُ. (Mṣb, Ḳ.) You say, فَرَجَ اللّٰهُ عَنْكَ غَمَّكَ and ↓ فَرَّجَ اللّٰهُ غَمَّكَ [*May God remove,* or *clear away, from thee thy grief,* or *sorrow;* and in like manner, suppressing the objective complement but meaning it to be understood, فَرَجَ عَنْكَ and ↓ فَرَّجَ عَنْكَ]. (Ṣ.) ═ See also 7, in two places. ═ فَرِجَ, [aor. ـَ,] inf. n. فَرَجٌ, *He had his pudendum* (فَرْج) *constantly uncovered* (Ṣ, TA) *when he sat.* (TA.) — [And, app., *He had buttocks which did not meet,* or *which scarcely met, by reason of their bigness.* (See فَرِجٌ and أَفْرَجُ.)] — فَرِجَتْ said of a she-camel: see 4. — [Freytag adds, as from the Ṣ, another signification of فَرِجَ, "Liberatus fuit curis, tristitia, laetatus fuit:" but for this I do not find any authority.]

2. فرّج: see the preceding paragraph, first sentence: — and again, in the latter half, in three places. ═ Also, (O, Ḳ,) inf. n. تَفْرِيجٌ, (Ḳ,) *He was,* or *became, extremely aged,* or *old and weak.* (O, Ḳ.) [From فَرَّجَ لَحْيَيْهِ, which see expl. voce فَكَّ.]

4. افرج النَّاسُ عَنْ طَرِيقِهِ *The people cleared themselves away from his road,* or *path; removed out of his way.* (Ṣ, O, Ḳ.*) And افرجوا عَنِ القَتِيلِ [as also ↓ انفرجوا (occurring thus in the Ṣ and Mṣb and TA in art. جلو)] *They cleared themselves away,* or *removed, from the slain person:* (Mgh, O, Mṣb, Ḳ:) implying that it was not known who had killed him. (Mṣb.) And افرجوا عَنِ المَكَانِ *They left, abandoned,* or *quitted, the place.* (O, Ḳ.) — افرج الغُبَارُ *The dust became dispersed.* (TA.) — And افرج signifies also *His shooting,* or *casting, became altered* [*for the worse*], *having been good.* (TA.) ═ افرج الوَلَدُ النَّاقَةَ *The young one caused the she-camel to be in the state in which one says of her* ↓ فَرِجَتْ, i. e. ↓ انْفَرَجَتْ فِى الوِلَادَةِ [app. meaning *She became unknit,* or *loosened,* in the joints of the hips *in parturition* (see explanations of فَرِيجٌ as applied to a ewe and to a woman)], *when bringing forth for the first time; whereby she was caused to suffer extreme distress:* whence ↓ فَارِجٌ signifies *Distressed.* (Mgh.)

5. تفرّج: see 7, in two places. — [It also signifies *He diverted, amused,* or *cheered, himself;* or *became diverted,* &c.; often followed by عَلَى شَىْءٍ, meaning *by viewing a thing,* i. e., some rare, or pleasing, object: but thus used, it is app. post-classical. (See also the next paragraph.)]

7. انفرج *It opened;* [and particularly *by diduction,* or *so as to form an intervening space,* or *a gap,* or *breach; it gaped; it became unclosed;* and so ↓ تَفَرَّجَ; (see exs. in art. فيص, voce أَفَاصَ, in three places;) and *it became unknit,* or *loosened,* said of a bone, and of a limb or member, and of a joint; (see فَرِيجٌ, in two places; and see also فَكَكْتُ, and انفكّ in three places, and فَكَكَ;)] syn. انفتح. (Mṣb in art. فتح; &c. [See also فُرْجَةٌ.]) — انْفَرَجَتْ سِيَتَاهَا is said of a bow such as is termed ↓ فَرُوجٌ, (O, Ḳ, TA,) as also انفجّت [i. e. انفجّت هِىَ, which shows that the meaning is, *Its two curved extremities were such as to have an open space between them and between the intermediate portion and the string*]. (TA.) — See also 4, second sentence: — and the same, last sentence; and فَرِيجٌ, in two places; and فَارِجٌ. — [انْفَرَجْتُ عَنِ الكَلَامِ occurs in the L, in art. فص, app. meaning *I broke off from,* or *intermitted, speaking.*] — انفرج said of grief, or sorrow, or anxiety, [and the like,] signifies *It was,* or *became, removed, cleared away,* or *dispelled;* (A, O, TA;) as also ↓ تفرّج; (Ṣ,* O,* TA;) and so ↓ فَرَجَ, aor. ـُ, inf. n. فُرُوجٌ. (TA.) Aboo-Dhu-eyb says,

وَلِلشَّرِّ بَعْدَ القَارِعَاتِ فُرُوجُ ↓

meaning [*And to evil, after striking and agitating calamities, there is,* or *shall be,*] *a removing, clearing away,* or *dispelling:* (Ṣ, O, TA:) the last word being the inf. n. of the last of the verbs above mentioned; or it may be a pl. of ↓ فُرْجَةٌ, like as صُخُورٌ is of صَخْرَةٌ. (TA.) — Also *He was,* or *became, happy,* or *cheerful.* (KL. [See also 5.])

فَرْجٌ: see فُرْجَةٌ. — *The space between the hind legs* of a horse or mare: (Ṣ, O, K:) so in the saying of Imra-el-Ḳeys,

لَهَا ذَنَبٌ مِثْلُ ذَيْلِ العَرُوسِ
تَسُدُّ بِهِ فَرْجَهَا مِنْ دُبُرْ

[*She has a tail like the skirt of the bride, with which she fills up the space between her hind legs, from behind*]. (Ṣ, O.) And *The space between the fore and hind legs* of a horse or the like. (L.) [Hence, app.,] one says, مَلَأَ فَرْجَهُ and فُرُوجَهُ, and سَدَّ فُرُوجَهُ [in which phrase مدّ is erroneously put for سدّ in one place in the TA], and جَرَى مِلْءَ فُرُوجِهِ, meaning † *He* (a horse) *ran swiftly.* (TA.) And مَلَأَ فُرُوجَ فَرَسِهِ † *He made his horse to run at the utmost rate of the pace termed* حُضْر. (TA in art. ملأ.) — *The pudendum,* or *pudenda;* the *part,* or *parts, of the person, which it is indecent to expose;* (Ṣ, O, Mṣb, Ḳ, &c.;) applied to the *pudenda of men* and *of women* and *of youths, with what is around them;* and so *of horses* and *the like:* (TA:) or the *anterior pudendum* [i. e. the *external portion of the organs of generation*] *of a man* and *of a woman,* by common consent of the lexicologists; and applied to *this* and the *posterior pudendum* [in the conventional language of the

297 •

law] because both belong to the same [legal] predicament [in certain cases]; (Mgh, Mṣb;) or because each of them is a place of opening; (Mṣb;) or because between the legs: (TA:) but in common parlance it is mostly applied to the *anterior pudendum:* (Mṣb:) or peculiarly, accord. to some, the *anterior pudendum of a woman* [i. e. the *vulva*, or *external portion of the organs of generation of a woman:* and the *vagina*]: (MF, TA:) pl. فُرُوجٌ. (Mṣb.) فُلَانٌ ٱبْنُ فَرْجِهِ means † *Such a one is solicitous for his* فرج. (Er-Rághib, TA in art. بنى.) —— And i. q. فَتْقٌ [app. as meaning *An open, wide, place*]: pl. فُرُوجٌ: (Mṣb:) which latter also signifies The *sides*, or *lateral parts, quarters*, or *tracts*, of a land. (TA.) And The *part between the two sides*, i. e. the بَطْن, of a valley: and hence used in relation to a road, as meaning its *entrance:* and a فَجّ [or *wide*, or *depressed, road*,] of a mountain. (ISh, TA.) And *A frontier-way of access to a country;* and [particularly *such as is*] *a place of fear;* (Ṣ, O, Ḳ, TA;) so called because not obstructed; (TA;) and so ▼ فَرْجَةٌ, (Mṣb,) [pl. فُرَجٌ, whence] one says, فُلَانٌ تُسَدُّ بِهِ الفُرَجُ, (A,) or الفُرُوجُ, which is the pl. of فَرْجٌ, (TA,) meaning [*Such a one, by him are obstructed*] *the frontier-ways of access* [*to the enemy's country*]. (A, TA.)

فِرْجٌ: } see فَرْجٌ; the latter in two places.
فُرُجٌ: }

فَرَجٌ inf. n. of فَرِجَ [q. v.]. (Ṣ, TA.) —— And [app. as such also, or] as a simple subst., The *having the pudendum* (الفَرْج) *constantly uncovered*, (Ḳ, TA,) *when sitting*. (TA.) —— Also a subst. [or quasi-inf. n.] from فَرَّجَ الغَمَّ; (Mṣb;) [as such signifying] The *removal*, or *clearing away, of grief*, or *sorrow:* or *freedom from grief*, or *sorrow:* (Ṣ,* O,* KL:) or i. q. رَاحَةٌ [i. e. *rest, repose*, or *ease;* or *cessation of trouble*, or *inconvenience, and of toil*, or *fatigue;* or *freedom therefrom*]: (MA:) and ▼ فَرْجَةٌ and ▼ فُرْجَةٌ accord. to ISk, and ▼ فِرْجَةٌ also accord. to Az, signify the same as فَرَجٌ: (Mṣb:) one says, مَا لِهٰذَا الغَمِّ مِنْ ▼ فَرْجَةٍ and ▼ فُرْجَةٍ and ▼ فِرْجَةٍ [*There is not for this grief any removal*, or *clearing away*]: (T, TA:) and لِكُلِّ غَمٍّ فُرْجَةٌ ▼ i. e. كَشْفَةٌ [*For every grief there is a removal, clearing away*, or *dispelling*]: (A:) or ▼ فَرْجَةٌ, of which فُرُوجٌ may be a pl., (see 7, in two places,) signifies *rest from grief*, or *mourning*, or *from disease:* (TA:) or *freedom from difficulty, distress*, or *straitness:* as also ▼ فُرْجَةٌ: (Mṣb:) or *freedom from anxiety;* (Ṣ, O, Ḳ;) as also ▼ فُرْجَةٌ and ▼ فِرْجَةٌ: (O, Ḳ:) or ▼ فَرْجَةٌ, with fet-ḥ, is an inf. n. [app. of unity]; and ▼ فُرْجَةٌ, with ḍamm, is a simple subst.: (IAṭr, Mṣb:) or ▼ فَرْجَةٌ relates to an affair or event; and ▼ فُرْجَةٌ, [which see expl. below,] to a wall, and a door; but the two [primary] significations are nearly the same: the authority for the three [syn.] forms of the word is taken by the author of the Ḳ from the statement in the T, cited above, that one says, مَا لِهٰذَا الغَمِّ مِنْ فَرْجَةٍ and فُرْجَةٍ and فِرْجَةٍ. (TA.) —— [Hence,] أُمُّ الفَرَجِ is a name of *The* جُوذَابَة [n. un. of جُوذَابٌ: see art. جذب]. (Ḥar p. 227.)

فَرِجٌ (Ṣ, O, TA) and ▼ أَفْرَجُ (Ḳ, TA) A man *whose pudendum* (فَرْج) *is constantly uncovered* (Ṣ, O, Ḳ, TA) *when he sits*. (TA.) —— مَكَانٌ فَرِجٌ *A place in which is* تَفَرُّج [app. as meaning *diversion, amusement*, or *cheering pastime; such a place as is termed in Pers.* تَفَرُّجْ گَاهْ]. (A, TA.)

فَرْجٌ (Ṣ, O, Ḳ) and ▼ فِرْجٌ, with kesr, (O,) or ▼ فُرُجٌ, (Ḳ,) and ▼ فَارِجٌ and ▼ فَرِيجٌ, (Ṣ, O, Ḳ,) [like فَرُوجٌ (see 7) and فَجَّآءُ,] A bow *wide apart from the string;* (Ṣ, O, Ḳ;) or *of which the string is distant from its* كَبِد [q. v.]. (TA.) —— And the first, A woman *wearing a single garment;* (O, L, Ḳ;) of the dial. of El-Yemen; (O, L;) like فُضُلٌ in the dial. of Nejd; (L;) as also ▼ فُرُجٌ. (Ḳ.) —— And, as also ▼ فُرُجٌ, One *who will not conceal a secret:* (O, Ḳ:) and ▼ فُرُجَةٌ a man *wont to reveal his secrets*. (Ḥam p. 49.)

فَرْجَةٌ: see فَرَجٌ, in five places. —— It is said in the T, that أَدْرَكُوا القَوْمَ عَلَى فَرْجَتِهِمْ or ▼ فُرْجَتِهِمْ occurs in a trad. as meaning عَلَى هَزِيمَتِهِمْ [i. e. *They overtook the people*, or *party, in their state of defeat*]: but it is also related as with قاف and حاء [app. قَرْحَتِهِمْ]. (TA.)

فُرْجَةٌ *An opening*, or *intervening space*, [or *a gap*, or *breach*,] *between two things;* (Mṣb, TA;) as also ▼ فَرْجٌ, (A,) of which the pl. is فُرُوجٌ only; (TA;) [and so ▼ مَفْرَجٌ, lit. *a place of opening*, occurring in the Ḳ in art. ودى, &c.;] and ▼ مُنْفَرَجٌ: (JK and Ḳ voce خَلَلٌ, &c.:) the pl. of the first is فُرَجٌ (Mṣb, TA) and فُرُجَاتٌ: (TA:) and it is also in a wall, (Ṣ, Mṣb, Ḳ,) and the like: (Ṣ, Mṣb:) and signifies also *an opening*, or *a space*, or *room, made by persons for a man entering among them*, in a place of standing or of sitting. (Mṣb.) One says, بَيْنَهُمَا فُرْجَةٌ, meaning ٱنْفِرَاجٌ [i. e. *Between them two is an opening*, or *intervening space*, &c.]. (Ṣ.) فُرَجُ الشَّيْطَانِ [*The Devil's gaps*], occurring in a trad., means *the gaps*, or *unoccupied spaces, in the ranks of men praying* [*in the mosque*]. (L.) —— See also فَرْجٌ, last sentence: —— and see فَرَجٌ, in seven places: —— and فَرْجَةٌ.

فِرْجَةٌ: see فَرَجٌ, in three places.

فُرُجَةٌ: see فُرُجٌ, last sentence.

فَرُوجٌ, applied to a bow [like فَرْجٌ &c.]: see 7.

فَرِيجٌ: see فَرْجٌ. —— Also A ewe *whose hips are unknit*, or *loosened*, [in the joints], (ٱنْفَرَجَ ▼ وَرِكَاهَا [see 4],) *when she brings forth*. (TA.) And A woman *whose bones are unknit*, or *loosened*, (ٱنْفَرَجَتْ ▼ عِظَامُهَا) *in consequence of parturition:* and hence, as likened thereto, ‡ a camel *that is fatigued, and drags his feet*, or *stands still:* (Skr, O:) or a woman *fatigued in consequence of parturition:* and hence, as being likened thereto, ‡ a she-camel *that is fatigued*. (Kr, TA.) And A she-camel *that has brought forth her first offspring*. (O, Ḳ.) [See also فَارِجٌ.] —— Also, accord. to the Ḳ, [and the O as on the authority of Ibn-'Abbád,] i. q. بَارِدٌ: but [SM says that] this is a mistake for بَارِزٌ, meaning *Uncovered, appearing*, or *apparent;* in which sense it is applied also to a fem. noun: (TA:) it is applied, in a verse of Aboo-Dhu-eyb, to a pearl (دُرَّة), as meaning *uncovered*, and *exposed to view*, for sale. (O, TA.)

فَرَّاجٌ One *who often removes, clears away*, or *dispels, grief*, or *anxiety, from those affected therewith;* or *who does so much*. (O.)

فَرُّوجٌ The *young of the domestic hen;* [the *chicken*, and *chickens;*] (Ṣ, Mgh, O, Ḳ; [but the explanation is omitted in one of my copies of the Ṣ;]) as also فُرُّوجٌ, (Ṣ, O, Ḳ,) like سُبُّوحٌ [q. v.], (Ḳ,) a dial. var., (Ṣ, O, TA,) mentioned by Lḥ: (TA:) n. un. with ة: (Ṣ:) pl. فَرَارِيجُ. (Ṣ, Mgh, O.) —— And hence, app., by a metaphorical application, (Mgh,) it signifies also *A* [*garment of the kind called*] قَبَآء, (Ṣ, Mgh, O, Ḳ, [but omitted in one of my copies of the Ṣ,]) *having a slit in its hinder part:* (Mgh, O, Ḳ:) or the *shirt of a child:* (O, Ḳ:) [but] the Prophet is related to have prayed in a فروج (Mgh, TA) of خَزّ (Mgh) or of silk; (TA;) or he pulled off one that he had put on. (O.)

فَارِجٌ: see فَرْجٌ. —— Also A she-camel *that has become unknit*, or *loosened*, [app. in the joints of the hips,] (ٱنْفَرَجَتْ ▼ [see 4],) *in consequence of parturition, and therefore hates the stallion*, (O, Ḳ,) *and dislikes his being near*. (O.) [See also فَرِيجٌ.] And see 4, last sentence.

أَفْرَجُ, in the phrase أَفْرَجُ الثَّنَايَا, i. q. أَفْلَجُ [q. v.]. —— And A man *whose buttocks do not meet*, (Ṣ, O, Ḳ,) or *scarcely meet*, (TA,) *by reason of their bigness:* (Ṣ, O, Ḳ:) fem. فَرْجَآءُ: it is mostly the case among the Abyssinians. (Ṣ, O.) —— See also فَرِجٌ.

تِفْرِجٌ, accord. to Akh, *A beater and washer and whitener of clothes;* syn. قَصَّارٌ. (O.) —— See also the next paragraph.

تِفْرِجَةٌ and ▼ تِفْرَاجٌ are sings. of تَفَارِيجُ, (O,) which signifies, (IAṭr, O, Ḳ,) as pl. of the first, (Ḳ,) or of the second, (IAṭr, O,) The *openings* [or *interstices*] *of the fingers:* (IAṭr, O, Ḳ:) and the *apertures*, (IAṭr, O,) or *clefts*, (Ḳ,) of a railing: (IAṭr, O, Ḳ:) and also, (O, Ḳ,) accord. to IDrd, as pl. of تِفْرِجَةٌ, (O,) the *slits* of the [kind of garment called] قَبَآء [and فَرُّوج]. (O, Ḳ.) ——

تفرجة as an epithet, applied to a man, signifies *Cowardly and weak*; as also ▼ تفراجة; (O, Ḳ;) and نفرجاة, with ن, (O,* Ḳ,) mentioned by IAmb, as imperfectly decl., and as signifying *cowardly*; (O;) or so, accord. to the T and L, ▼ تفرج and تفرجة, and نفرج and نفرجة: and the last two, and نفراج and نفرجاة, all with ن, signify one *who becomes defeated*, or *put to flight*, (يَنْكَشِفُ,) *on the occasion of war*, or *battle*. (TA.)

تفراج and تفراجة: see the next preceding paragraph.

مفرج: see فُرْجَة. [Hence] مَفْرَجُ الفَمِ [*The place of opening of the mouth*]. (TA in art. شجر.) مَفَارِج [is its pl.; and] signifies *Places of exit*, or *egress*. (TA.)

مُفْرَج, occurring in the saying, in a trad., لَا يُتْرَكُ فِى الإِسْلَامِ مُفْرَجٌ, [meaning that he who is thus termed shall not be left unbefriended among the Muslims,] is variously explained: Aṣ used to say that it is with ح; and disapproved of the saying مفرج, with ج: A'Obeyd says, I heard Moḥammad Ibn-El-Ḥasan say, it is related with ح and with ج; and he who says مفرج, with ج, means *A slain person found in a desert tract, not by a town or village*, [which signification is mentioned in the Ḳ,] the fine for whose blood is to be paid from the government-treasury: AO says that it means *one who becomes a Muslim and has no alliance of friendship with any one* [*among the Muslims*]; wherefore, if he commits a crime, [such as maiming another, &c.,] the government-treasury must make amends for it, because he has no relations or others bound to aid him by paying a bloodwit [or the like]: (Ṣ, O: and the like is also said in the Mgh and in the Ḳ:) or, accord. to Jábir El-Joạfee, it means *a man who is among a people to whom he does not belong*; wherefore they are bound to pay for him a bloodwit [or the like]: (O, TA:) or it means *one who has no kinsfolk, or near relations*: so accord. to IAạr: (Mgh, TA:) or *one who has no offspring*: or *one who has no wealth*, or *property*: and it is also said to mean *one burdened by the obligation to pay a bloodwit, or a ransom, or a debt that must be discharged*: and [in like manner] ▼ مَفْرُوج is said to mean *one who is burdened with a debt*: but it is correctly with ح [unpointed]; (TA;) [i.e.] such is termed مُفْرَح, with ح: (Aṣ, Mgh:) and مُفْرَج means *one burdened by his family*, although he be not in debt. (Az, TA voce مُفْرَح [q. v.].)

مُفْرِج One *whose shooting*, or *casting, has become altered* [*for the worse*], *having been good*. (AA, O,* Ḳ.) ═ And thus, without ة, A hen *having chickens*. (Ṣ, O, Ḳ.)

مُفَرَّج A camel (O) *whose elbow is distant from his armpit*: (O, Ḳ:) or *wide in step*: (O:) or, with ة, a she-camel *whose elbows are far from her chest, and whose armpits are* [*therefore*] *wide*. (Ḥam p. 783.) — And *A comb*. (O, Ḳ.)

مَفْرُوج An *opened* door. (TA.) — See also مُفْرَج, near the end.

مُنْفَرَج: see فُرْجَة.

فرجن

Q. 1. فَرْجَنَ الدَّابَّةَ *He curried the beast*; *removed the dust from it with the* فِرْجَوْن. (Ṣ, Ḳ.) But the etymologists assert that the ن is augmentative. (TA.)

فِرْجَوْن *A currycomb*; syn. مِحَسَّةٌ [q. v.]. (Ṣ, Ḳ.)

فرح

1. فَرِحَ, (Ṣ, A, L, Mṣb, Ḳ, &c.,) [aor. ـَ,] inf. n. فَرَحٌ, (Ṣ,* L,* Mṣb, &c.,) *He rejoiced*; *was joyful*, or *glad*; or *was happy*; (Ṣ, A, L, Mṣb, Ḳ, &c.;) syn. سُرَّ: (Ṣ, A, Mṣb,* &c.:) or *he experienced a sensation of lightness in his heart*: (Th, TA:) or *his bosom became dilated with delight*, or *pleasure, of short continuance, transitory*, or *fleeting, not lasting, as is the case in bodily and worldly pleasures*; فَرَحٌ differing from سُرُورٌ in the manner expl. below, though each is sometimes used as syn. with the other. (Er-Rághib, TA.) You say, فَرِحَ بِهِ *He rejoiced, was joyful*, or *glad*, or *was happy, by reason of him*, or *it*; syn. سُرَّ. (Ṣ, A, Mṣb.*) — And *He was*, or *became, well pleased*, or *content*. — And *He exulted*, or *rejoiced above measure*; or *he exulted greatly, and behaved insolently and unthankfully*, or *ungratefully*. (Ṣ, Mṣb, Ḳ.) The verb is used in this sense in the Ḳur xxviii. 76. (TA.)

2: see the paragraph here following.

4. افرحهُ, (Ṣ, A, Mṣb, Ḳ,) inf. n. إِفْرَاحٌ; (Ṣ;) and ▼ فرّحهُ, (Mṣb, Ḳ,) inf. n. تَفْرِيحٌ; (Ṣ;) *He*, or *it, rejoiced him*; *gladdened him*; *made him joyful*, or *glad*; or *made him happy*: (Ṣ, A, Mṣb, Ḳ:) [or *occasioned him a sensation of lightness of heart*: or *made his bosom to become dilated with delight*, or *pleasure, of short continuance, transitory*, or *fleeting, not lasting, as is the case in bodily and worldly pleasures*. See فَرَحٌ.] — And *He*, or *it, made him to be well pleased*, or *content*. (Mṣb.) — And *He*, or *it, made him to exult, or rejoice above measure*; or *to exult greatly, and to behave insolently and unthankfully*, or *ungratefully*. (Mṣb, Ḳ.) ═ Also *He*, or *it, grieved him*; or *made him unhappy*; lit. *deprived him of joy*; or *of happiness*: like as أَشْكَاهُ signifies "he made his complaint to cease." (L.) [Thus it has two contr. meanings.] — And *It* (a debt, AA, Ṣ, TA, or a thing, TA) *burdened him, burdened him heavily*, or *overburdened him*. (AA, Ṣ, Ḳ, TA.)

فَرَحٌ [inf. n. of فَرِحَ, q. v.: as a simple subst.,] *Joy, mirth*, or *gladness*; or *happiness*; (Ṣ, L, Mṣb, Ḳ;) syn. سُرُورٌ; (Mṣb, Ḳ;) *contr. of* حُزْنٌ, (L,) and *of* تَرَحٌ: (Ṣ and A in art. ترح:) or *a sensation of lightness of the heart*: (Th, TA:) or *dilatation of the bosom with delight*, or *pleasure, of short continuance, transitory*, or *fleeting, not lasting, as is the case in bodily and worldly pleasures*; whereas سُرُورٌ is dilatation of the bosom with delight, or pleasure, wherein is quiet or tranquillity or rest of mind, of short or of long continuance; but each is sometimes used as syn. with the other. (Er-Rághib, TA.) — And *A state of being well pleased*, or *content*, with a thing. (Mṣb.) — And *Exultation*, or *a rejoicing above measure*; or *a state of exulting greatly, and behaving insolently and unthankfully*, or *ungratefully*. (Ṣ, Mṣb, Ḳ.) — [Also *A festivity*, or *merry-making*; particularly, as used in the present day, *on the occasion of a marriage*. — Pl. أَفْرَاحٌ.] — In the saying of Muṭeeạ Ibn-Iyás,

قَدْ ظَفِرَ الحُزْنُ بِالسُّرُورِ وَقَدْ
أُدِيلَ مَكْرُوهُنَا مِنَ الفَرَحِ

[*Sorrow, or sadness, has overcome happiness, and the object of our dislike, or hatred, has been given a turn to prevail over the object of our love*], by مِنَ الفَرَحِ he means مِنَ المَفْرُوحِ بِهِ, i. e. المَحْبُوب. (Ḥam p. 391.)

فَرُحٌ: see the paragraph here following.

فَرِحٌ and ▼ فَرْحَانُ (Mṣb, Ḳ) and ▼ فَرُحٌ, as in some copies of the Ḳ and in the L and other lexicons, or ▼ فَرُوحٌ, as in other copies and mentioned by IJ, (TA,) and ▼ فَارِحٌ and ▼ مَفْرُوحٌ, (Ḳ,) the last mentioned by IJ; (TA;) fem. [of the first] فَرِحَةٌ and [of the second] فَرْحَى (Mṣb, Ḳ) and فَرْحَانَةٌ, (Ḳ,) but of the correctness of this last ISd was not certain: (TA:) pl. [of the first] فَرِحُونَ (Ṣ, Mṣb) and [of the second] فَرَاحَى and فَرْحَى: (Ḳ, TA:) *Rejoicing, joyful*, or *glad*; or *happy*: (Mṣb, Ḳ:) [or *experiencing a sensation of lightness in the heart*: or *having the bosom dilated with delight*, or *pleasure, of short continuance, transitory*, or *fleeting, not lasting, as is the case in bodily and worldly pleasures*. See فَرَحٌ.] Hence, in the Ḳur [iii. 164], فَرِحِينَ بِمَا آتَاهُمُ اللّٰهُ مِنْ فَضْلِهِ [*Rejoicing by reason of that which God has given them of his bounty*]. (Mṣb.) — And *Well pleased*, or *content*: whence, in the Ḳur [xxiii. 55 and xxx. 31], كُلُّ حِزْبٍ بِمَا لَدَيْهِمْ فَرِحُونَ [*Every sect is well pleased, or content, with that religion which it has*]. (Mṣb.) — And *Exulting*, or *rejoicing above measure*; or *exulting greatly, and behaving insolently and unthankfully*, or *ungratefully*: (Ṣ, Mṣb, Ḳ:) whence, in the Ḳur [xxviii. 76], إِنَّ اللّٰهَ لَا يُحِبُّ الفَرِحِينَ [*Verily God does not love those who exult, or rejoice above measure*; &c.]. (Ṣ, Mṣb.)

فَرْحَةٌ [*A joy, or gladness*; or *a happiness*]: see an ex. voce تَرْحَةٌ. — See also the next paragraph, in two places.

فُرْحَةٌ *A cause of joy* or *gladness*, or *of happiness*; *a thing whereby one is made joyful* or *glad*, or *happy*; as also ▼ فَرْحَةٌ; syn. مَسَرَّةٌ. (Ḳ.) —

And *A thing that thou givest to him that rejoices thee*; (L, Ḳ;) *a recompense that thou givest him*; (L;) [as also ▼ فُرْحَةٌ; for] you say, لَكَ عِنْدِى فَرْحَةٌ إِنْ بَشَّرْتَنِى, (Ṣ, A, [in one of my copies of the Ṣ أَىْ بَشَّرْتَنِى, as though this were an explanation, but the former is the right reading,]) and فُرْحَةٌ, (Ṣ,) meaning بُشْرَى [i. e. *There is for thee, with me, a gift for announcing a joyful event, if thou announce to me such an event*]. (A.)

فَرْحَانُ; fem. فَرْحَى, and accord. to the Ḳ فَرْحَانَةٌ also: see فَرِحٌ.

فَرْحَانَةٌ *White* كَمْأَة [or *truffles*]: (Ḳ:) from Kr: but ISd states the word transmitted to him to be with ق [i. e. قُرْحَانٌ, of which قُرْحَانَةٌ is mentioned as a n. un.]. (L, TA.)

فَرُوحٌ: }
فَارِحٌ: } see فَرِحٌ.

مُفْرَحٌ A man *burdened*, or *burdened heavily*, or *overburdened, by debt*, (A'Obeyd, Ṣ, TA,) or *by a fine*, or *the like, and unable to pay it*: (A'Obeyd, TA:) or *needy*, or *in want; overcome*; and *poor*: (Ḳ:) or *poor, possessing no property*: (TA:) one *who is not known to have any kinsfolk or near relations*; (Ḳ, TA;) but in a trad. in which it occurs in this sense as related by some, it is, as others relate the trad., with ج; and so in the sense next following: (TA:) and *a slain person found between two towns or villages*. (Ḳ.) In the trad. in which it is said لَا يُتْرَكُ فِى الإِسْلَامِ مُفْرَحٌ it has the first of the significations mentioned above accord. to A'Obeyd [i. e. the saying means *One who is burdened*, or *burdened heavily*, or *overburdened, by debt*, &c., *shall not be left unbefriended among the Muslims*]. (TA.) And in the writing that the Apostle of God wrote [as a covenant] between the Muhájirs and the Anṣár were the words, لَا يَتْرُكُوا مُفْرَحًا حَتَّى يُعِينُوهُ عَلَى مَا كَانَ مِنْ عَقْلٍ أَوْ فِدَآءٍ, in which مُفْرَحًا means مَفْدُوحًا, (Ez-Zuhree, Aṣ, Ṣ,) i. e. [*They shall not leave*] *one who is burdened*, or *burdened heavily*, or *overburdened, by debt*, [*until they aid him to acquit himself of what has become incumbent* on him, *of a bloodwit* or *a ransom*,] meaning that his debt shall be paid for him from the treasury of the state: so says Aṣ; and he disallowed the saying [in this case] مُفْرَجٌ, [q. v.,] with ج. (Ṣ.)

مُفْرِحٌ A thing *that makes joyful* or *glad*, or *that makes happy*: (T, L:) [and ▼ مَفْرُوحٌ بِهِ a thing *by which one is made joyful* or *glad*, or *by which one is made happy*:] one says, مَا يَسُرُّنِى بِهِ مُفْرِحٌ, (Aṣ, T, Ṣ, L,) and ▼ مَفْرُوحٌ بِهِ, for which one should not say مَفْرُوحٌ [alone], (Aṣ, Ṣ,) [i. e. *Nothing that makes joyful* &c., and *by which one is made joyful* &c., *renders me happy by means of it*,] relating to an affair, or event. (Ṣ.) [See also فُرْحَةٌ.]

مُفَرِّحٌ *A certain well-known* [*exhilarating*] *medicine*; (Ṣ, Ḳ;) *a certain medicine which is given to drink to him who is in grief, and in consequence of which he becomes happy; thus called by the physicians, and by others called* سُلْوَانٌ. (Ṣ in art. سلو.)

مِفْرَاحٌ One *who rejoices much*, or *often*: (Ḳ:) or one *who rejoices* [app. *much*] *whenever fortune renders him happy*. (Ṣ.)

مَفْرُوحٌ: see مُفْرِحٌ, in two places: = and see فَرِحٌ.

فرخ

1. فَرِخَ, aor. ـَ, (Ḳ,) inf. n. فَرَخٌ, (TḲ,) *He* (a man, TA) *became free from fright*, or *fear, and at ease*, or *calm*. (Ḳ.) [See also 4.] — And فَرِخَ إِلَى الأَرْضِ *He clave to the ground*; (Ḳ, TA;) as also ▼ فرّخ. (TA.)

2. فَرَّخَتْ, and ▼ أَفْرَخَتْ, said of a bird, (Ṣ, A, Mṣb, Ḳ, but in the Ṣ and Mṣb the verbs are in the masc. forms,) [inf. n. of the former تَفْرِيخٌ,] *She had* [or *she produced by hatching*] *a young one*, (Mṣb, Ḳ,) or *young ones*. (A.) [In the L, in one place, and so, accord. to the TA, in other lexicons, for صَارَ in the explanatory phrase صَارَ لَهَا فَرْخٌ, is put طَارَ; as though the verbs signified *She had a young one that flew*.] — And both verbs, said of an egg (بَيْضَةٌ), *It had* [or *produced*] *a young one*: (L, Ḳ:) or افرخت said of an egg, *it had in it a young bird*: (ISh, TA in art. بيض:) or *it broke open from over the young bird, which thereupon came forth from it*. (AHeyth, TA in art. روع; and Mṣb.) — See also the next paragraph, in two places. — فَرَّخَ الزَّرْعُ, (Ṣ, A, L, Ḳ,) inf. n. تَفْرِيخٌ, (Ṣ, L,) ‡ *The seed-produce*, or *corn, was ready to cleave open, when it had come up*: (Ṣ:) or *produced many shoots*: (A:) or *put forth its shoots*: (Ḳ:) or *shot forth into leaf from the grain, when the latter had cloven asunder*; as also ▼ افرخ. (L.) [See also قَصَّبَ.] And فَرَّخَ شَجَرُهُمْ فِرَاخًا كَثِيرَةً ‡ *Their trees produced many offsets*, or *shoots from their roots or stems*. (A.) — See also 1. — [Hence,] بَاضَ فِيهِمُ الشَّيْطَانُ وَفَرَّخَ, occurring in a trad., means ‡ *The devil made his fixed abode among them*; like as a bird keeps to the place of its eggs and young ones. (L.) And [in like manner] one says, فرّخ الشيطان فِى رَأْسِهِ ‡ *The devil took up an abode in his head*. (TA in art. فحص.) — فرّخ القَوْمُ means † *The people*, or *party, became weak*; i. e., *became like young birds*. (Ḳ.) And فرّخ said of a man, † *He was*, or *became, base, vile*, or *abject*. (T, TA.) And † *He* (a man) *was frightened*; or *he feared*, or *was afraid*. (Ḳ.) And فُرِّخَ, in the pass. form, said of a coward, and of a weak old man, inf. n. تَفْرِيخٌ, † *He was frightened, and made to tremble*. (L.)

4. أَفْرَخَتْ said of a bird: — and of an egg: see 2. — [Hence,] one says, أَفْرَخَ بَيْضَةُ القَوْمِ, meaning † *What was hidden, of the affair*, or *case, of the people*, or *company of men, became apparent*. (ISh, TA in art. بيض. [See also a similar phrase in what follows.]) And افرخ فُؤَادُهُ ‡ *His heart became free from fear*: fear in the heart being likened to a young bird in the egg. (L.) And افرخ الرَّوْعُ ‡ *Fright*, or *fear, departed*; (Ṣ, Ḳ, TA;) as also ▼ فرّخ, inf. n. تَفْرِيخٌ: (Ḳ, TA:) and one says, لِيُفْرِخْ رَوْعُكَ ‡ *Let thy fright*, or *fear, depart*; like as the young bird goes forth from the egg. (Ṣ, TA. [But see رُوعٌ: and see also a phrase similar to this in what follows.]) And أَفْرَخَ الأَمْرُ *The affair*, or *case, became manifest*, or *plain*, (Ṣ, A, L, Ḳ,) *as to its issue*, or *result*, (L,) *after having been confused*, or *dubious*; (Ṣ, A, L, Ḳ;) as also ▼ فرّخ. (L.) — افرخ القَوْمُ بَيْضَهُمْ, (Ṣ, L, Ḳ,) or بَيْضَتَهُمْ, (as in some copies of the Ḳ,) meaning ‡ *The people*, or *party, disclosed their secret*, (Ṣ, L, Ḳ, TA,) is said of those whose case has become apparent. (L.) [Hence it seems that افرخ البَيْضَةَ properly signifies *It* (a bird) *hatched the egg, and produced the young bird*.] أَفْرِخْ رَوْعَكَ ‡ *Calm thy mind*, (Ṣ, L, Ḳ, TA,) is a prov., mentioned by Az, from A'Obeyd, as said, on occasions of fear, to him who is cowardly. (L, TA.) And أَفْرَخَ رَوْعَهُ means † *He prayed for him that his fright*, or *fear, might become calmed, and depart*. (AO, TA.) — See also 2, latter half.

10. استفرخ الحَمَامَ *He took for himself the pigeons* (Ṣ, Ḳ) *for their young ones*, (Ṣ,) or *for* [*the purpose of their producing*] *young ones*. (Ḳ.)

فَرْخٌ The *young one of a bird*: (Ṣ, A, Mgh, L, Ḳ:) this is the primary signification: (L:) or, *of any creature that lays eggs*: (Mṣb:) fem. with ة: (Ṣ, A:) and, (L, Ḳ,) sometimes, (L,) the *young one of any animal*: (L, Ḳ:) pl. (of pauc., Ṣ, L) أَفْرُخٌ and أَفْرَاخٌ (Ṣ, Mgh, L, Mṣb, Ḳ) and أَفْرِخَةٌ, (L, Ḳ,) the last of which is extr. [with respect to rule], (IAạr,) and (of mult., Ṣ, L) فِرَاخٌ (Ṣ, L, Mṣb, Ḳ) and فِرْخَانٌ (L, Mṣb, Ḳ) and فُرُوخٌ (Mṣb, Ḳ) and فُرْخٌ. (L.) [See an ex. (from a poet) in which فِرَاخ is treated grammatically as a sing. in the first paragraph of art. خلف.] — [Hence,] † *A base, a vile*, or *an abject, man, who is driven away*. (Ḳ.) And one says, فُلَانٌ فَرْخٌ مِنَ الفِرَاخِ, (TA,) or مِنَ الفُرُوخِ, (so in two copies of the A,) meaning ‡ *Such a one is a bastard*: (A, TA:) said by El-Khafájee to be a phrase of the people of El-Medeeneh, peculiarly; but accord. to MF, it is a post-classical phrase common in El-Ḥijáz. (TA.) — And ‡ *A sucker, an offset*, or *a sprout, of any plant* (L, Ḳ) or *tree* &c.: (L:) or *a branch* of a tree: or, as some say, *a branch that is in the middle* of a tree: (Ḥam p. 347:) or [its pl.] فِرَاخٌ signifies *offsets*, or *shoots, from the roots* or *stems* of trees: (A:) and this is also said to signify *worms that are in herbs*. (Ḥam p. 491.) And ‡ *Seed-produce*, or *corn, shooting forth into leaf from the grain, when the latter has cloven* asunder: (Lth, TA:) or, *ready to cleave open,* (Ṣ, Ḳ,) *when it has come up:* (Ṣ:) or, *when it has shoots.* (L.) — And الفَرْخُ signifies ‡ *The fore part of the brain;* (Ḳ, TA;) thus called by way of comparison [to the young one of a bird], in like manner as it is called العُصْفُورُ; (TA;) or the عصفور is beneath the فَرْخ: (TA in art. عصفر:) the pl. is فِرَاخٌ: and الفَرْخُ signifies [also, particularly,] *the fore part of the brain of the horse.* (TA in the present art.) In the saying of El-Farezdaḳ,

• وَيَوْمَ جَعَلْنَا البِيضَ فِيهِ لِعَامِرٍ •
• مُصَمِّمَةً تَفْأَى فِرَاخَ الجَمَاجِمِ •

he means [*And a day in which we made the swords, penetrating into that which they smote, cleave*] *the brains* [lit. *brain* (الدِّمَاغ) *of the tribe of 'Ámir*]. (Ṣ, TA.)

فَرِخٌ, like كَتِفٌ, † A man *whose grounds of pretension to respect, or honour, are suspected.* (TA.)

فَرْخَةٌ fem. of فَرْخٌ [q. v.]. (Ṣ, A.) — Also † *A broad* سِنَان [or *spear-head*]. (Ḳ.) — فَرْخَةُ الدَّيْلَمِ: see ذُرَّاحٌ.

فُرَيْخٌ a dim. [of فَرْخٌ]: hence the saying, فُلَانٌ فُرَيْخُ قُرَيْشٍ ‡ [*Such a one is the honoured and cherished of Kureysh*]: فريخ being here a dim. (Ṣ, Ḳ) denoting magnification (Ḳ) [i. e.] denoting commendation: (Ṣ:) and فُلَانٌ فُرَيْخُ قَوْمِهِ ‡ *Such a one is the honoured* [*and cherished*] *of his people;* like a little young bird in the house of a people who rear it and treat it with kindness. (A.)

فُرَيْخِيَّةٌ [or, probably, فُرَخِيَّةٌ, agreeably with analogy,] an epithet applied to نِصَال [meaning "arrow-heads," &c., but app. a mistranscription for نِبَال i. e. "arrows"], which were so called in relation to الفُرَيْخ, a certain blacksmith in the Time of Ignorance: (TA:) or الفُرَيْخ was a man who used, in the Time of Ignorance, to pare, or shape, arrows: (Ṣ:) mentioned by a poet in the saying,

• وَمَقْذُوذَيْنِ مِنْ بَرْىِ الفُرَيْخِ •

[*And two feathered arrows of the paring, or shaping, of El-Fureykh*]. (Ṣ, TA.) [Freytag mentions فُرَّيْخِى, as applied to an arrow, meaning "ad virum فريخ appellatum referendus:" but he names no authority: and it has been shown above that the name of the man is without teshdeed; and so, therefore, is its rel. n.]

فُرُوخٌ *Ears of wheat of which the final condition has become apparent, and of which the grain has become organized and compact:* occurring in a trad., in which the selling of such for measured wheat is forbidden. (IAth, TA.)

مَفْرَخٌ: see مَفَارِخُ.

مُفْرِخٌ A hen-bird *having* [or *producing by hatching*] *a young one* [or *young ones* (see 2)]; (L, Ḳ;) as also ▼ مُفَرِّخٌ. (L.)

مُفْرَخٌ: see مَفَارِخُ.

مُفَرِّخٌ: see مُفْرِخٌ.

مَفَارِخُ, a pl. of which the sing. is not mentioned, (TA,) *Places where birds have* [or *produce by hatching*] *young ones.* (Ḳ.) [Such a place may be called, accord. to analogy, ▼ مُفْرَخٌ (which may be the sing. of مَفَارِخُ) and ▼ مُفَرَّخٌ.]

فرد

1. فَرَدَ, aor. ـُ, [inf. n. فُرُودٌ,] *He, or it, was, or became, single; sole; or one, and no more.* (Mṣb.) — See also 7, (with which two other forms of the unaugmented verb, namely, فَرِدَ and فَرُدَ, are also mentioned,) in four places.

2. فرّد, inf. n. تَفْرِيدٌ, *He applied himself to the study of practical religion, or the law, and withdrew from* [*the rest of*] *mankind, and attended only to the observance of the commands and prohibitions* [*of religion*]. (IAạr, T, L, Ḳ.) [See also the part. n., below.]

4. افرد as intrans.: see 7. — أَفْرَدَتْ *She* (a female, Ṣ, L, a pregnant female, A, or a woman, Ḳ) *brought forth one only:* (Ṣ, A, L, Ḳ:) opposed to أَتْأَمَتْ: (A:) not said of a she-camel, because she never brings forth more than one. (Ṣ, L, Ḳ.) — افردهُ *He made him, or it, to be single; sole; or one, and no more.* (Lth, T, M,* L, Mṣb.*) — And *He put, or set, him, or it, apart, aside, or away; he separated him, or it.* (Ṣ, Ḳ.) You say, افردهُ مِنْهُ [*He separated him from him, and rendered him solitary; or he left him solitary*]. (A and Mgh in art. وتر.) [See an ex. in a verse cited voce عَاذِبٌ.] — [Hence,] افرد فُلَانًا بِشَىْءٍ *He made such a one to have a thing to himself alone, with none to share, or participate, with him in it.* (A in art. فرز.) — And افرد الحَجَّ عَنِ العُمْرَةِ *He performed the rites and ceremonies of the pilgrimage separately from those of the* عُمْرَة [q. v.]. (Mṣb.) — And افرد إِلَيْهِ رَسُولًا (Ṣ, Ḳ) *He sent* [*away*] *a messenger to him.* (Ḳ.)

5: see the next paragraph, in two places.

7. انفرد and ▼ فَرَدَ signify the same: (Ṣ:) the latter, aor. ـُ, [inf. n. فُرُودٌ,] is expl. by Lth as signifying *He was, or became, alone, by himself, apart from others, or solitary:* (T, L:) and thus انفرد بِنَفْسِهِ signifies. (Mṣb.) And انفرد عَنْهُ *He, or it, was, or became, apart, or separate, from him, or it, and alone.* (L.) And انفرد بِفُلَانٍ and ▼ استفردهُ are syn. [as meaning *He was, or became, alone with such a one*]. (M, A, Ḳ.) And انفرد بِالأَمْرِ, (AZ, T, M, L, Ḳ,) and بِكَذَا, (Ṣ,) and بِرَأْيِهِ; (L;) and ▼ فَرَدَ, (AZ, T, M, L, Ḳ,) aor. ـُ, (AZ, T, M, L,) inf. n. فُرُودٌ; (AZ, L;) and ▼ فَرِدَ, and ▼ فَرُدَ, (M, L, Ḳ,) mentioned by Lḥ; (M, L;) and ▼ افرد, (L, Ḳ,) and ▼ تفرّد, and ▼ استفرد; (Ṣ, M, L, Ḳ;) signify alike; (AZ, T, Ṣ, M, L, Ḳ;) i. e. *He was, or became, alone; independent of others; without any to share, or participate, with him; in the affair,* and *in such a thing,* and *in his opinion:* (the lexicons passim: [see اِسْتَبَدَّ:]) and [in like manner] تفرّد ▼ بِالمَالِ [*he was without any to share, or participate, with him in the property*]. (Mṣb.) — لَأُقَاتِلَنَّهُمْ حَتَّى تَنْفَرِدَ سَالِفَتِى, occurring in a trad., means † *I will assuredly fight with them until I die;* lit., *until the side of my neck shall become separate* from my body; because its separation can be only by death. (L.)

10. استفرد as intrans.: see 7. — استفردهُ: see 7. — Also *He found him alone, having no second person with him.* (A.) [Hence, one says,] اِسْتَطْرَدَ لَهُمْ فَلَمَّا آسْتَفْرَدَ مِنْهُمْ رَجُلًا كَرَّ عَلَيْهِ فَجَدَلَهُ [*He fled, or wheeled about widely, from them, to turn again, by way of stratagem; and when he found a man of them alone, he returned against him, and threw him down upon the ground*]. (A, L.) And استفرد الدُّرَّةَ *He* (the diver) *found the pearl alone, having no other with it.* (A.) — And *He took it alone; by itself; without any other, or any like it.* (T, L.) *He took it forth from among the things that were with it.* (M, Ḳ.)

فَرْدٌ *Single; sole; only; one, and no more;* syn. وِتْرٌ; (Ṣ, A, L, Mṣb;) i. e. وَاحِدٌ: (Mṣb:) [and, used as a subst., *a single,* or *an individual, person* or *thing:*] fem. فَرْدَةٌ and ▼ فَرْدَى [which latter is anomalous, as though fem. of فَرْدَانُ]: (Mṣb:) pl. أَفْرَادٌ and ▼ فُرَادَى which latter is anomalous, as though pl. of فَرْدَانُ (Ṣ, L, Mṣb) and of فَرْدَى, like as سُكَارَى is pl. of سَكْرَانُ and of سَكْرَى. (Mṣb. See also فُرَادٌ, below.) You say, عَدَدْتُ الدَّرَاهِمَ أَفْرَادًا *I counted the dirhems one by one.* (T, A.) — And *Such as has no equal, or like:* (Lth, M, L, Ḳ:) pl. أَفْرَادٌ (M, Ḳ) and فُرَادَى [respecting which latter see above]. (Ḳ.) الفَرْدُ as an epithet applied to God means *The Single; the Sole; the One;* (T;) *He who has no equal, or like; the Unequalled:* (Lth, T, L:) but Az says, I have not found it so applied in the Sunneh; and no epithet should be applied to God except such as He has applied to Himself, or such as the Prophet has applied to Him. (L.) And one says سَيْفٌ فَرْدٌ, (Ḳ,) and ▼ فَرَدٌ, (T, L, Ḳ,) and ▼ فَرُدٌ, (L, Ḳ,) and ▼ فَرِدٌ, (Ḳ,) and ▼ فُرُدٌ, (T, Ḳ,) and ▼ فَرِيدٌ and ▼ فَرْدَدٌ, (Ḳ, but the third and fifth not in the text of the Ḳ as given in the TA,) *A sword having diversified wavy marks, streaks, or grain;* (ذُو فِرِنْدٍ, Ḳ, [in the TA وَفِرِنْدٌ, as though one said also سَيْفٌ فِرِنْدٌ, which is evidently a mistake,]) *unequalled* (T, L, Ḳ) *in excellence.* (T, L.) — And The *half* [meaning *one*] *of a pair* or *couple.* (M, L, Ḳ.) — And *Such as is alone, by himself* or *by itself,* or *apart from others; unconnected with,* or *unattended by, others; solitary,* or *separate;* syn. مُتَّحِدٌ, (M, L, Ḳ,) or مَا كَانَ وَحْدَهُ; (Lth, L;) *unmixed with others;* [in which sense it is] a word of more common application than

وِتْرٌ, and more special than وَاحِدٌ: (Kull p. 278:) pl. فِرَادٌ (M, L, Ḳ) [and فُرُودٌ and أَفْرَادٌ also, as will be shown below]: an ex. of the first of these pls. occurs in the saying, (cited by IAạr, L,)

تَخَطُّفَ الصَّقْرِ فِرَادَ السِّرْبِ

[*As the hawk's seizing*, or *carrying off by force, those that are apart from the others of the flock of birds*]. (M, L. See, again, فُرَادٌ.) [Hence,] one says ثَوْرٌ فَرْدٌ, (Ṣ,) and شَىْءٌ فَرْدٌ, (M, Ḳ,) and ▼ فَرَدٌ, (Ṣ, M, Ḳ,) and ▼ فَرِدٌ, and ▼ فَرُدٌ, (M, Ḳ,) and ▼ فُرُدٌ, (Ḳ,) and ▼ فَارِدٌ, (Ṣ, M, Ḳ,) and ▼ فَرِيدٌ, (Ṣ, Ḳ,) and ▼ فَرُودٌ, (M, Ḳ,) and ▼ فَرْدَانٌ, (Ḳ,) [and ▼ مُفْرَدٌ (see an ex. voce شَاةٌ, in art. شوه),] *A bull*, (Ṣ,) and *a thing*, (M, Ḳ,) *that is alone, by itself*, or *apart from others; solitary*, or *separate from others*. (Ṣ, M, Ḳ.) And سِدْرَةٌ ▼ فَارِدَةٌ *A lote-tree apart from others*. (Ṣ.) And شَجَرَةٌ ▼ فَارِدٌ, (M, Ḳ,) and فَارِدَةٌ, (M, TA.) *A tree apart from others*. (M, Ḳ,* TA.) And ظَبْيَةٌ ▼ فَارِدٌ *A gazelle apart*, or *separate, from the herd*. (Ṣ, M, Ḳ.) And نَاقَةٌ ▼ فَارِدٌ, and ▼ مِفْرَادٌ, and ▼ فَرُودٌ, *A she-camel that goes away alone, apart from others, in the pasture*, (M, L, Ḳ,*) *and at the water*; (M in explanation of the last, and L;) the epithet applied to the male being ▼ فَارِدٌ, only. (M, L.) And هُوَ ▼ فَارِدٌ بِهٰذَا الأَمْرِ *He is alone in this affair*. (A.) And it is said in a trad., لَا تُعَدُّ ▼ فَارِدَتُكُمْ, meaning *Your ewe*, or *she-goat, that ye have set apart from the flock*, or *herd, that ye may milk her in the tent*, or *house, shall not be reckoned* [among those for which ye are to pay the poor-rate]: (A:) or the meaning is, *what is over and above the* فَرِيضَة [or *fixed number of camels, &c., to be given in payment of the poor-rate*] *shall not be added to the latter and reckoned therewith*. (L.) And in another it is said, لَا يَغُلُّ ▼ فَارِدَتُكُمْ, expl. by Th as meaning *Such of you as shall segregate himself*, as, for instance, one or two, *and gain spoil, shall* resign it to the collective body, and *not act unfaithfully* by taking it for himself. (M, L.) And in another, فَمِنْكُمُ المُزْدَلِفُ صَاحِبُ العِمَامَةِ الفَرْدَةِ *And of you is El-Muzdelif, he of the solitary turban*: this was said of him because, when he rode, no one with him wore a turban, to show honour to him. (L.) — لَقِيتُهُ فَرْدَيْنِ means *I met him, we two being alone*. (Ṣ, L, Ḳ.) — أَفْرَادُ النُّجُومِ, (Ṣ, M, L, Ḳ,) as also فُرُودُهَا, (Ḳ,) signifies *The brightly-shining stars in the horizon* [*when other stars, there, are invisible*] (الدَّرَارِىُّ): so called because they are apart from the other [visible] stars. (M, L.) And الفُرُودُ, (T, M, L, and so in some copies of the Ḳ,) in some copies of the Ḳ ▼ الفَرْدُودُ, [and thus in the CḲ,] but the former is the right, (TA,) *Certain stars, disposed in a row, behind the Pleiades*; (Ḳ;) in some copies of the Ḳ, *around the Pleiades*: (TA:) *certain bright stars around the Pleiades*. (T, L.) And (L) *Certain stars around* حَضَارِ [q. v.], which is one of the two stars called المُحْلِفَانِ, (M, L, TA,) the other whereof is called الوَزْنُ; (TA;) *certain small stars with* حَضَارِ; so called because situate apart from the latter, by its side. (Kitáb Anwá el-'Arab, TA.) And الفَرْدُ is a name of *The star* (α) *in the hinder part of the neck of* الشُّجَاع [the constellation *Hydra*; which star is also called عُنُقُ الشُّجَاعِ]. (Ḳzw in his description of الشجاع.) — فَرْدٌ signifies also *One side of a jaw*: (M, L, Ḳ:) pl. أَفْرَادٌ. (M, L.) — And *A sandal such as is termed* سِمْطٌ, *not patched, nor having a second sole added to it*; (Ḳ;) *a sandal having a single sole; not having a sole composed of two pieces of leather sewed together, one beneath the other*; thus in the saying,

يَا خَيْرَ مَنْ يَمْشِى بِنَعْلٍ فَرْدِ

[*O best of such as walk with a single-soled sandal*], meaning O best of the great men of the Arabs; for sandals were worn by the Arabs, exclusively of the foreigners; and thin sandals, only by the kings and chief persons of the former. (L.) — Also, and ▼ فَارِدٌ, *A bull* [app. *a wild bull*]. (Lth, T, L. [See also مُفْرَدٌ.]) — [The pl.] الأَفْرَادُ as a conventional term in lexicology signifies *What have been transmitted by only one of the lexicologists*; what is thus transmitted, if the transmitter is a person of exactness (as Aboo-Zeyd and El-Khaleel and others), is admitted. (Mz, 5th نوع. [See also الآحَادُ, voce أَحَدٌ; a similar, but less restricted, term: and see المَفَارِيدُ.])

فَرَدٌ and فَرِدٌ and فَرُدٌ and فُرُدٌ: see the next preceding paragraph, first quarter: and again, in the second quarter: and for the first and second and third, see also فُرَادٌ.

فَرْدَةٌ fem. of فَرْدٌ [used as an epithet] in the first of the senses assigned to the latter above. (Mṣb.)

فُرْدَةٌ One *who goes away alone*, (Ḳ, TA,) *having left his companions*. (TA.)

فُرُدَاتٌ [*Hills*, or *the like, such as are termed*] آكَام [pl. of أَكَمَةٌ, q. v.]. (Ḳ.)

فَرْدَى: see فَرْدٌ, first sentence: — and see فُرَادٌ.

فَرْدَانٌ: see فَرْدٌ, second quarter: — and see فُرَادٌ.

فَرَادِ; see the paragraph here following.

فُرَادٌ [is most properly regarded as a quasi-pl. n., rather than as a pl., of فَرْدٌ; and فُرَادَ is similar to it in meaning]. One says, جَاؤُوا فُرَادًا, and ▼ فُرَادَى, (Ṣ, M, Ḳ,) with tenween and without it, (Ṣ,) and ▼ فُرَادَ, (Ḳ,) like ثُلَاثَ and رُبَاعَ, (TA,) and ▼ فَرَادِ, and فِرَادًا [a pl. of ▼ فَرْدٌ,] and ▼ فَرْدَى, (Ḳ,) [and ▼ فُرَّادًا, perhaps thus by poetic license, see an ex. in a verse cited voce مُوسِرٌ,] *They came one by one; one at a time*; (Ṣ;) *one after another*: (M, Ḳ:) AZ relates that the Kilábees said, جِئْتُمُونَا فُرَادًا [*Ye came to us one by one*; or *one after another*]: and هُمْ فُرَادٌ وَأَزْوَاجٌ [*They are separate persons and pairs*], with tenween: and the Arabs said قَوْمٌ فُرَادُ, imperfectly decl., likened to ثُلَاثُ and رُبَاعُ, [*A party composed of separate persons, disposed by ones, or one after another*,] and ▼ فُرَادَى, which latter is said by Fr to be a pl.: (T, L:) and the sing. [he adds] is ▼ فَرْدٌ and ▼ فَرِدٌ and ▼ فَرِيدٌ and ▼ فَرْدَانٌ: (T, Ḳ:) but ▼ فَرَدٌ, (so accord. to a copy of the T,) or ▼ فَرُدٌ, (so in the Ḳ accord. to the TA, [in the CḲ فُرُدٌ,]) in this sense, [i. e. in the pl. sense] is not allowable. (T, Ḳ.)

فَرُودٌ: see فَرْدٌ, second quarter, in two places.

فَرِيدٌ: see فَرْدٌ, former half, in two places: and see فُرَادٌ. — Also i. q. شَذْرٌ [app. as meaning *The beads that divide the other beads of a string*]; (T, A;) in the language of the 'Ajam [app. meaning Persians] called جَاوَرْسَق [a word I do not find in any dictionary]: accord. to Ibráheem El-Harbee, شَذْرٌ *of silver, like pearls*: (T:) or شَذْرٌ *that divide the pearls and gold*: (M, L, Ḳ:) and *pearls that are strung, and divided by other things interposed*: (Ṣ, L, Ḳ:) or *pearls that divide the pieces of gold in a necklace*: (A:) one thereof is termed ▼ فَرِيدَةٌ: (T, M, A, L:) pl. فَرَائِدُ. (T, M, Ḳ.) And *A precious*, or *highly-esteemed, gem*; (M, L, Ḳ;) as also ▼ فَرِيدَةٌ; (Ḳ;) as though it were the only one of its kind; (M, L;) or so called because unequalled; or because [it is a pearl] found alone in its shell: (MF:) and as some say, (Ṣ,) ▼ فَرَائِدُ الدُّرِّ signifies *the large pearls*. (Ṣ, L.) — Also The *intermediate vertebræ between the last of the six vertebræ that are next to the* دَأْى [q. v.] *of the neck and the six that are between these and the* [*rump-bone called the*] عَجْب; as also ▼ فَرَائِدُ: (M, L, Ḳ:) or ▼ فَرِيدَةٌ [the sing.] signifies the *vertebra that projects from the part, of the back of a horse, that is next to the lumbar vertebræ; intervening between the dorsal vertebræ and the lumbar*: it projects in some horses. (M, L.)

فَرِيدَةٌ, and the pl. فَرَائِدُ: see the next preceding paragraph, in five places.

فُرَادَى: see فَرْدٌ, first sentence: and see also فُرَادٌ, in two places.

فَرَّادٌ One *who sells*, (T, A, L, Ḳ,) and one *who makes*, (M, L, Ḳ,) *what are termed* فَرِيد, (A, L, Ḳ,) i. e. (A) شَذْر. (T, A.)

فُرَّادًا: see فُرَادٌ.

فَرْدَدٌ: see فَرْدٌ, first quarter.

الفَرْدُودُ: see فَرْدٌ, latter half.

فَارِدٌ, and its fem. (with ة): see فَرْدٌ, near the middle, in nine places: — and again, near the end. — سُكَّرٌ فَارِدٌ *Sugar of the best kind, and white*. (Ḳ.) — And إِبِلٌ فَوَارِدُ [*She-camels*] *which stallions do not resemble* (لَا تُشْبِهُهَا). (So in the O and Ḳ. [But the right reading is evidently I think, لا تَشْتَبِهُهَا, which the Turkish translator of the Ḳ appears to have found in a copy of that work; and the meaning, therefore, *which stallions do not desire.* فَوَارِدُ is pl. of فَارِدَةٌ.])

مُفْرَدٌ: see فَرْدٌ, second quarter. — [Hence, as a conventional term, *A single, simple, word* or *vocable;*] *an expression of which a portion does not denote a portion of its meaning:* (KT:) [pl. مُفْرَدَاتٌ. — And *Singular,* as distinguished from dual and plural. — And مُفْرَدَاتُ الطِّبِّ *The simples of medicine; medicinal simples.*] — And مُفْرَدٌ signifies also *A wild bull.* (L. [See, again, فَرْدٌ, near the end.])

مُفْرِدٌ A female, (Ṣ, L,) a pregnant female, (A,) or a ewe or she-goat, (M,) or a woman, (Ḳ,) *bringing forth one only:* (Ṣ, M, A, L, Ḳ:) like مُوحِدٌ and مُفِذٌّ: (Ṣ, L:) opposed to مُتْئِمٌ. (A.) [See its verb, 4.]

ذَهَبٌ مُفَرَّدٌ *Pieces of gold* (*in a necklace,* A) *divided, one from another, by* فَرِيد [q. v.], (M, A, L, Ḳ,) i. e., by pearls. (A.)

مُفَرِّدٌ A rider *having no other with him:* (A:) or a rider *having only his camel with him.* (Ḳ.) — طُوبَى لِلْمُفَرِّدِينَ, occurring in a trad., (L,) means *Good betide those who apply themselves to the study of practical religion,* or *the law, and withdraw from* [*the rest of*] *mankind, and attend only to the observance of the commands and prohibitions* [*of religion*]: (IAạr, T,* L, Ḳ, TA:) and (Ḳ, TA) it is also said to mean (TA) *those who are devoted to the commemoration of the praises of God:* (Ḳ, TA:) or, as expl. by the Prophet himself, *those men and women who commemorate the praises of God much,* or *frequently:* (TA:) also, (Ḳ,) or, as Ḳt says in explaining the trad., (TA,) [and as his words are cited in the T,] *those whose contemporaries in birth,* (Ḳ, TA,) *and the generation among which they were,* (TA,) *have perished,* or *died, while they themselves have remained,* (Ḳ, TA,) *commemorating the praises of God:* but Az holds the explanation of IAạr to be more correct than this of Ḳt. (TA.)

مِفْرَادٌ: see فَرْدٌ, near the middle of the paragraph.

المَفَارِيدُ as a conventional term in lexicology signifies *What have been uttered by only one of the Arabs:* differing from الأَفْرَادُ, which signifies what have been transmitted from the Arabs by only one of the leading lexicologists. (Mz, 15th نوع.)

فردس

Q. 1. فَرْدَسَهُ, (O, Ḳ,) inf. n. فَرْدَسَةٌ, (Kr, M, O,) *He threw him down, prostrate, on the ground,* (Kr, M, O, Ḳ,) *in an evil,* or *abominable, manner:* (Kr, M, O:) and *flung him upon the ground;* lit., *smote with him the ground.* (O, Ḳ.) — And فَرْدَسَ الجُلَّةَ *He filled,* or *stuffed, compactly, the* [*receptacle for dates, termed*] جُلَّة. (AA, O,* Ḳ.)

فَرْدَسَةٌ *Width; amplitude:* (M, O, Mṣb, Ḳ:) whence is derived the word فِرْدَوْسٌ, (Mṣb, Ḳ,) accord. to Fr. (Mṣb.)

فِرْدَوْسٌ *A garden:* (Ṣ, Mṣb:) so in the Greek language [παράδεισος]: (M:) or *a garden comprising everything that is in gardens:* (Zj, M, A, O, Ḳ:) such is the proper signification; (Zj, M, O;) and so with the people of every language: (Zj, M:) *and containing grape-vines:* (Fr, O, Ḳ:) or *a garden in which are grape-vines:* (IAmb, M, Mṣb:) or *a place in which are grape-vines:* (TA:) or *an ample, beautiful garden:* (A:) or *a garden comprising grape-vines and palm-trees:* (Bḍ in xviii. 107:) or with the Arabs it signifies *a valley abounding with herbage, like a garden:* (M:) or *a valley,* (Zj, Mṣb,) or *valleys,* (O, Ḳ,) *producing various sorts of plants* or *herbage:* (Zj, O, Mṣb, Ḳ:) in the Ḳ, for الأَوْدِيَةُ الَّتِى تُنْبِتُ, we should read مِنَ الأَوْدِيَةِ الَّتِى تُنْبِتُ; (TḲ;) [or rather, مِنَ الأَوْدِيَةِ مَا يُنْبِتُ, as in the Mṣb:] or *a meadow;* syn. رَوْضَةٌ: (Seer, M:) and the *greenness of grapes* (أَعْنَاب), (so in a copy of the M,) or *of herbs* (أَعْشَاب): (so in the TA:) masc. and fem.: (Mṣb:) sometimes the latter; (Ḳ;) as in the Ḳur xxiii. 11, because, by الفِرْدَوْس is there meant الجَنَّة: (O, TA:) it is an Arabic word, (Ṣ, O, Mṣb, Ḳ,) accord. to Fr, (Ṣ, O, Mṣb,) occurring in a verse cited voce ثَوَابٌ, which is by Ḥassán Ibn-Thábit, (O,) derived from فَرْدَسَةٌ, meaning "width" or "amplitude," (Mṣb, Ḳ,*) accord. to Fr: (Mṣb:) or it is Greek, (Zj, O, Mṣb, Ḳ,) transferred to the Arabic language; (Zj, O, Mṣb;) [i. e., arabicised: but as it occurs in the Ḳur (xviii. 107 and xxiii. 11), this is contr. to the opinion of Esh-Sháfi'ee and others, who deny that any arabicized word occurs therein: (see سُنْدُسٌ:)] or it is Syriac: (Zj, O, Ḳ:) the pl. is فَرَادِيسُ; (A, TA;) which is applied by the people of Syria to *gardens and grape-vines.* (TA.) — Hence, (Bḍ in xviii. 107,) الفِرْدَوْسُ [*Paradise:* or] *a garden of trees,* or *walled garden,* (حَدِيقَة,) *in* الجَنَّة [or *Paradise*]: (Ṣ:) or *the highest of the stages of* الجَنَّة: (Bḍ, ubi suprà:) or *the middle and highest part of* الجَنَّة. (Jel, ibid.)

فُرْدُوسٌ *Increase* (نَزَل, in the CḲ نُزُل,) *that is in* طَعَام [i. e. *wheat*]: (O, Ḳ:) mentioned by IDrd, as heard from some persons of El-Baḥreyn. (O.)

فُرَادِسٌ A man *big in the bones.* (Ibn-'Abbád, O, Ḳ.)

مُفَرْدَسٌ A *trellised* grape-vine; syn. مُعَرَّشٌ. (Lth, Ṣ, M.) — *A wide breast.* (O, K.) — *Wide-breasted; having a wide breast.* (M.) — And [A thing] *filled,* or *stuffed, compactly.* (O.)

فرز

1. فَرَزَهُ, (Ṣ, A, O, Mṣb, Ḳ,) aor. ـِ, inf. n. فَرْزٌ, (Ṣ, O, Mṣb, Ḳ,) *He put it,* or *set it, apart, away,* or *aside; removed it;* or *separated it;* from another thing, or from other things; (Ṣ, A, O, Mṣb, Ḳ;) as also ▾ افرزه, (Ṣ, O, Ḳ,) inf. n. إِفْرَازٌ: (Ḳ:) *he divided it* therefrom; (A, TA;) [and so ▾ افرزه:] *he divided it into parts,* or *shares;* as also ▾ افرزه: (Az, Mṣb, TA:) *he distributed it,* or *dispersed it.* (AO, AZ, TA.) You say, فَرَزَ لَهُ نَصِيبَهُ, aor. and inf. n. as above; and ▾ افرزه; *He set apart,* or *separated, for him his portion,* or *share.* (Mgh.) And فَرَزَ لَهُ مِنْ مَالِهِ نَصِيبًا [*He set apart,* or *divided, for him a portion,* or *share, of his property*]; as also ▾ افرزه. (A.) And ▾ افرز لَهُ نَصِيبًا مِنَ الدَّارِ [*He divided for him a share of the house*]. (A.) — See also 2. — [Also, app., *He made fringes,* or *similar decorations, to it;* namely, a garment, or piece of cloth, or the like: see the pass. part. n.] Aboo-Firás [El-Farezdaḳ] says,

• بُسُطٌ مِنَ الدِيبَاجِ قَدْ فُرِزَتْ •
• أَطْرَافُهَا بِفَرَاوِزٍ ▾ خُضُرِ •

[app. meaning, *Carpets of silk brocade, the extremities of which had been fringed with green fringes*]. (TA.)

2. فَرَّزَ عَلَىَّ بِرَأْيِهِ, (Ḳ,) or ▾ فَرَزَ, (thus, without teshdeed, in the O,) inf. n. تَفْرِيزٌ, [which may be of either of the verbs,] (Ḳ,) *He decided* (قَطَعَ) *against me by his opinion.* (Ibn-'Abbád, O, Ḳ. [See also 8.])

3. فارز شَرِيكَهُ *He separated himself from his partner, with the latter's concurrence;* syn. فَاصَلَهُ, (Ṣ, O, Ḳ,) and قَاطَعَهُ, (Ṣ, A, O, Ḳ,) and فَارَقَهُ. (A.)

4. افرزه: see 1, in six places. — أَفْرَزْتُ فُلَانًا بِشَىْءٍ *I made such a one to have a thing to himself alone, with none to share, or participate, with him in it.* (A.) — Also *It* (an object of the chase) *offered him an opportunity* (Ṣ, O, Ḳ) *so that he shot it, or shot at it,* (Ṣ, O,) *from within a short distance.* (Ṣ, O, Ḳ.)

6. تفارز الشُّرَكَآءُ *The partners separated themselves, one from another.* (A.)

7. انفرز بَعْضُهُمْ عَنْ بَعْضٍ *They went apart, away,* or *aside; removed;* or *separated; one from another,* or *one party from another.* (TA in art. عزل.)

8. افترز أَمْرَهُ دُونَ أَهْلِ بَيْتِهِ means قَطَعَهُ [i. e. *He decided his affair exclusively of the people of his house* or *tent,* or *of his wife and family*]. (O, Ḳ. [See also 2.])

Q. Q. 1. فَرْوَزَ *He died;* (IDrd, O, Ḳ;) said of a man: (IDrd, O:) like هَرْوَزَ. (TA.)

فَرْزٌ *A depressed tract of land* (Ṣ, O, Ḳ, TA) *between two hills:* (TA:) or *an intervening space between two mountains:* (TA:) [or] ▾ فُرْزَةٌ has the latter meaning; mentioned by Ibn-'Abbád. (O.)

فُرْزٌ: see فُرْزَةٌ, in two places: — and see also فَرْزٌ. — Accord. to Lth, الفُرْزُ is syn. with الفَرْدُ; but this is disallowed by Az. (TA.)

فُرْزَةٌ *A cleft in rugged ground.* (TA.)

فَرْزَةٌ *A road in, or upon, an* [*eminence such as is termed*] أَكَمَة; as also ▼ فَرْزٌ. (Ibn-'Abbád, O, Ḳ.) —— See also فَرْزٌ. ═ Also *i. q.* فُرْصَةٌ, i. e. نَوْبَةٌ [meaning *A turn*; or *time at which*, or *during which, a thing is*, or *is to be, done, or had, in succession*]. (O, Ḳ.*)

فِرْزَةٌ *A piece*, or *detached portion*, (Ṣ, O, Mṣb, Ḳ,) *of a thing that is put*, or *set, apart, away*, or *aside*, or *that is removed*, or *separated*; (Ṣ, O, Ḳ;) as also ▼ فِرْزٌ: pl. [of pauc.] أَفْرَازٌ and [of mult.] فُرُوزٌ: and ▼ فِرْزٌ signifies also *a portion*, or *share, that is put aside for the party to whom it pertains, whether one* [*person*] *or two*. (TA.)

فُرْزٌ A slave *sound*, or *healthy*, or *without defect* or *blemish*: or a free man *sound*, or *healthy*, or *without defect* or *blemish, and plump*. (Ibn-'Abbád, O, Ḳ.)

فَرْوَازٌ [an arabicized word, from the Pers. پَرْوَاز, app. as meaning *A fringe*, or *the like*; as the latter word does in Turkish, and probably, sometimes, in Persian]: accord. to some, it is of the measure فَعْلَالٌ from فَرْزٌ in the first of the senses expl. in this art.; therefore, if so, it is an Arabic word: the pl. is فَرَاوِيزُ. (TA.) See 1, last sentence.

فَارِزٌ A tongue *distinct* [in utterance]: (O, Ḳ, TA:) and *discriminating* language. (A,* O, Ḳ,* TA.) ═ Also *A species of ant, round and black, found in dates*: so says Ibráheem El-Ḥarbee: (O and TA in art. عقف:) or the *progenitor* (جَدّ) *of the black ants*: that of the red is termed عُقْفَان: (Ḳ:) but it has been before said by the author of the Ḳ, in art. فزر, that فَازِرٌ signifies "black ants in which is a redness:" and it may be a mistranscription. (TA.)

فَارِزَةٌ *A road taking its course in a tract of sand amid sands that are compact and cleaving to the ground, and soft*, (O, Ḳ,) *appearing like an extended natural cleft in the ground*: but this is mentioned in the book of Lth in art. فزر [as written فَازِرَة]. (O.)

أَفْرَزُ *Humpbacked*; as also أَفْرَصُ and أَفْرَسُ: so says Fr. (TA voce أَعْجَرُ.) [The same meaning is also assigned to أَفْزَرُ, q. v.]

إِفْرِيزٌ, of a wall, an arabicized word, (Ṣ, Mgh, O, Ḳ,) [of unknown origin, like our word "frieze," and the French "frise," &c., said in the TA to be from the Pers. پَرْوَاز, mentioned above, voce فَرْوَازٌ,] *A projecting appertenance* or *roof* or *covering* (جَنَاحٌ نَادِرٌ) thereof; (Mgh;) the طُنُف [q. v., app. meaning *a projecting coping*, or *ledge*, or *cornice*,] thereof; (O and Ḳ in the present art., and the same and Ṣ in art. طنف;) *surrounding the upper part*: (Kr, TA voce زِيفٌ:) [it is also expl. as meaning] *a hole*, or *an aperture, in a wall*. (KL. [But this is app. a mistake, caused by a misunderstanding of the word طَاقٌ, which is expl. as having this meaning and also as syn. with إِفْرِيزٌ; and the author of the KL evidently doubted its correctness, for he adds, "so we have heard."])

مُفْرَزٌ: see what next follows.

مَفْرُوزٌ and ▼ مُفْرَزٌ *Put*, or *set, apart, away*, or *aside*; *removed*; or *separated*: (Mgh:) *divided into parts*, or *shares*. (Mṣb.) ═ And the former, *Having the back broken*; like مَفْرُوسٌ. (TA in art. فرس.) ═ ثَوْبٌ مَفْرُوزٌ, (Ṣ, O, Ḳ,) by some written مُفْرَوْزٌ, (TA,) is from إِفْرِيزٌ, the افريز of a wall, (Ṣ, TA,) and signifies [*A garment*, or *piece of cloth*,] *having* تَطَارِيف [app. meaning *a fringe*, or *fringes*; likened to fingers, or the ends of fingers]. (O, Ḳ.) [See 1, last sentence.]

فرزن

Q. 2. تَفَرْزَنَ, said of a بَيْذَق [or pawn] in the game of شِطْرَنْج [or chess], *It became a* فِرْزَان. (TA.) [See an ex. voce دَسْتٌ.]

فِرْزَانُ الشِّطْرَنْجِ (Ḳ, TA) [*The queen of the game of chess*; or, as some say,] *what occupies the place of the wezeer to the sultán* [*in that game*]: (TA:) the former of these words is arabicized, from [the Pers.] فَرْزِين. (O and Ḳ in art. فرز, and Ḳ in the present art.)

فرس

1. فَرَسَهُ, aor. ـِ, inf. n. فَرْسٌ, (Ṣ, M, O, Mṣb, Ḳ, &c.,) *He* (a lion) *broke*, or *crushed so as to break, its neck*; (Ṣ, A,* Mgh,* O, Ḳ;) i. e., the neck of his فَرِيسَة; (Ṣ, O, Ḳ;) as also ▼ افترسهُ: (Ṣ:) this is the primary signification: (Ṣ, Mgh, TA:) or *he* (a beast of prey) *seized it*, (a thing,) *and broke*, or *crushed so as to break, its neck*; as also ▼ افترسهُ: (M:) or *he* (a lion) *broke it*; i. e., his فَرِيسَة: (Mṣb:) and *he bruised*, or *crushed, and broke, it*; namely, a thing. (M.) Accord. to ISk, (Ṣ,) you say, فَرَسَ الذِّئْبُ الشَّاةَ, (Ṣ, TA,) meaning *The wolf seized the sheep*, or *goat, and broke*, or *crushed so as to break, its neck*: (TA:) accord. to En-Naḍr (i. e. ISh), you say, أَكَلَ الذِّئْبُ الشَّاةَ [The wolf ate, or devoured, the sheep, or goat], but not ▼ افترسها. (Ṣ, O, TA.) —— Hence, (Ṣ, Mgh, O, Mṣb,) *He killed it, in any manner*; (Ṣ, Mgh, O, Mṣb, Ḳ;) as also افترسهُ: (TA:) or ▼ the latter, *he* (a lion, O, or a wolf, TA) *captured it*; or *made it his prey*. (O, Ḳ, TA. See also 2 [where a similar but tropical usage of the former verb is mentioned.]) You say, فَرَسَهُ الأَسَدُ *The lion killed him or it*. (Mgh.) —— فَرَسَ الذَّبِيحَةَ, (M, Mṣb,) aor. ـِ, (M,) inf. n. as above, (Ṣ, M, Mgh,) *He* (the slaughterer) *broke the bone of the neck of the slaughtered animal before it became cold*: (Ṣ, Mgh, O:) or *broke its neck before its death*: (Mṣb:) or *cut*, or *severed, its* نُخَاع [or *spinal cord*]: or *divided its neck*: (M, TA:) or *slaughtered it so as to reach to the* نخاع: (AO, TA:) the action thus [variously] expl. is forbidden. (Ṣ, Mgh, Mṣb, TA.) —— فَرَسَهُ فِرْسَةً ▼ قَبِيحَةً *He struck him* [*in an abominable manner*, app. *in the back*,] *so that the part between his hips became depressed and his navel protruded*. (M.) ═ فَرُسَ, aor. ـُ, (Ṣ, A, O, Ḳ,) inf. n. فُرُوسَةٌ (Ṣ, A, O, Ḳ*) and فَرَاسَةٌ (Ṣ, Ḳ,* in the O فِرَاسَة) and فُرُوسِيَّةٌ, (Ṣ,* A, O,* Ḳ,*) all of which ns. are mentioned as syn. by Aṣ, (TA,) [as they are also in the Ṣ and Ḳ,] and the first and last, in like manner, by IAạr, (TA,) [but the first is expressly said to be an inf. n. of فَرُسَ in the Ṣ and A only, and the second in the Ṣ only, and the third (which seems to be rather a simple subst.) in the A only,] *He was*, or *became, skilled in horsemanship*, or *in the management of horses*, (Ṣ, A, O, Ḳ, TA,) *and in riding them*, (O,* Ḳ, TA,) *and in urging them to run, and in remaining firm upon them*: (TA:) or فَرَاسَةٌ and فُرُوسَةٌ are inf. ns. having no verb: Lḥ only [says ISd] mentions فَرَسَ and فَرُسَ as signifying *he became a horseman*; and this is extr.: (M, TA:) but [beside what has been cited above, from the Ṣ and A and Ḳ,] IḲṭṭ also says that فَرَسَ الخَيْلَ, inf. n. فُرُوسَة and فُرُوسِيَّة, signifies *he rode horses well*; and in like manner فَرَسَ [but not followed by الخيل]. (TA.) —— Hence, † *He was*, or *became, skilled in anything that he endeavoured to do*. (TA.) ═ فَرَسَ بِالنَّظَرِ, [and بِنَظَرِهِ, and بِعَيْنِهِ, and فَرَسَ فِى النَّاسِ, (see فَارِسٌ,)] aor. ـِ, (Mṣb,) inf. n. فِرَاسَةٌ and فَرَاسَةٌ, (Aṣ, IAạr, Mṣb, TA,) accord. to the citation of the words of Aṣ and IAạr in the L, but this is at variance with the opinion generally held, [which is, that فَرَاسَةٌ is an inf. n. only of فَرُسَ, signifying as expl. above, and that فِراسَةٌ is a subst. from تَفَرَّسَ, having no proper verb of which it is an inf. n.,] (TA,) is said of a man [in the same sense as تَفَرَّسَ, (q. v.,) as will be seen from the explanations of فِرَاسَةٌ and فَارِسٌ, below]. (Mṣb.) See 5, latter part, in two places. ═ فَرِسَ *He kept continually*, or *constantly, to the eating of the dates called* فَرَاس. (O, Ḳ.) —— And *He pastured upon*, or *depastured, the plants called* فَرْس. (O, Ḳ.)

2. فرّس الغَنَمَ, (inf. n. تَفْرِيسٌ, TA,) *He* (a wild beast) *seized often the sheep* or *goats*, or *seized many of them, and broke*, or *crushed so as to break, their necks*. (M, TA.) ═ فَرَسَهُ الشَّىْءَ, (inf. n. as above, TA,) *He exposed to him* (namely a wild beast) *the thing*, [meaning the animal,] *that he might seize it, and break*, or *crush so as to break, its neck*: and ▼ أَفْرَسَهُ إِيَّاهُ *he threw*, or *cast, it to him, that he might do so to it*: (M:) and أَفْرَسَ ▼ الرَّجُلُ الأَسَدَ حِمَارَهُ *the man left his ass to the lion, that he might break his neck*, or *kill him*, or *make him his prey, while he himself should escape*. (Ṣ, Ḳ.) El-'Ajjáj uses the former verb in relation to the kind of flies called نُعَر, saying,

• ضَرْبًا إِذَا صَابَ اليَآفِيخَ ٱحْتَفَرْ •
• فِى الهَامِ دُحْلَانًا يُفَرِّسْنَ النُّعَرْ •

[*A beating which, when it falls upon the tops of heads, digs, in the pates, hollows that afford prey to the blue stinging flies*]; meaning, that these wounds are wide, and enable the نعر to obtain thence what they desire. (M.) And one of the poets uses it in relation to human beings, in the following verses, [which exhibit an instance of the license termed إِقْوَآء,] cited by IAạr:

• قَدْ أَرْسَلُونِى فِى الكَوَاعِبِ رَاعِيًا •
• فَقَدْ وَأَبِى رَاعِى الكَوَاعِبِ أُفْرِسَ ♦ •
• أَتَتْهُ ذِئَابٌ لَا يُبَالِينَ رَاعِيًا •
• وَكُنَّ سَوَامًا تَشْتَهِى أَنْ تُفَرَّسَا •

[*They had sent me among the girls with swelling breasts, as a guardian; and, by my father, while guardian of the girls with swelling breasts*, or *by the father of the guardian of the girls with swelling breasts, I was* (lit. *I am*) *made a prey: there came thither wolves not caring for a guardian, and those females were* (as) *pasturing camels eagerly desiring to be given as prey*]: he likens these women to pasturing camels, although differing from them inasmuch as the latter do not eagerly desire to be given as prey, since this would be a cause of their death, whereas women do eagerly desire it, since فَرْسُ الرِّجَالِ لِلنِّسَآءِ [lit. *men's making women their prey*] is in this case † *men's holding commerce of love with women*: أُفْرِسَ is for فُرِسْتُ; for, as Sb says, they sometimes put أَفْعَلَ in the place of فَعَلْتُ: أَبِى is in the gen. case as governed by وَ denoting swearing; and راعى الكواعب may be a denotative of state relating to the ت [the pronoun of the first person] understood [in أُفْرِسَ for فُرِسْتُ]; or وأبى may be prefixed to راعى الكواعب, governing it in the gen. case, and by the latter expression he may mean himself: by wolves not caring for a guardian, he means wicked men not caring for him who guarded these women: and he uses the word تشتهى to denote intense desire; for if he did not mean intenseness, he would have said تُرِيدُ. (M.)

3. فارسهُ, inf. n. مُفَارَسَةٌ and فِرَاسٌ, (M, TA,) [app., *He vied*, or *contended, with him in horsemanship*: this signification seems to be indicated by what immediately precedes in the M, which is, فَرُسَ and فَرِسَ "he became a horseman:" but perhaps it may signify *he vied*, or *contended, with him in* فِرَاسَة, meaning *insight*, &c.: or it may have both these significations.]

4. افرس *He* (a pastor) *had the neck of one of his sheep, or goats, broken*, or *had one of them killed*, (Ṣ, O,) or *taken*, (Ḳ,) *by the wolf*, (Ṣ, O, Ḳ,) *he being inadvertent*. (Ḳ.) — See also 2, in two places. — افرس عَنْ بَقِيَّةِ مَالٍ *He left a remainder of property* [*as a prey*], *having taken all beside thereof*. (AA, O, Ḳ.)

5. تفرّس *He pretended to others that he was a horseman*, or *one skilled in horsemanship*. (Aṣ, O, Ḳ.) ═ *He acted deliberately*, (Ṣ, O, Ḳ, TA,) *and considered*, or *examined*, a thing, or *did so repeatedly, in order to know it*, or *to obtain a clear knowledge of it*. (Ṣ,* Ḳ,* TA.) — تفرّس فِيهِ الشَّىْءَ [*He perceived in him the thing intuitively*; or *by a kind of thaumaturgic faculty, and by right opinion and conjecture*: or *by means of indications*, or *evidences, and experiments, and the make and dispositions*: (see فِرَاسَةٌ, below:) or] *he perceived in him the thing by forming a correct opinion from its outward signs*; syn. تَوَسَّمَهُ. (M.) You say, تَفَرَّسْتُ فِيهِ خَيْرًا, (Ṣ, O,) or الخَيْرَ, (Mṣb,) [*I perceived in him good*, or *goodness, intuitively*; &c.: or] *I discovered* (تَعَرَّفْتُ) *in him good*, or *goodness, by right opinion*. (Mṣb.) فَرَسَ ♦, and فِرَاسَةٌ and فَرَاسَةٌ, and بِعَيْنِهِ, and بِنَظَرِهِ, and بِالنَّظَرِ, inf. n. فِرَاسَةٌ and فَرَاسَةٌ, (respecting which, however, see 1, last quarter,) signifies the same as تفرّس; i. e., *He perceived*, or *discerned, the internal, inward*, or *intrinsic, state, condition, character*, or *circumstances, by examination* of outward indications, &c., and *by his eye*. And so فَرَسَ ♦ فِى النَّاسِ *He saw into the internal, inward*, or *intrinsic, states*, &c., *of men*. See فِرَاسَةٌ, below.]

8: see فَرَسَهُ, in five places.

Q. Q. 1. فَرْنَسَةٌ [an inf. n. of which the verb is فَرْنَسَتْ, as is shown by the mention of the part. n. مُفَرْنِسَةٌ,] A woman's *good managing of the affairs of her house*, or *tent*: (Lth, Ḳ, TA:) the ن is augmentative. (TA.)

فَارِسٌ: see الفَرْسُ.

فِرْسٌ *A species of plant*: (Yaạkoob, Ṣ, M, O, Ḳ:) the قُصْقَاص, (O, and so in copies of the Ḳ,) or قُضْقَاض, (so in the CḲ,) [each said to be a name of the أُشْنَان (or *kali*) *of Syria*, or of *a species of* حَمْض, q. v.,] accord. to Abu-l-Mekárim: (O:) or the حَبْن [q. v.]: or the بَرْوَق [q. v.]: (O, Ḳ:) or the [*small kind of thorny trees called*] شِرْس. (TA.)

فَرَسٌ [*A horse; and a mare;*] *one of what are called* خَيْل; (M;) the name فرس is given to it because it crushes and breaks the ground with its hoofs; (A, O;*) and is applied to the *male* and the *female*; (Ṣ, M, A, Mgh, O, Mṣb, Ḳ;) but mostly applied to the latter; (M;) the female not being called فَرَسَةٌ ♦; (Ṣ, O;) or the female is [sometimes] thus called: (Yoo, IJ, M, Mṣb, Ḳ:) it is applied also to the *Arabian*, (Mgh, Mṣb,) and to the *Turkish*, (Mṣb,) or that which is *not Arabian*: (Mgh:) or, accord. to Moḥammad [the Ḥanafee Imám], to the *Arabian only*; but for this [says Mṭr] I find no authority of a lexicologist, except that ISk, speaking of a solid-hoofed animal, says, "whether it be a بِرْذَوْن or a فَرَس or a بَغْل or a حِمَار:" (Mgh:) the pl. is أَفْرَاسٌ, (Ṣ, M, Mgh, O, Mṣb, Ḳ,) [a pl. of pauc. but used as a pl. of mult. also,] and أَفْرُسٌ, [a pl. of pauc. only,] (O,) and فُرُوسٌ: (Ḳ:) and as فَرَسٌ is originally fem., you say ثَلَاثُ أَفْرَاسٍ when you mean males [as well as when you mean females]: (M:) or you say ثَلَاثَةُ أَفْرَاسٍ, with ة, when you mean males; and ثَلَاثُ أَفْرَاسٍ, without ة, when you mean females: (Mṣb:) the dim. is فُرَيْسٌ, (Ṣ, O, Mṣb,) when applied to the male; (Mṣb;) and فُرَيْسَةٌ ♦, when applied to the female; (Ṣ, O, Mṣb;) agreeably with rule; (Mṣb;) accord. to Aboo-Bekr Ibn-Es-Sarráj: (Ṣ, O:) or فُرَيْسٌ ♦ when applied to the female [also], which is extr. (Sb, M. [See حَرْبٌ.]) — هُمَا كَفَرَسَىْ رِهَانٍ [*They two are like two horses running for a wager*] is a saying applied to two persons running a race to a goal, and being equal: (A, O, Ḳ:) the comparison relating to the beginning [of a contest], for the termination necessarily shows which outstrips; (O, Ḳ:) and to two who are equal, and two who are nearly equal, in excellence &c. (Ḥar p. 640.) It was said by a man who swore that he would abstain from his wife for four months, and then divorced her: for the period during which a woman may be taken back after a [first or second] divorce is that of three menstruations or three periods of purity from menstruation; and if it ended in this case before the end of the four months during which he swore to abstain from her, she became separated from him by that divorcement: so he likened the two periods to two horses running for a wager. (O,* TA.) — فَرَسُ البَحْرِ † [*The horse of the great river*; i. e., of the Nile;] *the hippopotamus*. (Dmr. [See also عَضْبٌ.]) — الفَرَسُ † *A well-known constellation*; so called because of its resemblance in form to a horse; (M;) [i. e.] الفَرَسُ الأَعْظَمُ † [*The Greater*, or *Greatest, Horse*;] *the constellation Pegasus*. (Ḳzw.) — قِطْعَةُ الفَرَسِ † [*The Piece of the Horse*;] *the constellation Equuleus*. (Ḳzw.) — الفَرَسُ التَّامُّ † [*The Complete horse*;] *a certain constellation composed of thirty-one stars, in which a portion of the constellation called* الفَرَسُ الأَعْظَمُ *is included*. (Ḳzw. [It is further described by him; but in a manner that does not enable me to identify it with any of the constellations named by our astronomers.])

الفَرْسَةُ, (IAạr, Ṣ, M, O, Ḳ, TA,) or الفُرْسَةُ ♦, (M, TA,) the former accord. to A'Obeyd, (M, TA,) or, accord. to A'Obeyd, it is with ص, and the vulgar, he says, pronounce it with س, (O,) *Gibbosity* [*of the back*]; syn. الحَدَبُ: (IAạr, O, TA:) or, (M, O, Ḳ, TA,) as also الفَرْصَةُ, (M, O,) which latter is the more approved in this sense, (M,) *the* رِيح [or *flatus*] *of gibbosity*; (M, O, Ḳ, TA;) [i. e.] *the* ريح *that renders gibbous*; (M;) as though it were breaking, or crushing so as to break, the back (كَأَنَّهَا تَفْرِسُ الظَّهْرَ أَىْ تَدُقُّهُ), and cleaving it (تَفْرِصُهُ أَىْ تَشُقُّهُ): (O:) [or الفَرْسَةُ signifies *the displacement of one of the vertebræ*; for,] accord. to Aṣ, one says أَصَابَتْهُ فَرْسَةٌ when one of the vertebræ of one's back has become displaced; but the flatus (الرِّيحُ) from which gibbosity results is termed الفَرْصَةُ, with ص: (TA:) or الفَرْسَةُ signifies *a flatus that attacks in the neck, and breaks it*: (Ṣ:) or, as some say, *an imposthume*, or *ulcer*, (قَرْحَة,) *that is in the neck, breaking it*: (M:) or *a breach* (فَرْجَة) *in the neck*; thus says AZ: or *a breach* (فرجة) *that is in* [*the case of*] *gibbosity*: the pl. is فَرَسَاتٌ, not

أَفْرِسَةٌ, which latter is said to be a pl. of فَرْسَةٌ, but is anomalous. (TA.)

فُرْسَةٌ and فُرْصَةٌ; the latter of which is the more approved in both of the following senses; *i. q.* نَوْبَةٌ [meaning *A turn; or time at which*, or *during which, a thing is*, or *is to be, done*, or *had, in succession*; as also فُرْزَةٌ: pl. فُرَسٌ]: فُرَسُ الوِرْدِ [*the turns*, or *times, for coming to water in succession*] means [*the occasions of*] *persons' being left free to come to water.* (M. [See فُرْصَةٌ.]) — And *i. q.* نُهْزَةٌ [meaning *An opportunity; a time at which*, or *during which, a thing may be done*, or *had*]. (IAạr, M, O.) So in the phrase أَصَابَ فُرْسَتَهُ [*He got*, or *obtained, his opportunity*]. (M.)

فِرْسَةٌ [an inf. n. of modality]: see 1, near the middle of the paragraph. ═ الفِرْسَةُ: see الفَرْسَةُ.

فَرَسَةٌ: see فَرَسٌ, near the beginning.

الفِرْسِنُ, of the camel, is *What corresponds to the* حَافِر [or *hoof*] *of the horse* (Ṣ, O, Mṣb, Ḳ) *and the like*: (Ṣ, O, Mṣb:) or *what corresponds to the* قَدَم [or *foot*] *of the man*: (El-Bári', Mṣb:) and † of the bovine animal in like manner: (IAmb, Mṣb:) and sometimes ‡ of the sheep or goat, (Ṣ, O, TA,) for الظِّلْف: (TA:) or it is only of the camel: (El-Bári', Mṣb:) or *the extremity of the* خُفّ [or *foot*] of the camel: (M:) of the fem. gender: (IAmb, M, O, Mṣb, Ḳ:) pl. فَرَاسِنُ, (M, Mṣb,) not فِرْسِنَاتٌ: (M:) it is of the measure فِعْلِنٌ; (Ṣ, O;) the ن being augmentative; (Aboo-Bekr Ibn-Es-Sarráj, Ṣ, O, Mṣb, Ḳ;) because it is from فَرَسْتُ. (Aboo-Bekr Ibn-Es-Sarráj, Ṣ.) See also art. فرسن.

فَرَاسٌ *A sort of black dates*; (IAạr, O, Ḳ;) *not the same as the* سِهْرِيز (O) or شِهْرِيز. (Ḳ.)

أَبُو فِرَاسٍ: } see الفَارِسُ.
الفَرُوسُ: }

فَرِيسٌ [originally *Having the neck broken*, or *crushed so as to be broken.* — And hence,] *Killed* [*in any manner*: see 1]: pl. فَرْسَى. (Ḳ.) It is applied in this sense to a bull, and in like manner [without ة] to a cow. (TA.) — And [hence] ▼ فَرِيسَةٌ signifies The *prey* of a lion [or other beast]: (TA:) *an animal that is seized*, (M,) *and that has its neck broken*, (Ṣ, M, Mṣb,*) by a lion [or other beast]; (Ṣ, Mṣb;) as also فَرِيسٌ: (M:) [pl. of the former فَرَائِسُ.] — See also مَفْرُوسٌ. ═ Also *A ring*, or *hoop, of wood*, (Ṣ, M, O, Ḳ,) *bent* [*into that form*], *and tied*, (M, O,) *at the end of a rope*; (M, O, Ḳ;) called in Pers. جَنْبَر [correctly چَنْبَر]. (Ṣ, O, Ḳ.) ═ See also فَرِيصُ العُنُقِ, in art. فرص.

فُرَيْسٌ, and with ة; dim. ns.: see فَرَسٌ, near the middle; the former in two places.

فَرَاسَةٌ: see what next follows.

فِرَاسَةٌ a subst. (Ṣ, M, O, Ḳ) from التَّفَرُّسُ, (O, Ḳ, TA,) signifying التَّوَسُّمُ, (TA,) or from تَفَرَّسْتُ تَفَرَّسَ فِيهِ الشَّىْءَ [q. v.], (Ṣ,) or from فِيهِ خَيْرًا [q. v.]: (M:) or, as also ▼ فَرَاسَةٌ, [said to be] an inf. n. of فَرَسَ بِالنَّظَرِ: [but see this verb:] (Mṣb:) فِرَاسَةٌ بِالعَيْنِ [or بِالنَّظَرِ (see 1, last quarter,)] signifies *Insight*; or *intuitive perception*; or the *perception*, or *discernment, of the internal, inward*, or *intrinsic, state, condition, character*, or *circumstances, by the eye* [or *by the examination of outward indications* &c.]: (IḲṭṭ:) or فِرَاسَةٌ signifies *a faculty which God puts into the minds of his favourites, in consequence whereof they know the states, conditions*, or *circumstances, of certain men, by a kind of what are termed* كَرَامَات [or *thaumaturgic operations*], *and by the right direction of opinion and conjecture*: and also *a kind of art* [*such as physiognomy*, which is especially thus termed in the present day,] *learned by indications*, or *evidences, and by experiments, and by the make and dispositions, whereby one knows the state, conditions*, or *circumstances, of men*: (IAth:) or the *discovery of an internal quality in a man by right opinion.* (Mṣb.) It is said in a trad., اِتَّقُوا فِرَاسَةَ المُؤْمِنِ [*Beware ye of the insight*, &c. *of the believer*]: (Ṣ, M, IḲṭṭ, IAth, Mṣb:) and the reason is added, فَإِنَّهُ يَنْظُرُ بِنُورِ ٱللّٰهِ [*for he looks with the light of God*]. (TA. [See also قُرَابَةٌ.])

فَرِيسَةٌ: see فَرِيسٌ. [It is a subst. formed from the latter by the affix ة.]

فَرَّاسٌ, and الفَرَّاسُ, and أَبُو فَرَّاسٍ: see الفَارِسُ, in four places.

الفِرْنَاسُ: see الفَارِسُ, in two places. — Also † *The strong and courageous*, (En-Naḍr, O, Ḳ,) of men, as being likened to the lion. (En-Naḍr, O, TA.) — And † *The headman*, or *chief, of the* دَهَاقِين [pl. of دِهْقَانٌ, q. v.], (IKh, O, Ḳ,) and *of the villages*, or *towns*: (IKh, O:) pl. فَرَانِسَةٌ. (IKh, O, Ḳ.)

الفِرْنَوْسُ: see الفَارِسُ.

الفُرَانِسُ: see the next paragraph, in two places.

فَارِسٌ act. part. n. of فَرَسَ [q. v.]. — الفَارِسُ *The lion*; [so called because he breaks the neck of his prey;] as also ▼ الفَرُوسُ, [which has an intensive signification,] and ▼ الفَرَّاسُ, (O, Ḳ,) which last [also] has an intensive signification, (TA,) and ▼ أَبُو فِرَاسٍ, (Ṣ, A, Ḳ,) and ▼ أَبُو فَرَّاسٍ, (O,) and ▼ المُفْتَرِسُ, (TA,) and ▼ الفِرْنَاسُ, (Ṣ, M, Ḳ,) and ▼ الفِرْنَوْسُ, a word of a measure not mentioned by Sb, (IJ, M,) and ▼ الفُرَانِسُ; (Ḳ;) or ▼ الفِرْنَاسُ, which is said by IKh to be applied to the lion because he is the chief of the beasts of prey, signifies, (O,) or signifies also, (Ṣ,) used as an epithet applied to the lion, (Ṣ,* M,* O,) and so ▼ الفُرَانِسُ, (Ṣ,* M, O,) *the thick-necked*, (Ṣ, O,) *that is wont to break the neck of his prey*; or the former of these two, *the rapacious* lion; (O;) and the ن in these words is augmentative: (Sb, Ṣ, M, O:) and you also say ▼ سَبُعٌ فَرَّاسٌ, (M,) or ▼ أَسَدٌ فَرَّاسٌ, (TA,) meaning *a rapacious beast*, (M,) or *lion*, (TA,) *that often seizes others and breaks their necks.* (M, TA.) ═ Also The *master*, or *owner, of a horse*; (Ṣ, M, Ḳ;) a possessive epithet; (M;) like لَابِنٌ (Ṣ, O, Ḳ) and تَامِرٌ: (Ṣ, O:) and *a horseman; a rider upon a horse*; (ISk, Ṣ, Mgh, O, Mṣb, Ḳ;) and *upon a mule*; (ISk, A, Mgh, Mṣb;) and *upon an ass*: (ISk, Mgh, Mṣb:) or a rider upon a mule is called فَارِسٌ عَلَى بَغْلٍ; (ISk, Ṣ, O, Mṣb, Ḳ;) or فَارِسُ بَغْلٍ; (A, O;) and a rider upon an ass, فَارِسٌ عَلَى حِمَارٍ; (ISk, Ṣ, Mgh, O, Mṣb;) and a rider upon any solid-hoofed beast, فَارِسٌ عَلَى ذِى حَافِرٍ: (Ḳ:) or these phrases are not used: (Ḳ:) 'Omárah Ibn-'Aḳeel Ibn-Bilál Ibn-Jereer says, (Ṣ,) or AZ, (Mṣb,) I do not call the owner of the mule, nor the owner of the ass, فَارِسٌ, but I call them بَغَّالٌ and حَمَّارٌ: (Ṣ, O, Mṣb:) [فَارِسٌ is often best rendered *a cavalier*:] the pl. is فُرْسَانٌ (Ṣ, M, Mṣb) and فَوَارِسُ, which latter is [more usual, but] anomalous, (Ṣ, M, O, Mṣb, Ḳ,) for فَوَاعِلُ is [regularly] the measure of the pl. of a sing. of the measure فَاعِلَةٌ, as ضَوَارِبُ, pl. of ضَارِبَةٌ, or of an epithet of the measure فَاعِلٌ applying to a female, as حَوَائِضُ, pl. of حَائِضٌ, or of a sing. of the measure فَاعِلٌ applying to a thing that is not a human being or not a rational being, as بَوَازِلُ, pl. of بَازِلٌ, and حَوَائِطُ, pl. of حَائِطٌ; and there are no instances like فَوَارِسُ except those of هَوَالِكُ and نَوَاكِسُ [and خَوَالِفُ and some other words enumerated in the Mṣb and TA]; (Ṣ, Mṣb;) and as فوارس is not applied to females, no ambiguity is feared from its usage: (Ṣ, O:) [ISd says,] we have not heard اِمْرَأَةٌ فَارِسَةٌ. (M.) — Also, (Aṣ,) or فَارِسٌ عَلَى الخَيْلِ, (Ṣ,) A man *skilful in horsemanship*, or *in the management of horses.* (Aṣ,* Ṣ.) — And hence, the former, (فارس,) † A man *skilful in anything that he endeavours to do.* (TA.) — الفَوَارِسُ is the name of † *Four stars of the constellation Cygnus.* (Ḳzw. See دَجَاجٌ.) ═ رَجُلٌ فَارِسُ النَّظَرِ, (Ṣ, O, TA,) and بِنَظَرِهِ, and بِعَيْنِهِ, (Aṣ,) *A man who acts deliberately, and examines*: (Ṣ, and so in Ḥr p. 356:) *who possesses* فِرَاسَة [i. e. *insight*, or *intuitive perception*, &c.]: (O:) or *knowing by means of examination.* (TA.) And فَارِسٌ فِى النَّاسِ [*Seeing into the internal, inward*, or *intrinsic, states*, &c., *of men*]. (IAạr.) ═ فَارِسُ, (Ṣ, M, Mgh, Ḳ,) or فَارِسٌ, (so in some copies of the Ḳ,) [the former if fem., as it is a proper name, the latter if masc.,] *A certain nation*; (Mgh, Mṣb;) [namely, the *Persians*;] *i. q.* ▼ الفُرْسُ: (Ṣ, O, Ḳ:) generally fem.: (Mṣb:) فُرْسٌ is pl. of ▼ فَارِسِىٌّ which is a rel. n. from فَارِسُ in the sense next following: (M:) [or, rather, فُرْسٌ is a coll. gen. n., and فَارِسِىٌّ is its n. un.] — Also, (Ṣ, O, but in the Ḳ "or") *The country of the* فُرْس; (Ṣ, O, Ḳ;) [i. e., *Persia*;] *a country of a certain nation.* (M.)

فَارِسِىٌّ [*Persian: a Persian*]: see فَارِسٌ. Hence, التَّمْرُ الفَارِسِىُّ *A certain sort of dates,* (Mgh, Mṣb,) *of good quality.* (Mṣb.)

أَفْرَسُ: see مَفْرُوسٌ. ═ It is also a noun of excess, or a comparative and superlative epithet, from فِرَاسَةٌ, used by Zj, in the phrase أَفْرَسُ النَّاسِ, meaning, *The best,* (M,) or *best and most true,* (TA,) *in* فِرَاسَة, [i.e., *insight,* or *intuitive perception, &c.,*] *of mankind.* (M, TA.) One says also, أَنَا أَفْرَسُ مِنْكَ *I am more endowed with mental perception,* [or *insight,* or *intuitive perception,*] *and more knowing, than thou.* (TA.)

مَفْرُوسٌ *Having the back broken:* (M, TA:) and so مَفْرُوزٌ. (TA.) — And *Humpbacked;* as also ▼ فَرِيسٌ, (M, TA,) and ▼ أَفْرَسُ (Fr in TA voce أَعْجَرُ) [and أَفْرَصُ and أَفْرَزُ].

المُفْتَرِسُ: see الفَارِسُ.

مُفْرِسَةٌ A woman *who manages well the affairs of her house,* or *tent.* (Lth, TA.)

فرسخ

فَرْسَخٌ, mentioned, but not explained, by J [in the Ṣ], (Ḳ,) [*A parasang,* or *league;*] *three Háshimee miles* (أَمْيَال هَاشِمِيَّة [see مِيلٌ]): or *twelve thousand cubits:* or *ten thousand cubits:* (Ḳ:) *three miles of the Háshimee measure,* i. e., accord. to the Bári' and the T [&c.], *twenty-five bow-shots; twenty-five times the measure termed* غَلْوَة [q. v.]: (Mṣb:) or *three miles,* i. e. *thirty bow-shots reckoning the bow-shot as four hundred cubits,* or *sixty bow-shots reckoning the bow-shot as two hundred cubits:* (Mṣb voce مِيلٌ:) the ancient Greeks said that it is *three miles, reckoning these* [*together*] *as about sixty bow-shots* [*of the shorter measure mentioned above*]: (Mṣb in the present art.:) or, accord. to some, *six miles:* (L: [but this is app. a mistake occasioned by finding it expl. as consisting of sixty bow-shots and supposing these to be bow-shots of four hundred cubits each:]) it is [said to be] from the same word as signifying "rest," or "ease;" (Ḳ, TA;) because, when a man walks the distance thus called, he sits down, and rests: or, accord. to the Mṣb, from فَرْسَخَة signifying "width;" the word having this meaning, however, is فَرْشَخَة, with ش: (TA:) [the truth is, that] it is a Pers. word [فَرْسَنگ], arabicized: (Ṣ, A:) the pl. is فَرَاسِخُ. (Ṣ, A, Mṣb.) The other meanings of this word, not mentioned by J, may have been regarded by him as not of established authority. (TA.) — It signifies also *An opening,* or *intervening space, between two things.* (Ḳ.) — And *A thing in which is no opening,* or *intervening space:* as though having two contr. significations. (Ḳ.) — Also *A thing that is lasting and abundant, that does not cease,* or *come to an end.* (IṢh, Ḳ.) — And *A long time* (Ḳ, TA) *of the night* or *of the day:* thus in the saying, اِنْتَظَرْتُكَ فَرْسَخًا [*I looked,* or *waited, for thee,* or *I have looked, &c., a long time &c.*]. (TA.) — And *A* سَاعَة [meaning *hour* or *time*] (Ḳ, TA) of the day: or *a time* of the night and of the day: pl. as above. (TA.) — And The *time,* (Ḳ, TA,) or *interval,* (TA,) *between stillness and motion.* (Ḳ, TA.) — And *Stillness,* or *quiet:* (Ḳ, TA:) a meaning mentioned by more than one of the authorities respecting strange words. (TA.) — And *Rest,* or *ease.* (Ḳ.)

فرسق

فِرْسِقٌ: see the art. here following.

فرسك

فِرْسِكٌ (Ṣ, O, Ḳ) [and فِرْسِقٌ (Ḳ in art. فرسق) The *peach:* or the sort thereof called the *nectarine:* from the Greek περσική or περσικόν; the *malum Persicum,* which is generally applied to the former fruit; or *amygdalus Persica* of Linn., (so in Forskål's Flora Aegypt. Arab. p. cxiii.,) which is applied to both of the fruits above mentioned: i. e.] the [*fruit called*] خَوْخ; (Ḳ, TA;) of the dial. of El-Yemen: (TA:) or *a sort thereof,* (Ḳ,) *i. q.* فِرْسِقٌ, which is *like the* خوخ *in size,* (Lth, O,) أَجْرَدُ [which here means *without down,* and for which Golius and Freytag appear to have read أَجْوَدُ], *smooth, red* [accord. to the CḲ "or red"], (Lth, O, Ḳ, TA,) *and yellow, the flavour of which is like that of the* خوخ: (Lth, O, TA:) or [*a cling-stone peach* or *nectarine;* i. e.] *a sort of* خوخ *that does not cleave asunder from its stone:* (Ṣ, O:) or [*a free-stone peach* or *nectarine;* i. e.] *such as cleaves asunder from its stone.* (Ḳ.)

فرسن

الفِرْسِنُ, of the camel, is *What corresponds to the* حَافِر [or *hoof*] *of the horse or a similar beast:* (Ṣ, Ḳ:) or *the part which is below the* رُسْغ [or *pastern*] *and in which are the bones called* سُلَامَى [q.v.]: and sometimes it is ‡ of the sheep or goat: it is of the fem. gender: and the pl. is فَرَاسِنُ: (TA:) accord. to Ibn-Es-Sarráj, the ن is augmentative, because it is from فَرَسْتُ, (Ṣ, TA,) and [therefore] it has been mentioned before [in art. فرس, in which see more]. (Ṣ.)

الفُرْسَانُ: see what next follows.

الفُرَاسِنُ *The lion;* (Ḳ, TA;) as also ▼ الفُرْسَانُ: and so [الفُرَانِسُ and] الفُرْنَاسُ. (TA.) See also the last paragraph below.

الفُرَاسِيُونُ, (Ḳ, TA,) with ḍamm, (TA,) *The* كُرَّاث جَبَلِىّ [lit. *mountain-leek*]: (Ḳ, TA:) so it is said to be: it is *a four-sided* أَصْل [app. meaning *stem*], *from which rise many white, four-sided, branches, whereon sometimes grow rough leaves like the thumb; and it has a blossom inclining to blueness and yellowness:* (TA:) *it has the property of clearing the complexion, dissolves thick humours, is diuretic, opens obstructions, and is beneficial as a remedy for the bite of the dog,* (Ḳ, TA,) i. e. *of the mad dog:* (TA:) [it is now applied in Cairo to *euphrasia:* (Forskål, Descr. Anim. &c., p. 145:) and *marrubium plicatum.* (Idem, Flora Aegypt. Arab., pp. lxviii. and 213.)]

مُفَرْسَنُ الوَجْهِ, with fet-ḥ to the س, *Having much flesh in the face.* (Ḳ.) Perhaps the lion is hence called ▼ فُرَاسِن. (TA.)

فرش

1. فَرَشَهُ, (Ṣ, A, O, Ḳ,) aor. ـُ, (Ṣ, O,) inf. n. فَرْشٌ (O, Ḳ) and فِرَاشٌ, (Ṣ, O, Ḳ,) *He spread it; expanded it.* (Ṣ, A, O, Ḳ.) You say, فَرَشْتُ لَهُ فِرَاشًا and فَرَشْتُهُ فِرَاشًا (A, TA) and ▼ أَفْرَشْتُهُ (TA) and ▼ اِفْتَرَشْتُهُ (A) [*I spread for him a bed:* or the last signifies *I spread it* (namely a bed) *for myself*]. And فَرَشْتُ فُلَانًا *I spread for such a one.* (Lth.) And فَرَشَ فُلَانًا بِسَاطًا, inf. n. فَرْشٌ; and ▼ فَرَّشَهُ بساطا; and ▼ أَفْرَشَهُ بساطا, inf. n. تَفْرِيشٌ; *He spread for such a one a carpet* (IAạr, Ḳ) in his entertainment. (IAạr.) And ▼ فَرَّشَ الثَّوْبَ, inf. n. تَفْرِيشٌ; and ▼ افترشه; [*He spread the garment,* or *piece of cloth:* or the latter signifies *he spread it for himself.*] (TA.) And ▼ افترش تَحْتَهُ تُرَابًا or ثَوْبًا [*He spread,* or *spread for himself, beneath him, dust,* or *a garment,* or *piece of cloth*]. (A.) And كُنْتُ أَفْتَرِشُ ▼ الرَّمْلَ وَأَتَوَسَّدُ الحَجَرَ [*I used to spread the sand for my bed, and make the stone my pillow*]. (A, TA.) And ▼ افترش ذِرَاعَيْهِ, (A, TA,) and بِذَيْهِ, (TA,) *He* (a lion, and a wolf, and a dog, TA, or a beast of prey, A, TA) *spread his fore legs upon the ground:* (TA:) and the former phrase, *he* (a man, Mṣb, TA) *spread his fore arms upon the ground,* (Ṣ, Ḳ, TA,) *in the same manner, not raising them from the ground;* the doing of which in prostrating oneself in prayer, is forbidden: (TA:) or *laid his fore arms upon the ground* (Mgh, Mṣb) *like a bed for himself.* (Mṣb.) فَرْشٌ [as an inf. n. of which the verb is فُرِشَتْ, as is shown by an explanation of إِقْعَادٌ in the Ṣ and L, and by the phrase مَفْرُوشَةُ الرِّجْلِ mentioned in the Ṣ and O and TA,] in the hind leg of a camel [and of a horse as is shown by the explanation above mentioned of اقعاد] signifies The *being a little expanded;* which is approved: (Ṣ, O, Ḳ:) when the width [between the shanks] is immoderate, so that the hock-joints knock together, which state is termed عَقَلٌ [inf. n. of عَقِلَ], it is disapproved: or, as some say, it signifies its *not being erect nor much expanded.* (Ṣ, O.) And فَرَشَ ٱللّٰهُ الفَرْشَ, (Fr, Ṣ,) inf. n. فَرْشٌ, (Fr, Ṣ, Ḳ,) means *God spread abroad the young camels;* syn. بَثَّ. (Fr, Ṣ, Ḳ.*) — [Hence,] فَرَشَهُ أَمْرَهُ, (Ṣ,) or أَمْرًا, (Ḳ,) ‡ *He made,* or *rendered, his state,* or *case,* or *affair,* (Ṣ,) or *a state, &c.,* (Ḳ,) *ample,* or *free from straitness, to him;* and *laid it open to him, altogether;* [as though he expanded it to him;] syn. أَوْسَعَهُ إِيَّاهُ, (Ṣ, Ḳ,) and بَسَطَهُ لَهُ كُلَّهُ. (TA.) And in like manner the saying of 'Alee,

فَرَشْتُكُمُ الْمَعْرُوفَ, is expl. by Ibn-Abi-l-Hadeed as signifying أَوْسَعْتُكُمْ إِيَّاهُ [meaning ‡ *I largely conferred upon you favour*, or *kindness*]: but MF deems this strange. (TA.) You say also, فَرَشْتُهُ أَمْرِى ‡ *I displayed*, or *laid open, to him my state*, or *case*, or *affair*; [and so أَفْرَشْتُهُ ▾ أَمْرِى; (see an ex. voce بَاطِنٌ;)] syn. بَسَطْتُهُ لَهُ. (A.) [And agreeably with this explanation, probably, the saying of 'Alee mentioned above should be rendered in the opinion of MF.] — [Hence also,] فُلَانٌ يَفْرُشُ نَفْسَهُ لِلنَّاسِ ‡ [*Such a one lays himself out for the service of men*]; (A;) and يَفْتَرِشُ ▾ نَفْسَهُ لَهُمْ: (TA:) [or perhaps, *makes himself like a victim for them*: (see مُتَفَرِّش, below:) for you say, فَرَشَهُ لِلذَّبْحِ, or أَفْرَشَهُ ▾, (which latter form is mentioned by Freytag in his Lexicon, but without any indication of the authority,) meaning, † *he threw him down* (namely a beast) *for slaughter*: (see فَرْش, below:)] and افترشه ▾ ‡ *he prostrated him, and got upon him*: (A:) or ‡ *he overcame him*, (meaning another man,) *and prostrated him*, (O, Ḳ, TA,) *and got upon him*. (TA.) — فَرَشَ الْمَكَانَ, aor. ـُ and ـِ, inf. n. فَرْشٌ, means *He spread the place* [with carpets or the like]; as also فَرَّشَهُ ▾, and افرشه ▾. (Mṣb.) And فَرَّشَ ▾ الدَّارَ, inf. n. تَفْرِيشٌ, *He paved the house*; (Lth, Ṣ, Ḳ;) *he spread in the house baked bricks*, or *broad and thin stones*. (Az, TA.) — هٰذَا فِرَاشٌ يَفْرُشُكَ [*This is a bed sufficiently large for thee*] is like the saying هٰذِهِ شَمْلَةٌ تَشْمَلُكَ i. e. تَسَعُكَ. (TA in art. شمل.) — فرش عَنْهُ [app. فَرَّشَ] [*He desired, and prepared himself for, it*, or *him*. (TA.) — And فَرَشَ, aor. ـُ, (O, TA,) inf. n. فَرْشٌ, (O, Ḳ, TA,) *He lied*: (O, Ḳ,* TA:) one says, كَمْ تَفْرُشُ i. e. [*How long*] *wilt thou lie?* (O, TA.)

2: see 1, in four places; two near the beginning and two near the end. — فَرَّشَ الزَّرْعُ, inf. n. تَفْرِيشٌ, ‡ *The seed-produce spread itself* (Ṣ, A, TA) *upon the surface of the earth*. (TA.) You say, فَرَّعَ الزَّرْعُ وَفَرَّشَ ‡ [*The seed-produce put forth its shoots, and spread itself upon the surface of the earth*]. (A.) And the latter of these two verbs is also *like the former* [*in signification*]. (TA.) — فَرَّشَ الطَّائِرُ, (A, Ḳ,) inf. n. as above; (Ḳ;) and تَفَرَّشَ ▾; (Ṣ, A, Ḳ;) ‡ *The bird expanded and flapped its wings*, (Ṣ, A, Ḳ,* TA,) عَلَى شَىْءٍ *over a thing*, (A, Ḳ, TA,) *without alighting*: (A, TA:) and ▾ the latter verb, *it* (a young locust) *spread its wings*. (Mgh.)

4: see 1, in five places. — افرشهُ also signifies ‡ *He spoke evil of him*; or *did so in his absence*: (IAạr, A,* O, Ḳ, TA:) and they say, أَفْرَشْتَ فِى عِرْضِى ‡ [*Thou spakest evil of me*; &c.]. (TA.) [See افترش عِرْضَهُ.] — And † *He made it thin*; or *thin, and fine in the edge*; namely, a sword. (O, Ḳ.) — افرش الشَّجَرُ ‡ *The trees put forth branches*; syn. أَغْصَنَ. (A, TA.) — افرش عَنْهُ ‡ *He*, or *it*, *left him*, or *quitted him*. (Ṣ, A, Ḳ.) You say, ضَرَبَهُ فَمَا أَفْرَشَ عَنْهُ حَتَّى قَتَلَهُ ‡ *He beat him*, or *smote him, and left him not until he slew him*. (A,* TA.) And افرش عَنْهُمُ الْمَوْتُ ‡ *Death quitted them*; *became withdrawn from them*. (IAạr, O.) — افرشت said of a mare, † *She desired to be covered*. (O.) — افرشهُ [from فَرْش signifying "young camels"] *He gave him young camels*, (O, Ḳ,) *small or large*. (O.) — And افرش [app. أَفْرَشَ, or perhaps أَشْرَفَ,] *He* (a man) *became a possessor of* فرش [app. فَرْش, and meaning *young camels*]. (IḲṭṭ, TA.) — And افرش said of a place, *It abounded with* فَرَاش, (O, Ḳ, TA,) i. e., [app., *moths*, or *butterflies*, and, as being the cause thereof,] *seed-produce*. (TA.) — أَقْفَلَ فَأَفْرَشَ [*He locked, and made fast by means of the catch*, or *catches*, (فَرَاشَة, or فَرَاش, which see below,) *of the lock*]. (Ṣ, TA.)

5: see 2, last sentence, in two places.

7: see 8, last signification.

8: see 1, first quarter, in five places; and latter half, in two places. — افترش لِسَانَهُ [lit.] *He expanded his tongue*: (Ṣ:) i. e. ‡ *he spoke in whatsoever manner he desired*. (Ṣ, A, Ḳ.) — افترشهُ ‡ *He trod upon him* or *it*: (Ṣ, Ḳ, TA:) [as though he made him or it a carpet or a bed:] from الفِرَاش and الفَرْش. (TA.) — [Hence,] افترش الطَّرِيقَ ‡ *He went*, or *travelled, along the road*. (TA.) — [Hence also,] افترش آمْرَأَةً † *He compressed a woman*. (TA.) — And † *He took to wife a woman*. (O.) One says, افترش كَرِيمَةً † *He took to wife a female of high birth*. (TA.) — [Hence also,] افترش عِرْضَهُ lit. *He made his honour as a bed for himself to tread upon*; (O, TA;) i. e., ‡ *he treated his honour as a thing which it was allowable to attack, by speaking evil of him*. (O, Ḳ, TA.) [See also 4, second sentence.] — And افْتَرَشَتْنَا السَّمَآءُ بِالْمَطَرِ ‡ *The sky assailed us with rain*. (A,* O.) — And افترش الْمَالَ ‡ *He took the* مال [i. e. *property*, or *cattle*, &c.,] *wrongfully*, or *by force*. (Ḳ, TA.) — And افترش أَثَرَهُ ‡ *He followed his footsteps*; *he tracked him*. (A, O, Ḳ.) — افْتَرَشَ [in one of my copies of the Ṣ, أُفْتُرِشَ, which is also allowable, as the verb in the act. form is trans. as well as intrans.,] *It became spread*, or *expanded*; (Ṣ, Ḳ, TA;) as also انفرش ▾; said of a garment or the like. (TA.)

فَرْشٌ [an inf. n. of 1, q. v. passim. — Also, used in the sense of a pass. part. n. in which the quality of a subst. is predominant,] *What is spread, of household furniture*, (Ṣ, Ḳ,) [such as *carpets* and *mattresses* and *the like*. See also فِرَاش.] — ‡ *Seed-produce when it spreads itself* (Ṣ, Ḳ, TA) *upon the ground*: (TA:) in [some of] the copies of the Ḳ, instead of إِذَا فَرَّشَ, which is the right reading, we find اذا فُرِشَ: accord. to some, the word signifies *seed-produce when it has become three-leaved*, or *four-leaved*. (TA.) — † *A place abounding with plants* or *herbage*. (O, Ḳ.) — ‡ *A wide*, or *spacious, plain*, or *tract of land*, or *place*: (Ṣ, Ḳ, TA:) or *land that is plain*, or *even, and soft, and unobstructed by mountains*: (TA:) or *a depressed tract of land in which are trees of the kinds called* عُرْفُط *and* سَلَم, (IAạr, O,) *which cause the mouths of the camels that eat them to become relaxed*. (O.) [Hence, app., the saying,] مِنَ الْعَرْشِ إِلَى الْفَرْشِ, meaning, [*From the highest sphere*, or *the empyrean, to*] *the earth*. (A in art. عرش.) — † *A collection of trees of the kind called* عِضَاه: and *a round plot of trees of the kind called* طَلْح. (TA.) — ‡ *Shrubs*, or *small trees*: (Lth, A, Ḳ:) and *small fire-wood*. (Lth, Ḳ.) — ‡ *Young camels*; or *the young of camels*; (Fr, Ṣ, A,* Ḳ;) and فَرِيش ▾ is said to have this meaning; but accord. to Aboo-Bekr, erroneously: (TA:) so the former signifies in the Ḳur vi. 143: (Ṣ, Ḳ:) Fr says, I have heard no pl. of it: and he adds, that it may here be an inf. n. used as a subst., from the saying, فَرَشَهَا اللّٰهُ فَرْشًا, meaning, بَثَّهَا بَثًّا: [see 1:] (Ṣ, TA:) but it is said in the Ḳ that in all of the above-mentioned senses that are assigned to it in that work, it has no sing.; meaning that it is used alike as sing. and pl.: (TA:) and *bulls* or *cows*: and *sheep* or *goats*: (Ḳ:) so accord. to some of the expositors of the Ḳur: (TA:) and *such as are fit for nothing but slaughter*, (Ḳ, TA,) of camels, and of bulls or cows, and of sheep or goats; as some say: (TA:) or *such as is thrown down* (يُلْقَى, i. e., يُفْرَشُ,) *for slaughter*, of the young of camels, and bulls or cows, and sheep or goats; used alike as sing. and pl.: (Mgh:) and فَرْشُ الإِبِلِ also signifies *old camels*. (Th, TA.)

فَرْشَةٌ *A track, somewhat depressed, extending to the distance* [*of the journey*] *of a day and a night*, and *the like thereof*, and *only in land that is wide and level and like the* [*desert termed*] صَحْرَآء: pl. فُرُوش. (AḤn, TA.)

فِرْشَةٌ *Form*; *appearance*; *garb*; or *the like*; syn. هَيْئَةٌ: so in the saying, هُوَ حَسَنُ الفِرْشَةِ [*He is goodly in form*, &c.]. (O, Ḳ.)

فَرْشِىٌّ *A seller of* فَرْش [meaning *household furniture such as carpets and mattresses and the like*]. (TA.)

فَرَاشٌ [*Moths*, and *the like, that fly into the flame of a lamp* &c.;] the *flying things* (Ṣ, TA) *that fall one after another into the lamp*, or *lighted wick*, (Ṣ, Ḳ, TA,) *to burn themselves*: (TA:) [and accord. to modern usage, *butterflies* also:] a pl., [or rather a coll. gen. n.,] of which the sing. [or n. un.] is ▾ with ة: (Ṣ, Ḳ:) the former mentioned in the Ḳur ci. 3: (TA:) or the former signifies *what one sees, resembling small gnats, falling, one after another, into the fire*: (Zj:) or *young locusts, when their wings grow*, (Fr, Mgh, Jel,) *and they spread them forth*, (Mgh,) *and mount, one upon another*: (Fr, Mgh:) and *silk-worms*; app. so called because they become like these when they come forth from the cocoon. (Mgh.) It is said in a prov., أَطْيَشُ مِنْ فَرَاشَةٍ ▾ [*More light*, or *unsteady*, or *light-witted, than a moth that flies into the flame of the lamp*]. (Ṣ.) And فَرَاشَةٌ ▾ is used to signify ‡ *A man who is light* (A, Ḳ) *in head;* (A, TA;) *light-witted,* or *unsteady;* (TA;) such being likened to the فراشة of the lamp, in respect of lightness, or unsteadiness, and contemptibleness. (A,* TA.) ═ Also *Thin pieces of bone, such as fly off from any bone when it is struck:* or *any crusts,* or *coverings, that are upon bone, exclusive of the flesh:* or the *bone of the eyebrow:* or *what is thin, of the bone of the head:* or the *bones that come forth from the head of a man when it is broken:* (TA:) or فَرَاشُ الرَّأْسِ signifies *certain thin bones that are next to the bone that covers the brain:* (Ṣ, TA:) and ▼فَرَاشَةٌ, *any thin bone:* (Ṣ, Ḳ:) and ▼فَرَاشَةُ الرَّأْسِ, *the thin bones,* or *pieces of bone, of the head, such as fly off in consequence of a blow.* (TA.) —— Also, فَرَاشُ الظَّهْرِ *The place where the upper parts of the ribs are infixed in* [*the spine of*] *the back.* (TA.) —— And الفَرَاشَانِ *The two extremities of the haunches, in* [or *at*] *the* نُقْرَة, q. v. (TA.) —— And *The parts of the upper portions* (فُرُوع) *of the two shoulder-blades that rise towards the base of the neck and the even part of the back.* (AO, O.) —— And *Two veins, green,* or *of a dark,* or *an ashy, dust-colour,* (أُخْضَرَانِ,) *beneath the tongue.* (En-Naḍr, O, Ḳ.* [In the last of these, this signification and the next are erroneously assigned to the sing. word. See also الفَرَاشُ.]) —— Also, (TA,) or فَرَاشَا اللِّجَامِ, (En-Naḍr, O,) or ▼فَرَاشَتَاهُ, (IDrd in his Book on the Saddle and Bridle,) *The two iron things with which are made fast the cheek-straps of the head-stall.* (En-Naḍr, O, Ḳ.) —— And فَرَاشٌ and ▼فَرَاشَةٌ also signify The *edge* of anything. (Aboo-Sa'eed, in TA, art. نسر.) ═ And The former, *Mud that has dried, after the water, upon the ground.* (Ṣ, O, Ḳ.) —— And it is said to signify *A little water in pools left by torrents:* n. un. ▼فَرَاشَةٌ [q. v.]. (TA.) —— And [*Little*] *bubbles* (حَبَب) *upon the surface* of [the beverage called] نَبِيذ: (Ṣ, O, Ḳ:) and likewise of the water of sweat: (Ṣ,* L:) or *a little sweat:* so says IAạr. (L.) ═ فَرَاشُ قُفْلٍ signifies *The* مَنَاشِب [or *catches*] *of a lock;* [app. meaning *the little pins which fall into corresponding holes in the bolt of the Arabian wooden lock of a door,* (which see figured and described in the Introduction to my work on the Modern Egyptians,) *when it is pushed into the hole or staple of the door-post, preventing its being drawn back until they are raised by the key, which has small pins, made to correspond with the holes, so that, being introduced into these, they push up the catching pins:*] n. un. ▼ with ة: (A'Obeyd, TA:) or فَرَاشَةُ ▼ قُفْلٍ signifies *what catches,* or *sticks fast, in a lock;* (Ṣ, Ḳ;) [or, as expl. in the Arabic Dictionary of Farḥát, *what enters into a lock and makes it fast;*] meaning *its teeth;* (TḲ;) [which are *the little pins described above:*] the word is thought by IDrd to be not Arabic: or, thus applied, it is from the same word as signifying "a thin bone," because of the thinness of the فراشة of the lock. (TA.)

فِرَاشٌ *A thing that is spread* (Mgh, Ḳ) *upon the ground:* (Mgh:) *a thing that is spread for one to sit or lie upon;* in which sense it is used in the Ḳur ii. 20: (TA:) and particularly, *a bed, upon which one sleeps:* (AA, Mgh:) pl. [of pauc.] أَفْرِشَةٌ (TA) and [of mult.] فُرُشٌ, (Ṣ, Ḳ,) for which one may say, in the dial. of the Benoo-Temeem, فُرْشٌ. (Sb.) [See also فَرْشٌ: and see what is quoted below from a trad.] —— Hence, (TA,) ‡ A man's *wife;* (AA, Ṣ, O, Ḳ;) as also إِزَارٌ and لِحَافٌ: (O, TA:) pl. فُرُشٌ; so used, accord. to some, in the Ḳur lvi. 33. (Ḳ.) —— Also ‡ A woman's *husband:* (AA, Er-Rághib:) and a female slave's *master,* or *owner.* (TA.) So, accord. to some, in the words of a trad., الوَلَدُ لِلْفِرَاشِ وَلِلْعَاهِرِ الحَجَرُ, meaning *The child is for the husband;* (Er-Rághib, TA;) or *for the master of the bed,* who is *the husband,* or *the owner of the woman;* (Mgh, TA;) or *for the bed,* so that there is no ellipsis; (TA;) *and for the adulterer,* or *fornicator, shall be stones,* like as you say he shall have dust, meaning, *nothing;* i. e., he shall have no right of relationship; or, accord. to some, *stoning.* (Mgh.) [See also عَاهِرٌ.] —— † The *nest of a bird.* (O, Ḳ,* TA.) —— † *A house,* or *tent.* (AA.) —— And الفِرَاشُ signifies *The place against which the tongue goes in the furthest,* or *innermost, part of the mouth;* (AA, O, Ḳ, TA;) or, as some say, *in the lower part of the* حَنَك [which word app. here, as it often does, means the *palate*]: or فِرَاشُ اللِّسَانِ signifies *the portion of skin* (الجِلْدَةُ) [to which is here added الشَّتَّاءُ, app. a mistranscription which I am unable to rectify,] *that covers the bases of the upper teeth.* (TA. [In the TA voce مَحَارَةٌ, in art. حور, q. v., it is written الفَرَاشَةُ.])

فَرِيشٌ A plant, or herbage, *that becomes spread upon the ground, not standing up upon a stem.* (TA.) [See also مُفْتَرِشٌ.] —— And † A girl, or young woman, *compressed by a man;* (O, Ḳ;*) an instance of فَعِيلٌ from اِفْتَعَلَ; (O;) [being from اِفْتَرَشَ;] but not heard by Az on any other authority than that of Lth. (TA.) —— And † *An Arabian Bull* [or perhaps it is properly an epithet applied to that animal as meaning] *having no hump:* (TA:) [see also مُفَرَّشٌ as applied to a camel:] or فِرَاشٌ, which is pl. of فَرِيشٌ, signifies *a sort of oxen, between the* دِرَاب *and* عِرَاب, *having small humps, and their* اعياب [a mistranscription for أَغْبَاب, i. e. *dewlaps,* pl. of غَبَبٌ] *are flaccid,* or *pendulous.* (TA voce دَرْبَانِيَّةٌ.) —— Also ‡ A mare, (Aṣ, O, Ḳ,) or any solid-hoofed animal, (Ṣ,) *seven days,* (Aṣ, Ṣ, Ḳ,) or *seven nights,* (O,) *after her having foaled;* (Aṣ, Ṣ, O, Ḳ, TA;) which is the best of times for putting a burden upon her: (O, Ḳ:) and *that has recently brought forth;* (O, Ḳ, TA;) so says Ḳṭ; like the نُفَسَاء of women; or like the عُوذ of she-camels: (TA:) pl. فَرَائِشُ. (Ṣ, O, Ḳ.) —— See also فَرْشٌ, latter half.

فَرَاشَةٌ: see فَرَاشٌ, in ten places. ═ Also ‡ *A small quantity of water:* (A, O, Ḳ, TA:) one says, لَمْ يَبْقَ فِي الإِنَاءِ إِلَّا فَرَاشَةٌ [*There remained not in the vessel save a small quantity of water*]. (O, TA.) And *A small quantity of water remaining in pools left by torrents, the ground beneath which is seen, by reason of its clearness:* and some say, *a place where water collects and remains in a smooth,* or *hard and smooth, rock.* (TA.) ═ And *Great stones, like mill-stones, which are laid first* [*as a foundation*] *and upon which is then built a* تَرْكِيب, i. e. *an enclosure for palm-trees.* (TA.) ═ And الفَرَاشَتَانِ signifies *Two cartilages near,* or *by, the* لَهَاة [which generally means the *uvula;* but also, the *arches,* or *pillars, of the soft palate;* or the *furthest part of the mouth*]. (TA.)

فَرَّاشٌ *One who spreads the carpets and similar furniture* [*such as beds, or mattresses,* and *the like, and keeps them in order:* app. a post-classical word: fem. with ة]. (KL.)

مُفْرَشٌ *A thing resembling the* شَاذَكُونَة [*a kind of thick quilted stuff made in El-Yemen*]; (O, Ḳ;) i. e. *a thing that is put upon the* صُفَّة [or *covering next the saddle*] *to sit upon;* (TA;) as also ▼مُفْرَشَةٌ: (A, TA:) or the latter is *smaller than the former,* (O, Ḳ,) *and is put upon the* صُفَّة *of the camel's saddle,* (A,) or *upon the camel's saddle* [*itself*], *to sit upon:* (O, Ḳ:) [pl. مَفَارِشُ.] —— [Hence,] مَفَارِشُ is applied to signify ‡ *Women,* or *wives.* (A, TA.) One says, فُلَانٌ كَرِيمُ المَفَارِشِ ‡ *Such a one is a person who has high-born wives or women;* (A;) or *who takes as his wives high-born women.* (Ṣ, O, Ḳ.) One says also of a man who has never married, إِنَّهُ لَهَالِكُ المَفْرَشِ, meaning † *Verily his life has passed away lost.* (TA.) And هُلْكُ المَفَارِشِ is said to mean † *Persons who will not die upon their beds, and will not die otherwise than by slaughter.* (TA.)

مُفْرَشَةٌ: see the next preceding paragraph.

جَمَلٌ مُفَرَّشٌ, (O, Ḳ,) [and] ▼ جَمَلٌ مُفْتَرِشُ الأَرْضِ, (T, TA,) or ▼ مُفْتَرِشُ الظَّهْرِ, (A, TA,) ‡ *A camel having no hump.* (T, A, O, Ḳ, TA.) [See also فَرِيشٌ.] And أَكَمَةٌ ▼ مُفْتَرِشَةُ الظَّهْرِ, (Ṣ, TA,) or ▼ مُفْتَرَشَةُ الظهر, (as in one of my copies of the Ṣ and in a copy of the A,) ‡ *A flat-topped* [*hill,* or *eminence, of the kind termed*] اكمة. (Ṣ, A, TA.)

مُفْتَرِشٌ Seed-produce *spreading itself* (Ṣ, Ḳ, TA) *upon the ground.* (TA.) [See also فَرِيشٌ.] —— شَجَّةٌ مُفْتَرِشَةٌ *A wound of the head that reaches to the* فَرَاش [q. v.]; as also ▼ مُفْتَرَشَةٌ: (L:) or *that cracks the bone but does not crush.* (Ṣ, O, Ḳ.)

مَفْرُوشَةُ الرِّجْلِ (Ṣ, O, TA) applied to a she-camel, (TA,) *Having what is termed* فَرْش *in the hind leg;* (thus, by implication, in the Ṣ and O; [see 1;]) or *having a* [*certain*] *bending in the hind leg.* (TA.)

مُفْتَرَشٌ; and its fem., with ة: see مُفَرَّشٌ.

مُفَرَّشٌ; and its fem., with ة: see مُفْتَرَشٌ: —— and for the latter, see also مُفْتَرِشٌ.

فُلَانٌ مُتَفَرِّشٌ لِلنَّاسِ ‡ *Such a one is a person who lays himself out for the service of men,* or *makes himself like a victim for them,* (يَفْرِشُ لَهُمْ نَفْسَهُ,) in kindness for them. (A.) And فُلَانٌ كَرِيمٌ مُتَفَرِّشٌ لِأَصْحَابِهِ ‡ *Such a one is a generous person, who lays himself out for the service of his companions,* &c.; expl. by the words يَفْتَرِشُ نَفْسَهُ لَهُمْ. (TA.)

فرشح

Q. 1. فَرْشَحَ, inf. n. فَرْشَحَةٌ (Ṣ, Ḳ) and فِرْشَحَى, (Ḳ,) *He* (a man, Ṣ) *parted his legs:* (Ḳ:) or *he parted his legs in sitting;* and so فَرْشَطَ: (Lḥ, Ṣ:) or *he spread his legs wide apart:* (A'Obeyd, TA:) and *he stood with his legs wide apart* in prayer; (Ks, Ṣ;) and so فرشح رِجْلَيْهِ: (Ṣ:) or *he sat in a relaxed state, with his thighs cleaving to the ground;* (Ḳ;) and so فَرْشَطَ: (TA:) or *he leaped,* or *jumped;* (Ḳ;) or *made short leaps* or *jumps.* (TA.) And فَرْشَحَتْ, (Ṣ, L, and so in some copies of the Ḳ,) or ▼ تَفَرْشَحَتْ, (thus in other copies of the Ḳ, and thus in the CḲ,) *She* (a camel) *parted her hind legs* to be milked (Ṣ, L, Ḳ) and to stale. (L.)

Q. 2. تَفَرْشَحَتْ: see what immediately precedes.

فِرْشَاحٌ *A broad,* or *wide,* land: (Ḳ, TA:) accord. to the Ḳ, *syn. with* فِرْسَاحٌ; but Sh says that the latter is a mistranscription; the former being the correct word, from فَرْشَحَ فِي جِلْسَتِهِ: and Az mentions the latter as from the Jm, but not found by him as on trustworthy authority. (TA in art. فرسح.) — And *A spreading,* or *wide,* solid hoof. (Ṣ, Ḳ.) — And Clouds (سَحَاب) *in which is no rain.* (Ḳ.) — And An *unseemly,* or *ugly,* and *old,* woman, and she-camel. (Ḳ.)

الفِرْشِيحُ ‡ *The penis:* (Ḳ, TA:) a tropical term. (TA.)

فرص

1. فَرَصَهُ, (M, Ḳ,) aor. ـُ, (TA,) or ـِ, (O in art. فرس,) inf. n. فَرْصٌ, (Ṣ, M,) *He cut it;* (Ṣ, M, Ḳ;) namely, skin, or a skin, (M,) [and metal; (see مِفْرَصٌ;)] or it signifies, (TA,) or signifies also, (Ṣ, Ḳ,) sometimes, (Ṣ,) *he slit it,* or *cut* or *divided it lengthwise:* and *he made a hole in it:* (Ṣ, Ḳ, TA:) namely, skin, or a skin: (TA:) or *he slit it,* namely, a skin, *with an iron instrument having a wide end, like as the maker of sandals slits the two ears of the sandal at the heel, to put into them the* شِرَاك [or *the two arms of the* شِراك]: (Lth, TA:) or فَرَصْتُ النَّعْلَ signifies *I made a hole in each of the two ears of the sandal, for the* شراك [or *for the two arms of the* شراك]. (Ṣ.) — Also, (Ṣ, M, Ḳ,) aor. ـِ, [so in a copy of the M, but accord. to a rule of the Ḳ it should rather be ـُ,] inf. n. as above, (M,) *He hit,* or *hurt, his* فَرِيصَة [q. v.]; (M, Ḳ; and so in a copy of the Ṣ;) or, accord. to [other copies of] the Ṣ, *his* فَرِيص [q. v.]; (TA;) which is a place where a wound causes death. (Ṣ.) — And فَرِصَ, [aor. ـَ,] inf. n. فَرَصٌ; and فُرِصَ, inf. n. فَرْصٌ; *He had a complaint of his* فَرِيصَة. (M.) — فَرَصَ الفُرْصَةَ: see 8.

2. تَفْرِيصُ أَسْفَلِ نَعْلِ القِرَابِ, (L,) or تَفْرِيصُ نَعْلِ القِرَابِ, (TA, [in the O بَعْدَ القِرَابِ, which is an evident mistranscription,]) signifies *The ornamenting,* or *engraving,* (تَنْقِيش, O, L, Ḳ, TA,) *of the* نعل [i. e. *shoe of iron* or *silver, at the bottom of the scabbard of a sword*], (L,) or *of the lower part of the* نعل (O, Ḳ, TA) *of the scabbard,* (O,* TA,) *with the extremity of the* [*instrument of*] *iron.* (O, L, Ḳ, TA.) [Note: the Ḳ reading is تَفْرِيصُ نَعْلِ القِرَابِ النَّعْلِ? — printed: نَعْلِ القِرَابِ النَّعْلِ (O, Ḳ, TA) [i. e.] نَعْلِ القِرَابِ]

3. فَارَصَنِي فِي المَآءِ, (A,) inf. n. مُفَارَصَةٌ, (Ḳ,) *He took of the water with me, each of us taking his turn.* (A.) The inf. n. signifies The *doing,* or *taking, with another, each in his turn.* (Ḳ.)

4. أَفْرَصَتْهُ الفُرْصَةُ *The opportunity gave him power* or *ability* [to do a thing]. (M, A, Ḳ.)

5. تفرّص الفُرْصَةَ: see 8.

6. تَفَارَصُوا المَآءَ *They shared the water among themselves by turns.* (M, A,* Mṣb.) And تفارصوا بِئْرَهُمْ *They took,* or *drew, of the water of their well by turns.* (Ṣ, Ḳ.)

8. افترص الفُرْصَةَ *He took,* or *seized, the opportunity;* or *he arose and hastened to be before another,* or *others, in taking,* or *seizing, the opportunity;* syn. اِنْتَهَزَهَا; (O, Ḳ;) or اِغْتَنَمَهَا: (TA:) or *he got,* or *took, the opportunity;* as also ▼ تفرّصها; and ▼ فَرَصَهَا, (M, TA,) aor. ـِ, (so in a copy of the M,) inf. n. فَرْصٌ. (TA.) You say also, افترص الأُمُورَ [*He took,* or *seized, opportunities to do things*]. (A.) And فُلَانٌ لَا يُفْتَرَصُ إِحْسَانُهُ وَبِرُّهُ [*Such a one's beneficence and kindness are not caught at*]; because there is no fear that his beneficence and kindness will become beyond one's reach. (A, TA. [See also 8 in art. فرط.]) — مَنِ افْتَرَصَ مُسْلِمًا ظُلْمًا, occurring in a trad., is an instance of the verb derived from فَرْصٌ signifying the "act of cutting," or from فُرْصَةٌ signifying "an opportunity;" and the meaning is [*Such as*] *detracts,* or, literally, *cuts off, somewhat* [*from the honour of a Muslim wrongfully*]: or *assumes authority over the honour of a Muslim wrongfully,* by speaking evil of him behind his back, or otherwise, or defaming him. (IAth, L, TA.*) = افترصت الوَرَقَةُ [from الفَرِيصَةُ, "the quivering muscle" so called,] *The leaf was caused to quiver.* (M, TA.)

فَرْصٌ The *stones of the* مُقْل [or *fruit of the Theban palm*]: n. un. with ة. (AA, O, Ḳ.)

فَرْصَةٌ: see فُرْصَةٌ. = Also, الفَرْصَةُ, *The* رِيح [or *flatus*] *from which results gibbosity* [*of the back*] (الحَدَب): (Ṣ, M, O, Ḳ:) and الفُرْصَةُ is a dial. var. thereof: (M, TA:) or, accord. to A'Obeyd, the latter [q. v.] is vulgar. (TA.)

فُرْصَةٌ *A turn; a time at which,* or *during which, a thing is,* or *is to be, done,* or *had, in succession:* (Ṣ, A, Ḳ:) or *a turn,* or *time, for persons' coming to water in succession,* (Yaạḳoob, Ṣ,* M, A,* Mṣb, Ḳ,*) *in the cases of the periodical drinkings of their camels, such as the* خِمْس *and the* رِبْع *and the* سِدْس *&c.,* (Yaạḳoob, M,) *when the water is little;* (Mṣb;) as also ▼ فَرْصَةٌ (M) and ▼ فَرِيصَةٌ: (Yaạḳoob, M:) a dial. var. of the same is with س; (IAạr, M;) and رُفْصَةٌ is another: (TA:) pl. فُرَصٌ. (M, Mṣb.) You say, جَآءَتْ فُرْصَتُكَ مِنَ البِئْرِ *Thy turn,* or *time, for watering from the well has come.* (Aṣ, Ṣ,* Mṣb.*) — *A portion,* or *share, of what falls to one's lot, of water;* syn. شِرْب. (Ṣ, Ḳ.) — *An opportunity; a time at which,* or *during which, a thing may be done,* or *had;* syn. نُهْزَة; (Ṣ, M, TA;) and قُرْصَةٌ is a dial. var. of the same. (M.) You say, اِنْتَهِزِ الفُرْصَةَ, i. e. اِغْتَنِمْهَا [expl. above: see 8]. (Ṣ.) And أَيَّامُكَ فُرَصٌ [*Thy days are opportunities*]. (A, TA.) = See also فُرْصَةٌ. = Also The *temper* (سَجِيَّة), and *outstripping,* and *strength,* of a horse. (M.)

فِرْصَةٌ *A piece of wool,* (Aṣ, M,) or *of cotton,* (Aṣ, Ṣ, M, O, Mṣb, Ḳ,) or *of rag,* (Ṣ, O, Mṣb, Ḳ,) *with which a woman wipes herself, to purify herself from the catamenia;* (Ṣ, M,* O, Mṣb, Ḳ;) as also ▼ فُرْصَةٌ and ▼ فَرْصَةٌ: (Kr, M:) from فَرَصَ meaning "he cut" a thing: (Aṣ, TA:) pl. فِرَاصٌ: (Ḳ:) or they say فِرَاصٌ, as though pl. of فَرْصَةٌ. (IDrd, O.) — And, accord. to AAF, *A piece,* or *bit, of musk.* (M.) = See also فُرْصَةٌ.

فَرْصَآءُ A she-camel *that remains aside, and when the trough for watering is vacant, comes and drinks:* (O, Ḳ,* TA:) from فُرْصَةٌ signifying نُهْزَة. (Az, TA.)

فِرَاصٌ *Strong;* (O, Ḳ;) as expl. by El-Umawee: (O:) and *thick and red;* (O, Ḳ;) as expl. by Ez-Ziyádee. (O.) = مَا عَلَيْهِ فِرَاصٌ, (O,) or مِنْ فِرَاصٍ, (Ḳ,) means *There is not upon him a garment:* (O, Ḳ:) so says El-Umawee. (O.)

فَرِيصٌ *One who shares in water with another, each taking of it in turn.* (Ṣ, Ḳ.) You say, هُوَ فَرِيصِى [*He is my sharer in water, each of us taking thereof in turn*]; and in like manner, ▼ مُفَارِصِى. (TA.) = فَرِيصٌ is also, like فَرَائِصُ, pl. of فَرِيصَةٌ; (Ṣ;) [or, rather, فَرِيصٌ is a coll. gen. n., whereof the n. un. is ▼ فَرِيصَةٌ;] which signifies The *portion of flesh* [or *muscle*] *between the side and the shoulder-blade which incessantly trembles,* or *quakes,* (Aṣ, Ṣ, Ḳ,) *in a beast:* (Aṣ, Ṣ:) or the *portion of flesh which is in the part extending from the* مَرْجِع [or *lower part, next the armpit,*] *of the shoulder-blade to the arm, on either side, and which trembles,* or *quakes, when the man,* or *beast, is frightened:* (Zj, in his "Khalḳ el-Insán:") or the *portion of flesh which is by the* نُغْض *of the* كَتِف, [which may app. be here rendered with sufficient exactness the *cartilage of the shoulder-blade; or the part of it where it moves to and fro;*] *in the middle of the side, by the place where the heart beats: there are two such portions, each of them thus called, which tremble, or quake, on an occasion of fright:* and the *piece of flesh that is between the breast* (ثَدْى) *and the* مَرْجِع [expl. above] *of the shoulder-blade,* of a man and of a beast: or, as some say, the *lower part* (أَصْل) *of the* مَرْجِعُ المِرْفَقَيْنِ [or *place to which either elbow returns,* in a beast, *when, having been removed from the usual place, it is brought back thereto*]: (M:) or *a small piece of flesh which is in the heart, and which trembles,* or *quakes, by reason of a calamity, when one is frightened:* (A'Obeyd:) or *a piece of flesh* [or *muscle*] *in the side, which trembles,* or *quakes, when one is frightened.* (A.) [Hence the saying,] هُوَ ضَخْمُ الفَرِيصَةِ ‡ *He is bold and strong.* (A, TA.) — فَرِيصُ العُنُقِ *The external jugular veins* (أَوْدَاج) *of the neck:* n. un. with ة: (A'Obeyd, Ṣ, Ḳ:) or *the tendons,* or *sinews,* (عَصَب,) *and veins, of the neck:* so, app., says A'Obeyd, in the following words of a trad.: إِنِّى لَأَكْرَهُ أَنْ أَرَى الرَّجُلَ ثَائِرًا فَرِيصُ رَقَبَتِهِ قَائِمًا عَلَى مُرَيْئَتِهِ يَضْرِبُهَا [*Verily I hate to see the man having the tendons,* or *sinews, and veins, of his neck swelling* with anger, *rising against his little wife, beating her*]: for these are what swell out in anger: (Ṣ:) or, accord. to IAạr, the meaning is, the hair of the فريص, which term is metaphorically used in relation to the neck, though it [really] has no فرائص, because anger causes its veins to swell out [like as fright causes the فَرِيص properly so called to tremble or quake]: (Az, TA:) فَرِيس is a dial. var. of the same. (TA.) [See فَرْصَةٌ, last signification.]

الفَرِيصَةُ: see فَرِيصٌ, in two places. — فَرِيصَةٌ i. q. أُمُّ سُوَيْدٍ, (IDrd, O, Ḳ,) i. e., الاِسْتُ. (TA.) — See also فُرْصَةٌ.

أَفْرَصُ *Humpbacked;* as also أَفْرَزُ and أَفْرَسُ. (Fr in TA voce أَعْجَرُ.)

مِفْرَصٌ: see what next follows.

مِفْرَاصٌ (IDrd, Ṣ, M, A, O, Ḳ) and مِفْرَصٌ ▼ (IDrd, Ṣ, O, Ḳ) *A thing with which silver is cut,* (Ṣ, A,) *and gold:* (A:) or *a broad iron instrument with which one cuts:* (M:) or the *iron with which iron is cut,* or *silver:* (Ḳ:) or *a broad iron instrument with which iron is cut:* (IDrd, O:) or the *iron with which silver is cut:* (O:) [see also مِقْرَاصٌ:] or, as some say, *i. q.* إِشْفَى [q. v.] *with a broad head, with which sandals are sewed.* (IDrd, O.) El-Aạshà says,

* وَأَدْفَعُ عَنْ أَعْرَاضِكُمْ وَأُعِيرُكُمْ *
* لِسَانًا كَمِفْرَاصِ الخَفَاجِىِّ مِلْحَبَا *

[*And I defend your honours, and lend to you a tongue like the* مفراص *of the Khafájee, sharp*]. (Ṣ.) And you say, بَيْنَ جَنْبَيْهِ مِفْرَاصُ الخَفَاجِىِّ ‡ [*Between his two sides is* an intellect sharp as *the* مفراص *of the Khafájee*]. (A.) [Hence it seems that among the tribe of Khafájeh were expert workers with the instrument thus called.]

هُوَ مُفَارِصِى: see فَرِيصٌ, second sentence.

فرصد

فِرْصِدٌ and فِرْصِيدٌ ▼ The *stones of raisins* and *of grapes;* (M, O, L, Ḳ;) as also فِرْصَادٌ ▼. (M, L, Ḳ.)

فِرْصَادٌ The [*mulberry called*] تُوت [q. v.]: (AO, AḤn, O, Mṣb:) or the [*tree called*] تُوت: or *its fruit:* (M, Ḳ:) or the *red* توت: (Ṣ, Mṣb:) [or, accord. to Zeyn el-'Aṭṭár, the *sweet and white mulberry:* so says Golius: see تُوتٌ:] Lth says that it is *a well-known tree;* that the people of El-Baṣrah call the tree thus, and call its fruit تُوتٌ: (T, O,* Mṣb:) and by فِرْصَادٌ the lawyers mean the *tree that bears the* [*fruit called*] تُوت. (Mṣb.) — Also *A red dye:* (Ḳ:) or *redness.* (M, L.) — See also فِرْصِدٌ.

فِرْصِيدٌ: see فِرْصِدٌ.

فرض

1. فَرَضَهُ, (Ṣ, A, O, Mṣb, &c.,) aor. ـِ, (Mṣb, TA, &c.,) inf. n. فَرْضٌ, (Ṣ, O, Mṣb, Ḳ, &c.,) *He made a mark in it,* or *upon it, by notching,* or *otherwise:* (O:) *he notched it; made a notch,* or *an incision, in it;* (Ṣ, O, Mṣb, Ḳ;) namely, a piece of wood, (Mṣb,) a زَنْد, [or rather فَرَضَهَا said of a زَنْدَة, from which fire is produced,] and a سِوَاك [or toothstick], (Ṣ, O,) and in like manner a bow; (A;) as also [افترضه ▼; (see this verb below;) and] فَرَّضَهُ ▼, inf. n. تَفْرِيضٌ: (Ḳ:) or this last signifies *he notched it much;* or *made notches in it;* (Ṣ, O, TA;) or you say, فَرَّضَ قَوْسَهُ and فَرَّضَ قِسِيَّهُ: (A:) and فَرَضَهُ signifies *he notched it with his teeth;* namely, a tooth-stick: (Aṣ:) and *he cut it;* namely, a thing; or a hard thing; which is said by some to be the primary signification: (TA:) and *he* (a tailor) *cut it out;* namely a garment: (Kull p. 275:) and *he cut it out and made it round;* namely a shield: (TA:) and فَرْضٌ also signifies the *cutting,* or *dividing, lengthwise; cleaving;* or *the like;* applied in a general manner; or the *making a trench,* or *an oblong excavation, in the middle of a grave;* فَرَضْتُ لِلْمَيِّتِ signifying *I made a trench,* or *an oblong excavation, in the middle of a grave, for the corpse.* (TA.) = فَرَضَ لَهُ, [aor. and] inf. n. as above, (Ḳ, &c.,) *He apportioned to him* [a thing]: *he appointed to him* [a thing]: (Bḍ in xxxiii. 38, and TA:*) because that which is apportioned, or appointed, [to a person] is cut off from the thing from which it is apportioned, or appointed: (TA:) *he made* [a thing] *lawful,* or *allowable, to him;* (Jel in xxxiii. 38, and Kull in p. 275, and TA;*) relating to a case into which a man has brought himself: (Kull:) this is said to be the meaning when the phrase فَرَضَ اللّٰهُ لَهُ occurs in the Ḳur: (TA:) *he appointed,* or *assigned, to him a definite portion;* (Ḳ;) as also افرض ▼ له. (O, L, Ḳ.) You say فَرَضَ لَهُ فِى العَطَآءِ [*He appointed,* or *assigned, to him a definite portion in the gift*]. (Aṣ, Ṣ.) And فَرَضَ لَهُ فِى الدِّيوَانِ (Aṣ, Ṣ, A) [*He appointed,* or *assigned, to him a definite portion in the register of soldiers* or *pensioners;* or] *he registered his stipend therein.* (Aṣ, A, TA.) And فَرَضَهُ, (Ṣ,) and افرضه ▼, (Ṣ, Ḳ,) *He gave to him.* (Ṣ, O, Ḳ.) — فَرَضَ, (Ṣ, A, Mgh, Mṣb,) aor. as above, (TA,) and so the inf. n., (Mṣb, TA,) also signifies *He* (God, Ṣ, A, Mgh, Mṣb) *made* a thing, (Ṣ, TA,) or prayer, (A, Mgh,) or statutes or ordinances, (Mṣb,) *obligatory,* or *binding,* syn. أَوْجَبَ, (Ṣ, A, Mgh, Mṣb, TA,) *by a known decree,* (TA,) [or *He imposed* a thing &c.,] عَلَى إِنْسَانٍ *on a man,* (TA,) or عَلَيْنَا *on us;* (Ṣ;) and so اِفْتَرَضَ ▼: (Ṣ, A, Mgh, O, Ḳ:) or فَرْضٌ is like إِيجَابٌ; but the latter is so termed in consideration of its befalling; and the former is so called in consideration of the sentence, or decree, respecting it: (B:) [this is said in books on the law, in explanation of the opinion of Aboo-Ḥaneefeh, as opposed to that of Esh-Sháfi'ee: for] accord. to Esh-Sháfi'ee, these two terms are alike; (L, TA;) but accord. to Aboo-Ḥaneefeh, the difference between الوَاجِبُ and الفَرْضُ is like the difference between heaven and earth: (TA:) this distinction, however, is founded upon contested derivations of the two terms: (Kull p. 276:) and it is said that wherever the phrase فَرَضَ اللّٰهُ عَلَيْهِ occurs, it means إِيجَابٌ. (TA.) Also *He* (the apostle of God) *instituted,* or *prescribed,* [a thing *as a statute,* or *an ordinance,* or *a command* or *prohibition;*] syn. سَنَّ; (O, Ḳ;) on the authority of IAạr alone: (O, TA:) but accord. to others, *he made necessarily obligatory* or *binding;* and this, says Az, is the obvious meaning. (TA.) Also *He* (a judge) *decreed,* or *adjudged,* [a thing, as, for instance,] expenses [&c.]. (Mṣb.) Also *He assigned,* or *appointed, a particular time for doing* a thing; or *he determined, defined,* or *limited,* a thing *as to time,* or *otherwise;* the inf. n., فَرْضٌ, being syn. with تَوْقِيتٌ: (Ibn-'Arafeh, A, O, Ḳ:) as in the phrase فَمَنْ فَرَضَ فِيهِنَّ الحَجَّ [*And whoso determineth the performance of the pilgrimage therein*]; (Ibn-'Arafeh, O, Ḳ;) occurring in the Ḳur [ii. 193]; and in like manner it is expl. by Ibn-'Arafeh as occurring in xxxiii. 38 of the Ḳur: (O, TA:) but the phrase quoted above is also expl. as meaning *and whoso maketh it obligatory,* or *binding, on himself to perform the pilgrimage therein,* by his entering upon the state of إِحْرَام. (TA.) — سُورَةٌ أَنْزَلْنَاهَا وَفَرَضْنَاهَا, (Ḳ,) in the Ḳur, [commencing chap. xxiv.,] (TA,) means [*This is a chapter which we have revealed and*] *in which we have set down the obligatory statutes:* (O, Ḳ:) or *in which we have bound you to do according to what is made obligatory therein:* (Az, O:) or, as some read, وَفَرَّضْنَاهَا ▼, (Ṣ, O, Ḳ,*) meaning *and in which we have set down obligatory statutes,* (O, L, Ḳ,) *one after another:* (O, Ḳ:) or *which we have distinctly explained:* (Az, Ṣ, O, Ḳ:) or we

have distinctly explained what is in it, of lawful and unlawful [*things*]. (T, TA.) — فَرْضٌ also signifies The act of *reading*, or *reciting*. (IAạr, O, Ḳ.) You say, فَرَضْتُ جُزْئِى *I read*, or *recited*, *my portion*. (O, TA.) ═ فَرُضَ, inf. n. فَرَاضَةٌ, *He was*, or *became*, *skilled in the* فَرَائِض; (A, O, Ḳ, TA;) i. e. *in the science of the division of inheritances*. (TA.) MF says that, accord. to IḲṭṭ, the verb is also written فَرِضَ, like كَتِبَ: but [says SM] what I find in his "Kitáb el-Abniyeh" is the mention of the two modes of writing in the instance of فرضت said of a cow; and the verb applied to a man he has not mentioned. (TA.) ═ فَرَضَتْ, aor. ـِ, inf. n. فُرُوضٌ; and فَرُضَتْ, inf. n. فَرَاضَةٌ; *She* (a cow) *became old, aged, far advanced in age*, (Ṣ, O, Ḳ,) or *extremely old*. (TA.) ═ And فَرُضَ, inf. n. فُرُوضٌ, signifies *It* (a thing) *became wide; it widened*, or *dilated*. (TA.)

2: see 1, first sentence: and again, in the last quarter of the paragraph. ═ فَرَّضَ, inf. n. تَفْرِيضٌ, said of a man, *He had a* فَرِيضَة [*to give from*] *among his camels*. (O, Ḳ.)

4. افرض لهُ: and افرضهُ: see 1, latter part of the first half of the paragraph. ═ أَفْرَضَتِ المَاشِيَةُ *The beasts amounted to the number which rendered it obligatory on the owner to give from among them a* فَرِيضَة. (Ṣ, O, Ḳ.*)

8. افترضهُ: see 1, first sentence. — لَمْ يَفْتَرِضْهَا وَلَدٌ, occurring in a trad., means [*A child had not been brought forth by her*; lit.] لَمْ يَحُزَّهَا, and لَمْ يُؤْثِرْهَا [a mistake for لم يُؤَثِّرْهَا]. (TA.) ═ See also 1, latter part of the first half of the paragraph. ═ افترض الجُنْدُ *The soldiers received their stipends*. (A, Ḳ.) ═ افترض القَوْمُ *The people*, or *company of men*, *perished, none of them remaining*; syn. انقرض. (Ḳ.)

فَرْضٌ *A mark* [*made by notching*, or *otherwise*; as is shown by the first explanation of 1]: (TA:) *a notch*, or *an incision*, in a thing: (O, TA:) of a bow, (Ṣ, A, Ḳ,) the *place of the string*; (Ḳ;) the *notch* (Ṣ, A, O) *in the curved extremity* thereof, (A,) *into which the string falls*; (Ṣ, O;) as also ↓ فُرْضَةٌ; (A, TA;) or this is the *place of the notch for the string thereof*: (Mṣb:) pl. of the former فِرَاضٌ (Ṣ, O, Ḳ) and فُرُوضٌ; (TA;) and of the latter فُرَضٌ (Mṣb, TA) and فِرَاضٌ: (Mṣb:) also, of a زَنْد, (Ṣ, Ḳ,) or [rather] of a زَنْدَة, (A,) the *notch*; (Ḳ;) or the *place*, or *part*, *whence the fire is produced*; (Ṣ, Ḳ;) the *hole*, or *perforation, that is made in the head* thereof, *into which the* زَنْد *is put, and then twisted round, in producing fire*; also called وَقْرٌ; (A;) and ↓ فُرْضَةٌ signifies the same: (TA:) and فُرُوضٌ also signifies *notches* in an unfeathered and headless arrow [such as is used in the game called المَيْسِر]. (TA.) ═ *I. q.* ↓ مَفْرُوضٌ (A, Mṣb, Ḳ) [*Apportioned: appointed: made lawful*, or *allowable*: and] a thing *made obligatory*, or *binding*, *by God*; (Ṣ, A, O, Ḳ;) *for neglecting which one will be punished*; like وَاجِبٌ; accord. to Esh-Sháfi'ee; (TA in art. وجب;) because it has marks and limits; (Ṣ, O, TA;) said to be from the same word signifying "a mark," because it inseparably pertains to a man, like a mark; (TA;) or, as some say, because it necessarily pertains to a man like as does the فَرْض, i. e. notch, to the arrow; (O, TA;) as also ↓ مُفْتَرَضٌ: (TA:) pl. فُرُوضٌ. (Mṣb.) As a law-term, it is of two sorts, فَرْضُ عَيْنٍ and فَرْضُ كِفَايَةٍ: the former is That *whereof the observance is obligatory on every one, and does not become of no force in respect of some in consequence of the observance* [*thereof*] *by some* [*others*]; as religious belief, and the like: the latter is That *whereof the observance is obligatory on the collective body of the Muslims, and, in consequence of the observance* [*thereof*] *by some, becomes of no force in respect of the rest*; as warring against unbelievers, and the prayer over the dead in the bier. (KT.) You say, هٰذَا أَمْرٌ فَرْضٌ عَلَيْهِمْ, and ↓ مَفْرُوضٌ, and ↓ مُفْتَرَضٌ, *This is* [a thing] *made obligatory*, or *binding, on them by God*. (TA.) And حَقُّكَ فَرْضٌ, and ↓ مَفْرُوضٌ, and ↓ مُفْتَرَضٌ, *Thy right*, or *due*, *is* [a thing] *made obligatory*, or *binding*, *by God*. (A.) ↓ نَصِيبًا مَفْرُوضًا, in the Ḳur [iv. 8 and 118], means *A share*, or *portion*, *determined, defined*, or *limited*, *as to time*, or *otherwise*: (Zj, Ibn-'Arafeh:) or, in iv. 118, *a share*, or *portion, cut off and limited*. (Ṣ, O.) [See also فَرِيضَةٌ.] — *A statute, an ordinance, a command* or *prohibition*, of the Apostle of God; syn. سُنَّةٌ. (IAạr, O, Ḳ.) [But فَرْضٌ is generally distinguished from سُنَّةٌ: the former, for instance, being applied to prayer appointed in the Ḳur-án; and the latter, to prayer appointed by Mohammad without allegation of a divine order.] — *A gift*, or *a soldier's stipend* or *pay*, syn. عَطَآءٌ, (A,) or عَطِيَّةٌ, (Ṣ, O, Ḳ,) *assigned*, or *appointed*. (Ṣ, O, Ḳ.*) In the copies of the Ḳ, مَوْسُومَة is put by mistake for مَرْسُومَة. (TA.) You say, مَا أَصَبْتُ مِنْهُ فَرْضًا وَلَا قَرْضًا *I did not obtain from him an assigned*, or *appointed*, *gift*, or *soldier's stipend*, (Ṣ, O, TA,) *nor a gift to be requited*, or *a loan*. (O, TA.) And فَرْضٌ also signifies *A thing which one makes obligatory*, or *binding*, *on himself, and freely gives*: or *a thing which one gives liberally, not for a recompense*. (IDrd, O, Ḳ.) ═ Also *Soldiers who receive stipends*: (Ḳ:) so accord. to Lth, as related by Az; but [Ṣgh says] I have not found it in the book of Lth: (O:) or *soldiers having definite portions assigned to them*: (A:) pl. فُرُوضٌ. (A, TA.) You say, عِنْدَهُ مِائَةٌ مِنَ الفَرْضِ *He has with him a hundred soldiers* &c. (A.) ═ *A shield*. (Ṣ, O, Ḳ.) Ṣakhr-el-Ghei says, describing lightning, (O, TA,) likening it to a light shield which an announcer of tidings was turning over and over with his hands that a party might see it and be gladdened [by the signal], (TA,)

* أَرِقْتُ لَهُ مِثْلَ لَمْعِ البَشِيرِ *
* يُقَلِّبُ بِالكَفِّ فَرْضًا خَفِيفَا *

[*I was sleepless by reason of it, it being* (in its flickering) *like the signalling of the announcer of tidings turning over and over with the hand a light shield*]: one should not say قُرْصًا خفيفا. (Ṣ, O, TA: but my copies of the Ṣ have قَلَّبَ instead of يُقَلِّبُ.) [See also what follows.] — And *A stick*, or *piece of wood*; syn. عُودٌ: thus [it means] in the verse (فِى البَيْتِ) accord. to El-Jumahee, (O, TA,) i. e. in the verse above-cited: (TA:) he says, الفَرْضُ فِى البَيْتِ عُودٌ: (O, TA:) whence the author of the Ḳ has been misled to explain الفَرْض as meaning عُودٌ مِنْ أَعْوَادِ البَيْتِ. (TA.) — And *An arrow before it has been furnished with feathers and a head*: (Akh, Ṣ, O, TA:) a meaning also heard by El-Jumahee: (O, TA:) and to this, in the hand of the player, 'Abeed El-Abraṣ has likened lightning, accord. to the Ṣ; but Ṣgh says, in the TṢ, that he did not find the verse cited by J in the poetry of 'Abeed. (TA.) — And *A piece of rag*: another explanation heard by El-Jumahee. (O.) — And *A garment*, or *piece of cloth*: (O, Ḳ:) a meaning mentioned by Aṣ on the authority of some one or more of the Arabs of the desert, of Hudheyl. (O.) [See also فِرَاضٌ.] — And it is said that in the verse cited above it means the notch in the زَنْد [or rather زَنْدَة, mentioned in the first sentence of this paragraph]. (O, TA.) ═ *A sort of dates* (Ṣ, O, Mṣb, Ḳ) *of 'Omán*: (Mṣb:) Aṣ says that the best dates of 'Omán are these and the بَلْعَق: (Ṣ, O:) and AḤn says, Certain of the desert-Arabs of 'Omán informed me that when the tree thereof has its fruit ripened, and the gathering is delayed, the fruit falls from its stones, and the raceme remains with nothing upon it but stones hanging to the تَفَارِيق [by which they are attached to the ends of the stalks]. (TA.)

فُرْضٌ The *fruit of the* دَوْم [or *Theban palm*] *while continuing red*. (AA, O,* Ḳ.)

فُرْضَةٌ: see فَرْضٌ, first sentence, in two places. — *A gap*, or *an opening*, in a wall and the like: pl. فُرَضٌ. (Mṣb.) — *A gap*, or *breach*, *in the bank* of a river, (Ṣ, Mgh, O, Mṣb, Ḳ,) *whence one draws water*, (Ṣ, O, Ḳ,) or *by which one descends to the water*, (Mgh, Mṣb,) *and by which the ships*, or *boats*, *ascend*; (Mṣb;) i. e. (Mgh) its مَشْرَعَة: (Aṣ, A, Mgh:) pl., in this and the following senses, فُرَضٌ (TA) and فِرَاضٌ. (A, TA.) Hence the saying, in a trad., فَاجْعَلُوا السُّيُوفَ لِلْمَنَايَا فُرَضًا † *Therefore make ye the swords to be* مَشَارِع [here used in the sense of *means of access*] *to death*; (O, TA;) and offer, or expose, yourselves to martyrdom. (TA.) Hence also, فِرَاضٌ is used in the sense of ثُغُورٌ [pl. of ثَغْرٌ, q. v.]. (TA.) — Of a sea, or great river, The *place where ships unload*; syn. مَحَطُّ السُّفُنِ: (Ṣ, O, Ḳ:) or *where they are stationed, near the bank of a river*, or *near the land*. (Mgh.) — Of a receptacle for ink, The *place of the ink*. (Ṣ, O, Ḳ.) — Of a door, The نَجْرَان [or *piece of wood in which is the foot*; i. e. *upon which turns the foot*]. (Ṣ, O, Ḳ.) — Of a mountain, *A part sloping down from the middle and side.* (TA.) — فُرْضَتَانِ i. q. فُرَيْضَتَانِ, q. v., accord. to ISk. (IB.)

فَرَضِىٌّ and ▼ فَارِضٌ (Ṣ, A, Mgh, O, Ḳ) and ▼ فَرَّاضٌ (A, Mgh, B) and ▼ فَرِيضٌ (A, O, L, Ḳ) A man *skilled in the science of the* فَرَائِض; (Ṣ,* A, Mgh, O, Ḳ,* B;) i. e. *in the science of questions relating to inheritance;* (Mgh;) or *in the science of the division of inheritances.* (TA.)

فِرَاضٌ The *mouth* of a river or rivulet. (Ṣ, O, Ḳ.*) — And *Roads,* or *ways.* (Lth, O, Ḳ.) [In this latter sense, app., (as well as in others shown above,) pl. of فُرْضَةٌ, q. v.] — Also The *fire that is elicited from the* زَنْدَة. (AḤn, TA.) [See also فَرْضٌ (of which it is a pl.), first sentence.] — And *Clothing:* (Ṣ, O, Ḳ:) one says, مَا عَلَيْهِ فِرَاضٌ *There is not upon him any clothing;* (Ṣ, O;) or, accord. to AHeyth, *covering.* (TA.) [See also فَرْضٌ, near the end.]

فَرِيضٌ An arrow *having its notch cut;* (Ṣ, A, O, Ḳ;) as also ▼ مَفْرُوضٌ. (TA.) — See also فَرَضِىٌّ: — and see فَارِضٌ. — Also The *cud of the camel;* accord. to Kr: but accord. to others this is called, قَرِيضٌ [q. v.], with ق. (TA.)

فَرِيضَةٌ, of the measure فَعِيلَةٌ in the sense of the measure مَفْعُولَةٌ: pl. فَرَائِضُ: said by some to be derived from فَرْضٌ signifying the act of "apportioning," or "appointing;" because فرائض are apportioned, or appointed: by others said to be from فَرْضٌ in relation to a bow. (Mṣb.) [These remarks apply to the word in all the senses here following.] — A subst. signifying *A thing made obligatory,* or *binding, on a person* or *persons,* (Ṣ, Mgh, TA,) *by God;* (Ṣ, TA;) *an obligatory statute* or *ordinance of God, in a general sense:* pl. as above. (TA.) — *A portion,* or *share, made obligatory,* or *binding,* (Ḳ,* TA,) on a man: (TA:) or *anything apportioned,* or *appointed:* [and particularly *a primarily-apportioned inheritance:* (see an ex. in the first paragraph of art. عول:)] and hence, فَرَائِضُ is applied to the *portions, or shares, of inheritances;* [i. e. the *fixed primary portions of inheritances assigned by the Ḳur-án;* which are a half, third, fourth, sixth, and eighth;] because they are apportioned, or appointed, to their several owners. (Mgh.) And hence, (Mgh,) عِلْمُ الفَرَائِضِ, and elliptically الفَرَائِضُ, (Ṣ,* Mgh, O,* Mṣb,) *The science of the division of inheritances;* (Ṣ, O, TA;) or *the science of questions relating to inheritance.* (Mgh.) It is said in a trad., (Mgh,) تَعَلَّمُوا الفَرَائِضَ وَعَلِّمُوهَا النَّاسَ فَإِنَّهَا نِصْفُ العِلْمِ, accord. to the relation commonly followed, with the pron. fem., referring to الفرائض; and وَعَلِّمُوهُ فَإِنَّهُ, with the pron. masc., referring to عِلْم understood as prefixed to الفرائض; [i. e. *Learn ye the science of the division of inheritances, &c., and teach ye it to* (other) *men, for it is the half of science:*] it is said to be called the half of science in consideration of the division of statutes into those which pertain to the living and those which pertain to the dead; or by way of amplification. (Mgh,* Mṣb.) The phrase الفَرِيضَةُ العَادِلَةُ [*The equitable portion of inheritance*], in a trad. of Ibn-'Omar, is that respecting which the Muslims have agreed: or that for which the authority is elicited from the Ḳur-án and the Sunneh without there being in these any express statute respecting it: or that is equitably divided, agreeably with the portions and shares mentioned in the Ḳur-án and the Sunneh. (TA.) — *What is made obligatory,* or *binding,* [*on the owner, to give,*] *of pasturing beasts,* [i. e. *camels,*] *in payment of the poor-rate;* (Ṣ, O, Ḳ;) the *camel that is taken in payment of the poor-rate:* so termed because it is made obligatory to be given, of a certain number of camels: the ة is added because the word is made a subst., not an epithet: pl. فَرَائِضُ: (TA:) فَرَائِضُ الإِبِلِ signifying *the dues of the poor-rate, of camels:* (A, Mgh:*) the فريضة of twenty-five camels is a بِنْتُ مَخَاضٍ, (Mgh,) or she-camel one year old; (AHeyth;) that of thirty-six, a بِنْتُ لَبُونٍ, (AHeyth, Mgh,) or she-camel two years old; (AHeyth;) that of forty-six, a حِقَّةٌ, or she-camel three years old; and that of sixty-one, a جَذَعَةٌ, or she-camel four years old. (AHeyth.) الفَرِيضَتَانِ signifies *The* جَذَعَة *of sheep,* or *goats, with the* حِقَّة *of camels;* (ISk, Ṣ, O, Ḳ;) and ▼ الفُرْضَتَانِ signifies the same, accord. to ISk. (IB.) And فَرِيضَةٌ, by an extension of its meaning, is applied to *A camel,* in other cases than those of the poor-rate. (TA.) — See also فَارِضٌ.

فِرْيَاضٌ *Wide,* or *broad.* (O, Ḳ.)

فَرَّاضٌ: see فَرَضِىٌّ.

فَارِضٌ: see فَرَضِىٌّ. — *Old, aged,* or *advanced in age;* applied to a cow; (Ṣ, A, O;) in the Ḳur ii. 63; (Ṣ, O;) and to a ram: (TA:) or *extremely aged;* or *old and weak;* applied to a cow; (Fr, Ḳatádeh;) as also فَارِضَةٌ and ▼ فَرِيضٌ (TA) and ▼ فَرِيضَةٌ: (Ḳ, TA: [but to what these are applied is not shown further than by their being mentioned as fem. epithets:]) or *large and fat;* applied to a cow: pl. فَوَارِضُ: (AZ:) and the pl. also signifies *sound,* or *healthy, and large;* (Ibn-'Abbád, O, TṢ, Ḳ;) *not small, nor diseased:* (Ibn-'Abbád, O, TṢ:) and, contr., *diseased.* (Ibn-'Abbád, O, TṢ, Ḳ.) — ‡ *Old, aged,* or *advanced in age, and large, big,* or *bulky;* applied to a man: (TA:) or *large, big,* or *bulky;* applied to a man; (Ṣ, A, O, Ḳ;) and to a full-grown unripe date (بُسْرَة); (A, TA;) and to the bursa faucium of a camel (شِقْشِقَة); and to a uvula (لَهَاة); (O, Ḳ;) and to a skin for water or milk (سِقَآء); (IB;) and to a beard (لِحْيَة); (A, O, Ḳ;) or, applied to this last, it is with ة; (Akh, Ṣ;) or with and without ة: (L:) and without ة, applied in the same sense to anything; (Ṣ, O, Ḳ;) being masc. and fem.: (Aṣ, O:) pl. فُرَّضٌ, (IAạr, Ṣ, A, O, Ḳ,) applied to men; (IAạr, Ṣ, A, O;) or this, so applied, signifies *goodly,* or *handsome:* (TA:) and فَوَارِضُ is applied to dates [&c.]. (A, TA.) Also † *Old,* or *ancient;* (Ḳ;) applied to a thing. (TA.) You say ضِغْنٌ فَارِضٌ ‡ *Great rancour,* or *malevolence,* or *malice;* (L;) as also ضَغِينَةٌ فَارِضٌ: (A, L:) or *old rancour, &c.* (O.) And ضَبٌّ فَارِضٌ ‡ *Great enmity.* (IAạr.)

أَفْرَضُ The *most* [and *more*] *skilled,* of men, *in the science of the* فَرَائِض; (Ṣ, Mgh, O, Ḳ;*) i. e. *in the science of the division of inheritances;* (Ṣ, O, TA;) or *in the science of questions relating to inheritance.* (Mgh.) It is said in a trad., أَفْرَضُكُمْ زَيْدٌ *The most skilled, of you, &c., is Zeyd.* (Ṣ, Mgh.)

مِفْرَضٌ *An iron instrument with which notches, or incisions, are made.* (Ṣ, O, Ḳ.)

مُفَرَّضٌ *Notched much,* or *in many places; serrated;* or *jagged.* (El-Báhilee.) — And hence, The [*kind of beetle called*] جُعَل: (El-Báhilee:) or the *male of the* [*beetles called*] خَنَافِس. (IAạr.)

مَفْرُوضٌ: see فَرِيضٌ: — and see also فَرْضٌ, as syn. with مَفْرُوضٌ, in four places.

مُفْتَرَضٌ: see فَرْضٌ, as syn. with مَفْرُوضٌ, in three places.

فرط

1. فَرَطَ, (O, Ḳ,) aor. ـُ, (TA,) inf. n. فُرُوطٌ, (Ḳ,) *He* (a man, TA) *preceded; went before; was,* or *became, before, beforehand, first,* or *foremost; had,* or *got, priority,* or *precedence;* (O, Ḳ, TA;) as also فَرِطَ, aor. ـَ, [inf. n. فَرَطٌ; which is therefore used as an epithet applied to one and to more;] (O, TA;) and so ▼ افترط, in the phrase افترط إِلَيْهِ فِى هٰذَا الأَمْرِ [*He was foremost in attaining to him in this affair*]. (TA.) [See مُفْتَرِطٌ.] — فَرَطَ القَوْمَ, (Ṣ, O, Mṣb, Ḳ, &c.,) aor. ـُ, (Ṣ, Mṣb,) or ـِ, (Ḳ,) inf. n. فَرْطٌ, (Ṣ,) or فُرُوطٌ, (Mṣb,) or both, (O,) or the former and فَرَاطَةٌ, (M, Ḳ,) *He preceded,* or *went before, the people,* or *company of men,* (Ṣ, M, O, Mṣb, Ḳ,) *to the water,* (Ṣ, O,) or *in search of water,* (Mṣb,) or *to come to water,* (M, Ḳ,) *for the purpose of preparing the buckets and ropes,* (Mṣb,) or *for the purpose of putting into a right state the watering-trough* (M, Ḳ) *and ropes* (M, O) *and buckets,* (M, O, Ḳ,) i. e. *to prepare these for them.* (TA.) [See also 5.] — An Arab of the desert said to El-Ḥasan, عَلِّمْنِى دِينًا وَسُوطًا لَا ذَاهِبًا فُرُوطًا وَلَا سَاقِطًا سُقُوطًا, meaning *Teach thou me a religion of the middle sort, not passing beyond the due mean, nor falling short of it.* (TA.) — فَرَطَ مِنْهُ *It proceeded from him hastily, before reflection,* or *without premeditation;* [*as though it preceded his judgment;*] syn. بَدَرَ, and سَبَقَ, and تَقَدَّمَ. (TA.) [See 3.] You say, فَرَطَ مِنْهُ كَلَامٌ, aor. ـُ, *Speech proceeded from him hastily, before reflection,* or *without premeditation;* syn. سَبَقَ, and تَقَدَّمَ. (Mṣb.) And فَرَطَ إِلَيْهِ مِنِّى قَوْلٌ *A saying proceeded to him from me hastily, before reflection,* or *without premeditation;* syn. سَبَقَ. (Ṣ.) And in like manner you say of an evil action. (TA.) — فَرَطَ عَلَيْهِ *He hasted to do him an evil action:* (O, TA:) *he acted hastily and unjustly towards him.* (Ṣ, O,

TA.) Hence, in the Ḳur [xx. 47], إِنَّا نَخَافُ أَنْ يَفْرُطَ عَلَيْنَا *Verily we fear that he may act hastily and unjustly towards us:* (Ṣ:) or *that he may hastily do to us an evil action:* (Ibn-'Arafeh, O:) or *that he may hasten to punish us.* (Fr, Bḍ, O, Jel.) [See also 4.] فَرَطَ عَلَيْهِ also signifies *He did to him what was disagreeable,* or *hateful,* or *evil; he annoyed him.* (TA.) And فَرَطَ, inf. n. فُرُوطٌ, *He reviled.* (IḲṭṭ.) You say also فَرَطَ عَلَيْهِ فِى الْقَوْلِ: see 4, latter half. — فَرَطَ فِيهِ: see 2, near the middle. — فَرَطَ فِى حَوْضِهِ: see 4, last sentence but one. — فَرِطَتِ النَّخْلَةُ *The palm-tree was left without being fecundated until its spadix became dry and hard* (عَسَا, in the CḲ عَشَا, and in the O يَعْسُو). (O, Ḳ,* TA.) — And فَرِطَتِ الْبِئْرُ *The well was left until its water had collected again.* (Sh, TA.) = فَرَطَ إِلَيْهِ رَسُولَهُ: see 2. — فَرَطَ وَلَدًا, or وَلَدًا, and فَرَطَ وَلَدَهُ: see 4.

2. فَرَّطَهُ, inf. n. تَفْرِيطٌ, *He, or it, made him to precede; to be, or become, before, beforehand, first,* or *foremost; to have,* or *get, priority,* or *precedence;* (TA;) as also ↓ افرطهُ. (O, TA.) — *He emboldened him,* in contention, or altercation; as also ↓ افرطهُ. (TA.) فَرَّطَ إِلَيْهِ رَسُولًا, (IDrd, O, Ḳ,) inf. n. as above, (IDrd,) *He sent to him a messenger* (IDrd, O, Ḳ) *among his particular,* or *special, friends; sent him forward,* or *in advance, to him:* (IDrd, O:) or *he made him his deputy in a litigation:* (O:) and ↓ افرط رَسُولًا *he sent a messenger specially and expressly respecting his needful affairs:* (IAạr, O, L, Ḳ:*) and فَرَّطَ ↓ إِلَيْهِ رَسُولَهُ *he sent forward,* or *in advance, his messenger to him, and hastened him:* (Ḳ, TA: [in the CḲ, instead of وَأَعْجَلَهُ, we find وَأَرْسَلَهُ:]) but [SM says,] I do not find this last form mentioned by any of the leading authorities. (TA.) — فَرَّطَهُ also signifies *He sent it before, remaining behind it:* or *he quitted it, and sent it before:* (TA:) *he left it, and quitted it:* (Ṣ:) *he left him;* (AA;) as also ↓ افرطهُ: (Ks, Ṣ:) *he left him, and became behind him;* as also ↓ افرطهُ: (TA:) *he left him, and went before him:* (Ṣ, O, Ḳ:) and ↓ افرطهُ [has a similar meaning,] *he left him behind, and forgot him:* (Fr:) and *he forgot it,* namely a thing, or an affair: (Ḳ:) فِرَاطٌ, also, [inf. n. of ↓ فارط,] signifies the act of *leaving:* (TA:) and فرّط عَنْهُ *he left, forsook,* or *relinquished, him,* or *it;* or *he abstained,* or *desisted, from it:* (TA:) and فرّط فيه *he neglected it; and preferred backwardness* (قَدَّمَ الْعَجْزَ) *in it,* or *with respect to it;* and *failed,* or *fell short, of doing what he ought,* or *flagged,* or *was remiss, with respect to it;* as also فَرَّطَهُ; (Ḳ; [but accord. to the TA, only the former of these two phrases signifies "he failed of doing what he ought," &c.;]) or simply *he neglected it;* (ISd, TA;) or *he failed of doing what he ought,* or *flagged,* or *was remiss, with respect to it, and neglected it,* (Ṣ, O, Mṣb,) *so that it escaped him;* (Ṣ, O;) as also ↓ فَرَطَ فيه, (Ṣ, O, Ḳ,* [in the Ḳ, the words rendered "so that it escaped him" are omitted,]) aor. ـُ, (Ṣ, O,) inf. n. فَرْطٌ: (Ṣ, O, Ḳ:) and فرط alone, *he flagged,* or *was remiss; was lazy,* or *indolent:* (TA:) its second pers. sing. is used in cautioning a man against a thing before him, or in commanding him to go forward, or to advance; and is intransitive. (Ṣb, TA.) Ṣakhr-el-Ghei says,

* ذٰلِكَ بَزِّى فَلَنْ أُفَرِّطَهُ *
* أَخَافُ أَنْ يَنْجِزُوا الَّذِى وَعَدُوا *

That is my weapon, and I will not send it before, remaining behind it: [*I fear lest they perform that which they have threatened:*] or *I will not quit it, nor send it before:* or *I will not be behind it:* (TA:) or *I will not neglect it.* (ISd, TA.) And Sá'ideh Ibn-Ju-eiyeh says,

* مَعَهُ سِقَآءٌ لَا يُفَرِّطُ حَمْلَهُ *

With him is a skin, the carrying of which he will not leave, nor quit. (Ṣ.) You say also, فَرَّطْتُكَ فِى كَذَا وَكَذَا *I left thee in such and such* [a state, &c.]: (AA, O:) and مَا أَفْرَطْتُ ↓ مِنَ الْقَوْمِ أَحَدًا *I did not leave, of the people,* or *company of men, any one.* (Ks, Ṣ, O.) And فرّط فِى جَنْبِ اللّٰهِ *He neglected the things of God, and did them not:* (TA:) or *the command of God.* (O, TA.) [See also art. جنب.] And it is said in a trad., لَيْسَ فِى النَّوْمِ تَفْرِيطٌ إِنَّمَا التَّفْرِيطُ أَنْ لَا يُصَلِّىَ حَتَّى يَدْخُلَ وَقْتُ الْأُخْرَى [*There is no falling short of one's duty in sleeping: the falling short of one's duty is only the not awaking until the time of the other* (prayer) *commences*]. (TA.) — Also *He let him alone, or left him, for a while;* or *granted him a delay,* or *respite;* [and so ↓ فارطهُ; for] أَمْلَلْتُ فِرَاطَهُمْ means *I long let them alone,* or *left them,* or *granted them delay* or *respite.* (TA.) — You say also, فرّط اللّٰهُ عَنْهُ مَا يَكْرَهُ *God put away,* or *removed,* or *averted, from him what he dislikes,* or *hates:* (Kh, Ṣ, O, Ḳ:) but this expression is seldom used except in poetry. (Ṣ, O.) = فرّطهُ, (O, Ḳ,) inf. n. تَفْرِيطٌ, (TA,) also signifies *He praised him immoderately;* (O, Ḳ, TA;) like قَرَّظَهُ: (O, TA:) Ṣgh has expressed, in the TṢ, his fear that the former may be a mistranscription for the latter; but seems to have afterwards conceded the correctness of the former, from his mention of it in the O. (TA.)

3. فَارَطَهُمْ, (Ṣ, O,* Ḳ,* in the O and Ḳ فارطهُ,) inf. n. مُفَارَطَةٌ and فِرَاطٌ, (Ṣ,) *He vied,* or *strove, with them, to precede them; to outgo,* or *outstrip, them; to get before them.* (Ṣ, O,* Ḳ.*) — تَكَلَّمَ فِرَاطًا, (Ṣ, O, Mṣb, Ḳ,) the latter word being an inf. n. of فارط, (TA,) *He spoke hastily; without premeditation;* expl. by سَبَقَتْ مِنْهُ كَلِمَةٌ; (Ṣ, O, Ḳ;) *he let fall hasty,* or *unpremeditated, sayings* or *expressions;* expl. by سَقَطَ مِنْهُ بَوَادِرُ. (Mṣb.) — See also 2, in two places: — and see 6. — فارطهُ also signifies *He found him;* syn. صَادَفَهُ: (O, Ḳ, TA:) and so فالطهُ and لافطهُ. (TA.)

4: see 2, in seven places. — أَفْرَطَتْ أَوْلَادًا, (Ṣ, O,) or افترطت ↓ اولادا, (TA,) said of a woman, *She sent children before her* [*to Paradise, by their dying in infancy*]; syn. قَدَّمَتْهُمْ: (Ṣ, O, TA:) and افترط ↓ اولادا, said of a man, in like manner signifies قَدَّمَهُمْ. (TA.) And you say also, فَرَطَ ↓ وَلَدُهُ *He was preceded by his child to Paradise.* (IḲṭṭ.) And فَرَطَ ↓ وَلَدًا, (Ḳ, TA,) or وَلَدًا, (CḲ,) *He lost children by their dying young:* (Ḳ, TA;) *as though they preceded him to Paradise;* (TA;) and so افترط ↓ وَلَدًا; (Mṣb;) and افترط ↓ فَرَطًا; which also signifies *he lost a young child by death:* (TA:) or the last of these phrases, (Ḳ,) or the last but one, (Ṣ, O,) signifies *he lost his child,* or *children,* (Ḳ,) or *a young child,* (Ṣ, O,) *by death before attaining to puberty.* (Ṣ, O, Ḳ.) [See اِحْتَسَبَ.] And أُفْتُرِطَ ↓ الْوَلَدُ *The child's death was hastened;* or *was made to happen early.* (Th.) — افرطهُ *He hastened him;* or *made him to hasten.* (Ṣ, O.) And you say also, السَّحَابَةُ تُفْرِطُ الْمَآءَ † *The cloud hastens and forwards the water* in the beginning of the [autumnal rain called] وَسْمِىّ. (TA.) And افرطت السَّحَابَةُ بِالوَسْمِىِّ ‡ *The cloud hastened with the* [rain called] وَسْمِىّ. (Ṣ, O, and the like is said in the Ḳ.) And افرط بِيَدِهِ إِلَى سَيْفِهِ لِيَسْتَلَّهُ *He put his hand hastily to his sword to draw it forth.* (IAạr, O, Ḳ.) And افرط [alone] *He hastened with an affair.* (Ḳ,* TA.) And *He advanced,* or *went forward, before tarrying,* or *waiting,* or *pausing,* فِى الْأَمْرِ *in the affair.* (TA.) — افرط also [very frequently] signifies *He exceeded the due bounds,* or *just limits;* or *acted extravagantly,* or *immoderately;* (Ṣ, O, Mṣb, Ḳ, TA;) فِى الْأَمْرِ *in the affair;* (Ṣ, O, TA;) and فِى حُبِّهِ *in loving him;* and فِى بُغْضِهِ *in hating him;* (O, TA;) and فِى مَدْحِهِ *in praising him:* (Ḳ:) it is likewise said of anything exceeding the due bounds; [meaning *it was,* or *became, excessive,* or *immoderate:*] and also signifies *he did more than he was commanded.* (TA.) You say also, فَرَطَ ↓ عَلَيْهِ فِى الْقَوْلِ *He exceeded the due bounds, or just limits, towards him in speech.* (Ḳ, TA.) And افرط فِى الْقَوْلِ *He talked* [*excessively, exceedingly, immoderately,* or] *much.* (TA.) [And, افرط عَلَيْهِ *He acted insolently,* or *presumptuously, towards him.*] — Also افرط عَلَيْهِ *He loaded him* (namely a camel, IḲṭṭ) *with that which he was unable to bear.* (IḲṭṭ, Ḳ.) And افرط *He filled* (Ṣ, O, Ḳ) a مَزَادَة (Ṣ) or a قِرْبَة (O) *so that he made the water to flow:* (O, Ḳ:) or a watering-trough or vessel (TA) *so that it overflowed:* (Ḳ, TA:) and فَرَطَ ↓ فِى حَوْضِهِ, (O, TA,) aor. ـُ, (O,) inf. n. فَرْطٌ, (TA,) *he filled his watering-trough:* (O, TA:) or *poured much water into it.* (TA.) — And افرط النَّخْلَةَ *He left the palm-tree without fecundation until its spadix became dry and hard.* (O, L, Ḳ. [See 1, near the end.])

5. تفرّط *He* (a horse) *outwent,* or *got before,* other horses. (Ṣ, TA.) [See also 1.] — See also the next paragraph.

6. تفارطوا *They vied,* or *strove, one with another, to precede, outgo, outstrip,* or *get before.* (Ṣ, O.*) Bishr says, [using the verb transitively,]

يُنَازِعْنَ الأَعِنَّةَ مُصْعَبَاتٍ
كَمَا يَتَفَارَطُ الثَّمَدَ الحَمَامُ

[*They contend with the reins, being unbroken and refractory, like as the pigeons vie, one with another, in striving to get first to the scanty remains of rain-water*]. (Ṣ.) — [Hence,] تفارط فُلَانٌ *Such a one preceded,* or *got before, and made haste.* (O, Ḳ, TA.) — And hence, (TA,) تَفَارَطَتْهُ الهُمُومُ, (O, Ḳ, TA,) and الأُمُورُ, (O, TA,) † *Anxieties,* and *affairs,* or *events, came to him* [*as though*] *vying, one with another, to be first:* (Ḳ, TA:) or *befell him at an indefinite time,* (O,* Ḳ,* TA,) *but only at such a time.* (O, TA.) You say also, ↑ فَارَطَتْهُ الهُمُومُ † *Anxieties ceased not to come to him at one indefinite time after another.* (TA.) — تفارط الشَّىْءُ *The time of the thing past;* as also ↑ تفرّط, which occurs in a trad., relating to a time of prayer, and meaning *its time passed before its being performed:* (TA:) and both of these verbs are used in the sense next following in relation to a warring, or warring and plundering, expedition. (O.) *The time of the thing became postponed,* or *delayed, so that he who desired it did not attain it.* (Ḳ.) You say, تَفَارَطَتِ الصَّلَاةُ عَنْ وَقْتِهَا *The prayer became delayed after its time.* (TA.)

8: see 1, first sentence: — and see 4, in five places. — فُلَانٌ لَا يُفْتَرَطُ إِحْسَانُهُ وَبِرُّهُ (Ṣ, Ḳ*) *Such a one's beneficence and kindness are not caught at,* (لَا يُفْتَرَصُ, as in a copy of the Ṣ and in the TA,) or *do not pass away,* (لَا يَنْقَرِضُ, as in another copy of the Ṣ,) *and* (Ṣ, TA) *their passing away, so that one cannot avail himself of them, is not to be feared:* (Ṣ, Ḳ, TA:) a saying of one of the Arabs of the desert. (TA.)

فَرْطٌ *Excess; extravagance; exorbitance; an exceeding degree; an exceeding of the due bounds,* or *just limits.* (Ṣ, O, Ḳ,* TA.) You say, إِيَّاكَ وَالفَرْطَ فِى الأَمْرِ [*Avoid thou,* or *beware thou of, excess in the affair*]. (Ṣ, O.) — *Mastery, ascendency, prevalence,* or *predominance:* (Ḳ, TA:) as, for instance, of eager desire, and of grief. (TA.) = *A time, whether long or short; an indefinite time;* syn. حِينٌ. (Ṣ, O, Ḳ.) You say, لَقِيتُهُ فِى الفَرْطِ بَعْدَ الفَرْطِ *I met him time after time.* (Ṣ, O.) And أَنَا آتِيهِ الفَرْطَ *I come to him,* or *will come to him, at some time.* (TA.) — It also denotes one's meeting a man, (TA,) or coming to him, (Ḳ,) *after some days,* (Ḳ, TA,) accord. to A'Obeyd; (TA;) *not more than fifteen days,* (Ḳ,) or *than fifteen nights,* accord. to the same, (Ṣ, O,) *nor less than three.* (Ḳ.) You say, أَنَا أَلْقَاهُ فِى الفَرْطِ [*I meet him,* or *will meet him,* or *shall meet him, after some days*]. (TA.) [But the above-mentioned restriction does not apply when it is prefixed to a noun signifying a period of time: for] you say also, أَتَيْتُهُ فَرْطَ يَوْمٍ أَوْ يَوْمَيْنِ [app. meaning *I came to him after a day or two days*]. (Ṣ, O.) [It is said in the TA that, accord. to ISk, it is used in the saying آتِيكَ فَرْطَ يَوْمٍ أَوْ يَوْمَيْنِ, and that it is *a day between two days;* but this seems to me to be a mistake for *between a day and two days:* it is afterwards said in the TA that فَرْطَ يَوْمٍ أَوْ يَوْمَيْنِ means *after two days;* but the complete explanation should doubtless be *after a day or two days.*] Lebeed says,

هَلِ النَّفْسُ إِلَّا مُتْعَةٌ مُسْتَعَارَةٌ
تُعَارُ فَتَأْتِى رَبَّهَا فَرْطَ أَشْهُرِ

[*Is the soul aught but a borrowed thing to be enjoyed, which is lent, and goes to its Lord after some months?*]. (Ṣ.) And an Arab said, مَضَيْتُ فَرْطَ سَاعَةٍ وَلَمْ أُومِنْ أَنْ أَنْفَلِتَ; and being asked "What is فرط ساعة?" he answered, "Like since thou begannest to speak:" he meant [*I went away after a little while,* or *a little while ago, and*] by لم and what follows it, *I did not feel sure of my escaping.* (TA.) = Also *A small mountain;* (Ḳ;) pl., accord. to Kr, فُرُطٌ [q. v.]: (TA:) or the *head of an* [*eminence such as is termed*] أَكَمَة. (Ḳ.) — And the same, (Ḳ,) or ↑ فُرُطٌ, (thus as written in the O,) *An erect way-mark,* or *thing set up for guidance to the right way:* (O, Ḳ:) pl. أَفْرُطٌ and أَفْرَاطٌ: (Ḳ:) [but] it is said in the A that بَدَتْ لَنَا أَفْرَاطُ المَفَازَةِ is a tropical saying, signifying مَا آسْتَقْدَمَ مِنْ أَعْلَامِهَا [as though meaning ‡ *The foremost of the way-marks of the desert,* or *waterless desert, appeared to us*]. (TA.)

فُرُطٌ: see فَرْطٌ, near the end.

فَرَطٌ *A person who goes before,* or *in advance of, others, to the water,* (Ṣ, Mgh, Ḳ,) or *who is sent before,* or *in advance, to seek water,* (Mṣb,) *and who prepares for them the ropes and buckets,* (Ṣ, O, Mṣb,) *and plasters with mud* [in one copy of the Ṣ *and fills*] *the watering-troughs, and draws water for them;* (Ṣ, TA;) as also ↑ فَارِطٌ; (Ṣ, Mgh, O, Mṣb, TA;) being of the measure فَعَلٌ in the sense of the measure فَاعِلٌ, (Ṣ, Mṣb, TA,) like تَبَعٌ in the sense of تَابِعٌ: (Ṣ, TA:) and *a number of persons who perform that office;* (Ṣ, O, Mṣb, Ḳ;) as also ↑ فُرَّاطٌ, (Ṣ, Mṣb, Ḳ, TA,) pl. of فَارِطٌ: (Mṣb, TA:) you say رَجُلٌ فَرَطٌ and قَوْمٌ فَرَطٌ. (Ṣ, Mṣb.) It is said in a trad., أَنَا فَرَطُكُمْ عَلَى الحَوْضِ [*I shall be your preceder to the pool of Paradise*]. (Ṣ, O.) — See also فَارِطٌ. — [Hence,] ‡ *A child* [*that dies*] *not having attained to puberty:* (Ḳ, TA:) [whence the phrase اِفْتَرَطَ فَرَطًا: see 4:] pl. أَفْرَاطٌ: or فَرَطٌ is both sing. and pl. [in this sense]. (TA.) — Hence also, (Ṣ, Mṣb,) ‡ *A reward,* or *recompense, prepared in advance,* or *beforehand:* (Ṣ, Mgh, Mṣb, Ḳ:) and *a work,* or *an action, of the same kind.* (Ḳ.) You say, of an infant that has died, (Ṣ, Mṣb,) اَللّٰهُمَّ آجْعَلْهُ لَنَا فَرَطًا *O God, make him to be a* [*cause of*] *reward,* or *recompense, prepared in advance,* or *beforehand, for us.* (Ṣ, Mgh, Mṣb.) — [Hence also,] ‡ *Water* [*at which one arrives*] *in advance of other waters.* (Ḳ, TA.) — [Hence also,] أَفْرَاطُ الصُّبْحِ, (Ṣ, O,) or الصَّبَاحِ, (Ḳ,) ‡ *The annunciations,* or *foretokens,* (Ḳ,) or *the beginnings of the annunciations* or *foretokens,* (Ṣ, O,) *of the daybreak:* (Ṣ, O, Ḳ:) sing. فَرَطٌ. (Lth, TA.) — See also فَرْطٌ, last sentence. = Also *Haste.* (TA.) — See also the next paragraph.

فُرُطٌ *A swift* horse; (Ṣ, O, Ḳ;) one *that precedes, outgoes, outstrips,* or *gets before, others:* (Ṣ, A, O:) pl. أَفْرَاطٌ. (L, TA.) — *A case,* or *an affair, in which the due bounds,* or *just limits, are exceeded:* (Ṣ, O, Ḳ:) or *neglected;* (Ṣ,* TA;) as also ↑ فَرْطٌ: (TA:) or *despised and neglected.* (AHeyth, O, TA.) You say, كُلُّ أَمْرِ فُلَانٍ فُرُطٌ *The whole of the case of such a person is one in which the due bounds,* or *just limits, are exceeded.* (A, TA.) And it is said in the Ḳur [xviii. 27], وَكَانَ أَمْرُهُ فُرُطًا, meaning, *And whose case is one in which the due bounds,* or *just limits, are exceeded:* (Ṣ, O:) or *in which obedience is neglected and unheeded:* (TA:) or [*one of*] *preference of backwardness* (تَقْدِيمُ العَجْزِ): (Zj:) or [*one of*] *repentance:* or, accord. to some, the meaning is that which here next follows: (O, TA:) *wrongdoing; injustice; transgression:* (O, Ḳ, TA:) some say also, that it means *hastening,* or *acceleration.* (TA.) = فُرُطٌ (Ṣ, O) and ↑ فُرْطٌ (O) *An* [*eminence such as is termed*] أَكَمَة, *resembling a mountain:* (Ṣ, O:) or the second, accord. to Zbd, the *base* (سَفْح) *of a mountain:* (TA:) pl. أَفْرَاطٌ (Zbd, Ṣ, O) and أَفْرُطٌ. (O.) [See also فَرْطٌ, last sentence but one.]

فَرْطَةٌ *A single act of going forth;* (Ṣ, O, Ḳ;) and *of preceding,* or *going before.* (Ṣ, O.) — [*A hasty,* or *an unpremeditated, saying,* or *action:* pl. فَرَطَاتٌ. (See 1 and 3.)] You say, اَللّٰهُمَّ آغْفِرْ لِى فَرَطَاتِى, i. e. مَا فَرَطَ مِنِّى [meaning, *O God, forgive me my hasty,* or *unpremeditated, sayings,* or *actions*]: (TA:) [or *my acts of hastiness,* or *forwardness, and transgression:* for] الفَرْطَةُ فِى الدِّينِ [unless we should in this instance read الفُرْطَة, as the Turkish translator of the Ḳ has done,] signifies *hastiness,* or *forwardness, and transgression, in religion.* (TA.)

فُرْطَةٌ The *act of going forth;* (Ṣ, O, Ḳ;*) and *of preceding,* or *going before.* (Ṣ, O.) Hence the saying of Umm-Selemeh, to 'Áïsheh, نَهَاكِ عَنِ الفُرْطَةِ فِى البِلَادِ [*He* (referring to Moḥammad) *forbade thee from going forth into the country,* or *provinces*]. (Ṣ, O.) And فُلَانٌ ذُو فُرْطَةٍ فِى البِلَادِ *Such a one is a person who makes many journeys.* (TA.)

فِرْطِىٌّ and فُرْطِىٌّ, (Ibn-'Abbád, Ḳ,) but the latter is said in the Moḥeeṭ to be with ḍamm, [which most probably means that it is فُرُطِىٌّ, and it is thus written in the O,] (TA,) applied to a camel and to a man, *Untractable, refractory,* or *stubborn;* (Ibn-'Abbád, Ḳ;) *not rendered manageable* or *submissive.* (TA.)

فِرَاطٌ (Ṣ, O) and ▼ فُرَاطَةٌ, like ثُمَامَةٌ, or ▼ فِرَاطَةٌ, (so in the O,) Water *that is for him, of the tribes, who first arrives at it;* (Ṣ, O;) water *that is common property among a number of tribes, and is for him who first arrives at it:* (O, Ḳ:) and in like manner the latter word applied to a well. (TA.) You say, هٰذَا مَآءٌ فُرَاطَةٌ ▼ بَيْنَ بَنِى فُلَانٍ وَبَنِى فُلَانٍ, meaning, [*This is water between the sons of such a one and the sons of such a one, so that*] *whichever of them arrives at it first waters* [*his beasts*] *and the others do not throng him.* (TA.)

فُرَاطَةٌ : see فِرَاطٌ, in three places.

فَارِطٌ *Preceding; going before; being,* or *becoming, before, beforehand, first,* or *foremost; having,* or *getting, priority,* or *precedence:* pl. فُرَّاطٌ. (TA.) — See the sing. and pl. voce فَرَطٌ, first sentence. — فُرَّاطُ القَطَا *The foremost of the* [*birds called*] قطا [meaning *sand-grouse*], *who precede the others to the valley and the water.* (Ṣ, TA.) — فَارِطٌ also signifies One *who goes before to dig the grave:* pl. as above, and also فَوَارِطُ, which latter is extr., like فَوَارِسُ, pl. of فَارِسٌ, as is said in the O. (TA.) — And hence, (Lth, TA,) الفَارِطَانِ, (Lth, Ṣ, O, Ḳ,) in the A ▼ الفُرْطَانِ, (TA,) ‡ *Two stars,* (Lth, Ṣ, O, Ḳ,) *separate, each from the other,* (Lth, Ṣ, O,) *before* [*the stars in the tail of the Bear,* app. meaning *the Greater Bear, called*] بَنَاتُ نَعْشٍ, (Ḳ,) or *before the bier* (سَرِير) *of* بنات نعش: [each] being likened to the فارط who goes before a company of men to dig the grave. (Lth, O, TA.)

مُفْرَطٌ *Sent before,* or *first,* or *foremost.* (TA.) Hence the saying in the Ḳur [xvi. 64], (TA,) وَأَنَّهُمْ مُفْرَطُونَ *And that they shall be sent before,* or *first,* or *foremost,* to the fire [of Hell], *and hastened* thither; (Az, O, Ḳ, TA;) this being the primary signification: (Az, O, TA:) or *forgotten* (Mujáhid, Fr, O) in the fire [of Hell]: (Fr:) or *neglected,* or *left:* (TA:) or *forgotten, and neglected* or *left,* in the fire: and another reading is ▼ مُفْرِطُونَ, meaning [they are] *exceeding the limits assigned to them:* (O, Ḳ:) and another is ▼ مُفَرِّطُونَ, meaning [*falling short of their duty*] to themselves, in respect of sins. (TA.) — [*Filled,* or] *full;* applied to a pool of water left by a torrent. (Ṣ, TA.)

مُفْرِطٌ *Exceeding the due bounds,* or *just limits; acting extravagantly;* applied to a man: *excessive;* applied to anything; as, for instance, tallness, and shortness. (TA.) It is said in a trad. of 'Alee, ▼ لَا تَرَى الجَاهِلَ إِلَّا مُفْرِطًا أَوْ مُفَرِّطًا *Thou wilt not see the ignorant otherwise than exceeding the due bounds in what he doth or falling short of what he ought therein.* (TA.) See also مُفْرَطٌ.

مُفَرِّطٌ : see مُفْرِطٌ and مُفْرَطٌ.

مَفَارِطُ The *extremities* of a country or the like. (TA.)

فُلَانٌ مُفْتَرِطُ السِّجَالِ إِلَى العُلَى [*Such a one's emulation is foremost in attaining to eminence*]; i. e. he has precedence therein: [see 1, first sentence:] (TA:) said in praise of a man. (TA in art. رنق.)

فرطح

Q. 1. فَرْطَحَ *He made broad,* or *wide,* (Ḳ,) or *he spread out,* or *expanded,* anything: and so فَلْطَحَ. (L.) Hence, فُرْطِحَ said of a round cake of bread, *It was made broad,* or *wide:* (Ṣ, L:) said by IB to be correctly فُلْطِحَ, and to be thus in a verse as related by El-Ámidee. (TA. [But see the pass. part. n., below.])

فِرْطَاحٌ : see what follows.

رَأْسٌ مُفَرْطَحٌ *A broad,* or *wide, head;* (Ṣ, Ḳ;) as also ▼ فِرْطَاحٌ: the former is thus accord. to J; but it is [said to be] correctly مُفَلْطَحٌ, with ل: (Ḳ:) [or] both are correct; ر being a letter which replaces ل. (MF.)

فرع

1. فَرَعَ [*He,* or *it, overtopped,* or *surpassed in height* or *tallness:* this seems to be the primary signification]. It is said in a trad., يَكَادُ يَفْرَعُ النَّاسَ طُولًا (O, TA) *He is,* or *was, near to overtopping the people,* or *surpassing them in tallness.* (TA.) And one says, فَرَعَ فِى قَوْمِهِ i. e. طَالَ [app. meaning *He surpassed in tallness among his people* or *party*]; as also ▼ افرع. (TA.) And فَرَعَ القَوْمَ, (Ḳ,) or فَرَعْتُ قَوْمِى, (Ṣ, O,) inf. n. فَرْعٌ and فُرُوعٌ, † *He was,* or *became, superior to the people* or *party,* (Ḳ,) or *I was,* or *became, superior to my people* or *party,* (Ṣ, O,) *in eminence,* or *nobility,* or *in beauty,* or *goodliness.* (Ṣ, O, Ḳ.) And فَرَعَ صَاحِبَهُ † *He was,* or *became, superior to his companion; he excelled him.* (IAạr, TA in art. برع.) [See also 5.] — And فَرَعَ, (O, Ḳ,) aor. َ, (Ḳ,) inf. n. فَرْعٌ (TḲ [as is indicated in the Ḳ, and, in the former of the two senses here following, فُرُوعٌ also, said in the TA to be syn. with صُعُودٌ]), ‡ *He* (a man, O) *ascended:* and also *he descended:* thus having two contr. significations: (O, Ḳ, TA:) or, accord. to IAạr, it has the former meaning, and ▼ افرع has the latter meaning: (TA: [but see what follows:]) you say, فَرَعْتُ الجَبَلَ (Ṣ, TA) and فِى الجَبَلِ, (TA,) *I ascended the mountain;* (Ṣ, TA;) as also ▼ فَرَّعْتُهُ, (Ṣ, O,* Ḳ,*) inf. n. تَفْرِيعٌ: (Ṣ, O, Ḳ:) and فَرَّعْتُ ▼ فِى الجَبَلِ *I descended the mountain;* as also ▼ أَفْرَعْتُ فِيهِ: (Ṣ, O, Ḳ:) or, as IB says, on the authority of A'Obeyd, افرع ▼ فِى الجَبَلِ means *he ascended the mountain:* and افرع ▼ مِنْهُ *he descended it.* (TA.) — And فَرَعْتُ رَأْسَهُ بِالعَصَا, (Ṣ, O, Ḳ,* TA,*) inf. n. فَرْعٌ; (O, TA;) as also قَرَعْتُهُ, (Ṣ, O,) inf. n. قَرْعٌ; (O;) ‡ *I smote his head,* [or *assailed it, smiting,*] syn. عَلَوْتُهُ (Ṣ, O, Ḳ,* TA) بِهَا (Ḳ, TA) ضَرْبًا, (TA,) [*with the staff,* or *stick*], and بِالسَّيْفِ [*with the sword*]. (TA.) — فَرَعْتُ فَرَسِى بِاللِّجَامِ, (Ṣ, O, Ḳ,*) aor. َ, inf. n. فَرْعٌ, (Ṣ, O,) † *I pulled in my horse by the bridle and bit, to stop him.* (Ṣ, O, Ḳ.) — فَرَعْتُ بَيْنَهُمَا, (Ṣ, O,) or بَيْنَهُمْ, (Ḳ, TA,) aor. َ, inf. n. فَرْعٌ, (TA,) ‡ *I interposed,* or *intervened as a barrier,* (Ṣ, O, Ḳ, TA,) *between them two,* (Ṣ, O, TA,) or *between them,* (Ḳ, TA,) and *restrained* (Ṣ, O, Ḳ, TA) *them two,* (Ṣ, O, TA,) or *them,* and *made peace,* or *effected a reconciliation, between them:* (Ḳ, TA:) and ▼ فرّع بَيْنَ القَوْمِ, inf. n. تَفْرِيعٌ, † *He made a separation, and interposed,* or *intervened as a barrier, between the people,* or *party:* and hence the saying in a trad., كَانَ يُفَرِّعُ ▼ بَيْنَ الغَنَمِ, i. e. *He was making a separation between the sheep,* or *goats:* IAth says that Hr has mentioned it as with ق; but, he adds, Aboo-Moosà says, it is one of his mistakes. (TA.) ═ هٰذَا أَوَّلُ صَيْدٍ فَرَعَهُ means *This is the first object of the chase of which he shed,* or *has shed, the blood.* (TA. [See also 4.]) — See also 8. ═ فَرِعَ الأَرْضَ: see 4. ═ فَرِعَ, [aor. َ,] (TA,) inf. n. فَرَعٌ, (Ṣ, O, Ḳ, TA,) *He* (a man) *was,* or *became, abundant,* (TA,) or *free from deficiency,* (Ṣ, O, K,) *in respect of the hair* [*of the head*]. (Ṣ, O, Ḳ, TA.) [See أَفْرَعُ.]

2: see 1, near the middle, in two places. ═ فَرَّعْتُ مِنْ هٰذَا الأَصْلِ مَسَائِلَ, (Mṣb, Ḳ, but in the latter فَرَّعَ,) inf. n. تَفْرِيعٌ, (TA,) ‡ *I derived,* or *deduced, questions,* or *problems,* or *propositions, from this fundamental axiom* or *principle;* (Mṣb;) or *made questions to be the* فُرُوع [i. e. the *branches,* meaning *derivatives,*] *of this fundamental axiom* or *principle:* (Ḳ, TA:) a tropical phrase. (TA.) ═ See again 1, latter half, in two places. ═ And see also 4, former half, in three places.

3. فارع الرَّجُلَ *He sufficed the man; and bore,* or *took upon himself, a responsibility for him.* (TA.)

4: see 1, in five places. — You say افرع بِهِمْ meaning *He alighted at their abode* [*as a guest*]; syn. نَزَلَ. (Ḳ.) And أَفْرَعْنَا بِفُلَانٍ فَمَا أَحْمَدْنَاهُ i. e. نَزَلْنَا بِهِ [*We alighted as guests at the abode of such a one, and we did not find him to be such as should be commended*]. (Ṣ, O.) — And افرع فى لومه [app. فِى لُؤْمِهِ] i. e. اِنْحَدَرَ [as though meaning ‡ *He lowered himself in his meanness,* or *sordidness;* but I suspect it to be a mistranscription]; a tropical phrase. (TA.) ═ افرع الأَرْضَ *He went round, or about,* or *round about,* (Ṣ, O, Ḳ, TA,) or *did so much,* (Ṣ, O, TA,) *in the land,* (Ṣ, O, Ḳ, TA,) as also ▼ فَرَّعَهَا, and ▼ فرعها, (TA,) *and consequently knew its state,* or *case,* or *circumstances.* (Ṣ, O, Ḳ, TA.) ═ افرعت الإِبِلُ *The camels brought forth the* [*firstlings,* or] *first offspring* (الفَرَع). (O, Ḳ.) — And أَفْرَعُوا, (O,) or افرع القَوْمُ, (Ḳ,) *They,* (O,) or *the people,* or *party*, (Ḳ,) *were*, or *became*, *persons whose camels had brought forth the first offspring.* (O, Ḳ.) —— And افرع القَوْمُ *The people*, or *party*, *sacrificed the* فَرَع [or *firstling of a camel*, or *of a sheep* or *goat*]: (Ṣ, Mṣb:) or افرع الفَرَعَةَ *he sacrificed the* فَرَعَة, (O, Ḳ,) which signifies the same as the فَرَع; (Mgh, Mṣb;) and so ▼ استفرع الفَرَعَةَ; (O;) or [simply] ▼ استفرع; (Ḳ;) and افرع [alone]; (O;) and ▼ فرّع, (O, Ḳ,) inf. n. تَفْرِيعٌ; (Ḳ;) *he sacrificed the* فَرَع; (O, Ḳ;) whence the trad., ▼ فَرِّعُوا إِنْ شِئْتُمْ وَلٰكِنْ لَا تَذْبَحُوا غَرَاةً حَتَّى يَكْبَرَ i. e. *Slaughter ye the firstling* [*of a camel*, or *of a sheep* or *goat*], *but slaughter not one that is little, whose flesh is like glue*, [*until it be full-grown.*] (O, TA.*) —— And [hence, perhaps,] أَفْرَعْتُهُ *I made him to bleed.* (Mṣb.) And أَفْرَعَتِ الضَّبُعُ الغَنَمَ, (O, Ḳ, TA,) so says Ibn-'Abbád, (O, TA,) or فِى الغَنَمِ, so in the L, (TA,) *The hyena*, or *female hyena*, *injured*, and *made to bleed*, (O, Ḳ, TA,) or *killed*, and *injured*, (L, TA,) *the sheep* or *goats.* (O, L, Ḳ, TA.) And افرع اللِّجَامُ الفَرَسَ *The bit made the mouth of the horse to bleed.* (O, Ḳ. [See also 1, near the end.]) And افرع المَرْأَةَ, said of menstruating, *It made the woman to bleed.* (TA.) And [hence, app.,] افرع العَرُوسَ *He accomplished his want in respect of the compressing of the bride.* (AA, O, Ḳ.* [See also 8.]) —— And افرعت *She* (a woman) *saw blood on the occasion of childbirth*: (O, Ḳ:) or, as some say, *before childbirth*: (A'Obeyd, TA:) or *at the first of her menstruating*: (Ibn-'Abbád, O, Ḳ:) or *she menstruated*: (A'Obeyd, L, TA:) or *she* (a woman, or a beast,) *first saw blood when taken with the pains of parturition, or near to bringing forth*: and افرع لَهَا الدَّمُ *the blood appeared to her.* (L, TA.) ═══ And افرع *He began*, or *commenced*, discourse, or a narration; (Ḳ;) and so ▼ استفرع; (Sh, O, Ḳ, TA;) and ▼ افترع: (Sh, TA:) and likewise, as also ▼ استفرع, a thing. (Ḳ.) One says, بِئْسَ مَا أَفْرَعْتَ بِهِ *Very evil is that with which thou hast begun*, or *commenced*: (Ṣ, O:) and نِعْمَ مَا أَفْرَعْتَ [or أَفْرَعْتَ بِهِ] [*Very good is that which* [or *with which*] *thou hast begun.* (Mṣb.) And افرع سَفَرَهُ, and حَاجَتَهُ, *He began, commenced*, or *entered upon, his journey, and his needful affair.* (TA.) And افرعوا مِنْ سَفَرِهِمْ *They came*, or *arrived, from their journey when it was not the proper time for their coming.* (TA.) —— And افرعوا *They sought after herbage in its place* (انْتَجَعُوا) *among the first*, or *foremost, of the people.* (Ṣ, O, Ḳ.) ═══ افرع أَهْلَهُ, thus in all the copies of the Ḳ, expl. as meaning كَفَلَهُمْ, and likewise in the O, is a mistranscription by Ṣgh, whom the author of the Ḳ has here followed: it is correctly, افرع الوَادِى أَهْلَهُ i. e. *The valley sufficed its people*; syn. كَفَاهُمْ. (TA.) ═══ أُفْرِعَ بِسَيِّدِ بَنِى فُلَانٍ, (O, Ḳ,) with ḍamm, (Ḳ,) means *The chief of the sons of such a one was taken* (O, Ḳ, TA) *and slain.* (TA.)

5. تفرّعت أَغْصَانُ الشَّجَرِ *The branches of the trees became abundant.* (Ṣ, O, Ḳ.*) —— And [hence,] تفرّع الوَادِى † [*The valley branched forth*]. (TA.) —— [See also an ex. in a verse cited voce فَظِيعٌ.] —— تَفَرَّعَتْ مِنْ هٰذَا الأَصْلِ مَسَائِلُ (O, Mṣb, Ḳ, TA) ‡ *Questions*, or *problems*, or *propositions, were derived*, or *deduced, from this fundamental axiom* or *principle*; (Mṣb;) or *were made to be the* فُرُوع [i. e. the *branches*, meaning *derivatives*,] *thereof*; (Ḳ, TA;) [*they ramified therefrom*;] is a tropical phrase. (TA.) ═══ تفرّعهم ‡ *He set upon them* (O, Ḳ, TA) *with reviling* and *the like*; as in the A and L: (TA:) and *he was*, or *became, superior to them*, (O, Ḳ, TA,) *in eminence*, or *nobility*; and *excelled them*: (TA: [see also 1:]) or it signifies, (Ṣ, Ḳ, TA,) or signifies also, (O,) ‡ *he married*, or *took to wife, the chief of their women*, (Ṣ, O, Ḳ, TA,) *and the highest of them*: (TA:) and تَفَرَّعْتُ بَنِى فُلَانٍ ‡ *I married among the noble and high of the sons of such a one*; like تَنَصَّيْتُهُمْ and تَذَرَّيْتُهُمْ. (TA.)

8. افترع: see 4, latter half. —— Hence, (TA,) *He devirginated* a maid; (Ṣ, O, Mṣb, Ḳ, TA;) as also ▼ فَرَعَهَا. (Ḳ.) —— And hence, افترع قَصِيدَةَ كَذَا ‡ [*He broached such an ode*], and مَعَانِىَ كَذَا [*such meanings*]: (Ḥar p. 61:) and يَفْتَرِعُ أَبْكَارَ المَعَانِى ‡ [*He broaches virgin meanings*]. (TA, and Ḥar ubi suprà.)

10: see 4, former half, in two places: ═══ and the same again, latter half, in two places.

فَرْعٌ The *upper*, or *uppermost, part* of anything; (Ṣ, O, Mṣb, Ḳ;) the فرع being *what branches forth* (يَتَفَرَّعُ) *from the lower*, or *lowest, part* thereof: (Mṣb:) pl. فُرُوعٌ only. (TA.) It is said in a trad. أَىُّ الشَّجَرِ أَبْعَدُ مِنَ الخَارِفِ قَالُوا فَرْعُهَا قَالَ وَكَذٰلِكَ الصَّفُّ الأَوَّلُ [*What part of trees is furthest from the plucker of the fruit? they said, The uppermost part thereof; he said, And such like is the first row* of the persons worshipping in the mosque]. (TA.) Thus فَرْعُ الأُذُنِ signifies *The upper*, or *uppermost, part of the ear*; (Ḳ,* MF, TA;) pl. as above. (TA.) And فُرُوعُ المُقْلَتَيْنِ *The upper*, or *uppermost, parts of the two eyeballs.* (TA.) —— [Hence,] *A branch of a tree* or *plant*: (KL, TA:) or the *head of a branch*: or *a great branch*: and *a branch of anything.* (MA.) —— [And hence, † *A branch*, or *subdivision*, or *derivative*, of anything that is regarded as a fundamental or a whole;] *a thing that is built*, or *founded, upon another thing*; opposed to أَصْلٌ: (Ḳ, TA:) [the pl. فُرُوعٌ, as opposed to أُصُولٌ meaning "fundamentals," signifies, in the conventional language of the lawyers and the men of science in general, the *derivative institutes of the law*, &c.: see 2:] عِلْمُ الفُرُوعِ [*the science of the derivative institutes of the law*] is what is commonly known by the appellation of عِلْمُ الفِقْهِ [*the science of jurisprudence*; because it is mainly concerned with institutes derived from fundamentals]. (Ḥájjee Khaleefeh.) —— And ‡ The *hair* of a woman: pl. as above [app. used in a collective sense like the French "cheveux"]: (Ḳ, TA:) one says اِمْرَأَةٌ طَوِيلَةُ الفُرُوعِ [meaning ‡ *A long-haired woman*]. (TA.) And (Ḳ) ‡ *Full* [or *abundant*] *hair.* (Ṣ, O, Ḳ, TA.) —— And ‡ The *noble*, or *man of eminence*, of a people or party: (Ṣ, O, Ḳ, TA:) pl. as above: (TA:) one says, هُوَ فَرْعُ قَوْمِهِ ‡ *He is the noble, or man of eminence, of his people* or *party*, (Ṣ, O, TA,*) and مِنْ فُرُوعِهِمْ *of their nobles*, &c. (TA.) —— And [app. from the same word as signifying "a branch of a tree,"] † *A valley branching off.* (TA.) And † *A channel in which water runs to the* شِعْب (Ḳ, TA) i. e. the وَادِى [here meaning the *water-course in a low tract* or *between the two acclivities of two mountains*]: (TA:) [but] in this sense its pl. is فِرَاعٌ. (Ḳ, TA.) ═══ Also [or قَوْسٌ فَرْعٌ] *A bow that is made from the extreme portion of a branch*, (Aṣ, Ṣ, O, Ḳ, TA,) *from the head thereof*: (Aṣ, TA:) and (Ḳ) *a bow that is not* [*made from a branch*] *divided lengthwise* (Ṣ, O, Ḳ, TA) is called قَوْسٌ فَرْعٌ; (Ṣ, O, TA;) such as is [made from a branch] divided lengthwise being called قَوْسٌ فِلْقٌ: (Ṣ, O:) or the فرع is [*one*] *of the best of bows*: (AḤn, Ḳ, TA:) and [this word is used as an epithet, i. e.] one says قَوْسٌ فَرْعٌ and فَرْعَةٌ. (Ḳ.) ═══ Also, i. e. فَرْعٌ, *Property that is beneficial*, or *serviceable, and made ready*, or *prepared*: (O, Ḳ, TA:) or, accord. to the Ṣ, it is ▼ فَرَعٌ which has this signification; but this is said by Ṣgh [app. in the TṢ], and after him by the author of the Ḳ, to be a mistake; and a verse in which it occurs with the ر quiescent is cited in the O and Ḳ as an ex. of it in this sense: it may be, however, that the poet has made the ر quiescent of necessity [by poetic license, for the sake of the metre]; or it may here [properly] signify "a branch," and be metonymically used as meaning *recent property.* (TA.) ═══ See also the next paragraph, latter half.

فَرَعٌ The *firstling of the camel*, (Ṣ, Mgh, O, Mṣb, Ḳ,) or *of the sheep or goat*, (L, Ḳ,) *which they used to sacrifice to their gods*, (Ṣ, Mgh, O, Mṣb, Ḳ,) *looking for a blessing thereby*; (Ṣ, O, Mṣb;) and ▼ فَرَعَةٌ signifies the same: (Mgh, Mṣb:) hence, (Mgh, O, Ḳ,) it is said in a trad., [implying the prohibition of this custom,] لَا فَرَعَ وَلَا عَتِيرَةَ, (Ṣ, O, Ḳ,*) or لَا فَرَعَةَ ▼ وَلَا عَتِيرَةَ: (Mgh: [see عَتِيرَةٌ:]) or *when the camels amounted to the number for which their owner wished, they sacrificed* [*a firstling*]: (TA:) or when one's camels amounted to a complete hundred, (Ḳ, TA,) he sacrificed a he-camel thereof every year, and gave it to the people to eat, neither he nor his family tasting it, or rather, it is said, (TA,) he sacrificed a young, or youthful, he-camel to his idol: and the Muslims used to do it in the first part of El-Islám: then it was abrogated: (Ḳ, TA:) accord. to the Bári' and the Mj, *the firstling of camels* and also *that of sheep* or *goats* are thus called: (Mṣb:) the pl. [of فَرَعٌ] is فُرُوعٌ, with two ḍammehs. (Ḳ.) It is said in a prov., أَوَّلُ الصَّيْدِ فَرَعٌ [*The first of what are taken by the chase* or *the like is a* فرع] as being likened to a firstling: so says Yezeed Ibn-Murrah. (TA. [See Freytag's Arab. Prov., i. 35.]) — The poet Ows Ibn-Ḥajar, (Ṣ, O,) or Bishr Ibn-Abee-Kházim, has used it as meaning The *skin of a* فرع; (Ṣ, O;*) suppressing the prefix جِلْد: (Ṣ:) for they used to clothe with its skin another young one of a camel, in order that the mother of the one sacrificed might incline to it [and yield her milk]. (O; and the like is said in the TA.) ═ Also, and ♦ فَرْعٌ, *Lice:* (Ṣ, Ḳ:) or, as some say, *small lice:* (TA:) and *one thereof* is termed ♦ فَرْعَةٌ and ♦ فَرَعَةٌ: (Ṣ, Ḳ:) or, accord. to some, فرعة signifies *a large louse.* (TA.) ═ And the former (فَرْعٌ), *Food that is prepared* [app. *for persons invited to partake of it*] *on the occasion of camels' bringing forth;* like as خُرْسٌ signifies such as is on the occasion of a woman's bringing forth. (TA.) — And *A portion,* or *share;* syn. قِسْمٌ: (O, Ḳ, TA:) accord. to some, peculiarly *of water.* (TA.) — See also فَرْعٌ, last quarter. ═ It is also the inf. n. of فَرِعَ. (TA. [See 1, last sentence.])

فَرْعَةٌ *A high,* or *an elevated, place* of a mountain: pl. فِرَاعٌ: so in the saying, اِيتِ فَرْعَةً مِنْ فِرَاعِ الجَبَلِ فَانْزِلْهَا [*Come thou to one of the high places of the mountain and descend it*]: (Ṣ, TA:) or, as some say, it signifies particularly the *head* of a mountain. (TA. [See also فَارِعَةٌ.]) — And فَرْعَةُ الجُلَّةِ *The highest,* or *uppermost, of the dates of the* [*receptacle called*] جُلَّة [q. v.]. (TA.) — And فرعة الطريق [i. e. فَرْعَةُ الطَّرِيقِ] and فرعته [sic, app. ♦ فَرَعَتُهُ,] and ♦ فَرْعَاؤُهُ and ♦ فَارِعَتُهُ all signify *The highest part of the road,* and *the place where it ends:* or *the conspicuous and elevated part thereof:* or ♦ فَارِعَتُهُ signifies *the sides,* or *borders, thereof.* (TA. [See also فَارِعَةُ الطَّرِيقِ.]) — And one says, أَتَيْتُهُ فِى فَرْعَةٍ مِنَ النَّهَارِ ‡ *I came to him in a first part of the day.* (TA.) ═ See also فَرْعٌ, latter half.

فُرْعَةٌ The *blood of the virgin on the occasion of devirgination.*

فَرَعَةٌ: see فَرْعَةٌ. ═ [Also] *A piece of skin that is added in the* قِرْبَة [or *water-skin*] *when the latter is not full-sized,* or *complete.* (O, Ḳ.) ═ See also فَرْعٌ, first quarter, in two places: ═ and the same again, latter half, in one place. ═ It is also a pl. of فَارِعٌ [q. v.]. (O, Ḳ.)

فُرُوعُ الجَوْزَآءِ means *The most intense degree of heat:* (Ṣ, O, TA:) [or rather الفُرُوعُ is a name of *a certain asterism of* الجَوْزَآء (which is an appellation of *Orion* and of *Gemini,* either whereof may be here appropriately meant,) *at the season of the auroral rising of which the heat becomes most intense:*] Aboo-Khirásh says,

وَظَلَّ لَهَا يَوْمٌ كَأَنَّ أُوَارَهُ
ذَكَا النَّارِ مِنْ نَجْمِ الفُرُوعِ طَوِيلُ

[*And a day continued to them, the heat whereof was as though it were the blazing of fire, from the asterism of the* فُرُوع; *a long* day]: (Ṣ,* O, TA:) in the Ṣ, وَظَلَّ لَنَا; but correctly لَهَا, meaning to the she-asses: (TA:) and Aboo-Sa'eed related it as above with the unpointed ع in الفروع: (Ṣ,* TA:) in the same manner, also, it is expl. by him as used in the phrase فَيْحُ نَجْمِ الفُرُوعِ [which I would render *the vehement raging* of the heat *of the asterism of the* فروع] in a verse of Umeiyeh Ibn-Abee-'Áïdh: El-Jumaḥee related it differently, with غ; but the فُرُوغ [or rather the فَرْغَانِ] are of the stars of Aquarius; and the season thereof [i. e. of their auroral rising] is cold; there is then no فيح. (TA.)

فُرَيْعٌ, occurring [with tenween, perfectly decl.,] in a verse of Umeiyeh Ibn-Abi-ṣ-Ṣalt, (O, Ḳ,) *i. q.* ♦ فِرْعَوْنُ, (O,) which is a proper name of such as was King of the Amalekites [or rather of the ancient Egyptians, in general], like as قَيْصَر was of the Room [or Greeks of the Lower Empire], and كِسْرَى of the Persians, (Ksh in ii. 46,) [and also] a foreign word, (Mṣb,) [wherefore it is imperfectly decl., in Hebr. פַּרְעֹה, i. e. *Pharaoh,*] a dial. var. of فِرْعَوْنُ, or used by poetic license: (Ḳ:) the pl. of the latter is فَرَاعِنَةٌ. (Mṣb.)

فُرْعُونٌ: see the next preceding paragraph.

فَارِعٌ [*Overtopping,* or *surpassing in height* or *tallness:* this seems to be the primary signification]. You say جَبَلٌ فَارِعٌ *A mountain higher,* or *taller, than what is next to it.* (Ṣ, O.) — And *High,* or *tall;* applied to a man, and to an extended gibbous piece of sand. (TA.) — And *High,* or *elevated; goodly in form* or *aspect* or *appearance; beautiful:* (Aboo-'Adnán, O, Ḳ:) or [simply] *high* [app. *in rank* or *dignity*]: (IAṭr, O:) and also *low, ignoble,* or *mean:* (IAṭr, O, Ḳ:) thus having two contr. significations. (O, Ḳ.) — And a man of the Arabs said, لَقِيتُ فُلَانًا فَارِعًا مُفْرِعًا ♦, meaning [*I met such a one*] one of us *ascending* and the other *descending.* (Ṣ, O, TA.) ═ Also sing. of فَرَعَةٌ, which signifies The *armed attendants,* or *guards, of the Sultán,* or *sovereign:* (O, Ḳ, TA:) it is like وَازِعٌ. (TA.)

فَارِعَةٌ The *higher,* or *highest, part* of a mountain [and of a valley]: one says, اِنْزِلْ بِفَارِعَةِ الوَادِى وَاحْذَرْ أَسْفَلَهُ [*Alight thou in the higher,* or *highest, part of the valley, and beware of its lower,* or *lowest, part*]. (Ṣ, O.) See also فَرْعَةٌ, in two places. — الفَارِعَةُ مِنَ الغَنَائِمِ means *The surplus that is deducted* [so I render المُرْتَفِعَةُ الصَّاعِدَةُ, app. *such things as cannot be divided and are therefore removed,*] *from the main stock of the spoils before they are divided into fifths.* (TA.) — And فَوَارِعُ, (pl. of فَارِعَةٌ, TA,) applied to تِلَاع, [a word variously explained, here, I think, used as signifying either high, or low, grounds, (see its sing. تَلْعَةٌ,)] (Ṣ, O,* Ḳ,*) means *Of which the channels wherein the torrents flow are in high,* or *elevated, parts.* (Ṣ, O, Ḳ.)

فَيْفَرَعٌ (Ḳ, TA) and فَيْفَرُوعٌ (TA) *A species of trees.* (Ḳ, TA.)

أَفْرَعُ *Free from deficiency in the hair* [*of the head*]; (Ṣ, O, Ḳ;) *contr. of* أَصْلَعُ; (IDrd, Ṣ, O, Ḳ;) used only in this sense; not applied to a man who is large in the beard or in the whole head of hair: (IDrd, Ṣ, O:) the Prophet was أَفْرَع, (Ṣ, O,) and so was Aboo-Bekr, (O, Ḳ,) and 'Omar was أَصْلَع: (O:) fem. فَرْعَآءُ; (Ṣ, O, Ḳ;) accord. to IDrd, applied to a woman as meaning *having much hair:* (Ṣ, O:) pl. فُرْعَانٌ, (O, Ḳ,) like its contr. صُلْعَانٌ; (O;) and also فُرْعٌ. (Ḳ.) 'Omar, being asked, "Are the صُلْعَان better or the فُرْعَان," said "The فرعان are better," meaning to assert the superior excellence of Aboo-Bekr over himself. (O.) — فَرْعَآءُ الطَّرِيقِ: see فَرْعَةٌ. ═ Also *i. q.* مُوَسْوَسٌ [app. as meaning *Such as is subject to diabolical promptings* or *suggestions*]: so in the trad., لَا يَؤُمَّنَّكُمُ الأَفْرَعُ [*The* افرع *shall by no means act as your Imám*]. (Nh, Ḳ, TA.)

مُفْرَعٌ Anything *tall.* (TA.) — مُفْرَعُ الكَتِفِ A man *broad in the shoulder-blades:* (Ṣ, O, TA:) or *high therein.* (TA.) And كَتِفٌ مُفْرَعَةٌ *A shoulder-blade high, projecting, and broad.* (TA.)

مُفْرِعٌ: see فَارِعٌ, last sentence but one.

مِفْرَعٌ *One who interposes as a restrainer between persons* [*at variance*], (O, Ḳ, TA,) *and makes peace,* or *effects a reconciliation, between them:* (TA:) pl. مَفَارِعُ. (Ṣ, O, Ḳ.)

فرعن

Q. 2. تَفَرْعَنَ *He* (a man, TA) *affected the nature,* or *disposition, of the* فَرَاعِنَة [pl. of فِرْعَوْنُ, and here meaning *such as are inordinately proud* or *corrupt* or *unbelieving,* &c., *as were the Pharaohs*]. (Ṣ,* Ḳ, TA.)

فَرْعَنَةٌ *Cunning;* i. e. *intelligence,* or *sagacity;* or *intelligence mixed with craft and forecast;* (Ṣ, Ḳ, TA;) and *pride, haughtiness,* or *insolence* (TA.)

فِرْعَوْنُ [*Pharaoh;*] *the surname of El-Weleed Ibn-Muṣ'ab, king of Egypt:* (Ṣ:) or *the surname of every king of Egypt:* (Ḳ:) or it signifies, (Ḳ,) or signifies also, (Ṣ,) [app. used as a proper name,] *anyone inordinately proud* or *corrupt* or *unbelieving;* (Ṣ, Ḳ;) *insolent and audacious in acts of rebellion* or *disobedience,* or *extravagant therein and in wrongdoing:* as also فِرْعَوْنٌ and فُرْعُوْنٌ; (Ḳ;) the last mentioned by IKh, from Fr, and anomalous: (TA:) pl. فَرَاعِنَةٌ. (Mṣb, Ḳ, TA.) It is said in a trad., أَحَدُنَا فِرْعَوْنُ هٰذِهِ الأُمَّةِ [app. meaning *One of us is the Pharaoh of this people,* or *nation*]. (Ṣ: in one of my copies of the Ṣ, أحدنا and فُرْعُوْنُ.) — And [it is said that] الفِرْعَوْنُ signifies *The crocodile,* (Ḳ, TA,) in the language of the Copts. (TA.)

الدُّرُوعُ الفِرْعَوْنِيَّةُ *Certain coats of mail so called in relation to the* فِرْعَوْن [or *Pharaoh*] *of Moses.* (Sh, TA.)

فرغ

1. فَرَغَ, [aor. ـُ; and app. فَرِغَ, aor. ـَ and ـُ, as below; inf. n. فُرُوغٌ and فَرَاغٌ; or, accord. to some, the latter is a simple subst., but it is more commonly used than the former;] said of a thing, *It was,* or *became, empty, vacant, void, devoid, destitute,* or *unoccupied;* syn. خَلَا. (Mṣb.) [You say, فَرَغَ مِنْ كَذَا *It was,* or *became, empty, vacant, void, devoid,* or *destitute, of such a thing;* or *unoccupied thereby.*] And فَرَغَ لَكَ الشَّىْءُ [*The thing was,* or *became, vacant,* or *unoccupied, for thee;* as though it were a place, or a vessel: and hence, *the thing was,* or *became, exclusively for thee*]. (TA voce خَلَا.) — [Hence,] فَرَغَ (O,* Ḳ,* TA) said of a man, (TA,) [and app. فَرِغَ also, as below,] inf. n. فُرُوغٌ, ‡ *He died;* (O, Ḳ, TA;) because his body became devoid of his soul, or spirit. (TA.) — And فَرَغَ مِنَ الشُّغْلِ, (Ṣ, O, Mṣb, Ḳ,*) aor. ـُ, inf. n. فُرُوغٌ (Ṣ, O, Mṣb, Ḳ) and [more commonly] فَرَاغٌ, (Ṣ, O, Ḳ,) or the latter is a simple subst.; (Mṣb;) and فَرَغَ, aor. ـَ, (O, Ḳ,) mentioned by Yoo; (O;) and فَرِغَ, aor. ـَ, (O, Mṣb, Ḳ,) of the dial. of Temeem; (Mṣb;) and فَرِغَ, aor. ـُ, a compound of two dial. vars.; (O, Mṣb;) *He was,* or *became, vacant from, devoid of,* or *free from, business, occupation,* or *employment; unoccupied, unemployed,* or *at leisure.* (Ḳ,* TA.) [See also 5.] — [And hence, فَرَغَ مِنَ الأَمْرِ *He ceased from, ended,* or *finished, the affair.*] — And فَرَغَ لَهُ and إِلَيْهِ, (O, Mṣb, Ḳ, TA,) aor. ـُ and ـَ; (TA;) and فَرِغَ, (O,* Mṣb, Ḳ,* TA,) aor. ـَ; inf. n. فُرُوغٌ and [more commonly] فَرَاغٌ; (TA;) *He made him,* or *it, his object,* or *the object to which he directed himself;* syn. قَصَدَ: (O, Mṣb, Ḳ, TA:) [or *he made him,* or *it, his exclusive object;* agreeably with an explanation of the phrase here following]: whence, in the Ḳur [lv. 31], سَنَفْرُغُ لَكُمْ *We will make you our object;* expl. by IAạr as meaning سَنَعْمِدُ [which is syn. with سَنَقْصِدُ]; (TA;) and some read سَنَفْرَغُ; (O, TA;) and some, سَنِفْرَغُ; (O;)

and some, سَنِفْرِغُ, asserting that Temeem say نِعْلِمُ; (O, TA;) and some, سَنَفْرُغُ إِلَيْكُمْ, meaning سَنَقْصِدُ; or سَنَفْرُغُ لَكُمْ means *We will apply ourself exclusively* (سَنَتَجَرَّدُ) *to* the reckoning with, and the requiting of, *you;* and it is said to be a threat; (Bḍ;) a metaphorical phrase, from a man's saying to him whom he threatens, سَأَفْرُغُ لَكَ, (Ksh, Bḍ,) meaning *I will apply myself exclusively to* the making an assault upon *thee:* (Ksh:) one says [also] in threatening, لَأَفْرُغَنَّ لَكَ [meaning in like manner *I will assuredly apply myself* &c.]. (TA.) [See, again, 5.] — فَرِغَ المَآءُ, (Ṣ, O, Ḳ,) aor. ـَ, (Ṣ, Ḳ,) inf. n. فَرَاغٌ, (Ṣ, TA,) *The water poured out* or *forth,* or *became poured out* or *forth.* (Ṣ, O, Ḳ.) = فَرُغَ, [aor. ـُ,] inf. n. فَرَاغَةٌ, ‡ *He* (a horse) *was easy,* or *good, and quick, in pace, and wide in step.* (TA.) — فَرُغَتِ الضَّرْبَةُ ‡ *The* [*wound made by a*] *stroke,* or *blow, was wide;* (O, Ḳ, TA;) likened to the فَرْغ of the leathern bucket. (TA.) — And فَرَاغَةٌ (as an inf. n. of which the verb is فَرُغَ, TḲ) signifies The *being impatient, and disquieted* or *disturbed* or *agitated.* (O, Ḳ.) = فَرَغَ as trans.: see 4.

2. فَرَّغْتُهُ *I made it empty, vacant, void, devoid, destitute,* or *unoccupied;* as also ↓ أَفْرَغْتُهُ. (Mṣb.) تَفْرِيغُ الظُّرُوفِ signifies *The making the receptacles empty.* (Ṣ, O, Ḳ.) And some read [in the Ḳur xxxiv. 22], حَتَّى إِذَا فُرِغَ عَنْ قُلُوبِهِمْ, (O, TA,) expl. as meaning *Until, when their hearts shall be made void of fear,* or *fright:* or, accord. to IJ, فُرِغَ and فُزِّعَ and ٱفْرَنْقَعَ [which are all mentioned as readings in the same passage] have one meaning. (TA. [See 2 in art. فزع.]) — [Hence one says, فَرَّغَهُ لِكَذَا *He made him to be,* or *become,* or *he left him, vacant from, devoid of,* or *free from, business, occupation,* or *employment;* or *made him to be unoccupied, unemployed,* or *at leisure; so that he might apply himself exclusively to such a thing.*] — See also the next paragraph.

4: see 2, first sentence. — افرغهُ, (Ṣ, O, Ḳ,) inf. n. إِفْرَاغٌ and مُفْرَغٌ, (O,) signifies [also] *He poured it out,* or *forth;* (Ṣ, O, Ḳ;) namely, water [&c.]; (Ṣ;) as also ↓ فَرَّغَهُ, (Ṣ, O, Ḳ,) inf. n. تَفْرِيغٌ; (Ṣ, O;) and افرغ likewise signifies *he poured forth* blood; (Ṣ, O, Ḳ;) and ↓ فَرَغَ عَلَيْهِ المَآءَ, meaning *he poured out,* or *forth, upon him, the water,* is mentioned by Th, who has cited as an ex.,

• فَرَغْنَ الهَوَى فِى القَلْبِ ثُمَّ سَقَيْنَهُ •
• صُبَابَاتِ مَآءِ الحُزْنِ بِالأَعْيُنِ النُّجْلِ •

[*They* (referring to women) *poured desirous love into the heart; then they gave him to drink the remains of the water of grief,* by looking *with the wide eyes:* but perhaps فَرَغْنَ is here used for فَرَّغْنَ, by poetic license, for the sake of the metre]: (TA:) إِفْرَاغَةٌ signifies *A single act of* إِفْرَاغ; and hence the trad. كَانَ يُفْرِغُ عَلَى رَأْسِهِ ثَلَاثَ إِفْرَاغَاتٍ [*He used to pour upon his head three pourings*]. (TA.) — [Hence,] رَبَّنَا أَفْرِغْ عَلَيْنَا صَبْرًا, in the Ḳur [ii. 251 and vii. 123], means ‡ *O our Lord, pour forth upon us patience,* like as [the water of] the leathern bucket is poured forth: (O, TA:) or *send down upon us patience* (Mṣb,* TA) *that shall envelop us:* (TA:) or أَفْرَغَ ٱللّٰهُ عَلَيْهِ الصَّبْرَ means † *God inspired him with patience.* (Mṣb in art. ربط.) — [Hence, also,] أَفْرَغَ عَلَيْهِ ذَنُوبًا [lit. *He poured forth upon him a bucketful of water*] means ‡ *he talked with him of that in consequence of which he was confounded,* or *perplexed, by shame.* (TA.) — افرغ also signifies *He poured* metal, such as gold and silver &c., *in a molten state, into a mould.* (TA.) And *He cast* a thing, i. e. *formed it by pouring molten metal into a mould.* (Mṣb. [See its pass. part. n., مُفْرَغٌ.]) — And افرغ عِنْدَ الجِمَاعِ *He poured forth his* مَآء [or *sperma*] *on the occasion of* جماع. (TA.)

5. تفرّغ *He was,* or *became,* or *he made himself to be, vacant from, devoid of,* or *free from, business, occupation,* or *employment; unoccupied, unemployed,* or *at leisure;* syn. تَخَلَّى مِنَ الشُّغْلِ. (O, Ḳ.) [See also فَرَغَ مِنَ الشُّغْلِ.] Hence the trad. of the Prophet, تَفَرَّغُوا مِنْ هُمُومِ الدُّنْيَا مَا ٱسْتَطَعْتُمْ [*Be ye,* or *make yourselves to be, vacant,* or *free, from the anxieties of the present state of existence as much as ye are able*]. (O.) — And تَفَرَّغْتُ لِكَذَا [*I was,* or *became,* or *I made myself to be, vacant,* or *free, from business, occupation,* or *employment;* or *unoccupied, unemployed,* or *at leisure; for such a thing:* and *I applied myself exclusively to such a thing*]: (Ṣ: [these meanings are there indicated, but not expressed; and are well known:]) one says, تفرّغ لِلْعِبَادَةِ [*He applied himself exclusively to religious service*]: (Mṣb in art. بتل:) and تَفَرَّغْتُ لِلْأَمْرِ means [also, simply,] تَصَدَّيْتُ لَهُ [i. e. *I addressed,* or *applied,* or *directed, myself,* or *my regard,* or *attention,* or *mind, to the affair*]. (Mṣb in art. صد.) [See also فَرَغَ لَهُ and إِلَيْهِ.] — And تفرّغ بِهِ signifies تَخَلَّى بِهِ [meaning *He confined himself exclusively to it;* or *contented himself with it exclusively of other things*]. (Ḳ and TA in art. خلو.)

8. اِفْتَرَغْتُ *I poured forth upon myself* (Ṣ, O) water: (Ṣ:) [and so افترغت عَلَى نَفْسِى; for one says,] رَأَيْتُهُ يَغْتَرِفُ المَآءَ ثُمَّ يَفْتَرِغُهُ عَلَى نَفْسِهِ [*I saw him taking,* or *lading out, the water; then pouring it forth upon himself*]. (A, TA.) And اِفْتَرَغْتُ لِنَفْسِى مَآءً *I poured out for myself water.* (O, Ḳ.)

10. استفرغ [*He drew forth* water &c.]. One says, استفرغ مَا فِى الرَّاوِيَةِ مِنَ المَآءِ [*He drew forth what was in the leathern water-bag,* or *pair of leathern water-bags, of water*]. (TA in art. عزل.) El-Akhṭal said respecting Esh-Shaạbee, meaning to denote the largeness of the latter's retentive faculty, أَنَا أَسْتَفْرِغُ مِنْ إِنَآءٍ وَاحِدٍ وَهُوَ يَسْتَفْرِغُ مِنْ أَوَانِى شَتَّى ‡ [*I draw from one vessel, and he*

draws from divers vessels]. (TA.) —— Also *He vomited intentionally*; or *constrained himself to vomit*: (O, Ḳ:) thus it signifies in the conventional language of the physicians. (O.) —— اِسْتَفْرَغَ فُلَانٌ مَا فِى صَحْفَتِهِ is a prov., meaning *Such a one* [*exhausted*, or] *chose for himself, as his share,* [*the whole of*] *what was in his* صحفة [or *large bowl*]. (TA in art. صحف.) —— And one says, اِستفرغ فُلَانٌ مَجْهُودَهُ ‡ *Such a one exhausted his power*, or *ability*; or *exerted it unsparingly*, or *to the utmost*; (Ṣ,* O, Mṣb,* Ḳ,* TA;) فِى كَذَا [*in such a thing*]. (Ṣ, TA.)

فَرْغٌ *Width, breadth*, or *ampleness*. (Ṣ, O, TA.) —— And The *place whence the water pours forth, between the cross-pieces of wood* (العَرَاقِى), of the leathern-bucket; (Ṣ, O, Ḳ;) as also ↓ فِرَاغٌ: (Ḳ: [expl. in the O as signifying the *side* of the leathern bucket *from which the water pours forth*:]) pl. of the former فُرُوغٌ (TA) and مَفَارِغُ, [which is anomalous, like مَشَابِهُ and مَحَاسِنُ &c.,] (A, TA,) or this is pl. of ↓ مَفْرَغٌ. (TA.) —— Hence فَرْغُ الدَّلْوِ المُقَدَّمُ and فَرْغُ الدَّلْوِ المُؤَخَّرُ, (Ṣ, O,) الفَرْغَانِ, and الفَرْغُ الأَوَّلُ and الفَرْغُ الثَّانِى, (Ṣ, O, Ḳ,) or (Ḳzw,) *Two of the Mansions of the Moon*, (Ṣ, O, Ḳ,) *the Twenty-sixth Mansion* and *the Twenty-seventh*; *four stars, wide apart, forming the corners of a square*, or *four-sided figure*; (Ḳzw;) *each consisting of two stars*, (Ṣ, O, Ḳ, and Ḳzw,) *of two bright stars*, (Ṣ,) *the apparent distance between each two stars being the measure of five cubits*, (Ṣ, O, L,) or *the measure of a spear*; (Ḳ;) [see ذِرَاعٌ and رُمْحٌ; *the former pair consists of the stars* α *and* β *of Pegasus*; and *the latter, of* γ *in Pegasus together with the bright star in the head of Andromeda*; as is shown by what here follows:] the Arabs name الدَّلْوُ the four bright stars in Pegasus which form a square, or four-sided figure; i. e., that at the extremity of the neck, which is called مَتْنُ الفَرَسِ, and that which is called مَنْكِبُ الفَرَسِ, and that which is called جَنَاحُ الفَرَسِ, and the star that belongs to both Pegasus and Andromeda: (Ḳzw, descr. of Pegasus:) [these two pairs of stars are what are commonly known as the فَرْغَانِ; and are plainly indicated by the periods assigned to the auroral settings thereof: but the periods assigned to their auroral risings would lead us to apply the appellation of the فرغان to some other stars, not easily determinable, in Aquarius: see نَوْءٌ: and see also مَنَازِلُ القَمَرِ, in art. نزل.] The pl. الفُرُوغُ is said to be applied to *The* فَرْغَانِ *with the stars around them*: (O, TA:) and (accord. to El-Jumaḥee, O, TA) الفُرُوغُ [in the CḲ erroneously written الفَرُوغ] signifies [*The constellation called*] الجَوْزَآء. (O, Ḳ, TA. [But see فُرُوعُ الجَوْزَآءِ, in art. فرع.]) —— فَرْغٌ also signifies *A vessel in which is* [*the exuded*, or *expressed, juice termed*] دِبْسٌ, (O, Ḳ,) and صَقْرٌ. (O.) —— Also *Land affected with drought*, or *barrenness*. (IB, TA.) —— See also the next paragraph.

فِرْغٌ: see فَارِغٌ. —— ذَهَبَ دَمُهُ فِرْغًا and ↓ فَرْغًا mean *His blood went for nothing, as a thing of no account, unretaliated, and uncompensated by a mulct*, (Ṣ, O, Ḳ,) *and retaliation for it was not sought*: (Ṣ, O:) and in like manner one says, ذَهَبَتْ دِمَاؤُهُمْ فِرْغًا [*Their bloods went for nothing*, &c.]. (Z, TA.) Hence, in the Ḳur xxviii. 9, accord. to one reading, وَأَصْبَحَ فُؤَادُ أُمِّ مُوسَى فِرْغًا (Ksh and Bḍ) i. e. *And the heart*, or *mind, of the mother of Moses became* [*as though it were*] *a thing that was lost*, or *that had gone away*. (Ksh. [See فَارِغٌ.])

فُرْغٌ: see فَارِغٌ, first quarter.

فُرُغٌ i. q. مُفْرَغٌ [*Made empty, vacant, void*, &c.]: (O, TA:) so in the phrase إِنَآءٌ فُرُغٌ [*An emptied vessel*]: (TA:) and so in the saying [in the Ḳur xxviii. 9], accord. to the reading of Kh, وَأَصْبَحَ فُؤَادُ أُمِّ مُوسَى فُرُغًا [*And the heart of the mother of Moses became rendered void* of patience, or of anxiety, &c.: see فَارِغٌ]. (O, TA.) —— Applied to a bow, as also ↓ فِرَاغٌ, it means *Without a string*: or, as some say, *without an arrow*. (TA.)

فَرْغَانٌ [whether with or without tenween is not shown] A *wide*, or *capacious*, vessel. (TA.)

فَرَاغٌ [generally mentioned as an inf. n., and much used as such; but accord. to the Mṣb, a simple subst.: as a simple subst., it means *Emptiness, vacancy*, or *vacuity*, &c.: —— and *vacancy*, or *freedom*, from business, &c.; or *contr. of* شُغْلٌ, as is said in the Ḳ, in art. شغل: and *cessation* from an affair: —— &c.: see 1]. —— بَيْتُ الفَرَاغِ means *The privy*.]

فِرَاغٌ *A great bowl, that cannot be carried*: pl. أَفْرِغَةٌ. (Ibn-'Abbád, O, Ḳ.) —— *A wide*, or *capacious, large, watering-trough, of hides*. (Aṣ, O, Ḳ.) —— *A vessel* (IAạr, T, O, Ḳ) *of any kind*. (IAạr, T, O.) —— *An udder*. (O.) —— The *half of a load, such as is on either of the two sides of a camel*: (AA, O, Ḳ:) so in the dial. of Ṭeiyi. (AA, O.) —— See also فَرْغٌ, second sentence. ═══ [As a pl.,] *Valleys*, or *torrent-beds*: from IAạr, who has not mentioned a sing. thereof, nor the derivation. (TA.) —— And [probably as pl. of ↓ فَرِيغٌ, agreeably with analogy,] *Broad* نِصَال [or *arrow-heads*; the word نصال being app. understood]. (O, Ḳ.) ═══ [As a sing. epithet,] A she-camel *having no brand*, or *mark made with a hot iron*. (TA.) —— Also A she-camel *having much milk, ample in the integument of the udder*. (AZ, O, L, Ḳ.) —— And A bow *of which the arrow-head makes a wide wound*: or *of which the arrow goes far*. (O, Ḳ.) —— See also فُرُغٌ. —— And see the next paragraph, in two places.

فَرِيغٌ *Broad*, or *wide*. (TA.) See فِرَاغٌ. [Hence,] ضَرْبَةٌ فَرِيغٌ (Ṣ) or فَرِيغَةٌ (O, Ḳ) ‡ *A wide* [*wound made by a*] *stroke*, or *blow*; (Ṣ, O, Ḳ, TA;) likened to the فَرْغ of the leathern bucket: (TA:) and ↓ طَعْنَةٌ فَرْغَآءُ, likewise, signifies ‡ *a wide* [*wound made by a*] *piercing* [with a spear &c.], (Ṣ, O, Ḳ, TA,) *of which the blood flows*. (TA.) —— And ‡ A مَزَادَةٌ فَرِيغَةٌ [or leathern water-bag] *that takes in much water*; (O, Ḳ, TA;) as though having فَرْغ, i. e. width. (TA.) —— And فَرِيغٌ signifies also ‡ Land, or ground, *that is even*, or *flat, as though it were a road*, (O, Ḳ, TA,) *and wide*: (TA:) or *that is marked by much treading*: to such Aboo-Kebeer El-Hudhalee likens the whiteness of the أُثْر, i. e. فِرِنْد, of a sword. (O, TA.) ═══ And ‡ A horse *wide in step*, (Ṣ, O, Ḳ, TA,) *easy*, or *good, and quick, in pace*; as also ↓ فِرَاغٌ: (O, Ḳ, TA:) or *swift and excellent, wide in step*: or *quick in pace, wide in step*, applied to a horse or the like; and so ↓ فِرَاغٌ, applied to an ass, and likewise to a man: and, accord. to Z, فَرِيغٌ applied to an ass signifies *wide in step*. (TA.) —— Also *Sharp*, applied to an arrow, and likewise to a knife. (TA.) And † *Sharp-tongued*, applied to a man. (TA.)

فُرَاغَةٌ The *sperma of a man*. (Ṣ, ISd, Ḳ.)

فَارِغٌ *Empty, vacant, void, devoid, destitute*, or *unoccupied*; syn. خَالٍ; as in the phrase إِنَآءٌ فَارِغٌ [*an empty vessel*]: (O, TA:) and likewise applied to a man, (O, TA,*) meaning *vacant* from, *devoid* of, or *free* from, business, occupation, or employment; (K,* TA;) as also ↓ فَرِغٌ: (O, Ḳ, TA:) [and often, used elliptically, meaning *vacant from, devoid of*, or *free from, business* &c., and *care* or *anxiety* or *disquietude*; *unoccupied, unemployed*, or *at leisure*:] and ↓ أَفْرَغُ is *syn. with* فَارِغٌ; (O, Ḳ;) as in the phrase, of Ru-beh, مَا المَشْغُولُ مِثْلُ الأَفْرَغِ [*The busied is not like the free from business*]: (O, TA:) [فُرَّاغٌ is pl. of فَارِغٌ: and] ↓ فُرْغٌ is *syn. with* فُرَّاغٌ; (O, Ḳ; [in the former, as is often the case, the sign of teshdeed in this word has been carelessly omitted; and in the CḲ, الفَرْغُ is put for الفُرَّاغُ, and has been erroneously supposed to be for الفَرَاغُ;]) for ex., Ṭuleyḥah Ibn-Khuweylid El-Asadee says, in relation to the slaying of his brother's son, Ḥibál Ibn-Selemeh Ibn-Khuweylid,

• فَمَا ظَنُّكُمْ بِالقَوْمِ إِذْ تَقْتُلُونَهُمْ •
• أَلَيْسُوا وَإِنْ لَمْ يُسْلِمُوا بِرِجَالِ •
• فَإِنْ تَكُ أَذْوَادٌ أُصِبْنَ وَنِسْوَةٌ •
• فَلَنْ تَذْهَبُوا فُرْغًا بِقَتْلِ حِبَالِ •

[*And what is your opinion of the party when ye slay them? Are they not (though they have not become Muslims) men? And if some small numbers of camels have been smitten* (*and carried off*), *and some women, ye will not go away free from care by reason of the slaying of Ḥibál*]. (O, TA.) It is said in the Ḳur [xxviii. 9], وَأَصْبَحَ فُؤَادُ أُمِّ مُوسَى فَارِغًا, meaning *And the heart*, or *mind, of the mother of Moses became devoid of patience*: or *devoid of everything except remembering* of Moses: or *devoid of anxiety*; because of God's having promised to restore him to her, (O, TA,) by words in the next but one of the preceding verses. (O.) [See also another reading voce فَرِغٌ; and another, voce فُرُغٌ.] And it is said in a form of prayer, اَللّٰهُمَّ إِنِّى أَسْأَلُكَ العَيْشَ الرَّافِغَ وَالمَالَ الفَارِغَ [*O God, I ask of Thee ample*, or *abundant, and pleasant*, or *good, means of subsistence, and cattle free from labour*]. (TA.) And one says, فُلَانٌ فَارِغٌ مَشْغُولٌ, meaning † *Such a one is devoted to that which is unprofitable.* (TA in art. شغل.) And هٰذَا كَلَامٌ فَارِغٌ ‡ [*This is empty talk* or *language*]. (TA.)

أَفْرَغُ [*More*, and *most, empty* &c.: and *more*, and *most, free* from business &c.]. أَفْرَغُ مِنْ فُؤَادِ أُمِّ مُوسَى [*More void than the heart*, or *mind, of the mother of Moses*] is a prov. (Meyd. [See فَارِغٌ, latter half.]) See also another prov., voce حَجَّامٌ. — Also *i. q.* فَارِغٌ, q. v.: (O, Ḳ:) fem. فَرْغَآءُ: see فَرِيغٌ.

مُفْرَغٌ *A place of pouring out* or *forth:* (O, TA:) and [particularly] the *part* of the leathern bucket *that is next to the fore part of the watering-trough.* (TA.) See فَرْغٌ, second sentence. — Also *i. q.* سيلان [app. سَيَلَانٌ i. e. The *flowing* of water &c.; as an inf. n. of فَرَغَ said of water]. (TA.)

دِرْهَمٌ مُفْرَغٌ *A dirhem* [cast, i. e.] *poured into a mould; not* مَضْرُوبٌ [*coined* or *minted*]. (TA.) And حَلْقَةٌ مُفْرَغَةٌ *A ring that is solid* (Ṣ, O, Ḳ, TA) *in the sides* [that compose the round], (Ṣ, O,) *and* [*continuous,*] *not cut.* (TA.) One says, هُمْ كَالْحَلْقَةِ المُفْرَغَةِ لَا يُدْرَى أَيْنَ طَرَفَاهَا [*They are like the solid and continuous ring, of which it is not known where are the two ends*]: (A, TA:) a prov., applied to a company of men united in words and action. (TA in art. حلق.) — مُفْرَغٌ is also an inf. n. of أَفْرَغَهُ [q. v.]. (O.)

مُسْتَفْرِغَةٌ A she-camel *having much milk.* (O, Ḳ. [See also فِرَاغٌ.]) — And مُسْتَفْرِغٌ ‡ A horse *that does not reserve aught of his run* [i. e. *of his power of running*, for the time of need; *that exhausts his power thereof*]. (O, Ḳ, TA.)

فرفخ

فَرْفَخٌ (Ṣ, A, L, Ḳ) and ▼ فَرْفَخَةٌ, (L,) [the former app. a coll. gen. n., and the latter the n. un., *Purslane*, or *garden purslane*;] the *herb called* البَقْلَةُ الحَمْقَآءُ, (Ṣ, A, L,) *which does not grow in Nejd,* (L,) *also called* فَرْفِينٌ, (Ṣ, A,) *i. q.* رِجْلَةٌ: (Ṣ, L, Ḳ:) an arabicized word, from the Pers. پَرْپَهْن, which signifies "broad-winged." (AḤn, L, Ḳ.) — Also, the former, The كُعَابِر [which are *things that are taken forth*, or *picked out, and thrown away, in the clearing*] *of wheat.* (Ḳ.)

فَرْفَخَةٌ: see the preceding paragraph.

فرق

1. فَرَقَ بَيْنَ الشَّيْئَيْنِ, (Ṣ, Mgh, O, Mṣb, Ḳ,*) aor. ـُ, (Ṣ, Mgh, O, Mṣb,) and in one dial. ـِ, (Mṣb, TA,) inf. n. فَرْقٌ and فُرْقَانٌ, (Ṣ, O, Mṣb, Ḳ,) the latter of which has a more intensive signification, (TA,) *He made a separation*, or *a distinction*, or *difference,* (Mṣb, Ḳ, TA,) *between the two things,* (Ḳ,* TA,) or *between the parts of the two things:* (Mṣb:) relating alike to objects of sight and to objects of mental perception: (TA:) IAṣr, by exs. that he mentions, makes it to relate particularly to objects of the mind, such as sayings; and ▼ فَرَّقَ, to persons, or material things: (Mṣb: [and it is stated in the Mgh that the same distinction is mentioned by Az:]) others, however, state that the two verbs are syn.; but that the latter has an intensive signification. (Mṣb.) It is said in the Ḳur [v. 28], فَافْرُقْ بَيْنَنَا وَبَيْنَ القَوْمِ الفَاسِقِينَ [*Therefore decide Thou*, or *make Thou a distinction, between us and the unrighteous people*]: accord. to one reading, فَافْرِقْ. (Mṣb, TA.) فِيهَا يُفْرَقُ كُلُّ أَمْرٍ حَكِيمٍ, in the Ḳur [xliv. 3], means [*Wherein*] *is made distinct* [*every firm decree*]: (Lth, TA:) or *is decided;* (O, Ḳ, TA;) thus expl. by Ḳatádeh. (O, TA.) And in the phrase وَقُرْآنًا فَرَقْنَاهُ, (Ṣ, O, Ḳ, TA,) in the same [xvii. 107], (Ṣ, O, TA,) by فَرَقْنَاهُ is meant *We have made it distinct,* (Ṣ, O, Ḳ, TA,) *and rendered it free from defect,* (O, Ḳ, TA,) *and explained the ordinances therein:* (TA:) but some read ▼ فَرَّقْنَاهُ, meaning *We have sent it down in sundry portions, in a number of days.* (Ṣ, TA.) وَإِذْ فَرَقْنَا بِكُمُ البَحْرَ, (O, Ḳ, TA,) in the Ḳur [ii. 47], (O, TA,) means *And when we clave because of you the sea;* i. q. فَلَقْنَاهُ: (O, Ḳ, TA:) another reading, ▼ فَرَّقْنَا, meaning *we divided into several portions*, is mentioned by IJ; but this is unusual. (TA.) It is also said that الفَرْقُ is for rectification; and ▼ التَّفْرِيقُ, for vitiation: and IJ says that إِنَّ الَّذِينَ فَرَّقُوا ▼ دِينَهُمْ, in the Ḳur [vi. 160, and the like occurs in xxx. 31], means *Verily those who have divided their religion into sundry parts, and dismembered it, and have disagreed respecting it among themselves:* but that some read فَرَقُوا دِينَهُمْ, without teshdeed, meaning, *have severed their religion from the other religions* [app. *by taking it in part*, or *parts, therefrom*]; or this, he says, may mean the same as the former reading, for sometimes فَعَلَ has the same meaning as فَعَّلَ. (TA.) IJ also says that فَرَقَ لَهُ عَنِ الشَّىْءِ signifies *He made the thing distinct*, or *plain, to him.* (TA.) — فَرَقَ الشَّعَرَ بِالمُشْطِ, aor. ـُ and ـِ, inf. n. فَرْقٌ, *He separated his hair with the comb:* and ▼ فَرَّقَ رَأْسَهُ بِالمُشْطِ, inf. n. تَفْرِيقٌ, *He separated the hair of his head with the comb.* (TA.) [And it is implied in a trad. cited in the O and TA that فَرَّقَهُ signifies the same as the latter of the two phrases in the next preceding sentence.] — فَرَقَ لَهُ الطَّرِيقُ, (Ṣ, O, Ḳ,) inf. n. فُرُوقٌ, (Ḳ,) *The road presented itself to him divided into two roads:* (Ṣ, O, Ḳ, TA:) or [it means] *an affair presented itself*, or *occurred, to him, and he knew the mode*, or *manner, thereof:* (TA, as from the Ḳ: [but not in the CḲ nor in my MS. copy of the Ḳ:]) and hence, in a trad. of I'Ab, فَرَقَ لِى رَأْىٌ *An idea*, or *opinion, appeared* [or *occurred*] *to me:* (TA:) [or] one says, فَرَقَ لِى هٰذَا الأَمْرُ, inf. n. فُرُوقٌ, *This affair became*, or *has become, distinct, apparent*, or *manifest, to me:* and hence the saying, فَإِنْ لَمْ يَفْرُقْ لِلْإِمَامِ رَأْىٌ [*And if an idea*, or *an opinion, appear not*, or *occur not, to the Imám*]. (Mgh.) — فَرَقَتْ said of a she-camel, and of a she-ass, (Ṣ, O, Ḳ,) aor. ـُ, (Ṣ, O,) inf. n. فُرُوقٌ, *She, being taken with the pains of parturition, went away at random in the land.* (Ṣ, O, Ḳ.) — فَرَقَ, (O, Ḳ,) aor. ـُ, (Ḳ,) *He voided dung;* syn. ذَرَقَ [which is said of a bird, and sometimes of a man]. (O, Ḳ. [See also أَفْرَقَ.]) — And *He possessed a* فِرْق [q. v.] (O, Ḳ, TA) *of sheep* or *goats:* (O, TA:) accord. to the Ḳ, *of date-stones with which to feed camels:* but the former explanation is the right. (TA.) — فَرَقَهَا, (Ḳ,) inf. n. فَرْقٌ, (TA,) *He fed her* (i. e. a woman) *with* فَرِيقَة [q. v.]; as also ▼ افرقها, (Ḳ,) inf. n. إِفْرَاقٌ. (TA.) — فَارَقَنِى ▼ فَفَرَقْتُهُ, aor. ـُ, [*He vied with me in fear and*] *I exceeded him in fear.* (Lḥ, L, TA.) — See also 2, last sentence. — فَرِقَ, (Ṣ, O, Mṣb, Ḳ,) aor. ـَ, (Mṣb, Ḳ,) inf. n. فَرَقٌ, (Ṣ, O, Mṣb,) *He feared;* or *was*, or *became, in fear, afraid*, or *frightened.* (Ṣ, O, Mṣb, Ḳ.) You say, فَرِقْتُ مِنْكَ [*I feared thee*, or *was in fear of thee*]: (Ṣ, O, Mṣb:*) but you should not say, فَرِقْتُكَ: (Ṣ, O:) Sb [however] mentions فَرِقَهُ, suppressing مِنْ. (TA.) And you say also, فَرِقَ عَلَيْهِ [*He feared for him*]. (TA.) — And فَرِقَ, aor. ـَ, *He entered into a wave,* [which is termed فِرْق,] *and dived therein.* (Ḳ.) — And the same verb accord. to the Ḳ, but accord. to Ṣgh [in the O] it seems, from the context to be فَرَقَ, (TA,) *He drank* (O, Ḳ) *the measure called* فَرَق, (O,) or *with the* فَرَق. (Ḳ, TA.)

2. فرّقه, inf. n. تَفْرِيقٌ and تَفْرِقَةٌ, (Ṣ, O, Ḳ,) *He separated it* [*into several*, or *many, portions*]; *disunited it* [i. e. a thing, or a collection of things]; or *dispersed*, or *dissipated, it;* or did so *much* [or *greatly* or *widely*]; syn. بَدَّدَهُ. (Ḳ.) And فَرَّقَ بَيْنَ الأَشْيَآءِ [*He made*, or *caused, a separation* &c., or *much*, or *a wide, separation*, &c., *between the things*]. (Mgh.) [And فرّقه فِيهِمْ and عَلَيْهِمْ *He scattered*, or *distributed, it among them*, and *to them.*] See 1, former half, in five places. It is said in a trad. of 'Omar, فَرِّقُوا عَنِ المَنِيَّةِ وَاجْعَلُوا الرَّأْسَ رَأْسَيْنِ, (Mgh, O,*) meaning *Separate ye* your cattle by way of preservation *from death,* [*and make the one head two head,*] by buying two animals with the price of one, that, when one dies, the second may remain. (Mgh, O.) And it is said in a trad. respecting the poor-rate, لَا يُفَرَّقُ بَيْنَ مُجْتَمِعٍ وَلَا يُجْمَعُ بَيْنَ مُفْتَرِقٍ *There shall be no separating what is put together, nor shall*

there be a putting together what is separate. (TA. [The reason is, that by either of these acts, in the case of cattle, the amount of the poor-rate may be diminished.]) يُفَرِّقُونَ بِهِ بَيْنَ ٱلْمَرْءِ وَزَوْجِهِ [in the Ḳur ii. 96, meaning *Whereby they might dissolve, break up, discompose, derange, disorganize, disorder,* or *unsettle, the state of union subsisting between the man and his wife, in respect of affairs and of the expression of opinion,* or, briefly, *whereby they might cause division and dissension between the man and his wife,*] is from التَّفْرِيقُ as meaning تَشْتِيتُ الشَّمْلِ وَالكَلِمَةِ. (El-Iṣbahánee, TA.) One says also, فَرَّقَ الأَمْرَ, meaning شَتَّتَهُ [i. e. *He discomposed, deranged, disorganized, disordered,* or *unsettled, the state of affairs*]. (Ṣ in art. شت.) And فَرَّقَ عَلَيْنَا الكَلَامَ [lit. *He scattered speech* (app. meaning *he jabbered*) *at us,* or *against us*]. (Ḳ in art. بق: see R. Q. 1 in that art.) In the saying in the Ḳur [ii. 130 and iii. 78], لَا نُفَرِّقُ بَيْنَ أَحَدٍ مِنْهُمْ [*We will not make a distinction between any of them*], the verb is allowably made to relate to احد because this word [in negative phrases] imports a pl. meaning. (TA. [See p. 27, 3rd col.]) See, again, 1, near the middle. ═ فَرَّقَهُ, (O, TA,) inf. n. تَفْرِيقٌ, (O, Ḳ, TA,) also signifies *He made him to fear,* or *be afraid; put him in fear;* or *frightened him:* (O, Ḳ,* TA:) and ▼ أَفْرَقْتُهُ مِنْهُ *I made him to fear,* or *be afraid of, him,* or *it:* (Mṣb:) and Lḥ mentions ▼ فَرَقْتُ الصَّبِىَّ as meaning *I frightened the boy,* or *child;* but ISd says, I think it to be فَرَّقْتُ. (TA.)

3. فَارَقَهُ, inf. n. مُفَارَقَةٌ and فِرَاقٌ, (Ṣ, Mṣb, TA,) *He separated himself from him,* or *it;* or *left, forsook,* or *abandoned, him,* or *it:* or *he forsook,* or *abandoned, him, being forsaken,* or *abandoned, by him:* syn. بَايَنَهُ; (TA;) and قَاطَعَهُ, and فَارَزَهُ; (A in art. فرز;) and تَرَكَهُ. (Mṣb in art. ترك.) And فارق آمْرَأَتَهُ *He separated himself from his wife.* (TA.) — فَارَقْتُ فُلَانًا مِنْ حِسَابِى عَلَى كَذَا وَكَذَا *I released such a one from my reckoning with him on such and such terms agreed upon by both:* and so صَادَرْتُهُ عَلَى كَذَا وَكَذَا. (TA.) And فُورِقَ عَلَى مَالٍ يُؤَدِّيهِ *He* (an agent) *was released from being reckoned with on the condition of his paying certain property for which he became responsible.* (TA in art. صدر.) ═ فَارَقَنِى فَفَرَقْتُهُ: see 1, last quarter.

4. افرقوا إِبِلَهُمْ *They left their camels in the place of pasture, and did not assist them in bringing forth, nor have them got with young.* (IAạr, O, Ḳ.) — And افرق غَنَمَهُ *He made,* or *caused, his sheep,* or *goats, to stray; and neglected them,* or *caused them to become lost,* or *to perish.* (TA.) — And افرق *He lost a portion of his sheep* or *goats.* (IKh, TA.) — And *His sheep,* or *goats, became a* فِرِيقَة [q. v.]. (IKh, TA.) ═ افرق *He recovered;* (Lth, Aṣ, Az, Ṣ, O, Ḳ;) or *recovered, but not completely;* (Aṣ, O, Ḳ;) to which IKh adds, *quickly;* (TA;) i. e., a sick person from (مِنْ) his sickness; (Aṣ, Az, Ṣ, O, Ḳ;) and one fevered from his fever; (Aṣ, Ṣ;) and one smitten with the plague: (Lth, TA:) or (Ḳ) it is not said except in the case of a disease that does not attack one more than once, as the small-pox, (O, Ḳ,) and the measles. (O.) — افرقت *She* (a camel) *had a return of some of her milk.* (O, Ḳ.) ═ افرق said of a man, and of a bird, and of a beast of prey, and of a fox, *He voided dung,* or *thin dung.* (Lḥ, TA. [See also 1, last quarter.]) — And افرقهُ *He,* or *it, caused him to void dung;* syn. أَذْرَقَهُ. (Ḳ. [But I do not find اذرق mentioned except as an intrans. v.]) See also فَرَّقَهُ, last sentence. ═ افرقها: see 1, last quarter. ═ أَفْرَقْتُهُ مِنْهُ: see 2, last sentence.

5. تعرق, inf. n. تَفَرُّقٌ (O, Ḳ) and تِفِرَّاقٌ, (Ḳ, TA,) with two kesrehs, but accord. to the "Nawádir" of Lḥ تَفْرِيقٌ, (TA,) [and in the CḲ تَفْرَاق,] *It was,* or *became, separated,* or *disunited:* or *separated much,* or *greatly,* or *widely,* or *into several,* or *many, portions;* or *dispersed,* or *dissipated:* contr. of تَجَمَّعَ: and ▼ افترق signifies the same: (Ḳ, TA:) and so does ▼ انفرق: (TA:) all are quasi-pass. of فَرَّقْتُهُ: (Ṣ,* TA:) [or rather the second and third have the former of the meanings mentioned above: and تفرّق has the latter of those meanings:] or ▼ اِفْتَرَقَا is said of two sayings, as quasi-pass. of فَرَقْتُ بَيْنَهُمَا: and تَفَرَّقَا, of two men, as quasi-pass. of فَرَّقْتُ بَيْنَهُمَا: (Mgh,* Mṣb, TA:) so says IAạr: (Mṣb:) [but] one says also, افترق القَوْمُ [*The party,* or *company of men, became separated;* or *they separated themselves:*] (Mṣb:) and Esh-Sháfi'ee has used ▼ اِفْتَرَقَا as relating to two persons buying and selling; (Mṣb, TA;) and so have Aḥmad [Ibn-Ḥambal] and Aboo-Ḥaneefeh and Málik and others. (TA.) It is said in a trad., البَيِّعَانِ بِالخِيَارِ مَا لَمْ يَتَفَرَّقَا i. e. [*The buyer and seller have the option* to annul their contract] *as long as they have not become separated* bodily; (Mgh, Mṣb;) originally, مَا لَمْ يَتَفَرَّقْ أَبْدَانُهُمَا; for this is the proper meaning. (Mṣb.) تَفَرَّقَتْ بِهِمُ الطُّرُقُ [properly *The roads became separate with them,*] means *every one of them went one* [*separate*] *way.* (TA.) [And one says, تفرّقت الأَغْصَانُ (Ṣ in art. شذب, &c.,) *The branches were,* or *became,* or *grew out, apart, one from another; divaricated; diverged; forked; straggled;* or *spread widely and dispersedly.* And تفرّق أَمْرُهُ *His affair,* or *state of affairs, became discomposed, deranged, disorganized, disordered,* or *unsettled, so that he considered what might be its issues,* or *results, saying at one time, I will do thus, and at another time, I will do thus:* see أَجْمَعَ; and شَتَّ: and ▼ افترق signifies the same: see an ex. voce فَشَا, in art. فشو. And تفرّقت كَلِمَتُهُمْ (Ḳ voce شَالَ, in art. شول,) *Their expression of opinion was,* or *became, discordant:* and تفرّقت آرَاؤُهُمْ *Their opinions were,* or *became, so.*]

6. تفارقوا *They separated themselves, one from another;* or *left, forsook,* or *abandoned, one another.* (TA.)

7. انفرق, of which مُنْفَرَقٌ may be an inf. n. [like اِنْفِرَاقٌ], as well as a n. of place, *It was,* or *became, separated,* or *divided.* (O, Ḳ.) See also 5. [Hence,] اِنْفَلَقَ i. q. انفرق الفَجْرُ [*The dawn broke*]. (TA.)

8. افترق: see 5, first sentence, in three places: and also in the last sentence but one.

فَرْقٌ [is originally an inf. n.: but is often used as a simple subst. meaning *A distinction,* or *difference, between two things.* — Hence,] The *line* [or *division*] *in the hair of the head:* (Ḳ: [see also مَفْرِقٌ:]) or, as some say, the *part,* of the head, *extending from the side of the forehead to the spiral curl upon the crown:* an ex. occurs in a verse of Aboo-Dhu-eyb cited voce مُطْرَبٌ. (TA.) — [And app. *A blaze on a horse's forehead.* (See an ex. voce مُعْتَدِلٌ.)] — And [hence, perhaps,] one says, بَانَتْ فِى قَذَالِهِ فُرُوقٌ مِنَ الشَّيْبِ i. e. أَوْضَاحٌ [app. meaning *There appeared in the back of his head portions of white,* or *hoary, hair, distinct from the rest*]. (TA.) — One says also of the female comber and dresser of the hair, تَمْشُطُ كَذَا وَكَذَا فَرْقًا i. e. [*She combs and dresses* the hair] *with such and such a mode* or *manner* [app. *of combing and dressing* or *of dividing*]. (L. [But the last word, which seems to be in this case an inf. n., is there written without any vowel-sign.]) ═ Also *A certain bird* or *flying thing;* (طَائِرٌ O, Ḳ;) not mentioned by AḤát in "the Book of Birds." (O, TA.) ═ And *Flax.* (Ḳ.) ═ See also فَرَقٌ, in nine places.

الفُرْقُ: see الفُرْقَانُ. — It also signifies *A certain vessel with which one measures.* (TA. [See also فَرَقٌ.]) — And [it is said that] الفُرْقَانُ signifies قدحان مفترقان [app. meaning *Two separate bowls,* or *milking-vessels,* supposing the former word to be قَدَحَانِ; the latter word being مُفْتَرِقَانِ]. (TA. [This is app. said in explanation of فُرْقَانٌ ending a verse in which it means "milking-vessels:" but it is said in the Ṣ, and in one place in the TA, that it is in that instance pl. of فَرْقٌ or فَرَقٌ, q. v.])

فِرْقٌ *A piece,* or *portion, that is split from a thing,* or *cleft therefrom;* (Ṣ, O, Ḳ;) whence its usage in the Ḳur xxvi. 63: (Ṣ, O:) and *a portion of anything* (Ḳ, TA) *when it is separated;* and the pl. is فِرَقٌ: (TA:) or *a portion that is separated,* or *dispersed, of a thing;* and thus it is said to mean in the Ḳur ubi suprà; and the pl. is أَفْرَاقٌ, like أَحْمَالٌ as pl. of حِمْلٌ. (Mṣb.) See also فِرْقَةٌ. — Also *A great flock* or *herd, of sheep* or *goats:* (Ṣ, O, Ḳ:) and (as some say, TA) *of the bovine kind:* or *of gazelles:* or *of sheep,* or *goats, only:* or *of straying sheep* or *goats;* as also ▼ فَرِيقٌ, (Ḳ, TA,) and ▼ فَرِيقَةٌ: (TA:) or *less than a hundred,* (Ḳ, TA,) *of sheep or goats.* (TA.) فِرْقَانِ مِنْ طَيْرٍ صَوَافَّ, occurring in a trad., in which the second and third chapters of the Ḳur-án are likened thereto, (L,) means *Two flocks* [*of birds expanding their wings without moving them in flight*]. (L, TA: but the first word, in both, is without any vowel-sign.) See, again, فِرْقَةٌ. — And *A set of boys.* (O, Ḳ.) An

Arab of the desert said of some boys whom he saw, هٰؤُلَآءِ فِرْقُ سَوْءٍ [*These are a bad set of boys*]. (O.) —— And *A distinct quantity of date-stones with which the camel is fed.* (Ḳ.) —— [And app. *Any feed* for one's beast: see an ex. in art. جل, conj. 4.] ▬ Also *A mountain.* (IAạr, O, Ḳ.) And *A* [*hill, or mountain, or the like, such as is termed*] هَضْبَة. (IAạr, O, Ḳ.) —— And *A wave, billow, or surge.* (IAạr, O, Ḳ.) —— And الفِرْقُ is the name applied by the Arabs to *The star* [*a*] *upon the right shoulder of Cepheus.* (Ḳzw.)

فَرَقٌ *Wideness of the space between the two central incisors,* (IKh, Ṣ, O, Ḳ, TA,) *of a man:* (TA:) and likewise *between the two toe-nails of the camel.* (Yaạkoob, Ṣ, O, Ḳ, TA.) And *A division in the* عُرْف [or *comb*] *of the cock:* and likewise *in the forelock,* and *in the beard, of a man:* (Ṣ, O, Ḳ:) pl. أَفْرَاقٌ. (Ṣ, O.) And *sparseness,* or *a scattered state,* of the plants, or herbage, of a land. (Ṣ, O, Ḳ.) —— In a horse, The *state of the hips when one of them is more prominent than the other;* which is disapproved: (Ṣ, O, Ḳ, TA:) or *a deficiency in one of the thighs, in comparison with the other:* or *a deficiency in one of the hips.* (TA.) —— Also The *dawn:* or الفَرَقُ signifies فَلَقُ الصُّبْحِ: (Ḳ:) or *what has broken of the bright gleam of dawn; of the dawn that rises and spreads, filling the horizon with its whiteness;* (مَا انْفَلَقَ مِنْ عَمُودِ الصُّبْحِ [which is one of the explanations of الفَلَقُ in the Ḳ];) because it has become separated from the blackness of the night: (TA:) one says, أَبْيَنُ مِنْ فَرَقِ الصُّبْحِ a dial. var. of فَلَقِ الصُّبْحِ [i. e. *More distinct than what has broken of the bright gleam of dawn*]. (Ṣ, O, Mṣb,* TA.) ▬ It is also the inf. n. of فَرِقَ [q. v.: when used as a simple subst., signifying *Fear,* or *fright*]. (Ṣ, O, Mṣb.) ▬ Also, and ▼ فَرْقٌ, (Ṣ, Mgh, O, Mṣb, Ḳ,) the latter accord. to the usage of the relaters of traditions, (Az, Mgh, O, Mṣb, TA,) but the former accord. to the usage of the Arabs, (Az, Mgh, O,* TA,) or the former is the more chaste (Ḳ, TA) accord. to Aḥmad Ibn-Yaḥyà and Khálid Ibn-Yezeed, (TA,) *A certain vessel,* (T, Mgh, O, Mṣb,) *a measure of capacity,* (Ṣ, O, Ḳ, TA,) *of large size,* (TA,) *well known,* (Ṣ,) *in El-Medeeneh,* (Ṣ, Mṣb, Ḳ,) *holding three* آصُع [a pl. of صَاعٌ], (Mgh, O, Mṣb, Ḳ, TA,) or, (Ḳ, [app. referring to ▼ فَرْقٌ only,]) which is the same quantity, *sixteen pints,* (Ṣ, Mgh, O, Mṣb, Ḳ,* TA,) i. e. *twelve times the quantity termed* مُدّ *by the people of El-Ḥijáz:* (TA:) or, accord. to El-Ḳutabee, the ▼ فَرْقٌ is *sixteen pints,* and the صاع is one third of the فَرَق; but the فَرَق is *eighty pints:* or the ▼ فَرْق, he adds, is, as some say, *four pints:* (Mgh:) or it is *four* أَرْبَاع [pl. of رُبْعٌ, q. v.]; (Ḳ, TA;) thus accord. to AḤát: and IAth says, the فَرَق is said to be *five* أَقْسَاط; [or *six;* (see قِسْطٌ;)] the قِسْط being the half of a صاع: but the ▼ فَرْق is *a hundred and twenty pints:* (TA:) in the "Nawádir" of Hishám, on the authority of [the Imám] Moḥammad, the ▼ فَرْق is said to be *thirty-six pints;* but [Mṭr says] this I have not found in any of the lexicons in my possession; and so what is said in the Moheeṭ, that it is *sixty pints:* (Mgh:) the pl. is فُرْقَانٌ, (Ṣ, Mgh, O, Ḳ, TA,) which is of فَرَقٌ ▼ and of فَرْقٌ; (Ṣ, Mgh, O, TA;) and أَفْرُقٌ occurs in a trad. as a pl. [of pauc.] of فَرَقٌ meaning the measure thus called. (TA.) 'Áisheh is related to have said that she and the Prophet used to wash themselves from a vessel called the ▼ فَرْق. (O, Mṣb.) [In a verse of which a hemistich is cited in the Ṣ and TA, the pl. فُرْقَان is used as meaning *Milking-vessels.* (See also الفُرْقُ.) Respecting a modern signification of ▼ فَرْق (*A bale,* or *sack,* of merchandise), see De Sacy's Chrest. Ar., sec. ed., iii., 378-9 and 382.]

فَرْقٌ: see فَرُوقَةٌ, in two places.

فَرِقٌ is applied to plants, or herbage, (نَبْتٌ,) as meaning [*In a sparse,* or *scattered, state;* or] *small, not covering the ground:* (AḤn, Ḳ, TA:) or (Ḳ) فَرِقَةٌ is applied to land, (أَرْضٌ,) meaning *of which the plants,* or *herbage, are in a sparse,* or *scattered, state;* (Ṣ, O, Ḳ, TA;) *not contiguous:* (Ṣ, O, TA:) thus used, it is a possessive epithet, having no verb. (TA.) ▬ See also فَرُوقَةٌ, in two places.

فُرْقَةٌ the subst. from فَارَقَهُ; (Ṣ, MA,* TA;) or from افْتَرَقَ, (Mṣb,) [i. e.] a quasi-inf. n. used in the sense of افْتِرَاقٌ; (TA;) signifying *Separation, disunion,* or *abandonment;* (MA, KL, PṢ;) and ▼ فِرَاقٌ is syn. therewith, whence the reading [in the Ḳur xviii. 77], هٰذَا فِرَاقُ بَيْنِي وَبَيْنِكَ [*This shall be the separation of my and thy union*]; and so is ▼ فَرَاقٌ, (O,* Ḳ, TA,) which [is an inf. n. of فارقه, and], in the Ḳur lxxv. 28, means the *time of the quitting of the present world by death.* (TA.)

فِرْقَةٌ *A* طَائِفَة [or *party, portion, division, sect,* or *distinct body* or *class,*] of men, (Ṣ, O, Mṣb, Ḳ,) and of other things; as also ▼ فِرْقٌ; (Mṣb;) and so, accord. to IB, ▼ فَرِيقٌ: (TA: [but see this last word:]) [and *a separate herd* or *the like* of cattle:] pl. فِرَقٌ (O, Mṣb, Ḳ) and أَفْرَاقٌ (Ṣ, O, Ḳ) is pl. of فِرْقٌ (O, Ḳ) and أَفَارِيقُ is pl. of أَفْرَاقٌ, (Ṣ, O, Ḳ,) and أَفَارِقَةٌ occurs in poetry; (O, Ḳ;) or أَفَارِيقُ may be of the class of أَبَاطِيلُ, a pl. without a sing. (O, TA.) —— Also *A portion of a thing in a state of dispersion;* and so ▼ فِرْقٌ and ▼ فَرِيقٌ. (L, TA.) ▬ And *A skin that is full* [*of milk*], *that cannot be agitated to make butter* حَتَّى يُفْرَقَ ▼ أَىْ يُفْرَقَ [app. a tropical phrase meaning *until it is made to void some of its contents*]. (Ḳ.)

فُرْقَانٌ, originally an inf. n. (Mṣb. [See 1, first sentence.]) *Anything that makes a separation,* or *distinction, between truth and falsity.* (Ṣ, O, Ḳ.) —— Hence, (TA,) الفُرْقَانُ signifies *The Ḳur-án;* (Ṣ, O, Mṣb, Ḳ;) as also ▼ الفُرْقُ. (Ṣ, O, Ḳ.) —— And The *Book of the Law revealed to Moses,* (Az, O, Ḳ,) in which a distinction is made between that which is allowable and that which is forbidden. (O.) —— And *Proof, evidence,* or *demonstration.* (O, Ḳ.) —— And *The time a little before daybreak:* (AA, O, Ḳ:) or *the dawn.* (O, Ḳ.) One says, طَلَعَ الفُرْقَانُ [*The dawn rose*]. (O.) —— And *Aid,* or *victory:* (IDrd, O, Ḳ:) so, accord. to IDrd, in the phrase يَوْمَ الفُرْقَانِ in the Ḳur [viii. 42]: (O:) or by this phrase is meant *The day of Bedr,* (O, Ḳ,) in which a distinction was made between right and wrong. (O.) —— And *The cleaving of the sea:* so it means [accord. to some] in the Ḳur ii. 50. (O, Ḳ.) —— And *Boys:* (O, Ḳ:) such the people of the olden time used to make witnesses [in law-suits or the like]. (O.) ▬ It is also pl. of فَرَقٌ (Ṣ, M, O, Ḳ) and of فَرْقٌ. (Ṣ, Mgh, O.)

فَرْقَةٌ and فِرَاقٌ: see فُرْقَةٌ.

فَرُوقٌ: see فَرُوقَةٌ, in two places: ▬ and أَفْرَقُ, last sentence but two.

فَرِيقٌ *A* طَائِفَة [or *party,* &c.,] (Ṣ, Mṣb, Ḳ) *more in number,* (Ṣ, Ḳ,*) or *larger,* (Mṣb,) *than a* فِرْقَة: (Ṣ, Mṣb, Ḳ:) pl. [of pauc.] أَفْرِقَةٌ and [of mult.] أَفْرِقَاءُ and فُرُوقٌ (Ḳ, TA) and فُرُقٌ: (CḲ:) see also فِرْقَةٌ, in two places; and see فِرْقٌ: AḤei says that it is itself a quasi-pl. n., applied to *few* and to *many:* 'Abd-el-Ḥakeem, that it occurs in the sense of *a* طَائِفَة [or *party,* &c.], and in the sense of *a single man:* and El-Iṣbahánee, that it signifies *a company of men apart from others* [i. e. *a party of men*]: (MF, TA:) or [simply] *a company* [*of men*]. (O.) —— And *A separator of himself.* (IB, TA.) Hence the saying, هُوَ أَسْرَعُ مِنْ فَرِيقِ الخَيْلِ i. e. [*He is swifter*] *than the outgoer,* or *outrunner, of the horses.* (TA.) —— نِيَّةٌ فَرِيقٌ means مُفَرِّقٌ [i. e. *A place to which one purposes journeying that separates widely*]: a poet says,

• أَحَقٌّ أَنَّ جِيرَتَنَا ٱسْتَقَلُّوا •
• فَنِيَّتُنَا وَنِيَّتُهُمْ فَرِيقُ •

[*Is it true that our neighbours have gone away, so that the place to which we purpose journeying and the place to which they purpose journeying are such as separate widely*]: he says فَرِيق in like manner as one applies [the epithet] صَدِيق to a company of men. (Sb, TA.) ▬ Also *A palm-tree* (نَخْلَة) *in which is* [app. meaning *out of which grows*] *another.* (AA, AḤn, O, TA.)

فَرُوقَةٌ, applied to a man and to a woman, (IDrd, Ṣ, O, Ḳ,) and having no pl., (Ṣ, O,) and ▼ فَرُوقَةٌ, applied to a man (Ibn-'Abbád, O, Ḳ) and to a woman, (Ḳ,) and ▼ فَارُوقَةٌ, applied to a man (O, Ḳ) and to a woman, or, as epithets applied to a man, فَرُوقَةٌ, (Ḳ,) and ▼ فُرُّوقَةٌ, (CḲ,) and ▼ فَارُوقَةٌ, and ▼ فَرُوقٌ, (Ḳ,) but this last is also applied to a woman, (IB, TA,) and ▼ فَرُّوقٌ, and ▼ فَارُوقٌ, One *who fears much,* or *vehemently;* [or rather the epithets with the affix ة are doubly intensive, meaning one *who fears very much;*]

(Ṣ,* O,* Ḳ, TA;) and ▼ فَرِقٌ and ▼ فُرُقٌ signify the same as the other epithets above; or ▼ فَرُوقٌ signifies *fearing*, or *fearful, by nature*; and ▼ فَرِقٌ, [simply,] *fearing* a thing. (Ḳ.) It is said in a prov., رُبَّ عَجَلَةٍ تَهَبُ رَيْثًا وَرُبَّ فَرُوقَةٍ يُدْعَى لَيْثًا وَرُبَّ غَيْثٍ لَمْ يَكُنْ غَيْثًا [*Many an act of haste causes* (lit. *gives*) *slowness, and many a very fearful* man *is called a lion, and many a collection of clouds has not been* productive of *rain*]: (Ṣ,* O:) said by Málik Ibn-'Amr Ibn-Mohallam, when Leyth, his brother, looked hopefully at the clouds from afar, and desired to avail himself of the benefit thereof; whereupon Málik said to him, "Do not, for I fear for thee some of the troops of the Arabs:" but he disobeyed him, and journeyed with his family; and he had not stayed [away] a little while when he came [back], and his family had been taken. (O. [See also Freytag's Arab. Prov. i. 535.]) ▬ And الفَرُوقَةُ signifies الحُرْمَةُ [meaning *Honour*, or *reputation*; or *that which one is under an obligation to respect and defend*]: (O, Ḳ, TA: [in the CḲ الحَزْمَةُ:]) so Sh was told: and [so, app., ▼ الفَرُوقُ, for] he cites as an ex.,

* مَا زَالَ عَنْهُ حُمْقُهُ وَمُوقُهُ *
* وَاللُّؤْمُ حَتَّى ٱنْتُهِكَتْ فَرُوقُهُ *

[*His foolishness and his stupidity quitted him not, and meanness, so that his honour, &c., was violated*]. (O, TA.) ▬ And *The fat of the kidneys*: (O, Ḳ:) so says A'Obeyd, on the authority of El-Umawee; but Sh disallowed this meaning, and knew it not. (O, TA.)

فَرِيقَةٌ: see فِرْقٌ. — Also *Some* (Ṣ, O, Ḳ) *one* or *two* or *three* (Ṣ, O) *of a flock* or *herd, of sheep* or *goats, becoming separate therefrom*, (Ṣ, O, Ḳ,) *being shut out from the rest by the like of a mountain or a space of sand or some other thing*, as is said in the "Kitáb Leysa," (TA,) *and going away*, (Ṣ, O, Ḳ,) in the "Kitáb Leysa" *straying*, (TA,) *in the night, from the main aggregate*. (Ṣ, O, Ḳ.) ▬ And *Dates cooked with fenugreek* (حُلْبَة), *for the woman in the state following childbirth*: (Ṣ, O, Ḳ:) or *fenugreek* (حُلْبَة) *cooked with grains* (حُبُوب) [or *kernels*?], (O, Ḳ, TA,) *such as* مَحْلَب [q. v.], *and* بر [app. a mistranscription], *and other things*, (TA,) *for her*: (Ḳ, TA:) or, accord. to IKh, *a soup that is made for him who is affected with a chronic disease*, or *emaciated by disease so as to be at the point of death*. (TA.) [See also فَلِيقَةٌ.]

فُرُوقٌ: see فَرُوقَةٌ, first sentence.

فُرُوقَةٌ: see فَرُوقَةٌ, first sentence, in two places.

فَارِقٌ [act. part. n. of فَرَقَ, q. v.]. الفَارِقَاتُ, mentioned in the Ḳur lxxvii. 4, means *Those angels that descend with what makes a distinction between truth and falsity*: (Fr, O, Ḳ:) or *that distinguish between that which is allowable and that which is forbidden*: (Th, TA:) or *that make a distinction between things according as God has commanded them*. (Er-Rághib, TA.) — Also, فَارِقٌ, A she-camel, and a she-ass, *in consequence of her being taken with the pains of parturition, going away at random in the land*; (Ṣ, O, Ḳ;) and so فَارِقَةٌ, as in the "Mufradát:" or a she-camel *that separates herself from her mate, and brings forth alone*: or a she-camel *that runs* (تَشْتَدُّ), *and then casts her young one by reason of the pain that befalls her*; thus expl. by IAạr: (TA:) pl. فَوَارِقُ and فُرَّقٌ (Ṣ, O, Ḳ) and فُرُقٌ (Ḳ) and فُرَّاقٌ, which is thus used by El-Aạshà, applied to she-camels, and ▼ مَفَارِيقُ is [an irreg. pl.] likewise applied to she-camels as syn. with فَوَارِقُ. (TA.) — And hence, as being likened to such a she-camel, applied to a cloud (سَحَابَة) as meaning ‡ *Apart from the other clouds*; (Ṣ, O, Ḳ;) *cut off from the main aggregate of the clouds*: (ISd, TA:) or an *isolated* cloud, *that will not break its promise* [*of giving rain*], *and sometimes preceded by thunder and lightning*: (TA:) thus applied, also, having for pl. فَوَارِقُ and فُرَّقٌ [&c.]. (O.)

فَارُوقٌ A thing *that makes a distinction between two things*: and a man *who makes a distinction between truth and falsity*: (TA:) or one *who makes a distinction between affairs*, or *cases*. (Mṣb.) الفَارُوقُ is an appellation that was given to 'Omar Ibn-El-Khaṭṭáb, (Ṣ, O, Ḳ, TA,) the second of the Khaleefehs; (TA;) because a distinction was made by him between truth and falsity. (Ibráheem El-Ḥarbee, O, Ḳ,* TA.) — التِّرْيَاقُ الفَارُوقُ, (O,) or تِرْيَاقٌ فَارُوقٌ, (Ḳ,) *The most approved sort of theriac*, (O, Ḳ,) and *the most esteemed of compounds*; because it makes a distinction between disease and health: (Ḳ:) called by the vulgar تِرْيَاق فَارُوقِى. (TA.) ▬ See also فَرُوقَةٌ, first sentence.

فَارُوقَةٌ: see فَرُوقَةٌ, first sentence, in two places.

أَفْرَقُ, applied to a man, *Having a wide space between the two central incisors*: (IKh, TA:) [or] *i. q.* أَفْلَجُ [app. as meaning the same, or having a similar meaning]: (Ḳ, TA: [but the CḲ has الأَفْلَحُ instead of الأَفْلَجُ:]) or, accord. to Lth, the أَفْرَقُ is *like the* أَفْلَج, except that the افلج is such as has been rendered so, and the افرق is such *naturally*. (O, TA.) And A camel *having a wide space between the two toe-nails*. (Yaạḳoob, TA.) And *Having a wide space between the buttocks*. (TA.) And A he-goat *having a wide space between his horns*. (IKh, TA.) And A ram, or he-goat, *having a wide space between his testicles*: and [the fem.] فَرْقَآءُ a ewe, or she-goat, *having a wide space between the two teats*. (Lth, O, Ḳ, TA.) — A camel *having two humps*. (TA.) — A man *whose forelock is as though it were divided*; and in like manner, *whose beard is so*. (Ṣ, O, Ḳ.*) A cock *whose* عُرْف [or *comb*] *is divided*: (Ṣ, O, Ḳ:) and (accord. to Lth, O) a *white* cock: (O, Ḳ:) or, as some say, *having two combs* (ذُو عُرْفَيْنِ). (O.) — A horse *having one of the hips more prominent than the other*; which is disapproved: (Ṣ, Ḳ, TA:) or *having a deficiency in one of his thighs, in comparison with the other*: or *having a deficiency in one of the hips*: or, accord. to the T, a beast *having one of his elbows prominent, and the other depressed*. (TA.) And A horse *having one testicle*. (Lth, O, Ḳ, TA.) The pl. is فُرْقٌ. (TA, in which it is here mentioned: also mentioned in the Ḳ after أَفْرَقُ as applied to a ram or he-goat: in the CḲ [erroneously] فُرُقٌ.) And ▼ فُرُوقٌ applied to a horse signifies the same as أَفْرَقُ. (O, TA.) — طَرِيقٌ أَفْرَقُ *A road that is distinct, apparent*, or *manifest*. (TA.) And سَيْلٌ أَفْرَقُ *A torrent that is as though it were the* فرق [app. as meaning *wave, billow*, or *surge*]. (TA.)

تَفَارِيقُ [*Sundry*, or *separate*, or *scattered, portions* or *things*: and *sundry times*]. You say, أَخَذْتُ حَقِّى مِنْهُ بِالتَّفَارِيقِ (Ṣ, O, Ḳ,* TA) i. e. [*I took my right*, or *due, from him in sundry portions*: or] *at sundry times*. (TA.) And ضَمَّ تَفَارِيقَ مَتَاعِهِ i. e. [*He put together*] *what were scattered* [*of his household goods*, or *furniture and utensils*]. (TA.)

* إِنَّكَ خَيْرٌ مِنْ تَفَارِيقِ العَصَا *

[*Verily thou art better than the several portions of the staff*], (Ṣ, O, Ḳ,) which is a prov., (O,) was said by a poet, (Ṣ,) or by Ghaneeyeh, (O,) or Ghuneiyeh, (Ḳ,) El-Aạrábeeyeh, to her son; for he was evil in disposition, [عازما in the CḲ is a mistake for عَارِمًا,] very mischievous, notwithstanding his weakness, (O, Ḳ,) and slenderness of bone; (O;) and he assaulted one day a young man, who thereupon cut off his nose, and his mother took the mulct for it; so her condition became good after abasing poverty; then he assaulted another, who cut off his ear; and another, who cut off his lip; and his mother took the mulct for each; and when she saw the goodness of her condition, (O, Ḳ,) the camels and the sheep or goats and the household goods that she had acquired, (O,) she said thus: (O, Ḳ:) for from the staff (Ṣ, O, Ḳ) when it is broken (Ṣ) is made a سَاجُور [q. v.], and from this are made tent-pegs, and from the tent-peg is made an عِرَان [q. v.], and from this are made تَوَادٍ [pl. of تَوْدِيَةٌ, q. v.]. (Ṣ, O, Ḳ.)

مَفْرِقٌ (Ṣ, O, Ḳ) and مَفْرَقٌ (Ṣ, O, Mṣb, Ḳ) The *middle* of the head; (Ṣ, O, Ḳ;) the *place where the hair* of the head *is separated*: (Ṣ, O, Mṣb, Ḳ:) pl. مَفَارِقُ; which is used also in the sense of the sing., as though the sing. applied to every part thereof: (Ṣ, O:) one says, شَابَتْ مَفَارِقُ رَأْسِهِ [meaning *The place* (lit. *places*) *of the separation of the hair of his head became white*, or *hoary*]. (Mgh voce ذَكَرٌ.) [See also فَرْقٌ.] — Also The *place*, of a road, *where another road branches off*: (Ṣ, O, Mṣb, Ḳ:) both words are used in this sense likewise: (Ṣ, O, Ḳ:*) pl. as above. (Ḳ.) — And [hence] one says, وَقَفْتُهُ عَلَى مَفَارِقِ الحَدِيثِ ‡ [*I made him to know*] *the modes*, or *manners*, [*of the narrative*, or *discourse*,] or *the manifest, plain*, or *obvious, modes* or *manners* [*thereof*]. (TA.)

مُفْرِقٌ A she-camel *whose young one has become separated from her*, (Ṣ, O, Ḳ, TA,) as some say, (TA,) *by death:* (Ṣ, O, Ḳ, TA:) pl. ▼ مَفَارِيقُ. (TA. [Thus in my original, not مَفَارِقُ.]) — And A she-camel *that tarries two years*, or *three, without conceiving.* (TA.) — And A she-camel *having a return of some of her milk.* (TA.) — And Anyone *recovering from his disease.* (Lḥ, TA.) — And *Deviating from the right way* or *course*, or *from that which is right.* (TA.) — And مُفْرِقُ الجِسْمِ, (thus accord. to the Ḳ, there said to be like مُحْسِنٌ,) or ▼ مُفَرَّقُ الجِسْمِ, (thus in the O,) A man (O) *having little flesh:* or *fat*, or *plump:* (O, Ḳ:) two contr. meanings. (Ḳ.)

مُفَرَّقُ الجِسْمِ : see what next precedes.

مُفَرِّقُ النَّعَمِ [*The disperser of the camels* or *cattle;*] *the* [*small, stinking beast called*] ظَرِبَان ; because when it emits a noiseless wind from the anus among the cattle, they disperse themselves. (Ṣ, O, Ḳ.)

مَفَارِيقُ : see مُفْرِقٌ : — and فَارِقٌ, latter half.

مُنْفَرَقٌ is a n. of place, as well as an inf. n. [of اِنْفَرَقَ]: (O, Ḳ:) and is used by Ru-beh as meaning *A place where a road divides.* (O.)

فرقد

فَرْقَدٌ *A calf:* (Ṣ:) accord. to Aboo-Kheyreh, *after he has become about two months old:* (TA voce عِجْلٌ:) or *the calf of a wild cow;* as also ▼ فُرْقُودٌ : (IAạr, O, L, Ḳ:) fem. فَرْقَدَةٌ. (L.) — And الفَرْقَدُ (O, L, Ḳ) and ▼ الفُرْقُودُ (O, Ḳ) † *The asterism* (نَجْم) *by which one directs his course* (O, Ḳ) *by sea and by land;* (O;) *two stars* [β *and* γ *of Ursa Minor*]; (L, Ḳ;) *also called* (in poetry, O, Ḳ, [and generally in prose,]) الفَرْقَدَانِ ; (O, L, Ḳ;) thus in a verse cited voce إِلَّا ; (O;) they are *two stars near the* قُطْب [or *pole-star*]; (Ṣ, L;) *two stars that never set, revolving round the* جَدْى [or *pole-star*], *both in Ursa Minor;* (L;) *the two bright stars of the four that form the angles of a quadrilateral figure in Ursa Minor;* (Ḳzw;) *also called by the Arabs* الفَرَاقِدُ [which is the pl. of الفَرْقَدُ]. (L.) == And فَرْقَدٌ signifies also *A level*, or *an even, land.* (Ibn-'Abbád, O.)

فُرْقُودٌ : see above, first and second sentences.

فرقع

Q. 1. فَرْقَعَ الأَصَابِعَ *i. q.* نَقَّضَهَا, (Ṣ,* O,* Ḳ, [in copies of the Ḳ written نَقَضَهَا, but correctly with teshdeed, as is shown by what here follows,]) inf. n. فَرْقَعَةٌ *i. q.* تَنْقِيضٌ (Ṣ, O) and تَفْقِيعٌ, (TA,) [*He cracked the joints of his fingers;*] i. e. *he pressed his fingers so that a sound was heard to proceed from their joints:* (TA:) the doing of which is forbidden, (O, TA,) in prayer. (TA. [See also 2 in art. فقع.]) And one says, سَمِعْتُ صَرْقَعَةً and فَرْقَعَةً لِرِجْلٍ [*I heard a cracking of the joints of the fingers of a man*]: both signify the same. (TA.) — And فَرْقَعَهُ *He twisted his* (a man's, Ḳ) *neck.* (O, Ḳ.) == فَرْقَعَ [as an intrans. v.], (O, Ḳ, TA,) inf. n. as above, (TA,) *He ran vehemently*, (O, Ḳ, TA,) *going back*, or *retreating:* so in the Tekmileh. (TA.) — And فِرْقَاعٌ (as an inf. n. of which the verb is فَرْقَعَ, TḲ) signifies The *emitting of wind from the anus with a sound:* (O, Ḳ:) mentioned by IDrd as from some one or more of the Arabs. (O.) — See also فَرْقَعَةٌ in what next follows.

Q. 2. تَفَرْقَعَتِ الأَصَابِعُ *The fingers produced a sound* or *sounds* [*by their joints' being cracked*]; (O;) quasi-pass. of 1 in the first of the senses expl. above; (Ṣ, Ḳ;) as also ▼ اِفْرَنْقَعَت, (Ḳ, TA,) inf. n. اِفْرِنْقَاعٌ and [quasi-inf. n., being app. the inf. n. in this case of فُرْقِعَت,] ▼ فَرْقَعَةٌ, (TA,) [and this is app. what is meant by its being said that] ▼ الاِفْرِنْقَاعُ is [syn. with] الفَرْقَعَةُ. (Ḳ.) — Accord. to IDrd, تَفَرْقُعٌ signifies The *sounding of two things striking against each other.* (O.) — And تفرقع الرَّجُلُ *The man drew himself together*, or *shrank;* like تَقَرْعَفَ [which is mentioned in the Ḳ in the same sense, as also تَقَرْفَعَ]. (L, TA.)

Q. 3: see Q. 2, in two places. — الاِفْرِنْقَاعُ also signifies *The withdrawing*, or *removing*, and *going away*, from a thing (عَنْ شَيْءٍ); (Ḳ;) and *the dispersing of itself*, or *becoming dispersed.* (IAth, TA.) اِفْرَنْقِعُوا عَنِّى, a phrase used by 'Eesà Ibn-'Omar, (Ṣ, O,) to people who had congregated about him on an occasion of his having fallen from his ass, (O,) means *Withdraw ye*, or *remove*, (Ṣ,) or *disperse yourselves*, (O,) *from me*, (Ṣ,) and *go away.* (Ṣ, O.) And 'Eesà Ibn-'Omar is related to have read, [in the Ḳur xxxiv. 22,] حَتَّى إِذَا افْرَنْقَعَ عَنْ قُلُوبِهِمْ ; meaning, كُشِفَ ; [الفَزَعُ, or the like, being understood;] but the common reading is فُزِّعَ, q. v. (TA.)

اِسْتُ الفَرْقَعَةِ *The* [here app. meaning *anus* (see 1)]; (Lth, IAạr, Ḳ;) of the dial. of El-Yemen: (O:) also called الفُرْقُعَةُ. (TA.)

فرك

1. فَرْكٌ, as expl. by Lth, signifies (O, TA) primarily (TA) One's *rubbing*, or *rubbing and pressing*, a thing [with the hand] *so that its integument becomes stripped off* (O, TA) *from its kernel;* as, for instance, a [shelled] walnut. (TA.) One says, فَرَكَ السُّنْبُلَ, (Ṣ, O, Mṣb, Ḳ,) aor. ـُ, inf. n. فَرْكٌ, (Ṣ, Mṣb,) *He rubbed*, or *rubbed and pressed, the ears of corn* (Ḳ, TA) with his hand [*so that the kernels became divested of their husks*]. (Ṣ, O, Mṣb, TA.) And فَرَكَ الثَّوْبَ (Ṣ, O, Mṣb, Ḳ) *He rubbed*, or *rubbed and pressed, the garment* (Ḳ, TA) with his hand [*to remove a soil*]. (Ṣ, O, Mṣb, TA.) And فَرَكَ المَنِىَّ مِنَ الثَّوْبِ (Mgh, O, Mṣb,) aor. and inf. n. as above, (Mgh,) *He rubbed*, (Mṣb,) or *rubbed and pressed*, (Mgh,) *with his hand, the* [dry soil of] *sperma, so that it crumbled, and came off from the garment;* (Mgh, Mṣb;) like حَتَّهُ : and in like manner الطِّينَ [i. e. *the* dry *mud*]. (Mṣb.) [And فَرَكَ القَمْلَةَ *He rubbed*, or *rubbed and pressed, the louse, between his finger and thumb, or otherwise*, to kill it. (See the pass. part. n., below.)] == فَرِكَتْ زَوْجَهَا, and فَرِكَهَا زَوْجُهَا, aor. ـَ ; (Ṣ, O, Ḳ;) and فَرَكَتْهُ, and فَرَكَهَا, aor. ـُ, but this form of the verb is extr.; (Ḳ;) inf. n. فِرْكٌ (Ṣ, O, Ḳ) and فَرْكٌ and فُرُوكٌ ; (Ḳ;) *She hated her husband, and her husband hated her;* (Ṣ, O;) or *she hated her husband vehemently, and her husband hated her vehemently:* (Ḳ:) the verb has not been heard otherwise than as relating to the husband and wife: (Ṣ, O:) Lḥ has mentioned فَرَكَتْهُ, aor. تَفْرُكُهُ ; but it is not well known: (TA:) all of the nouns mentioned above as inf. ns. signify [hatred, or] vehement hatred, in a general sense, as also ▼ فُرْكَانٌ, (Ḳ, TA,) which is [app. a simple subst.] mentioned on the authority of Seer, and also mentioned as with two kesrehs and the teshdeed [i. e. ▼ فِرِكَّانٌ]: (TA:) or all relate peculiarly to the hatred of the husband and wife; (Ḳ, TA;) i. e., to the man's hating his wife; or to her hating him, which is the better known: it is said in a trad. of Ibn-Mes'ood, إِنَّ الحُبَّ مِنَ اللّٰهِ وَالفِرْكَ مِنَ الشَّيْطَانِ [*Verily love* of the husband *is from God, and hatred* of the husband *is from the Devil*]: A'Obeyd says that الفِرْك signifies the woman's hating *her husband;* that it relates peculiarly to the wife and the husband, and that it had not been heard by him as used in relation to any but them two: and IAạr says that the sons of a man by a wife who hates him, which sons are termed أَوْلَادُ الفِرْكِ, possess generosity, because the sons thus called are most like to their fathers, and do not resemble her: and when the husband hates the wife, one says صلفها [i. e. صَلِفَهَا or صَلَفَهَا] and صلفت عنده [i. e. صَلِفَتْ عِنْدَهُ]. (TA.) == فَرِكَتِ الأُذُنُ, aor. ـَ, (Ḳ,) inf. n. فَرَكٌ, (Ṣ, O, Ḳ,) *The ear had a flaccidity in its* أَصْل [or *base*, meaning the *part surrounding the entrance of the meatus auditorius*]. (Ṣ,* O,* Ḳ.)

2. تَفْرِيكٌ [inf. n. of فرّك] The *causing to be hated*, or *much hated.* (O.)

3. فَارَكَهُ, (AZ, O, Ḳ, TA,) inf. n. مُفَارَكَةٌ, (TA,) *i. q.* تَارَكَهُ [i. e. *He left, forsook*, or *abandoned, him;* or *he did so being left* &c. *by him*]; (AZ, O, Ḳ, TA;) namely, his companion; (AZ, O;) said by IF to be formed by substitution [of ف for ت]: (O, TA:) expl. in the A as meaning فَارَقَهُ [which is syn. with تاركه]. (TA.)

4. افرك السُّنْبُلُ *The ears of corn became* ▼ فَرِيك, i. e. *in the state in which they were fit to be rubbed*, or *rubbed and pressed, with the hand* [*so as to divest the kernels of their husks*], *and then to be eaten:* (Ṣ, O:) and افرك الزَّرْعُ, (TA,) and الحَبُّ, (Ḳ,) *The seed-produce*, and *the grain, attained to the state in which it was fit to be rubbed*, or *rubbed and pressed*, (Ḳ, TA,) *with the*

hand: or *the grain became hard,* or *firm, and attained to its utmost state of growth;* before which it is forbidden to sell it. (TA.)

5. تفرّك *He* (an effeminate man, O) *affected languor,* or *languidness,* (تَكَسَّرَ) *in his speech,* (O, Ḳ,) *and in his walk:* (Ḳ:) so says IDrd. (O.)

7. انفرك السُّنْبُلُ *The ears of corn were rubbed,* or *rubbed and pressed,* (Ḳ, TA,) with the hand [*so that the kernels became divested of their husks*]. (TA.) And انفرك الثَّوْبُ *The garment became rubbed,* or *rubbed and pressed,* (Ḳ, TA,) with the hand [*to remove a soil*]. (TA.) [See 1.] — And انفرك المَنْكِبُ *The shoulder-joint became lax,* or *slack:* (Ṣ,* TA:) or انفرك مَنْكِبُهُ, (Lth, O, Ḳ,*) as also انفركت وَابِلَتُهُ, (Lth, O,) signifies *the* وَابِلَة [or *head*] *of his humerus became dislocated* (Lth, O, Ḳ) *from the* صَدَفَة [or *socket*] *of the scapula, so that the shoulder-joint became lax,* or *slack:* but when the like thereof happens in the وابلة of the femur, one does not say انفرك, but حُرِقَ, and the epithet مَحْرُوقٌ is applied to it [i. e. to the hip-joint]. (Lth, O.) — And انفرك عَنْ عَهْدِهِ *He became released from his compact, engagement,* or *promise;* syn. انْفَكَّ. (TA.)

10. استفرك الحَبُّ فِى السُّنْبُلَةِ *The grain became full* (سَمِنَ [q. v.]), *and hard,* or *firm,* [as though demanding to be rubbed with the hand so as to be divested of the husks, and eaten,] *in the ear of corn.* (Ḳ,* TA.)

فَرْكٌ: see what next follows.

فَرِكٌ, (O, Ḳ,) like كَتِفٌ, (Ḳ,) or correctly, as written in the L and A, ▼ فَرْكٌ, (TA, [but this I think doubtful,]) [A fruit or the like] *of which the integument becomes rubbed off* [with the hand]: (O, Ḳ: [I read المُنْفَرِكُ قِشْرُهُ, as in the CḲ, for المُتَفَرِّكُ قِشْرُهُ in other copies of the Ḳ and in the O:]) thus applied to an almond, and likewise to a peach. (TA.) — See also what next follows.

أُذُنٌ فَرْكَآءُ *An ear having a flaccidity in its* أَصْل [or *base*]; as also ▼ فَرِكَةٌ. (Ṣ, O, Ḳ. [See 1, last sentence.])

فِرِكَّانٌ and **فُرُكَّانٌ**: see 1, latter half.

فَرَاكِ a term for حَيْض [or *Menstruation*]: mentioned by MF. (TA.)

فَرُوكٌ: see فَارِكٌ, first sentence.

فَرِيكٌ, applied to grain (حَبٌّ), *i. q.* ▼ مَفْرُوكٌ [i. e. *Rubbed,* or *rubbed and pressed,* with the hand, *so that the integument becomes stripped off from the kernel*]: (Ḳ:) or wheat (بُرّ) *that is rubbed,* &c., *and picked,* or *cleared.* (O.) See also 4. — And *Wheat rubbed,* &c., *and moistened with clarified butter &c.;* (Ḳ, TA;) also termed ▼ مَفْرُوكَةٌ. (TA.) — The فَرِيكَانِ, or, as in some copies of the Ḳ, ▼ فَرِيكَتَانِ, (TA,) *Two bones* [app. *the two greater cornua of the os hyoides*] *in,* or *at,* (فِى) *the root of the tongue.* (Ḳ, TA.)

فَرِيكَتَانِ: see what next precedes.

فَارِكٌ A woman *hating,* or *who hates, her husband;* [app. accord. to the Ḳ, *vehemently;*] as also ▼ فَرُوكٌ [but app. in an intensive sense]: (Ṣ, O, Ḳ:) pl. of the former فَوَارِكُ. (O,* TA.) Dhu-r-Rummeh says, (O, TA,) describing camels, (TA,)

* إِذَا اللَّيْلُ عَنْ نَشْزٍ تَجَلَّى رَمَيْنَهُ *

* بِأَمْثَالِ أَبْصَارِ النِّسَآءِ الفَوَارِكِ *

[*When the night clears away from an elevated piece of ground, they cast at it the like of the eyes of the women that hate their husbands*]: (O, TA:) he likens them to the women that hate their husbands because these raise their eyes towards men, not confining the look to the husbands: he says, these camels enter upon the time of dawn, having journeyed all their night; and whenever an elevated piece of ground becomes within their view, they cast their eyes at it by reason of sprightliness and strength for the journeying. (TA.)

مُفَرَّكٌ [*Caused to be hated,* or *to be much hated:* see its verb. And] A man *hated by women:* (Ṣ, O, Ḳ:) such was Imra-el-Ḳeys: (Ṣ, O:) [and accord. to Freytag, ▼ مَفْرُوكٌ occurs in this sense in the Deewán of Jereer.] And مُفَرَّكَةٌ A woman *hated by men.* (IAạr, Ḳ.) — Also *Left, forsaken,* or *abandoned, and hated.* (Fr, TA.)

مَفْرُوكٌ: see فَرِيكٌ. One says also قَمْلَةٌ مَفْرُوكَةٌ [*A louse rubbed,* or *rubbed and pressed, between the finger and thumb,* or *otherwise,* to be killed]. (Ṣ, O.) — Applied to a camel, (En-Naḍr, O, Ḳ,) it means *Such as is termed* أَفَكُّ [q. v.]; (En-Naḍr, O;) *whose shoulder is slit* [so I render انْخَرَمَ, but I incline to think that it here means *is splayed,* or *dislocated,* as though rent without being separated (see تَخَرَّمَ)], *and the* عَصَبَة [which I suppose to signify in this case either *tendon* or *ligament*] *that is in the interior of the* أَخْرَم [q. v., app. here meaning the *glenoid cavity of the scapula*] *detached.* (En-Naḍr, O, Ḳ. [See also انفرك مَنْكِبُهُ.]) — And A garment, or piece of cloth, (TA,) *strongly dyed* (Ḳ, TA) with saffron &c. (TA.) — See also مُفَرَّكٌ.

مَفْرُوكَةٌ, as a subst.: see فَرِيكٌ.

فرم

2. تَفْرِيمٌ [as an inf. n. of which the verb is فَرَّمَتْ] signifies A woman's *contracting her* قُبُل (or قُبُل, TA) [i. e. *vulva or vagina*] *with the stones of raisins* [which were supposed to have an astringent property, or *with some other medicament:* see فَرْمٌ: and see also 10]: and so تَفْرِيبٌ. (IAạr, T.)

3. فِرَامٌ [app. as an inf. n. of which the verb is فَارَمَتْ] signifies A woman's *menstruating, and stuffing her vulva with a piece of rag:* and one says of her who has done this, ▼ اِفْتَرَمَتْ [and app. also فَارَمَتْ]. (T, Ḳ.) [See also فِرَامَةٌ.] — It occurs in a trad. [as an inf. n.] used in the sense of مُجَامَعَة [meaning ‡ The act of *compressing*]. (IAth, TA.)

4. افرم *He filled* (T, Ṣ, Ḳ) a watering-trough (T, Ḳ) or a vessel: (Ṣ:) of the dial. of Hudheyl. (T, Ṣ.)

8. اِفْتَرَمَتْ, said of a woman: see 3.

10. اِسْتَفْرَمَتْ *She* (a woman) *applied a medicament to her vulva,* or *vagina, to contract it:* (Ṣ, Ḳ:*) or *she stuffed her vulva,* or *vagina,* (T, TA,) *with the stones of raisins, and the like:* (TA:) the women of [the tribe of] Thaḳeef, having a wideness in that part, made this use of the stones of raisins, desiring thereby to contract it: (M, TA:*) [see also 2: and see فَرْمٌ:] the epithet ▼ فَرْمَآءُ is applied to her who does thus; as also ▼ مُسْتَفْرِمَةٌ. (M, Ḳ.) — And [hence] one says of a mare, اِسْتَفْرَمَتْ بِالحَصَى, meaning † *She caused the pebbles to enter her vulva by her vehement running.* (TA. [And the same is implied in the Ṣ by an ex. and explanation of the part. n.])

فَرْمٌ, (T, Ṣ, M, Ḳ,) and ▼ فَرْمَةٌ, (Ṣ, Ḳ,) and ▼ فِرَامٌ, (M, Ḳ,) *A medicament,* or *remedial application,* (T, Ṣ, M, Ḳ,) *such as the stones of raisins,* (T, M,) *used by a woman for the purpose of contracting her vulva,* or *vagina.* (T, Ṣ, M, Ḳ.)

فَرْمٌ The *rag that is used on the occasion of menstruation:* (IAth, TA:) and ▼ مَفَارِمُ signifies the *rags used on the occasion thereof;* and [may be an irreg. pl. of فَرْمٌ, like as مَشَابِهُ is held to be of شَبَهٌ, but it is said that it] is a pl. having no sing.: (M, TA:) [in the Ḳ, in art. حشو, the ▼ مَفَارِمُ (there in the CḲ erroneously written مَقَاوِمُ) are said to be *used by the* مُسْتَحَاضَة: see 8 in that art.]

فَرْمَةٌ: see فَرْمٌ.

فَرْمَآءُ: see 10.

فِرَامٌ: see فَرْمٌ: = and see also the next following paragraph.

فِرَامَةٌ The *piece of rag which a woman bears* [*stuffed*] *in her vulva,* or *vagina:* (AZ, T, Ḳ:) or her *menstruating, and stuffing her vulva with a piece of rag;* like ▼ فِرَامٌ [as expl. above: see 3]. (Ḳ.)

أَفْرَمُ A man (TA) *whose teeth become much broken.* (Ḳ, TA.)

مُفْرَمٌ *Filled with water* (T, M) &c.: (M:) mentioned by A'Obeyd, as applied to a watering-trough: (T:) and applied also to a شِعْب [or road in a mountain, &c.,] as meaning *filled with men,* or *people:* (M:) of the dial. of Hudheyl. (T, M.)

مَفَارِمُ: see فَرْمٌ, in two places.

مُسْتَفْرِمَةٌ: see 10.

فرن

فُرْنٌ [app. from, or cognate with, the Latin

"furnus"] *An oven*, (IDrd,* Ṣ,* M, Ḳ,) syn. مَخْبَزٌ, (M, Ḳ,) [or *one*] *in which one bakes bread such as is termed* فُرْنِىّ; (Ṣ, Ḳ;) *differing from the* تَنُّور [q. v.]: (Ṣ:) a word of the dial. of Syria: (M:) thought by IDrd to be not Arabic [in origin]: (TA:) pl. أَفْرَانٌ. (M.)

فُرْنِىٌّ *Thick*, (Ṣ, Ḳ,) *round*, or *circular*, (Ḳ,) *bread*; (Ṣ, Ḳ;) so called in relation to its place [in which it is baked, i. e. the فُرْن]: (Ṣ:) or (Ḳ) *a sort of bread having a raised and pointed*, or *hollowed, head, the lateral portions thereof being drawn together to*, or *towards, the middle*, (M, Ḳ,) *and being intermingled, one part thereof in another*, (M,) *roasted*, or *fried*, (Ḳ,) *then well moistened with milk and clarified butter and sugar*: (M, Ḳ:) n. un. ▾ فُرْنِيَّةٌ: which signifies also *a round*, or *circular, great cake of bread*: (M:) [whence, app.,] فَإِذَا هِىَ مِثْلُ الفُرْنِيَّةِ الحَمْرَآءِ [*And lo, she*, or *it, was like the red* فرنيّة; but to what this refers I know not]: a saying of some of the Arabs. (Ṣ, TA.) — And (as being likened thereto, TA) ‡ *A thick, bulky, man*: (M, Ḳ, TA:) and (Ḳ) *a bulky dog*. (IB, Ḳ, TA.) — Also *A baker*; as a rel. n. of فُرْنٌ: (Mṣb:) and so ▾ فَرَّانٌ, in the dial. of the vulgar. (TA.)

فُرْنِيَّةٌ: see the next preceding paragraph.

فَرَّانٌ: see فُرْنِىٌّ, last sentence. [It is applied in the present day to *A baker of bread* and *of meat &c.*]

فَارِنَةٌ *A female baker* (T, Ḳ) *of the bread termed* فُرْنِىّ. (T.)

فرنب

فِرْنِبٌ *A rat*, or *mouse*; syn. فَأْرَةٌ: (IAạr, O, Ḳ:) or the *young one generated between it and a jerboa*: (Ḳ:) or [as a coll. gen. n.] the *rat*, or *mouse*; syn. فَأْرٌ. (T.) [See also قِرْنِبٌ.]

فرنج

الفِرَنْجُ, n. un. فِرَنْجِىٌّ: see what follows.

الإِفْرَنْجَةُ (O, Ḳ) [and الإِفْرَنْجُ, which is the more common,] and ▾ الفِرَنْجُ, (MF, TA, [but in the Commentary of MF written without any of the syll. signs,]) in which last manner it is correctly written accord. to the sheykhs of El-Andalus, who are the nearest to, and the best acquainted with, the country of the people thus called, and so written by Suh, (MF,) *A certain people*; [*the Franks*; an appellation given originally, by the Arabs, to *the French*; and afterwards to *all Europeans except those of the Turkish Empire*:] an arabicized word from إِفْرَنك, (Ḳ,) or افرنگ (O,) or from فرنك [or فرنگ]: (Suh, MF:) accord. to general analogy, it should be الإِفْرِنْجَة, with kesr to the ر: (O, Ḳ:) so called because the seat of their dominion is [named] فرنجة or فرانسة [i. e. France]; and their king is called الفرنسيس, [more properly الفَرَنْسِيسُ,] which is likewise an arabicized word. (Suh, as cited by MF.) [The n. un., or appellation given to a single person of this people, is إِفْرَنْجِىٌّ and فِرَنْجِىٌّ.]

فرند

فِرِنْدٌ *A sort of cloth*, or *garment*, (Lth, T, O, Ḳ,) *well known*: (Ḳ:) an adventitious word, (Lth, T, O,) [from the Pers. پَرَنْد,] arabicized. (O, Ḳ.) — And [hence, app.,] فِرِنْدُ السَّيْفِ, (T, Ṣ, M, O, Ḳ,) and ▾ إِفْرِنْدُهُ, (Ṣ, O, Ḳ,) *The diversified wavy marks, streaks, grain*, or *water, of the sword*; syn. وَشْيُهُ, (T, Ṣ, M, O, Ḳ,) and جَوْهَرُهُ, (T, O, Ḳ,) and رُبَدُهُ [q. v.], (Ṣ, O,) and طَرَائِقُهُ, (T, O,*) and مَاؤُهُ الَّذِى يَجْرِى فِيهِ, (T, O,) i. e. سَفَاسِقُهُ. (T.) — And الفِرِنْدُ signifies *The sword itself*. (M, L, Ḳ.) — And *The* حَوْجَم; (Ḳ, TA;) i. e. (TA) *the red rose*. (M, TA.) — And *The grains of the pomegranate*. (AA, O, Ḳ.)

فِرِنْدٌ i. q. أَبْزَارٌ [*Seeds that are used in cooking, for seasoning food*; &c.]: pl. فَرَانِدُ. (IAạr, O, Ḳ.)

فِرِنْدَاةٌ *A* قَطَاة [or *sand-grouse*]. (Ibn-'Abbád, O, Ḳ.)

إِفْرِنْدُ السَّيْفِ: see فِرِنْدٌ, second sentence.

فرنس

For words mentioned in some of the lexicons under this head, see art. فرس.

فرنق

Q. 2. تَفَرْنَقَ *He was*, or *became, bad*; (Ḳ, TA;) said of a camel: (TA:) and so تَفَرْنَقَتْ said of a sheep or goat (شَاة). (Ibn-'Abbád, O, TA.) ═ And تَفَرْنَقَتْ أُذُنُهُ *His ear became raised*. (Ibn-'Abbád, O, Ḳ.)

فُرْنُقٌ *Bad*; (Ibn-'Abbád, O, Ḳ;) applied to the عَرِيف [or chief, superintendent, or manager of the affairs,] of a people or party: and so ▾ مُتَفَرْنِقٌ applied to a camel. (Ibn-'Abbád, O.)

فُرَانِقٌ The بَرِيد, i. e., (IDrd, Ṣ, O,) the *warner before the lion*; (Ṣ, O, Ḳ;) *a certain beast of prey*, [sometimes called by us the *lion's provider*,] *that cries out before the lion, as though warning men of his presence*; *said to resemble the jachal* (ابْنُ آوَى); (IDrd, TA;) and said to be the *jachal* [itself]; but some say otherwise: (TA voce بَرِيد:) a Pers. word, (IDrd, Ṣ, O,) arabicized, (IDrd, Ṣ, O, Ḳ,) originally پَرْوَانَه [or پَرْوَانَك], (IDrd, TA,) or originally پَرْوَانَك: (Ṣ, O, Ḳ:) said by AḤát to be [also] called the وَعْوَع. (TA.) — And (hence, TA) The *guide of the messenger on a beast of the post*. (O, Ḳ, TA.) And sometimes The *guide of an army* was thus called. (Ṣ, TA.) — And, (O, Ḳ,) accord. to some, (O,) it signifies The *lion* [himself]. (O, Ḳ.)

مُتَفَرْنِقٌ: see فُرْنُقٌ.

فره

1. فَرُهَ, aor. ـُ, (Ṣ, Ḳ,) inf. n. فَرَاهَةٌ and فَرَاهِيَةٌ (Ḳ) [and app. also فُرُوهَةٌ, expl. below as a simple subst.], *He was*, or *became, skilled*, or *skilful*. (Ṣ, Ḳ.) — And فَرُهَ and فَرِهَ, aor. of each ـَ, [inf. n. app. فُرُوهَةٌ and فَرَاهَةٌ and فَرَاهِيَةٌ, expl. below as simple substs.,] said of a horse or similar beast, &c., *He was*, or *became, brisk, lively, sprightly, active, agile*, or *light*. (Mṣb.) — [And فَرُهَ, inf. n. فَرَاهَةٌ, (of which see an explanation below,) probably signifies *He was*, or *became, beautiful, comely, pretty*, or *elegant*; like صَبُحَ, inf. n. صَبَاحَةٌ.] — And فَرِهَ, (Ṣ, Ḳ,) aor. ـَ, (Ḳ,) inf. n. فَرَهٌ, (TḲ,) *He exulted*, or *rejoiced above measure*; or *he exulted greatly, and behaved insolently and unthankfully*, or *ungratefully*: (Ṣ, Ḳ:) the ه in this verb, accord. to Fr, is substituted for the ح in فَرِحَ, which has this meaning. (TA.)

2: see what next follows.

4. أَفْرَهَتْ *She* (a camel) *brought forth* [*young ones such as are termed*] فُرْه (Ṣ) or فُرَّه (Ḳ) [i. e. *such as were brisk, lively, sprightly, active, agile*, or *light*]; as also ▾ فَرَّهَتْ, inf. n. تَفْرِيهٌ. (Ḳ.) — And *She* (a woman) *brought forth beautiful children*. (TA.) — And افره *He* (a man) *took for himself a* غُلَام [i. e. *youth, young man*, or *male slave*,] *such as is termed* فَارِه (IAạr, Ḳ) meaning *beautiful*, or *comely, of countenance*. (IAạr, TA.)

10. هُوَ يَسْتَفْرِهُ الأَفْرَاسَ means يَسْتَكْرِمُهَا [i. e. *He seeks the horses*, or *mares, that are of generous race*]: (Ḳ, TA:) and the like is said in the A, but with الدَّوَابّ in the place of الافراس. (TA.)

فَرِهٌ [part. n. of فَرِهَ, meaning *Exulting*, or *rejoicing above measure*; &c.]. In the Ḳur xxvi. 149, some read فَرِهِينَ, from فَرِهَ, signifying as expl. above: others reading فَارِهِينَ, which is from فَرُهَ: (Ṣ, TA:) — but فَرِهٌ is also *syn. with* فَارِهٌ, as an epithet applied to a youth, or young man, or male slave; and thus the reading of فرهين in the Ḳur has been expl. as meaning *Possessing skill*. (TA.)

فُرَاهٌ i. q. فُرَاتٌ, as an epithet applied to water, signifying *Sweet*, &c.: both are chaste forms, and well known, like تَابُوهٌ and تَابُوتٌ: so in the Towsheeḥ. (MF and TA in art. فرت.)

فَرَاهَةٌ [mentioned in the first paragraph as an inf. n. is also expl. as a simple subst.]: see فُرُوهَةٌ. — Also *Beauty*, or *comeliness*. (Mṣb, TA.)

فُرُوهَةٌ [app. an inf. n., but mentioned as a simple subst., meaning] *Skilfulness*. (Ḳ.) — And فُرُوهَةٌ and ▾ فَرَاهَةٌ and ▾ فَرَاهِيَةٌ denote a quality of a hackney and of a mule and of an ass, (Ṣ,) or of a horse, or similar beast, &c., (Mṣb,) all signifying *Briskness, liveliness, sprightliness, activity, agility,* or *lightness.* (Mṣb, TA.*)

فَرَاهِيَةٌ [mentioned in the first paragraph as an inf. n.]: see what next precedes.

فَارِهٌ *Skilful,* or *possessing skill;* (Ṣ, Mṣb, Ḳ;) part. n. of فَرُهَ, irregularly formed, for by rule it should be فَرِيهٌ: (Ṣ:) accord. to Z, it is applied to a man; and also, without ة, to a قَيْنَة [i. e. female slave, or slave-songstress]. (Mṣb.) — And it is applied as an epithet to a hackney, (Az, Ṣ, Mṣb,) and a mule, (Ṣ,) and an ass, (Az, Ṣ, Mṣb,) or to a horse, or similar beast, (Az,) meaning *Brisk, lively, sprightly, active, agile,* or *light;* (Az,* Mṣb;) *sharp; strong; that goes,* or *journeys, much; a great goer:* (Az, TA:) it is not applied to a فَرَس, (Az, Ṣ,) i. e. to an Arabian horse; (Az, Mṣb;) such being termed جَوَادٌ, (Az, Ṣ, Mṣb,) and رَائِعٌ: (Ṣ:) 'Adee Ibn-Zeyd has applied it to the latter; but Aṣ has charged him with error in so doing; saying that he possessed not knowledge of horses: (Ṣ:) the pl. is فُرْهٌ, (Ṣ, Mṣb,) like بُزْلٌ and حُولٌ pls. of بَازِلٌ and حَائِلٌ, (Ṣ,) or فُرُهٌ, like كُتُبٌ, (Ḳ,) and فَرَهَةٌ, with two fet-ḥahs, (Mṣb,) or فُرْهَةٌ, (Ṣ, Ḳ,) but this is held by Sb to be a quasi-pl. n., (ISd, TA,) and فُرَّهٌ, like رُكَّعٌ, and فُرْهَةٌ, like سُكْرَةٌ, (Ḳ,) as in the A, but MF says that no pl. of this measure is known. (TA.) — Also, applied to a غُلَام [i. e. youth, young man, or male slave], *Beautiful,* or *comely, of countenance.* (IAạr, TA.) And [the fem.] فَارِهَةٌ signifies *A beautiful,* or *comely,* girl, or young woman: (Ḳ:) [and] so ▼ فُرْهَاةٌ, [of which the masc. is أَفْرَهُ, and] of which the pl. is فُرْهٌ; but Az says, I do not think that they use this word in relation to girls, or young women, though they may apply it peculiarly to female slaves like as they apply فَارِهٌ and فَارِهَةٌ peculiarly to hackneys and mules and jades, exclusively of Arabian horses. (Mṣb.) — And فَارِهَةٌ is also syn. with فَتِيَّةٌ [i. e. *A youthful* female, or one *in the prime of life*]: (thus accord. to several copies of the Ḳ and accord. to the TA:) or قَيْنَةٌ [i. e. *a female slave,* or *a slave-songstress:* see the first sentence of this paragraph]. (Thus in the CḲ.) — And it signifies also [A woman] *who eats vehemently:* (Ḳ:) and فَارِهٌ applied to man, *A vehement eater.* (IAạr, TA.)

أَفْرَهُ: see its fem., فُرْهَاةٌ, in the next preceding paragraph. — فُلَانٌ أَفْرَهُ مِنْ فُلَانٍ means *Such a one is more beautiful,* or *comely, than such a one.* (Mṣb.)

مُفْرِهٌ and مُفْرِهَةٌ (Ṣ, Ḳ) and مُفَرِّهَةٌ (Ṣ) are epithets applied to a she-camel, meaning *Bringing forth* [*young ones such as are termed*] فُرْهٌ (Ṣ) or فُرَّهٌ. (Ḳ.) [See 4.]

فرهد

Q. 2. تَفَرْهَدَ, said of a boy, or youth, not of a man, *He became fat.* (TA. [See also فُرْهُدٌ, and مُفَرْهَدٌ.])

فَرْهَدٌ: see the next paragraph, in three places.

فُرْهُدٌ (Ṣ, M, O, L, Ḳ) and ▼ فُرْهُودٌ (M, L, Ḳ) A boy, or youth, (L,) *fat,* or *compact in make,* (حَادِرٌ,) *and thick;* (Ṣ, M, O, L, Ḳ;) as also ▼ فَرْهَدٌ: (O:) and *soft, thin-skinned, and plump:* (M, O,* Ḳ:) some assign this meaning to قُرْهُدٌ, but others say that this is a corruption, and it is correctly with ف: and one says also غُلَامٌ فُلْهُدٌ, meaning *a plump boy* or *youth:* (L:) also, (Ḳ,) or فُرْهُدٌ [only], (TA,) or ▼ فُرْهُودٌ, (IDrd, O,) a boy, or youth, (IDrd, O, Ḳ, TA,) not a man, (IDrd, O,) *plump* (IDrd, O, Ḳ, TA) *in body,* (TA,) *and beautiful* (IDrd, O, Ḳ, TA) *in face;* (TA;) as also ▼ فَرْهَدٌ: (Ḳ:) and فُرْهُدٌ and ▼ فَرْهَدٌ signify a boy, or youth, *that has nearly attained to puberty.* (O. [See also فُلْهُدٌ and قُوْهَدٌ.]) — Also, i. e. the first and second, (L, Ḳ,) or ▼ فُرْهُودٌ, which is of the dial. of Azd, (O,) The *whelp of a lion;* (O, L, Ḳ;) of the dial. of 'Omán: the pl. [of ▼ فُرْهُودٌ, or] of فُرْهُدٌ, accord. to Kr, is فَرَاهِيدُ; but ISd distrusts his authority on a matter of this kind. (L.)

فُرْهُودٌ: see the next preceding paragraph, in four places. — Also *A young mountain-kid.* (L, Ḳ.) — And [the pl.] فَرَاهِيدُ signifies *Young lambs* or *kids.* (O, Ḳ.)

مُفَرْهَدٌ A *fat* boy or youth. (TA.)

فرو

[2. فَرَّى الجُبَّةَ, inf. n. تَفْرِيَةٌ, *He furred,* or *lined with fur, the garment called* جُبَّة: see the pass. part. n., below.]

4. افرى *He was,* or *became, abundant in cattle,* or *other property:* like أَثْرَى. (M in art. ثرو. [See فَرْوَةٌ, last sentence.])

8. افترى فَرْوًا *He wore* فَرْو [i. e. *fur*]: (Ṣ, M, Ḳ:) [and so, app., افترى alone: see مُفْتَرٍ, below.]

فَرْوٌ signifies *A certain thing that is worn;* (Ṣ, Mṣb;) as also ▼ فَرْوَةٌ: (Mṣb:) each of these is a word of well-known meaning: (M:) [but the former is properly a coll. gen. n., and ▼ فَرْوَةٌ is its n. un.; agreeably with what here follows:] الفَرْوُ is well known [as being *fur*]; and ▼ فَرْوَةٌ is the appellation applied when it is [*a furred garment*] *like the* جُبَّة: (Lth, T:) and signifies also *a skin,* but not unless *having upon it* وَبَر [i. e. *fur,* or *soft hair,*] or *wool:* (T:) [in general,] this latter word signifies, (Ḳ, TA,) and some say the former also, (TA,) *a kind of garment, well known,* (Ḳ, TA,) *lined with the skins of various species of animals, the most highly esteemed whereof is the* سَمُّور [or *sable*], *tanned, and sewed together; this garment being worn for preservation from the cold:* (TA:) فِرَآءٌ is the pl. (Ṣ, M, Mṣb, TA) of mult., and the pl. of pauc. is أَفْرٍ: so says Aboo-'Alee El-Ḳálee. (TA.)

فَرْوَةٌ: see the next preceding paragraph, in three places. — Also The *scalp,* or *skin of the head:* (Ṣ, Mṣb, Ḳ:) or فَرْوَةُ الرَّأْسِ signifies *the scalp,* or *skin of the head, with the hair thereof,* (Lth, T, M, Mgh,) of a man, and of other than man: (M:) or *the upper part of the head:* (M, TA:) and one says, ضَرَبَهُ عَلَى أُمِّ فَرْوَتِهِ meaning [*He struck him upon*] *his* هَامَة [*crown,* &c.]. (TA.) [Hence,] it is metaphorically applied, in a trad., to ‡ The *skin* of the face. (TA.) — And ‡ A woman's [*head-covering such as is called*] خِمَار, (Mgh, Ḳ, TA,) or [*such as is called*] قِنَاع; occurring in a trad.; (Mgh, TA;) metaphorically applied thereto. (Mgh.) — And † *A crown, such as is worn by a king:* (Z, Ḳ,* TA:) [said to be] so called because made of skins. (TA.) — And *A* [*garment of the kind called*] جُبَّة *of which the two sleeves have been tucked up.* (Ḳ.) — And *The half of a* [*garment such as is called*] كِسَآء *made of the soft hair of camels;* (Ḳ, TA;) *now known by the appellation of* جبة [evidently a mistranscription, app. for خَبَّة, q. v.]. (TA.) — And *A* [*bag such as is termed*] وَفْضَة [q. v.], (Ḳ, TA,) [i. e.] *like the* خَرِيطَة, *made of skin,* (TA,) *in which the beggar puts his alms.* (Ḳ, TA.) And hence, (TA,) ذُو الفَرْوَةِ means *The beggar.* (Ḳ, TA.) — And *A portion of herbage collected together and dry.* (Ṣ, Ḳ.) — And *Waste,* or *uncultivated, land, having in it no herbage* (T, Ḳ) *and no* بَرَش [or *maculæ,* or *spots differing in colour from the rest*]. (T.) — أَبُو فَرْوَةَ signifies *The* بَلُّوط [here meaning *chestnut,* which is called in Egypt ابو فروة in the present day]; of the dial. of Egypt: it is thus called because within its husk is what resembles the soft hair of camels. (TA.) = Also *i. q.* ثَرْوَةٌ, (Fr, Aṣ, ISk, T, Ṣ, M, Mṣb, Ḳ,) and غِنًى; (Ṣ, Ḳ;) [i. e. *Abundance,* and *richness* &c.;] accord. to Yaạḳoob [i. e. ISk], (M,) formed from ثَرْوَةٌ by substitution (Ṣ, M) of ف for ث: (M:) one says, إِنَّهُ لَذُو ثَرْوَةٍ مِنَ المَالِ and فَرْوَةٍ, both meaning the same [i. e. *Verily he is a possessor of abundance of property*]; (T, Ṣ; [in some copies of the latter, فِى المَالِ;]) so says ISk, (T,) or Fr; (Ṣ;) and Aṣ says the like: (Ṣ:) the latter says, فُلَانٌ ذُو فَرْوَةٍ and ثَرْوَةٍ, meaning *Such a one is a possessor of abundant property.* (T.)

فَرَّآءٌ *A manufacturer of* فِرَآء [i. e. *furs,* or *furred garments*]: — and *A seller thereof.* (TA.)

جُبَّةٌ مُفَرَّاةٌ [*A furred* جُبَّة;] *a* [*garment of the kind called*] جُبَّة *upon which is a* فَرْوَة [or *fur,* i. e., *that is lined therewith*].

مُفْتَرٍ [act. part. n. of 8]. المُفْتَرِى لَا يَجِدُ البَرْدَ [*The wearer of fur will not feel the cold*] is a saying of the Arabs. (TA.)

Quasi فروز

Q. Q. 1. فَرْوَزَ see in art. فرز.

فرى

1. فَرَاهُ, (M, Ḳ,) aor. يَفْرِيهِ, (Ḳ,) inf. n. فَرْىٌ, (Ḳ,) *He slit it,* or *cut it lengthwise, ill,* or *improperly;* or *well,* or *properly;* as also ▼ فرّاه and ▼ افراه [both relating to both of the foregoing explanations]: (Ḳ:) or *he slit it,* or *cut it lengthwise, and made it bad,* or *improper;* as also ▼ فرّاه: or, accord. to the sound lexicologists, the former has this meaning: but ▼ افرى signifies *he slit,* or *cut lengthwise, and made good,* or *proper:* (M:) or ▼ افراه (M, Ḳ) signifies, (M,) or signifies also, (Ḳ,) *he made it good,* or *proper:* or *he ordered* [another] *to make it so:* (M, Ḳ:) as though he removed from it unsoundness, or imperfection: but some say that this signifies *he slit it,* or *cut it lengthwise, and made it bad,* or *improper:* and when you mean *he measured it, and cut it, to make it good,* or *proper,* you say فَرَاهُ, inf. n. فَرْىٌ: (M:) [thus, accord. to J,] فَرَى, aor. and inf. n. as above, signifies *he cut* a thing *in order to make it good,* or *proper:* (Ṣ:) or *he cut* a skin, or hide, *in a good,* or *proper, manner:* (Ks, Ṣ, Mṣb:) and ▼ افرى *he cut* it *in a bad,* or *an improper, manner:* (Ks, Ṣ:) or this signifies *he slit much, in a bad,* or *an improper, manner:* and افرى الجِلْدَ, accord. to Aṣ, *he rent, tore,* or *slit, the skin, and made holes in it, and spoiled it:* and افرى signifies also *he slit* a thing (Ṣ, M, Mṣb) of any kind; (M; [as also ▼ فرّاه:]) thus you say, افرى الأَوْدَاجَ *he slit the* اوداج [or *external jugular veins*], (T, M, Mgh, Mṣb,) *and made what was in them, of the blood, to come forth;* (T, Mgh, Mṣb;) and in like manner one says of a garment, or piece of cloth, and of a جُلَّة [or receptacle for dates, made of palm-leaves woven together]; (T;) or *he cut the* اوداج: (Ṣ:) IAạr alone mentions فَرَى أَوْدَاجَهُ and ▼ افراها: (M:) [but it is also said that فَرَى signifies *he cut* a نِطْع [or the like]: (Ḳ in art. خلق: [see an ex. in a verse cited in the first paragraph of that art.; also cited in the T after the first of the explanations here following, and in the M after the second thereof:]) or فَرَى, aor. and inf. n. as above, signifies *he measured, and worked,* or *manufactured,* and *made good,* or *proper,* a thing, such as a sandal, or a نِطَع [q. v.], or a water-skin, and the like: (T:) or *he measured* it, *and cut it, to make it good,* or *proper:* (M:) and *he measured and manufactured* a مَزَادَة [or leathern water-bag]: (Ṣ, Ḳ:) or *he sewed, and made well,* or *properly,* a مزادة: (T:) [it is said that] the difference between ▼ الإِفْرَآء and الفَرْىُ is this, that the former signifies *the cutting so as to render bad,* or *improper,* and *the slitting like as the slaughterer and the wild beast slit* [*their victims*]; and the latter, *the cutting so as to make good,* or *proper,* like the act of cutting of the sewer of the hide, or of leather: but فَرَى sometimes occurs in the sense of افرى: (Mgh:) one says, ▼ أَفْرَيْتُ رَأْسَهُ, meaning *I split,* or *clave, his head* with a sword; like أَفْرَرْتُهُ: (Yz, T &c. in art. فر:) and افرى الجُرْحَ *he slit the wound:* (T:) and افرى الذِّئْبُ بَطْنَ الشَّاةِ [*the wolf slit,* or *rent, the belly of the sheep,* or *goat*]: (Ṣ:) and one says, قَدْ أَفْرَيْتَ وَمَا فَرَيْتَ i. e. *thou hast done ill,* or *improperly, and hast not done well,* or *properly.* (A, TA.) — فَرَاهُ, aor. as above, [and so the inf. n.,] is sometimes metonymically used [as meaning ‡ *He slaughtered him,* or *butchered him;* i. e.] as denoting vehemence, or excess, in slaying. (TA.) — And it means also † *He cut him with censure,* or *satire:* (TA:) and ▼ افرى means *he blamed,* or *censured,* a man. (M, Ḳ.) — And you say, فَرَيْتُ الأَرْضَ ‡ *I traversed,* or *crossed,* (lit. *travelled and cut,*) *the land,* or *country;* (T, Ṣ, Ḳ, TA;) inf. n. as above. (TA.) — هُوَ يَفْرِى ▼ الفَرِىَّ means † *He effects what is wonderful in his deed.* (Ṣ, Ḳ.) مَا يَفْرِى فَرِيَّهُ ▼ أَحَدٌ, thus, with teshdeed [to the ى in فريه] as related by A'Obeyd, is said of a courageous man [as meaning *No one does his deed,* or the like]: but it is said [by Kh] to be correctly فَرْيَهُ, [as an inf. n.,] without teshdeed. (M. [See, however, what follows.]) They say, تَرَكْتُهُ يَفْرِى ▼ الفَرِىَّ, meaning [*I left him*] *doing well,* or *excellently, in a deed,* or *in watering:* [an explanation relating to what here follows:] the Prophet said, respecting 'Omar, whom he saw in a dream drawing water at a well with a great bucket, فَلَمْ أَرَ عَبْقَرِيًّا يَفْرِى فَرِيَّهُ ▼ [*And I have not seen a chief of a people do his deed,* &c.]: (T:) or, as some relate it, he said فَرْيَهُ: (TA:) [but] A'Obeyd says, this is like thy saying يَعْمَلُ عَمَلَهُ and يَقُولُ قَوْلَهُ; and Fr cited to us [as an ex.]

قَدْ كُنْتِ تَفْرِينَ بِهِ الفَرِيَّا ▼

meaning [*Verily*] *thou didst multiply and magnify thy words respecting it:* (T: and in like manner this hemistich [which shows, by the measure, that الفَرِيَّا cannot be here a mistake for الفَرْيَا,] is expl. in the Ṣ:) it is said that ▼ فَرِىٌّ thus used is of the measure فَعِيلٌ in the sense of the measure مَفْعُولٌ, from فَرَى signifying "he cut" [or "cut lengthwise" or "slit"] a hide, or leather; (Ḥar p. 257; [where see more;]) [and this assertion is corroborated by the fact that] one says of a man strenuous, or vigorous, in an affair, and strong, تَرَكْتُهُ يَفْرِى ▼ الفَرِىَّ وَيَقُدُّ [lit. *I left him slitting,* or *cutting, the slit,* or *cut, thing, and shaping*]. (T.) — فَرَى is also synonymous with افترى: see the latter, in two places. — فَرَى البَرْقُ, aor. and inf. n. as above, signifies *The lightning shone,* or *glistened,* or *shone with flickering light, and continued, in the sky.* (T, TA.) = فَرِىَ, (T, Ṣ, M, Ḳ,) aor. يَفْرَى, (T, Ṣ,) inf. n. فَرًى, (T, Ṣ, Ḳ, but omitted in the CḲ,) *He was,* or *became, confounded,* or *perplexed, and unable to see his right course;* syn. بَهِتَ, (T,) and دَهِشَ, (T, Ṣ, M, Ḳ,) and تَحَيَّرَ, (Ṣ, Ḳ,) and بَطِرَ: (Skr, on the verse here following:) El-Aalam El-Hudhalee says,

وَفَرِيتُ مِنْ فَزَعٍ فَلَا
أَرْمِى وَلَا وَدَّعْتُ صَاحِبْ

[*And I became confounded,* &c., *by reason of fright, so that I did not shoot* an arrow, *nor bade I farewell to a friend*]: (T, M:) or, accord. to Aṣ, فَرِىَ, aor. يَفْرَى, signifies *he looked, and knew not what he should do:* (T:) and فَرِيتُ signifies also *I wondered;* from ▼ الفَرِىّ meaning "that which is wonderful." (Skr, on the verse above-cited.)

2: see 1, first quarter, in three places.

4: see 1, former half, in seven places: — and also in the latter half, near the middle of the paragraph.

5. تفرّى *It became slit,* or *cut lengthwise;* (Ṣ, M, Mṣb, Ḳ;) as also ▼ انفرى; (Ṣ, M, Mṣb;) both said of a skin, (M,) or of a thing: (Ṣ:) or *it became much slit,* or *rent;* said of the sewing of a leathern water-skin. (T.) And تفرّى عَنْهُ ثَوْبُهُ *His garment became much slit,* or *rent, from him.* (T.) And تفرّت العَيْنُ ‡ *The spring of water burst forth:* (Ḳ, TA:) or تفرّت الأَرْضُ بِالعُيُونِ ‡ *The earth,* or *ground, burst with the springs.* (Ṣ, M, A, TA.) — [Hence,] the saying of Ḳabeeṣah Ibn-Jábir,

تَفَرَّى بَيْضُهَا عَنَّا فَكُنَّا
بَنِى الأَجْلَادِ مِنْهَا وَالرِّمَالِ

i. e. † *Its eggs* (the pronoun in بيضها denoting the earth) *burst from us* [so as to disclose us], *so that we were the sons of the hard tracts thereof and of the soft tracts,* or *plains,* [or *of the sands,*] means only their numerousness, and the wide extent of their districts. (Ḥam p. 341.) — And تفرّى اللَّيْلُ عَنْ صُبْحِهِ ‡ [*The night became distinct, as though cleft, from its dawn*]. (TA.)

7: see the next preceding paragraph.

8: افترى كَذِبًا *He forged,* or *fabricated, a lie,* or *falsehood;* (T, Ṣ, M, Mgh, Mṣb, Ḳ;) you say, افترى عَلَيْهِ كَذِبًا [*he forged against him a lie*]; (Mgh, Mṣb;) and كَذِبًا ▼ فَرَى signifies the same, (T, Ṣ, M, Mṣb, Ḳ,) aor. يَفْرِى, (Mṣb,) inf. n. فَرْىٌ; (M;) and this verb likewise is followed by عَلَيْهِ: (Mṣb:) ▼ فرى in this sense is mentioned as said by Lth; others saying افترى. (T.) افترى is used in the Ḳur in relation also to the attributing a copartner to God: thus in the saying [in iv. 51], وَمَنْ يُشْرِكْ بِٱللّٰهِ فَقَدِ ٱفْتَرَى إِثْمًا عَظِيمًا [*And whoso attributeth a copartner to God, hath devised an enormous sin*]. (Er-Rághib, TA.)

فَرْيَةٌ *Clamour;* or *a confusion,* or *mixture, of cries* or *shouts* or *noises.* (M, Ḳ, TA. [الحَلْبَةُ in the CḲ is a mistake for الجَلَبَةُ.])

فِرْيَةٌ *A lie,* or *falsehood;* (Ṣ,* M, Mgh,* Mṣb,* Ḳ, TA;) a subst. from افترى: (Ṣ, Mgh, Mṣb, TA:) and meaning [also] *a defamation:* (Mgh:) pl. فِرًى. (TA.) — And *An affair,* or *a case, of great magnitude* or *moment* or *gravity.* (M, TA.)

فَرِىٌّ *Slit,* or *cut lengthwise;* applied to a skin (جِلْدٌ): and so فَرِيَّةٌ [app. as applied to a قِرْبَة or the like, as being fem. of فَرِىٌّ]. (M, TA.) — And A *wide* دَلْو [or leathern bucket]; (M, Ḳ;) as though it were slit; (M;) as also فَرِيَّةٌ. (Ḳ.) — And A thing *forged,* or *fabricated;* (Ṣ, Ḳ, TA;) thus [or rather as hence meaning *unknown,* or *unheard of,*] in the saying, لَقَدْ جِئْتِ شَيْئًا فَرِيًّا, in the Ḳur [xix. 28], (Ṣ, TA,) i. e. [*Thou hast done*] *a thing hitherto unknown; a thing deemed strange:* (Bḍ:) or a thing *of great magnitude* or *moment* or *gravity;* (Ṣ, Ḳ, TA;) and thus it is said to mean in the phrase above cited: (Ṣ, TA:) or *wonderful;* (T, TA;) thus as expl. by Er-Rághib; (TA;) and thus it is also said to mean in that phrase. (T, TA.) — See also 1, latter half, in eight places. == Also, applied to a man, *A forger,* or *fabricator, of lies;* and so ▾ مِفْرًى. (Lḥ, M, TA.) == And Milk *of the time when it is milked.* (Ḳ.) == And they say, الفَرِىَّ الفَرِىَّ, meaning العَجَلَةَ العَجَلَةَ [i. e. *Haste: haste:* used in an imperative sense; as inf. ns. are often thus used; but they are] both like غَنِىّ [in measure]: mentioned by Ṣgh. (TA.)

أَفْرَى الفِرَى occurs in a trad. as meaning *The most lying of lies:* الفِرَى is the pl. of فِرْيَةٌ. (TA.)

مِفْرًى: see فَرِىٌّ.

مَزَادَةٌ مَفْرِيَّةٌ A [or leathern water-bag] *made in a good,* or *proper, manner; well made.* (T, TA.)

فز

1. فَزَّ, (A, O, Ḳ,) aor. ـِ, inf. n. فَزٌّ, (TA,) *He* (a gazelle) *was,* or *became, frightened,* or *afraid.* (A, O, Ḳ.) — فَزَّ قَلْبُهُ *His heart heaved* by reason of fear. (O.) — فَزَّ عَنْهُ *He* (a man, O) *turned away from him.* (A, O, Ḳ.) And *He separated himself from him, and became alone.* (A, O, Ḳ.) == فَزَّ, aor. ـِ, inf. n. فَزَازَةٌ and فُزُوزَةٌ, *He* (a man, O) *became excited with ardour,* or *eagerness.* (O, Ḳ.) == فَزَّ فُلَانًا عَنْ مَوْضِعِهِ, (A, O,* Ḳ,) inf. n. فَزٌّ, (O,) *He disturbed, removed,* or *unsettled, such a one from his place:* (A, O,* Ḳ:) or *he frightened, and disturbed,* or *removed,* or *unsettled, such a one from his place, and made his courage* (lit. *his heart*) *to fly away:* (IDrd, TA:) and [in like manner] ▾ أَفَزَّهُ *he frightened him;* (Ḳ;) or, as in some copies of the Ḳ, *he disturbed* or *disquieted him;* (TA;) or *he frightened him, and disturbed* or *disquieted* or *unsettled him, and made his courage* (lit. *his heart*) *to fly away.* (Ṣ, O.*) [See also 10.] == فَزَّ, aor. ـِ, inf. n. فَزِيزٌ (Ṣ, O, Ḳ, TA) and فَزٌّ, (TA,) said of a wound, *It became moist, and flowed,* (Ṣ, O, Ḳ, TA,) *discharging its contents;* and so فَصَّ: and in like manner it is said of water [app. as meaning *it oozed forth*]: (TA:) and of sweat, meaning *It exuded;* and so فَصَّ. (TA in art. فص.)

2. فزّزهُ *He* (a man) *rendered him powerful,* or *strong, and made him to overcome.* (Ibn-'Abbád, O.)

4: see 1, latter half.

8. افتزّ *He* (a man, O) *overcame;* (Ḳ;) or *was,* or *became, powerful,* or *strong, and overcame:* (O:) and ابتزّ and ابتلّ signify the same: so in the Nawádir. (O, TA.)

10. استفزّهُ *It* (fear, Ṣ, A, O) *excited him to lightness and unsteadiness; unsettled him.* (Ṣ, A, O, Ḳ.) وَٱسْتَفْزِزْ مَنِ ٱسْتَطَعْتَ مِنْهُمْ بِصَوْتِكَ, in the Ḳur [xvii. 66], is expl. by Fr as meaning *And excite thou to lightness and unsteadiness,* or *unsettle thou, when thou canst, with thy voice.* (O, TA.) And in like manner, وَإِنْ كَادُوا لَيَسْتَفِزُّونَكَ مِنَ الأَرْضِ, in the same [xvii. 78], is expl. by him (O, TA) as meaning, *And verily they were near to unsettling thee from the land:* (TA:) but some say the meaning is, *they were near to frightening thee so as to excite thee to promptness of flight from the land.* (O, TA.) And استفزّهُ عَنْ رَأْيِهِ *He incited him,* or *excited him, to ignorance, foolishness,* or *wrong conduct, and levity,* or *unsteadiness, so as to make him swerve from his right sentiment, opinion,* or *judgment;* like اِسْتَخَفَّهُ عن رأيه. (Az and TA in art. خف.) — *He incited him,* or *excited him, to be promptly obedient and submissive to him and to that which he desired of him;* like استخفّهُ. (Ksh in xliii. 54.) — *He expelled him* (Jel in xvii. 105, and Ḳ) from the land, (Jel,) or from his abode, *and disturbed,* or *disquieted,* or *unsettled, him,* (Ḳ,) *so as to excite him to lightness and unsteadiness.* (TA.) [See also 1, latter half.] — *He,* or *it, deceived him,* or *beguiled him, so as to cast him into destruction.* (TA.) — *He slew him:* so the verb is expl. by some in the Ḳur xvii. 78, quoted above. (TA.)

فَزٌّ *A light,* or *an active,* man. (Ṣ, A, O, Ḳ.) — And The *offspring of the cow;* (Ṣ;) [meaning,] *of the wild cow:* (O, Ḳ:) because of its restlessness: (TA:) pl. أَفْزَازٌ. (Ṣ, O, Ḳ.)

فَزَّةٌ *A leap with disquietude* [or *fright*]. (TA.)

قَعَدَ مُسْتَفِزًّا [so in a copy of the Ṣ, but without the vowel-signs: in two other copies of the same, مُسْتَوْفِزًا, which belongs to art. وفز:] *He sat in an uneasy posture.* (Ṣ.) — فَرَسٌ مُسْتَفِزٌّ لِلْوَثْبِ وَالعَدْوِ [so in two copies of the Ṣ, in art. طمر; in the O, in that art., مُسْتَفِزُّ الوَثْبِ وَالعَدْوِ; probably a mistake for مُسْتَفَزٌّ; app. meaning, *A horse in a state of excitement to leap and run.*]

فزر

1. فَزَرَ, (Ṣ, O, Mṣb, Ḳ, &c.,) aor. ـُ, (M, O, TA,) or ـِ, (Mṣb,) inf. n. فَزْرٌ, (Ṣ,* O,* Mṣb,) *He rent,* or *slit,* a garment, or piece of cloth: (Ḳ:) *he dissundered* (Ṣ,* O,* Mṣb) the same. (Ṣ, O.) — *He split, slit,* or *cracked,* a thing. (Ṣ, O, TA.) — *He struck* a man's nose *with a thing so as to split it.* (O,* TA.) — *He struck* one with a stick, or staff: (TA:) or *he struck* him with a stick, or staff, *on his back,* (Ḳ, TA,) *so as to break it.* (TA.) — *He separated, disunited, sundered,* or *dispersed,* a thing. (TA.) — *He separated,* or *divided,* a thing from another thing. (TA.) — *He broke* [a thing]. (Sh, O, Mṣb.) Sh says, I was in the desert, and, seeing some small round tents (قِبَاب) pitched, I said to an Arab of the desert, "To whom belong these قباب?" and he answered, لِبَنِى فَزَارَةَ فَزَرَ ٱللّٰهُ ظُهُورَهُمْ: whereupon I said to him, "What meanest thou by it?" and he answered, "[*To Benoo-Fezárah:*] *may God break* [*their backs*]." (TA.) — *He crumbled,* or *broke into small pieces,* a جُلَّة [or round piece of camel's or similar dung]; as also ▾ فزّر, (TA,) and ▾ افزر. (O, Ḳ, TA. [In the CḲ, الجُلَّة is put for الجِلَّة.]) == See also 5. == Also, as implied in the Ḳ, but correctly فَزِرَ, aor. ـَ, inf. n. فَزَرٌ [q. v.], *He was,* or *became, such as is termed* أَفْزَرُ [expl. below]. (TA.)

2 and **4:** see 1, last signification but one.

5. تفزّر *It* (a garment, or piece of cloth,) *became rent,* or *slit;* (Ḳ;) as also ▾ انفزر; (O,* Ḳ;) and ▾ فَزَرَ, inf. n. فُزُورٌ; (Mṣb; [but see فَزْرٌ, below;]) and so the like thereof; (Mṣb;) and the same is said of a wall: (TA:) and *it* (a garment, or piece of cloth,) *became dissundered, ragged, tattered,* or *shabby, and old and worn out;* (Ṣ, TA;) as also ▾ انفزر. (TA.)

7: see 5, in two places.

فَزْرٌ inf. n. of the trans. v. فَزَرَ. (Mṣb.) — [And app. used as a simple subst., having for its pl. فُزُورٌ: see فِزْرٌ.] == [Also] A man *possessing little,* or *no, good,* or *goodness;* or *little,* or *no, wealth;* like نَزْرٌ. (AZ, TA in art. نزر.)

فِزْرٌ *A flock of sheep,* or *herd of goats:* (Ṣ, O:) or *a flock of sheep from ten to forty:* (AZ, A'Obeyd, Ṣ, O, Ḳ:) or *from three to ten;* thus in the copies of the Ḳ; but in the L, *to twenty:* (TA:) and *two,* and *more:* (Ṣ, O, Ḳ:) and hence, (Ṣ, O,) الفِزْرُ was a surname of Saad Ibn-Zeyd-Menáh: he came to the مَوْسِم [or fair, and place of meeting, app. of the pilgrims,] with some goats, and allowed them to be taken as spoil, saying, "Whoso takes of them one, it shall be his, but a فِزْر [i. e. *a pair* or *more*] of them shall not be taken;" فِزْر here meaning *two* and *more:* whence the prov., لَا آتِيكَ مِعْزَى الفِزْرِ, meaning [*I will not come to thee*] until *the goats of El-Fizr* shall become gathered together; and [that means *never,* for] those goats will never become gathered together: (Ṣ, O, Ḳ:) or, accord. to ISd, this surname was given to him because he said to his sons, one after another, "Pasture ye these goats," and they were incompliant to him; so he called to the people, "Collect yourselves together;" and they did so; and he said, "Take ye them as spoil; but I do not allow to any one more than one;" therefore they separated them at once, and they became scattered in the country: this was the origin of the prov.: and one of their provs. relating to leaving a thing undone is the saying, لَا أَفْعَلُ ذٰلِكَ مِعْزَى الفِزْرِ [*I will not do that* until *the goats of El-Fizr* shall become gathered together. (TA.) Accord. to AO, (Ṣ, O, TA,) فِزْرٌ means The *kid* (Ṣ, O, Ḳ, TA) itself: (Ṣ, O, TA:)

and one says, لَا أَفْعَلُهُ مَا نَزَا فُزْرٌ [*I will not do it as long as a kid leaps*]. (TA.) — And The *male young one of the* نَمِر [or leopard]: (TA:) or the *male young one of the* [*beast of prey called*] بَبْر [q. v.], (O, Ḳ, TA, [in the CḲ, erroneously, بَبْر,]) as is said in the T, and likewise in the Tekmileh: (TA:) and فُزْرَةٌ signifies the *female young one thereof*; (O, Ḳ, TA;) or, as some say, the *sister thereof*: (TA:) and ▼ فَزَارَةٌ signifies the *female of the* بَبْر; (O, Mṣb, TA;) thus says IAạr, (O,) [and] thus is said in the T: (TA:) or the *mother of the* بَبْر is called فزارة; and also the *female of the* نَمِر; (Ḳ, TA;) thus says IAạr. (TA.) = Also The أَصْل [or *origin*, &c.,] (O, Ḳ) of a thing. (O.) = And *A small thing*, (O, Ḳ,) *like a* نَفْخَة [or *blister*], *in the root of the thigh*, (O,) *below the extremity of the pubes, resembling a* غُدَّة [or *ganglion*], *from an ulcer that comes forth in a man*, (O, Ḳ,) or *from a wound*. (O.)

فَزْرٌ an inf. n. [of which the verb, accord. to a general rule, is فَزِرَ], A garment's *being old and worn out*; and *rent*, or *slit*. (KL. [See also 5, with which the verb فَزِرَ, inf. n. فُزُورٌ, is mentioned in a similar sense.]) — And [app. The *being open*, or *wide*, or *broad*,] meaning in Pers. فراخ شدن. (KL.) = Also The *being such as is termed* أَفْزَرُ [expl. below]. (Ṣ. [See 1, last sentence.])

فُزْرٌ *Slits, rents*, or *fissures*: (Ḳ:) but this word perhaps occurred to the author of the Ḳ mistranscribed; for it is said in the L that فُزُورٌ [a pl. of which the sing. is app. فَزْرٌ, originally an inf. n.,] signifies *slits, rents*, or *fissures*, and *clefts*, or *cracks*. (TA.)

فُزْرَةٌ: see فَازِرٌ. = Also *A great protuberance* upon the back, or upon the chest. (Ḳ.)

فَزَارَةٌ: see فُزْرٌ, last quarter of the paragraph.

فَازِرٌ A *wide* road; (Ṣ, O, Ḳ;) as also ▼ فُزْرَةٌ: (O, Ḳ:) or a *wide and conspicuous* road: or, accord. to ISh, *a road that passes over the* [*eminences termed*] نِجَاف [pl. of نَجْف] *and the* [*hills*, or *small mountains termed*] قُور [pl. of قَارَةٌ], *and cleaves them as though it made furrows upon their heads*: you say, أَخَذْنَا طَرِيقَ الفَازِرِ and أَخَذْنَا الفَازِرَ, meaning [*We took*] *the road that made a track upon the heads and the base of the mountains*. (TA.) And ▼ فَازِرَةٌ [or طَرِيقٌ فَازِرَةٌ] signifies *A road taking its course in a tract of sand amid sands that are compact and cleaving to the ground*, (Ḳ, TA,) *and soft; appearing like an extended, long, natural cleft in the ground*: (TA:) the same meaning is also assigned to فَازِرَةٌ. (Ḳ* and TA in art. فرز.) = Also *A species of ants*, (O,) *black ants*, (Ḳ,) *in which is a redness*: (O, Ḳ:) mentioned also among words of which the final radical is ز [as being called فَازِزٌ]. (TA.) — And The *round black thing* [app. *a species of animalcule*] *found in* [*dried*] *dates*. (O.)

فَازِرَةٌ: see the next preceding paragraph.

أَفْزَرُ and ▼ مَفْزُورٌ A man *humpbacked*; (Ṣ, O;) *having a great protuberance upon his back*; (Ṣ, O, Ḳ:) or *having such a protuberance upon his chest*: (Ḳ:) or, accord. to Ibn-'Abbád, the former signifies the same as أَقْعَسُ [*having a protuberant breast*, or *chest, and a hollow*, or *receding, back*]. (O. [See also أَفْزَرُ.]) — And [the fem. of the former] فَزْرَآءُ A female, (Ḳ,) or girl, or young woman, (TA,) *full of fat and flesh*: or *that has nearly attained to puberty*. (Ḳ, TA.)

مَفْزُورُ الأَنْفِ A man *having his nose struck with a thing so as to be split*. (TA.) = See also أَفْزَرُ.

فزع

1. فَزِعَ, (Ṣ, O, Mṣb, Ḳ,) and فَزَعَ, (Ḳ,) aor. ـَ, of the former verb, (Mṣb, Ḳ,) and of the latter also, (Ḳ,) inf. n. فَزَعٌ, (Ṣ, O, Mṣb, Ḳ,) which is of the former verb, (Ṣ,* O, Mṣb, TA,) and [of the latter verb] فَزْعٌ [فَزْعًا in the CḲ being a mistake for فَزَعًا] and فِزْعٌ, (Ḳ, TA,) *He feared*; or *was*, or *became, in fear, afraid, frightened*, or *terrified*; (Ṣ, O, Mṣb, Ḳ, TA;) and so ▼ تفزّع: (TA in art. روع:) you say, فَزِعَ مِنْهُ *he feared him*, or *it*; or *was*, or *became, in fear*, &c., *of him*, or *it*: (MA, Mṣb, TA:) accord. to Er-Rághib, فَزَعٌ signifies *a shrinking*, and *an aversion*, that comes upon a man, *from a thing causing fear* or *fright*; and is *a kind of* جَزَع [q. v.]; and one should not say فَزِعْتُ مِنَ اللّٰهِ like as one says خِفْتُ مِنْهُ: or, as Mbr says, in the "Kámil," its primary signification is the *fearing*, or *being in fear* or *afraid* or *frightened* or *terrified*: then, by a metonymical application, it signifies a people's *going forth quickly to repel an enemy*, or *the like, that has come upon them suddenly*; and this meaning has become [conventionally regarded as] proper. (TA.) — فَزَعٌ signifies also The *seeking*, or *demanding, aid*, or *succour*: (Az, Ḳ, TA:) and the *aiding*, or *succouring*; (Az, Ṣ, O, Ḳ, TA;) this latter being likewise a signification of ▼ إِفْزَاعٌ: (Ṣ, O:) an ex. of the former word (Ṣ, O, TA) in the latter sense (O, TA) occurs in the saying of the Prophet to the Anṣár, إِنَّكُمْ لَتَكْثُرُونَ عِنْدَ الفَزَعِ وَتَقِلُّونَ عِنْدَ الطَّمَعِ [*Verily ye are many on the occasion of aiding*, or *succouring, and ye are few on the occasion of coveting*, or *greed*]; (Ṣ, O, TA;) or in this saying the implied meaning may be, *on the occasion of men's betaking themselves to you in fear* (عِنْدَ فَزَعِ النَّاسِ إِلَيْكُمْ) *in order that ye may aid* or *succour them* [which is virtually the same as *their seeking your aid* or *succour*]: (TA:) thus [it is said] فَزَعٌ has two contr. significations: (Ḳ:) and both of these significations are expressed by the verb فَزِعَ: (O:) you say فَزِعَ إِلَيْهِ and فَزِعَ مِنْهُ; (Ḳ in continuation of what has been last cited therefrom above, and TA; [app. meant to indicate that both of these phrases signify *he sought*, or *demanded, aid*, or *succour, of him*; and *he aided*, or *succoured, him*; or that the former phrase has the former signification; and the latter phrase, the latter signification; though accord. to the TḲ, both phrases have the former signification, and the former phrase has also the latter signification;]) but you should not say فَزَعَهُ, (Ḳ, TA,) i. e. like مَنَعَهُ: (TA:) [or] from الفَزَعُ as signifying "fear," or "fright," you say فَزِعْتُ إِلَيْكَ and فَزِعْتُ مِنْكَ; [app. meant to indicate that the former phrase signifies *I betook myself to thee in fear*, which is a meaning thereof well known, and nearly agreeing with an explanation of the verb followed by إِلَيْهِ which will be found below in this paragraph; and that the latter phrase signifies *I feared thee*, or *I was*, or *became, in fear*, &c., *of thee*, the only meaning, of this phrase, for which I find any explicit authority, and one for which I have given three authorities in the first sentence of this art.;] but you should not say فَزِعْتُكَ: (Ṣ: [thus in my copies, فَزِعْتُكَ, not فَزَعْتُكَ:]) or فَزِعَ إِلَيْهِمْ signifies *he sought*, or *demanded, of them, aid*, or *succour*; and فَزَعَهُمْ and فَزِعَهُمْ signify *he aided*, or *succoured, them*, syn. أَغَاثَهُمْ [in the CḲ أَعَانَهُمْ] and نَصَرَهُمْ, like ▼ أَفْزَعَهُمْ: (Ḳ, TA:) accord. to IB, فَزِعْتُهُ meaning أَغَثْتُهُ is originally فَزِعْتُ لَهُ [primarily signifying *I feared*, or *became in fear* &c., *for him*]; then the ل was dropped; for one says فَزِعْتُهُ and فَزِعْتُ لَهُ: (TA:) or فَزِعَ, like فَرِحَ, signifies اِنْتَصَرَ: (Ḳ: [thus in the copies of the Ḳ, and hence in the TA, app. a mistranscription for اِسْتَنْصَرَ, *he sought*, or *demanded, aid*, or *aid against an enemy*:]) and فَزِعَ إِلَيْهِ *he betook himself*, or *had recourse, to him*, or *it, for refuge, protection*, or *preservation*, (Ṣ, O, Mṣb, Ḳ, TA,) *by reason of fear*, or *fright*, (Ṣ,) *and sought*, or *demanded, aid*, or *succour, by him*, or *it*; whence, in a trad. respecting the eclipse of the sun, فَافْزَعُوا إِلَى الصَّلَاةِ i. e. *Then betake yourselves*, &c., *to prayer, and seek*, or *demand, aid*, or *succour, by it*. (TA.) — فَزِعَ مِنْ نَوْمِهِ means *He became roused from his sleep*; (O, Ḳ;) because he who is roused is not free from some fear, or fright: occurring in a trad. in this sense. (O.) And one says, فَزِعْتُ بِمَجِىْءِ فُلَانٍ, meaning *I prepared* [or *roused*] *myself by reason of the coming of such a one, by a change of state*, or *condition, like as the sleeper passes from the state of sleeping to that of waking*. (TA.) = فَزَعَهُ in the phrase فَازَعَهُ ▼ فَفَزَعَهُ means *He exceeded him in fear*, or *fright*. (TA.) = فُزِّعَ عَنْ قُلُوبِهِمْ: see the next paragraph.

2. فَزَّعَهُ: see 4. — [It also app. signifies *He made a fearful event*, or *fearful events, to befall him*: see its pass. part. n. below.] — فَزَّعَ عَنْهُ *He removed from him fear*, or *fright*: (O, in two places:) it is implied by the context in the Ḳ that ▼ افزع عنه has this meaning; but in the O and other lexicons it is فَزَّعَ. (TA.) And فُزِّعَ عَنْهُ, (Ṣ, Ḳ,) inf. n. تَفْزِيعٌ, (Ḳ,) *Fear*, or *fright, was removed from him*. (Ṣ, Ḳ.) It is said in the

Ḳur [xxxiv. 22], حَتَّى إِذَا فُزِّعَ عَنْ قُلُوبِهِمْ, meaning *Until, when fear, or fright, shall be removed from their hearts*: (Ṣ, O:) this is the common reading: another reading is فَزَّعَ اللّٰهُ, i. e. فَزَّعَ: and El-Ḥasan reads ▼ فُزِعَ: and he says that in this reading and the first, the prep. with its noun are [regarded as supplying the place of the agent and therefore virtually] in the nom. case, as in the phrase سِيرَ عَنِ البَلَدِ: (TA:) some read فُرِّغَ [q. v.]: (O and TA in art. فرغ:) and 'Eesà Ibn-'Omar is related to have read إِذَا ٱفْرَنْقَعَ. (TA in art. فرقع.)

3. فازعهُ ففزعهُ [*He vied with him in fear, or fright,*] *and he exceeded him therein.* (TA. See 1, last sentence but one.)

4. افزعهُ, (Mṣb, Ḳ,) inf. n. إِفْزَاعٌ, (Ṣ, O,) *He made him to fear*, or *to be afraid*; *frightened him*; or *terrified him*; (Ṣ,* O,* Mṣb, Ḳ;) as also ▼ فزّعهُ, (Ṣ, O, Mṣb, Ḳ,) inf. n. تَفْزِيعٌ. (Ṣ, O.) And you say, يُفْزَعُ مِنْهُ [*One is made to fear*, or *be afraid of*, or *is frightened*, or *terrified*, *at, it*, or *him*], (Ṣ, O, Ḳ,) and مِنْ أَجْلِهِ [*on account of him*, or *for the sake of him*], (O, Ḳ,) and بِهِ [*by him*, or *by means of him*]. (O.) — [Hence,] *He housed him* from his sleep. (Ḳ, TA. [See 1, last quarter.]) — Also *He aided*, or *succoured, him.* (Ṣ, Ḳ.) See 1, former half; and again, in the latter half. — See also 2.

5: see 1, first sentence.

فَزَعٌ *Fear*, or *fright*: (Ṣ, O, Ḳ:) originally (Ṣ) an inf. n.; but notwithstanding this, (Ṣ,* O, Ḳ,) sometimes, (Ṣ, O,) having a pl., which is أَفْزَاعٌ. (Ṣ, O, Ḳ.) — [And, as seems to be indicated by an explanation of مَفْزَعٌ (q. v.), *A fearful event*: pl. as above.]

فَزِعٌ *Fearing*; *being afraid* or *frightened* or *terrified*; (Er-Rághib, MA, Mṣb, TA;) thus in a verse cited voce ظُنْبُوبٌ; (Er-Rághib, TA;) and ▼ مُفَازِعٌ is syn. therewith: (O, Ḳ:) and one says also ▼ رَجُلٌ فَازِعٌ, pl. فَزَعَةٌ; and ▼ مَفْزُوعٌ; meaning *a man put in fear*; *made afraid*; *frightened*, or *terrified*. (TA.) And *In a state of disquiet, disturbance*, or *agitation*: whence an extraordinary reading, of four readers, in the Ḳur xxviii. 9, [i. e. فَزِعًا] for فَارِغًا, relating to the heart of the mother of Moses, meaning *in a state of disquiet*, &c., *almost quitting its pericardium.* (TA.) It has no broken pl.; its only pl. being فَزِعُونَ. (TA.) — Also *Seeking*, or *demanding, aid*, or *succour*; and Ṣgh thus explains it [in the O] as used in the verse above mentioned; but Er-Rághib says that this is an explanation of the intended meaning, not of the literal signification: (TA:) and it has also the contr. meaning, *aiding*, or *succouring*; thus being trans., though of the measure فَعِلٌ; but it may be altered from ▼ فَازِعٌ, like as حَذِرٌ is [said to be] altered from حَاذِرٌ. (IB, TA,)

فَزْعَةٌ: see فُزَعَةٌ.

فُزَعَةٌ A man *whom one is made to fear, of whom one is made afraid*, or *at whom one is frightened*: (O, Ḳ:) [like مَفْزَعَةٌ as expl. by Lth and others:] and *by whom*, or *by means of whom, one is made afraid*, or *frightened.* (O.)

فَزَعَةٌ sing. of فَزَعَاتٌ in the phrase فَزَعَاتُ الرَّوْعِ [app. meaning *The fears*, or *frights, of the heart*]. (TA. [The sing., as well as the pl., is there said to be thus, بِالتَّحْرِيك; but if the former be, as I think it is, an inf. n. un., it should by rule be ▼ فَزْعَةٌ.])

فُزَعَةٌ One *who fears men*, or *is frightened at them*: (Ḳ:) or one *who fears*, or *is frightened, much*, or *often*; (O;) [and] so ▼ فَزَّاعَةٌ. (TA. [But see what next follows.])

فَزَّاعَةٌ *One who makes men to fear*, or *frightens them, much*, or *often.* (O, Ḳ.) See also فُزَعَةٌ.

فَازِعٌ: see فَزِعٌ, in two places.

مَفْزَعٌ i. q. مَلْجَأٌ [as meaning *A refuge*, i. e. *a place to which*, or *a person to whom, one betakes himself*, or *has recourse, for refuge, protection*, or *preservation*,] (Ṣ, O, Mṣb, Ḳ, TA,) *on the occasion of the befalling of an affliction* or *a calamity*; (TA;) applied to a sing. and a pl. (Ṣ, O, Ḳ) and a dual (Ṣ, O) and a masc. and a fem.; (Ṣ, O, Ḳ;) one says, فُلَانٌ مَفْزَعٌ لِلنَّاسِ *Such a one is a refuge to men when an event comes upon them suddenly*, and هُمَا مَفْزَعٌ لِلنَّاسِ, and هُمْ مَفْزَعٌ, &c.; (Ṣ, O;) and ▼ مَفْزَعَةٌ is the same in signification and in its applications; (Ḳ;) expl. by IF as signifying *a place to which one who is in fear*, or *frightened, betakes himself*, or *has recourse, for refuge, protection*, or *preservation*: (TA:) or مَفْزَعٌ signifies one of whom aid, or succour, is sought, or demanded: (Ḳ:) and ▼ مَفْزَعَةٌ, [*a cause of fear* or *fright*; being a word of the class of مَبْخَلَةٌ and مَجْبَنَةٌ; i. e.] *a thing that one is made to fear*, or *at which one is frightened*; (Ṣ;) or *a person whom one is made to fear*, or *at whom one is frightened*; [like فُزَعَةٌ;] or *on account of whom*, or *for the sake of whom, one is made to fear*, or *is frightened*: (Lth, O, Ḳ:) you say, فُلَانٌ لَنَا مَفْزَعَةٌ [*Such a one is to us a person whom we are made to fear*, &c.], and in like manner you say of a female, and of a pl. number. (O.)

مُفْزَعَةٌ: see the next preceding paragraph, in two places.

مُفَزَّعٌ *Cowardly*; (Fr, O, Ḳ;) as being made to fear, or to be frightened at, everything: (Fr, O:) and *courageous*; (Fr, O, Ḳ;) as being one the like of whom fearful events are made to befall (بِمِثْلِهِ تُنْزَلُ الأَفْزَاعُ). (Fr, O. [But what here follows suggests another reason, and I think a better, for the latter meaning.]) مُفَزَّعَةٌ applied by 'Amr Ibn-Maadee-Kerib as an epithet to his اِسْت, in replying to a threat of El-Ash-'ath, who had said to him, لَوْ دَنَوْتَ لَأَضْرِطَنَّكَ, means *Secure from being overcome by fear*, or *fright*, *and* [*therefore*] *not lax so as to break wind* [*in consequence of fear*]; being from فُزِّعَ عَنْهُ meaning "he removed fear, or fright, from him;" or it may be for the same reason as that for which مُفَزَّعٌ is applied to a courageous man. (O.)

مَفْزُوعٌ: }
مُفَازِعٌ: } see فَزِعٌ, first sentence.

فس

فَسْفَسَةٌ *i. q.* فَصْفَصَةٌ, i. e. رَطْبَةٌ: (Ḳ:) the second of these is more known than the first; both of which are arabicized, from the Persian إِسْپِسْت [or إِسْفِسْت]. (TA.)

فسأ

1. فَسَأَهُ: see 2. — Also, (M, Ḳ,) or فَسَأَهُ بِالعَصَا, (AZ, O,) aor. ـَ, inf. n. فَسْءٌ, (M,) *He struck*, or *beat*, (AZ, M, O, Ḳ,) *him*, (O,) or *his back*, (AZ, M, Ḳ,) *with the staff*, or *stick*; (AZ, M, O, Ḳ;) as also ▼ تَفَسَّأَهُ, (Ḳ,) or تفسّأهُ بالعصا. (O.) — And فَسَأَ فُلَانًا عَنْهُ *He restrained, withheld*, or *debarred, such a one from him.* (O,* Ḳ.) = فَسِئَ, aor. ـَ, [inf. n., app., فَسَأٌ, q. v. infrà,] *He was*, or *became, such as is termed* أَفْسَأُ [q. v.]. (Ḳ.)

2. فسّأهُ, namely, a garment, or piece of cloth, (Ṣ, M, O, Ḳ,) inf. n. تَفْسِئَةٌ (Ṣ, O) and تَفْسِىءٌ, (Ṣ,) *He stretched it so that it rent*, or *became ragged*, or *dissundered*: (Ṣ, O:) or *he rent it*; as also ▼ فَسَأَهُ, aor. ـَ, (M, Ḳ,) inf. n. فَسْءٌ. (M.)

5. تفسّأ, said of a garment, or piece of cloth, (Ṣ, M, O, Ḳ,) *It became ragged*, or *dissundered*, (Ṣ, O,) *and worn out*: (Ṣ:) like تقضّأ, or تفصّأ: (accord. to different copies of the Ṣ: the latter in the L:) or *it became rent.* (M, O.) — تفسّأ فيهم, (Ḳ,) or بِهِمْ, (O,) said of a disease, *It spread among them*, (O, Ḳ,) and *became common among them*: (TA:) like تفشّأ. (O, Ḳ.) = تفسّأهُ: see 1.

6. تفاسأ, and تفاسى, (M, O, TA,) *He* (a man) *protruded* (M, O, TA) *his posteriors*, (M,) or *his back*, (O,) or *both.* (TA.)

فَسَأٌ a subst. signifying The *state of such as is termed* أَفْسَأُ [q. v.]: (M, TA:) or *a hollowness*, or *incurvity, of the spine.* (TA in art. فقأ.) [See also 1, last sentence.]

أَفْسَأُ *i. q.* أَبْزَخُ [i. e. *Having a protuberant breast*, or *chest, and hollow back*; &c.]: or *having a protuberant breast*, or *chest, and the lower part of the belly prominent*: (M, Ḳ:) fem. فَسْآءُ: (M:) and (M, in the Ḳ "or") he *who, when he walks, is as though his posteriors were in pain* (in the M تَوَجَّعُ; in some copies of the Ḳ تُوجِعُ [as though for تَتَوَجَّعُ], and in some يرجع); as also ▼ مَفْسُوءٌ: (M, Ḳ:) or he *who, when he sits, cannot rise but with an effort*: (O, Ḳ:) or *whose spine enters into* [or *turns inwards between*] *his haunches.* (Ḳ.)

مَفْسُوءٌ: see the next preceding paragraph.

فسط and فست

فُسْتَاتٌ, also written فِسْتَاتٌ: see فُسْطَاطٌ.

فُسْتَاطٌ, also written فِسْتَاطٌ: see فُسْطَاطٌ, in art. فسط, to which it belongs; for the ت is a substitute for the [former] ط in فسطاط, or for the [latter] س in فُسَّاطٌ. (M and TA in art. فسط.)

فستق

فُسْتُقٌ and فُسْتَقٌ, (O, Mṣb, Ḳ,) the latter the more agreeable with the original, (O,) which is پِسْتَه, (O, Ḳ,) a Pers. word, (O,) for from this each is arabicized; (O, Mṣb,* Ḳ;) [The *pistachio-nut, pistacia vera* of Linn.;] *a certain fruit;* (O;) [in the Mṣb بقل; perhaps a mistranscription for نقل, i. e. نُقْلٌ, *a certain fruit that is eaten with wine;*] *well known:* (Ḳ:) said in a verse of Aboo-Nukheyleh to be مِنَ البُقُولِ: thus, and thus only, with ب, the phrase is related: if it were مِنَ النُّقُولِ, the mistake would be removed: (O:) Az says that the فستقة [which is the n. un.] is *a fruit of a well-known tree:* and AḤn says, "It has not come to my knowledge that it grows in the land of the Arabs:" (TA:) it is good for the liver, and the mouth of the stomach, and the colic, and the odour of the mouth. (Ḳ. [In the CḲ, النَّهْكَة is put for النَّكْهَة.]) The vulgar pronounce the word with fet-ḥ [to the ف, saying فَسْتَق: and many of them say فِسْتَق]. (Mṣb.)

ثَوْبٌ فُسْتُقِىٌّ [meaning *A garment of the colour of the* فُسْتُق] is [thus] with ḍamm [to the ف and ت]. (Mṣb.)

فسح

1. فَسُحَ, (MA, Mṣb, Ḳ, [in the CḲ فَسَحَ, a misprint,]) with ḍamm, (Mṣb,) like كَرُمَ, (Ḳ,) [aor. ـُ,] inf. n. فُسَاحَةٌ, (L,) or فَسَاحَةٌ [for which the former is app. a mistranscription] and فُسْحَةٌ, (MA,) *It* (a place) *was,* or *became, spacious, roomy, wide,* or *ample;* (MA, Mṣb, Ḳ;) as also ▼افسح, (Mṣb, Ḳ,) and ▼تفسّح, and ▼انفسح. (Ḳ.) = فَسَحَ لَهُ, (Ṣ, MA, Mṣb, Ḳ,) aor. ـَ, (Mṣb, Ḳ,) inf. n. فَسْحٌ (MA, Mṣb, TA) and فُسُوحٌ; (TA;) as also ▼تفسّح, (A, Ḳ,) and ▼افسح; (A;) *He made room,* or *ample room, for him,* (Ṣ, MA, Mṣb, Ḳ,) فِى المَجْلِسِ (Ṣ, MA, Mṣb) *in the sitting-place,* or *in the assembly.* (MA.) You say, تَفَسَّحُوا ▼ فِى المَجْلِسِ, (Ṣ, Mṣb,*) and ▼تَفَاسَحُوا, (Ṣ, Ḳ,) *Make ye room,* or *ample space,* [*in the sitting-place,* or *in the assembly,*] syn. تَوَسَّعُوا: (Ṣ, Ḳ:) both of these verbs have nearly the same signification: [each may be rendered, but the latter more properly, *make ye room,* or *ample space, one for another:*] the latter occurs, accord. to the reading of El-Ḥasan, and the former accord. to that of others, in the Ḳur lviii. 12. (Fr, TA.) — And اِفْسَحْ عَنِّى *Remove thou, withdraw,* or *retire to a distance, from me.* (Ksh and Bḍ in lviii. 12.) — فَسْحٌ [as inf. n. of فَسَحَ] also signifies The *making wide steps;* and so فَيْسَحَى. (Ḳ.) [Hence,] اِفْسَحِ الخُطَى, said by an Arab of the Desert, of the Benoo-'Okeyl, to one who was sewing for him a water-skin, and mentioned in the T, as heard by its author, meaning †*Make wide the spaces between each two punctures of the needle,* lest the punctures should rend. (L.) — And فَسَحَ لَهُ الأَمِيرُ فِى السَّفَرِ means *The commander,* or *governor, wrote for him a* فَسْحٌ [q. v.]. (Ḳ.)

2. فسّح *He made* a place *spacious, roomy, wide,* or *ample.* (Mṣb.)

4: see 1, first and second sentences.

5: see 1, in three places. — [تفسّح also signifies *He expatiated,* or *ranged at large:* and *he had ample room* or *scope:* see مُتَفَسَّحٌ.]

6: see 1, third sentence.

7: see 1, first sentence. — [Hence,] انفسح مُرَاحُهُمْ [lit. *The nightly resting-place of their camels was,* or *became, spacious,*] means † *their camels became numerous.* (TA.) — And انفسح صَدْرُهُ † *His bosom became dilated* [*with joy*]. (Ṣ, A.) — And انفسح طَرْفُهُ † *His eye had an unobstructed view, nothing hindering its seeing far.* (L.)

Q. Q. 2. تَفَيْسَحَ: see تَفَيْحَسَ, in art. فحس.

فَسْحٌ *A writing like a* جَوَاز [or *traveller's pass*]. (Ḳ.) [See 1, last sentence.]

فُسُحٌ: see فَسِيحٌ, in three places.

فُسْحَةٌ *Spaciousness, roominess, width,* or *ampleness;* (Ṣ, A, L, Ḳ;) [particularly, or generally,] with respect to the ground. (L.) [In the MA it is mentioned as an inf. n. of فَسُحَ.] — And [*Ample scope for action* &c.] in an affair. (Mṣb in art. رخو.) [And *A state in which is ample scope for acting* &c.: see نَفَسٌ.] — الفُسْحَتَانِ signifies *The two spaces without hair on the two sides of the hair that grows immediately beneath the middle of the lower lip.* (L.)

فُسْحُمٌ: see فَسِيحٌ, in two places. — فُلَانٌ ابْنُ فُسْحُمٍ is a phrase mentioned by Lḥ, thought by him to be from الفُسْحَة and الإِنْفِسَاح, but the meaning is unknown. (L.) = Also The *glans of the penis.* (Ḳ in art. فسحم; where the word is mentioned again in the Ṣ likewise.)

فُسَاحٌ: see the paragraph here following.

فَسِيحٌ (Ṣ, A, Mṣb, Ḳ) and ▼فُسَاحٌ, (Ḳ,) like طَوِيلٌ and طُوَالٌ, (TA,) *Spacious, roomy, wide,* or *ample;* applied to a place; (Ṣ, A, Mṣb, Ḳ;) as also ▼فُسُحٌ and ▼فُسْحُمٌ: (Ḳ:) or ▼فُسُحٌ signifies thus applied to a sitting-place: (Ṣ:) and ▼فُسْحُمٌ, (Ṣ, Ḳ,) in which the م is augmentative, (Ṣ,) signifies (Ṣ, Ḳ) also (Ḳ) وَاسِعُ الصَّدْرِ [meaning *free from distress of mind* or *from narrowness of mind*], (Ṣ, Ḳ,) as does also ▼فُسُحٌ [in the CḲ in this sense written فُسْحٌ]; both being applied in this sense to a man. (Ḳ.) — سَيْرٌ فَسِيحٌ [means *A pace in which the steps are wide:* see 1, latter half].

جَمَلٌ مَفْسُوحُ الضُّلُوعِ i. q. مَسْفُوح [i. e. *A camel wide in the ribs*]. (TA.)

مَا لَكَ فِى هٰذَا مُتَفَسَّحٌ [*There is not for thee ample scope* (lit. *a place in which one has ample scope*) *in this*]. (A.)

مُنْفَسَحُ وَادٍ [*The place of expanding of a valley*]. (JK and Ḳ in art. خرق, &c.)

مُرَاحٌ مُنْفَسِحٌ † *A nightly resting-place of camels,* or *of camels and other cattle, in which they are numerous.* (Aṣ, Ḳ.)

فسخ

1. فَسَخَ, (Ṣ, A, L, Ḳ,) aor. ـَ, (Ṣ, L, Ḳ,) inf. n. فَسْخٌ; (Ṣ, L;) and ▼فسّخ; (L; [but this has an intensive signification;]) *He dislocated, luxated,* or *disjointed,* (A, L, Ḳ,) one's arm, or hand, (Ṣ, A, L, Ḳ,) or a limb, *without breaking:* (L:) [and] فَسَخْتُ المَفْصِلَ عَنْ مَوْضِعِهِ *I removed the joint from its place.* (Mṣb.) — And the former v., aor. and inf. n. as above, *He removed* a stick, or twig, or branch, *from its place with his hand.* (Mṣb.) — And the same v., (Ṣ, Mṣb,) aor. as above, (A,) and so the inf. n., (Ḳ,) *He cast,* or *cast off,* (Ṣ, Mṣb, Ḳ,) a garment, (Ṣ, Mṣb,) or his garments. (A.) You say, فَسَخْتُ عَنِّى ثَوْبِى *I cast,* or *cast off, from me my garment.* (Ṣ.) — And the same v., (L, Mṣb,) [aor. and] inf. n. as above, (Ḳ,) *He separated, disunited, sundered, dissundered,* or *dispersed,* (L, Mṣb, Ḳ,) a thing. (L, Mṣb.) — Also, the same verb, (Ṣ, A, L, Mṣb,) aor. as above, (L,) and so the inf. n., (L, Mṣb, Ḳ,) ‡ *He undid, dissolved,* or *annulled,* (Ṣ, A, L, Mṣb, Ḳ,) a sale, (Ṣ, A, L, Mṣb,) and a determination, resolution, or decision, (Ṣ,) and a marriage, (Ṣ, A, L,) and a contract, compact, or covenant, and an affair. (Mṣb.) — And the same v., (L, Mṣb,) [aor. and] inf. n. as above, (L, Ḳ,) † *He* (a man, Mṣb) *corrupted,* or *disordered,* the judgment, or opinion. (L, Mṣb, Ḳ.) = فَسِخَ, aor. ـَ, (L, Ḳ,) inf. n. فَسَخٌ; (L;) or فَسَخَ, this v. being intrans. as well as trans.; (Mṣb;) † *It* (the judgment, or opinion,) *was,* or *became, corrupt,* or *disordered.* (L, Mṣb, Ḳ.) — [And, accord. to the TḲ, فَسِخَ, (but this I think to be a mistake for فَسُخَ,) inf. n. فَسْخٌ, signifies ضَعُفَ († *He was,* or *became, weak,* app. *in intellect and in body;* see فَسْخٌ below); said of a man: and جَهِلَ (app. intrans., meaning † *He was,* or *became, ignorant;* but accord. to the TḲ trans., meaning *he knew not* a thing).] — In the conventional language of the philosophers, الفَسْخُ [as an inf. n.] signifies † *The transmigration of the rational soul of a human being from his body to* [*some one of*] *the inanimate,*

not increasing, bodies, such as the minerals, or *metals, and the simple elements:* (Dict. of Technical Terms used in the Sciences of the Musalmans:) or, *to a plant:* the former meaning being that of ٱلرَّسْخُ. (So in a marginal note in a copy of the TK.)

2: see the preceding paragraph, first sentence.

3. فَاسَخَهُ البَيْعَ ‡ [*He agreed with him in undoing, dissolving,* or *annulling, the sale*]. (A. [See **6**.])

4. افسخ القُرْآنَ † *He forgot the Kur-án.* (Fr, Ṣ.)

5: see **7**, in two places. — تفسّخ الشَّعَرُ عَنِ الجِلْدِ *The hair fell off and became scattered from the skin,* peculiarly of a dead body: (L, K:) and in like manner, اللَّحْمُ عَنِ العَظْمِ *the flesh from the bone.* (A, L.) And تَفَسَّخَتِ الفَأْرَةُ فِى المَآءِ *The rat,* or *mouse, became dissundered,* [or *fell in pieces, through putrefaction,*] *in the water.* (Ṣ.) — تفسّخ تَحْتَ الحِمْلِ الثَّقِيلِ, said of a [young camel such as is termed] رُبَع, (Ṣ, K,*) *He was,* or *became, weak beneath the heavy load,* (K,) *and unable to bear it:* (Ṣ, K:) and [in like manner] one says of a man, تفسّخ تَحْتَ العِبْءِ الثَّقِيلِ. (A.)

6. تفاسخوا العَقْدَ † *They agreed together in undoing, dissolving,* or *annulling, the contract, compact,* or *covenant.* (Mṣb.) And تفاسخا البَيْعَ ‡ [*They two agreed in dissolving,* or *annulling, the sale*]. (A.) — And تفاسخت الأَقَاوِيلُ ‡ *The sayings annulled,* or *contradicted, one another.* (TA.)

7. انفسخ *It* (a limb, L, such as an arm, or a hand, A, L) *became dislocated, luxated,* or *disjointed;* (A, L;) as also ▾تفسّخ. (L.) One says, وَقَعَ فُلَانٌ فَٱنْفَسَخَتْ قَدَمُهُ *Such a one fell, and his foot became dislocated.* (L. [And the like is said in the A.]) — *It* (a stick, or twig, or branch,) *became removed from its place by the hand.* (Mṣb.) — *It* (flesh) *became dissundered by putrefaction;* as also ▾تفسّخ. (L.) — And, said of a sale, (Ṣ, A, K,) and a determination, resolution, or decision, (Ṣ, K,) and a marriage, (Ṣ, A, K,) [and a contract, compact, or covenant, (see **1**,)] and an affair, (L,) ‡ *It became undone, dissolved,* or *annulled.* (Ṣ, A, L, K.) — Also said of a weak man, [app. as meaning † *He became unnerved,*] on an occasion of difficulty. (L: see فَسِيخ.)

فُسْخٌ [mentioned above as the inf. n. of **1** in most of its senses] † *Weakness* (L, K) *in intellect and in body;* as also ▾فُسْخَةٌ. (L.) — And † *Ignorance:* (K:) which is referrible to weakness of intellect. (TA.) ═ And † *Weak in intellect and in body;* as also ▾فُسْخَةٌ. (K.) — See also فَسِيخ.

فَسِخٌ † A *corrupt,* or *disordered,* judgment, or opinion. (L.)

فُسْخَةٌ: see فُسْخٌ, in two places.

فَسِيخٌ [applied to flesh-meat, *Parting in pieces, and easily resolvable, by reason of much cooking.* (Golius, from Meyd.) — And] † A *weak* man, *who becomes unnerved* (▾يَنْفَسِخُ) *on an occasion of difficulty:* (L:) a man *who does not attain that which he wants,* (Ṣ, L, K,) *and is not fit for his affair,* or *business;* as also ▾فُسْخٌ [q. v.]. (K.)

ثَوْبٌ فَاسِخٌ [† *A faded garment:* so in the language of the present day: perhaps post-classical]. (A in art. رمد.) ═ [الفَاسِخُ is a name given by the Jews to their festival of *The Passover:* see De Sacy's Chrest. Ar., sec. ed., i. 291, and p. 97 of the Ar. text: and see also الفِصْح.]

فسد

1. فَسَدَ, aor. ُ, (Ṣ, M, A, O, L, Mṣb, K, &c.,) which is the aor. commonly known, (TA,) and ِ, (IDrd, M, O, L, K,) which is of weak authority; (IDrd, O, TA;) and فَسُدَ, aor. ُ; (Ṣ, M, O, L, K;) inf. n. فَسَادٌ (Ṣ, M, A, O, L, K) and فُسُودٌ, (M, O, L, K,) the former being inf. n. of فَسَدَ, aor. ُ, (Ṣ, A, O,) and so the latter, and the former being also inf. n. of فَسَدَ, (O,) or the former is of فَسَدَ and the latter is of فَسُدَ, (TA,) or the former is a simple subst., and the latter is the inf. n.; (Mṣb;) *It* (a thing, Ṣ, A, O) [and *he* (a man)] *was,* or *became, bad, evil, corrupt, unsound, wrong, wrongful, improper, unrighteous, wicked, vitious, depraved,* or *dishonest; devoid of virtue,* or *efficacy; in a corrupted, vitiated, perverted, marred, spoiled, injured, impaired, deteriorated, tainted,* or *infected, state; in a state of disorder* or *disturbance, destruction, annihilation, consumption, waste,* or *ruin;* (MA, KL, PṢ, &c.;) and so ▾استفسد: (KL:) *contr. of* صَلَحَ: (M,* L, K:) *it became altered in its state* [*for the worse*]: and *it became null, void, of no force,* or *of no account;* or *it came to nought,* or *perished;* accord. to the explanation by most of the expositors of the ex. in the Kur xxi. 22. (MF.)

2: see **4**, first sentence.

3. فاسدهُ *He became at variance with him; he cut, severed,* or *broke, the tie of friendship* [or *kindred*] *with him.* (L in art. كشح.) And فُلَانٌ يُفَاسِدُ رَهْطَهُ [*Such a one cuts the ties of friendship,* or *kindred, with his people, tribe,* or *near kinsfolk*]. (A.)

4. افسد, (Ṣ, M, O, L, Mṣb, K, &c.,) inf. n. إِفْسَادٌ and [quasi-inf. n.] فَسَادٌ; (L;) and ▾فسّد, (O, L, Mṣb, K,) inf. n. تَفْسِيدٌ; (O, K;) *He,* or *it, made,* or *rendered, bad, evil, corrupt, unsound, wrong, wrongful, improper, unrighteous, wicked, vitious, depraved,* or *dishonest; deprived of virtue,* or *efficacy; corrupted, vitiated, perverted, marred, spoiled, injured, impaired, deteriorated, tainted,* or *infected;* [*constituted, disposed, arranged,* or *qualified, ill, wrongly,* or *improperly;*] *disordered,* or *disturbed,* [*disorganized,*] *destroyed, annihilated, consumed, wasted,* or *ruined;* (MA, KL, &c.;) *contr. of* أَصْلَحَ. (M, L, K.) One says, افسد المَالَ [*He rendered the property in a bad state; marred, impaired, consumed,* or *wasted, it*]. (L.) [And افسد عَلَيْهِمْ *He corrupted, perverted,* or *marred, their state, case, affair, scheme, plot,* or *the like;* أَمْرَهُمْ, or the like, being understood. And افسدهُ عَلَىَّ *He corrupted him and rendered him disaffected towards me.*] إِفْسَادُ صَبِىٍّ, occurring in a trad., means *The injuring a child by rendering its mother pregnant while she is suckling it and so vitiating her milk:* which act is also termed الغِيلَةُ. (L.) [And افسد as contr. of أَصْلَحَ signifies also *He acted in a bad, an evil,* or *a corrupt, manner; acted ill, corruptly, wrongly, wrongfully, improperly, unrighteously, wickedly, vitiously,* or *dishonestly;* or *did evil,* or *mischief;* إِلَيْهِ *to him:* and *he created,* or *excited, disorder, disturbance, disagreement, discord, dissension, strife,* or *quarrelling;* or *made,* or *did, mischief;* بَيْنَ القَوْمِ *between,* or *among, the people,* or *party.* (See also **10**.)]

6. تفاسدوا *They became at variance, one with another;* (M, L;) *they cut, severed,* or *broke, the tie of kindred,* (M, L, K,) *and of friendship,* (L,) *one with another.* (M, L, K.)

7. انفسد [as quasi-pass. of أَفْسَدَهُ] is not allowable, (Ṣ, L,) or has not been heard. (K.)

10. استفسد *contr. of* اِسْتَصْلَحَ. (Ṣ, O, L, K.) [Hence, *He regarded,* or *esteemed,* a thing, or man, *as bad, evil, corrupt, unsound, wrong, wrongful, improper, unrighteous, wicked, vitious, depraved,* or *dishonest;* &c.: see **1**. — And] *He wished,* or *desired,* [a thing, or man,] *to be bad, evil, corrupt,* &c. (KL.) — [And *He sought to render bad, evil, corrupt,* &c. — And hence, *He treated in such a manner as to render disaffected,* or *rebellious.*] One says, الأَمِيرُ يَسْتَفْسِدُ رَعِيَّتَهُ [*The prince,* or *governor, treats his subjects in such a manner as to render them disaffected,* or *rebellious*]. (A.) And استفسد السُّلْطَانُ قَائِدَهُ *The Sultán provoked the leader of his forces to rebellion by his evil conduct to him.* (L.) — [And *He sought to act in a bad, an evil,* or *a corrupt, manner; to act ill, corruptly, wrongly, wrongfully, improperly, unrighteously,* or *dishonestly.*] One says, استفسد فُلَانٌ إِلَى فُلَانٍ [*Such a one sought to act in a bad, an evil,* or *a corrupt, manner,* or *to act ill,* &c., *to such a one*]. (M.) — [And *He sought discord,* or *dissension.* — And *It* (an event) *happened in a bad,* or *an evil, manner.*] — See also **1**.

فَسَادٌ an inf. n. of **1**: (Ṣ, M, A, &c.:) or a simple subst.: (Mṣb:) [as a subst. signifying] *Badness, evilness, corruptness, unsoundness, wrongness, wrongfulness, impropriety, unrighteousness, wickedness, vitiousness, depravity,* or *dishonesty;* the state of being *devoid of virtue* or *efficacy;* a *corrupted, vitiated, perverted, marred, spoiled, deteriorated,* or *tainted, state;* a *state of disorder* or *disturbance,* or *of destruction, annihilation, consumption, waste,* or *ruin:* (MA, KL, PṢ, &c.:) *contr. of* صَلَاحٌ. (Lth, M, Mṣb.) And it is also [frequently used as a quasi-inf. n.] *syn. with* إِفْسَادٌ

[signifying The *making*, or *rendering*, *bad*, *evil*, *corrupt*, &c.: (see 4:) and, oftener, the *acting ill*, *corruptly*, *wrong*, *wrongfully*, *improperly*, *unrighteously*, *wickedly*, *vitiously*, or *dishonestly*; *doing evil*, or *mischief*; and *creating*, or *exciting*, *disorder*, *disturbance*, *disagreement*, *discord*, *dissension*, *strife*, or *quarrelling*]: (L:) and [particularly] the *taking property wrongfully*. (O, Ḳ.) [Hence,] حَرْبُ الفَسَادِ [*The war of evildoing*]: thus was termed a war that happened between [the two sub-tribes] بَنُو شلك [in which the latter word is app. a mistranscription for شِبْلٍ] and غَوْث, of the tribe of طَىِّء: it was so termed because one party patched their sandals with the ears of the other, and one party drank wine out of the skulls of the other. (MF.) — Also *Drought*, *barrenness*, *dearth*, or *scarcity of good*: (M, L, Ḳ:) so in the Ḳur [xxx. 40], ظَهَرَ ٱلْفَسَادُ فِى ٱلْبَرِّ وَٱلْبَحْرِ i. e. *Drought, &c., hath appeared in the land, and in the cities that are upon the rivers*; (M, L, TA;) accord. to Zj; (M;) or accord. to Ez-Zejjájee. (L, TA.)

فَسِيدٌ: see the next paragraph.

فَاسِدٌ, (Ṣ, M, A, O, L, Mṣb, Ḳ, &c.,) part. n. of فَسَدَ; (Ṣ, M, A, &c.;) and ▼فَسِيدٌ, (Ṣ, M, O, L, Ḳ,) part. n. of فَسُدَ; (Ṣ, O;) *Bad, evil, corrupt, unsound, wrong, wrongful, improper, unrighteous, wicked, vitious, depraved*, or *dishonest*; *devoid of virtue*, or *efficacy*; *in a corrupted, vitiated, perverted, marred, spoiled, injured, impaired, deteriorated, tainted*, or *infected, state*; *in a state of disorder* or *disturbance, destruction, annihilation, consumption, waste*, or *ruin*: (MA, KL, PṢ, &c.: [contr. of صَالِحٌ and صَلِيحٌ, as is indicated in the Ṣ and M &c.:]) pl. (of the former, Ṣ, O, Mṣb, [dev. from general analogy, and of the latter agreeably therewith,]) فَسْدَى, (Ṣ, M, O, Mṣb, Ḳ,) applied to a people, (Ṣ, M, O,) like as they said سَاقِطٌ and سَقْطَى; (Ṣ, O;) the pl. being made of the same form as هَلْكَى because these two words are nearly the same in meaning. (Sb, M.)

أَفْسَدُ is [a noun denoting the comparative and superlative degrees] from الفَسَادُ; as in the prov., أَفْسَدُ مِنْ بَيْضَةِ البَلَدِ i. e. [*More corrupt*, or *unsound*, &c.,] *than the egg that the ostrich leaves in the desert, not returning to it*, in consequence of which it becomes corrupt, or unsound, &c.: and, anomalously, from الإِفْسَادُ; as in the prov., أَفْسَدُ مِنَ الجَرَادِ [i. e. *More corrupting*, or *marring*, &c., *than the locust*], because it strips the trees and the herbage; and as in other provs. (Meyd.)

مَفْسَدَةٌ *A cause*, or *means*, or *an occasion*, *of* فَسَاد [i. e. *badness, evilness, corruptness, unsoundness*, &c.; or *making*, or *rendering, bad, evil, corrupt*, &c.]; (M, A;) *contr. of* مَصْلَحَةٌ: (Ṣ, O, Mṣb, Ḳ:) pl. مَفَاسِدُ. (A, Mṣb.) One says, هٰذَا الأَمْرُ مَفْسَدَةٌ لِكَذَا [*This affair, or event, is cause of evil, &c., to such a thing*]. (M.) And هُمْ مِنْ أَهْلِ المَفَاسِدِ لَا المَصَالِحِ [*They are of the people who do actions that are causes of evil, not actions that are causes of good*]. (A.)

فسر

1. فَسَرَ, aor. ـِ (Ṣ, M, O, Mṣb, Ḳ) and ـُ, (M, Ḳ,) inf. n. فَسْرٌ; (Ṣ, M, O, Mṣb, Ḳ;) and ▼فَسَّرَ, (Ṣ, M, Ḳ,) inf. n. تَفْسِيرٌ; (Ṣ, Ḳ;) which latter is the more common; (IḲṭṭ;) or the latter has an intensive signification; (Mṣb;) *He discovered, detected, revealed, developed*, or *disclosed*, a thing that was concealed or obscured; (IAạr, O, Ḳ;) or a meaning perceived by the intellect: (B:) *he rendered* a thing *apparent, plain*, or *clear*; *explained, expounded*, or *interpreted*, it: (Ṣ, M, O, Mṣb, Ḳ:) accord. to Th (O, Ḳ, TA) and IAạr, (TA,) ▼تَفْسِيرٌ and تَأْوِيلٌ signify the same; (O, Ḳ, TA;) and so these and مَعْنًى: (O, TA:) or ▼تفسير signifies the *discovering, detecting, revealing, developing*, or *disclosing, what is meant by a dubious expression*; and تأويل signifies the "reducing one of two senses, or interpretations, which an expression bears, or admits, to that which suits the apparent meaning:" (O, L, Ḳ, TA:) or the latter, the "turning a verse of the Ḳur-án from its apparent meaning to a meaning which it bears, or admits, when the latter is agreeable with the Ḳur-án and the Sunneh:" for instance, in the phrase in the Ḳur [vi. 95, &c.], يُخْرِجُ ٱلْحَىَّ مِنَ ٱلْمَيِّتِ, if the meaning be [thus explained], "He produceth the bird from the egg," this is ▼تفسير: and if the meaning be [thus explained], "He produceth the believer from the unbeliever," or "the knowing from the ignorant," this is تأويل: (KT:) or ▼تفسير signifies the *expounding, explaining*, or *interpreting, the narratives that occur collected without discrimination in the Ḳur-án, and making known the significations of the strange words or expressions, and explaining the occasions on which the verses were revealed*; and تأويل, the "explaining the meaning of that which is مُتَشَابِه, [or what is equivocal, or ambiguous,] i. e., what is not understood without repeated consideration." (TA.) — Also فَسَرَ, inf. n. فَسْرٌ; and ▼فَسَّرَ, inf. n. تَفْسِرَةٌ, (Ṣ, O, Ḳ,) like تَذْكِرَةٌ; (TA;) or تَفْسِرَةٌ has the last of the significations assigned to it below as a subst.; (O, Ḳ, TA;) or it is post-classical; (Ṣ, O, Ḳ;) *He* (a physician) *examined*, or *inspected, urine*, (Ṣ, O, Ḳ, [but the inf. ns. only are mentioned,]) *that he might judge, by its colour, of the disease of the person from whom it came*. (TA.)

2: see the preceding paragraph, in six places.

5: see the next following paragraph.

10. استفسرهُ كَذَا *He asked him to explain, expound*, or *interpret, such a thing to him*: (Ṣ, Mṣb, TA:) and ▼تَفَسَّرَهُ is like اِسْتِفْسَارٌ. (TA.)

تَفْسِرَةٌ *Anything by which is known the explanation and meaning* of a thing: (O, TA:) or *anything which interprets*, or *explains, the state*, or *condition*, of a thing. (B, TA.) — *Urine by means of which*, (M, O, Ḳ,) or *by means of the colour of which*, (TA,) *one seeks to obtain an indication of the disease* (M, O, Ḳ, TA) *of a patient*: (O, TA:) or it is an inf. n., as mentioned above. (O, Ḳ.) [See 1, last sentence.]

عَاهِنٌ: see أَوْرَدَ كَلَامَهُ غَيْرَ مُفَسَّرٍ.

فسط

فُسْطَاطٌ and فِسْطَاطٌ (Ṣ, M, Mṣb, Ḳ) and فُسَّاطٌ and فُسْتَاطٌ and فِسْتَاطٌ and فِسَّاطٌ, (Ṣ, M, Ḳ,) the ت in the last two, as it is not found in the pl., being a substitute for the [former] ط in فسطاط, or rather for the [latter] س in فسّاط, because it is more regular to change the latter of two identical letters than to change the former, and because the two identical letters in فسّاط are together, whereas the two identical letters in فسطاط are separated, (M,) and فُسْتَاتٌ and فِسْتَاتٌ, (Ḳ,) altogether eight different forms, but MF observes that Esh-Shiháb El-Ḳastalánee gives twelve, [which, however, he does not transcribe, the remaining four being probably with fet-ḥ to the ف,] (TA,) *A tent of hair*[*-cloth*]: (Ṣ, Mṣb:) or *a great tent*: (Mgh:) or *a kind of structure* (M, Z) *used in travelling, less than the* سُرَادِق: (Z:) or the *kind of structure called* سُرَادِق: (Ḳ:) pl. فَسَاطِيطُ; (M, Mṣb, TA;) for which they did not say فَسَاتِيطُ. (M, TA.) — Hence فُسْطَاطٌ is applied to *A city*: (Z, TA:) *any city*: and particularly *a city in which is the general place of assemblage of people*: (TA:) *a populous*, or *comprehensive, city*; accord. to some: (Mṣb:) the *place of assemblage of the people of a* كُورَة [which means a *city*, and a *district*, or *region*], (Lth, Az, Ḳ,) *around their general mosque*: (Az, TA:) or you say, فُسْطَاطُ المِصْرِ, meaning *the place of assemblage of the people of the* مصر [or *city*], *around their congregational mosque*. (M.) فُسْطَاطٌ [so in two copies of the Ṣ] is [a name of] The city of مِصْر [the metropolis of Egypt]: (Ṣ:) or الفُسْطَاطُ is also the proper name of مِصْرُ العَتِيقَةُ, (Ḳ, TA,) the city so called, (TA,) which was built by 'Amr Ibn-El-'Áṣ; (Ḳ, TA;) the city of مصر in old times; as also الفِسْطَاطُ: (Mṣb:) and البَصْرَةُ. (TA.)

فسق

1. فَسَقَ is said to signify primarily *It* (a thing) *went forth*, from another thing, *in a bad*, or *corrupt, manner*. (Mṣb.) One says, فَسَقَتِ الرُّطَبَةُ, (Ṣ, O, Mṣb,) or فَسَقَتِ الرُّطَبَةُ عَنْ قِشْرِهَا, (Ḳ,) *The fresh ripe date came forth from its skin*; (Ṣ, O, Mṣb, Ḳ;) as also ▼انفسقت: (IDrd, O, Ḳ:) and in like manner فَسَقَ is said of anything as meaning *it came forth from its integument*: so says Es-Saraḳusṭee. (Mṣb.) — [Hence] فَسَقَ, aor. ـُ and ـِ, (Ṣ, O, Mṣb, Ḳ) the latter aor. mentioned by Akh, (Ṣ, O, Mṣb,) inf. n. فُسُوقٌ (Ṣ, Mgh, O, Mṣb, Ḳ) and فِسْقٌ, (Ṣ, O, Ḳ,) or this latter is a simple subst.; (Mṣb;) and likewise فَسُقَ, like كَرُمَ, (Ḳ, TA,) mentioned by Lḥ, but not known by Ks; (TA;) *He went forth from, departed from*, or *quitted*, (Mgh, Mṣb, Ḳ,) *the right way*, (Mgh, Ḳ,) or *the way of truth*, (Ḳ,) and *the limits of the law*, (Mgh,) [or *the bounds of*] *obedience*; (Mṣb;) *he forsook, relinquished*, or *neglected, the command of God*; *he disobeyed*; (Ḳ;) or *i. q.* فَجَرَ [meaning

as above; or *he transgressed;* or *acted unrighteously, sinfully, wickedly, vitiously,* or *immorally*]. (Ṣ, O, Ḳ. [See also فِسْقٌ below.]) فَسَقَ عَنْ أَمْرِ رَبِّهِ (in the Ḳur [xviii. 48], O, TA) means *He departed* (خَرَجَ) *from the command of his Lord:* (Th, Ṣ, O, Ḳ:) or *from the obeying* [*of the command*] *of his Lord:* (Fr, O, TA:) and Akh says that this phrase is like اِتَّخَمَ عن الطَّعَامِ, (Ṣ, O,) meaning عَنْ أَكْلِهِ الطَّعَامَ, (Ṣ,) or عَنْ مَأْكَلِهِ; but Th says that there is no need of this [explanation]: or, accord. to AO, it means *he declined,* or *deviated, from obeying the command of his Lord:* (O:) for فَسَقَ signifies also *he declined,* or *deviated:* (Ḳ:) and hence the saying, فَسَقَتِ الرِّكَابُ عَنْ قَصْدِ السَّبِيلِ i. e. [*The ridden camels*] *declined* [*from the right direction of the way*]. (TA.) Sometimes فُسُوقٌ may mean The *believing in a plurality of gods:* and it may mean the *committing sin.* (A Heyth, O.) And it is said to mean The *calling one another by names of reproach:* (Zj,* Mgh, TA:) or the *saying* "*O Jew,*" and "*O Christian,*" after one has become a believer: thus in the Ḳur xlix. 11. (TA.) — One says also, فَسَقَ فِى الدُّنْيَا, inf. n. فِسْقٌ, meaning *He had a wide,* or *an ample, range in respect of worldly things, and made them light and easy to himself, being without restraint in his management of them, not making them strait to him.* (Ḳṭr, Sh, TA.) — And فَسَقَ مَالَهُ *He made away with his property;* and *disposed of it,* or *spent it.* (TA.)

2. تَفْسِيقٌ is the *contr. of* تَعْدِيلٌ: (O, Ḳ, TA:) one says فَسَّقَهُ, (O, TA,) inf. n. تَفْسِيقٌ, (TA,) *He* (the judge) *pronounced him to be characterized by* فِسْق [q. v.]: (O, TA:) *he attributed to him* فِسْق. (TA.)

7: see 1, second sentence. — [Hence,] انفسق مِنَ الخَيْرِ, said of the فَاسِق, *He divested himself,* or *became divested, of good.* IDrd, O.)

فِسْقٌ is an inf. n., (Ṣ, O, Ḳ,) or a simple subst., (Mṣb,) from فَسَقَ [q. v]: (Ṣ, O, Mṣb, Ḳ:) unless as signifying [simply] *A going forth,* or *a departure,* it is said to be a word unknown before El-Islám, and to have become so much used in its legal acceptation as to be, when so used, conventionally regarded as proper (MF, TA:) [thus used,] it signifies *a going forth,* or *departure, from the right way,* (Ḳ, TA,) which is said to be the primary meaning, (TA,) or *from the way of truth;* (Ḳ, TA;) or *from the truth,* or *that which is right,* as in the phrase وَإِنَّهُ لَفِسْقٌ, (O, Ḳ, [in the CḲ لَفَسْقٌ, a strange mistake,]) in the Ḳur [vi. 121]; (O;) or *a relinquishment,* or *neglect, of the command of God;* (Lth, O, Ḳ;) and *an inclining to disobedience;* (Lth, O;) or also *disobedience* [itself]; (Ḳ;) or *i. q.* فُجُور [meaning as above; or *transgression;* or *unrighteous, sinful, wicked, vitious,* or *immoral, conduct*]: (O, Ḳ:) it is said by El-Iṣbaháneo to be a more general term than كُفْر; applying to *few sins, misdeeds, transgressions,* or *acts of disobedience,* or to *little thereof;* and also, to *many,* or *much thereof;* but is commonly known as applying to the latter: and it is related on the authority of Málik that in the Ḳur vi. 146 it means *such as is slaughtered:* (TA:) [being used as a subst.,] it sometimes has a pl., which is فُسُوقٌ. (TA.)

فُسَقُ (Lth, O, Ḳ) and ▼ فِسِّيقٌ, (Lth, Ṣ, O, Ḳ,) applied to a man, *Always characterized by* فِسْق. يَا أَيُّهَا الفَاسِقُ means يَا فُسَقُ — (Lth, Ṣ, O, Ḳ.) [*O thou* فَاسِق]; (Ṣ, O, Ḳ;) like يَا خُبَثُ, meaning يَا أَيُّهَا الخَبِيثُ; فُسَقُ being determinate, as is shown by their saying يَا فُسَقُ الخَبِيثُ, thus prefixing ال to خبيث: (Ṣ, O:) and to a woman they say ▼ يَا فَسَاقِ, like قَطَامِ, (Ṣ, O, Ḳ,) meaning يَا فَاسِقَةُ (Ḳ) [or rather يَا أَيَّتُهَا الفَاسِقَةُ].

فَسْقِيَّةٌ, with fet-ḥ, [often pronounced فِسْقِيَّة,] a post-classical word, [arabicized, from the Lat. "piscina,"] *i. q.* مُتَوَضَّأٌ [properly *A place,* here meaning *a tank,* or *basin, in which the ablution termed* وُضُوء *is performed:* now commonly applied *to a basin,* or *shallow pool, of water, in the court of a house,* or *in a room, generally having in the centre a fountain that throws up water:*] pl. فَسَاقِىُّ. (TA.)

فَسَاقِ: } see فُسَقُ
فِسِّيقٌ: }

فَاسِقٌ *Going forth,* or *departing,* or one *who goes forth,* or *departs,* [*from the right way,* or *the way of truth,* and *the limits of the law,* or] *from* [*the bounds of*] *obedience;* (Mṣb;) *disobedient* [*to God*]; (Mgh, TA;) [*transgressing,* or *a transgressor; unrighteous, sinful, wicked, vitious,* or *immoral;*] mostly applied to one *who has taken upon himself to observe what the law ordains, and has acknowledged its authority, and then fallen short of observance in respect of all,* or *of some, of its ordinances:* and when the person fundamentally, or utterly, an unbeliever is thus termed, it is because he falls short of observing the ordinance that the intellect renders obligatory on him and that the natural constitution with which he was created in his mother's womb requires to be conceded; hence the believer is contrasted with him in the Ḳur xxxii. 18; so فَاسِقٌ is a more general term than كَافِرٌ; and ظَالِمٌ is a more general term than فَاسِقٌ: (El-Iṣbahánee, TA:) accord. to IDrd, (O,) the فاسق is thus called because of his divesting himself, or becoming divested, of good: (O, Ḳ:) the word has not been heard in the speech of the people of the Time of Ignorance, (IAạr, Ṣ, O, Mṣb, Ḳ,) nor in their poetry, (IAạr, Ṣ, O, Ḳ,) though it is an Arabic word, (IAạr, Ṣ, O, Mṣb, Ḳ,) and a chaste one, and the Ḳur-án has used it: (IAạr, Mṣb:) the pl. is فَسَقَةٌ and فُسَّاقٌ: (Mṣb:) فَوَاسِقُ, [pl. of فَاسِقَةٌ,] applied to women, signifies فَوَاجِرُ [generally meaning *adulteresses,* or *fornicatresses*]. (TA.) — The five animals, or living things, (الحَيَوَانَاتُ الخَمْسُ, [specified voce حَيَوَانٌ,]) are metaphorically termed فَوَاسِقُ [as though meaning ‡*Transgressors*] (Mgh, Mṣb) because of their noxiousness, (Mgh,) or because of their much, or frequent, noxiousness and harmfulness, so that they may be killed in the case of freedom from إِحْرَام and in the state of إِحْرَام, and in prayer, which is not rendered ineffectual thereby: (Mṣb:) or because of their being out of the pale of inviolability: or, as some [unreasonably] say, because the eating of them is forbidden. (Mgh.)

فَاسِقِيَّةٌ *A certain mode of attiring oneself with the turban.* (Z, O, Ḳ.) One says, تَعَمَّمَ فُلَانٌ الفَاسِقِيَّةَ [*Such a one attired himself with the turban in the mode termed* الفاسقيّة]. (TA.)

الفُوَيْسِقَةُ *The rat,* or *mouse;* syn. الفَأْرَةُ: (Ṣ, O, Ḳ:) so called because it comes forth from its hole upon people: (O, Ḳ:) or, accord. to Z, because it does mischief in houses: and it is said in a trad. that it is to be killed: the word is the dim. of فَاسِقَةٌ. (TA.)

أَفْسَقُ [*More,* or *most, characterized by* فِسْق]. The Arabs say, لَعَنَ ٱللّٰهُ أَفْسَقِى وَأَفْسَقَكَ, meaning, الأَفْسَقَ مِنَّا [i. e. *May God curse the more characterized by* فِسْق, *of us,* or *of me and thee*]. (Fr, O.)

فسكل

Q. 1. فَسْكَلَهُ *He postponed him;* i. e., *made him,* or *asserted him, to be behind,* or *posterior,* or *last,* (Sh, O, Ḳ,) *in rank,* or *estimation.* (O.) — And فَسْكَلَ *He was,* or *became, behind,* &c.: the verb being intrans. as well as trans. [unless فَسْكَلَ be a mistake for فُسْكِلَ, the pass. form, of which an ex. occurs in the O and TA]. (Ḳ.) — Accord. to IAạr, a foreign word (عَجَمِيَّة), arabicized. (O.)

فُسْكُلٌ: see the next paragraph, in two places.

فِسْكِلٌ The *last, in coming in, of the horses in a race;* (Ṣ, O, Ḳ;) as also ▼ فُسْكُلٌ and ▼ فُسْكُولٌ and ▼ فِسْكَوْلٌ: (Ḳ:) also called the سُكَيْت [q. v.] and the قَاشُور. (Ṣ, O. [In a copy of the Ṣ, in art. سكت, الفِسْكَل is put for الفِسْكِل.]) — And hence, (Ṣ, O,) applied to a man, † *Low, base, ignoble, vile,* or *mean:* (Ṣ, O, Ḳ:) the vulgar say ▼ فُسْكُلٌ. (Ṣ, O.)

فُسْكُولٌ and فِسْكَوْلٌ: see فِسْكِلٌ. — Both also signify † *Occupying the hinder,* or *latter,* or *last, place* [*in rank,* or *estimation:* see Q. 1, above]; (Ḳ, TA;) as epithets applied to a man. (TA.)

فسل

1. فَسُلَ, (Ṣ, M, O, Ḳ,) with ḍamm, (Ṣ, O,) like كَرُمَ; (Ḳ;) and فَسِلَ, (M, Ḳ,) like عَلِمَ; (Ḳ;) and فُسِلَ, (M, Ḳ,) of the form of that whereof the agent is not named, (M,) like عُنِىَ; (Ḳ;) inf. n. فَسَالَةٌ and فُسُولَةٌ (Ṣ, M, O, Ḳ) and فُسُولٌ; (M, TA;) *He* (a man, Ṣ, O) *was,* or *became, low, base, ignoble, vile,* or *mean;* (Ṣ, M, O, Ḳ;) *such as had no manliness,* or *manly virtue,* (M, Ḳ,) *and no hardiness.* (TA.) = And فَسَلَ الصَّبِىَّ *He weaned the boy;* (AA, O, Ḳ;) as though a dial. var. of فَصَلَ. (TA.)

2: see the paragraph here following.

4. افسل عَلَيْهِ مَتَاعَهُ *He pronounced against him* (i. e. against another man, Lth, O) *that his goods* *were bad;* syn. ارذله: (Lth, O, Ḳ:) and افسل عَلَيْهِ دَرَاهِمَهُ *he pronounced against him that his dirhems,* or *pieces of money, were bad,* or *were such as are termed* زُيُوف; (Lth, O, Ḳ;*) syn. زَيَّفَهَا, (Lth, O, Ḳ, TA,) and أَرْذَلَهَا: (TA:) and [in like manner] ♦ فَسَّلَهُ, inf. n. تَفْسِيلٌ, signifies أَرْذَلَهُ and زَيَّفَهُ. (TA.) ═ See also what next follows.

8. افتسل الفَسِيلَةَ, (M,) inf. n. اِفْتِسَالٌ; (O, TA;) or ♦ أَفْسَلَهَا; (Ḳ; [app. a mistranscription for اِفْتَسَلَهَا, as it is outweighed by the latter in authority;]) *He plucked the young palm-tree from its mother, and planted it* (M, O, Ḳ) *in another place.* (O.)

فَسْلٌ and ♦ مَفْسُولٌ, (Ṣ, M, O, Mṣb, Ḳ,) as epithets applied to a man, (Ṣ, O, Mṣb,) *Low, base, ignoble, vile,* or *mean;* (Ṣ, M, O, Mṣb, Ḳ;) *such as has no manliness,* or *manly virtue,* (M, Ḳ,) *and no hardiness:* (TA:) pl. [of pauc.] أَفْسَالٌ, (Ṣ, O,) or أَفْسُلٌ, (M, Ḳ,) or both, (TA,) and [of mult.] فِسَالٌ and فُسُولٌ (Ṣ, M, O, Ḳ) and فُسُولَةٌ (Kr, M, Ḳ) and فُسْلٌ (M, Ḳ) and فُسَلَآءُ, (Ṣ, M, O, Ḳ,) which last is anomalous, as though they imagined it to have as its sing. فَسِيلٌ. (M.) — Also, the former, Anything *bad, corrupt, vile, base, abominable,* or *disapproved.* (TA.) [The pl.] فُسُولٌ, applied to dirhems, or pieces of money, means *Bad;* or *such as are termed* زُيُوف. (TA.) ═ And فَسْلٌ signifies also *Cuttings from grape-vines, for planting.* (AḤn, M, Ḳ.*)

فِسْلٌ *Foolish, stupid,* or *unsound in intellect* or *understanding.* (AA, O, Ḳ.)

فَسِيلٌ The *young ones,* or *small ones, of palm-trees,* like وَدِىٌّ; (Ṣ, O, Mṣb;) as also ♦ فَسِيلَةٌ: (Ṣ, O:) [or] the former signifies *such as are cut from the mother-tree,* or *plucked from the ground,* (Mgh,* Mṣb,) *of the young ones,* or *small ones, of palm-trees,* (Mgh,) *and then planted;* (Mgh, Mṣb;) and ♦ فسيلة signifies *one thereof:* (Mṣb:) [i. e.] ♦ فَسِيلَةٌ signifies [*a sucker,* or *an offset, of a palm-tree:* or] *a small palm-tree:* and فَسِيلٌ is its pl., as also فَسَائِلُ, (M, Ḳ,) and فُسْلَانٌ, (Ṣ, O, Ḳ,) or this last is a pl. pl., (M,) or [rather] it is pl. of فَسِيلٌ [which is properly speaking a coll. gen. n.], like as رُغْفَانٌ is pl. of رَغِيفٌ. (Mṣb.)

فُسَالَةٌ The *filings* (سُحَالَة) of iron: (Ṣ, O:) or the *portions that become scattered about, on the occasion of beating* [or *hammering*], *in the manufacturing,* of iron and the like thereof. (M, Ḳ.)

فَسِيلَةٌ: see فَسِيلٌ, in three places.

مُفَسِّلَةٌ A woman *who, when her husband is desirous of compressing her,* (Ṣ, M, O, Ḳ,) *urges an excuse to him,* (Ṣ, O,) or *says to him* أَنَا حَائِضٌ, (M, Ḳ,*) and *the like thereof,* (M,) *in order to repel him* (M, Ḳ) *thereby:* (M:) such, and the مُسَوِّفَة [which belongs to the same category] the Prophet cursed. (O.)

مَفْسُولٌ: see فَسْلٌ.

فسو

1. فَسَا, (aor. يَفْسُو, Mṣb,) inf. n. فَسْوٌ (Ṣ, M, Mṣb, Ḳ) and فُسَآءٌ, (M, Ḳ,) or this latter is a simple subst., (Ṣ, Mṣb,) *He emitted a noiseless wind* [or *a puff of wind*] (Mṣb, Ḳ, TA) *from his anus.* (Ḳ,* TA.) [Hence the saying, فَسَا بَيْنَنَا الظَّرِبَانُ, or بَيْنَهُمْ, expl. in art. ظرب.]

6. تفاسى, said of a man, *He protruded his posteriors:* (M, TA:) and تَفَاسَتْ, said of the [beetle called] خُنْفُسَآء, *It protruded its podex for the purpose of emitting a noiseless wind:* (Ṣ, TA:) but Aṣ says that it is with hemz. (TA. See 6 in art. فسأ.)

الفَسَا is a dial. var. of الفَسْأُ [i. e. فَسَا is a dial. var. of فَسَأَ, expl. in art. فسأ]. (Ḳ.)

الفَسَآءُ: see the paragraph here following.

فَسْوَةٌ [is the inf. n. of unity of فَسَا, as such signifying *A single noiseless emission of wind from the anus:* and] has for its pl. [فَسَوَاتٌ, agreeably with rule, and also] فُسًى, which is [anomalous,] like شُهًى pl. of شَهْوَةٌ, which see. (TA.) — لَيْسَ لَهُ إِلَّا فَسْوَةُ الضَّبُعِ [the lit. signification of which is sufficiently plain] occurs in a trad. as meaning † *There is not any benefit,* or *profit,* or *utility, attributable to it;* [or rather, *it is worse than useless;*] the ضبع [or hyena] being particularized because of its stupidity and its evil nature: or, some say, it [i. e. فسوة الضبع, and app. ♦ الفَسَآءُ also (mentioned among the addenda to this art. in the TA),] is *a plant* (شَجَرَةٌ) *like the* خَشْخَاش [or *poppy*], *from the fruit of which no great utility is derived:* so says IAth. (TA.) [See also خَمْطٌ, in two places.] — فَسَوَاتُ الضِّبَاعِ is an appellation of *Certain truffles* (كَمْأَةٌ); (Ḳ;) *a species of* كَمْأَة; (M;) said by AḤn to be *the species thereof called* القَعْبَلُ; (M, TA;) and the like is said in the Minháj; and further, that it is *a plant of disagreeable odour, having a head which is cooked, and eaten with milk; and when it dries, there comes forth from it what resembles* وَرْس [q. v.]. (TA.)

فُسَآءٌ an inf. n. of 1; (M, Ḳ;) or a subst. therefrom [signifying *A noiseless wind from the anus*]. (Ṣ, Mṣb.)

فَسُوٌّ A man *who often emits a noiseless wind from the anus;* (Ṣ, M, Ḳ;) as also ♦ فَسَّآءٌ. (M, Ḳ.)

فُسَيَّةٌ [originally فُسَيْوَةٌ] dim. of فَسْوَةٌ. (TA.)

فَسَّآءٌ: see فَسُوٌّ. — And الفَسَّآءَةُ: see what here follows.

الفَاسِيَةُ (Ṣ, M, Ḳ) and ♦ الفَاسِيَآءُ (M, Ḳ) and ♦ الفَسَّآءَةُ (TA) *The* [*beetle called*] خُنْفُسَآء; (Ṣ, M, Ḳ;) which emits a noiseless wind, and makes the party to stink by its foul odour: (M:) the pl. of the first is الفَوَاسِى. (TA.) Hence the prov., أَفْحَشُ مِنْ فَاسِيَةٍ i. e. [*More foul than*] *a* خنفساء. (Ṣ, M.)

الفَاسِيَآءُ: see the next preceding paragraph. — [اِبْنُ الفَاسِيَآءِ] is an appellation of *The insect called* قَرَنْبَى, *resembling the beetle called* خُنْفُسَآء, *or somewhat larger than the latter, with long hind legs, and with a speckled back:* for القَرَنْبَى, as the explanation of اِبْنُ الفَاسِيَآءِ, the TA, in art. بنى, has القرينى; and the TT, in that art., as from the T, القَرْنَى: what I have here substituted for these is evidently, in my opinion, right.]

أَفْسَى مِنَ الظَّرِبَانِ [*More wont to emit noiseless wind from the anus than the* ظربان, a small stinking beast, described in art. ظرب,] is a saying of the Arabs. (TA.)

المَفْسَى *The anus* [as being *the place of emission of the* فُسَآء]. (TA.) مَا أَقْرَبَ مَحْسَاهُ مِنْ مَفْسَاهُ [*How near is his mouth to his anus!*] is a prov. [expressive of wonder at a man's shortness: see مَحْسًى, in art. حسو]. (Ṣ.)

فش

1. فَشَّ الوَطْبَ, (Ṣ, A, Ḳ,) aor. ـُ, inf. n. فَشٌّ, (Ṣ, TA,) *He made the wind,* (Ṣ, A, Ḳ,) *and the butter,* (TA,) *to come forth from the milk-skin,* or *butter-skin,* (Ṣ, A, Ḳ, TA,) *by loosing the tie round its mouth.* (TA.) And فَشَّ السِّقَآءَ *He loosed the tie of the skin, and opened its mouth, after blowing into it, so that the wind came forth from it.* (Mgh.) [Hence the prov.,] لَأَفُشَّنَّكَ فَشَّ الوَطْبِ † *I will assuredly make thine anger to come forth from thy head, as one makes the wind to come forth from the milk-skin,* or *butter-skin:* said to a man who is angry: (T, Ṣ:) or *I will assuredly remove thy boastfulness,* &c.: (TA:) or *I will assuredly take away thy pride, and thy vanity,* or *vain glory,* or *conceit,* &c.: (Th:) or the meaning is لَأَحْلُبَنَّكَ [*I will assuredly mulct thee,* &c.; lit., milk thee]. (Kr.) See also فَشَاشِ. — [Hence,] فَشَّ النَّاقَةَ, (Ṣ, Ḳ,) aor. as above, (TA,) and so the inf. n., (Ṣ, TA,) *He milked the she-camel quickly.* (Ṣ, Ḳ.) And فَشَّ الضَّرْعَ *He exhausted all the milk of the udder.* (TA.) — [Hence also, فَشَّ الوَرَمَ *It* (a medicament) *caused the swelling,* or *tumour, to subside.*] (See also 7.) — And فَشَّ القُفْلَ, (IḲṭṭ, L,) or البَابَ, (Mgh, Mṣb,) [aor. ـُ,] inf. n. فَشٌّ, (IḲṭṭ, L,) *He opened the lock,* (IḲṭṭ, L,) or *the lock of the door, by artifice,* (Mgh, Mṣb,) *without a key,* (IḲṭṭ, L,) or *without its key:* (Mṣb:) from فَشَّ السِّقَآءَ. (Mgh.) — And according to Lth, (O,) تَتَبُّعُ السَّرِقَةِ الدُّونِ signifies الفَشّ [app. meaning *The seeking repeatedly,* or *in a leisurely manner, after pilfering,* or *petty theft*]: (O, Mṣb, Ḳ:) it is the inf. n. of فَشَّهُ, aor. ـُ: (O, Mṣb:) and Lth, (O,) or Az, (Mṣb,) cites as an ex.,

* نَحْنُ وَلِينَاهُ فَلَا نَفُشُّهُ *

[which seems to mean *We have had charge of it, and we will not seek repeatedly,* or *in a leisurely manner, bit by bit, after pilfering from it*]. (O, Mṣb.) — And فَشَّ, aor. ـُ, inf. n. فَشٌّ, *He compressed* a woman. (IḲṭṭ, TA.) — And *He ate;* as a trans. verb. (TA.) — And فَشَّ الرَّجُلُ, (Ṣ, O, Ḳ,) aor. ـِ, (O,) [inf. n. فَشٌّ,] *The man eructed,* or *belched.* (Ṣ, O, Ḳ. [A meaning assigned by Freytag to 4 also, as on the authority of the Ṣ, in which I find it assigned to فَشّ only.]) — And الفَشّ also signifies *The blowing gently*, or *softly*. (TA.) — And *The breaking wind gently*, or *softly*. (IAạr, TA.) — And *The uttering calumny*; (O, Ḳ;) thus accord. to IAạr, with ف, (O,) بَيْنَ النَّاسِ [*among the people*]. (TḲ.) — And فَشَّ القَوْمُ, inf. n. فُشُوشٌ, *The people*, or *party, became in good condition*, or *fat, after leanness*: mentioned here, and also in art. قش, in the L. (TA.) — And فَشَّ is *syn. with* فَاشَ as meaning *He gloried*, or *boasted, and magnified himself, imagining* [*in himself*] *what he did not possess*. (TA in art. فيش.)

4. افشّ القَوْمُ *The people*, or *party, went away, and fled quickly*: and so with ق. (TA.)

7. انفشّت الرِّيَاحُ *The blasts of wind came forth* from the skin, (Ṣ, Mgh,*) on its being felt, (Mgh,) and from the like thereof. (Ṣ.) — انفشّ اللَّبَنُ *The milk flowed forth* by reason of the wideness of the orifice of the teat. (TA.) — انفشّ الجُرْحُ [and الوَرَمُ, and likewise ▾ فَشَّ accord. to modern usage,] *The wound* [and *the swelling* or *tumour*] *ceased to swell*, or *be inflated*. (ISk, Ṣ) — انفشّ عَنِ الأَمْرِ *He* (a man) *became remiss and indolent in the affair*: (Ṣ:) *he turned back from it through weakness and impotence*; like تفيّش. (TA in art. فيش.) — And انفشّ *He was*, or *became, cowardly; weak-hearted*. (TA.)

R. Q. 1. فَشْفَشَ, (Ḳ,) inf. n. فَشْفَشَةٌ, (Fr, O,) *He was*, or *became, weak in judgment*. (Fr, O, Ḳ.) — And *He was*, or *became, extravagant, immoderate*, or *excessive, in lying*: (IDrd, O, Ḳ:) or so فشفش فِى قَوْلِهِ. (TA.) — And فشفش بِبَوْلِهِ *He sprinkled his urine*; (IDrd, O, Ḳ;) as also شَفْشَفَ. (IDrd, O.)

فَشٌّ The *fruit of the* يَنْبُوت [q. v., *a kind of trees*, of which one species is said to be also called خُرُوب; but see the next sentence]; (Ṣ, O, Ḳ;) not mentioned by AḤn in the Book of Plants: (O, TA:) n. un. فَشَّةٌ: and pl. فِشَاشٌ. (TA.) — And The [*species of trees called*] خُرُوب [which name is now commonly applied to the *carob*, or *locust-tree*; *ceratonia siliqua*]; as also ▾ فُشُوشٌ, (O, Ḳ,) and ▾ فُشْفُشَةٌ, (TA as from the Ḳ, but not in the CḲ nor in my MS. copy of the Ḳ,) or this last signifies *a* خُرُوبَة [n. un. of خُرُوب], accord. to AA. (O.) — Also *Foolish*, or *stupid*. (IAạr, O, Ḳ.) — And *Places in which water collects and remains*: and *a depressed piece of ground into which water pours and where it remains*: (O, Ḳ:) so says Ibn-'Abbád: [but] ISh says that هَجْلٌ فَشٌّ means [*a wide, depressed, piece of ground*,] *such as is not very deep*. (O.) — Also, and ▾ فَشُوشٌ, and ▾ فَشْفَاشٌ, [this last said in the TA to be written by Ṣgh with kesr, but it is not so in the O,] *A* [*garment of the kind called*] كِسَآء *such as is thick* (IAạr, O, Ḳ, TA) *in texture*, (TA,) *fine in the yarn*; (IAạr, O, Ḳ, TA;) called by the vulgar ▾ فَشَّاشٌ; (O; in the TA فشّاش;) or, as some say, ▾ فَشَّاشٌ signifies *a thick* كِسَآء; and ▾ فَشُوشٌ, *a thin*, or *flimsy*, كِسَآء, *such as is scanty in the yarn*. (TA.)

فَشَاشِ, like قَطَامِ, [indecl.,] means ▾ الفَاشَّةُ [i. e. *She who makes the wind to come forth from a skin, by loosing the tie round its mouth*: in the TA expl. only as signifying الضَّرُوطُ عِنْدَ الجِمَاعِ, which may be a secondary meaning, but is not the meaning in what here follows]. (O, Ḳ.) فَشَاشِ فُشِّيهِ ▾ مِنْ آسْتِهِ إِلَى فِيهِ [lit. *O woman discharging the confined wind* of the skin, *discharge thou its confined wind, from its anus to its mouth*, i. e., from end to end], (Meyd, O, Ḳ,) which is a prov., (Meyd, O,) means † [O woman] *do thou with it*, or *him, what thou wilt, for it*, or *he, has no means of self-defence* (Meyd, O, L, Ḳ) *nor of becoming altered*; and it is said in relation to an angry man who is not able to become altered: (L:) الفَشّ is the making the wind to come forth from a وَطْب. (Meyd.)

فَشَاشٌ: see the next paragraph.

فَشُوشٌ A female slave *who emits noiseless wind from the anus*; as also فاشاة [an evident mistranscription for ▾ فَاشَّة]: (IAạr, in TA:) [or] a woman *from whom wind issues on the occasion of* الجِمَاع: (IDrd, O, Ḳ, TA:) or, accord. to the Ḳ, applied to a woman, *sonum submissum genitalibus edens in congressu*: and also, applied to a man, *who glories*, or *boasts, vainly*: but these two explanations are there wrongly assigned: (TA:) the former of them applies to نَجَّاخَة; and the latter, to فَيُوش; two epithets occurring, with فَشُوش, in a verse of Ru-beh. (O, TA.) — And, applied to a woman, *i. q.* خَلَّابَةٌ [i. e. *Very deceitful*]: (O, CḲ, TA:) thus correctly, with خ: in some copies of the Ḳ with ح; and in others, with ج. (TA.) — And A woman *who sits upon the* جُرْدَان. (TA.) — Also, (O, Ḳ,) applied to a she-camel, (Ṣ, O, TA,) and to a ewe, or she-goat, (O, TA,) it signifies مُنْتَشِرَةُ الشُّخْبِ, (Ṣ, O, Ḳ, TA,) meaning *Whose milk flows forth without its being drawn, by reason of the wideness of the orifice of the teat*: or *whose milk flows forth in separate jets, like the rays of the rising sun, into the vessel, so as not to make froth*: and ▾ فَشَاشٌ signifies the *quality*, or *state, that is denoted by this epithet thus applied*. (TA.) — And A skin, such as is used for water or milk, *that sweats*, or *exudes moisture*. (O, Ḳ.) — See also فَشٌّ, in three places.

فَشِيشٌ The *sound of a gentle emission of wind from the anus*. (TA.) — And The *sound of the skin* of a viper when it moves along upon a dry, or rigid, substance. (TA.)

فَشَّاشٌ One *who opens locks by artifice*, (Mgh, Mṣb,) *without their keys*. (Mṣb.) — See also فَشٌّ, last sentence, in two places.

فَاشَّةٌ: see فَشَاشِ and فَشُوشٌ.

فُشْفُشَةٌ: see فَشٌّ, second sentence.

فَشْفَاشٌ A man *who inflates himself with lying, and arrogates to himself that which belongs to another*. (TA.) — See also فَشٌّ, last sentence.

مُنْفَشُّ المَنْخِرَيْنِ A man *inflated in the nostrils, with shortness and expansion of the cartilaginous portion of the nose*, which are characteristics of the noses of the Zenj. (TA.)

فشأ

1. فَشَأَ, (O, Ḳ,) aor. َ, (Ḳ,) [inf. n. فَشْءٌ;] as also ▾ افشأ; *He magnified himself*; or *behaved proudly*, or *haughtily*: (O, Ḳ:) [or *he gloried*, or *boasted*: for] الفَشْءُ is from الفَخْرُ, (Ibn-Buzurj, O,) [or] *syn. with* الفَخْرُ. (Ḳ.)

4: see what here precedes.

5. تفشّأ *It* (a thing) *spread*. (Ṣ, O.) One says of a disease, تفشّأ بِهِمْ, (AZ, Ṣ, O,) or فِيهِمْ, (Ḳ,) [and تفشّى, and تفشّا,] *It spread among them*: (AZ, Ṣ, O, Ḳ:) and تفشّأهم *it became common*, or *general*, or *universal, among them*. (O.) — تفشّأ بِهِ *He mocked at him*, or *derided him*. (O, Ḳ.)

فشج

1. فَشَجَ, aor. ِ, (Ṣ, O, Ḳ,) inf. n. فَشْجٌ, (A'Obeyd, TA,) *He parted his legs*, or *made an opening between them*, (A'Obeyd, Ṣ, O, Ḳ,) *but less than is denoted by* تَفَاجَّ, (A'Obeyd, TA,) previously to making water; as also ▾ فشّج, (Ṣ, O, Ḳ,) inf. n. تَفْشِيجٌ; (Ṣ, O;) or the latter signifies *he did so* [*much*, i. e.,] *in a greater degree than is denoted by the former verb*: (TA:) [and فَشَحَ and فشّح signify the same:] and ▾ تفشّج [likewise] is syn. with تَفَحَّجَ [signifying the same as فَشَجَ]; (Lth, Ṣ, Ḳ;) or he did so at the fire. (Lth, L.) And فَشَجَتْ (T, TA) and ▾ تفشّجت and ▾ انفشجت, (T, O, TA,) as also انفشحت, with ح, (IAạr, O,) are said of a she-camel, (T, O, TA,) meaning *She parted her* [*hind*] *legs widely*, to be milked or to stale. (T, TA.) — And فَشَجَ عَنْهُ, and ▾ فشّج, *He declined, deviated*, or *turned aside* or *away, from him*, or *it*; like فَشَحَ and فشّح. (TA in art. فشح.)

2: see the foregoing paragraph, in two places.

5: see the same paragraph, in two places.

7: see the same paragraph.

فشح

1. فَشَحَ, aor. َ, (Ḳ,) inf. n. فَشْحٌ, (TḲ,) *He* (a man, TḲ) *parted his legs*, or *made an opening between them*; (Ḳ;) like فَشَجَ; both mentioned by Th, on the authority of IAạr; (TA;) as also ▾ فشّح, (Ḳ,) inf. n. تَفْشِيحٌ; and likewise with ج, as mentioned by Th. (TA.) — And فَشَحَ عَنْهُ, and ▾ فشّح, *He declined, deviated*, or *turned aside* or *away, from him*, or *it*; (Ḳ;) and so فَشَجَ and فشّج. (TA.)

2: see above, in two places: — and see also what here follows.

5. تفشّحت *She* (a camel) *parted her* [*hind*] *legs widely*; syn. تَفَاجَّتْ; (Ḳ, TA;) [to be milked, or] to stale; as also ↓ فشّحت; (TA;) and so ↓ انفشحت. (Ḳ.) — And تفشّح جَارِيَتَهُ *He compressed his young woman.* (Ḳ.)

7: see the next preceding paragraph.

فَشَاحِ, [indecl.,] like قَطَامِ, *The* ضَبُع [or *hyena*, or *female hyena*]. (Ḳ.)

فشغ

1. فَشَغَهُ, (Ṣ, O, Ḳ,) aor. َ, (Ḳ,) inf. n. فَشْغٌ, (TA,) *It overspread it and covered it*; (Ṣ, O, Ḳ;) as also ↓ فشّغهُ, (Ḳ,) inf. n. تَفْشِيغٌ. (TA.) And فَشَغَتْ said of the نَاصِيَة [or forelock (of a horse)], and of the قُصَّة [which has the same, or a similar, meaning], *It covered the eye.* (TA.) And فَشَغَ *It* (a thing) *was, or became, wide and spreading*; as also ↓ انفشغ: and ↓ تَفَشَّغَتْ said of the غُرَّة [or blaze on a horse's forehead] is like فَشَغَتْ [signifying *it was wide and spreading*]. (TA.) [See also 5.] — فَشَغَهُ بِالسَّوْطِ, (Ṣ, O, TA,) inf. n. as above, (Ṣ,) *He set upon him,* or *assailed him,* or *struck him, with the whip,* syn. عَلَاهُ بِهِ, (Ṣ, O, TA,) and ضَرَبَهُ بِهِ; (TA;) and افشغهُ ↓ بِالسَّوْطِ signifies in like manner *he struck him with the whip*; (Ṣ;) or so افشغهُ ↓ السَّوْطَ. (O, Ḳ.)

2: see 1, first sentence. — [Hence,] فشّغهُ النَّوْمُ, inf. n. تَفْشِيغٌ, *Sleep came upon him and overpowered him*; (Aṣ, O, Ḳ,* TA;) and *rendered him heavy, lazy,* or *torpid.* (O, TA.)

4: see 1, last sentence.

5. تفشّغها, said of the he-camel, *He overcame her, and mounted upon her*; namely, the she-camel. (O.) — And in like manner, تفشّغهُ, said of debt, (O,) *It overcame him, and lay as a burden upon him.* (O, Ḳ.) — And, said of hoariness, *i. q.* تشيّعهُ and تَشَيَّمَهُ and تَسَنَّمَهُ [i. e. *It became abundant upon him, and spread*]: (IAạr, TA:) or تفشّغ فِيهِ said of hoariness, or of the blood, *it spread in him, and became abundant*: (Ḳ:) or this, said of hoariness, *it became abundant in him, and spread*: and, said of the blood, *it overcame him, and pervaded his body.* (Ṣ, O.) See also 1. تفشّغ الوَلَدُ, occurring in a trad., means *Children were,* or *became, numerous.* (O.) And in another trad. occur the words, مَا هٰذِهِ الفُتْيَا الَّتِى قَدْ تَفَشَّغَتْ, meaning [*What is this judicial decision*] *that has spread abroad?* (O: [and the like is said in the Mgh, in which the verb thus used is said to be from فَشَاغٌ signifying a certain plant:]) but this is differently related; some saying thus; and some, تشغّفت [q. v.]; and some تشعّبت [app. a mistranscription, perhaps for شَعَبَتْ, q. v.]. (TA.) One says also, تفشّغ الخَيْرُ فِى بَنِى فُلَانٍ i. e. [*Good,* or *prosperity,*] *became abundant,* and *arose,* or *betided, among the sons of such a one.* (TA.) — And تفشّغ البُيُوتَ *He* (a man, Ṣ, O) *entered among the houses,* or *tents*; (Ṣ, O, Ḳ;) and *disappeared among them.* (Ḳ,* TA.) — And تفشّغ المَرْأَةَ *He devirginated the woman.* (Ṣ, O, Ḳ: more fully expl. in all of these by the words دَخَلَ بَيْنَ رِجْلَيْهَا وَافْتَرَعَهَا.)

7. انفشغ *It* (a thing, TA) *appeared, and became abundant.* (O, Ḳ, TA.) See also 1.

فَشْغَةٌ *A* [*substance like*] *cotton* (قُطْنَة [in the L قَصَبَة]) *in the interior of the reed,* or *cane*: and also *a substance that flies about from the interior of the* صوصلاة [in the O صَوْصَلَّاة, and in the Ḳ without the teshdeed], i. e. *the plant,* or *herb, thus called,* (Lth, O, Ḳ,) *which is the* صَاصُلَّى; (O;) *and this is that whereof the children of El-'Irák eat the interior.* (TA.) — And The [*species of convolvulus called*] لَبْلَاب [q. v.], (Ḳ, TA,) *which mounts upon trees, and twines upon them.* (TA.)

فَشَاغٌ, (Ṣ, [thus written in my copies and others also,] and so in the Mgh,) or ↓ فُشَاغٌ and ↓ فُشَّاغٌ, (O, Ḳ, said in the former to be like صُرَاخ and مُكَّآء, and in the Ḳ to be like غُرَاب and also with teshdeed,) thus accord. to IB on the authority of Az, and thus also accord. to Hr, but mentioned by Z as with the unpointed ع, (TA,) *A certain plant,* (Ṣ, Mgh, O, Ḳ,) [said by Golius to be the *rough smilax,*] *that spreads,* (Ṣ, Ḳ,) or *mounts,* (Mgh, O,) *and twines, upon trees,* (Ṣ, Mgh, O, Ḳ,) *and mars them,* (O, Ḳ, [in some copies of the latter of which it is mentioned in two places,]) *and has no leaves* [?]. (Mgh.)

فُشَاغٌ: see the next preceding paragraph. — Also *A piece of hide,* or *leather, with which a skin for water or milk is patched.* (O, Ḳ.)

فُشَّاغٌ: see فَشَاغٌ.

نَاصِيَةٌ فَاشِغَةٌ: see the following paragraph.

أَفْشَغُ A ram (Ḳ) *whose horns go this way and that* [app. meaning *widely,* or *dissimilarly*]. (O, Ḳ.) — And نَاصِيَةٌ فَشْغَآءُ *A spreading forelock* [of a horse]; (Ṣ, O, Ḳ;) as also ↓ فَاشِغَةٌ. (O, Ḳ.) — And رَجُلٌ أَفْشَغُ الثَّنِيَّةِ *A man having the fore tooth projecting.* (Lth, O, Ḳ.) And أَفْشَغُ الأَسْنَانِ *Having the teeth disparted*; (Lth, O, Ḳ;) *having wide interstices between the teeth.* (Lth, O.)

فشل

1. فَشِلَ, (Ṣ, O, Mṣb, Ḳ,) aor. َ, (O, Mṣb, Ḳ,) inf. n. فَشَلٌ; (Ṣ, O, Mṣb;) a verb of which exs. occur in the Ḳur iii. 118 and viii. 48; and فَشَلَ, aor. ُ; and فَشُلَ, aor. ُ; two dial. vars., the former of these agreeable with a reading of the latter verse of the Ḳur-án, and the latter agreeable with a reading of the same verse by El-Ḥasan El-Baṣree; (O;) *He was,* or *became, cowardly,* (Ṣ, O, Mṣb, Ḳ,) and *weak,* (O, Ḳ,) or *weak-hearted,* (Mṣb,) and *flagging, remiss,* or *languid,* (Ḳ,) and *timorous.* (TA.) — فَشَلَتْ, and فَشَلَتْ فِشْلَهَا, (O,) or فَشَلَتْ مِفْشَلَهَا, (Ḳ,* TA, [in the CḲ ↓ فَشَّلَتْهُ, the pronoun relating to الفِشْل,]) inf. n. فَشْلٌ; (TA;) and ↓ افْتَشَلَتْهُ, (O, Ḳ,* TA,) thus accord. to the M as well as the O, (TA,) i. e. مِفْشَلَهَا, (O,) or فِشْلَهَا; (TA;) [in the Ḳ افْتَشَلَتْ alone, i. e. without any complement, as though it were intrans.; or ↓ افشلت, which is said in the TA to be the reading in the copies of the Ḳ, but which I have not found in any;] and ↓ تفشّلت [mentioned without any complement, as though intrans.]; (Ḳ, TA;) said of a woman, (O, Ḳ, TA,) in relation to the فِشْل, (Ḳ,) which is also called مِفْشَل, (IAạr, O,) meaning *She hung a* ثَوْب [or *piece of cloth*] (thus in the O, in the TA *her* ثوب,) *upon the* [*camel-vehicle called*] هَوْدَج, *then put it* [or *drew it,* or *the main part thereof,*] *within it, and bound its extremities to the* قَوَاعِد [or *four pieces of wood that form a square frame upon which it is fixed* (see its sing. قَاعِدَة)]; this being [beneath her (see فِشْل) so as to be to her] a preservative from the heads of the [curved pieces of wood called] أَحْنَآء [pl. of حِنْو q. v.] and the [apparatus called] أَقْتَاب [pl. of قَتَب q. v.] and the knots of the cord called عُصُر [pl. of عِصَام q. v.]: (O, TA:) so says ISh. (TA.)

2 and 4: see the preceding paragraph.

5. تفشّل, said of water, *It flowed.* (Ṣ, O, Ḳ.) — And *He took a wife* (ISh, O, Ḳ) مِنْهُمْ [*from among them,* probably meaning persons not of his own kindred: see مِفْشَل]. (ISh, O.) — See also 1.

8: see 1, latter sentence.

فَشِلٌ *Weak*; (Ṣ, O, Ḳ;) or *weak-hearted*; (Mṣb;) *cowardly*; (Ṣ, Mṣb, Ḳ;) *flagging, remiss,* or *languid*; (Ḳ;) and accord. to the Ḳ, ↓ فَشْلٌ signifies the same, and one says, رَجُلٌ خَشْلٌ فَشْلٌ and ↓ خَشِلٌ فَشِلٌ; but [SM says that] this is a mistake, and [incorrectly] taken from a passage of the M, in which it is stated that one says رَجُلٌ خَسْلٌ فَسْلٌ and خَشْلٌ فَشْلٌ; i. e., with ش in both and with س in both; not that it is with fet-ḥ in both and like كَتِف: (TA:) [I find, however, ↓ خَشِلٌ فَشِلٌ mentioned in art. خشل in the Ḳ, and also, as from Ibn-'Abbád, in the same art. in the O; and as ↓ فَشِلٌ is agreeable with a general rule as part. n. of فَشِلَ, I think it probably correct:] the pl. is أَفْشَالٌ, (Ṣ,) or فُشْلٌ, (Ḳ,) or both. (TA.) In the following verse, occurring in a trad. respecting the prayer for rain, (O, TA,) uttered to the Prophet by an Arab of the desert, (O,)

• وَلَا شَىْءَ مِمَّا يَأْكُلُ النَّاسُ عِنْدَنَا •
• سِوَى الحَنْظَلِ العَامِىِّ وَالعِلْهِزِ الفَسْلِ •

by العِلْهِزُ الفَسْلُ is meant العِلْهِزُ الفَسْلُ آكِلُهُ, i. e. الضَّعِيفُ مُدْخِرُهُ, (O, TA;*) the phrase being like الشَّجَرَةَ المَلْعُونَةَ in the Ḳur [xvii. 62], i. e., آكِلُوهَا: [so that the verse means, *And there* *is nothing, of what men eat, in our possession, save the colocynth that is a year old, and therefore dry,* or *that has been laid up for the year of drought or barrenness, and the food made of blood and the fur of camels, the eater, and the storer, whereof is weak*]: (O, TA:) but it is also related with س, [i. e. الفَسْل,] and thus does not need any paraphrastic interpretation. (TA.) — See also what next follows.

فِشْلٌ, (O, Ḳ,) or ♦ فَشْلٌ, (Ṣ,) [but said to be] with kesr, (O, K,) *A certain thing* (Ṣ, Ḳ) *of the apparatus of the* [*women's camel-vehicle called*] هَوْدَج, (Ṣ,) *which the woman puts beneath her in the* هودج: (Ḳ:) or the *curtain* (سِتْر) *of the* هودج; as also ♦ مِفْشَل. (IAạr, O, Ḳ.) [See a description thereof in the latter sentence of the first paragraph.]

فَشِلٌ: see فِشْلٌ, in four places.

فَيْشَلٌ: see the paragraph here following.

الفَيْشَلَةُ *The* حَشَفَة; (Ḳ;) [i. e.] *the head* [or *glans*] *of the penis*: (Ṣ, O:) and *the head of any* مُحَوَّق [or *penis having a large glans*]: (CḲ: in the text of the Ḳ as given in the TA, مُجَوَّف: [and thus in my MS. copy of the Ḳ; but it has been there altered, app. to agree with the TA, as have many other words in that copy; and the former reading is evidently, I think, the right:] some say that its ل is augmentative, like the ل in عَبْدَلٌ and in [the proper name] زَيْدَلٌ: but it may be from some other word than فَيْشَةٌ, though this has nearly the same meaning, [or, as is said in the TA in art. فيش, both have the same meaning,] and, if so, the ى may be augmentative, which is more agreeable with analogy: (TA:) the pl. is فَيَاشِلُ, (Ḳ,) and ♦ فَيْشَلٌ is another pl. [or rather a coll. gen. n.] thereof, used as such in a verse of Jereer. (TA.) — [The pl.] فَيَاشِلُ signifies also a name of *Certain trees*. (Ḳ.) — [Freytag adds as other meanings what belong to a description of the proper name of a certain water and of hills surrounding it, called الفَيَاشِلُ.]

تَفْشِيلٌ *Milk remaining in the udder*: (Fr, O, Ḳ:) and so تَمْشِيلٌ. (Fr, O.)

مِفْشَلٌ: see فِشْلٌ. — Also *One who takes a wife from among persons not of his own kindred, lest the offspring should come forth spare in body,* or *weak*. (IAạr, O, Ḳ, TA.)

مِفْشَلَةٌ The كَيَارِجة [i. e. كَيَارِجَة], (ISh, TA,) which is an arabicized word from the Pers. كراجه, in Turkish قورسق [also written قُورْصَق, i. e. the *gizzard*, or the *crop, of a bird*]. (TḲ voce مِشْفَلَةٌ [which is said in the Ḳ to signify thus, and also the *stomach of a ruminant animal*: one of the two words thus expl. may be a mistranscription for the other].)

فشو

1. فَشَا, (aor. يَفْشُو, Ṣ,) inf. n. فُشُوٌّ (Ṣ, MA, Mṣb, Ḳ) and فُشِىٌّ (Ḳ) and فَشْوٌ, (Mṣb, Ḳ,) *It* (a thing, Mṣb, or a secret, MA, or information, news, or tidings, Ṣ, Ḳ, and a man's beneficence, or bounty, Ḳ) *became revealed, disclosed,* or *divulged,* (Ṣ, MA, Mṣb, Ḳ,*) and *spread*. (Ṣ,* Mṣb, Ḳ.) — [*It* (a saying or the like) *became common*; or *obtained extensively*.] — فَشَتِ المَاشِيَةُ *The cattle pastured* [*at large*], *where they pleased.* (Mṣb.) — فَشَتْ عَلَيْهِ ضَيْعَتُهُ, (TA in art. ضيع,) or فَشَتْ عَلَيْهِ الضَّيْعَةُ, (TA in the present art.,) or فَشَتْ ضَيْعَتُهُ, (Ḥam p. 33,) said to mean *His property was,* or *became, large,* or *abundant,* [or *widespread,*] *so that he was unable to collect it together*: and [hence] *his means of attaining his object,* or *his affairs, became disordered so that he knew not with which of them to begin*: (TA in art. ضيع and in the present art.:) or *he took to doing an affair that did not concern him.* (TA in art. ضيع, and Ḥam p. 33.) — And فَشَتْ أُمُورُ النَّاسِ *The affairs of the people became discomposed,* or *disordered*; syn. اِفْتَرَقَتْ. (Mṣb.)

4. افشاهُ *He revealed, disclosed,* or *divulged, it,* (Ṣ, MA, Mṣb, Ḳ,) and *spread it*; (Ṣ,* Mṣb, Ḳ;) namely, a thing, (Mṣb,) or a secret, (MA,) or information, news, or tidings, (Ṣ, Ḳ,) and a man's beneficence, or bounty. (Ḳ.) — افشى اللّٰهُ ضَيْعَتَهُ, occurring in a trad., means *God made,* or *may God make, his means of subsistence to be abundant.* (TA in art. ضيع.) — And افشى, said of a man, *He had numerous cattle,* (T, Ḳ, TA,) *such as sheep* or *goats, and camels, &c., pasturing at large,* (Ḳ, TA.)

5. تفشّى *It* (a thing) *became wide.* (Ṣ.) And تفشّت القَرْحَةُ *The ulcer,* or *sore, became wide,* (Ḳ, TA,) *and blistered, and corrupt, by reason of thick purulent matter.* (TA.) — تَفَشَّاهُمْ, and تفشّى بِهِمْ, said of a disease, *It became much among them,* (Ḳ, TA,) *and spread*: or, as in the T, *became common,* or *general,* or *universal, among them*: AZ mentions the verb as with hemz. (TA. [See 5 in art. فشأ.]) — And تفشّى الحِبْرُ فِى الكَاغِدِ *The ink infiltrated into the paper* upon which one had written, it (the paper) being thin. (TA.)

فَشْيَانٌ, accord. to the Ḳ, but in the book of Az [i. e. the T] فَشَيَانٌ, (TA,) *A swoon* (غَشْيَةٌ) *that betides a man*; termed in Pers. تَاسًا: (Ḳ, TA:) mentioned by Lth. (TA.)

فَشَآءٌ *The multiplication by propagation,* and the *numerousness, of cattle.* (Ḳ.)

فَاشِيَةٌ sing. of فَوَاشٍ, (TA,) which signifies *Such as spread themselves, of cattle pasturing at large, of sheep* or *goats, and of camels, &c.* (Ṣ, Ḳ, TA.) Hence, (TA,) it is said in a trad., ضُمُّوا فَوَاشِيَكُمْ حَتَّى تَذْهَبَ فَحْمَةُ العِشَآءِ [*Draw ye together your cattle pasturing at large, until the darkness,* or *intense blackness, of,* or *after, nightfall pass away*]. (Ṣ, TA.) — Also *A sleep which a person takes during a portion of the night, after which he rises.* (TA.)

فص

1. فَصَّهُ, [aor., accord. to rule, ـُ, and inf. n., accord. to Golius, فَصٌّ,] ‡ *He separated it* from (مِنْ) another thing; (Ṣ, A, Ḳ;) as also ♦ افتصّهُ: (Ṣ, Ḳ:) and *he pulled it out,* or *up,* or *off*; or *removed it*; or *displaced it*; from another thing; (Ṣ, Ḳ;) as also ♦ the latter. (Ṣ.) — فَصَّ, inf. n. فَصِيصٌ: see 7. — فَصَّ الجُرْحُ, aor. ـِ, inf. n. فَصِيصٌ, (Ṣ, M, O, Ḳ,) like فَزَّ; (Ṣ, O;) *The wound became moist, and flowed*: (Ṣ, O, Ḳ:) or *flowed*: or *flowed with somewhat, not much.* (M.) And فَصَّ العَرَقُ *The sweat exuded*; (M, TA;) and so فَزَّ. (TA.) — فَصَّ said of the [locust, or cricket, called] جُنْدُب, (Sh, O, Ḳ,) inf. n. فَصِيصٌ (M, O) and فَصٌّ, (M,) *It uttered a sound.* (Sh, M, O, Ḳ.) And, said of a child, (AA, O, Ḳ,) inf. n. فَصِيصٌ, (AA, O,) *He uttered a weak weeping,* (AA, O, Ḳ, TA,) *like whistling.* (TA.) — And فَصِيصٌ signifies also The *being in a state of commotion*; and *twisting,* or *winding.* (M.) — And one says, مَا فَصَّ فِى يَدِى شَىْءٌ, (IAạr, M, O, Ḳ,) aor. ـِ, inf. n. فَصٌّ, (M,) *Nothing remained,* or *became permanent,* (IAạr, O, Ḳ,) or *accrued,* (M,) [*in my hand,*] مِنْهُ, [*thereof,* or *therefrom*]. (M.)

2. فصّص الخَاتَمَ [*He set a* فَصّ (q. v.) *in the ring,* or *signet*]. (A.) — فصّص بِعَيْنِهِ, (A,) inf. n. تَفْصِيصٌ, (O, Ḳ,) ‡ *He looked intently,* or *hardly*: (A:) or *he opened his eyes and looked intently,* or *hardly.* (Ibn-'Abbád, O, Ḳ.)

4. افصّ إِلَيْهِ مِنْ حَقِّهِ شَيْئًا † *He produced,* or *gave forth,* (Fr, Ṣ, Ḳ,) or *gave,* (M,) *to him somewhat of his right,* or *due.* (Fr, Ṣ, M, Ḳ.)

7. انفصّ ‡ *It became separated* from (مِنْ) another thing: (Ṣ, M, Ḳ, TA:) *it became parted asunder, severed, disjoined,* or *disunited*: (TA:) and *i. q.* اِنْفَرَجَ [app. as meaning *it opened, so as to form an interval, an interstice,* or *a gap*]; (L;) [and so, app., ♦ فَصَّ, aor. ـِ, inf. n. فَصِيصٌ; for] فَصِيصٌ is *syn. with* اِنْفِرَاجٌ. (TA.) And [hence,] † *He got out of* or *from* (مِن) a thing, *and severed himself* therefrom. (Mṭr, in De Sacy's Chrest. Arabe, 2nd ed., tome iii., p. 232.) And اِنْفَصَصْتُ عَنِ الكَلَامِ means اِنْفَرَجْتُ [i. e., app., *I broke off from,* or *intermitted, speaking*]. (L.)

8: see 1, in two places.

10. مَا استفصّ مِنْهُ شَيْئًا † *He did not extract, get out,* or *elicit, from him,* or *it, anything.* (Ṣ, Ḳ.)

R. Q. 1. فَصْفَصَ *He told a narrative,* or *story, truly*; (IAạr, Ḳ, TA;) as though from its فَصّ, [q. v.,] and كُنْه. (TA.) — And [the inf. n.] signifies The *being hasty* in speech, (Ibn-'Abbád, O, Ḳ,) *and quick* therein. (Ibn-'Abbád, O.) — Also *He fed* a beast, or horse or the like, *with* فِصْفِصَة [q. v.]. (M.)

R. Q. 2. تَفَصْفَصُوا عَنْهُ, (Ḳ, TA,) مِنْ حَوَالَيْهِ, (O, TA,) *They dispersed themselves, and took themselves away, from him,* (Ḳ, TA,) *from around him*; *and took fright, and ran away at random.* (O, TA.)

فَصّ, of a ring, or signet, (Ṣ, M, A, Mṣb, Ḳ,) signifies [The *stone*, or *gem*, or] *what is set* therein, (Lth, M, L, Mṣb,) *of a different substance* therefrom; (Mṣb;) and is also written ▼ فِصّ, (M, A, Ḳ,) thus pronounced by the vulgar, (Lth, Ṣ,) but J's saying this does not necessarily mean that it is incorrect, which, as in opposition to what is said by J, it is asserted not to be in the Ḳ [and A], (TA,) or the latter form is bad, accord. to ISk and El-Fárábee; (Mṣb;) and ▼ فُصّ; (A, Ḳ;) all of which three forms are mentioned by Ibn-Málik and others; but they assert that the first is the most correct and the most commonly known: (TA:) pl. [of pauc.] أَفُصّ (Lth, M) and [of mult.] فُصُوص (Ṣ, M, A, Mṣb, Ḳ) and فِصَاص. (Lth, M.) — [Also, *Any gem*, or *similar stone, rare* or *common*, and *natural* or *factitious:* and *any hard stone cut for inlaying* or *for construction.* — *A die, such as is used in the game of tables*, or *backgammon:* and *an ossicle that is used in like manner:* see كَعْب.] — ‡ *A clove* (سِنّ) of garlic; (Lth, A, O, Ḳ;) [and] so ▼ فَصَّة. (Ṣ and L in art. سن.) — † The *yolk* of an egg. (M, voce مُحّ.) — † The *bubbles* of water. (M.) — † *What leaps*, or *leap, up*, [i. e., the *particles that leap up, in effervescence*,] of wine. (M.) — ‡ The *black* (حَدَقَة) of the eye: (M, Ḳ:) [or the *pupil:* for] you say, عَرَفْتُ البَغْضَآءَ فِى فَصِّ حَدَقَتِهِ ‡ [*I knew vehement hatred in the pupil of the black of his eyes*]: and رَمَوْهُ بِفُصُوصِ أَعْيُنِهِمْ ‡ [*they cast piercing glances at him with their eyeballs*]. (A, TA.) — ‡ *A joint*, or *place of separation between two parts of an animal:* (M, A:) or *any joint*, (AZ, M,) or *any place of meeting of two bones*, (ISk, Ṣ, Mṣb, Ḳ,) *except* [*of*] *the fingers*, (AZ, M,) for the joints thereof are not so called: (M:) pl., in this and all the other senses which we have mentioned, [of pauc.] أَفُصّ (M) and [of mult.] فُصُوص: (Ṣ, M, A, Mṣb:) or, as some say, contradicting AZ, the فصوص are the بَرَاجِم and the سُلَامَيَات: [see these two words:] (Sh, TA:) and ISh says, in the "Book of Horses," that the فصوص of the horse are the *joints of the knee and pasterns*, in which latter are the سُلَامَيَات, these being the bones of the pasterns. (TA.) One says of a horse, إِنَّ فُصُوصَهُ لَظِمَآءٌ ‡ *Verily his joints are hard; not flabby nor fleshy.* (Ṣ, A.) [And hence, app., from the place in which it is mentioned by Z in this art., the saying,] فُلَانٌ حَزَّازُ الفُصُوصِ [in a copy of the A, حَزَّار; and in the TA, ضرار; but I have no doubt that the right reading is that which I have given; lit., *Such a one is the great cutter of joints;*] meaning, ‡ *Such a one is often right in his judgment*, or *opinion, and in his answer.* (A, TA.) — Hence, [immediately,] accord. to Abu-l-'Abbás; or [originally] from فَصّ in the first of the senses expl. above, accord. to IDrd; (Mṭr, cited in De Sacy's Chrest. Arabe, sec. ed. iii. 232;) فَصُّ أَمْرٍ ‡ *The point upon which a thing, or an affair, turns*, or *hinges;* or *the point in which it is distinguished*, or *discriminated, from other things;* syn. مَفْصِلُهُ; (Abu-l-'Abbás ubi suprà, Ṣ, Mṣb, Ḳ;) or مَحَزُّهُ: (Mṭr ubi suprà:) [or *its utmost point*, or *particular;* syn. مُنْتَهَاهُ: (Mṣb in art. فصل, in explanation of مَفْصِلُ أَمْرٍ:)] or *its origin*, or *source;* syn. أَصْلُهُ; (M; and Mṭr ubi suprà, and L;) and مَخْرَجُهُ الَّذِى قَدْ خَرَجَ مِنْهُ: (L, TA:) and *its essence*, or *very essence; its substance; its most essential*, or *elementary, part; its pith; the ultimate element to which it can be reduced* or *resolved;* syn. حَقِيقَتُهُ, (M, L, TA,) and كُنْهُهُ, i. e. جَوْهَرُهُ, and نِهَايَتُهُ: (L, TA:) or *its real, as opposed to its apparent, state;* syn. مَخْبُرهُ. (A, TA.) Hence the saying, (Ṣ, Mṣb, TA,) of a poet, (Ṣ, TA,) or of Ez-Zubeyr Ibn-El-'Owwám, (TA,) or of 'Abd-Allah Ibn-Jaafar Ibn-Abee-Ṭálib, (Mṭr ubi suprà, and TA,)

* وَيَأْتِيكَ بِالأَمْرِ مِنْ فَصِّهِ *

‡ [*And he will tell thee the thing*, or *affair*, tracing it *from the point on which it turns*, or *hinges;* &c.: but it appears to be originally without وَ; forming an incomplete hemistich: see Freytag's Arab. Prov. ii. 918]: (Ṣ, M,* A,* Mṭr, TA:) or *he will tell thee the thing*, or *affair, distinctly.* (Mṣb, TA.*) You say also, قَرَأْتُ فِى فَصِّ الكِتَابِ كَذَا ‡ [*I read, in the most essential part of the book* or *writing, such a thing*]. (A, TA.) And hence, فُصُوصُ الأَخْبَارِ ‡ [*The most essential parts* or *particulars of narrations*]. (A.)

فِصّ: } see فَصّ, first signification.
فُصّ: }

فَصَّة: see فَصّ, former half.

فَصِيص [as an inf. n.: see 1. ═ Also] Date-stones (نَوًى) *clean, as though oiled.* (Ibn-'Abbád, O, Ḳ.)

فَصَّاص [*A cutter*, or *an engraver*, or *a seller, of* فُصُوص, or *stones*, or *gems, for rings* or *signets*]. (TA.)

فِصْفِص: see what next follows.

فِصْفِصَة (Ṣ, M, Mṣb, Ḳ) and ▼ فِصْفِص (M) *A certain plant;* (Ḳ;) *i. q.* رَطْبَة [*a species of trefoil*, or *clover*], (Ṣ, M, Mṣb,) *a food for beasts*, or *horses and the like*, (TA,) *before it dries up;* after which it is called قَتّ: (Mṣb:) or *i. q.* قَتّ: or قَتّ *in its fresh state:* (M:) also written with س: (TA:) originally, (Ṣ, M,) in Pers., (Ṣ, M, Ḳ,) إِسْبِسْت, (so in copies of the Ṣ,) or إِسْفِسْت, (so in a copy of the Ṣ and one of the M) or إِسْبَسْت, (Ḳ, and so, accord. to the TA, in the handwriting of Az,) or إِسْپِسْت: (CḲ:) pl. فَصَافِص. (Ṣ, M, Mṣb.)

فُصَافِص *Hardy; strong;* (O, Ḳ, TA;) applied to a man. (TA.)

الفُصَافِصَة *The lion.* (O, Ḳ.)

خَاتَمٌ مُفَصَّص [*A ring*, or *signet, having a* فَصّ *set in it*]. (A.)

فصح

1. فَصُحَ, (Ṣ, A, Mz in the 9th نوع, and so in some copies of the Ḳ as stated in the TA,) [aor. ـُ,] inf. n. فَصَاحَة, (KL,) or فَصْح; (Mz ubi suprà, on the authority of Er-Rághib;) or ▼ فَصَّح; (so in other copies of the Ḳ;) or the latter also; (A;) and ▼ افصح; (A, Ḳ, Mz;) said of milk, *It became divested of the froth*, (Ṣ, A, Ḳ, Mz,) which is the primary signification accord. to Er-Rághib; (Mz;) and *clear of its biestings:* (A:) or ▼ افصح has this latter signification. (Ṣ, L, Ḳ.) And فَصْح, accord. to Er-Rághib, signifies [also] *A thing's becoming clear of what was mixed with it.* (Mz ubi suprà.) — And [hence] فَصُحَ, (Ṣ, Mṣb, Ḳ, and Mz ubi suprà,) [aor. ـُ,] inf. n. فَصَاحَة (Ṣ, Ḳ) and فَصْح, (Ḳ,) ‡ *He* (a man) *was*, or *became, good in his language*, or *dialect;* a metaphorical signification from the same verb as said of milk; so accord. to Er-Rághib: (Mz: see also 4: [and see فَصَاحَة below:]) or *he* (a foreigner) *was*, or *became, good and correct in his language*, or *dialect:* (Ṣ, Mṣb:) or *he* [a man] *was*, or *became, clear, perspicuous*, or *distinct, in speech*, or *language:* and *he* (a foreigner) *spoke Arabic intelligibly:* but this signification seems to belong more properly to أَفْصَحَ, q. v.: or *he* [a man] *was an Arab* [*by birth, and therefore in speech*], *and he increased in* فَصَاحَة [q. v.]; like ▼ تفصّح: (Ḳ:) and *he was*, or *became, eloquent;* (L;) thus used as syn. with بَلُغَ [from which it is properly distinct]. (MF.) ═ قَدْ فَصَحَكَ الصُّبْحُ [is said to mean] † *Daybreak has become apparent to thee, and its light has overcome thee:* (Ḳ,* TA:) and some say, فَضَحَكَ: [or,] accord. to Lḥ, فَصَحَهُ الصُّبْحُ means *daybreak came upon him suddenly.* (TA.)

2. فصّح: see 1, first sentence. — Also, ‡ *He* (a foreigner) *made his tongue to speak Arabic.* (A.)

4. افصح: see 1, first sentence, in two places. — It is also said of urine, (Ḳ, TA,) as mentioned by IAạr, but not expl. by him, (TA,) meaning *It became clear*, or *free from turbidness.* (Ḳ.) — And افصحت is said of a ewe, or she-goat, (Ṣ, A, Ḳ,) and of a she-camel, (TA,) meaning *Her milk became free from admixture;* (Ḳ;) or *free from froth, and clear of its biestings:* (A:) or *her biestings ceased, and the milk came after:* (Lḥ, TA:) or *her biestings ceased, and her milk became free from admixture.* (Ṣ.) — And [hence] افصح signifies also ‡ *He spoke with* فَصَاحَة; (Ḳ, TA;) [i. e. *clearness, perspicuousness*, or *distinctness;* accord. to the explanation of فصاحة in the Ḳ, and the usage of this verb in numerous exs.; or *with chasteness*, or *correctness;*] as also افصح بِهِ and افصح الكَلَامَ and افصح القَوْلَ; but when the verb became in frequent use, and commonly known, the objective complement became dropped, as in the case of أَحْسَنَ, &c.: (TA:) † *he spoke clearly*, or *plainly*, (A,* Ḳ,*

TA,) to another; (A, TA;) *without indistinctness*, or *without concealment*: (TA:) [and] ‡ *he* (a foreigner) *spoke Arabic*: (Ṣ, A, Mṣb:) or † *spoke Arabic correctly*: (ISk, Mṣb:) [and] † *he* (a man of barbarous or vitious or indistinct speech) *spoke intelligibly*. (L.) And one says, افصح فى مَنْطِقِهِ ‡ *He* (a child) *began to speak intelligibly*. (A, L.) And افصح فُلَانٌ ثُمَّ فَصُحَ ↓ ‡ [*He spoke Arabic, and then became good in his language*, or *dialect*: so accord. to Er-Rághib, as cited in the Mz, 9th نوع; in which it is said that some, but not so correctly, use these two verbs in the converse manner: or *he spoke clearly*, or *intelligibly*, *and then became chaste*, or *good and correct*, or *eloquent*, *in his speech*, or *language*]. (A.) And افصح is also used in poetry as signifying † *He* (an animal not endowed with speech) *uttered a sound*, or *cry*, *clearly*. (L.) And one says, افصح عَنْ شَىْءٍ, inf. n. إِفْصَاحٌ [in this and the preceding senses], meaning ‡ *He explained a thing*. (A,* TA.) And افصح عَنْ مُرَادِهِ † *He showed* or *revealed* [*his desire* or *his meaning*]. (Mṣb.) — Also † *It* (a thing) *became clearly apparent*, *manifest*, or *evident*. (Ḳ.) One says, افصح الصُّبْحُ ‡ *The daybreak became clearly apparent*; (A,* Ḳ;) *the light of daybreak appeared*. (Ṣ.) — And افصح الرَّجُلُ مِنْ كَذَا † *The man got clear out of such a thing*; or *escaped from it*. (Ṣ, TA.) You say, نُفْصِحُ مِنْ شِتَائِنَا ‡ *We shall get clear out of our winter*. (A.) — And أَفْصَحُوا ‡ *They* (the Christians, Ṣ, A, Ḳ) *entered upon*, (Ṣ, Ḳ,) or *celebrated*, (A,) *the festival called* الفِصْح [or *Easter*], (Ṣ, A, Ḳ,) *and broke their fast, eating flesh-meat*. (TA.) [And said also of Jews, meaning *They celebrated the Passover*: see الفِصْح.]

5. تفصّح ‡ *He affected* (تَكَلَّفَ) *the faculty*, or *quality*, *of* فَصَاحَة [q. v.] (Ṣ, A, TA) فِى كَلَامِهِ [*in his speech*]; as also ↓ تفاصح: (Ṣ:) or *he made use of the faculty of* فَصَاحَة: or, as some say, [but accord. to general analogy, this signification seems to belong more properly to ↓ تفاصح,] *he affected a resemblance to those endowed with that faculty*; [or *made a show of* فصاحة;] like تَحَلَّمَ as meaning "he made a show of الحِلْم" [i. e. "forbearance," &c.; in which sense تَحَالَمَ is more commonly used]. (TA.) See also 1, latter part.

6: see the next preceding paragraph, in two places.

10. [استفصحهُ † *He deemed it* فَصِيح as meaning *chaste*, or *free from barbarousness*, &c.; namely, a word, or phrase: and probably used in a similar sense in relation to a man: but perhaps post-classical: its pass. part. n. occurs in the Mgh, in art. بنى.] — اِسْتَفْصَحْتُهُ عَنْ كَذَا † [*I asked him*, or *desired him*, *to explain such a thing*: see 4, latter half]. (O and Ḳ in art. سنح.)

فَصْحٌ: see فَصِيحٌ.

فِصْحٌ: see فَصِيحٌ, first sentence. — Also ‡ A day *cloudless by reason of cold*; (ISh, T, TA;) or a day *without clouds and without cold*; as also ↓ مُفْصِحٌ. (Ḳ.) — And الفِصْحُ [or عِيدُ الفِصْح] (vulgarly pronounced الفَصْح, ISk, Mṣb) ‡ *The festival of the Christians*, (Ṣ, A, Mṣb, Ḳ,) [namely, *Easter*,] *when they break their fast, and eat flesh-meat*, (Ṣ, Mṣb,) *after having fasted eight and forty days, the Sunday after these days being their festival*: (TA:) [and *the Passover of the Jews*; also called الفَاسِخُ; thus with س and خ: more properly called عِيدُ الفَطِيرِ:] pl. فُصُوحٌ. (Mṣb, TA.)

فَصِيحٌ Milk *divested of the froth*, (Ṣ, A,) and *clear of its biestings*: (A:) or milk *that has come after the ceasing of the biestings*; as also ↓ فِصْحٌ. (Lḥ, TA.) — [And hence, ‡ *Chaste*, as meaning *free from barbarousness*: applied in this sense to a word, or an expression, and to language in general, and to a speaker, or writer: i. e.,] as applied to a word, or an expression, it means [*free from an incongruous combination of letters and from strangeness and from contrariety to analogy not sanctioned by frequency of usage among the Arabs of pure speech*: (see فَصَاحَة, below:) or] *of which the beauty is perceived by hearing*: (Ḳ:) and as applied to language in general, [*free from weakness of construction and from incongruity of words, with* فَصَاحَة (which see again) *in the words themselves*:] as used by the vulgar, it means *in which the rules of desinential syntax are observed*; syn. مُعْرَبٌ: (L:) [and sometimes it means] *eloquent*; syn. بَلِيغٌ [from which it is properly distinct]: (Ṣ:) and as applied to a man, [*possessing a faculty whereby he is enabled to express what he desires, with* فَصَاحَة (which see again) *in language*: or] *clear*, *perspicuous*, or *distinct*, *in speech*, or *language*; as also ↓ فَصْحٌ; (Ḳ;) but this latter is an intensive epithet, [being originally an inf. n.,] like عَدْلٌ: (TA:) [and sometimes it signifies] *eloquent*; syn. بَلِيغٌ [respecting which see what precedes]: (Ṣ, A:) or مُنْطَلِقُ اللِّسَانِ [i. e. *free from impediment of the tongue*, or *eloquent*, or *chaste*,] *in speech*, *who knows how to distinguish what is good in language from what is bad*: (TA:) the pl. as applied to men is فُصَحَآءُ and فِصَاحٌ and فُصُحٌ, (Ḳ, TA,) the last formed in the manner of the broken pl. of a subst., like قُضُبٌ pl. of قَضِيبٌ: (Sb, TA:) the fem. is فَصِيحَةٌ; of which the pl. is فِصَاحٌ and فَصَائِحُ. (Ḳ, TA.) And you say رَجُلٌ فَصِيحُ اللِّسَانِ † *A man whose tongue speaks Arabic correctly*. (Mṣb.) And لِسَانٌ فَصِيحٌ i. q. طَلْقٌ † [*A tongue free from impediment*, or *eloquent*, or *chaste in speech*]: (Ṣ:) or ‡ *an eloquent tongue*. (A.) And فَصِيحٌ signifies also † Any one *having the faculty of speech*; (Ṣ;) [i. e.] *a human being*: (TA:) أَعْجَمُ meaning that which is "destitute of the faculty of speech;" (Ṣ;) [i. e.] "a beast;" as also صَامِتٌ: whence the saying, لَهُ مَالٌ فَصِيحٌ وَصَامِتٌ ‡ [as though meaning *He has property consisting of human beings and of beasts*: but see صَامِتٌ]. (TA.) And it also occurs in poetry as meaning † *Clear*, applied to the cry of an ass. (L.)

فَصَاحَةٌ, [an inf. n. of فَصُحَ, q. v.: as denoting a quality of a word, and of language in general, and of a speaker or writer, from the same word as relating to milk, it signifies ‡ *Chasteness*, as meaning *freedom from barbarousness*: i. e.,] in a word, *freedom from an incongruous combination of letters and from strangeness and from contrariety to analogy* [*not sanctioned by frequency of usage among the Arabs of pure speech*]; (KT, and Mz in the 9th نوع;) [for] the point upon which it turns is the frequency of the use of a word by the Arabs [of pure speech]; (Mz ibid.;) a word being known to have this quality by its being frequently used by the Arabs in whose Arabic confidence is placed, or by its being used by them more frequently than one synonymous therewith: (El-Ḳazweenee in the "Eedáḥ," cited in the same نوع of the Mz:) and in language [in general], *freedom from weakness of construction* (ضَعْفُ التَّأْلِيفِ q. v.) *and from incongruity of words, combined with* فَصَاحَة *in the words themselves*: (KT:) and in a speaker [or writer] *a faculty whereby one is enabled to express what he desires, with* فَصَاحَة *in language*: (KT:) or *goodness and correctness in language*, or *dialect*: (Ṣ:) or *clearness*, *perspicuousness*, or *distinctness*, *in speech*, or *language*: (Ḳ:) and [agreeably with an explanation of فَصِيحٌ in the Ṣ and A &c.] it is sometimes used as meaning *eloquence*; syn. بَلَاغَةٌ [from which it is properly distinct]. (MF.)

أَفْصَحُ [*More*, and *most*, *chaste*, as meaning *free from barbarousness*; &c.]: in the Ḳur xxviii. 34, it means *more clear* or *perspicuous* or *distinct* [in tongue]. (Jel.)

[أَفْصَحِيَّةٌ The *quality of being more*, and *most*, *chaste*, as meaning *free from barbarousness*; &c.]

مَفْصَحٌ [or as a n. of place from أَفْصَحُوا (see 4, last two sentences)] *A place where the Christians celebrate the festival called* الفِصْح [or *Easter*]. (A.) [And app. also *A place where the Jews celebrate the festival so called by them*, i. e. *the Passover*.]

مُفْصِحٌ: see فِصْحٌ. — Also Anything *clearly apparent*, *manifest*, or *evident*. (Ṣ.)

فصد

1. فَصَدَ, (Ṣ, O, Ḳ,) aor. ـِ, (Ḳ,) inf. n. فَصْدٌ (Ṣ, O, Ḳ) and فِصَادٌ, (O, Ḳ,) [or the latter is a simple subst.,] *He cut*, (Ṣ, O,) or *slit*, (Ḳ,) [or *opened*,] *a vein*; (Ṣ, O, Ḳ;) as also ↓ افتصد. (Ṣ,* Ḳ.) — And فَصَدَهُ, aor. ـِ, inf. n. فَصْدٌ (M, L, Mṣb) and فِصَادٌ, (M, L,) or the latter is a simple subst., (Mṣb,) *He cut*, or *slit*, [or *opened*,] *it*, namely, a vein. (M, L.) [And app., accord. to

the Mṣb, *He bled him by opening a vein*; agreeably with what here follows.] And one says also, فَصَدَ النَّاقَةَ *He slit* [or *opened*] *a vein of the she-camel to draw forth the blood therefrom and to drink it* [or *to put it in a gut and broil it*: see فَصِيدٌ]. (M, L.) —— لَمْ يُحْرَمْ مَنْ فُصْدَ لَهُ *He has not been denied the entertainment of a guest for whom a camel has been bled by the slitting* [or *opening*] *of a vein and who has had the blood so obtained*, (M, A,* Ḳ,) is a prov.; (Ṣ, M, A, O;) فُصْدَ being for فُصِدَ, (Ṣ, M, O, Ḳ,) like ضُرْبَ for ضُرِبَ, and قُتْلَ for قُتِلَ; (M;) and some, also, say فُزْدَ; (Ṣ, M, O, Ḳ;) for every quiescent ص before د may be changed into ز; and every movent ص before د may have somewhat of the sound of ز given to it, (Ṣ, M, O,) but may not in this case be altogether changed into ز; so that for صَدَفَ and صَدَرَ you may not say زَدَفَ and زَدَرَ: (M:) some, also, say مَنْ قُصْدَ لَهُ, with ق, meaning مَنْ أُعْطِىَ قَصْدًا i. e. [who has been given] a little: (Ṣ, O, Ḳ:) the origin of the saying was this: two men passed the night at the abode of an Arab of the desert, and, meeting in the morning, one of them asked his companion respecting the entertainment given by the host, and the latter answered, "I was not entertained as a guest, but only a vein [of a camel] was slit [or opened] to draw blood for me;" whereupon the other replied in the words above: (O, Ḳ:) or a man used to entertain another as his guest in a time of scarcity, and, having no food to offer him, and being unwilling to slaughter his camel, bled it by slitting [or opening] a vein, and heated the blood that came forth, for his guest, until it became thick, and gave it to him to eat; and hence this prov.: (M, L:) it is applied to him who has obtained a part of that which he wanted. (Yaạḳoob, M, O, L, Ḳ.) [See فَصِيدٌ.] —— One says also, فَصَدَ لَهُ عَطَآءً, (O, L, Ḳ,) aor. ـِ, inf. n. فَصْدٌ, (L,) meaning *He apportioned to him a gift, or stipend, and caused it to be transmitted to him.* (O, L, Ḳ.)

2. رَأَيْتُ فِى الأَرْضِ تَفْصِيدًا مِنَ السَّيْلِ means *I saw, in the ground, a cleft*, or *furrowed, state, resulting from the torrent.* (ISh, O, L, Ḳ.* [Here تَفْصِيدًا is a pass. inf. n., used as a subst.]) —— And تَفْصِيدٌ, also, signifies The *macerating* [a thing] *with a little water.* (ADḳ, O, Ḳ.)

4. افصد الشَّجَرُ, and ▾ انفصد, *The trees opened their gems*, (M, Ḳ,) *and disclosed the extremities of their leaves.* (M.)

5: see 7. [Hence,] تفصّد جَبِينُهُ عَرَقًا *His* جبين [i. e. *forehead*, or *side of the forehead*,] *flowed with sweat*: (M, O:) the last word is here put in the accus. case as a specificative; and has the force of an agent; the meaning being, the sweat of his جبين flowed. (M.)

7: see 4. —— Also, and ▾ تفصّد, *It flowed*: (Ṣ, O:) or both signify *it flowed in small quantity*; said of blood. (A.) —— See also what next follows.

8. *He* (a man) *had his vein cut* [or opened]; i. e. *he had blood taken from him by the opening of a vein*; and so ▾ انفصد as used in the present day]. (Lth, L, Mṣb.*) —— See also 1, first sentence.

فُصْدَةٌ: see فَصِيدَةٌ.

فِصَادٌ an inf. n. of 1 [q. v.]: (M, O, L, Ḳ:) or a simple subst. [signifying The *act of bleeding by opening a vein*]. (Mṣb.)

فَصِيدٌ and ▾ مَفْصُودٌ A vein *slit* [or *opened*]. (M, Ḳ.) —— And both signify also A man *bled by the opening of a vein.* (TḲ.) —— Also, the former, *Blood* (Ṣ, M, O, L, Ḳ) *obtained by the cutting* [or *opening*] *of a vein* (Ṣ, O, L) *of a camel*, (L,) *and put into a gut*, (Ṣ, M, O, Ḳ,) *in the Time of Ignorance*, (M,) *and broiled*: (Ṣ, M, Ḳ:) the Arabs in the Time of Ignorance used to eat it, (M, A,* L,) and to give it to the guest to eat, in a season of dearth. (Ṣ, O,* L.)

فَصِيدَةٌ *Dates kneaded and mixed with blood*; (Ibn-Kuthweh, O, L, Ḳ;) as also ▾ فُصْدَةٌ; (O, Ḳ;) thus termed by Ibn-'Abbád: (O:) a medicine given to children. (Ibn-Kuthweh, O, L.)

فَصَّادٌ *A phlebotomist*, or *bleeder*. (MA. [See also what next follows.])

فَاصِدٌ [*Bleeding*, or (like فَصَّادٌ) *one who bleeds, by opening a vein*]. (Mṣb.) —— And الفَاصِدَانِ signifies *The place* [or *the two places*] *of the running of the tears upon the cheek.* (O.)

اِعْصِبْ مَفْصِدَهُ [*Bind thou his place of blood-letting*]. (A.)

مِفْصَدٌ [*A lancet*;] *the instrument with which a vein is slit* [or *opened*]. (O, Mṣb, Ḳ.)

مَفْصُودٌ: see فَصِيدٌ.

مُتَفَصِّدٌ: see what follows.

مُنْفَصِدٌ and ▾ مُتَفَصِّدٌ *Flowing*; (M, Ḳ;) *running*: (Ḳ:) [or *flowing in small quantity*: see 7.]

فصع

1. فَصَعَ, aor. ـَ, (Lth, O, Ḳ,) inf. n. فَصْعٌ, (Lth, Ṣ, O,) *He squeezed*, or *pressed*, a fresh ripe date, (Lth, Ṣ, O, Ḳ,) *with his two fingers* [or *his thumb and a finger*], (Lth, O,) *so that it should become divested of its skin*; (Lth, Ṣ, O;) and in like manner, a fig: (Lth, O:) or *he made* it (i. e. a fresh ripe date) *to come forth from its skin*, (A'Obeyd, O,) [to which SM adds, as from A'Obeyd,] *in order that it might ripen quickly.* (TA.) The act thus explained is forbidden in a trad.; [but I have not found for what reason.] (Ṣ, O.) —— And *He rubbed* a thing *with his two fingers*, (in the Ḳ, erroneously, *with his finger*, TA,) *in order that it might become soft, and open so as to disclose what was in it.* (IDrd, O, Ḳ, TA.) —— And *He pulled* or *stripped*, or *put off*, [a garment or the like]. (O, TA.) You say, فَصَعَ عِمَامَتَهُ (O, Ḳ) عَنْ رَأْسِهِ (Ḳ) *He removed*, or *took off, his turban from his head.* (O, Ḳ.) —— Said of a boy [not yet circumcised], *He withdrew his prepuce from his glans*; and so ▾ افتصع. (Ṣ, O, Ḳ.) —— فَصَعَتْ said of a mare; *She disclosed and concealed alternately her vulva on the occasion of staling.* (Ibn-'Abbád, O, Ḳ.) —— فَصَعَ لِى بِكَذَا, (Ḳ,) inf. n. فَصْعٌ, (TA,) *He gave to me such a thing*: (Ḳ:) [or] فصّع ▾ لِى بِحَقِّى, inf. n. تَفْصِيعٌ, *he gave to me my right*, or *due*: (Ibn-'Abbád, O:) and فَصَعَ لَهُ بِالْمَالِ *he gave to him the property*; as also ▾ فصّع. (Ḳ.)

2. فَصَّعْتُهُ مِنْ كَذَا, inf. n. تَفْصِيعٌ, *I made it to go*, or *come, forth from such a thing.* (IAạr, Ṣ, L, TA.) —— See also 1, last sentence, in two places. —— Accord. to Lth, فصّع, inf. n. as above, is also used in relation to a stink, and the ordure of a child, and a noiseless emission of wind from the anus: (O:) [or] it means *He emitted wind from the anus with a sound*: or *without a sound.* (Ḳ.)

7. انفصع *It went*, or *came, forth* from a thing; or *was made to do so*; quasi-pass. of فَصَّعْتُهُ مِنْ كَذَا (Ṣ.)

8. اِفْتَصَعْتُ مِنْهُ حَقِّى *I took from him my right*, or *due*, (O, Ḳ,*) *all of it*, (Ḳ,) *by force*, (O, Ḳ,) *not leaving of it anything*: (O:) or *I took from him my right, or due, all of it, on the spot.* (Ṣ, O.) —— See also 1, latter half.

فُصْعَةٌ The *prepuce of a boy*, (IDrd, T, O, Ḳ, TA,) *when it is wide, so that the glans protrudes from it*, (IDrd, O, Ḳ, TA,) or *when he withdraws it from over the glans, before he is circumcised.* (T, TA.)

فَصْعَانُ *Having the head always uncovered, by reason of heat and inflammation.* (IAạr, O, Ḳ.)

أَفْصَعُ A boy *having the prepuce appearing* (Ṣ, O, Ḳ) *withdrawn from the glans.* (Ṣ, O.) ═ And الفَصْعَآءُ [fem. of الأَفْصَعُ] signifies الفَأْرَةُ [app. as n. un., or fem., of الفَأْرُ q. v.; but it may here have some other of the meanings expl. in art. فأر]. (IAạr, Ḳ.)

فصل

1. فَصَلَ, (Ṣ, M, O, Mṣb, Ḳ,) aor. ـِ, inf. n. فَصْلٌ, (M, Mṣb, Ḳ,) *He separated*, or *divided*, (Ṣ, O, Mṣb, Ḳ,) and *put apart*, (Mṣb,) a thing, (Ṣ, O, Mṣb,*) عَنْ غَيْرِهِ [*from another thing*], (Mṣb,) and بَعْضَهُ مِنْ بَعْضٍ [or عَنْ بَعْضٍ] i. e. *part thereof from part*]. (M and TA in art. ميز.) And (Ḳ,) *He made a separation*, or *partition*, (M, Ḳ, TA,) بَيْنَهُمَا (M, TA*) i. e. *between them two*, meaning, two things, *making it known that the former had come to an end*: so says Er-Rághib: (TA:) and فَصَلَ الحَدُّ بَيْنَ الأَرْضَيْنِ, [aor. and] inf. n. as above, *The limit*, or *boundary, made*, or *formed, a separation between the two lands*: (Mṣb:) and فَصَلْتُ بَيْنَ القَوْمِ *I made a division*, or *separation, between*, or *among, the people*, or *party.* (O.) —— [Hence,] فَصَلَ الرَّضِيعَ عَنْ أُمِّهِ, (Ṣ, Mgh, O,) or المَوْلُودَ (M, Ḳ) عَنِ الرَّضَاعِ, (M,) aor. as above,

(M, Ḳ,) inf. n. فِصَالٌ, (Ṣ, O,) or فَصْلٌ, and the former is a simple subst., (M, Ḳ,) or both, (Mgh,) *He weaned* [*the suckling from his mother, or the young infant from sucking the breast*]; (Ṣ, M, Mgh, O, Ḳ;) as also ↑ افتصلهُ: (Ṣ, M, O:) or فَصَلَتِ المَرْأَةُ رَضِيعَهَا, inf. n. فَصْلٌ, and فِصَالٌ is the subst., *the woman weaned her suckling.* (Mṣb.) — Hence also, i. e. from فَصَلَ as first expl. above, فَصْلُ الخُصُومَاتِ *The deciding of litigations, altercations, or disputes:* like فَصْلُ الخِطَابِ: (Mṣb:) or this latter means *distinct, or plain speech; which he to whom it is addressed distinctly, or plainly, understands; which is not confused, or dubious, to him:* (Ksh in explanation of it in the Ḳur xxxviii. 19, and Mgh:) or *such as decides, or distinguishes, between what is true and what is false,* (Ksh ibid., Mgh, O, Ḳ,) *and what is sound and what is corrupt,* (Ksh, Mgh,) *and what is correct and what is erroneous:* (Ksh:) or *such as decides the judgment, or judicial sentence:* (Er-Rághib, TA:) or *the evidence, or proof, that is obligatory* [as a condition of his justification] *upon the claimant, or plaintiff,* and *the oath that is obligatory* [in like manner] *upon him against whom the claim, or plaint, is urged;* (Ksh, O, Ḳ; [an explanation of which a part is dropped in the CḲ;]) thus accord. to 'Alee: (Ksh:) or *the* [*using of the*] *phrase* أَمَّا بَعْدُ. (Ksh, O, Ḳ. [Respecting this phrase, and for other explanations, see 3 in art. خطب.]) كَلِمَةُ الفَصْلِ in the Ḳur xlii. 20 means *The sentence of* God's *deciding between mankind* on the day of resurrection, (O,) which is called يَوْمُ الفَصْلِ. (TA.) And الفَصْلُ [alone] means *The deciding judicially between what is true and what is false;* (M, O, Ḳ;) and, (O, Ḳ,) sometimes, (O,) so ↑ الفَيْصَلُ; (Ṣ, O, Ḳ;) or this latter is [a simple subst., i. e.,] a name for such decision; (TA;) and is also an epithet [expl. below]. (M, O, Ḳ.) هٰذَا يَوْمُ ٱلدِّينِ هٰذَا يَوْمُ ٱلْفَصْلِ, in the Ḳur xxxvii. 20 and 21, means [*This is the day of requital:*] *this is the day wherein a decision, or a distinction, shall be made* (يُفْصَلُ فِيهِ) *between the doer of good and the doer of evil, and every one shall be requited for his work and with that wherewith God will favour his servant the Muslim.* (M.) And إِنَّ رَبَّكَ هُوَ يَفْصِلُ بَيْنَهُمْ يَوْمَ ٱلْقِيَامَةِ فِيمَا كَانُوا فِيهِ يَخْتَلِفُونَ, in the Ḳur xxxii. 25, means [*Verily thy Lord*] *He shall decide* [*between them*], *and distinguish what is true from what is false,* [*on the day of resurrection,*] *by distinguishing the speaker of what is true from the speaker of what is false, in respect of that wherein they used to disagree,* of what concerned religion. (Bḍ.) And one says also فَصَلَ الحُكْمَ [He decided *the judgment,* or *judicial sentence*]. (M.) فَصَلَ النَّظْمَ, in the Ḳ, is a mistake: see 2. (TA.) ═ فَصَلَ مِنَ النَّاحِيَةِ, (Ṣ, O,) or مِنَ البَلَدِ, (Ḳ,) or عَنْ بَلَدِ كَذَا, aor. ـِ, (M,) inf. n. فُصُولٌ, (M, Ḳ,) *He went forth* [*from the part of the country, or from the town or country, or from such a town or country*]. (Ṣ, O, Ḳ.) And فَصَلَ العَسْكَرُ عَنِ البَلَدِ [*The army went forth from the town or country*]: whence the saying of the Prophet respecting Ibn-Rawáḥah, كَانَ أَوَّلَنَا فُصُولًا وَآخِرَنَا قُفُولًا i.e. *He was the first of us in going away* (↑ انْفِصَالًا) from his house and his family *and the last of us in returning* to [it and] them. (Mgh.) And فَصَلَ فُلَانٌ مِنْ عِنْدِى, inf. n. فُصُولٌ, *Such a one went forth* [*from my presence* or *vicinage,* or *from me*]. (TA.) And فَصَلَ مِنِّى كِتَابٌ إِلَيْهِ [*A letter*] *passed from me to him.* (TA.) Thus the verb is intrans. as well as trans.; its inf. n. when it is trans. being فَصْلٌ; when intrans., فُصُولٌ. (TA.) — And فَصَلَ الكَرْمُ *The vine put forth small grapes, resembling lentils* or *a grain similar thereto.* (M, Ḳ.)

2. فَصَّلَ النَّظْمَ, (M, TA,) thus correctly, with teshdeed, but in the Ḳ فَصَلَ, like نَصَرَ, (TA,) [inf. n. تَفْصِيلٌ,] *He put between every two of the strung beads* [or *pearls*] *a bead such as is termed* فَاصِلَةٌ [q. v., or what is described voce مُفَصَّلٌ as an epithet applied to a necklace]. (M, Ḳ, TA.) — And فَصَّلْتُ الشَّىْءَ, inf. n. تَفْصِيلٌ, *I made the thing to consist of distinct portions* or *sections.* (Mṣb.) — And فَصَّلَ الشَّاةَ, (inf. n. as above, TA,) *He* (a butcher) *divided the sheep,* or *goat, into limbs,* or *members.* (Ṣ, O, TA.) — [Hence فصّل means also *He cut* a piece of cloth for a garment: and *he cut out* a garment: — whence تَفْصِيلٌ means The *cut* of a garment. (See also De Sacy's Chrest. Ar., sec. ed., i. 86-7.)] — And [hence, likewise,] تَفْصِيلٌ also signifies [The *dissecting,* or *analyzing,* of speech, or language: the *explaining distinctly,* or *in detail:* and] the *making distinct, clear, plain, manifest,* or *perspicuous; i. q.* تَبْيِينٌ. (Ṣ, O, Ḳ.) فَصَّلْنَاهُ in the Ḳur vii. 50 [referring to the book of the Ḳur-án] means بَيَّنَّاهُ [*Which we have made distinct,* &c.]: or, as some say, *whereof we have divided the verses by means of the* فَوَاصِل [pl. of فَاصِلَةٌ, q. v.]. (TA.)

3. فاصل شَرِيكَهُ, (Ṣ, Ḳ, TA,) inf. n. مُفَاصَلَةٌ, (TA,) *He separated himself from his partner, with the latter's concurrence;* syn. بَايَنَهُ, (Ḳ, TA,) and فَارَزَهُ. (Ṣ and O and Ḳ in art. فرز.)

7. انفصل *It became separated,* or *divided,* (Ṣ, M, O, Mṣb, Ḳ,) and *put apart.* (Mṣb.) — [And *He went forth,* or *away;* like the intrans. فَصَلَ.] See 1, near the end.

8: see 1, former half. — افتصل النَّخْلَةَ عَنْ مَوْضِعِهَا *He transplanted the palm-tree.* (AḤn, M, Ḳ.) A man of Hejer [which is famous for its dates] said that the best of palm-trees is that of which the young one has been removed from its place of growth, which young one is called ↑ فَصْلَةٌ. (TA.)

فَصْلٌ inf. n. of the trans. v. فَصَلَ [q. v. passim]. (M, Mṣb, Ḳ, TA.) [As a simple subst., it has various significations here following: and is] sing. of فُصُولٌ. (Ṣ, O.) — *A separation, division,* or *partition,* between two things. (M, Ḳ.) — The *place of the* مَفْصِل [i. e. *joint,* or *articulation,* and therefore *of the division, of two bones*] of the body: between every one such and another [that is the next to it] is a وِصْل [or limb, in the CḲ, erroneously, وَصْل]. (Lth, O, Ḳ.) See also مَفْصِلٌ. — As used by the Baṣrees, [in grammar,] it is [*A disconnective*] *like* عِمَادٌ as used by the Koofees: (O, Ḳ:) thus in the saying in the Ḳur [viii. 32], إِنْ كَانَ هٰذَا هُوَ ٱلْحَقَّ مِنْ عِنْدِكَ [lit. *If this, it, be the truth from Thee*], هو is termed فصل and عماد, [more commonly the former,] and الحقّ is in the accus. case as being the predicate of كان. (O.) — Also sing. of فُصُولٌ in the phrase فُصُولُ السَّنَةِ [*The four divisions of the year;* namely *autumn, winter, spring,* and *summer*], expl. in art. زمن. (Mṣb: see زَمَنٌ.) — And *A division,* or *section, of a* باب [or *chapter*]; as being divided from others, or as forming a division between itself and others, so that it has the meaning of the measure مَفْعُولٌ or that of the measure فَاعِلٌ. (MF, TA.) — And The *contr. of* أَصْلٌ [as denoting relationship]: there are أُصُول of relationship and فُصُول thereof; [the former meaning the *stocks* and] the latter meaning the *branches.* (Mṣb. [See also other explanations of فَصْلٌ as opposed to أَصْلٌ under the latter of these words.]) ═ [It is also used as an epithet.] One says قَوْلٌ فَصْلٌ *A true say* or *saying;* (M, Ḳ;) *not false:* thus in the Ḳur [lxxxvi. 13]: (M:) or فَصْلٌ there means *distinguishing between what is true and what is false;* and relates to the Ḳur-án [itself]. (Ksh, Bḍ, Jel.) And it is said of the speech of the Prophet that it was فَصْلٌ لَا نَزْرٌ وَلَا هَذَرٌ, (O, TA, but in the latter هَذْرٌ [to assimilate it in form to نَزْرٌ],) meaning *Distinct,* (O, TA,) *clear,* or *plain, distinguishing between what is true and what is false;* (TA;) *not little nor much.* (O.) ═ And *A general* طَاعُون [i. e. *plague* or *pestilence*]. (TA.)

فَصْلَةٌ *A transplanted palm-tree;* (AḤn, M, Ḳ;) *a young palm-tree removed from its place of growth* [meaning *from its mother-tree*]: pl. فَصَلَاتٌ. (TA.) See 8.

فِصَالٌ an inf. n., (Ṣ, Mgh, O,) or a simple subst., (M, Mṣb, Ḳ,) The *weaning* of a sucking infant. (Ṣ, M, Mgh, O, Mṣb, Ḳ.) It is said in the Ḳur [xlvi. 14], وَحَمْلُهُ وَفِصَالُهُ ثَلَاثُونَ شَهْرًا, (O, TA,) meaning *And the period of the bearing of him in the womb and* thenceforward to the end of the time of *the weaning of him is thirty months.* (TA.) And one says, هٰذَا زَمَنُ فِصَالِهِ *This is the time of the weaning of him.* (Mṣb.)

فَصِيلٌ *A young camel when weaned from his mother:* (Ṣ, M, Mgh,* O, Ḳ, TA:) and sometimes *such a young one of the bovine kind:* (TA:) [and by a proleptic application,] *a young camel* [in a general sense], because he is, or will be, weaned from his mother: (Mṣb:) [in the T, voce حُوَارٌ,

and in other lexicons &c., it is applied to *a young, newly-born, camel:* and in the L, voce سُخْد, to a fœtus in a she-camel's belly: see an ex. of its meaning *a young sucking camel* (one of many such exs.) in the first paragraph of art. رجل; and a strange similar usage of the first of the following pls. in a verse cited voce خَسْفٌ:] the pl. is فُصْلَانٌ, (Sb, Ṣ, M, Mgh, O, Mṣb, Ḳ,) agreeably with rule, (Sb, M,) and فِصْلَانٌ, (Sb, Fr, M, Mṣb, Ḳ,) formed by likening the sing. to غُرَابٌ, of which غِرْبَانٌ is a pl., (Sb, M,) and فِصَالٌ, (Sb, Ṣ, M, Mṣb, Ḳ,) as though it were an epithet, (Sb, M, Mṣb,) like كَرِيمٌ, of which كِرَامٌ, is a pl.: (Mṣb:) and the female is termed فَصِيلَةٌ. (M, Ḳ.) — Also *A* حَائِط [or *wall of enclosure*], (M, O, Ḳ,) *having little height,* (O, Ḳ,) *before,* or *in front of, a fortress;* (M, Ḳ;) or (Ḳ) *before,* or *in front of, the* [*main*] *wall of a city* or *town.* (O, Ḳ.) One says, وَثَّقُوا سُورَ المَدِينَةِ بِكِبَاشٍ وَفَصِيلٍ [*They strengthened the wall of the city by means of buttresses and a low wall in front of it*]. (TA.) — And *A piece* of stone; of the measure فَعِيلٌ in the sense of the measure مَفْعُولٌ. (TA.)

فَصِيلَةٌ *A piece of the flesh of the* فَخِذ [or *thigh*]: (Hr, IAth, O, Ḳ, TA:) or, accord. to Th, (O, in the Ḳ "and") *a piece of the limbs,* or *members, of the body.* (O, Ḳ, TA.) — And *A man's nearer, or nearest,* رَهْط (Ṣ, M, O, Ḳ) and عَشِيرَة (M, Ḳ) [i. e. *kinsfolk,* or *sub-tribe,* &c.]: or [*some*] *of the nearest of the* عَشِيرَة of a man: from the first of the significations mentioned in this paragraph: (IAth, TA:) it signifies *less than the* فَخِذ: (Mgh, Mṣb:) or *less than the* قَبِيلَة: (TA:) [see شَعْبٌ in two places:] or the *nearest to him of the* آبَاء [meaning *male ancestors* and *including paternal uncles*] *of a man:* (Th, M, Ḳ, TA:) [or *any one of such persons;* for] El-'Abbás [one of Mohammad's paternal uncles] was called فَصِيلَةُ النَّبِىِّ: the term is like the مَفْصِل in relation to the human foot. (TA.) جَاؤُوا بِفَصِيلَتِهِمْ means *They came, all of them,* or *all together.* (Ṣ, O.)

فَصَّالٌ an epithet applied to a man, (O,) *Who praises men much in order that they may bestow upon him:* an adventitious, not indigenous, word: (O, Ḳ:) [and] *loquacious in every place.* (MA.)

فَاصِلٌ [as an act. part. n.] *Separating; dividing;* or *making a separation,* or *partition.* (Mṣb.) — It is said in a trad., مَنْ أَنْفَقَ نَفَقَةً فَاصِلَةً فِى سَبِيلِ اللّٰهِ فَبِسَبْعِمِائَةِ ضِعْفٍ, (Ṣ,* O, Ḳ,*) meaning [*Whoso expends expense*] *such as distinguishes between his belief and his unbelief* [i. e. *such as distinguishes him as a believer, it shall be* rewarded *with seven hundred fold*]: (Ṣ, O, Ḳ, TA:) or, as some say, *such as he cuts off from his property.* (TA.) And one says كَلَامٌ فَاصِلٌ (Ḳ and TA in art. فرز) and ↓ فَيْصَلٌ (A ibid.) *i. q.* فَارِزٌ (O and Ḳ, and TA ibid.) i. e. *Discriminating language.* (TA ibid.) And حُكْمٌ فَاصِلٌ and ↓ فَيْصَلٌ [*A judgment,* or *judicial sentence, that is decisive,* and therefore meaning,] *that has effect;* and in like manner, ↓ حُكُومَةٌ فَيْصَلٌ: and ↓ طَعْنَةٌ فَيْصَلٌ [*An act of piercing* or *thrusting* with a spear or the like] *that decides between the two antagonists.* (M, Ḳ, TA.) As an epithet applied to God, الفَاصِلُ means *The Decider between the* خَلْق [i. e. the *human race,* or *these and other created beings,*] *on the day of resurrection.* (Zj, TA.)

فَيْصَلٌ: see 1, near the middle. It also signifies *A cut,* or *severance,* (O, TA,) *such as is complete,* (TA,) between two persons. (O, TA.) — And it is also an epithet: see فَاصِلٌ, in four places. — And [hence] it signifies † *A judge, one who decides judicially, an arbiter,* or *arbitrator;* (Ṣ, O, Ḳ;) and so ↓ فَيْصَلِىٌّ: (Ibn-'Abbád, O, Ḳ:) in the Expos. of the "Miftáḥ" [of Es-Sekkákee] by the seyyid [El-Jurjánee] it is implied that it is in this sense a tropical intensive appellation. (TA.)

فَاصِلَةٌ *A bead* [or *a bead of gold* or *a gem*] *that forms a separation, or division, between the pair of* [*other*] *beads* [i. e. *between every two other beads*] *in a string thereof.* (M, Ḳ. [See also مُفَصَّلٌ.]) — And [hence] فَوَاصِلُ, of which it is the sing., † The *final words of the verses of the Ḳur-án,* (O, Ḳ,) and *of the clauses of rhyming prose* [in general], (Mṣb and Ḳ and TA in art. سجع,) *that are like the rhymes of verses;* (O and Ḳ in the present art., and Mṣb and TA in art. سجع;) and [the *final words*] *of verses.* (TA in art. سجع.)

فَيْصَلِىٌّ: see فَيْصَلٌ.

مَفْصِلٌ *Any place of meeting* [or *juncture,* as being *a place of separation,*] *of two bones of the body and limbs* or *members;* as also ↓ فَصْلٌ: (M, Ḳ:) *a single one of the* مَفَاصِل *of the limbs* or *members:* (Ṣ, O, Mṣb, Ḳ:) [*a joint such as the elbow* and *knee* and *knuckle:* and sometimes *a joint* as meaning *a bone having an articulation at each end,* or *at one end, together with the flesh that is upon it:*] in a trad. in which it is said that the mulct for any مَفْصِل of a human being is the third of the mulct for the [whole] finger, it means the مَفْصِل of any of the fingers or toes; i. e. the *portion between any* أُنْمُلَتَانِ [here meaning *two knuckles;* but this is a loose and an imperfect explanation; for to it should be added, and also the *ungual portion,* or *portion in which is the nail;* for the word is here applied to denote *any of the phalanges with the flesh that is upon it:* in the T &c., in art. نمل, one of the explanations of الأُنْمُلَة is "the مَفْصِل in which is the nail"]. (TA.) — And [hence] one says, يَأْتِيكَ بِالأَمْرِ مِنْ مَفْصِلِهِ † [*He will tell thee the thing,* or *affair,* tracing it *from the point on which it turns,* or *hinges;* (like as one says, مِنْ فَصِّهِ, q. v.;) or], *from its utmost point* or *particular,* i. e., مُنْتَهَاهُ. (Mṣb.) [This saying may be originally a hemistich, thus:

* وَيَأْتِيكَ بِالأَمْرِ مِنْ مَفْصِلِهْ *

like the similar saying ending with فَصِّه.] — In the following saying of Aboo-Dhu-eyb, [the former half of which I give from art. طفل in the Ṣ, the latter half only being cited in the present art. in the Ṣ and M and O,]

* وَإِنَّ حَدِيثًا مِنْكِ لَوْ تَبْذُلِينَهُ *
* جَنَى النَّحْلِ فِى أَلْبَانِ عُوذٍ مَطَافِلِ *
* مَطَافِيلَ أَبْكَارٍ حَدِيثٍ نِتَاجُهَا *
* تُشَابُ بِمَآءٍ مِثْلِ مَآءِ المَفَاصِلِ *

[*And verily discourse from thee, if thou wouldst bestow it, would be* (like) *gathered honey of bees in the milk* (lit. *milks*) *of* camels *such as have recently brought forth, having young ones with them, such as have young ones with them* [and] *that have brought forth but once, whose bringing forth has been recent,* such milk being *mixed with water like the water of the* مفاصل], المَفَاصِل (which is pl. of مَفْصِلٌ, Ṣ, O) signifies (accord. to Aṣ, Ṣ, O) *the place of separation* (↓ مُنْفَصَل) *of the mountain from the tract of sand, these two having between them crushed and small pebbles, so that the water thereof is clear,* (Ṣ, M, O,) *and glistens,* (وَيَبْرُقُ, Ṣ, O,) or *and is shallow;* (وَيَرِقُّ:) the poet meaning to describe the clearness of the water because of its descending from the mountain and not passing by dust nor earth: (M:) or it signifies *hard stones* (M, Ḳ) *compactly disposed,* or *heaped up:* (M, Ḳ: in the former, مُتَرَاصِفَة: in the latter, مُتَرَاكِمَة:) and (M, Ḳ) it is said to signify (M) *what is between two mountains,* (M, Ḳ,) *consisting of sand and crushed pebbles, the water whereof is clear:* (Ḳ:) or, accord. to AO, *the water-courses* of a valley: (O:) accord. to Abu-l-'Omeythil, *the clefts in mountains, from which water flows;* and only said of *what are between two mountains:* in the T, the مَفْصِل is said to be *any place, in a mountain, upon which the sun does not rise:* (TA:) and it is said that مَآءُ المَفَاصِلِ means *what flows from between the two joints* (مِنْ بَيْنِ المَفْصِلَيْنِ) *when one of them is cut from the other; like clear water;* and the sing. is مَفْصِلٌ: (M:) AA says that the مفاصل in the verse are *the* مفاصل *of the bones;* and that it likens that water to the مَآء of the flesh: (O, TA:) and IAạr says the like thereof. (TA.)

المِفْصَلُ † *The tongue;* (Ṣ, M, O, Mṣb, Ḳ;) as being likened to an instrument. (Mṣb.)

عِقْدٌ مُفَصَّلٌ *A necklace between every two pearls* [or *other beads*] *of which is put a bead* [*of another kind*], (Ṣ, O, TA,) or *a* شَذْرَة [or *bead of gold,* &c.], or *a gem, to form a division between every two of the same colour,* or *sort.* (TA.) — آيَاتٌ مُفَصَّلَاتٌ, in the Ḳur [vii. 130] means [*Signs,* or *miracles,*] *between every two whereof was made a separation by a period of delay:* or *which were made distinct, plain,* or *manifest.* (TA.) — And المُفَصَّلُ is an appellation of *The portion of the Ḳur-án from* [*the chapter entitled*] الحُجُرَات [i. e. ch. xlix.] *to the end;* accord. to the most correct opinion: or *from* الجَاثِيَة [ch. xlv.]: or *from* القِتَال [ch. xlvii.]:

or *from* قاف [ch. l.]: or *from* الصَّافَّات [ch. xxxvii.]: or *from* الصَّفّ [ch. lxi.]: or *from* تَبَارَكَ [ch. lxvii.]: or *from* إِنَّا فَتَحْنَا [ch. xlviii.]: or *from* سَبِّحِ ٱسْمَ رَبِّكَ [ch. lxxxvii.]: or *from* الضُّحَى [ch. xciii.]: (Ḳ:) this portion is thus called because of its many divisions between its chapters: (Mṣb, Ḳ:) or because of the few abrogations therein: (Ḳ:) accord. to the A, it is the portion next after that called المَثَانِى. (TA.)

مُنْفَصَلٌ: see مَفْصِلٌ, latter half.

فصم

1. فَصَمَهُ, (Ṣ, M, Mṣb, Ḳ,) aor. ـِ, (M, Mṣb, Ḳ,) inf. n. فَصْمٌ, (Ṣ, M, Mṣb,) *He broke it* (Ṣ, M, Mṣb, Ḳ) *without separating:* (Ṣ, M, Mṣb:) [i. e. *he cracked it:*] and ↓ فصّمهُ [*he cracked it much, or in several places*], (M, TA,) inf. n. تَفْصِيمٌ. (TA.) And فَصَمَ الخُرْزَةَ [*He cracked, or tore without separating, the seam, or suture, of a skin*]. (Ḳ and TA in art. خرم: in the CḲ قَصَمَ and الخَرَزَةَ.) القَصْمُ, with ق, signifies "the breaking so as to separate. (TA.) — See also 4. — فُصِمَ, said of a house, or tent, (Ḳ,) or of the side thereof, (M,) *It became thrown down, or demolished.* (M, Ḳ.) — And وَصْمٌ signifies A thing's *being cracked.* (A'Obeyd, TA.)

2: see the preceding paragraph.

4. افصم المَطَرُ *The rain passed away, or ceased.* (Ṣ, M, Ḳ.) And افصمت عَنْهُ الحُمَّى *The fever quitted him:* (Ṣ, Ḳ,* TA:) in the Ḳ, erroneously, افصم الحُمَّى. (TA.) And one says, دَآءٌ ↓ يَفْصِمُ وَلَا يُفْصِمُ *A disease that breaks and does not pass away.* (TA.) — And افصم is said of a stallion [camel], meaning *He ceased, or abstained, from covering.* (TA.)

5: see the next paragraph.

7. انفصم *It broke* (Ṣ, M, Mṣb, Ḳ) *without becoming separated:* (Ṣ, M, Mṣb:) [i. e. *it became cracked:*] and ↓ تفصّم has a similar meaning [i. e. *it became cracked much, or in several places*]. (Ṣ, M, Ḳ.) You say, انفصم ظَهْرُهُ *His back cracked.* (TA.) And انفصمت الدُّرَّةُ *The pearl cracked in one part thereof.* (TA.) — And *It broke; or became severed, or cut off.* (Ḳ.) It is said in the Ḳur [ii. 257], لَا ٱنْفِصَامَ لَهَا (Ṣ, M, Mṣb, TA) meaning *There shall be no breaking incident to it.* (M, TA.) — And *It opened so as to form an interstice, or a gap.* (TA in art. شظى.)

فصم السِّوَاكِ [app. فَصْمٌ, originally an inf. n., but probably, I think, a mistranscription for قَصْمٌ,] *A fragment* [*of the stick with which the teeth are cleaned*]. (TA.)

فَصْمَةٌ *A crack in a wall.* (TA.)

فَأْسٌ فَصِيمٌ *A large* [*hoe, or adz, or the like*]. (Fr, Ḳ.)

أَفْصَمُ An anklet *much cracked.* (El-Hejeree, M, Ḳ.*)

دُمْلُجٌ مَفْصُومٌ [*A cracked armlet* of silver: to this, thrown down and neglected, Dhu-r-Rummeh likens a sleeping gazelle]. (Ṣ, TA.)

فصى

1. فَصَى الشَّىْءَ مِنَ الشَّىْءِ, (M, Ḳ,) or عَنِ الشَّىْءِ, (Mṣb, and so in the TA,) improperly written in the copies of the Ḳ فصا, (TA,) aor. يَفْصِيهِ, (Mṣb, Ḳ,) inf. n. فَصْىٌ, (M, Mṣb,) *He separated the thing from the thing;* (M, Ḳ;) or *removed it therefrom:* (Mṣb:) whence فصى اللحم عن العظم [evidently meaning فَصَى اللَّحْمَ عَنِ العَظْمِ i. e. *He separated,* or *removed, the flesh from the bone*]: (TA:) [but in both of my copies of the Ṣ, I find فَصَى اللَّحْمُ عَنِ العَظْمِ, as though فَصَى were used as syn. with تفصّى and انفصى, meaning *The flesh became freed,* or *cleared, from the bone:* perhaps a mistake of copyists; though it is immediately added,] and ↓ فَصَّيْتُهُ مِنْهُ, inf. n. تَفْصِيَةٌ, i. e. *I freed it,* or *cleared it, from it;* (Ṣ, Ḳ;) or, accord. to Fr, this signifies *I separated it from it,* i. e., anything from another thing. (Ḥar p. 640.)

2: see the preceding paragraph.

3. فاصاهُ, inf. n. مُفَاصَاةٌ, as is related on the authority of Er-Rázee, but accord. to analogy, not on the ground of received usage, means *He separated himself from him; left, forsook,* or *abandoned, him;* or *forsook,* or *abandoned, him, being forsaken,* or *abandoned, by him;* syn. فَارَقَهُ. (Ḥar p. 640.)

4: see 5. — افصى عَنْكَ الحَرُّ means *The heat departed,* or *has departed, from thee:* but you do not say افصى عنك البَرْدُ: (ISk, Ṣ, M: but in the M, عنك is omitted in both phrases:) or you say, الحَرُّ, and افصى عَنَّا الشِّتَآءُ, *the winter,* and *the heat, departed from us;* or *left,* or *quitted, us;* (Ḳ, TA;) so says Az, on the authority of IAạr: (TA:) or, accord. to IAạr, افصى عَنْكَ الشِّتَآءُ [*the winter departed,* or *has departed, from thee*]; and سَقَطَ عَنْكَ الحَرُّ. (M, TA.) And افصى المَطَرُ *The rain cleared away.* (Ṣ, M, Ḳ.) — افصى said of a sportsman, *He had no game caught in his snare.* (Ḳ.)

5. تفصّى, said of flesh, or flesh-meat, *It became separated,* or *detached,* عَنِ العَظْمِ [*from the bone*]; as also ↓ انفصى; (M;) which is said of anything that was sticking. (Lth, TA.) *He became freed, free,* or *released,* [and in like manner said of a thing of any kind,] مِنْهُ [*from him,* or *it*]; (Ṣ, M, Mṣb, Ḳ;) i. e., from another man, (Ṣ,) from his adversary, or antagonist; (Mṣb;) from a thing; (M;) from debts; (Ṣ, Mṣb;*) from straitness, or difficulty, (Ṣ, Mṣb, TA,) or from trial, or affliction; (Ṣ, TA;) or from good, or evil; as also ↓ افصى. (Ḳ.) And *He,* or *it, went forth,* or *departed,* مِنَ الشَّىْءِ [*from the thing*]; as also ↓ انفصى, and ↓ استفصى. (Mṣb.) أَشَدُّ تَفَصِّيًا means أَشَدُّ تَفَلُّتًا: (Mṣb, TA:) thus in the trad. respecting the Ḳur-án, لَهُوَ أَشَدُّ تَفَصِّيًا مِنْ قُلُوبِ الرِّجَالِ مِنَ النَّعَمِ [*Verily it is more apt to escape from the breasts of men than are pasturing camels,* or *cattle, from their pastor*]. (TA. [In my original, the last word in this saying is without any vowel-sign; but it is not doubtful, as the trad. is well known.])

7: see the next preceding paragraph, in two places.

10: see 5, last sentence but one.

فَصًى, (M, Ḳ,* TA,) incorrectly written in the copies of the Ḳ with ا, (TA,) The *stones* (حَبّ) *of raisins:* (M, Ḳ:) also mentioned in the Ḳ [and M] as with ض: (TA:) n. un. فَصَاةٌ: (M, Ḳ:) of the dial. of El-Ḥijáz: and they also call the *stones of dates* فصية [app. فِصْيَةٌ, pl. of فَصًى, like as فِتْيَةٌ is pl. of فَتًى]. (TA.)

فَصْيَةٌ the subst. from تَفَصَّى as syn. with تَخَلَّصَ; (Ṣ, M, Mṣb, Ḳ;) [thus signifying *Freedom,* or *release,* from a thing or state;] primarily denoting one's *being in a thing and then coming,* or *going, forth,* or *departing, from it;* (Ṣ;) as also ↓ فُصْيَةٌ. (Ḳ.) Hence the saying, قَضَى ٱللّٰهُ لِى بِالفَصْيَةِ مِنْ هٰذَا الأَمْرِ [*God decreed for me,* or *may God decree for me, freedom,* or *release, from this affair,* or *case*]. (A, TA.) — فَصْيَةٌ مَا بَيْنَ الحَرِّ وَالبَرْدِ means *An intermission* (سَكْتَةٌ, lit. *a quiescence,*) *between heat and cold:* and one says لَيْلَةٌ فَصْيَةٌ and يَوْمٌ فَصْيَةٌ [*A night* that is, or that was, *one of intermission,* and *a day* &c.], and لَيْلَةٌ فَصِيَةٌ and يَوْمٌ فَصِيَةٌ [meaning the same]. (M, Ḳ.)

فُصْيَةٌ: see the next preceding paragraph.

فض

1. فَضَّهُ, (Ṣ, Mgh, O, Mṣb,) aor. يَفُضُّ, (Ṣ, O, Mṣb,) inf. n. فَضٌّ, (Ṣ, A, Mgh, O, Mṣb, Ḳ,) *He broke it;* namely, the seal (A, Mgh, Mṣb, Ḳ) of a letter; (A, Ḳ;) and any other thing: (TA:) *he broke it asunder,* or *into several pieces; he dissundered it;* (Ṣ, Mgh, O, Ḳ;) for instance, the seal from a letter. (Ṣ, O.) فَضَّ الخَاتَمَ is also a metonymical phrase, meaning ‡ *Inivit:* (TA:) [or rather, *i. q.*] فَضَّ البَكَارَةَ ‡ *he destroyed the virginity:* the virginity being likened to a seal: or this phrase is from فَضَضْتُ اللُّؤْلُؤَةَ *I bored,* or *perforated, the pearl.* (Mṣb.) [See also 8.] You say also, فَضَّ ٱللّٰهُ فَاهُ, (Mṣb, TA,) and, accord. to IḲṭṭ, ↓ أَفَضَّهُ, which J disallows, (TA,) *God broke,* or *may God break, his teeth:* (TA:) or *God scattered,* or *may God scatter, his teeth.* (Mṣb.) The phrase لَا يَفْضُضِ ٱللّٰهُ فَاكَ, (Ṣ, A,) meaning *May God not break thy teeth,* (TA,) occurs in a trad.: (Ṣ, A:) and J says, (TA,) you should not say ↓ يُفْضِضْ; (Ṣ, TA; [but in

one copy of the Ṣ, I find يَفْضِضُ;]) though some allow it: and some say that إِفْضَاء [evidently a mistake for إِفْضَاض] means the *falling out* of the teeth *from above and below;* but the former explanation is the more common. (TA.) — *He separated it; dispersed it; scattered it; broke it up;* (Ṣ, A, Mṣb, TA;) namely, a thing; (Mṣb;) or a party of men; (Ṣ, O;) or a ring of men, (A, TA,) after they had collected together. (TA.) You say also, فَضَّ المَالَ عَلَى القَوْمِ (Mgh,* TA) *He distributed the property among the people,* or *party of men.* (Mgh, TA.*) — فَضَضْتُ مَا بَيْنَهُمَا *I cut* [*the tie,* or *bond, that was between them*]. (TA.) — فَضَّ المَآءَ, [aor. and] inf. n. as above, *He poured out,* or *forth, the water;* (TA;) and so الدُّمُوعَ *the tears.* (Ḥar p. 57.) [See also 8.] = فَضَّ المَآءُ, [aor., accord. to rule, يَفِضُّ,] *The water flowed:* (TA:) and انفضّت ↓ الدُّمُوعُ *The tears poured forth.* (Ḥar p. 57.)

2. فضّض [*He silvered* a thing: *he ornamented* a bit or bridle *with silver:* from فِضَّةٌ: see the pass. part. n., below.]

4: see 1, in two places. — افضّ العَطَآءَ *He made the gift large.* (TA.)

5: see 7. = تَفَضَّيْتُ from الفِضَّةُ, for تَفَضَّضْتُ, has been mentioned by Sb; but ISd says, I know not what he meant thereby; whether *I took for myself,* or *acquired,* فِضَّة, [i. e. *silver*], or *I made use of it.* (TA.)

7. انفضّ *It broke;* or *became broken;* (Ṣ, Mgh;) said of a seal, (Mgh,) or thing. (Ṣ.) — انفضّ مِمَّا صُنِعَ بِٱبْنِ عَفَّانَ, occurring in a trad., means *His connections became cut,* or *sundered,* [*so that he became clear*] *from what was done to* ['Othmán] *Ibn-'Affán,* through grief and regret: (O, TA:) but accord. to one relation, the verb is [انقضّ,] with ق. (TA.) — انفضّ also signifies *It became separated, dispersed, scattered,* or *broken up;* or *it separated, dispersed,* or *scattered, itself,* or *it broke up;* (Ṣ, Mgh, O, Mṣb;) said of a thing, (Mṣb,) and of a party of men; (Ṣ, Mgh, O, Mṣb;) as also ↓ تفضّض, said of a thing, (Ṣ,) and of a party of men. (TA.) One says, انفضّ المَجْلِسُ [*The assembly of persons sitting together broke up*]. (Mṣb in art. جلس.) — See also 1 last sentence.

8. افتضّها *He devirginated her:* (O, Ḳ:) and so اقتضّها, with ق. (O, TA.) [See also 1, second sentence.] — افتضّ المَآءَ *He poured out,* or *forth, the water by little and little, successively:* (O, Ḳ:) *or he obtained the water at the time of its coming forth* (Ṣ, O, Ḳ,) *from the spring* or *from the clouds.* (TA.) [See also 1, near the end.] — افتضّت said of a woman, *She broke* [i. e. *ended*] *her* عِدَّة, (O, Ḳ, TA,) meaning a widow's عِدَّة [during which she may not marry again, nor use perfumes &c., and] which is a period of four months and ten nights, but was before the Prophet's time a year: (TA:) this she did by touching perfume, or by some other act, (Ḳ, TA,) such as paring the nail, or plucking out the hair from the face: (TA:) or she rubbed her body with [or against] a beast, (Ḳ, TA,) i. e. an ass, or a sheep or goat, (O in art. حفش,) thereby to quit the state of the عِدَّة: or it was customary with them for her to wipe her قُبُل with a bird, and to throw it away; in consequence of which it hardly ever, or never, lived: (Ḳ, TA:) she used to enter a حِفْش [or small tent], and wear the worst of her clothing until a year passed, when a beast or bird was brought to her, and by means thereof she broke her عِدَّة; then she went forth, and a بَعْرَة [or piece of camel's or similar dung] was given to her, and she threw it: (TA: [see 1 in art. بعر:]) she used not to wash herself, nor to touch water, nor to pare a nail, nor to pluck out hair from her face; then she would go forth, after the year, with the foulest aspect, and break her عِدَّة by means of a bird, wiping her قُبُل with it, and throwing it away. (O, TA.) The verb, thus used, occurs in a trad., but, as some relate it, with ق and ب [i. e. saying تَقْبِضُ instead of تَفْتَضُّ]; and Az mentions that Esh-Sháfi'ee related this trad. [in like manner] pronouncing the word with ق and ض, from القبض. (TA.)

R. Q. 1. فَضْفَضَ *He made* a garment, and a coat of mail, *wide,* or *ample.* (TA.) = [Also, probably, *It* (a garment, and a دِرْع and † the means of subsistence,) *was,* or *became, wide,* or *ample:* see فَضْفَضَةٌ, below.]

R. Q. 2. تَفَضْفَضَ بَوْلُ النَّاقَةِ *The urine of the she-camel became sprinkled upon her thighs.* (TA.)

فَضٌّ, (Ḳ,) or فَضٌّ مِنَ النَّاسِ, (O, TA,) *A small number of men* (نَفَرٌ) *in a state of dispersion.* (O, Ḳ, TA.) And تَمْرٌ فَضٌّ *Dates in a separate state, not sticking together.* (IAar. [See also فَتٌّ.]) And حَرِيرٌ فَضٌّ *Silk scattered, strewn,* or *thrown dispersedly.* (A, TA.) [See also فَضَضٌ, and فُضَاضٌ.]

فَضَّةٌ: see the next paragraph, in two places.

فِضَّةٌ [*Silver;*] *a certain thing well known:* (Ṣ, O, Ḳ:) or *wrought silver:* (IAar, T and Ḳ voce تِبْرٌ, q. v.:) pl. فِضَضٌ. (TA.) The phrase قَوَارِيرَ مِنْ فِضَّةٍ, in the Ḳur [lxxvi. 16], means *Such* [*flasks*] as, *notwithstanding their clearness,* or *transparency, will be secure from being broken, and capable of being restored to a sound state if broken,* (Az, O, Ḳ,) *like silver:* (Az, O,) being, as Zj says, *originally of silver, yet transparent, so that what will be within them will be seen from without;* whereas the قوارير of this world are originally from sand. (Az, O.) [See also art. قر.] = Also *An elevated* [*stony tract such as is termed*] حَرَّة; and so ↓ فَضَّةٌ: pl. فِضَضٌ and فِضَاضٌ. (Ibn-'Abbád, O, Ḳ.) — And فِضَاضُ الجِبَالِ signifies *Rocks scattered* (مَنْثُورٌ, in the CḲ مَنْشُورٌ), *one upon another:* (Ibn-'Abbád, O, Ḳ:) sing. ↓ فَضَّةٌ. (TA.)

فَضَضٌ *What is separated, dispersed,* or *scattered;* (Ṣ, O, Ḳ;) as also ↓ فَضِيضٌ; (O, Ḳ, TA;) of rain-water, and of hail, and of sweat: (TA:) and *sprinkled:* (Ḳ:) and particularly *what is sprinkled,* of water, *when one performs ablution with it,* (A, O, Ḳ,) *and what flows upon the limbs on that occasion;* (A;) as also ↓ فَضِيضٌ. (Ḳ.) The saying of 'Áïsheh to Marwán, فَأَنْتَ فَضَضٌ مِنْ لَعْنَةِ ٱللّٰهِ, (A, O, Ḳ,) or ↓ فَضِيضٌ, (A,) or ↓ فُضُضٌ, or ↓ فُضَاضٌ, accord. to different relations, (Ḳ,) means *So thou art a part* [*of the object*] *of the curse of God:* (Sh, A, O, Ḳ:) for the Apostle of God had cursed the father of Marwán, the latter being at the time [essentially] in his father's loins: (A:) or it means that he came forth in sprinkled seed from his father's loins: (Th, Ṣ,* TA:) or, accord. to another relation, she said فُظَاظَةٌ [see فَظِيظٌ]. (TA.) [See also فَضٌّ and فُضَاضٌ.]

فُضُضٌ: see فَضَضٌ [and فَضِيضٌ].

فُضَاضٌ *What is separated, dispersed,* or *scattered,* of a thing, *when it is broken;* (Ṣ, O, Ḳ;) as also ↓ فِضَاضٌ; (O, Ḳ;) and ↓ فُضَاضَةٌ. (TA.) You say, طَارَتْ عِظَامُهُ فُضَاضًا *His bones became scattered in fragments* on the occasion of the blow. (TA.) See also فَضَضٌ.

فِضَاضٌ: see the next preceding paragraph.

فَضِيضٌ: see مَفْضُوضٌ: — and see فَضَضٌ, in three places. — Also *What is cast forth from the mouth,* of date-stones. (TA.) — And *Sweet water:* (Ṣ, O, Ḳ:) or *flowing water:* (A'Obeyd, Ṣ, O, Ḳ:) or *fresh water when it comes forth from the spring* or *from the clouds:* (O:) or *water such as is termed* غَرِيضٌ: pl. فُضُضٌ. (TA in art. فظ.) And a place *abounding with water.* (TA.) — نَاقَةٌ كَثِيرَةُ فَضِيضِ اللَّبَنِ *A she-camel having much milk:* and رَجُلٌ كَثِيرُ فَضِيضِ الكَلَامِ *a man of much speech* or *talk.* (TA.) = And accord. to El-Khaṭṭábee and others, [and among them the author of the Ḳ,] *A* طَلْع [or *spadix of a palm-tree*] *when it first comes forth:* but this is a mistranscription; correctly غَضِيضٌ, with غ (O, TA.)

فُضَاضَةٌ: see فُضَاضٌ.

فَاضَّةٌ *A calamity; a misfortune:* (Fr, Ṣ, O, Ḳ:) as though breaking and demolishing that which it befalls: (O, TA:) pl. فَوَاضُّ. (O, Ḳ.)

فَضْفَضَةٌ *Wideness,* or *ampleness,* of a garment, and of a دِرْع [see فَضْفَاضٌ], and † of the means of subsistence. (Ṣ, O, Ḳ.) [See R. Q. 1.]

فَضْفَاضٌ *Wide,* or *ample:* (Ṣ, O, Ḳ:) in this sense applied to a garment; (Ṣ, O;) and to a دِرْع; (O, Ḳ;) the درع [or shift] of a woman, and the درع [i. e. coat of mail] used in war; (O;) as also فَضْفَاضَةٌ, (Ṣ, A, O, Ḳ,) and ↓ فُضَافِضَةٌ; (TA;) and † to the means of subsistence: (Ṣ:) also *much*, or *abundant, and ample:* (TA:) and [in this sense] applied to water. (TA.) فَضْفَاضُ الرِّدَآءِ وَالبَدَنِ, in a trad. of Sateeh, means ‡ *Liberal*, or *generous, in disposition:* or *a large giver:* (TA:) and رَجُلٌ فَضْفَاضٌ means ‡ *a man who gives much;* likened to water to which the same epithet is applied. (TA.) You say also, جَارِيَةٌ فَضْفَاضَةٌ *A fleshy, corpulent, tall, girl.* (O, K.) And سَحَابَةٌ فَضْفَاضَةٌ *A cloud abounding with rain.* (TA.) And أَرْضٌ فَضْفَاضٌ *Land overspread with water from abundance of rain.* (O, TA.)

فُلَانٌ فَضْفَاضَةُ وَلَدِ أَبِيهِ, accord. to Lth, means *Such a one is the last of the children of his father;* but Az says that the word known in this sense is نَضْنَاضَة, with ن. (TA.)

فُضْفَاضٌ : see فُضَافِضَةٌ.

مِفَضَّةٌ *A thing with which clods of earth are broken;* (S, O, K;) as also ▼ مِفْضَاضٌ. (O, K.)

مُفَضَّضٌ A thing *silvered:* (TA:) a bridle (لِجَام) *ornamented with silver.* (S, TA.)

مِفْضَاضٌ : see مِفَضَّةٌ.

مَفْضُوضٌ *Broken;* as also ▼ فَضِيضٌ. (TA.)

فضح

1. فَضَحَهُ, (S, A, &c.,) aor. َ, inf. n. فَضْحٌ, (Msb,) *He exposed his vices, faults,* or *evil qualities* or *actions; disgraced him;* or *put him to shame.* (S, A, L, Msb,* K.) لَا تَفْضَحْنَا بَيْنَ خَلْقِكَ, occurring in a prayer, means *Expose not Thou our vices,* or *faults, among thy creatures:* or the meaning may be, *protect Thou us, that we may not be disobedient, and so deserve to have our vices,* or *faults, exposed among thy creatures.* (Msb.) — [Hence,] فَضَحَ القَمَرُ النُّجُومَ ‡ [*The moon put to shame the stars;* i. e.] *the light of the moon predominated over that of the stars,* (A, TA,) *so that they were not apparent,* or *distinct:* (TA:) and in like manner, الصُّبْحُ *the dawn.* (A, TA.) — And فَضَحَكَ الصُّبْحُ, said to a person sleeping at daybreak, (TA,) ‡ *Daybreak has shone forth, so as to discover thee to him who may see thee, and to expose thee to shame:* (L, TA:) or *i. q.* فَصَحَكَ [i. e. *daybreak has become apparent to thee, and its light has overcome thee:* or *daybreak has come upon thee suddenly*]. (K.) — And فَضَحَ الصُّبْحُ, (so in the S, and in some copies of the K,) or ▼ فَضَّحَ, (so in other copies of the K,) and ▼ افضح, (S, K,) † *The daybreak appeared,* (S, K, TA,) *and shone forth.* (TA.) = فَضِحَ, aor. َ, (K,) inf. n. فَضَحٌ, (TK,) *It was,* or *became, of the colour termed* فُضْحَةٌ [q. v.]. (K.)

2 : see the last sentence but one above.

3. فاضحهُ [*He exposed his vices, faults,* or *evil qualities* or *actions, the other doing the like to him:* see also 6]. (A.)

4 : see 1, last sentence but one. — افضح البُسْرُ † *The full-grown unripe dates showed in them a redness.* (S.) And افضح النَّخْلُ † *The palm-trees became red* and *yellow* [*in their fruit*]. (K.)

6. تفاضح المُرْتَجِزَانِ [*The two composers,* or *reciters, of verses of the metre termed* رَجَز *exposed each other's vices, faults,* or *evil qualities* or *actions*]. (A.) And أَرَادُوا أَنْ يَتَنَاصَحُوا فَتَفَاضَحُوا [*They desired,* or *meant, to give sincere,* or *faithful, advice* or *counsel, one to another, and they exposed one another's vices, faults,* or *evil qualities* or *actions*]. (A.)

8. افتضح *His vices, faults,* or *evil qualities* or *actions, became exposed; he became disgraced,* or *put to shame:* (S, L, K:) *he did evil, and became disgraced thereby.* (L.) — And [hence] افْتَضَحْنَا فِيكَ *We have been negligent,* or *have failed of our duty, in respect of visiting thee, and seeking for thee.* (A, TA.)

الصُّبْحُ الفَضَحُ *The dawn that is overspread with redness:* (K, TA:) because of its shining forth. (TA.) = See also what next follows.

فُضْحَةٌ, a subst. from فَضِحَ, (L, K, TA,) and ▼ فَضَحٌ, (S, L, TA,) the inf. n. of فَضِحَ, (TK,) *Whiteness, but not in an intense degree:* (K, TA: [and the same is implied in the S:]) or, as some say, *dust-colour inclining to* طُحْلَة [which is *a hue between that of dust and whiteness, with a little blackness,* or *between that of dust and blackness, with a little whiteness*], (S, L, TA,) *intermixed with an ugly hue; one of the colours of camels and of pigeons:* the epithet is ▼ أَفْضَحُ; fem. فَضْحَآءُ: said by an Arab of the desert, in answer to a question of AA respecting it, to be the *colour of cooked flesh-meat.* (L, TA.) فُضْحَةُ الصُّبْحِ means *The whiteness of the dawn.* (TA.)

فَضِيحَةٌ : see فَضَّاحٌ.

فَضُوحٌ One *who exposes* [*much,* or *habitually,* or *often,*] *the vices, faults,* or *evil qualities* or *actions, of others; who* [*so*] *disgraces them,* or *puts them to shame;* as also ▼ فَضَّاحٌ. (TA.) One says, الخَمْرُ فَضُوحٌ لِشَارِبِهَا [*Wine is a thing that exposes much the vices, faults,* or *evil qualities* or *actions, of the drinker thereof*]. (A.) — يَا فُضُوحُ means *O thou who art rendered notorious by thy evil character* or *conduct.* (K,* TA.)

فُضُوحٌ : see فَضِيحَةٌ, in two places.

هُوَ فَضِيحٌ فِى المَالِ *He is a bad manager of property,* or *cattle;* (K, TA;) *not taking good care thereof.* (TA.)

فَضَاحَةٌ :
فُضُوحَةٌ : } see the paragraph here following.

فَضِيحَةٌ a subst. from فَضَحَهُ, as also ▼ فُضُوحٌ, (S, A, L, K,) and ▼ فُضُوحَةٌ, and ▼ فَضَاحَةٌ, (L, K,) and ▼ فِضَاحٌ; (K;) *Disgrace, shame,* or *ignominy;* (PS, TA;) *a state of exposure of the vices, faults,* or *evil qualities* or *actions,* of a man: (Har p. 3:) *any evil thing that exposes its author to disgrace* or *shame; any disgraceful,* or *shameful, thing:* (L:) *a vice,* or *fault,* or *the like;* syn. عَيْبٌ: pl. فَضَائِحُ: (Msb:) [and] *a disgracing; putting to shame;* or *rendering ignominious.* (MA and KL; in both of which it is mentioned as an inf. n.) It is said in a trad., فُضُوحُ ▼ الدُّنْيَا أَهْوَنُ مِنْ فُضُوحِ الآخِرَةِ [*The disgrace of the present world is easier to bear than the disgrace of the world to come*]. (A, TA.)

فَضُوحٌ : see فَضَّاحٌ.

فَاضِحٌ [act. part. n. of 1]. It is said in a prov., الظَّمَأُ الفَادِحُ أَهْوَنُ مِنَ الرِّيِّ الفَاضِحِ [*Oppressing thirst is easier to bear than the state of satisfaction with drinking that disgraces,* or *puts to shame*]: and you say, إِذَا كَانَ العُذْرُ وَاضِحًا كَانَ العِتَابُ فَاضِحًا [*When the excuse is manifest, reproof is disgracing*]. (A, TA.) — And الفَاضِحُ signifies † *The daybreak,* or *dawn:* because it exposes and manifests everything. (Har. p. 556.)

أَفْضَحُ *White, but not intensely so:* (S, L, K:) see also explanations of فُضْحَةٌ, indicating other meanings: fem. فَضْحَآءُ. (L, TA.) — Hence, because of their colours, (S,) الأَفْضَحُ signifies *The lion:* and *The camel.* (S, K.)

فضخ

1. فَضَخَ, aor. َ, (Msb, K,) inf. n. فَضْخٌ, (Mgh, Msb,) *He broke* a hollow thing [or the like], (Mgh, Msb, K, TA,) such as a head, and a melon; (A, TA;) syn. كَسَرَ; (Msb, K, TA;) as also ▼ افتضخ: (K, TA:) *he broke,* or *crushed,* syn. شَدَخَ, (S, K, TA,) a person's head, (S, TA,) and a fresh ripe date, and the like; (TA;) as also ▼ افتضخ: (K, TA:) or *he struck* a person's head [*and wounded it*] *so that the brains came forth:* (Msb:) and [particularly] *he crushed* (شَدَخَ) full-grown unripe dates [to make the beverage called فَضِيخ]; and so ▼ افتضخ: (S:) or ▼ افتضخ البُسْرَ *he made,* or made for himself, *the beverage called* نَبِيذ [or فَضِيخ] *of the full-grown unripe dates.* (A.) — And *He ruptured,* or *broke,* or *rent open,* an eye, (AZ, K, TA,) and a belly, and any receptacle containing oil or beverage. (AZ, TA.) — And فَضْخُ المَآءِ signifies *The pouring forth of water,* (K, TA,) and *of the seminal fluid;* occurring in the latter sense in a trad. (TA.) — And يَفْضَخُ شَارِبَهُ, said of a beverage, (K, TA,) such as is termed فَضِيخ, (TA,) means † *It subdues* (يَكْسِرُ) *and intoxicates its drinker.* (K, TA.)

4. افضخ, said of a raceme, or bunch, (عُنْقُود,) [of dates or the like,] *It attained to the time,* (L, K,) *and became in a fit state, for the crushing of the fruit and* (L) *for the expressing of the juice.* (L, K.)

7. انفضخ [*It* (a hollow thing or the like, such as a head, and a melon,) *became broken,* or

crushed: (see 1:) or] it (a person's head) *was struck* [*and wounded*] *so that the brains came forth:* (Mṣb:) and *it* (a camel's hump) *became broken,* or *crushed.* (Ṣ, Ḳ.) — انفضخت *It* (an eye) *became ruptured, broken,* or *rent open.* (L.) And انفضخ *It* (a full skin) *slit,* or *burst, and let flow its contents.* (L.) And the former, *It* (a قَارُورَة [i.e. flask, or bottle,]) *broke, and became empty.* (L.) And *It* (a دَلْو [or leathern bucket]) *poured forth the water that was in it:* (L, Ḳ:) and so انفضخت. (L.) And *It* (a قَرْحَة [i.e. purulent pustule, or the like,]) *opened,* (A, L, Ḳ,) *and discharged its fluid,* (L,) or *and became wide.* (Ḳ.) — And انفضخ said of a man, *He wept much,* (Ḳ, TA,) *and shed copious tears.* (TA.) — And *It* (anything) *became wide.* (L.)

8: see 1, in four places.

فَضُوخٌ Beverage *that subdues* (يَكْسِرُ) *and intoxicates its drinker.* (L, Ḳ.) See the next paragraph.

فَضِيخٌ *A beverage* (Ṣ, A, Mgh, Ḳ) *of the kind called* نَبِيذ (A) *prepared from full-grown unripe dates,* (Ṣ, A, Mgh, Ḳ,) *crushed,* (Ḳ,) *without its being touched* [i.e. *boiled or heated in any degree*] *by fire:* (Ṣ:) or *prepared by putting dried dates into a vessel, and then pouring upon them hot water, which extracts their sweetness, after which the preparation is boiled, and becomes strong:* it is like بَاذَق in respect of the legal predicament to which it belongs: but if cooked in the least degree, it is like مُثَلَّث. (KT.) A rájiz says,

• بَالَ سُهَيْلٌ فِى الفَضِيخِ فَفَسَدْ •

expl. in art. بول. (L.) Ibn-'Omar, being asked respecting فَضِيخ, said, "It is not فَضِيخ, but ✱ فَضُوخ;" meaning that it subdues and intoxicates its drinker. (Mgh,* L.) — Also *Expressed juice of grapes.* (L, Ḳ.) — And *Milk mixed with a greater quantity of water,* (Ḳ, TA,) *so that it has become thin, and is white, like* ضَيْح *and* خَضَار &c. (TA.)

مِفْضَخَةٌ *A stone with which full-grown unripe dates are crushed.* (Ḳ.) — And مَفَاضِخُ [of which it is app. the sing.] signifies *Vessels for the beverage called* فَضِيخ, (L, Ḳ,) *in which it is left to become* [*fermented and*] *strong.* (L.) — And the former signifies also *A wide* دَلْو [or *leathern bucket*]. (Ḳ.)

فضل

1. فَضَلَ, aor. ـُ; and فَضِلَ, aor. ـَ; and فَضِلَ, aor. ـُ; three syn. dial. vars.; (Ṣ, O, Mṣb, Ḳ;) the second mentioned by ISk; and the third [said to be] anomalous and unparalleled; (Ṣ, O;) [but] it is a compound of two thereof, (Ṣ, O, Mṣb, Ḳ,) accord. to the companions of Sb, (Ṣ, O,) i.e. a compound of the second and the third, (Ḳ,) like نَعِمَ having for its aor. يَنْعُمُ, (Sb, Ṣ, O, Mṣb,) and نَكِلَ, aor. يَنْكُلُ, [but this I do not find in its proper art.,] and حَضِرَ, aor. يَحْضُرُ, [but this is disallowed by some,] and فَرِغَ, aor. يَفْرُغُ, among perfect verbs, (Mṣb,) and مِتُّ, aor. تَمُوتُ, and دِمْتَ, aor. تَدُومُ, (Sb, Ṣ, O, Mṣb,) and كِدْتَ, aor. تَكُودُ; (Sb, Ṣ;) inf. n. فَضْلٌ: (Ṣ,* O,* Mṣb, Ḳ:*) all signify *It exceeded;* or *was,* or *became, redundant,* or *superfluous;* [syn. زَادَ;] being used in relation to الفَضْلُ (Ḳ, MF, TA) meaning الزِّيَادَةُ, as Ibn-Es-Seed says, (MF, TA,) [i.e.] as meaning the contr. of النَّقْصُ: (Ḳ, TA:) or the first of the three, i.e. فَضَلَ, aor. ـُ, inf. n. فَضْلٌ, signifies thus, *i. q.* زَادَ, (Mṣb,) and فَضْلٌ and فُضُولٌ are also inf. ns. [of the same, i.e.] signifying زِيَادَةٌ, as in the saying, in a trad., accord. to different relaters, إِنَّ لِلّٰهِ مَلَائِكَةً سَيَّارَةً فُضْلًا عَلَى المَلَائِكَةِ and فُضُلًا المُرَتَّبِينَ مَعَ الخَلَائِقِ [i.e. *Verily to God belong angels who occupy themselves in ranging about, in addition to the angels who are stationed among the created,* or *human and other, beings*]: (TA:) and all the three dial. vars. mentioned above signify *it remained* [of a greater quantity or number]; syn. بَقِىَ; (Ṣ,* O,* Mṣb;) you say, فَضَلَ مِنْهُ شَىْءٌ, aor. ـُ; and فَضِلَ, aor. ـَ; and فَضِلَ, aor. ـُ; *somewhat remained thereof:* (Ṣ, O:) or from الفَضْلُ as meaning البَقِيَّةُ, you say فَضَلَ like نَصَرَ, [i.e. aor. ـُ,] and فَضِلَ like حَسِبَ, [implying that the aor. is ـَ and ـِ,] (Ḳ,) [accord. to the TḲ meaning *it had somewhat remaining,* but accord. to SM,] using these verbs [which are said by him to be like نَصَرَ and سَمِعَ and حَسِبَ, the last as mentioned by Lḥ,] in the phrase فَضَلَ مِنْهُ شَىْءٌ [expl. above]. (TA.) — [فَضَلَ is trans. as well as intrans.] One says, فَضَلَهُ and فَضَلَ عَلَيْهِ, [aor. ـُ,] inf. ns. فَضْلٌ and فُضُولٌ, [but see a distinction made between these two words voce فَضْلٌ, below,] meaning *He,* or *it, exceeded,* or *excelled, him,* or *it.* (MA.) See also 4. [And see فَضْلٌ below, last signification.] الفَضْلُ as meaning *The overcoming,* or *surpassing, in highness, elevation,* or *eminence, of rank, condition,* or *estimation,* has but one form of verb, فَضَلَ, aor. ـُ, like قَعَدَ, aor. يَقْعُدُ: he who relates the saying of the poet,

• وَجَدْنَا نَهْشَلًا فَضِلَتْ فُقَيْمًا •

[*We found,* or *have found, that Nahshal* (the tribe so called) *overcame* &c., or *have overcome* &c., *Fuḳeym* (another tribe)], pronouncing the ض [in فضلت] with kesr, errs; not distinguishing between the two meanings: so says Ibn-Es-Seed, in the book entitled "Kitáb el-Farḳ:" and Eṣ-Ṣeymuree says, in his book entitled "Kitáb et-Tebṣireh," فَضَلَ, aor. يَفْضُرُ, like نَصَرَ, aor. يَنْصُرُ, is from الفَضْلُ meaning *the ruling* [others] *as a chief, lord,* or *master.* (TA.) And فَضَلَهُ signifies also [simply] *He overcame him; surpassed him;* or *gained ascendency,* or *the mastery, over him.* (TA.) See also 3.

2. فَضَّلَهُ (Ḳ, TA) عَلَى غَيْرِهِ, (TA,) inf. n. تَفْضِيلٌ, *i. q.* مَزَّاهُ, (Ḳ, TA,) i.e. *He attributed to him an excellence distinguishing him from* [or *above*] *another,* or *others:* (TA:) or فَضَّلْتُهُ عَلَى غَيْرِهِ, inf. n. as above, *I judged him* (Ṣ, O, Mṣb,* TA) *to be more excellent than another,* or *others:* (Ṣ,* O,* Mṣb, TA:*) or *I made him* (Ṣ, O, Mṣb,* TA) *to be so.* (Ṣ,* O,* Mṣb, TA.) وَفَضَّلْنَاهُمْ عَلَى كَثِيرٍ مِمَّنْ خَلَقْنَا, in the Ḳur [xvii. 72, i.e. *And we have made them to excel many of those that we have created*], has been expl. as meaning that the excellence of the son of Adam consists in his walking erect, whereas the beasts, the camels and the asses and the like, walk pronely; and the son of Adam takes food with his hands, whereas the other animals take it with the mouth. (TA.) And وَاللّٰهُ فَضَّلَ بَعْضَكُمْ عَلَى بَعْضٍ, in the Ḳur [xvi. 73, i.e. *And God hath made some of you to excel some others*], means, in ability, and wealth, and rank or station, and power; which are excellences that may be acquired. (Er-Rághib, TA.) And you say, فَضَّلَهُ بِهِ, meaning خَصَّهُ [i.e. *He distinguished him particularly, peculiarly,* or *specially, by it,* namely, a thing]. (A and Ḳ in art. خص.) And فَضَّلَ فِى العَطَآءِ *He gave to some more than to others.* (Ṣ in art. افق.) — [An explanation of فضّل given by Golius, as on the authority of the Ḳ, ("i. q. وسّخ, *Sordibus infecit,* vel *pro sordida habuit,* quotidianam vestem,") is a strange mistake; app. caused by his finding in a copy of the Ḳ التَّفْضِيلُ التَّوْسِيخُ instead of التَّفَضُّلُ التَّوَشُّحُ: see 5.] — اِسْمُ التَّفْضِيلِ *The noun of the attribution of excess* or *excellence* is a term applied to *the comparative and superlative noun* or *epithet;* also called أَفْعَلُ التَّفْضِيلِ, because it is regularly of the measure أَفْعَلُ: see exs. voce خَيْرٌ.]

3. الفِضَالُ [and المُفَاضَلَةُ inf. ns. of فَاضَلَ] and ✱ التَّفَاضُلُ [inf. n. of 6 (of which see an ex. in art. سوى, conj. 6,)] signify التَّمَازِى فِى الفَضْلِ [i.e. *The contending for superiority in excellence*]; (Ḳ,* TA;) التَّمَازِى being of the measure تَفَاعُل from المَزِيَّةُ. (TA.) And you say, فَاضَلْتُهُ فَفَضَلْتُهُ ✱, (Ṣ, O, Ḳ,* in the last فَاضَلَنِى,) aor. of the latter ـُ, (TA,) inf. n. فَضْلٌ, (O, TA,) *I contended with him for superiority,* or *vied with him, in excellence,* (O, TA,) *and I surpassed him,* or *outvied him, therein.* (Ṣ, O, Ḳ, TA.) — And فاضل بَيْنَ الشَّيْئَيْنِ [app. *He made the relation between the two things to be unequal in respect of excellence;* i.e. *he made the two things to be unequal,* or *unlike each other, in excellence; contr. of* سَاوَى بَيْنَهُمَا: see also 6]. (TA.)

4. افضل فِى تِجَارَتِهِ *He gained;* or *made gain,* or *profit; in his traffic;* syn. رَبِحَ. (Az and Mṣb in art. ربح.) — افضل عَنْهُ [and ✱ فَضَلَ عَنْهُ, aor. ـُ, inf. n. فَضْلٌ, (see فَضْلٌ below, last signification, and see also فَاضِلٌ,)] *It exceeded it.* (Ḳ, TA. [See also 1, latter half.]) Ows says, describing a bow,

• كَقَوْسِ طِلَاعِ الكَفِّ لَا دُونَ مِلْئِهَا •

• وَلَا عَجْسُهَا عَنْ مَوْضِعِ الكَفِّ أَفْضَلَا •

[*Like a bow of which the part that is grasped is sufficient in size for the filling of the hand, not less than suffices to fill it, nor does the part that is grasped thereof extend beyond the place of the hand*: the pret. being here used for the aor. to suit the metre]. (TA. [But my original has كَفُوَمْ, an evident mistranscription.]) — افضل أَفْضَلْتُ مِنْهُ الشَّىْءَ : see 5, in two places. ═ أَفْضَلْتُ مِنْهُ الشَّىْءَ and ♦ اِسْتَفْضَلْتُ signify the same, (Ṣ, O, Ḳ, TA,) i. e. *I left of it the thing remaining*, or *redundant*. (O, TA.)

5. تفضّل عَلَيْهِ [in the CḲ (erroneously) فَضَّلَ] *i. q.* تَمَزَّى, (Ḳ, TA,) both of which signify *He thought himself to be superior to him in excellence*; (TA in art. مزو ;) whence the saying in the Ḳur [xxiii. 24], يُرِيدُ أَنْ يَتَفَضَّلَ عَلَيْكُمْ, meaning *He desireth that he may have superiority over you in rank and station*: (TA in the present art.:) or *i. q.* ♦ افضل عليه, (Ṣ, O, Mṣb, Ḳ, TA,) inf. n. إِفْضَالٌ, (Mṣb, TA,) i. e. *he bestowed*, or *conferred, a benefit*, or *benefits, upon him*, syn. أَحْسَنَ, (Ṣ, TA,) or تَطَوَّلَ, (Ḳ, TA,) and *gave him of his bounty*: (TA:) [and each, followed by بِشَىْءٍ, *he presented him*, or *favoured him, with a thing*:] or تفضّل signifies, (Ḳ,) or signifies also, (Ṣ,) *he laid claim to superiority of excellence* over his equals, or fellows; (Ṣ, Ḳ;) whence [accord. to some] the saying in the Ḳur quoted above: (Ṣ:) and [you say] ♦ افضل عَلَيْهِ فِى الحَسَبِ, (Ḳ, TA,) meaning *he became possessed of eminence*, [or *superiority, over him, in the grounds of pretension to respect or honour*,] as in a verse of Dhu-l-Iṣba' cited voce عَنَّ, [q. v., p. 2164,] ending with فَتَخْزُونِى for فَتَخْزُونِى, [which latter reading I have there given,] because the rhyme of the whole ode requires the former. (TA.) ═ التَّفَضُّلُ also signifies التَّوَشُّحُ [generally meaning *The throwing a portion of one's garment over his left shoulder, and drawing its extremity under his right arm, and tying the two extremities together in a knot upon his bosom*]: and *the putting*, or *disposing, the extremities of his two garments*, or *pieces of cloth, contrariwise*, or *in contrary directions, upon his* عَاتِق [or *part between the shoulder and the neck*]. (Ḳ, TA: but in the former, عَلَى عَاتِقَيْهِ is erroneously put for على عاتقه. TA.) — And تَفَضَّلَتْ said of a woman in her tent or chamber or house, *She was in a single garment*; (Ṣ, O, TA;) [*she wore a single garment*;] *such as is termed* مِفْضَل [q. v.]: (Ṣ, TA:) or *she* (a woman) *wore the garments of her service*. (TA.)

6: see 3. — التَّفَاضُلُ بَيْنَ القَوْمِ means *The differing in superiority*, or *excellence, of some over others, among the people*, or *party*. (TA.) And one says, الأَشْيَآءُ تَتَفَاضَلُ [meaning *The things are unequal*, or *unlike, one to another, in respect of excellence*; contr. of تَتَسَاوَى : see also 3]. (TA.)

10. استفضل أَلْفًا *He took a thousand* [dirhems] *in excess of his right*, or *due*. (TA.) — See also 4.

فَضْلٌ [an inf. n.: (see 1, throughout:) and also a simple subst., signifying] *An exceeding, a redundant*, or *a superfluous, quantum* [of anything, good or evil]; *an excess, a redundance*, or *a superfluity*; syn. زِيَادَةٌ ; (Mgh, Mṣb;) *contr. of* نَقْصٌ : (Ṣ, O, Ḳ:) [and often meaning *superabundance*, or *exuberance*; and *surpassingness, superiority*, or *excellence*, عَلَى غَيْرِهِ *over another*, or *others, than him*, or *it*: and *preponderance*:] the pl. is فُضُولٌ : (Mgh, Mṣb, Ḳ:) and this is sometimes used as a sing.; (Er-Rághib, Mṣb;) and [thus used] relates to a thing [or quality] in which is no good; (Er-Rághib, Mgh, Mṣb;) by a predominant application; whence the saying فُضُولٌ بِلَا فَضْلٍ [*excess without excellence*]: (Mgh:) and hence the rel. n. ♦ فُضُولِىٌّ is formed from it: (Er-Rághib, Mṣb, TA:) [see this last word, one of the explanations of which shows that a particular meaning of فُضُولٌ is the *quality of busying oneself with that which does not concern him*:] accord. to Er-Rághib, فَضْلٌ signifies *an excess* [in respect of a property or quality, or of an acquisition,] *above moderateness*: and this is of two sorts; such as is commended, as the فضل of knowledge, or science; and such as is discommended, as the فضل of anger at that whereat it is not necessary: but فَضْلٌ is more used in relation to that which is commended; and [the pl.] فُضُولٌ, in relation to that which is discommended: when the former is used of an excess [in respect of some attribute] of one of two things above the other, it is of three sorts; فضل of kind, as of the animal kind above the vegetable kind; and of species, as of man above other animals; and of the individual, as of one man above another; the first and second of which three are essential attributes, such that he who is deficient in [either of] them cannot do away with his deficiency and acquire فضل, as, for instance, the horse, and the ass, which cannot acquire the excellence (فَضِيلَة) of the human being; but the third may be accidental, such that the way may be found to acquire it, and of this sort are ability, wealth, rank or station, and power: and it signifies also *any gift whereof the giving to the recipient thereof is not obligatory*; [i. e. *a free gift*, or *gratuity*; and *an act of bounty* or *grace*; *a favour*; *a benefit*; and *bounty* as an abstract term;] as in the saying [in the Ḳur iv. 36], وَٱسْأَلُوا ٱللّٰهَ مِنْ فَضْلِهِ [*And ask ye God of his free gift*, or *of his bounty*, or (as expl. in the Ksh and by Bḍ) *of his exhaustless treasures*]; and in the saying in the Ḳur [v. 59 and lvii. 21 and lxii. 4], ذٰلِكَ فَضْلُ ٱللّٰهِ يُؤْتِيهِ مَنْ يَشَآءُ [*That is the free gift of God; He giveth it to whom He willeth*]; which comprises the three sorts of excellences (فَضَائِل) [mentioned above]: thus says Er-Rághib: El-Munáwee says, [explaining one of its meanings,] in the "Towḳeef," that it is the *commencing*, or *originating, of an act of beneficence without an efficient cause* [i. e., app., *not by reason of any obligation*]. (TA.) — Also *A portion remaining*, (Ḳ, TA,) of a thing, such as food &c., and of water in the leathern water-bag, and of wine or beverage in the vessel; (TA;) and ♦ فَضْلَةٌ and ♦ فُضَالَةٌ signify the same, (Ḳ, TA,) or *a redundant portion* (Ṣ and O and Mṣb in explanation of these two words) of a thing: (Ṣ, O:) whence the saying of the vulgar, الفَضْلَةُ ♦ لِلْفَضِيلِ i. e. *The remaining portion* of the wine or beverage [*is for the excellent*]. (TA.) It is said in a trad., لَا يُمْنَعُ فَضْلُ المَآءِ لِيُمْنَعَ بِهِ الكَلَأُ [*The redundance of water shall not be denied that the herbage be thereby denied*]: (TA, in the present art.:) meaning that when there is a well in the desert, with herbage near it, and a person prevents others from drawing water, he thereby prevents the latter from availing themselves of the herbage; for when a man comes with his camels, and pastures them upon that herbage, and does not then water them, thirst kills them. (TA in art. كلأ.) And it is said in another trad., فَضْلُ الإِزَارِ فِى النَّارِ [*The redundant portion of the waist-wrapper is in the fire* of Hell]; meaning what one drags [thereof] upon the ground, by reason of pride. (TA.) And one says, فِى يَدِهِ فَضْلُ الزِّمَامِ, meaning [*In his hand is*] *the end of the* زمام [or *nose-rein* of the camel]. (TA.) الفُضُولِ ♦ and ذَاتُ الفُضُولِ, with ḍamm and with fet-ḥ, [*The thing having redundant portions*] is the name of the coat of mail of the Prophet, which was thus called because having redundance and ampleness. (TA.) فُضُولُ الغَنَائِمِ means *The remains of the spoils when they are divided*; (TA;) such as a single horse, or a single camel. (KL.) And by the فُضُول of women are meant The *remains of the menstrual discharge*. (Ḥam p. 107: see, there, explanations of a verse in which this occurs.) حِلْفُ الفُضُولِ [*The confederacy*, or *covenant, of the* فضول, a word which is here of uncertain meaning,] is thus explained: Háshim and Zuhrah and Teym [accord. to the CḲ Teymà] went in to 'Abd-Allah Ibn-Jud'án, and united in a confederacy to repel wrongdoing, and to exact the due from the wrongdoer; and it was thus called because they bound themselves by their confederacy not to leave in the possession of any one aught remaining [of property] whereof he might despoil any one, without their taking it for him [i. e. the latter] from him [i. e. the former]: (O, Ḳ, TA: [in the CḲ, يَظْلِمُهُ أَحَدٌ is a mistake for يظلمه أَحَدًا :]) or it was thus called as being likened to a confederacy, or covenant, which was made of old, at Mekkeh, in the days of Jurhum, to act with mutual equity, and to take for the weak from the strong, and for the stranger from the resident, and in which three men, every one of whom was named El-Faḍl, joined: and it was also called that of the مُطَيَّبُون. (TA. [See art. طيب.]) — The saying لَا يَمْلِكُ دِرْهَمًا فَضْلًا عَنْ دِينَارٍ, and the like may be said of other sayings similar to it, means *He does not possess a dirhem nor a deenár* [or rather *much less a deenár*]: it is as though one said, *he does not possess a dirhem: how then should he possess a deenár?* for the negation of that which is much is a necessary consequence of the negation of that which is little: فَضْلًا is here in the accus. case as an inf. n.; the implied meaning being فَقَدَ مِلْكَ دِرْهَمٍ فَقْدًا

يَفْضُلُ عَنْ فَقْدِ مِلْكِ دِينَارٍ [or rather يَفْقِدُ &c., i. e. *he lacks the possession of a dirhem with a lacking exceeding the lacking of the possession of a deenár*]: (Mṣb:) Ḳuṭb-ed-Deen Esh-Sheerázee says, (Mṣb, TA,) in the Expos. of the "Miftáḥ," (TA,) فَضْلًا is used in a case in which the inferior [of two things] is deemed a thing of which the existence is improbable, and the impossibility of the existence of a thing that is above it is meant thereby; wherefore it occurs between two phrases differing in meaning; and it is mostly used after a particle of negation: (Mṣb, TA:) AḤei says that he had not found any authority for it in the [classical] language of the Arabs. (Mṣb. [See also بَلْهَ, which is used in a somewhat similar manner.])

فُضُلٌ *Wearing a single garment, such as is termed* مِفْضَلٌ; an epithet applied to a woman; (Ṣ, Mgh,* O, Ḳ;) and also to a man; (Ṣ, O, Ḳ;) like ▼ مُتَفَضِّلٌ: (O, Ḳ:) it is of the dial. of Nejd; like فُرُجٌ in the dial. of El-Yemen. (L in art. فرج.) — And A woman *proud*, or *self-conceited*, or *so in her gait; who makes a portion of her skirt to be redundant* [*so that it drags upon the ground when she walks*]. (TA.) — See also مِفْضَلٌ, in three places.

فَضْلَةٌ: see فَضْلٌ, former half, in two places. — [Hence, as used by grammarians,] *A dispensable member of a proposition*; such as the objective complement of a verb, when the suppression thereof is not detrimental [to the meaning]; *contr. of* عُمْدَةٌ. (I'Aḳ, p. 143) [The pl. is فَضَلَاتٌ.] — And The *clothes that are used for sleeping* [*therein*]: (Ḳ, TA:) [so called] because they are an addition over and above the clothes that are used on various [other] occasions. (TA.) — And *Wine*; and so ▼ فِضَالٌ [which see also in what here follows]: (O, Ḳ:) الفَضْلَةُ is mentioned by A'Obeyd as *a name for wine*: (O:) or it signifies, accord. to AḤn, *the wine that alters* [or *has become altered*] *in colour after oldness*; and ISd says that it is so called because the choice, or best, or most excellent, part thereof [for لِأَنَّ حميمها in my original (an obvious mistranscription) I read لِأَنَّ صَمِيمَهَا] is what remains: (TA:) the pl. is فَضَلَاتٌ and فِضَالٌ [the latter word mentioned above as a syn. of فَضْلَةٌ]. (Ḳ.)

فِضْلَةٌ is a n. of the same kind as جِلْسَةٌ and رِكْبَةٌ: (AZ, Ṣ, O, TA:) one says, إِنَّهُ لَحَسَنُ الفِضْلَةِ, meaning [*Verily he is comely in respect of*] *the manner of wearing a single garment*. (Ṣ,* O,* Ḳ,* TA.)

فِضَالٌ: see فَضْلَةٌ: — and see also مِفْضَلٌ.

فُضُولٌ: see فَضْلٌ, latter half.

فَضِيلٌ; pl. فُضَلَآءُ: see فَاضِلٌ; and see an ex. voce فَضْلٌ, former half.

فُضَالَةٌ: see فَضْلٌ, former half.

فَضِيلَةٌ *An excellence*, or *excellent quality*; *contr. of* نَقِيصَةٌ; (Ṣ, O, Mṣb;) and *contr. of* رَذِيلَةٌ (M and Ḳ in art. رذل:) or *a high degree in* [or *of*] *excellence*: (Ḳ:) [differing from فَاضِلَةٌ, q. v.:] pl. فَضَائِلُ. (MA.)

فُضَالَى [a pl. of which the sing. is not mentioned] *i. q.* ▼ مُتَفَضِّلُونَ, (O, Ḳ, TA,) i. e. [Men] *who bestow*, or *confer, benefits*. (TA.)

فُضُولِيٌّ a rel. n. formed from فُضُولٌ as pl. of فَضْلٌ but used as a sing.: (Er-Rághib, Mṣb, TA:) see فَضْلٌ, near the beginning: *One who busies himself with that which does not concern him*. (Er-Rághib, Mgh, O, Mṣb, TA.) In the conventional language of the lawyers, *One who is not a commissioned agent*, (Mgh, O, KT, TA,) *nor a guardian* (وَلِيّ), (KT, TA,) *nor a proprietor*, (TA,) *nor a person of firm judgment* (أَصِيل), *in a contract*. (KT.) The pronunciation with fet-ḥ to the ف is a mistake. (Mgh, O.) — Also *A tailor*. (IAạr, O, Ḳ.)

فَضَّالٌ: see مِفْضَالٌ.

فَاضِلٌ [act. part. n. of فَضَلَ: as such signifying *Exceeding*; &c.]. One says, مَالُ فُلَانٍ فَاضِلٌ i. e. [*The wealth*, or *property*, *of such a one is superfluous*; or] *abundant*, or *much in quantity, such as has exceeded the supply of food sufficient to sustain life* (فَضَلَ عَنِ القُوتِ). (TA.) — And [*Excelling*; or *excellent*, as also ▼ فَضِيلٌ, of which the pl. is فُضَلَآءُ, but which is probably post-classical: or it is] applied to a man as [a possessive epithet] meaning *possessing* فَضْل [i. e. *excellence*]. (TA.) [And conventionally, *Erudite*; or *excellent in learning*.] — See also مَفْضُولٌ.

فَاضِلَةٌ is a subst. from فَضِيلَةٌ [app. as a concrete term, signifying *An excellent thing*, or *an excellent action*; each as distinguished from an excellent quality]; (Ḳ, TA;) pl. فَوَاضِلُ: (TA:) [but generally] it signifies *a gift*, or *thing that is given*: (Ḥam p. 431, and Ḥar p. 184:) or *a benefit*, or *benefaction*: or *such as is continual*, or *uninterrupted*: (MA:) pl. as above: (Ḥam and Ḥar, ubi suprà; and MA:) [or] فَوَاضِلُ signifies *benefits*, or *benefactions, that are goodly*, or *pleasing*, (IDrd, O, Ḳ,) or *such as are great*, or *large*. (Ḳ.) And فَوَاضِلُ المَالِ signifies *What accrues to one of the proceeds and profits of property*, (O, Ḳ, TA,) *of the increase of lands and palm-trees and the like*, and *the gains of commercial transactions*, and *the milk and wool of cattle and sheep*. (TA.) The Arabs say, إِذَا عَزَبَ المَالُ قَلَّتْ فَوَاضِلُهُ (O, Ḳ,) meaning *When the estate is distant, the profits of its owner, accruing therefrom, are small in quantity*. (O.)

أَفْضَلُ [*More*, and *most excellent*, &c.]; fem. فُضْلَى: (TA:) pl. masc. أَفَاضِلُ; and pl. fem. فُضْلَيَاتٌ and فُضَلٌ. (Mṣb in art. احر.)

مِفْضَلٌ: see مِفْضَالٌ. — Also *A single garment that is worn* [*without any other*] *by a woman* (Ṣ, O, Ḳ, KL) *in her tent* or *house* or *chamber, such as is called* خَيْعَلٌ [a garment variously described], or *the like of this*, (Ṣ,) and *by a man*; (KL;) also called ▼ مِفْضَلَةٌ, (Ḳ,) and ▼ فُضُلٌ; (Fr, O, Ḳ;) or ▼ ثَوْبٌ فُضُلٌ signifies *a single garment, a* مِلْحَفَة [q. v.], or *the like thereof, with which a woman wraps herself* (تَتَوَشَّحُ بِهِ); (Mgh;) and accord. to Lth, ▼ فِضَالٌ signifies *a single garment that is worn by a man in his tent* or *house* or *chamber*: (TA:) and مِفْضَلٌ signifies [also] *an every-day-garment*: (MA:) ▼ فِي ثِيَابٍ فُضُلٍ occurring in a trad. of 'Áïsheh requires consideration [as being questionable]. (Mgh.)

مِفْضَلَةٌ: see the next preceding paragraph.

مُفَضَّلٌ: see what next follows.

رَجُلٌ مِفْضَالٌ and ▼ مِفْضَلٌ and ▼ مُفَضَّلٌ and ▼ فَضَّالٌ *A man possessing much excellence*, or *superiority*, (Ḳ, TA,) *and beneficence, and goodness, and liberality*, or *bounty*. (TA.) And (Ḳ) رَجُلٌ مِفْضَالٌ عَلَى قَوْمِهِ, (Ṣ, O, Ḳ) and امْرَأَةٌ مِفْضَالَةٌ عَلَى قَوْمِهَا, (Ḳ,) *A man, and a woman, possessing excellence*, or *superiority*, [or *much thereof*, agreeably with the former explanation, *over his*, and *her, people*,] *and liberal* or *bountiful* [or *very liberal* or *bountiful*]. (Ṣ, O, Ḳ.)

مَفْضُولٌ [pass. part. n. of فَضَلَ: as such signifying *Exceeded*; &c.: and *excelled*: and *overcome*, or *surpassed, in highness, elevation*, or *eminence*, *of rank*, &c.: and simply] *overcome*, or *surpassed*: whence the saying, قَدْ يُوجَدُ فِي المَفْضُولِ مَا لَا يُوجَدُ فِي ▼ الفَاضِلِ [*Sometimes*, or *often, what is not found in the overcomer is found in the overcome*]. (TA.)

مُتَفَضِّلٌ One *who lays claim to superiority of excellence* over his equals, or fellows. (Ṣ.) [See also its verb: and] see فُضَالَى. — See also فُضُلٌ.

فضو and فضى

1. فَضَا, (M, Mṣb, Ḳ,) aor. يَفْضُو, (M, Mṣb,) inf. n. فُضُوٌّ (M, Mṣb, Ḳ) and فَضَآءٌ, (M, Ḳ,) *It* (a place) *was*, or *became, wide*, or *spacious*; (M, Mṣb, Ḳ;) as also ▼ افضى; (TA as from the Ḳ, in which I do not find it;) the latter occurring in a trad., and expl. in the Nh as signifying *it became a* فَضَآء [q. v.]. (TA.) — [And *It was*, or *became, empty, vacant*, or *void*; (for it is said in the TA that الفضو, by which الفُضُوُّ is evidently meant, signifies الخُلُوُّ;) as also ▼ افضى, as appears from an explanation of the part. n. مُفْضٍ, q. v.] — فَضَا الشَّجَرُ بِالمَكَانِ, inf. n. فضو [i. e. فُضُوٌّ], *The trees became numerous*, or *abundant*, [*so as to occupy much space*,] *in the place*. (IḲṭṭ, TA.) — And فَضَا دَرَاهِمَهُ *He did not put his dirhems*, or *money, into the purse* [app. meaning that *he left his money strewn*]. (Ḳ.)

4. افضى: see the preceding paragraph, in two places. — Also *He went forth*, (Ṣ,) or *came*, (TA,) *to the* فَضَآء [q. v.]. (Ṣ, TA.) — [Hence] افضى فُلَانٌ إِلَى فُلَانٍ *Such a one came to*, or *reached, such a one*: (M, Mgh, TA:) originally, *became in the space*, or *the place*, or *quarter, of*

such a one: (M:) or properly, *became in the* فَضَآء *of such a one.* (Mgh.) And in like manner, افضى إِلَيْهِ الأَمْرُ [*The thing,* or *event, came to,* or *reached, him*]. (M.) And أَفْضَيْتُ إِلَى الشَّىْءِ *I came to,* or *reached, the thing.* (Mṣb.) Accord. to IAạr, (TA,) الإِفْضَآءُ properly signifies الاِنْتِهَآءُ [i. e. *The coming at last,* or *ultimately,* or *the reaching,* to a person or thing]. (IAạr, T, Mṣb, TA.) Hence the saying [in the Ḳur iv. 25], وَقَدْ أَفْضَى بَعْضُكُمْ إِلَى بَعْضٍ i. e. *When one of you hath come,* and *betaken himself, to the other;* (TA;) in which the verb is made trans. by means of إِلَى because having the meaning [of اِنْتَهَى or] of وَصَلَ: (M:) or this means, *when one of you hath become alone with the other,* agreeably with the original derivation; or, accord. to some, it is an allusion to mutual contact, skin to skin: or to copulation. (Mgh.) You say, افضى إِلَى آمْرَأَتِهِ [*He went in to his wife:* or] *he became in contact with his wife, skin to skin:* (Ṣ, Mṣb:) or it signifies, (M, Ḳ,) or signifies also, (Ṣ, Mṣb,) ‡ *he compressed his wife:* (Ṣ, M, Mṣb, Ḳ:) or *he was,* or *became, with her alone in private, whether he compressed her or not.* (M, Ḳ.) — افضى بِهِمْ *He reached with them,* or *brought them to, a wide,* or *spacious, place.* (TA.) And افضى بِهِ الطَّرِيقُ إِلَى وَعْرٍ مِنَ الأَرْضِ [*The road brought him to a rugged tract of land*]. (Ḳ* and TA in art. وعر.) — افضى بِيَدِهِ إِلَى الأَرْضِ *He touched the ground with the palm of his hand* (IF, Ṣ, Mṣb, Ḳ) in his prostration [in prayer]. (Ṣ, Ḳ.) And أَفْضَيْتُ إِلَيْهِ بِيَدِى مِنْ غَيْرِ حَائِلٍ *I put my hand to it without anything intervening;* i. q. مَسِسْتُهُ (Mṣb in art. مس.) — أَفْضَيْتُ إِلَى فُلَانٍ بِسِرِّى [*I communicated,* or *made known, to such a one my secret*]: (Ṣ:) or أَفْضَيْتُ إِلَيْهِ بِالسِّرِّ *I acquainted him with the secret.* (Mṣb, TA.) — افضى also signifies † *He became poor:* so says IAạr: as though he came to the ground. (TA.) ═ لَا يُفْضِى ٱللّٰهُ فَاكَ, occurring in a trad., is a phrase expressive of a prayer, meaning *May God not make thy mouth wide and empty.* (TA.) — Hence the saying of IAạr, الإِفْضَآءُ أَنْ تَسْقُطَ الثَّنَايَا مِنْ تَحْتُ وَمِنْ فَوْقُ [app. meaning that إِفْضَآء is the inf. n. of أُفْضِىَ signifying *His central incisors, below and above, fell out;* or *he was caused to lose them*]: and hence [the epithet] المُفْضَاةُ [and therefore hence also what here follows]. (TA.) — افضى المَرْأَةَ *He made the woman's* مَسْلَكَانِ (i. e. her *vagina and rectum,* Mṣb) *to become one,* (Ṣ, M, Mgh, Mṣb, Ḳ, TA,) in devirginating her, (Mṣb,) or in compressing her; (TA;) the intervening part becoming rent: (Mgh, TA:) and so أَفَاضَهَا: (M, in which it is mentioned in art. فضى:) the epithet applied to her is ↓ مُفْضَاةٌ, (M, Mgh, Mṣb, Ḳ,) which is *syn. with* شَرِيمٌ. (Ṣ.)

5. تَفَضَّيْتُ for تَفَضَّضْتُ see in art. فض (conj. 5). — [التَّفَضِّى in a passage of the Fákihet el-Khulafà accord. to several copies thereof is an obvious mistake for التَّقَضِّى, with the unpointed ص: see Freytag's Critical Annotations and Corrections in his edition of that work, p. 6.]

فَضًا, (Ṣ, M, Ḳ,) also written فَضًى, (TA,) *A thing* (Ṣ, Ḳ) *mixed.* (Ṣ, M, Ḳ.) You say طَعَامٌ فَضًا *Mixed food:* (Ṣ:) and تَمْرٌ فَضًا *dates mixed,* (AA,* Ṣ, M,) as, for instance, (Ṣ, TA,) with raisins, (Lḥ, Ṣ, M, TA,) in one vessel, or bag; thus says El-Ḳálee; (TA;) or *scattered,* or *strewn, and mixed:* (M:) and تَمْرَانِ فَضَيَانِ [*two sorts of dates mixed*]: and تُمُورٌ أَفْضَآءٌ [*several sorts of dates mixed*]. (AA, TA.) And مَتَاعُهُمْ فَوْضَى فَضًا *Their goods are mixed together:* (M:) or *are shared in common.* (TA.) And أَمْرُهُمْ فَضًا بَيْنَهُمْ [*Their case is mixed,* or *promiscuous,* &c., like أَمْرُهُمْ فَوْضَى بَيْنَهُمْ (q. v. in art. فوض); or] *their case among themselves is alike;* (M, TA;) i. e. *they have no commander over them.* (Ṣ, TA.) And تَرَكَ الأَمْرَ فَضًا i. e. [*He left the affair*] *in an unsound* [or *a disordered*] *state.* (TA.) And أَلْقَى ثَوْبَهُ فَضًا [*He threw down his garment in a disorderly,* or *careless, manner;*] *he did not commit his garment to any one's care.* (M, TA.) — [Also *One;* a *single* thing or person: and *alone; by itself* or *himself; not having any other with it* or *him; apart from others:* thus it has two contr. meanings.] You say سَهْمٌ فَضًا *One,* or *a single, arrow:* (Ḳ:) or *an arrow that is alone, by itself, not having any other with it, in the quiver.* (AA, TA.) And بَقِيتُ فَضًا *I remained alone,* (Az, Ḳ, TA,) *of such as were fellows:* (Az, TA:) or *apart from my brethren and my family.* (Akh, TA.) ═ Also, i. e. فَضًا, (M, Ḳ,) or correctly with ى [i. e. فَضًى], as written by El-Ḳálee, (TA,) The *stones* (حَبّ) *of raisins;* (M;) i. q. فَضًا [or فَضًى]. (Ḳ.) ═ See also what next follows.

فَضْيَةٌ *Water collecting and stagnating:* pl. فِضَآءٌ, with medd, accord. to Kr; and also ↓ فَضًى and فِضًى, with fet-ḥ and with kesr, the former of these like حَلَقٌ as pl. [or rather a quasi-pl. n.] of حَلْقَةٌ, and the latter like بِدَرٌ as a pl. of بَدْرَةٌ; occurring in different relations of a verse of 'Adee Ibn-Er-Riḳáạ. (M in art. فضى, and TA.)

فَضَآءٌ is an inf. n.: (M, Ḳ, TA:) and is expl. by Aboo-'Alee El-Ḳálee as signifying *Width,* or *spaciousness.* (TA.) — [It is also used as an epithet:] see فَاضٍ. — And [as a subst., or an epithet in which the quality of a subst. is predominant,] it signifies *A court, an open area,* or *a yard,* of a house; syn. سَاحَةٌ: (Ṣ, Ḳ:) and *a wide,* or *spacious, tract of land:* (ISh, Ṣ, M, Ḳ:) or *a plain and wide expanse of land:* (Sh, TA:) the pl. is أَفْضِيَةٌ. (ISh, TA.)

فِضَآءٌ *Water running upon the ground:* (Ḳ:) or, accord. to Aboo-'Alee El-Ḳálee it is [in measure, but not exactly in meaning,] like حِسَآءٌ [a pl. of حِسْىٌ], signifying *water running upon the surface of the earth;* [or rather *waters* &c.; for he adds,] and its sing. is ↓ فَضْيَةٌ: in the M, [in art. فضى,] it is said to be a pl. of فَضْيَةٌ, [q. v.,] on the authority of Kr. (TA.)

فَضْيَةٌ: see the next preceding paragraph.

فَاضٍ (Mṣb, TA) and ↓ مُفْضٍ (M,* TA) *Wide,* or *spacious,* (M,* Mṣb, TA,) as also ↓ فَضَآءٌ, (Az, Er-Rághib, Mgh, Mṣb, TA,) *open and plain, and vacant.* (TA.) — [The first of these words, in the present day, pronounced فَاضِى, is commonly used in the sense of فَارِغٌ as meaning *Unoccupied, unemployed,* or *at leisure.*]

مَفْضًى i. q. مُتَّسَعٌ [*A place of width* or *spaciousness,* &c.]. (TA.)

مُفْضٍ: see فَاضٍ. [And see also its verb, 4.]

مُفْضَاةٌ: see 4, last sentence.

فطأ

1. فَطَأَهُ is like حَطَأَهُ in its [various] meanings. (Ḳ.) Like the latter it signifies *He struck him on the back.* (AZ, Ṣ, O.) — And *He broke it,* or *crushed it.* (Ṣ, O, Ḳ.) — And فَطَأَهَا, (Ṣ, O, TA,) aor. ـَ, inf. n. فَطْءٌ, (TA,) *He compressed her;* (Ṣ, O, TA;) namely, a woman. (TA.) — And فَطَأَ بِهِ الأَرْضَ *He threw him down,* or *prostrated him, on the ground.* (Ṣ, O.) — And فَطَأَ بِسَلْحِهِ *He cast forth his excrement,* or *ordure;* sometimes occurring with ث; (Ṣ, O;) which is a dial. var.; or an instance of mispronunciation. (O.) — And فَطَأَتِ الغَنَمُ بِأَوْلَادِهَا *The sheep,* or *goats, brought forth their young ones.* (Ṣ, O.) And لَعَنَ ٱللّٰهُ أُمًّا فَطَأَتْ بِهِ *May God curse a mother who cast him forth* [*from her womb*]: like شَطَأَتْ بِهِ. (TA in art. شطأ.) — And فَطَأَ بِهَا *He broke wind* [app. *with a sound;* like حَطَأَ بِهَا]. (Ṣ, O.) — فَطَأَ القَوْمَ *He did to the people,* or *party, what they did not like.* (O, Ḳ.) — And فَطَأَ ظَهْرَ بَعِيرِهِ *He loaded his camel with a heavy burden, so that his back became hollow,* or *depressed.* (Ḳ.) ═ فَطِئَ, aor. ـَ, (Ḳ,) inf. n. فَطَأٌ, (TA,) [app., i. q. فَطِسَ, i. e. *He had the bone of his nose wide and depressed;* or *depressed and expanded;* or *he had his nose spreading upon his face:* see فَطَأٌ below. — And] *He had a hollow back, and a protuberant breast,* or *chest.* (Ḳ.) — And فَطِئَ البَعِيرُ *The camel was, by nature, low,* or *depressed, in his back.* (Ṣ, O.)

4. افطأ *He copulated much,* or *often.* (IAạr, O, Ḳ.) — And *He became ample in his state,* or *circumstances.* (IAạr, O, Ḳ.) — And *His nature,* or *disposition, became evil, after having been good.* (IAạr, O, Ḳ.) ═ افطأهُ *He fed him; gave him to eat;* or *gave him food.* (O, Ḳ.)

6. تفاطأ, (Ḳ, TA,) said of a man, (TA,) is *syn. with* تَقَاعَسَ [q. v.; app. in a sense similar to the senses here following]: or it signifies *more than* تقاعس. (Ḳ, TA.) تفاطأ عَنْهُ means *He held back,* or *receded, from him,* or *it.* (Ḳ,* TA.) And تفاطأ عَنْهُمْ *He was defeated, and retreated from them,* (O, Ḳ,) after he had charged, or made an assault or attack, upon them. (O.)

فَطَأٌ [mentioned above as inf. n. of فَطِئَ, and in the O erroneously written فُطْء,] *i. q.* فَطَسٌ [i. e. *A depression and expansion of the bone of the nose; or a spreading of the nose upon the face*]; (Ṣ,* O,* Ḳ;) and ▾ فَطَأَةٌ is *syn. with* فَطْسَةٌ [which is a subst. signifying as above] (Ṣ, O: but in one of my copies of the Ṣ, the former of these words is written فُطَأَةٌ; and in the O, the latter is written فُطْسَة). —— And *Hollowness of the back,* (Ḳ, TA,) or, as some say, *of the middle of the back,* (TA,) *and protuberance of the breast,* or *chest;* as also ▾ فُطْأَةٌ. (Ḳ, TA.)

فُطْأَةٌ: } see the next preceding paragraph.
فَطَأَةٌ: }

أَفْطَأُ *i. q.* أَفْطَسُ [i. e. *Having the bone of his nose depressed and expanded;* or *having his nose spreading upon his face*]. (Ṣ,* O,* TA.) It is said that Museylimeh the Liar was أَفْطَأ, (O,) or أَفْطَأَ الأَنْفِ: so in a trad. (TA.) —— And *Having a hollow back, and a protuberant breast,* or *chest.* (Ḳ.) And أَفْطَأُ الظَّهْرِ A camel *low,* or *depressed, in the back, by nature.* (TA.)

فطح

1. فَطَحَهُ, (Ṣ, Ḳ,) aor. ـَ, (Ḳ,) inf. n. فَطْحٌ; (Ṣ;) and ▾ فَطَّحَهُ, (Ṣ,* Ḳ,) inf. n. تَفْطِيحٌ; (Ṣ;) *He made it broad,* or *wide.* (Ṣ, Ḳ.) —— And فَطَحَ العُودَ وَغَيْرَهُ, (Ḳ, TA,) inf. n. as above; and ▾ فَطَّحَهُ, inf. n. as above; (TA;) *He pared,* or *fashioned by cutting, the stick,* or *piece of wood,* &c., *and made it broad,* or *wide.* (Ḳ, TA.) And فَطَحَ الحَدِيدَةَ, and ▾ فَطَّحَهَا, *He made the piece of iron broad,* or *wide, and even,* or *flat,* for a مِسْحَاة, or a مِعْزَق, or some other thing. (L.) —— And فَطَحَ بِالعَصَا ظَهْرَهُ, (Ḳ,* TA,) aor. and inf. n. as above, (TA,) *He struck his back with the staff,* or *stick.* (Ḳ,* TA.) —— And فَطَحَتْ بِالوَلَدِ, said of a woman, *i. q.* رَمَتْ بِهِ [*She cast forth the child,* or *the fœtus*]. (Ḳ, TA.) [Compare طَفَحَتْ.] ═ فَطِحَ, aor. ـَ, inf. n. فَطَحٌ, [app., *He* (a man) *had a broad,* or *wide, head:* (see أَفْطَحُ:) or it signifies, or signifies likewise, and so app. ▾ فَطَّحَ, inf. n. تَفْطِيحٌ, (see فَطَحٌ below, and أَفْطَحُ,)] said of the head, and of the end of the nose, *It was,* or *became, broad,* or *wide.* (TḲ.) ═ فَطِحَ النَّخْلُ *The palm-trees became fecundated.* (Kr, Ḳ.)

2: see the preceding paragraph, in four places.

فَطَحٌ [inf. n. of فَطِحَ, q. v.: and, as a simple subst.,] *Breadth,* or *width, of the head,* (Ṣ, Ḳ, TA,) *in the middle;* as also تَفْطِيحٌ: (TA:) and *breadth,* or *width, of the end of the nose,* (L, Ḳ,) *so that it sticks close to the face;* as in the bull, which is termed أَفْطَحُ. (L.)

فَطُوحٌ A she-camel *bulky in the belly,* (Ḳ, TA,) *broad,* or *wide, in the ribs.* (TA.)

أَفْطَحُ A man *having a broad,* or *wide, head.* (Ṣ.) And A *broad,* or *wide,* head; (A, L;) as also ▾ مُفَطَّحٌ (Ṣ, A, L) and ▾ مَفْطُوحٌ. (A.) And أَرْنَبَةٌ فَطْحَآءُ *A broad,* or *wide, end of a nose:* (A, L:) and so قَدَمٌ [i. e. *foot*]. (A.) —— الأَفْطَحُ *The bull:* so called because of the breadth of the end of his nose: (L, Ḳ:) an epithet in which the quality of a subst. predominates. (L.) —— And *The chameleon* (Ḳ, TA) *whose back and colour the sun makes to glisten so that it becomes white by reason of the heat thereof.* (TA.) —— And الفَطْحَآءُ *The broad,* or *wide, part of a bow.* (L.) ═ Also *i. q.* أَقْدَعُ [q. v.]. (Ḳ.)

مُفَطَّحٌ: } see the next preceding paragraph.
مَفْطُوحٌ: }

فطحل

الفِطَحْلُ, (Ṣ, O, Ḳ,) and accord. to the expositors of the Fṣ, الفَطَحْلُ also, (TA,) [or زَمَنُ الفِطَحْلِ,] *A* [or *the*] *time in which mankind had not as yet been created* (لَمْ يُخْلَقْ فِيهِ بَعْدُ): (Ṣ, O, Ḳ:) or *the time of Noah:* (Ḳ:) or *a* [or *the*] *time in which the stones were moist,* or *soft:* (Ṣ, O, Ḳ:) thus said Ru-beh, when asked respecting it; (TA;) and thus the Arabs of the desert accord. to AO: (Ṣ, O, TA:) a poet said,

زَمَنَ الفِطَحْلِ إِذَا السِّلَامُ رِطَابُ

[*In the time of the* فطحل, *when the stones were moist,* or *soft*]: (TA:) and El-'Ajjáj is related to have said, (Ṣ,) or, correctly, Ru-beh, as in the O, or Ru-beh Ibn-El-'Ajjáj, in replying to a woman whom he desired to take to wife, and who had asked him what was his age, and what was his property, &c., (TA,)

فَقُلْتُ لَوْ عُمِّرْتُ عُمْرَ الحِسْلِ
أَوْ عُمْرَ نُوحٍ زَمَنَ الفِطَحْلِ
وَالصَّخْرُ مُبْتَلٌّ كَطِينِ الوَحْلِ
صِرْتُ رَهِينَ جَدَثٍ أَوْ قَتْلِ

[*And I said, If I were made to live the life of the new-born young one of the ḍabb* (which is said to be seven hundred years), *or the life of Noah in the time of the fiṭaḥl, when the rocks were moist like the clay of the mire, I should become the pledge of a grave or of slaughter*]: (Ṣ,* O, TA: but the last has هَرَمٍ in the place of جَدَثٍ:) and one says, كَانَ ذٰلِكَ زَمَنَ الفِطَحْلِ [*That was in the time of the fiṭaḥl*]; a prov., in which the last word is said to have the first, or the third, of the meanings expl. in this art.; and which is said of a thing that happened long ago: (Meyd: [see also Freytag's Arab. Prov. ii. 340:]) and أَتَيْتُكَ عَامَ الفِطَحْلِ, and الهِدَمْلَةِ, expl. by AḤn as meaning [*I came to thee*] *in the time* [or *year*] *of abundance of herbage, and of food and drink.* (TA.) —— And فِطَحْلٌ also signifies *A torrent.* (Sh, O, Ḳ.) —— And A camel *large, big,* or *bulky.* (Fr, Sh, Ḳ.) —— And *Plump and big.* (Ibn-'Abbád, O, Ḳ.)

فطر

1. فَطَرَهُ, (Ṣ, M, Ḳ,) aor. ـُ, (M, Ḳ, TA,) and, accord. to the Ḳ, ـِ also, but this latter form requires consideration, for it is related by Ṣgh, from Fr, in another sense, that of milking a camel, and not unrestrictedly, (TA,) inf. n. فَطْرٌ; (Ṣ, M;) and ▾ فَطَّرَهُ, (M, TA,) inf. n. تَفْطِيرٌ; (TA;) [but the latter is with teshdeed to denote muchness, or frequency, or repetition, of the action, or its application to many objects;] *He clave, split, slit, rent,* or *cracked, it.* (Ṣ, M, Ḳ.) —— Hence, (Ṣ,) فَطَرَ, (Ṣ, Mṣb, Ḳ,) aor. ـُ, (Mṣb, TA,) inf. n. فَطْرٌ (Mṣb, Ḳ) and فُطُورٌ, (Ḳ,) *It* (the tooth called نَاب, of a camel,) *came forth;* (Ṣ, Ḳ;) *it clave the flesh and came forth.* (TA.) —— See also 7. ═ فَطَرَهُ, (Ṣ, Mgh, Mṣb, Ḳ,) aor. ـُ, inf. n. فَطْرٌ, (Ṣ, Mgh, Mṣb,) *He* (God, Mṣb, Ḳ) *created it,* (Ṣ, Mṣb, Ḳ,) namely, the creation: (Mṣb, Ḳ:) *he caused it to exist, produced it,* or *brought it into existence, newly, for the first time, it not having existed before; originated it; commenced,* or *began it;* (Ṣ, M, A, Mgh, Ḳ;) as also ▾ افتطره, relating to an affair. (TA.) I'Ab says, I did not know what is [the meaning of] فَاطِرُ ▾ السَّمٰوَاتِ [*The Originater,* or *Creator, of the heavens*] until two Arabs of the desert came to me, disputing together respecting a well, and one of them said أَنَا فَطَرْتُهَا, meaning, *I originated,* or *began, it.* (Ṣ.) فُطِرَ عَلَى الشَّىْءِ: see طُبِعَ. [The explanation there given is confirmed by explanations of فِطْرَةٌ.] ═ فَطَرَ العَجِينَ, (Lth, Ṣ, Ḳ,) aor. ـُ, inf. n. فَطْرٌ; (Ṣ;) and ▾ فَطَّرَهُ; (Ks, TA;) *He made the dough into bread,* or *baked it, without leavening it,* or *leaving it until it should become good* [or *mature*]; (Ḳ;) *he kneaded the dough and made it into bread,* or *baked it, immediately;* (Lth;) *he hurried the dough,* or *prepared it hastily, so as to prevent its becoming mature.* (Ṣ.) You say فَطَرَتِ ٱلْمَرْأَةُ العَجِينَ حَتَّى ٱسْتَبَانَ فِيهِ الفُطْرُ [*The woman hurried the dough,* or *prepared it hastily, so that immaturity,* or *want of leaven, was manifest in it*]. (Ṣ.) —— And in like manner, فَطَرَ الطِّينَ *He prepared,* or *kneaded, the clay,* or *mud,* [*without leaving it until it should become mature,*] *and plastered with it immediately.* (Lth, TA.) —— And فَطَرَ الجِلْدَ, (IAạr, Ḳ,) inf. n. فَطْرٌ; (TA;) and ▾ افطره; (Ḳ;) *He did not saturate the skin with the tanning liquid:* (IAạr, Ḳ:) or *he did not put it therein.* (A.) ═ And فَطَرَ, (Fr, O, Ḳ,) aor. ـُ and ـِ, (Fr, O, Ḳ,* TA,) inf. n. فَطْرٌ, (Fr, Ṣ, O, Ḳ,) *He milked a she-camel,* (Fr, Ṣ, O, Ḳ,) and a ewe or goat, (TA,) *with the fore finger and the thumb:* (Fr, Ṣ, O, Ḳ, TA:) or *with the ends of the fingers:* (Ḳ, TA:) or, as one does in indicating the number thirty, i. e., *with the two thumbs and the two fore fingers:* [but this is app. a mistake for what next follows:] (L, TA:) or, accord. to IAth, *with two fingers* [*and*] *with the end of the thumb.* (TA. See also خَبَّ النَّاقَةَ.)

— And [hence, app.,] فَطَرَ أَصَابِعَهُ *He pressed,* or *squeezed, his fingers.* (TA.) And *He struck his* (another's) *fingers so that they burst forth with blood* (انْفَطَرَتْ دَمًا). (TA.) — See also 2: — and 4, first sentence.

2. فَطَّرَهُ: see 1, first sentence. — Also, (inf. n. تَفْطِيرٌ, Ṣ,) *He made him to break his fast;* or *to eat and drink;* (Ṣ,* Mgh,* Ḳ;) as also ↓ افطرهُ, and ↓ فَطَرَهُ: (Ḳ:) *he gave him breakfast: he,* or *it,* (namely, the action termed إِسْتِمْنَآءٌ, and a clyster, [&c.,] Mṣb,) *broke,* or *vitiated, his fast.* (Mṣb.) And you say also هٰذَا كَلَامٌ يُفَطِّرُ الصَّوْمَ, [and, more commonly, يُفْطِرُهُ,] *This is speech which breaks,* or *vitiates, the fast.* (TA.) — فطّر العَجِينَ: see 1.

4. افطر *He broke his fast;* (Ṣ,* Mgh;*) *he breakfasted; he ate and drank after fasting;* (Mṣb,* Ḳ;) as also ↓ فَطَرَ, (Ḳ,) aor. ـُ, (TA,) inf. n. فُطُورٌ: (Mṣb, TA:) *his fast became vitiated.* (Mṣb.) افطر as quasi-pass. of فَطَّرْتُهُ is extr., (Sb,) like أَبْشَرَ as quasi-pass. of بَشَّرْتُهُ. (Sb, Mgh.) You say افطر عَلَى تَمْرٍ [*He breakfasted upon dates,* or *dried dates;*] *he made dates,* or *dried dates, his breakfast, after sunset* [*in Ramaḍán*]. (Mṣb.) In the saying صُومُوا لِرُؤْيَتِهِ وَأَفْطِرُوا لِرُؤْيَتِهِ [*Fast ye after the sight of it,* namely, the new moon commencing Ramaḍán, *and break ye your fast after the sight of it,* namely, the new moon commencing Showwál], the ل is in the sense of بَعْدَ, i. e., بَعْدَ رُؤْيَتِهِ. (Mṣb.) — *It was time for him to break his fast:* (Ḳ:) *he entered upon the time of breaking his fast;* (Mgh, Mṣb, Ḳ;) like أَصْبَحَ and أَمْسَى as meaning "he entered upon the time of morning" and "upon the time of evening:" (Mgh,* Mṣb:) or *he became in the predicament of those who break their fast, and so though he neither ate nor drank:* whence the trad., أَفْطَرَ الحَاجِمُ وَالْمَحْجُومُ *The cupper and the cupped place themselves in the predicament of those who break their fast: or it is time for the cupper and the cupped to break their fast:* or it is used after the manner of a harsh expression, and an imprecation against them. (IAth.) — افطرهُ: see 2. — افطر الجِلْدَ: see 1.

5: see the next paragraph, in six places.

7. انفطر, and ↓ تفطّر, (Ṣ, M, Ḳ,) and ↓ فَطَرَ, (M,) [but the second is with teshdeed as quasi-pass. of 2, to denote muchness, or frequency, or repetition, or application to many subjects of the action, as is indicated in the Ṣ by its being expl. by تَشَقَّقَ,] *It became cleft, split, slit, rent,* or *cracked.* (Ṣ, M, Ḳ.) إِذَا ٱلسَّمَآءُ ٱنْفَطَرَتْ [in the Ḳur lxxxii. 1] means *When the heaven shall become cleft.* (Bḍ, TA.) And تَكَادُ ٱلسَّمٰوَاتُ يَتَفَطَّرْنَ ↓ مِنْهُ [in the Ḳur xix. 92] *The heavens are near to becoming repeatedly rent in consequence thereof.* (Bḍ.) And تَفَطَّرَتْ ↓ قَدَمَاهُ *His feet became cracked:* [or *much cracked.*] (TA, from a trad.) And ↓ تَفَطَّرَتِ الأَرْضُ بِالنَّبَاتِ *The earth became cracked* [*in many places by the plants coming forth*]. (TA.) And تَفَطَّرَ ↓ الشَّجَرُ بِوَرَقٍ [*The trees broke forth with leaves;* as also انفطر, often occurring in this sense; see Ḥar p. 58; and see فَطْرٌ]. (Ṣ and Ḳ, voce رَاحَ; &c.) And تَفَطَّرَتْ ↓ قَدَمَاهُ دَمًا [and انفطرت (see 1, last sentence but one,)] *His feet* [*burst forth* or] *flowed with blood.* (TA.) — And انفطر الصُّبْحُ † *The dawn broke.* (TA in art. صدع.)

8: see 1. And see also 8 in art. شرع.

فَطْرٌ [as an inf. n.: see 1: — as a subst.,] *A cleft, split, slit, rent,* or *crack:* (Ḳ:) or, accord. to some, *a first cleft* &c.: (MF:) pl. فُطُورٌ: (Ḳ:) occurring in the saying هَلْ تَرَى مِنْ فُطُورٍ [*Dost thou see any clefts?*], in the Ḳur [lxvii. 3]. (TA.) — 'Omar, being asked respecting [the discharge termed] المَذْى, answered, It is الفَطْرُ: (O, Ḳ:) thus as related by A'Obeyd: (TA:) it is said that he likened it, in respect of its paucity, to what is drawn from the udder by means of the milking termed الفَطْرُ: (O, Ḳ:) or, as some say, it is from تَفَطَّرَتْ قَدَمَاهُ دَمًا [expl. above]: (TA:) or he likened its coming forth from the orifice of the ذَكَر to the coming forth of the نَاب of the camel: or, as it is related by En-Naḍr, he said ↓ الفُطْرُ, with ḍamm; meaning *the milk that appears upon the orifice of the teat of the udder.* (O, Ḳ.)

فَطْرٌ *Such as has broken forth* [with buds or leaves] (مَا تَفَطَّرَ), of plants. (TA.) See also فِطْرٌ. — And, (Ṣ, Ḳ,) as also ↓ فُطُرٌ, (Ḳ,) the latter used in poetry, (TA,) [*The toadstool;*] *a species of* كَمْأَة [or *fungus*], (Ṣ, Ḳ,) *white and large,* (Ṣ,) *and deadly:* (Ḳ:) [so called] because the ground cleaves asunder from it: (TA:) n. un. فَطْرَةٌ. (Ṣ.) [Also applied in the present day to The *common mushroom; agaricus campestris.* And *Any fungus.*] — [Also, the former, *Immaturity,* or *want of leaven,* in dough:] see the explanation of فَطَرَتِ المَرْأَةُ العَجِينَ. — And فُطْرٌ and ↓ فُطْرٌ signify also *Somewhat of that which remains of milk* [*in the udder*], *which is then milked:* (L, Ḳ:) *or a small quantity of milk when it is milked:* (TA:) or *milk at the time when it is milked.* (AA, TA.) See also فَطْرٌ, last sentence.

فِطْرٌ *Grapes when the heads thereof appear;* (Ḳ, TA;) [so called] because the [fruit-] stalks [then] break forth (تَنْفَطِرُ); (TA;) as also ↓ فَطْرٌ. (Ḳ, TA.) — Also a subst. from أَفْطَرَ; (Ṣ;) [as such] it signifies The *breaking of a fast; contr. of* صَوْمٌ. (TA.) [Hence, عِيدُ الفِطْرِ *The festival of the breaking of the fast,* immediately after Ramaḍán; sometimes called الفِطْرُ alone.] ↓ الفِطْرَةُ means صَدَقَةُ الفِطْرِ [*The alms of the breaking of the fast*], (O, Ḳ, TA,) which is a صَاع [q. v.] of wheat: the prefixed noun (صدقة) is rejected, and ة is affixed to its complement (الفطر) to indicate that such has been done: but it is a word used by the lawyers; not of the classical language. (TA.) — See also مُفْطِرٌ.

فُطُرٌ: see فُطْرٌ, in two places.

فِطْرَةٌ *Creation:* (Mṣb:) the *causing* a thing *to exist, producing* it, or *bringing* it *into existence, newly, for the first time; originating* it. (TA.) — The *natural constitution with which a child is created in his mother's womb;* (AHeyth, Ḳ;) *i. q.* خِلْقَةٌ. (Ṣ, Mgh.) It is said to have this signification in the Ḳur xxx. 29. (TA.) And so in the saying of Moḥammad, كُلُّ مَوْلُودٍ يُولَدُ عَلَى الفِطْرَةِ *Every infant is born in a state of conformity to the natural constitution with which he is created in his mother's womb,* either *prosperous* or *unprosperous* [*in relation to the soul*]; and if his parents are Jews, they make him a Jew, with respect to his worldly predicament; [i. e., with respect to inheritances &c.;] and if Christians, they make him a Christian, with respect to that predicament; and if Magians, they make him a Magian, with respect to that predicament; his predicament is the same as that of his parents until his tongue speaks for him; but if he die before his attaining to the age when virility begins to show itself, he dies in a state of conformity to his preceding natural constitution, with which he was created in his mother's womb. (AHeyth, TA.) [See another explanation of the word, as occurring in this trad., below.] — *Nature; constitution;* or *natural, native, innate,* or *original, disposition,* or *temper* or other *quality* or *property; idiosyncrasy.* (Th, TA.) — The *faculty of knowing God, with which He has created mankind:* (TA:) the *natural constitution with which a child is created in his mother's womb, whereby he is capable of accepting the religion of truth:* this is a secondary application: and this is [said to be] the signification meant in the trad. mentioned above. (Mgh.) — Hence, The *religion of el-Islám:* (Mgh:) the *profession whereby a man becomes a Muslim, which is the declaration that there is no deity but God, and that Moḥammad is his servant and his apostle, who brought the truth from Him,* and this is (AHeyth, TA) *religion.* (AHeyth, Ḳ, TA.) This is shown by a trad., in which it is related that Moḥammad taught a man to repeat certain words when lying down to sleep, and said فَإِنَّكَ إِنْ مُتَّ مِنْ لَيْلَتِكَ مُتَّ عَلَى الفِطْرَةِ [*And then, if thou die that same night, thou diest in the profession of the true religion*]. (AHeyth, TA.) Also by the saying, قَصُّ الأَظْفَارِ مِنَ الفِطْرَةِ *The paring of the nails is* [*a point*] *of the religion of el-Islám.* (Mgh.) — Also *i. q.* سُنَّةٌ [app. meaning The *way, course, mode,* or *manner, of acting,* or *conduct,* or *the like, pursued, and prescribed to be followed, by Moḥammad*]. (TA.) — In the Ḳur xxx. 29, accord. to some, The *covenant received,* or *accepted, from Adam and his posterity.* (Bḍ.) — The pl. is فِطَرَاتٌ and فِطِرَاتٌ and فِطْرَاتٌ. (TA.) — See also فِطْرٌ.

الإِيمَانُ الفِطْرِىُّ [*The faith to which one is disposed by the natural constitution with which he is created*]. (Mṣb.)

فُطَارٌ A sword *having in it cracks*; (Ṣ, Z, O, Ḳ;) and (Ḳ) *that will not cut*: (IAạr, O, Ḳ:) or *recently made*. (TA.)

فَطُورٌ (Ṣ, Mṣb, Ḳ) and ↓ فَطُورِىٌّ, (Ṣ, Ḳ,) as though the latter were a rel. n. from the former, (Ṣ,) *A breakfast; a thing* [i. e. *food* or *beverage*] *upon which one breaks his fast*. (Ṣ, Mṣb, Ḳ.)

فَطِيرٌ Dough *unleavened*; or *not left until it has become good* [or *mature*]; *contr. of* خَمِيرٌ: (Ṣ, TA:) and in like manner clay, or mud. (TA.) [Hence,] عِيدُ الفَطِيرِ [*The feast of unleavened bread; also called, of the Passover;*] *a festival of the Jews*, [*commencing*] *on the fifteenth day of their month* نِيسَان, *and lasting seven days*. (Mṣb. [See also الفِصْحُ.]) — Anything *prepared, made*, or *done, hastily*, or *hurried, so as to prevent its becoming mature*: (Lth, Ṣ, Ḳ:) *fresh; recent; newly made*: (Ṣ, TA:) pl. فُطْرَى: (Ṣgh, IAth, TA:) for أَطْعَمَهُ فَطِيرًا, in the Ḳ, expl. as meaning [*He fed him*] *with* فَطِير, is a gross mistake, a mistranscription of أَطْعَمَهُ فُطْرَى, as the phrase stands in the handwriting of Ṣgh himself, in well-formed letters, and with the syll. signs, meaning *meats* [*newly prepared*, &c.]. (TA.) You say عِنْدِى خُبْزٌ خَمِيرٌ وَحَيْسٌ فَطِيرٌ [*I have leavened bread, and*] *fresh, recent*, or *newly made*, حيس [q. v.]. (Ṣ, TA.) You say also إِيَّاكَ وَالرَّأْىَ الفَطِيرَ ‡ *Beware thou of a hastily formed, immature, opinion*. (Ṣ.) And شَرُّ الرَّأْىِ الفَطِيرُ ‡ [*The worst opinion is the hastily formed, and immature*]. (TA.) — A skin *not saturated with the tanning liquid*: or *not put therein*: (TA:) a whip *not tanned*: *not softly tanned*: (TA:) or *not newly tanned*. (L.) — Also *A calamity*; syn. دَاهِيَةٌ. (O, Ḳ, TA.)

فُطُورَةٌ: see what next follows.

فَطِيرَةٌ and ↓ فُطُورَةٌ *A sheep*, or *goat, that is slaughtered on the day of* [*the festival of*] *the* فِطْر: (Ḳ, TA:) mentioned by Ṣgh, and in the B. (TA.)

فُطَارِىٌّ A man *possessing neither good nor evil*; (IAạr, O, Ḳ,* TA;) *such as is termed* فَدْم [*impotent in speech* or *actions, heavy*, or *dull*; &c.]: (TA:) from فُطَارٌ applied to a sword, meaning that will not cut. (IAạr, O, TA.*)

فَطُورِىٌّ: see فَطُورٌ.

فَاطِرٌ A camel *whose* نَاب [or *tush*] *is coming forth*, (Ṣ,) or *cleaving the flesh and coming forth*. (TA.) — فَاطِرُ ٱلسَّمٰوَاتِ وَٱلْأَرْضِ [in the Ḳur xlii. 9, &c.,] means *The Originater* [or *Creator*] *of the heavens and of the earth*. (I'Ab, Ṣ,* TA.) See 1.

فُوطِيرٌ a subst. for الجِمَاع, in Syriac. (TA.)

أُفْطُورٌ, and the pl. أَفَاطِيرُ: see the next paragraph.

تَفَاطِيرُ, a word similar to تَعَاشِيبُ and تَعَاجِيبُ and تَبَاشِيرُ [q. v.], none of which four words has a sing., *Pimples that come forth in the face of a boy* or *young man*, and *of a girl* or *young woman*; as also ↓ نَفَاطِيرُ: thus correctly, with ت and ن: the author of the Ḳ, following Ṣgh [in the O], says that ↓ أَفَاطِيرُ is the pl. of ↓ أُفْطُورٌ, and signifies *a cracking*, or *chapping, in the nose of a young man*, and *in his face*. (TA.) — Also, thus correctly, with ت, The *first of* [*the herbage of the rain called*] *the* وَسْمِىّ [q. v.]; and in this sense also it has no sing.: but it is said in the Ḳ that ↓ نَفَاطِيرُ is pl. of ↓ نُفْطُورَةٌ, with ن; [in the O, that it is pl. of ↓ نُفْطُورٌ;] and [in both] that it signifies *scattered herbage*; (TA;) and Lḥ says, as is stated by AḤn, that نَفَاطِيرُ ↓ مِنْ عُشْبٍ means *small quantities of herbage* in land: (O, TA:) it is also added in the Ḳ, in explanation of ↓ نَفَاطِيرُ, or it signifies the *first herbage of* [the rain called] the وَسْمِىّ: (TA:) [and it is said that] تَفَاطِيرُ نَبَاتٍ signifies *what break forth of*, or *from, plants*, or *herbage*. (TA voce تَبَاشِيرُ.)

مُفْطِرٌ A man *breaking his fast; eating and drinking after fasting*: (Ṣ,* Mṣb,* Ḳ, TA:) pl. مَفَاطِيرُ, (Sb, Ṣ, Mṣb, Ḳ,) like as مَيَاسِيرُ is pl. of مُوسِرٌ, (Ṣ,) and مَفَالِيسُ of مُفْلِسٌ: (Mṣb:) and ↓ فِطْرٌ signifies the same, as sing. and pl., (Ṣ, Mṣb, Ḳ,) being originally an inf. n. (Ṣ, Mṣb.)

مُنْفَطِرٌ is used in the Ḳur [lxxiii. 18], in the phrase ٱلسَّمَآءُ مُنْفَطِرٌ بِهِ [*The heaven* shall be *with rents by reason of it*], in the manner of a possessive noun, [not as an act. part. n.,] like مُعْضِلٌ in the phrase دَجَاجَةٌ مُعْضِلٌ. (TA.)

نُفْطُورٌ and نُفْطُورَةٌ, and the pl. نَفَاطِيرُ: see تفاطير, in six places.

فطس

1. فَطَسَ, (Ṣ, M, A, Mṣb, Ḳ,) aor. ـِ (Ṣ, Mṣb, Ḳ) and ـُ, (Mṣb,) inf. n. فُطُوسٌ, (Ṣ, M, &c.,) *He died*; (Ṣ, M, &c.;) as also طَفَسَ: (TA:) or *he died without disease*: (M:) or *without any apparent disease*. (TA.) — فَطَسَ الحَدِيدَ, (A, O, Ḳ, TA,) aor. ـِ, (Ḳ,* TA,) inf. n. فَطْسٌ, (TA,) *He made the iron broad* (A, O, Ḳ) with the great hammer called فِطِّيس: (A:) or *he beat the iron*. (TA.) — And الفَطْسُ signifies *The treading vehemently*, or *the compressing vehemently*. (M, TA: the word thus doubly rendered is الوَطْءُ.) — And you say, فَطَسْتُهُ عَنْ كَذَا meaning *I repelled him in a most evil manner from such a thing*: and likewise *I beat him* [app. *away from such a thing*]. (Ibn-'Abbád, O, Ḳ.) — And فَطَسَهُ بِالكَلِمَةِ, (Ibn-'Abbád, O, Ḳ,) and بِالخَبَرِ, (Ibn-'Abbád, O,) aor. ـِ, (Ḳ,) *He uttered in his face* [*the word*, or *sentence*, and *the tidings*, or *information*]; as also ↓ فَطَّسَهُ, (Ibn-'Abbád, O, Ḳ,) inf. n. تَفْطِيسٌ. (Ibn-'Abbád, O.) — فَطِسَ, aor. ـَ, inf. n. فَطَسٌ, (Ṣ, M, A, Ḳ,) *He had the bone of his nose wide and depressed*; (M;) or *depressed and expanded*: (Ṣ, A, Ḳ:) *he had his nose spreading upon his face*. (A, Ḳ.) [And فَطِنَ app. signifies the same.]

2. فَطَّسَهُ *He killed him*. (Mṣb.) — See also 1.

فَطْسٌ (with fet-ḥ, O, in a copy of the M written فُطْس,) The *berries of the myrtle*: n. un. with ة. (Lth, M, O, Ḳ.)

فَطْسَةٌ: see فَطْس.

فَطْسَةٌ The *skin of an animal that has not been slaughtered in the manner prescribed by the law*. (Ibn-'Abbád, O, Ḳ.) — [See also فَطْسٌ.] — Also *A certain bead used for fascinating and restraining* [*men*]; (Lḥ, Ṣ, M, Ḳ;) *one of the beads of the Arabs of the desert, with which women are asserted by the Arabs to fascinate and restrain men*. (O.) They (i. e. women, O, Ḳ) say,

• أَخَذْتُهُ بِالفَطْسَهْ • بِالثُّوَبَا وَالعَطْسَهْ •

[*I captivated and restrained him by means of the fatseh, by means of yawning and of sneezing*]: (Ṣ, O, Ḳ: [in some copies of the Ṣ and Ḳ بالثُّوَبَآءِ:]) they shorten الثوبآء on account of the metre, which is رَجَز with the third foot of each hemistich suppressed. (O.)

فَطَسَةٌ a subst. from فَطِسَ [as such signifying *A state of depression and expansion of the bone of the nose*; or *a spreading of the nose upon the face*]: (Ṣ, O, Ḳ:) or the same word, (M, L,) or ↓ فَطَسٌ, (TA, [but this is the inf. n. of فَطِسَ, and seems to be here a mistranscription,]) the *place of a width and depression of the bone of the nose*. (M, L, TA.)

فِطِّيسٌ *A great hammer*, (Ṣ, M, A, O, Ḳ,) *such as is used by a blacksmith*: (A, TA:) or, (Ḳ,) accord. to IDrd, (O,) it is either Greek or Syriac, (O, Ḳ,) not genuine Arabic. (O.) — And *A great* فَأْس [i. e. *hoe* or *adz* or *axe*]. (M, TA.)

فِطِّيسَةٌ The *snout of the swine*; as also ↓ فِنْطِيسَةٌ: (Ṣ, M,* Ḳ:) or its *nose with what is next thereto*: (IDrd, O, Ḳ:) and, (Ḳ,) accord. to Th, (O,) it [app. meaning the *lip*] is [called] the شَفَة of man, and of camels the مِشْفَر, and of beasts of prey the خَطْم and the خُرْطُوم, and of the swine the ↓ فِنْطِيسَة, (O, Ḳ,* [in the latter of which it is plainly stated that فِطِّيسَة is used in relation to man and to camels and to beasts of prey, whereas Th seems evidently to mean that what is called the شَفَة of man, and of camels the مِشْفَر, &c., is called the فِنْطِيسَة of the swine,]) which word he [thus] mentions, with ن, as of the measure فِنْعِيلَة, the ن being augmentative. (O.)

فَاطِسٌ *Dying*, or *dead*. (IAạr, M.)

فِنْطِيسَةٌ: see فِطِّيسَةٌ, in two places: and see also art. فنطس, in two places.

أَفْطَسُ A man (Ṣ) *having the bone of his nose wide and depressed*; (M;) or *depressed and ex-*

panded: (Ṣ, Ḳ:) *having his nose spreading upon his face:* (Ḳ:) fem. فَطْسَآءُ. (M, Ḳ.) And it is also applied as an epithet to the nose itself [as meaning *Having its bone wide and expanded;* &c.]. (A in art. نفس.) — تَمْرَةٌ فَطْسَآءُ means *A date small in the drupe, having the base cleaving* [*to it*]. (TA.)

فطم

1. فَطَمَهُ, (Ṣ, Mṣb, Ḳ,) aor. ـِ, (Mṣb, Ḳ,) inf. n. فَطْمٌ, (Mṣb,* TA,) *He cut it,* or *severed it;* (Ṣ, Mṣb, Ḳ, TA;) namely, a rope, (Ṣ, Mṣb, TA,) or a stick, or piece of wood, and the like. (TA.) — And فَطَمَهُ, (Ḳ,) or فَطَمَتْهُ (Ṣ, Mṣb) said of a mother (Ṣ) or of a suckling woman, (Mṣb,) aor. and inf. n. as above, (Mṣb, TA,) *He,* (Ḳ,) or *she,* (Ṣ, Mṣb,) *weaned,* or *ablactated, him,* (Ṣ, Mṣb, Ḳ,) namely, a child, (Ṣ, Ḳ,) or suckling. (Mṣb.) And فُطِمَتِ السَّخْلَةُ *The lamb,* or *kid, was weaned,* or *ablactated.* (Ḳ.) [And in like manner one says of other animals.] — And [hence, or] from the first of the significations expl. above, (Mṣb,) one says, فَطَمْتُهُ عَنْ عَادَتِهِ ‡ *I* [*weaned him,* or] *disengaged him,* (TA,) or *withheld him,* (Mṣb,) namely, a man, (Ṣ, Mṣb, TA,) [*from his custom,* or *habit.*] And لَأَفْطِمَنَّكَ عَمَّا أَنْتَ عَلَيْهِ ‡ [*I will assuredly wean thee from the state in which thou art,* or *from that which thou art pursuing:* or] *I will assuredly cut short thy eager desire.* (TA.)

4. افطم *He* (a child) *entered upon the time for his being weaned,* or *ablactated.* (Mṣb, TA.) And in like manner one says of a lamb, or kid. (IAạr, Ḳ, TA.)

6. تفاطموا *Their lambs,* or *kids,* (سِخَالُهُمْ, [in the CḲ, erroneously, سِخَالُهُمْ,]) *kept to their mothers after the weaning,* or *ablactation;* (Ḳ, TA;) *therefore this* [*person*] *gave,* or *delivered, his lambs,* or *kids, to this; and this* [*person*], *his lambs,* or *kids, to this.* (TA.)

7. [انفطم *He* (a child, or young one,) *was,* or *became, weaned,* or *ablactated:* commonly used in this sense in the present day. — And] انفطم عَنْهُ ‡ *He desisted from,* or *left,* or *relinquished, him,* or *it.* (Ḳ, TA.)

فِطَامٌ The *act of weaning,* or *ablactation,* of a child or young one: (Ṣ, Mṣb,* Ḳ:) a subst. in this sense. (Ḳ.) == And [it is also, app., an epithet:] you say نَاقَةٌ فطام [app. نَاقَةٌ فَطَامِ, like as you say نَاقَةٌ فَاطِمٌ, q. v.], meaning *A she-camel whose young one has been weaned from her:* thus in the A. (TA.) — [And hence it seems to be used as a proper name of a woman; like فَاطِمَةُ; for it is said,] and the woman is named فَطَامِ, like حَذَامِ, [in form]. (TA.)

فَطِيمٌ A child *weaned,* or *ablactated;* (Ṣ, Mṣb, Ḳ;) as also ↑ مَفْطُومٌ: (Ḳ:) pl. of the former فُطُمٌ, (Ṣ, Mṣb, Ḳ,) which is of a rare form as pl. of an epithet of the measure فَعِيلٌ, and more particularly of such as is used in the sense of the measure مَفْعُولٌ. (IAth, TA.) And سَخْلَةٌ فَطِيمٌ [in the CḲ فَطِيمَةٌ] and ↑ فَاطِمٌ and ↑ مَفْطُومَةٌ *A lamb,* or *kid, weaned,* or *ablactated,* (Ḳ, TA,) *which is the case two months from its birth, and it ceases not to be thus termed until it becomes a* جَفْر [q. v.]. (TA.)

فَطِيمَةٌ [a subst., rendered so by the affix ة,] *A sheep,* or *goat, weaned,* or *ablactated.* (TA.)

فَاطِمٌ [act. part. n. of 1, q. v.] — [Hence,] فَاطِمَةٌ A suckling woman *weaning,* or *ablactating,* a suckling. (Mṣb.) And فَاطِمٌ A she-camel *whose young one has become a year old and been weaned,* or *ablactated.* (Ṣ, TA.) And A she-camel *that weans,* or *is weaning, from her, her young one.* (TA.) [See also فِطَامٌ.] — [Hence,] in a trad. cited voce مُرْضِعٌ [q. v.], الفَاطِمَةُ signifies † *Death.* (TA in art. رضع.) == See also فَطِيمٌ.

مَفْطُومٌ; and its fem., with ة: see فَطِيمٌ.

فطن

1. فَطِنَ, [aor. ـَ,] inf. n. فِطْنَةٌ and فَطَانَةٌ and فَطَانِيَةٌ [&c. as in the next sentence, *He was,* or *became, intelligent, understanding, knowing, sagacious,* or *skilful:* see the explanations of فِطْنَةٌ below]; (Ṣ;) and فَطُنَ signifies [the same, i. e.] *he became such as is termed* فَطِنٌ. (Lth, TA.) You say, فَطِنَ لَهُ, (Mṣb, Ḳ,) and إِلَيْهِ, and بِهِ, (Ḳ,) aor. ـَ; (Mṣb, Ḳ;) and فَطَنَ, aor. ـُ; (Mṣb, Ḳ;) and فَطُنَ, aor. ـُ; (Ḳ;) inf. n. فِطْنٌ (Mṣb, Ḳ) and فَطْنٌ and فُطْنٌ and فَطَنٌ and فَطُنٌ (Ḳ) and فِطْنَةٌ and فِطَانٌ (Mṣb) and فُطُونَةٌ and فَطَانَةٌ and فَطَانِيَةٌ; (Ḳ;) *He was,* or *became,* [*intelligent, understanding, knowing,* or *sagacious, respecting it;* (agreeably with explanations above;) or] *skilled of it,* i. e. *skilful in it;* (Ḳ;) namely, an affair: (Mṣb:) [and *he understood,* or *knew,* it; often used in this sense:] and sometimes they said فَطِنَهُ, making the verb trans. by itself, because it implies the meaning of فَهِمَ; (TA;) or فَطَنْتُ الشَّىْءَ, with fet-ḥ, signifies *I understood,* or *knew, the thing:* (Ṣ:) and some say that فَطَانَةٌ [as inf. n., agreeably with analogy, of فَطُنَ, which see in what follows,] signifies [the *possessing*] *excellence in respect of readiness of intelligence for the perception of what comes to one from another.* (TA.) [فَطِنَ لَهُ also signifies *He took notice of,* or *paid attention to, him,* or *it:* see Ḥar p. 626, and Ḥam p. 695.] And فَطُنَ signifies [also] *He became one of whom* فِطْنَةٌ [i. e. *intelligence,* &c., as expl. below,] *was a* سَجِيَّة [meaning *faculty,* or *quality, firmly rooted in the mind*]. (Mṣb.)

2. فَطَّنَهُ لِلْأَمْرِ, (Mṣb, TA,) inf. n. تَفْطِينٌ, (Ḳ, TA,) *He made him to understand,* or *know, the affair:* (Ḳ,* TA:) or *he made him knowing in the various modes of the affair, and skilful therein.* (Mṣb.) Hence the prov., لَا يُفَطِّنُ القَارَةَ إِلَّا الحِجَارَةُ i. e. [*Nothing will make*] *the she-bear* [*to understand, except stones*]. (TA.) And فَطَّنَهُ المُعَلِّمُ means *The teacher rendered him* فَطِن [i. e. *intelligent,* &c.,] *by the disciplining of his mind and the correcting him.* (TA.)

3. مُفَاطَنَةٌ is of the measure مُفَاعَلَةٌ from فِطْنَ: (Ṣ:) [as such it signifies The *contending,* or *vying, one with another, in intelligence, understanding, knowledge, sagacity,* or *skill;* whence فَاطَنْتُهُ is used in the Ḳ (in art. حجو) as a syn. of حَاجَيْتُهُ, q. v.: or] it signifies [sometimes] the *showing intelligence, understanding, knowledge, sagacity,* or *skill, one with another.* (PṢ.) [Agreeably with the former explanation,] one says, فَاطَنَهُ فِى الكَلَامِ, i. e. *He held a dialogue* or *colloquy,* or *a disputation* or *debate, with him* [*with the view of trying which of them would prove superior in intelligence,* &c.]; syn. رَاجَعَهُ. (Ḳ) [See also 3 in art. لحن.]

5. تفطّن لَهُ *He understood it,* or *knew it,* [*quickly,* or] *with quickness of intelligence;* namely, what was said. (TA.)

فَطْنٌ: } see what next follows.
فَطُنٌ:

فَطِنٌ (Ṣ, Mṣb, Ḳ, KL) and ↑ فَطُنٌ (Ṣ, Ḳ, KL) and ↑ فَطْنٌ and ↑ فَطِينٌ and ↑ فَطُونٌ and ↑ فَاطِنٌ (Ḳ) are epithets (Ṣ, Ḳ, TA) applied to a man, (Ṣ, TA,) signifying *Intelligent, understanding, knowing, sagacious,* or *skilful;* (Ṣ,* Ḳ,* KL;) the first expl. by Lth as signifying *possessing* فِطْنَة *respecting things:* (TA:) and it signifies one *of whom* فِطْنَة *has become a* سَجِيَّة [meaning *faculty,* or *quality, firmly rooted in the mind*]: (Mṣb:) the pl. [of this] is فُطْنٌ, (Ḳ,) or فُطُنٌ, with two dammehs, (Mṣb,) or both: (TA:) and the fem. is فَطِنَةٌ. (Ḳ.) فَطِنٌ بِخُصُومَتِهِ means A man *knowing in the various modes of his disputation,* or *litigation, and skilful therein.* (Mṣb.)

فِطْنَةٌ [mentioned above as an inf. n. seems to be regarded by some as a simple subst., and] signifies *Intelligence, understanding, knowledge, sagacity,* (Ṣ,* KL, PṢ,) or *skill;* (Ḳ, KL, PṢ;) *contr. of* غَبَاوَةٌ: (TA:) or, accord. to some, *such* [*intelligence,* &c.,] *as is instinctive* [or *natural; infused into the mind by God*]; *not acquired.* (TA.) [See also ذِهْنٌ.]

فَطُونٌ: } see فَطِنٌ.
فَطِينٌ:
فَاطِنٌ:

فظ

1. فَظَّ, (Mṣb,) sec. pers. فَظِظْتَ, (Ṣ, M, Mṣb,) inf. n. فَظَاظَةٌ (Ṣ, M, Mṣb, Ḳ) and فَظَظٌ, (M, Ḳ,) but the former is the more common because of the difficulty of pronouncing the doubled letter in the latter, (M,) and ↑ فِظَاظٌ is syn. with these, (M, Ḳ,) and so is ↑ فَظَاظٌ, but these two are simple substs., (M,) *He* (a man) *was,* or *became, such as is termed* فَظٌّ [i. e. *rough, coarse, rude,* &c., as expl. below]; (Ṣ, M, Mṣb, Ḳ;*) or *rough,* &c., *so as to be unduly feared.* (Mṣb.) == فَظَّهُ, (M, Ḳ,)

aor. ـُ, inf. n. فَظٌّ; (TḲ;) and ▼ افتظّهُ; (M, Ḳ;) *He let it out,* namely the water termed فَظٌّ, *by cutting open the stomach* [of a camel]: (M, TA:) or *he pressed it,* or *squeezed it, out,* namely the water so termed, (M, Ḳ,) *from the stomach,* (M, TA,) *and drank it:* (TḲ:) and ▼ افتظّ كَرِشَ بَعِيرٍ *he slaughtered a camel, and pressed out,* or *squeezed out, the water of its stomach, and strained it:* (Esh-Sháfi'ee, T:) or ▼ افتظّ signifies *he gave his camel to drink, then bound his mouth in order that he might not ruminate, and, when attacked by thirst, cut open his belly, and pressed out,* or *squeezed out, the fluid of the feces of his stomach, and drank it:* (Ṣ:) and ▼ أَفْظَظْتُ الكَرِشَ *I pressed out,* or *squeezed out, the water of the stomach.* (Z, TA.)

4: see فَظَّهُ. — افظّهُ, inf. n. إِفْظَاظٌ, also signifies *He turned him back,* or *away, from the object of his desire.* (TA.) — And افظّهُ is also said of a man when he has inserted the thread into the eye of the needle: [if the affixed pronoun refer to the eye of the needle, the meaning is, *He inserted the thread into it:* if to the thread, *he inserted it into the eye of the needle:*] mentioned by AA. (TA.)

8: see فَظَّهُ, in three places.

فَظٌّ, applied to a man, (T, Ṣ, M, &c.,) *Rough; coarse; rude; unkind; hard; churlish; uncivil; surly; hard to deal with; incompliant; unobsequious;* (Ṣ, M, O, Ḳ, and Bḍ in iii. 153;) *evil in disposition; illnatured;* (O, Ḳ, and Bḍ and Jel ubi suprà;) *hard-hearted; hard,* or *severe; rough, coarse,* or *the like, so as to be unduly feared;* (Mṣb;) *rough,* or *coarse, in speech;* (Lth, T, M, Ḳ;) *sour,* or *austere, therein:* (Lth:) [said in the T to be from the same word in the sense next following; but accord. to the M, the reverse seems to be the case:] pl. أَفْظَاظٌ. (M.) You say, إِنَّهُ لَفَظٌّ بَظٌّ [*Verily he is rough, coarse,* or *the like*]; the latter word being an imitative sequent; (M, Ḳ;) as such we regard it because Th, who mentions it, does not explan it; (M;) and ▼ فَظِيظٌ بَظِيظٌ [app. signifies the same]. (TA in art. بظ.) — Also The *water of the stomach* [*of a camel*], (T, Ṣ, Ḳ,) *which is pressed,* or *squeezed, out, and drunk,* (T, Ḳ,) *on an occasion of want of water,* (T,) *in the waterless deserts;* (T, Ḳ;) the *water that comes forth from the stomach* [*of a camel*]; because it is a coarse, or bitter, beverage: (M:) it may not be used for the purpose of religious purification: (Esh-Sháfi'ee, T:) also, the *urine of horses which is drunk on an occasion of thirst:* pl. فُظُوظٌ: thus used by Mutemmem Ibn-Nuweyreh. (M, L.)

فَظَاظٌ and فِظَاظٌ: see 1, first sentence.

فَظِيظٌ The *seminal fluid of a woman:* or *of a stallion:* (M, Ḳ:) so they assert: but it is not of established authority: (M:) and so say IDrd and Fr: (TA:) accord. to Kr, the *seminal fluid of a stallion, in a she-camel's womb:* (M,* TA:) or this is the explanation given by Fr: (T:) and ▼ فُظَاظَةٌ is of the measure فُعَالَةٌ from this word; (Ḳ;) as signifying the *seminal fluid of a stallion,* or the *water of the stomach;* but El-Khaṭṭábee disallows the latter meaning; or from فَظٌّ: (TA:) and hence the saying of 'Áïsheh to Marwán, وَلٰكِنَّ ٱللّٰهَ لَعَنَ أَبَاكَ وَأَنْتَ فِى صُلْبِهِ فَأَنْتَ فُظَاظَةٌ مِنْ لَعْنَةِ ٱللّٰهِ [*But God cursed thy father when thou wast* essentially *in his loins; so thou art seed of the* object *of the curse of God*]; (Ḳ;) i. e., نُطْفَةٌ مِنْهَا; (TA;) or عُصَارَةٌ مِنْهَا [*produce thereof,* as though *expressed therefrom*]: (Z:) or, accord. to one relation, فُضُضٌ; (Ḳ;) pl. of فَضِيضٌ, which means water such as is termed غَرِيضٌ: or, accord. to another relation, فُضَضٌ, meaning نُطْفَةٌ: and accord. to another, فَضِيضٌ. (TA.) — See also فَظٌّ.

فُظَاظَةٌ: see the next preceding paragraph.

هُوَ أَفَظُّ مِنْ فُلَانٍ *He is* [*more rough, coarse, rude,* or *the like,* (see فَظٌّ,) or] *more difficult in disposition, evil in disposition, illnatured,* or *perverse, than such a one.* (TA.)

فظع

1. فَظُعَ الأَمْرُ, (Ṣ, O, Mṣb, Ḳ,) aor. ـُ, (O,) inf. n. فَظَاعَةٌ, (Ṣ, O, Mṣb,) and perhaps فَظْعٌ [respecting which see فَظَعَ]; (Mbr, TA;) as also ▼ افظع; (Ṣ, O, Mṣb, Ḳ;) *The affair,* or *event, was,* or *became, hard, difficult,* or *distressing; bad, evil, abominable, foul,* or *unseemly; excessive,* or *exorbitant:* (Ṣ:) or *excessively bad, evil, abominable, foul,* or *unseemly.* (O, Mṣb, Ḳ.) — And فَظِعَ الأَمْرَ, (Ḳ, TA,) thus in the copies of the Ḳ, and in like manner in the O, [where I find, AZ says, فَظِعْتُ الأَمْرَ, aor. أَفْظَعُهُ,] but [SM says] in the "Nawádir" of AZ, فَظِعَ بِالأَمْرِ, inf. n. فَظَاعَةٌ, (TA,) *He reckoned the affair,* or *event,* or *judged it to be, great, hard, difficult,* or *distressing,* syn. ٱسْتَعْظَمَهُ, (Ḳ,) or *was made to fear,* or *be frightened, and was overcome, by it,* (AZ, O, TA,) *and trusted not that he had power to accomplish it,* or *to bear it:* (AZ, O, Ḳ, TA:) it is said in a trad., أُرِيتُ أَنَّهُ وُضِعَ فِى يَدَىَّ سِوَارَانِ مِنْ ذَهَبٍ فَفَظِعْتُهُمَا [*I was made to see,* meaning *I imagined,* or *dreamt, that two bracelets of gold were put upon my arms, and I regarded them with fear*]; in which instance, as IAth says, the verb is thus made trans. in accordance with its meaning, which is أَكْبَرْتُهُمَا, and خِفْتُهُمَا: but the phrase commonly known is فَظِعْتُ بِهِ and مِنْهُ: (TA:) you say, فَظِعْتُ بِكَذَا *I was unable to do,* or *accomplish such a thing:* (Ibn-'Abbád, O, Ḳ:*) and فَظِعْتُ بِأَمْرِى occurs in a trad. as meaning [*I found that*] *my affair,* or *case, was hard, difficult,* or *distressing, to me, and I regarded it with fear,* or *dread:* فَظِعَ بِالأَمْرِ, inf. n. فَظَاعَةٌ and فَظَعٌ, means *He saw the affair,* or *event,* or *case, to be* فَظِيع [q. v.]: Mbr says, فَظَعٌ is an inf. n. of فَظِعَ بِهِ: or it may be an inf. n. of فَظُعَ, like as كَرَمٌ is of كَرُمَ: but I have not heard it save in the saying of the poet,

• قَدْ عِشْتُ فِى النَّاسِ أَطْوَارًا عَلَى خُلُقٍ •
• شَتَّى وَقَاسَيْتُ فِيهِ اللِّينَ وَالفَظَعَا •

[*I have lived among men during several periods, conforming to disposition differing in kind,* (عَلَى خُلُقٍ شَتَّى being like the phrase إِنَّ سَعْيَكُمْ لَشَتَّى in the Ḳur xcii. 4, meaning إِنَّ مَسَاعِيَكُمْ لَأَشْتَاتٌ, as is said in the Ksh and by Bḍ,) *and I have endured therein softness and hardness*]. (TA.) — فَظَعَ, (O, Ḳ,) aor. ـَ, inf. n. فَظْعٌ, (O,) said of a vessel, (Ḳ,) *It became full.* (O, Ḳ.)

[2. فظّع, inf. n. تَفْظِيعٌ, accord. to Freytag, signifies *He described* a thing *as great:* but for this he names no authority: by "great" is here meant *hard, difficult,* or *distressing;* &c.: see 1, first sentence.]

4. افظع as intrans.: see 1, first sentence. — أَفْظَعَنِى الأَمْرُ *The affair,* or *event, made me to fear,* or *frightened me: made me to fall into a hard, difficult,* or *distressing, case:* (TA:) *made me to be without power,* or *strength,* or *ability; disabled,* or *incapacitated, me.* (Ḥam p. 32.) — And أُفْظِعَ *He* (a man, Ṣ, O, Mṣb) *suffered the befalling of a hard, difficult,* or *distressing, event.* (Ṣ, O, Mṣb, Ḳ.) — See also 10.

5: see what next follows.

10. استفظعهُ (Ṣ, O, Ḳ) and ▼ افظعهُ (Ṣ, Ḳ) and ▼ تفظّعهُ (O, Ḳ) *He found it* (a thing, Ṣ) *to be* فَظِيع [i. e. *hard, difficult,* or *distressing;* &c.]. (Ṣ, O, Ḳ.)

فَظْعٌ: see فَظِيعٌ. — Also *Full;* applied to a vessel. (O, TA.)

فَظِيعٌ (Ṣ, O, Mṣb, Ḳ) and ▼ مُفْظِعٌ (Ṣ, Mṣb, TA) and ▼ فَظْعٌ, which last is a possessive epithet, (TA,) applied to an affair, or event, *Hard, difficult,* or *distressing; bad, evil, abominable, foul,* or *unseemly; excessive,* or *exorbitant:* (Ṣ, TA:) or *excessively bad, evil, abominable, foul,* or *unseemly.* (O, Mṣb, Ḳ.*) — And the first, *Much,* or *abundant:* so in the saying of 'Amr Ibn-Maadee-Kerib,

• وَقَدْ عَجِبَتْ أُمَامَةُ أَنْ رَأَتْنِى •
• تَفَرَّعَ لِمَّتِى شَيْبٌ فَظِيعُ •

[*And Umámeh wondered that she saw me such that much,* or *abundant, hoariness had spread in,* or *overspread, my hair descending below the ears,* or *upon the shoulders:* فِى is app. understood before لِمَّتِى]. (O, TA.) — فَظِيعٌ applied to water signifies *Sweet:* (Lth, O, Ḳ:) or *clear; limpid;* or *cool, sweet, and clear* or *limpid.* (IAạr, O, Ḳ, TA.)

مُفْظِعٌ: see فَظِيعٌ.

فعل

1. فَعَلَهُ, (Ṣ, O, Mṣb, Ḳ,*) aor. ـَ, (Ṣ, O, Ḳ,) inf. n. فَعْلٌ (Ṣ, O, Mṣb, Ḳ) and فَعَالٌ, (Ṣ, O, Mṣb,) and ▼ فِعْلٌ is the subst. therefrom, (Ṣ, O, Mṣb, Ḳ,*) but, accord. to Ibn-Kemál, it has become commonly used as the inf. n.; MF, however, says that its being thus used requires consideration; and it is said that there is no instance like فَعَلَهُ, aor. يَفْعَلُهُ, inf. n. فِعْلٌ, except سَحَرَهُ, aor. يَسْحَرُهُ, inf. n. سِحْرٌ; or, to these may be added as sometimes occurring, خَدَعَ, aor. يَخْدَعُ, inf. n. خَدْعٌ and خِدْعٌ, and صَرَعَ, aor. يَصْرَعُ, inf. n. صَرْعٌ and صِرْعٌ; (TA;) [*He did it*]; namely, a thing. (Ṣ, O. [For further explanation see فِعْلٌ below.]) [In the Ḳur. xxi. 73,] some read وَأَوْحَيْنَا إِلَيْهِمْ فَعْلَ ٱلْخَيْرَاتِ [*And we suggested to them the doing of good works*]; (Lth, Ṣ, O;) others reading ▼ فِعْلَ الخيرات. (Lth, O.) —— And one says also فَعَلَ بِهِ [*He did to him* something]. (TA.) [فَعَلَ ٱللّٰهُ بِهِ is a form of imprecation, meaning *May God do to him* what He will do; i. e. may God punish him: see an ex. voce أَظْلَمُ. —— And فَعَلَ بِالْمَرْأَةِ often occurs in trads. &c. as meaning *He compressed the woman.*]

2. تَفْعِيلٌ [inf. n. of فَعَّلَ] is used by IJ as metonymically signifying The *scanning* of a verse; because the names of the measures of its feet, all of them, have the letters ف and ع and ل for constituents, as when you say فَعُولُنْ and مَفَاعِيلُنْ and فَاعِلُنْ and فَاعِلَاتُنْ &c. (TA.)

3. [فَاعَلَا, inf. n. فِعَالٌ, if used, app. signifies *They two did* a thing *together.*] See فِعَالٌ below.

7. انفعل quasi-pass. of 1: you say, فَعَلْتُهُ فَٱنْفَعَلَ [*I did it, and it was done*]; (Ṣ, Mṣb;) like your saying كَسَرْتُهُ فَٱنْكَسَرَ. (Ṣ.) [الِانْفِعَالُ signifies *The suffering*, or *receiving, the effect of an act, whether the effect is intended by the agent* or *not:* or, accord. to some, particularly *when the effect is not intended;* for it is implied in a passage in the TA, that it is held by some to be used particularly in cases in which the effects are such as the blushing in consequence of confusion, or shame, affecting one from the seeing a person, and the emotion, or excitement, ensuing from the hearing of singing, and the agitation of the passionate lover at his seeing the object of his love: as a term of logic, it is one of the ten predicaments, i. e. *passion*, or *suffering.*] It is said that to every فِعْل there is an انْفِعَال, except to the act of creation, which proceeds from God; for this is the bringing into existence from a state of non-existence, not from matter [already existing to receive the effect of the act]. (TA.)

8. افتعل عَلَيْهِ كَذِبًا (Mgh,* O, Mṣb,* Ḳ) and زُورًا (O) *He forged against him a lie.* (Mgh,* O, Mṣb,* Ḳ.) —— Hence the phrase الخُطُوطُ تُفْتَعَلُ i. e. [*Handwritings*] *are forged*, or *falsified.* (Mgh.) —— And [hence] it used to be said, أَعْذَبُ الأَغَانِي مَا ٱفْتُعِلَ i. e. [*The sweetest of songs is*] *such as has been composed with originality, not in imitation of any model:* and أَظْرَفُ ٱلشِّعْرِ مَا ٱفْتُعِلَ [*The most eloquent of poetry is such as has been so composed*]. (TA.)

فَعْلٌ an inf. n. of 1. (Ṣ, O, Mṣb, Ḳ.) ═ And The *vulva of the she-camel*, and *of any female.* (Ḳ.)

فِعْلٌ: see 1, in two places: [as a subst. from فَعَلَهُ] it signifies [*A deed*, or *an action:* or] *a motion* (حَرَكَة) *of a human being:* (Ḳ:) or, as Ṣgh says, the *origination of anything, whether it be what is termed* عَمَل [which means *work* or *labour* or *service* as well as *a deed* or *an action*] or *other than it;* so that it is more general in application than عَمَل: (TA:) or it is a metonymical term for *any* عَمَل [meaning *deed* or *action*] *that is transitive* (M, Ḳ, TA) or *intransitive* (M, TA:) or *a mode that is accidental to the producer of an effect upon another* [*person* or *thing*] *by reason of the producing of the effect at the first; as the mode that ensues to the cutter by reason of his being cutting:* or, as Er-Rághib says, the *production of an effect considered with reference to an agent thereof;* and it is *common to that which is by his*, or *its, origination or otherwise, and to that which is with knowledge or otherwise, and to that which is by intention or otherwise, and to what proceeds from the human being or the animal* [*of any kind*] *or the inanimate thing;* and عَمَل and صُنْع are more particular in application: El-Ḥarállee says that the فِعْل is *what has become apparent in consequence of a motive of the efficient, whether from knowledge or otherwise, by reason of premeditation* [for لِتَدَيُّن (an obvious mistranscription in my original) I read لِتَدَبُّر] *or otherwise:* and El-Juweynee says that it is *what is within the limits of a small space of time, without repetition*, or *reiteration;* whereas the عَمَل is what has been repeated, or reiterated, and whereof the time has been long; but this is repugned by the trad. [in which occurs the saying], مَا فَعَلَ ٱلنُّغَيْرُ [expl. in art. نغر]: (TA:) the pl. is فِعَالٌ (Ṣ, O, Mṣb, Ḳ) and أَفْعَالٌ [a pl. of pauc.], (O, TA,) [and أَفَاعِيلُ is app. a pl. pl., i. e. pl. of أَفْعَالٌ, like أَقَاوِيلُ pl. of أَقْوَالٌ which is pl. of قَوْلٌ, and many other instances]: you say, إِنَّ ٱلرُّشَا تَفْعَلُ ٱلأَفَاعِيلَ وَتُنْسِي إِبْرَاهِيمَ وَإِسْمَاعِيلَ [*Verily bribes do* great *deeds, and cause* the receivers *to forget* the principles of *Ibráheem and Ismá'eel*, who are esteemed models of true religion]. (TA. [This saying is written in my original without any vowel-signs, perhaps because well known: and it is there added that الافاعيل may be pl. of افعول (which has been altered by the copyist and is probably a mistranscription for أُفْعُولَة) or of افعال; with other remarks equally doubtful and unimportant.]) [Hence, بِالفِعْلِ meaning *Actually;* as opposed to بِالقُوَّةِ i. e. potentially, or virtually.] —— As used by the grammarians, it means [*A verb;* i. e.] *what denotes a meaning in itself together with any one of the three times* [*past and present and future;* but it should be observed that it includes the مَصْدَر, or *infinitive noun;* and also that there is what is termed فِعْلٌ نَاقِصٌ *an incomplete*, i. e. *non-attributive, verb* (as كَانَ coordinate to صَارَ, &c.); as well as what is termed فِعْلٌ تَامٌّ *a complete*, i. e. *attributive, verb*]. (TA.)

فَعْلَةٌ *A single* فِعْل [i. e. *deed* or *action*], (Mṣb, TA,) with fet-ḥ. (Mṣb.) Thus in the saying in the Ḳur [xxvi. 18], وَفَعَلْتَ فَعْلَتَكَ ٱلَّتِى فَعَلْتَ [lit. *And thou hast done thy one deed that thou hast done*]; as though the speaker said, قَتَلْتَ ٱلنَّفْسَ قَتْلَتَكَ: in which Esh-Shaạbee read ▼ فِعْلَتَكَ [*thy kind of deed*], with kesr, as meaning قَتَلْتَ القِتْلَةَ ٱلَّتِى قَدْ عَرَفْتَهَا: so says Zj; but he adds that the former reading is better. (TA.) And [hence also] one says, كَانَتْ مِنْهُ فَعْلَةٌ حَسَنَةٌ or قَبِيحَةٌ [*A good single deed proceeded from him* or *a bad* one]. (Ṣ, O, TA.)

فِعْلَةٌ: see the next preceding paragraph.

فِعْلَةٌ *A custom, manner, habit*, or *wont.* (Ḳ.)

[فِعْلِيٌّ *Of*, or *relating to, a verb.*]

[فِعْلِيَّةٌ The *quality of a verb.*]

فَعَالِ, like نَزَالِ, has sometimes occurred as meaning اِفْعَلْ [*Do thou*]. (O, Ḳ.*)

فَعَالٌ, (O, Ḳ,) accord. to Lth, (O,) is a name for *A good doing*, such as *liberality*, or *bounty*, (O,) and *generosity*, (O, Ḳ, [the only meaning assigned to it in the Ṣ,]) and *the like of these:* (O:) or, (O, Ḳ,) accord. to IAạr, (O,) the *doing of a single person*, peculiarly, [as distinguished from فِعَال, q. v.,] (O,) *relating to good* and *to evil;* (O, Ḳ;) one says, فُلَانٌ كَرِيمُ الفَعَالِ [*Such a one is generous in respect of doing* or *doings*], and فُلَانٌ لَئِيمُ الفَعَالِ [*Such a one is mean in respect of doing* or *doings*]; (O; [and the like is said in the T and in the Mṣb;]) and Az says that this is the correct explanation; not that of Lth; and Mbr [likewise] says, it is used in commendation and in discommendation; (O;) and it is *used only of a single agent.* (O, Ḳ.) —— It is also an inf. n. (Ṣ, O, Mṣb. [See 1, first sentence.])

فِعَالٌ, as distinguished from فَعَالٌ, signifies *A doing that is between two* [*agents*]; (IAạr, O, Ḳ, TA;) and therefore it is an inf. n. of ▼ فَاعَلَ [a verb of which I have not found any ex.]. (TA.) —— It is also a pl. of فِعْلٌ. (Ṣ, O, Mṣb, Ḳ.) ═ Also The *handle*, (Ḳ,) or *piece of wood that is inserted into the hole*, (IAạr, IB, O,) *of the axe*, or *adz*, or *hoe:* (IAạr, IB, O, Ḳ:) pl. فُعُلٌ. (Ḳ.)

فُعَالَةٌ (with ḍamm, O, TA, [in the CḲ, erroneously, فَعالَة,]) A metonymical appellation substituted for خُزَاعَة, (O, Ḳ, TA,) the well-known tribe [thus named]. (TA.)

فَعَّالٌ [*Wont to do*]. (Ḳur xi. 109 and lxxxv. 16. [Thus in the phrase فَعَّالٌ لِمَا يُرِيدُ *Wont to do what He willeth:* relating to God.])

فَاعِلٌ [act. part. n. of 1, *Doing:* and, used as a subst., *a doer:* and hence] *a carpenter* is thus called; accord. to IAạr: but it is now peculiarly applied to *such as works with clay, [and builds, and plasters,] and digs foundations:* (TA:) and [the pl.] فَعَلَةٌ, (Mgh, Ḳ, TA,) as an epithet in which the quality of a subst. predominates, is applied to *workers in clay* and *digging* and *the like;* (Ḳ, TA;) or *such as work with their hands in clay* or *building* or *digging;* like عَمَلَةٌ [pl. of عَامِلٌ]. (Mgh.) — وَكُنَّا فَاعِلِينَ, in the Ḳur [xxi. 79], means *And we were able to do what we willed.* (O, TA.) And وَٱلَّذِينَ هُمْ لِلزَّكٰوةِ فَاعِلُونَ, in the same [xxiii. 4], means *And who give the* زكوة [or *poor-rate*]: (Zj, O, TA:) or, as some say, *who do that which is good,* or *righteous.* (O, TA.)

مُفْتَعَلٌ A writing *forged,* or *falsified.* (Mgh.) — And Poetry *composed with originality, not in imitation of any model.* (TA.) — جَآءَ بِٱلْمُفْتَعِلِ, meaning *It produced a grievous,* or *distressing, effect,* (Ḳ, TA,) is a phrase mentioned by IAạr, as used by Ed-Dubeyree when asked respecting a wound that he had received and that rendered him sleepless, and as used by him in respect of anything [unprecedented]: thus one says, عَذَّبَنِى وَجَعٌ أَسْهَرَنِى فَجَآءَ بِٱلْمُفْتَعِلِ i. e. [*A malady that rendered me sleepless, tormented me,*] *and produced pain that had not been known before.* (TA.)

فغم

1. فَغَمَ, aor. ـَ, inf. n. فَغَامَةٌ and فُغُومَةٌ, *It was,* or *became, full;* said of the سَاعِد [or fore arm]; (Ṣ, Ḳ;) and of a vessel. (Ḳ.) — And فَغُمَتْ, said of a woman, *She was,* or *became, full-formed, and thick in her shank.* (Ḳ.) — See also 4, in three places.

2: see what next follows.

4. افغم; [like أَفْأَمَ;] (Ṣ, Ḳ;) and so افغر; (Ḳ in art. فغر;) as also ▼ فَغَمَ; (thus in some of the copies of the Ḳ;) or ▼ فَغَّمَ, (thus accord. to other copies of the Ḳ and accord. to the TA,) aor. ـَ, inf. n. فَغْمٌ; (TA;) *He filled* a vessel; (Ṣ, Ḳ, TA;) and *exceeded the usual degree,* or *strove,* or *laboured,* or *did not fall short of what was requisite, in filling* it. (TA.) — And أَفْغَمْتُ ٱلْبَيْتَ بِرِيحِ ٱلْعُودِ [*I filled the house,* or *chamber,* or *tent, with the odour of aloes-wood*]. (Ṣ.) It is said in a trad., لَوْ أَنَّ ٱمْرَأَةً مِنَ ٱلْحُورِ ٱلْعِينِ أَشْرَفَتْ لَأَفْغَمَتْ مَا بَيْنَ ٱلسَّمَآءِ وَٱلْأَرْضِ رِيحَ ٱلْمِسْكِ i. e. [*If a woman* (of Paradise) *of those having eyes like the eyes of gazelles rose into view,*] *she would fill* [*the space between the heaven and the earth with the odour of musk*]: thus related: and also لَأَفْغَمَتْ, and لَفَغَمَتْ: but Az says that the right relation is لافعمت, with ع. (TA in this art. and in art. فعم.) And one says, افغم ٱلْمِسْكُ ٱلْبَيْتَ *The musk filled with its odour,* (Ṣ,) or *perfumed,* (Ḳ,) [*the house,* or *chamber,* or *tent.*] — And افغم ٱلرَّجُلَ *He filled the man with anger;* (Ṣ, TA;) mentioned by Az on the authority of Aboo-Turáb: (TA:) or *he angered him:* or *he filled his nose with odour,* (Ḳ, TA,) i. e. *with sweet odour:* (TA:) as also ▼ فَغَمَهُ and ▼ فَغَّمَهُ, aor. of both ـَ, (Ḳ, TA,) inf. n. فَغْمٌ; but better known with the pointed غ. (TA.) — And افعمه and افغمه *He filled him with joy,* or *happiness.* (Aboo-Turáb, TA.)

12. افْعَوْعَمَ *It became full, and overflowed.* (Ḳ.) — And افعوعم طِيبًا *It* (a house, or chamber, or tent,) *became filled with perfume.* (TA.)

فَعْمٌ *Full;* applied in this sense to a سَاعِد [or fore arm]; (Ṣ, Ḳ;) and to a vessel; as also ▼ فَعْمَلٌ, in which the ل is augmentative: (Ḳ:) and *full of flesh;* applied to the place of the anklet. (TA.) It is said of the Prophet, in a trad., كَانَ فَعْمَ ٱلْأَوْصَالِ i. e. *He was full in respect of the limbs.* (TA.) And one says ٱمْرَأَةٌ فَعْمَةٌ *A woman full-formed, and thick in her shank.* (Ḳ.) And حَاضِرٌ فَعْمٌ *A* [*great*] *tribe filled with its people.* (TA.) [See also مُفْعَمٌ: and see أَفْعَمُ.] — And *A species of tree:* or the *rose.* (Ḳ.)

فَعْمَلٌ: see the next preceding paragraph.

أَفْعَمُ *Full* [like فَعْمٌ]: or *overflowing by reason of fulness.* (TA.)

مُفْعَمٌ *Filled;* applied in this sense to a skin for water or milk; as also مُفْأَمٌ: but as to ▼ مَفْعُومٌ, IAạr asserts that he had not heard it except in a verse of Kutheiyir: Az, however, mentions it as signifying *full* [like فَعْمٌ], applied to a river, or rivulet: and Aboo-Sahl cites an ex. of it from the verses of the Fṣ as signifying *full of flesh.* (TA.) — The phrase سَيْلٌ مُفْعَمٌ may be of the same category as هَمٌّ نَاصِبٌ [for هَمٌّ ذُو نَصَبٍ], the meaning being *A torrent having the quality of filling;* though the possessive epithet in most instances has the form of the act. part. n., such as طَالِقٌ [for ذَاتُ طَلَاقٍ] and مُرْضِعٌ [for ذَاتُ رَضِيعٍ]: or it may be that مُفْعَمٌ in this case is expressive of muchness, or abundance, like the latter word in the phrase شِعْرٌ شَاعِرٌ and in مَوْتٌ مَائِتٌ. (Ḥam p. 106.)

مَفْعُومٌ: see the next preceding paragraph.

فعو or فعى

1. فَعَا شَيْئًا i. q. فتته [so in my original, app., if not a mistranscription, فَتَّتَهُ i. e. *He crumbled a thing much*]; said of a man. (TA.)

2. فَعَّى, inf. n. تَفْعِيَةٌ, *He branded* a camel *with a mark in the form of the viper* (ٱلْأَفْعَى). (TA.)

4. افعى *He* (a man) *became possessed of* [or *characterized by*] *evil after good* or *goodness.* (TA.)

5. تفعّى *He* (a man, Ṣ) *became like the viper* (ٱلْأَفْعَى, Ṣ, Ḳ) *in evil:* (Ṣ, TA:) or, as in the A, *he made himself to resemble the viper* (تَشَبَّهَ بِٱلْأَفْعَى) *in the evilness of his disposition.* (TA.)

فَاعٍ *Angry* and *foaming* [*with anger*]. (IAạr, M, Ḳ.) — And [the fem.] فَاعِيَةٌ A woman (TA) *wont to calumniate;* syn. نَمَّامَةٌ. (Ḳ, TA: in the CḲ ٱلشَّمَامَةُ is put for ٱلنَّمَّامَةُ.)

فَاعِيَةٌ [as a subst.] The *flower of the* حِنَّآء [i. e. *Lawsonia inermis,* or *Egyptian privet*]: (Ḳ:) [said to be] a dial. var. of فَاغِيَةٌ [q. v.]. (TA.)

أَفْعًى, (Ṣ, Mṣb, Ḳ) of the fem. gender, but with tenween, (Ṣ, Mṣb,) because it is a subst., not an epithet; (Mṣb;) [said in the Ṣ and Mṣb to be like أَرْوًى; but this is a mistake, for اروى is without tenween;] or it is an epithet and a subst.; (Ḳ, TA;) but mostly a subst.; (TA;) [if used as an epithet, it is without tenween, written أَفْعَى, being also of the measure of a verb;] *A certain serpent,* (Ṣ, Mṣb, Ḳ,) *of a malignant kind;* [i. e. the *viper;*] also called ▼ أُفْعُوٌّ, (Ḳ, TA, [in the CḲ, erroneously, أُفْعُوان, which see in what follows,]) occurring in a trad., in which it is said that there is no harm in the killing of the أُفْعُوّ and the حُدُوّ by the مُحْرِم, the [final] alif being changed into و in both of these words in the dial. of El-Ḥijáz: (TA:) *it is spotted, black and white; slender in the neck; broad in the head; it is said that it will not quit its place;* (TA;) *always coiling itself round; and neither antidote nor charm is of any avail against it:* (Mṣb, TA:) *sometimes it has two horns* [i. e. it sometimes signifies the *cerastes,* or *horned viper*]: (TA:) ▼ أُفْعُوَانٌ signifies the *male:* (Ṣ, Mṣb, TA:) [see also خَشَاشٌ:] the pl. is أَفَاعٍ. (Ṣ, Mṣb, Ḳ.* [In the Ḳ, the pl. is written أَفَاعِى, which, when indeterminate, is wrong.]) — [Hence,] by way of comparison [to vipers], (TA,) ٱلْأَفَاعِى signifies ‡ *Certain veins* (عُرُوق) *that branch off from the* حَالِبَانِ [q. v.]. (Ḳ.)

أُفْعَآءٌ [a pl. of which the sing. is not mentioned] *Sweet,* or *pleasant, odours.* (IAạr, M, Ḳ.)

أُفْعُوٌّ, and أُفْعُوَانٌ: see أَفْعًى.

أَرْضٌ مَفْعَاةٌ *A land in which are vipers* (أَفَاعٍ): or, abounding therewith. (Ḳ.)

مُفَعًّى A camel *branded with a mark in the form of the viper* (ٱلْأَفْعَى): (Ḳ:) and [the fem.] مُفَعَّاةٌ camels (إِبِلٌ) *branded therewith.* (TA.)

مُفَعَّاةٌ [as a subst.] *A brand in the form of the viper* (ٱلْأَفْعَى). (Ṣ, Ḳ.)

فغر

1. فَغَرَ, (Ṣ, Mgh, Mṣb, Ḳ,) aor. ـَ (Mṣb, Ḳ) and ـُ, (AZ, Ḳ,) inf. n. فَغْرٌ (Mṣb, TA) and فُغُورٌ, (TA,) *He opened* his mouth; (Ṣ, Mgh, Mṣb, Ḳ;) as also ▼ افغر. (Zj, Ṣgh, Ḳ.) — [Also, both verbs, فَغَرَ and ▼ افغر, *He,* or *it, made,* or *caused, to open the mouth.* And hence,] فَغَرَ ٱلنَّجْمُ, (T, TA,) or ٱلثُّرَيَّا, (Ṣ, O,) i. e. أَفْغَرَ ٱلنَّجْمُ, (T, Ṣ, O,) *The*

asterism, meaning *the Pleiades, became overhead:* [lit., *made one to open his mouth:*] (T:) this is in the winter: (Ṣ, O:) for when the Pleiades are in the midst of the sky, he who looks at them opens his mouth: (T, Ṣ, O:) or *the Pleiades began to rise* [*after sunset, so as to be overhead in the middle of the night*], in the winter. (TA.) —— فَغَرَ also signifies *It* (the mouth) *opened;* (Ṣ, Mgh, Mṣb, Ḳ;) as also ↑انفغر: (Ḳ:) and the latter is said of a blossom, or flower, in the same sense. (Ṣ, Mṣb, TA.) — And فَغَرَتِ السِّنُّ †*The tooth showed its point;* as though it broke forth to grow: but some say that its ف is substituted for ث, and Az inclines to think so [though ثَغَرَ differs much in meaning from فَغَرَ]. (TA.)

4: and 7: see 1; the former in three places.

هُوَ وَاسِعُ فَغْرِ الفَمِ *He is wide in the opening of the mouth.* (Lth, O, Ḳ.) — And accord. to Lth, (O,) فَغْرٌ signifies also *A rose when it opens:* (O, Ḳ:) but it is thought by Az to be, in this sense, a mistake for فَغْوٌ, with و. (O.)

وُلِدَ بِالْفَغْرَةِ *He was born at the commencement of the rising of the Pleiades* [*after sunset*]; (O, Ḳ;) which is in the winter. (TA.) See 1.

فُغْرَةٌ The *mouth of a valley:* pl. فُغَرٌ. (O, Ḳ.)

طَعْنَةٌ فَغَارِ, the latter word like قَطَامِ, [*A spear-wound, or the like,*] *that passes through.* (O, Ḳ.)

فَاغِرٌ, an epithet in which the quality of a subst. is predominant, (TA,) *A* [*certain*] دُوَيْبَّة [i. e. *small animal, or small creeping thing, or insect*], (O, Ḳ, TA,) *always opening its mouth:* (O, TA:) and *another, black and white in the* أَنْف [or *snout*], *that stings men.* (TA.)

فَاغِرَةٌ *A sort of perfume:* (Ṣ, Ḳ, TA:) or (Ḳ, TA) the *roots of the* [*lotus called*] نَيْلُوفَر [q. v.] (Ṣ, Ḳ, TA) *of India:* (Ṣ, TA:) or the كَبَابَة [or *cubeb*] (Ḳ, TA) *of China;* because, when a man eats it, he opens his mouth. (TA.)

مَفْغَرَةٌ A wide tract of land. (Ṣ, Ḳ.) — And *An opening, or a hollow, in a mountain, smaller than a* كَهْف. (Ḳ.)

فغفور

فَغْفُورِىّ [*China-ware, or porcelain,*] the [*sort of*] خَزَف *that is brought from China;* so called from فَغْفُور, [the title of] the king of China: vulgarly فَرْفُورِىّ. (TA in art. فر.)

فغم

1. فَغَمَهُ الطِّيبُ, (Ṣ, Ḳ,) aor. ـَ, inf. n. فَغْمٌ and فُغُومٌ, (Ḳ,) *The perfume stopped the air-passages of his nose.* (Ṣ, Ḳ.) — And فَغَمَتِ الرَّائِحَةُ السُّدَّةَ *The odour opened the obstruction of the nose:* thus the verb has two contr. significations. (Ḳ.) — See also a trad. cited in art. فعم, conj. 4. —— فَغَمَ said of a rose, or flower, (Ṣ, TA,) aor. ـَ, inf. n. فُغُومٌ, (TA,) *It opened;* as also ↑تفغّم. (Ṣ, TA.) —— فَغَمَ, (Ṣ, Ḳ, TA,) inf. n. فَغْمٌ; (TA;) and ↑فاغم, (Ṣ,* Ḳ, TA,) inf. n. فِغَامٌ (Ṣ, TA) and مُفَاغَمَةٌ; (Ṣ;) *He kissed* (Ṣ, Ḳ, TA) him, or it, (Ṣ,) or a woman. (Ḳ, TA.) — And فَغِمَ said of a kid, (Ḳ, TA,) inf. n. فَغَمٌ, (TA,) *He sucked* (Ḳ, TA) *the dug of his mother.* (TA.) —— فَغِمَ بِهِ, (Ṣ, Ḳ,) aor. ـَ, (Ḳ,) inf. n. فَغَمٌ, (Ṣ,) *He was,* or *became, attached to it, fond of it,* or *eagerly desirous of it.* (Ṣ, Ḳ.) And فَغَمُ الكَلْبِ signifies *The dog's being attached,* or *accustomed,* or *habituated, to the chase.* (TA.) — And فَغِمَ بِالمَكَانِ, (Ḳ, TA,) inf. n. فَغَمٌ, (TA,) *He resided, stayed, dwelt,* or *abode, in the place;* and *kept,* or *clave, to it;* (Ḳ, TA;) *not quitting it.* (TA.)

3: see the preceding paragraph.

4. افغم *He filled* a vessel: (Ḳ:) and so افعم. (TA.) — And *It filled* its place *with its odour;* (Ḳ;) as also افعم [q. v.]. (TA.)

5: see 1.

7. انفغم, said of a زُكَام [or defluxion from the head], *It was,* or *became, removed, cleared away,* or *dispelled;* syn. اِنْفَرَجَ; (Ḳ;) as also ↑افتغم. (TA.)

8: see what next precedes.

فَغَمٌ *What one extracts from the interstices of his teeth,* (Ḳ, TA,) *of what has clung thereto.* (TA.) It is said in a trad., كُلُوا الوَغْمَ وَاطْرَحُوا الفَغَمَ [*Eat ye the* وغم *and throw ye away the* فغم]; in which, accord. to IAth, by the فغم is meant what is expl. above; and by the وغم, *what falls, portion after portion, of the food:* but some, he adds, say that the converse is the case. (TA.)

فَغْمٌ and ↑فَغَمٌ The *mouth, altogether:* or the *chin with the two lateral portions of its jaw;* (Ḳ, TA; [i. e. بِلَحْيَيْهِ; for which the CḲ has بِلِحْيَتِهِ;]) and so ↑فُغْمٌ: (TA:) or, accord. to Sh, فَغْمٌ signifies the *nose:* but accord. to Kr, it is ↑فَغَمٌ that has this meaning. (TA.) أَخَذَ بِفَغْمِهِ, a phrase mentioned by AZ, is expl. as meaning *He took hold of his chin together with the two lateral portions of its jaw:* or, accord. to Sh, it means *he took hold of his nose:* (TA:) or it means †*he distressed, afflicted, troubled,* or *molested, him.* (Ḳ, TA.)

فَغَمٌ: see the next preceding paragraph.

هُوَ فَغِمٌ بِهِ (Ṣ, TA) and ↑مُفْغَمٌ بِهِ (Ḳ, TA) *He is attached to it, fond of it,* or *eagerly desirous of it.* (Ṣ, Ḳ, TA.) And كَلْبٌ فَغِمٌ عَلَى الصَّيْدِ [*A dog attached, &c., or accustomed, or habituated,* (see 1,) *to the chase*]: (Ṣ:) or كَلْبٌ فَغِمٌ [alone] *a dog eagerly desirous of the chase.* (TA.)

فُغْمٌ: see فَغْمٌ.

فَغْمَةُ الطِّيبِ *The odour of perfume:* (Ṣ, TA:) and so فَغْوَتُهُ. (TA.) And فَغْمَةُ رِيحِ الخَمْرِ *The fragrance of the odour of wine*]. (Z, TA voce عَصْفَة.)

مُفْغَمٌ: see فَغِمٌ.

مَفْغُومٌ *A thing perfumed with aromatics.* (TA.) —— And [A man] *affected with a* زُكَام [or *defluxion from the head*]. (TA.)

فغى and فغو

1. فَغَا, (Ḳ, TA,) inf. n. فَغْوٌ, (TA,) *It* (a thing) *became revealed, disclosed,* or *divulged;* syn. فَشَا. (Ḳ, TA.) — And *Its odour became perceptible,* or *perceived:* occurring in a trad. in this sense, said of saffron: or, as some relate it, the verb in that instance is ↑افغى, which means *it flowered,* or *blossomed.* (TA.) — And, said of seed-produce (زَرْع), *It dried, became dry,* or *dried up.* (Ḳ.) —— فَغِىَ, aor. يَفْغَى, inf. n. فَغًا, said of dates (تَمْر), *i. q.* حشف, [app. a mistranscription, unless there be such as حَشِفَ, which seems to be not improbable, as one says تَمْرٌ حَشِفٌ, and حَشَفٌ also; but it can hardly be doubted that the meaning is, *They became bad, such as are termed* حَشَف or حَشَف, or, which is nearly the same, *such as are termed* فَغًا]: so says Aboo-'Alee El-Ḳálee. (TA.)

4. افغى *It* (a plant, Ṣ, [app., accord. to the Ḳ, the plant حِنَّاء,]) *put forth its* فَاغِيَة [i. e. *flower,* or *blossom*]. (Ṣ, Ḳ.) See also 1. — افغت النَّخْلَةُ *The palm-tree became in a bad, or corrupt, state* [*with respect to its fruit,* as is implied in the Ṣ; i. e. *bore dates such as are termed* غفا]. (Ṣ, Ḳ.) — And [hence, app.,] افغى (said of a man, TA) *He became poor after being rich:* and *He became ugly after being handsome:* and *He rebelled after being obedient:* (Ḳ, TA:) all from IAạr: as though his state became bad, or corrupt, like as do unripe dates. (TA.) — And, said of a man, *He kept constantly to the eating of* فَغًا, (Ḳ, TA,) i. e. *unripe dates in an altered state.* (TA.) —— And افغى فُلَانًا *He angered such a one.* (Ḳ, TA.) One says, مَا الَّذِى أَفْغَاكَ [*What is it that angered thee? or, hath angered thee?*]. (TA.)

فَاغِيَةٌ: see فَغْوٌ.

فَغًا [or فَغًى] *i. q.* غَفًا [or غَفًى] in its several meanings (Ḳ, TA) that have been mentioned [in art. غفو and غفى]: and among these it has that of The *bad* of anything. (TA.) And The [*refuse termed*] حُثَالَة [q. v.] of wheat. (TA.) And *A dust that comes upon unripe dates, spoiling them, and rendering them* [*in the skin*] *like the wings of the* [*locusts, or the like, called*] جَنَادِب [pl. of جُنْدَب]. (TA.) And Unripe dates [themselves] (Ṣ, TA) *such as are bad and* مُغْبَرّ [i. e. *of a hue like dust*]; (Ṣ;) or *such as are* مُتَغَيِّر [i. e. *altered* for the worse]. (TA.) — And فَغَا الإِبِلِ *The small, or young, of camels.* (TA.) —— And accord. to the Ḳ, الفغا signifies مَيَلٌ فِى العلبة والجفنة; but this is a mistake; correctly it signifies مَيَلٌ فِى الفَمِ وَالعُلْبَةِ وَالجَفْنَةِ, meaning فِى العُلْبَةِ والجَفْنَةِ [i. e. *A distortion in the mouth,* and *in the kinds of bowl called* عُلْبَة *and* جَفْنَة], as expl.

by ISd: Kr says that it signifies *a certain malady*, which ISd thinks to be *a distortion in the mouth*, an explanation given by IAạr. (TA.)

فَغْوَةُ الطِّيبِ *The odour of perfume*; like فَغْمَةٌ: (TA in art. فغم:) or *the state of spreading of the odour of perfume*. (TA in the present art.)

فَاغِيَةٌ and ↓ فَغْوٌ The *flower of the* حِنَّآء [i.e. *Lawsonia inermis*, or *Egyptian privet*]; (Fr, Ṣ, Ḳ;) as also فَاغِيَةٌ: (Ḳ in art. فغو or فغى:) or both signify the *flower*, or *blossom, of anything* [i. e. *of any plant*, or, app., *of any fragrant plant*: see Ḥam p. 713]: or, as is said in a trad., the فاغية is the *prince*, or *chief, of the sweet-smelling plants of Paradise*: Sh says that ↓ الفَغْوُ signifies نَوْرٌ وَرَائِحَةٌ طَيِّبَةٌ [*a flower*, or *blossom*; and *a sweet odour*: but I think that we should read نَوْرٌ ذُو رَائِحَةٍ طَيِّبَةٍ *a sort of flower*, or *blossom, having a sweet odour*]: and IAạr says that the فاغية is the *best and* the *most fragrant of sweet-smelling plants*: (TA:) or it is the *flower produced by a branch of the* حِنَّآء *that has been planted inverted, and which is sweeter than* [*that of*] *the* [*common*] حِنَّآء. (Ḳ.)

فقا

1. فَقَأَ العَيْنَ, (Ṣ, Mgh, O, Mṣb, Ḳ,) aor. َ, (Mṣb, Ḳ,) inf. n. فَقْءٌ, (Ṣ, Mgh, O,) *He put out the eye*; or *blinded it*; or *made it to sink in its socket*; syn. بَخَقَهَا; (Lḥ, Ṣ, O, Ḳ;) as also ↓ فَقَّأَهَا, (Ṣ, O, Ḳ,) inf. n. تَفْقِئَةٌ: (Ṣ, O:) or, accord. to the Mṣb, بَخَصَهَا; which is said by Es-Saraḳusṭee to mean *he put his finger into the eye and pulled it out*; and by IḲṭṭ to mean *he extinguished its light*; and by some to mean *he slit it*, or *rent it*: (TA:) or *he slit*, or *rent, the portion of the eye that is surrounded by the white thereof*: (Mgh:) or *i. q.* قَلَعَهَا; (Ḳ, TA;) i. e. [*he pulled out the eye*; or], as some say, *he pulled out the portion of the eye which is surrounded by the white, and with which one sees*: (TA: [and the like is said in the Mgh in explanation of القَلْعُ, but this is there said to differ from الفَقْءُ:]) or, as some say, *he put his finger into the eye and so slit*, or *rent, it*: (TA:) or *he broke*, or *ruptured, the eye*; syn. كَسَرَهَا; and so البَثْرَةَ [*the pimple*, or *the small*, or *purulent, pustule*]; and the like of these: (Ḳ: [and to all of these the two other explanations mentioned above as from the Ḳ are likewise there, improperly, made to relate:]) this last explanation, in the Ḳ, is said by MF to be unknown; but it is mentioned in the A and L, and by more than one of the leading lexicologists: (TA:) [accord. to Mṭr,] فَقَأْتُ البَثْرَةَ means *I slit the pimple*, &c., or *rent it* [*open*]. (Mgh, Mṣb.) Among the Arabs in the Time of Ignorance, when a man's camels amounted to a thousand, he put out (فَقَأَ) an eye of one of them (a بَعِير), and set it free to pasture where it would, and made no use of it. (TA.) — فَقَأَ اللّٰهُ عَنْكَ عَيْنَ الكَمَالِ is a tropical saying [app. meaning *May God prevent from seeing thee the fatal eye*: the term عين الكمال being applied to an eye believed to have the power of killing by its glance]. (A, TA.) — And فَقَأَ نَاظِرَيْهِ, (O, Ḳ,) likewise said to be a tropical phrase, (TA,) means ‡ *He dispelled his anger*. (O, Ḳ.) — And فَقَأَ عَيْنَهُ also means [sometimes] ‡ *He struck him*; or *struck him vehemently with a broad thing*, or *with anything*; or *slapped him with his hand*: or *he was rough, rude*, or *ungentle, to him in speech*. (TA in art. عين.) — And فَقَأَتِ البُهْمَى, inf. n. فُقُوءٌ, (O, Ḳ, TA,) or, accord. to the L, فَقْءٌ, (TA,) *The* [*barley-grass termed*] بهمى *was rendered dusty by rain, or by a torrent, so that the cattle would not eat it until it became clean*: (O, Ḳ, TA:) and in like manner one says of any plant. (O, TA.) [See also 1 in art. فقا.] — And, as some say, (TA,) or ↓ تفقّأت, (Ṣ, O, TA,) ‡ *The envelopes* [or *glumes*] *of the* بُهْمَى *burst open so as to disclose* (Ṣ, O, TA) *its fruit* [or *seeds*], (Ṣ, O,) or *its flower*. (TA.)

2: see 1, first sentence. — لَا يُفَقِّئُ البَيْضَ, (IJ, TA,) or لَا يَتَفَقَّأُ ↓ البَيْضَ, (A, TA,) † [*He will not break*, or *burst, eggs*, or *the eggs*,] is said of a weak and quiet man, (IJ, TA,) or of an impotent man. (A, TA.)

4. افقأ *His breast*, or *chest, became depressed* (انْخَسَفَ), *in consequence of a malady, or an accident*; (IAạr, O, TA;) said of a man. (IAạr, O.) [But see فَقَأٌ and أَفْقَأُ.]

5: see 7, in two places. — It is also said of the corpse that has lain long upon the field of battle, meaning *It rent*, or *burst*. (Mgh.) And one says, تَفَقَّأْتُ شَحْمًا † [*I almost burst with fat*]: (Ṣ:) [and] تَفَقَّأَتِ الشَّاةُ شَحْمًا [*the sheep*, or *goat, almost burst with fat*]: (O:) شحما being in the accus. case as a specificative. (Ṣ, O.) And أَكَلَ حَتَّى كَادَ بَطْنُهُ يَتَفَقَّأُ † *He ate until his belly almost burst*. (A, TA.) And أَكَلَ حَتَّى كَادَ ↓ يَنْفَقِئُ † [*He ate until he almost burst*]. (O: in the TA with بَكَى [*he wept*] in the place of اكل, and with بَطْنُهُ after ينفقئ.) — And تَفَقَّأَتِ السَّحَابَةُ عَنْ مَائِهَا ‡ *The cloud burst with its water*. (Ṣ,* O,* TA.) — See also 1, last sentence. = And see 2.

7. انفقأت العَيْنُ and ↓ تفقّأت, quasi-pass. vs., [the former] of فَقَأَ العَيْنَ and [the latter] of فَقَّأَهَا as expl. in the first sentence of this art.; (Ḳ, TA;) [thus signifying *The eye became put out*; or *blinded*; or *made to sink in its socket*: &c.: or *it broke*; or *became broken*, or *ruptured*:] and so البَثْرَةُ [*the pimple*, or *the small*, or *purulent, pustule*]: and the like of these: (Ḳ, TA:) the former, (Mgh,) or each, (Mṣb,) said of a بَثْرَة, means *it* [*broke*, or] *rent*, or *burst*: (Mgh, Mṣb:) and thus ↓ تفقّأ said of [a pustule such as is termed] a دُمَّل, (Ṣ, Mgh, O,) and of [such as is termed] a قَرْح. (Ṣ, O.) — See also 5.

8. افتقأ الخَرْزَ is expl. in the Ḳ as meaning أَعَادَ عَلَيْهِ وَجَعَلَ بَيْنَ الكُلْبَتَيْنِ كُلْبَةً أُخْرَى; [and in like manner in the O, except that the latter has كُلْبَةً and الكُلْبَتَيْنِ; and so have several copies of the Ḳ;] but this meaning is assigned by Lḥ to اقتفأ, which see for a fuller explanation. (TA.)

فَقْءٌ (Ṣ, O, Ḳ) and (O, Ḳ) accord. to Ks and Fr (O) ↓ فُقَأَةٌ [in the CḲ فَقَاةٌ] and ↓ فَقَاةٌ (O, Ḳ) and in some copies of the Ḳ ↓ فُقَّاءَةٌ (TA) and ↓ فَاقِيَآءُ, (Ḳ,) originally فَاقِئَآءُ, (TA,) The [*membrane called*] سَابِيَآء (Ṣ, O, Ḳ) *which comes forth* عَلَى رَأْسِ الوَلَدِ [*upon the head of the young one*, meaning *at the time of bringing forth*,] (Ṣ, O,) or *which rends open from off the head of the young one* [*at the time of bringing forth*]: (Ḳ:) pl. [of the first] فُقُوءٌ: (TA:) or *a small, thin, piece of skin, which is upon the nose of the young one, and which, if not removed from it*, (O, Ḳ,) *at the birth*, (O,) *causes its death*, (O, Ḳ,) is thus termed, (Ḳ,) or is termed ↓ فُقَأَةٌ, by IAạr: (O:) or, accord. to Aṣ, the *water* [or *fluid*] *that is* عَلَى رَأْسِ الوَلَدِ [app. meaning that is *discharged at the time of the birth* (see 2 in the arts. ربق and رمد)]: and accord. to IAạr, the *water* [or *fluid*] *that is in the* مَشِيمَة [or *membrane enclosing the fœtus in the womb*] is termed فَقْءٌ and سُخْدٌ and سُخْتٌ and نُخْطٌ: (TA:) it is also said that فَقْوٌ signifies *a certain white thing that comes forth from the woman or the she-camel in parturition, and which is an envelope wherein is much water* or *fluid*; mentioned by A'Obeyd as with hemz [i.e. written فَقْءٌ], and said by him to be the سَابِيَآء [q. v.]. (TA in art. فقو.) — And فَقْءٌ signifies also *A small hollow*, or *cavity, in stone*, or *a rugged place, that collects water*: (Ḳ:) or it is [*a hollow*, or *cavity*,] *like a* حُفْرَة or جُفْرَة, *in the midst of a* [*stony place such as is termed*] حَرَّة, (Sh, O, TA,) or *in the midst of a mountain*: (TA:) and ↓ فَقِئٌ signifies the same: (Ḳ:) the pl. (of the former, O, or of the latter, TA) is فُقْآنٌ. (O, TA.)

فَقَأٌ *A protuberance*, or *swelling out*, (O, TA,) *of the back*, (O,) or *of the breast*, or *chest*. (TA.) [But see 4, and see also أَفْقَأُ.]

فَقَاةٌ: see فَقْءٌ, in two places. — Also ‡ *A cloud in which is neither thunder nor lightning, and the rain of which is* مُتَقَارِب [app. meaning *drawing near*: as though likened to the membrane thus called]. (O,* TA. [In the former written, in this instance, فُقَاءَة, which I think to be a mistranscription by the copyist.])

فُقَّاءَةٌ: see فَقْءٌ.

فَقْآى: see the next paragraph.

فَقِئٌ A he-camel *affected with a disease termed* حَقْوَة [q. v.], *in consequence of which he voids not his urine nor his dung*; (O, Ḳ;*) *and sometimes*, or *often, his veins and his flesh become choked with blood, and swollen; and if slaughtered and cooked, the cooking-pot becomes full of blood; and sometimes*, or *often, his stomach becomes so much inflated*, or *swollen, that it rends*, or *bursts*: and it is likewise applied to a she-camel: (O:) and ↓ فَقْآى signifies the same applied to a she-camel. (Ḳ.) — Also (i. e. فَقِئٌ) The *disease above-*

mentioned, itself. (O, Ḳ.) ═ See also فَقْءٌ, latter sentence.

فُقَآءَةٌ : } see فَقْءٌ.
فَاقِيَآءُ :

أَفْقَأُ *Having a protuberant breast*, or *chest*. (IAạr, TA in art. فسأ.) [But see 4, and see also فَقًا.]

مُفَقِّئَةٌ Valleys, or water-courses, or torrent-beds, (أَوْدِيَةٌ,) *that cleave the earth.* (O, Ḳ.)

فقح

1. فَقَحَ : see 2. — Said of a plant, *It became tall*, or *full-grown, and blossomed.* (Ḳ.) ═ فَقَحَ فُلَانًا *He*, or *it, hit*, or *struck, such a one in his* فَقْحَة [q. v.]. (Ḳ.) ═ And فَقَحَ الشَّىْءَ, (Ḳ,) aor. ـَ, inf. n. فَقْحٌ, (TA,) *i. q.* سَفَّهُ [i. e. *He took the thing into his mouth, not moistened,*] *like as one does medicine:* (Ḳ, TA:) of the dial. of El-Yemen. (TA.)

2. فقّح, (Ṣ, Ḳ,) inf. n. تَفْقِيحٌ, (Ṣ,) *He* (a whelp) *opened his eyes for the first time;* (Ṣ, Ḳ;) as also ▼ فَقَحَ, aor. ـَ, (Ḳ,) inf. n. فَقْحٌ. (TA.) It is said in a trad., فَقَّحْنَا وَصَأْصَأْتُمْ, (Ṣ, TA) ‡ *We have opened our eyes for the first time, and ye have kept your eyes closed;* (TA;) meaning *the truth has become manifest to us, and ye have been blind to it;* (AO, A,* TA;) or *we have seen our right course, and ye have not seen* [*yours*]. (IB, TA.) And فقّح الشَّجَرُ *The trees burst their buds, and made the extremities of their leaves to appear.* (L.)

5. تفقّح *It opened;* syn. تَفَتَّحَ: (Ḳ:) it is said in this sense of a rose, (Ṣ, A, TA,) and of any flower, or blossom: (TA:) some say that it signifies تفتّح absolutely: others, peculiarly فِى الكَلَامِ. (Az, as quoted in the L. [See تَفَتَّحَ فِى الكَلَامِ (a well-known phrase) in art. فتح: but فى الكلام in the present case appears, from what precedes, to be evidently a mistranscription for فِى الكِمَامِ, i. e., *in relation to calyxes.*])

6. تفاقحوا *They put* [or *turned*] *their backs one towards another;* (Ṣ, Ḳ;) [from فَقْحَةٌ, q. v.;] like as you say تَظَاهَرُوا [and تَدَابَرُوا] and [in the contr. sense] تَقَابَلُوا. (Ṣ, TA.)

فَقْحَةٌ : see فُقَّاحٌ. — Also The *anus:* (Ṣ, Ḳ:) because it opens in the case of need: (Ḥam p. 677:) or *a wide*, or *an ample, anus:* (Ḳ, MF:) or *a wide* دُبُر: or *a* دُبُر *with what it comprises:* and afterwards, by reason of frequency of usage, applied to signify *any* دُبُر: (L:) pl. فِقَاحٌ. (Ṣ, Ḳ.) — And The *palm of the hand;* as also ▼ فَقَاحَةٌ: (Ḳ:) of the dial. of El-Yemen: so called because of its width. (TA.) — And The *napkin* (مِنْدِيل) *of* الإِحْرَام [i. e., *which is used by one performing the rites of the* حَجّ or *of the* عُمْرَة]: (Ḳ:) of the dial. of El-Yemen. (TA.)

فَقَاحَةٌ : see the next preceding paragraph.

فُقَّاحٌ *A certain herb,* (Ḳ, TA,) *resembling the* أُقْحُوَان [or *chamomile*] *in its growth and its place of growth;* n. un. with ة: it is *one of the plants growing in the sands; and it is said that its flower is more contracted than that of the chamomile, and that the dust, or earth, sticks to it as it does to the* [*herb called*] حَمَصِيص: (TA:) or the *flower of the* إِذْخِر [or *juncus odoratus*]; (Ṣ, Ḳ, TA;) said by Az to be *a sort of perfume, sometimes put into medicine, called* فُقَّاحُ الإِذْخِرِ; and it is the *flower of the* إِذْخِر *when its calyx opens:* (TA:) or the *flower*, or *blossom, of any plant,* (Ḳ, TA,) *when it opens, whatever be its* لَوْن [i. e. *colour*, or *kind*]; (TA;) as also ▼ فَقْحَةٌ, (Ḳ, TA,) thus with fet-ḥ and sukoon. (TA. [Written by Golius فُقْحَةٌ.]) — Also ‡ *A woman of goodly*, or *beautiful, make*, or *form.* (Kr, Ḳ, TA.)

عَلَى فُلَانٍ حُلَّةٌ فُقَّاحِيَّةٌ *Upon such a one is a* حُلَّة [q. v.] *of the colour of the rose when it is about to open.* (Ṣ.)

هُوَ مُتَفَقِّحٌ لِلشَّرِّ † *He is in a state of preparation for evil*, or *mischief.*

فقد

1. فَقَدَهُ, (Ṣ, A, MA, Mgh, O, L, Mṣb, Ḳ,) aor. ـِ, (Ṣ, A, O, &c.,) inf. n. فَقْدٌ and فِقْدَانٌ (Ṣ, MA, O, L, Mṣb, Ḳ) and فُقْدَانٌ (Ṣ, O, F) and فُقُودٌ; (IDrd, O, L, Ḳ;) and ▼ افتقده; (Ṣ, A, MA, Mgh, O;) *He found it not,* (L, TA,) *lost it,* (MA, PṢ, &c.,) *saw it not,* (JK in explanation of the latter verb,) [*missed*, or *failed of finding* or *seeing, it,*] *it was*, or *became, absent from him,* (Mgh,) or *he had it not, was destitute of it, was without it, lacked it,* or *wanted it*, syn. عَدِمَهُ; (Mṣb, L, Ḳ;) but accord. to Er-Rághib, الفَقْدُ has a more special signification than العَدَمُ, this latter being the contr. of الوُجُودُ; (TA;) [whereas] الفَقْدُ [as inf. n. of فُقِدَ, though often used as meaning *the being non-existent*, properly] signifies *the thing's being absent from the range of perception by sense so that its place is not known.* (Bḍ in xii. 71.) [فُقِدَ signifies *It was not found, was lost, was not seen,* &c.] It is related of Abu-d-Dardà that he said, مَنْ يَتَفَقَّدْ ▼ يَفْقِدْ, [lit. *He who seeks will not find,*] meaning *he who seeks after good in mankind will not find it;* for he saw good to be rare in mankind: or *he who seeks to acquaint himself with the circumstances of men will not find what will please him.* (L.)

4. أَفْقَدَهُ اللّٰهُ إِيَّاهُ *God caused him to lose*, or *fail of finding, him*, or *it.* (L, Ḳ.) One says, أَفْقَدَكَ اللّٰهُ كُلَّ حَمِيمٍ [*May God cause thee to lose every relation*, or *loved and loving relation*]. (A.) [Or] الإِفْقَادُ is not of established authority: as to the saying الجُنُونُ يُفْقِدُ شَهْوَةَ الجِمَاعِ [meaning *Insanity causes to lose*, or *annuls, the desire of coïtus*], the correct word is يُعْدِمُ or يُزِيلُ. (Mgh.)

5. تفقّدهُ *He sought it*, or *sought for it* or *after it;* or *did so leisurely* or *repeatedly;* (A,* Mgh, L;) as also ▼ افتقدهُ: (Mgh, L:) or *he sought it*, or *sought for it* or *after it, it being absent from him;* (Ṣ, O, L, Mṣb, Ḳ;) as also ▼ افتقدهُ: (Ḳ:) or *he sought*, or *sought leisurely* or *repeatedly, to obtain knowledge of it, having lost it:* so accord. to Er-Rághib and many others; but this expression and تَعَهَّدَهُ are used, by some, each in the place of the other, and the latter, accord. to Er-Rághib and many others, [properly] signifies *he sought*, or *sought leisurely* or *repeatedly, to obtain knowledge of it, having known it before.* (MF.) You say, مَا تَفَقَّدْتُهُ مُنْذُ ▼ ٱفْتَقَدْتُهُ, meaning منذ فَقَدْتُهُ [i. e. *I have not sought for*, or *after, him*, or *it, since I lost him*, or *it.* (B, TA.) See also 1, last sentence. — [Also *He investigated it.*]

6. تفاقدوا means فَقَدَ بَعْضُهُمْ بَعْضًا [i. e. *They lost one another*]. (Ṣ, O, Ḳ.)

8 : see 1: — and see also 5, in three places.

الفَقْدُ, (O, Ḳ,) by Az, (Ḳ,) or in a number of the copies of the work of Az, (O,) erroneously written الفَقَدُ, (O, Ḳ,) *A certain plant,* (Ḳ,) *resembling the* [*species of cuscuta, or dodder, called*] كَشُوث: (TA:) and *a beverage prepared from raisins* or *honey* or [*the plant*] كشوث, as also ▼ الفُقْدُدُ: (Ḳ:) or, as AḤn says, *a certain plant which is thrown into the beverage of honey, which beverage consequently becomes strong, and is then called* الفَقْدُ: he says, the فَقْد is *what is called in Pers.* فَنْجَنْكُشْت: IAạr says, ▼ الفِقْدَةُ [or الفَقَدَةُ? the n. un.] is *the* كشوث: and *a beverage prepared from raisins and honey;* and it is said that *a beverage* (نَبِيذ) *is made of honey, and then the* فَقْد *is thrown into it, and causes it to become strong:* so says Lth: and he says that the فَقْد is *a plant resembling the* كشوث: and ▼ الفُقْدُدُ is *the* نَبِيذ *of the* كشوث. (O.)

الفِقْدَةُ : see the next preceding paragraph.

الفُقْدُدُ : see الفَقْدُ, in two places.

فَقِيدٌ and ▼ مَفْقُودٌ signify the same, (O, Mṣb, Ḳ,) [*Not found, lost, not seen, missed, non-existent,*] *absent from one,* (Mgh in explanation of the latter,) *not had, lacking* or *lacked, wanting* or *wanted.* (Mṣb, Ḳ.) One says, مَاتَ غَيْرَ فَقِيدٍ وَلَا حَمِيدٍ, (A, Ḳ,) and غَيْرَ ▼ مَفْقُودٍ وَلَا مَحْمُودٍ, (A,) [*He died unmissed and unpraised;* or,] *without his loss being cared for* [*and without being praised*]. (A, Ḳ.)

فَاقِدٌ [as act. part. n. of 1 signifies *Not finding* a thing, *losing* it, *not seeing* it, *missing* it, *not having* it, *being destitute* of it, *lacking* it, or *wanting* it; or *having failed to find* it, *having lost* it, or *having failed to see* it. — And hence,] A woman *who is bereft of her child* [*by death*]: (A'Obeyd:) or *who loses* (تَفْقِدُ) *her husband* or *child:* (Ṣ, O:) or *whose husband*, or *child,* (L, Ḳ, TA,) or *relation*, or *loved and loving relation,* (TA,) *has died:* (L, Ḳ, TA:) or *who marries after the death of her husband.* (Lth, L, Ḳ.) The Arabs say, لَا تَتَزَوَّجَنَّ فَاقِدًا وَتَزَوَّجْ مُطَلَّقَةً [*Do not thou marry a woman whose husband has died, but* [rather] *marry thou a divorced woman*]. (Lḥ, L.) —— And in like manner, (O,) it is applied also to a she-gazelle, (Ṣ, O, L,) and to a cow [app. a wild cow], (O, L, Ḳ,) as also ▼ فَاقِدَةٌ, (O,) meaning *Whose young one has been devoured by a beast*, or *bird, of prey*; (O, L, Ḳ;) and to a pigeon (حَمَامَة) likewise. (L.)

مَفْقُودٌ : see فَقِيدٌ, in two places.

فقر

1. فَقَرَ, (TA,) [aor., app., ـُ and ـِ,] inf. n. فَقْرٌ, (O, Ḳ, TA,) *He dug* the ground; (O,* Ḳ,* TA;) as also ▼ فقّر, (TA,) inf. n. تَفْقِيرٌ. (Ḳ, TA.) And *He dug* a well *to draw forth the water*. (TA.) —— And فَقْرٌ signifies The *boring*, or *perforating*, of beads for the purpose of stringing; (Ḳ;) [as also ▼ تَفْقِيرٌ; for one says] ▼ فَقَّرْتُ [as well as فَقَرْتُ], meaning *I bored*, or *perforated*, beads. (Ṣ.) —— And The act of *cleaving*, *slitting*, or *rending*. (O.) [See also 8.] —— And فَقَرَ أَنْفَ البَعِيرِ, (Ṣ, O, Ḳ,*) [and فَقَرَ البَعِيرَ also, as is indicated in the TA,] aor. ـُ and ـِ, inf. n. فَقْرٌ, (Ḳ,) *He made an incision in the nose* [or *muzzle*] *of the camel*, (Ṣ, O, Ḳ, TA,) the beast being refractory, (TA,) *with an iron instrument*, (Ṣ, O, TA,) *so as to reach to the bone*, (Ḳ, TA,) or *nearly so*, (TA,) *then put upon the place of the incision the* [*cord called*] جَرِير, (Ṣ, O, TA,*) *with a* [*string such as is termed*] وَتَر *wound upon it*, (Ṣ, O,) *to render him tractable*, or *to train him*, *thereby*: (Ṣ, O, Ḳ, TA:) sometimes the refractory camel has three incisions made in his muzzle; and when his owner desires to render him tractable, and to prevent him from being brisk above measure, he puts the جرير upon the incision that is next to his lip, and in consequence he governs him as he will; and if he be between the refractory and the tractable, he puts the جرير upon the intermediate incision, and in consequence he exceeds in his pace; and if he desire that he should stretch forth and go without inconvenience to his owner, he puts the جرير upon the uppermost incision. (Aboo-Ziyád, L.) [The incision above mentioned is termed ▼ فُقْرَةٌ.] —— Hence, app., by a tropical usage, فَقَرَ signifies † *He stigmatized* a man: Freytag has mentioned it as occurring in the Deewán of the Hudhalees, and meaning "*satyra perstrinxit eius vitia commemorans* aliquem."] ═══ [فَقَرَهُ, aor. ـُ, inf. n. فَقْرٌ, *He*, or *it*, *broke the* فَقَار (or *vertebræ*) *of his back*. —— Hence the phrase,] فَقَرَتْهُ الفَاقِرَةُ, (Ṣ, O,) or الدَّاهِيَةُ, aor. ـِ, inf. n. فَقْرٌ, (Mṣb,) [lit.] *The calamity broke the vertebræ of his back*: (Ṣ, O:) [meaning] *the calamity befell him*. (Mṣb.) ═══ فَقُرَ, with ḍamm, [aor. ـُ,] *He had a complaint of his vertebræ*: and فَقِرَ, aor. ـَ, inf. n. فَقَرٌ, *He had a complaint of his vertebræ arising from fracture* or *disease*. (Mṣb.) —— فَقُرَ or فَقِرَ in the sense of افْتَقَرَ: see 8.

2: see 1, first and third sentences. —— فَقَّرَ لِلْوَدِيَّةِ, (Ṣ, TA,*) or لِلْفَسِيلَةِ, (Ḳ, TA,) inf. n. تَفْقِيرٌ; [and accord. to Golius, ▼ تفقّر, but for this I have not found any authority;] *He dug a hollow such as is termed* فَقِير [q. v.] *for the shoot*, or *offset*, *of a palm-tree*. (Ṣ, Ḳ, TA.) —— And فُقِّرَ, said of anything, *It was incised*, or *notched*; and *impressed*, or *marked*. (TA.) —— Lth has erroneously assigned to تَفْقِيرٌ, a meaning belonging to تَقْفِيزٌ, q. v. (TA.)

4. افقر *He* (a colt) *became fit for riding upon his* فَقَار [or *vertebræ*]; like أَرْكَبَ: (O:) or *he* (a colt, Mṣb), or *it* (the back of a colt, L), *became* [*strong in the vertebræ and*] *fit for being ridden*. (L, Mṣb.) ═══ افقرهُ نَاقَتَهُ, (Ṣ, O,) or بَعِيرَهُ, (ISk, Ḳ,) or ظَهْرَ بَعِيرِهِ, (TA,) or بَعِيرًا, (Mgh,) or دَابَّتَهُ, (A'Obeyd, TA,) or المُهْرَ, (Mṣb,) *He lent him the vertebræ* [meaning *the back*] *of his she-camel, that he might ride thereon*: (Ṣ, O:) and *he lent him the back of his camel* (ISk, Ḳ, TA) *during a journey*, (ISk, TA) *for carrying a burden*, and *for riding*, (ISk, Ḳ, TA,) *to be returned afterwards*: (ISk, TA:) and *he lent him a camel, that he might ride thereon*; from فَقَار signifying the "vertebræ" of the back: (Mgh:) and *he lent him his beast to ride as long as he pleased during a journey and then to return it to him*: (A'Obeyd, TA:) and *he lent him the colt to ride upon its vertebræ* [or *back*]. (Mṣb.) —— Hence, افقرهُ أَرْضَهُ ‡ *He lent him his land for sowing*. (TA, from a trad.) —— أَفْقَرَكَ الصَّيْدُ means *The object of the chase has enabled thee to have its vertebræ within thy power*; therefore shoot it, or shoot at it: (O, TA:) or *has enabled thee to have its side* [which is sometimes termed فَقْر] *within thy power*: (Ḳ:) or *has become near to thee*. (TA.) [The Khaleefeh] El-Weleed the son of Yezeed the son of 'Abd-El-Melik is related to have said, أَفْقَرَ بَعْدَ مَسْلَمَةَ الصَّيْدُ لِمَنْ رَمَى i. e. *The object of the chase has enabled the shooter at it to have its vertebræ within his power after Meslemeh*; meaning that, since the death of his paternal uncle Meslemeh, the territory of the Muslims had become assailable to him who might attempt it. (TA.) ═══ افقرهُ also signifies *He* (i. e. God, Ṣ, O, Ḳ, or a man, Mṣb) *rendered him* فَقِير [meaning *poor*, or *needy*, &c.]. (Ṣ, O, Mṣb, Ḳ.) ═══ مَا أَفْقَرَهُ [i. e. *How poor*, or *needy*, &c., *is he!*] and مَا أَغْنَاهُ [which has the contr. meaning] are [said to be] anomalous; for their [respective primitive] verbs are افْتَقَرَ and اسْتَغْنَى, from either of which the verb of wonder is not properly [or regularly] formed. (Ṣ, O. [But see 8.])

5. ظَهَرَ قِبَلَنَا نَاسٌ يَتَفَقَّرُونَ العِلْمَ, occurring in a trad., as some relate it, means [*There appeared before us men*] *eliciting what was recondite*, or *obscure*, *of knowledge*, and *opening what was closed thereof*; from فَقَرْتُ البِئْرَ meaning "I dug the well to draw forth the water:" but the reading commonly known is [يَتَقَفَّرُونَ, q. v.,] with the ق before the ف. (IAth, TA.) —— See also 2.

6. تفاقر *He feigned the lowliness*, or *submissiveness*, *of poverty*, *humbling*, or *abasing*, *himself with men*. (Ḳ* and TA in art. بأس.)

8. افتقر *He clave*, *slit*, or *rent*; and *opened*: [see also 1, fourth sentence:] hence its usage in a trad. of 'Omar, in which, after his saying that Imra-el-Ḳeys was the foremost of the poets, and had made the source of poetry to well forth abundantly to them, [see خَسَفَ,] he is related to have added, وَافْتَقَرَ عَنْ مَعَانٍ عُورٍ أَصَحَّ بَصَرٍ: in saying this, he attributed a sound and an opened sight to the poetry, [which he thus personified,] and in like manner he described obscure and occult meanings by applying to them the epithet عُور [generally meaning "blind of one eye"]: he meant that Imra-el-Ḳeys had made the meanings of poetry clear and perspicuous, and unveiled them, and shunned substitution and obscure diction: عَنْ with what is [to be understood as] antecedently connected with it occupies the place of a noun in the accus. case as a denotative of state: it is as though he said, فَتَحَ لِلشِّعْرِ أَصَحَّ بَصَرٍ مُجَاوِزًا لِلْمَعَانِى العُورِ مُتَخَطِّيًا لَهَا [lit. *He opened*, *to poetry*, *a most sound vision*, *passing over half-blind meanings*]. (O.) ═══ Also, (O,) *He was*, or *became*, فَقِير [meaning *poor*, or *needy*, &c.]; (Ṣ, O, Mṣb, Ḳ, &c.;) and so ▼ فَقُرَ, aor. ـُ, inf. n. فَقْرٌ; (Mṣb;) and ▼ فَقِرَ, aor. ـَ; (Ḳ;) or they said افتقر, (Sb, Mṣb, TA,) like as they said اشْتَدَّ, (Sb, TA,) but they did not say فَقُرَ, (Sb, Mṣb, TA,) like as they did not say شَدُدَ, (Sb, TA,) افتقر serving them instead of فَقُرَ; (Mṣb;) nor did they use any unaugmented form of this verb. (Sb, TA.) —— And one says, افتقر إِلَيْهِ *He*, or *it*, *wanted*, *needed*, or *required*, *him*, or *it*; [a phrase of frequent occurrence; like فَقِيرٌ إِلَيْهِ;] i. q. اِحْتَاجَ اليه. (TA in art. حوج.)

10. استفقر بَعِيرًا [*He borrowed*, or *asked for the loan of*, *the back of a camel*, *for carrying a burden* or *for riding*]. (See أَرْمَلَ.)

فَقْرٌ and ▼ فُقْرٌ signify the same, (Ṣ, O, Mṣb, Ḳ,) but the latter is bad, (Lth, TA,) and sometimes they said ▼ فُقُرٌ, (MF, TA,) *Poverty*, *want*, or *need*; *contr. of* غِنًى: (Ḳ:) or the *state of a man when he has* [*only*] *what suffices for his household*, or *those who dwell with him and whose maintenance is incumbent on him*: (ISd, Ḳ:) [other meanings are indicated by explanations of the epithet فَقِيرٌ, q. v.:] ▼ مَفَاقِرُ [signifying *needs*, or *wants*,] is said by some to be a pl. of فَقْرٌ, anomalous, like مَشَابِهُ [pl. of شَبَهٌ] and مَلَامِحُ [pl. of لَمْحَةٌ]: or it may be a pl. of ▼ مَفْقَرٌ, an inf. n. of فَقُرَ; or pl. of ▼ مُفْقِرٌ; or it has no sing.: (TA:) you say, سَدَّ اللّٰهُ مَفَاقِرَهُ ▼ *God rendered him*, or *may God render him*, *free from want*; (Ṣ, Mṣb, Ḳ;) [lit.] *God supplied*, or *may God supply*, *his various needs*, or *wants*. (Ṣ, Ḳ.) —— And فَقْرٌ signifies also *Anxiety*; or *disquietude*, or *trouble*, *of mind*: pl. فُقُورٌ: (O, Ḳ, TA:) one says, شَكَى إِلَيْهِ فُقُورَهُ *He complained to him of his anxieties*; &c.:

and it means also, *his circumstances*, and *wants*: (TA:) [for,] accord. to IAạr, the phrase فُقُورُ النَّفْسِ is like شُقُورُهَا. (O.) ═ See also فِقْرَةٌ.

فَقْرٌ : see the next preceding paragraph. ═ Also The *side*: pl. فُقُورٌ, (Ḳ, TA,) which is extr. [in respect of analogy]: mentioned by Kr. (TA.) [See أَفْقَرَكَ الصَّيْدُ.]

فَقْرٌ : see فِقْرَةٌ.

فَقُرٌ : see فَقِيرٌ, former half, in two places.

فُقْرٌ : see فَقْرٌ.

فِقْرَةٌ : see فَقَارٌ. ═ Accord. to the Ḳ, it signifies also *A certain plant*; and its pl. [or rather the coll. gen. n.] is † فِقَرٌ: but the sing. [or n. un.] is correctly † فَقُرَةٌ, with fet-ḥ and then ḍamm, mentioned by Sb as a word of a rare form, of which the pl. [or coll. gen. n.] is † فَقُرٌ, as it has no broken pl.; and expl. by Th. (TA.)

فُقْرَةٌ *A hollow dug in the ground*: pl. فُقَرٌ. (O, Ḳ, TA.) — And The [*incision termed*] قُرْمَةٌ (IAạr, O, TA) *that is made in the nose* [or *muzzle*] (IAạr, O) *of the camel*, (IAạr, O, TA,) [*in order to render him tractable*, (see 1, near the beginning,)] *after which* [*if necessary*] *another is made*, [*above it*,] *and then another, until he becomes gentle*: (IAạr, O:) pl. [of pauc. أَفْقُرٌ, occurring in the L, evidently as a pl. of فُقْرَةٌ in this sense, and, of mult., but also used as a pl. of pauc.,] فُقَرٌ. (O, TA.) Hence the saying of 'Áïsheh, in relation to [the murder of] 'Othmán, [app. alluding to its involving three violations, namely, the violation of the sacredness of the city in which it was perpetrated and of the month in which it occurred and of the person of the Khaleefeh,] بَلَغْتُمْ مِنْهُ الفُقَرَ الثَّلَاثَ, meaning ‡ *Ye have done to him the like of your deed to the camel above mentioned* [*upon which ye have inflicted the three* فُقَر]: thus expl. by AZ. (TA.) Accord. to AHeyth, فُقَر means † *Great*, or *grievous*, or *formidable, events*. (O.) And the three فُقَرَات of the son of Adam are said to be † *The day of birth and the day of death and the day of resurrection*. (O.) — Also The *part, of a shirt, that is the place into which the head is inserted*. (Ḳ.) ═ Also *Nearness*. (Ḳ.) And one says, هُوَ مِنِّى فُقْرَةً, meaning *He is near to me*. (Ḳ,* TA.) ═ See also مُفْقِرٌ.

فِقْرَةٌ : see فَقَارٌ. — [Hence] الفِقَرَاتُ is a name of † *The star* [or *stars*] *in the* خَرَزَات [meaning *joints of the tail*] *of Scorpio*. (Ḳzw in his descr. of Scorpio.) And فِقَرٌ signifies † *Certain ornaments, moulded*, or *fashioned, in the form of the vertebræ of the back*: (A, KT, TA, and Ḥar p. 34:) one of which is termed فِقْرَةٌ. (Ḥar ibid.) — And hence, (KT,) or as being likened to a vertebra of the back, (Ṣ, O, KT,) ‡ The *best verse in an ode* is termed فِقْرَةٌ. (Ṣ, O, Ḳ, KT.) — And hence, as being likened to the best verse in an ode, فِقْرَة means ‡‡ *Any choice phrase* or *sentence*: (KT:) one says, مَا أَحْسَنَ فِقَرَ كَلَامِهِ i. e. [*How beautiful are*] *the points*, or *points of wit*, (نُكَت [pl. of نُكْتَةٌ]) *of his speech*, or *language!* (A, TA.) — And in like manner it is applied to signify † The *end* [or *final word*] *of every verse of an ode* and [*of every clause*] *of a* خُطْبَة [which is in rhyming prose]. (Mṣb.) — And † [*A pair of clauses of rhyming prose, both ending with the same rhyme*; i. e.] the فِقْرَة is *that which in* [*rhyming*] *prose is like the verse in poetry*. (Kull p. 208.) ═ Also *A piece of land, such as is termed* قَرَاح [q. v.], *for sowing*. (O, Ḳ.) ═ And *A thing that serves as a mark*, or *sign*, (Lth, Ḳ, TA,) *to men contending*, or *competing, in shooting*, or *casting*, (Lth,) *such as a mountain*, (Ḳ,) or *such as a hill*, or *a hollow dug in the ground*, (Lth,) or *a* هَدَف [or *butt*, &c.], (Lth, Ḳ, TA,) and *the like*: (Ḳ, TA:) they say, in such contending or competing, أُرَامِيكَ مِنْ أَدْنَى فِقْرَةٍ [*I will contend, or compete, with thee in shooting*, or *casting, from the nearest* فقرة] and مِنْ أَبْعَدِ فِقْرَةٍ [*from the furthest* فقرة]. (Lth, TA.)

فَقْرَةٌ : see فِقْرَةٌ.

فُقْرَى [The *lending one a camel*, &c., *to be ridden* or *to carry a burden*;] a subst. [similar to رُقْبَى and عُمْرَى] from أَفْقَرَهُ نَاقَتَهُ (Ṣ) or بَعِيرَهُ. (Ḳ.)

فَقَارٌ The *vertebræ of the back*; (Ṣ,* Mṣb, Ḳ;) the *bones of the spine, which are set in regular order, one upon another, from the part where is the* كَاهِل *to the* عَجْب: (Ḳ,* TA:) [it is sometimes used as a sing., as in the Ṣ and O and Ḳ voce طَبَقٌ: but properly] the sing., (Mṣb, Ḳ,) or n. un., (Ṣ, TA,) is † فَقَارَةٌ, (Ṣ, Mṣb, Ḳ,) for which one should not say فِقَارَةٌ, with kesr: (ISk, Mṣb:) and † فِقْرَةٌ, of which the pl. is فِقَرٌ and فِقَرَاتٌ and فِقْرَاتٌ, and فِقِرَاتٌ, signifies the same as فَقَارَةٌ: (Ṣ, Mṣb, Ḳ;) as does also † فَقْرَةٌ. (Ḳ.) — [Hence,] فَقَارُ الجَوْزَاءِ † *The three very bright stars* [δ and ε and ζ] *disposed obliquely in the midst of the constellation* الجوزاء [i. e. *Orion*]. (Ḥar p. 456. [See art. جوز.]) — And [hence also,] ذُو الفَقَارِ † the name of *A* [*celebrated*] *sword of the Prophet*, (Ṣ, O, Ḳ,) and afterwards, *of 'Alee*: it had previously belonged to El-'Áṣ Ibn-Munebbih, who was slain at Bedr, (O, Ḳ,) by 'Alee, by whom his sword was given to the Apostle: (O:) accord. to Abu-l-'Abbás [i. e. Th], it was thus named because there were in it small beautiful hollows [app. meaning small scallops in the edge, such as some modern swords have, for the more easy cleaving of coats of mail]: it is also, accord. to some, called ذو الفِقَار; but this is said by El-Khaṭṭábee to be vulgar. (TA.) — It (i. e. ذو الفقار) is also used, metaphorically, as meaning ‡ *The spear*. (TA.)

فَقِيرٌ *A hollow that is dug around the shoot*, or *offset, of a palm-tree, when it is planted*: (Ṣ, O:) or *a well* [or *the like thereof*] *in which the shoot*, or *offset, of a palm-tree is planted*, (Ḳ, TA,) *then alluvial soil with dung of camels or the like is pressed down around it*: (TA:) pl. فُقُرٌ, with two ḍammehs: (Ḳ, TA:) or this [app. the pl., but accord. to the TA the sing.,] signifies *wells*, (Ḳ, TA,) *three, and more, together*, (TA,) or *communicating, one with another*. (Ḳ, TA.) The sing. signifies also *A well*: (Mgh, O:) or *an old well*: (O:) or *a well having little water*: (TA:) pl. as above. (Mgh.) — And *A plain*, or *soft, place, in which wells are dug forming a regular series*. (O, Ḳ.) And رَكِيَّةٌ فَقِيرَةٌ signifies *A dug well*. (TA.) And فَقِيرُ بَنِى فُلَانٍ فِى الرَّكَايَا is expl. by A'Obeyd as meaning *The share of the sons of such a one of the wells*. (TA.) — Also The *mouth*, (Ḳ, TA,) or the *place whence the water issues*, (Ṣ, O, TA,) *of a subterranean channel*, or *conduit*: (Ṣ,* O,* Ḳ,* TA:) pl. as above. (TA.) — And it is said to signify *A* [*hollowed*] *trunk of a palm-tree, by means of which one ascends to an upper chamber*: but the word commonly known in this sense is نَقِيرٌ [q. v.], with ن. (IAth, TA.) ═ As an epithet applied to a camel, it means *Having an incision* [or *two incisions* or *three*] *made in his nose* [or *muzzle*] *in the manner explained in the first paragraph of this art.*; and so † مَفْقُورٌ. (Ḳ, TA.) ═ Also, applied to a man, (TA,) *Having the vertebræ of the back broken*; (Ṣ, O, Ḳ,* TA;) and so † فَقِرٌ and † مَفْقُورٌ: (Ḳ:) or *having a complaint of the vertebræ of his back, arising from fracture* or *from disease*: (Mṣb:) or *having his vertebræ pulled out from his back, so that his spine is interrupted*: (T, L:) and † فَقِرٌ, a man *having a complaint of his vertebræ*: (Ṣ, O, TA:) and فقير and † مَفْقُورٌ, a man *afflicted* [lit. *having the vertebræ of his back broken*] *by a calamity*. (Mṣb.) ═ Hence, as though having the vertebræ of his back broken, (IDrst, TA in art. جبر,) [but said to be irregularly formed from اِفْتَقَرَ, like مَا أَفْقَرَهُ, q. v.,] *Poor*; or *needy*; contr. of غَنِىٌّ; (as implied in the Ḳ;) *having* [*only*] *what suffices for his household*, or *those who dwell with him and whose maintenance is incumbent on him*: (ISd, Ḳ:) or one *who finds food sufficient to sustain life*: (Ḳ:) or one *who possesses only what is sufficient for life*: (ISk, Ṣ, Ḳ:*) or one *whose property is*, or *has become, little*: further expl. in art. سكن: (Mṣb:) or one *who has what to eat*; (Aboo-'Amr Ibn-El-'Alà;) differing from مِسْكِينٌ, which signifies one who possesses nothing; altogether destitute: (Aboo-'Amr Ibn-El-'Alà, ISk, Ṣ, O, Ḳ:) or both mean *destitute*, i. e. *possessing nothing*: (IAạr, Ṣ, O:) Aboo-Ḥaneefeh holds the opinion of ISk, (TA,) who cites the following verse from a poem of Er-Rá'ee in praise of 'Abd-El-Melik Ibn-Marwán;

أَمَّا الفَقِيرُ الَّذِى كَانَتْ حَلُوبَتُهُ *
وَفْقَ العِيَالِ فَلَمْ يُتْرَكْ لَهُ سَبَدُ *

[*As to the* فقير *whose milch camel was sufficient for his household, and nothing* (more) *was left to him*:] (Ṣ, O, TA:) Aṣ says that the مسكين is better in condition than the فقير: and Yoo says that the فقير is better in condition than the مسكين; and adds, I asked an Arab of the desert, Art thou فقير? and he answered, No, by God, but rather مسكين: (Ṣ, O, TA:) or the former signifies *needy, needing*, or *wanting*; *a needer*; and the latter, one abased by need or want, or otherwise; (Ibn-'Arafeh, O, Ḳ;) who, if abased by need or want, may lawfully receive of the poor-rate; but if abased otherwise than by need or want, he may not receive of the poor-rate; for he may be rich: (Ibn-'Arafeh:) [الفَقِيرُ إِلَى ٱللّٰهِ *the needer of God*, i. e., of God's help, &c., and الفَقِيرُ إِلَى رَحْمَةِ ٱللّٰهِ *the needer of the mercy of God*, are epithets which a man often writes before his name:] it is said in the Ḳur [xxxv. 16], أَنْتُمُ الفُقَرَآءُ إِلَى ٱللّٰهِ وَٱللّٰهُ هُوَ ٱلْغَنِىُّ ٱلْحَمِيدُ, which is explained as meaning *Ye are the needers*, or *they who stand in need, of God*: [*and God, He is the Self-sufficient, the Praised in every case*:] (O,* TA: [see also the Ḳur xxviii. 24:]) or فقير signifies one *who is crippled*, or *deprived of the power of motion, by disease*, or *who suffers from a protracted disease, being weak, and who has no trade*; and one *who has a mean trade that does not suffice for his need*; and مسكين, a beggar, who has a trade that stands in some stead, (حِرْفَةٌ تَقَعُ مَوْقِعًا,) but does not cause him and his household to be without want; (Esh-Sháfi'ee, T, O, Ḳ;) so that the former is in a harder condition than the latter accord. to Esh-Sháfi'ee; (T;) and it seems that he is called فقير because of crippleness, or protracted disease, which prevents his freely employing himself in making gain: (Khálid Ibn-Yezeed:) Aṣ also says that the latter is in a better condition than the former; (Ṣ, O, Ḳ;) and so says Aḥmad Ibn-'Obeyd: (TA:) and as to the verse of Er-Rá'ee, cited above, it is said to mean that the person there mentioned had a milch camel in former times, but possessed it no longer, and that لَمْ يُتْرَكْ لَهُ سَبَدٌ means that nothing was left to him: (Mgh:) the pl. of the latter epithet is also applied in the Ḳur xviii. 78 to men possessing a ship, or boat, which is worth a considerable sum; (Mgh;) whence Aboo-Bekr holds the opinion of Aṣ to be correct: (TA:) but it is urged in reply, that these men were hirers, not owners, of the vessel, as appears from one reading, [app. يُعَمِّلُونَ for يَعْمَلُونَ,] with teshdeed: (TA:) or the former signifies one *who has neither property nor gain that suffices for his need*; and the latter, one who has property or gain not sufficient for him: or, as some say, the converse is the truth: (Bḍ in ix. 60:) or both signify the same, (IAạr, Ṣ, Ḳ,) one *who possesses nothing*: (IAạr, Ṣ:) or when they are used together, they differ in signification; and when used separately, they both [sometimes] signify the same: (El-Bedr El-Ḳaráfee:) [see more voce مِسْكِينٌ:] fem. with ة: (Mṣb, Ḳ:) pl. masc. فُقَرَآءُ; (Mṣb, Ḳ;) pl. fem. فَقَائِرُ, (Ḳ,) and فُقَرَآءُ (Lḥ, Mṣb, TA) like the masc., [said to be] the only instance of the kind except سُفَهَآءُ as pl. of سَفِيهَةٌ; (Mṣb;) [though فُقَهَآءُ, and perhaps some other instances, should be added;] but ISd says, I know not how this is. (TA.)

فَقَارَةٌ: see فَقَارٌ.

فَيْقُرٌ: see the next paragraph.

فَاقِرَةٌ [*An act that breaks*, or *will break, the vertebræ of the back*: and hence,] † *a calamity*, or *misfortune*; (Ṣ, O, Ḳ;) as also ▼ فَيْقُرٌ: (Ṣ, O, Ḳ:) or, accord. to Lth and others, *such as breaks the vertebræ of the back*: (TA:) pl. فَوَاقِرُ. (Ḥar p. 399.) عُمِلَ بِهِ الفَاقِرَةُ is a prov., meaning *He did to him an act breaking*, or *that would break, his vertebræ*; or *a calamity*, or *misfortune*, as in the Ḳur lxxv. 25: (Meyd:) [or, accord. to J, it app. means *he did to him that which would render him tractable*; for he says,] it is from the phrase فَقَرْتُ أَنْفَ البَعِيرِ. (Ṣ. [This phrase in the Ṣ has been strangely misunderstood by Golius; who has consequently, after mentioning the meaning "infortunium," added "et Habena seu capistrum, de quo in Conj. 1."]) — And [hence] الفَاقِرَةُ signifies † *The resurrection*. (TA.)

أَفْقَرُ [*More*, and *most*, *poor* or *needy* &c.: said to be formed irregularly from اِفْتَقَرَ, not from an unaugmented form of the verb; like مَا أَفْقَرَهُ]. (See Ḥam pp. 573-4.)

مُفْقَرٌ: see فَقْرٌ.

مُفْقِرٌ, applied to a man, (O, TA,) *Strong* (O, Ḳ, TA) *in the vertebræ of the back*; (TA;) and thus ▼ مُفَقَّرٌ, applied to a camel; and [in like manner] ▼ ذُو فُقْرَةٍ, so applied, *strong to be ridden*: (O, TA:) and مُفْقِرٌ signifies also *strong in the back*; applied to a colt: (TA:) and, thus applied, *that has attained to the time when he may be ridden*. (Ḳ.) — And [hence] one says, إِنَّهُ لَمُفْقِرٌ لِهٰذَا الأَمْرِ † *Verily he is equal to this affair, possessing firmness of mind*, or *strength*, or *power, for it*; (ISh, O, L, Ḳ;) and لِهٰذَا العَزْمِ *for this determination*, or *resolution*; and لِهٰذَا القِرْنِ *for this adversary*, or *opponent*. (L.) And رَجُلٌ مُفَقَّرٌ ▼ † *A man sufficient for everything that he is ordered to do*; (O, Ḳ, TA;) as though by reason of the strength of his vertebræ. (TA.) — See also فَقْرٌ.

مُفَقَّرٌ A sword *having notches*, or *indentations, in its* مَتْن [q. v.], (Ṣ, Ḳ,) *forming depressions therein*. (Ḳ.) — See also مُفْقِرٌ, in two places.

مَفْقُورٌ: see فَقِيرٌ, in three places.

مَفَاقِرُ: see فَقْرٌ, in two places.

أَرْضٌ مُتَفَقِّرَةٌ *Land in which are many* فُقَر, meaning *hollows*. (O, Ḳ.)

مُتَفَاقِرٌ A man *asserting himself to be in a state of* فَقْر [i. e. *poverty*, or *need*, &c.]. (A, TA.)

فقص

1. فَقَصَ, aor. ـِ, (Lth, Lḥ, M, O, Ḳ,) inf. n. فَقْصٌ; (Lth, Lḥ, IDrd, M, O;) *He broke*; (Lth, Lḥ, M, O, Ḳ;) or *crushed*; (Lḥ, O, Ḳ;) an egg, (Lḥ, IDrd, M, O, Ḳ,) and the like thereof, (IDrd, O,) and any hollow thing; (Lth, M, O;) as also ▼ فقّص, inf. n. تَفْقِيصٌ: (M, TA:) and *he* (a bird) *broke asunder* an egg from over the young bird: (A and TA in explanation of the former verb:) and فَقَسَ, aor. ـِ, inf. n. فَقْسٌ, signifies the same as فَقَصَ. (Lḥ, O.) — فَقَصَ فُلَانٌ بَيْضَ الفِتْنَةِ [lit. *Such a one broke asunder the eggs of sedition*, or the like,] is a tropical phrase [meaning ‡ *such a one originated sedition*, &c.]. (A, TA.) — [Golius has assigned to فَقَصَ, constr. with an accus., another signification ("*assecutus fuit* rem"), as on the authority of the Ḳ; app. from a mistranscription in the explanation of المِفْقَاص, in a copy of that lexicon.]

2: see the preceding paragraph.

5: see what next follows.

7. انفقصت البَيْضَةُ and ▼ تفقّصت *The egg broke* [or *broke asunder*] عَنِ الفَرْخِ [*from over the young bird*].

بَيْضَةٌ فَقْصَةٌ: see مَفْقُوصَةٌ.

فَقِيصٌ as an epithet: see its fem. voce مَفْقُوصَةٌ. — Also *An iron thing like a ring, among the apparatus of the tiller of land*, (Lth, O, Ḳ,) *which clasps together* [app. *at the upper parts, so as to form a support like a trevet, for his provisions &c.,*] *several separate sticks*, or *pieces of wood, set over against one another*. (Lth, O.)

فَقُّوصٌ, (Lth, O, Ḳ,) or فَقُّوصَةٌ, (M,) [the former a coll. gen. n., and the latter its n. un.,] *A melon* (بِطِّيخَة) *before it has become ripe*: (Lth, M, O, Ḳ:) a word of the dial. of Egypt: (Lth, O, Ḳ:) [but now applied in Egypt to the *cucumis sativus* (or *common cucumber*); (Forskål's Flora Aegypt. Arab., pp. lxxvi., 169;) or, particularly, *cucumis sativus fructu albo*: (Delile's Floræ Aegypt. Illustr., no. 929:)] also mentioned as with س for the last letter. (TA.)

مِفْقَاصٌ [*A kind of mace*;] *a thing like a pomegranate, at the end of an iron rod, that breaks*, or *crushes, everything that it reaches*. (Ibn-'Abbád, O, Ḳ.)

بَيْضَةٌ مَفْقُوصَةٌ and ▼ فَقِيصَةٌ (IDrd, O, Ḳ) and ▼ فَقْصَةٌ (CḲ [but not found by me elsewhere]) *An egg broken*, or *crushed*. (IDrd, O, Ḳ.)

فقع

1. فَقَعَ, aor. ـَ and ـُ, inf. n. فُقُوعٌ (Ṣ, O, Ḳ) and فَقْعٌ, (Ḳ,) said of the colour of a thing, (Ṣ, O,) *It was intensely yellow*: (Ṣ, O, Ḳ:) or *its yellowness was free from admixture*. (Ḳ, TA. [See also فَقْعٌ below.]) [And] فَقَعَ said of a skin, or hide, or a tanned, or red, skin or hide, (أَدِيم,) *It was beautiful and clear* [*in colour*]. (Ḥam p. 562.) — فَقَعَ said of a boy, *He became active, and grew, grew up*, or *became a young man*; (Ḳ,* TA; [in both of which it is implied that the aor. of the verb in this and the next two senses is ـَ and ـُ, as above;]) and so ▼ تفقّع. (TA.) — And فَقَعَ (Ḳ, TA) said of a man, (TA,) *He died from*, or *in consequence of, the heat*. (Ḳ, TA.) — فَقَعَتِ الفَوَاقِعُ فُلَانًا *The calamities of time*, or *fortune, crushed such a one*. (Ḳ,* TA.) — فَقَعَ, aor. ـَ, (Ḳ,) inf. n. فَقْعٌ, (O,) *He stole*. (O, Ḳ. [Accord. to the TḲ, trans. in this sense.]) — And *He emitted wind from the anus, with a sound*; (Ḳ, TA;) in which sense the inf. n. is

likewise فَقَعَ; accord. to some, peculiarly said of an ass: and فَقَّعَ ▼ بِهِ, and ▼ بِمِفْقَعٍ, and ▼ بِمِفْقَاعٍ, inf. n. تَفْقِيعٌ, *he did so vehemently.* (TA.) ═ فَقِعَ, i. e. like فَرِحَ, (Ḳ, TA,) inf. n. فَقَعٌ, (TḲ,) said of a man, (TA,) *He became red.* (Ḳ, TA.)

2. فقّع, (TA,) inf. n. تَفْقِيعٌ, (O, Ḳ, TA,) *He twisted the sides of his mouth,* or *opened his mouth and was diffuse, in speech,* (O, Ḳ, TA,) *and uttered speech that had no meaning.* (TA.) —— And فقّع أَصَابِعَهُ, (Ṣ, O,* TA,) inf. n. as above, (Ṣ, O, Ḳ, TA,) *i. q.* فَرْقَعَهَا, (Ṣ, O,* Ḳ,* TA,*) [*He cracked the joints of his fingers;*] i. e. *he pressed his fingers so that a sound was heard to proceed from their joints:* (TA:) the action signified thereby is forbidden to be performed in prayer: (O, TA:) [but it is said that] this is *the contracting of the fingers to the inner side of the hand and making a sound with the outer side* [app. *by pressing the fist upon the ground so as to make the joints of the fingers crack,* when rising; for I think that any action more irregular than this would be too obviously wrong to need prohibition]. (O.) —— And فقّع الوَرْدَةَ, inf. n. تَفْقِيعٌ, *He made the rose into a round form* (أَدَارَهَا), *and then struck it so that it rent open,* or *asunder, producing a sound:* (O:) or التَّفْقِيعُ signifies *the striking a rose with the hand,* (O, Ḳ,) or *the making a rose-leaf into a round* [and app. *hollow*] *form, and pressing it with the fingers,* (TA,) *so that it produces a sound,* (O, Ḳ, TA,) *when rending open,* or *asunder.* (TA.) —— [And فقّع signifies also *It cracked with a sound:* and *it crackled:* said of a flint-stone in fire: see صَوَّانٌ: and said of salt thrown into a fire: see نَارٌ.] —— See also 1, last sentence but one. ═ فقّع الأَدِيمَ, (O, TA,) inf. n. as above, (Ḳ,) *He made the hide red.* (O, Ḳ, TA.)

4. افقع, (TA,) inf. n. إِفْقَاعٌ, (O, Ḳ, TA,) *He was,* or *became, poor,* or *needy;* (TA;) or *in an evil state* or *condition.* (O, Ḳ, TA.)

5: see 1. —— [Reiske, as stated by Freytag, has explained this verb as signifying *It was,* or *became, contracted;* said of a hand: but probably, I think, in consequence of his having found تفقّعت erroneously written for تَقَفَّعَت.]

6. تفاقعت عَيْنَاهُ *His eyes became white:* (O, Ḳ, TA:) or *became cleft,* or *fissured:* or *had in them foul,* or *foul white, matter.* (TA.)

7. انفقع *It became cleft,* or *fissured,* or *rent open* or *asunder.* (O, Ḳ.)

فَقْعٌ [an inf. n., of فَقَعَ, q. v. Used as a subst.,] *Intense whiteness.* (TA.) [But it seems to signify more commonly, *Intense yellowness:* or *yellowness free from admixture:* see 1, first sentence.] ═ And *i. q.* حُصَاصٌ [app. as meaning *An emission of wind from the anus, with a sound*]. (Ṣ, O, TA. [See 1, last sentence but one.]) ═ Also, and ▼ فِقْعٌ, (Ṣ, O, Ḳ,) the latter mentioned by ISk, (Ṣ, O,) *A species of* كَمْأَة [or *truffles*]; (Ṣ, O;) accord. to A'Obeyd, (Ṣ, O,) the *white and soft thereof;* (Ṣ, O, Ḳ;) which is the *worst thereof;* or, as IAth says, *a species of the worst* [*kind*] *of* كمأة; accord. to AḤn, *it comes forth from the ground so as to appear, white, and is bad;* the good being that which is extracted by digging: Lth says, it is *a* كَمْء [or *truffle*] *that comes forth from the base of the plant called* إِجْرِد [q. v.], and is *of the worst of* كمأة, *and the quickest in becoming corrupt:* (TA:) the pl. is فِقَعَةٌ, (Ṣ, O, Ḳ,) which is of both forms of the sing.; (Ṣ, O, TA;) and فَقَعٌ, with fet-ḥ, has for pls. أَفْقُعٌ [a pl. of pauc.] and فُقُوعٌ [a pl. of mult.]. (AḤn, TA.) A vile man is likened thereto: (Ṣ, O, Ḳ:*) one says, هُوَ أَذَلُّ مِنْ فَقْعٍ قَرْقَرٍ, (Ṣ,) or مِنْ فَقْعٍ بِقَرْقَرَةٍ, (O, Ḳ,) [*He is more vile than the* فقع *of,* or *than* فقع *in, a low and soft tract of ground,*] because the beasts kick it along, (Ṣ,) or because it offers not resistance to the gatherer thereof, or because it is trodden with the feet, (O, Ḳ,) and the beasts kick it along. (O.) —— [From a mention of the pl. فُقُوعٌ in art. ذأن, and in the present art. in the TA, it appears that فَقْعٌ is also applied to The *species of fungus called* ذُؤْنُونٌ, and to the *species called* طُرْثُوثٌ, &c.] —— And [hence, perhaps,] فَقْعٌ [as a coll. n.] signifies also †*Pointed toes* (خَرَاطِيم) of a sort of boots. (O, TA.)

فِقْعٌ: see the next preceding paragraph.

فَقَاعٌ: see what next follows.

فُقَاعٌ; (O, and thus in my MS. copy of the Ḳ; in other copies of the Ḳ فَقَّاعٌ or فُقَّاعٌ; and in all the copies is added كُرَبَاعٍ or بِالضَّمِّ كُرْبَاعٍ; [but there is no such word as كُرْبَاعٍ, nor رُبَّاعٌ; whence it seems to be meant that we should read كُرَبَاعٍ; i. e. فُقَاعٌ, like رُبَاعُ, imperfectly decl.; but see what follows;]) so says Ibn-Buzurj: (O:) or, (O, Ḳ,) accord. to AZ, (O,) ▼ فَقَاعٌ, (O, Ḳ,*) like كُثْمَانٍ) ثَمَانٍ): رَبَاعٍ, (O,) [i. e.] with fet-ḥ, like (Ḳ:) [which suggests that كُـرْبَـاعٍ may be an early mistranscription for كَرَبَاعٍ, and that فُقَاع is wrong, and only فَقَاع right, though it is said in one place in the TA that فُقَاع is like سَحَاب, i. e. that it is فَقَاعٌ:] or it is ▼ فَقِيعٌ, like أَمِيرٌ; (Ḳ, TA;) so accord. to El-Jáḥiḍh, as mentioned by Az: (TA:) applied to a man, as meaning *Red;* (O, Ḳ, TA;) *intensely so; by reason of* إِغْرَاب [i. e. app., *goodliness of condition*]: (O, TA:) and ▼ فُقَاعِىٌّ, as an epithet applied to a man, signifies *red.* (TA.)

فَقِيعٌ, (so in the O,) or ▼ فِقِّيعٌ, like سِكِّيتٌ, (Ḳ,) but the former, like أَمِيرٌ, is the right, [a coll. gen. n.,] and its n. un. is with ة, (TA,) The *white, of pigeons;* (Ḳ, TA;) said by El-Jáḥiḍh to be *such, of pigeons, as are like the* صَقَالِبِىّ [or *Sclave*] *of men;* (O, TA;) *a kind of white pigeon;* so called as being likened to a [white] species of truffle [i. e. the فقع]. (TA.) —— أَبْيَضُ فَقِيعٌ, (so in the O,) or ▼ ابيض فِقِّيعٌ, like سِكِّيتٌ, (Ḳ,) *White that is intense* (O, Ḳ) *in whiteness.* (O.) [See also فَاقِعٌ.] —— فَقِيعٌ as an epithet applied to a man: see فُقَاعٌ.

فُقَاعِىٌّ: see فُقَاعٌ: —— and see فَاقِعٌ, in two places.

فَقَّاعٌ One *who emits wind from the anus, with a sound, much,* or *frequently.* (TA.) —— And *Strong,* or *vehement;* and *bad, corrupt,* or *wicked.* (Lth, O, Ḳ.)

فُقَّاعٌ *A certain beverage,* (Ṣ, O, L, Ḳ,) [*a sort of beer,*] *made from barley:* (L, TA:) [but there are several sorts thereof, perhaps peculiar to post-classical times: (see De Sacy's Chrest. Arabe, sec. ed., vol. i., pp. 149-154:)] so called because of the froth that rises upon its head. (O, Ḳ. [See فُقَّاعَةٌ.]) —— And *A certain plant,* (AḤn, O, Ḳ,) *such as is termed* ▼ مُتَفَقِّعٌ, i. e., (AḤn, O, Ḳ*) *which, when it dries up, becomes hard, and as though it were horns.* (AḤn, O, Ḳ.) [Now applied in North-Western Africa to The *toadstool,* which is called in other parts فُطْر.]

فِقِّيعٌ: see فَقِيعٌ, in two places.

فُقَّاعَةٌ, like رُمَّانَةٌ, sing. of فَقَاقِيعُ, (TA,) which signifies The *bubbles that rise upon water,* (Ṣ, O, Ḳ, TA,) and *upon wine,* (O,) [&c.,] *round,* [or *globular,*] (TA,) *like* قَوَارِير [or *vessels of glass*]. (Ṣ, O, TA.)

فُقَّاعِىٌّ *A seller of* [*the beverage called*] فُقَّاع. (TA.)

فَاقِعٌ (Ṣ, O, Ḳ) and ▼ فُقَاعِىٌّ (Ḳ) Yellow *intensely yellow;* (Ṣ, O, Ḳ;) thus both signify: (Lḥ, Ḳ, TA:) or red *intensely red:* (Ḳ:) or red *free from an admixture of whiteness:* or *purely red:* (TA:) or فَاقِعٌ is applied to white and to any other colour as signifying *free from admixture;* (Ḳ;) and ▼ فُقَاعِىٌّ is applied in this sense to white: (TA:) and ▼ أَفْقَعُ, of which the pl. is فُقْعٌ, signifies *intensely white.* (Ḳ.)

فَاقِعَةٌ *A calamity,* or *misfortune:* (Ṣ, O, Ḳ:) pl. فَوَاقِعُ. (Ṣ, O, Ḳ.*)

أَفْقَعُ; pl. فُقْعٌ: see فَاقِعٌ.

فَقْرٌ مُفْقِعٌ, accord. to the Ḳ, signifies مُدْقِعٌ [as though meaning *Poverty causing to cleave to the dust* or *earth*]: but the right phrase is فَقِيرٌ مُفْقِعٌ, signifying مُدْقِعٌ [i. e. a *poor* person *cleaving to the dust* or *earth:* for أَدْقَعَ is intrans. as well as trans.]; which denotes the worst condition, like مَجْهُودٌ. (TA.) [See 4.]

مِفْقَعٌ and ▼ مِفْقَاعٌ [The *anus* (as being the instrument) *with which wind is emitted vehemently, with a sound*]: see 1, last sentence but one.

خُفٌّ مُفَقَّعٌ i. q. مُخَرْطَمٌ (O, Ḳ) i. e. *A boot having its fore part pointed.* (TA in art. خرطم.)

المُفَقِّعَةُ *A certain black bird of which the base of the tail is white,* (O, Ḳ,) *that pecks camels', or similar, dung.* (O.)

مِفْقَاعٌ: see مِفْقَعٌ; and 1, last sentence but one.

مُتَفَقِّعٌ: see فُقَّاعٌ.

فقم

1. فَقِمَ, (Ṣ, Ḳ,* TA,) aor. ـَ, (TA,) inf. n. فَقَمٌ, *It, or he, was, or became, full:* (Ṣ, Ḳ, TA:) it is said of a vessel: (TA:) and one says [also] أَصَابَ مِنَ المَآءِ حَتَّى فَقِمَ [*He obtained, or took, of the water until he became full*]; mentioned by IDrd. (Ṣ, TA.) — And أَكَلَ حَتَّى فَقِمَ *He ate until he became affected with indigestion, or oppressed by much eating.* (Ḳ.) — فَقِمَ مَالُهُ *His property, or wealth, became much, or abundant:* or it has the contr. meaning, i. e., *passed away; came to an end; or became spent, exhausted, or consumed.* (Ḳ, TA.) ═ فَقِمَ, aor. ـَ, (Ḳ, TA,) inf. n. فَقَمٌ (Ṣ, Ḳ, TA) and فُقْمٌ, (Ḳ, TA,) *He had the lower central incisors prominent,* (Ṣ, TA,) *so that they did not close against the upper,* (Ṣ,) or *so that the upper did not close against them when he* (the man) *closed his mouth:* so in the L: or *he had the lower jaw long and the upper short:* but accord. to the Ḳ, *he had the upper central incisors prominent, so that they did not close against the lower:* (TA:) the epithet applied to him is ↓ أَفْقَمُ; (Ṣ, Ḳ, TA;) fem. فَقْمَآءُ. (TA [in which it is added that one says رَجلٌ فُقْمٌ; but رجل is app. here a mistranscription for رِجَالٌ].) — And [hence] فَقِمَ فُلَانٌ i. q. بَطِرَ and أَشِرَ ‡ [i. e. *Such a one exulted; or exulted greatly, or excessively; and behaved insolently and unthankfully, or ungratefully:* &c.]: (Ḳ, TA:) because البَطَرُ and الأَشَرُ are departure from the limit of rectitude. (TA.) — And فَقِمَ الأَمْرُ, (Ḳ, TA,) aor. ـَ, (TA,) inf. n. فَقَمٌ and فُقْمٌ and فُقُومٌ, ‡ *The affair did not proceed in a right course.* (Ḳ, TA.) — And فَقِمَ and فَقُمَ are *syn. with* تفاقم, q. v. (Ḳ.) — And فَقِمَ signifies also *It (a thing) was, or became, wide, or ample.* (TA.) ═ فَقِمَ المَرْأَةَ: see 3. ═ فَقَمَ الكَلْبَ *He took hold of the* فُقْم [i. e. *muzzle*] *of the dog;* (Ḳ;) as also ↓ تفقّمهُ. (Z, Ḳ.)

3. فاقم المَرْأَةَ, (Ṣ,* Ḳ, TA,) inf. n. مُفَاقَمَةٌ and فِقَامٌ, (Ṣ, TA,) *He compressed the woman;* (Ṣ, Ḳ, TA;) as also ↓ فَقَمَهَا. (Ḳ.)

5: see 1, last sentence.

6. تفاقم *It (an affair, or a case,) was, or became, great, or formidable;* (Ṣ, Mgh, Ḳ, TA;) and *hard, or difficult;* (Mgh;) said of what is disliked, or hated; (TA;) and ↓ فَقِمَ and ↓ فَقُمَ signify the same. (Ḳ.)

فَقْمٌ: see what next follows.

فُقْمٌ (Ṣ, Ḳ) and ↓ فَقْمٌ (Ḳ) The لَحْى [meaning *lateral portion of the lower jaw*]; (Ṣ, Ḳ;) or *either one of the* لَحْيَان. (Ḳ.) Hence the trad., مَنْ حَفِظَ مَا بَيْنَ فُقْمَيْهِ وَرِجْلَيْهِ دَخَلَ الجَنَّةَ [*He who keeps from evil what is between his two lateral portions of the lower jaw* (i. e. his tongue), *and* what is between *his two legs* (i. e. his ذَكَر), *enters Paradise*]. (Ṣ,* TA.) — [And] The *upper part* [*of the interior*] *of the mouth:* the lower part is the حَنَك. (IAạr, T in art. حنك.) — See also فَقْمٌ.

فُقْمٌ The *mouth.* (Sh, Ḳ, TA. [See also فُقْمٌ.])

أَفْقَمُ; fem. فَقْمَآءُ: see 1. — Hence, † *Anything crooked, distorted, or uneven.* (TA.) And أَمْرٌ أَفْقَمُ ‡ *An affair, or a case, of a crooked kind; contrary to what is right.* (Ṣ,* Ḳ,* TA.) — [And Freytag adds, from the Deewán of the Hudhalees, *Difficult,* as an epithet applied to a thing: — and, as a signification of the fem., *A calamity, or misfortune.*]

فقه

1. فَقِهَ, aor. ـَ, (Ṣ, Mṣb, Ḳ, &c.,) inf. n. فِقْهٌ, the verb being like عَلِمَ and the inf. n. like عِلْمٌ, in measure and in meaning, (TA,) or فَقَهٌ; (JK; [and the same seems to be implied in the Mṣb and the Ḳ;]) and فَقُهَ; (Mṣb, Ḳ;) *He had, or possessed, what is termed* فِقْه, meaning *understanding,* (Ṣ, Ḳ,) and *knowledge,* and *intelligence,* and especially *knowledge of the law* (عِلْمُ الدِّينِ): (Ḳ:) or both are *syn. with* عَلِمَ: (Mṣb, TA:) or فَقُهَ, of which the inf. n. is فَقَاهَةٌ, (Ṣ, TA,) or فِقْهٌ, (JK,) signifies [peculiarly] *he had, or possessed, knowledge of the law* (عِلْمُ الشَّرِيعَةِ): (Ṣ:) or this latter verb signifies *he had, or possessed, what is termed* فِقْه *as a faculty firmly rooted in his mind:* (Mṣb, TA:) or, accord. to IB, *i. q.* ↓ تَفَقَّهَ [q. v., as intrans.]: and *he was, or became,* [*a* فقيه, q. v., or] *equal to the* فُقَهَآء. (TA in art. علم: see علم.) One says, فُلَانٌ لَا يَفْقَهُ وَلَا يَنْقَهُ [which may be rendered *Such a one will not understand nor comprehend:* but the two verbs are exactly syn.]. (Ṣ.) And to the witness one says, كَيْفَ فَقَاهَتُكَ لِمَا أَشْهَدْنَاكَ [app. meaning *How is thy understanding of* (or *how understandest thou*) *what we have made thee to witness?*]: it is not said to any other than the witness: (Ḳ, TA:) thus in the M: (TA:) or, accord. to Z, it is said to other than the witness. (Ḳ,* TA.) — And فَقِهَهُ, (Mgh, Ḳ,) aor. ـَ, inf. n. فِقْهٌ, (Ḳ,) *He understood it,* (Mgh, Ḳ,) namely, a meaning, (Mgh,) or a thing that one explained to him; (TA;) as also ↓ تفقّههُ. (Ḳ.) — See also 3.

2. فقّههُ, (Ṣ, Ḳ,) inf. n. تَفْقِيهٌ, (Ḳ,) *He* (God) *made him to know or have knowledge* [or *to understand,* or *instructed him*], or *taught him;* (Ṣ,* Ḳ, TA;) and (Ḳ) so ↓ افقههُ, (Mṣb, Ḳ,) or *he made him to understand.* (Ṣ, Mgh.) It is said in a trad., اَللّٰهُمَّ عَلِّمْهُ الدِّينَ وَفَقِّهْهُ فِى التَّأْوِيلِ i. e. *O God, teach him* الدين [app. here meaning *the science of the law*] and [*instruct him in*] *the* تأويل [*or interpretation,* &c.,] *and the meaning thereof.* (TA.) And you say, أَفْقَهْتُكَ ↓ الشَّىْءَ *I made thee to understand,* (Ṣ, Mṣb,*) or *I taught thee,* (Mṣb,) *the thing.* (Ṣ, Mṣb.) And ↓ أَفْقَهْتُهُ *I explained to him the learning of* الفقه [meaning *the science of the law*]. (T, TA.)

3. فاقههُ *He searched with him into* [*matters of*] *science, disputing with him,* (Ṣ, Ḳ,) ↓ فَفَقَهَهُ, aor. ـُ, [inf. n. فَقْهٌ,] *and he overcame him therein.* (Ḳ.)

4: see 2, in three places.

5. تفقّه *He learned knowledge, or science:* (M voce سَوَّدَ:) [and particularly] *he learned* الفِقْه [meaning *the science of the law*]: (JK:) or *he took, or applied himself, to the acquisition of* الفقه [meaning thus]. (Ṣ, TA.) And تفقّه فِى العِلْمِ is like تَعَلَّمَ [meaning *He became, or made himself, learned, or thoroughly learned, in science*]. (Mṣb.) لِيَتَفَقَّهُوا فِى الدِّينِ, in the Ḳur ix. 123, means *That they may task themselves to obtain understanding in* الدِّين [i. e. *the law,* or *religion* in general], *imposing upon themselves the difficulties attendant on the acquisition thereof.* (Ksh, Bḍ.) See also 1, in two places; in the latter of which it is mentioned as transitive.

فِقْهٌ [as a simple subst.] signifies *Understanding* (Ṣ, Mṣb, Ḳ) of a thing; (Mṣb, Ḳ;) and *knowledge* thereof; (Mṣb, Ḳ;) and *intelligence:* (Ḳ:) accord. to IF, *any knowledge* of a thing is thus termed: (Mṣb:) [hence فِقْهُ اللُّغَةِ *The science of lexicology* is the title of a work written by him; and of another work, by Eth-Tha'álibee:] and, as used by the lawyers [and others], الفقه denotes a particular science; (Mṣb;) it signifies particularly, (Ṣ, TA,) or predominantly, (Ḳ, TA,) *The science of the law;* [*jurisprudence;*] (Ṣ, Ḳ, TA;) syn. عِلْمُ الشَّرِيعَةِ, (Ṣ, TA,) or عِلْمُ الدِّينِ, [which is the same as علم الشريعة,] because of its preëminence (Ḳ, TA) above the other kinds of science: (TA:) and more particularly, *the science of the* فروع [or *derivative institutes*] *of the law.* (TA.)

فَقِهٌ; and its fem., with ة: see the next paragraph.

فَقِيهٌ Any one *possessing knowledge* of a thing. (TA.) فَقِيهُ العَرَبِ signifies *The* عَالِم [or *man of knowledge*] *of the Arabs;* (TA;) and was an appellation given to El-Ḥárith Ibn-Keledeh (الحٰرِثُ بْنُ كَلَدَةَ), who was also called طَبِيبُ العَرَبِ [as is said in the Ṣ in art. ازر], because this appellation is syn. with the former; but IKh and El-Ḥareeree do not mean by فقيه العرب any particular person. (Mz, close of the 39th نوع.) — [Particularly and predominantly,] فقيه signifies *One possessing knowledge of the law;* [*a lawyer;*] (Ṣ, Ḳ;) as also ↓ فَقُهٌ; (Mṣb, Ḳ;) fem. فقيهة and ↓ فَقُهَةٌ: pl. [of فَقِيه] فُقَهَآءُ; and [of فَقِيهَة] فَقَائِهُ and فُقَهَآءُ;

(Ḳ;) the last of these pls. mentioned by Lḥ, and anomalous, as applied to women: ISd says, "in my opinion, he, of the Arabs, who says فُقَهَآءُ [in speaking of women] takes no account of the fem. ة: it is like فُقَرَآءُ applied to women." (TA.) [In Egypt, the appellation فِقِى, a vulgar corruption of فَقِيه, is now applied to *A schoolmaster;* and to *a person who recites the Ḳur-án &c. for hire.*] — فَحْلٌ فَقِيهٌ means *A stallion* [*camel*] *expert in covering,* (Ḳ, TA,) *that knows well the she-camels that are lusting, and the pregnant.* (TA.)

المُسْتَفْقِهَةُ *The female companion of the wailing woman, who responds to her* (Ḳ, TA) *in what she says;* because she catches and retains quickly, and understands, what she [the former] says, and to reply to it: [as though it signified "she who seeks, or desires, to understand:"] it is said in a trad. that each of these persons is cursed by God. (TA.)

فقو

1. فَقَوْتُ أَثَرَهُ or إِثْرَهُ *I followed his track,* or *footsteps;* i. q. قَفَوْتُهُ; (Ḳ, TA;) mentioned by Yaạḳoob among the words formed by transposition: so in the M. (TA.)

فَقْوٌ: see its syn. فَقْىٌ, in art. فقا.

فُقْوَةٌ The فُوق [or *notch*] of the arrow; (Ṣ, Ḳ, TA;) i. e. the *part which is the place of the bowstring:* (TA:) [also called فُوقَةٌ, from which it is app. formed by transposition, like the other words mentioned in this art.:] pl. فُقًى, (Ṣ, Ḳ,) also written فقًا. (TA.) An ex. of the pl. occurs in a verse cited in art. عرقب, voce عُرْقُوبٌ. (Ṣ.)

فك

1. الفَكُّ, accord. to Er-Rághib, primarily signifies التَّفْرِيجُ [i. e. The *opening* a thing; and particularly *by diduction,* or *so as to form an intervening space,* or *a gap,* or *breach*]. (TA.) You say, فَكَّ, first pers. فَكَكْتُ, (Ṣ, O, Mṣb, Ḳ,) aor. ـُ, inf. n. فَكٌّ, (O, Mṣb,) *He separated* (Ṣ, O, Mṣb, Ḳ) a thing (Ṣ, O, Ḳ) from another thing; and any two things knit together, or intricately intermixed: (Ṣ, O:) or فَكَّكْتُهُ *I separated one part of it from another part thereof:* (Mṣb:) and ▼ تَفْكِيكٌ likewise signifies the *separating* two things knit together, or intricately intermixed. (Lth, Ṣ, TA.) And *He broke* [or *broke open*] a seal, i. e. a sealed piece of clay or wax; (Mgh, Mṣb,* TA;) in relation to which ▼ يَفْتَكُّهُ occurs as meaning يَفُكُّهُ, though we have not heard it [as a classical expression in this sense]. (Mgh.) — And فَكَّ العَظْمَ, (Mgh, Mṣb,) aor. and inf. n. as above, (Mṣb,) *He dislocated the bone; put it out of joint.* (Mgh, Mṣb.) [This, or the like, is what is meant by its being said that] الفَكُّ in the hand, or arm, is [i. e. denotes] less than الكَسْرُ. (Ḳ.) — And فَكَّ يَدَهُ, (Ḳ, TA,) aor. and inf. n. as above, (TA,) *He opened,* or *unclosed, his hand from what was in it:* (Ḳ, TA:) so in the M. (TA.) — And فَكَّ الرَّهْنَ, (Ṣ, Mgh, O, Mṣb, Ḳ,) aor. ـُ, (TA,) inf. n. فَكٌّ and فُكُوكٌ; (Ḳ;) and ▼ افتكّهُ; (Ṣ, Mgh, O, Ḳ;) ‡ *He redeemed the pledge;* (Ṣ, Mgh, O, Mṣb, Ḳ, TA;) *got it out from the hand of him to whom it was pledged.* (Mgh.) — And فَكَكْتُ signifies also *I loosed, set loose* or *free,* or *let go,* anything. (Mṣb.) — [Hence,] فَكَّ الأَسِيرَ, (Mṣb, Ḳ,) aor. ـُ, (TA,) inf. n. فَكٌّ and فَكَاكٌ and فِكَاكٌ, (Ḳ,) ‡ *He liberated,* or *set free, the captive.* (Mṣb, Ḳ, TA.) And فَكَّ الرَّقَبَةَ, (Ṣ, O, Mṣb, Ḳ,) aor. ـُ, inf. n. فَكٌّ, (TA,) [lit. *He loosed the neck,*] means ‡ *he emancipated* [*the slave*]. (Ṣ, O, Mṣb, Ḳ, TA.) فَكُّ الرَّقَبَةِ is expl. in a trad. as meaning † *The assisting in paying the price* [*of the slave* when one is unable to pay the whole of the price]. (O, TA.) In the Ḳur [xc. 13], فَكُّ رَقَبَةٍ is said by some to mean † *The emancipating of a slave:* and by some, † *the man's emancipating himself from subjection to God's punishment by the confession of the unity of God and by righteous doing and then by teaching the same to others.* (TA.) فُكَّ فُلَانٌ means † *Such a one was set free, and at rest, from a thing.* (IAạr, Th, TA.) — [Hence also,] one says, هُوَ يَفُكُّ المَشَاكِلَ † [*He solves*] *the things,* or *affairs, that are dubious,* or *confused.* (TA in art. شكل.) — قَدْ فَكَّ وَفَرَجَ is said of a very old man, meaning فَرَّجَ لَحْيَيْهِ [i. e. *He has parted his jaws,* by hanging the lower jaw in consequence of weakness]; as is the case in extreme old age. (Ṣ, O.) And [hence,] فَكَّ, (AZ, Ṣ, O, Ḳ,) aor. ـِ, inf. n. فَكٌّ and فُكُوكٌ, (AZ, Ṣ, O,) said of a man, means † *He was,* or *became, extremely aged,* or *old and weak.* (AZ, Ṣ, O, Ḳ.) [Or فَكَّ thus used may be from الفَكُّ signifying "the jaw:" and so what next follows.] — فَكَكْتُ الصَّبِىَّ *I put medicine into the mouth of the boy* or *young male child* [opening his jaws for that purpose]. (Ṣ, O.) ═ فَكِكَ, [third pers. فَكَّ,] aor. يَفَكُّ, inf. n. فَكَكٌ, قَدْ فَكِكْتَ *Thou hast become such as is termed* أَفَكُّ i. e. *one whose* مَنْكِب [here meaning *shoulder-bone*] *has become unknit,* or *loosened,* (انفرج,) *from its joint, in consequence of weakness and flaccidity.* (Ṣ.) [See also فَكَكٌ below.] — And قَدْ فَكِكْتَ, aor. تَفَكُّ; (Ṣ, O, Ḳ;) and فَكُكْتَ, (O, Ḳ,) a verb of a very rare form, [respecting which see دمّ, last sentence,] (MF, TA,) aor. تَفَكُّ; (O, Ḳ;) inf. n. فَكَّةٌ (Ṣ, O, Ḳ) and فَكٌّ also; (TA;) ‡ *Thou hast become foolish,* or *stupid, and soft, flaccid,* or *languid.* (Ṣ, O, Ḳ, TA.)

2: see the preceding paragraph, second sentence.

4. افكّت *She* (a camel) *being near to bringing forth, her* صَلَوَان [app. meaning *two parts on the right and left of the tail* (see صَلًا in art. صلو)] *became lax,* or *flaccid, and her udder became large;* (Ḳ, TA;) and so أَفْكَهَتْ; (TA;) so too ▼ تفكّكت: or this last signifies *she became vehemently desirous of the stallion.* (O, Ḳ.) — And افكّ مِنَ الحِبَالَةِ *He* (a gazelle) *got loose from the snare* into which he had fallen. (TA: also mentioned, but not expl., in the O.)

5. تفكّك *It* (a thing) *became much,* or *widely, separated; and became unclosed.* (O, TA.) — تفكّكت السَّفِينَةُ *The ship parted asunder; became disjointed; became separated in its places of joining.* (Mgh in art. خلع.) — See also 7. — And see 4. — You say also, هُوَ يَتَفَكَّكُ meaning ‡ *He is* [or *acts*] *without power of self-restraint, in consequence of stupidity,* or *unsoundness of intellect,* (Ṣ, O, Ḳ, TA,) in his gait, and in his speech: (TA:) or تَفَكَّكَ in walking is *syn. with* تَخَلَّعَ, (Ṣ and Ḳ and TA in art. خلع,) i. e. [*he was,* or *became, loose in the joints;* or] *he shook his shoulder-joints and his arms, and made signs with them.* (TA in that art.)

7. انفكّ *It became separated:* you say, انفكّ الشَّىْءُ مِنَ الشَّىْءِ *The thing became separated from the thing:* (O, TA:) and انْفَكَكْتُ مِنْكَ [*I became separated from thee*]. (TA.) — And, said of a bone, *It became dislocated,* or *out of joint;* (MA, Mgh,* Mṣb;*) *it unknit,* or *loosened, and separated;* syn. اِنْفَرَجَ وَٱنْفَصَلَ; as also ▼ تفكّك. (Mgh.) [And it is also used in relation to a member of the body:] one says, سَقَطَ فُلَانٌ فَٱنْفَكَّتْ قَدَمُهُ أَوْ إِصْبَعُهُ i. e. اِنْفَرَجَتْ وَزَالَتْ [*Such a one fell, and his foot,* or *his finger, became unknit,* or *loosened, and dislocated*]: (Ṣ, O:) [or] انفكّت قَدَمُهُ means زَالَتْ [i. e. *his foot became dislocated*]; and انفكّت إِصْبَعُهُ means اِنْفَرَجَتْ [i. e. *his finger became unknit,* or *loosened* in a joint]. (Ḳ.) — One says also, انفكّت رَقَبَتُهُ مِنَ الرِّقِّ, meaning ‡ *He became freed* [lit. *his neck became loosed*] *from slavery.* (Ṣ,* O,* TA.) — And انفكّ عَنْ عَهْدِهِ † [*He became released from his compact, engagement,* or *promise*]. (TA voce انفرك.) — And لَا يَنْفَكُّ عَنْ قُبْحِ فِعْلِهِ † [*He will not desist from his evil doing*]. (O and Ḳ in art. عرف.) ═ [It is also used in the sense and manner of the non-attributive verb زَالَ; respecting which see art. زيل.] One says, مَا ٱنْفَكَّ فُلَانٌ قَائِمًا, meaning مَا زَالَ قَائِمًا [i. e. *Such a one ceased not to be,* or *continued to be, standing*]. (Ṣ, O.) And مَا زِلْتُ, مَا ٱنْفَكَكْتُ عَنْ أَذْكُرُكَ, meaning *I ceased not,* or *I continued, remembering thee*]. (Fr, TA.) And it occurs in a verse of Dhu-r-Rummeh, immediately followed by إِلَّا, which is [said by Aṣ and IJ and others to be] redundant. (Ṣ, O. [See that verse, and the remarks upon it, in art. الا, p. 78, col. i.])

8: see 1, former half, in two places.

الفَكُّ The لَحْىُ [meaning *jaw;* and also *either of the two lateral portions of the lower jaw*], (Ṣ, O, Mṣb, Ḳ,) i. e. (Mṣb) *each of the* لَحْيَانِ;

(Mgh, Mṣb;) as also ▼ الأَفَكُّ: (O, Ḳ:) or this latter signifies *the* مَجْمَع [or *part in which is the commissure*] *of the* خَطْم [generally meaning *muzzle*]; (Lth, O, Ḳ;) as also الفَكُّ; (TA;) that is, (Lth, O, in the Ḳ "or" [as if to denote a different meaning],) [*the part in which is the symphysis*] *of the* فَكَّانِ [or *two lateral portions of the lower jaw*]: (Lth, O, Ḳ:) [see الفَنِيكُ:] and الفَكَّانِ is said to mean *the place* [*on either side with that on the other side*] *where the two jaws meet* [*and are articulated*] *next the temple, above and below;* of a human being and of a horse or the like: (TA:) and, in the Bári', (Mṣb,) or in the T, (TA,) *the place of meeting of the two sides of the mouth* (مُلْتَقَى الشِّدْقَيْنِ) *on both sides:* (Mṣb, TA:) [but this last explanation is strange, and app. little known:]) pl. فُكُوكٌ. (Mṣb.) One says, مَقْتَلُ الرَّجُلِ بَيْنَ فَكَّيْهِ [which may be best rendered *The man's slayer is between his two jaws, or two lateral portions of his lower jaw*]; (Ṣ, O, TA;) meaning the man's tongue: (TA:) a prov., in which مقتل may be [properly] an inf. n., or a noun of place, or an inf. n. used in the place of an act. part. n.: accord. to the third of these explanations, [which most nearly denotes the meaning intended,] it is as though one said, قَاتِلُ الرَّجُلِ بَيْنَ فَكَّيْهِ. (Meyd. [See Freytag's Arab. Prov., ii. 597.]) See also فَكَكٌ.

فَكَّةٌ [an inf. n.: see 1, last sentence]. — الفَكَّةُ is the name of *One of the northern constellations,* [*Corona Borealis,*] (Ḳzw,) *certain stars,* (Ṣ, O, Ḳ,) *eight stars, called in Pers.* كاسه درويشان, (Ḳzw,) *behind* السِّمَاكُ الرَّامِحُ [i. e. *Arcturus*], (Ṣ, O, Ḳ,) [*near*] *behind the staff of* الصَّيَّاح [which is a name of *Bootes*], (Ḳzw,) *having a circling form,* (Ṣ, O, Ḳ, and Ḳzw,) *but with a gap,* or *breach, in the circling, for which reason,* [agreeably with the Pers. appellation mentioned above,] *it is called* قَصْعَةُ المَسَاكِينِ [*the bowl of the paupers*], (Ḳzw,) this being *the name given to it by the children.* (Aṣ, Ṣ, O, Ḳ.)

فَكَكٌ *An unknit, or a loosened, state* (انْفِرَاج) *of the* مَنْكِب [or *shoulder-joint*]. (Ḳ. [But see 1, last explanation but one, where it is mentioned as an inf. n.]) — And (Ḳ) *A state of dislocation of the foot:* (Ṣ, O, Ḳ:) hence the phrase, in a verse of Ru-beh, كَمُنْهَاضِ الفَكَكْ: (Ṣ, O:*) but (in this instance, O), accord. to Aṣ, الفَكَك is used by poetic license for الفَكّ [meaning "the jaw," so that the phrase signifies *like him whose jaw has become broken after its having been set*]. (Ṣ, O.) — And *A state of fracture of the jaw:* (Ḳ, TA:) or *of dislocation thereof.* (TA.)

فَكَاكُ الرَّهْنِ and فِكَاكُهُ, (Ṣ, O, Mṣb,* Ḳ,) the latter mentioned by Ks (Ṣ, O, Mṣb) and ISk, (Mṣb,) *That wherewith the pledge is, or is to be, redeemed:* (Ṣ, O, Mṣb,* Ḳ:) so in a verse cited voce غَلِقَ. (Ṣ, O.)

فَكَّاكٌ [One *who separates, &c., much,* or *often*]. — [And hence,] فَكَّاكٌ هَكَّاكٌ ‡ One *who does not make his words and their meanings congruous,* or *consistent, by reason of his foolishness,* or *stupidity.* (Z, TA.)

فَاكٌّ [as an act. part. n., *Separating,* &c. — And] † *Extremely aged,* or *old and weak;* applied in this sense to a man; (AZ, Ṣ, O, Ḳ;) and also to a camel: (Ḳ:) or, applied to a camel, *disabled,* or *fatigued, by leanness,* or *emaciation:* fem. with ة. (En-Naḍr, TA.) — And ‡ *Foolish,* or *stupid:* (Ṣ, O:*) or *very foolish,* or *stupid:* (IAạr, Ḳ, TA:) and you say فَاكٌّ تَاكٌّ, (IAạr, Ṣ, O, TA,) making تاكّ an imitative sequent: or, accord. to Yaạḳoob, you say شَيْخٌ فَاكٌّ وَتَاكٌّ: thus he makes تاكّ a substitute, not an imitative sequent. (TA.) And أَحْمَقُ فَاكٌّ وَهَاكٌّ ‡ [*A foolish,* or *stupid, person,*] one *who talks of that which he knows and of that which he knows not, and is more,* or *oftener, incorrect than correct.* (El-Ḥoseybee, TA.) Pl. فَكَكَةٌ and فِكَاكٌ. (IAạr, Ḳ.)

أَفَكُّ, (Ṣ, Ḳ,) or أَفَكُّ المَنْكِبِ, (Ḳ,) One *whose* مَنْكِب [here meaning *shoulder-bone*] *has become unknit,* or *loosened,* (انْفَرَجَ,) *from its joint, in consequence of weakness and flaccidity.* (Ṣ, Ḳ.* [See also مَفْرُوكٌ.]) — And رَجُلٌ أَفَكُّ [*A man having the jaw broken*]. (TA. [There expl. as signifying مَكْسُورُ الفَكِّ; a mistranscription, for مَكْسُورُ الفَكِّ: see فَكَكٌ, last sentence.]) ═ See also الفَكُّ.

مُفِكَّةٌ, applied to a she-camel, part. n. of أَفَكَّتْ [q. v.]: (O, TA:) and مُفْكِهَةٌ and مُفْكِهٌ are syn. therewith. (TA.)

مُتَفَكِّكَةٌ A mare *desiring the stallion,* (AO, O, Ḳ,) *not offering opposition to him.* (AO, O.)

مُنْفَكِّينَ in the Ḳur [xcviii. 1], (O, TA,) followed by the words حَتَّى تَأْتِيَهُمُ الْبَيِّنَةُ, (O,) means, accord. to Mujáhid (O, TA) and Zj, (TA,) *In the condition of desisting* (O, TA) from their infidelity; (TA;) or, as Akh says, *ceasing* from their infidelity: (TA:) or, accord. to another, (O,) namely, Niftaweyh, (TA,) *quitting the present state of existence,* (O, TA,) i. e., *sharing, one with another, in perdition, until the evidence came to them* (O, TA) that had been affirmed to them in the Towráh, with respect to the description of Mohammad &c.; تَأْتِيَهُم being lit. an aor., but in its meaning a pret.: (O:) Az says that it is not from مَا انْفَكَّ meaning مَا زَالَ, but from انْفِكَاكُ الشَّىْءِ مِنَ الشَّىْءِ meaning "the thing's becoming separated from the thing:" accord. to IAạr, as mentioned by Th, فُكَّ فُلَانٌ means "Such a one was set free, and at rest, from a thing;" and hence منفكّين in the Ḳur means *experiencing rest:* accord. to Er-Rághib, it means *separated,* or *separated into several parties;* for all [to whom the word, preceded by a negative, relates] were assenting to error. (TA.)

فكر

1. فَكَرَ فِيهِ, (O,* Mṣb, Ḳ,) aor. ـِ, (O, TḲ,) or ـُ, (Mṣb,) inf. n. فَكْرٌ; (Ṣ, O, Mṣb, Ḳ;*) and ▼ أَفْكَرَ; (Ṣ, O, Mṣb, Ḳ;) and ▼ فكّر, (Ṣ, O, Ḳ,) [which is more common than either of the first and second,] inf. n. تَفْكِيرٌ; (O, TA;) and ▼ تفكّر; (Ṣ, O, Mṣb, Ḳ;) and ▼ افتكر, (Mṣb, TA,) but this last is vulgar; (TA;) *He thought upon it, considered it,* or *examined it* [*mentally*]; (Mṣb;) *he considered it in order to obtain a clear knowledge of it;* (Ṣ, O,* TA;) *he employed his mind,* (M, TA,) or *his consideration,* (Ḳ, TA,) *upon it.* (M, Ḳ, TA.) [See also فِكْرٌ.]

2, 4, 5, and 8: see the preceding paragraph.

فَكْرٌ inf. n. of 1 [q. v.]. — لَيْسَ لِى فِى هٰذَا الأَمْرِ فَكْرٌ, (Yaạḳoob, Ṣ, O, Ḳ,*) which is more chaste than ▼ فِكْرٌ, [in this case,] (Yaạḳoob, Ṣ, O,) but the latter is sometimes used, (Ḳ,) means *I have no want,* or *need, of this thing:* (Yaạḳoob, Ṣ, O, Ḳ:*) or, as is said in the A, لَا فَكْرَ لِى فِى هٰذَا i. e. *I have no want, or need, of this, nor do I care for it.* (TA.)

فِكْرٌ and ▼ فِكْرَةٌ (Ṣ, O, Mṣb, Ḳ) and ▼ فِكْرَى, (Lth, O, Ḳ,) are simple substs., (Ṣ, O, Mṣb,*) but the last is of rare occurrence, (Lth, O,) signifying *Thought, consideration,* or [*mental*] *examination,* فِى أَمْرٍ [*respecting a thing*]; (Mṣb;) *consideration* [of a thing] *in order to obtain a clear knowledge* [of it]; (Ṣ, TA;) the *employment of the mind,* (M, TA,) or *of the consideration,* (Ḳ, TA,) upon a thing: (M, Ḳ, TA:) or *repeated consideration for the purpose of seeking* [*to discover*] *meanings:* or the *arranging of things in the mind in order, by them, to arrive at some object of which the attainment is desired, though it be but a preponderating opinion:* (Mṣb:) or the *arranging of known things* [*in the mind*] *in order to attain to* [*the knowledge of*] *an unknown* [*thing*]: (KT:) pl. of the first أَفْكَارٌ; (IDrd, Ḳ;) but Sb says that neither فِكْرٌ nor عِلْمٌ nor نَظَرٌ has any pl.: (TA:) the pl. of ▼ فِكْرَةٌ is فِكَرٌ. (Mṣb.) One says, لِفُلَانٍ فِكَرٌ كُلُّهَا فِقَرٌ [*Such a one has thoughts all of which are points of wit*]. (A, TA.) ═ See also فَكْرٌ.

فِكْرَةٌ: } see the next preceding paragraph; the
فِكْرَى: } former in two places.

فِكِّيرٌ [*Thoughtful;*] *having much* فِكْر; (IF, Ṣ, O, Ḳ;) as also ▼ فَيْكَرٌ. (Kr, Ḳ.)

فَيْكَرٌ: see what next precedes.

فكل

8. افتكل فى فعله i. q. اِحْتَفَلَ [*He strove, laboured,* or *exerted himself,* &c., *in his doing*]; (IAạr, O, Ḳ;) said of a man. (IAạr, O.)

أَفْكَلٌ *A tremour,* (Ṣ, O, Ḳ,) from cold or from fear: (Ṣ:) hence, in a trad., أَخَذَنِى أَفْكَلٌ [*A tremour seized me*]: (Ṣ,* O:) and in another, فَبَاتَ وَلَهُ أَفْكَلٌ [*And he passed the night having a* *tremour*, or *shivering*]: (O:) thus used, as indeterminate, it is perfectly decl.; but if used as a [proper] name of a man, it is imperfectly decl. because determinate and also of the measure of a verb: (Ṣ, O:) some say, (IF, O,) no verb is formed from it; (IF, Ṣ, O;) but such is not the case, for they said رَجُلٌ مَفْكُولٌ [which shows that it had a verb though none is known to have been in use]. (IF, O.) [أَخَذَتْ بِى نَاقَتِى أَفْكَلًا مِنَ السَّيْرِ is a saying mentioned in the O and Ḳ, (in the former as from Ibn-'Abbád,) but the meaning is not expl., nor indicated by the context, in either of them; and the strangeness of its phraseology convinces me that it presents a mistranscription: I believe that the first word is mistranscribed for أَحْدَثَتْ, and, consequently, that the meaning is, *My she-camel produced in me a tremour* arising *from the* rate of *journeying*: some copies of the Ḳ, as is stated in the TA, for مِنَ السَّيْرِ, have مِنَ السَّبْقِ, *from the outstripping.*] — Also The [*bird commonly called*] شِقِرَّاق [generally meaning the *green wood-pecker*]; (O, Ḳ;) because they regard it as of evil omen; so that when it presents itself to them, they are frightened at it, and tremble. (O.) ═ And *A company*, or *collective body*, of men: one says, جَاؤُوا بِأَفْكَلِهِمْ *They came with their company* [i. e. *all together*]. (Ibn-'Abbád, O, Ḳ.) أَفَاكِيلُ [is app. a pl. thereof, and, as such,] signifies أَفْوَاجٌ [pl. of فَوْجٌ, q. v.]: thus in the phrase أَفَاكِيلُ مِنْ كَذَا [app. meaning *Multitudes of such a kind of thing*]: (Ḳ:) [or] thus in the saying, mentioned by Ibn-'Abbád, عِنْدَهُ أَفَاكِيلُ مِنْ كَلَامٍ [app. meaning *He has multitudes of sayings*, or *words*; for كَلَامٌ (q. v.) is used in a pl. sense as well as in a sing. sense]. (O. [The difference of these two exs. in respect of the last word suggests that there may be in one of them a mistranscription.])

مَفْكُولٌ [the pass. part. n. of a verb which is not mentioned,] *Affected with a tremour.* (IF, O, Ḳ, TA. [See أَفْكَلُ, first sentence.])

فكه

1. فَكِهَ, aor. ـَ, inf. n. فَكَاهَةٌ (Ṣ, Mgh, Ḳ) and فَكَهٌ, (Ḳ, TA,) [the latter inf. n. correctly thus, agreeably with a general rule, in the CḲ with the ك quiescent, but said in the TA to be بالتحريك,] † *He was*, or *became, cheerful, happy*, or *free from straitness*; (Ṣ, Mgh, Ḳ;) *jocose*, or *given to jesting*, (Ṣ, Mgh,) *and to laughing*: (Mgh, Ḳ:) or *one who talked to his companions and made them to laugh.* (Ḳ.) — See also 5.

2. فَكَّهَهُمْ, inf. n. تَفْكِيهٌ, *He brought to them* فَاكِهَة [i. e. *fruit*]. (Ḳ.) — And [hence] فَكَّهَهُمْ بِمُلَحِ الكَلَامِ, inf. n. as above, ‡ *He entertained them in a novel manner with facetious sayings or talk.* (Ḳ, TA.)

3. فَاكَهَهُ, (Ḳ,) inf. n. مُفَاكَهَةٌ, (Ṣ,) ‡ *He jested*, or *joked, with him*; (Ṣ, Ḳ, TA;) *indulged in pleasantry with him.* (TA.) It is said in a prov., لَا تُفَاكِهْ أَمَةً وَلَا تَبُلْ عَلَى أَكَمَةٍ ‡ [*Jest not thou with a female slave, and make not water upon a hillock*, i. e. *and publish not what is secret of thine affair*: see art. اكم]. (Ṣ, TA.) [See also an ex. in a verse cited voce تَزَنَّدَ.]

4. أَفْكَهَتْ *She* (a camel) *yielded her milk plentifully on the occasion of eating the* [*herbage called*] رُبَع, *before her bringing forth*: (Ṣ, TA:) or *she being near to bringing forth, her* صَلَوَانِ [app. meaning *two parts on the right and left of the tail* (see صَلًا in art. صلو)] *became lax*, or *flaccid, and her udder became large*; like أَفْكَّتْ. (TA in art. فك. [See also the part. n., below.])

5. تَفَكَّهَ *He ate fruit* (فَاكِهَة): (Mṣb, Ḳ:) and *He took fruit with his hand*; [*he helped himself to it*;] syn. تَنَاوَلَ الفَاكِهَةَ: and hence, as is said in the A, (TA,) the saying in the Ḳur [lvi. 65], فَظَلْتُمْ تَفَكَّهُونَ is ironical, meaning [*And then ye would be in the condition of*] *making your fruit to be your saying* إِنَّا لَمُغْرَمُونَ *Verily we are burdened with debt* (which words occur in the next verse)]: or تَفَكَّهَ here [or rather in a case of this kind] means *He threw away from himself the fruit*: thus says Ibn-'Aṭeeyeh, (Ḳ, TA,) in his exposition: (TA:) [but see other explanations in what follows:] and it signifies also *He abstained from fruit*: thus it bears two contr. meanings. (Ḳ.) — And sometimes [it means] ‡ *He amused himself with talk*; like as one amuses himself with the eating of fruit after a meal; i. e.] التَّفَكُّهُ is metaphorically used as meaning التَّنَقُّلُ بِالحَدِيثِ. (Bḍ in lvi. 65.) — And † *He affected jesting*, or *joking*. (TA.) — And تَفَكَّهُوا بِفُلَانٍ † *They spoke evil of such a one*; or *did so in his absence*; and *defamed him*; and *did thus with jesting, one with another.* (TA.) — And تَفَكَّهَ بِهِ † *He enjoyed it*: (Ṣ, Mṣb, Ḳ:) and [particularly] (Mṣb) *he enjoyed the eating of it.* (Mgh, Mṣb.) — And تَفَكَّهَ also signifies † *He wondered*, (Ṣ, Mṣb, Ḳ,) مِنْهُ *at it*; and so ↓ فَكِهَ, followed likewise by مِنْهُ. (Ḳ.) And hence [accord. to some] the saying in the Ḳur cited above, فَظَلْتُمْ تَفَكَّهُونَ i. e. † [*And then ye would be in the condition of*] *wondering* at what had befallen you in respect of your seed-produce. (TA.) — And *He repented, grieved, lamented*, or *regretted*: (IAạr, Ṣ, Ḳ:) and the words of the Ḳur cited in the last sentence above, (Ṣ, TA,) as expl. by some, (TA,) mean [*And then ye would be in the condition of*] *repenting*, &c.: (Ṣ, TA:) and so تَفَكَّنُونَ, which is of the dial. of 'Okl; or, accord. to Lḥ, Temeem say تَتَفَكَّنُونَ, and Azd-Shanoo-ah say تَتَفَكَّهُونَ. (TA.)

6. تَفَاكُهٌ signifies The *jesting*, or *joking*, [or *indulging in pleasantry*, (see 3,) of a number of persons,] *one with another.* (Ḳ.) [You say, تَفَاكَهُوا *They jested*, &c., *one with another.*]

فَكِهٌ *Eating*, or *an eater of*, فَاكِهَة [i. e. *fruit*]; (Ḳ, TA;) a possessive epithet; applied to a man. (TA.) — Also, (Ṣ, Mgh, Ḳ,) and ↓ فَاكِهٌ, (Ḳ, TA, in the CḲ فَاكِهَةٌ,) and ↓ فيكهان [app. فَيْكَهَانٌ or فَيْكِهَانٌ, like تَيِّهَانٌ], (AZ, TA,) † *Cheerful, happy*, or *free from straitness*; (AZ, Ṣ, Mgh, Ḳ;) *jocose*, or *given to jesting*, (AZ, Ṣ, Mgh,) *and to laughing*: (Mgh, Ḳ:) or the first, (Ḳ, TA,) and second, (Ḳ,) one *who talks to his companions and makes them to laugh*: (Ḳ, TA:) and فَكِهَاتٌ, applied to women, *cheerful, happy*, or *free from straitness.* (TA.) — And فَكِهٌ signifies also † *Exulting*, or *rejoicing above measure*; or *exulting greatly, and behaving insolently and unthankfully*, or *ungratefully*: (Ṣ, TA:) and thus the pl. فَكِهِينَ signifies in the Ḳur (Ṣ, Mgh) xlix. 26 [as some there read]: (Ṣ:) ↓ فَاكِهِينَ [is the more common reading and] means *enjoying an easy and a pleasant life*; or *enjoying ease and plenty.* (Ṣ, Mgh.) — And † *Wondering*: and thus some explain the pl. فَكِهُونَ in the Ḳur xxxvi. 55. (TA.) — هُوَ فَكِهٌ بِأَعْرَاضِ النَّاسِ means ‡ *He is one who delights in speaking evil of men, or in doing so in their absence.* (Ḳ, TA.)

[فَكِيهٌ is said by Golius to signify "Qui proloqui non potest," on the authority of the KL: but in my copy of the KL, I find that the word to which this meaning is assigned is فَهِيهٌ.]

فُكَاهَةٌ, a subst. [as distinguished from the inf. n. فَكَاهَةٌ], (Ṣ, Ḳ,) *A jesting*, or *joking*; (Ṣ, Mgh, Mṣb, Ḳ;) as also ↓ فُكَيْهَةٌ. (Ḳ.)

فُكَيْهَةٌ: see what next precedes.

فَاكِهٌ *Possessing* فَاكِهَة [i. e. *fruit*]; (Ḳ, TA;) an epithet of the same class as تَامِرٌ and لَابِنٌ: or, accord. to Aboo-Mo'ádh the grammarian, one *whose fruit has become abundant.* (TA.) — See also فَكِهٌ, in two places. — And [the fem.] فَاكِهَةٌ, † A palm-tree (نَخْلَةٌ) *inducing wonder*, or *admiration, and pleasure*, or *joy*; or *pleasing*, or *rejoicing*; [*app. by its having much fruit*;] syn. مُعْجِبَةٌ. (Ḳ.)

فَاكِهَةٌ a word of well-known meaning, (Ṣ,) *Fruit, of any kind*; (Ḳ;) *a thing*, or *things, the eating whereof is enjoyed*, (Mgh, Mṣb,) whether *moist* or *dry*, as *figs* and *melons* and *raisins* and *pomegranates*: (Mṣb:) [the words, of the Ḳur lv. 68, فِيهِمَا فَاكِهَةٌ وَنَخْلٌ وَرُمَّانٌ have caused it to be much and vainly disputed whether dates and pomegranates be, or be not, included among the things termed فَاكِهَة: it seems to be the general opinion of the lexicologists that they are included; but the contrary opinion is held by many of the lawyers, and by the Imám Aboo-Ḥaneefeh among them:] the pl. is فَوَاكِهُ, meaning *kinds thereof.* (Ṣ.) — And (by way of comparison [thereto], TA) ‡ *Sweetmeat*; syn. حَلْوَآءُ; (Ḳ;) which is also applied by some to "fruit" (فاكهة), (T in art. حلو,) or to "sweet fruit." (Ḳ in that art.) — And فَاكِهَةُ الشِّتَآءِ [lit. *The fruit of winter*] is metonymically used as meaning ‡ *the fire.* (Ḥar p. 594.)

فَاكِهَانِىٌّ: see فَاكِهِىٌّ.

فيكهان : see فَكِهٌ, second sentence.

فَاكِهَانِىٌّ A seller of فَاكِهَة [i. e. *fruit*]; (Ṣ, Ḳ;) as also ↑ فَاكِهِىٌّ ; (TA;) but not فَكَّاهٌ. (Sb, TA.)

كَانَ مِنْ أَفْكَهِ النَّاسِ occurs in two trads. [as meaning † *He was of the most cheerful and jocose of men*]. (TA [in which the meaning is indicated by the context].)

أُفْكُوهَةٌ i. q. أُعْجُوبَةٌ † [*A wonderful thing*]. (Ḳ.) You say, جَآءَ فُلَانٌ بِأُفْكُوهَةٍ † [*Such a one did*, or *uttered, a wonderful thing*]. (TA.)

مُفْكِهٌ (AZ, Ṣ, Ḳ) and مُفْكِهَةٌ (Ḳ) A she-camel *whose milk is thick*, (Ḳ, TA,) *like biestings*: (TA:) or *that yields her milk plentifully on the occasion of eating the* [*herbage called*] رِبْع, *before her bringing forth*: (Ṣ:) or *whose milk pours forth on the occasion of parturition, before her bringing forth*: or, accord. to Sh, the meaning is that indicated by the second explanation of the verb, 4 [q. v.]. (TA.)

فل

1. فَلَّهُ, (M, Ḳ,) aor. ـُ, inf. n. فَلٌّ, (M, TA,) *He broke it*, or *notched it, in its edge*, (M, Ḳ,) namely, [a sword or the like, or] anything; (M;) and so ↑ فَلَّلَهُ, (Ḳ, TA,) [or this signifies he did so *much*, or *in many places*,] inf. n. تَفْلِيلٌ. (TA.) —— And i. q. كَسَرَهُ [app. as meaning *He broke it*, in an unrestricted sense; as well as in another sense; as will be shown by what follows]. (Ṣ.) وَلَا فَلُّوا لَهُ صَفَاةً, i. e. [lit.] *Nor did they break a stone* (كَسَرُوا حَجَرًا) *belonging to him*, was said by 'Áïsheh in describing her father: she alluded thereby to his strength in religion. (TA. [See also قَرَعَ صَفَاتَهُ, in art. صفو; and see also مَغْمَزٌ.]) And [in like manner] one says, استفلّ ↑ غَرْبَهُ meaning كَسَرَهُ [i. e. † *He broke his sharpness*, or *vehemence*, or *valour*]. (TA.) And فَلَّ الجَيْشَ, (Ṣ, O, Mṣb,) or القَوْمَ, (M, Ḳ,) aor. and inf. n. as above, (M, O, Mṣb,) *He defeated* (هَزَمَ, Ṣ, M, O, Ḳ, or كَسَرَ, Mṣb) *the army*, or *military force*, (Ṣ, O, Mṣb,) or *the people*, or *party*. (M, Ḳ.) And مَنْ قَلَّ ذَلَّ وَمَنْ أَمِرَ فَلَّ, (Ṣ, Meyd, O,) a prov., (Meyd, O,) meaning *He who has few aiders is overcome*, [or *becomes abased*], *and he who has many relations* [or *who possesses authority to command*] *defeats* (فَلَّ) *his enemies*. (Meyd. [In Freytag's Arab. Prov., ii. 683, a different (and I think a wrong) reading is given, with قَلَّ in the place of فَلَّ; though the reading with فَلَّ is added.]) شَجَّكِ أَوْ فَلَّكِ أَوْ جَمَعَ كُلًّا لَكِ, in the story of Umm-Zara, is said to mean, *Whether he wound thee by smiting thy head, or break a limb* [*of thee*], *or combine the two deeds to thee*: or by فلّك is meant *altercate*, or *wrangle, with thee*: (TA, in two places:) or the meaning [of فلّك] is *defeat thee* [so I render كَسَرَكِ]; or *take away thy property*; or *defeat thee* (كَسَرَكِ) *with his altercation and his censure*. (O.) —— فَلَّ عَنْهُ عَقْلُهُ, aor. ـِ, [in the CḲ (erroneously) ـُ,] *His intellect*, or *intelligence, departed from him, and then returned*. (M, Ḳ.)

2: see above, first sentence. —— تَفْلِيلٌ [as inf. n. of the pass. v. فُلِّلَ] means The *state of being broken*, or *notched*, [*much*, or *in many places*,] *in the edge* of a knife, or *in the edges* of the teeth, (T, TA,) and the like, (T,) [i. e.] and also *in* [*the edge of*] a sword. (TA.)

4. افلّت الأَرْضُ *The land became such as is termed* فِلّ [q. v.]. (AḤn, M.) —— And أَفَلَّ, (Fr, T,) and أَفْلَلْنَا, (Ṣ, O,) *He* (a man, Fr, T,) and *we*, (Ṣ, O,) *became in a land such as is termed* فِلّ, (Fr, T, Ṣ, O,) *upon which rain had not fallen*: (Fr, T:) or the latter means *we trod a land* (M, Ḳ) *such as is termed* فِلّ (M) or *such as is termed* فَلّ. (Ḳ.) —— And افلّ † *He* (a man, Ṣ, M, O) *lost*, or *became deprived of, his property*: (Ṣ, M, O, Ḳ:) from فِلٌّ applied to land. (M.) —— And in like manner, one says, افلّ الدَّهْرُ مَالَهُ † [*Time*, or *fortune, deprived him of his property*]. (O.)

5: see the next paragraph, in three places: —— and see also R. Q. 1, in two places [in each of which the verb is most probably, I think, mistranscribed].

7. انفلّ *It became broken*, or *notched, in its edge*; as also ↑ افتلّ, and ↑ تفلّل; (M, Ḳ, TA;) said of [a sword or the like, or of] anything; (M;) the first quasi-pass. of فَلَّهُ, as is also the second; but the third is quasi-pass of فَلَّلَهُ [and implying that it was so *much*, or *in many places*, or said of several things or of several parts of a thing]; (TA;) [therefore] one says [of a sword], تَفَلَّلَتْ ↑ مَضَارِبُهُ, meaning تَكَسَّرَتْ [i. e. *Its edges* (for the swords of the Arabs in the older times were generally two-edged), or *its parts for striking, became broken*, or *notched, much*, or *in many places*]; (Ṣ, TA;) and one says, انفلّ سِنُّهُ, (T, TA,) meaning [simply] *His tooth became broken*, or *notched, in its edge*. (TA.) And انفلّوا *They became defeated*; (Ṣ,* M, Mṣb, Ḳ;) as also ↑ تفلّلوا [but this has an intensive signification]. (M, Ḳ.)

8: see the next preceding paragraph.

10: see 1, former half. —— استفلّ الشَّىْءَ *He took of the thing the least portion*, (M, Ḳ,) *because of its difficulty* (لِعُسْرِهِ), (M,) or *such as the tenth part thereof* (كَعُشْرِهِ): (Ḳ:) or الإِسْتِفْلَالُ signifies *the obtaining a little thing from a difficult place*; *from a place of the seeking of a right*, or *due*, or *of a gift*; it having no other object than a thing of little account. (T.)

R. Q. 1. فَلْفَلَ *He walked with an elegant and a proud and self-conceited gait, with an affected inclining of the body from side to side*; (T, O, TA;) as also ↑ تَفَلْفَلَ: (TA:) or both signify *he walked thus, with short steps*: (Ḳ:) or ↑ تفلفل signifies [simply] *he went with short steps*; (En-Naḍr, O;) or so ↑ تفلّل. (T accord. to the TT.) —— And *He rubbed and cleaned his teeth with the* [*stick called*] سِوَاك; (T, O, Ḳ;) as also ↑ تفلفل; (IAạr, O, Ḳ;) or so ↑ تفلّل. (T accord. to the TT.) —— فلفل الطَّعَامَ and الشَّرَابَ *He peppered the food* and *the wine or beverage*. (M.) —— [And فلفل الشَّعَرَ *He made the hair very crisp*, or *such as we term woolly, like that of the negro*: see the pass. part. n., below.]

R. Q. 2. تَفَلْفَلَ: see R. Q. 1, in three places. —— Said of the hair of a negro, *It became very crisp* [or *such as we term woolly*]. (M, TA.) —— And تفلفل قَادِمَتَا الضَّرْعِ *The two anterior teats of the udder became black*. (Ṣ, O, Ḳ.)

يَا فُلُ, (Ṣ in this art. and in art. فلن, and Ḳ and TA in the latter art.,) meaning يَا فُلَانُ [*O such a one*], (Ṣ &c.,) with refa and without tenween, (TA,) is sometimes said to one person, [i. e. to a man,] and يَا فُلَانِ to two persons, and يَا فُلُونَ to a pl. number; and يَا فُلَةُ to a female, and يَا فُلَتَانِ to two females, and يَا فُلَاتُ to a pl. number of females, (Ḳ, TA,) and sometimes يَا فُلَاةُ, (Ḳ,* TA,) thus correctly, of the dial. of some of the tribe of Temeem, in the copies of the Ḳ erroneously written يا فُلَاتُ, (TA,) is said, and some say يَا فُلَ, [in the CḲ يا فلُ, but correctly يَا فُلَ, i. e., as is said in the TA, بِنَصْبِ اللَّامِ,] meaning يَا فُلَةُ: (Ḳ, TA:) [J says,] يَا فُلُ, without teshdeed, said in calling to a person, is apocopated from يَا فُلَانُ; not formed in the way of تَرْخِيم, for if it were an instance of ترخيم they would say يَا فُلَا: (Ṣ in this art.:) [or,] accord. to Sb, يَا فُلُ is not held to be an instance of a word from which is elided something that is retained when it is not [thus] used in calling to a person, but the noun in this case is made to be of two letters in the manner of دَمٌ [which is originally دَمَوٌ or دَمَىٌ or دَمْىٌ], and it is thus made to be of two letters because a word that is used in calling to a person or thing is a subject for elision: (M in this art.:) and sometimes فُلُ was used otherwise than in calling to a person, by poetic license, as in the saying of Abu-n-Nejm,

* فِى لَجَّةٍ أَمْسِكْ فُلَانًا عَنْ فُلِ *

(Ṣ and M in this art.,) meaning عَنْ فُلَانٍ [i. e. *In*, or *amid, a multitude of cries*, or *noises*: (thus expl. in the Ṣ:) *withhold thou such a one from such a one*]: (Ṣ in art. فلن:) and Sb disallowed the saying فُلُ as meaning فُلَانٌ [in the CḲ (erroneously) يا فُلُ as meaning يا فُلَانُ] except [in the vocative form of speech and] in poetry: (M and Ḳ and TA in art. فلن:) [but] they said [also] فُلُ بْنُ فُلٍ, [said to be] an instance of an elision, (T and M in art. فلن,) i. e. of the elision of a final و [accord. to some, who hold فُلَانٌ to be originally فُلْوَانٌ]; (T;) like as they said هَىُّ بْنُ بَىٍّ: (T, M:) and أَىْ فُلُ, with the ل quiescent, occurs in a trad. respecting the resurrection; meaning يَا فُلَانُ: (TA:) Ibn-Buzurj says that some of the tribe of اسد [i. e. Asd or Asad] say يا فل [app. يَا فُلُ, without any variation,] in calling to a man and to two men and to a pl. number of men and to a female: (TA in art. فلن:) accord. to Aṣ, one says يَا فُلُ and يَا فُلَاهْ; he who says يَا فُلُ saying thus [when he pauses after it and] when he goes on, making the noun marfooạ without tenween; whereas he who says يَا فُلَاهْ says thus when he is silent after it, retaining the ه [which is termed the ه of pausation], but when he goes on he rejects the ه and makes the noun to be manṣoob, saying [for ex.] يَا فُلَا قُلْ [*O such a one, say*]. (T and TA in art. فلن.) [See also مُضَمَّنٌ (in art. ضمن), last sentence.]

فَلٌّ *A break*, or *notch, in the edge*, (ISk, T, Ṣ, M, O, Mṣb, Ḳ,) of a sword, (ISk, T, Ṣ, O, Mṣb, Ḳ,) [or the like,] or of anything; (M;) and so ✦ فَلَّةٌ [i. e. a *single break*, or *notch, in the edge*,] of a sword: (TA:) pl. of the former فُلُولٌ, (ISk, T, Ṣ, M, O, Mṣb, Ḳ,) of which an ex. occurs in a verse cited voce بَيْدَ: (O, TA:) it has been said that فُلُولٌ is an inf. n.; but it is more correctly said to be pl. of فَلٌّ. (M.) — And *A portion that has fallen off from a thing, like the filings of gold and of silver, and the sparks of fire*: (M, Ḳ, TA:) pl. فُلُولٌ. (M, TA.) ═ And *A company* (M, Ḳ, TA) of men; (TA;) as also ✦ فَلِيلٌ: (M, Ḳ, TA:) pl. of the former فُلُولٌ. (TA.) ═ And it is [an epithet] applied to a number of men, (Ṣ, M, O, Ḳ, [in the CḲ in this case, erroneously, فُلٌّ,]) and to a single man, (Ṣ, O,) signifying *Defeated*; (Ṣ, M, O, Ḳ;) and ✦ فُلَّى also signifies thus, applied to a كَتِيبَة [i. e. a military force, or troop, &c.]; (AA, T, O, Ḳ;) like فُرَّى: (AA, T, O:) one says رَجُلٌ فَلٌّ and قَوْمٌ فَلٌّ, and sometimes [when speaking of a number of men] they said فُلُولٌ and فِلَالٌ; (Ṣ, O;) accord. to the copies of the Ḳ, the pl. is أَفْلَالٌ and فُلُولٌ; but correctly the latter is فُلَّالٌ, like رُمَّانٌ, as in the M; (TA;) [i. e.] the pl. is فُلُولٌ and فُلَّالٌ: and [of فَلٌّ used in a pl. sense it is said that] it must be either a quasi-pl. n. or [originally] an inf. n.: if the former, the sing. should by rule be فَالٌّ, the case being like شَارِبٌ and شَرْبٌ, [of which the former is a sing. and the latter is a quasi-pl. n.,] and فَالٌّ is of the measure فَاعِلٌ in the sense of the measure مَفْعُولٌ: and فلول is not necessarily pl. of فَلٌّ, but is rather pl. of فَالٌّ; for the pl. of the quasi-pl. n. is extr., like the pl. of the pl.: (M, TA:*) and as to فُلَّالٌ, it is necessarily pl. of فَالٌّ, for فَعْلٌ is not of the forms that have فُعَّالٌ as the measure of a pl.: (M, TA:) if it [i. e. فَلٌّ] be [originally] an inf. n., [this accounts for its being applied alike to a number of men and to a single man, which is not mentioned in the M, or] it is like نَسْجٌ in the sense of مَنْسُوجٌ in the phrase نَسْجُ اليَمَنِ. (M.) ═ Also Land *affected with drought* or *barrenness*; as also ✦ فِلٌّ: or [i. e. the former accord. to the Ḳ, but app. each accord. to the text of the M as given in the TT,] *such as is rained upon but does not produce plants* or *herbage*: (AO, M, Ḳ:) or *such as the rain has failed to fall upon during several years*: or *such as is not rained upon between two lands that have been rained upon*: (M, Ḳ:) or, accord. to AO, this is termed فَلٌّ خَطِيطَةٌ; having the second of the meanings expl. in this sentence: (M:) or *upon which rain has not fallen*: (TA:) [in this sense, in the TT, as from the T, written فِلٌّ [for ✦ فِلٌّ]: and so in the same, as from the T and M, in the sense here following:] or *in which is nothing*; (T, M,* Ḳ:*) so says IAạr; whence, he adds, الفَلَاةُ; but [Az says] I do not think that it is taken thence: (T:) the pl. is like the sing., [or rather the word used as a sing. is likewise used as a pl.,] and أَفْلَالٌ, (M, Ḳ,) this pl. form being sometimes used: (M:) or the pl. of ✦ الفِلُّ is أَفْلَالٌ; and one says also أَرْضٌ أَفْلَالٌ. (T.) ═ And *A sort of cloth made of the hard fibres of flax*. (TA.)

فُلٌّ a term for يَاسَمِين مُضَاعَف [*Double jasmine*], *which is* [*rendered so*] *either* بِالتَّرْكِيب [an expression meaning, as used in the present day, *by grafting*], or *by slitting the stem thereof and inserting into it the* [*additional*] *jasmine* [app. meaning *by budding*]: *it is a flower of pure whiteness; and the rubbing oneself with its leaves perfumes the body*: (TA:) [this name, or, more commonly, ✦ فُلّ, is now applied to the *Arabian jasmine* (*jasminum sambac*), or, as Forskål says (Flora Aegypt. Arab. p. cii.), *nyctanthes sambac*, mentioned by him among the plants cultivated in El-Yemen.] — [Freytag, misled by the CḲ, has assigned to this word a meaning belonging to فَلّ.]

فِلٌّ Land *in which is no herbage*; (Ḳ;) or land *not rained upon, and in which is no herbage*. (Ṣ, O.) See also فَلٌّ, in three places. — غَدَا فِلًّا مِنَ الطَّعَامِ, with kesr, means [*He went forth early in the morning*] *devoid of food*. (O.) — And فِلٌّ مِنَ الخَيْرِ occurs in a verse, (Ṣ, O,) in the poetry of 'Abd-Allah Ibn-Rawáḥah and in that of Ḥassán, (Ṣ, O,) meaning *Devoid of good*. (Ṣ, TA.) [See عَلٌّ.] ═ And *Such as has become thin*, of hair. (Ḳ.) ═ See also فُلّ.

فَلَّةٌ: see فَلٌّ, first sentence.

فَلَلٌ, in a sword [or the like], The *state of having breaks*, or *notches, in the edge*. (Ṣ, O.)

فَلِيلٌ: see أَفَلُّ. — Applied to the tusk, or canine tooth, of a camel, *Broken* (Ṣ, M, O, Ḳ) *in the edge*. (Ṣ, O.) ═ See also فَلٌّ, first quarter. ═ Also, and ✦ فَلِيلَةٌ, *a quantity of hair collected together*: (Ṣ, M, O, Ḳ:) the two words are either of the class of سَلٌّ and سَلَّةٌ [which are exactly syn., each with the other,] or are an instance of the pl. [or rather coll. gen. n.] that does not differ from its sing. [or n. un.] except in [its not having] the [affix] ة: (M:) in one instance, occurring in a trad., the latter is said to signify *a* كُبَّة [or *portion convolved*, or *glomerated*, or *formed into a ball*] *of hair*, or, as Z says, app. *of* [*the silk called*] دِمَقْس: the pl. [of either] is فَلَائِلُ. (TA.) Hence, (O,) ✦ فَلِيلَةٌ signifies also The *mane of the lion*. (O, TA.) In the saying of Sá'ideh Ibn-Ju-eiyeh,

• وَغُودِرَ ثَاوِيًا وَتَأَوَّبَتْهُ •
• مُذَرَّعَةٌ أُمَيْمَ لَهَا فَلِيلُ •

[*And he was left remaining, and a hyena having stripes upon its arms*, (thus مُذَرَّعَةٌ as used in this verse is expl. in the TA in art. ذرع, q. v.,) *a young mother*, (أُمَيْمَ being an instance of تَرْخِيم, used by poetic license, for أُمَيْمَةُ, a dim. of أُمّ,) and therefore unusually fierce, *having a mane*, or *having convolved*, or *glomerated, hair, came to him at night*, or *in the beginning of the night*], the last word is expl. by Suh, in the R, as meaning the عَرْف [so in my original, an obvious mistranscription for عُرْف, with ḍamm]; but by Skr as meaning شَعَر مَكْبُوب. (TA.) — And فَلِيلٌ signifies also [The *membranous fibres that grow at the base of the branches of the palm-tree*, called] لِيف: (M, Ḳ:) so in the dial. of Hudheyl: (TA:) and ✦ فُلْفُلٌ signifies the same. (Ḳ.)

فَلِيلَةٌ: see the next preceding paragraph, in two places.

فُلَّى: see فَلٌّ, in the former half.

فَلِيَّةٌ, (T,* Ḳ, TA,) like عَلِيَّةٌ, (TA,) or فَلِيَّةٌ, (O,*) [in the TT, as from the T, and in the O, written without the sign of teshdeed to the ل (app. because it is sufficiently indicated by the heading of the art. and by the pl. of this word), and in the CḲ, erroneously, فَلِيَةٌ,] Land *upon which the rain* [*that should have been that*] *of its year has not fallen until the falling of the rain of the next year upon it*: pl. فَلَالِيُّ: (ISh, T, O, Ḳ:) [and Az says,] I have heard them call thus (i. e. by the sing.) land *in which is nothing*; like فِلٌّ as expl. by IAạr. (T.)

فُلْفُلٌ, (Ṣ, M, O, Mṣb, Ḳ,) also pronounced ✦ فُلْفُلٌ, (Ḳ,) but the vulgar pronounce it [thus] with kesr, (O,) and the pronouncing it with kesr is said to be not allowable, (Mṣb,) a word of Pers. origin, (M,) arabicized, from پِلْپِل, with kesr, (O,) [or پِلْپِل; i. e. *Pepper*;] *a sort of berry*, (حَبّ, Ṣ, O, Ḳ,) *brought from India*, (O, Ḳ,*) *well known*, (Ṣ, M, O,) *not growing in the land of the Arabs, but often mentioned in their language*: AḤn was informed by one who had seen it that *its tree is just like the pomegranate*; (M, TA;) *but* Dáwood the ḥakeem adds that *it is taller*; (TA;) *between the pair of leaves thereof are two fruit-stalks, regularly disposed, each fruit-stalk of the length of the finger; and it is green, and is then plucked, and spread in the shade, and becomes black and shrivelled; and it* [*the tree*] *has thorns, like those of the pomegranate*: *when it* [i. e. *the fruit*] *is fresh and moist, it is preserved* *with water and salt until it becomes mature, when it is eaten like as preserved herbs are eaten upon the tables of food, and it is a digestive*: the n. un. is ▼ فُلْفُلَةٌ [app. meaning *a peppercorn*, like حَبَّةُ فُلْفُلٍ: and حَبُّ فُلْفُلٍ means *peppercorns*, collectively]: (M, TA:) Dáwood says, in the "Tedhkireh," that *its leaves are thin, red next the tree and green in the other direction, and its wood is lank and soft*: and *it is white and black*: (TA:) *the white is the better*. (TA.) [A long description of its properties, with additions in the TA, some of them well known and others fanciful, I omit as being needless.] — دَارُفُلْفُل, or ▼ دَارْفُلْفُل, (accord. to different copies of the Ḳ,) [app. دَارُفُلْفُلٍ, or perhaps دَارُفُلْفُلٌ, a compound of two words (both originally Pers.) made one, as such written in the Ḳ with the article (الدارفلفل), and perfectly declinable, because (although a compound of two nouns) it is not a proper name,] is The *tree of the* فُلْفُل *when it first bears fruit*, accord. to the Ḳ; but several writers declare that the tree of [the] دارفلفل is not the same as the tree of the فلفل: (MF, TA:) [دارفلفل is one of the names now applied to *long pepper*, and is commonly pronounced دَارْفِلْفِل:] it is [generally] known in Egypt by the name of عِرْقُ الذَّهَبِ, [another term, now used, for long pepper,] and is called in Pers. پلپل دراز [i. e. پِلْپِل دَرَاز, the latter of which words signifies "long"]: (TA:) *it increases the venereal faculty, causes the food to digest; removes colic*, (Ḳ, TA,) *and flatulence*; (TA;) *and is beneficial as a remedy against the bite*, or *sting, of venomous reptiles, applied as a liniment, with oil*. (Ḳ, TA.) — فُلْفُلٌ is also a name sometimes applied to The *fruit of the* بَرْوَق [q. v., in art. برق]; likening it to the فلفل mentioned before [i. e. to peppercorns]: he who pronounces it, when thus applied, ▼ فِلْفِلٌ errs; for this signifies the *fruit of certain trees of the* [*kind called*] عِضَاه; and the people of El-Yemen call thus [particularly] the *fruit of the* [*species of* عضاه *termed*] غَاف [q. v.]. (M.) — فُلْفُلُ المَآءِ is the name of *A certain plant growing in the neighbourhood of water, lank, soft*, or *smooth, in the leaves, having berries* (حَبّ) *in bunches*. (TA.) — فُلْفُلُ القُرُودِ is *The same as* حَبُّ اللَّيمِ [but what this is I do not find]. (TA.) — فُلْفُلُ الصَّقَالِبَةِ is *What is called* [*in Pers.*] فنجنكشت [i. e. فَنْجَنْكُشْت: see الفَقْدُ]. (TA.) — فَلَافِلُ is pl. of فُلْفُلٌ.] And فَلَافِلُ السُّودَانِ is the name of *Certain berries* (حَبّ), *round and smooth, in sheaths*, or *cases*, (غُلُف,) *and in receptacles* (أَبْيَات) *like the* صَنَوْبَر [or *cone of the pine*, app. *in form*]. (TA.) — See also فَلِيلٌ, last sentence. — فُلْفُلٌ signifies also *A sharp*, or *clever, servant*; (T, O, Ḳ;) and ▼ فِلْفِلٌ is said to signify thus likewise by Mullà 'Alee, in his "Námoos," and even more commonly: but this requires consideration. (MF, TA.)

فِلْفِلٌ: see the next preceding paragraph, first sentence: and the same again, in three places.

فُلْفُلَةٌ n. un. of فُلْفُلٌ; q. v., former half.

أَفَلُّ, applied to a sword [or the like], (T, Ṣ, O, Ḳ,) *Having breaks*, or *notches, in its edge*; (T, Ṣ,* O;*) or *broken*, or *notched, in its edge*; as also ▼ مَفْلُولٌ and ▼ مُنْفَلٌّ. (M, Ḳ.) الأَفَلُّ was the name of a sword of 'Adee Ibn-Ḥátim (O, Ḳ) Eṭ-Ṭá-ee. (O.)

مُفَلَّلٌ, applied to a نَضِىّ [app. as meaning an arrow-head] *Broken by having hit stones*. (Ṣ.) And, applied to front teeth (ثَغْر) *Serrated*. (T.)

مَفْلُولٌ }
مُنْفَلٌّ } see أَفَلُّ.

مُفَلْفَلٌ, applied to food, (TA,) and to wine, (T, TA,) [*Peppered*, i. e.] *having* فُلْفُل *put into it*, (T, M,* TA,) *and consequently burning the tongue*: (T, TA:) or wine *that burns* [*the tongue*] *like* فُلْفُل. (Ṣ, O, Ḳ, TA.) — And A garment, or piece of cloth, *figured with round forms resembling* فُلْفُل [or *peppercorns*] *in roundness and smallness*; (T, O, TA;) i. e. (TA) *figured with the like of the* صَعَارِير [pl. of صُعْرُورَة] *of* فُلْفُل. (M, Ḳ, TA.) — And *Very crisp* hair, [*such as we term woolly*,] (T, O, Ḳ, TA,) *like that of the negro*. (TA.) — And A hide *worn*, or *eroded, by the tan*, (نَبِكَهُ الدِّبَاغُ, M, Ḳ, in the CḲ نَبَكَهُ الدَّبّاغُ,) *the like of* فُلْفُل [or *peppercorns*] *appearing in it*. (TA.)

فلت

1. فَلَتَ, intrans. and trans., syn. with أَفْلَتَ, q. v. (Mṣb.) See also 8.

3. فَالَتَهُ بِهِ, (A, TA,) inf. n. مُفَالَتَةٌ (A, O, TA) and فِلَاتٌ, (O, Ḳ, TA,) *He came upon him suddenly, at unawares*, or *unexpectedly, with it*. (A, O,* Ḳ,* TA.)

4. افلت, (T, Ṣ, O, Mṣb, TA,) inf. n. إِفْلَاتٌ; (T, Mṣb, TA;) and ▼ انفلت; (T, Ṣ, O, TA;) and ▼ تفلّت; (Ṣ, O, TA;) and ▼ فَلَتَ, aor. ـِ, inf. n. فَلْتٌ; (Mṣb;) signify the same; (T, Ṣ, O, Mṣb, TA;) i. e. *He*, or *it*, (a bird, &c., Mṣb, or a thing, Ṣ, O,) *escaped; got away*; or *became*, or *got, loose, clear, quit, free*, or *at liberty*; (O, Mṣb, TA;) [or *did so*] *suddenly*: (TA:) or ▼ تَفَلُّتٌ and ▼ انفلات and إِفْلَاتٌ signify a thing's *going forth suddenly*: (Mgh:) or ▼ انفلت signifies *he*, or *it, went forth quickly*: (Mṣb:) and one says أَفْلَتَنِى, (M, Ḳ,) for افلت مِنِّى [*he escaped*, &c., *from me*]; (Ṣgh, TA in art. جرع;) and ▼ تفلّت مِنِّى, and ▼ انفلت; (M, Ḳ;) all signifying the same. (TA.) [See exs. voce جُرْعَةٌ; and another ex. in art. حص, conj. 7.] — See also 5. — افلتهُ; (T, Ṣ, M, O, Mṣb, Ḳ;) and ▼ فَلَتَهُ, aor. ـِ, inf. n. فَلْتٌ; both verbs being trans. as well as intrans.; (Mṣb;) *He made him*, or *it*, [and *he suffered him*, or *it*,] (namely, a man, M, or a bird, &c., Mṣb,) *to escape*, or *get away*, or *to become*, or *get, loose, clear, quit, free*, or *at liberty*; *he set him*, or *it, loose, free*, or *at liberty*; (T, M, O, Mṣb, TA;) *he saved him*, or *freed him*, from destruction. (T, TA.) [See, again, جُرْعَةٌ.]

5: see 4, in three places. — تفلّت عَلَيْنَا, (Mgh,) or عَلَيْهِ, (O, Ḳ, TA,) *He seized*, (Mgh, O, Ḳ, TA,) or *came suddenly*, (TA,) *upon us*, (Mgh,) or *upon him*. (O, Ḳ, TA.) Hence, in a trad. of Umm-Háni, فَتَفَلَّتَ عَلَيْهِمَا لِيَقْتُلَهُمَا [*And he seized upon them both to slay them*]. (Mgh.) — And تفلّت إِلَيْهِ *He was desirous of it*, or *he longed for it*; (M, O, Ḳ, TA;) as also ▼ أَفْلَتَ; namely, a thing. (M, TA.) Hence the saying, أَرَاهُ يَتَفَلَّتُ إِلَى صُحْبَتِكَ [*I see him to be desirous of thy companionship*]. (TA.) And one says, لَا أَرَى لَكَ أَنْ تَتَفَلَّتَ إِلَى هٰذَا وَلَا أَنْ تَتَفَلَّتَ عَنْهُ [*I am not of opinion that thou shouldst be desirous of this, nor that thou shouldst be averse from it*]. (TA.)

7: see 4, in four places.

8. افتلتهُ *He took it quickly*, or *hastily*; namely, a thing: (M, TA:) or *he seized it*, or *carried it off, by force*; or *took it hastily and openly*; or *snatched it at unawares*. (Aṣ, O.) And it is doubly trans.: you say, افْتَلَتَهَا ٱللّٰهُ نَفْسَهَا [*God took away from her suddenly her soul*]: and hence, أُفْتُلِتَتْ نَفْسَهَا [lit. *She had her soul taken away from her suddenly*]; (O, TA;) a phrase occurring in a trad., (T, O, TA,) meaning *she died suddenly, without disease*: (T, TA:) you say, أُفْتُلِتَ نَفْسَهُ, meaning *He died suddenly*; (M, TA;) and أُفْتُلِتَ نَفْسُهُ; (Ṣ, TA;) with the نفس in the accus. case and in the nom. case; (TA;) and أُفْتُلِتَ alone; meaning *he died suddenly*. (Ṣ, O, Ḳ, TA.) [See also أُفْتُتِتَ, in art. فت; and أُفْتِيتَ in the same.] And افْتَلَتَهُ المَوْتُ; and ▼ فَلَتَهُ; as also فَلَّتَهُ; *Death took him away suddenly*. (IAạr, T, TA.) — And أُفْتُلِتَ بِأَمْرٍ كَذَا *He was taken suddenly by such a thing, before his preparing for it*. (O, Ḳ, TA: omitted in the CḲ.) — And أُفْتُلِتَ عَلَيْهِ *The affair was decided against him exclusively of him* [i. e. *without his having any part in the decision*]. (TA.) [See also 8 in art. فوت.] — أُفْتُلِتَ also signifies *It* (any affair) *was done without pausing*. (T, TA.) — And one says, افْتَلَتَ الكَلَامَ, meaning *He extemporized the speech; spoke it without consideration*, or *thought*, or *preparation*, or *without pausing*, or *hesitating*. (Ṣ, M, O, Ḳ.)

فَلْتٌ *Escape*: one says, لَيْسَ لَكَ مِنْ هٰذَا الأَمْرِ فَلْتٌ *There is no escape for thee from this affair*, or *event*, or *case*. (En-Naḍr, T, Ḳ,* TA.*)

فَلْتَانٌ and فُلْتٌ: see فَلَتَانٌ.

فَلْتَةٌ *A sudden*, or *an unexpected, event*; or *a thing that comes upon one suddenly*, or *at unawares*: and *anything done without consideration*: (IAth, L, TA:) and *an affair*, or *event, that happens without its being soundly, thoroughly*, or *well, performed* or *effected*: pl. فَلَتَاتٌ: it has no broken pl.: (M, TA:) and فَلَتَاتٌ signifies *slips*, or *faults*, *of an assembly*, or *a company of men sitting together*. (T, O, Ḳ, TA.) One says, مَاتَ فَلْتَةً [*He died suddenly*]. (M.) And كَانَ ذٰلِكَ فَلْتَةً *That* (meaning an affair, or event, Ṣ, O) *was sudden*, or *unexpected*; (Ṣ, M, O, Mṣb, Ḳ, TA;) *without premeditation*, (Ṣ, O, Mṣb, Ḳ, TA,) *and without a wavering in opinion*: (Ṣ, O, Ḳ, TA:) or, as some say, *it was* [*like*] *a thing hastily and forcibly seized*, or *snatched*: (L, TA:) and, accord. to some, it is derived from فَلْتَةٌ in the sense next following. (O,* TA.) — The *last night of any of the sacred months, of which night people differ as to whether it be lawful to war therein or not, wherefore the avenger of blood hastens to obtain retaliation*: (O, TA:) or the *last night of the month*; (Ṣ, M, O, Ḳ, TA;) i. e., *of any month*: (Ṣ, O, Ḳ, TA:) or the *last day of a month after which is a sacred month*; (Ṣ, M, O, Ḳ, TA;) as the last of Jumáda-l-Ákhireh; because a man might see therein him on whom he would take his blood-revenge, and if he delayed to do so, and the next day arrived, the sacred month commenced, and the opportunity escaped him: (M, TA:) or *an hour observed by the Arabs in the Time of Ignorance*; namely, the *last hour of the last day of Jumáda-l-Ákhireh*: they made hostile attacks, or incursions, during this hour, even when the new moon of Rejeb had risen; Rejeb not commencing until sunset: (AHeyth, T, TA:) or لَيْلَةُ فَلْتَةٍ (or accord. to MF الفَلْتَةِ, TA,) *the night by* [*the deducting of*] *which the month becomes deficient, and by* [*the addition of*] *which it becomes complete*; for sometimes some persons see the new moon when others do not see it, and these latter make a hostile attack, or incursion, upon the others; and it is thus called because it is like a thing that has been let loose after having been bound. (M, TA.) ═ See also فَلُوتٌ.

فُلَتَةٌ : } see the next paragraph.
فِلْتَانٌ :

فَلَتَانٌ i. q. تَفَلَّتٌ: (M:) [or] it is from التَّفَلُّتُ, (T,) like صَلَتَانٌ (T, Ṣ) from الاِنْصِلَاتُ: (T:) an epithet signifying *Brisk, lively*, or *sprightly*, (Lth, T, Ṣ, O, Ḳ,) *and sharp of spirit*; (Lth, T, Ṣ, O;) applied to a man, (Lth, T,) or to a horse, (Ṣ, O,) as also ↓ فَلَتٌ and ↓ فُلُتٌ and ↓ فِلْتَانٌ, (O,) the last of which is said by Kr to be pl. of فَلَتَانٌ signifying *swift, fleet*, or *quick*; (M;) or all are applied in this latter sense to a horse: (Ḳ:) and ↓ فُلَتَةٌ, كُلَتَةٌ, applied to a horse, *that leaps, springs*, or *bounds, with his whole body and limbs*. (Ḳ in art. كلت.) Also, i. e. فَلَتَانٌ, *Strong, sturdy, hard*, or *hardy*; (T, O, Ḳ;*) applied to a man. (T, O.) And *Bold*, or *daring*; (T, O, Ḳ;) applied to a man: (T:) and so فَلَتَانَةٌ applied to a woman. (T, O.) And *Desirous of evil*, or *mischief*. (M, TA.) And, some say, *Fleshy*; *having much flesh*. (M.) ═ Also *A certain bird*, (M, Ḳ, TA,) *of which they assert that it preys upon birds*, (M,) or that preys upon apes, or monkeys, (Ḳ, TA,) *said* by AḤát *to be the* زُمَّج, (TA,) which, accord. to him, is the *male eagle*: (TA in art. زمج:) *it is of a colour inclining to yellow; and sometimes it seizes the lamb*, or *kid*, *and the young child*: thus in the "Ḥayát el-Ḥayawán" &c. (TA.)

فَلُوتٌ A garment *of which the two edges cannot be drawn together, by reason of its smallness*; (A'Obeyd, T, Ṣ, O, Ḳ;) *of which the two edges cannot be drawn together in the hand*, (M, L,) *so that they escape from the hand of the wearer when he wraps himself in the garment*: (L:) applied as an epithet to a بُرْدَة; as also ↓ فَلْتَةٌ: (O, L:) or فَلُوتٌ signifies a garment *that does not remain fixedly upon its wearer, by reason of its roughness* or *coarseness*, or *its smoothness* or *softness*. (IAạr, O.)

مُنْفَلِتٌ, for which one should not say مُفْلَتٌ, as an epithet applied to a camel, *That has got loose*. (ISh, T.)

فلج

1. فَلَجَ, aor. ـُ, (Ṣ, M, O, L, Mṣb, Ḳ,) and ـِ, (Ḳ,) or the latter only [when the verb is trans. as] in فَلَجَ القَوْمَ, (TA,) inf. n. فَلْجٌ, (Ṣ, O, K,) or فُلُوجٌ, (Mṣb,) or both, and, accord. to Kr, فَلْجٌ and فَلَجٌ, but it is said in the L that these two are simple substs.; (TA;) and ↓ افلج, inf. n. إِفْلَاجٌ; (Ḳ, TA;) the latter verb authorized by AO and Ḳṭr and others, but omitted by Th in the Fṣ; (TA;) *He succeeded; succeeded in an enterprise* or *a contest; overcame, conquered*, or *gained a victory*: (Ṣ, O, Ḳ, &c.:) or *he attained his object; gained what he sought*. (Mṣb.) One says, مَنْ يَأْتِ الحَكَمَ وَحْدَهُ يَفْلُجْ [*He who comes to the judge by himself will succeed*, or *overcome*, or *gain his cause*]: a proverb. (Ṣ, O.) And فَلَجَ عَلَى خَصْمِهِ, (Ṣ, O,) and ↓ افلج, (TA,) *He* (a man) *succeeded against*, or *overcame, his adversary*; (Ṣ, O, TA;) and *got before him*, or *got precedence of him*. (TA.) And فَلَجَ بِحُجَّتِهِ, (Mṣb, TA,) and فِى حُجَّتِهِ, (TA,) *He established*, (Mṣb,) or *he overcame by* and *in*, (TA,) *his argument, plea, allegation*, or *proof*. (Mṣb, TA.) And فَلَجَتْ حُجَّتُهُ [*His argument*, &c., *was successful*]. (A.) And فَلَجَ سَهْمُهُ, and ↓ افلج, *His arrow was successful*. (O, TA.) And فَلَجَتْ بِقَلْبِى *She* (a woman) *took away* [or *captivated*] *my heart*. (A, TA.) — And فَلَجَ القَوْمَ, in which case only one says يَفْلِجُ and يَفْلُجُ, and فَلَجَ أَصْحَابَهُ, *He* (a man) *succeeded against*, or *overcame, the people*, or *party*, and *his companions*. (TA.) — فَلَجَ, aor. ـِ, (Ṣ, M, O, L, Ḳ,) and ـُ, (Ḳ,) or the former only, (MF, TA,) inf. n. فَلْجٌ, *He divided* a thing; *parted* it; *divided* it *in parts* or *shares*; or *distributed* it; (Ṣ, O, Ḳ;) as also ↓ فلّج, inf. n. تَفْلِيجٌ: (O, Ḳ:) *he divided* property, (Mgh, TA,) or running water; (TA:) and *he divided* a thing *in halves*. (M, L, Mṣb, TA.) One says, فَلَجْتُ الشَّىْءَ بَيْنَهُمْ *I divided, parted*, or *distributed, the thing between them*, or *among them*. (Ṣ, O.) And فَلَجَ الشَّىْءَ بَيْنَهُمَا *He divided the thing between them two in halves*. (M, L, TA.) And فَلَجْتُ الْفًا, aor. ـِ, inf. n. فَلْجٌ and فُلُوجٌ, *I divided, parted*, or *distributed, a thousand* [dirhems] *by means of the* فِلْج, a well-known measure of capacity. (Mṣb.) — And فَلَجْتُ الشَّىْءَ, (Ṣ, Mṣb, Ḳ,*) aor. in this case and in other cases following ـُ and ـِ, (Ḳ,) or ـُ only, (TA,) [but it is implied in the Ṣ and O and Mṣb that it is ـِ,] inf. n. فَلْجٌ, (Ḳ,) *I split the thing, clave it*, or *divided it lengthwise*: (Ṣ, O:) or *I split the thing*, &c., *into two halves*: (Mṣb, Ḳ:) or فَلَجْتُ الشَّىْءَ فِلْجَيْنِ has this latter meaning. (Ṣ, O.) — And فَلَجْتُ الأَرْضَ لِلزِّرَاعَةِ, (Ṣ, O, Ḳ,*) inf. n. فَلْجٌ, (Ḳ,) [like فَلَحْتُهَا,] *I furrowed*, or *ploughed, the land for sowing*. (Ṣ, O, Ḳ.) — And هُوَ يَفْلُجُ الأَمْرَ *He looks into, and divides*, or *distributes, and manages, the thing*, or *affair*. (L, TA.) — And فَلَجَ, inf. n. فَلْجٌ, *He imposed* the [tax called] جِزْيَة. (Ḳ.) One says, فَلَجَ الجِزْيَةَ عَلَى القَوْمِ, (T, Ṣ, Mgh,* O, &c.,) and فَلَجَ القَوْمَ, (TA,) *He imposed the* جزية *upon the people*, or *party*; (T, Ṣ, Mgh, O, &c.;) *he divided the* جزية *among the people*, or *party, imposing upon each person his portion*; (Aṣ, Mgh;*) and فَلَجَ الجِزْيَةَ بَيْنَهُمْ: (A:) [said to be] from فِلْج, or فَالِج, (Aṣ, Mgh,) or القَفِيزُ الفَالِجُ; (A'Obeyd, Ṣ, O;) signifying a certain measure of capacity; because the جزية used to be paid in wheat, or corn: (Aṣ, Mgh:) or the verb in this sense is an arabicized word. (Shifá el-Ghaleel.) ═ فَلِجَ, aor. ـَ, inf. n. فَلَجٌ and فَلْجَةٌ, *He had what is termed* فَلَجٌ, meaning [as expl. below, i. e.] *width between the teeth*, and *feet* [or *legs*, and *arms*], &c. (Lḥ, TA.) ═ فُلِجَ, (Th, Ṣ, O, Mṣb, Ḳ,) inf. n. فَالِجٌ, one of the [few] inf. ns. of the measure فَاعِلٌ; (ISd, TA;) and فَلِجَ, aor. ـَ, mentioned by IḲṭṭ and Es-Saraḳusṭee and others; (MF, TA;) but the former alone is mentioned by Th in the Fṣ, and by other celebrated lexicologists; (TA;) [and vulg. ↓ انفلج;] *He had the disease termed* الفَالِجُ [expl. below]. (Th, Ṣ, O, Mṣb, Ḳ.)

2: see 1, former half: — and see also فَلَجَ, in two places.

3. فالجهُ *He contended with him, trying which of them should succeed*, or *overcome*. (TA.) Hence one says, (TA,) أُفَالِجُكَ أُمُورًا مِنَ الحَقِّ *I will contend with thee, trying which of us shall succeed, to accomplish affairs of right*. (A, TA.)

4. افلج as intrans.: see 1, former half, in three places. ═ افلجهُ اللّٰهُ عَلَيْهِ *God made him to succeed against him*; *to overcome him, conquer him*, or *gain the victory over him*: (Ṣ, O, Ḳ:*) and *made him to excel him*. (TA.) — And خَاصَمْتُ

فَأَفْلَجَنِى *I contended in an altercation, disputed, or litigated, and he decided in my favour, and judged me to have prevailed against,* or *overcome, my adversary.* (TA, from a trad.) — And افلج ٱللّٰهُ حُجَّتَهُ, (Ṣ, O, Mṣb,) or بُرْهَانَهُ, (Ḳ,*) *God made his argument, plea, allegation,* or *proof, right, and manifest,* or *clear:* (Ṣ, O, Ḳ:*) or *established it.* (Mṣb.)

5. تفلّجت قَدَمُهُ *His foot became cracked,* or *chapped.* (Ṣ, O, Ḳ.) [See also مُتَفَلِّح, in art. فلح.] — [And تفلّجت said of a woman, *She made open spaces between her front teeth:* see the part. n., voce أَفْلَجُ.]

7. انفلج الصُّبْحُ i. q. انبلج [*The daybreak shone,* or *shone brightly*]. (TA.) ═ See also 1, last sentence.

10. استفلج فُلَانٌ بِأَمْرِهِ *Such a one mastered,* or *became master of, his affair:* and so استفلح, with ح. (A, TA.) [See the latter verb.]

فَلْجٌ an inf. n. of فَلَجَ [q. v.]. (Ṣ, O, Ḳ, &c.) — And [probably as such] i. q. قَمْرٌ [app. as meaning *An overcoming in a game of hazard*]; as also ↓ فُلْجٌ. (L.) ═ See also فَالِجٌ, in two places. ═ Also, and ↓ فِلْجٌ, (Ṣ, O, Ḳ,) and ↓ فُلْجٌ, [q. v.,] (Seer, L,) [or perhaps this is a mistranscription for فَلْجٌ or فِلْجٌ,] *The half of a thing:* (Ṣ, O, Ḳ:) pl. of the first and second فُلُوجٌ. (Ṣ, O.) One says, هُمَا فَلْجَانِ *They two are two halves.* (Ḳ.) — And one says, فِى رِجْلِهِ فُلُوجٌ, [pl. of فَلْجٌ,] *In his foot are fissures,* or *cracks;* as also فُلُوحٌ. (Ṣ in art. فلح.) — See also فَلَجٌ.

فُلْجٌ (Ṣ, O, Ḳ) and ↓ فَلَجٌ (L) and ↓ فُلْجَةٌ, (O, Ḳ,) substs., (or, accord. to some, the first and second are inf. ns., TA,) *Success; success in an enterprise* or *a contest; conquest;* or *victory.* (Ṣ, O, L, Ḳ.) One says, لِمَنِ ٱلْفُلْجُ and ↓ ٱلْفَلَجُ *To whom belongs success,* or *the conquest,* or *victory?* (Lḥ, L.) — See also فَلْجٌ.

فِلْجٌ: see فَلْجٌ. — Also, (Ṣ, O, Mṣb, Ḳ,) and ↓ فَالِجٌ, (TA,) or قَفِيزٌ فَالِجٌ, (AO, Ṣ, O,) *A certain measure of capacity,* (AO, Ṣ, O, Mṣb, Ḳ,) *well known,* (Mṣb, Ḳ,) *with which things are divided,* (TA,) *of large size, said to be the same as the* قَفِيز [q. v.]; and ↓ فَالِجٌ is said to be an arabicised word, from the Syriac فالغا: (L: [but see فُلْجٌ:]) it is said that the ↓ فالج [thus in my copy of the Mgh, but it is there strangely added that it is "with fet-ḥ," as though فَالَج,] is *two fifths of what is termed* ٱلْكُرُّ ٱلْمُعَدَّلُ, [see art. كر,] and, by 'Alee Ibn-'Eesà, that it is *larger than the* فِلْج: in the T, the ↓ فَالِج is said to be *the half of the great* كُرّ; and the فِلْج is *the measure of capacity that is called in Syriac* فَالْغَا. (Mgh.)

فَلَجٌ: see فُلْجٌ, in two places. ═ It is also an inf. n. of فَلِجَ [q. v.]: (Lḥ, TA:) and signifies *Distance,* or *width, between the teeth;* (Ḳ;) as also ↓ تَفْلِيجٌ: (TA:) or, *between the medial and lateral incisors,* (T, Ṣ, O,) *when natural;* and تَفْلِيجٌ, *distance,* or *width, between those teeth when it is the effect of art.* (T.) فَلَجٌ in all the teeth is disapproved, and not at all beautiful; but it is esteemed goodly when only between the two middle teeth. (TA.) — Also *Distance,* or *width, between the feet,* (Lth, O, Ḳ, TA,) *in the posterior direction:* (O, TA:) or, *between the shanks;* like فَحَجٌ: (ISd, TA:) or *crookedness,* or *curvature,* [or *a bowing outwards,*] *of the arms.* (TA. [See أَفْلَجُ.]) And *The turning over of the foot upon the outer side, and displacement of the heel;* in a neuter sense. (L.) ═ Also, (Ṣ, Ḳ,) and, accord. to the Ṣ, فَلْجٌ, but this is a mistake, (IB, Ḳ,) *A river:* (A'Obeyd, TA:) or *a small river:* (Ṣ, O, Ḳ:) *a rivulet,* or *streamlet;* syn. جَدْوَلٌ: (A:) or *a running spring of water:* or *running water:* (R, TA:) or *a large well:* (Ibn-Kunáseh, TA:) pl. أَفْلَاجٌ (Ṣ, O) and فَلَجَاتٌ (R, TA) [or فُلْجَانٌ, for] فُلْجَانٌ signifies *rivulets, streamlets,* or *small channels, for the irrigation of seed-produce:* and ↓ فُلُجٌ, with two dammehs, signifies *a rivulet, streamlet,* or *small channel, for irrigation, running to every part of a garden.* (L.) — فَلَجٌ is also sometimes used as an epithet: one says مَآءٌ فَلَجٌ meaning *Running water:* and عَيْنٌ فَلَجٌ *a running spring of water.* (L.) ═ And ٱلْفَلَجُ signifies *The daybreak.* (TA.)

فَلِجٌ [part. n. of فَلِجَ]: see an ex. voce أَفْلَجُ.

فُلُجٌ: see فَلَجٌ, last sentence but two. — It is also a pl. of فَلِيجٌ [q. v. voce فَلِيجَةٌ].

فَلْجَةٌ: see فَلِيجَةٌ.

فُلْجَةٌ: see فُلْجٌ.

فَلَجَاتٌ *Fields,* or *lands, sown,* or *for sowing.* (TA. [See also فَلْجَةٌ, in art. فلح.]) — See also فَلَجٌ, last sentence but two.

فُلْجٌ, [thus in the L,] accord. to Sb, *A sort of men:* one says, ٱلنَّاسُ فُلْجَانِ *The people,* or *men, are two sorts;* [for ex.,] consisting of entering and going out: [but I think it most probable that فُلْجٌ and فُلْجَانِ are mistranscriptions for فِلْجٌ and فِلْجَانِ, for] Seer says that فلج signifying "a half" and "a sort" is derived from فِلْجٌ syn. with قَفِيزٌ: thus he makes فِلْجٌ an Arabic word. (L.) See also فَلْجٌ.

فِلْجَانٌ, [said to be] from فِلْجٌ signifying "a certain measure of capacity," [but app. from the Pers. فِنْجَان,] *A* [*small porcelain* or *earthenware*] *cup out of which coffee &c. is drunk;* commonly pronounced by the vulgar فِنْجَان and فِنْجَال [from the Pers. پِنْگَان and پِنْگَال, and also called ↓ فِلْجَانَةٌ, vulgarly فِنْجَانَة; and ↓ فِيَالَجَةٌ: (see سُومَلَةٌ:) pl. فَلَاجِينُ and فَنَاجِينُ and فَنَاجِيلُ]. (TA.)

فِلْجَانَةٌ: see the next preceding paragraph.

فَلِيجٌ: see the paragraph here following.

فَلِيجَةٌ *One of the oblong pieces of cloth of a tent:* (TA:) or, *of a* [*tent of the kind called*] خِبَآء: (Aṣ, Ṣ, O, Ḳ:) Aṣ says, I know not in what part it is: (TA:) ↓ فَلِيج appears to be used for it by poetic license; or the word may be one of those pronounced with and without ة; or without ة it may be a pl. [or coll. gen. n.] of which the sing. [or n. un.] is with ة: (M, TA:) [or] فَلِيجٌ signifies *a single oblong piece of a* بِجَاد [q. v.]; and its pl. is فُلُجٌ: (L and TA in art. بجد:) and [in like manner] ↓ فَلْجَةٌ signifies *a piece of a* بِجَاد. (TA in the present art.) — See also فَلِيحَةٌ, with ح.

فَلُّوجٌ *A writer.* (Ibn-Jembeh, O, Ḳ.) And *A manager and reckoner:* from the phrase هُوَ يَفْلُجُ ٱلْأَمْرَ, expl. above. (TA.)

فَلُّوجَةٌ *Land that is put into a right,* or *proper, state for sowing;* (Ṣ, O, Ḳ;) *good, clear, land prepared for sowing:* (TA:) pl. فَلَالِيجُ. (Ṣ, O, Ḳ.) And [hence, app.,] *Any one town,* or *village, of the Sawád:* (O, Ḳ:*) pl. as above. (O.)

رَجُلٌ فَالِجٌ فِى حُجَّتِهِ *A man who succeeds,* or *overcomes, in his argument, plea, allegation,* or *the like;* as also ↓ فَلْجٌ. (TA.) And ٱلسَّهْمُ ٱلْفَالِجُ *The arrow that is successful:* (Ṣ, O, Ḳ:) *the winning arrow in the game called* ٱلْمَيْسِر: or it may mean *the arrow that is successful in a contest at archery.* (TA.) ═ See also فِلْجٌ, in four places. — فَالِجٌ (Ṣ, O, L, Ḳ) and ↓ فَلْجٌ (L) also signify *A large,* or *bulky, camel, with two humps, that is brought from Es-Sind for the purpose of covering:* (Ṣ, O,* Ḳ:) or *a camel with two humps, between the Bukhtee* (ٱلْبُخْتِىّ) *and the Arabian:* so called because his hump is divided in halves, or because his two humps have different inclinations: (L:) pl. of the former فَوَالِجُ. (Ṣ, M, Ḳ; all in art. صر.) — And ٱلْفَالِجُ signifies [*Palsy,* or *paralysis,* whether *partial* or *general; hemiplegia* or *paraplegia:*] *a disease arising from a flaccidity in one of the lateral halves of the body;* (A;) or *a flaccidity in one of the lateral halves of the body,* (Ḳ, TA,) *arising suddenly,* (TA,) *occasioned by an efflux of a phlegmatic humour, and causing the passages of the spirit to become obstructed;* (Ḳ, TA;) *this being its first effect; it deprives the patient of his senses and his motion; and is sometimes in one member:* (TA:) or *a flatus* (رِيحٌ, Ṣ, O, L, TA) *which attacks a man, and deprives him* [*of the use*] *of one lateral half of the body;* (thus in the L, and the like is said in the 'Eyn; TA;) whence it is thus called:

(IDrd, Ṣ, O:) or *a disease that arises in one of the lateral halves of the body, occasioning the loss of the senses and of motion, and sometimes in both lateral halves, and sudden in its attack; on the seventh* [*day*] *it is dangerous; but when it has passed the seventh, its acuteness ceases; and when it has passed the fourteenth, it becomes a chronic disease:* (Mṣb:) it is called in a trad. of Aboo-Hureyreh دَآءُ الأَنْبِيَآءِ [*the disease of the prophets*]: and is said by Et-Tedmuree, in the Expos. of the Fṣ, to be *a disease that attacks a man when the venters* (بُطُون) *of the brain become filled with certain moistures, or humours, occasioning the loss of sensation and of the motions of the members, and rendering the patient like a dead person, understanding nothing.* (TA.) ═ أَنَا مِنْ هٰذَا الأَمْرِ كَفَالِجِ بْنِ خَلَاوَةَ, or فَالِجُ بْنُ خَلَاوَةَ, is a saying expl. in art. خلو.

فَيْلَجٌ [The *cocoon of a silk-worm;*] the *thing from which* قَزّ *is obtained:* an arabicized word; [from the Pers. پِيلَه *pílah;* but said to be] originally فَيْلَق, and thus some pronounce it. (Mṣb.)

فَيَالَجَةٌ: see فُلْجَانٌ. [فَيَالِجَة occurs in art. قز in the TA, as its pl.; being there expl. as meaning *small cups* (فَنَاجِين) *in which wine* (شَرَاب) *is drunk:* but I think that this may be taken from a mistranscription for فَيَالَجَة.]

أَفْلَجُ, (TA,) or أَفْلَجُ الأَسْنَانِ, (Ṣ, Mgh, O, Ḳ, TA,) applied to a man, and فَلْجَآءُ الأَسْنَانِ applied to a woman, (Ṣ, O,) for the teeth must be mentioned, (IDrd, Ṣ, O, Ḳ,) [but MF disputes this,] and ▼مُفَلَّجُ الأَسْنَانِ, applied to a man, accord. to one reading of a trad., (TA,) *Having the teeth separate, one from another:* (TA:) or, *distant,* or *wide apart, one from another:* (Mgh,* Ḳ:) or *having the medial and lateral incisors distant, one from another,* or *wide apart.* (Ṣ, O.) [See also أَفْرَقُ.] And ▼مُفَلَّجُ الثَّنَايَا A man *having an interstice between the middle pair of teeth;* (Ṣ, O, Ḳ;) as also ▼فَلِجُ الثَّنَايَا; (A;) *contr. of* مُتَرَاصُّ الثَّنَايَا. (Ṣ, O.) And ▼مُتَفَلِّجَةٌ A woman *that makes open spaces between her front teeth,* for the purpose of improving their appearance. (L, from a trad., in which a curse is pronounced against her who does this.) And ثَغْرٌ أَفْلَجُ *Front teeth that are separate,* or *distant,* or *wide apart, one from another;* and ▼مُفَلَّجٌ signifies the same [app. *when they are rendered so artificially:* see فَلَجٌ]. (TA.) — And أَفْلَجُ applied to a man, *Having a crookedness,* or *curvature,* [or *bowing outwards,*] *in the arms:* when it is in the legs, the person is termed أَفْحَجُ: (L:) or *wide between the arms:* (O, Ḳ:) or *wide between the paps;* (Ṣ, L;) which last explanation is said in the Ḳ to be erroneous; but he who is wide between the paps is also wide between the arms. (MF.) — هَنٌ أَفْلَجُ *A vulva, of a woman, whereof the labia majora are wide apart.* (L.) — فَرَسٌ أَفْلَجُ *A horse having the prominent parts of the haunch-bones wide apart.* (IDrd, O, L.)

[أُفْلُجِيٌّ *Having the fingers wide apart.* (Freytag, from the Deewán of the Hudhalees.)]

مُفْلَجٌ [*Rendered*] *successful,* or *victorious;* and *safe,* or *secure.* (KL.) [See also its verb.]

مُفَلَّجٌ: see أَفْلَجُ, in three places. — أَمْرٌ مُفَلَّجٌ *An affair not rightly disposed or directed.* (O, Ḳ.)

مَفْلُوجٌ *Having the disease termed* الفَالِجُ. (Ṣ, Mgh, O, Mṣb, Ḳ.)

مُتَفَلِّجَةٌ: see أَفْلَجُ.

فلح

1. فَلَحَ, aor. ـَ, inf. n. فَلْحٌ, *He clave, split, slit,* or *cracked;* and *he cut:* (Ḳ: [compare فَلَجَ, and فَلَقَ, and فَلَذَ:]) *he clave,* and *cut, iron.* (T, Mṣb.) Hence, the saying of a poet, (T, TA,)

• إِنَّ الحَدِيدَ بِالحَدِيدِ يُفْلَحُ •

Verily iron with iron is cloven, and *cut.* (T, Ṣ, Mgh,* Ḳ.*) And فَلَحَ رَأْسَهُ, inf. n. as above, *He clave, split,* or *cracked, his head.* (TA.) And فَلَحَ شَفَتَهُ, aor. and inf. n. as above, *He slit,* or *cracked, his lip.* (L.) And فَلَحَ الأَرْضَ, (Ṣ, Mṣb,) aor. and inf. n. as above, (Mṣb,) *He furrowed,* or *ploughed, the land, to cultivate it; he tilled the ground.* (Ṣ, Mṣb. [And فَلَجَهَا has a similar meaning.]) ═ Also, aor. and inf. n. as above, *He acted with artifice, fraud,* or *guile;* (Ḳ, TA;) and so ▼فَلَّحَ, inf. n. تَفْلِيحٌ. (Ḳ, TA.) You say, ▼فَلَّحَ بِهِمْ *He acted with artifice, fraud,* or *guile, towards them, and said what was not true.* (TA.) And ▼فَلَّحَ بِهِ *He mocked at him,* or *derided him, and acted with artifice, fraud,* or *guile, towards him.* (L, Ḳ.*) — And, aor. as above, inf. n. فَلْحٌ and فِلَاحَةٌ, *He defrauded him in a sale;* syn. of the inf. n. بَخْسٌ فِى بَيْعٍ: (so in the CḲ:) or *he bade high for an article of merchandise in order to inveigh another into purchasing it at a high price;* syn. of the inf. n. نَجْشٌ فِى بَيْعٍ. (So in other copies of the Ḳ, and in the L and TA.) You say, فَلَحَ بِهِ [*He so acted towards him in a sale*]: this is when one trusts to thee, and says to thee, "Sell to me a slave," or "an article of merchandise," or "buy it for me," and thou comest to the merchants, and buyest it at a high price, and sellest by defrauding, and obtainest something from the merchant: or, accord. to the T, فَلْحٌ signifies a hirer's *exceeding* [*in an offer*] *in order that another may do so; thus inciting* him. (L.) ═ فَلِحَتْ شَفَتُهُ السُّفْلَى, [aor. ـَ,] inf. n. فَلَحٌ, *His under lip was slit,* or *cracked.* (MA.) See also فَلَحٌ below.

2. see 1, former half, in three places.

4. افلح *He prospered; was successful; attained,* or *acquired, that which he desired* or *sought,* (MA, L, Mṣb,) or *what was good,* or *felicity,* or *that whereby he became in a happy and good state:* (L:) *he was,* or *became, fortunate, happy,* or *in a happy and good state.* (MA.) It is commonly known as an intrans. verb; but Ṭalḥah Ibn-Muṣarrif and 'Amr Ibn-'Obeyd, read قَدْ أُفْلِحَ المُؤْمِنُونَ, [the first verse of ch. xxiii. of the Ḳur-án,] with the verb in the pass. form. (MF.) [See also 10.] — *He was,* or *became, in a state of safety.* (L.) — *He continued in a good,* or *prosperous, state,* (MA, L,) and *in the enjoyment of ease, comfort,* or *the blessings of life.* (L.) — افلح بِالشَّىْءِ *He lived* [or *continued in life*] *by means of the thing.* (Ḳ.) The saying of 'Abeed,

• أَفْلِحْ بِمَا شِئْتَ فَقَدْ يُبْلَغُ بِالْـ •
• ـنُّوكِ وَقَدْ يُخَدَّعُ الأَرِيبُ •

means *Live thou by what thou wilt;* whether by stupidity or by intelligence; *for* [*one's object is sometimes attained by stupidity, and the intelligent,* or *sagacious, is sometimes deluded,* or *much deluded;* or] *the stupid is sometimes supplied with the means of subsistence, and the intelligent is* [*sometimes*] *denied:* (T, L:) or the meaning is *prosper thou,* &c. (L.)

10. اِسْتَفْلِحِى بِأَمْرِكِ, said by a man to his wife, (Ṣ,) a form of words used in divorcing (L, Ḳ) in the Time of Ignorance, (L,) *Prosper thou in thy case,* (AO, Ṣ, Mgh, TA,) *and be independent therein:* (AO, Mgh, TA:) when a man says thus to his wife and she consents, his saying so once separates her from him so that he cannot take her back: (L, from a trad.:) but as it is merely an allusive expression, intention is necessary to render it binding: as some relate the trad., it is with ج [i. e. استفلجى: see art. فلج]. (MF.) [See also 4, above.]

فَلْحٌ *A fissure, cleft, slit,* or *crack:* pl. فُلُوحٌ. (Mṣb.) One says, فِى رِجْلِهِ فُلُوحٌ *In his* (a man's, Ṣ) *foot are fissures,* or *cracks,* (Ṣ, Ḳ, TA,) *produced by cold:* (TA:) as also فُلُوجٌ. (Ṣ, TA.)

فَلَحٌ *A fissure,* or *crack, in the under lip;* (T, Ḳ;) [or] ▼فَلْحَةٌ has this meaning; (Ṣ;) or signifies the *place of such a fissure* or *crack:* (L:) [or the former is a coll. gen. n.; and the latter, its n. un.:] that which is in the upper lip is termed عَلَمٌ: (T, TA:) or فَلَحٌ signifies *a fissure,* or *crack, in the lip:* or, *in the middle of the lip, less than what is termed* عَلَمٌ: or *a slitting,* or *cracking, in the lip, such as happens to the lips of the* [*Africans called*] زَنْج. (L.) — [And] The *having the under lip slit,* or *cracked.* (Ṣ. [App. an inf. n. of which the verb is ▼فَلِحَ; like as it is of فَلِحَتْ said of the under lip as mentioned above.]) ═ See also فَلَّاحٌ.

فَلْحَةٌ: see فَلَحٌ. — Also *A* [*field,* or *land, such as is termed*] قَرَاح, (AḤn, L, Ḳ,) *furrowed,* or *ploughed, for cultivation:* its pl., فَلَحَات, occurs in a verse of Ḥassán, as some relate it; but as others relate it, it is فَلْنْجَمات, with ج (AḤn, L.)

فَلَاحٌ (Ṣ, A, Mgh, L, Mṣb, Ḳ, &c.) and ▼ فَلَحٌ (Ṣ, L, Ḳ) the latter a contraction of the former, (L,) *Prosperity; success;* the *attainment,* or *acquisition, of that which one desires or seeks,* (Ṣ, A, Mgh, L, Mṣb, Ḳ,) or *of that whereby one becomes in a happy and good state.* (L.) And *Safety,* or *security.* (Ṣ, L, Ḳ.) And *Continuance,* or *permanence, in a good,* or *prosperous, state,* (A, L, Ḳ,) and *in the enjoyment of ease, comfort,* or *the blessings of life;* and the *continuance of good:* (L:) and simply *continuance, permanence, lastingness, duration,* or *endurance.* (ISk, Ṣ, L.) There is not in the language of the Arabs any word more comprehensive in its significations of what is good in the present life and in the final state than الفَلَاحُ. (TA.) حَىَّ عَلَى الفَلَاحِ, in the call to prayer, means *Come ye to the means of the attainment of Paradise, and of permanence therein:* (IAth, L:) or *hasten to the attainment of everlasting life:* (L:) or *come to safety,* or *security:* (Ṣ:) or *come ye to the way of safety and prosperity:* (Mṣb:) or *come to the continuance of good.* (L.) And you say, لَا أَفْعَلُ ذٰلِكَ فَلَاحَ الدَّهْرِ *I will not do that while time lasts.* (L.) A poet says,

وَلٰكِنْ لَيْسَ لِلدُّنْيَا فَلَاحُ

meaning [*But there is not to the present state of existence*] *lastingness,* or *endurance.* (Ṣ, L.) —— Also (both words) ‡ The [*meal,* or *food, called*] سَحُور [*that is eaten a little before daybreak previously to commencing a day's fast*]: (Ṣ, A, L, Ḳ:) so called because thereby is the continuing of the fast; (Ṣ, A;) or because of the lastingness of its utility. (L.)

فَلَاحَةٌ: see what next follows.

فِلَاحَةٌ, (thus in my copies of the Ṣ, and in the L and Mṣb,) with kesr, (Mṣb,) [agreeably with general analogy,] or ▼ فَلَاحَةٌ, with fet-ḥ, (Ḳ, [but I think that fet-ḥ is here a mistake for kesr, because فَلَاحَةٌ deviates from general analogy, and because it is a general rule of the author of the Ḳ to omit the mention of the vowel of a word when it is fet-ḥ,]) *Agriculture;* or the *art, work,* or *occupation, of ploughing, tilling,* or *cultivating, land.* (Ṣ, L, Mṣb, Ḳ.)

فَلِيحَةٌ The *pericarp* (سِنْفَة) *of the* [*tree called*] مَرْخ, *when it splits:* (Ḳ, TA:) also mentioned as with ج [i. e. فَلِيجَةٌ]. (TA.)

فَلَّاحٌ *A plougher, tiller,* or *cultivator, of land;* [*a peasant;*] (Ṣ, Mṣb, Ḳ, TA;) because he cleaves (يَشُقُّ i. e. يَفْلَحُ) the land: (TA:) [pl. فَلَّاحُونَ:] coll. gen. n. فَلَّاحَةٌ. (A, TA.) —— And [hence, as being likened to a plougher,] *A seaman,* or *sailor;* (Ḳ, TA;) *a servant of ships* or *boats.* (TA.) —— And *One who lets asses, or other beasts, on hire;* syn. مُكَارٍ: (T, Ḳ, TA:) so called as being likened to the plougher, &c., of land. (TA.) —— And *One who defrauds in a sale, in the manner described in the explanation of the phrase* فَلَحَ بِهِ. (L.)

أَفْلَحُ *Having a fissure,* or *crack, in the under lip:* (Ṣ, Mgh:) or a man *having what is termed* فَلَحٌ *in his lip:* fem. فَلْحَآءُ. (L.) 'Antarah El-'Absee was surnamed الفَلْحَآءُ because of a fissure in his under lip; the fem. form of the epithet being used because الشَّفَةُ (the lip) is fem.; (Ṣ, L;) or because his name is fem. (L.) [See also أَعْلَمُ.]

قَوْمٌ أَفْلَاحٌ [*i. q.* مُفْلِحُونَ] *A people prospering; successful; attaining,* or *acquiring, that which they desire or seek,* or *what is good,* or *that whereby they become in a happy and good state:* افلاح is a pl. of which ISd says, "I know not any sing. of it." (L.)

مَفْلَحَةٌ *A cause,* or *means, of prosperity* or *success;* or *of the attainment,* or *acquisition, of that which one desires or seeks,* or *of what is good,* or *of that whereby one becomes in a happy and good state.* (L, from a trad.)

رَجُلٌ مُتَفَلِّحُ الشَّفَةِ, and اليَدَيْنِ, and القَدَمَيْنِ, *A man having the lip chapped,* or *cracked, much, by cold,* and so *the hands,* and *the feet.* (L.) [See also 5 in art. فلج.]

فلذ

1. فَلَذَ, aor. ـِ, inf. n. فَلْذٌ, *He cut,* or *cut off.* (Mṣb.) One says, فَلَذَ لَهُ قِطْعَةً مِنَ المَالِ *He cut off for him a portion of the property:* (T:) and فَلَذْتُ لَهُ مِنْ مَالِى, (Ṣ, M, O, L,) aor. as above, (M, L,) and so the inf. n., (M, L, Ḳ,) *I cut off for him* [*a portion*] *of my property:* (Ṣ, O, L:) or *gave him* [*a portion*] *of it at once:* or *gave him* [*a portion*] *of it without delay, and without promising:* or *gave him much thereof.* (M, L, Ḳ.*) —— See also the next paragraph, in two places.

2. فلّذ, (T, L,) inf. n. تَفْلِيذٌ; (T, O, L, Ḳ;) as also ▼ فَلَذَ, inf. n. فَلْذٌ; (L, TA;) *He cut in pieces* (T, O, L, Ḳ) flesh-meat. (T, L.) Hence, in a trad., إِنَّ الفَرَقَ مِنَ النَّارِ فَلَذَ ▼ كَبِدَهُ [*Verily the fear of the fire* of Hell *cut in pieces his liver;* but perhaps فَلَذَ is here a mistranscription for فَلَّذَ]; said, by the Prophet, of one who had died from fear of the fire [of Hell]. (L.)

3. فالذ النِّسَآءَ, inf. n. مُفَالَذَةٌ, *He bandied words,* or *held colloquies, with women.* (O,* Ḳ.) One says, فُلَانٌ ذُو مُطَارَحَةٍ وَمُفَالَذَةٍ *Such a one has a habit of bandying words,* &c., *with women.* (Ḳ,* TA.)

8. افتلذ مِنْهُ قِطْعَةً مِنَ المَالِ *He cut off,* or *took, for himself, from him, a part,* or *portion, of the property.* (T.) And اِفْتَلَذْتُ مِنْهُ حَقِّى *I cut off,* or *took, for myself, from him, my right,* or *due.* (A, TA.) And اِفْتَلَذْتُهُ المَالَ *I took from him a part,* or *portion, of the property.* (Ṣ, O, L, Ḳ.)

فِلْذٌ The *liver of a camel:* (Ṣ, M, O, L, Ḳ:) pl. أَفْلَاذٌ [also said to be a pl. of فِلْذَةٌ, q. v.]. (Ṣ, M, O, L.)

فِلْذَةٌ *A piece,* or *portion,* of liver, (Ṣ, M, O, L, Ḳ,) *cut in an oblong form,* (O,) and of flesh-meat, (Ṣ, O, L, Ḳ,) and of property, (Ṣ, O, L,) and of gold, and of silver, (M, L, Ḳ,) &c.: (Ṣ, O, Mṣb:) *a piece of flesh-meat cut in an oblong form:* (Aṣ, T, M, L:) pl. [of mult.] فِلَذٌ (T, Ṣ, L, Ḳ) and [of pauc.] أَفْلَاذٌ, (T, M, L, Ḳ,) the latter irregular, as though the augmentative letter [in the sing.] were elided; or فِلْذٌ may be a dial. var. of فِلْذَةٌ, and so this pl. may be regular. (M, L.) —— أَفْلَاذُ الأَرْضِ, (M, L, Ḳ,) or أَفْلَاذُ كَبِدِ الأَرْضِ, occurring in a trad., (Aṣ, T, A, L,) relating to the signs of the day of resurrection, accord. to different relations thereof, (L,) means ‡ *The buried treasures of the earth,* (Aṣ, T, M, L, Ḳ,) and *its riches.* (L.) —— And أَفْلَاذُ كَبِدِ مَكَّةَ means ‡ *The principal and choicest persons of the inhabitants of Mekkeh; of the tribe of Ḳureysh:* so called because the liver is one of the noble parts of the body. (L.) —— الفِلَذَاتُ [(not to be mistaken for الفِلِزَّاتُ) is a pl. of الفِلْذَةُ, and] signifies الأَجْسَامُ السَّبْعَةُ [i. e. † *The seven material substances;* namely, *the four elements,* (*fire, air, earth, and water,*) *and the three products composed of these* (which are *minerals, vegetables, and animals*)]. (MF. [But in the copy of his work which I use, الاجساد is erroneously put for الاجسام.])

فَالُوذٌ (T, Ṣ, M, O, L, Ḳ) and ▼ فَالُوذَقٌ, but, accord. to Yaạkoob, not ▼ فَالُوذَجٌ, (Ṣ, O, L,) or this is the proper form, because the ه in the original Pers. word is regularly changed into ج, (MF,) [the word being] arabicized, (T, Ṣ, O, L,) from the Pers. (M, O,* L) پَالُودَه [or فَالُودَه or پَالُوده], (O,) *A kind of sweet food,* (M, O,* L, Ḳ,) *well known,* (Ḳ,) *prepared of the purest substance of wheat* (لُبُّ الحِنْطَةِ), (T, L,) or *of starch,* (TA in art. نشو,) [*with water and honey:*] pl. فَوَالِيذُ [of which see an ex. in the next paragraph]. (A.) —— Also i. q. فُولَاذٌ, q. v. (M, L, Ḳ.)

فُولَاذٌ, (T, M, O, L, Mṣb, Ḳ,) an arabicized word, (T, O, Mṣb,) from the Pers. پُولَاد [or فُولَاد or پولاد], (O,) and ▼ فَالُوذٌ also, (M, L, Ḳ,) *Steel;* i. e. *purified and refined iron;* or the *pure part of iron;* (T, M, O, L, Mṣb, Ḳ;) *which is added in other iron:* (M, L:) pl. فَوَالِيذُ. (A.) One says, الضَّرْبُ بِالفَوَالِيذِ خَيْرٌ مِنَ الضَّرْبِ فِى الفَوَالِيذِ [*The smiting with the weapons of steel* in battle *is better than the thick white honey in the sweet messes of the kind called* فالوذ]. (A.)

فَالُوذَقٌ and فَالُوذَجٌ: see فَالُوذٌ, above.

مُفَلْوَذٌ A sword *made of* فُولَاذ [i. e. *steel*]. (O, Ḳ.)

فلز

فِلِزٌّ (Lth, IDrd, Ṣ, A, O, Ḳ, &c.) and فِلَزٌّ and فُلُزٌّ, (Ibn-'Abbád, O, Ḳ,) the first of which is what is commonly known, (TA,) *White copper* (نُحَاس أَبْيَض) [app. *a sort of bronze in which the relative quantity of the tin is unusually large*] *whereof are made cast cooking-pots* (Lth, O, Ḳ, TA) *of large size, and mortars in which substances are pounded*: (TA:) or the *metals*; *gold* and *silver* and *copper* and *the like*: (A'Obeyd, A, O, Ḳ:*) or the *substance* [i. e. *recrement*] *that is removed* [or *blown away*] *by the blacksmith's bellows from molten metals*: (Ṣ, O, Ḳ:) or the *dross*, or *recrement*, *of iron*, (O, Ḳ,) *that is removed* [or *blown away*] *by the blacksmith's bellows*: (O:) or *stones*: (O, Ḳ:) its primary meaning is [said to be] *hardness*, and *ruggedness*. (IDrd, O.) الفِلِزَّات [pl. of الفِلِزّ (not to be mistaken for الفَلَذَات)] signifies *The seven metals*; namely, *gold*, *silver*, *copper*, *iron*, *lead*, *tin* [thus I here render الأُسْرُبّ], *and tutenag* [thus I render الخَارصينى, following De Sacy and others]. (Ḳzw.) —— And hence, as being likened to the فلز above described, (TA,) ‡ *A strong, hard, and thick*, or *coarse*, *man*. (Ḳ,* TA.) And ‡ *A niggard*: (Ibn-'Abbád, O, Ḳ, TA:) as though he were hard iron, upon which nothing would make any impression. (TA.) —— And *A thing upon which swords are tested by striking it therewith*. (Ibn-'Abbád, O, Ḳ.)

فلس

2. فلّسه, (Ṣ, A, O, Mṣb, Ḳ,) inf. n. تَفْلِيس, (Ṣ, O, Mṣb, Ḳ,) *He* (a judge) *proclaimed him*, (Ṣ, A, O, Mṣb,) or *pronounced him*, (O, Ḳ,) *to be*, or *to have become*, *in a state of* إِفْلَاس [meaning *bankruptcy*, or *insolvency*], (Ṣ, A, O, Ḳ,) or *to have become* مُفْلِس [meaning *bankrupt*, or *insolvent*], *and paraded him among the people as such*. (Mṣb.) —— And [hence] one says, فُلِّسَ مِنْ كُلِّ خَيْرٍ [app. meaning *He was pronounced destitute of all good*, or *of all property*]. (TA.) ═ فُلِّسَ *It was marked with spots differing in colour from the rest, resembling* فُلُوس, or *small copper coins*. (See مُفَلَّس.) تَفْلِيسُ اللَّوْنِ [used as a subst. properly so termed] signifies *Spots in a colour, differing therefrom in colour, resembling* فُلُوس. (M.)

4. افلس, [inf. n. إِفْلَاس,] *He became* مُفْلِس [which in the common legal acceptation means *bankrupt*, or *insolvent*]: (Ṣ:) or *he had no property remaining*: (O, Ḳ:) as though his دَرَاهِم [or pieces of silver] had become فُلُوس [or small copper coins], (Ṣ, O, Ḳ,) and base money: like as أَخْبَثَ signifies "his companions, or friends, became bad, wicked, or deceitful:" (Ṣ, O:) or *he became in such a state that it was said he had not a* فَلْس [or *small copper coin*]; (Ṣ, O, Ḳ;) like as أَقْهَرَ signifies "he became in a state in which to be overcome, or subdued:" (Ṣ, O:) or as though he became in a state in which to be overcome, or subdued: (Mṣb:) or *he became a possessor of* فُلُوس *after he had been a possessor of* دَرَاهِم: (M, Mṣb:) but properly, [so in the Mṣb, but I would rather say secondarily, or tropically,] *he became reduced from a state of ease*, or *competence*, or *richness*, *to a state of difficulty*, or *poverty*. (Mṣb.) ═ افلس الرَّجُلَ *He sought the man and missed his place*. (AA, O.)

فَلْس [*A small copper coin*;] *a thing well known*, (M, A, Ḳ,) *used in buying and selling*; (Mṣb;) the *forty-eighth part of a dirhem*: [i. e., *about half a farthing of our money*:] so in Egypt: (Ibn-Faḍl-Allah, cited by Es-Suyooṭee in his Ḥusn el-Moḥáḍarah:) pl. (of pauc., Ṣ, O) أَفْلُس, and (of mult., Ṣ, O) فُلُوس. (Ṣ, M, O, Mṣb, Ḳ.) [The dim. of the former of these pls. is أُفَيْلِس ▼: see an ex. below, voce مُفْلِس. The pl. فُلُوس is the common term for *Money* in Egypt and some other parts in the present day.] —— [Hence, *Anything resembling a small coin*: as —— *A counter of metal*: —— and *A scale* of a fish: as Ṣgh says,] فُلُوسُ السَّمَكِ signifies *what are on the back of the fish, resembling the* [*coins called*] فُلُوس. (O.) —— And The *seal of the* جِزْيَة [or *tax paid by the free non-muslim subject of a Muslim government*], (T, Ṣ, Ḳ,) *which was hung upon the neck*, (T, Ṣ, TA,) or *upon the throat*. (O, Ḳ.)

الفَلْس *A certain idol which belonged to the tribe of Ṭeiyi*, (IDrd, M, O, Ḳ,) *in the Time of Ignorance*; which 'Alee, being sent by Moḥammad, destroyed, taking away the two swords, مِخْذَم and رَسُوب, that El-Ḥárith Ibn-Abee-Shemir had given to it. (O, TA.)

فَلَس, from أَفْلَسَ, [app. signifying *Bankruptcy* or *insolvency*: or *a state of indigence* or *destitution*: and] *lack of obtainment*: (Ḳ, TA:) and *failure of finding him whom* [or *that which*] *one seeks*. (TA.) You say, وَقَعَ فِى فَلَسٍ شَدِيدٍ [*He fell into a severe state of indigence* or *destitution*]. (TA.) And one says, فِى حُبِّهَا فَلَسٌ, meaning *With her love*, or *the love of her*, *is no obtainment*: and the phrase حُبُّهَا فَلَسٌ, occurring in a verse of El-Mo'attal El-Hudhalee, or of Aboo-Ḳilábeh, [in which the love thus described is afterwards termed حُبٌّ مُفْلِسٌ ▼, so that فَلَس is here used for مُفْلِس, or the phrase is elliptical,] *Her love*, or *the love of her*, *is such that nothing is obtained from it*. (O.)

فَلَّاس *A seller of* فُلُوس, pl. of فَلْس. (M, O, Ḳ.)

أُفَيْلِس: see فَلْس and مُفْلِس.

مُفْلِس act. part. n. of 4 [q. v.]: pl., (Mṣb,) or quasi-pl. n., (A,) مَفَالِيسُ ▼; (A, Mṣb;) like as مَفَاطِيرُ is of مُفْطِر, [and مَيَاسِيرُ of مُوسِر;] or pl. of مِفْلَاس ▼ [which signifies the same as مُفْلِس but in an intensive degree]. (A, TA.) [The dim. is مُفَيْلِس ▼.] You say, فُلَانٌ مُفَيْلِسٌ مَا لَهُ إِلَّا أُفَيْلِسٌ [*Such a one is nearly a bankrupt*, or *nearly destitute*; *he has nothing but a few small copper coins*]. (A, TA.) —— See also فَلَس.

مُفَلَّس *Proclaimed* [or *pronounced*] *by the judge to be in a state of* إِفْلَاس. (A.) [See 2.] ═ Also, (Mgh,) or مُفَلَّسُ اللَّوْنِ, (O, Ḳ,) *A horse*, (Mgh,) or other thing, (O, Ḳ,) *having upon his skin spots differing in colour from the rest, resembling* فُلُوس [or *small copper coins*]. (Mgh, O, Ḳ.)

مِفْلَاس: see مُفْلِس.

مَفَالِيس, a pl. or quasi-pl. n.: see مُفْلِس.

مُفَيْلِس dim. of مُفْلِس, q. v.

فلسف

Q. 2. تَفَلْسَفَ *He was*, or *became*, *a* فَيْلَسُوف [or philosopher]. (M.) —— *He affected to be a philosopher*. (PU.)

فَلْسَفَة, a foreign word, *Science*; (M;) [*philosophy*; or] *love of science*: from the word here following. (O and Ḳ in art. سوف.)

فَيْلَسُوف *A man of science*; (M;) [*a philosopher*;] a word meaning in Greek *a lover of science*. (O and Ḳ in art. سوف.)

فلطح

Q. 1. فَلْطَحَ *He expanded*, and *made broad*, or *wide*, a round cake of bread; (Ḳ, TA;) as also فَرْطَحَ; both mentioned by Abu-l-Faraj: [see art. فرطح: both are app. correct; but the former seems to be the more approved:] and *he made broad*, or *wide*, anything. (TA.)

فِلْطَاح: see the following paragraph.

مُفَلْطَح A cake of bread [*expanded*, and *made broad*, or] *wide*: (IAạr, TA:) and a thing [of any kind (see the verb)] *having breadth and width*. (TA.) حَسَكَةٌ مُفَلْطَحَةٌ occurs in a trad. [meaning *A broad*, or *wide*, *head of a thistle* or *the like*]. (TA.) And رَأْسٌ مُفَلْطَحٌ means *A broad*, or *wide*, *head*; as also فِلْطَاحٌ ▼. (Ḳ.) —— إِذَا ضَنُّوا عَلَيْهِ بِالمُفَلْطَحَةِ, occurring in a trad., is expl. by El-Khaṭṭábee as meaning [*If they be niggardly*, *to him*, *of*] *the expanded cake of bread*: and it is also expl. as meaning *the dirhems* [or *money*]: (TA:) or the phrase [accord. to one relation] is إِذَا ضَنُّوا عَلَيْكَ بِالمُطَلْفَحَةِ, in which both of the meanings above mentioned are assigned to the last word. (L and TA in art. طلفح.)

فلع

1. فَلَعَهُ, (Ṣ, Ḳ,) aor. ـَ, (Ḳ,) inf. n. فَلْع, (Ṣ,) *He clave*, *split*, or *rent*, *it*, (Ṣ, Ḳ,) i. e., a thing; (Ṣ;) or it signifies, or signifies also, (accord. to different copies of the Ḳ,) *he cut it*, (Ḳ,) with a sword, &c.; and *he broke*, or *crushed*, *it*; like as one does the hump of a camel, with a knife: (TA:) and one says also فلّعهُ ▼, (Ṣ, Ḳ,) inf. n. تَفْلِيع; (Ṣ;) meaning the same; (Ḳ;) or this has an intensive signification. (O, TA.) —— And فَلَعْتُهُ [also] signifies *I made it apparent*, or *manifest*; or *exposed it to view*. (Sh, TA.)

2: see the preceding paragraph.

5: see the paragraph next following, in three places.

7. انفلع (Ṣ, Ḳ) and [in an intensive sense] ▼ تفلّع (Ḳ) *It became cleft, split,* or *rent; &c.* (Ṣ, Ḳ.) One says, انفلعت البَيْضَةُ, and [in an intensive sense] ▼ تفلّعت, *The egg became cleft, split,* or *cracked asunder.* (IF, O.) And ▼ تفلّعت قَدَمُهُ *His foot became cleft in several,* or *many, places;* or *cracked,* or *chapped:* syn. تَشَقَّقَت. (Ṣ.)

فَلْعٌ and ▼ فِلْعٌ *A fissure,* or *crack,* in the foot, (Ṣ, O, Ḳ,) &c.: (Ḳ:) pl. فُلُوعٌ; (Ṣ, O, Ḳ;) like فُلُوجٌ and فُلُوحٌ. (O.)

فِلْعٌ: see what next precedes.

فَلْعَةٌ *A piece of the hump of a camel:* (O, Ḳ, TA:) pl. فِلَعٌ. (TA.) — لَعَنَ ٱللّٰهُ فِلْعَتَهَا (Ṣ, O, Ḳ) is a foul phrase, (Ṣ,) a phrase used in reviling; (O, Ḳ;) or, as in the T, one says in reviling a female slave, قَبَّحَ ٱللّٰهُ فِلْعَتَهَا, meaning [*May God remove far from all that is good*] *her rima vulvæ;* or *what is cleft,* or *cracked,* or *chapped, of her heel:* or, as Kr says, ▼ فَلْعَتَهَا, app. meaning فَرْجَهَا [*her vulva*]; for فَلَعَة, [thus] مُحَرَّكَة, means the فَرْج. (TA.)

فَلَعَةٌ: see what next precedes.

فَلُوعٌ A *very sharp* sword; one *that cuts much:* pl. فُلُعٌ. (Ḳ. [See also مِفْلَعٌ.])

فَالِعَةٌ *A calamity,* or *misfortune:* pl. فَوَالِعُ. (O, Ḳ.)

مِفْلَعٌ A *sharp,* or *cutting,* sword. (TA. [See also فَلُوعٌ.])

مَزَادَةٌ مُفَلَّعَةٌ [*A leathern water-bag composed*] *of several pieces of skins sewed together.* (O, Ḳ.)

فلق

1. فَلَقَهُ, aor. ـِ, (Ṣ, Mgh, O, Mṣb, Ḳ,) inf. n. فَلْقٌ, (Ṣ, Mgh, O, Mṣb,) *He split it, clave it,* or *divided it lengthwise;* (Ṣ, Mgh, O, Mṣb, Ḳ;) as also ▼ فلّقهُ, (Ṣ,* Ḳ,) inf. n. تَفْلِيقٌ; (Ṣ;) or the latter has an intensive signification [or relates to a number of objects]. (O,* Mṣb.) 'Alee used often to swear by saying, وَٱلَّذِى فَلَقَ ٱلْحَبَّةَ وَبَرَأَ ٱلنَّسَمَةَ [*By Him who clave the grain,* making it to germinate, *and created,* or *produced, man,* or *the soul*]. (TA.) — [Hence,] فَلَقَ ٱلصُّبْحَ, (Ṣ,) or ٱلْفَجْرَ, (TA,) said of God, (Ṣ,* TA,) *He made the dawn* [*to break,* or] *to appear.* (TA.) — فلقت النَّخْلَةُ [app. فَلَقَت, the part. n. being فَالِقٌ, q. v.,] means *The palm-tree split,* or *clave, from* [*around,* i. e. *so as to disclose,*] *the spathe.* (TA.) — And فَلَقَ فِى ٱلْأَرْضِ, aor. ـِ, inf. n. فَلْقٌ, *He went far into the land;* like غَلَقَ. (Ibn-'Abbád, O and TA in art. غلق.) ═ And فَلْقٌ, (Ḳ,) as inf. n. of فَلَقَ in the phrase فَلَقَ صُوفَ ٱلْجِلْدِ, (TḲ,) signifies The *plucking* of the wool of the hide *when it has become stinking;* like مَرْقٌ. (Ḳ, TA. [كَالْمَرَقِ, in the CḲ, is a mistake, for كَالْمَرْقِ.])

2: see above, first sentence.

4. افلق *He did,* or *performed,* or *he uttered, what was admirable,* or *wonderful;* (Ṣ, O, Mṣb, Ḳ, TA;) said of a man, (Ṣ, O, TA,) and (TA) of a poet, (Ṣ,* O,* Mṣb, Ḳ, TA,) in his poetry; (TA;) as also ▼ افتلق. (Ṣ, Ḳ.) [From فِلْقٌ, q. v.] — And *He brought to pass that which was a calamity;* (Ḳ;) as also ▼ افتلق. (Lḥ, TA.) One says to a man, جِئْتَ بِعُلَقَ فُلَقَ i. e. أَعْلَقْتَ وَأَفْلَقْتَ, meaning [*Thou hast brought to pass*] *that which is a calamity.* (Ṣ, O, Ḳ.*) — And افلق فِى ٱلْأَمْرِ *He was,* or *became, skilled in the affair.* (TA.)

5: see 7, first sentence. [Hence] one says, تَصَدَّعَتِ ٱلْبَيْضَةُ وَلَمْ تَتَفَلَّقْ [*The egg cracked,* or rather *cracked in several places, but did not split apart,* or *did not split much*]. (Az, Ṣ in art. قيض.) And of milk such as is termed رَائِب [q. v.] one says تفلّق meaning *It became dissundered,* or *curdled, by reason of intense sourness:* or, as heard by Az from some of the Arabs, *it, being collected in a skin, and smitten by the heat of the sun, became dissundered,* or *curdled, so that the milk* [or *curds*] *became separate* [*from the whey*]: and of such milk they loathe the drinking. (TA.) — And تفلّق ٱلصُّبْحُ: see 7. — تفلّق said of a boy: see Q. Q. 2. — See also 8, in two places.

7. انفلق *It became split, cleft,* or *cloven,* or *divided lengthwise; it split, clave,* or *clave asunder;* (Ṣ, Mgh, O, Mṣb, Ḳ;) as also ▼ تفلّق; (Ṣ, Mgh,* Ḳ;) [or] the latter signifies تَشَقَّقَ [i. e. *it became split, &c., much,* or *in pieces,* or *in several* or *many places*]. (O, Mṣb.) The former occurs in the Ḳur xxvi. 63, said of the sea [as meaning *It clave asunder*]. (O.) — [Hence,] انفلق ٱلصُّبْحُ (Ṣ and Ḳ in art. عطس) and ▼ تفلّق (TA in the present art.) *The dawn broke.* (TA in explanation of the latter.)

8. افتلق *He* (a man, TA) *strove,* or *exerted himself, so that he excited wonder by reason of his vehemence* in running; as also ▼ تفلّق and ▼ تَفَيْلَقَ. (Ḳ.) One says, مَرَّ يَفْتَلِقُ فِى عَدْوِهِ, (Ṣ, O,) and ▼ يَتَفَلَّقُ فيه, and ▼ يَتَفَيْلَقُ, (O,) *He passed along doing what was wonderful by reason of his vehemence in his running.* (Ṣ, O.) See also 4, in two places.

Q. Q. 2. تَفَيْلَقَ, said of a boy, *He became big,* or *bulky, and fat,* or *plump;* (O, Ḳ, TA;) as also ▼ تفلّق; both mentioned in the "Nawádir." (TA.) — See also 8, in two places.

فَلْقٌ, (AHeyth, TA,) or ▼ فَلَقٌ, (Ṣ, O, TA,) the former said by AHeyth to be the more correct, (TA,) *A split, fissure, cleft,* or *longitudinal division;* syn. شَقٌّ: pl. فُلُوقٌ: (Ṣ, O, TA:) and ▼ فَلَقٌ (Lḥ, Ḳ, TA) [or فَلْقٌ ?] signifies also [particularly] *a fissure,* or *cleft,* (شَقٌّ) *in a mountain;* (Lḥ, Ḳ, TA;) and so ▼ فَالِقٌ: (Ḳ, TA:) and *a* شِعْب [app. meaning *gap,* or *ravine,* or *pass*]. (TA.) One says, مَرَرْتُ بِحَرَّةٍ فِيهَا فُلُوقٌ, meaning شُقُوقٌ [i. e. *I passed by a stony tract such as is termed* حَرَّة *in which were fissures,* or *clefts*]. (Ṣ, O.) And فِى رِجْلِهِ فُلُوقٌ i. e. شُقُوقٌ [*In his foot,* or *leg, are fissures* or *clefts*]. (Aṣ, Ṣ, O,* Ḳ.) And كَلَّمَنِى مِنْ فَلْقِ فِيهِ (Lḥ, Ṣ, O, Ḳ) and ▼ فِلْقِ فِيهِ, (Lḥ, Ṣ, Ḳ,) the former of which is the more known, (TA,) meaning مِنْ شَقِّهِ [*He spoke to me from out the fissure of his mouth,* i. e., *with his lips,* not by means of a spokesman]. (Ḳ.) And ضَرَبَهُ عَلَى فَلْقِ رَأْسِهِ *He struck him on the place where his hair was separated, the middle of his head.* (TA.) — See also فَلَقٌ. ═ And see the paragraph here following, last quarter.

فِلْقٌ: see the next preceding paragraph. ═ See also فِلْقَةٌ, in two places. — Also *A rod,* or *branch, that is split in two,* (Ṣ, O, Ḳ,) [i. e., *in halves,*] *and of which are then made two bows, each whereof is termed* فِلْق, (Ṣ, O,) [or] *each half* (كُلُّ شِقٍّ [in the CḲ شَقِّ]) *of what is thus split is termed* فِلْق: (Ḳ, TA:) and thus is termed *a bow that is made of the half of a branch,* (Ḳ, TA,) *the branch being split in two;* and it is also termed قَوْسٌ فِلْقٌ, the latter word being thus used as an epithet, on the authority of Lḥ: or, as AHn says, the bow termed فِلْق is one *of which the wood whereof it has been made has been previously split in two,* or *three, pieces:* and he also says that ▼ فَلِيقٌ [app. for قَوْسٌ فَلِيقٌ] signifies *a bow of which the piece of wood has been split in two pieces.* (TA.) [See also شَرِيجٌ, in two places: and see فَرْعٌ.] ═ Also *A wonderful thing* or *affair* or *case;* (Ṣ, O, Mṣb, Ḳ;) as also ▼ فَلِيقٌ, (Ḳ,) and ▼ فَيْلَقٌ, (TA,) and ▼ فَلِيقَةٌ, (O,* TA,) of which last an ex. occurs in the prov.,

• يَا عَجَبِى لِهٰذِهِ ٱلْفَلِيقَهْ •

• هَلْ تَغْلِبَنَّ ٱلْقُوَبَاءُ ٱلرِّيقَهْ •

[*O my wonder at this wonderful thing! Does the ringworm indeed overcome the spittle?*]: AA says, the meaning is, that he was in wonder at the alteration of usual occurrences; for the spittle usually dispels the ringworm, so he spat upon his ringworm, but it did not become healed: القوباء is made an agent; and الريقة, an objective complement. (O, TA.) — And *A calamity,* or *misfortune;* (Ṣ, O, Ḳ;) as also ▼ فِلْقَةٌ, (Ḳ, TA, accord. to the CḲ ▼ فَلْقٌ,) and ▼ فَلِيقٌ, (O, Ḳ,) and ▼ فَلِيقَةٌ, (Ṣ, O, Ḳ,) and ▼ فِلْقَى (Ḳ, TA) or ▼ فَلْقَى, (TA,) and ▼ فَيْلَقٌ, (O and CḲ,) and ▼ مُفْلِقَةٌ. (IDrd, O, Ḳ.) The Arabs say, ▼ يَا لَلْفَلِيقَةِ *O* [come with succour] *to the calamity.* (Ṣ, O.) And ▼ جَآءَ بِعُلَقَ فُلَقَ, (Ṣ, O, Ḳ,) imperfectly decl., (Ṣ, O,) i. e. [*He brought to pass*] *that which was a calamity:* (Ṣ, O, Ḳ:) and ▼ بِعُلَقٍ فُلَقٍ: (O, Ḳ:) or this means *a very wonderful thing.* (TA.)

فَلَقٌ: see فِلْقٌ, first sentence, in two places. — Also The *daybreak,* or *dawn;* (Ṣ, O, Ḳ;) as also ▼ فَلَقٌ, mentioned by Z and others; (TA;) and thus the former has been expl. as signifying in the Ḳur cxiii. 1: (Ṣ, O, TA:) or *what has broken* (انفلق) *of the* عَمُود *of the dawn;* (Fr, Ḳ, TA;) i. e. [*of the bright gleam of dawn; of the dawn that rises and spreads, filling the horizon with its whiteness;* or] the *extending light that is like the* [*long tent called*] عَمُود: (TA:) or [simply] the *light of daybreak* or *dawn:* (Mṣb, Ḳ:*) or the *appearing of the daybreak* or *dawn:* (Zj, TA:) and فَلَقُ الصُّبْحِ signifies *the light,* and *shining,* or *bright shining, of the daybreak* or *dawn:* (TA:) one says, هُوَ أَبْيَنُ مِنْ فَلَقِ الصُّبْحِ and فَرَقِ الصُّبْحِ [*It is more distinct than what has broken of the bright gleam of dawn*]. (O, TA.) — And [hence,] The *plain appearing of the truth after its having been dubious.* (TA.) ═ Also *A low,* or *depressed, place of the earth, between two hills,* or *elevated grounds;* (Aṣ, Ṣ, O, Ḳ;) as also ▼ فَالِقٌ, (Ṣ, O, Ḳ,) and ▼ فَالِقَةٌ, (Ḳ,) which last is said by Aboo-Kheyreh, or some other, of the Arabs of the desert, to be *in the midst of mountains, giving growth to trees, a place where people alight and where camels,* or *other cattle, remain during the cold night,* saying that the ▼ فالق is *of hard,* or *hard and level, ground;* (TA;) and the pl. of فَلَقٌ is فُلْقَانٌ (Ṣ, Ḳ, TA) and أَفْلَاقٌ also: (TA:) or فَلَقٌ, (Ḳ,) or ▼ فَالِقٌ, (TA,) signifies *a wide tract of land* or *ground, between two extended tracts of sand;* (Ḳ, TA;) and the pl. of the latter word is فُلْقَانٌ, like as حُجْرَانٌ is pl. of حَاجِرٌ. (TA.) ═ And الفَلَقُ signifies *Hell;* syn. جَهَنَّمُ: (Ḳ:) or *a certain well* (جُبٌّ) *therein.* (Es-Suddee, O, Ḳ.) ═ And *The whole creation; all the beings,* or *things, that are created.* (Zj, Ṣ, O, Ḳ.) This, accord. to some, is the meaning in the Ḳur cxiii. 1. (Ṣ, O.) ═ And *What remains, of milk, in the bottom of the bowl;* whence one says, (in reviling a person, attributing to him meanness, TA,) يَا ٱبْنَ شَارِبِ الفَلَقِ [*O son of the drinker of what remains* &c.]. (Ḳ, TA.) — And The milk *that is in a dissundered,* or *curdled, state, by reason of sourness;* as also ▼ مُتَفَلِّقٌ. (Ḳ.) ═ And *The* مِقْطَرَة *of the keeper of a prison;* (Ṣ, O,* Ḳ;) i. e. [*a kind of stocks;*] *a piece of wood in which are holes of the size of the shank, wherein men are confined,* (Ḳ, TA,) i. e. *thieves and waylayers,* (TA,) *in a row:* (Ḳ, TA:) whence the saying of Z, بَاتَ فُلَانٌ فِى الشَّفَقِ وَالفَلَقِ مِنَ الشَّفَقِ إِلَى الفَلَقِ i. e. [*Such a one passed the night*] *in fear and the* مقطرة [*from* the time of *the redness of the region of sunset after the setting of the sun until the dawn*]. (TA.) See also فَلَقَةٌ.

جَآءَ بِعُلَقَ فُلَقَ: and بِعُلَقٍ فُلَقٍ: see فِلْقٌ, last sentence.

الفَلَقَةُ *A certain brand, beneath the ear of a camel,* (O, Ḳ,) *in the form of a ring in the middle of which is a perpendicular line dividing it* [*from top to bottom, and,* in some copies of the Ḳ, *extending downwards so that about half of its length is below the ring*]. (O, Ḳ.* [In some copies of the latter it is figured, but somewhat differently in different copies.]) — See also فَلَقَةٌ.

فِلْقَةٌ *A piece* [properly *that has been split off*] (Mgh, Mṣb, KL) of a thing; as also ▼ فِلْقٌ: (KL:) or *a fragment,* or *piece broken off,* (Ṣ, O, Ḳ, TA) of bread, or of a [bowl such as is termed] جَفْنَة, (TA,) or of this latter the *half,* (Ṣ, O, Ḳ, TA,) as in the saying أَعْطِنِى فِلْقَةَ الجَفْنَةِ [*Give thou to me the half of the bowl,* perhaps meaning, *of its contents*], (Ṣ, O, TA,) or, as some say, *one of the divided halves thereof:* (TA:) the pl. of فِلْقَةٌ is فِلَقٌ: (Mgh, TA:*) and ▼ فِلَاقٌ is app. a pl., like أَفْلَاقٌ, (and perhaps فُلُوقٌ, mentioned voce فِلَاقٌ,) and ▼ فُلَاقٌ a quasi-pl. n., of ▼ فِلْقٌ, all agreeably with analogy; whence] one says, صَارَ البَيْضُ فِلَاقًا ▼, and ▼ فُلَاقًا, meaning أَفْلَاقًا, (Ṣ, O, Ḳ,) i. e. [*The eggs became fragments;* or it means, *became cleft in pieces;* or] *became much cleft,* or *cleft in many places.* (Ḳ, TA. [See also فُلَاقٌ and فِلَاقٌ below.]) ═ See also فِلْقٌ, last quarter.

فَلَقَةٌ [signifies, in the present day, *A thick staff, to the ends of which are attached the two ends of a rope, by means whereof a man's legs are secured, between the rope and the staff, when he is bastinaded;* and it is also called ▼ فَلَقٌ: this may perhaps be meant by its being said in the TA, on the authority of Lḥ, that الفَلَقَةُ signifies الخَشَبَةُ; as also ▼ الفَلْقَةُ].

فَلْقَى, or فَلَقَى: see فِلْقٌ, last quarter.

فَلْقَآءُ الضَّرَّةِ A ewe, or she-goat, (شَاةٌ,) *wide,* or *ample, in the udder.* (Ibn-'Abbád, O, Ḳ.)

فُلْقَانٌ *A sheer,* or *an unmixed, lie.* (IAạr, O, Ḳ.) [It is also a pl.: see فَلَقٌ, in two places.]

فِلَاقٌ: see فِلْقَةٌ, in two places. — Also, (O, Ḳ,) and فُلُوقٌ, (thus in the O,) or ▼ فَلُوقٌ, like صَبُورٌ, (thus in the Ḳ, [but this I think questionable,]) Milk *becoming,* or *become, like cheese:* (O, Ḳ:) [or فِلَاقٌ may be here a quasi-pl. n. of فِلْقٌ (q. v. voce فِلْقَةٌ), so that the meaning may be, *that has become cleft portions of curd;* and فُلُوقٌ may also mean thus as a pl. of فِلْقٌ. See also the next paragraph.]

فُلَاقٌ: see فِلْقَةٌ, in two places. — Also The *state of* milk's *becoming thick and sour,* so that it curdles, or becomes dissundered: (IAạr, Ḳ, TA:) [or it may be here a pl. of فِلْقٌ (q. v. voce فِلْقَةٌ), for in a verse cited by IAạr the milk in this case is termed ذُو فُلَاقٍ, so that it may mean the *separate portions of curd* of milk that has become thick and sour; though it is said in the TA that its pl. is فُلُوقٌ, for this I think very questionable. See also the next preceding paragraph.]

فَلُوقٌ: see فِلَاقٌ.

فَلِيقٌ: see فِلْقٌ, former half. — Also The *depressed place in the* جِرَان [or *under part of the neck*] *of the camel, where is the passage of the windpipe:* (Ṣ, O, Ḳ:) or, accord. to Lth, the *part that is* [*as though it were*] *cleft, of the interior of the neck of the camel:* (O, TA:) or, as some say, the *part between the* [*two sinews called the*] عِلْبَاوَانِ, *when the fur between these is* [*as though it were*] *cleft:* and it is not said in relation to a human being. (TA.) — And الفَلِيقُ also signifies [*The cephalic vein;*] *a certain vein in the upper arm,* (O, Ḳ,) *that runs to the* [*cartilage called*] نُغْض *of the shoulder-blade:* it is *the vein of the* وَاهِنَة; and is [*also*] *called* الجَائِفُ [q. v., and see also الوَرِيدُ]. (O.) And *A certain vein that swells up in the neck.* (Ḳ.) ═ See, again, فِلْقٌ, in two places.

فُلَاقَةُ آجُرٍّ *A piece of baked brick:* (Lḥ, Ḳ:) pl. فِلَاقٌ. (So in copies of the Ḳ. [Probably a mistranscription for ▼ فُلَاقٌ, which, if correct, is properly a coll. gen. n.])

فُلَيْقَةٌ: see فِلْقٌ, in three places. ═ Also *A quantity collected together,* (فَلِيلَةٌ, Ḳ, TA, in the O without any point to the first letter,) or *a small quantity,* (قُلَيلَةٌ, thus in some copies of the Ḳ,) *of hair:* (O, Ḳ, TA:) mentioned by Ibn-'Abbád. (O, TA.) ═ And *A sort of broth;* thus termed by the people of El-Medeeneh; occurring in a trad. as related by Ibráheem El-Ḥarbee; (O;) or *a pottage* (قِدْر) *that is cooked, and into which fragments* (فِلَق, i. e. كِسَر,) *of bread are crumbled:* (TA:) but accord. to AA, it is called فَرِيقَةٌ only. (O, TA.)

فُلُوقٌ: } see مُفَلَّقٌ.
فُلَّيْقٌ: }

فَالِقٌ *Splitting, cleaving,* or *dividing lengthwise.* (TA.) فَالِقُ الحَبِّ وَالنَّوَى, (O, Ḳ,*) in the Ḳur [vi. 95], (O,) means *The Cleaver of the dry grain* so as to produce therefrom green leaves [*and of the date-stone*]: or, as some say, *the Creator thereof.* (O, Ḳ.*) And hence the saying of 'Áisheh, إِنَّ البُكَآءَ فَالِقٌ كَبِدِى [*Verily weeping is cleaving my liver*]. (TA.) — Hence, also, in the Ḳur [vi. 96], فَالِقُ الإِصْبَاحِ *He who causeth the dawn to break:* in which instance, also, فالق has reference to the meaning of *Creator:* (O, TA:) so says Zj. (TA.) — نَخْلَةٌ فَالِقٌ means *A palm-tree splitting,* or *cleaving from* [*around,* i. e. *so as to disclose,*] *the spathe:* (O, Ḳ,* TA:) pl. فُلْقٌ. (TA.) — الفَوَالِقُ as pl. of الفَالِقُ signifies *The veins that divide* [*so as to form ramifying veins* (thus I render ▼ العُرُوقُ المُتَفَلِّقَةُ)] *in the human being.* (Ibn-'Abbád, O, TA.) — See also فَلَقٌ, first sentence. — And see فِلْقٌ, former half, in three places. — خَلَّيْتُهُ بِفَالِقَةِ ▼ الوَرِكَةِ, or, as in the T, بِفَالِقِ الوَرِكَآء, [thus in the TA, but I think that الوركة and الوركآء are evidently mistranscriptions, and that the right reading is الوَدْكَآءِ, with دال,] meaning [*I left him in the low, or depressed, tract in the midst of*] the sand [called *El-Wedkà*]. (TA.)

فَيْلَقٌ *An army; a military force:* (Ṣ, O, Ḳ:) or *a great* [*military force such as is termed*] كَتِيبَة: (Ḳt, Mṣb, TA:) this is the primary signification, and the only one known to Ḳt: (TA:) pl. فَيَالِقُ. (Ṣ, Ḳ.) One says, رَمَاهُمْ بِفَيْلَقٍ شَهْبَآءَ, meaning [*He assailed them*] *with a formidable* [*great*] كَتِيبَة. (TA.) — And *A great, big,* or *large,* man: (O, Ḳ:) occurring in this sense in a trad., as an epithet applied to Ed-Dejjál: Ḳt doubted whether it were thus or فَيْلَمٌ; but Az affirms that both have this meaning. (O.) And one says, بُلِىَ فُلَانٌ بِٱمْرَأَةٍ فَيْلَقٍ, meaning [*Such a one was tried,* or *afflicted, with a woman,* or *wife,*] *cunning, evil, and clamourous.* (TA.) — See also فِلْقٌ, in two places. = Also [The *cocoon of a silk-worm;*] the *thing from which* قَزّ *is obtained;* an arabicized word. (Mṣb voce فَيْلَج, q.v.: mentioned also in the Mgh, in art. فرش.)

فَالِقَةٌ, as a subst.: see فِلْقٌ, former half: and see also فَالِقٌ, last sentence.

قُتِلَ فُلَانٌ أَفْلَقَ قِتْلَةٍ means *Such a one was slain with the hardest,* or *most violent, sort of slaughter.* (Lḥ, TA.) — And مَا رَأَيْتُ سَيْرًا أَفْلَقَ مِنْ هٰذَا *I have not seen a journey further in extent than this.* (Lḥ, TA.)

مُفْلِقٌ A poet *who poetizes admirably,* or *wonderfully.* (Ṣ, O.)

مَفْلَقَةٌ: see فِلْقٌ, last quarter.

مُفَلِّقٌ, applied to a peach, and an apricot, and the like, *that splits,* or *cleaves, from* [*around,* i.e. *so as to disclose,*] *its stone, and becomes dry:* and ↓فُلُّوقٌ, with ḍamm to the ف, and also to the ل, with teshdeed, signifies *such as does not become dry:* (Mṣb:) or ↓فُلَّيْقٌ, (Ṣ, O, Ḳ,) with ḍamm and [then] teshdeed, (Ṣ,) like قُبَّيْطٌ, (O, Ḳ,) signifies, applied to a peach, *that splits,* or *cleaves, from* [*around*] *its stone:* and مُفَلَّقٌ, *such as becomes dry.* (Ṣ, Ḳ.)

مِفْلَاقٌ A man *low, ignoble,* or *mean, and poor,* or *destitute:* (Lth, O, Ḳ:) or one *who possesses no property:* pl. مَفَالِيقُ: and to such is likened such as possesses no knowledge nor understanding of a juridical decision. (O.) And A man *who does,* or *utters, evil,* or *disliked,* or *hateful, things.* (TA.)

مَفْلُوقٌ A camel *marked with the brand termed* فَلْقَة [q.v.]. (O, Ḳ.)

مُتَفَلِّقٌ: see فِلْقٌ, last quarter: — and see فَالِقٌ.

فلقس

فَلْقَسٌ: see the following paragraph, latter sentence.

فَلَنْقَسٌ *One whose mother is Arab, but not his father:* (Lth, O, Ḳ:) or *one whose father is such as is termed* مَوْلًى [i.e. *a freedman under the patronage of his emancipator*], *and whose mother is Arab;* (Ṣ, O, Ḳ;) thus says A'Obeyd, (Ṣ, O,) and thus Sh: (TA:) or *one whose father and mother are Arabs, and whose two grandmothers are slaves;* (O, Ḳ;) thus accord. to AZ and AHeyth (O) and ISk, and this is [said to be] the right explanation: (TA:) or *one whose father is a* مولى [expl. above], *and his mother the like,* i.e. *a* مَوْلَاة; (Ṣ, O, Ḳ;) thus accord. to Abu-l-Ghowth. (Ṣ, O.) — Also, (O, Ḳ,) and ↓فَلْقَسٌ, (Ḳ,) *Niggardly,* or *a niggard;* and *vile,* or *ignoble.* (O, Ḳ.*)

فلك

1: see the next paragraph, in two places.

2. فَلَّكَ, (Ṣ, O, Ḳ,) inf. n. تَفْلِيكٌ, (Ṣ,) said of a girl's breast, *It became round,* (Ṣ, O, Ḳ, TA,) *like the* فَلْكَة [or *whirl* (*of a spindle*)], but less than is denoted by نُهُودٌ [inf. n. of نَهَدَ, q.v.]; (TA;) as also ↓تفلّك, (Ṣ, O, Ḳ,) and ↓افلك, (Th, O, Ḳ,) and ↓فَلَكَ. (Ibn-'Abbád, O, Ḳ.) — And فلّكت, (Ḳ,) inf. n. as above, (TA,) *She became round in the breast;* as also ↓فَلَكَتْ. (Ḳ, TA. [For the latter verb, the CḲ has فَلِكَت.]) = See also فَلْكَةٌ, second sentence. — التَّفْلِيكُ also signifies The pastor's *making, of coarse hair* (هُلْب), *a thing like the* فَلْكَة (AA, T, Ṣ, O, TA) *of the spindle,* (AA, T, TA,) *and inserting it into the tongue of the young unweaned camel,* (AA, T, Ṣ, O, TA,) *having perforated the tongue* [*for that purpose*], (AA, T, TA,) *in order that he may not suck:* (AA, T, Ṣ, O, TA:) accord. to Lth, فَلَّكْتُ الجَدْىَ signifies *I put a twig around the tongue of the kid in order that it might not suck:* but Az says that the right explanation of التفليك is that of AA [given above]. (TA.) [See also 4 in art. جر, and 4 in art. لبج.] = And فلّك, inf. n. as above, *He* (a man) *persisted,* or *persevered,* (لَجَّ,) in an affair; (Ḳ, TA;) and so ↓افلك. (TA.) = And فلكت *She* (a bitch) *desired copulation, and discharged blood from the womb;* syn. اجعلت وحاضت. (O, Ḳ.)

4: see 2, first sentence: — and فَلْكَةٌ, second sentence: = and see also 2, last sentence but one.

5: see 2, first sentence.

فُلْكٌ *A ship:* (Ṣ, O, Mṣb, Ḳ, &c.:) [also particularly applied to the *ark* of Noah; as in the Ḳur-án vii. 62, &c.:] the word is generally thus only; but some say ↓فُلُكٌ also, with two ḍammehs; and it is held that this may be the original form; and that فُلْكٌ may be a contraction, like as عُنْقٌ is [of عُنُقٌ accord. to Sb]: (MF, TA:) it is masc. and fem., (Ṣ, O, Ḳ,*) and sing. and pl., (Ṣ, O, Ḳ,) and Ibn-'Abbád says that it has فُلُوكٌ also for a pl.: (O:) [it is said that] it may be sing., and in this case masc.; and pl., and in this case fem.: (IB, Mṣb:) [but see what here follows:] it occurs in the Ḳur-án in the following (and other) places: in xxvi. 119, &c.; where it is sing. and masc.: (Ṣ, O, TA:) and in [xvi. 14 and] xxxv. 13; where it is pl. [and fem.]: (TA:) and in ii. 159; where it is fem., and may be either pl. or sing.: it seems that, when it is sing., it is regarded as meaning the مَرْكَب, and is therefore made masc.; or the سَفِينَة, and is therefore made fem.: (Ṣ, O, TA:) or, (Ḳ,) as Sb used to say, (Ṣ, O, TA,) the فُلْك that is a pl. [in meaning] is a broken pl. of that, (Ṣ, O, Ḳ, TA,) i.e. of the فُلْك, (IB, O, Ḳ, TA,) that is a sing. [in meaning]: and it is not like الجُنُب, which is sing. and pl. [in meaning], and the like thereof (Ṣ, O, Ḳ, TA) among substs., such as الطِّفْل &c.; (Ṣ, O, TA;) for فُلْكَانِ has been heard from the Arabs as dual of فُلْك, but not جُنُبَانِ [or the like] as dual of جُنُب [or the like]; and they say that what has not been dualized is not a pl. [form], but [is, or may be,] a homonym, and what has been dualized [is, or may be,] a pl. [form]: (MF, TA:) Sb then says in continuation, (TA,) for فُعْلٌ and فَعَلٌ share in application to one thing [or meaning], as العُرْبُ and العَرَبُ, (Ṣ, O, Ḳ, TA,) &c.; (Ṣ, O, TA;) and as it is allowable for فَعَلٌ to have for its pl. فُعْلٌ, as in the instance of أُسْدٌ and أَسَدٌ, so too فُعْلٌ may have for its pl. فُعْلٌ. (Ṣ, O, Ḳ, TA.) ↓فُلُكِىٌّ is a dial. var. of فُلْكٌ; and Abu-d-Dardà read, [in the Ḳur x. 23,] إِذَا كُنْتُمْ فِى ٱلْفُلُكِىِّ [*When ye are in the ships;* where others read فى الفُلْكِ; and where the context shows that the pl. meaning is intended]. (IJ, TA.) = [It may also be a pl. of the word next following].

الفَلَكُ *The place of the revolving of the stars;* (O, Ḳ, TA;) [*the celestial sphere:* but generally imagined by the Arabs to be a material concave hemisphere; so that it may be termed *the vault of heaven;* or *the firmament:*] the astronomers say that it is [a term applied to *every one, by itself, of*] *seven* أَطْوَاق [by which they mean *surrounding spheres*], *exclusive of the* سَمَآء [or *sky, as meaning the region of the clouds*]; *wherein have been set the seven stars* [i.e. *the Moon, Mercury, Venus, the Sun, Mars, Jupiter, and Saturn*], *in every* طَوْق [or *surrounding sphere*] *a star, some being higher than others; revolving therein:* (TA:) [it is also commonly imagined that above these is an eighth sphere, called by the astronomers فَلَكُ الثَّوَابِتِ (*the sphere of the fixed stars*), and by others فَلَكُ الكُرْسِىِّ; and above this, a ninth, called فَلَكُ العَرْشِ and فَلَكُ الأَطْلَسِ, and also called الأَثِيرُ (q.v.):] the pl. is أَفْلَاكٌ [a pl. of pauc.] (Ṣ, O, Mṣb, Ḳ, TA) and فُلُكٌ (Ḳ, TA) and فُلْكٌ may be another pl., like as أُسْدٌ and خُشْبٌ are pls. of أَسَدٌ and خَشَبٌ. (Ṣ, O, TA. [Thus accord. to both of my copies of the Ṣ, as well as the O and TA: but it may be that أُسْدٌ and خُشْبٌ are mistranscriptions for أُسُدٌ and خُشُبٌ; and therefore that for فُلْكٌ (which is not mentioned as a pl. of فَلَكٌ in the Ḳ) we should read فُلُكٌ.]) And فَلَكُ السَّمَآءِ signifies *The pole of heaven*; [generally *the north celestial pole*;] likened to the pivot, or axis, of the mill-stone. (TA.) — Also (i. e. الفَلَكُ) *The revolving of the heaven* [or *celestial sphere*]. (TA.) — And فَلَكٌ signifies also *The circuit*, and *main part*, of anything. (K.) — And *Waves of the sea in a state of commotion*, (O, K, TA,) *circling*, (TA,) *and going to and fro*. (O, TA.) This, (O, TA,) or what is next mentioned, (TA,) or the place of revolving of the stars, (O,) or the pole of heaven, (TA,) is meant in a trad. where it is said of a horse smitten by the [evil] eye, that he was as though he were turning in a فَلَك. (O, TA.) And *Water put in motion by the wind*, (O, K, TA,) *going to and fro, in a state of commotion*: (O, TA:) mentioned by Z. (TA.) — Also *A hill*, or *mound, of sand, having around it a wide expanse of land*: (IAar, O, K, TA:) or فَلَكٌ مِنَ الرَّمْلِ signifies *rugged, round* أَجْوِبَة [app. a pl. of جَوْبَة (though I do not find it mentioned as such), and meaning *depressed and clear places*], *of the sands, like* [*tracts of*] *what are termed* كُذَّان [or *soft stones resembling dry pieces of clay*], *hollowed out by the gazelles*. (TA.) — And *Pieces of land*, (S, O, K, TA,) or of sand, (S,) *having a circular form, and elevated above what is around them*, (S, O, K, TA,) *with ruggedness and evenness*; (TA;) one whereof is termed ▼ فَلْكَةٌ, (S, O, K, TA,) with the ل quiescent; pl. فِلَاكٌ; (K, TA;) i. e. [this is pl. of فَلْكَة,] like قَصْعَةٌ and قِصَاعٌ: (TA:) in [the book entitled] El-Ghareeb El-Musannaf, [by Aboo-'Amr Esh-Sheybánee, we find] ▼ فَلْكَة and فَلَكٌ, [each] بِالتَّحْرِيك; [accord. to which, فَلَكَة is a n. un., and فَلَك is a coll. gen. n.;] but in "the Book" of Sb, [agreeably with the K, we find] ▼ فَلْكَةٌ [as a sing.] and فَلَكٌ [as a quasi-pl. n.], like حَلْقَةٌ and حَلَقٌ. (IB, TA.) — See also فَلْكَةٌ, in two places.

فَلْكٌ A slave (AA, O) *having a buttock like the* فَلْكَة [or *whirl*] *of a spindle* (AA, O, K) *in shape*; (AA, O;) *resembling the Zenj*; (K;) [for] the buttocks of the Zenj are round: (AA, O:) or *large in the buttocks*. (TA.) And (O, K) it is said to signify (O) *Thick, or coarse of make, in the joints*: (O, K:) and loose in the bones; (K;) or *weak, loose in the bones, and flaccid*; thus expl. by Ibn-'Abbád: (O:) and *having a pain in his patella* (فِى فَلْكَةِ رُكْبَتِهِ). (O, K.)

فُلْكٌ: *i. q.* فُلْكٌ, q. v. — And a pl. of فَلَكٌ. (K, TA.)

فَلْكَةٌ The *whirl* of a spindle: (MA:) [this is what is meant by the saying that] the فَلْكَة of the مِغْزَل is well known; (K;) [and] is thus called because of its roundness: (S, O:) [it is *a piece of wood, generally of a hemispherical form*, or *nearly so, through the middle of which the upper part of the spindle-pin is inserted*:] also pronounced ▼ فَلَكَةٌ: (O, K:) the pl. [of the former] is ▼ فَلَكٌ [or rather this is a quasi-pl. n.] and [that of the latter sing. is] فِلَكٌ. (TA.) — And *A thing that is made round*, or *hemispherical*, (▼ يُفَلَّكُ, or ▼ يُفْلَكُ, accord. to different copies of the K,) *like the* فَلْكَة *of the spindle, of coarse hair* (هُلْب), *then the tongue of the young unweaned camel is perforated*, [*and this thing is inserted into it*, (see 2, and see also 4 in art. لهج,)] *in order that he may be prevented from sucking*. (K. [For فَتَخْرِقُ لِسَانَ الفَصِيلِ in the CK, I read فَيُخْرَقُ لِسَانُ الفَصِيلِ, as in other copies of the K and in the TA: after these words, the copies of the K have فَيُغْضَدُ بِهِ, app. a mistranscription for some phrase meaning فَيُجْعَلُ فِيهِ, which is necessary to complete the explanation.]) — And *An* [*eminence such as is termed*] أَكَمَة [*formed*] *of one mass of stone*; (K, TA;) accord. to ISh, [*of*] *the smaller of the* [*eminences termed*] إِكَام, *compact in its head, as though this were the* فَلْكَة *of a spindle, not giving growth to anything, in height of the measure of two spears or a spear and a half*. (TA.) — See also فَلَكٌ, near the end, in two places. — Also *Anything circular*. (K.) — And [particularly] The *joint* [or *cartilaginous disk*] *between the two vertebræ* [i. e. *between any one of the vertebræ and that next to it*] *of the camel*: (K, TA:) and the pl. [or rather quasi-pl. n.] thereof, in this sense and in the last two of the senses following, is ▼ فَلَكٌ. (TA.) — [And The *cap* of the knee; (see فَلْكٌ;) فَلْكَةُ الرُّكْبَةِ signifying *the patella*: so in the present day.] — And The *small thing* (الهَنَةُ) [app. the *foramen cæcum*, from its round form, for, though the TA adds the epithet النَّاشِئَةُ, which means "rising," I think that this addition may be conjectural,]) *upon the head of the root of the tongue*. (K.) — And The *side of the* [*portion of the breast called the*] زَوْر [q.v.], and the *part thereof that is round*, or *circular*. (K. [But see بَلْدَة; where it is said that "*the* فَلَك *of the* زَوْر *of a horse are six in number*:" what they are I have been unable to determine: I incline to think that they may be spiral curls, such as are termed دَوَائِر, pl. of دَائِرَة.])

فَلَكَةٌ: see فَلْكَةٌ, first sentence.

فَلَكَةٌ: see فَلَكٌ, near the end.

فُلْكِىٌّ: see فُلْكٌ, last sentence but one.

فَلَكِىٌّ [*Of*, or *relating to, the* فَلَك as meaning the *celestial sphere*. — And] *One who occupies himself* [*as an astronomer*, or *astrologer*] *with the science of the stars*. (TA.)

فُلَيْكَةٌ [dim. of فُلْكٌ, which is sometimes fem. when used as a sing. as well as when used as a pl.,] *A small ship*: the vulgar say فلوكة [i. e. فَلُوكَة; whence the Italian "feluca"]. (TA.)

فَالِكٌ and ▼ مُفَلِّكٌ A girl *whose breast is becoming round*, (K, TA,) *like the* فَلْكَة [or *whirl* (*of a spindle*)]. (TA.) [And the former is also applied as an epithet to the breast: for] AA says that [the pl.] فَوَالِكُ is applied to breasts (ثُدِىّ) that are less than such as are termed نَوَاهِد. (TA.)

فَيْلَكُونٌ The شُوبَق [or *baker's rolling-pin*: see the latter word]: (O, K, TA: [in the CK, السَّوِيقُ is erroneously put for الشُّوبَقُ:]) Az holds both of these words to be arabicized. (O.) — And (TA) The بَرْدِىّ [or *papyrus*]. (S; and K in art. فلكن.) — And *Tar*, or *pitch*; syn. قَارٌ, or زِفْتٌ. (K in art. فلكن.) — And قَوْسٌ فَيْلَكُونٌ *A great bow*. (TA in art. فلكن.)

أَفْلَكُ One *who goes round about the* فَلَك, (IAar, O, K,) i. e. the *hill*, or *mound, of sand that has around it a wide expanse of land*. (IAar, O.)

الإِفْلِيكَانِ *Two portions of flesh which border, on each side, the* لَهَاة; (IDrd, O, K;) i. e. they are *the* غُنْدُبَتَانِ [q. v.]. (IDrd, O.)

فَالِكٌ: see مُفَلِّكٌ.

فلن

فُلَانٌ is a substitute for the proper name of a human being, (S, Msb,* K, TA,) i. e. of a male; (S, TA;) and in like manner ▼ فُلَانَةُ, (Msb, K, TA,) for that of a female; (TA;) each without ال: (Msb:) [the former may be rendered *Such a one*, or *Such a man*; and the latter, *Such a woman*:] and الفُلَانُ and ▼ الفُلَانَةُ for other than a human being, (S, K, TA,) i. e. for a [particular] camel, (Lth, TA,) or for a [particular] beast, as in the saying, رَكِبْتُ الفُلَانَ [*I rode such a beast*, i. e. *such a male beast*], and ▼ حَلَبْتُ الفُلَانَةَ [*I milked such a beast*]: (Msb, TA:) فُلَانٌ has no dual nor pl.: (IB, TA:) [but] sometimes one says to a single person, masc., يَا فُلُ; and to two, يَا فُلَانِ; and to a pl. number, يَا فُلُونَ: and in the fem., يَا فُلَةُ; &c.: (K: [see more in art. فل:]) accord. to Kh, فُلَانٌ is of the measure فُعَالٌ; and its dim. is ▼ فُلَيْنٌ: (TA:) or, as some say, it is of the measure فُعْلَانٌ, [originally فُلْوَانٌ,] with و rejected, therefore its dim. is ▼ فُلَيَّانٌ [originally فُلَيْوَانٌ]; (T, L, TA;) like as إِنْسَانٌ is [said by some to be] إِنْسِيَانٌ, of which the ى is rejected, and therefore its dim. is أُنَيْسِيَانٌ. (T, L.)

فُلَيْنٌ: see the preceding paragraph.

فُلَانَةُ, and الفُلَانَةُ: see فُلَانٌ, in three places.

فُلَانِىٌّ the rel. n. of فُلَانٌ: it is rendered indeterminate by the affix ى; and by means of the article أَلْ, it becomes determinate; therefore you say فُلَانٌ الفُلَانِىُّ [meaning *Such a one, the person named in relation to such a one*]. (TA.)

فُلَيَّانٌ: see فُلَانٌ, near the end.

فلهد

فَلْهَدٌ and فُلْهُدٌ A boy, or youth, *compact in make* (حَادِر), *fat, that has nearly attained to puberty*; as also ▼ فُلْهُودٌ and ▼ مُفَلْهَدٌ: (K:) or فلهد [i. e. فَلْهَدٌ or فُلْهُدٌ] signifies a *fat* boy or youth, *that has nearly attained to puberty*; thus expl. by AA: [and so فُرْهُدٌ is expl. by him: and فُرْهُدٌ and فُرْهُدٌ are similarly expl.:] or, as some say, a *plump* boy or youth: and accord. to Kr, a boy *that fills the cradle*. (TA.)

فُلْهُودٌ: } see the preceding paragraph.
مُفَلْهَدٌ:

فلو

1. فَلَاهُ, (M, Ḳ,) first pers. فَلَوْتُهُ, (Ṣ, M, Mṣb,) aor. ـُ, (TA,) inf. n. فَلْوٌ, (M, Ḳ, TA,) with fet-ḥ, and فِلَآءٌ accord. to the M, or فِلَآءٌ accord. to the Ḳ, (TA,) *He withdrew him from sucking*; namely, a colt, (M, Ḳ,) and a young ass, (M,) and a child; (M, Ḳ;) as also ↓ افلاه, and ↓ افتلاه: (M, Ḳ:*) or *he weaned*, or *ablactated, him*, as also ↓ افلاه, and ↓ افتلاه: (Ḳ:) or فَلَاهُ عَنْ أُمِّهِ and ↓ افتلاه signify thus; relating to a colt and a young ass: (Ṣ: [and in a similar manner both are expl. in the T, on the authority of ISk:]) or فَلَاهُ, (M,) or فَلَاهُ عَنْ أُمِّهِ, relating to a colt and a young ass, (T,) signifies thus; (T, M;) but ↓ افتلاه, (M,) or افتلاه لِنَفْسِهِ, (T,) signifies *he took him for himself* [app. *from his mother*]: (T, M:) or فَلَوْتُهُ and ↓ أَفْلَيْتُهُ signify *I separated him from his mother*; namely, a colt: and فُلِيَتْ is said of a filly [meaning *she was separated* &c.]. (Mṣb.) [Hence,] the ↓ فَلَاة [q. v.] is [said to be] thus called لِأَنَّهَا فُلِيَتْ عَنْ كُلِّ خَيْرٍ, [*Because it is as though it were weaned*, and *removed, from everything good*]. (M.) — And فَلَوْتُهُ *I reared him*, or *brought him up*; [namely, a youth, or boy;] as also ↓ افْتَلَيْتُهُ: a poet says,

* وَلَيْسَ يَهْلِكُ مِنَّا سَيِّدٌ أَبَدًا *
* إِلَّا ٱفْتَلَيْنَا ↓ غُلَامًا سَيِّدًا فِينَا *

[*And a chief of us does not ever perish but we rear a youth* to be *a chief among us*]. (Ṣ.) ═ فَلَاهُ بِالسَّيْفِ, (M, Ḳ,) first pers. فَلَوْتُهُ and فَلَيْتُهُ, (T, Ṣ,) inf. n. فَلْوٌ and فَلْىٌ, (M in this art. and in art. فلى,) *He struck* (Ṣ, M, Ḳ) *him*, (Ḳ,) or *his head*, (Ṣ, M,) *with the sword*: (Ṣ, M, Ḳ:) or *he struck*, or *cut, it*, i. e. one's head, *with the sword*. (T* and M in art. فلى.) — And فَلَوْتُ القَوْمَ *I entered amid the breaks*, or *interspaces, of the people*; like فَلَيْتُهُمْ. (T, TA.) ═ فَلَا as intrans., said of a man, *He journeyed*, or *went forth to journey*. (IAạr, T, Ḳ.) — And *He became intelligent after being ignorant*. (IAạr, T, Ḳ.)

4: see 1, first sentence, in three places. — افلت said of a mare, (M, Ḳ,) and of a she-ass, (M,) means *She was one whose colt had attained to the age for his being weaned*. (M, Ḳ.) And the phrase قَدْ أَفْلَيْنَ أَمْهَارًا, ending a verse of 'Adee Ibn-Zeyd, and referring to wild animals, means, as expl. by AḤn, *that had become in the state in which their young ones were full-grown and in no need of their mothers*. (M.) ═ And افلى القَوْمُ *The people*, or *party, came to the* فَلَاة [or *desert*, &c.]: (Ṣ, Ḳ:*) or, as Z says, *entered it*; which is nearly the same as the former explanation. (TA.)

8: see 1, in six places: ═ and see also art. فلى.

فَلًا [a coll. gen. n.]: see فَلَاةٌ.

يَا فُلَا and يَا فُلَاةُ: see يَا فُلُ, in art. فل.

فِلْوٌ: see فَلُوٌّ.

فَلَاةٌ *A* [*desert such as is termed*] قَفْر; (M, Ḳ;) so called for a reason mentioned above, in the first paragraph, q. v.; (M;) or [*such as is called*] مَفَازَة; (T, Ṣ, Ḳ;) *in which is no water*; or, *in the fewer cases, in which there is an interval of two days with a portion of the day preceding them and of the day following them between the waterings of camels and of one day between the waterings of asses and of sheep* or *goats* لِلْإِبِلِ رِبْعٌ وَلِلْحَمِيرِ وَالغَنَمِ غِبٌّ: (M, Ḳ:) or *a land in which is no water*: (Mṣb:) or *a wide* [*desert such as is termed* صَحْرَآء]: (M, Ḳ:) pl. فَلَوَاتٌ, (T, Ṣ, M, Ḳ,) a pl. of pauc., (TA,) and ↓ فَلًا, (T, Ṣ, M, Mṣb, Ḳ,) [or rather this is a coll. gen. n. of which فَلَاةٌ is the n. un.,] and فُلِىٌّ, (M, Ḳ,) or this is pl. of فَلًا, (Ṣ,) and [so are] فِلِىٌّ (M, Ḳ) and فُلُوٌّ [which is the original of فُلِىٌّ and فِلِىٌّ], (CḲ,) أَفْلَآءٌ is [likewise] pl. of فَلًا. (Ṣ, M, Mṣb, Ḳ.*) — أَخُو الفَلَاةِ *A man of the desert*: or *one who travels in the desert* or *deserts*.] — And ٱبْنُ الفَلَاةِ *The* حِرْبَآء [or *male chameleon*]. (T in art. بنى.)

فِلَآءٌ, mentioned in the paragraph here following as a pl. of فِلْوٌ, signifies also *Bones*. (TA.)

فَلُوٌّ (Ṣ, M, Mgh, Mṣb, Ḳ) and فُلُوٌّ (M, Ḳ) and ↓ فِلْوٌ (Ṣ, M, Mṣb, Ḳ) *A colt*, (Ṣ, Mgh,) because he is weaned; (Ṣ;) or *a colt*, and *a young ass*, (M, Mṣb, Ḳ,) *when weaned*, (M, Ḳ,) or *separated from his mother*: (Mṣb:) or *when a year old*; (Ḳ;) or فَلُوٌّ signifies also *a colt that is a year old*: (M: [see قَارِحٌ:]) and *a light*, or *an active, ass*: (IAạr, TA voce يَعْفُورٌ:) and sometimes (Ṣ) the female is called فَلُوَّةٌ: (Ṣ, Mṣb:) the pl. is أَفْلَآءٌ, (Ṣ, M, Mgh, Mṣb, Ḳ,) like أَعْدَآءٌ as pl. of عَدُوٌّ, (Ṣ, Mgh, Mṣb,) and like أَحْبَارٌ as pl. of حِبْرٌ, (TA,) and also فَلَاوَى, (Ṣ, Ḳ,) and فُلُوٌّ, mentioned by Fr, (M, TA,) and فِلَآءٌ is mentioned as a pl. of فِلْوٌ signifying *a colt* by Aboo-'Alee El-Ḳálee. (TA.)

بَدَوِيَّةٌ فَلَوِيَّةٌ are epithets applied to a woman [each signifying *Of*, or *belonging to, the* فَلَاة, or *desert*]. (TA.)

مُفْلٍ and مُفْلِيَةٌ A mare *having a* فَلُوّ. (Ṣ, TA.)

فلى

1. فَلَى رَأْسَهُ, (M, Mgh, Ḳ,) and ثِيَابَهُ, (Mgh,) [aor. ـِ,] inf. n. فَلْىٌ; (M, Mgh;) and ↓ فَلَّى رَأْسَهُ also; (Ḳ; [but not in my copy of the TA;]) *He searched his head*, (M, Mgh, Ḳ,) and *his clothes*, (Mgh,) *for lice*: (M, Mgh, Ḳ:) [and it appears from an explanation below (see 8) that افتلى رأسه perhaps signifies the same:] or one says, فَلَيْتُ رَأْسَهُ مِنَ القَمْلِ [*I searched his head for lice*]: (Ṣ:) or فَلَيْتُ رَأْسِى, aor. as above, and so the inf. n., signifies *I cleared my head of lice*. (Mṣb.) [See also الفَلَآء, below.] In the saying of 'Amr Ibn-Maạdee-kerib,

* تَرَاهُ كَالثَّغَامِ يُعَلُّ مِسْكًا *
* يَسُوْءُ الفَالِيَاتِ إِذَا فَلَيْنِى *

[*Thou seest it* (meaning the white hair intermixing with black) *like the thagham* (the plant so called) *inserted in musk, grieving the lousing women when they louse me*], فَلَيْنِى is for فَلَيْنَنِى, (T, Ṣ,) the two ن being deemed difficult of utterance; (T;) as Akh says, he has rejected the latter ن because it is merely a preservative to the verb [lest its affix should be supposed to form an essential part of it], whereas the former ن may not be rejected, because it is the pronoun of the verb. (Ṣ.) — [Hence,] فَلَى الشِّعْرَ, (ISk, T, Ṣ, Ḳ,) aor. and inf. n. as above, (TA,) ‡ *He considered, and endeavoured to understand, the poetry, and elicited its meanings*, (ISk, T, Ṣ, Ḳ, TA,) *and what was strange of it*: (ISk, Ṣ, TA:) or, accord. to the A, *he investigated the meanings of the poetry*: one says, اِفْلِ هٰذَا البَيْتَ فَإِنَّهُ صَعْبٌ ‡ [*Investigate thou the meaning of this verse, for it is difficult*]. (TA.) [Freytag has mentioned فَلَا, in art. فلو, as signifying "Disquisivit," and as followed by عن; from the Deewán of the Hudhalees.] And فَلَى الأَمْرَ † *He considered*, or *examined, the various modes of the affair*, or *case, endeavouring to obtain a clear knowledge of them, and looked to its result*. (T, TA.) And فَلَيْتُ القَوْمَ بِعَيْنِى † [*I examined the people*, or *party, with my eye, in order to know them*]: and فَلَيْتُ خَبَرَهُمْ † [*I examined their state*, or *case, in order to know it*]. (TA.) And فَلَاهُ فِى عَقْلِهِ, (T, M, Ḳ, TA,) aor. as above, (T, TA,) and so the inf. n., (M, TA,) ‡ *He looked*, or *examined, to see what was his intelligence*: (T, TA:) or *he tried*, or *tested, him, in respect of his intelligence*. (M, Ḳ, TA.) — فَلَيْتُ القَوْمَ *I entered amid the breaks*, or *interspaces, of the people*; (T, TA;*) as also ↓ افْتَلَيْتُهُمْ; (T;) and so فَلَوْتُهُمْ. (TA.) And فَلَى المَفَازَةَ *He passed through the* مفازة [i. e. *desert*, or *waterless desert*]. (TA.) — فَلَاهُ بِالسَّيْفِ, aor. يَفْلِيهِ, (Ḳ, TA,) inf. n. فَلْىٌ, (TA,) signifies the same as فَلَاهُ, aor. يَفْلُوهُ, (Ḳ, TA,) inf. n. فَلْوٌ. (TA.) See the latter verb in art. فلو. ═ فَلَى i. q. اِنْقَطَعَ [*It*, or *he, was cut*, or *cut off*, &c.]. (IAạr, T, Ḳ.)

2: see the first sentence above.

4: see 1, near the end of the paragraph.

5. تفلّى *He applied himself, as to a task, to the act of searching his head for lice*. (T,* M, TA.)

6. تفالت الحُمُرُ *The asses scratched, scraped, or rubbed, one another;* as though they were lousing one another. (M, TA.) —— See also 10.

8. يَفْتَلُونَ الفَلَاةَ, (T,) or المَكَانَ, (Ḳ,*) ‡ *They depasture the herbage* (T, Ḳ*) *of the* فلاة [or *desert, or waterless desert, &c.*], (T,) or *of the place,* (Ḳ,) *and seek for the portions of herbage that are beginning to dry up therein;* like as [is done when] the head is searched for lice (كَمَا يُفْتَلَى الرَّأْسُ or كما يُفْلَى الرأس accord. to two transcripts from the T). (T in arts. فلو and فلى of the TT.) [This meaning of the verb is expl. (imperfectly) in art. فلو, to which it does not belong.]

10. استفلى رَأْسَهُ, and ♦ تفالى, (Ṣ, Ḳ,) i. e. تفالى هُوَ [not تفالى رأسه], (Ṣ,) *He desired that his head might be searched for lice.* (Ṣ, Ḳ.) ═ And استفلاهُ *He exposed himself to have his head struck and cut with the sword:* (M, TA:) a poet says,

أَمَا تَرَانِي رَابِطَ الجَنَانِ
أَفْلِيهِ بِالسَّيْفِ إِذَا ٱسْتَفْلَانِي

[*Dost thou not see me to be strong of heart? I will strike and cut his head with the sword when he exposes himself to be so struck* &c.]

[فِلْيَةٌ, mentioned in this art. by Freytag, with فَلَالِىُّ as its pl., is taken by him from a mistranscription in the CḲ in art. فل: see فَلِيَّةٌ in that art.]

الفَلَاةُ, like كِسَآءٌ [in measure], means فلاة الشعر [evidently, I think, فَلَآءُ الشَّعَرِ, or the first word may be a mistranscription for فَلْىُ,] i. e. اخذك ما فيه [lit. *Thy taking what is in it,* in which "it" refers to *the* شعر: app. a euphemism for *the taking of lice from the hair:* if so, it may be an inf. n., like فَلْىٌ; (see 1, first sentence;) or it may be a simple subst., like what here follows]: mentioned by IAmb, from his companions. (TA.)

فَلَايَةٌ [The *act of searching the head for lice;*] the subst. from فَلَى رَأْسَهُ signifying "he searched his head for lice." (Lth,* T,* Ḳ.) [See also the next preceding paragraph.]

[فَالٍ act. part. n. of 1: fem. فَالِيَةٌ.] فَالِيَاتٌ and فَوَالٍ [are pls. of فَالِيَةٌ and] signify Women *who search the head for lice.* (T, TA.) See an ex. of the former pl. in the verse cited in the first paragraph. —— فَالِيَةُ الأَفَاعِى (in which the former word is a pl. [in meaning], M, TA) signifies [lit. *The lousers of the vipers;* meaning,] accord. to the A, *certain species of the kind [of beetles] called* خنافس [pl. of خُنْفُسَآء], *speckled, found at the holes of the serpents, which they louse:* (TA:) or *a certain* خنفساء, *speckled* (M, Ḳ) *with* [*the colour termed*] صُحْمَة, *which is found at the holes* [*of serpents &c.*], *and is the mistress of* خنافس; (M;) *which is familiar with scorpions and serpents; so that when it comes forth from a hole* [*thereof*], *it makes known their existence* [*therein*]: (Ḳ:) or *certain small things like* خنافس, *speckled; which are familiar with scorpions and serpents; so that when they are seen in the hole* [*thereof*] *it is known that behind them are scorpions and serpents:* (T:) or *certain insects* (دَوَابُّ) *that are found at the holes of the* [*lizards called*] ضِبَاب [pl. of ضَبٌّ]; *so that when they come forth, it is known that the* ضَبّ *is coming forth inevitably.* (M.) Hence one says, اتتكم فَالِيَةُ الأَفَاعِى, (IAạr, T, M, Ḳ,*) meaning † *The beginning of evil to be looked for* [*has come to you*], (IAạr, T,) or *the beginnings of evil* [*have come to you*]; (Ḳ;) which is a prov. (IAạr, T.) —— And [hence] اِبْنُ الفَوَالِى means *The* جَانّ; i. e. *the serpent* [*so called*]. (T in art. بنى.)

فَالِيَةٌ [fem. of فَالٍ, q. v. —— And also] *A knife.* (T.)

فم

فَمٌ The *mouth:* (MA, KL, &c.:) it is originally فَوْهٌ, (Ṣ, Ḳ, and Mṣb in art. فوه,) with two fet-ḥahs, (Mṣb in that art.,) or فَوْهٌ; (so in some copies of the Ṣ;) the ه being cut off from it, the و is not susceptible of declension, because it is quiescent, therefore م is substituted for it; but when you form the dim. or the pl., you restore it to its original state, saying [in the former case] فُوَيْهٌ and [in the latter case] أَفْوَاهٌ, and not أَفْمَآءٌ [in some of the copies of the Ṣ not أَفْمَامٌ]: but when you form the rel. n., you say ♦ فَمِىٌّ; and, if you will, ♦ فَمَوِىٌّ, combining the substitute and the letter for which it is substituted, like as they say in the dual فَمَوَانِ; this being held to be allowable because of there being therein another letter rejected, i. e. the ه, as though they made the م in this case to be a substitute for the ه, not for the و; (Ṣ, TA;) and one says also فَمَيَانِ, which, like فَمَوَانِ, is anomalous; (IAạr, Ḳ in art. فوه;) but one says فَمَانِ also, as well as فَمَوَانِ: (Mṣb in art. فوه:) it has three forms, فَمٌ and فُمٌ and فِمٌ: (Ṣ, Ḳ, TA:) and some decline it doubly; saying in the nom. case فُمٌ, accus. فَمًا, and gen. فِمٍ; (Ṣ, TA;) like اِمْرُؤٌ and اِبْنُمٌ, which have been said to be the only other instances of the kind: (TA:) when it is prefixed to the [pronominal] ى, one says فَمِى and فِىَّ; but when to [a pronoun] other than the ى, it is declined with the letters و and ا and ى, so that one says فُوهُ and فَاهُ and فِيهِ; but one also says فَمُهُ: (Mṣb. in art. فوه:) and sometimes the م is musheddedeh, (Ṣ, Ḳ,) in poetry, as in the saying, (Ṣ, TA,) of Moḥammad Ibn-Dhu-eyb El-'Ománee El-Fuḳeymee, the rájiz, (TA in this art. and in art. طسر,) addressing Er-Rasheed, or, accord. to IKh, said in relation to Suleymán Ibn-'Abd-El-Melik and 'Abd-El-'Azeez, (TA in art. طسر,)

يَا لَيْتَهَا قَدْ خَرَجَتْ مِنْ فُمِّهِ
حَتَّى يَعُودَ المُلْكُ فِى أُسْطُمِّهِ

(Ṣ, TA) or أُطْسُمِّهِ i. e. [*O, would that it had gone forth from his mouth, so that the dominion might return*] *to its rightful owner;* (Ṣ in art. سطم, and TA in art. طسر;) and it would have been allowable, (Ṣ, TA,) accord. to ISk, (Ṣ,) or accord. to Fr, (TA,) if he had said ♦ مِن فَمِّهِ, with fet-ḥ to the ف: (Ṣ, TA:) the pl. of فَمّ, with teshdeed, is أَفْمَامٌ; and its dim. is ♦ فُمَيْمٌ, mentioned by Lh. (TA.) MF says that many of the expositors of the Tes-heel have collected the dial. vars. of this word, compounded and uncompounded, and they have exceeded twenty; that with fet-ḥ, they say, being the most common and the most chaste. (TA.) [See more in art. فوه.] —— [Hence,] الفَمُ is metonymically applied to ‡ *The teeth.* (Ḥam p. 242.) —— [Hence also,] فَمُ الحُوتِ † *The star* [α] *in the mouth of Piscis Australis.* (Ḳzw &c.: see art. حوت.) And فَمُ الفَرَسِ † *The star* [ε] *upon the lip of Pegasus.* (Ḳzw.) —— [And فَمُ الرَّحِمِ † *The mouth of the womb.*] —— And فَمُ النَّهرِ † *The mouth of the river.* (MA.) —— And [hence likewise,] فَمٌ is also used as meaning † *Branch;* opposed to اسْتٌ meaning "root." (TA in art. سته; in which see اسْتٌ, last quarter.) ═ فَمٌ مِنَ الدِّبَاغِ means The *quantity that is used at one time, of tan;* (Fr, Ḳ,* TA;) like نَفْسٌ مِنْهُ. (Fr, TA.)

فَمِىٌّ and فَمَوِىٌّ: see the preceding paragraph, near the beginning.

فُمَّ a dial. var. of the conjunction ثُمَّ [q. v.]: (Ḳ:) or the ف in the former is a substitute for the ث in the latter: one says, رَأَيْتُ عَمْرًا فُمَّ زَيْدًا and ثُمَّ زَيْدًا, both meaning the same [i. e. *I saw 'Amr: then Zeyd*]: (TA:) and in like manner one says فُمَّتَ and فُمَّتْ, meaning ثُمَّتَ and ثُمَّتْ. (M and TA voce ثُمَّ.)

فَمٌّ and فُمٌّ, فُمَيْمٌ: see the first paragraph, latter half.

فن

1. فَنَّهُ, (M,) or فَنَّ الإِبِلَ, (T, Ṣ,) aor. ـُ, (T, M,) inf. n. فَنٌّ, (T, Ṣ, M, Ḳ,) *He drove away* (T, Ṣ, M, Ḳ*) *him,* (M,) or *the camels.* (T, Ṣ.) —— And [فَنَّهُ also signifies *He delayed,* or *deferred, with him,* or *put him off,* in the matter of his debt, *by promising time after time to pay him;* for] one of the significations of الفَنُّ is المَطْلُ. (T, Ḳ.) —— And فَنَّهُ, aor. ـُ, (M,) inf. n. فَنٌّ, (M, Ḳ,) *He cheated, deceived, overreached,* or *defrauded, him;* or *made him to suffer loss* or *damage* or *detriment;* syn. of the inf. n. غَبْنٌ. (M, Ḳ.) —— And *He caused him to suffer difficulty, distress,* or *trouble;* or *fatigue,* or *weariness;* syn. عَنَّاهُ; (M;) or the syn. of الفَنُّ is العَنَآءُ [which is the subst. from عَنَّاهُ; and signifies *difficulty, distress,* or *trouble*]. (T, Ḳ.) —— [And *He,* or *it, adorned,* or *decorated, him,* or *it;* for] الفَنُّ signifies التَّزْيِينُ. (Ḳ.)

2. فَنَّنَ النَّاسَ *He made the men,* or *peoples, to consist of different sorts,* or *of a medley, not of*

one tribe. (M, Ḳ, TA.) —— فنّن الحَدِيثَ *He diversified the narrative,* or *discourse.* (MA.) And فنّن الكَلَامَ [*He diversified the speech,* or *language:* or] *he branched off into one mode after another* [*in speech*]: and so ↓ تفنّن [alone, this verb being intrans.]. (T, TA.) And فنّن رَأْيَهُ *He varied his opinion, not keeping steadily to one opinion.* (T, TA.) —— And [the inf. n.] تَفْنِينٌ signifies The *mixing* or *confusing* [a thing or things]; or *a state of confusion* or *disorder;* syn. تَخْلِيطٌ. (Ṣ, Ḳ.) [Hence, as inf. n. of فَنَّنَ,] in a garment, or piece of cloth, [the *having*] *streaks differing from the rest:* (Ṣ, Ḳ:) or the *state of becoming dissundered,* (T, M,) *one part from another,* (T,) *when old and worn out, without becoming much rent:* (T, M:) or *difference* (M, Ḳ) *in its make* (M) or *in its texture,* (Ḳ,) *by thinness in one place and thickness in another:* (M, Ḳ:) or التَّفْنِينُ signifies [*there being*] *what is a thin,* or *flimsy, unseemly place in the garment,* or *piece of cloth, that is* [*in other parts*] *thick,* or *compact.* (T.) —— And فنّن signifies also *He sought many* [or *various*] *things.* (Ḥar p. 612.)

5. تفنّن *It was,* or *became, of various sorts,* or *modes,* or *manners.* (KL.) —— See also 2. You say likewise تفنّن فِى الكَلَامِ [*He practised,* or *took to, various modes,* or *manners, in speech; he diversified therein*]. (TA in art. طرق, conj. 3. [Thus used, it is like افتنّ, q. v.]) —— And تفنّن فِى العُلُومِ *He was,* or *became, possessed of various acquirements in the sciences.* (MA.) ═ Also *It was,* or *became, in a state of commotion:* thus expl. by some; others add, *like the* فَنَن [or *branch*]. (M.)

8. افتنّ *He began, commenced,* or *entered upon, various sorts of speech.* (M, Ḳ.) And افتنّ فِى حَدِيثِهِ and فِى خُطْبَتِهِ *He produced,* or *gave utterance to, various sorts and ways of speech,* [i. e. *he diversified,*] *in his narration,* or *discourse,* and *in his oration,* or *harangue:* (Ṣ, TA:) it is like اشْتَقَّ [meaning *he branched off* in it]. (Ṣ. [See also 5.]) And افتنّ فِى خُصُومَتِهِ *He expatiated, and practised versatility, in his altercation,* or *disputation,* or *litigation.* (TA.) —— And افتنّ الحِمَارُ بِأُتُنِهِ *The he-ass betook himself to driving away his she-asses to the right and to the left and in a direct and an indirect course.* (TA.)

10. استفنّهُ *He incited, urged,* or *made, him to practise various sorts,* or *modes,* or *manners, of pacing.* (Ḳ.)

R. Q. 1. فَنْفَنَ *He* (a man, IAạr, T) *caused his camels to become dispersed, by reason of indolence and remissness.* (IAạr, T, Ḳ.)

فَنٌّ *A sort,* or *species,* syn. ضَرْبٌ, (T, M, Ḳ,) or نَوْعٌ, (Ṣ, Mṣb,) of a thing; (Mṣb;) as also ↓ أُفْنُونٌ [in this sense and in the senses here following; in the CḲ, erroneously, أَفْنُون]: (M, Ḳ:) and *a state,* or *condition;* syn. حَالٌ: (M, Ḳ:) [and *a way:* (see what follows:)] and *a mode,* or *manner:* (MA:) pl. [of mult.] فُنُونٌ (T, Ṣ, M, Mṣb, Ḳ) and [of pauc.] أَفْنَانٌ. (T, M, Ḳ.) One says, رَعَيْنَا فُنُونَ النَّبَاتِ [*We pastured* our cattle *upon the various sorts of herbage*]: and أَصَبْنَا فُنُونَ الأَمْوَالِ [*We obtained the various sorts of possessions*]: and a poet says,

* قَدْ لَبِسْتُ الدَّهْرَ مِنْ أَفْنَانِهِ *
* كُلَّ فَنٍّ نَاعِمٍ مِنْهُ حَبِرْ *

[*I have enjoyed of the various sorts of fortune, every pleasant, soft, sort thereof*]. (T.) [↓ أُفْنُونٌ has for its pl. أَفَانِينُ, which may also be regarded as pl. of أَفْنَانٌ pl. of فَنٌّ like as it is said to be a pl. pl. of فَنَنٌ: and] أَفَانِينُ [alone], (Ṣ,) or أَفَانِينُ كَلَامٍ, (TA,) signifies *kinds* [or *sorts*], and *ways,* or *modes,* or *manners,* [i. e. *diversities,* or *varieties,*] *of speech;* (Ṣ, TA,* PṢ;) like أَسَالِيبُ [pl. of أُسْلُوبٌ]. (Ṣ, TA.) And فُنُونٌ signifies *Different sorts of men,* or *a medley thereof, not of one tribe.* (M.) —— Also *A wonderful thing* or *affair* or *case.* (Ṣ, TA.)

هُوَ فَنُّ عِلْمٍ *He is* [*a good student of science,* i. e.] *one who occupies himself well with science.* (Ḳ.)

فَنَّةٌ مِنَ الدَّهْرِ *A particular period of time;* [or *a particular time;*] as also فَيْنَةٌ. (T, Ḳ.*) The Arabs say, كُنْتُ بِحَالِ كَذَا وَكَذَا فَنَّةً مِنَ الدَّهْرِ and فَيْنَةً مِنَ الدَّهْرِ [*I was in such and such a state,* or *condition, at,* or *during, a particular time*]. (T.)

فُنَّةٌ *Much,* or *abundance, of herbage.* (IAạr, Ḳ.)

فَنَنٌ *A branch of a tree:* (Ṣ, M, Mṣb, Ḳ:) or *such as is of just proportion in length* or *in breadth:* (T:) said to be syn. with غُصْنٌ; but this latter signifies "such as has been cut off" i. q. قَضِيبٌ meaning مَقْضُوبٌ: (M:) pl. أَفْنَانٌ; (T, Ṣ, M, Mṣb, Ḳ;) said by Sb to be its only pl.; (M;) occurring in the Ḳur lv. 48; where some explain it as pl. of فَنٌّ, and meaning "sorts," or "species"; others, as pl. of فَنَنٌ: (T, Bḍ:) and أَفَانِينُ is a pl. pl., (T, Ṣ, Ḳ,) i. e. pl. of أَفْنَانٌ. (T, Ṣ.) —— And as a branch shelters like as does darkness, a poet uses it metaphorically, saying,

* أَغَاثَ شَرِيدَهُمْ فَنَنُ الظَّلَامِ *

‡ [*The shelter of the darkness aided him,* or *them, who fled*]. (M.) —— And [in like manner also] the pl. pl. is used in a trad. describing the inmates of Paradise, as meaning ‡ *Locks of hair;* these being likened to branches: and El-Marrár says,

* أَعَلَاقَةً أُمَّ الوَلِيدِ بَعْدَمَا *
* أَفْنَانُ رَأْسِكَ كَالثَّغَامِ المُخْلِسِ *

‡ [*Dost thou feel attachment of love to Umm-El-Weleed after that the locks of thy head have become like the hoary thagham?*]; meaning the locks of the hair of his head when he had become hoary. (T. [See ثَغَامٌ.])

فَنِينٌ *A humour in the armpit* [of a camel], *with pain.* (M, Ḳ.) —— And *A camel having the tumour thus called;* as also ↓ مَفْنُونٌ. (M, Ḳ.)

شَجَرَةٌ فَنَّآءُ and فَنْوَآءُ, which latter is anomalous, *A tree having branches;* (Ṣ;) the latter thus expl. by AA; but by rule it should be فَنَّآءُ: (A'Obeyd, T:) or the latter, which is anomalous, signifies *having long branches:* (M:) or both signify *having many branches.* (Ḳ.) —— And [hence] اِمْرَأَةٌ فَنْوَآءُ † *A woman having much hair:* but in this case, as in the former, the epithet, by rule, should be فَنَّآءُ. (M.) [See also فَيْنَانٌ.]

فَنَّانٌ *A wild ass that has various sorts,* or *modes, of running:* (Ṣ, Ḳ:) used in this sense in the poetry of El-Aạshà. (Ṣ.) [See also مِفَنٌّ.]

شَعَرٌ فَيْنَانٌ † *Hair having locks* [lit. *branches*] (M,* Ḳ) *like the* أَفْنَان *of trees;* [the latter word properly signifying *having many branches,* (see Ḥam p. 622,) of the measure فَيْعَالٌ, not فَعْلَانٌ;] therefore it is perfectly decl.: so says Sb: (M:) or it signifies *long and beautiful hair;* the latter word being of the measure فَيْعَالٌ from الفَنَنُ, and the ى augmentative. (T.) —— And one says also, agreeably with analogy, رَجُلٌ فَيْنَانٌ, (M,) and اِمْرَأَةٌ فَيْنَانَةٌ, (M, Ḳ,) meaning [*A man,* and *a woman,*] *having much hair;* (Ḳ;) for فَيْنَانٌ is perfectly decl., derived from أَفْنَانُ الشَّجَرِ: IAạr has mentioned اِمْرَأَةٌ فَيْنَى meaning [*a woman*] *having much hair;* and if the phrase be thus, فَيْنَان must be imperfectly decl.; but [ISd says] I regard this as a mistake of IAạr. (M.) [See also art. فين.]

أُفْنُونٌ: see فَنٌّ, in two places. ═ Also *A tangled,* or *luxuriant,* or *dense, branch.* (T, Ḳ.) —— And *Obscure, indistinct,* or *confused, speech,* (T, Ḳ,) *of a foolish, stupid,* or *dull, person.* (T.) —— And *A mixed,* or *confused, run,* of a horse and of a she-camel. (T, Ḳ.) ═ Also *A serpent.* (T, M, Ḳ.) —— And *An old woman:* so some say: (M:) or *an old woman advanced in age:* (T, Ḳ:) or *one who is flaccid,* or *flabby:* (Ḳ:) Yaạḳoob has explained it as having the first of these three meanings; but IB regards this as improbable, because a verse of Ibn-Aḥmar which is cited as an ex. thereof is preceded by what shows that it is applied to his beloved. (TA.) [It is said in the M to be also the proper name of a certain woman; and as such it may be used by Ibn-Aḥmar.] —— And *i. q.* دَاهِيَةٌ [*A calamity,* or *misfortune,* &c.]: (M, Ḳ:) so some say. (M.) ═ And The *first part* of youth, or youthfulness; and of clouds. (M, Ḳ.)

مِفَنٌّ A man *who has various sorts,* or *modes,* [i. e. *diversities,* or *varieties,*] *of speech;* (T, TA;) and so ↓ مُتَفَنِّنٌ: (Ṣ:) or a man *who utters,* or *performs, wonderful things:* (Ṣ, Ḳ, TA:) fem. with ة. (T, Ṣ, Ḳ.) —— And A horse *that performs various sorts,* or *modes, of running.* (TA.)

مُفَنَّنٌ A garment, or piece of cloth, *diversified; not uniform.* (M, TA.) — And *Old, and evil in disposition,* as an epithet applied to a man: (M:) and so with ة applied to a woman. (M, Ḳ.) — Also, with ة, A she-camel *that seems to one to have been ten months pregnant,* ثُمَّ تَنْكَشِفُ مِنَ الكِشَافِ [app. meaning *then suffers,* or *exposes, herself to be compressed;* from الكِشَافُ as inf. n. of كَشَفَت said of a she-camel: compare تنكشف as here used with تَكَشَّفُ said of a woman]. (Ḳ.)

فَنِينٌ : see مَفْنُونٌ.

مِفَنٌّ : see مُتَفَنِّنٌ.

فنتق

فُنْتُقٌ *A* خَان *of the way* or *road;* (Ibn-'Abbád, O, Ḳ;) a dial. var. of فُنْدُقٌ [q. v.]; disapproved by El-Khafájee; but heard by Fr from a desert-Arab of Ḳudá'ah, as meaning *a* فُنْدُق, i. e. خَان. (TA.)

فنجان

فِنْجَانٌ and فِنْجَانَةٌ : see فِلْجَانٌ, in art. فلج.

فنخ

1. فَنَخَ, aor. ـَ, (L,) inf. n. فَنْخٌ, (L, Ḳ,) *He bruised* a bone *without splitting,* or *cleaving,* it, *and without causing to bleed:* (Ḳ:) or فَنَخَ رَأْسَهُ بِشَىْءٍ *he bruised the bone of his head with a thing without making an apparent cleft or causing blood to flow:* or *he struck his head with a thing,* meaning a staff, or stick, *cleaving it* or *not cleaving it.* (L.) And فَنَخَ رَأْسَهُ, and ↓ فنّخهُ, *He broke his head, and rendered him submissive,* or *abased him.* (L.) And فَنَخَهُ, aor. ـَ, inf. n. فَنْخٌ and فُنُوخٌ, *He weakened him, rendered him languid,* or *enervated him.* (L.) And فَنَخَهُ, (Ṣ, L,) aor. ـَ, (L,) inf. n. فَنْخٌ; (L, Ḳ;) and ↓ فنّخهُ, inf. n. تَفْنِيخٌ; (Ṣ, L, Ḳ;) and ↓ تفنّخهُ; (L;) *He,* or *it,* (an affair, or event, Ṣ,) *overcame him, overpowered him, subdued him, and rendered him submissive,* or *abased him:* (Ṣ, L, Ḳ:) or *did so in the worst,* or *most abominable, manner.* (L.)

2 : see the preceding paragraph, in two places.

5 : see 1, last sentence.

فَنِيخٌ A man *overcome, overpowered, subdued, and rendered submissive,* or *abased:* or *overcome,* &c., *in the worst,* or *most abominable, manner.* (L.) And An *old* man: (L:) [a man] *flaccid,* or *flabby, and weak.* (L, Ḳ.)

مِفْنَخٌ A man *who abases his enemies, and breaks their heads, much,* or *often.* (Ṣ, Ḳ.) In explaining this word, J uses رَأْسُهُمْ for رُؤُوسَهُمْ; and the author of the Ḳ does the same, though in art. سلع he charges J with error for using a similar expression. (MF.) [Or, perhaps, the meaning here intended may be, *and defeats their head,* or *chief.*]

غَيْرُ مَفْنُوخٍ, occurring in a trad., applied to a [garment of the kind called] بُرْد, means *Not old and worn out, nor weak.* (TA.)

فند

1. فَنَدَ, aor. ـِ, (TḲ,) inf. n. فَنْدٌ; (Ṣ, M, A, O, L, Ḳ, TA;) or فند, [perhaps فَنَدَ, not فَنِدَ,] inf. n. فُنُودٌ; (IḲṭṭ, TA;) and ↓ افند, (Ṣ, IḲṭṭ, L,) inf. n. إِفْنَادٌ; (Ṣ, L, Ḳ;) *He lied; uttered a falsehood; said what was untrue:* (Ṣ, M, IḲṭṭ, A, O, L, Ḳ:) this is [said to be] the primary signification. (L.) ↓ قَوْلٌ إِفْنَادٍ is used by a poet for قَوْلٍ ذِى إِفْنَادٍ [*A saying having,* or *characterized by, lying,* or *falsehood*]. (M, L.) — And فَنِدَ, aor. ـَ, (TḲ,) inf. n. فَنَدٌ, (M, O, Ḳ,) *He erred,* or *committed a mistake* or *mistakes,* (M, O, Ḳ, TḲ,) *in extreme old age,* (O,) in speech, or in judgment, or opinion: (M, Ḳ, TḲ:) and ↓ افند *he made many mistakes in his speech.* (Aṣ, TA in art. سهب.) — And فَنِدَ, aor. ـَ, (IḲṭṭ, TA, TḲ,) inf. n. فَنَدٌ; (T, Ṣ, M, IḲṭṭ, A, O, L, Ḳ;) and ↓ افند; (Ṣ, M, IḲṭṭ, L;) *He became weak in judgment by reason of extreme old age:* (Ṣ, IḲṭṭ, A, O, L:) or *he became unsound in mind,* (M, L, Ḳ,) [*in such a state that*] *his intellect,* or *intelligence, was denied,* or *disapproved,* (T, M, Ḳ, TḲ, الفَنَدُ being expl. in the T and M and Ḳ by إِنْكَارُ العَقْلِ, and فَنِدَ in the TḲ by انكر عقله [meaning أُنْكِرَ عَقْلُهُ], and in like manner افند [of which see the part. n., مُفْنِدٌ, below, as expl. in the A],) *by reason of extreme old age,* (T, M, Ḳ, TḲ,) or *disease;* (M, Ḳ, TḲ;) primarily thus restricted to the case of old age, but sometimes used without the being so restricted: (M:) and ↓ افند is also expl. as signifying *he became weak in intellect,* or *doted:* (IḲṭṭ, TA:) and as signifying *he became extremely aged,* because he who has become so speaks perverted language; from the same verb as signifying *he lied.* (L.) — [And فَنِدَ, inf. n. فَنَدٌ, app. signifies also *He was,* or *became, impotent:* and *unthankful for the favour of God:* see فَنَدٌ.]

2. فنّدهُ, inf. n. تَفْنِيدٌ, *He pronounced him to be a liar, an utterer of falsehood,* or *a sayer of what was untrue.* (Fr, M, Ḳ.) — See also 4. — *He blamed him,* (Ṣ, O, L,) and *pronounced his judgment to be weak:* (Ṣ, A, O, L:) or *he pronounced him,* (Fr, T,) or *it,* i. e. his judgment, (IAạr, T,) *to be weak.* (Fr, IAạr, T.) And *He pronounced him to be impotent,* or *lacking in ability.* (Fr, M, L, Ḳ.) ═ فند فَرَسًا *He acquired,* or *got for himself, a horse:* (T, O, TA:) so says Háróon Ibn-'Abd-Allah, as mentioned by Sh: but (Az says) I know it not in this sense: thus in the T: (TA:) or [rather] *he took him for the purpose of tying him,* or *keeping post, on the enemy's frontier,* (T, TA,) and *as a refuge to which to have recourse* (T, O, TA) *when suddenly attacked by the enemy;* (T, TA;) from فِنْدٌ, (T, O, TA,) signifying "a شِمْرَاخ," (O,) or "a great شمراخ," (T, TA,) "of a mountain," (T, O, TA,) or as signifying "a great mountain:" (O:) or i. q. ضَمَّرَهُ [as meaning *he made him light of flesh for military service*], (O, Ḳ, TA,) *so as to be like the branch of a tree,* termed فِنْد. (O, TA.) ═ فند فُلَانًا عَلَى الأَمْرِ *He desired, of such a one,* [*the performance of*] *the affair;* (Ḳ, TA;) as also ↓ فانده, (O, Ḳ, TA, in the O فِى الأَمْرِ,) inf. n. مُفَانَدَةٌ; (TA;) and ↓ تفنّدهُ. (O, Ḳ, TA.) ═ فند فِى الشَّرَابِ *He kept constantly,* or *perseveringly, to the beverage,* or *wine.* (AḤn, M, Ḳ, TA.) ═ And فنّد (inf. n. تَفْنِيدٌ, TA) *He sat upon a* فِنْد, (T, L,) i. e. *a* شِمْرَاخ *of a mountain.* (T, O, Ḳ.)

3 : see 2, near the end of the paragraph.

4. افند, inf. n. إِفْنَادٌ, as intrans.: see 1, in five places. ═ افندهُ (inf. n. as above, TA) *He charged him with error in judgment,* or *opinion;* as also ↓ فنّدهُ. (M, Ḳ.) — And *It* (old age) *rendered him weak in judgment,* or *unsound in mind:* (L:) or *it* (extreme old age) *caused him to have little understanding;* [or *to be*] *like a stone.* (A.)

5. تفنّد *He repented,* (Ḳ, B, TA,) مِنْهُ [*of it*]. (T, Ḳ.) ═ تفنّدهُ : see 2, near the end.

8. اُفْتُنِدَ *He was caused to perish by reason of extreme old age.* (O.)

فَنَدٌ : see the next paragraph, first sentence.

فِنْدٌ (T, Ṣ, M, A, O, L, Ḳ) and ↓ فَنَدٌ (Ibn-'Abbád, O, Ḳ) *A great mountain:* (IF, O, Ḳ:) or *a mountain apart from others:* (Ibn-Abi-l-Ḥadeed, TA:) or *a portion of a mountain,* (Ibn-'Abbád, Ṣ, O, Ḳ,) or *a great portion thereof,* (M, TA,) *having tallness,* or *length,* [app. the former,] (Ibn-'Abbád, Ṣ, O, Ḳ, TA,) and some add, *with slenderness:* (TA:) or *a head,* or *round and tall and slender head,* or *peak,* (شِمْرَاخ,) *of a mountain:* (T, A:) or *a great peak* or *head* (شمراخ, T, L, or رَأْس, M, L,) *of a mountain:* (T, M, L:) or *a* رُكْن [i. e. *a side,* or *an outward part,* or the *strongest side* or *outward part,*] *of a mountain:* (L:) pl. أَفْنَادٌ. (M, L.) One says of a bulky and heavy man, كَأَنَّهُ فِنْدٌ, meaning *As though he were a head,* or *peak,* (شِمْرَاخ,) *of a mountain.* (A.) — And the former (فِنْدٌ) is the sing. of أَفْنَاد in the phrase أَفْنَادُ اللَّيْلِ, (T,) which means *The component parts,* or *portions, of the night.* (T, O, Ḳ, TA.) — And *A congregated party* (T, O, Ḳ, TA) *of men.* (T, O.) One says, هُمْ فِنْدٌ عَلَى حِدَةٍ *They are a party by itself.* (T, TA.) And it is said in a trad., (T,) respecting the Prophet, (T, O, Ḳ,) that, when he died, (O,) صَلَّى النَّاسُ عَلَيْهِ أَفْنَادًا أَفْنَادًا i. e. [*The people prayed for him,* or *invoked blessing upon him,*] *one by one, without an Imám;* (Th, T, O, Ḳ;) or *companies after companies:* (O, Ḳ:) and they were computed to be thirty thousand, with sixty thousand angels; two angels to every one (T, O, Ḳ) of the believers. (T, O.) And the Prophet said, (T, O, Ḳ,) after announcing that he would be among the first that should die, (T, O,) تَتَّبِعُونِى أَفْنَادًا أَفْنَادًا يُهْلِكُ بَعْضُكُمْ بَعْضًا, meaning [*Ye will follow me*] *in scattered companies, company after company;* [*killing one another;*] أَفْنَادًا being pl. of فِنْد; (Nh, TA;) and in like manner is expl. a similar phrase in a trad. of 'Áïsheh: (T, TA:) or the former means ✝ ذَوِى فَنَد i. e. [*impotent;* and *unthankful;* lit.] *having impotence;* and *unthankfulness for* [*God's*] *favour.* (O, Ḳ, TA.) — And *A sort,* or *species:* (Ḳ, TA:) pl. أَفْنَادٌ: one says, جَآءُوا أَفْنَادًا *They came being diverse sorts.* (TA.) — And *A branch of a tree.* (T, O, Ḳ.*) — And *Land upon which rain has not fallen;* (T, O, Ḳ;) also termed ✝ فندية [app. فِنْدِيَّةٌ]. (T.)

فَنَدٌ [inf. n. of فَنِدَ, q. v.: as a subst.,] i. q. فُحْشٌ [app. as meaning *Exorbitance in speech*]; and *error in judgment:* pl. أَفْنَادٌ. (Ḥam p. 112.) — See also فِنْدٌ, near the end.

فِنْدَةٌ *A complete branch from which a bow is made.* (O.)

فندية [app. فِنْدِيَّةٌ]: see فِنْدٌ, last sentence.

فِنْدَأْوَةٌ (in the O and CḲ without hemz) A *sharp* قَدُوم [or adz]. (Ṣ, O, K.) — And A *bold,* or *fearless,* she-camel. (IAạr and Sh, TA in art. عدأ.)

فِنْدَأْيَةٌ *An adz,* or *an axe,* or *a hoe;* syn. فَأْسٌ: (IAạr, T, L:) or *a broad-headed* فأس: (M, L:) pl. فَنَادِيدُ, which is anomalous. (IAạr, T, L.)

فَانِيذٌ *A sort of sweetmeat, made of concrete juice of the sugar-cane* (قَنْد, q. v.,) *and starch* (نَشًا): a foreign word; for the measure فَاعِيلٌ is not found in Arabic; and therefore the lexicographers have not mentioned it: (Mṣb:) it is also written with ذ; (MF;) and is an arabicized word, from [the Pers.] پَانِيدْ [or پَانِيذْ]: (Ḳ voce فانيذ:) but is more properly with ذ. (MF.)

مُفْنِدٌ, (T, Ṣ, L, Ḳ,) or ✝ مُفْنَدٌ, [meaning *Weak in judgment,* or *unsound in mind,* &c., (see 1,) *by reason of extreme old age,* or *disease,*] an epithet applied to a man only: you do not use the fem. form, with ة, applying it to an old woman, because [it is held that] she has not possessed judgment (T, Ṣ, M, L, Ḳ) in her youth (T, Ṣ, M, L) or at any time: (Ḳ:) or both مُفْنِدٌ and ✝ مُفْنَدٌ signify [as above: or] one *whose intellect,* or *intelligence, is denied,* or *disapproved,* (أُنْكِرَ عَقْلُهُ,) *by reason of extreme old age:* or *who confounds* [*things*] *in his speech:* (A:) or the former, or ✝ the latter, signifies *loquacious by reason of unsoundness of mind:* (Aṣ, T:) and the former signifies *weak in intellect:* (L:) [and *extremely aged:* (see 1:)] and the same, (T,) or ✝ the latter, (L,) *weak in judgment;* notwithstanding he may be strong in body: and *weak in body;* notwithstanding he may be right in judgment: and *weak in judgment and in body.* (Fr, T, L.)

مُفْنَدٌ: see the next preceding paragraph, in four places.

فندر

فَنْدَرٌ and فُنْدُرٌ, applied to a boy or youth, *Plump:* and *wanting in courage and generosity; stupid and heavy.* (Ibn-'Abbád, O.)

فِنْدِيرٌ and ✝ فِنْدِيرَةٌ (Ḳ in this art., and Ṣ in art. فدر,) *A great mass of rock that becomes detached* (Ṣ, Ḳ) *from the head* (Ṣ) or *from the side* (Ḳ) *of a mountain:* (Ṣ, Ḳ:) pl. فَنَادِيرُ. (TA.) — And, both words, *A large lump* of dates (Ḳ, TA) *compacted together;* as also فِدْرَةٌ. (TA.)

الفُنْدُورَةُ *The anus.* (IAạr, T, O, TA.)

فِنْدِيرٌ: see فِنْدِيرَةٌ.

Accord. to some, the ن in the words mentioned in this art. is augmentative. (O.)

فندق

فُنْدُقٌ The *fruit of a certain tree,* (Lth, O, Ḳ,) the *same as the* بُنْدُق, which has been mentioned before, [i. e. *hazel-nut,* or *hazel-nuts,*] (Ḳ,) or *round, like the* بُنْدُق, *having a covering which, being removed, discloses a kernel* (حَبّ), *like the* فُسْتُق. (Lth, O.) ═ And, (Lth, O, Ḳ,) in the dial. of the people of Syria, *A* [*building of the kind called*] خَان [q. v.], *where men alight and lodge,* [*and in which they deposit their goods,*] *of the* خَانَات *that are in the roads,* (Lth, O, Ḳ,*) *and in the cities:* (Lth, O:) [said to be] a Pers. word, [app. from the Greek πανδοχεῖον, occurring in Luke x. 34, as remarked by Golius,] mentioned by Sb: pl. فَنَادِقُ. (TA.)

فُنْدَاقٌ *A register of accounts:* (O, Ḳ:) thought by Aṣ to be an arabicized word: but the word commonly known [in this sense] is with ق [i. e. قُنْدَاق]. (TA.)

فنزج

فَنْزَجٌ *A leaping, jumping, springing,* or *bounding;* and so ✝ فَنْزَجَةٌ: (L:) or the *game,* or *sport, called* دَسْتَبَنْد, [or دَسْتْبَنْد, a Pers. word,] meaning the *dance of the Magians,* (Lth, O, L,) or *a dance of the Persians* (العَجَم), (Ṣ, Ḳ,) *in which the performers hold one another by the hand;* (Lth, Ṣ, O, Ḳ;) arabicized from [the Pers.] پَنْجَه [app. as meaning "a gripe with the hand"]: (Ṣ, Ḳ:) or *a game,* or *sport, of the Nabathæans, called in Pers.* پَنْجَكَانْ [app. from پَنْجَه and گَانْ, from the joining of hands]; (ISk, O;) *a game, or sport, played by the Nabathæans in joyous exultation:* (IAạr, O:) occurring in a saying of El-'Ajjáj cited in art. عكف. (TA. See 1 in that art.) — And, as some say, The *five embolismal, or supplementary days, which are added at the end of the twelfth month of the Persians* [*and called by them* پَنْجَهٔ دُزْدِيدَهْ]. (IDrd, O, L.)

فَنْزَجَةٌ: see the preceding paragraph.

فنطس

فِنْطَاسٌ [The *bottom of the hold* of a ship or boat; i. e.] the *part* of a ship or boat *where the water that is drawn out* therefrom *collects:* (AA, O, Ḳ, TA:) this is the primary signification: (O, TA:) pl. فَنَاطِيسُ. (TA.) — Hence, (O,) *A tank made of boards,* (O, Ḳ,) *and tarred,* (O,) *borne in sea-going vessels,* (O, Ḳ,*) *and containing sweet water for drinking.* (O,* Ḳ.) — And, (O, Ḳ,) accord. to IAạr, (O,) *A bowl* (O, Ḳ) *of wood, the exterior of which is coloured with yellow and red and green,* (O,) *with which the sweet water is distributed* (O, Ḳ) *among the ship's crew.* (O.) ═ It is also applied to a nose, as signifying *Broad.* (IDrd, M, TA. [See also what next follows.])

فِنْطِيسٌ A nose *wide in the nostril, and expanded in the end:* (Ibn-'Abbád, O, Ḳ:) pl. فَنَاطِيسُ. (Ḳ. [See also what next precedes.]) — And, (O, Ḳ,) accord. to IDrd, (O,) A man *broad in the nose.* (O, Ḳ.) — And *Low, ignoble,* or *ungenerous,* (O, Ḳ, TA,) accord. to some, in an absolute sense, (TA,) or *in respect of birth;* (O, Ḳ, TA;) thus accord. to Ibn-'Abbád: pl. as above. (O.) ═ Also The *penis;* (O, Ḳ;) and so فِرْطِيسٌ: accord. to some, peculiarly of the swine. (TA.)

فِنْطِيسَةٌ The *snout* of the swine: (O, Ḳ: [mentioned also in art. فطس; the ن being held by some to be augmentative:]) and so فِرْطِيسَةٌ. (TA.) And The *nose* of the wolf. (O.) And one says, إِنَّهُ لَمَنِيعُ الفِنْطِيسَةِ (O, Ḳ*) and الفِرْطِيسَةِ, (O,) meaning † [*Verily he is*] *one who defends,* or *guards, from encroachment,* or *invasion,* or *attack, what is in his possession,* or *occupation; who refuses to submit to wrongful treatment:* (O, Ḳ:) thus mentioned on the authority of Aṣ; and Aboo-Sa'eed [meaning Aṣ] says that his فِنْطِيسَة and فِرْطِيسَة [properly] signify his *nose.* (TA.)

فنع

1. فَنِعَ, aor. ـَ, (Ṣ, O,* Ḳ,) inf. n. فَنَعٌ, (Ṣ, O,) *He abounded, and increased, in wealth.* (Ṣ, O, Ḳ.) مَنْ قَنِعَ فَنِعَ is a prov., (O, TA,) meaning [*He who is contented*] *is free from want,* or *is rich.* (TA.)

فَنَعٌ [as a simple subst.] *Increase, and abundance, of wealth:* (Ṣ:) *increase* (O, Ḳ, TA) *in wealth* and *in what is little in quantity:* (TA:) and i. q. خَيْرٌ [*good, moral or physical; wealth,* or *much wealth; prosperity, welfare,* or *wellbeing;* &c.]: and *generosity:* (O, Ḳ, TA:) and *large,* or *ample, liberality* or *bounty* or *munificence:* (TA:) and *excellence;* (O, Ḳ;) or *much,* or *abundant, excellence.* (TA.) One says مَالٌ ذُو فَنَعٍ and فَنَعًا, but the former is more common and more known, i. e. *Abundant wealth.* (TA.) And فَرَسٌ ذُو فَنَعٍ فِى سَيْرِهِ *A horse having increase* [*in his rate of going*], or *having excess* [*therein*]. (TA.) — And *Strength of odour* of musk. (Ḳ.) مِسْكٌ ذُو فَنَعٍ means *Musk of which the odour is strong.*

(Ṣ, O.) —— And *Good report.* (IDrd, O, Ḳ.) And The *spreading,* or *diffusion, of eulogy.* (TA.) ═══ Also *Much* of anything; and so ▼ فَنِيعٌ, and ▼ فَنَعٌ. (IAạr, TA.)

فَنِعٌ *Abounding, and increasing, in wealth;* as also ▼ فَنِيعٌ. (O, Ḳ.) —— See also فَنَعٌ, last sentence.

فَنِيعٌ: see فَنِعٌ: —— and see also فَنَعٌ, last sentence.

مِفْنَعٌ A man (A'Obeyd, O) *having a good report.* (A'Obeyd, O, Ḳ.)

فنق

2. فَنَّقَهُ, (Ṣ,) inf. n. تَفْنِيقٌ; (O, Ḳ;) and ▼ فانقه, (Ṣ, O,) inf. n. فِنَاقٌ; (TA;) *He made him to enjoy,* or *lead, a plentiful, and a pleasant* or *an easy, and a soft* or *delicate, life;* or *a life of ease and plenty.* (Ṣ, O, Ḳ.)

3: see the preceding paragraph.

4. افنق *He* (a man, O) *enjoyed,* or *led, a plentiful, and a pleasant* or *an easy, and a soft* or *delicate, life;* or *a life of ease and plenty; after straitness of the means of subsistence.* (O, Ḳ.) [See also what next follows.]

5. تفنّق *He* (a man, Ṣ) *enjoyed,* or *led, a plentiful, and a pleasant* or *an easy, and a soft* or *delicate, life;* or *a life of ease and plenty.* (Ṣ, O, Ḳ.) —— And تَفَنَّقْتُ فِى أَمْرِ كَذَا *I affected daintiness, nicety,* or *refinement, and cleanliness, in such an affair.* (TA.)

فَنَقٌ *Plentifulness, and pleasantness* or *easiness, and softness* or *delicacy, in living;* as also ▼ فُنَاقٌ. (TA.)

فُنُقٌ (Ṣ, O, Ḳ, TA) and ▼ مِفْنَاقٌ (O, Ḳ, TA) A woman, (Ṣ,) or young woman, (O, Ḳ, TA,) *that has been made to enjoy,* or *lead, a plentiful, and a pleasant* or *an easy, and a soft* or *delicate, life;* (Ṣ, O, Ḳ, TA;) *large in body, beautiful, and youthful:* Aṣ says that the former, applied to a woman, signifies *having little flesh;* but Sh knew not this, and he cites El-Aạshà as applying this epithet to a woman whom he describes as one whose elbows are unapparent, and such, he says, is not one having little flesh: IAạr says that it is applied to one who is as though she were a stallion-camel such as is termed فَنِيقٌ. (TA.) —— And the former, applied to a she-camel, signifies *Youthful, fat* or *plump,* (Ṣ, O, Ḳ, TA,) *fleshy, and bulky.* (TA.) —— See also فَنِيقٌ. —— It is also pl. of فَنِيقٌ. (Ṣ, O, Ḳ.)

فُنَاقٌ: see فَنَقٌ.

فَنِيقٌ *A stallion,* (Ṣ, O, Ḳ,) [i. e.] *a stallion-camel,* (IAạr, TA,) *that is highly regarded,* (Ṣ, O, Ḳ,) *and is not molested, because of the high estimation in which he is held by his owner,* or *owners, nor is ridden:* (O, Ḳ:) it is said by AZ to be one of the names for such a stallion: (Ṣ, TA:) or it is an epithet applied to a camel, meaning *such as is acquired for covering:* (TA:) the pl. is فُنُقٌ (Ṣ, O, Ḳ) accord. to AZ, and أَفْنَاقٌ accord. to IDrd, (Ṣ,) or the latter is pl. of the former pl.: (O, Ḳ:) and ▼ فُنُقٌ is applied as an epithet to a [single] camel, like فَنِيقٌ. (TA.)

فَنِيقَةٌ A [*sack such as is called*] غِرَارَة [q. v.]: (AA, O, Ḳ:) or a *small* غرارة: or a receptacle smaller than the غرارة: (TA:) [said by Meyd to be *a sack in which clay,* or *mud, is carried away:* (Golius:)] pl. فَنَائِقُ. (O, Ḳ.)

عَيْشٌ مُفَانِقٌ, (Ṣ, O, Ḳ,) and some say مُفَانَقٌ, (TA,) *A life that is plentiful, and pleasant* or *easy, and soft* or *delicate;* or *a life of ease and plenty.* (Ṣ,* O,* Ḳ, TA.)

مِفْنَاقٌ: see فُنُقٌ.

فنك

1. فَنَكَ بِالمَكَانِ, [aor. ـُ, (TḲ,)] inf. n. فُنُوكٌ, *He remained, stayed, dwelt,* or *abode, in the place.* (El-Umawee, Ṣ, O, Ḳ.) —— فَنَكَ فِى الأَمْرِ, (Ṣ, O, Ḳ,*) aor. as above, (Ṣ,) and so the inf. n., (Ṣ, O,) *He persisted,* or *persevered, in the affair;* (Ṣ, O, Ḳ;*) as also ▼ افنك. (Ḳ.) [See also فَنَكٌ; and see other explanations below.] And فَنَكَ فِى الكَذِبِ *He persisted,* or *persevered, in lying:* asserted by Yaạḳoob to be formed by transposition from فَكَنَ: and Aboo-Ṭálib says that ▼ فانك and ▼ فنّك, of which latter the inf. n. is تَفْنِيكٌ, signify *he persisted,* or *persevered,* in lying, and in evil; not in good; and denote the like of consecutiveness. (TA.) [See also فَنَكٌ, which may be an inf. n. of فَنَكَ in this sense, and in others.] And فَنَكَ عَلَيْهِ, (Ḳ, TA,) inf. n. as above, (TA,) signifies [in like manner] *He kept,* or *applied himself, constantly, perseveringly,* or *assiduously, to it;* as also ▼ افنك. (Ḳ, TA.) —— And فَنَكَ فِى الطَّعَامِ, (Ibn-'Abbád, Ṣ, O, Ḳ,) aor. as above, (Ṣ,) and so the inf. n., (Ṣ, O,) *He continued constantly, uniformly,* or *regularly, in the eating of the food, not loathing aught thereof;* (Ibn-'Abbád, Ṣ, O, Ḳ;) as also فَنِكَ, (Ṣ, O, Ḳ,) with kesr, (Ṣ, O,) like عَلِمَ, (Ḳ,) inf. n. فُنُوكٌ; (Ṣ, O, Ḳ;) and so ▼ فانك: (Ibn-'Abbád, O, Ḳ:) and ▼ فَانَكْتُ الطَّعَامَ وَالشَّرَابَ signifies [simply] *I kept continually,* or *constantly, to the food and the beverage:* and also *I loathed them,* or *turned away from them with disgust.* (Ibn-'Abbád, O.) —— And فَنَكَ فِى الأَمْرِ [not فانك as in the lexicons of Golius and Freytag, the latter of whom gives both forms of the v. in the sense here following, as does also the TḲ,] signifies also *He entered into the affair.* (Ḳ.) —— And *He mastered the affair, and overcame it.* (O.) —— فَنَكْتَ فِى لَوْمِى, and ▼ افنكت فيه, (both in the TA, but the latter only in the O,) *Thou wast,* or *hast become, skilled in the blaming,* or *censuring, of me, and profuse,* or *immoderate, therein:* so says Fr. (O, TA.) —— And فَنَكَتْ and ▼ أَفْنَكَتْ *She* (a woman) *blamed,* or *censured, and kept continually,* or *constantly, to blaming,* or *censuring,* or *to some other thing* [or *act*]. (Lth, O, TA.*) —— And the former, said of a girl, or young woman, *She cared not for what she did nor for what was said to her.* (Ibn-'Abbád, O, Ḳ.) This meaning has also been assigned to ▼ فَنَّكَتْ. (TA.) —— And فَنَكَ, (Ḳ,) inf. n. as above, (TA,) *He lied,* or *said what was untrue;* as also ▼ افنك. (Ḳ.)

2: see above, near the beginning.

3: see 1, first quarter: and near the middle, in two places.

4: see 1, in five places.

فَنْكٌ i. q. عَجَبٌ: (IAạr, O, Ḳ, TA:) [it app. means *A wonderful thing:* for] IAạr cites as an ex.,

* وَلَا فَنْكَ إِلَّا سَعْىُ عَمْرٍو وَرَهْطِهِ *

* بِمَا ٱخْتَشَبُوا مِنْ مِعْضَدٍ وَدَدَانِ *

[*And there is not anything wonderful except the conduct of 'Amr and his near kinsfolk in their having taken without selection a sword commonly used for lopping trees, and one that was blunt*]: (TA:) and ▼ فَنَكٌ signifies the same. (Ḳ, TA.) ═══ Also *Persistence,* or *perseverence;* or the act of *persisting,* or *persevering.* (TA.) [In this and the following senses, it seems to be an inf. n., of which the verb is فَنَكَ; as is indicated in the TA.] —— And The act of *overcoming.* (O, Ḳ, TA. [Accord. to the TA, from IAạr; but said in the O to be from another, not there named.]) —— And The *acting wrongfully, unjustly, injuriously,* or *tyrannically.* (IAạr, O, Ḳ, TA.) —— And The *lying,* or *saying what is untrue.* (IAạr, O, Ḳ, TA.)

فَنَكٌ *A certain beast,* (Kr, O, Ḳ,) *of the skin of which the furred garment is made;* (Kr, Ṣ, O;) [the *marten;*] *the furred garment whereof is the best sort of such garments, and the highest in estimation,* and *the most equable, and is suitable to all temperate constitutions:* (Ḳ:) it is said to be *a species of the Turkish fox's cubs;* and therefore Az and others say that the word is arabicized: some of the travellers relate that it is applied to the *young-one of the jackal* (اِبْنِ آوَى) in the country of the Turks: (Mṣb:) it is also said to mean *a certain skin that is worn;* and to be an arabicized word: [in Pers. a furred garment is called فَنَكْ:] IDrd says, "I do not think it to be Arabic:" and MF mentions ▼ فَنِيكٌ as signifying *an animal like the fox;* an arabicized word; from [a work entitled] غَايَةُ البَيَانِ; and he says that it appears to be the فنك that is mentioned in the Ḳ. (TA.) —— See also فَنْكٌ.

The مَجْمَعُ اللَّحْيَيْنِ [or *part in which is the symphysis*] *of the* لَحْيَانِ [or *two lateral portions of the lower jaw*], (Lth, O, Ḳ, TA,) *in the middle of the chin,* (Lth, O, TA,) *of a man;* (Lth, O, Ḳ, TA;) this is when the word is used in the sing. form; (Lth, O; [see also الفَلْكُ;]) and it is also called ▼ الإِفْنِيكُ; (Lth, O;) [and in like manner Aboo-'Amr Esh-Sheybánee explained what is meant by the upper فَنِيك as is stated by IF and in the O:] or *the extremity* [*of each*] *of the* لَحْيَانِ, *at the place of the* عَنْفَقَة [or *tuft of hair that is between the lower lip and the chin;*] (Ṣ, Ḳ;) also called ↑ الإِفْنِيكُ; but Ks knew not this: (Ṣ:) or the فَنِيكَانِ are *the two extremities of the* عَنْفَقَة: (O:) or (Ḳ, TA, in the CḲ "and") the sing. signifies *a bone* [*beneath the temple,*] *to which the shaving of the head reaches* (عَظْمٌ يَنْتَهِى إِلَيْهِ حَلْقُ الرَّأْسِ): (Ḳ, TA:) and accord. to Lth, the dual signifies *the two extremities of the* [*lower*] *jaw,* of whatever has a jaw, *that move in the act of chewing, below the temples:* (O:) or, accord. to Sh, *the two thin, rising bones,* [app. *the two coronoid processes of the jaw,*] *lower than the ears, between the temple and the ball of the cheek.* (TA.) The lower فنيك is [app. *The symphysis of the pubes;* being] said by Aboo-'Amr Esh-Sheybánee to be *the part where the two hip-bones meet together:* (IF, O:) [hence, perhaps, and therefore it may be erroneously,] the فنيك is said by AA to be *the root,* or *base, of the tail:* (TA:) and it signifies, as also ↑ الإِفْنِيكُ, (IDrd, O, Ḳ,) *the* زِمِكَّى, (Ḳ,) or زِمِجَّى, [i. e. the *place of growth,* or the *root,* or the *whole, of the tail, of a bird,* or] *of a young bird;* as they assert; (IDrd, O;) but IDrd says, "I will not pronounce it to be correct:" (O:) and the dual signifies *two bones cleaving together: when, in the female pigeon, they are broken, she does not retain her eggs* [*sufficiently*], *but excludes them prematurely.* (Lth, O.) ═ See also فَنَكٌ.

الإِفْنِيكُ: see the next preceding paragraph, in three places.

مُتَفَنِّكَةٌ *A foolish,* or *stupid,* woman. (Ibn-'Abbád, O, Ḳ.)

فنو

فَنْوٌ, said to be sing. of أَفْنَآءٌ: see the latter, below.

فَنًا: see the next paragraph: ═ and see also فَنًى, in art. فنى.

فَنَاةٌ *A bull* or *cow;* syn. بَقَرَةٌ; (AA, T, Ṣ, M, Ḳ;) [i. e.] *a* بَقَرَة وَحْشِيَّة [or *wild bull* or *cow; an antelope of the bovine kind*]: so says Aboo-'Alee El-Ḳálee: (TA:) it occurs in a verse of Lebeed; and is said, as on the authority of IAạr, to be قَنَاة, with ق: (TA in art. قنو:) pl. فَنَوَاتٌ (AA, T, Ṣ, M, Ḳ) and [coll. gen. n.] ↑ فَنًا. (Aboo-'Alee El-Ḳálee, TA.)

أَفْنَى *i. q.* فَيْنَانٌ [i. e. *Hair having locks like the branches of trees;* or *long and beautiful hair*]; (M, Ḳ, TA;) [or] meaning *long hair.* (TA.) [The fem. of أَفْنَى is فَنْوَآءُ. Hence,] اِمْرَأَةٌ فَنْوَآءُ *A woman having much hair:* (IAạr, M, Ḳ:) and شَجَرَةٌ فَنْوَآءُ *A tree having* أَفْنَان [or *branches*]; (AA, T, Ṣ, M;) or *a tree having wide shade:* (Ḳ:) by rule it should be فَنَّآءُ [q. v. in art. فن]. (Ṣ, M, Ḳ.)

أَفْنَآءٌ مِنَ النَّاسِ means *Mixed sorts of men* or *people;* like أَغْنَآءٌ: and the sings. are [said to be] فِنْوٌ and عِنْوٌ: (IAạr, T:) one says, هُوَ مِنْ أَفْنَآءِ النَّاسِ when it is not known of whom he is: (Ṣ:) or رَجُلٌ مِنْ أَفْنَآءِ القَبَائِلِ, meaning *a man such that one knows not of what tribe he is:* but some hold that one says only, قَوْمٌ من افناء القبائل; not رَجُلٌ; and that there is no sing. of أَفْنَآءٌ: (M in art. فنى:) accord. to AHeyth, one says, هٰؤُلَآءِ مِنْ أَفْنَآءِ النَّاسِ, meaning *these are of the strangers from this and that place:* but one does not say, speaking of one person, رَجُلٌ من افناء الناس: and Umm El-Heythem knew not a sing. of أَفْنَآءٌ. (T in art. فنى.)

فنى

1. فَنِىَ, (T, Ṣ, M, Mṣb, Ḳ, &c.,) aor. يَفْنَى; (T, M, Mṣb, Ḳ;) and فَنَى, aor. يَفْنِى, (M, Ḳ,) which is extr., mentioned by Kr, and said by him to be of the dial. of Belḥárith Ibn-Kaạb; (M;) the former of the two verbs being that which is commonly known; (TA;) inf. n. فَنَآءٌ, (T, Ṣ, M, Mṣb, Ḳ, &c.,) which is of both of the verbs; (TA;) *It* (i. e. a thing, Ṣ, Mṣb, TA) *passed away and came to an end; vanished away; became spent,* or *exhausted; failed entirely; ceased, perished,* or *came to nought;* or *was,* or *became, transitory, evanescent,* or *non-existent;* the inf. n. being *syn. with* نَفَادٌ; (Aboo-'Alee El-Ḳálee, TA;) *contr. of* بَقَآءٌ; (M, TA;) and the pret. being *syn. with* عُدِمَ: (Ḳ, TA:) it is said of every created thing that it is subject to الفَنَآء. (Mṣb.) [Hence] دَارُ الفَنَآءِ [*The abode of transitoriness, evanescence,* or *perishableness,*] means *the present world.* (T in art. دور.) — And, said of a man, (T, M, Ḳ,) i. e. فَنِىَ, aor. and inf. n. as above, (M,) ‡ *He was,* or *became, extremely aged;* or *old and infirm;* syn. هَرِمَ: (M, Ḳ:) or *he became on the verge of death by reason of extreme age* or *of age and infirmity.* (T.) Lebeed says,

> • حَبَائِلُهُ مَبْثُوثَةٌ بِسَبِيلِهِ •
>
> • وَيَفْنَى إِذَا مَا أَخْطَأَتْهُ الحَبَائِلُ •

(T, M,) meaning [*His snares are spread in his way, and when the snares fail to catch him*] *he becomes old and infirm and so dies:* (T:) or it means, *when death misses him he becomes old and infirm.* (M.)

3. فاناهُ, (T, Ṣ, M, Ḳ,) inf. n. مُفَانَاةٌ, (T, TA,) *He* (a man, Ṣ, M) *soothed,* or *coaxed, him:* (AA, T, Ṣ, M, Ḳ:) and, (M,) accord. to El-Umawee, (T, Ṣ,) *he stilled,* or *quieted, him.* (T, Ṣ, M.) El-Kumeyt says, (Ṣ, M,) mentioning anxieties, (M,)

> • تُقِيمُهُ تَارَةً وَتُقْعِدُهُ •
>
> • كَمَا يُفَانِى الشَّمُوسَ قَائِدُهَا •

[*They rouse him at one time, and* at another time *they render him sedate like as her leader soothes,* or *coaxes,* or like as he *stills,* or *quiets, the refractory mare*]. (Ṣ, M: in the T, accord. to the TT, the verse ends with رَائِدُهَا [her pastor], instead of قَائِدُهَا.) Accord. to IAạr, فاناهُ signifies واجاهُ [app. a mistranscription for وَآخَاهُ, originally آخَاهُ, *He fraternized with him;* or *acted with him in a brotherly manner*]. (TA.) [Hence the phrase] أُزَجِّى الزَّمَانَ i. e. أُفَانِى الأَيَّامَ [meaning *I make the time to pass away easily;* as though beguiling it]. (Ḥar p. 607.) — And one says, بَنُو فُلَانٍ مَا يُعَانُونَ مَالَهُمْ وَلَا يُفَانُونَهُ i. e. *The sons of such a one do not tend,* or *take care of, their cattle,* or *camels,* or [*other*] *property, and do not manage the same well.* (T.)

4. افناهُ *He,* or *it, caused it,* or *him, to pass away and come to an end; to vanish away; to become spent,* or *exhausted; to fail entirely; to cease, perish,* or *come to nought; he,* or *it, did away with, destroyed,* or *annihilated, it,* or *him;* (T, Ṣ,* M, Mṣb,* Ḳ, TA;) trans. of فَنِىَ. (T, Ṣ, Mṣb, Ḳ.) The saying of a rájiz, (T, TA,) namely, Abu-n-Nejm, (TA,) describing a pastor of sheep or goats,

> • يَقُولُ لَيْتَ ٱللّٰهَ قَدْ أَفْنَاهَا •

(T, TA,) may mean an imprecation against them, i. e. *He says, would that God had destroyed them:* (T:) — or it means, *would that God had made to grow for them* [*the plant called*] الفَنَى, i. e. عِنَبُ الثَّعْلَبِ; so that they might have abundance of milk, and become fat. (T, TA.)

6. تَفَانَوْا, (Ṣ, Ḳ,) or تفانوا قَتْلًا, (M,) *They destroyed one another,* (Ṣ, M, Ḳ,) [or *they shared, one with another, in destruction,* (see an ex. in a verse cited voce دَقَّ,) *by slaughter,*] in war, or battle. (Ṣ.)

الفَنَى, thus, with ى, in the M, and thus it should be written accord. to Aboo-'Alee El-Ḳálee, in the T and Ṣ with ا, and in like manner in the Ḳ, in which it is [mentioned in art. فنو, and] written without the article ال (فَنًا), and said to be a pl., of which the sing. is ↑ الفَنَاة, (TA,) [*The plant called*] عِنَبُ الثَّعْلَبِ; [see art. ثعلب; and see also الأَفَانِى, in this art.;] (T, Ṣ, M, Ḳ;) whereof one is called ↑ فَنَاةٌ: (Ṣ:) or, as some say, *another plant;* (T;) [i. e.,] as some say, *a species of trees,* or *plants,* (شَجَرٌ,) *having red berries,* (حَبٌّ,) (Ṣ,) *of which necklaces are made,* (Ṣ,) or *the unbroken of which are made use of as* قَرَارِيط [meaning *carat-weights*] *with which to weigh, every berry* (حَبَّة) *being a* قِيرَاط: and some say that it is *a herb that grows in rugged places, rising from the ground to the height of the measure of a finger, and less, and depastured by the cattle.* (M.)

فَنَاةٌ: see the next preceding paragraph, in two places: ═ and see also art. فنو.

فِنَآءٌ *A yard,* or *an exterior court,* i. e. *a wide space,* (T, Ṣ, M, Mgh, Mṣb, Ḳ,) *in front,* (T, M, Mgh, Mṣb, Ḳ,) or *extending from the sides,* (Ṣ, Mṣb,) of a house: (T, Ṣ, M, Mgh, Mṣb, Ḳ:) pl. أَفْنِيَةٌ (T, Ṣ, M, Mṣb, Ḳ) and فُنِىٌّ: (Ḳ:) and ثِنَآءٌ [q. v.] signifies the same. (T, M.)

فَانٍ part. n. of فَنِىَ [i. e. signifying *Passing away and coming to an end*; &c.]. (T.) — And ‡ An old man *extremely aged*, or *old and infirm*; (M,* Mṣb, Ḳ,* TA;) so called because of his nearness to passing away, or perishing: (Mṣb:) or an old man *whose faculties have entirely failed*. (Mgh.) And فَانِيَةٌ occurs in a trad., applied to a she-camel, or to camels, as meaning †*Advanced in age*. (TA.) — [فَانٍ فِى ٱللّٰهِ, in the language of the mystics, means † *Lost in contemplation of God, and insensible to all else*.]

أَفْنَآءٌ مِنَ النَّاسِ is expl. in art. فنو.

الأَفَانِى [without the article أَفَانٍ] is the name of *A species of plant*, (T, Ṣ, Ḳ,) *yellow, and red*; (T;) [*said to be so called*] *while fresh and succulent*; (Ṣ;) accord. to AA, (T,) *when it has dried up, it is called* الحَمَاطُ; (Ṣ, T;) but this is a mistake; for الافانى signifies *a particular species of plant by itself, of the herbs*, or *leguminous plants, termed* ذُكُور, *which dries up, and becomes scattered*; whereas the حماط is the حَلبة [a mistranscription for حَلَمَة], and this does not dry up, because it is of the [kind called] جَنْبَة and عُرْوَة: (T:) the n. un. is أَفَانِيَةٌ, (T, Ṣ,) like ثَمَانِيَةٌ [in measure]. (Ṣ.) And it is said to signify also [*The plant called*] عِنَبُ الثَّعْلَبِ. (Ṣ. [See also الفَنَى, above.])

مُفْنَاةٌ A land (أَرْضٌ) *suitable to those who alight and abide therein*: (Ḳ, TA:) it occurs, in a verse of Ḳeys Ibn-El-'Eyzár El-Hudhalee, with ق, [as some relate that verse,] but Aṣ says that in the dial. of Hudheyl it is with ف. (TA in art. قنى.)

فه

1. فَهِهَ, (Ḳ,) [or perhaps فَهَّ, but originally فَهِهَ], like فَرِحَ, (Ḳ,) sec. pers. فَهِهْتَ, [aor. ـَ,] inf. n. فَهَهٌ (Ṣ, TA) [and app. فَهَّةٌ and فَهَاهَةٌ], *He* (a man, Ṣ) *lacked power* or *ability*. (Ṣ, Ḳ.) And فَهَّ, inf. n. فَهَاهَةٌ and فَهَّةٌ, *He made a slip*, or *committed a fault, from lack of power* or *ability, &c.* (TA.) And فَهَّ فِى خُطْبَتِهِ, and حُجَّتِهِ, *He* (a man) *failed of being thoroughly effective* [*in his discourse*, or *oration*, or *harangue*, and *his argument*, or *plea*, or *evidence*]. (TA.) — And فَهِهْتُ الشَّىْءَ *I forgot the thing*. (ISh, Ḳ,* TA. [In the Ḳ the third pers. is mentioned, as being فَهِهَ; but I think it should be contracted (agreeably with a general rule), as in what here follows.]) And فَهَّ عَنِ الشَّىْءِ, inf. n. فَهٌّ [probably, I think, a mistake for فَهَهٌ], *He forgot the thing*. (TA.) See also 4.

2: see what next follows.

4. افهّهُ *He* (i. e. God) *made him to lack power* or *ability*; as also ▾ فهّههُ. (Ṣ, Ḳ. [The former is omitted in one of my copies of the Ṣ.]) — And *He* (another person) *made him to forget*. (TA.) One says, خَرَجْتُ لِحَاجَةٍ فَأَفَهَّنِى فُلَانٌ عَنْهَا حَتَّى ▾ فَهِهْتُ i. e. [*I went forth for a needful affair, and such a one*] *made me to forget it* [*so that I did forget it*]. (Ṣ, TA. [Or افهّنى may be here better rendered agreeably with the explanation next following.]) Accord. to IDrd, أَفَهَّنِى عَنْ حَاجَتِى signifies *He busied me so as to divert me* [*from my needful affair*, or *the object of my want*]. (TA.)

R. Q. 1. فَهْفَهَ *He fell from a high station to a lower one*. (IAạr, TA.)

فَهٌّ, (Ṣ, Ḳ,) applied to a man, (Ṣ,) *Lacking power* or *ability*; (Ṣ, Ḳ;) as also ▾ فَهِهٌ, (CḲ, but omitted in other copies of the Ḳ,) and ▾ فَهِيهٌ, (Ṣ,* Ḳ,) and ▾ فَهْفَهٌ, (Ḳ,) which last is mentioned by IDrd as signifying *dull of tongue, lacking power*, or *ability, to accomplish the object of his want*: (TA:) and فَهَّةٌ is applied, in the sense first mentioned, to a woman; (Ṣ;) or as meaning *lacking power*, or *ability, to accomplish the object of her want*. (TA.) And كَلِمَةٌ فَهَّةٌ means [*A word*, or *a sentence*, &c.,] *having* فَهَاهَة [i. e. *a lack of power*, &c.]. (TA.)

فَهَّةٌ and ▾ فَهَاهَةٌ [each of which has been mentioned above as an inf. n.] *Lack of power* or *ability*; (Ṣ, Ḳ;) as also ▾ فَهْفَهَةٌ. (Ḳ.) — The first signifies also *A case*, or *an instance, of* فَهَاهَة: and [*a case*, or *an instance, of*] *unmindfulness* or *forgetfulness*: (TA:) and *a slip*, or *fault*: and *a case*, or *an instance, of ignorance*: and *the like thereof*. (A'Obeyd, Ṣ, TA.*)

فَهِهٌ: see فَهٌّ.

فَهِيهٌ *i. q.* فَهٌّ, q. v.: (Ṣ,* Ḳ:) or *unable to speak*. (KL. [See فَكِيهٌ.]) One says سَفِيهٌ فَهِيهٌ [*Lightwitted, lacking power* or *ability*]. (Ṣ, TA.)

فَهَاهَةٌ: see فَهَّةٌ.

فَهْفَهٌ: see فَهٌّ.

فَهْفَهَةٌ: see فَهَّةٌ.

هُوَ فَهْفَاهٌ عَلَى المَالِ means *He is a good manager* or *tender* or *superintendent* [*of the camels* or *cattle* &c.]. (Ḳ.)

فهد

1. فَهِدَ, (Ṣ, A, O, L, Ḳ,) aor. ـَ, (A, Ḳ,) inf. n. فَهَدٌ, (L,) *He* (a man, Ṣ, A, O) *resembled the* فَهْد [or *lynx*] (Ṣ, A, O, L, Ḳ) *in his stretching himself and his sleeping*, (L, Ḳ,) or *in his much sleeping, and stretching himself*. (Ṣ, A, O.) And *He slept, and was*, or *feigned himself, heedless of what was requisite*, or *necessary to be done*. (L, Ḳ.) Hence the saying, (Ṣ, L,) of a woman describing her husband, as related in the story of Umm-Zara, (L,) إِنْ دَخَلَ فَهِدَ وَإِنْ خَرَجَ أَسِدَ وَلَا يَسْأَلُ عَمَّا عَهِدَ (Ṣ,* L,) i. e. *If he come in* and be with me in the tent, or house, *he is* gentle and quiet *like the* فَهْد, which is described as sleeping much; and is, or feigns himself, heedless of the things that are amiss therein, and that I ought to put into a right, or proper, state; such is his generosity, and goodness of disposition; *and if he go out*, and see his enemy, *he is like the lion* [in boldness; *and he will not ask respecting what he has ordered*]. (L.) And one says, فَهِدْتَ عَنِّى, inf. n. فَهَدٌ, *Thou wast*, or *hast been, heedless*, or *negligent, of me*. (A.) — فَهَدَ لَهُ, (O, L, Ḳ,) aor. ـَ, (Ḳ,) *He did well*, or *kindly, in his affair in his absence*: (O, L, Ḳ:) like قَادَ, and مَهَدَ. (O, L.)

فَهْدٌ [The *lynx*; *lupus cervarius*;] *a well-known beast of prey*; (L, Mṣb, Ḳ;) *with which one hunts*; *and which sleeps much*; (L;) *called in Pers.* يُوز: (Mgh:) fem. فَهْدَةٌ: (L, Mṣb:) pl. of the masc. فُهُودٌ (Ṣ, Mgh, O, L, Mṣb, Ḳ) and أَفْهُدٌ (O, L, Ḳ) which is a pl. of pauc.; (O;) and the pl. of the fem., accord. to analogy, is فَهْدَاتٌ. (Mṣb.) أَنْوَمُ مِنَ الفَهْدِ [*More sleepful than the lynx*] is a proverb. (A.) — And *A nail in the* وَاسِط [or *fore part*] *of the* [*camel's saddle called*] رَحْل; (O, L, Ḳ;) *also termed* كَلْبٌ [q. v.]. (L.) To the creaking sound of this nail the similar sound of a stallion-camel's tushes is likened.

فَهِدٌ and فِهِدٌ [A man] *resembling the* فَهْد [or *lynx*] *in his stretching himself and his sleeping* [or *in his doing thus much*, or *often*]: and [a man] *being*, or *feigning himself, heedless of what is requisite*, or *necessary to be done*. (Ḳ.)

فَهْدَةٌ fem. of فَهْدٌ [q. v.]. (Mṣb.) — The ابنت فَهْدَة [i. e. *podex*, or *anus*]. (L, Ḳ.) — *A small piece of butter*. (L in art. نهد.) — الفَهْدَتَانِ, (Ṣ, A, O,) or فَهْدَتَا صَدْرِ الفَرَسِ, (AO, TA,) or فَهْدَتَا الفَرَسِ, (L, Ḳ,) *Two prominent portions of flesh in the* [*part of the breast called*] زَوْر [q. v.] *of the horse*, (Ṣ, A, O, Ḳ,) *like two stones of the kind termed* فِهْر: (Ṣ, O:) or *the prominent flesh in the breast of the horse, on its right and left*: (L:) or *two portions of flesh on the right and left of the breast of the horse*. (AO, TA.) — And فَهْدَتَا البَعِيرِ *Two protuberant bones behind the ears of the camel*; (O, L, Ḳ;) *the same that are termed* الخُشَّشَاوَانِ. (O, L.)

فَهَّادٌ *The owner*, or *master, of a* فَهْد [or *lynx*]: (L:) or *one who trains the* فَهْد *for hunting*. (T, O, L, Ḳ.)

فَوْهَدٌ *A fat boy or youth*, (AA, Ṣ, O, L,) *that has nearly attained to puberty*; (AA, Ṣ, L;) *i. q.* فَلْهَدٌ; (AA, L;) [and فُرْهُدٌ and ثَوْهَدٌ;] and فُرْهُدٌ; (O, Ḳ;) as also ▾ أُفْهُودٌ: (O, Ḳ:) Yaạḳoob asserts that the ف in فوهد is a substitute for the ث in ثوهد, or that the converse is the case; and both signify a boy *perfect in make*: or, accord. to AA, *soft and plump*: or both signify *perfect, and soft, thin-skinned, and plump*: (L:) fem. فَوْهَدَةٌ. (Ṣ, O, L, Ḳ).

أُفْهُودٌ: see the next preceding paragraph.

فهر

1. فَهَرَ, aor. ـَ, (Mṣb, Ḳ,) inf. n. فَهْرٌ (Ṣ, O, Mṣb,

Ḳ) and فَهَرَ; (Ṣ, O, Ḳ;) and ▾ افهر, (IAạr, O,* Ḳ,) inf. n. إِفْهَار; (TA;) *He compressed a woman,* (IAạr, Ṣ, O, Mṣb, Ḳ,) *one of his young women,* (IAạr,) *without consummating the act,* i. e. *without* إِنْزَال, (IAạr, Ṣ, O, Mṣb,) *and then removed to another and consummated the act* (IAạr, Ṣ, O, Mṣb, Ḳ) *with the latter,* (IAạr, O, Mṣb,) *who was with him in the house,* or *chamber;* (IAạr;) the doing of which is forbidden (Ṣ, O, Mṣb) by the Prophet: (O:) and ▾ the latter verb signifies also *He was alone with one of his young women,* (Ḳ, TA,) لِقَضَآءِ حَاجَتِهِ, (TA,) *when another of them heard the sound proceeding from him,* which [sound] is termed الوَجْسُ, (Ḳ, TA,) and الخَفْخَفَةُ, and الرِّكْزُ; (TA;) which [also] is forbidden. (Ḳ, TA.)

2. فهّر, inf. n. تَفْهِيرٌ, *He compressed without consummating the act,* i. e. *without* إِنْزَال, *by reason of weariness and languor.* (Mṣb in art. عزل. [See also 1.]) — Also, inf. n. as above, *He* (a man) *was,* or *became, weary,* or *fatigued.* (Ṣ, TA.) Said of a horse, as also ▾ فَيْهَرَ and ▾ تَفَيْهَرَ, *He was,* or *became, out of breath by reason of fatigue* or *running;* (Ḳ, TA;) *and interrupted,* or *stopped short, in running; and jaded:* (TA:) or *he fell back by degrees from running, by reason of weakness, and being interrupted,* or *stopped short, in running:* (Ḳ, TA:) or the first deficiency of the rate of running of the horse is termed التَّرَادُّ [the falling back by degrees]; the next, الفُتُورُ [the becoming languid]; and the next, التَّفْهِيرُ. (Ṣ, TA.)

4: see 1, in two places. — افهر بَعِيرُهُ *His camel became jaded, and broke down with him,* or *perished, so that he was unable to prosecute his journey.* (IDrd, O, Ḳ.) — And افهر (said of a man, TA) *His flesh became compacted and lumpy* (O, Ḳ*) *and wrinkled by reason of fatness:* (O:) when such is the case, it is the ugliest sort of fatness. (O, Ḳ.) — Also *He was present at the festival of the Jews,* (IDrd, O, Ḳ, TA,) *called* الفُهْر: (TA:) or *he came to their synagogue:* (Ḳ, TA:) or it signifies also *he was present in their synagogue.* (IDrd, O.) — And أُفْهِرَتْ, said of a girl, *She was circumcised.* (Ibn-'Abbád, O, Ḳ.)

5. تفهّر فِى المَالِ *He became,* or *made himself, ample,* or *abundant, in wealth,* or *in camels,* or *the like;* (Ṣ, O, Ḳ;) as also ▾ تَفَيْهَرَ; (Ḳ;) as though the former verb were formed by substitution from تَبَحَّرَ: or it may mean *he was,* or *became, weary, fatigued,* or *jaded,* and *languid,* or *remiss.* (Ṣ, O.) And تفهّر فِى الكَلَامِ *He took a wide,* or *an ample, range in speech.* (TA.)

Q. Q. 1. فَيْهَرَ: see 2.

Q. Q. 2. تَفَيْهَرَ: see 2: — and see also 5.

الفُهْرُ, (Mṣb, Ḳ,) or فُهْرُ اليَهُودِ, (Ṣ, Mgh, O,) *The synagogue of the Jews,* (Ṣ, Mgh, O, Mṣb, Ḳ,) *in which they assemble* (O, Mṣb, Ḳ) *for prayer* (Mṣb) *on the occasion of their festival:* (Ḳ:) or *a certain day on which they eat and drink:* (Ḳ:) or it signifies also *a certain festival of the Jews:* (O:) [app. *the feast of Purim* (written in the Book of Esther פורים pl. of פור)]: accord. to A'Obeyd, (O, Mṣb,) a Hebrew word, (Ṣ, O, Mṣb,) or Nabathæan; (Mṣb;) arabicized; (Ṣ, Mṣb;) originally بُهْر; (Ṣ, O, Mṣb;) and the Christians say فُخْر. (TA.)

فِهْرٌ, (Ṣ, O, Ḳ,) masc. and fem.; (Fr, Ṣ, O, Ḳ;) or, accord. to Lth, the Arabs in general made it fem.; but it occurs in the Ḳ as masc.; (TA;) *A stone such as fills the hand:* (Ṣ, O, Ḳ:) or *a stone of the size of that with which one crushes walnuts* (Ḳ, TA) *and the like:* (TA:) or *a round stone with which one bruises,* or *brays, perfume:* (Ḥam p. 643:) or *a stone,* absolutely: (TA:) pl. [of pauc.] أَفْهَارٌ (Ṣ, O, Ḳ) and [of mult.] فُهُورٌ: (O, Ḳ:) Aṣ used to say فِهْرٌ and ▾ فِهْرَةٌ, (Ṣ, O,) [indicating the former to be a coll. gen. n. and the latter to be the n. un.,] like سِدْرٌ and سِدْرَةٌ: (O:) the dim. is ▾ فُهَيْرَةٌ. (Ṣ, O.)

فِهْرَةٌ: see the next preceding paragraph.

فَهِيرَةٌ *Pure, unmixed, milk, into which heated stones are put; and when it boils, flour is sprinkled upon it, and it is mixed, and stirred about, and beaten, therewith; and is then eaten:* (ISk, Ṣ, O, Ḳ:) it has also been mentioned as with ق. (TA.)

فُهَيْرَةٌ [dim. of فِهْرٌ and of فِهْرَةٌ]: see فِهْرٌ.

نَاقَةٌ فَيْهَرَةٌ and فَيْهَرٌ, (O, Ḳ,) the former mentioned by IDrd, and the latter by Ibn-'Abbád, *A she-camel that is hard and strong,* (O,) or *hard and large.* (Ḳ.)

أَرْضٌ مَفْهَرَةٌ *Land having in it* [*stones such as are termed*] أَفْهَار [pl. of فِهْرٌ]. (O, TA.)

مَفَاهِرُكَ, (Ḳ, TA,) thus we find it, with fet-ḥ, but in some copies of the Ḳ with ḍamm, (TA,) *The flesh of thy breast.* (Ḳ, TA.)

IF says that there is not in the original language [of the Arabs] more than one word having in it the letters ف and ه and ر, and that is الفِهْرُ. (O.)

فهرس

Q. 1. فَهْرَسَ الكُتُبَ [*He made,* or *wrote, a catalogue of the books* or *writings*], (O,) or فهرس كِتَابَهُ [*he made an index,* or *a table of contents, to his book* or *writing*], (Ḳ,) inf. n. فَهْرَسَةٌ. (TA.) See what follows.

فِهْرِسٌ *A book,* or *writing, in which* [*the names* or *titles* or *descriptions*] *of* [*other*] *books,* or *writings, are collected;* [i. e. *a catalogue of books* or *writings:* but more commonly, accord. to modern usage, the *index,* or *table of contents,* of a book or writing; in an Arabic book, generally placed at the beginning:] an arabicized word; (Lth, O, Ḳ;) from [the Pers.] فِهْرِسْت: (O, Ḳ:) pl. فَهَارِسُ. (TA.)

فهم

1. فَهِمَهُ, aor. ـَ, inf. n. فَهْمٌ (Ṣ, Mṣb, Ḳ, &c.) and فَهَمٌ, (Mṣb, Ḳ,) which is the more chaste, (Ḳ,) but the former is a dial. var. [more] extensively obtaining, or, as some say, it is a subst. used as an inf. n., (Mṣb,) and فَهَامِيَةٌ (Ṣ, Ḳ) and فَهَامَةٌ and فِهَامَةٌ, (Ḳ,) *He understood it,* or *knew it with the mind; he apprehended its meaning;* syn. عَقَلَهُ, (JK,) and عَلِمَهُ (Ṣ, Mṣb, Ḳ) and عَرَفَهُ بِالقَلْبِ. (Ḳ.) And فَهِمَ عَنْهُ [*He understood what he* (another) *said*]. (A in art. خرس; &c.) [See also فَهِيمٌ below.] — فَهُمَ, meaning *He was,* or *became, such as is termed* فَهِيمٌ [i. e. *one having much understanding*], is like عَلُمَ, meaning "he was, or became, such as is termed عَلِيمٌ." (TA.)

2: see what next follows.

4. أَفْهَمَهُ and ▾ فَهَّمَهُ, (Ṣ, Mṣb, Ḳ, TA,) inf. n. of the latter تَفْهِيمٌ, (Ṣ, TA,) *I made him to understand,* or *know,* a thing; (Ṣ,* Mṣb,* Ḳ,* TA;) syn. جَعَلْتُهُ يَفْهَمُهُ. (TA.)

5. تفهّمهُ *He understood it,* or *knew it,* (فَهِمَهُ,) *one thing* [or *one particular thereof*] *after another;* (Ṣ, Ḳ;) namely, speech, or language. (Ṣ.) — [And *He endeavoured to understand it.* (See its inf. n. as used in the former half of the second paragraph of art. دبر.)] And ▾ التَّفَاهُمُ signifies the same as التَّفَهُّمُ [app. as meaning *The endeavouring to understand;* or *the affecting,* or *pretending, to understand*]. (TA.)

6: see what next precedes.

7. انفهم, (Ḳ, TA,) as quasi-pass. of فَهِمَهُ, inf. n. فَهْمٌ, [or of أَفْهَمَهُ, i. e. as meaning *He was made to understand,* or *know,*] (TA,) is an incorrect word. (Ḳ, TA.)

10. اِسْتَفْهَمَنِى الشَّىْءَ *He sought,* or *desired, of me, the understanding of the thing* [i. e., *that he might be made to understand it*]; (Ṣ,* Ḳ,* TA;) syn. طَلَبَ مِنِّى فَهْمَهُ. (TA.)

فَهْمٌ is an inf. n. of 1, (Ṣ, Mṣb, Ḳ, &c.,) or a subst. used as an inf. n.: (Mṣb:) [see 1, first sentence:] it is expl. as signifying The *conception of the meaning from the word, or expression:* or the *quickness of the transition of the mind from extrinsic to other* [i. e. *intrinsic*] *things:* or *a condition of the mind whereby it ascertains what is approvable:* or, as in the "Aḥkám" of El-Ámidee, *excellence of intelligence in respect of its readiness to apprehend quickly subjects of inquiry that present themselves to it.* (TA.)

فَهِمٌ, an epithet applied to a man, (Ṣ,) *Quick of understanding;* syn. سَرِيعُ الفَهْمِ. (Ḳ.)

فَهِيمٌ *Having much understanding;* syn. كَثِيرُ الفَهْمِ; an intensive epithet; like ▾ فَهَّامَةٌ [except that the latter is doubly intensive]. (TA.)

فَهَّامَةٌ: see what next precedes.

فَاهِمٌ [act. part. n. of فَهِمَ; *Understanding*, or *knowing*, a thing].

مَفْهُومٌ [pass. part. n. of فَهِمَ; *Understood*, or *known*. — And hence, مَفْهُومُ لَفْظٍ *The acceptation of a word* or *an expression*; i. e. *the meaning*, or *sense*, *in which it is understood*: see also مَعْنًى, in art. عنى].

فهو

1. فَهَوْتُ عَنْهُ, (JK, Ḳ,) aor. أَفْهُو, inf. n. فُهُوٌّ, (JK,) *I was unmindful*, *forgetful*, or *neglectful*, *of it*. (JK, Ḳ.) — ISd says, فَهَا فُؤَادُهُ is like هَفَا, [which, said of the heart, accord. to explanations in the TA in art. هفو, means *It fluttered*, or *palpitated*: and *it was flurried* by reason of grief or of beating:] and no inf. n. of it has been heard, therefore I think it to be formed by transposition. (TA.) — And فَهَا signifies also *He spoke clearly*, or *distinctly*, *after doing the contrary thereof*. (TA.)

3. فاهاهُ, inf. n. مُفَاهَاةٌ; *i. q.* فاوهه, inf. n. مُفَاوَهَةٌ; i. e. *He talked*, or *discoursed*, *with him*: and *he contended with him for superiority in glory*, or *excellence*. (TA in art. فوه.)

4. افهى *He was weak*, or *erroneous*, *in his judgment*, or *opinion*. (IAạr, Ḳ, TA.)

فَاهٍ, formed by transposition from فَائِهٌ, A man *who reveals*, or *discloses*, *everything that is in his mind*; like فَاوُوهَةٌ; (Fr, in Ṣ and TA, art. فوه;) and so فَاهٌ: (Fr, in TA ibid.:) and فَاهٍ بِجُوعِهِ one *who reveals his hunger*. (TA ibid.)

[الافهبان, said by Freytag to signify *The elephant and the buffalo*, is a mistranscription for الأَقْهَبَانِ.]

أَفْهَآءٌ [a pl. of which the sing. is not mentioned] *i. q.* بُلْهٌ [pl. of أَبْلَهُ; signifying *Heedless*; or *heedless of evil by reason of their goodness*; &c.]. (IAạr, TA.)

فو

فُو, with the و quiescent, [*Valerian*;] *a certain medicine*, (Ḳ, TA,) *a diuretic*, (CḲ,) *beneficial as a remedy for pain of the side and for alopecia*. (Ḳ, TA.) ═ As a prefixed noun, signifying The *mouth*, see voce فُوهٌ, in art. فوه.

فُوَّةٌ, (T, Ṣ, M, Ḳ,) like قُوَّةٌ [in form], (Ṣ, Ḳ,) [*Madder*; the *species thereof used by dyers*; *rubia tinctorum*;] *certain roots* (Lth, T, Ṣ, M, Ḳ) *of a plant* (M) *which are extracted from the earth*, (Lth, T, M,) *with which they dye* (Lth, T, Ṣ, M, Ḳ) *clothes*, or *garments*: (Lth, T:) AḤn says, *red roots of a plant which rises slender*, *having upon its head berries intensely red and having much juice used for writing therewith and variegating*: (M:) *called in Pers.* رُوِين: (PṢ: [in a copy of the T رُوِين or رُوِين: and in my copies of the Ṣ رويته and رُوِينَه:]) *it is* [*also used as*] *a medicine*, *having the property of causing abortion*, (Ḳ,) *producing a flow of the urine and of the menstrual discharge*, (Ḳ,* TA,) *aperient*, *clearing the complexion* or *skin*, *clearing the skin from every mark of the ringworm and of the white* [*species of leprosy termed*] بَهَق: (Ḳ:) it has been mentioned also in the Ḳ as ending with [a radical] ه [i. e. written فُوَّهٌ, in art. فوه]; but, as is said by Lth, [and in the T,] the final letter is that which denotes the fem. gender. (TA.)

مَفْوَاةٌ; pl. مَفَاوٍ: see the following paragraph.

مُفَوًّى *Dyed with* فُوَّة; applied to a garment; (T, Ṣ, M, Ḳ;) and to a hide. (M.) — And مَفْوَاةٌ A land (أَرْضٌ) *abounding with* فُوَّة: (AḤn, M, Ḳ:) or having in it فُوَّة: (M:) and مَفْبَاةٌ signifies the same: (TA in art. غبى:) or you say ارض مفواة من المفاوى [i. e. ▼ مَفْوَاةٌ; of which the pl., without the article, is مَفَاوٍ]; (T;) المَفَاوِى signifying the lands (الأَرَضُونَ) *that give growth to* فُوَّة. (TA.)

فوت

1. فَاتَ الأَمْرُ, aor. يَفُوتُ, inf. n. فَوْتٌ and فَوَاتٌ, originally signifies فَاتَ وَقْتُ فِعْلِهِ [i. e. *The time*, or *opportunity*, *of the doing*, or *performing*, *of the affair passed*, *passed away*, *elapsed*, or *escaped*, *neglected by him*, *without his doing it* or *performing it*]; and hence the phrase فَاتَتِ الصَّلَاةُ, meaning *The time of prayer passed*, *passed away*, *elapsed*, or *escaped*, *without his performing it therein*: (Mṣb:) and ▼ افتات is syn. with فَاتَ. (M, O.) [And both of these verbs are trans.:] one says فَاتَهُ الشَّىْءُ, (Ṣ, O, Mṣb,) or الأَمْرُ, (M, Ḳ,) aor. as above, (O,) and so the inf. ns.; (Ṣ,* M, O,* Mṣb, Ḳ;) and ▼ افتاته; (Ḳ;) *The thing*, or *affair*, *passed*, or *passed away*, *from him* [*neglected by him*]; (M, Ḳ;) [or *the time*, or *opportunity*, *of the doing*, or *performing*, *thereof passed*, or *passed away*, *from him neglected by him*;] or *the thing escaped him*, [or *became beyond his reach*,] *so that he was unable to attain it*, or *to do it*, or *to accomplish it*. (Mṣb.) But this explanation is not applicable except in the case of prayer, and the like: in other cases, فَاتَهُ signifies *He*, or *it*, *preceded him*; *was*, or *became*, or *got*, *before him*; *outwent him*; *passed beyond him*; or *had*, *got*, or *took*, *precedence of him*: and *went*, or *passed*, *away from him*: and *the like*. (MF, TA.) One says, فَاتَنِى كَذَا, meaning سَبَقَنِى [i. e. *Such a thing preceded me*, &c., app. *so as to become beyond my reach*]: and فُتُّهُ [*I preceded it*, &c.]: (T:) and جَارَيْتُهُ حَتَّى فُتُّهُ أَنَا *I ran with him until I passed beyond him*, or *outwent him*: (A, TA:) and فَاتَهُ فُلَانٌ بِذِرَاعٍ *Such a one preceded him*, or *outwent him*, *by a cubit*. (Mṣb.) فَلَا فَوْتَ, in the Ḳur xxxiv. 50, means فَلَا فَوْتَ لَهُمْ مِنَّا [*And there shall be for them no escaping from us*], i. e. لَا يَفُوتُونَنَا [*they shall not escape us*]. (Jel. [And Bḍ says the like; adding, "by flight, or fortifying themselves."]) An Arab of the desert is related to have said, الحَمْدُ لِلّٰهِ الَّذِى لَا يُفَاتُ وَلَا يُلَاتُ [expl. in art. ليت]. (T.) And they assert that a man went forth from his family, and when he returned, his wife said to him, "If thou hadst been present with us, we would have related to thee what hath happened;" whereupon he said to her, لَمْ تُفَاتِى فَهَاتِى (M, Meyd) i. e. *It has not escaped thee* [lit. *thou hast not been escaped*], *so adduce* what thou hast [to tell]: the saying is a proverb. (Meyd.) — See also 5: and see 8, in three places. — فَاتَ is also *syn. with* فَادَ [as signifying *He died*; in which sense the aor. is يَفُوتُ, and the inf. n. فَوْتٌ]. (A in art. فيد.) And ▼ أُفْتِيتَ signifies *He died suddenly*. (TA in art. فات, q. v.)

4. افاتهُ الشَّىْءَ, (Ṣ, MA,) or الأَمْرَ, (Ḳ,) *He made the thing*, or *affair*, *to pass*, or *pass away*, *from him* [*neglected by him*; or *he made the time*, or *opportunity*, *of the doing*, or *performing*, *thereof to pass*, or *pass away*, *from him neglected by him*; or *he made the thing to escape him*, or *become beyond his reach*, *so that he was unable to attain it*, or *to do it*, or *to accomplish it*: see 1, second sentence]. (M, A, Ḳ.)

5. فَاتَهُ ▼ به means تفوّت عَلَيْهِ فِى مَالِهِ, (A'Obeyd, T, Ṣ, M, O, Ḳ,) i. e. *He acted exclusively of him*, (M,) [or *passed him over*], namely, his father, (A'Obeyd, T, M, O,*) *in respect of his property*, (A'Obeyd, T, &c.,) i. e. his own property, (A'Obeyd, T,) by giving it away, (A'Obeyd, T, M, O,) and squandering it, (A'Obeyd, T, M,) *without consulting him*, or *asking his permission*: (O, TA:) occurring in a trad., relating to a case in which the Prophet ordered the father to cause the property to be restored to his son; and informed him that the son had no right to act thus to his father. (A'Obeyd, T, O.*) — See also 8, latter half, in two places: — and see the paragraph here following, in two places.

6. تفاوت has for its inf. n. تَفَاوُتٌ and تَفَاوَتٌ and تَفَاوِتٌ, (Ṣ, M, O, Ḳ,) the second and third of which are mentioned by AZ; the second is said by ISk (who mentions this and the third, M) to be of the dial. of the Kilábees, and the third is mentioned by El-'Ambaree; both anomalous, for the inf. n. of a verb of the measure تَفَاعَلَ is تَفَاعُلٌ, [in the copies of the Ṣ بتفاعل, and said to be so in J's handwriting,] with ḍamm to the ع, except in this instance: (Ṣ, O:) but Sb said that there is not among inf. ns. an instance of تَفَاعَلٌ nor of تَفَاعِلٌ. (M.) مَا تَرَى فِى خَلْقِ الرَّحْمٰنِ مِنْ تَفَاوُتٍ, (T, M, O, Ḳ,) or ▼ تَفَوُّتٍ, (T, O, Ḳ,) [the former in the CḲ and the latter in other copies of the Ḳ,] the latter being the reading of Ḥamzeh and Ks, in the Ḳur [lxvii. 3], (O,) means *Thou seest not in the creation of the Compassionate*, (M, O,) i. e. in his creation of the heaven, (M,) *any incongruity*, or *discordance*; (T, M, O;) or *any fault*, *defect*, or *imperfection*, so that the beholder might say, "If it were thus, it were better;" (T, O, Ḳ;) thus the latter reading is expl. by Es-Suddee; (T, O, TA;) and Fr says that both readings have one meaning: (T, TA:) you say of a thing ▼ تفوّت and تفاوت. (M.) — And one says, تفاوت الشَّيْئَانِ *The two things were far apart*, *one from the other*; or *widely distinct* or *separated*: (Ṣ, O, Ḳ:) or

differed, or *were different*. (Mṣb.) And تَفَاوَتَا فِى الفَضْلِ *They two were distinct*, or *dissimilar*, *in respect of excellence*, (Mṣb,) or فِى الشَّرَفِ [*in eminence*, or *nobility*]. (A.)

8: see 1, first and second sentences. — Aṣ, relating the verse of Ibn-Muḳbil,

• يَا حُرَّ أَمْسَيْتُ شَيْخًا قَدْ وَهَى بَصَرِى •
• وَٱفْتِيتَ مَا دُونَ يَوْمِ لبَعْثِ مِنْ عُمُرِى •

[which may be rendered *O ingenuous* woman, (حُرَّ being an abbreviation of حُرَّةُ,) *I have become an old man, my sight has become weak, and what is anterior to the day of resurrection, of my life, has been passed*, or *has run out* like water poured forth (فُرِغَ)], says, it is from الفَوْتُ, and الإِفْتِيَاتُ [app. as the inf. n. of the pass. v. افتيت used in this verse] signifies الفَرَاغُ. (T.) — See also 1, last sentence. — الإِفْتِيَاتُ signifies also *The betaking oneself*, or *applying oneself*, *before another* or *others*, or *hastily*, (Ṣ, O, Mṣb,) *to a thing*, (Ṣ, O,) or *to the doing of a thing*, (Mṣb,) *without obeying him who should be obeyed*, (Ṣ, O,) or *following his own opinion only*, *without consulting him who had the best right to order in the case*: (Mgh,* Mṣb:) you say, افتات عَلَيْهِ بِأَمْرِ كَذَا i. e. فَاتَهُ ▾ بِهِ [app. meaning *He so betook himself*, &c., *in opposition to him*: or فاته به may be here used in the sense in which it is expl. above voce تَفَوَّتَ]. (Ṣ, O.) And you say, فُلَانٌ لَا يُفْتَاتُ عَلَيْهِ *Such a one, nothing is to be done without his order*; (Ṣ, O, Ḳ;*) and so لَا يُفَاتُ ▾ عليه; (Ḥar p. 63;) or لَا يُفْتَاتُ عَلَيْهِ شَىْءٌ دُونَ أَمْرِهِ [which means the same]. (Mṣb.) أَمِثْلِى يُفْتَاتُ عَلَيْهِ فِى بَنَاتِهِ, (T, M, O,) or فِى أَمْرِ بَنَاتِهِ, (Ṣ, TA,) occurs in a trad., (Ṣ, M, Mgh, O, TA,) meaning *Shall such a one as I* [am] *have anything done in respect of his daughters without his order?* (Mgh,* TA;) and was said by 'Abd-Er-Raḥmán the son of Aboo-Bekr to his sister 'Áisheh, on the occasion of her having given in marriage his daughter, the elder Ḥafṣah, during his absence, to El-Mundhir the son of Ez-Zubeyr. (T,* O, TA.*) And you say, افتات عَلَيْهِ فِى شَىْءٍ, and فَاتَهُ ▾ بِشَىْءٍ, meaning *He brought to pass a thing exclusively of him* [i. e., of another person, without the latter's having any part therein]. (TA.) And افتات عَلَيْهِ فِى كَذَا, and تفوّت ▾ عَلَيْهِ فِيهِ, *He followed his own opinion only*, *exclusively of him* [i. e., of another], *in the disposal*, or *management*, *of such a thing*: the verbs being trans. by means of عَلَى because implying the meaning of التَّغَلُّب. (TA.) And افتات عَلَيْهِ فِى الأَمْرِ, (M, Ḳ,* TA,) and تفوّت ▾ عَلَيْهِ فِيهِ, (MA,) *He decided against him in the affair*. (M, MA, Ḳ,* TA.) — And افتات بِأَمْرِهِ *He effected*, or *executed*, *his affair without consulting any one*: thus accord. to Aṣ, without hemz: (T, TA:) and, as is related on the authority of ISh and ISk, one says, افتأت بأمره, with hemz, meaning *he was alone in his affair*; and in like manner one says, برأيه *in his opinion*. (TA. [See also art. فأت.]) — And افتات الكَلَامَ *He originated*, or *excogitated*, *the speech*: (O, Ḳ, TA:) and *he extemporized the speech*; *spoke it without consideration*, or *thought*, or *preparation*, or *without pausing*, or *hesitating*; as also اِفْتَلَتَهُ. (TA.)

فَوْتٌ an inf. n. of 1. (Ṣ,* M, &c.) — فَوْتَ فَمِهِ and فَوْتَ رُمْحِهِ and فَوْتَ يَدِهِ [lit. *Beyond the reach of his mouth* and *of his spear* and *of his hand*, or *arm* (in several copies of the Ḳ erroneously written فَوْتُ)] mean *where he sees it but will not* [*be able to*] *reach it*, or *attain it*. (Ḳ, TA.) A man said to another, reviling him, [or rather said of him,] جَعَلَ ٱللّٰهُ رِزْقَهُ فَوْتَ فَمِهِ i. e. [*May God make his sustenance to be beyond the reach of his mouth*,] *where he shall see it and shall not attain it*. (Ṣ, O. [And the like is said in the M and A.]) And one says, هُوَ مِنِّى فَوْتَ الرُّمْحِ [*He*, or *it*, *is*] *where my spear will not reach him*, or *it*. (Ṣ, A, O.) And هُوَ مِنِّى فَوْتَ اليَدِ [*He*, or *it*, *is*] *beyond the reach of my hand*, or *arm*: mentioned by Sb among what are peculiarly adverbial expressions. (M.) And أَفْلَتَنَا فُلَانٌ فَوْتَ اليَدِ and فَوْتَ الظُّفُرِ [*Such a one escaped from us beyond the reach of a hand*, or *an arm*, and *beyond the reach of a finger-nail*]. (A. [Golius, as on the authority of the A, has فُوَيْتَ ▾ ظُفُرٍ, which he explains as syn. with فَوْتَ يَدٍ; but it signifies *A little beyond the reach of a finger-nail*.]) — أَسْمَعُ صَوْتًا وَأَرَى فَوْتًا means *I hear a sound*, or *voice*, *but I see not a deed*, or *no deed*. (TA in art. صوت.) — فَوْتٌ signifies also The *space between two fingers* [*when they are extended apart* (see بُصْمٌ)]: (Ṣ, M, O, Ḳ:) pl. أَفْوَاتٌ. (Ṣ, M, O.) — And you say, بَيْنَهُمَا فَوْتٌ فَائِتٌ ▾ like as you say بَوْنٌ بَائِنٌ [i. e. *Between them two* (meaning two men) *is a wide distance*; app. in respect of rank or estimation: the last word being in this case a corroborative, like the latter word in مَوْتٌ مَائِتٌ and لَيْلٌ لَائِلٌ]. (M.)

فَوَاتٌ an inf. n. of 1. (Ṣ,* M, &c.) — [Hence,] مَوْتُ الفَوَاتِ *Sudden death*: (Ṣ, M, A, O, Ḳ:) likewise termed المَوْتُ الفُوَاتُ and المَوْتُ الفَوَاتُ. (IAạr, TA.) You say, مَاتَ مَوْتَ الفَوَاتِ *He died a sudden death*. (Ṣ, O.) The Prophet, passing by a leaning wall, quickened his pace; and being asked wherefore he did so, answered, أَخَافُ مَوْتَ الفَوَاتِ [*I fear sudden death*]. (O.)

فُوَيْتٌ One *who follows his*, or *her*, *own opinion only*, (M, O, Ḳ,) *not consulting any one*: (O:) applied alike to a man and to a woman: (M, O, Ḳ:) on the authority of Er-Riyáshee: pronounced by AZ with hemz. (O.) — See also فَوْتٌ [of which it is the dim.]

فَائِتٌ act. part. n. of 1 [q. v.]. (T.) — See also فَوْتٌ, last sentence.

فوج

1. فَاجَ, [aor. يَفُوجُ,] said of musk, *i. q.* فَاحَ [i. e. *It diffused*, or *exhaled*, *its odour*]. (O, Ḳ.) — And, said of the day, ‡ *It became cool*. (O, Ḳ, TA.) And one says, فَاجَتِ الشَّمْسُ عِنْدَ بَرْدِ النَّهَارِ †[*The sun became moderated at the cool time of the day*]. (O.)

2. لَسْتُ بِرَائِحٍ حَتَّى أُفَوِّجَ means [*I am not going in the evening*] *until I refresh myself by the coolness of the air*. (Ḳ: there expl. by the words أَىْ أُبَرِّدَ عَنْ نَفْسِى [in which, for أُبَرِّدَ, I read أُبْرِدَ]: in some copies [erroneously] عَلَى نفسى.)

4. افاج, (Ḳ,) inf. n. إِفَاجَةٌ, (Ṣ,) *He hastened*, or *went quickly*; (Ṣ, Ḳ, and O and Mṣb in art. فيج:) and *he ran*. (Ṣ, Ḳ.) — And افاج القَوْمُ فِى الأَرْضِ *The people*, or *party*, *went away*, *and spread*, or *dispersed themselves*, *in the land*. (L in art. فيج.) — And افاج فِى عَدْوِهِ *He was slow in his running*. (L in art. فيج.) [Thus افاج has two contr. significations.] — Also *He sent the camels to the watering-trough*, or *tank*, *drove by drove*. (O,* Ḳ.)

10. أُسْتُفِيجَ فُلَانٌ *Such a one was desired*, or *incited*, *to be* [*quick*, or] *brisk*, or *prompt*; syn. أُسْتُخِفَّ. (Ḳ, and O in art. فيج.)

فَوْجٌ *A company*, *congregated body*, *party*, or *group*, *of men*; (Ṣ, A, O, L, Mṣb, Ḳ;*) as also فَائِجٌ ▾, (L,) and فَائِجَةٌ ▾, (Ḳ,) and فَيْجٌ ▾, (O, Ḳ, and Mṣb in art. فيج, q. v.,) which last is said by Az to be originally فَيِّجٌ, from فَاجَ, aor. يَفُوجُ, like هَيِّنٌ from هَانَ, aor. يَهُونُ, for which they say also هَيْنٌ: (O, and Mṣb* in art. فيج:) or *a crowd*, or *dense company* &c.: (so accord. to an explanation of the first of the following pls. by Z in the Ksh and by Bḍ, both in Ḳur cx. 2:) or *a company*, &c., *of the followers*, or *dependants*, *of chiefs*: or *a great crowd of men*: (L:) [and app. † *a multitude* of things: (see an ex. voce أَفْكَلٌ, in art. فكل:)] pl. [of pauc.] أَفْوَاجٌ [also used as a pl. of mult.] (Ṣ, O, Mṣb, Ḳ) and [of mult.] فُؤُوجٌ and pl. pl. أَفَاوِيجُ (Ṣ, O, Mṣb, Ḳ) and أَفَاوِجُ (Ṣ, O, Ḳ) and أَفَائِجُ, as though pl. of أَفِيجَةٌ. (O.)

فَيْجٌ: see the next preceding paragraph: — and see also art. فيج.

فَائِجٌ: see فَوْجٌ. One says, مَرَّ بِنَا فَائِجُ وَلِيمَةِ فُلَانٍ, meaning *The company* (فَوْج) *of those that were at the repast of such a one* [*passed by us*]. (TA.) — It is said that فَائِجٌ, applied to a she-camel, signifies *Fat*: or *such as is termed* حَائِلٌ, *and fat*: but the word commonly known [thus used] is فَاثِجٌ [q. v.]. (TA.)

فَائِجَةٌ: see فَوْجٌ: — and see also art. فيج.

فوح

1. فَاحَ المِسْكُ, (Mṣb, Ḳ,) aor. يَفُوحُ and يَفِيحُ; (Mṣb;) or فَاحَتْ رِيحُ المِسْكِ, aor. تَفُوحُ and تَفِيحُ; (Ṣ;) inf. n. فَوْحٌ (Ṣ, Mṣb, Ḳ) and فُؤُوحٌ and فَوَحَانٌ, (Ṣ, Ḳ,) and فَيْحٌ (Ṣ, Mṣb, Ḳ) and فَيَحَانٌ; (Ṣ, Ḳ;) *The musk diffused* [or *exhaled*] *its odour*; (Mṣb, Ḳ;) or *the odour of the musk diffused itself* [or *became exhaled*]; and فاح الطِّيبُ *the perfume diffused* [or *exhaled*] *its odour*; (Ṣ;) or this last signifies *the perfume became perceptible*; or *it clung and remained*; [in a garment or person;] syn. عَبِقَ: (Mṣb in art. فيح:) the verb is not used in relation to a foul, or disagreeable odour or thing: (Ṣ, A, Mṣb, Ḳ:) of such an odour one says خَبُثَتْ: (Mṣb:) or the former verb is common to both: (Ḳ:) but this assertion is outweighed [by the other]: (TA:) فَوْحٌ signifies the *giving forth*, and *exhaling, a sweet*, or *pleasant, odour*: (KL:) and the *perceiving such an odour*: Fr says that فَاحَتْ رِيحُهُ and فَاخَتْ are syn.; but AZ says the فَوْخ is attended by sound. (TA.) — For other significations of this verb, see art. فيح.

4. افاح: for this verb, see art. فيح.

6. نَزَلْنَا فِى بُسْتَانٍ تَنَاوَحَتْ أَطْيَارُهُ وَتَفَاوَحَتْ أَنْوَارُهُ [*We alighted in a garden the birds of which warbled plaintively, one to another, and the flowers of which exhaled sweet odours, one with another*]. (A.)

فَوْحُ الحَيْضِ *The chief and first portion of the menstrual discharge.* (L.)

فَوْحَةٌ [*A spreading*, or *an exhalation*], of perfume. (TA in art. عصر.)

فوخ

1. فَاخَتِ الرِّيحُ, aor. تَفُوخُ, inf. n. فَوَخَانٌ; (Ḳ;) as also فاخت, aor. تَفِيخُ, (Ḳ in art. فيخ,) inf. n. فَيْخٌ and فَيَخَانٌ; (TA in art. فيخ;) *The wind*, or *odour, rose*, or *diffused itself*: (Ḳ:) you say, فَاخَتْ مِنْهُ رِيحٌ طَيِّبَةٌ, aor. تَفُوخُ and تَفِيخُ, *a sweet odour diffused itself from him*, or *it*; like فاحت: (AO, Aṣ, Ṣ:) or فاخت الرِّيحُ, aor. تَفُوخُ, (AZ, Ṣ, Ḳ,) inf. n. فَوْخٌ (AZ, TA in art. فوح,) or فَوَخَانٌ, (AZ, TA in the present art.,) signifies *the wind made a sound*, or *noise*, (AZ, Ṣ, Ḳ, TA,) *in its blowing*. (AZ, TA.) — And فاخ الحَرُّ *The heat became allayed*, or *assuaged*. (L.) = See also the next paragraph, in two places.

4. افاخ, (AZ, Ṣ, Ḳ,) inf. n. إِفَاخَةٌ, (Lth, AZ, Ṣ, IAth,) *He* (a man) *emitted wind*, (Lth, AZ, Ṣ, Ḳ,) *with a sound*, (AZ, Ṣ,) *from the anus*; (Lth;) and ↓ فاخ, aor. يَفُوخُ, inf. n. فَوَخَانٌ (Ḳ, TA) and فَوْخٌ, (TA,) signifies the same: (Ḳ, TA:) or the former, *he voided excrement with an emission of wind*: (IAth, TA:) [mentioned also in art. فيخ:] and *he* (a man, or a beast,) *emitted wind in voiding urine*: (ISh, Ṣ:) and ↓ فاخ, aor. يَفُوخُ, *it* (the emission of excrement) *made a sound*. (L.) — افاخ بِبَوْلِهِ *He emitted his urine from a dilated aperture*. (L.) And افاخت *She* (a camel) *made a sprinkling* with her urine. (L.) — افاخ الزِّقَّ, inf. n. as above, *He opened the mouth of the* زِقّ [or *skin for wine &c.*] *to give vent to the air within it*: thus accord. to Fr; who says that he heard a sheykh, of those having knowledge in the Arabic language, explain this phrase as meaning *he smeared the inside of the* زِقّ *with* رُبّ [or *rob*]. (L.) — أَفِخْ عَنْكَ مِنَ الظَّهِيرَةِ, (L, TA,) in the Ḳ عَنَّا, but correctly عنك, as in other lexicons, (TA,) [as also أَفِخْ,] means أَبْرِدْ, (L, Ḳ,) i. e. *Stay thou until the mid-day heat shall have become assuaged, and the air be cool*. (L, TA.)

فود

1. فَادَ, aor. يَفُودُ, (Ṣ, Mgh, O, Ḳ, and T in art. فيد,) inf. n. فَوْدٌ; (AA, Ḳ, and T in art. فيد;) as also فَادَ, aor. يَفِيدُ, (Ṣ, O, Ḳ, and T &c. in art. فيد,) inf. n. فَيْدٌ; (IAạr, Ḳ, and T in art. فيد;) *He died*. (T, Ṣ, Mgh, O, Ḳ.) = And فاد, aor. يَفُودُ, (M,) inf. n. فَوْدٌ, (Ḳ,) *It* (property) *continued*, or *belonged*, or *appertained*, syn. ثَبَتَ, (M, Ḳ,) لِصَاحِبِهِ *to its owner*; (M;) as also فاد, aor. يَفِيدُ, (Ṣ, L, Ḳ, in art. فيد,) inf. n. فَيْدٌ: (Ḳ:) or (so in the Ḳ) *it went away, passed away*, or *departed*; (Ḳ;) as also فاد, aor. يَفِيدُ, (Ḳ in art. فيد,) inf. n. فَيْدٌ. (Ḳ. [See also art. فيد.]) = فادهُ, (Aṣ, Yaạḳoob, T, M, L,) aor. يَفُودُهُ, (Yaạḳoob, M,* L,) inf. n. فَوْدٌ, (Ḳ,) *He mixed it*, (M, L, Ḳ,) namely, saffron [&c.], (M, L,) or perfume &c., (Aṣ, T,) or *moistened it with water &c.*; (L;) syn. دَافَهُ; (Aṣ, Yaạḳoob, T, M, L;) from which it is formed by transposition [accord. to the lexicologists; but not accord. to the grammarians, because it has an inf. n.]: (M, L:) and so فادهُ, aor. يَفِيدُهُ, (Ṣ, L, Ḳ, in art. فيد,) inf. n. فَيْدٌ. (L. [See also art. فيد.])

4. أَفَدْتُهُ *I killed him; destroyed him*. (O, Ḳ. [See also art. فيد.]) = And *I gave him property*. (M, L, Ḳ.) It belongs to this art. and to art. فيد [q. v.]. (L.) — See also 10.

5. تفوّد فَوْقَ الجَبَلِ *He* (a mountain-goat) *ascended* (أَشْرَفَ) *upon the mountain*. (O,* L, Ḳ.)

6. هُمَا يَتَفَاوَدَانِ العِلْمَ (ISh, Ḳ) is a phrase used by the vulgar, (ISh,) but the correct expression is يَتَفَايَدَانِ, meaning *They two impart knowledge, each to the other*: (Ḳ:) or يتفايدان بِالمَالِ بَيْنَهُمَا *They two give, of the property, each to the other*; or *profit*, or *benefit, each other therewith*: (ISh:) or, in the opinion of MF, each is allowable. (TA. [See also art. فيد.])

10. استفادهُ, (M, L, Ḳ,) and ↓ افادهُ, (M, Ḳ,) [respecting which latter see 10 in art. فيد,] as also تفيّدهُ, (Ḳ, [but this belongs to art. فيد only,]) *He gained it, acquired it*, or *got it, for himself*, namely, property [&c.]. (M, L, Ḳ.) [See more in art. فيد.]

فَوْدٌ *Each of the two sides of the head*: (Aṣ, Ṣ, M, A, O, L, Mṣb, Ḳ:) pl. أَفْوَادٌ: (M, L, Mṣb:) one says, بَدَا الشَّيْبُ بِفَوْدَيْهِ [*Hoariness appeared in the two sides of his head*]. (Ṣ, O, L.) And The *main*, or *chief, portion of the hair of the head, next the ear*; (M, L, Ḳ;) or *of the hair that descends below the lobe of the ear, next the ear*: (IF, L, Mṣb:) or فَوْدَانِ signifies [*two locks*, or *plaited locks, of hair, such as are termed*] ضَفِيرَتَانِ (ISk, Ṣ, O, L, Mṣb) of a man (ISk, Ṣ, O, L) and of a woman. (O.) — † The *side* (Ḳ, TA) of anything; (TA;) *each of the two sides* (M, L) of a thing. (L.) You say, اِرْفَعْ فَوْدَ الخِبَآءِ ‡ *Raise thou the side of the tent*. (A.) And نَزَلُوا بَيْنَ فَوْدَيِ الوَادِى ‡ [*They alighted*, or *abode, between the two sides of the valley*]. (A.) — ‡ *Each of the two equiponderant halves of the load of a beast*: (Ṣ, M, O, L, Ḳ, TA:) one says, قَعَدَ بَيْنَ الفَوْدَيْنِ ‡ [*He sat between the two equiponderant halves of the load of the beast*]. (Ṣ, O, L, TA.) And [hence, app.,] † *A* [*sack such as is termed*] جُوَالِق. (Ḳ.) — † The *part that is abundant in plumage* of each of the wings of the eagle: (M:) [or *each of the wings*; for] one says, أَلْقَتِ العُقَابُ فَوْدَيْهَا عَلَى الهَيْثَمِ ‡ [*The eagle cast* its *wings* [*upon*, or *over, the eaglet*]. (A.) — One says also, جَعَلْتُ الكِتَابَ فَوْدَيْنِ, meaning ‡ *I doubled the upper part of the letter*, or *writing, over the lower part, so that it became two halves*. (A, O.) — And اِسْتَلَمْتُ فَوْدَ البَيْتِ ‡ [*I touched, by kissing*, or *with the hand*,] *the corner of the House* [*of God*; i. e., of the Kaạbeh]. (A.) = Also *A company, congregated body, party*, or *group, of men*; or *a crowd*, or *dense company* &c.; or *a great crowd of men*; syn. فَوْجٌ: (Ibn-'Abbád, O, Ḳ:) pl. أَفْوَادٌ. (Ibn-'Abbád, O.)

فُؤَادٌ, (O, Ḳ,) with fet-ḥ to the ف, (O,) like سَحَابٌ [in form], (Ḳ,) i. q. فُؤَادٌ [generally meaning The *heart* (see other explanations in art. فأد)]; (O, Ḳ;) a dial. var. of the latter word. (O.)

فَائِدَةٌ a subst. from فَادَ المَالُ, (M, Ḳ, and L in art. فيد,) in the sense of ثَبَتَ: (M, and L in art. فيد:) it belongs to this art. and to art. فيد. (TA. [See the latter art.])

مَفُودٌ, applied to perfume &c., i. q. مَدُوفٌ [*Mixed*, or *moistened with water &c.*]; (Aṣ, T;) as also مَفِيدٌ. (Ṣ and O and L in art. فيد.)

رَجُلٌ مِتْلَافٌ مِفْوَادٌ *A destructive man*; as also مِفْيَادٌ. (Ibn-'Abbád, O, Ḳ.)

فور

1. فَارَ, (M, Mṣb, Ḳ,) aor. يَفُورُ, said of water; (Mṣb;) and فَارَتْ, aor. تَفُورُ, said of a قِدْر [or

cooking-pot]; (T, Ṣ;) inf. n. فَوْرٌ and فَوَرَانٌ (T, Ṣ, M, Mṣb, Ḳ) [the latter of which is the more common] and فُؤُورٌ (M, Ḳ) and فُوَارٌ; (M, TA;) *It boiled*, or *estuated*. (T, Ṣ, M, Mṣb, Ḳ.) — [فار said of a liquor, *It fermented*. (See نَبِيذٌ.) — Said of blood, and of wine, *It flushed*, or *mantled*, in the cheeks or head.] — فارت نَفْسُهُ *His soul* [or *stomach*] *heaved*; or *became agitated by a tendency to vomit*; *i. q.* ثارت [q.v.]. (T in art. ثور.) — فار فائره ♦ *i. q.* ثار ثائرهُ (T, Ṣ, Ḳ) *His anger boiled* [or *became roused* or *excited*]; (Ṣ;) or *he was*, or *became*, *angry*. (TA.) — [And ♦ the same phrase is expl. in the M, accord. to the transcript in the TT, as signifying انْتَشَرَ غَضَبُهُ; but I think that the right reading is evidently عَصَبُهُ; and the meaning, *His sinews became swollen*; said of a horse or the like: see art. نشر; and see also فَائِرٌ, below.] — فار العِرْقُ, inf. n. فَوَرَانٌ, *The vein became excited*, or *in a state of commotion, and flowed forth* [*with blood*]: (M, Ḳ, TA:) to which is added in the Ḳ, وَضَرْبٌ; but this is a mistake, occasioned by a false reading of the next words in the M, which are وَضَرْبٌ فَوَّارٌ رَغِيبٌ وَاسِعٌ. (TA. [See فَوَّارٌ.]) — فَوْرُ العِرْقِ, in a horse means *The vein's having inflations*, or *knots*, [or *a varicose condition*,] *apparent in it*; which is disapproved. (ISk, TA.) — فار said of water signifies also *It welled*, and *came forth*, from the earth, or ground: (Mgh:) *it appeared, pouring forth*, from the spring, or source. (TA.) — فاروا is said of men assembled in market-places [app. as meaning *They bustled*, or *were in a state of commotion*]. (TA.) — فار المِسْكُ, inf. n. فُوَارٌ and فَوَرَانٌ, [*The odour of*] *the musk spread*. (M, Ḳ.) = فُرْتُهُ: see 4. = Also (فُرْتُهُ) *I made for it*, i. e. the balance, *what are termed* فِيَارَانِ [dual of فِيَارٌ, q. v.]. (Th, M, Ḳ.)

2. فوّر للنُّفَسَآءِ *He made what is termed* فِيرَةٌ [q. v.] *for the woman in the state following childbirth*. (M, Ḳ.)

4. أَفَرْتُهُ and ♦ فُرْتُهُ *I made it to boil*, or *estuate*. (IAạr, M, Ḳ.)

الفَارُ *The muscles* of a man: (M, Ḳ:) also mentioned in art. فأر, as written with ء. (TA.) أَبْرِزْ نَارَكَ وَإِنْ هَزَلْتَ فَارَكَ [*Put forth thy fire*, that passengers may see it and be attracted by it, *though thou make lean thy muscles*,] is a saying meaning † *give food though thou injure thy body* [by doing so]. (M, L.) = See also فَأْرٌ (with which it is syn. in other senses), in art. فأر.

فَوْرٌ [originally an inf. n.: see 1.] The *burning*, or *heat, and boiling*, of Hell. (TA.) And *Intenseness*, or *vehemence*, of heat; (TA;) as also ♦ فَوْرَةٌ. (Ṣ.) — فَوْرُ الشَّفَقِ *The remains of the redness in the western horizon after sunset*: as also ♦ فَوْرَةٌ. (TA.) [See also فَوْرَةٌ.] = And *A time*: (TA:) [or rather] the *present time in which is no delaying*. (Mṣb.) Thus in the saying, الشُّفْعَةُ عَلَى الفَوْرِ [*The right of pre-emption is to be had*] *in the present time in which is no delaying*. (Mṣb.) — And hence, *A state in which is no delay*. (Mṣb.) You say, جَآءَ فُلَانٌ فِى حَاجَتِهِ ثُمَّ رَجَعَ مِنْ فَوْرِهِ [*Such a one came for the object of his want*,] *then returned immediately*, or *at once*: or, as some say, *with the same motion with which he came, not ceasing from motion after it*; properly, *conjoining what was before the coming with what was after it, without tarrying*. (Mṣb.) And أَتَوْا مِنْ فَوْرِهِمْ, meaning مِنْ وَجْهِهِمْ [i. e., app., *They came in a headlong manner*; like the phrase مَضَى عَلَى وَجْهِهِ]; (M, Ḳ, TA; but the M has جَاؤُوا instead of أَتَوْا;) and this is said by Zj to be the meaning of مِنْ فَوْرِهِمْ in the Ḳur iii. 121: (M, TA:) or قَبْلَ أَنْ يَسْكُنُوا [*before their resting*, or *ceasing from motion*]: (Ḳ, TA:) or مِنْ فَوْرِهِمْ in the Ḳur ubi suprà means *in the commencement of their procedure*: (O:) or *in*, or *at*, *their instant of time*; (Ksh, Bḍ;) i. e. [*in*, or *at*, *the same instant*, or] *immediately*: (Bḍ:) and أَتَيْتُ فُلَانًا مِنْ فَوْرِى, meaning قَبْلَ أَنْ أَسْكُنَ [i. e. *I came to such a one before my resting*, or *ceasing from motion*]. (Ṣ, O.) And you say, فَعَلْتُهُ مِنْ فَوْرِى, meaning *I did it at once*, or *instantly*. (T, TA.)

فُورٌ *Gazelles*: (T, Ṣ, M, Ḳ:) a word having no sing.; (T, Ṣ, M, TA;) accord. to IAạr and Yaạḳoob: (TA:) or its sing. is ♦ فَائِرٌ; (M, Ḳ, TA;) accord. to Kr. (TA.) One says, لَا أَفْعَلُ كَذَا مَا لَأْلَأَتِ الفُورُ *I will not do such a thing while the gazelles wag their tails*. (IAạr, T, Ṣ.)

فَارَةُ المِسْكِ *The odour of musk*: or the *bag*, or *receptacle*, [i. e. *the follicle*, or *vesicle*,] thereof: (M, L:) [Ṣgh says that] this and what next follows have been mentioned in art. فأر, [q. v.,] but should more properly be mentioned in the present art., both being from فَارَ, aor. يَفُورُ. (O.) — فَارَةُ الإِبِلِ means *The sweet exhalation from the skins of the camels when they are moist after returning from the water*. (M, Ḳ.)

فَوْرَةٌ: see فَوْرٌ: — and فُوَارَةٌ. — Also *An ebullition of anger, rage, or passion*; syn. هَائِجٌ. (Ṣ and Ḳ in art. هيج.) — And *Freshness*, or *newness*: so in the saying أَخَذْتُ الشَّىْءَ بِفَوْرَتِهِ [*I took the thing in its fresh*, or *new*, *state*]. (TA.) — [And hence,] فَوْرَةُ النَّهَارِ *The first part*, or *beginning, of the day*. (T, TA.) And فَوْرَةُ العِشَآءِ *The time* [*next*] *after the* عشآء [or *nightfall*]. (Ṣ, TA.) — فَوْرَةُ النَّاسِ *The place where people congregate, and where they bustle*, or *are in a state of commotion*, (يَفُورُونَ,) *in their market-places*. (TA.) — فَوْرَةُ الجَبَلِ *The higher*, or *highest, part*; and *the elevated and hard*, or *elevated and plain* or *level, part*; *of the mountain*. (Ḳ.)

فُورَةٌ *i. q.* فُؤْرَةٌ [expl. in art. فأر] meaning *A certain flatus in the pastern of a horse* [&c.]. (O, Ḳ.) — And *i. q.* كُوفَةٌ [*A round piece*, or *collection, of red sand*; or *a piece*, or *collection, of sand mixed with pebbles*; &c.]. (Kr, M, Ḳ.)

فِيرَةٌ *Fenugreek* (حُلْبَةٌ) *mixed* [in the manner described voce فَثِيرَةٌ (q. v.) in art. فثر] *for the woman in the state following childbirth*. (M, Ḳ.)

فِيَارٌ sing. of فِيَارَانِ, (T,) which signifies The *two things* (T, Ṣ, M, O, Ḳ) *of iron* (M, Ḳ) *between which is the tongue of the balance*: (T, Ṣ, M, O, Ḳ:) originally with و in the place of the ى, (M, O,) changed into ى because of the kesreh before it. (O.)

فُوَارَةٌ The *froth*, or *foam, that boils*, or *boils over*, of a cooking-pot: (Ṣ and Ḳ in this art. • and voce طُبَاخَةٌ:) and ♦ مَفَاوِرُ signifies the same, mentioned by Ibn-'Abbád. (O.) And [in like manner] ♦ فَوْرَةٌ signifies The *mantling foam upon the surface* of wine. (TA.)

فَوَّارٌ [an intensive epithet from فَارَ; signifying *Boiling much*; &c.: — and Water, &c., *welling forth abundantly*; *gushing*]. — [Hence,] ضَرْبٌ فَوَّارٌ *A smiting* [*that inflicts a wound*] *such as is wide*, (IAạr, M, TA,) *so that the blood flows* [*abundantly*]: (M:) a poet says,

• بِضَرْبٍ يُخْفِتُ فَوَّارَهُ •
• وَطَعْنٍ تَرَى الدَّمَ مِنْهُ رَشِيشَا •
• إِذَا قَتَلُوا مِنْكُمُ فَارِسًا •
• ضَمِنَّا لَهُ بَعْدَهُ أَنْ يَعِيشَا •

(IAạr, M, TA. [The text of the M as given in the TT, for تَرَى الدَّمَ, has يُرى الدم; and for أَنْ يَعِيشَا, it has او يعيشا: and the right reading of the first hemistich seems to be, بِضَرْبٍ تُخْفِتُ فَوَّارَةٍ; for an inf. n. is sometimes made fem.: see an instance of ضَرْبٌ as fem. in the EM p. 157: the poet means, *With a smiting that silences*, or *kills, inflicting a wide and gushing wound; and a piercing* with the spear *in consequence of which thou seest the blood sprinkled: when they slay a horseman of you, we are responsible for him after it that he shall live*: i. e., as is said in the M, his blood shall be revenged, so that he will be as though he had not been slain: and it is also there said that by يخفت فواره is meant لنا واسعة فدمها يسيل ولا صوت له; in which the two fem. pronouns and the fem. epithet all relate to the word ضَرْبٌ, agreeably with what I have stated to be in my opinion the right reading of the first hemistich.])

فَيُّورٌ *Sharp*, as an epithet applied to a man; syn. حَدِيدٌ. (O, Ḳ.) See also طَيُّورٌ.

فُوَّارَةٌ, (accord. to the Ḳ,) or ♦ فَوَّارَةٌ, (accord. to a copy of the M,) *A source*, or *spring*, of water: (M, Ḳ:) [the latter word is app. the right in this case; for] IAạr says that ♦ فَوَّارَةٌ is applied to a *wave*: and to a بِرْكَة [i. e. *watering-trough*, or *the like*; or *basin, pool, pond*; &c.]: and فَوَّارَةٌ, to *anything that is not water*: and in one place he says that دَوَّارَةٌ and فَوَّارَةٌ are applied to *anything that does not move nor turn round*; and دُوَّارَةٌ and ♦ فُوَّارَةٌ to *such as moves and turns round*. (T,

TA.) — فَوَّارَةُ الوَرِكِ, with fet-ḥ and teshdeed, signifies *The hole,* or *perforating aperture, of the* ورك [or *haunch*]: (Ṣ, O:) or the فَوَّارَة, (Ḳ,) or ▼ فُوَارَة, (so in a copy of the M,) is *an aperture in the* وَرِك [or *haunch*], *to the belly,* or *interior of the body, not obstructed by bone:* (M, Ḳ:) [these two explanations plainly apply to *the sacro-ischiatic foramen:* but what here follows is consistent with what precedes, though somewhat less clear:] or the فَوَّارَتَانِ, (Ḳ,) or ▼ فُوَارَتَانِ, (accord. to a copy of the M,) are [*two parts, in the region of the pelvis, described as being*] سُكْتَانِ [a word which I do not find to have any proper meaning that would be here apposite, but which seems to be applied in this case, by a kind of catachresis, to *two parts through which a weapon or the like may pass,*] *between* [*each of*] *the haunch-bones* or *hip-bones* (بَيْنَ الوَرِكَيْنِ) *and the* قُحْقُح [or *ischium*], *towards the side of the* وَرِك [or *hip-bone*], (M, Ḳ,) *not intervening as obstacles in the way to the belly,* or *interior of the body; and they are what become in a state of commotion in the act of walking,* or *going along.* (M.) [See also الفَائِلُ, in art. فيل.] And accord. to Lth, the term فَوَّارَتَانِ, (O, and so in a copy of the T,) or ▼ فُوَارَتَانِ, (so in another copy of the T,) is applied to *Two appertenances of the* كَرِش [or *stomach,* properly *of a ruminant animal*], *having within them two small nodous lumps* (غُدَّتَانِ), *which latter are not eaten, and each of which is a piece of flesh in the midst of red flesh.* (T, O.)

فُوَارَة: see the next preceding paragraph, in six places.

فَائِرٌ [part. n. of 1: — hence, فَارَ فَائِرُهُ]: see 1, in two places. — Applied to a beast, of the equine and other kinds, *Swollen in the sinews;* syn. مُنْتَشِرُ العَصَبِ. (Ḳ. [In the TA, this is said to be a mistake for مُنْتَشِر الغَضَب, and thus I find it to be written in the L, and in a copy of the M accord. to the TT: but see what I have said, in the first paragraph of this art., respecting the phrase above mentioned.]) — See also فَوْز.

مَفَاوِرُ: see فُوَارَة.

فوز

1. فَازَ, aor. يَفُوزُ, inf. n. فَوْزٌ (Ṣ, A, O, Mṣb, Ḳ) and مَفَازٌ and مَفَازَةٌ, (TA,) *He attained, acquired, gained,* or *won, good,* or *good fortune,* (Ṣ, A, O, Mṣb,* Ḳ,) or *his wish* or *desire,* or *what he desired* or *sought;* (Bḍ in iii. 182, and TA;) *he met with,* or *experienced, that for which one would be regarded with a wish to be in the like condition, without its being desired that it should pass away from him; he became far from what was disliked,* or *hated,* or *evil:* (TA:) *he succeeded,* or *was successful: he won,* or *gained the victory:* (Mṣb:) [*he had his arrow drawn,* or] *his arrow came forth* [*from the* رِبَابَة], *in the game called* المَيْسِر: and ‡ *it* (an arrow) *won;* or *came forth before its fellow* [or *fellows in that game*]. (O,* TA.) You say, فَازَ بِهِ *He attained it, acquired it, gained it,* or *won it;* (Kh, A, O, Mṣb, Ḳ;) namely, good, or good fortune; (Kh, O;) or reward: (A:) and *he took it away; went away with it.* (Ṣ, Ḳ.) — *He became safe,* or *secure; he escaped.* (Ṣ, A, O, Mṣb, Ḳ.) You say, فَازَ مِنْهُ *He became safe,* or *secure, from it; he escaped it;* (A, O, Ḳ;) namely, evil; (TA;) or punishment. (A, O, TA.) And طُوبَى لِمَنْ فَازَ بِالثَّوَابِ وَفَازَ مِنَ العِقَابِ *A happy end is his who gains reward and escapes punishment.* (A.) — And فَازَ, (Ṣ, O, Ḳ,) aor. يَفُوزُ, (TA,) inf. n. فَوْزٌ, (Ṣ, A, Ḳ,) ‡ *He perished:* (Ṣ, A, Ḳ:) *he died;* and so ▼ فَوَّزَ: (Ṣ, A, O, Mṣb, Ḳ:) thus the former bears two contr. significations: (A, Ḳ:) but IB says that, accord. to some, the latter is not used in this sense unless preceded by another phrase such as in the following ex.: مَاتَ فُلَانٌ وَفَوَّزَ ▼ فُلَانٌ بَعْدَهُ [*Such a one died and such a one died after him*]: and accord. to others, ▼ فَوَّزَ signifies ‡ *he became in the* مَفَازَة [or *state of temporary safety*] *which is between the present life and that which is to come.* (TA.) [This last signification is given in the A.] — See also 2.

2. فَوَّزَ † *He went,* or *his course brought him, to the* مَفَازَة: (IAạr, TA:) or ‡ *he went upon the* مفازة: (A, TA:) or † *he went away:* (IAạr, O, Ḳ:) or ‡ *he went away into the* مفازة: (A:) and ▼ فَازَ signifies † *he traversed the* مفازة. (Mṣb.) You say, فَوَّزَ بِإِبِلِهِ (Ṣ, A, O, Ḳ) ‡ *He entered upon the* مفازة *with his camels.* (Ṣ, O, Ḳ.) — Also † *He went forth from one land or country to another:* and ▼ تَفَوَّزَ signifies the same as فَوَّزَ. (TA.) — See also 1, latter part, in three places. — And, said of a road, *It was,* or *became, apparent:* (O, Ḳ:) and Ṣgh adds, [but not in the O,] and *it stopped,* or *came to an end.* (TA.)

4. افازه بِكَذَا *He* (God, Ṣ, O, Ḳ, or a man, Mṣb) *caused him to attain, acquire, gain,* or *win, such a thing.* (Ṣ, O, Mṣb, Ḳ.)

5: see 2.

فَازٌ: see what next follows.

فَازَةٌ *A* [*tent such as is called*] مِظَلَّة, (Ṣ, Ḳ,) with two poles, (Ḳ,) or *that is extended with a pole:* (Ṣ; in which is added, "it is in my opinion an Arabic word:") pl. [or rather coll. gen. n.] ▼ فَازٌ. (ISd, TA.)

فَائِزَةٌ ‡ *A thing that rejoices one, and by which one attains good* or *the object of his desire:* you say, فَازَ بِفَائِزَةٍ ‡ *He attained, acquired, gained,* or *won, a thing that rejoiced him,* &c. (A, O,* TA.)

مَفَازٌ: see the following paragraph, near the end.

مَفَازَةٌ *A place of safety, security,* or *escape.* (Ṣ, A, O, Ḳ.) So in the Ḳur [iii. 185], فَلَا تَحْسَبَنَّهُمْ بِمَفَازَةٍ مِنَ العَذَابِ [*Do thou by no means reckon them to be in a place of security from punishment*]: (Ṣ, A,* O:) or, accord. to Fr, the meaning here is, *far from punishment.* (TA.) — *A cause,* or *means, of prosperity,* or *success,* or *of the attainment or acquisition of that which one desires or seeks,* or *of what is good,* or *of that whereby one becomes in a happy or good state;* syn. مَفْلَحَة. (A.) — ‡ [*The state of temporary safety which is between the present life and that which is to come.* See 1, last signification.] — ‡ *A place of perdition,* or *destruction:* (Mṣb, Ḳ:*) or *i. q.* فَلَاة: (A:) [i. e.] *a desert;* syn. بَرِّيَّة; *any* [*desert such as is called*] قَفْر: (TA:) or *a desert in which is no water:* (ISh, O, Ḳ:) and *a desert in which is no water for the space of a journey of two nights or more:* when there is none for the space of a journey of a night and a day, it is not thus called: (ISh, O, TA:) or *a tract in which two watering-places are so far apart that camels are kept from drinking two days, with a portion of the day preceding them and of the day following them,* [accord. to that which is generally preferred of the explanations of the term رِبْع which is here employed,] *and other animals* [that journey quicker] *drink on alternate days;* as also فَلَاة: or *such as is between that in which camels are kept from drinking two days &c. as above, and that in which other animals drink on alternate days;* as also فَيْفَاةٌ: (TA:) so called to prognosticate good fortune, and safety, (Aṣ, IF, Ṣ, A, O, Mṣb,) as meaning a place of safety, (A,) from فَازَ signifying "he became safe:" (Mṣb:) or from فَوَّزَ, (IAạr, Ṣ, O,* Mṣb,) or فَازَ, (AḤei, TA,) signifying "he perished," (IAạr, Ṣ, O,* AḤei,) or "he died:" (Mṣb, TA:) AḤei condemns the former of these assertions; but Az and ISd say that it is the more commonly approved, though the latter is the more agreeable with analogy: (TA:) or it is so called because he who comes forth from it, having traversed it, is safe: (IAạr, TA:) the pl. is مَفَاوِزُ: (Ṣ:) and ▼ مَفَازٌ signifies the same as مَفَازَةٌ: so in a trad. of Kaạb Ibn-Málik; فَاسْتَقْبَلَ سَفَرًا بَعِيدًا وَمَفَازًا [*And he saw before him,* or *looked forward to, a far journey and a desert,* or *a waterless desert,* &c.]. (TA.)

فوص

3. المُفَاوَصَةُ signifies *The being clear,* or *perspicuous,* syn. البَيَانُ, (Ṣ, O, Ḳ,) in talk or discourse (فِى الحَدِيثِ). (Ṣ. [In the O, and Ḳ, مِنَ الحَدِيثِ; and hence it is said in the TḲ that فَاوَصَ الحَدِيثَ بَيَّنَهُ signifies *He made the talk,* or *discourse, clear,* or *perspicuous:* but for this I do not find any authority.]) Some say المُفَايَصَةُ. (IB, TA in art. فيص.) [See also 4 in art. فيص.]

4. مَا أَفَاصَ بِكَلِمَةٍ: see art. فيص. [It seems to be indicated in the Ṣ that this is from المُفَاوَصَةُ, expl. above: and the like of this is app. said by IB.]

6. التَّفَاوُصُ signifies التَّبَايُنُ [*The being,* or *becoming, separated, one from another*]; from البَيْنُ, not from البَيَانُ: (O, Ḳ:) originally التَّفَايُصُ; mentioned also [in a different sense] in art. فيص. (TA.) See the latter art.

فوض

2. فوّض إِلَيْهِ الأَمْرَ, (Ṣ, M, A, O, Mṣb, Ḳ,) inf. n. تَفْوِيضٌ, (Mgh, O, Mṣb,) *He committed to him the thing, affair, or case;* syn. رَدَّهُ, (Ṣ, A, O, Ḳ,) or صَيَّرَ, (M,) or سَلَّمَ; (Mgh, Mṣb;) *abstaining from contention, or litigation;* (Mgh;) *and made him arbiter thereof.* (TA.) It is said in the Ḳur [xl. 47], (TA,) وَأُفَوِّضُ أَمْرِى إِلَى ٱللّٰهِ (A, TA) *And I commit my case unto God, making Him arbiter thereof.* (TA.) — التَّفْوِيضُ فِى النِّكَاحِ, (Ṣ, O,) or نِكَاحُ التَّفْوِيضِ, (TA,) is *The giving* [a woman] *in marriage without* [*requiring*] *a dowry.* (Ṣ, O, TA.) You say, فوّض المَرْأَةَ *He gave the woman in marriage without* [*requiring*] *a dowry.* (Ḳ.) And فَوَّضَتْ بُضْعَهَا إِلَى زَوْجِهَا, (Mgh,) or نِكَاحَهَا إِلَى الزَّوْجِ, (Mṣb,) *She married herself to her husband without a dowry:* (Mgh, Mṣb:) or فَوَّضَتْ signifies *She gave up, or renounced, the ordinance of the dowry.* (Mṣb.)

3. مُفَاوَضَةٌ signifies The *being copartner, or copartners, in everything;* (O, Ḳ;) [as though each of two persons, or every one of more than two, committed all that he had to the other, or others;] as also ▼ تَفَاوُضٌ. (Ḳ.) [See 6.] Hence, (TA,) شَرِكَةُ المُفَاوَضَةِ *Copartnership in everything;* (Lth, M, Ṣ, A,* Mgh,* TA;) *in which everything is common property;* (Lth, M, TA;) opposed to شِرْكَةُ العِنَانِ, which is copartnership in one thing: (Lth:) or *copartnership of two persons in all that they possess:* (Mṣb:) or *copartnership of two persons in all that is in their hands, or that they may afterwards acquire;* which is null and void accord. to Esh-Sháfi'ee, but allowable accord. to Aboo-Ḥaneefeh and his two companions [Aboo-Yoosuf and Moḥammad]. (TA.) You say, شَارَكْتُهُ شَرِكَةَ مُفَاوَضَةٍ *I was copartner with him in all the property that we both together possessed.* (Az, TA.) Hence also, (TA,) مُفَاوَضَةُ العُلَمَآءِ *The conversing and conferring of the learned on matters of science; each of two persons receiving what the other had* [*to communicate*], *and giving what he himself had to the other;* as though each committed what he had to his companion. (O,* TA.) — The *commixing* [*in social intercourse*]. (A.) — The *being coequal.* (A, O, Ḳ.) — The *competing* (مُجَارَاةٌ) in an affair. (Ḳ.) You say, فَاوَضَهُ فِى أَمْرِهِ, (Ṣ, O, TA,) or فِى كَذَا, (Mgh,) *He competed with him,* (جاراه, Ṣ, Mgh, O, TA, [for which Golius has read جازاه, whence he has been led to assign to فاوض a wrong meaning, which Freytag has inadvertently copied,]) *and did like as he did,* (Mgh,) *in his affair,* (Ṣ, TA,) or *in such an affair.* (Mgh.) And فَاوَضْتُهُ *I competed with him;* syn. جَارَيْتُهُ: and كَانَ بَيْنَهُمَا مُفَاوَضَةٌ [*There was, between them two, competing*]. (A.)

6: see 3. You say, تَفَاوَضَ الشَّرِيكَانِ فِى المَالِ *The two partners were sharers in the property altogether:* (Ṣ, O, TA:) or تفاوض الشريكان signifies *the two partners were coequal.* (A, Mgh.) — [Hence, تفاوضوا *They conversed and conferred together; every one receiving what the others had to communicate, and giving what he himself had to the others:* see 3. — And *They mixed together in social intercourse:* see, again, 3.] — تفاوضوا الحَدِيثَ *They* [*discoursed together;* or] *began, or commenced, or entered upon, discourse.* (M, Mṣb.) [See an ex. in a verse cited in the first paragraph of art. زهو.] — Also, تفاوضوا فِى الأَمْرِ *They competed* (فَاوَضَ بَعْضُهُمْ بَعْضًا, [*every one doing like as the others did,*]) *in the affair.* (Ṣ, O, Ḳ.)

فَوْضَةٌ a subst. from مُفَاوَضَةٌ (O, TA) [signifying, app., *Copartnership:* &c.].

قَوْمٌ فَوْضَى *A party, or company, of men who are equals, having no chief:* (Ṣ, O, Mṣb, Ḳ:) or *separated,* or *in a state of dispersion;* (Lth, O, Ḳ;) فوضى being pl. of فَائِضٌ, which is not in use: (Lth, O:) or *mixed,* (Ṣ, O, M, Ḳ,) *one with another;* (Ṣ, O, Ḳ;) in which sense, also, فوضى is applied to a number of ostriches: (Ṣ, O:) or *having no commander, nor any to collect them together:* (M:) or *mixed, and having no commander over them.* (A.) You say, النَّاسُ فَوْضَى فِى هٰذَا *The people are equals in this; there is no distinction to be made between them.* (Mgh.) And جَآءَ القَوْمُ فَوْضَى *The party, or company, of men came mixed together.* (Ṣ.) And الوَحْشُ فَوْضَى *The wild animals are in a state of separation,* or *dispersion,* (O, TA,) *going to and fro.* (TA.) أَمْوَالُهُمْ فَوْضَى بَيْنَهُمْ *Their possessions are property which they share among themselves;* as also ▼ فَيْضُوضَآءُ and ▼ فَيْضُوضَى. (Ṣ.) And مَتَاعُهُمْ فَوْضَى بَيْنَهُمْ, and فَوْضَى فَضًا, *Their goods are common property among them.* (M.) And المَالُ فَوْضَى بَيْنَهُمْ *The property is promiscuous among them: whosoever desireth of them a thing taketh it.* (Mṣb.) And كَانَتْ خَيْبَرُ فَوْضَى *Kheyber was promiscuous* (Mgh) *common property* (Mgh, Mṣb) among the Companions; *not divided.* (Mṣb.) — أَمْرُهُمْ فَوْضَى, and ▼ فَوْضَآءُ, (M,) or فَوْضَى بَيْنَهُمْ, and فَيْضَى, (TA,) *Their case is mixed, or promiscuous:* or *is equal among them:* (Lḥ, M, TA:) or أَمْرُهُمْ فَوْضَى بَيْنَهُمْ, (AZ, O, Ḳ,) or ▼ فَوْضُوضَآءُ بَيْنَهُمْ, (TA,) or both, (O, TA,) *Their case is mixed,* or *promiscuous,* (AZ, O, Ḳ,) *every one of them making free use of that which belongs to another,* (Ḳ,) *one wearing the garment of another, and one eating the food of another, none of them consulting his companion respecting that which he does without his order.* (AZ, O.) [See a similar phrase voce مَشُورَةٌ.]

فَوْضَآءُ: and فَوْضُوضَآءُ: } see فوضى, last sentence.

تَفْوَاضَةٌ *Remains of life:* (O, TA:) so in the saying, رَأَيْتُ التَّفْوَاضَةَ لِفُلَانٍ (O) or بِفُلَانٍ (TA) [*I saw the remains of life pertaining to,* or *in, such a one*].

مُفَوِّضَةٌ A woman *who marries herself to her husband without a dowry:* (Mgh, Mṣb:) or *who gives up, or renounces, the ordinance of the dowry:* (Mṣb:) or, accord. to some, the word is مُفَوَّضَةٌ, (Mgh, Mṣb,) meaning *married* by her guardian *without the naming of the dowry:* (Mgh:) or meaning *having the affair of the dowry committed to her by the law, so that she may make it obligatory or annul it:* (Mṣb:) or meaning *married without the mention of a dowry, or on the condition of her having no dowry.* (KT.)

فوط

2. فَوَّطَهُ, inf. n. تَفْوِيطٌ, *He clad him,* or *attired him, with a* فُوطَة. (TA.)

فُوطَةٌ sing. of فُوَطٌ, which signifies *Cloths that are brought from Es-Sind,* (Lth, O, Ḳ, TA,) *thick,* or *coarse, and short, used as waist-wrappers:* (Lth, O, TA:) or *striped waist-wrappers:* (Ḳ:) Az says, I have not heard this word in aught of the language of the Arabs, and I know not whether it be an Arabic word or of the language of the foreigners, but I have seen in El-Koofeh *striped waist-wrappers, which are sold, and are bought by the camel-drivers and the Arabs of the desert and the servants and the people of the lowest sort, who use them as waist-wrappers, and call them thus;* sing. فُوطَةٌ: IDrd says that it is not an Arabic word: (O, TA:) it is added in the Ḳ, or it is a word of the language of Es-Sind: Ṣgh says, (TA,) فوطه is a word of the language of Es-Sind, arabicized, from پوتَه, with a ḍammeh not fully sounded: (O, TA:) [and SM adds,] it is called with us in El-Yemen, أَزْهَرِيَّة: and by reason of frequency of usage, they have derived from it the verb above-mentioned. (TA.) The dim. of فُوطَةٌ is ▼ فُوَيْطَةٌ. (Ḥar p. 294.) [See also De Sacy's Chrest. Arabe, sec. ed., i. 195.] — It (the pl.) is also applied to *Short napkins, with striped extremities, woven at El-Maḥalleh El-Kubrà, in Egypt, which a man puts upon his knees to preserve himself therewith* [*from being soiled*] *at meals* [*and with which the hands are wiped after washing*]. (TA.)

فُوطِىٌّ *Blue, but not of a clear blueness.* (TA.)

فُوَيْطَةٌ dim. of فُوطَةٌ, q. v.

فَوَّاطٌ *A weaver, or seller, of* فُوَط, pl. of فُوطَة. (TA.)

مُفَوَّطٌ A man *clad,* or *attired, with a* فُوطَة. (TA.)

فوظ

1. فَاظَ, aor. يَفُوظُ, inf. n. فَوْظٌ and فُوَاظٌ: see فَاظَ in art. فيظ.

فوف

1. مَا فَاقَ بِخَيْرٍ, (T, M, O,) or مَا فَاقَ عَنِّى بِخَيْرٍ, (Ḳ,) وَلَا زَنْجَرَ, (T, O, Ḳ,) aor. يَفُوفُ, (Ḳ,) inf. n. فَوْفٌ, (T, M, O, Ḳ,) [may be rendered *He did* *not benefit*, or *he did not benefit me, with what might be taken between the nail of his thumb and that of his forefinger, nor did he with what might be taken by the inside of the nail of the thumb from the extremity of the fore tooth*; i. e., *with a thing inconceivably small*; or *with anything*; being] a phrase meaning one's answering (T, M, O, Ḳ) a person who has asked for a thing (T, O, Ḳ) by putting his thumb-nail upon the nail of his fore finger, (T, M, O, Ḳ,) and by taking away the inner side of the nail [of the thumb] from the extremity of the fore tooth, (T, O,) and saying "Not [even] this [will I give thee]," (T, O, Ḳ,) or "Not [even] the like of this." (M.)

فَوْف : see the next paragraph, in two places.

فُوف The *whiteness that is upon the nails of young persons*; (Ṣ, M, O, Ḳ;) as also ↓ فَوْف; (T, M, Ḳ;) the latter mentioned by Fr, but not known by IAạr; (T;) or the former is the more common: (Ḳ:) n. un. with ↓ ة; (M, Ḳ;) meaning *a portion thereof*. (M.) — And The *integument* [or *pellicle*] *that is upon* [what is termed] *the core of the heart, and the stone of the date*, (عَلَى حَبَّةِ القَلْبِ وَالنَّوَاةِ,) *beneath the flesh* [or *pulpy substance*] *of the date*: (M, Ḳ:) or the *white grain* [i. e. the *embryo*, which resembles a white grain,] *in the interior of the date-stone, from which the palm-tree grows forth* [or *germinates*]: and it is said that ↓ فُوفَةٌ signifies the *integument* [or *pellicle*] *that is upon the date-stone*: (Ṣ, O:) [i. e.] the *thin integument that is upon the date-stone*; also called the قِطْمِير. (T.) — [Hence, or from one of the significations mentioned above,] one says, مَا أَغْنَى عَنِّى فُوفًا i. e. [*He* (a man, Ṣ, O) *did not avail me*] *aught*. (Ṣ, O, Ḳ.) And مَا ذَاقَ فُوفًا [*He tasted not*] *aught*. (T, Ḳ.) — And فوف signifies also *Any integument*; (M, Ḳ;) and so ↓ فُوفَةٌ. (Ḳ.) — And The *bladder of an animal of the bovine kind*; as also ↓ فَوْف: (Ḳ:) mentioned by Ṣgh in the TṢ. (TA.) — Also *A sort of the* [*garments called*] بُرُود *of El-Yemen*: (M, Ḳ:) *thin, variegated*, or *figured, garments of El-Yemen*: (IAạr, T:) and one says also بُرْدٌ ↓ فُوفِىٌّ, and ثُوثِىٌّ, which is formed by substitution, and mentioned by Yaạḳoob, and بُرْدُ أَفْوَافٍ, meaning *a* بُرْد *having white stripes*, (M,) and so ↓ بُرْدٌ مُفَوَّفٌ; (Ṣ, M, Ḳ;) or this last and بُرْدُ أَفْوَافٍ signify *a thin* بُرْد; (Ṣ, O, Ḳ, TA;) and in like manner one says حُلَّةُ أَفْوَافٍ: (TA:) أَفْوَاف is pl. of فُوف: (Ṣ, O:) and accord. to Lth, the أَفْوَاف are *of the* [بُرُود *called*] عَصْب [q. v.] *of El-Yemen*. (O.) — Also *Flowers*, or *blossoms*; syn. زَهْرٌ; [in the CḲ زَهَر;] used in this sense by Ibn-Aḥmar; being likened by him to the garments called فُوف. (T, Ḳ, TA.) — And *Portions of cotton*: (O, Ḳ, and so in some copies of the Ṣ:) [perhaps meaning] *a white thing* [*resembling cotton*] *which is in the* عُشَر [q. v.]. (Ḥam p. 784.) — [And Freytag mentions its signifying The *extreme portion* of the penis; as on the authority of the Ḳ: but he seems to have confounded فوف with فوق.]

فُوفَةٌ the subst. denoted by the verb فَافَ: (M, TA:) [as such,] it is coupled by a poet with زِنْجِير [which is similar to it in meaning: see this last word]. (Ṣ, O, TA.) — Also n. un. of فُوف. (Ṣ, M, O, Ḳ.) See this latter word, in three places.

بُرْدٌ فُوفِىٌّ : see فُوف, latter half.

بُرْدٌ مُفَوَّفٌ : see فُوف, latter half. — غُرْفَةٌ مُفَوَّفَةٌ, the mention of which occurs in a trad. of Kaạb, means [*An upper chamber*] *whereof one brick is of gold and another of silver* [i. e. *constructed of gold and silver bricks alternately*]. (TA.)

فوفل

الفوفل, (Ḳ, [there said to be بِالضَّمِّ وَالفَتْحِ, app. indicating that it is الفُوفَلُ and الفَوْفَلُ, but accord. to the CḲ and TḲ الفُوفَلُ, and thus only, as though it were said to be بِالضَّمِّ فَالفَتْحِ,]) or شَجَرَةُ الفَوْفَلِ, (thus written in the O, [in the TT, as from the M, شجر الفوفل, thus, without the affix ة to the former word, and without any vowel-sign,]) accord. to AḤn, (M,) or Aboo-Ziyád, (O,) *A palm-tree*, [*the areca catechu*, or *betel-nut palm*,] *like the cocoa-nut palm, that bears racemes upon which are the* فوفل, *resembling dates*, (M, O, Ḳ,) *of which some are black and some are red, not of the growth of the land of the Arabs*: (O:) [in one of my copies of the Ṣ, the فَوْفَل (thus the word is there written) is said to be *a tree like the cocoa-nut*: in the other copy it is not mentioned:] the فوفل is said by AḤn to be *the fruit of a certain palm-tree, hard as though it were wood*: (M:) in the Tedhkireh of Dáwood it is said to be *a fruit like the Syrian* جَوْز [or *walnut*], *of an astringent quality, found upon trees resembling the cocoa-nut*: (TA:) *it is good for hot and gross humours*, (Ḳ, TA,) *prepared as a liniment*; (TA;) *and for inflammation of the eye*, (Ḳ, TA,) *as a dressing and collyrium*; *and has great efficacy for drying up the seminal fluid, and as a digestive*. (TA.)

فوق

1. فَاقَهُمْ, (Ṣ, Mgh, O, Mṣb, Ḳ,) derived from فَوْق as signifying the contr. of تَحْت, (Mgh,) aor. يَفُوقُهُمْ, (Ṣ, O,) inf. n. فَوْقٌ (O, Ḳ) and فَوَاقٌ (Ḳ) and فَوَقَانٌ, (CḲ,) *He* (a man, Ṣ, O, Mṣb) *was*, or *became, above them*, or *superior to them*, or *he excelled them*, or *surpassed them*, (Ṣ, Mgh, O, Mṣb, Ḳ,) namely, his companions, (Ṣ, O, Mṣb, Ḳ,) or others, (Mgh,) *in eminence*, or *dignity*, or *nobility*; (Ṣ, O, Ḳ;) and *he overcame them*; (Mṣb, TA;) and *did so in*, or *by, an argument* or *the like*. (Mṣb.) And فُقْتُ فُلَانًا *I became better than such a one*, and *higher*, and *more eminent* or *noble*; as though above him in station. (TA.) And فَاقَتِ الجَارِيَةُ بِالجَمَالِ [*The young woman excelled in beauty*, or *comeliness*]. (Mṣb.) It is said in a trad., حُبِّبَ إِلَىَّ الجَمَالُ حَتَّى مَا أُحِبُّ أَنْ يَفُوقَنِى أَحَدٌ بِشِرَاكِ نَعْلٍ [*Comeliness has been made lovely to me so that I love not that any one should excel me in the thong of a sandal*]. (TA.) — فاق, (Ṣ, O, Ḳ,) aor. يَفُوقُ, (O,) inf. n. فُوَاقٌ, (Ṣ, O, Ḳ,) said of a man, (Ṣ,) means that *The wind rose from his chest*; (Ṣ, O, Ḳ;) [i. e. *he hiccoughed*, or *hickuped*; a signification indicated by its being said that] فُوَاق means the *reiterating of an overpowering* [or *involuntary*] *sobbing sound*: (Mṣb, TA:) and ↓ فُوَاق [as a subst.] signifies also the *wind* [itself] *that rises from the chest* (Ṣ, O, Ḳ) *of a man*. (Ṣ, O.) — And, accord. to Az, (Mṣb,) فاق, (Mṣb, TA,) aor. يَفُوقُ, (Mṣb,) inf. n. فُوَاقٌ (Mṣb, TA) and فُؤُوقٌ, (TA,) *He was affected*, or *taken, with a panting*, or *breathing* [*shortly*, or] *uninterruptedly*. (Mṣb, TA.) — And فاق بِنَفْسِهِ, (Ṣ,* O, Ḳ,) aor. يَفُوقُ, (Ṣ, O,) inf. n. فُوُوقٌ [or فُؤُوقٌ] (Ṣ, O, Ḳ) and فُوَاقٌ, (Ḳ,) said of a man, (Ṣ,) *His spirit was about to pass forth*: (Ṣ, O, Ḳ:) or *he gave up his spirit*; (Ṣ,* O,* Ḳ;) as also فاق [alone] aor. يفيق: (IAạr, O and Ḳ in art. فيق:) or *he died*: (Ḳ:) or ↓ فُوَاق [is app. held by some to be a simple subst., and] accord. to IAạr signifies *death itself*: (TA:) or it signifies, (Ṣ, O, Mṣb,) or signifies also, (Ḳ,) *an affection* [i. e. *a gasping*, or *short catching of the breath*,] *incident to a man at the point of death*: (Ṣ, O, Mṣb, Ḳ:) and one says [of the man], فاق, aor. يَفُوقُ, inf. n. فوق [app. فَوْقٌ]; the verb being of the class of طَلَبَ [of which the inf. n. most commonly used is طَلَبٌ; or, if the saying that the verb is of the class of طَلَبَ be not meant to indicate the form of its inf. n. as well as that of its aor., فوق may be a mistranscription for فُوُوقٌ or فُؤُوقٌ]. (Mṣb.) — فاقت, (O, Ḳ,) aor. تَفُوقُ, inf. n. فُوَاقٌ, (TA,) *She* (a camel) *had in her udder the* فِيقَة, or *milk that had collected between two milkings*; (O, Ḳ, TA;) and (Ḳ) so ↓ أَفَاقَتْ: (Ṣ, O, Ḳ:) or the latter verb signifies *she* (a camel) *attained to the time for her being milked*; and the inf. n. is إِفَاقَةٌ and [quasi-inf. n.] ↓ فُوَاقٌ: (IAạr, TA:) or إِفَاقَة in relation to the she-camel means her *being driven*, or *led, back from the pasturing, and left until she rests, and recovers* [*her milk*]: (ISh, TA:) and إِفَاقَةُ الدِّرَّةِ signifies *the returning of the milk*. (Zeyd Ibn-Kethweh, TA.) [See also فُوَاق, below.] — فَوَقٌ signifies *A bending*, or [thus in the TA as from the Ḳ, but in copies of the Ḳ "and,"] *a breaking*, (Ḳ, TA,) *in the notch* (فِى الفُوقِ), (Ḳ,) or *in one of the two cusps of the notch*, (TA,) *of an arrow*: (Ḳ, TA:) or its verb, said of an arrow, is فَاقَ, aor. يَفَاقُ, inf. n. فَاقٌ and فَوْقٌ, in which the و is then made movent with fet-ḥ, [so that the word becomes فَوَقٌ,] because this verb is of the class of فَعِلَ, aor. يَفْعَلُ: (Ḳ, TA:) or one says of an arrow فَوِقَ, [aor. يَفْوَقُ,] inf. n. فَوَقٌ, meaning *its notch broke*; (Mṣb;) and ↓ انفاق said of an arrow signifies thus; (Ṣ, Mṣb;) or *its notch became much broken*; (O, Ḳ, TA;) or *became split*, or *cracked*. (TA.) — And فُقْتُ السَّهْمَ, (Ṣ, O, Mṣb, Ḳ,) inf. n. فَوْقٌ, (Mṣb,) *I broke the notch of the arrow*. (Ṣ, O, Mṣb, Ḳ.) And فاق الشَّىْءَ, aor. يَفُوقُ, *He broke the thing*. (TA.) —

فاق in the sense of افتاق [from فَاقَةٌ] is not allowable. (Ṣ, O.)

2. فَوَّقَهُ, inf. n. تَفْوِيقٌ, *He made him,* or *judged him, to excel,* or *to have excelled.* (TA.) ═ فوّق الفَصِيلَ, (Ṣ, O, Ḳ,) inf. n. as above, said of the pastor, (TA,) *He gave to the young unweaned camel to drink the quantities of milk that had collected in the udder between two milkings time after time.* (Ṣ, O, Ḳ, TA. [See فُوَاقٌ.]) — And [hence] one says, فَوَّقَنِى الأَمَانِىَّ وَأَرْضَعَنِى أَفَاوِيقَ ▾ بِرِّهِ † [*He made me to obtain on repeated occasions the things wished for, and nourished me with the recurrent supplies of his bounty*]. (TA.) And it is said in a trad. of 'Alee, إِنَّ بَنِى أُمَيَّةَ لَيُفَوِّقُونَنِى تُرَاثَ مُحَمَّدٍ, meaning † [*Verily the sons of Umeiyeh*] *give to me by little and little of the property* [*constituting the heritage of Moḥammad*]. (TA.) — See also 10. ═ فَوَّقَ السَّهْمَ, (inf. n. as above, Mṣb,) *He made to the arrow a* فُوق [i. e. *notch for the bow-string*]. (Ṣ, O, Mṣb, Ḳ.) — And [hence,] فَوَّقَ المَرْأَةَ † *He slit the vulva of the woman.* (TA in art. سوس.) — See also the next paragraph, last sentence.

4. إِفَاقَةٌ, (O, Ḳ, TA,) some say, (O, TA,) signifies *A resting;* (O, Ḳ, TA;) from ▾ فُوَاقٌ signifying *a resting between two milkings;* (O, TA;) which latter meaning, as well as the former, the Ḳ erroneously assigns to the former word. (TA.) — And أَفَاقَتْ said of a she-camel, signifies the same as فَاقَتْ expl. above: see 1, latter half. (O, Ḳ, TA.) — And [hence, perhaps,] افاق مِنْ مَرَضِهِ, (Ṣ, O, Ḳ, TA,) and مِنْ سُكْرِهِ, (Ṣ, O,) and مِنْ غَشْيَتِهِ, (O, TA,) inf. n. إِفَاقَةٌ; (TA;) and ▾ استفاق; both signify the same; (Ṣ, O, Ḳ;) i. e. *He returned to a healthy,* or *sound, state* [*of body* and *of mind, from his disease,* and *from his intoxication,* and *from his swoon,* or *fit of insensibility*]: (O, Ḳ, TA:) or one says of the diseased, افاق and ▾ استفاق meaning *he became convalescent;* or *recovered, but not completely, his health and strength:* and the subst. [or quasi-inf. n.] is ▾ فُوَاقٌ: (TA:) and one says of the insane, or possessed, افاق, inf. n. إِفَاقَةٌ, meaning *he recovered his intelligence;* and of the intoxicated, likewise, افاق, originally افاق مِنْ سُكْرِهِ, like as one says اِسْتَيْقَظَ مِنْ نَوْمِهِ: (Mṣb:) [and it is said that] ▾ الإِسْتِفَاقَةُ as syn. with الإِفَاقَةُ is derived from فَوْقٌ meaning the contr. of تَحْتٌ, like as تَعَلَّى مِنْ مَرَضِهِ and تَمَاثَلَ are from العُلُوُّ and المُثُولُ: (Ḥar p. 132:) but accord. to 'Alee Ibn-'Eesà, ▾ استفاق signifies *he sought,* or *desired,* الإِفَاقَة. (Ḥam p. 541.) — And [hence,] افاق الزَّمَانُ ‡ *The time became abundant in herbage after barrenness* or *drought.* (O, Ḳ, TA.) ═ أَفَقْتُ السَّهْمَ, (inf. n. إِفَاقَةٌ, Mṣb,) *I put the* فُوق [or *notch*] of the arrow *upon the bowstring,* (Ṣ, O, Mṣb,* Ḳ,) *to shoot with it;* (Ṣ, O, Mṣb;) as also أَوْفَقْتُهُ: but أَفْوَقْتُهُ is extr., (Ṣ, O, Ḳ,) and should not be said, (Ṣ, O,) or, accord. to Yoo, one says أَفْوَقْتُهُ also: (O:) and, accord. to the A, ▾ فَوَّقَ السَّهْمَ signifies [in like manner] *he put the bow-string into the notch of the arrow on the occasion of shooting.* (TA.)

5. تفوّق عَلَى قَوْمِهِ *He exalted himself above his people,* or *party.* (O,* Ḳ,* TA.) ═ تفوّق said of a young unweaned camel, *He drank* [or *sucked*] *the quantities of milk that had collected in the udder between two milkings time after time.* (Ṣ, O, Ḳ.) — And تَفَوَّقَهَا *He milked her,* namely, a camel, *drawing from her the quantities of milk that had collected in her udder time after time;* (O, Ḳ;) as also ▾ استفاقها. (Ḳ. [But see this latter below.]) — Hence the trad. respecting Aboo-Moosà, that he was discoursing with Ma'ádh, of reciting the Ḳur-án, and said, أَمَّا أَنَا فَأَتَفَوَّقُهُ تَفَوُّقَ اللَّقُوحِ [*As for me, I draw it forth in the manner of the drawing forth of the milk of the milch camel at the times when it has collected in her udder*], meaning ‡ *I do not recite my set portion at once, but piecemeal, in my night and my day.* (Ṣ, O, TA.) — One says also تفوّق شَرَابَهُ i. e. ‡ *He drank his wine,* or *beverage, part after part.* (TA.) Sb has mentioned that يَتَجَرَّعُهُ and يَتَفَوَّقُهُ are said of that which is not a labouring to do a thing at once, but is an act after an act, performed in a leisurely manner. (O, TA.)

7. انفاق *It* (a thing) *broke,* or *became broken;* quasi-pass. of فَاقَ الشَّىْءَ meaning كَسَرَهُ. (TA.) — See also 1, near the end. — Said of a camel, *He became lean,* or *emaciated:* — and *He perished,* or *died.* (O, Ḳ.)

8. افتاق *He was,* or *became, poor,* or *in want,* or *need:* (Ṣ, O, Mṣb, Ḳ:) فَاقَ in this sense is not allowable. (Ṣ, O.) ═ And *He died with much* فُوَاق [which may here mean either *hiccoughing* (which often occurs at the close of a fatal fever &c.), or *gasping,* or *short catching of the breath*]. (O, Ḳ.)

10: see 4, in four places. ═ استفاقها: see 5. [It signifies as there explained: or it signifies, or signifies also,] *He delayed the milking her,* namely, a camel, *until her milk collected in her udder,* or *in order that it might collect;* and so ▾ فوّقها, inf. n. تَفْوِيقٌ. (TA.) One says, اسْتَفِقِ النَّاقَةَ *Milk not thou the she-camel before the time.* (O,* Ḳ.) — — And مَا يَسْتَفِيقُ مِنَ الشَّرَابِ *He does not abstain* [*from drinking wine*]: (O, Ḳ, TA:) or *he does not drink it in the set time:* or *he does not appoint a time for drinking it, but drinks it always.* (TA.)

فَاقٌ *A* [*large bowl such as is termed*] جَفْنَة, *filled with food.* (Lth, T, O, Ḳ.) ═ And *Cooked olive-oil.* (O, Ḳ, TA.) So in the saying of Shemmákh, (O, TA,*) describing the hair of a woman, (TA,)

قَامَتْ تُرِيكَ أَثِيثَ النَّبْتِ مُنْسَدِلاً
مِثْلَ الأَسَاوِدِ قَدْ مُسِّحْنَ بِالفَاقِ

[*She stood showing to thee* hair *abundant and luxuriant,* or *abundant and long, in respect of growth, let down, like the black serpents that have been anointed with cooked olive-oil*]: or, as some say, meaning الإِنْفَاق, meaning *fresh olive-oil* [from إِنْفَاق, a Pers. word signifying "olive-oil"]: or, as AA relates it, the poet said, قَدْ شُدِّخْنَ بِالفَاقِ [*that have been crushed in the* فاق]; and accord. to him the last word has the meaning here next following. (O, TA.) ═ And The *desert;* syn. صَحْرَآءُ: (O, Ḳ, TA:) so says AA: and on one occasion he says that الفاق means *a certain land:* (O: a meaning also mentioned in the Ḳ:) or *a certain wide land.* (TA.) ═ It is also expl. as signifying بَان [i. e. *Oil of ben*]: and also *A comb:* on the authority of Th: and it may have either of these meanings in the verse cited above. (TA.) ═ And accord. to the Ḳ, it signifies *Tall, and incongruous in make;* and so ▾ فُوقَةٌ and ▾ فُوقٌ and ▾ فُوَاقٌ and ▾ فَيِّقٌ and ▾ فَيَاقٌ: but these words are all correctly, in this [or a similar] sense with two ḳáfs. (TA.) ═ Also, accord. to the Ḳ, *A certain aquatic bird, long in the neck:* but this, likewise, is correctly with two ḳáfs. (TA.)

فَوْقٌ is the *contr. of* تَحْتٌ; (Ṣ, Mgh, O, Mṣb, Ḳ;) [primarily signifying The *location that is above,* or *over;*] and is an adv. n. (Mgh, Mṣb, Ḳ) of place; (Mgh, Mṣb;) and a simple noun, indecl., [with ḍammeh for its termination, when the noun to which it should be prefixed is suppressed, and the meaning of this is intended to be understood, but not the word itself;] but when it is prefixed to another noun [which is either expressed or itself (and not merely its meaning) meant to be understood, and when the noun to which it should be prefixed is suppressed and neither this nor its meaning is meant to be understood,] it is declinable. (Ḳ. [For the words يَكُونُ ٱسْمًا وَظَرْفًا مَبْنِىٌّ, the reading of the Ḳ in the TA and CḲ, my MS. copy of the Ḳ (which I follow in this case) has يكون ظرفا واسما مبنيًّا.]) One says, زَيْدٌ فَوْقَ السَّطْحِ [*Zeyd is above,* or rather *upon, the house-top*]. (Mgh, Mṣb.) And العِمَامَةُ فَوْقَ الرَّأْسِ [*The turban is above,* or *upon, the head*]. (Mgh.) And طَفَا فَوْقَ المَآءِ *It floated upon the water.* (Ṣ &c. in art. طفو.) Ks has mentioned the saying, أَفَوْقَ تَنَامُ أَمْ أَسْفَلَ [*Dost thou,* or *wilt thou, sleep in the part that is above* of the house &c., *or in the part that is below?* i. e., *in the upper part,* or *in the lower part?*] with fet-ḥ, as suppressing the noun to which فوق is [meant to be understood as] prefixed. (TA.) Lth says that he who uses it as a صِفَة [by which (like other old writers) he means an adv. n. of place] should use the accus. case, as when one says, عَبْدُ ٱللّٰهِ فَوْقَ زَيْدٍ [*Abd-Allah is above Zeyd*]: but if you make it simply a noun, you use the nom. case, and say, فَوْقُهُ رَأْسُهُ [*His superior* (meaning *upper*) *part is his head*]; for in this instance it is the head itself, and you make each to be governed in the nom. case by the other. (TA.) In the saying in the Ḳur [xvi. 28], فَخَرَّ عَلَيْهِمُ ٱلسَّقْفُ مِنْ فَوْقِهِمْ [*And the roof fell on them from above them*], the utility of the phrase من فوقهم is hardly apparent, because عليهم sometimes serves in its stead: but IJ says that من فوقهم may here have a useful office; for عَلَى is sometimes used in relation to deeds [or events] that are difficult, and deemed onerous; [for instance,] you say, قَدْ سِرْنَا عَشْرًا وَبَقِيَتْ عَلَيْنَا لَيْلَتَانِ [*We have journeyed ten* nights *and* the journeys *two nights have remained* as though incumbent *on us*]; &c.; so that if it were said فخرّ عليهم السقف without the adding من فوقهم, it might be supposed to be like the saying قَدْ خَرِبَتْ عَلَيْهِمْ دَارُهُمْ [*Their abode had become in a state of ruin* as a punishment *upon them*]; but when He [referring to God] says من فوقهم, that meaning which was supposable ceases to be so; and the meaning becomes this, that it [the roof] fell when they were beneath it. (TA.) إِذْ جَاؤُوكُمْ مِنْ فَوْقِكُمْ وَمِنْ أَسْفَلَ مِنْكُمْ [*When they came to you from above you and from below you*], in the Kur [xxxiii. 10], relates to Benoo-Kureydhah, who came to them from above them; and to Kureysh and Ghatafán, who came from the district of Mekkeh, from below them. (TA.) وَٱلَّذِينَ ٱتَّقَوْا فَوْقَهُمْ يَوْمَ ٱلْقِيَامَةِ, in the Kur [ii. 208], means † [*But those who have been careful of their religious duties*] *shall be above them in station* [*on the day of resurrection*]. (O.) And one says, [agreeably with what has been stated in the first sentence of this paragraph, أَخَذَهُ مِنْ فَوْقُ, and] أَخَذَهُ مِنْ فَوْقٍ, [meaning † *He overcame him*, or *overpowered him*, and in like manner أَتَاهُ من فوق, as expl. in the Ham p. 128, i. e. قَهَرَهُ,] namely, his adversary; and so a hawk, his prey, or quarry. (M and K in an expl. of أَدَلَّ عَلَيْهِ, in art. دل.) And [in a similar manner] فَوْقَ is metaphorically used as denoting excess, (Mgh, Msb,) and excellence: (Msb:) thus one says, العَشَرَةُ فَوْقَ التِّسْعَةِ (Mgh, Msb) i. e. ‡ *Ten is above nine*; meaning *ten exceeds nine*: (Msb:) and هٰذَا فَوْقَ ذَاكَ (Mgh, Msb) i. e. ‡ [*This is above*, or *superior to, that*;] meaning *this is more excellent than that*; (Msb:) and hence, (Mgh, Msb,) in the Kur [ii. 24], (S, O,) بَعُوضَةً فَمَا فَوْقَهَا i. e. ‡ [*A gnat and*] *what exceeds it* (Mgh, Msb) *in smallness*, or *in largeness*; (Mgh, Msb, K;) *what is smaller than it*, (AO, S, O,) or *what is larger than it*, by the latter being meant the fly [mentioned in the Kur xxii. 72] and the spider [mentioned in xxix. 40], (Fr, S, O,) and the phrase as expl. in the former sense being like the reply to him who says "Such a one is small" وَفَوْقَ ذٰلِكَ i. e. † *And smaller than that*: (AO, O:) hence also, in the Kur [iv. 12], فَإِنْ كُنَّ نِسَآءً فَوْقَ ٱثْنَتَيْنِ (Mgh, Msb) i. e. ‡ [*And if they are women*,] *exceeding two*. (Msb.)

فُوقٌ The *part, of the arrow, which is the place of the bow-string*; [i. e. the *notch* thereof;] (S, O, Msb, K;) as also ٭ فُوقَةٌ: (Msb, K:) the former is masc., and also, like the latter, fem.: (IAmb, Msb:) and الفُوقَانِ signifies *the* زَنَمَتَانِ [or *two cusps of the* فُوق, *between which is put the bow-string*]; (O, K;) thus these are termed by the tribe of Hudheyl; but a poet who has used the dual form is said by AO to have meant thereby a single فُوق: (O:) the pl. [of mult.] is فُوَقٌ and [of pauc.] أَفْوَاقٌ; (S, O, Msb, K;) or, accord. to ISk, these are pls. of فُوقَةٌ; (TA;) and فُقًا also is a pl., formed by transposition; [see an ex. in a verse cited voce عُرْقُوبٌ;] (K, TA;) one says فُقْوَةٌ and فُقًا [for فُوقَةٌ and فُوَقٌ]. (TA.) سَهْمٌ ذُو فُوقٍ means *An arrow* rendered complete by its *having a* فُوق: — and hence ذَا فُوقٍ occurring in a trad. [as meaning † *A complete share*; for سَهْمٌ signifies "a share" as well as "an arrow"]. (A'Obeyd, O.) And أَعْلَاهُمْ فُوقًا, meaning ‡ *He*, or *they, of them, having the largest share of religion*, is a metaphorical phrase, from the فُوق of the arrow. (TA.) — And they say, أَقْبِلْ عَلَى فُوقِ نَبْلِكَ, [or, app., فُوقَ نَبْلِكَ,] for نَبْلٌ is a coll. n., meaning "arrows," or "Arabian arrows,"] meaning † *Betake thyself to thy affair, and that which concerns thee*. (TA.) — And رَمَيْنَا فُوقًا, (O, K,) or فُوقًا وَاحِدًا, (TA,) meaning رِشْقًا [i. e. ‡ *We shot in one direction*; or *we shot one bout, in one direction*]. (O, K, TA.) — [Hence, app.,] one says, كان فُلَانٌ لِأَوَّلِ فُوقٍ, meaning ‡ *Such a one was* [for the first discharge from the bow, i. e.,] *the first shot and dying*. (A, TA.) — And [hence, perhaps,] فُوقٌ signifies also ‡ *A mode*, or *manner, of speech*: (A, O, K:) pl. فُوَقٌ. (TA.) One says to a man when he enters upon a mode, or manner, of speech, خُذْ فِي فُوقٍ أَحْسَنَ مِنْهُ ‡ [*Enter upon a mode*, or *manner, of speech better than it*]. (A, TA.) — And ‡ The *first way*. (AA, O, K, TA.) — [Hence, app.,] they say, ‡ ارْجِعْ إِنْ شِئْتَ فِي فُوقٍ *Return thou, if thou wilt, to the state of close, or loving, communion in which we were*. (Ibn-'Abbád, Z, O, TA.) — And the Arabs say, in imprecating, لَا رَجَعَ فُلَانٌ إِلَى فُوقِهِ i. e. † *May such a one die*: so says AA; and he cites the following verse of El-'Uleykim El-Kindee,

مَا بَالُ عِرْسِى شَرِقَتْ بِرِيقِهَا •
• ثُمَّتَ لَا يَرْجِعُ لَهَا مِنْ فُوقِهَا

meaning † [*What is the case of my wife* that *she is choked by her spittle? Then*, or *afterward*,] *may it* (her spittle) *not return to its channel* [i. e. *her throat, the way whence it came*; so that she may be suffocated]. (O.) — And one says (O, K) of a man when he has gone away, (O,) مَا ٱرْتَدَّ عَلَى فُوقِهِ, meaning † He went away and *he did not return* [*to the place whence he departed*]. (O, K.) — فُوقٌ also signifies, (O, K,) accord. to Ibn-'Abbád, (O, TA,) † The *vulva of a woman*: (O, K, TA:) but As says that this is with ق [in the place of the ف]: (TA:) [it is, however, also said that] فُوقُ الرَّحِمِ signifies ‡ *the rima of the vulva*, by way of comparison [to the notch of the arrow]. (TA, in the supplement to this art.) — [And app. † The *front edge of the lobe* of the ear: see 1 in art. خرم, where it is mentioned in such a manner as seems to preclude the supposition of its being a mistranscription for قُوف.] — And (as Ibn-'Abbád says, O) † The *place of opening* (مَفْرَج, O, TA, in the K, erroneously, مَخْرَج, TA, and جَوْبَة, O, K, TA) *of the mouth*: or (as some say, O) the *extremity of the tongue*. (O, K, TA.) — And † The *uppermost part of the penis*, (En-Nadr, O, K, TA,) or *of the glans thereof*. (TA.) = And, accord. to the K, *A certain bird*; meaning *a certain aquatic bird*: but this is correctly [قُوق,] with two káfs. (TA.) — See also فَاقٌ, last sentence but one.

فِيقٌ [originally فُوقٌ]: see فِيقَةٌ. = Also, as mentioned in this art. and in art. فيق, in the K: see فَاقٌ, last sentence but one.

مُفِيقٌ and فِيَقٌ: see فِيقٌ.

فَاقَةٌ *Poverty*, (S, O, K,) *want*, or *need*. (S, O, Msb, K.) One says, هُوَ ذُو فَاقَةٍ *He is one who is in* [*poverty* or] *want* or *need*. (Msb.) [See 8.] It has no [unaugmented] verb. (TA.)

فُوقَةٌ: see فُوقٌ, first sentence. = And see also فَاقٌ, last sentence but one.

فَوَقَةٌ: see فَائِقٌ [of which, as a part. n., it is a pl.].

فَيْقَةٌ: see what next follows.

فِيقَةٌ, (S, O, &c.,) originally فِوْقَةٌ, (TA,) the و having become ى because of the kesreh before it, (S, O, TA,) The *milk that collects* (S, O, K) *in the udder* (K) *between two milkings*: (S, O, K:) and [or this is a mistake for ابن السَّرَّاج] سراج has mentioned ٭ فَيْقَةُ النَّاقَةِ, with fet-h; but ISd says, "I know not how that is:" (TA:) pl. ٭ فِيَقٌ, (S, O, K,) [or rather this is a coll. gen. n. and فَاقَةٌ is its n. un.,] and فِيَقٌ (IB, K) and فِيقَاتٌ (K) and أَفْوَاقٌ, [a pl. of pauc.,] (S, O, K,) or this may be pl. of the pl. فِيَقٌ, (IB, TA,) and أَفَاوِيقُ, (S, O, K,) which is a pl. pl. (O, K) [or pl. of أَفْوَاقٌ]. [See also عُرَاكَةٌ.] — See also above, conj. 2, an ex. of أَفَاوِيق in a tropical sense. — أَفَاوِيقُ also signifies ‡ The *water that has collected in the clouds and then falls in rain*, (S, O, K, TA,) *time after time*. (S, K, TA.) — Also, i. e. أَفَاوِيقُ, ‡ The *greater part* of the night: (Lh, O, K, TA:) so in the saying, خَرَجْنَا بَعْدَ أَفَاوِيقَ مِنَ اللَّيْلِ [*We went forth*] *after the greater part of the night had passed*: (Lh, O:) or, accord. to Th, *after portions* (أَقْطَاع) *of the night*. (TA.) — فِيقَةُ الضُّحَى means ‡ *The period of the* [*early portion of the forenoon called the*] ضحى *when the sun has become high*: (Ibn-'Abbád, O, K, TA:) or, accord. to Z, *the first part of the* ضحى. (TA.)

فَوْقَانِيٌّ [*Of*, or *relating to, the location that is above*, or *over*; *superior*; *upper*;] rel. n. of فَوْقُ, like as تَحْتَانِيٌّ is of تَحْتُ: ا and ن being very often added in the rel. n. (TA in art. تحت.) — And [hence, but more commonly فَوْقَانِيَّةٌ,] *A garment worn by a man over that which is next the body*; [*an upper-coat*; generally *long, reaching to the heels, ample in width, and with long sleeves*: it seems to have been formerly peculiar to men of the learned professions:] of the dial. of Mekkeh: post-classical. (TA. [See Dozy's Dict. des Noms des Vêtements chez les Arabes, p. 343.])

فُوَاقٌ The *returning supply of milk after sucking* or *milking*. (TA.) — See also the next paragraph, in three places.

فُوَاقٌ: see 1, former half, in two places: = and see 1 again, latter half: — and 4, in two places. — Also ‡ The *time between two milkings*; (Ṣ, O, Mṣb, Ḳ;) for the she-camel was milked, and then left a little while for her young one to suck her in order that she might yield her milk copiously, after which she was milked again; (Ṣ, O;) and likewise the *time between two suckings*; (Ksh in xxxviii. 14;) and ↓ فَوَاقٌ signifies the same: (Ṣ, O, Mṣb, Ḳ:) or, (Mṣb, TA,) accord. to IF, (Mṣb,) the فواق of the she-camel is the *returning of the milk into the udder after the milking*: (Mṣb, TA:) or فُوَاقٌ signifies the *time between the opening of one's hand and the grasping with it the udder* (Ḳ, TA) of the camel: or *when the milker grasps the udder and then lets it go, in milking*: (TA:) the pl. is أَفْوِقَةٌ and آفِقَةٌ; (O, Ḳ;) and Fr says that فواق has for its pl. أَفِيقَةٌ, originally أَفْوِقَةٌ, the kesreh of the و being transferred to the ف, and the و being then changed into ى because of the kesreh before it; and أَفْوِقَةٌ has for its pl. أَفْوِقَاتٌ. (TA.) One says, مَا أَقَامَ عِنْدَهُ إِلَّا فُوَاقًا ‡ [*He did not remain at his abode save as long as the time between two milkings*]. (Ṣ, O, TA.) And it is said in a trad., العِيَادَةُ قَدْرُ فُوَاقِ النَّاقَةِ † [The period of *the visiting* of a sick person *is the space of time between the two milkings of the she-camel*]. (Ṣ.) And in a trad. of 'Alee occurs the saying, قَالَ لَهُ الأَسِيرُ أَنْظِرْنِى فُوَاقَ نَاقَةٍ i. e. † [*The captive said to him,*] *Grant thou me a delay*, or *respite, as long as the time between two milkings* [*of a she-camel*]. (TA.) مَا لَهَا مِنْ ↓ فَوَاقٍ and فُوَاقٍ in the Ḳur [xxxviii. 14], accord. to different readings, (Ṣ,) the latter the reading of the Koofees except 'Áṣim, and the former that of the rest, (O,) means † [*There shall not appertain to it*] *any postponement*, or *delay*, and *resting*: (Ṣ:) or, accord. to AO, the latter is the meaning of the former reading; and the latter reading means, *any waiting*, or *expecting*: (TA:) or [both mean] *any pausing as much as the time between two milkings*, (Ksh, Bḍ,) or *two suckings*: (Ksh:) or *any returning*, and *repeating*; (I'Ab, Ksh, Bḍ;) from أَفَاقَ "he (a sick man) returned to a healthy, or sound, state"; and the فواق of the she-camel, when the supply of milk returns to her udder; (Ksh;) or because in it [i. e. the فواق] the milk returns to the udder; (Bḍ;) i. e. the blast [to which the words refer] shall be one only; it shall not be repeated. (Ksh.) The saying (Mgh, O, TA) of the Prophet, (O,) related in a trad., (O, TA,) قَسَمَ غَنَائِمَ خَيْبَرَ عَنْ فُوَاقٍ (Mgh,) or قَسَمَ الغَنَائِمَ يَوْمَ بَدْرٍ عَنْ فَوَاقٍ ↓ (O, TA) and فُوَاقٍ, (TA,) means † *He divided the spoils* [*of Kheyber*, or *on the day of Bedr*,] *in the space of the rest between two milkings* of a she-camel: (TA:) or *quickly*; (Mgh, O;) عن فواق meaning صَادِرًا عَنْ سُرْعَةٍ [i. e. قَسْمًا صَادِرًا عَنْ سُرْعَةٍ *with a dividing proceeding from quickness*]: (Mgh, O:*) or, as some say, the meaning is, *making some* of them [i. e. of those who composed his army] *to be more highly distinguished* (↓ أَفْوَق) *than others* (O, TA*) in the proportion of their spoils and of the trial undergone by them. (TA.) = See also فَاقٌ, last sentence but one.

فَيَاقٌ, mentioned in this art. in the Ḳ: see فَاقٌ, last sentence but one.

فَائِقٌ *Superior, excellent*, or *surpassing*: (Mgh, Mṣb:*) anything *excellent*, or *choice*, (O, Ḳ, TA,) and *pure, in its kind*. (TA.) You say, هُوَ فَائِقٌ فِى العِلْمِ [*He is superior, excellent*, or *surpassing, in knowledge*], and فِى الغِنَى [*in wealth*, &c.]. (Mgh.) And جَارِيَةٌ فَائِقَةٌ [*A young woman excelling* in beauty, or comeliness]. (Mṣb.) And فُوَقَةٌ [an irreg. pl. of فَائِقٌ, like as خَوَنَةٌ is of خَائِنٌ, for by rule these pls. should be فَاقَةٌ and خَانَةٌ,] signifies *Elegant scholars*, and *orators*. (IAạr, O, Ḳ.) = Also The *place of junction of the neck with the head*: (Ṣ, O, Ḳ:) therefore when this is high, the neck is long. (Ṣ, O.)

أَفْوَقُ: see فُوَاقٌ, last sentence but one. = Also An arrow *of which the* فُوق [or *notch*] *is broken*: (Ṣ, O, Mṣb, Ḳ, TA:) [and] an arrow *having no* فُوق: (L voce أَقْذُّ:) pl. فُوقٌ [perhaps a mistranscription for the regular form of pl., i. e. فُوقٌ; or it may be that the و is with fet-ḥ to distinguish it from فُوق signifying "a notch" of an arrow]: but IAạr explains this as signifying arrows *of which the heads have fallen*. (TA.) One says, رَجَعَ فُلَانٌ بِأَفْوَقَ نَاصِلٍ † *Such a one returned with an arrow having a broken notch and without a head upon it*; meaning, *with an incomplete share of good fortune*: (Ṣ, O:) or, *disappointed of attaining what he desired*, or *sought*: a proverb. (TA.) And رَدَدْتُهُ بِأَفْوَقَ نَاصِلٍ † [*I turned him back*, or *away, with a paltry benefit*; or] *I made his share of good fortune to be little*, or *incomplete*. (TA.) And مَا بَلِلْتُ مِنْ فُلَانٍ بِأَفْوَقَ نَاصِلٍ, expl. in the first paragraph of art. بل. — مَحَالَةٌ فَوْقَاءُ [*A large sheave of a pulley*] *of which every* سِنّ [or *tooth*, perhaps meaning *cog*, though I do not remember to have met with any description of a cogged مَحالة,] *has two cusps* (فُوقَانِ), (O, Ḳ,) *like the* فوقان [*of the notch*] *of the arrow*. (O.) [The strangeness of this explanation induces me to think that فَوْقَاءُ is here a mistranscription for فَوْهَاءُ, (see مَحَالَةٌ فَوْهَاءُ, in art. فوه,) and that the explanation is partly conjectural.] — And كَمَرَةٌ فَوْقَاءُ *A glans of a penis whereof the extremity is tapering in form*, (O, Ḳ,) *like that which is termed* حَوْقَاءُ. (O.)

مُفِيقٌ and مُفِيقَةٌ A she-camel *having in her udder the milk that had collected between two milkings*: (AA, Ṣ, O, Ḳ:) pl. مَفَاوِيقُ (Ṣ, O, Ḳ) and مَفَاوِقُ, (Akh, TA,) and ↓ فُيُقٌ also is pl. of مُفِيقٌ signifying as expl. above, mentioned by AA in the third vol. of his "Nawádir," and said by IB to be, accord. to analogy, pl. of فُوُوقٌ, and to be originally فُوُقٌ; but accord. to one relation of a verse in which it occurs, it is ↓ فِيَقٌ, which is more agreeable with analogy. (TA.) = And the former, applied to a poet, is *syn. with* مُفْلِقٌ [i. e. One *who poetizes admirably*, or *wonderfully*.]. (Aboo-Turáb, Ḳ. [But its verb is mentioned in the O and Ḳ in art. فيق.])

مُفَوَّقٌ ‡ Food, and beverage, *that is taken by little and little*. (IAạr, O, Ḳ, TA. [See its verb.]) = Applied to an arrow, [*Having a notch made for the bow-string*. (See 2.) — And] *Having the bow-string put into its notch on the occasion of shooting*: [see 4, last sentence:] — whence the saying, لَا زِلْتَ فِى الخَيْرِ مُوَفَّقًا وَسَهْمُكَ فِى الكَرَمِ مُفَوَّقًا †[*Mayest thou not cease to be rightly disposed in beneficence, and thine arrow made ready with the bow-string put into its notch in generosity*]. (A, TA.)

مُسْتَفِيقٌ A man *who sleeps much*: (O, Ḳ, TA:) mentioned by IAạr; but this is strange.

فول

فُولٌ [*Beans*; or the *bean*; *faba sativa* of Jussieu; *vicia faba* of Linnæus; i. e.] *i. q.* بَاقِلَّى [q. v.]: (T, IF, Ṣ, Mṣb:) or *i. q.* حِمَّص [i. e. *chick-peas*; or the *chick-pea*]: (so in one of my copies of the Ṣ: [in most of the copies of the Ṣ, this word is mentioned at the end of art. فيل; but in the older of my copies, before that art.:]) or *a certain grain*, or *seed*, (حَبّ,) *like the* حِمَّص: but with the people of Syria [and of Egypt], *i. q.* بَاقِلَّى: or (as some say, M) specially the *dry* [*thereof*]: n. un. with ة: (M, Ḳ:) mentioned by Sb. (M.)

فَوَّالٌ *A seller of* فُول. (TA.)

فولاذ

فُولَاذٌ: see art. فلذ.

فوم

2. فَوَّمْتُ الخُبْزَ *I made bread*, or *the bread*. (IJ, M.) [And] فَوِّمُوا لَنَا *Make ye bread for us*: (T, Ṣ:) a phrase said by Fr to have been heard from the Arabs as meaning thus. (T.)

فُومٌ, a word occurring in the Ḳur ii. 58, (T, Ṣ, M, &c.,) is expl. as signifying the same as ثُومٌ [which generally means *Garlic*; but is said to have also the meaning here next following]; (T, Ṣ, M, Mṣb, Ḳ;) said to be a dial. var. of the latter word, but app. [if meaning "garlic"] formed, as IJ says, by the substitution of ف for ث; (M;) and 'Abd-Allah [Ibn-Mes'ood] read [in the Ḳur ubi suprà] وَثُومِهَا [instead of وَفُومِهَا]: (Fr, T, Ṣ:) it is also expl. as signifying *wheat*; (T, Ṣ, M, Mṣb, Ḳ;) which is said by Lḥ to be a meaning of ثُومٌ and فُومٌ; and if Ibn-Mes'ood read the word as ثُوم, the meaning is فُوم, i. e. "wheat;" (T;) accord. to Fr, it is an old word, signifying thus, (T, Ṣ,*) and also *bread*; (T, Ṣ, Ḳ;) Zj says that there is no difference of statement among the lexicologists as to its having the former of these two meanings, that it is said to have the latter also, and that it also signifies the *other grains, beside wheat, whereof bread is made* [which last meaning is also mentioned in the Ḳ]; (T;) and IJ holds that it is rightly expl. as having the first of these three meanings (i. e. "wheat") and the last of them: (M:) another meaning assigned to it is حِمَّصٌ [i. e. *cicer arietinum; or chick-peas*]; (Ṣ, Ḳ;) which is of the dial. of Syria: (Ṣ:) and it signifies also *any* عُقْدَة [app. meaning *head* of a plant, such as that] *of an onion*, or *of a garlic*: or *a great gobbet of food*: (Ḳ: [for أَوْ لُقْمَة عَظِيمَة in the CḲ, I read او لُقْمَةٌ عَظِيمَةٌ as in other copies of the Ḳ:]) in the dial. of Azd-es-Saráh, it is applied to *ears of corn*; and ▼ فُومَةٌ is its n. un.; (M;) this latter signifying *an ear of corn*, (Ṣ, Ḳ, TA,) as expl. by IDrd: (TA:) فُومٌ has فُومَانٌ [of the measure فُعْلَانٌ] for a pl., this being [virtually] a pl. pl.; mentioned by IJ, who says that the ḍammeh in فُوم is different from the ḍammeh in فُومَانٌ. (M, TA.)

فُومَةٌ: see the next preceding paragraph, near the end. —— Also *A thing that one carries between his two fingers.* (Ḳ.)

قَطَّعُوا الشَّاةَ فُومًا فُومًا (M, Ḳ,*) means [*They cut the sheep*, or *goat*,] *into a number of pieces*; (M;) like فُوَمًا. (Ḳ.)

فَامِىٌّ, altered from فُومِىٌّ, *A seller of* فُوم [app. *in any of its senses*, but accord. to the TA as meaning *wheat*, or *chick-peas*]: (Ṣ, Ḳ:) [or] *a seller of fruit*: (MA:) accord. to Az, (TA,) الفَامِىُّ means السُّكَّرِىُّ, (Mgh, TA,) who is called by the vulgar البَيَّاع [generally signifying the *seller*, or *vender*; perhaps here meaning *the seller of sugar*, though I do not anywhere find السُّكَّرِىُّ thus explained]; (Mgh;) but he says, "I do not think it genuine Arabic." (TA.)

فوه

1. فَاهَ بِهِ, (Ṣ, Mṣb, Ḳ,) aor. يَفُوهُ (Ṣ, Mṣb) and يَفِيهُ also, (ISd, TA,) inf. n. فَوْهٌ, (MA,) [and inf. n. of unity فَوْهَةٌ, (see Ḥar p. 434,)] *He uttered it*, or *pronounced it*, (Ṣ, Mṣb, Ḳ,) namely, a saying; (Ṣ;) as also ▼ تفوّه. (Ṣ, Ḳ.) One says, مَا فُهْتُ بِكَلِمَةٍ, and ▼ مَا تَفَوَّهْتُ, i. e. *I opened not my mouth with a word*, or *sentence.* (Ṣ.) فَاهَ لِسَانٌ, a phrase used by El-Ḥareeree, the Arabs did not say: they only said, فاه الرَّجُلُ بِكَذَا [*The man opened his mouth with such a thing*, i. e., with such a saying, &c.]. (Ḥar p. 191.) And هٰذَا أَمْرٌ مَا فُهْتُ عَنْهُ, inf. n. فووه [or فُؤُوهٌ ?], is a saying mentioned by Fr, as meaning *This is a thing*, or *an affair, which I mentioned not*, or *have not mentioned.* (TA.) —— See also 2. ═ فَوِهَ, aor. يَفْوَهُ, [inf. n. فَوَهٌ,] *He* (a man) *had what is termed* ▼ فَوَه, (Ṣ, TA,) which means *width of the mouth*, (Ṣ, Ḳ, TA,) *and largeness thereof*: (TA:) or *protrusion and length of the upper central incisors*: (Ṣ, TA:) or *length of all the teeth*; length of the upper central incisors being termed رَوَقٌ: (IB, TA:) or *protrusion of the teeth from the lips, with length thereof.* (Ḳ, TA.)

2. فَوَّهَهُ *He* (i. e. God) *made him to be* أَفْوَه [or *wide in the mouth*, &c.]. (Ṣ, Ḳ.) —— شَدَّ مَا فَوَّهْتَ فِى هٰذَا الطَّعَامِ, [thus accord. to the TA, but an explanation of مُفَوَّه seems to show that the right reading is فُوِّهْتَ, in the pass. form,] and ▼ تَفَوَّهْتَ, and ▼ فُهْتَ, means شَدَّ مَا أَكَلْتَ [app. *Much indeed*, or *greatly indeed, didst thou eat*, or *hast thou eaten, of this food*: see شَدَّ: and see also 10]. (TA.)

3. فاوهه, (Ḳ, TA,) inf. n. مُفَاوَهَةٌ; (TA;) and فَاهَاهُ, [formed from the former by transposition,] (Ḳ, TA,) inf. n. مُفَاهَاةٌ; (TA;) *He talked*, or *discoursed, with him*: [see also 6:] and *he contended with him for superiority in glory*, or *excellence.* (Ḳ, TA.)

5. تفوّه *He spoke.* (KL.) See also 1, first and second sentences. —— And see 2. ═ تفوّه المَكَانَ †*He entered the* فُوهَة *of the place*; (Ḳ, TA;) i. e., *the mouth thereof*; likened to the فم [properly thus called] as being *the first place of ingress to the interior thereof.* (TA.)

6. تفاوهوا *They talked* [app. *one to another*: see 3]. (Ḳ.)

10. استفاه, (Ṣ, Ḳ,) inf. n. اِسْتِفَاهَةٌ and اِسْتِفَاهٌ, (Ḳ,) the latter mentioned by Lḥ, (TA,) *He* (a man, Ṣ) *ate*, (Ṣ, Ḳ,) or *drank*, (Ḳ,) *vehemently, after scantiness*, (Ṣ, Ḳ,) or *after weakness*; (so in a copy of the Ṣ;) but seldom used in relation to drinking: or you say, استفاه فِى الطَّعَامِ, meaning *he ate much of the food*: so says IAạr, not particularizing the act as being after scarcity or not. (TA.) [See also 2.] —— And *He quenched his thirst by drinking.* (Ḳ.)

فَاهٌ: see what next follows: and see the next paragraph again, in the latter half: ═ and the same word, and فَاهٍ, (the latter in two places,) see voce فَاوُوهَةٌ.

فُوهٌ and ▼ فَاهٌ and ▼ فِيهٌ (Ḳ, TA) and, accord. to the copies of the Ḳ, فُوهَةٌ, [or, as in the CḲ, فَوْهَة,] but correctly ▼ فُوَّهَةٌ, (TA,) and فَمٌ, all signify the same [i. e. The *mouth*]: (Ḳ, TA:) the pl. is أَفْوَاهٌ, (Ṣ, Ḳ, TA,) pl. of فُوهٌ, (Ṣ, TA,) and as such its case is plain; as pl. of فِيهٌ, it is like أَرْوَاحٌ as pl. of رِيحٌ; as pl of فَاهٌ, it is allowable as having و for its original medial radical; but as pl. of فُوَّهَة, it is anomalous: (TA:) and another pl. is أَفْمَامٌ, (Ḳ, TA,) said by some to be pl. of فُمٌّ or فَمٌّ, with teshdeed, of which an ex. occurs in a verse cited in the first paragraph of art. فم; but some disallow this pl.; and accord. to some, (TA,) it has no sing. (Ḳ, TA) agreeable with rule, (TA,) for فَمٌ is originally فَوَهٌ, (Ḳ, TA,) with the و movent by fet-ḥ, or [فَوْهٌ, as in some copies of the Ṣ,] with the و quiescent, on the authority of IJ; (TA;) the ه is elided, and the و becomes a movent final, therefore it must be changed into ا, because of the fet-ḥah preceding it, so the word becomes فا; but a noun may not be of two letters whereof one is [the ن of] the tenween, (Ḳ, TA,) thus the passage is expressed in the M, but MF remarks that correctly we should say whereof one is the ا, (TA,) and therefore a hard letter is substituted for it, one similar to it in kind, which is م, for they are both labials, and in the م is a sort of humming sound (هُوِىٌّ, in the CḲ هَوِىٌّ,) in the mouth, [or rather in the nose,] resembling [the sound of] the prolongation of the و: (Ḳ, TA:) [several similar disquisitions, added in the TA, respecting the change from فوه to فم, I omit, regarding them as needless: what is said on this subject in the Ṣ, in art. فم, I have mentioned in that art.:] in the present art., J says that the م of فم is a substitute for the ه, not for the و, of فوه; but this is a mistake: (IB, TA:) the dual of فَمٌ is فَمَانِ and فَمَوَانِ (IAạr, Ṣ, Mṣb, Ḳ) and فَمَيَانِ, the second and third of which are anomalous: (IAạr, Ḳ:) of the second, which occurs in a verse of El-Farezdaḳ, [and respecting which see the first paragraph of art. فم,] Sb says that it is used by poetic license. (TA.) In using it as a prefixed noun, in the phrase هٰذَا فُوهُهُ, they deemed the combination of the two هs difficult in respect of utterance; therefore they suppressed the [radical] ه thereof [in this case, and then in other, similar, cases], and said, هٰذَا فُوهُ, and فُو زَيْدٍ, and رَأَيْتُ فَا زَيْدٍ, and مَرَرْتُ بِفِى زَيْدٍ: and when prefixing it to [the pronoun denoting] thyself, thou sayest, هٰذَا فِىَّ; and this thou dost alike in using it in the nom. case and in the accus. and in the gen., because the و [of فُو] is changed into ى and is then incorporated [into the pronominal ى]: (Ṣ, and the like is said in the Mṣb:) and sometimes, though rarely, they did the like in other cases, when not prefixing it; for instance, فَا occurs at the end of a verse of El-'Ajjáj, without an affix, in this case for فَاهَا. (Ṣ.) —— In the saying كَلَّمْتُهُ فَاهُ إِلَى فِىَّ, meaning *I spoke to him, his mouth being near to my mouth*, فاه is in the accus. case as a denotative of state: (Ṣ, TA:*) or by reason of the derivative [مُكَلِّمًا] meant to be understood: or, as Sb says, it is an instance of one of the nouns that are put in the place of inf. ns., and it is not to be separated from what should follow it, so that you may not say كَلَّمْتُهُ فَاهُ [alone], for you tell of your nearness to the person, and that there is not any one between you and him: and if you will, you may use the nom. case, meaning وَهٰذِهِ حَالُهُ [*this being his state*], (Sb, TA,) i. e. فُوهُ إِلَى فِىَّ [*his mouth was near to my mouth*], the clause [following كلّمته] occupying the place of a denotative of state. (TA.) —— The saying فَاهَا لِفِيكَ, (Meyd, Ḳ, TA,) which is a prov., (Meyd, TA,) means *May God make the mouth of misfortune to cleave to thy mouth*; (Meyd, Ḳ,* TA;) [but lit. signifies, only, *her*, or *its, mouth* *to thy mouth;* and is [likewise] an instance of one of the nouns that are used in the manner of inf. ns. expressive of imprecation, by reason of a verb not mentioned: Sb says, فاها is without tenween, meaning فَا الدَّاهِيَةِ, as is shown by the saying,

* وَدَاهِيَةٍ مِنْ دَوَاهِى المَنُو
* نِ يَرْهَبُهَا النَّاسُ لَا فَا لَهَا

[*Many a misfortune is there, of the misfortunes of time, which men fear, that has no mouth,* wherewith to bite]: (Sb, TA:) A'Obeyd says that its primary meaning is, *may God make the ground to be in thy mouth;* that it is like the sayings بِفِيكَ الأَثْلَبُ and بِفِيكَ الحَجَرُ; (Ṣ, Meyd;) and [hence] it means *disappointment* [cleave] *to thee:* (Ṣ,* Meyd:) a man of Belhujeym, (Ṣ, Meyd,) cited by A'Obeyd, (Ṣ,) addressing a wolf that sought to get his she-camel, (Meyd,) says,

* فَقُلْتُ لَهُ فَاهَا لِفِيكَ فَإِنَّهَا
* قَلُوصُ آمْرِئٍ قَارِيكَ مَا أَنْتَ حَاذِرُهْ

[*And I said to him,* فاها لفيك, *for she is the youthful she-camel of a man who will give thee as a guest's entertainment that which thou fearest*]; (Ṣ, Meyd; but in the Ṣ, as IB has observed, فَإِنَّهُ is erroneously put for فَإِنَّهَا;) i. e. [who will entertain thee with] the shooting of arrows; (Meyd;) [by قَارِيكَ] he means يَقْرِيكَ, from قِرَى الضَّيْفِ: (Ṣ:) it is also said that فَاهَا is metonymically used as meaning the dust of the earth, which is termed the mouth of the earth because it drinks the water; and it is as though the saying meant *the dust be in thy mouth:* (Meyd:) Sh is related to have said, I heard IAạr say فَاهًا ▾ لِفِيكَ, with tenween, meaning *may God make thy mouth to cleave to the ground;* [or rather, *ground to thy mouth;* lit., simply, *a mouth to thy mouth;*] and some say فَاهَا لِفِيكَ, without tenween, as an imprecation meaning ↕ *may God break thy* فم [i. e. thy *teeth,* to which فم is often metonymically applied, as is also فوه]. (TA.) — One says also, سَقَى فُلَانٌ إِبِلَهُ عَلَى أَفْوَاهِهَا, meaning ↕ *Such a one drew for his camels the water when they came to it, while they were drinking;* not having stored it for them in the drinking-trough: and جَرَّ فُلَانٌ إِبِلَهُ عَلَى أَفْوَاهِهَا ↕ *Such a one suffered his camels to pasture while going along* [*by his driving them gently:* see art. جر]: so says Aṣ: and so accord. to the A and other lexicons; but the author of the Ḳ, by an omission, has assigned the latter explanation to the former phrase. (TA.) — لَوْ وَجَدْتُ إِلَيْهِ فَا كَرِشٍ, meaning أَدْنَى طَرِيقٍ, (Ḳ, TA,) has [with other, similar, phrases] been explained in art. كرش [q. v.]. (TA.) — فُو فَرَسٍ حَمِرٍ [*Mouth of a horse that is suffering indigestion in consequence of his having eaten barley and so made it to stink*] is an appellation applied to him who has stinking breath. (TA. [An ex. of it occurs in a verse of Imra-el-Ḳeys cited in the TA in art. حمر as in Ahlwardt's "Divans of the Six Ancient Arabic Poets," p. 125; and differently in De Slane's "Diwan d'Amro-'lkaïs," p. 36 of the Arabic text.]) — And فُو جُرَذٍ [*Mouth of a large field-rat*] and فُو دَبًا [*Mouth of a sort of small wingless locust,* or perhaps correctly فُو دَبَاةٍ *mouth of a small wingless locust,*] are nicknames applied to a little man. (TA.) — One says also, لَا فُضَّ فُوهُ, meaning ↕ *May his teeth,* or *front teeth, not be broken.* (Ḳ,* TA.) And سَقَطَ فُوهُ † *His teeth fell out.* (TA in art. فض [q. v.]) — And مَاتَ لِفِيهِ i. e. لِوَجْهِهِ [meaning ↕ *He died upon his face; prone:* like سَقَطَ لِوَجْهِهِ † *He fell upon his face:* the ل in both being used in the sense of عَلَى; as it is in the phrase خَرُّوا لِأَذْقَانِهِمْ (expl. in art. خر), &c.]. (A, Ḳ, TA. [The explanation in the TḲ, being somewhat ambiguous (though correct), has misled Freytag in this case.]) And [in like manner, using لِ in the sense of عَلَى,] كَبَّهُ ٱللّٰهُ لِفِيهِ, one of their forms of imprecation, meaning † *May God cause him to die:* or *prostrate him* [*upon his face;* as also كَبَّهُ لِوَجْهِهِ]. (TA.) — [See also فُوهَةٌ as syn. with فُوهٌ; like which it has أَفْوَاهٌ for a pl.] ═ فُوهٌ also, having for its pl. أَفْوَاهٌ, and pl. pl. أَفَاوِيهُ, (Ṣ, Mgh, Mṣb, Ḳ,) [which last is of very frequent occurrence,] signifies *Perfume,* or *an odoriferous substance:* (Mgh, Mṣb:) or *a thing,* or *substance, with which a perfume,* or *an odoriferous substance, is compounded* or *prepared* (يُعَالَجُ); like as تَوَابِلُ signifies things, or substances, with which sorts of food are compounded or prepared: (Ṣ, Mgh:) or *the* تَوَابِل [or *seeds used in cooking*] *with which food is compounded* or *prepared* (يُعَالَجُ) are also called أَفْوَاهُ الطِّيبِ: (Mṣb:) [the pl. and pl. pl. are now generally applied to *spices,* or *aromatics:*] or الأَفْوَاهُ, the pl. mentioned above, signifies [the seeds called] التَّوَابِلُ: and also *what diffuse fragrance* [I read نَوَافِح, as in my MS. copy of the Ḳ, pl. of نَافِحٌ, q. v., instead of نَوَافِج (with جيم), the only reading that I find in other copies of the Ḳ, regarding the latter as indubitably a mistranscription,] *of perfumes,* or *odoriferous substances:* (Ḳ:) and *the sorts,* or *species,* of flowers; (Ḳ, TA;) thus says AḤn; and in one place he says that الافواه signifies *what are prepared for perfume, of sweet-smelling flowers;* and sometimes they are of herbs, or leguminous plants: (TA:) and also *sorts,* or *species,* of a thing [app. of any kind]: (Ḳ:) and one says, هُوَ مِنْ أَفْوَاهِ الطيب, and أَفْوَاهِ البُقُولِ, meaning *It is of the sorts,* or *species,* and *of the mixtures,* or *compounds, of perfume,* and *of herbs,* or *leguminous plants:* (Mgh:) but فُوه is not applied to anything that is termed عَقَّار. (AHeyth, TA in art. عقر.)

فَوَهٌ: see 1, last sentence. — Also The *quality of a* مَحَالَة [or *large sheave of a pulley*] *such as is termed* فَوْهَاءُ, fem. of أَفْوَهُ, q. v. (TA.)

فِيهٌ: see its syn. فُوهٌ.

فُوهَةٌ: see فُوَّهَةٌ, in five places.

فُوَّهٌ *Certain slender, long, red roots, with which one dyes; beneficial for the liver and the spleen and the* نَسَا [app. as meaning *sciatica* or the *sciatic nerve*] *and pain of the hip and of the flank, powerfully diuretic, and kneaded with vinegar and applied as a liniment it cures the* [*leprosy termed*] بَرَص: (Ḳ, TA:) but the word was not known to Az in this sense, [which is the only meaning, except one which I think doubtful, that I find assigned to it;] and it is said to be the فُوَّة [which see in art. فو, i. e. *madder*]. (TA.) ═ See also فُوَّهَةٌ.

فَيِّهٌ, originally فَيْوِهٌ: see مُفَوَّهٌ.

فُوَّهَةٌ: see its syn. فُوهٌ. — [Hence] it signifies also ↕ The فم [i. e. *mouth*] of a place; likened to the فم [properly so called] as being the *first place of ingress,* or *entrance, to the interior:* (TA:) [and so too as being the *place of egress,* or *exit, from the interior:*] it is of a river, or rivulet, (Lth, Ṣ, Mṣb, TA,) and of a valley, or water-course, or torrent-bed, (Ḳ, TA,) and of a street, and of a road; (Ṣ, Mṣb, Ḳ, TA;) signifying the فم [or *mouth*]; as also ▾ فُوهَةٌ, (Ḳ, TA,) without teshdeed; mentioned by IAạr: (TA:) or it signifies thus in relation to a river, or rivulet; (Lth, Mṣb, TA;) the *foremost part* thereof: or, as some say, the *place of* its *pouring into the* كِظَامَة [q. v.]: and accord. to Lth, in relation to a valley, or water-course, or torrent-bed, its رَأْس [or *head,* as though in this case having one, or each, of two contr. meanings, unless, as I believe it to be, the mouth, or outlet, of a valley or water-course or torrent-bed be sometimes called its رأس as being its *foremost part*]: (TA:) and of a street, it is the *place of egress,* or *exit;* (Mṣb;) the *foremost part* thereof: (TA:) and of a road, it is the فم [or *mouth*], which is the *upper part* thereof (اعلاه): (Mṣb: [thus in my copy; but I think that اعلاه is a mistranscription, in my copy, for أَوَّلُهُ, and that the correct meaning is therefore the *foremost part* thereof, agreeably with what is said above in relation to a road and to a river or rivulet:]) but accord. to some, ▾ فُوهَةٌ, without teshdeed, is not allowable; and one should say, قَعَدَ عَلَى فُوَّهَةِ الطَّرِيقِ, and ▾ فُوهِهِ [probably, I think, a mistranscription for فُوهِهِ, with the و quiescent, both meaning *He sat at the mouth of the road*]; not ▾ فُوهَتِهِ, without teshdeed: (TA:) and فُوَّهَةٌ signifies also † the *first,* or *foremost, part,* of a thing; (Ḳ, TA;) like that of the street and that of the river or rivulet: [whence] one says, طَلَعَ عَلَيْنَا فُوَّهَةُ إِبِلِكَ i. e. ↕ *The first,* or *foremost, portion of thy camels* [*came to us,* or *came forth upon us*]; like the phrase فُوَّهَةُ الطَّرِيقِ: (TA:) the pl. of فُوَّهَةٌ is أَفْوَاهٌ, (Ks, Ṣ, Mṣb, TA,) which is anomalous, (Ṣ, Mṣb, TA,) and (TA) فَوَاهٌ [in the CḲ فُوهَاتٌ] and فَوَائِهُ. (Ḳ, TA.) [Hence] one says, دَخَلُوا فِى أَفْوَاهِ البَلَدِ وَخَرَجُوا مِنْ أَرْجُلِهِ, (A, Ḳ,* TA,) in the copies of the Ḳ أَرْجُلِهَا, which is wrong, (TA,) i. e. ↕ *They entered into the foremost parts of the country,* or *town,* *and went forth from the hindermost parts thereof:* (A, Ḳ, TA:) the sing. of أَفْوَاهٌ as here used is فُوَّهَةٌ. (TA.) —— It signifies also *A say,* or *saying,* or *speech;* (Ṣ, Ḳ, TA;) from 1 in the first of the senses assigned to it above: hence one says, إِنَّ رَدَّ الفُوَّهَةِ لَشَدِيدٌ (Ṣ, TA) *Verily the retracting of that which has been said is difficult:* (Ḥar p. 434:) and [hence] one says also, هُوَ يَخَافُ فُوَّهَةَ النَّاسِ [*He fears the say,* or *speech, of men*]. (TA.) —— And The Muslims' *rending one another's reputation by evil speech,* or *by backbiting;* (Ḳ, TA;) as also ↓ فُوهَةٌ. (TA.) —— إِنَّهُ لَذُو فُوَّهَةٍ means *Verily he is strong in speech, and free,* or *unconstrained, in tongue.* (TA.) —— And one says, مَا أَشَدَّ فُوَّهَةَ بَعِيرِكَ فِى هٰذَا الكَلَإِ, meaning [*How vehement is*] *thy camel's eating* [*of this herbage*]! and in like manner, فُوَّهَةَ فَرَسِكَ [*the vehement eating of thy horse*]: whence their saying أَفْوَاهُهَا مَجَاسُّهَا [which may be well rendered as it has been in art. جس, q. v.], meaning *Their good eating shows thee their fatness, causing thee to be in no need of feeling them to test their condition.* (TA.) —— And *Milk, as long as there remains in it the taste of sweetness;* (Ḳ,* TA;) as also ↓ فُوهَةٌ; and sometimes correctly said with ق, i. e. [قُوهَةٌ,] without teshdeed. (TA.)

فَاوُوهَةٌ A man *who reveals,* or *discloses, everything that is in his mind;* as also ↓ فَاهٍ, (Fr, Ṣ, TA, [but omitted in one of my copies of the Ṣ,]) and ↓ فَاهٌ: (Fr, TA:) and ↓ فَاهٍ بِجُوعِهِ one *who reveals his hunger;* originally فَائِهٌ, like as they said هَارٍ and هَائِرٌ. (TA.)

أَفْوَهُ *Having what is termed* فَوَهٌ, meaning as expl. in the last sentence of the first paragraph [i. e. *width of the mouth,* &c.]; fem. فَوْهَآءُ; (Ṣ, Ḳ, TA;) the former applied to a man, and the latter to a woman; (Ṣ, TA;) and in like manner to horses. (TA.) فَوْهَآءُ شَوْهَآءُ, applied to a woman, means *Wide-mouthed, ugly:* and, applied to a mare, *wide-mouthed, long-headed:* or *sharp in spirit.* (TA.) —— [Hence,] بِئْرٌ فَوْهَآءُ *A wide-mouthed well.* (Ḳ.) —— And طَعْنَةٌ فَوْهَآءُ *A wide wound made by piercing.* (Ḳ.) —— And مَحَالَةٌ فَوْهَآءُ [*A large sheave of a pulley*] (Ṣ, Ḳ, TA) *that is wide* (Ḳ, TA) *and* (TA) *whereof the teeth between which runs the well-rope are long.* (Ṣ, TA.) [See also مَحَالَةٌ فَوْقَآءُ, in art. فوق.]

مُفَوَّهٌ and ↓ فَيِّهٌ, (Ṣ, Ḳ,) the latter originally فَيْوِهٌ, (Ṣ,) *Eloquent;* (Ṣ, Ḳ, TA;) and so فَيِّهَةٌ applied to a woman; (Ṣ, TA;) *able in speech; an able speaker:* or فَيِّهٌ signifies *good in speech; a good speaker:* (TA:) or both signify *good and eloquent in speech;* as though taken from الفَوَهُ meaning "width of the mouth:" (IAạr, TA:) or *having an inordinate desire,* or *appetite, for food; a vehement eater;* (Ḳ, TA;) applied to a man and to other than man: (TA:) and the latter (فَيِّهٌ), *having an inordinate and insatiable desire,* or *appetite, for food:* (TA:) and this also signifies a man *who eats much;* syn. أَكُولٌ; (Ṣ, Ḳ;) and so does ↓ مُسْتَفِيهٌ: (Ḳ [in some copies of which, كوفى is strangely put in the place of اكول in the explanation here given]:) or ↓ مُسْتَفِيهٌ signifies a man *eating vehemently after scantiness,* (Ṣ,) or *after weakness:* (thus in a copy of the Ṣ:) and مُفَوَّهٌ is also expl. as meaning a man *who eats vehemently.* (TA.) And one says مِنْطِيقٌ مُفَوَّهٌ (Ḳ, TA) meaning [*Very*] *eloquent in speech:* (TA:) and مَنْطِقٌ مُفَوَّهٌ (Ḳ, TA) *Good,* or *excellent, speech,* or *diction.* (TA.) —— شَرَابٌ مُفَوَّهٌ means [*Beverage,* or *wine,*] *perfumed* (Ḳ, TA) *with* [*the odoriferous substances called*] أَفَاوِيهُ [pl. pl. of فُوهٌ, q. v.]. (TA.) —— And ثَوْبٌ مُفَوَّهٌ (Lth, Ḳ) and مُفَوًّى (Ḳ) *A garment,* or *piece of cloth, dyed with* فُوهٌ [or فُوَّةٌ, i. e. *madder*]. (Lth, Ḳ.)

مُسْتَفِيهٌ: see the next preceding paragraph, in two places.

فى

فِى is a particle governing the gen. case [and used in the manners and senses expl. in what here follows]. (T, Ṣ, M, Mughnee, Ḳ.) —— It relates to a receptacle; (Sb, Ṣ, M;) and, when used in a wider sense, to that which has some near resemblance thereto; (Sb, M;) [i. e.,] and also to what is considered as a receptacle: (Ṣ:) [in other words,] it denotes inclusion, or inbeing, (Mṣb, Mughnee, Ḳ, TA,) either in relation to place or in relation to time; (Mughnee, Ḳ, TA;) properly and tropically. (Mṣb, Mughnee, TA.) غُلِبَتِ الرُّومُ فِى أَدْنَى الأَرْضِ وَهُمْ مِنْ بَعْدِ غَلَبِهِمْ سَيَغْلِبُونَ فِى بِضْعِ سِنِينَ [*The Greeks have been overcome in the nearer,* or *nearest, part of the land, and they, after the overcoming of them, shall overcome in some few years*], in the Ḳur [xxx. 1—3], is an ex. of its relation to place and to time. (Mughnee.) And وَلَكُمْ فِى القِصَاصِ حَيٰوةٌ ‡ [*And there is, to you, in retaliation, life,* or *an advantage,* (respecting the meaning of which see art. حى,) in the Ḳur ii. 175,] is an ex. of its being used tropically. (Mughnee.) أَدْخَلْتُ الخَاتَمَ فِى أُصْبُعِى is an ex. of its relation to place, but the proposition is inverted [i. e. the meaning is *I inserted my finger into the signet-ring*]. (Mughnee.) [Using it properly,] you say, المَآءُ فِى الإِنَآءِ [*The water is in the vessel*]: (Ṣ:) and هُوَ فِى الجِرَابِ [*It is in the wallet,*] and فِى الكِيسِ [*in the purse*]: and هُوَ فِى بَطْنِ أُمِّهِ [*He is in the belly of his mother*]: and هُوَ فِى الغُلِّ [*He is in the shackle for the neck*]: (M:) and زَيْدٌ فِى الدَّارِ [*Zeyd is in the house*], (Ṣ, M,* Mṣb,) or *within the house,* and *in the midst of it,* for فِى الدَّارِ means دَاخِلَهَا, and وَسْطَهَا: (T:) and [using it tropically, you say,] الشَّكُّ فِى الخَبَرِ † [*Doubt,* or *uncertainty, is in the information*]. (Ṣ.) The saying فِيهِ عَيْبٌ [*In him is a fault,* or *blemish*], if relating to a real عَيْب, is proper; and if relating to an ideal عَيْب, tropical: the former is such as the amputation of the hand of the thief, and the redundance of a hand; and the latter, such as the running-away of a slave. (Mṣb.) [When relating to time, it may in some cases be rendered *In,* or *during;* as in the phrase فِى أَيَّامٍ مَعْدُودَاتٍ, in the Ḳur ii. 139, i. e. *In,* or *during,* certain *numbered days.* إِنَّ أَصْحَابَ الجَنَّةِ اليَوْمَ فِى شُغُلٍ فَاكِهُونَ, in the Ḳur xxxvi. 55, may be rendered † *Verily the inmates of Paradise this day shall be in the midst of diverting occupation, cheerful,* or *happy.* The phrase أَمَّا قَوْلُهُ كَذَا فَفِيهِ مَا فِيهِ, lit. † *As to his saying thus, in it is what is in it,* is used as a polite expression of objection, or contradiction; like فِيهِ تَأَمُّلٌ, q. v. In many instances, فِى may be rendered *Of,* or *concerning,* or *in respect of;* as in قَالَ فِيهِ كَذَا † *He said of,* or *concerning, him,* or *it, thus;* for قَالَ فِى ذِكْرِهِ كَذَا † *He said in mentioning him,* or *it, thus;* or فِى وَصْفِهِ *in describing him,* or *it;* or the like: hence, for ex., one says كَتَبَ كِتَابًا فِى عِلْمِ اللُّغَةِ † *He wrote a book of,* or *concerning, the science of lexicology:* and hence, in the Ḳur ii. 133, أَتُحَاجُّونَنَا فِى اللّٰهِ † *Do ye argue with us concerning,* or *in respect of, God?*] —— It also denotes concomitance, (Mughnee, Ḳ,) and (Ḳ) in this case (Mughnee) it is syn. with مَعَ. (Mṣb, Mughnee, Ḳ.) Thus in the phrase, قَالَ ادْخُلُوا فِى أُمَمٍ [*He shall say, Enter ye with peoples*], (Mṣb, Mughnee, TA,) in the Ḳur [vii. 36]: (Mṣb, TA:) or, as some say, the meaning is, فِى جَمَاعَةِ أُمَمٍ [*in the company of peoples*]. (Mughnee.) Thus, too, in the phrase, in the Ḳur [xlvi. 15], فِى أَصْحَابِ الجَنَّةِ [*With the inmates of Paradise*]. (Mṣb, TA.) [Or in these and similar instances, فِى may be rendered, more agreeably with the primary signification, as meaning *Among.*] In the Ḳ, the meaning as denoting concomitance and that which is identical with مَعَ are made distinct: and it has been said that بِ denotes the continuance of concomitance and مَعَ denotes its commencement; though this is not invariably the case. (MF, TA.) [Hence it is used to denote a combination of two qualities: as in the phrase طُولٌ فِى اسْتِرْخَآءٍ † *Length together with laxness:* (occurring in the Ḳ voce طَنَبٌ:) and سَوَادٌ فِى حُمْرَةٍ † *Blackness blending with redness:* and the like. And in like manner it is used to denote the combination of the length and breadth of a thing: as in the phrase طُولُهُ عِشْرُونَ ذِرَاعًا فِى ثَلَاثِ أَذْرُعٍ عَرْضًا *Its length is twenty cubits with* (or as we say *by*) *three cubits in breadth:* in which case the number of square cubits is expressed by the phrase عِشْرُونَ فِى ثَلَاثٍ, as though meaning *Twenty* as a multiplicand *with three* as its multiplier; i. e. *twenty multiplied by three:* see ضَرَبَ as signifying "he multiplied."]. —— It also denotes the assigning of a cause. (Mṣb, Mughnee, Ḳ.) Thus in the phrase فِى أَرْبَعِينَ شَاةً i. e. *On account,* or *because, of* completing [the possession of] *forty sheep* or *goats,* [the giving of] *a sheep or goat* [for the poor-rate] is incumbent [on the possessor: or this may be rendered, *in the case of* the possession *of forty, a sheep or goat* is to be given]. (Msb.) And thus in the saying, [in the Ḳur xii. 32,] فَذٰلِكُنَّ ٱلَّذِى لُمْتُنَّنِى فِيهِ [*And that is he because of whom ye blamed me*]. (Mughnee.) Thus also in the saying, in a trad., إِنَّ ٱمْرَأَةً دَخَلَتِ ٱلنَّارَ فِى هِرَّةٍ حَبَسَتْهَا [*Verily a woman entered the fire* of Hell *because of a she-cat which she confined* without food]. (Mughnee.) [And thus in the phrase أَسْلَفَ فِى كَذَا *He paid in advance*, or *beforehand, for*, or *on account of, such a thing.*] — It also denotes superiority; (Mughnee, Ḳ, TA;) i. e. (TA) it is used in the sense of عَلَى. (T, Ṣ, M, Msb, TA.) Thus in the saying, in the Ḳur [xx. 74], وَلَأُصَلِّبَنَّكُمْ فِى جُذُوعِ ٱلنَّخْلِ [*And I will assuredly crucify you upon the trunks of palm-trees*]. (T, Ṣ, Msb, Mughnee, TA.) And so in the verse of 'Antarah cited voce سَرْح. (T, M, Mughnee, TA.) And Yoo asserts that the Arabs say, نَزَلْتُ فِى أَبِيكَ, meaning عَلَيْهِ [i. e. *I alighted*, or *descended and stopped*, &c., *at the abode of thy father*]. (Ṣ.) — It is also *syn. with* بِ, (T, Ṣ, M, Mughnee, Ḳ,) sometimes. (Ṣ.) Thus in the saying of Zeyd-el-Kheyl,

• وَيَرْكَبُ يَوْمَ ٱلرَّوْعِ فِيهَا فَوَارِسٌ •
• بَصِيرُونَ فِى طَعْنِ ٱلْأَبَاهِرِ وَٱلْكُلَى •

(Ṣ, Mughnee, TA,) meaning, بطعن الاباهر والكلى [i. e. *And horsemen skilful in piercing the aortas and the kidneys ride in the day of fear therein*]. (Ṣ, TA.) And thus in a verse cited by Fr, أَرْغَبُ is made trans. by فِى and عَنْ instead of بِ and عَنْ. (T, TA.) [Thus, also, لَيْسَ فِى شَىْءٍ is sometimes used for لَيْسَ بِشَىْءٍ, meaning *It is nought; or not of any account or weight*; &c.: see more in art. شيأ.] — It is also *syn. with* إِلَى. (Mughnee, Ḳ.) Thus in the Ḳur [xiv. 10], فَرَدُّوا أَيْدِيَهُمْ فِى أَفْوَاهِهِمْ [*And they put their hands to their mouths*]. (Mughnee, TA.) — It is also *syn. with* مِنْ. (M, Mughnee, Ḳ, TA.) Thus in the Ḳur [xxvii. 12], فِى تِسْعِ آيَاتٍ [*Of*, or *among, nine signs*]. (M, TA.) And in the saying, خُذْ لِى عَشْرًا مِنَ ٱلْإِبِلِ فِيهَا فَحْلَانِ [*Take thou for me ten of the camels; of*, or *among, them let there be two stallions*. (M, TA.) [Thus too in the saying هُوَ فِى أَصْلِ قَوْمِهِ *He is of*, or *among, the purest in race*, &c., *of his people*: and the like thereof.] — It also denotes comparison; and this is when it occurs between a preceding [mention of a] thing excelled and a following [mention of a] thing excelling: as in the saying, [in the Ḳur ix. 38,] فَمَا مَتَاعُ ٱلْحَيٰوةِ ٱلدُّنْيَا فِى ٱلْآخِرَةِ إِلَّا قَلِيلٌ [*But the enjoyment of the present life, in comparison with that which is to come, is no other than little*]. (Mughnee, Ḳ.) — It is also used for compensation; and this is when it is redundant as a compensation for another [فِى] which is suppressed: as in the saying, ضَرَبْتُ فِيمَنْ رَغِبْتَ for ضَرَبْتُ مَنْ رَغِبْتَ فِيهِ [*I beat*, or *struck, him whom thou desiredst*]: (Mughnee, Ḳ:) but this is allowed by Ibn-Málik alone. (Mughnee.) — And it is used for corroboration: (Mughnee, Ḳ:) this is when it is redundant without its being for compensation: and this El-Fárisee allows in a case of necessity in verse; citing as an ex.,

• أَنَا أَبُو سَعْدٍ إِذَا ٱللَّيْلُ دَجَا •
• تَخَالُ فِى سَوَادِهِ يَرَنْدَجَا •

[*I am Aboo-Saad; when the night becomes dark, thou imagining its blackness to be black leather*]. (Mughnee.) And it is thus used in the saying, in the Ḳur [xi. 43], وَقَالَ ٱرْكَبُوا فِيهَا [for ٱرْكَبُوهَا, i. e. *And he said, Embark ye therein*, the like of which occurs also in xviii. 70 and xxix. 65], (Mughnee, Ḳ,) accord. to some. (Mughnee.) — فِى as a prefixed noun in the gen. case, *syn. with* فَمِ, and فِىَّ as *syn. with* فَمِى, see voce فُوهٌ, in art. فوه.

فَىَّ is a word expressive of wonder: they say, يَا فَىَّ مَا لِى أَفْعَلُ كَذَا [*O my wonder! What has happened to me* that *I do thus?*]: or it is expressive of regret on account of a thing that is passing away [so that this exclamation may be rendered *Oh! What has happened to me* &c.]: Ks says that it is not to be written with ء [though it is so written in several of the lexicons in art. فيأ, i. e. فَىْءَ]; and that it means يَا عَجَبِى [as first expl. above]: and in like manner one says, يَا فَىَّ مَا أَصْحَابُكَ [*O my wonder! What are thy companions?* i. e. *what manner of men are thy companions?* ما here denoting interrogation respecting qualities, or attributes; as in the Ḳur xxvi. 22]: and he says that ما in this case occupies the place of a noun in the nom. case. (M, TA.) Ks is also related to have said that some of the Arabs express wonder by فَىَّ and هَىَّ and شَىْءَ; and some add مَا, saying يَا فَيَّمَا and يَا هَيَّمَا and يَا شَيَّمَا, meaning *How good*, or *beautiful, is this!* the Ḳ is faulty here; mentioning only يَا فَيَّمَا, and explaining it as denoting wonder. (TA.)

تَفِيَّةٌ: see تَفِيئَةٌ, in art. فيأ.

فيأ

1. فَآءَ, aor. يَفِىءُ, inf. n. فَىْءٌ (Ṣ, O, Msb) and فُيُوءٌ, (O,) *He* (a man, Msb) *returned*; (Ṣ, O, Msb;) and so ↓ افآء, and ↓ استفآء: (M, TA:) فَىْءٌ, as also ↓ فَيْئَةٌ and ↓ فِيئَةٌ, [or the former of these, accord. to analogy, is an inf. n. of unity, and the latter an inf. n. of modality,] and إِفَاءَةٌ and ٱسْتِفَاءَةٌ all signify رُجُوعٌ: (Ḳ:) or, accord. to some, فَآءَ signifies particularly *he returned to a good state or condition*. (MF, TA.) One says, فَآءَ مِنْ غَضَبِهِ *He returned* [*to a good state, or recovered, from his anger*]: (M, TA:) and فُلَانٌ سَرِيعُ ٱلْفَىْءِ مِنْ غَضَبِهِ [*Such a one is quick in respect of the returning* &c. *from his anger*]: (Ṣ, M,* O:) and إِنَّهُ لَسَرِيعُ ٱلْفَيْئَةِ ↓, (M,) or لَحَسَنُ ٱلْفِيئَةِ ↓, (Ṣ, O,) i. e. [*Verily he is quick*, or *good, in respect of*] *the returning* [to a good state, or from his anger, or *in respect of the manner of returning* &c.]: (Ṣ, M, O:) and هُوَ سَرِيعُ ٱلْغَضَبِ سَرِيعُ ٱلْفِيئَةِ ↓ [*He is quick in respect of anger, quick in respect of returning*, or *recovering*, therefrom]. (A, TA.) And فَآءَ إِلَى ٱلْأَمْرِ, [i. e. فَآءَ ٱلْأَمْرَ] and فَآءَهُ, inf. n. فَىْءٌ and فُيُوءٌ, *He returned* [*to the affair*, or *to the command*, i. e. *to that which was commanded*]. (M, TA.) حَتَّى تَفِىءَ إِلَى أَمْرِ ٱللّٰهِ, in the Ḳur xlix. 9, means *Until it* [referring to a party (طَائِفَة) before mentioned] *return to the ordinance of God*, or *to that which God has commanded*: (Bd:) or *until it return* (T, Msb) *to obedience*, (T,) or *to that which is right*. (Msb.) And فَآءَ إِلَى ٱلْأَمْرِ, inf. n. فَىْءٌ, signifies also *He reconsidered the affair*, or *case*. (TA.) — فَآءَ ٱلْمُوْلِى (M, Msb, Ḳ) مِنِ ٱمْرَأَتِهِ, (M, Ḳ,) inf. n. فَىْءٌ, (TA,) or فَيْئَةٌ ↓, (Msb,) means *The man who had sworn to abstain from conjugal intercourse with his wife expiated his oath and returned to her*. (M, Msb,* Ḳ. [See Ḳur ii. 226.]) But MF observes that this usage of فَآءَ to signify *He expiated an oath* belongs to the conventional language of the law. (TA.) In the case of a man who has sworn that he will abstain from conjugal intercourse with his wife, a period of four months is appointed to him in the Ḳur-án; and if he have such intercourse with her in the four months, it is said of him, قَدْ فَآءَ, meaning *He has returned* [or *reverted*] from his oath, to the doing that which he swore that he would not do, and is bound to expiate his oath: if he have not had such intercourse with her until the end of the four months from the day of his swearing, then, Ibn-'Abbás and a number of the Companions pass upon her a single sentence of divorce, making the [said sentence of] divorce to have effect at the end of the months; but many of the Companions and others say that in this case he must return, and expiate his oath, or he must divorce. (T, TA.) And [hence] one says لَهُ عَلَى ٱمْرَأَتِهِ فَيْئَةٌ ↓ *He has the right of returning to his wife*: (Msb, TA:) and هُوَ يَمْلِكُ فَيْئَتَهَا ↓ *He possesses the right of returning to her*; namely, a wife whom he has divorced. (A, TA.) — ٱلْفَىْءُ عَلَى ذِى ٱلرَّحِمِ occurs in a trad. as meaning *The being favourably inclined*, or *affectionate, to the relation*; and *returning to kind treatment of him*. (TA.) — فَآءَ said of the shade, (M, Msb,) aor. يَفِىءُ, (Msb,) inf. n. فَىْءٌ, (M, Msb, Ḳ,*) *It shifted*, or *removed*; (M, Ḳ:*) or [rather] *it returned from the side of the west to the side of the east*: (Msb:) and تَفَيَّأَتِ ↓ ٱلظِّلَالُ *The shades became changed in their manner of being*; (Ṣ, O;) or [rather] *they returned* [*towards the east*] *after midday*. (T, TA. [See the Ḳur-án xvi. 50.]) — And فَآءَتِ ٱلشَّجَرَةُ; and ↓ تفيّأت; (M;) and ↓ فيّأت, inf. n. تَفْيِئَةٌ; (Ṣ, O, TA;) *The tree had much shade*. (M, TA.) فَآءَتِ ٱلْحَدِيدَةُ *The iron implement became blunt after its being sharp*. (T, TA.)

— فِئْتُ الغَنِيمَةَ, (mentioned, but not expl., in the Ḳ,) inf. n. فَىْءٌ, (TA,) means *I took the spoil.* (TḲ.) [See also 10.]

2. فيّأ الظِّلَّ, and افاءه*, *He* (God) *made the shade to return* [*in the afternoon*]. (El-Khafájee, MF, TA.) — فيّأت said of a tree: see 1, near the end. — Said of the wind, *It put in motion* the seed-produce, or standing corn, and the trees. (M, TA.) And, said of a woman, *She put in motion* her hair, from self-conceit, or vanity. (M, TA.)

4. أَفَأْتُهُ *I made it to return.* (O.) See also 2. — [Hence,] one says, أَفَآءَ ٱللّٰهُ عَلَى ٱلْمُسْلِمِينَ مَالَ ٱلْكُفَّارِ [*God restored to the Muslims*, as though it were theirs by right, or *gave to them as spoil, the property*, or *wealth, of the unbelievers*]; (Ṣ, O;) inf. n. إِفَآءَةٌ. (Ṣ.) And أَفَآءَ ٱللّٰهُ عَلَيْهِمُ ٱلغَنَائِمَ [*God restored*, or *gave, to them the spoils*]. And أَفَآءَ عَلَى قَوْمٍ فَيْئًا *He took for a party the spoil of another party and brought it to them:* and *he took for a party spoil that had been taken from them.* (T, TA.) — And أَفَأْتُ كَذَا *I made such a thing to be a* فَىْء [or *spoil*]. (TA.) — And أَفَأْتُ فُلَانًا عَلَى ٱلأَمْرِ *I turned him to the thing*, or *affair, when he had desired another thing*, or *affair.* (AZ, T.) — See also 1, first sentence.

5. تفيّأت الشَّجَرَةُ — and تفيّأت الظِّلَالُ: see 1, near the end. — تفيّأ فِيهِ means *He shaded himself in it;* i. e., in the shade termed فَىْء. (M.) One says, تَفَيَّأْتُ فِى فَىْءِ الشَّجَرَةِ [*I shaded myself in the afternoon-shade of the tree*]. (Ṣ, O.) And تفيّأ بِالشَّجَرَةِ [*He shaded himself by means of the tree;* or] *he entered into the* أَفْيَآء [or *afternoon-shades*] *of the tree:* (MA:) and [it is said that] تَفَيَّأْتُ الشَّجَرَةَ signifies *I entered into the* أَفْيَآء *of the tree, and shaded myself thereby:* (Ḥar p. 500:) and Aboo-Temmám has made it trans. by itself [i. e. without a prep.] in his saying,

* فَتَفَيَّأْتُ ظِلَّهُ مَمْدُودَا *

[as though meaning *And I protected myself from the sun by its shade, when it was extended*]: but [perhaps he has thus used the verb in the last of the senses here following, for] it is said that this is irregular. (TA.) — [Hence] one says, تَفَيَّأْتُ بِفَيْئِكَ meaning ‡ *I have had recourse to thee for protection.* (A, TA.) — تفيّأ is said of a branch or twig [as meaning *It bent, in a languid manner*]. (T, M, L, Ḳ, voce تَرَأَّدَ; &c.) And one says, تفيّأت لِزَوْجِهَا, meaning *She bent herself over her husband, and affected languor*, or *languidness, to him, feigning coyness*, or *opposition, and threw herself upon him:* (T,* TA:) from الفَىْءُ signifying "the act of returning:" and some say تفيّقت, with ق; but Az says that this is a mistake, and that it is correctly with ف. (TA.) — تفيّأ signifies also تَتَبَّعَ [*He sought a thing time after time*, or *repeatedly*, &c.]. (Ḥar p. 500.) And one says, فُلَانٌ يَتَفَيَّأُ ٱلأَخْبَارَ and يَسْتَفِيئُهَا* [app. meaning *Such a one seeks after news*, or *tidings, time after time*, or *repeatedly*, &c.]. (A, TA.)

10. استفآء *He took as spoil.* (Ṣ, M,* O, Ḳ.) One says, ٱسْتَفَأْتُ هٰذَا ٱلْمَالَ *I took this property as spoil.* (Ṣ, O.) — See also 5. — As intrans., see 1, first sentence.

فَىْءٌ *Afternoon-shade; shade after the declining of the sun from the meridian;* (T,* Ṣ, O;) [i. e.] the فَىْء *is what was sun, and has been annulled*, or *superseded, by shade;* (M, Ḳ;) or *that from which the sun has departed:* so called because of its "returning" from side to side: (Ṣ, O: [see 1, first sentence:]) ISk says, (Ṣ, O,) the ظِلّ is what sun has annulled, or superseded; [correctly, what sun annuls, or supersedes; (see ظِلّ;)] and the فَىْء is *what has annulled*, or *superseded, sun:* (Ṣ, Mgh, O:) but AO says, on the authority of Ru-beh, *that on which the sun has been and from which it has departed* is فَىْء and ظِلّ; and that on which the sun has not been is ظِلّ: (Ṣ, O:) [see more under this latter word:] pl. [of pauc.] أَفْيَآءٌ and [of mult.] فُيُوءٌ. (Ṣ, M, Mgh, O, Mṣb, Ḳ.) — And *Spoil, booty*, or *plunder;* syn. غَنِيمَةٌ [q. v.]; (Ṣ, M, Mgh, O, Mṣb, Ḳ;) thus called, by the inf. n., because it returns from one party to another; (Mṣb;) and فَىّ in this sense is not allowable; (Mgh, Mṣb;) nor is it in the preceding sense: (Mgh:) or *such as is obtained without difficulty;* and therefore likened to shade. (MF.) And The [*tax*, or *tribute, termed*] خَرَاج [q. v.]: (Ṣ, O, Ḳ:) frequently occurring in trads. as meaning *such, of the possessions of the unbelievers, as accrues to the Muslims without war:* (TA:) or *such as is obtained from the believers in a plurality of gods after the laying-down of arms:* (A'Obeyd, Mgh and Mṣb voce غَنِيمَةٌ:) or *such as God has restored* [as though it were theirs of right] *to the people of his religion, of the possessions of those who have opposed them, without fighting, either by the latter's quitting their homes and leaving them vacant to the Muslims, or by their making peace on the condition of paying a poll-tax or other money or property to save themselves from slaughter:* such is termed فَىْء in the Ḳur-án. (T. [See more under غَنِيمَةٌ.]) — Also *A flock of birds:* (O, Ḳ:) [or *a number of birds disposed in a row:*] also termed عَرَقَةٌ and صَفٌّ. (O, TA.) — يَا فَىْءُ, (M, O, Ḳ, in the CḲ [erroneously] يا فَىْءُ,) or, accord. to Ks, correctly يَا فَىَّ [q. v.], (M,) [*Oh!* or *O my wonder!*] an expression of regret, (M, O, Ḳ,) accord. to most, (TA,) or of wonder, (Ks, M, Ḳ, TA,) meaning يَا عَجَبِى (Ks, M.) [See شَىْءٌ, last three sentences.]

فِئَةٌ *A* [*party, portion, division*, or *distinct body*, of men, *such as is termed*] طَائِفَةٌ: (Ṣ, O, Ḳ, TA:) or *a company* (Mṣb, TA) *of soldiers who fight in the rear of an army, and to whom the latter has recourse in the case of fear or defeat:* (TA:) or *a company of men who* [*in war*] *have recourse, for aid, one to another:* (Er-Rághib, TA:) a word having no proper sing.: (Mṣb, TA:) originally فِىءٌ; (Ṣ, O, Ḳ;) the ة being substituted for the medial ى, which is dropped: (Ṣ, O:) or its original form is فِئْوٌ [or فِئَىٌ or فِئْوَةٌ or فِئْيَةٌ (see art. فاو and فاى)]; the final [radical] letter being that which is elided; for it is from فَأَوْتُ [or فَأَيْتُ] "I divided;" and فِئَةٌ is *syn. with* فِرْقَةٌ: (IB, L, TA:) pl. فِئَاتٌ and فِئُونَ, (Ṣ, O, Mṣb, Ḳ,) in which latter the و and ن are for the making good what is deficient [in the sing.]. (Mṣb.)

فَيْئَةٌ: see 1, in four places. — [Hence] ذُو فَيْئَةٍ a term applied to *Date-stones* (نَوَى ٱلتَّمْرِ) *when they are hard:* [because,] being given as fodder to cattle, and eaten by them, they pass forth as they were at first. (T, TA.) — Also *A time;* syn. حِينٌ. (Ḳ.) One says, جَآءَهُ بَعْدَ فَيْئَةٍ *He came to him after a time.* (TA.) — And The حِدَأَة [or *kite*], *that seizes as its prey the chickens from the dwellings:* (O:) or *a certain bird resembling the eagle*, (L, Ḳ,) *which, when it fears the cold, migrates to El-Yemen.* (L.)

فِيْئَةٌ: see 1, first quarter, in four places.

تَفِيئَةٌ, (M and Ḳ in art. تفأ,) as also تَفِئَةٌ, both mentioned by Lḥ, and the latter reckoned as a dial. var. of the former, (M in that art.,) [and أَفَانٌ and إِفَّانٌ and أَفَّةٌ and إِفَّةٌ and إِفٌّ and تَئِفَّةٌ, (see art. اف,)] The *time* of a thing: (M and Ḳ in art. تفأ:) one says, أَتَيْتُهُ عَلَى تَفِيئَةِ ذٰلِكَ *I came to him at the time of that:* (M in that art.:) and [by extension of the signification] one says, دَخَلَ عَلَى تَفِيئَةِ فُلَانٍ meaning أَثَرِهِ [i. e. *He entered near after such a one; as though treading in his footsteps*]: (Ḳ in the present art.:) the ت in تَفِيئَةٌ is an augmentative letter; the word being [originally] of the measure تَفْعِلَةٌ, but formed by transposition: Z says that the ت would not be augmentative if the composition of the word were as it is here, without transposition: that it is not of the measure تَفْعِلَةٌ from الفَىْءُ; for, if it were, it would be of the same measure as تَهْيِئَةٌ [i. e. it would be تَفْيِئَةٌ]; therefore, if not formed by transposition, it would be of the measure فَعِيلَةٌ [i. e. it would be from تفأ, as some hold it to be], because of the إِعْلَال [or alteration for the sake of alleviating the sound, such as takes place in يَسِيرٌ for يَيْسِرٌ, which cannot be in a noun of the measure تَفْعِلَةٌ from a triliteral root like فيأ, whose medial radical is infirm], the last radical being hemzeh: but its formation by transposition from تَئِفَّةٌ [originally تَأْفِفَةٌ] to تَفِئَةٌ, which is then changed to تَفِيئَةٌ, as Z says in the "Fáïḳ," is what determines the ت to be augmentative, and the [original] measure to be تَفْعِلَةٌ. (L and TA* in arts. فيأ and تفأ.)

مُفَآءٌ A thing *that has been made a* فَىْء [or *spoil*, &c.]. (TA.) And A person *whose country*, or *province*, or *town, has been conquered, and become a* فَىْءٌ *to the Muslims.* (IKt, O, TA.) It is in a trad. of some of those who have gone before, لَا يُؤَمَّرُ مُفَآءٌ عَلَى مُفِىْءٍ ♦, meaning *An emancipated slave shall not be made governor over an Arabian*; (Ḳ, TA;) or, as in the Nh [and O] and L, لا يَلِيَنَّ [*shall by no means rule*]; (TA;) as though it were said, none of the people of the Sawád (which was conquered by force and became a فَىْءٌ to the Muslims) shall rule over the Companions (O, TA) and their next successors. (TA.)

مُفِىْءٌ A person *who makes a thing* [or *a country* or *the like*] *to be a* فَىْءٌ. (TA.) See also مُفَآءٌ.

مَفْيَئَةٌ: } see the paragraph here following.
مَفْيَاةٌ: }

مَفْيُؤَةٌ *A place of* فَىْءٌ, i. e. *of the shade thus termed*; [*a place of afternoon-shade*;] (M, Ḳ;) as also ♦ مَفْيَأَةٌ; (Ḳ;) and, as AAF says, on the authority of Th, ♦ مَفْيَئَةٌ; (M, L, TA;) and so ♦ مَفْيُوءَةٌ, like مَسْمُوعَةٌ [in measure]: (L, TA:) accord. to Lth, (TA,) مَفْيُؤَةٌ is syn. with مَقْنُؤَةٌ, (Ṣ, TA,) which signifies *a place on which the sun does not come*: so says Az; and he adds that it is probably correct, but that he had not heard it on any other authority than of Lth. (TA.)

مَفْيُوءٌ *i. q.* مَعْتُوهٌ [*Idiotic*, or *an idiot*, i. e. *deficient*, or *wanting, in intellect*; &c.]: so called from his keeping long [or much] in the shade. (M, TA.)

مَفْيُوءَةٌ: see مَفْيُؤَةٌ.

فيج

1. فَاجَتْ بِرِجْلِهَا, aor. تَفِيجُ, *She* (a camel) *kicked with her hind legs, backwards.* (TA.)

4. افاج, mentioned in the O and L and Mṣb in this art.: see art. فوج.

فَيْجٌ *A foot-messenger*; *a courier who journeys on foot*: (Ṣ:) or *a Sultán's foot-messenger*: (L, Mṣb:) or *one who journeys with letters*: (L:) or *a quick courier who carries tidings*, or *communications, from one town*, or *country, to another*: (Nh, TA:) originally Pers., (Ṣ, O,) arabicized, (Ṣ, O, Ḳ,) from پَيْك: (O, Ḳ:) pl. فُيُوجٌ. (Ṣ, TA.) It is also expl. as meaning *One going*, or *journeying, alone*: thus in a verse of 'Adee Ibn-Zeyd, in which it is opposed to زَرَافَةٌ meaning "a company [of men]." (TA.) And [the pl.] فُيُوجٌ, (O, Ḳ,) as used in a verse of 'Adee Ibn-Zeyd, (O,) means *Men who enter the prison and go forth from it, keeping guard.* (O, L, Ḳ: in some copies of the Ḳ, *and keep guard.*) — And *A company* [*of men*]; (Mṣb;) *syn. with* فَوْجٌ: (O and Ḳ in art. فوج:) and sometimes applied to *a single person*: pl. [of pauc.] أَفْيَاجٌ and [of mult.] فُيُوجٌ. (Mṣb.) — Also *A low*, or *depressed, place, such as is termed* وَهْدٌ, of the earth, or ground. (AA, O, Ḳ.) — And *A state of dispersion*; as also ♦ فَيْجٌ. (TA. [See 4 in art. فوج.])

فِيجٌ: see what next precedes.

فَيَّاجَةٌ A she-camel *that kicks with her hind legs* [*much* or *often*], *backwards.* (TA. [See 1.])

فَائِجٌ *A wide* [*expanded and even tract such as is termed*] بَسَاط, of land. (AA, O in art. فوج.)

فَائِجَةٌ *A wide tract between two elevated portions*, (Ṣ, O, Ḳ, all in art. فوج,) *of rugged ground*, or *of sand*: (Ṣ, O:) or *what has the form of a valley between two mountains*, or *between two rugged tracts containing stones and sand and earth, like a* خَلِيف [q. v.], *but wider*: thus expl. by ISh: pl. فَوَائِجُ. (TA in art. فوج.)

فيح

1. فَاحَ, aor. يَفِيحُ, inf. n. فَيْحٌ and فَيَحَانٌ: see art. فوح. — فَاحَ الدَّمُ, inf. n. فَيْحٌ (L, Mṣb) and فَيَحَانٌ, (L,) *It poured out*, or *forth*: (L:) or *it flowed*; as also ♦ افاح, inf. n. إِفَاحَةٌ: or, accord. to AZ, the latter is trans., and signifies as expl. below in relation to blood. (Mṣb.) — And فَاحَتِ الشَّجَّةُ, (Ṣ, A, Mṣb, Ḳ,) aor. تَفِيحُ, inf. n. فَيْحٌ, (TA,) ‡ *The wound upon the head spirted forth blood*; (Ṣ, Mṣb, Ḳ;) or *poured forth much blood.* (A.) — And فَاحَ الحَرُّ, aor. يَفِيحُ, inf. n. فَيْحٌ; and aor. يَفُوحُ, inf. n. فَوْحٌ; † *The heat rose*, or *diffused itself, and raged vehemently.* (L.) It is said in a trad., شِدَّةُ القَيْظِ مِنْ فَيْحِ جَهَنَّمَ ‡[*The intenseness of the heat of summer is from the vehement raging of the heat of Hell*]. (TA.) And one says, الحُمَّى مِنْ فَيْحِ جَهَنَّمَ ‡ *The fever is from the vehemence of the heat of Hell.* (A.) — And فَاحَتِ القِدْرُ, (Ṣ, Ḳ,) aor. تَفِيحُ (Ṣ, TA) and تَفُوحُ, (TA,) † *The cooking-pot boiled*; (Ṣ, Ḳ, TA;) as though it were the fire of Hell, in its heat. (TA.) — And فَاحَتِ النَّارُ † *The fire spread.* (Mṣb.) And [hence, app.,] فَاحَتِ الغَارَةُ, aor. تَفِيحُ, i. e. ‡ [*The troop of horsemen making an attack*, or *incursion, upon a people*] *spread themselves.* (Ṣ, TA.) See فَيَاحِ. — And فَاحَ, (L, Mṣb, TA,) aor. يَفَاحُ, (L, TA,) [inf. n., app. فَيَحٌ, which signifies "width" accord. to the Ṣ and Ḳ, and is agreeable with general analogy in this case, as the aor. of the verb is originally يَفْيَحُ, though it seems to be implied in the Mṣb that the aor. is not يَفَاحُ, but يَفِيحُ,] *It* (a sea, Ṣ,* L, Ḳ,* TA, and a place, L, or a valley, Mṣb) *was*, or *became, wide.* (Ṣ,* L, Mṣb, Ḳ,* TA.)

2. لَوْ مَلَكْتَ الدُّنْيَا لَفَيَّحْتَهَا فِى يَوْمٍ وَاحِدٍ means ‡ [*If thou possessedst all that the world contains,*] *thou wouldst dissipate it*, or *squander it away, in one day.* (A, TA.*)

4. افاح *He poured forth, spilled*, or *shed*, blood. (Ṣ, Mṣb, Ḳ.) See also 1, first sentence. — افاح القِدْرَ † *He made the cooking-pot to boil.* (Ṣ, Ḳ.) — أَفِحْ عَنْكَ مِنَ الظَّهِيرَةِ i. q. أَبْرِدْ, (Ḳ,) i. e. † *Stay thou until the mid-day heat shall have become assuaged, and the air be cool*: (M, L, TA:) [as also افِحْ:] the medial radical letter is both و and ى. (M.)

فَيْحٌ and ♦ فُيُوحٌ *Abundance of herbage of the* [*rain*, or *season, called*] رَبِيع, *with ample extent of land*: (Ḳ:) [accord. to the TḲ, both are inf. ns., of which the verb is فَاحَ, and the agent is الرَّبِيعُ: but this, I think, is rendered doubtful by what here follows:] فيوح occurs in a verse [as some relate it]; but accord. to the relation of IAạr, it is فَتُوح, with ت, [and with fet-ḥ to the ف,] and this, which signifies "rain," is said by Az to be the right reading: the pl. [of فَيْحٌ] is فُيُوحٌ. (TA.)

أَفْيَحُ: see فَيَّاحٌ.

فَيَاحِ, like قَطَامِ, [indecl.,] (T, Ṣ, L, Ḳ,) of the fem. gender, (L,) a name for *The* غَارَة, (T, Ṣ, L, Ḳ,) meaning *troop of horsemen making a hostile attack*, or *incursion, upon a people.* (T, L.) فِيحِى ♦, فَيَاحِ, (Ṣ, A, Ḳ, &c., [in the CḲ, erroneously, فَيْحِى,]) said by the people of the Time of Ignorance, (Ṣ,) when they impelled horses making a hostile attack, or incursion, and they spread out, (L,) means *Spread out, O attacking troop of horsemen*: (Ṣ, A, Ḳ:) or *spread out upon them*, or *against them, and disperse yourselves*, &c. (Sh, L.)

فُيُوحٌ: see فَيْحٌ.

فَيَّاحٌ: see أَفْيَحُ, in two places. — Also ‡ *Profuse in bounty*: (Ṣ, A:) so in the saying, إِنَّهُ لَجَوَادٌ فَيَّاحٌ ‡[*Verily he is liberal, munificent*, or *generous*; *profuse in bounty*]. (Ṣ.) — And نَاقَةٌ فَيَّاحَةٌ ‡ *A she-camel that yields much milk*, (A, Ḳ,) *and has a large udder.* (Ḳ.)

أَفْيَحُ A sea, (Ṣ, L, Ḳ,) and a valley, (Mṣb,) and any place, (L,) *wide*, or *extensive*; (Ṣ, L, Mṣb, Ḳ;) as also ♦ فَيَّاحٌ: (Ṣ, L, Ḳ:) ♦ فَيَّاحٌ occurs in the story of Umm-Zarạ, accord. to A'Obeyd, applied to a بَيْت [i. e. *house*, or *tent*]; but accord. to others, it is ♦ فَيَاحٌ, without teshdeed: (L:) [the fem. of أَفْيَحُ: and pl. فِيحٌ:] one says دَارٌ فَيْحَآءُ *A wide*, or *an ample, house* or *abode*: (Ṣ, Ḳ:) and in like manner رَوْضَةٌ [*a meadow*, &c.]. (L, Mṣb.) — And فَيْحَآءُ signifies also *A sort of thin cooked food, such as is supped*, or *sipped*, (حَسَآء,) *seasoned with seeds such as are used in cookery.* (Ṣ, Ḳ.)

فيخ

1. فَاخَتِ الرِّيحُ, aor. تَفِيخُ, inf. n. فَيْخٌ and

فَيَخَانٌ: see 1 in art. فوخ. Accord. to Kr and the Ḳ, فَيْخٌ signifies *A spreading*, or *becoming diffused*; like فَوْخٌ: (TA:) but ISd expresses doubt of the correctness of this: (L, TA:) it is [said to be] an inf. n. in this sense. (TḲ.) — See also 4.

2. فَيَّخَ العَجِينَ *He made the dough like the* سُكُرُّجَة [or فَيْخَة (q. v.) in form]. (TA.)

4. افاخ, (L,) inf. n. إِفَاخَةٌ, (L, Ḳ,) *He* (a man, L) *emitted wind from the anus, with a sound*; (L, Ḳ;) as also ▼ فَاخَ: (L:) or *he voided excrement with an emission of wind*. (L, Ḳ.) [See also art. فوخ.] — افاخ, said of a man, signifies also سُقِطَ فِى يَدِهِ [i. e. *He repented of what he had done*; &c.]. (Ḳ.) — And افاخ مِنْ فُلَانٍ *He* (a man, TA) *turned away from, avoided, shunned, and left, such a one*; syn. صَدَّ عَنْهُ. (Ḳ.)

فَيْخَةٌ *A state of dilatation of the place of exit* of the urine. (IAạr, Ḳ.) — And *A tangled, luxuriant, or dense, and abundant, state* of herbage. (Ḳ.) — And *Vehemence*, or *intenseness*, of heat. (Ḳ, TA.) = And *A* [*kind of small saucer, or cup, such as is called*] سُكُرُّجَة [q. v.]: (Ḳ:) pl. فَيْخَاتٌ. (O and Ḳ voce شُفَارِج.)

فيد

1. فَادَتْ لَهُ فَائِدَةٌ, (T, Ṣ, A, O, L, Mṣb, Ḳ,) aor. تَفِيدُ, (Ṣ, A, O, &c.,) inf. n. فَيْدٌ, (Mṣb,) [*Profit*, or *advantage*, or *the like*, (see فَائِدَةٌ,)] *accrued to him*; (T,* Ṣ,* A, O,* L,* Mṣb, Ḳ;) or *came to him*. (IḲṭṭ, TA.) — And فاد, aor. يَفِيدُ, (T, Ṣ, M, O, L, Ḳ,) inf. n. فَيْدٌ, (M, O, L,) said of property, *It continued*, or *belonged* or *appertained*, syn. ثَبَتَ, (T, Ṣ, M, O, L, Ḳ,) لَهُ *to him*; (T, Ṣ, M, O, L;) as also فاد, aor. يَفُودُ, (M in art. فود,) inf. n. فَوْدٌ: (Ḳ in that art.:) or *went away*, *passed away*, or *departed*. (Ḳ. [But this last meaning, which I find only in the Ḳ, in relation to فاد, in this art. and in art. فود, may be taken from what next follows, and relate to property as applied to cattle.]) — And فاد, aor. as above, (T, M, L, Ḳ, and Ṣ &c. in art. فود,) and so the inf. n., (IAạr, T, L, and Ḳ in art. فود,) *He* (a man, M, TA) *died*; (T, M, L, Ḳ, and Ṣ &c. in art. فود;) as also فاد, aor. يَفُودُ, (Ṣ and Ḳ &c. in art. فود,) inf. n. فَوْدٌ; (Ḳ &c. in that art.;) and so فَاظَ and فَازَ; (TA;) i. q. فَاتَ. (A.) One says, مَا فَادَ حَتَّى بَلَغَ رِزْقُهُ النَّفَادَ, meaning مَا فَاتَ [i. e. *He did not die until his means of subsistence became exhausted*]. (A.) — And فاد, aor. as above, (Ṣ, M, O, L, Ḳ,) and so the inf. n., (Ṣ, O, L,) *He walked with an elegant and a proud and self-conceited gait, with an affected inclining of his body from side to side*; (Ṣ, M, O, L, Ḳ;) as also ▼ تفيّد. (T, Ṣ, M, L, Ḳ.) — And, (M, L, Ḳ,) accord. to some, (M, L,) *He was cautious of a thing, and turned aside from it*. (M, L, Ḳ.) [See also 2.] = فاد said of saffron, and of the plant called وَرْس, *It became pulverized, or reduced to powder by its being bruised* or *brayed*. (IḲṭṭ, TA.) = فادهُ, aor. يَفِيدُهُ, (Ṣ, L, Ḳ,) inf. n. فَيْدٌ, (L,) *He mixed it*, (namely, saffron, Ḳ,) or *moistened it with water* &c.; syn. دَافَهُ; (Ṣ, L, Ḳ;) from which it is formed by transposition [accord. to the lexicologists; but not accord. to the grammarians, because it has an inf. n.]; (TA;) as also فادهُ, aor. يَفُودُهُ, (T, M, L, &c., in art. فود,) inf. n. فَوْدٌ: (Ḳ in that art.:) and *he bruised*, or *brayed, it*, (namely, saffron, and the plant called وَرْس,) *and then wetted it with water*: (L in art. فود:) and فَادَتْهُ *she* (a woman) *rubbed it* (namely perfume) *in water, in order that it might dissolve*. (M, L.) = فاد المَلَّةَ عَنِ الخُبْزَةِ, inf. n. فَيْدٌ; and ▼ افادها; *He removed the hot ashes from the cake of bread*; syn. أَزَالَهَا. (TḲ. [In the O and Ḳ, this meaning of these two verbs is vaguely intimated, only by the words, الفَيْدُ أَنْ تُفِيدَ بِيَدِكَ المَلَّةَ عَنِ الخُبْزَةِ.])

2. فَيَّدَ مِنْ قِرْنِهِ (Th, M, L) *He turned away from*, or *avoided, his adversary*: (Th, L:) or *he fled from him*. (M.) [See a similar meaning of فاد, above.] = And فيّد, (T, O, Ḳ,) inf. n. تَفْيِيدٌ, (L, Ḳ,) *He augured evil from the cry of the* [*bird called*] فَيَّاد. (T, O, L, Ḳ.)

4. افادهُ *He gave it*, namely, property, (AZ, Ks, T, Ṣ, M, O, L, Ḳ,) to another: (AZ, Ks, T, Ṣ, M, L:) and افادهُ مَالًا, inf. n. إِفَادَةٌ, *He gave him property*. (Mgh, Mṣb.) It belongs to this art. and to art. فود. (Mṣb in art. فود.) — [And *He*, or *it*, *profited, advantaged*, or *benefited, him*; فَائِدَةٌ being understood. Hence,] one says, إِنْ أَفَدْتَنِى حَرْفًا فَقَدْ أَصْفَدْتَنِى أَلْفًا [*If thou teach me a word, thou givest me* what is worth *a thousand* dirhems]. (A in art. صفد.) — [Hence, also, افاد said of a word, and a phrase, *It had*, or *performed, a useful office, as expressive of a meaning*, or *as contributing to the expression thereof*, or *as adding to a meaning previously expressed*. And hence, *It imported*, or *conveyed, a meaning*; and particularly, when said of a phrase, *a complete meaning, such that a pause might be well made after* [the uttering] *it*; فَائِدَةٌ being understood.] = See also 10. — And see 1, last signification. — Also, افاده, inf. n. as above, *He killed him*; *destroyed him*; *slaughtered him*; namely, a man, and a beast. (T,* L, and Ḳ* in art. فود.)

5. تفيّد, as intrans.: see 1, latter half. = تفيّدهُ: see 10.

6. هُمَا يَتَفَايَدَانِ بِالمَالِ بَيْنَهُمَا *They two give, of the property, each to the other*; or *profit*, or *benefit, each other therewith*: (ISh, T, O, Ḳ:) you should not say يَتَفَاوَدَانِ: (Ḳ:) and هما يتفايدان العِلْمَ *They two impart knowledge, each to the other*: (Ḳ in art. فود [q. v.]:) or, in the opinion of MF, both of these verbs are allowable. (TA.)

10. استفادهُ (T, Ṣ, M, &c.) *He gained it, acquired it, or got it, for himself*, namely, property [&c.]; (T,* M,* Mgh, Mṣb, and L and Ḳ in art. فود;) and ▼ افادهُ is syn. therewith, (Ṣ, M, A, Mgh, O, L, Mṣb, Ḳ,) as used by some, (Mṣb,) having two contr. significations, (Ḳ,) though disallowed by others, (Mṣb,) or it is more chaste than the former; (Mgh;) and ▼ تفيّدهُ signifies the same. (M, and Ḳ in art. فود.) — [And *He derived it*, *learned it*, or *inferred it*. — And استفاد مِنْهُ *He gained*, or *derived, profit, advantage*, or *benefit, from him*, or *it*; فَائِدَةٌ being understood.]

فَيْدٌ *Saffron*: (IAạr, TA voce مَلَابٌ:) or the *leaves of saffron*: (L:) or *saffron mixed*, or *moistened with water* &c. (Ṣ, O, L, Ḳ.) — And The *hair upon a horse's lip*. (T, Ṣ, O, Ḳ.)

[فَيِيدٌ expl. by Golius as signifying (on the authority of Meyd) *Vir pusillanimus pavidusque*, is app. a mistake for فَئِيدٌ.]

فَيَّادٌ (T, Ṣ, M, A, O, L, Ḳ) and ▼ فَيَّادَةٌ, (T, Ṣ, O, L, Ḳ,) in which latter the ة is added to render the epithet intensive, (T, L,) A man *who walks with an elegant and a proud and self-conceited gait, with an affected inclining of his body from side to side*. (T, Ṣ, M, A, O, L, Ḳ.) One says, فُلَانٌ يَمْشِى عَلَى الأَرْضِ فَيَّادًا مَيَّادًا [*Such a one walks upon the ground*] *with an elegant and a proud and self-conceited gait*, &c. (A.) — Hence, الفَيَّادُ is said to signify *The lion*. (O.) — And *The male of the* بُوم [or *owl*]: (T, Ṣ, M, O, Ḳ:) or *i. q.* الصَّدَى [which is also said to signify the male of the بُوم: for other explanations see صَدًى]. (Ṣ, O.) — And ▼ فَيَّادَةٌ, (M,) or this and فَيَّادٌ, (T, Ṣ, O, Ḳ,) *One who collects together what he can, and eats it*. (Lth, T, Ṣ, M, O, Ḳ.)

فَيَّادَةٌ: see the next preceding paragraph, in two places.

فَائِدَةٌ a subst. from فَادَ المَالُ, (M, L, and Ḳ in art. فود,) in the sense of ثَبَتَ; (M, L;) or an act. part. n. from فَادَتْ لَهُ فَائِدَةٌ; (Mṣb;) *Profit, advantage, benefit*, or *good, which God bestows upon a man, and which he* [*the latter, consequently*] *gains*, or *acquires*, and *which he produces*: (T, L:) *an accession which accrues to a man*: (Mṣb:) *what one gains*, or *acquires, of knowledge*, (Ṣ, A, O, L, Mṣb, Ḳ,) and *polite accomplishments*, (Mṣb,) and *property*: (Ṣ, A, O, L, Ḳ:) *what one has recently acquired, of property, of gold or silver, or a slave, or the like*: (AZ, Mṣb:) and [simply] *profit, advantage, benefit*, or *utility*: and *good*: and *knowledge*: and *wealth*, or *property*: (KL:) pl. فَوَائِدُ: (T, O, L, Mṣb, Ḳ:) it belongs to this art. and to art. فود: (TA:) some improperly derive it from الفُؤَادُ. (MF.) — [Hence, *Utility as expressive of a meaning*, or *as contributing to the expression thereof*, or *as adding to a meaning previously expressed*, of a word or phrase. And hence, *A meaning*, or *an import*, of a word or phrase; and particularly *a complete meaning* of a phrase, *such that a pause may be well made after the uttering* thereof.]

مَفِيدٌ [Perfume, &c.] *mixed*, or *moistened with water* &c.; (Ṣ, O, L;) as also مَفُودٌ. (Aṣ, T in art. فود.)

رَجُلٌ مِتْلَافٌ مِفْيَادٌ *A destructive man*; as also ↓ مِفْوَادٌ. (Ibn-'Abbád and O and Ḳ in art. فود.)

فيروزج

فِيرُوزَجٌ [an arabicized word from the Pers. پيروزه or فِيرُوزَه *The turquoise*;] *a well-known kind of stone.* (TA.) — And *A certain sort of dye* [probably *of the colour of the stone so called*]. (TA.)

فيش

1. فَاشَ, (O, Ḳ,) aor. يَفِيشُ, inf. n. فَيْشٌ, (O, TA,) *He gloried,* or *boasted,* (O, Ḳ,) *and magnified himself, imagining* [*in himself*] *what he did not possess;* (Ḳ;) as also فَشَّ; like as you say دَامَ, aor. يَدِيمُ; and دَمَّ, aor. يَدُمُّ; (TA;) *he was boastful,* or *proud, pretending to possess a thing and not being as he pretended;* (TA;) and ↓ فايش [signifies the same; or] *he gloried,* or *boasted, vainly, and praised himself for that which was not in him.* (AHeyth, in L, art. طرمذ.) [See also 5.] — فاش الأَتَانَ, aor. as above, (IDrd, O, Ḳ,) and so the inf. n., (IDrd, O,) *He* (the ass) *mounted the she-ass:* (IDrd:) said by Yoo to be from الفَيْشَةُ. (O, Ḳ.*)

3. فايشهُ, (TA,) inf. n. فِيَاشٌ (Ṣ, O, Ḳ) and مُفَايَشَةٌ, (O, Ḳ,) *He vied,* or *contended, with him in glorying,* or *boasting,* or *in glory,* or *excellence.* (Ṣ,* O,* Ḳ,* TA.) — Also, (TḲ,) inf. n. مُفَايَشَةٌ, (Ibn-'Abbád, O, Ḳ,) *He threatened him much in fight, and then was pronounced a liar.* (Ibn-'Abbád, O, Ḳ, TḲ.) — See also 1.

5. تفيّش الشَّىْءَ *He arrogated the thing falsely;* (Ibn-'Abbád,* O,* Ḳ,* TA;) *without merit.* (Ibn-'Abbád, O, TA.) — تفيّش عَنِ الشَّىْءِ *He turned back from the thing* (Ibn-'Abbád, O, Ḳ) *through weakness and impotence;* (TA;) like انفشّ. (TA.)

فَيْشٌ and ↓ فَيْشَةٌ The *head* [or *glans*] *of the penis:* (Ṣ, O, Ḳ:) or *a swollen penis:* (TA:) or ↓ the latter word has the former me...ing; and فَيْشٌ is its pl., [or rather coll. gen. n.,] like as تَمْرٌ is of تَمْرَةٌ: (O:) and ↓ فَيْشَلَةٌ signifies the same as فَيْشَةٌ; and some say that its ل is augmentative: (TA:) or فَيْشٌ signifies *a weak* فَيْشَلَة. (Lth, TA.)

فَيْشَةٌ: see فَيْشٌ, in two places. — Also *The uppermost part of the head.* (TA.)

فِيَاشٌ: see فَيْشُوشَةٌ. — [See also 3.]

فَيُوشٌ: see the next paragraph, in two places.

فَيَّاشٌ A man *who glories,* or *boasts, and magnifies himself, imagining* [*in himself*] *what he does not possess;* (Ḳ;) *vainly boastful, without merit;* (TA;) *who contends for superiority in that which he does not possess;* (Ḳ;) and [in like manner] ↓ فَيُوشٌ one *who pretends to possess a thing, not being as he pretends;* (TA;) both signify one *who glories,* or *boasts, vainly, and praises himself for that which is not in him:* (AHeyth, in L, art. طرمذ:) and ↓ the latter is said to signify *a cowardly and weak* man. (TA.) — Also, *A chief,* or *lord, abounding in excellence,* or *generosity,* or *bounty,* (Ibn-'Abbád, O, Ḳ,) *who vies with others in glory.* (TA.)

فَاشُوشٌ *A weak and lax man.* (TA.)

فَيْشُوشَةٌ *Weakness and laxness;* (O, Ḳ;) and so ↓ فِيَاشٌ. (TA.)

فَيْشَلَةٌ: see فَيْشٌ.

فيص

1. فَاصَ فِى الأَرْضِ, aor. يَفِيصُ, (Ṣ, O, Ḳ,) inf. n. فَيْصٌ, (TA,) *He went away into the country,* or *in the land.* (Ṣ, O, Ḳ.) In the following verse of Imra-el-Ḳeys,

مَنَابِتُهُ مِثْلُ السُّدُوسِ وَلَوْنُهُ
كَشَوْكِ السَّيَالِ فَهْوَ عَذْبٌ يَفِيصُ

respecting which Aṣ said, I know not what is [the meaning of] يَفِيصُ, this word is said to be from فاص signifying as expl. above: (Ṣ, O:) [but I do not see what meaning that would be apposite in this case could be thence derived without straining:] but فاص signifies also *it shone,* or *glistened;* syn. بَرَقَ; (TA;) and some say that يفيص in this verse means يَبْرُقُ; (O, TA;) and the pronoun in مَنَابِتُهُ relates to the front teeth; (O,* TA;) by عَذْبٌ يَفِيصُ being meant the lustre (مَآء) thereof: (O:) [accordingly, the verse may be rendered, *The places of growth thereof,* i. e. *their gums,* were *like the* (*garment called*) سُدُوس, *and their colour* was *like the thorns of the* سَيَال (q. v.), *so that they were sweet* and *glistening:* (see the context in "the Divans of the six ancient Arabic poets," edited by Prof. Ahlwardt:) or, as some relate the verse, the last word is ↓ يُفِيصُ, (IB, O, TA,) from مَا أَفَاصَ بِكَلِمَةٍ [q. v.], (O,) so that it is a denotativ. of state, the meaning being فِى حَالِ كَلَامِهِ [i. e. *sweet when* [displayed in] *speaking*]; rather, *clearly uttering;* but it will be seen b... that يَفِيصُ, as well as يُفِيصُ, may, accord. to the M and Ḳ, be used in this sense:] (IB, TA:) see 4. — مَا ٱسْتَطَعْتُ أَنْ أَفِيصَ مِنْهُ, meaning *I was not able to turn aside,* or *away, from,* or *to avoid, him,* or *it.* (Ṣ, O.) [See also مَفِيصٌ: and see 4.] — And وَٱللّٰهِ مَا فِصْتُ, like as one says والله ما بَرِحْتُ [perhaps meaning *By God I did not quit my place;* as well as *I did not cease:*] (Ṣ, O, Ḳ:*) mentioned on the authority of AHeyth: (TA:) [that it has the latter meaning is clear; for] one says, مَا فِصْتُ أَفْعَلُ *I did not cease* (مَا بَرِحْتُ) *doing* [such a thing]: (M:) and ↓ استفاص, likewise, signifies بَرِحَ. (IB, TA.)

3: see 3 in art. فوص.

4. افاص الضَّبُّ عَنْ يَدِهِ [*The lizard called* ضَبّ *escaped,* or *slipped, from his hand,* is expl. as meaning] *his fingers became unclosed* (انْفَرَجَتْ) *from* [the grasp of] *the* ضبّ, *so that it escaped from him.* (M, TA.) And one says, قَبَضْتُ عَلَيْهِ فَلَمْ يُفِصْ *I grasped him and he did not escape,* or *get loose.* (AHeyth, TA.) And قَبَضْتُ عَلَى ذَنَبِ الضَّبِّ فَأَفَاصَ مِنْ يَدِى حَتَّى خَلَّصَ ذَنَبَهُ [*I grasped the tail of the* ضبّ *and it slipped from my hand so that it freed its tail*]: (Lth, Ṣ, O, TA: [but in the O, مِنْ is omitted before يَدِى; not intentionally, for the verb before من is there masc., as above:]) this is when thy fingers become unclosed (تَتَفَرَّجُ) from the grasp of its tail: (Lth, O:) and this [state of the fingers] is termed ↓ التَّفَاوُصُ. (TA.) [It is also said that] أَفَاصَتِ اليَدُ signifies *The fingers of the hand became unclosed* (تَفَرَّجَتْ) *from the grasp of the thing.* (Ḳ, TA. [But I doubt the correctness of this.]) — And الإِفَاصَةُ signifies *The being clear,* or *perspicuous;* syn. البَيَانُ; (O, Ḳ;) like المُفَاوَصَةُ, expl. in art. فوص; and *the being fluent.* (O.) [And also *The making* speech *clear,* or *perspicuous.*] One says, فُلَانٌ ذُو إِفَاصَةٍ إِذَا تَكَلَّمَ *Such a one is a person endowed with clearness,* or *perspicuity, and fluency, when he speaks.* (O.) And افاص لِسَانُهُ بِالكَلَامِ *His tongue made speech,* or *the speech, clear,* or *perspicuous;* and so ↓ فَاصَ, aor. يَفِيصُ; (M;) and مَا يَفِيصُ بِهِ لِسَانُهُ, (Ḳ, TA,) inf. n. فَيْصٌ, (TA,) *his tongue does not make it clear,* or *perspicuous* (Ḳ, TA.) And مَا أَفَاصَ بِكَلِمَةٍ *He did not make clear,* or *distinct,* or *perspicuous, a word,* or *a sentence.* (Yaḳḳoob, Ṣ, O, TA.) See also 4 in art. فوص: and see 1 in the present art. [And it is said that مَا أَفَاصَ بِكَلِمَةٍ signifies the same. Or, accord. to Mṭr, if he be correctly cited in Ḥar p. 447, the verb in this sense, and app. as thus used in all the phrases mentioned above, is correctly with ض, and not so with ص: but this I greatly doubt.] — One says also, افاص بِبَوْلِهِ *He ejected his urine:* (O, Ḳ:) or افاص بِهِ. (El-Ghooree, in Ḥar ubi suprà.)

6. التَّفَايُصُ is said to be the original and regular form of التَّفَاوُصُ, which signifies *The speaking, talking,* or *discoursing, each to another,* or *each with another:* the ى being changed into و because of the dammeh. (M in this art. and in art. فوص, and TA.) — See also another explanation in art. فوص: and see 4 in the present art.

10: see 1, last sentence.

مَا عَنْهُ مَفِيصٌ *There is not any place to which to turn aside,* or *away, from it:* or *there is not any turning aside,* or *away, from it:* syn. مَحِيدٌ [which may be meant either as a n. of place or as an inf. n.]: (Aṣ, Ṣ, O, Ḳ:) or مَعْدِلٌ. (IAạr, M.)

فيض

1. فَاضَ, (Ṣ, M, Mgh, &c.,) aor. يَفِيضُ, inf. n. فَيْضٌ (Ṣ, M, O, Mṣb, Ḳ) and فُيُوضَةٌ (Ṣ, O, Ḳ)

and فُيُوضٌ (M, O, Ḳ) and فُيُوضٌ and فَيُوضَةٌ (M, Ḳ) and فَيَضَانٌ, (M, O, Ḳ,) *It* (water) *overflowed; poured out,* or *forth, from fulness:* (Mgh:) *it* (water, Ṣ, O, Ḳ, or a torrent, Mṣb) *became abundant,* (Ṣ, O, Mṣb, Ḳ) *and flowed from* [*over*] *the brink of the valley,* (Mṣb,) or *so as to flow over the side of the valley,* (Ṣ, O,) or *so as to flow like a valley;* (Ḳ;) and ▼ افاض signifies the same: (Mṣb, TA:) *it* (water) *became abundant:* (TA:) [*contr. of* غَاضَ, aor. يَغِيضُ:] *it* (water, and that of the eyes, and the like, M, or anything fluid, Mṣb) *ran,* or *flowed:* (M, Mṣb:) or *it poured out,* or *forth;* or *poured out,* or *forth, vehemently; gushed out,* or *forth:* (M:) and *it* (water, and blood,) *fell in drops.* (Mṣb.) — *It* (a vessel) *became full:* (Mṣb:) [or *it overflowed:* for you say,] فَاضَ النَّهْرُ بِمَائِهِ *The river overflowed with its water:* and فَاضَ الإِنَآءُ بِمَا فِيهِ *The vessel overflowed with what was in it:* (Mṣb:) and a poet says,

* شَكَوْتُ وَمَا الشَّكْوَى لِمِثْلِى عَادَةٌ *
* وَلٰكِنْ تَفِيضُ الكَأْسُ عِنْدَ آمْتِلَائِهَا *

[*I complained; and complaint is not a custom of the like of me; but the cup overflows on the occasion of its being full*]. (A.) You say also, فَاضَتْ عَيْنُهُ, aor. as above, inf. n. فَيْضٌ, *The eye flowed* [with tears]. (TA.) And فَاضَ عَرَقًا, said of a man, [*He sweated;*] *sweat appeared upon his body,* on an occasion of grief. (IḲṭṭ.) — † *It* (a thing) *was,* or *became, much, abundant, many,* or *numerous.* (O, Ḳ.) You say, فَاضَ اللِّئَامُ † *The mean became many:* (Ṣ, O:) opposed to غَاضَ, q. v. (Ṣ and A in art. غيض.) And فَاضَ الخَيْرُ ‡ *Good,* or *wealth,* &c., *became abundant,* (A, Mṣb,) فِيهِمْ *among them.* (A.) — Aor. as above, (Ṣ,) inf. n. فَيْضٌ, (TA,) ‡ *It* (a piece of news, or a story,) *spread abroad;* (Ṣ, M, Ḳ;) as also ▼ استفاض; (Ṣ, M, A, Mṣb, Ḳ, TA;) *it spread abroad among the people,* (Mṣb and TA in explanation of the latter verb,) *like water.* (TA.) ▼ The latter is also said of a place, meaning ‡ *It became wide,* or *ample.* (A.) And you say, فَاضَ عَلَيْهِ الدِّرْعُ ‡ [*The coat of mail spread over him;* or *covered him*]. (A.) — Aor. as above, inf. n. فَيْضٌ and فُيُوضٌ, ‡ *He* (a man, Ṣ, O, Ḳ) *died:* (Ṣ, M, O, Ḳ:) and, (Ṣ, M, O, Ḳ,) in like manner, (Ṣ, O,) فَاضَتْ نَفْسُهُ, (Ṣ, M, A, Mgh, O, Mṣb, Ḳ,) aor. as above, (M,) inf. n. فَيْضٌ, (M, Mṣb,) ‡ *his soul departed,* or *went forth;* (Ṣ, M, A,* Mgh,* O, Mṣb, Ḳ;) of the dial. of Temeem; (Ṣ, M, O;) on the authority of AO and Fr; and AZ says the like; but Aṣ says that one should not say, فَاضَ الرَّجُلُ, nor فاضت نفسه, for فاض is only said of tears and of water: (Ṣ, O:) to which is added in the O, but one says, فَاظَ, with ظ, [as is also said in the Mgh,] as meaning "he died," and not فاض, with ض, decidedly: (TA:) [see, however, the remarks of IB below:] or the more chaste expression is فاظ, with ظ, without the mention of the نفس; and some do not allow any other: (Mṣb:) but in the L we find as follows: IAạr says. فاض الرجل and فاظ, meaning "the man died:" and Abu-l-Ḥasan says, فاظت نفسه, the verb relating to the نفس; and فاض الرجل and فاظ: but Aṣ says, I heard AA say that one should not say, فاظت نفسه, but فاظ, meaning "he died;" and not فاض, with ض, decidedly. IB, however, says that what IDrd has cited from Aṣ is different from that which J has ascribed to him; for IDrd cites the words of Aṣ thus: the Arabs say, فاظ الرجل, meaning "the man died;" but when they speak of the نفس, they say فاضت نفسه, with ض; and he quotes the ex.

* فَفُقِئَتْ عَيْنٌ وَفَاسَتْ نَفْسُ *

[*And an eye was put out, and a soul departed*]: and he [IB] adds that this is what is commonly known to be the opinion of Aṣ: but J has committed an error; for Aṣ quotes from AA that one should not say, فاظت نفسه, but فاظ, meaning "he died;" not فاض, decidedly: and he also says, nor does it necessarily follow from what he relates that he firmly believed it: AO says that فاظت نفسه is of the dial. of Ḳeys; and فاضت, of the dial. of Temeem: and AḤát says, I heard AZ say that Benoo-Ḍabbeh alone say, فاضت نفسه: in like manner also El-Mázinee says, on the authority of AZ, that all the Arabs say, فاظت نفسه, except Benoo-Ḍabbeh, who say, فاضت نفسه with ض. (TA.) [See also art. فيظ. It is further said, that] الفَيْضُ signifies *Death;* (A, Ḳ;) as occurring in a trad. respecting Ed-Dejjál, where it is said, ثُمَّ يَكُونُ عَلَى أَثَرِ ذٰلِكَ الفَيْضُ [*Then shall be, after that, death*]: (A, TA:) Sh says, I asked El-Bekráwee respecting this, and he asserted الفيض, in this case, to signify "death;" but I have not heard it from any other; unless it be from فَاضَتْ نَفْسُهُ signifying *His slaver collecting upon his lips at the departure of his soul* [*flowed*]. (TA.) — You say also فَاضَ صَدْرُهُ مِنَ الغَيْظِ ‡ [*His bosom overflowed with wrath,* or *rage*]. (A, TA.) And فَاضَ صَدْرُهُ بِالسِّرِّ † *His bosom disclosed,* or *revealed, the secret;* (Ṣ, O, Ḳ;) *his bosom could not conceal the secret;* (M;) *his bosom was full with the secret, and disclosed it, not being able to conceal it.* (TA.) — And فَيْضٌ is used as meaning † God's *suggesting* (إِلْقَآء) [of a thing]: what the Devil suggests (يُلْقِيهِ) is termed الوَسْوَسَةُ. (Kull p. 277.) — فَاضَ البَعِيرُ بِجِرَّتِهِ: see 4, latter half.

4. افاض: see 1, first sentence. = *He filled* a vessel *so that it overflowed:* (Ṣ, M, O, Ḳ:) or [simply] *he filled* a vessel, (M, Mṣb,) accord. to Lḥ; but the former, [says ISd,] in my opinion, is the correct signification. (M.) — *He made* water, and tears, and the like, *to run,* or *flow;* or *to pour out,* or *forth;* or *to pour out,* or *forth, vehemently; to gush out,* or *forth:* (M:) *he poured* [water &c.] *out,* or *forth:* (A, TA:) or *he poured* water *out,* or *forth, copiously.* (Mgh.) You say, افاض المَآءَ عَلَى نَفْسِهِ, (Ṣ, O, Ḳ,) or على جَسَدِهِ, (Mṣb,) *He poured the water* (Ṣ, O, Mṣb, Ḳ) *upon himself,* (Ṣ, O, Ḳ,) or *upon his body.* (Mṣb.) And افاض دُمُوعَهُ, (Ṣ,) or دَمْعَهُ, (Mṣb,) *He poured forth his tears.* (Mṣb.) And افاضت العَيْنُ الدَّمْعَ [*The eye poured forth tears*]. (TA.) — افاض آللّٰهُ الخَيْرَ ‡ *God made good,* or *wealth,* &c., *to abound.* (Mṣb.) — افاض عَلَيْهِ الدِّرْعَ ‡ *He put on him the coat of mail:* like as you say صَبَّهَا [lit. he poured it]. (A, TA.) — أَفَاضُوا مِنْ عَرَفَاتٍ ‡ *They pushed on, pressed on,* or *went quickly,* syn. دَفَعُوا, (Ṣ, Mgh, O, Mṣb, Ḳ,) or آنْدَفَعُوا, (M, A,) *with multitude,* (M, Mgh, O,) *from 'Arafát,* (Ṣ, M, A, Mgh, O, Mṣb, Ḳ,) to Minè, (Ṣ, M, O,) exclaiming لَبَّيْكَ: (M:) or *they returned, and dispersed themselves, from 'Arafát:* (O, Ḳ:) or *they hastened from 'Arafát* to another place: (Ḳ:) the last rendering is taken from Ibn-'Arafeh; and agreeably with all of these renderings, the phrase in the Ḳur [ii. 194], فَإِذَا أَفَضْتُمْ مِنْ عَرَفَاتٍ, has been explained: (TA:) and [in like manner,] you say, افاضوا مِنْ مِنًى إِلَى مَكَّةَ ‡ *They returned from Minè to Mekkeh;* on the day of the sacrifice: (Mṣb:) إِفَاضَةٌ signifies ‡ the *advancing, and pushing on,* or *pressing on,* in journeying, or pace, (A,* TA,) and the like, (A,) *with multitude,* and is only after a state of separation and congregation: (TA:) it is from the same word as signifying the "pouring out, or forth;" (A, O, TA;) or from افاض المَآءَ signifying "he poured the water out, or forth, copiously:" (Mgh:) and the original expression is افاض نَفْسَهُ, or رَاحِلَتَهُ; but they omit the objective complement, and hence the verb resembles one that is intrans.: (O, TA:) or افاضة signifies the *quickly impelling* or *urging* [a beast] *to run, with one's foot or leg,* or *feet or legs:* and افاض, *he* (a rider) *made his camel to exert himself beyond measure, to go a quick run, between the utmost rate and what is less than that;* افاضة denoting *the half* [*of the full rate*] *of the run of camels having riders upon them;* and being only applied when they have riders upon them: (Khálid Ibn-Jembeh:) and every دَفْعَة [or *act of pushing on,* or *pressing on,*] is termed إِفَاضَةٌ. (Ṣ, Mṣb, Ḳ.) Hence, طَوَافُ الإِفَاضَةِ, signifying *The circuiting* [around the Kaabeh] *on the return from Minè to Mekkeh;* (Mṣb, TA;) on the day of the sacrifice: (TA:) or *the circuiting of visitation.* (Mgh.) — افاضوا فِى الحَدِيثِ ‡ *They pushed on,* or *pressed on, in discourse;* syn. آنْدَفَعُوا: (Lḥ, Ṣ, M, A, O:) *they entered thereinto; launched forth,* or *out, thereinto;* (Lḥ, M, O;) *they were large,* or *copious,* or *profuse, therein:* (O, TA:) or *they dilated therein:* (M:) or *they began, commenced,* or *entered upon, discourse;* (Mṣb;) as also ▼ استفاضوه, (M, Mṣb,) accord. to some; (Mṣb;) but this latter is disallowed by most; (M;) or by the skilful. (Mṣb.) You say also, افاض فِى عَمَلٍ † *He entered into an action,* or *employment;* and *pushed on,* or *pressed on, therein:* (Bḍ in x. 62:) or *he began it, commenced it,* or *entered upon it.* (Jel, ibid.) — افاض بِالشَّىْءِ *He impelled,* or *thrust, with the thing:* (M:) *he cast,* or *threw, the thing.* (M, TA.) — افاض البَعِيرُ بِجِرَّتِهِ, (Lḥ, Ṣ, M, A, O,) and (Ṣ, O) افاض alone, (Ṣ, O, Ḳ,) and ▼ فَاضَ بِجِرَّتِهِ, (TA,) ‡ *The camel propelled his cud* (Lḥ, Ṣ, M, A, Ḳ) *from his inside,*

(Lḥ, M, A,) or *from his stomach,* (Ṣ, Ḳ,) *and expelled it,* or *ejected it:* (Ṣ:) or *cast it forth in a scattered and copious state:* or it means [*he made to be heard*] *the sound of his cud, and of his chewing.* (M.) — مَا افاض بِكَلِمَةٍ † *He did not make clear,* or *distinct,* or *perspicuous, a word,* or *sentence.* (Mṣb, TA.) [And ما افاض بكلمة signifies the same.] — افاض بِالقِدَاحِ, (Ṣ, M, A, O, Ḳ,) and عَلَى القِدَاحِ, meaning بِالقِدَاحِ, for prepositions stand in the places of other prepositions, (Ṣ, O,) and افاض القِدَاحَ, (O, Ḳ,) ‡ i. q. ضَرَبَ بِالقِدَاحِ [which has two significations: *He turned about,* or *shuffled, the gaming-arrows:* and *he played with the gaming-arrows*]: (Ṣ, M, A, O, Ḳ:) and أَجَالَهَا [which has the former of the above significations]: or *he dealt them forth.* (TA.) Aboo-Dhu-eyb says, describing a [wild] he-ass and his she-asses,

* فَكَأَنَّهُنَّ رِبَابَةٌ وَكَأَنَّهُ *
* يَسَرٌ يُفِيضُ عَلَى القِدَاحِ وَيَصْدَعُ *

(Ṣ, TA) ‡ [*And it was as though they were a bundle of gaming-arrows, and as though he were a shuffler thereof, shuffling* or] *dealing out the arrows, and deciding, and making known* what he produced: (TA:) or, accord. to Kh, *and speaking with his loudest voice,* saying "The arrow of such a one has won," or "This is the arrow of such a one:" or, accord. to some, *distributing,* or *dispensing,* by means of the arrows: (TA in art. صدع:) by عَلَى القِدَاحِ is meant بِالقِدَاحِ. (Ṣ voce عَلَى.) One relation of this verse substitutes يَخُوضُ for يُفِيضُ. (TA.) Az says that إِفَاض [a mistranscription for إِفَاضَة] is always a consequence of a state of separation, or dispersion, and abundance, or copiousness. (TA.) — Hence the saying in a trad. respecting a thing picked up from the ground, ثُمَّ أَفِضْهَا مِنْ مَالِكَ, [app. a mistake for فِي مَالِكَ,] i. e. † *Then put thou,* or *throw thou, it, and mix it, among thy property.* (TA.) — أُفِيضَتْ *She* (a woman) *became wide in the belly:* [as though spread out:] or *she became large in the belly, and flabby in flesh.* (M.) = افاض المَرْأَةَ *He made the* مَسْلَكَانِ [i. e. *vagina and rectum*] *of the woman to become one,* on the occasion of devirgination; (M;) i. q. أَفْضَاهَا [from which it is app. formed by transposition, as is indicated in the M.]. (O, TA.)

5. تفيّض *It flowed.* (Ḥar p. 610. [But this I do not find elsewhere.])

10. استفاض *He asked for the pouring out* (إِفَاضَة) *of water,* (Ḳ, TA,) *&c.* (TA.) = Said of a piece of news: and of a place: see 1, in the first half of the paragraph. You say also, استفاض الوَادِى شَجَرًا ‡ *The valley became wide, and abundant in trees.* (Ṣ, O, Ḳ, TA.) = استفاضوا الحَدِيثَ: see افاضوا فِى الحَدِيثِ. [It seems to be indicated in the Ṣ and O that it signifies *They spread abroad the story among the people;* as used by some: see مُسْتَفِيضٌ.]

فَيْضٌ *A river,* (M, TA,) in general: (TA:) pl. [of pauc.] أَفْيَاضٌ and [of mult.] فُيُوضٌ: the pluralization thereof shows that it is not an inf. n. used as a subst.: (M, TA:) [and *a river,* or *water, that overflows.*] الفَيْضُ is [hence] applied to The Nile of Egypt: (Ṣ, O, Ḳ:) or, accord. to the Tekmileh, to a place in the Nile of Egypt: (TA:) and to the river of El-Baṣrah: (Aṣ, Ṣ, Ḳ:) or this last is called فَيْضُ البَصْرَةِ, because of its greatness. (M.) You say also أَرْضٌ ذَاتُ فُيُوضٍ *Land in which is water:* (Lḥ, M:) or *in which are waters that overflow.* (Ṣ, Ḳ, TA.) — A horse ‡ *that runs much;* (Ṣ, M, O, Ḳ;) *that is fleet,* or *swift;* (M;) *that runs vehemently;* likened to water pouring forth; as also سَكْبٌ. (Eth-Thaalebee, in TA, art. سكب.) — A man ‡ *bountiful,* or *munificent;* as also ▼ فَائِضٌ, (A,) and ▼ فَيَّاضٌ: (Ṣ, O:) or, as also ▼ the last, a man *abounding* [or *profuse*] *in beneficence* or *bounty.* (M.) — *Much,* or *abundant,* water. (M.) — ‡ *Much,* or *abundance:* as in the saying, أَعْطَاهُ غَيْضًا مِنْ فَيْضٍ ‡ *He gave him little from much.* (Ṣ, M, O.) *Anything much in quantity.* (KL.) — † *A large gift:* [and simply *a gift, favour,* or *grace:*] pl. فُيُوضٌ. (KL.) — [See also 1, last sentence but one. Hence بِطَرِيقِ الفَيْضِ meaning † *By way,* or *means, of instinct; instinctively.*] — ‡ *Death:* [as being the outpouring of the soul:] see 1. (Sh, on the authority of El-Bekráwee; and Ḳ.) — ذَهَبْنَا فِى فَيْضِ فُلَانٍ † *We went with the corpse and bier of such a one.* (M.)

فَاضَةٌ: see مُفَاضٌ.

أَمْرُهُمْ فَيْضَى بَيْنَهُمْ: i. q. فَوْضَى, q. v. (TA in art. فوض.)

فَيْضُوضَآءَ, and فَيْضِيضَى, and أَمْرُهُمْ فَيْضُوضَى بَيْنَهُمْ, and فَيْضِيضَآءَ, and ▼ فَيُوضَى, i. q. فَوْضَى, q. v. in art. فوض. (AZ, Ḳ.)

فَيُوضٌ: see مُفَاضٌ.

فَيُوضَى: see أَمْرُهُمْ فَيُوضَى بَيْنَهُمْ.

فَيَّاضٌ A river *containing much water:* (Ṣ:) or *that flows much.* (Ḥam p. 375.) — Applied to a man: see فَيْضٌ, in two places.

فَائِضٌ A watering-trough *full:* a sea, or great river, [*overflowing:* see 1: or] *pouring,* or *pouring vehemently.* (TA.) — Applied to a man: see فَيْضٌ.

مُفَاضٌ pass. part. n. of 4 [q. v.]. — حَدِيثٌ مُفَاضٌ فِيهِ ‡ *Discourse in which people have pushed on,* or *pressed on:* (Ḳ:) [or *into which they have entered:* or *in which they have been large,* or *copious:* or *in which they have dilated:* or *begun:* see 4; and see also مُسْتَفِيضٌ.] — دِرْعٌ مُفَاضَةٌ ‡ *A wide,* or *an ample, coat of mail;* (Ṣ, M, A, O, Ḳ;) as also ▼ فَاضَةٌ (IJ, M) and فَيُوضٌ. (M.) [In the CḲ, this word is erroneously written مُفَاوَضَة, as applied to a coat of mail and to a woman.] مُفَاضٌ applied to a man, ‡ *Wide in the belly:* fem. with ة: (M:) or the latter, a woman *large in the belly,* (Ṣ, M, A, O, Ḳ,) *and flabby in flesh,* (M, A,) *and,* as some add, *inordinately tall:* (TA:): or, as some say, the latter signifies a woman *having her* مَسْلَكَانِ [i. e. *vagina and rectum*] *united;* as though formed by transposition from مُفْضَاةٌ: (M:) and, accord. to some, مُفَاضٌ signifies *having a fulness.* (TA.) It is said of the Prophet, كَانَ مُفَاضَ البَطْنِ, meaning ‡ *He had the belly even with the breast:* (O, Ḳ:) or *he had a fulness in the lower part of the belly.* (TA.)

مُسْتَفَاضٌ: see the next paragraph.

مُسْتَفِيضٌ One *who asks for the pouring out* (إِفَاضَة) *of water &c.* (Ṣ, O.) = A story, or a piece of news, ‡ *spread abroad* (Ṣ, M, A,* O, Mṣb, Ḳ) *among the people,* (Ṣ, O, Mṣb,) *like water;* (TA;) as also مُسْتَفَاضٌ فِيهِ; (Ṣ, O, Ḳ;) but you should not say مُسْتَفَاضٌ [alone], (Aṣ, Fr, ISk, and the lexicologists in general, and Az, Ṣ, O, Mṣb, and Ḳ,) for this is a mistake of the inhabitants of the towns and villages: (Aṣ, Fr, ISk, &c., and Mṣb:) or this last is a word of weak authority: (Ḳ:) it is, however, used by some; (Ṣ, O;) for instance, by Aboo-Temmám; (TA;) as meaning *begun, commenced,* or *entered upon;* but most disallow it unless followed by فِيهِ. (M.)

فيظ

1. فَاظَ, aor. يَفِيظُ, inf. n. فَيْظٌ (ISk, T, Ṣ, M, Ḳ) and فُيُوظٌ and فَيَظَانٌ (Ṣ, M, Ḳ) and فَيْظَانٌ (Lḥ, TA) and فَيْظُوظَةٌ, (Lth, M, Ḳ,) *He* (a man, Ṣ) *died;* (ISk, T, Ṣ, M, Ḳ;) as also, (sometimes, Ṣ) ▼ فَاظَ, aor. يَفُوظُ, inf. n. فَوْظٌ (ISk, T, Ṣ, M, Ḳ) and فَوَاظٌ; (Ṣ, Ḳ, TA; but in the CḲ, فُوَاظٌ, and there said to be with ḍamm;) or, accord. to IJ, only the inf. n., فَوْظٌ, of the latter verb is used, though the verb itself is allowable on the ground of analogy. (M.) You say also, حَانَ فَيْظُهُ and ▼ فَوْظُهُ, [in the CḲ فُوْظُهُ,] *The time came for his dying.* (M, Ḳ.) In like manner, (Ṣ,) you say also, فَاظَتْ نَفْسُهُ *His soul departed,* or *went forth;* Lth, T, Ṣ, M;) on the authority of AO and Ks; and the like is related on the authority of AZ; (Ṣ;) aor. تَفِيظُ, (M,) inf. n. فَيْظٌ (Lth, T, M) and فَيْظُوظَةٌ; (Lth, T;) and [accord. to some,] فَاظَتْ نَفْسُهُ, inf. n. فَوْظٌ: (M:) or, when the نفس is mentioned, you say, فَاضَتْ, with ض: (Ḳ:) Aṣ says, I heard Aboo-'Amr Ibn-El-'Alà say that one should not say فَاظَتْ نَفْسُهُ, (T,* Ṣ, M,*) but فاظ, (Ṣ, M,) meaning "he died;" and not فَاضَ, with ض, decidedly; (Ṣ;) or not فَاضَتْ: (T:) [but what was said by Aṣ respecting these two verbs has been stated more fully, and variously, in art. فيض, q. v.:] AO says that فاظت نَفْسُهُ is of the dial. of Keys; and فاضت, of the dial. of Temeem: Fr says that the people of El-Ḥijáz and Ṭeiyi say the former; and Ḳuḍá'ah and Temeem and Ḳeys say the latter: AḤát says, I heard AZ say that Benoo-Ḍabbeh alone say the latter; and El-Mázinee relates the like on the authority of AZ.

(TA.) — You say also, فَاظَ نَفْسَهُ, (Ks, Ṣ, M, Ḳ,) aor. يَفِيظُ, (Ks, T,) *He vomited forth his soul:* (Ks, Ṣ, M, Ḳ:) the verb being trans. as well as intrans. (Ks, Ṣ.)

4. افاظهُ *He* (God) *caused him to die.* (Ḳ, TA.) And you say also, ضَرَبْتُهُ حَتَّى أَفَظْتُ نَفْسَهُ [*I beat him, or smote him, until I made his soul to depart, or go forth*]. (Ṣ.) And لَأُفِيظَنَّ نَفْسَكَ [*I will assuredly cause thy soul to depart, or go forth*]. (M.) And افاظهُ ٱللّٰهُ نَفْسَهُ [*God caused him to vomit forth his soul*]. (Ks, T, Ṣ, M.)

تَفَيَّظُوا أَنْفُسَهُمْ *They constrained themselves to vomit forth their souls.* (Ṣ, TA.) [But in one copy of the Ṣ, I find يُفِيظُوا أَنْفُسَهُمْ, expl. as meaning *They cause to vomit forth their souls;* which suggests that the right reading may perhaps be يُفِيظُوا: or it may be يَفِيظُوا, from فَاظَ نَفْسَهُ.]

فيف

فَيْفٌ *A place that is even, level,* or *flat:* (Ṣ, O, Ḳ:) or, (Ḳ,) accord. to Lth, (T, O,) *a waterless desert,* (T, M, O, Ḳ,) *such as is even, level,* or *flat, and wide,* or *spacious;* (T, O;) and ▼ فَيْفَاةٌ and ▼ فَيْفَآءُ (M, Ḳ) and ▼ فَيْفَى (Ḳ) also signify [thus, or] *a waterless desert:* (M, Ḳ:) and, (Ḳ,) accord. to El-Mu-arrij, (T, O,) فَيْفٌ signifies a portion of the earth that is *a place whereof the winds are variable;* (T, O, Ḳ;) and this is the explanation that is preferred by Sh: (T:) and accord. to AA, it signifies [also] *any road between two mountains:* (T, TA:) its pl. is أَفْيَافٌ [a pl. of pauc.] and فُيُوفٌ [a pl. of mult.]. (T, Ṣ, M, O, Ḳ.)

فَيْفَى: see the preceding paragraph.

فَيْفَاةٌ: see فَيْفٌ: and see also مَفَازَةٌ, in art. فوز.

فَيْفَآءُ is *syn. with* فَيْفٌ, q. v.: therefore its ا is augmentative, (Ṣ, M,) accord. to Sb (M) and Mbr: (Ṣ:) and it signifies (Ṣ, M, O,) also (M) *a smooth* [*desert such as is termed*] صَحْرَآء: (Ṣ, M, O:) its pl. is فَيَافٍ. (Ṣ, M, O, Ḳ. [In the CḲ, this pl. is written فياف, as though it were a pl. of فَيْف.])

فيق

1. فَاقَ, aor. يَفِيقُ: see فاق بِنَفْسِهِ, in art. فوق.

4. أَفْيَقَ, said of a poet, *i. q.* أَفْلَقَ: (Ḳ:) or an imitative sequent thereto. (Aboo-Turáb, O.)

فِيقٌ:	see art. فوق.
فَيِّقٌ and فُيُقٌ:	
فِيقَةٌ and فَيِّقَةٌ:	
فُيَاقٌ:	
مُفِيقٌ:	

فيل

1. فَالَ رَأْيُهُ, aor. يَفِيلُ, (Ṣ, M, O, Ḳ,) inf. n. فُيُولَةٌ, (Ṣ,) thus in some copies of the Ḳ and in the A, (TA,) or فَيْلُولَةٌ, (M, O,) thus in other copies of the Ḳ, (TA,) and فَيَالَةٌ, thus in the O, but in the copies of the Ḳ فَيْلَةٌ, (TA,) *His judgment, or opinion, was weak,* (Ṣ, M, O, Ḳ,) and *erroneous;* (M, Ḳ;) as also ▼ تَفَيَّلَ; (M, Z, Ḳ, TA;) and [in like manner] فَيَّلَ ▼ فِى رَأْيِهِ [not فُيِّلَ] *he was incorrect in his judgment, or opinion;* and ▼ فَيَّلُوا occurs in a trad. as meaning فال رَأْيُهُمْ: (TA:) [and فَالَ alone, said of a man, signifies the same as فَالَ رَأْيُهُ, as is shown by a verse of El-Kumeyt cited in the T and M and O and TA: but it seems from what here follows (taken from a passage unconnected with the foregoing) that the first and third of what are mentioned above as inf. ns. are regarded by some as simple substs.:] and one says, ▼ فِى رَأْيِهِ فَيَالَةٌ, (T, M, Ḳ, TA,) the last word like سَحَابَةٌ, (TA, [in the CḲ, erroneously, فِى رِوايَةٍ فِيالَةٌ,]) and ▼ فُيُولَةٌ, (M, Ḳ, TA,) meaning [*In his judgment, or opinion, is*] *a weakness.* (TA.) — And فال signifies also *He* (a man) *magnified himself, and became like the elephant* (الفِيل): or *he showed a morose aspect:* (TA:) [or it may so signify: IAar cites the following verse:

مِنَ ٱلنَّاسِ أَقْوَامٌ إِذَا صَادَفُوا ٱلْغِنَى
تَوَلَّوْا وَفَالُوا لِلصَّدِيقِ وَفَخَّمُوا

which may mean [*Of mankind are folks who, when they find riches, turn the back, and*] *magnify themselves and become like the elephant* [*to the friend, and aggrandize themselves*]: or *show a morose aspect to the friend* [&c.]; for the elephant is morose in aspect. (M.)

2. فَيَّلَ رَأْيَهُ, (Ṣ, M, Ḳ,) inf. n. تَفْيِيلٌ, *He declared* [or *esteemed*] *his judgment, or opinion, to be weak,* (Ṣ,) or *bad,* and *erroneous.* (M, Ḳ.) Umeiyeh Ibn-Abee-'Áïdh says,

فَلَوْ غَيْرَهَا مِنْ وُلْدِ كَعْبِ بْنِ كَاهِلٍ
مَدَحْتَ بِقَوْلٍ صَادِقٍ لَمْ تُفَيَّلِ

meaning لَمْ يُفَيَّلْ رَأْيُكَ (Skr, M) i. e. [*But hadst thou praised other than her, of the children of Kaab Ibn-Káhil, with a true saying,*] *thy judgment, or opinion, would not have been declared weak.* (Skr.) — See also 1, in two places.

3. فَايَلَ, [inf. n. مُفَايَلَةٌ and فِيَالٌ, (see الفِيَالُ, below,)] *He played* [*at the game called* الفِيَال: see its part. n. below]. (O.)

5. تَفَيَّلَ: see 1. — Also *He* (a man, Ḳ, [or a camel, as is indicated in the O,]) *became fat,* (O, Ḳ,) *as though he were a* فيل [*or an elephant*]. (O.) [See also 10.] — And, said of youth, or young manhood, (الشَّبَاب,) *It increased,* (Lth, T, M, O, Ḳ,) *and became in its prime and fulness.* (Lth, T, O.) — And, said of herbage, *It became tall, and full-grown;* or *became of its full height, and blossomed.* (Th, M, Ḳ.)

10. اِسْتَفْيَلَ *He* (a camel) *became like the* فيل [or *elephant*] (M, Ḳ, TA) *in bigness:* (TA:) mentioned by IJ among the class of اِسْتَحْوَذَ and the like: part. n. مُسْتَفْيِلٌ. (M.) [See also 5.]

فَالٌ: see فِيلٌ, latter half: — and the paragraph commencing with فَائِلُ الرَّأْيِ, near its end: — and see also فَأْلٌ, in art. فأل.

فَيْلٌ: see the paragraph here following.

فِيلٌ [The *elephant;* Pers. پيل;] *a certain animal,* (TA,) *well known:* pl. [of pauc.] أَفْيَالٌ and [of mult.] فُيُولٌ and فِيَلَةٌ; (Ṣ, M, O, Mṣb, Ḳ;) not أَفْيِلَةٌ: (ISk, Ṣ, O, Mṣb:) accord. to Sb, فِيلٌ may be originally of the measure فُعْلٌ, (Ṣ, M, O,) pronounced with kesr because of the ى, like as they said أَبْيَضُ and بِيضٌ; but Akh says, this is not the case in the sing., but only in the pl.: (Ṣ, O:) fem. with ة. (M, Ḳ.) — Hence, لَيْلَةٌ مِثْلُ لَوْنِ ٱلْفِيلِ [lit. *A night like the colour of the elephant;*] meaning *a night that is black,* (M, TA,) *and dust-coloured;* (M;) *in which one knows not the right course to pursue:* the colours of the فيل being of this kind. (M, TA.) — [Hence, also, دَآءُ الفِيلِ *The disease called by us the tumid Barbadoes leg;* because the leg of the patient resembles that of the elephant by reason of its enormously-swollen state: not (as some have supposed it to be) elephantiasis; this latter being termed جُذَام (q. v.)]. — And [hence, likewise, used as an epithet,] فِيلٌ signifies also ‡ *Heavy* [or *dull*]; and *low, ignoble,* or *mean.* (Ḳ, TA.) — And one says رَجُلٌ فِيلُ الرَّأْيِ, meaning *A man weak in respect of judgment,* or *opinion;* (T, Ṣ, M, O, Ḳ;) and so ▼ فِيلُهُ (M, Ḳ;) and ▼ فَيِّلُهُ; (T, M, O, Ḳ;) and ▼ فَائِلُهُ, (ISk, T, Ṣ, M, O, Ḳ,) of the measure فَيْعِل; (O;) and ▼ فَالُهُ, (T, M, O, Ḳ,) and فَالٌ alone, (Ṣ, Ḳ,) meaning *weak in respect of judgment, or opinion;* (T, Ṣ, M, O, Ḳ;) *erring in insight:* (Ṣ:) pl. [of the first] أَفْيَالٌ: (Ṣ, M, O, Ḳ:) but AO says, the ▼ فَائِلٌ is *one who, inspecting, forms an opinion and errs;* if he err after examining a horse in all its states or conditions and forming an opinion respecting it from his inspection, [not while doing so,] he is not reckoned to be فائل. (TA.)

الفِيَالُ and الفَيَالُ, (Lth, T, M, O, Ḳ,) the former a subst. and the latter an inf. n. [of 3], (Lth, T, O,) and ▼ المُفَايَلَةُ [which is likewise an inf. n. of 3], (M, Ḳ,) *A certain game,* (Lth, T, M, O, Ḳ,) *well known,* (O,) *of the children,* (T,) or *of the youths,* or *young men, of the Arabs* (M, Ḳ) *of the desert,* (M,) *with earth,* or *dust:* (Lth, T, M, O:) *a thing is hidden in earth, or dust, which is then divided* (T, M) *into two portions; then the hider says to his companion, In which of them twain is it?* (T;) *and if he* [*who is thus questioned*] *mistake, the hider says to him* فَالَ رَأْيُكَ: (T, M,* Ḳ:*) ISk termed it الفِئَالُ, with ء; (O;) and it has been mentioned before in art.

فَالٌ: (T, O, Ḳ:) accord. to some, (TA,) this game is called السُّدَّرُ and الطَّبَنُ. (T, TA. [But see the former of these two words.])

فَيَالَةٌ: } see the first paragraph.
فُيُولَةٌ: }

فَيِّلُ اللَّحْمِ A man *having much flesh*: (T, O,* Ḳ:) some pronounce it with ء, (T, O,) saying فَيْأَلٌ, (T,) or فَيْئِلٌ; (O;) both mentioned before [in art. فأل]. (TA.) — فَيِّلُ الرَّأْيِ: see فِيلٌ, latter half.

فَيَّالٌ The *attendant*, or *master*, (Ṣ, M, O, Mṣb, Ḳ,) or the *keeper*, or *driver*, (MA, KL,) *of the* فيل [or *elephant*], (Ṣ, MA, O, Mṣb, KL,) or *of the* فِيلَة. (So in the M and Ḳ.)

فَائِلُ الرَّأْيِ: see فِيلٌ, latter half, in two places. — الفَائِلُ [as a subst.] signifies *The flesh that is upon the* خُرْبَة, (Ṣ, O,) or خُرْب, (Ḳ, [in the M, accord. to the TT, حرف, app. a mistranscription,]) *of the* وَرِك; (Ṣ, M, O, Ḳ;) [which, I think, will be plainly seen from what follows to mean *the flesh that is upon the sacro-ischiatic foramen*; though خُرْبُ الوَرِكِ and خُرْبَةُ الوَرِكِ are said in the TA, in art. خرب, to mean "the hole where the head of the thigh-bone is inserted;"] so says A'Obeyd: (Ṣ, O:) or, (Ṣ, M, O, Ḳ,) as some say, so adds A'Obeyd, (Ṣ, O,) *a certain vein* (T, Ṣ, M, O, Ḳ) *in the* خُرْبَة *of the* وَرِك, *descending into the leg*, (T,) or *in the thigh*: (Ṣ, O:) Aṣ says, in "the Book of the Horse," in the وَرِك is the خُرْبَة, which is a نُقْرَة wherein is flesh, no bone being in it; and in that نُقْرَة is the فَائِل, and there is no bone between the said نقرة and the belly, but only skin and flesh; (T,* Ṣ, O;) and he cites the saying of El-Aạshà,

• قَدْ نَخْضِبُ العَيْرَ فِى مَكْنُونِ فَائِلِهِ •
• وَقَدْ يَشِيطُ عَلَى أَرْمَاحِنَا البَطَلُ •

[*Oft we stain the ridge of the spear-head in what is concealed in the interior of his* فائل, *and oft the man of valour dies by means of our spears*]; مَكْنُون الفَائِل means his blood: he says [by implication], we are skilful in respect of the place of piercing: (Ṣ, O:) but Aṣ said مِنْ in the place of فِى; and AA, قَدْ نَطْعَنُ; which has been pronounced to be wrong: (O:) or the فَائِلَانِ, (T, M,) or the فَائِلَتَانِ ↓, (so in the Ḳ, [app. a mistranscription,]) are *two veins entering into the interior parts of the thighs*, (T, M, Ḳ,) *in the hinder parts thereof*; (M, Ḳ;) and they adduce as an evidence thereof the verse of El-Aạshà cited above, saying that the epithet مكنون would not have been used if the فائل were not a vein; but others say that [the poet meant that] he made the spear-head to become concealed in the furthest part of the flesh; and if the فائل were a vein, it would not have been mentioned as it has been in a phrase of Imra-el-Ḳeys which will be cited in what follows: (M:) [hence it is said,] or they are *two portions of flesh* [*between which is the lower part of the os sacrum*, i. e.] *the lower parts of which are upon the* صَلَوَانِ [dual of صَلًا], *from the region of the lower portions of the* حَجَبَتَانِ *to the* عَجْب, *bordering upon the* عُصْعُص *on either side, descending in the two sides of the two thighs*; [so in a human being,] and thus in the horse: (M, Ḳ: [for the meanings of the words that I have here left untranslated, I must refer to their several proper arts.; as they are variously explained:]) الفَالُ ↓ is a dial. var. of الفَائِلُ; (M, Ḳ, TA;) which is expl. by Ṣgh [in the O] as meaning *a certain vein issuing from the* قَوَّارَة *of the* وَرِك [i. e. *from the sacro-ischiatic foramen*]: (TA:) [but the assertion that الفال is a dial. var. of الفائل seems to be founded only upon what here follows:] Imra-el-Ḳeys says, [describing a horse,]

• لَهُ حَجَبَاتٌ مُشْرِفَاتٌ عَلَى الفَالِ •

(Ṣ, M; or على الفَالِى, as in the O and TA;) [i.e. *He has edges of the haunch-bones projecting above*, or *beyond*, *the* فائل; for] he means على فَائِلٍ, having altered the latter word by transposition. (T, Ṣ, O, TA.)

فَائِلَةٌ: see its dual in the next preceding paragraph, near the middle.

أَفْيَلُ [*More*, and *most*, *weak*, or *erroneous*; relating to a judgment, or an opinion]. أَفْيَلُ مِنَ الرَّأْيِ الدَّبَرِيِّ is a prov., meaning [*More weak*] *than an opinion* that is given *after the affair* [to which it relates] *has passed*. (Meyd.)

مُفَايِلٌ [in the Ṣ and O in art. فأل, with ء, i.e. مُفَائِلٌ,] *Playing at the game called* الفَيَالُ. (M, O.)

المُفَايَلَةُ expl. as a subst.: see الفَيَالُ.

مَفْيُولَآء [a quasi-pl. n. (like مَشْيُوخَآء &c.), but one of which the sing. (if it have one) is not mentioned,] The *young ones of the* فيل [or *elephant*]. (O, Ḳ.)

مُسْتَفْيِلٌ part. n. of 10, q. v. (M.)

فين

1. فَانَ, aor. يَفِينُ, (Ḳ,) inf. n. فَيْنٌ, (TA,) *He*, or *it*, *came*. (Ḳ.)

فَيْنَةٌ *A time*; syn. وَقْتٌ مِنَ الزَّمَانِ, or وَقْتٌ; (T;) or حِينٌ; (T, Ṣ, M, Ḳ;) and سَاعَةٌ. (Ṣ, Ḳ.) You say, لَقِيتُهُ الفَيْنَةَ بَعْدَ الفَيْنَةِ [*I met him time after time*]: (AZ, Ṣ, M, Ḳ; but some copies of the Ḳ omit the words بعد الفينة:) and لَقِيتُهُ فَيْنَةً [*I met him at a certain time*]: (AZ, Ṣ, M, Ḳ; but in some copies of the Ṣ and Ḳ, فَيْنَةَ:) thus فينة is made determinate in two different ways; by its having the article ال prefixed to it [in the former case], and as a proper name [in the latter case; with which compare what is said of بُكْرَة &c.]: (AZ, M:) and you say, إِنِّى لَآتِى فُلَانًا الفَيْنَةَ بَعْدَ الفَيْنَةِ i. e. [*Verily I come to such a one*] *time after time*; not continually repairing to him: (AZ, T:) and, accord. to ISk, مَا أَلْقَاهُ إِلَّا الفَيْنَةَ, i. e. [*I do not meet him save occasionally*, or] *time after time*. (TA.) [See also فَتَّةٌ.]

فَيْنَانٌ *Having beautiful and long hair*: (Ḳ:) or so فَيْنَانُ الشَّعَرِ; applied to a man: (Ṣ:) فَيْنَان [is also applied as an epithet to hair; and] has been mentioned in art. فن q. v.: (Ḳ:) if it be from فَنَنٌ, meaning "a branch," it is [of the measure فَيْعَالٌ, and therefore] perfectly decl. when indeterminate, and likewise when determinate [as a proper name]; but if from فَيْنَةٌ, meaning "a time," [which seems to be hardly reasonable,] it is [of the measure فَعْلَانٌ, and therefore] perfectly decl. in the former case and imperfectly decl. in the latter case. (Lḥ, T.) — One says also ظِلٌّ فَيْنَانٌ, meaning *Wide, extensive, shade*. (TA.)

أَفْيُونٌ, also written أُفْيُونٌ and إِفْيُونٌ, held by some to belong to this art. and by others to belong to art. افن, has been mentioned in page 70.

فيه

1. فَاهَ, aor. يَفِيهُ: see فَاهَ, aor. يَفُوهُ, in art. فوه.

فيهج

فَيْهَجٌ *A wine-measure*: (Ṣ, O, Ḳ:) a Pers. word arabicized [and therefore all its letters are regarded as radical]. (Ṣ.) — And *A strainer* (O, Ḳ, TA) *for wine*. (TA.) — And (sometimes, Ṣ, O) a name for *Wine*: (Ṣ, Ḳ:) or *clear wine*: (O, TA:) or an epithet applied to wine [app. signifying *clear*]: (TA:) or *wine such as is* مختلق [app. a mistranscription for مُخَلَّق, a word now used as signifying *aromatized*]; like قِنْدِيدٌ [q. v.] and أُمُّ زَنْبَقٍ. (IAmb, TA.)

END OF THE SIXTH PART OF BOOK I.